My
Generation

ALSO BY MICHAEL GROSS
   Model: The Ugly Business of Beautiful Women
   Bob Dylan: An Illustrated History

BY MICHAEL GROSS AND STEPHEN
DEMOREST (AS D. G. DEVON)
   Precious Objects
   Shattered Mask
   Temple Kent

My

FIFTY YEARS OF SEX, DRUGS, ROCK,
REVOLUTION, GLAMOUR, GREED,
VALOR, FAITH, AND SILICON CHIPS

Generation

MICHAEL GROSS

Cliff Street Books
An Imprint of HarperCollins*Publishers*

Portions of *My Generation* have been previously published in much different form in *New York*, GQ, and *British Vogue*.

MY GENERATION. Copyright © 2000 by Michael Gross. All rights reserved. Printed in the United States of America. No part of this book may be used or reproduced in any manner whatsoever without written permission except in the case of brief quotations embodied in critical articles and reviews. For information address HarperCollins Publishers Inc., 10 East 53rd Street, New York, NY 10022.

HarperCollins books may be purchased for educational, business, or sales promotional use. For information please write: Special Markets Department, HarperCollins Publishers Inc., 10 East 53rd Street, New York, NY 10022.

FIRST EDITION

Designed by Elina D. Nudelman

Printed on acid-free paper.

Library of Congress Cataloging-in-Publication Data

Gross, Michael.
    My generation: fifty years of sex, drugs, rock, revolution, glamour, greed, valor, faith
    and silicon chips/by Michael Gross—1st ed.
       p.   cm.
    Includes bibliographical references and index.
    ISBN 0-06-017594-X
    1. Baby boom generation—United States. 2. United States—Social conditions—
1960–1980. 3. United States—Social conditions—1980– 4. Gross, Michael. I. Title
Hn59 .G77 2000
305.24—dc21   99-055384

00 01 02 03 04 ❖/RRD 10 9 8 7 6 5 4 3 2 1

In Memory of Milton Gross (b.1912)
and for Estelle Gross (b. 1915)

I'm not trying to cause a great s-s-s-sensation,
I'm just talkin' 'bout my g-g-generation.

—*The Who, "My Generation"*

Contents

Cast of Characters

CYNTHIA BOWMAN—Runaway hippie turned PR executive.

STEVE CAPPS—Nerd turned software superstar.

JIM FOURATT—Hippie turned Yippie! turned gay activist and new music impresario.

MICHAEL FUCHS—Media maven turned multimillionaire retiree.

JOHN GAGE—Free Speech Movement activist turned computer-evangelist.

NINA HARTLEY—Red diaper baby turned bisexual feminist porn star.

VICTORIA LEACOCK—Second-generation celebrity turned AIDS activist.

BARBARA LEDEEN—Marxist turned right-wing conspirator.

DAVID MCINTOSH—Eagle Scout turned conservative maverick.

DOUG MARLETTE—Southern racist turned Pulitzer-winning political cartoonist.

MARK RUDD—Radical bomber turned vocational school teacher.

TIM SCULLY—LSD chemist turned turned software designer.

CAMERON SEARS—Environmental activist turned Grateful Dead manager.

RUSSELL SIMMONS—Ghetto pot dealer turned urban entrepreneur.

LESLIE CROCKER SNYDER—Radcliffe preppie turned hanging judge.

KATHRYN BOND STOCKTON—Jesus freak turned Queer Theorist.

DONALD TRUMP—Military school cut-up turned Ur-Yuppie.

THOMAS VALLELY—Vietnam War hero turned Asian redevelopment expert.

MARIANNE WILLIAMSON—Wild child turned spiritual celebrity.

Bethel, New York

AUGUST 14, 1998: I'm driving along a back road in rustic upstate New York when a *déjà vu* of an intensity I've experienced only once before overwhelms me. That time, en route to a meeting in Dallas, I drove into an open expanse called Dealy Plaza and didn't understand why it felt so eerie until I was alongside the Texas School Book Depository, approaching a triple underpass imprinted in my memory from repeated television news broadcasts. I sensed more than saw that I was driving where John F. Kennedy was killed in 1963.

This is different. I've been here before. In front of me is a huge natural amphitheater full of people arrayed before a great wooden stage, amassed for a three-day rock and folk concert called A Day in the Garden. This "garden," once a farm belonging to a man named Max Yasgur and long ago an Indian gathering ground, was also the site of a gentle, auspicious music and arts event called the Aquarian Exposition, better known as Woodstock, where at age seventeen I spent three near-sleepless days in August 1969.

Never trust anybody over thirty, people used to say in the years after Kennedy was killed. So this, the twenty-ninth anniversary of Woodstock, may be the last chance to trust in the Age of Aquarius.

In 1969, the bacchanal of 400,000 people was front-page news. "HIPPIES MIRED IN SEA OF MUD," sneered New York's then-conservative *Daily News.* Perhaps we were. But we were also enjoying the biggest coming-out party ever for America's biggest generation ever, the Baby Boom. And everyone wanted to be there.

Our youngest member was about four and a half that day. The oldest participants were gray-haired bohemian-era precursors and young-at-heart boomer pretenders. We were all caught up in the excitement of the moment when a window of opportunity—for drugs, for sex, for "liberation"—opened up and about 76 million of us scampered through before it slammed shut. It's no wonder the generation that followed resents us. Youth ruled, and if it still seems to, that's largely because we cannily repackage our youth and sell it over and again. But there's a lot of gray hair at Woodstock 1998, onstage and off.

Don Henley (b. 1947) of the 1970s band The Eagles is playing an age-appropriate, elegiac song, "The Boys of Summer," as I park my car and wade into the crowd past concession stands emblazoned with peace symbols. "Everybody knows the war is over," Henley sings. "Everybody knows the good guys lost." But did they? Here they are, grown up into wrinkled, happy people, in neat rows of beach chairs, lawn furniture, Mayan cherry-wood chairs ($20 a day, $120 if you want to take one home), and Indian-print bedspreads scattered with Beanie Babies for their brood.

It's a generational Rorschach. You can see what you want here.

Hippies? Woodstock '98's got 'em, even if some are a little shopworn. Head shops still line the road, and beatific teenage girls with daisies in their hair dance waving tinsel in the hay fields. Everywhere are tie-dye, suede, and patchwork clothes that look as if they just emerged from ruck-sacks circa Woodstock '69.

Drugs? Occasional wisps tell you marijuana is still around, but far harder to find (and of far better quality) than it used to be. "We went *hmmm*," says young mother Susan Kaufer, eyeing her three kids, six, eight, and eleven, and the cloud of pot above their heads. "They haven't said anything, thank god."

Yuppies? There's a BMW 733i passing a Jaguar with a vanity plate that says INTRNET on Hurd Road. The only psychedelic Volkswagen in sight is a New Beetle painted with the logo of a local radio station. The satellite ATM van is as busy as the Port-a-sans. The concession stands offer pasta caprese, focaccia, mixed baby green salads and cappuccino alongside the burgers and beer. Henley launches into a song called "The End of Innocence." There are Woodstock '69 and Woodstock '98 T-shirts for sale, Woodstock license plate frames, Woodstock mouse pads, even Yasgur's Farm Ice Cream.

"My wife brought me," says Ken Adamyk, who was nine years old the first time around and didn't go to Woodstock '69. "My older brother went. He doesn't have hair now, but he did." A couple in their fifties walks by with laminated backstage passes marked FOH, for friends of the house, I assume. I ask them what the initials mean anyway. "Fucking Old Hippie," he says. She laughs. "Old hippies fucking," she says brightly.

But we've grown up. Really, we have. Even if Jim Farber (b. 1957), who's covering the event for today's more sympathetic *Daily News*, complains that every time he asks a boomer his age the answer is thirty-seven, most people I talk to are glad to proffer their birthdate.

"I'm one of the people who held onto the beliefs, and some of the products—I don't have to go into specifics," says Stephen Biegel (b. 1950), a builder from Hoboken, New Jersey. "I'm still proud we stopped a war. But you have to go with the flow. I grew up, had children; you have to support them. That's not a contradiction. The contradictions are either dead or wandering the streets."

Bill Lauren, a Woodstock '69 veteran wearing Oakley sunglasses and a gnomic red hat, is selling those Mayan chairs. "The first time, I liked the mud," he says. "Been there, done that."

At the first Woodstock, drugs were in everyone's eyes and the scent of sex was in the air. "You can get away with a lot of things in a cornfield," Don Henley is saying onstage. Not anymore, though, not in this cornfield. Overnight camping is banned. There are no drug dealers in sight. Visible skinny bra straps have replaced visible bralessness as the women's fashion. The lake where people skinny-dipped is fenced and posted PRIVATE LAND.

On day two, one of the performers, Joni Mitchell (b. 1943), will note another change. "Free love?" she asks from the stage. "There's no such thing now." She lets out a high, wild laugh. "Pay later," she adds wryly before hitting the first notes of "Woodstock," the song that gave this day in the garden its name.

Stevie Nicks (b. 1948), a former singer with Fleetwood Mac, performs after Henley and sings the lyric, "Thunder only happens when it's raining," just as it starts to rain—to general mirth. I remember the rain from 1969, how it turned the grassy bowl into a muddy tangle of blankets, sleeping bags, food wrappers, underground newspapers, discarded clothes and filthy, half-awake teens. In 1998 I glance down. At my feet is a trampled copy of *Seventeen*. Lying nearby, a *Harper's Bazaar*. Otherwise it could be a New York Philharmonic concert on the great lawn in Central Park, so polite and well-ordered is the crowd.

It starts to rain harder, though, and people leave in droves. "We're going to the Hamptons," a friend from the music business says as he heads for the parking lot. "We're going to shop the outlets," adds another who flees, a one-time hippie with a teenage daughter in tow. I didn't know anyone who walked out of the first Woodstock, rain notwithstanding. But a couple of my friends were there and escaped it anyway, they were so high on LSD.

Woodstock '98 is aimed at two separate audiences. Friday and Saturday are for baby boomers. Sunday will be Generation X day; it will feature a much bigger crowd of much younger people, traffic jams, an all-day mosh pit, more than a dozen drug arrests, the sudden appearance of designer labels like CK, lots more piercings, tattoos, and dog collars, a much-remarked-on beer ban, and newer musicians such as Janis Joplin-style belter Joan Osborne and several pop bands: Goo Goo Dolls, Third Eye Blind, and Marcy Playground. That last band's lead singer mentions LSD—indeed, he admits taking it. Hardly anyone cheers.

Acid flashes aside, Day Two is the real nostalgia day, starring three Woodstock '69 veterans: Melanie (b. Melanie Safka, 1947), Richie Havens (b. 1941) and Pete Townshend (b. 1945), along with Donovan (b. 1946) and Mitchell, who wrote "Woodstock" even though she wasn't there. Lou Reed (b. 1942)—the former Velvet Underground leader who probably wouldn't have been caught dead at Woodstock '69—is the swizzle stick in the day's mixed drink.

By this time in 1969, the first Woodstock's fences had been torn down and the concert officially acknowledged to be free. So I go up to the main gate and find it fully operational. State troopers are everywhere, as they were the first time around; this time, though, they seem to be running things. A rumor has swept the press tent that Michael Lang (b. 1945), an organizer of the first Woodstock, is on site and furious at Allan Gerry, the sixty-nine-year-old cable television millionaire who now controls the thirty-seven-acre site and acreage around it through a charitable foundation. Gerry has turned it all into a Baby Boom Disneyland with three miles of gravel roads, five miles of freshly cut split-rail fences, and, of course, focaccia. Protesters from the Woodstock Nation Foundation are angry with Gerry, too. They've filed lawsuits and committed acts of civil disobedience against what they consider the illegal taking of a sacred piece of public land. But is this site really sacred anymore? In 1998 Lang was planning a thirtieth-anniversary concert, aimed at the young rock audience, not boomers; it took place a year later on a decommissioned air force base in Rome, New York, and by the end, degenerated into an orgy of burning, looting and rape that left concertgoers and nostalgia buffs alike declaring the Woodstock ideal dead.

That concert, as it happened, took place just a few days after John F. Kennedy Jr. (b. 1960), his wife and her sister died in a small-plane crash off Martha's Vineyard. For the youngest boomers, the tragedy was an opportunity to experience the sort of mass mourning via media surrounding the 1963 assassination of President John F. Kennedy.

With their picture-perfect parents, John Jr. and his sister, Caroline (b. 1957), were idealized symbols of the Baby Boom. And in strange synchronicity with the Kennedy progeny, our generation has proved to be as tragic as it was blessed, as late-blooming as it was prematurely admired, as reckless as it was adventurous, as pitiable as it was enviable.

The young Kennedy's death and the retread concert that immediately followed had the impact but not the import of the originals they so eerily echoed. The thirty-nine-year-old was not yet the man his father was, and Woodstock '99 was more *Lord of the Flies* than the event on which it was based. It is the peculiar curse of the baby boom that the shadows of its youth often seem brighter than its present.

I MISS DONOVAN'S show because I head to the rock-and-roll mall, a high-tech tented pavilion full of merchandise and memory at the rim of the concert bowl. You can buy a lot here: photos of Jimi Hendrix (b. 1942) and Janis Joplin (b. 1943), hippie bags, handmade brooms, Catskill Mountain Farm goat cheese. Cornelius Alexy (b. 1943) sells peace symbols made from pieces of the storm fence that surrounded the site in 1969. Farmers had carted most of it away, but Alexy kept the gate.

"It's funny," says Cindy Beno Persico (b. 1953). "I was standing right next to that fence. I had a ticket. I walked to the gate and four hundred people knocked it down. Now I'm back with my eight-year-old daughter. I've met a lot of people who were there. We've changed—we're maybe not living in communes—but we've still got the spirit of youthfulness."

"I was here for the first one too," John Sharp chimes in. "I had a blast. I was fourteen. This was all woods. This was Gentle Way and Groovy Path," the intersection where people bought and sold drugs. "I've changed, too," he says. "I'm married. I have a son. I work every day, but I still love adventure." I ask whether he's finding any here. "It's a lot more organized," he says. "It's a lot more commercialized."

Want peace in the world? Buy a badge or a bumper sticker. Want to chill out? Get a massage for a dollar a minute. Want to wave your freak flag? Have your hair braided with beads for a dollar an inch, or, for something more permanent, get pierced.

"It's the new thing, a tribal, instinctual thing," says Lisa Sampson, who's working the piercing booth. "The pierced people are the children of the freaks," piercer Danny Domino says. "They don't do it for a reason. Reasons go away. This doesn't."

"A fifty-five-year-old just pierced his belly button," Sampson adds.

Next door, you can buy books by boomer heroes like Ken Kesey and Allen Ginsberg, and videos of druggie idols like Timothy Leary and Neal Cassady, the star of Jack Kerouac novels and Kesey's traveling Merry Pranksters troupe. The Grateful Shed is selling hemp (marijuana plant) clothing, twine, hats, sandals, and even hemp "Aware Bear" teddy bears. John's Rocking Ride, based in Dayton, Ohio, is hawking tie-dye Jerry Garcia posters and Cuban cigars at $20 each. "The government's gone berserk," the salt-and-pepper-bearded proprietor storms. "We do business with butchers in China, but poor Castro can't get toilet paper!"

A few stalls away, Marcia Weiss (b. 1948) is one of several people selling original Woodstock ephemera. "Every generation had a best time of its life," is her explanation for why people buy it.

"They want to stay in touch with who they are, how it used to be," adds a browser, Greg Packer (b. 1964). Randy Smith (b. 1955) overhears him. "I drive a '69 Dodge Charger," Smith says. "I still have an eight-track tape player." He buys tapes for it on the Internet.

A copy of the programs given away at the first Woodstock will run you $125. Unused three-day tickets are $100. For some, these things mean more than money. "Money is a drug," says one man selling old tickets, Bill Burnham (b. 1943). "Most people can be bought. But it wasn't bullshit, it was real." By *it*, he seems to mean the Woodstock spirit. "It'll come back. There'll be a resurgence. We meant it and we've survived."

THE GENERATION THAT lived the Who lyric "Hope I die before I get old"—sung at the first Woodstock—has on the whole opted to do neither. And let people jokingly refer to the event as Geezer Woodstock; boomers are the backbone of this production, running not only the 1960s-style rock show, but also the very 1990s live Internet broadcast. Now that they finally control the culture they once merely dominated, boomers are determined to stay on top of it. Educated, worldly, raised on breached barricades, broken rules and new paradigms, they—we—are uniquely qualified to deal with the new global society we were instrumental in creating. So we've become the aging rulers of a culture of youth.

When the first demographic boomers turned fifty in 1996, far closer to their sixties than to the 1960s, as many have said, the media portrayed a generation still dancing away from maturity, and mortality, as fast as it could. "Sales of skin creams, suntan lotions, hair coloring, cosmetics, vitamins, and nutritional supplements are surging as millions of boomers join the battle against aging," said *American Demographics* magazine, which invented a new stage of life just for us—Mid-Youth, "a new and vibrant midlife marketplace"—and pointed out that boomers would not comprise the majority of Americans over age fifty until 2005.[1] *Life* printed a special edition honoring the generation, but its list of the fifty most influential boomers rang curiously hollow beyond the childlike arenas of sports, computers and the arts.

Some journalists pointed out that the boomers, just reaching their peak earning years, were poised to begin inheriting what economists refer to as a "$10 trillion legacy," history's largest transfer of wealth from one generation to another. Much of that will be spent by the boomer elite on power toys (from tiny cell phones and Palm Pilots to huge sport utility vehicles), travel and entertainment. But average boomers earn less than their parents in real dollars and will soon become financially responsible for those parentson top of mortgages and college tuition for children, and without a solid base of savings to rest on—so they will likely defer retirement and continue to work and create wealth well past retirement age, whether they want to or not.[2]

The shaky state of Social Security only adds to our social insecurity and desire to stay vital as long as possible. As Peter G. Peterson pointed out in *Atlantic Monthly* that year, by 2030, when the last boomers turn sixty-five, the country won't be able to afford them. "We deal with aging and mortality as reluctantly as the Victorians dealt with sex," Peterson said.[3]

I may get old, but I'll never be old.

The new siren song of the generation is sung by many of the musicians who visit the press tent to answer questions. "I don't think it's about giving up being young," says Melanie, whose treacly "Beautiful People" was one of the songs of the summer of '69. She's pudgy now in her embroidered velvet hippie frock, a shock of white hair sprouting above her still little-girl face. "They're not ever gonna grow up," she continues, gesturing out at the crowd. "They grew up with Peter Pan. It's too late."

"You have to look at the sixties as a renaissance thing," says Donovan Leitch, whose namesake son, a sometime model/rock musician, was quite appropriately one of the visual symbols of the 1960s revival in the 1990s. "Woodstock was symbolic of the way ideas that came out of jazz clubs, bookstores, and bohemia took over the arts. What we are seeing here are the consequences. We're not reliving but continuing what began then. This tradition, whatever you want to call it, should continue."

Guitarist and songwriter Peter Townshend (b. 1948), formerly of The Who, is next up to the microphone. Slightly stooped, with a pouchy face and sad eyes, he's no longer the guitar-smashing firebrand of Woodstock '69; he looks like a Dickensian clerk. Why return to Woodstock? "What brought me back was a sense of wanting to look at the reality of the whole thing," he says. "It was the single most important concert in our career. I'm fifty years old now. I know what makes the world go 'round. History is fucking important."

He recalls arriving at the first festival. "There were people everywhere, wandering in the woods like ghosts on drugs," he says. Doesn't it bother him, someone asks, that this latest Woodstock has no unifying theme, no politics? "The very fact that somebody has bought this land and wants to make music here says a lot about what really was important about the original occasion," he replies. "That's what the festival was really about. Everything else turned out slightly flawed."

Like his creation the pinball wizard Tommy and his one-time guru Meyer Baba ("Don't Worry, Be Happy"), Townshend is often treated like a seer, even though his rock star status and sudden, early wealth effectively separated him from his peers. Now he's asked to comment on the encampment just up the highway that includes local Woodstock Nation purists and members of the Rainbow Family, a band of caravaning vegetarian pacifists who come to the area every summer and are boycotting the concert. Townshend's answer is short and sweetly sensible. "I know what paid my rent," he says. "It was my father working."

Someone tells him Joni Mitchell is about to go onstage, and he excuses himself to go listen. I follow him out and ask one more rushed question.

Earlier, Townshend had said that after the first Woodstock, the kids who attended realized they had to take destiny into their own hands. "It was no longer about drugs or the generation gap," he'd said. "It was, 'What do we do?'"

So what did they do, I ask, all those Baby Boom kids? "What actually happened was, people took responsibility," he says. "They got jobs. They had families. And they started to live."

Conception

THIS IS THE story of the Baby Boom generation, the 900-pound gorilla of twentieth-century America, of how it grew up, and of its profound impact on the culture and history of its times. The Boom is usually defined as the 75 million-odd people born during the American fertility explosion from January 1, 1946, to December 31, 1964. That strict demographic excludes Americans born in the second trimester of the 1940s, after Pearl Harbor but before V-J Day, those members of the Silent or Swing generation whose beliefs, experiences, and cultural references formed the cutting edge of the Baby Boom.[1] And that definition also includes early 1960s babies closer culturally to the *next* generation, the spiky-haired kids snickering in the back of the Boom room, the so-called Generation X.

This book focuses on the lives of nineteen quintessential boomers, each of whom embodies or epitomizes a moment, idea, accomplishment, trend or tendency intrinsic to the larger narrative of this extraordinary, controversial generation. In order to single out these individuals, more useful generational cutoff dates had to be set. Clearly, a person born in 1942 has as much or more in common with someone born in 1946 than with the children of the late 1930s. So the day the Japanese bombed Pearl Harbor—December 7, 1941—seems as good as any to mark the start of the boom, and November 22, 1963, the day of John Kennedy's assassination, is an equally appropriate end.

The loose shoe fits. Many back-end members of the preceding Silent Generation were anything but silent and prefer, indeed demand, to be identified with boomers, their younger brothers and sisters. Though some late boomers look on the generation with disdain, many children born in the early 1960s grew up relating more to their immediate elders than to the often disaffected, cynical group that followed.

The oldest people in this book, New York State Supreme Court Justice Leslie Crocker Snyder, and John Gage, the chief science officer of Sun Microsystems, both born in 1942, are hardly silent types, and the youngest, filmmaker and AIDS activist Victoria Leacock (b. 1963), is anything but disaffected. All three identify themselves as Baby Boomers.

WE ARE NOT what you think. Although often referred to interchangeably, the Baby Boom is not the self-styled counterculture that flowered in the 1960s. The groupings do overlap, often to the detriment of the boom in general, which is more diverse and accomplished than the sex, drugs, and rock 'n' roll-driven counterculture it ushered in. Conventional wisdom has it that the Baby Boom peaked as a social force in summer 1969 with Woodstock, and began a descent into drug-induced paralysis and irrelevancy that winter, after the famously murderous Rolling Stones concert at Altamont, California. In fact, it was only the counterculture alliance of anti-establishment radicals and freaks that ended in those eventful months. And radical youth were a tiny—if highly visible—minority.

At the close of the century most of the counterculturalists' revolutionary pipe dreams have been overturned or co-opted. The agents of that overthrow, it now appears, were the generational majority, who turned out to be vastly different than anyone expected. Like First Baby Boomer Bill Clinton (b. 1946), we are not so much committed moralists as morally flexible, ambition-driven pragmatists far more like the parents we rebelled against than we may care to admit.

This distinction eludes many boomers, as well as those who pontificate about them, which has kept discussions of the generation mired in misconception. Ask an early (b. 1942–1949) or middle (b. 1950–1957) boomer to cite generational heroes, and you'll likely hear the names of political figures like Gloria Steinem, Tom Hayden and Abbie Hoffman, or of musicians like Joan Baez, John Lennon and Bob Dylan. In fact, these folks' birthdates precede even a loosely defined start of the boom. Steinem was born in 1934, Hoffman in 1936, Hayden in 1939, Lennon in 1940, and Baez and Dylan (then Robert Zimmerman) in 1941. Indeed, none of the major figures of the civil rights, antiwar or feminist movements were boomers. But this stands to reason. Youth typically admires and makes role models out of slightly older trailblazers.

Despite their constant evolution, those six icons remain tethered to the past. Though Hayden moved off the political fringe and became a Democratic party politician and officeholder, and Hoffman an environmentalist, they will always be remembered as the firebrand leaders of the 1968 youth revolt. The popular image of Steinem is freeze-framed in 1972, the year she founded *Ms.* magazine. And Baez, Dylan and Lennon will be forever linked to the mid-1960s. In truth, theirs is not the story of the generation that followed. If the boom was forged in the fires of the 1960s, its true and lasting accomplishments came later.

Baby boomers have reinvented themselves time and time again. When the hookah-smoking caterpillars of the 1960s turned into butterflies in the early 1980s, our flight patterns were informed by strong recollections—accepted or rejected—that affected everything we've done since. "If you remember, you weren't there," we say. But we were there, and loath as we are to admit it, we remember plenty.

I WAS BORN smack in the middle of the Baby Boom, in 1952, and grew up in one of the Levitt-built neighborhoods of Long Island, just outside New York City, that sprang up after the war to house new families of returning veterans. My parents—a former nurse and a newspaper columnist who served in the World War II Coast Guard—were both born in the second decade of the century. I was raised in the relative prosperity and surface calm of the Eisenhower-era economic boom, when abundance and upward mobility seemed assured. My first pair of baby shoes was bronzed. The Beaver and Eddie Haskell, Clarabell, the Mouseketeers, Mr. Wizard, Princess Summerfall Winterspring, Howdy Doody and Topo Gigio were beamed to me from the tiny, flickering screen of a huge wooden-cased black-and-white television set. I wore a Davy Crockett coonskin cap and carried a Roy Rogers lunchbox, and lived amid the ceaseless wonders of the American century.

I studied science and "new math" because we were lagging behind the Russians. The Cold War and its deadly symbol, the Bomb, which we'd created to end World War II, were constant threats. I was regularly forced to crouch under my desk in elementary school during air raid drills because the Russians were supposedly coming (they'd developed their own bomb in 1949, and though only we had dropped one, *they* couldn't be trusted). At age eight, I wore a Kennedy for President button and worried about Francis Gary Powers, whose U-2 spy plane had been shot down over Russia. At nine, I faked a stomachache to stay home to watch Alan Shepherd become the first American in space; at ten, I was sure the world was ending during the Cuban Missile Crisis; and at eleven, I spent four days watching the aftermath of Kennedy's assassination on television. Like millions of others, I saw Jack Ruby shoot Kennedy's alleged killer, Lee Harvey Oswald, live on TV, a defining moment at the Baby Boom family hearth—the end of the last generation's America, the beginning of ours.

Three short months later, the Beatles arrived and the world began to change at an ever-accelerating clip to a subversive soundtrack of Top 40 hits. Two years later, I discovered Bob Dylan, the first pop musician to tie high-minded ideas like peace, justice and surrealism to the lowest form of music around. By 1967, I was wearing bell bottoms, boots and protest buttons, listening to Malcolm X speeches at the local Economic Opportunity Council office, and marching for peace in Vietnam on Fifth Avenue in New York City. I read about Timothy Leary in *Life* magazine, tuned in to FM radio, bought Mothers of Invention, Jefferson Airplane and Jimi Hendrix records, and smoked my first marijuana, shortly after finding a pack of Zig Zag rolling papers in the street while hitchhiking. When I brought home the exotic little folder and asked my father what it was for, he knocked it out of my hand. Needless to say, I found out, fast.

In summer 1968, my concerned parents refused to let me go to the Democratic party convention in Chicago, so I watched on TV as Hubert Humphrey defeated Minnesota Senator Eugene McCarthy, and Chicago's Mayor Richard Daley and his blue-clad police force beat back the children's crusade behind McCarthy's peace candidacy, destroying any lingering belief my friends and I and thousands like us had in traditional electoral politics. Chicago clarified the curious disaffection that had lingered in the psyche of the Baby Boom ever since those shots were fired in Dallas in 1963. We were now in open opposition, and anyone our age who didn't agree was excommunicated, demonized, *not young.*

The following summer, in July 1969, mankind—American mankind, in fact—set foot on the moon. But I didn't watch; I didn't care. And neither did my new friends. By fall my suburban peers were taking everything from LSD to speed to Seconol, occupying the high school auditorium to protest the National Guard's shooting of students at Kent State University, and putting out an underground newspaper full of innocent poetry, protest and four-letter words. Though I took my share of drugs, politics was still what got me high—until the day a fellow marcher pulled an apple out of my hand at a demonstration, yelled, "Don't waste it!" and tossed the fruit through the window of a stock brokerage. That was the moment I realized the counterculture might be moving farther and faster than I wanted to go.

Still, in one of the first college classes defined by affirmative action goals, I managed to become a sort of pioneer. Of course, only at a formerly all-women's school could a relatively but not spectacularly intelligent white male from Long Island be a member of a minority. When I arrived at Vassar College in 1970 as a member of its first coeducational freshman class, the sexual revolution was nearly a decade old. I made it my business to catch up. Luckily, in those days, the worst thing you could catch from promiscuity was a shot of penicillin.

My freshman year ended with another building takeover—this one inspired by the school's decision to deny tenure to Vassar's more vocally left-wing faculty members and to open a technology school on our Poughkeepsie, New York, campus, in concert with the local computer giant, IBM. Like savage little latter-day Luddites, we dubbed it V.I.T.—the Vassar Institute of Technology—and drove a spike through its cyberheart. But we couldn't save the radical faculty. Their day was done.

We'd lost the war in the streets. Richard Nixon was president, and his Silent Majority had routed our ragtag troops of wannabe revolutionaries, sending the most radical among us underground to blow things up in increasingly futile gestures against a powerful state that could not win the war it was waging but knew how to kill students and Black Panthers. The rest of us began an unorganized retreat into the self. Tom Wolfe's Me Decade had dawned, and though some called it spiritual awakening, we were actually putting our former selves to sleep.

Midway through 1971, whatever was left of the "Movement" at Vassar began to disappear. Our politics weren't so much repudiated as simply left behind like so many Herman's Hermits records. We took drugs and had fun, instead. The campus soon split between two types of "heads." On one side were fans of Quaaludes, the suddenly fashionable soporific both renowned for enhancing sex (before delivering users into a near-coma) and disparaged as a CIA plot to quash opposition. Then there were the speed freaks and acidheads, whose edgy disdain for those who took downs knew no bounds. In between were a small core of if-it-feels-good-do-it experimenters who were up one night, down the next, bedding boys, girls, and both if they had the chance. If we had a movement, it was hedonism. In the words of the politician George Washington Plunkett, "We seen our opportunities and we took 'em."

Within a matter of months, I'd evolved from head of the New Student

Union—the successor to the Vassar chapter of the radical group Students for a Democratic Society—to rock critic for the school newspaper. Like all good college sophomores of the time, I'd discovered decadence. I read Huysmans, Baudelaire and Rimbaud; listened to T. Rex, David Bowie, the New York Dolls and Patti Smith; made my first pilgrimage to Max's Kansas City, the New York City bar where bohemia blended into glam rock; and had my first taste of cocaine and first—and last—of heroin. (I'm not running for president, so I can just admit it.)

Through the rest of the 1970s, I worked but mostly played as a rock writer and magazine editor, extending my adolescence by making a living out of what was once an enthusiasm. By the end of the decade, when corporate rock and disco made music mechanistic and soulless, it was time to get serious. I cut my hair, bought a suit, and began a series of nine-to-five jobs. Though I affected to despise Yuppies, the materialistic back-end boomers who'd come of age well after the economic expansion of the 1960s, I was in training to become one.

The transition wasn't easy. Others used communes, eastern religions, or self-actualization movements like *est* as their way out of the 1960s. Sex and drugs had been my escapes, rock music my refuge. Now I began to repudiate them all. In 1980, I made a portentous move from a loft downtown to an apartment on the edge of the canyons of midtown Manhattan. I started to care about a career and making money. I still spent time with druggies, but now saw their pathos. I kept playing the field, but worried about herpes, a new sexually transmitted disease with no cure. I began seeing the woman I would later marry; my penultimate lover went on to contract AIDS.

By 1984, at age thirty-two, I'd finally begun to focus. I'd identified a journalism beat—fashion and society and celebrity—that suited my taste for the prevailing *Zeitgeist*, found a job, joined a gym, bought some stocks and a co-op apartment, and sold half my record collection. As "dinks"— double income, no kids—my wife and I were financially stable. Like Madonna (b. 1958), whom I soon interviewed for *Vanity Fair*, I was living happily in the material world. And that November, in what seems in retrospect a significant rite of passage, I voted for my first Republican presidential candidate, Ronald Reagan (although I hedged my bet by writing in *my* dream ticket of Reagan and the Democratic candidate for vice president, Geraldine Ferraro).

I bought my first personal computer, a Kaypro 2, in 1984. A year later, I found myself, to use a 1960s phrase, in the belly of the beast when I went to work as a fashion columnist for the *New York Times*. Clothing designers, the new imagicians, had replaced rock stars as cultural locomotives. Many were baby boomers, as were most fashion photographers and editors and the bulk of their market. And now, the same techniques that once sold us records were being used to shrink-wrap us all in name-brand products from underwear to perfume. By the 1990s, when a new fashion market from the next generation emerged, we were ready to sell them our youth—the swinging Anna Sui 1960s! the glam Gucci 1970s!—cannily repackaged and emptied of bothersome social and political meaning. Our sacred signifiers—sex, drugs and rock songs—had devolved into sales tools for Detroit car makers and Seventh Avenue jeans manufacturers. As long as we could dress the new youth up to look like us, we could sustain the illusion that we were still young ourselves.

This book was born about six years later. I'd moved to *New York* magazine and discovered that what I loved was deconstructing the carefully cultivated images of the seemingly superficial people and worlds I covered. Then I was asked to write a profile of the lawyer representing Ivana Trump in her divorce from her boomer billionaire builder husband, Donald. Though ten years too old to be a boomer, attorney Michael Kennedy was a true cultural curiosity—and one of those members of the preceding generation who had set the tone for those of us who followed. An officer in the army training troops bound for Vietnam at Fort Knox, he left the service, left his wife and ran off with his best friend's, and ended up remarried and radicalized in 1960s San Francisco. There he gained fame as a leftist lawyer representing the Chicago 8 and Los Siete de la Raza, then defended drug dealers in the 1970s and gained underground renown for purportedly helping LSD guru Timothy Leary break out of federal prison. Michael Kennedy re-created himself yet again in the 1980s, moving to New York, where he had a grand Manhattan apartment and a beautiful Hamptons beach house, and made a move on Manhattan's high society with Ivana as his vehicle. Examining his journey, I somehow saw my own reflected in it—and wanted to deconstruct that feeling.

How had he gotten from there to here?

How, for that matter, had any of us?

THE STORY OF a generation's cultural impact is best told not through the lives of average members but through those who achieved or failed or both, extravagantly. So a portrait of this generation necessarily focuses on the affluent, the well-educated, the accomplished and the lucky, the bulk of the group that sets the generational agenda.[2] For this American generation, that group was generally, though not exclusively, white and, to a lesser extent, male. Boomers perfected the notion of politically correct colorblindness, but they were not raised with it; other races didn't mix much with the white boomers. Only for back-end boomers like hip-hop impresario Russell Simmons was a truly integrated society a fact of life, not a preacher's dream.[3] This, then, is unabashedly the story of an elite, a story of the city, not the country, of the coasts, not the core, of public life, not quotidian existence, of the coming things, not where they ended, of the ambitious, not the content, of the culturally noisy, not the silent majority.

"Donald Trump isn't a baby boomer," an editor friend balked when I said I planned to include him. Others were surprised at the selection of Simmons, who is responsible for so much of the hip-hop rage that cut the Baby Boom off from the cultural cutting edge. And Republican Congressman David McIntosh of Indiana is not typically associated with the generation whose excesses he eschewed. The point is, not all boomers came from the suburbs, grew their hair long, protested, smoked joints, listened to folk and rock, were sexually promiscuous and wound up in *est*. The differences between the individuals who comprise the generation are as significant as the similarities.

YOUNG ADULTS TODAY still dance to the boom's tune. Obvious stylistic differences (from piercing to rap) aside, their music and dress are about rebellion—kinder and gentler, perhaps, but rebellion nonetheless.

Celebrated by a now all-pervasive media as the prime movers of American culture in our youth, my generation continues to seduce the young with an adolescent solipsism clung to throughout our failures, maturing tragedies brought on by an awesome and sometimes awful self-centeredness. Told from birth we were special, unique, a bit above it all, we've come to believe it. As we move through middle age toward the end game, our sense of importance remains self-fulfilling.

It is no surprise to find baby boomers behind movements like post-modernism and hip-hop music. We relish making once-"subversive" notions mainstream and have certainly institutionalized the notion of our defiant, alienated adolescence. Yet we've now acquiesced to precisely those things we railed against in our youth: labels, brands, corporations, celebrities, the establishment, the machine.

In a world where war has been reduced to the third or fourth item on the network news, boomers are preternaturally inured to the low-level chaos. The first generation to grow up with remote controls, we invented channel-surfing and attention-deficit living. That taught us to be infinitely adaptable, even in the face of the Baby Boom cliché of "diminished expectations." We expect a lot. Which is why it is our hands and brains behind Microsoft, Apple, online trading and Web surfing. In an act of stunning cultural jujitsu, we have turned those diminished expectations into a thriving new economy. Or, at least, we want to believe we have.

Experts in imagery, we sometimes grant those illusions more value than we do actual substance—which partly explains why we fall for quixotic movements and false idols, intensely marketed charlatans, rock stars and fashion designers offering instant gratification of desire. We were raised on instant oatmeal. We want what we want when we want it, and generally speaking, we want it now. To a great extent, we've gotten it.

Despite growing older, settling down, marrying, having children, and giving up some if not all of our youthful indulgences, our absolute unwillingness to be middle-aged still marks us. Finally, we're at the point when we must translate experience into wisdom. And it's likely we will, if only because most of all, we intend to keep history's stage as long as we can.

THE NIGHT AFTER Woodstock 1998 ended, Bill Clinton, our "Rock-and-Roll President," as the *New York Times* referred to him in 1997[4], went on television for four closely watched minutes two nights before his fifty-second birthday. The man who'd let the good economic times roll finally admitted, after seven months of heated denials, that instead of saving Social Security, let alone establishing a new moral order, he'd been letting his own *bon temps roulez* by engaging in adulterous, one-way oral copulation in the White House Oval Office with a woman less than half his age—Monica Lewinsky (b. 1973), the pulpy, sexually adventurous daughter of two Baby Boomers. The seamy affair seemed an apt representation of something larger, for here was youth fellating the man chosen to symbolize the generation that became the very font of Youth, reinforcing that he and those he stood for ("We elected Bill Clinton, and he is us," wrote Rob Morse in the San Francisco *Examiner*[5]) are still potent, attractive, vigorous—*young*. Boomers could forgive Clinton a last burst of selfish stupidity. But they regretted it in the morning, disgusted by his weakness and their need to defend it. We are often graced with guilt over the advantage we have taken.

Clinton was hardly the first president to engage in extramarital sex during his term, but he was the first to be pursued by a pack of radical fundamentalists intent on repudiating the last fifty years of American history and returning us to Puritanism. The first to have his private life made so brutally public (ironically via an instrument, the Internet, that in many ways embodies the liberation ethic of his generation). The first to be forced by an inquisition to confess to his adulterous sexual escapades. Pundits of all ages leapt on that admission and used it to tar Clinton and everyone his age, declaring that he represents the worst traits of the Baby Boom, a generation that, in the prophetic words of Clinton's future wife, Hillary Rodham (b. 1947), at her college graduation in 1969, has spent its lifetime "searching for a more immediate, ecstatic, and penetrating mode of living."[6]

Here was proof, they said, that by defying all tradition, by letting it all hang out, the Baby Boom has been responsible for a plague of generally agreed-upon modern pathologies, notably drug abuse, promiscuity and lawlessness, and other subjects of debate: abortion, alternative sexual behavior, the coddling of criminals, political correctness, the cults of grievance and victimization, identity politics, declining standards of decency, discourse and education, and general incivility.

Whichever side of these battles boomers are on, one thing is sure: they are absolutely certain they're right.

Boomers, who now form the bulk of the country's adult population, chose to support their good-times guy. We sent out a clear message about using Baby Boom foibles as fuel for the politics of personal destruction and saved Clinton's presidency, even if many of us had to hold our noses to do it. That's how the generation has usually dealt with its overripe past. It wants forgiveness, not reminders. Jann Wenner (b. 1946), the publisher of *Rolling Stone*, whose drug-taking and carousing are the stuff of legend, and who celebrated his midlife crisis by leaving his wife for a younger man, neatly summed up the Boom's attitude toward Zippergate in an editorial.

"It's been fun," Wenner snickered. "Enough."[7]

Deny or dodge: that's the way we've done things. "I didn't inhale," Clinton claimed. I did inhale and remember anyway. We did drugs, had sex, dodged the draft, and indulged in oedipal fantasies of a bloodless "revolution" fought to the beat of The Rolling Stones record *Beggar's Banquet*. We lived like libertarians while supporting social engineering—for everyone else but us. We had a thoroughly irresponsible blast. Sure, we did good—a lot—in opening America up in a hundred different ways, creating a more inclusive and tolerant society, but that was counterbalanced by, as Neil Young (b. 1945) put it, "the damage done." Along with the rules, we shucked too many standards and hard-earned lessons of history.

So Clinton's lowly acts attained the status of generational apotheosis. "Suddenly," wrote Maureen Dowd (b. 1952) of the *New York Times*, "Baby Boomers realize that, despite a buzzing economy and a passel of luxury goods, we are going to die without experiencing the nobility that illuminated the lives of our parents and grandparents."[8]

If the president did not represent the best of us, he was a fair approximation in 1996, when we reelected him, and again in November 1998, when, though ambivalent about it, we punished the Republicans and, reaffirmed our allegiance to the president.

The Clinton-Lewinsky scandal hovered in the background of all the conversations contributing to the story that follows. They began just after Woodstock 1998 and ended in February 1999, just after the impeached president was found not guilty by the U.S. Senate. Some characters in the story know the Clintons personally. Some support them. Others hate them passionately. All found their situation symbolic. And none seemed terribly surprised that our First Boomers had ended up in such an unholy mess.

It hasn't been easy for the Baby Boom to grow up.

Childhood

JOHN GAGE (B. 1942), chief science officer for the Palo Alto, California-based computer giant Sun Microsystems, is driving through the warehouse district of San Francisco in his used Volvo. As he makes his way to an appointment with a startup software company, the evangelist for this $10 billion manufacturer of networking computers talks to me on his cell phone about Sun customers, "people who are creating brand-new things, making orchestras play inside the computer," he says. "They need tools, and they don't just want them to work; they want to know how they work."

Gage parks his car. "I'm going to walk in, and there will be six people who are writing software to make smart cards to move money around the world," he tells me. "This small company will develop the software, and then they will deliver it on a really tiny embedded consumer device that costs fifty cents. Here's the loading dock. I'm going in." And with that, he snaps his cell phone shut like postmodern punctuation.

Gage's father, a Texan prodigy, graduated from UCLA at nineteen, served as a lieutenant in the World War II navy and then became head of logistics for California-based Douglas Aircraft (later McDonnell-Douglas), moving his wife and son to Hollywood. In 1950s Los Angeles, pop music drove the city's tawny youth, and songs like "Sh-boom" told of worlds beyond the manicured lawns and perfect facades of Beverly Hills, where Gage had a paper route. L.A. was a blenderized city. Someone from Ohio lived next to someone from Massachusetts who lived next to someone from Mexico, creating a strange new sense of freedom. Like many his age, Gage got the feeling anything was possible.

Just as Gage was about to enter Hollywood High, his father moved the family to Newport Beach, a center of America's new space program, where he was building a factory to manufacture the McDonnell-Douglas Atlas rockets that would carry America's first astronauts into space. The space program symbolized modern American civilization, and its soul, Gage says, resided in Southern California—before the population explosion crunched the place under loop-de-loops of freeways.

Young Gage was Big Man on Campus: student body president at Newport Harbor Union High School and a three-time all-American swimmer. He also worked as a lifeguard at a body-surfing beach, and at night ran the parking lot at the Rendezvous Ballroom, where Jan & Dean played and beach music like "Wipe-Out" and "Pipeline" poured from tinny dashboard radios. "Swim, surf, study, sail—I had a rich life," Gage recalls. Not much different from any prosperous white war baby growing up in a nation of victors.

Despite superficial homogeneity, Newport Beach had its divisions. The school Gage attended attracted students from rich coastal towns, adjacent working-class neighborhoods and agricultural areas; the 4-H Club crowd was as big as the surfer clique. Yet Gage's family were Texas Democrats amid the conservative Republicans of Orange County who felt that their riches meant they were never wrong. Watching his father operate with calm and reason in that six-martini right-wing world, Gage grew curious about what lay beyond. The conjunction of popular culture and technology fed that desire. Gage listened to the radio deejay Wolfman Jack broadcasting rock 'n' roll that was out of control from somewhere below the Mexican border; it was out of control of advertisers and of the mechanisms of power that had run the country for almost 200 years.

By the time Gage graduated from high school in 1960—just before John F. Kennedy was elected president—he wanted out of Orange County. That fall, he entered the University of California at Berkeley, planning to follow in his father's footsteps; Berkeley was a national center for mathematics and physics, home of Nobel laureates, the place to be if you were inspired by Kennedy's can-do optimism about new frontiers in science and space.

After a year, though, Gage dropped out. He was restless, tired of school. He ended up in a beach town—he knew beach towns—only this time it was St.-Tropez, France, where he ran a seaside concession for a time. He was back in Berkeley when Kennedy was killed in Dallas, Texas, a year later, on November 22, 1963. That moment riveted his attention. It seemed like the death of something far greater than one man.

* * *

"IT WAS EXHILARATING," Jim Fouratt (b. 194?)[1] says breathlessly. "This twenty-one-year-old, five foot-two gay boy gets murdered and the cops say it's not a hate crime—they have yet to admit it's a hate crime. But to feel all that energy and youth excitement, and all those older people there, and running in the streets . . ."

The night before, Fouratt, a professional trend-hopper who's been everything from a Yippie! to an AIDS activist, had gone to a demonstration protesting a gay-bashing murder in the Midwest. He'd brought an Indian drum and beat it, just as he did in the 1960s. "Last night meant to me that no matter how many times the homophobes, the right wing, the Republican party, the Democrats and the liberals abandon the expression of freedom, people are not going to roll it back," he says. "It's this thing in the human spirit. For all the decadence, the depression, the Prozacing of our culture, there's still a vibrant energy that's about transformation. Could I debate some of those young kids with their tattoos and their anger? Of course. But I knew which side I was on."

He pauses a moment. "I'm not a relic."

Fouratt is the oldest offspring of an unmarried teenage mother and a wealthy man twenty years her senior who left soon after their third child was born. When Fouratt was three, his mother moved to Washington State, where *her* mother lived, and shuttled her children back and forth before marrying an Irish World War II veteran working as a short-order cook in Rhode Island, a widower with a child of his own.

Fouratt remembers spending a lot of his youth taking care of his mother. But he was sickly himself, between the ages of six and ten suffering from rheumatic fever, leukemia and polio. ("I'm one of the first cases cured through massive doses of cortisone, a wonder drug at the time," he says.) He missed third through fifth grade and watched television instead—everything from soap operas to the hearings of red-baiting Senator Joseph McCarthy, whose search for Communists in every nook and cranny of American life created national hysteria and intrigued Fouratt. When the boy heard about a Committee of One Million Americans supporting McCarthy, he toted petitions for the cause around the neighborhood. "Nobody would sign, and when I told my mother, she ripped them up."

Fouratt was enrolled in a Christian Brothers private school. A good dancer and a member of the Rhode Island chapter of Junior Achievement, he ran for class office but failed, he thinks, because his fellow students knew before he did that he was gay. Fouratt finally realized he was attracted to boys when he was thirteen. His sexual experience was limited to fleeting encounters while hitchhiking. ("You can do it to me," as he puts it.) His mother and stepfather, highly permissive, took him to a strip club for his sixteenth birthday. The boy was mortified.

But Fouratt's interests were catholic for a Catholic: he admired Dorothy Day, the Berrigans and other religious antiwar activists, and was fascinated by the outsider culture of beatniks and bohemians. College didn't interest him, so at sixteen he entered a Paulist seminary to become a priest. His motivation, he now thinks, came from "being a gay kid who wanted to feel good about himself and didn't quite know how."

Fouratt spent eighteen months in the seminary. Toward the end he went to a beatnik reading in nearby Baltimore and was instantly attracted to one of the poets. They had sex, and three weeks later, Fouratt contracted crab lice—a mystery to him but not, unfortunately, to the head of the seminary, a former Marine chaplain, who quickly deduced how he'd gotten them. The timing couldn't have been worse. Two other students had just been discovered as lovers and thrown out of the seminary. In the inquisitorial atmosphere that followed, one of Fouratt's classmates searched his dresser drawers, where he found photos of nude men Fouratt had clipped from magazines—for an art project, he says. He was given six hours to pack and a bus ticket home. He got off the bus in New York and headed straight to Greenwich Village. It was 1961. He was still a teenager and looked years younger.

When he stepped off the Greyhound bus, Fouratt headed to Sheridan Square, where the bohemian demimonde shaded imperceptibly into New York's still-secretive homosexual underground. "When I came to New York, like many young artist types, it wasn't to be gay," he says. "It was to be a bohemian, a beatnik, those were code words." Fouratt stayed in the city through the summer, and then moved to Cambridge, Massachusetts, where a friend had a dorm room at Harvard. The following spring, New York's experimental Phoenix Theater set up shop in Cambridge. Fouratt fell in love with one of the actors.

Unfortunately, when he followed the fellow back to New York, Fouratt discovered his love object was otherwise engaged. Since theater folk nonetheless gave him the sense of community he craved, he got a job at the Phoenix, decided to become an actor, lived on Coca-Cola and pizza, and joined the Village social scene, hanging out in West 10th Street bars like Julius and The Knight's Inn, where the artistic clientele could not care less who went home with whom. "Julius wasn't a gay bar," he says. "Everybody was gay and yet nobody was gay, you know?"

Fouratt's new friends provided entrée to New York's thriving underground theater scene. Jim began performing in minor roles at Caffe Cino, a legend on the Off-Off Broadway circuit, and with the Living Theater, an avant-garde operation known for its radical political agenda, interracial company and experimental productions. "Being in that world was exciting," he says. "People smoked marijuana, and there were black people and jazz musicians and poets, and the poets were attracted to the folk music scene, and there was all this crossover going on. We didn't want to be mainstream. It wasn't about politics. It was about other kinds of values."

Fouratt soon became a minor player in major events. He scored heroin for the comedian Lenny Bruce. In 1963, when the Internal Revenue Service seized the Living Theater's performance space commune on 14th Street, Fouratt was sent to get bail money from Mickey Ruskin. Ruskin owned Les Deux Megots, a Beat poet coffeehouse, and had just taken over The Knight's Inn and turned it into a jazz club.

Fouratt met Communists, anarchists and Beatniks committed only to antimaterialism. Saul Gottlieb, a radical and Living Theater fund-raiser, invited Jim on a cross-country drive to San Francisco, where Fouratt got a taste of North Beach bohemianism. In November 1963, back in New York, studying at Lee Strasberg's Actor's Studio, he was en route to class in an elevator in Carnegie Hall when someone boarded and said, "The President has just been shot." The elevator got stuck between floors. By the time it started moving again, it was confirmed that Kennedy had been killed, "and one of the women in that elevator had slept with Kennedy," Jim says with impish pride.

"SHE'S GREAT STUFF, she really is," a New York City detective says as she heads into Acting Supreme Court Justice Leslie Crocker Snyder's heavily guarded courtroom. The guards are necessary; Snyder (b. 1942), a soft-spoken blonde with fine features, brown eyes and pale pink nails, has gained a reputation as a hanging judge in her sixteen years on the bench. She's been nicknamed "Ice Princess" and "213," for the total years in jail she gave the leader of a drug gang called the Jheri Curls. In 1998 glassine bags of heroin stamped with her picture and the brand name "25 to Life"—after the maximum sentence for drug dealing—went on the market. It is a condition of her cooperation that I not give details about her family. She's about to demonstrate why.

Judge Snyder is sentencing a drug gang leader, Carl Dushain, and his chief enforcer, Danny "Cash" Green, who murdered a Harlem building superintendent as he begged for his life because they thought, mistakenly, that he'd snitched on them. They'd kidnapped and hung another victim from a pipe in a rat-infested dungeon, all in the course of running a multimillion-dollar crack and PCP trade in New York's slums. The slogan of their Dushain's Crew, gangsta band, was "Drugs, Sex, Murder."

Dushain stands before Snyder in chains. He has recently ripped a steel door off its hinges to smash a window in a failed escape attempt. He claims he was framed. Quietly, in a tone as sharp as a stiletto, Snyder calls him a monster, "grotesquely deviated from the norm." He stares back coldly. Decrying Dushain's release from jail in 1991, a mere three years after he shot his seventeen-year-old girlfriend in the head, Snyder catalogues his crimes: intimidating a witness with a photograph of a dismembered body, turning young girls into drug accountants-cum-sex toys while claiming to be helping them with penmanship. "I don't know whether you are sociopaths or psychopaths or if you had deprived backgrounds and *I don't care!*" Snyder nearly spits. "You've set a subhuman standard that's hard to achieve. Listening to you has made me sick." She gives Dushain a minimum 150-year sentence and Green 91 years in prison.

Snyder grew up in a family of scholars; her father was a professor of eighteenth-century French philosophy and literature. Leslie spent her infancy in the Virginia countryside, then at age eight moved to Baltimore, where she attended a private country day school on full scholarship. Their academic lifestyle—hopping from school to school, grant to fellowship—made their lives rich but kept them relatively poor. Summers were spent in Europe, where relatives owned hotels in Monte Carlo and London.

Snyder's father was usually immersed in his work. Her mother, who had a master's degree in French literature, was her inspiration. Though she worked as her husband's editor and assistant, she made sure her daughter understood that wasn't the only way for a woman. "My mother was a feminist before her time," Snyder says. "She would say to me, 'You can do anything you want. Aim high.' She was frustrated and wanted me to have a more satisfying existence."

Snyder's childhood was insular, "almost a time warp," she says. Her parents were New Deal Democrats, beliefs they expressed only in the voting booth. On trips to New York, where her family had more rich relations, she was cosseted, dining in posh restaurants and attending the theater. In Baltimore, she often felt like the odd girl out, the only Adlai Stevenson supporter among the young Eisenhower-era elite, a *New York Times* reader in a school full of debutantes. So though she acted the all-around girl, playing lacrosse every afternoon and cracking the books all night, Snyder always felt different. "That made me even more determined to have my own career," she says. In 1954, Snyder's parents moved to France while her father wrote a book. She attended a lycée, learned to speak French, Greek and Latin, went to museums, and lived in a bubble. Back in New York at fourteen, her protective shell cracked. She saw Elvis Presley on *The Ed Sullivan Show* and "absolutely flipped," she says. "I had a little inexpensive record player and I started collecting forty-fives, so I associate that music with sexual stirrings, real adolescent feelings." Snyder had another secret vice, one fewer of her contemporaries shared. On Sunday nights, she would go to bed early and tune her clock radio to a weekly show about the FBI's Ten Most Wanted List. "I'd take notes," she says. "Very strange." But very real. "As opposed to the eighteenth century," she says with a laugh.

Her family got a television in 1950 and Leslie was allowed to watch for fifteen minutes a night. "But on Friday and Saturday we could watch half an hour," she says. She chose a show called *Man Against Crime*. And when her parents asked what she wanted to be, she had a ready answer. "At five, I was saying, 'I want to be a lawyer.'" By eight, she'd chosen a specialty: criminal law.

By the time Snyder was a teenager, she'd skipped two grades, "although I would say socially I was not particularly mature." She liked boys and harbored secret crushes. But they never got very far. When she started dating a college boy, her father cross-examined him "to the point that was totally inappropriate," she says ruefully. Not until she'd graduated first in her class and headed to Radcliffe at sixteen, in 1958, could she indulge those interests. The school's association with Harvard—sharing every-thing except dormitories—made it virtually coed. In 1961 the birth con-trol pill first became available and caused a sea-change in sexual attitudes and behavior, drastically lowering the potential price of sex just as the first baby boomers reached puberty.

Snyder was young, very young, and essentially unsupervised. "I went a little boy-crazy," she admits. Then she found a smart, good-looking Harvard jock boyfriend who represented everything her parents dis-dained. They got engaged. Her Bachrach portrait ran atop a *New York Times* engagement announcement.

Her fiancé had competition of a sort: John F. Kennedy—the Elvis of pol-itics—who while speaking informally at Harvard would look the Cliffies over, Snyder recalls. "I was just totally smitten," she says. "He was so hand-some and charismatic. I started getting a lot more interested in politics."

* * *

THE TALL, THIN man has a long graying beard, distant eyes, and a pixilated smile. "I was born in Berkeley; I wasn't one of those outside agitators," says Tim Scully (b. 1944). He's still in Berkeley, or near enough, working at the Alameda-based software company Autodesk, where he runs design teams. He's lucky to be here. In 1974 he was sentenced to twenty years in a federal penitentiary. Asked to sum up his life, Scully quotes the Grateful Dead, for whom he once built sound equipment.

"It's been a long, strange trip," he says.

The Scully family came to the Sierra foothills in the 1840s Gold Rush. Scully's father married young and unhappily the first time, and his Irish Catholic parents wouldn't recognize the divorce. So when as an engineering student at Berkeley he married Tim's mother—an English Protestant and the daughter of a major in the Philippine constabulary—he was disinherited and had to drop out and work in a gas station.

Scully was raised in the northern California countryside. His mother was a clinical lab technician, and his dad, after the war, went to work at an oil refinery and later became a federal firefighter. "He felt he was underusing his intelligence," Scully says. "So the family script was, 'Get your Ph.D., get your security clearance, do government research. Don't join any organizations, don't dig girls, because you might get sidetracked.'"

As a child, Scully liked to visit his mother at the lab where she worked, and was fascinated with electronics, flashing lights and lit-up dials. He read science fiction writers Robert Heinlein and Arthur C. Clarke and *Amazing*, a magazine filled with short stories that projected future problems readers would solve. Realizing he'd only get to a good college on scholarship, Scully entered science fairs and in the eighth grade built a small computer that won him a summer job at the University of California's Lawrence Radiation Lab in Berkeley; he stayed in the attic of his grandparents' shingled house there. Back at school, Scully set out on a two-year project he hoped would get him to the University of Chicago: the construction of a linear accelerator designed to bombard mercury with neutrons and create gold. "It's good physics, but it's also alchemy," he says, laughing. His teachers gave him a spare classroom to work in and forgot about him. Their mistake. "I'm sure I was wiping out radio reception for miles around when I turned the thing on," he says. He was about to start making radiation—what a linear accelerator does—when his teachers abruptly called a halt to the project and encouraged him to apply to Berkeley for early admission. He didn't mind moving on. "I was a real wiseass twerp, too obviously smart and socially inept," Scully says. "I hadn't learned how to get along with people." He was too busy dreaming up ways to harness thermonuclear power, although he did make a few friends selling time-delay stink bombs to fellow students.

"They never proved it was me," he says, smirking.

MICHAEL FUCHS'S GRANDFATHER was an immigrant butcher on East 12th Street in lower Manhattan. Today Fuchs (b. 1946) lives a mere block away, but in a multilevel penthouse of glass and dark wood, surrounded by pre-Columbian and modern art and scrapbooks and photos commemorating a stellar career as a corporate maverick in what has come to be called convergent media. Though trained as a lawyer, Fuchs spent nineteen years, most of them as a top executive, at Home Box Office (HBO), the prototypical cable television brand. Named its chairman in 1984, he turned it into the first modern independent movie studio before being forced to resign in 1995 in a corporate shakeup that left him retired and rich, thanks to a multimillion-dollar "golden parachute"—the last in a lifetime of holy grails for aging baby boomers.

Though his name still comes up for top jobs at movie studios or television networks, he says he's having too much fun to take them seriously, driving race cars one day, flying off to Hawaii with his latest flame the next. At the start of an interview in his retirement office on 57th Street, Fuchs paces restlessly before settling in. Though his office is massive and has a drop-dead view of Central Park, it is somehow still confining.

The youngest of three children, Fuchs was born and raised in the Bronx, where his father managed the family business—real estate holdings like the Concourse Plaza Hotel, accommodation of choice for the New York Yankees. So young Fuchs gleaned not only the confidence born of being your own boss but a lifelong devotion to sports.

A precocious child, Fuchs read his first newspaper headline, TRUMAN FIRES MACARTHUR, during the Korean war, when he was four years old. Fuchs's brother, four years his senior, frightened the little boy by telling him that invading Communist Chinese soldiers had spread to Yonkers as a result. Politics seemed important; by age ten, Fuchs was handing out literature for Adlai Stevenson in his second run against President Dwight D. "Ike" Eisenhower.

Although Fuchs was to become a cable TV pioneer, the pioneering days of television—"the fakeness of the sets" of programs like *Captain Video*, which he watched on the family's five-inch black-and-white

Dumont—held little interest for him. Plus, he notes, "television didn't babysit kids in those days. They said, 'Go outside and play.'"

Early on, Fuchs decided he was part of a different generation than his older brother. "His generation expected to go to a good school and just fit in, and the sixties changed all that," he says. "We experienced an enormous amount of volatility, and it became part of our lives. We didn't expect things to just turn out normal."

One thing he and his brother shared, was rock 'n' roll. "I was there at the beginning," Fuchs says. The boys were listening in 1954 when Alan Freed, the Ohio radio disc jockey who gave the sound its name, first broadcast on the New York radio station WINS. Three years earlier in Cleveland, Freed had aired previously banned rhythm and blues "race records," sending record producers across America on the hunt for a white "crossover" artist who sounded black.

That act emerged from Chester, Pennsylvania, led by a hulking singer with a spit curl in the middle of his broad forehead. Bill Haley and the Comets were a modest success until 1955, when their song "Rock Around the Clock" was used in the film *The Blackboard Jungle*. Rioting ensued in movie theaters when it played over the title credits. Soon rock 'n' roll was everywhere. Fuchs and his brother would bring a transistor radio to the dinner table, claiming school news was being broadcast, until their father caught on and put an end to their ruse. But Mr. Fuchs could not stop rock from rolling. Pop music would never be the same. And neither would his teenage sons, who now had a sound entirely their own.

Fuchs entered high school in Mount Vernon, an ethnically diverse, middle-class town on the New York City border, in 1960. Though "the sixties sort of kicked in" while he was there, he says, "there was nothing like what you read about now, with kids and drugs and weapons." Though a good student, Fuchs was no academic star, "because I really didn't work at it," he says. "I used to short-cut everything and was hardly ever prepared." The only place he shined was on the basketball court. Mount Vernon was a basketball town, his high school a local athletic power, and Fuchs practiced and played almost every day. When his parents offered to send him to a private school in New York City, he declined. Young Fuchs had met the privileged kids on the basketball court. He thought they played "like girls."

Fuchs carried his competitive spirit into the realm of current events. "I was disappointed when the Sputnik beat us into space," he says. "I had a public school education that taught us America was the biggest and best at everything." He chuckles. "We were really so provincial."

Fuchs began to think about going into politics. "Kennedy lit it up for me," he says. "He was the president and a movie star and he said the right things." In spring 1963, Alabama governor George C. Wallace tried to stop two black students from entering the state's university. "I remember Kennedy sending [Attorney General Nicholas] Katzenbach down South to face Wallace. They seemed much more activist than the Eisenhower administration. I traveled overseas at that age—I was in Israel the summer of 1962, when I was seventeen—and everyone loved Kennedy. That was the last time working in Washington seemed glamorous." Curiously, Fuchs doesn't remember the Cuban Missile Crisis as anything out of the ordinary. "We grew up having air raid drills, so it was in our mental DNA. I remember many times hearing noises that would make me say, 'Could that be . . . ?' "

Fuchs finished high school in June 1963, and headed to Union College in Schenectady, New York, that fall. He'd wanted to go to Cornell but wasn't admitted. Aiming to be a professional athlete, he was "very casual about college," he says. "I filled out my application on the last night. Everything came to me pretty easily. And coming from a family with a family business—not that I wanted to go into that business—I knew I would be okay."

Years after the fact, Michael Fuchs had a fresh take on Kennedy's assassination, which took place just three months after he started college. He was supervising an HBO documentary on violence when he realized that before JFK's death, random, senseless killing was a rarity in America. By July 1966, when Richard Speck killed eight nurses one night in Chicago and Charles Whitman climbed a tower at The University of Texas and went on a ninety-four-minute shooting rampage that left sixteen dead and many more wounded, these events had begun to seem the eerie norm.

"Something was unleashed that year that was never put back in the bottle," Fuchs says. "It's not a theory that stands up to a lot of questioning, but post-'63 these things happened, and pre-'63 they didn't. If you could kill the prince, anyone could die."

GAZING DOWN FROM where Donald Trump lives and works, New York's Central Park looks like a doormat. In the 1980s, Trump (b. 1946) became a symbol of the small but highly visible group of young men and women who garishly displayed their awesome, often leveraged new wealth. Many have since learned to curb their egos and keep their consumption inconspicuous, but Trump has never been one to hide or be humble.

His office is full of trophies and testimonials—framed magazine covers, keys to cities, sports memorabilia, autographed photographs and drawings of his many properties, some bought, some built, some still in planning. "Take a look at that," the blond, blue-eyed tycoon instructs as I try to begin our interview. "That's my new building opposite the U.N." He doesn't mention that it has so outraged its neighbors, they have launched a public campaign against it.

Trump's career builds on his father Fred's, who before and after World War II constructed millions of lower- and middle-class dwellings in New York's outer boroughs that now house people likely to live their entire lives without seeing the New York Donald Trump inhabits. Like Abraham Levitt, the Russian-Jewish immigrant who built much of nearby Long Island, Fred Trump, the son of a Swedish immigrant, developed the brick pillbox houses many veterans moved into with their families when they came home from the war.

"My dad went down to Newport News, Virginia, where they had the biggest shipyard, and built some quite low-income housing for sailors coming home," Trump says. Then he developed single-family houses and some apartment houses in New York's boroughs. "It was a niche, and he did it really well."

Fred Trump owned about 20,000 rental units and was worth $20 million by the time Donald was born. Fred and his wife raised their five children in a twenty-three-room house in Jamaica Estates, an unusual 500-acre tract of large private residences in New York City that was developed at the beginning of the century and was home to doctors, lawyers, and politicians.[2] "But I didn't view us as out of the norm," Trump says, "and I think that's the way my parents wanted it."

Even as a child, Trump wanted to go farther faster. From the roads and rooftops of the outer boroughs, he would stare at the glittering Manhattan skyline. "I didn't like my father's business; I wanted to be over here," he says, gesturing out his window. "Brooklyn was a rough way to make a buck. If you raised the rent a dollar and a half you'd have people leave buildings. I'd rather sell an apartment for six million dollars."

Trump started going to building sites at age five, drove his first bulldozer at thirteen, and began working as a rent collector for his father soon thereafter. "Building is still my greatest asset," he says. "I get more credit for promotion and finance, but the truth is, what I do best is conceive of something and get it built."

He was a better student on construction sites than at Key Forest, the school he attended in Kew Gardens, Queens. "I was bored in school, understimulated," he says. "I wanted an energy release." He found it harassing his teachers, even punching one,[3] though he'd rather talk about throwing chalk at blackboards when they'd turned their backs. "It used to explode if you'd throw it hard," he recounts with glee.

In 1960 young Trump was sent to New York Military Academy, on the Hudson River near West Point. He still remembers a drill sergeant who brooked no nonsense. "This wasn't like school, where a teacher would say, 'Now, Donald, that's not very nice to do.' This guy would go crazy. He would grab you and throw you out a window. This was a rough group. And I don't say it in a negative way. I thought they were great. This was before you had prohibitions on stuff. Today, he couldn't do that." By the time he graduated, Trump had been made captain of cadets, "rather hard to believe for anybody that knows me," he concedes.

"**TODAY IS THE** anniversary of the Cuban Missile Crisis," Mark Rudd (b. 1947) tells me from his home in Albuquerque, New Mexico. It's been almost twenty years since he's given an interview about his life. And he's been waffling about whether to do one ever since I tracked him down at the junior college where he teaches math. But Rudd has a sense of history—and a new wife, his second, who says that since he likes shooting his mouth off so much at home, he ought to do it for a larger audience. "Fire away," the former firebrand of the Weather Underground finally e-mails. "No, better do that nonviolently."

Rudd's father was brought to America at age eight during the great wave of Jewish migration from Eastern Europe at the start of the last century. He grew up in Elizabeth, New Jersey, two houses away from his future wife, then studied to be an electrical engineer. After graduating college in the depths of the Depression ("the fear of poverty really defined them," Rudd says), Rudd's father couldn't find a job, so he joined the Civilian Conservation Corps and ended up in Utah working with the Navajo. Serving in the infantry in World War II, Jacob Rudd was stationed in the Philippines, preparing to invade Japan, when America dropped the first atomic bombs in 1945. "So I guess Hiroshima saved his life and brought me into the world," Rudd says.

Rudd grew up in a Newark neighborhood shared by blacks, Irish and Jews. They all mixed at his grandmother's candy store. "I was there almost every day behind the counter," he says. Rudd's grandmother worshiped the liberal hero Franklin Delano Roosevelt, and his parents were New Deal Democrats, but the family wasn't political. Neither were they religious. Though they attended services at a Conservative synagogue, the priority was education, based on the principle that "it's necessary to know what's going on because there's always danger lurking," Rudd says.

The upwardly mobile family soon moved to Maplewood, a suburb. Rudd's father ran his own real estate business, so Mark got whatever he wanted. "But they weren't nouveau riche conspicuous consumers," he says. "And I defined myself not as wealthy but lower-middle-class. I always worked odd jobs, mowing lawns and stuff." Rudd was overweight, a loner—"I didn't fit in; I thought I was more mature than the other kids." He preferred his ham radio to sports and read constantly. "That really was my passion," he says. "History. Biographies. Novels. I remember being thirteen or fourteen and my mother saying, 'Don't read Dostoyevsky. It will make you depressed!'" He read the multivolume *World Book* encyclopedia for fun. Years later, he saw himself in the hero of Phillip Roth's *Portnoy's Complaint*, "who was from Newark and knew all the names of the president's cabinet," he recalls. "I didn't know all the names, but I knew a lot of them."

He also knew he didn't like them. As a teenager, he already had a radical bent. He was reading Allen Ginsberg, Lawrence Ferlinghetti and the *Village Voice* by the time he went into Manhattan alone at twelve to take the ham radio operator's exam. By high school, Rudd had like-minded friends. They were all in their school's advanced classes, and none of them worried about college or careers—unthinkable today. When the young teenager heard that John Kennedy had been killed, he was unmoved. "I can't explain it, but I recognized that he was ultimately an American militarist," Rudd says.

The Cuban Missile Crisis had scared the Maypo out of him. And he was worried about Vietnam. There had been only 1,000 American advisers there in January 1961, but within a year that force had tripled. Then it tripled again. Then came June 11, 1963, the day Alabama's Governor Wallace blocked the door of the state's university, President Kennedy announced his support of a civil rights bill, and a civil rights worker named Medgar Evers was shot dead by a sniper in Mississippi. That same, momentous day, a Buddhist protester burned himself to death in Saigon. Copycat self-immolations followed. Rudd was more shocked by the distant events than those closer to home.

He took no pleasure from the Beatles, thinking them trivial compared to American rock, Motown, rhythm and blues and the new protest song movement. He'd started listening to folk musicians like Woody Guthrie and Pete Seeger in junior high. A few years later, he and his first girlfriend started taking the train into New York to see foreign films. Rudd decided that they were a release valve for America's simmering discontent, as were the Beats; James Dean and Marlon Brando; Norman Mailer; the phony-hating protagonist of J. D. Salinger's *Catcher in the Rye*, Holden Caulfield; the incendiary books published by Grove Press; and the "sick" comedy of Lenny Bruce and *Mad* magazine.

Rudd enrolled in Columbia University—mostly because his girlfriend would be close by at Sarah Lawrence, but also because he'd first tasted hot-and-sour soup at a Chinese restaurant near the campus, he says. Through his girlfriend, he'd already met his future: people like Michael Neumann, son of a German philosopher, Franz Neumann, and the stepson of another, Herbert Marcuse, the writer whose synthesis of Freud and Marx would soon make him a hero of what would be called the New Left.

BARBARA LEDEEN (B. 1948) works in a tiny warren of Formica-floored basement offices in a townhouse in Washington, D.C. All around the blowsy, frizzy-haired fifty-one-year-old are political buttons, signs and stickers—almost all bearing slogans making fun of President William Jefferson Clinton: "O.J. Clinton." "Don't Blame Me—I Cooperated with Ken Starr." Then there's a cartoon of three members of the National Organization for Women, with little Willy Clinton sucking his thumb, a brassiere sneaking out of his pocket, over the caption, "You leave our Billy alone . . . the little pervert's strengths outweigh his flaws."

Ledeen, executive director of the Independent Women's Forum (IWF), has been called a Judas wife and a she-wolf by feminists outraged over her opposition to affirmative action, which the IWF refers to as "feminist pork," part of the "victimhood industry." Ledeen embodies what's been called the Second Thoughts movement—a loose agglomeration of former members of the New Left who have rediscovered patriotism after deciding that American democracy not only tolerated but incorporated aspects of their radicalism. That made Ledeen part of what First Lady Hillary Clinton called the "vast right-wing conspiracy" aimed at bringing down her husband's administration.

Ledeen returns the compliment, excoriating feminists and the First Lady for supporting Clinton despite his affair with a White House intern. "Hillary Clinton represents that part of the Baby Boom that dug in for the long march through [America's] political institutions," Ledeen says. "Hillary Clinton is now where she was in 1968. We were wrong then, and they're wrong now."

Ledeen's father was an Orthodox Jew whose family had left Russia and settled in Rochester, New York. Her father spent World War II in uniform, erecting telephone poles along the Northwest coast, building infrastructure to guard against a Japanese invasion. "He loved the army, the heroism, the telephone poles; he loved the West and the mountains and how majestic and beautiful they were," his daughter recalls. "He loved America. Love it or leave it; that was my dad."

Back in Rochester after the war, he worked for his father's painting business and courted his future wife, the daughter of a wealthy German-Jewish doctor. "So obviously this is not a marriage made in heaven, right?" Ledeen says. Shortly after she was born, her mother's parents moved in with them when the doctor, who'd conducted X-ray experiments on himself, developed cancer and had a stroke. An already tense household became "miserable." Her father couldn't support them all, let alone in the style to which her mother's family was accustomed.

Her grandparents had kept some trappings of wealth; Ledeen's grandmother had a concert piano, and Barbara first watched television on a huge Dumont set with a tiny screen in her grandparents' apartment, upstairs in the duplex house they all shared. Though he could hardly speak, as they watched the Army-McCarthy hearings, in which the right-wing senator's accusations that the military was harboring communists led to his own downfall, her grandfather muttered, "Shame. Shame."

After inheriting the family painting company, Ledeen's father, a Stevenson-style liberal, became anti-union and entrepreneurial, and joined one of the Jewish country clubs in the area, "the nouveau country club, which was orange and chartreuse," she says. Ledeen had become a tightly wound coil of resentment. She was the only Jewish girl in her school. She seethed because her parents were always fighting, because they were stuck living with her grandparents. Looking at Jacqueline Kennedy, who accompanied her husband on a Rochester campaign stop in 1960, all she wanted was "to grow up and look like her and not like a Jew," she recalls. "I was a behavior problem; I didn't respond well to people telling me what to do," she adds. "Some things don't change."

An explosion was inevitable. Although she was secretary of her seventh-grade class in 1962, she got expelled for organizing a demonstration against enforced curfews. Her mother promptly took her to her own alma mater, the local private school. When the headmaster asked why she wanted to come there, Barbara said she didn't. "You're just a bunch of rich, spoiled kids," Ledeen snapped.

"You're accepted," the headmaster shot back. "We need you to liven this place up." The world outside only added to Ledeen's melancholy. The Cuban Missile Crisis that fall was "scary as hell," she says. "We used to sit under desks and wait for a nuclear bomb." Then Kennedy was killed. "That was *our* day that would live in infamy."

Private school wasn't easy. Ledeen's family was looked down on by the rich kids. "Dad wasn't a professional man, and I was a wild animal," she observes. "I get to this school and they had expectations about work and intellectual achievement, which I had never been exposed to before." Her parents were called in but couldn't change her behavior. So the school imposed a schedule: "From four to six, do your homework, from six to seven, set the table and eat, from seven to eight you'll be in your room, no telephone calls, no visiting, no radio, no TV," she recites. "And they said to me, 'We don't care if you don't do your homework, but you will not leave your room.'"

For a month, she refused to work. Then, while her friends were discovering the Beatles, she stumbled on *Beowulf*, the Old English epic poem about the adventures of a Scandinavian warrior. "I had never seen a poem," Ledeen says. "I did not know meter or rhyming or rhythm; I didn't know anything about the beauty of language. And I was totally seduced. I could not stop reading and writing. I wrote one poem and then another and another, and eventually I became the star student in literature. I was civilized by this."

"YOU KNOW, THE problem is, they don't remember things," Cynthia Bowman (b. 1949) says of her old friends who once called themselves Jefferson Airplane. The Airplane's singer, Grace Slick (b. 1939), has just released an autobiography. Bowman dismisses it as "mostly fantasy."

"She can't remember," Bowman insists. "She had to call all of us to be reminded. I had to reconstruct her wedding for her entirely. And they're all the same. Marty Balin, Jack Casady, Paul Kantner—they were at the same place at the same time, but the interpretation is entirely different."

Bowman remembers more than they do because it was long her job to be on top of things when the Airplane and its successor group, Jefferson Starship, were flying high. Although the tall, slim, well-coiffed blonde drives a slick sport utility vehicle and wears a tailored black-and-white nailhead suit appropriate for a woman running a million-dollar public relations business, her ragged voice hints at a raffish past. So does her office in the rickety wooden building that once housed The Black Cat, one of San Francisco's legendary bohemian bars, a hangout for homosexuals, artists and writers. She landed here by accident, having once told an employee to find her a new office just before taking off on a trip to Mexico. "I never made a plan in my life, but I end up where I'm supposed to be," she says.

Bowman's parents divorced when she was five. Her father, a radio operator in the Air Force during the war, fled to New York. She, her brother, and their mother moved from their middle-class Ohio neighborhood into a housing project in the Cleveland flats. Their descent from postwar prosperity was abrupt. "Sometimes we had Cheerios for breakfast, lunch and dinner," she recalls. Bowman's mother waited tables and finally moved the family to a better, if still impoverished, neighborhood in 1960.

Meanwhile, her father remarried and prospered, scaling the heights of corporate public relations at Mobil, where he worked on the oil company's sponsorship of public television, and later ran a similar program at United Technologies. Cynthia and her brother spent several weeks each summer in New York. "I remember seeing *Peter Pan* with Mary Martin on my sixth birthday and just being mesmerized," Bowman says. Although she recalls feeling "completely out of sync with that lifestyle," it became her own in fall 1963, when the kids moved in with Dad.

Cynthia was enrolled at St. Hilda's and St. Hugh's, a prestigious Episcopal private school near Columbia University. Bowman wasn't prepared for its rigors or for students far better educated and richer than she. "One girl's father was a vice president at NBC and she'd be delivered to school in a limousine," Bowman says. "I was schlepping on the subway. My experience was so different." She felt unattractive, too. "Very tall, really thin. Everybody had a flip in their hair, a Patty Duke thing. My hair wouldn't do that at all."

No love was lost between Bowman and her stepmother. "She couldn't have any kids of her own and certainly didn't want two miscreants from Cleveland, but she was stuck with us," Bowman recalls. And though he'd eventually stop, her father drank too much. Trouble was all around. Her brother, also in private school, hooked up with a member of the Vanderbilt clan, who introduced him to heroin; he was soon thrown out of school. "Having grown up in the projects, I'd always thought the *solution* was money," Bowman says wryly.

Though she found ways to fit in to her new environment—"I wasn't academically successful, but I was socially successful because I was pretty funny. And I didn't mind being made fun of, either"—she adds that she "was as dysfunctional as a kid can be." By ninth grade, she had become disruptive. One morning, when the girls were having a giggle over a nun with a stutter who was conducting the daily mass, the joke wound up being on Bowman. "I started laughing so hard I peed," she says. "And I got thrown out of St. Hilda's for disrupting chapel, for urinating."

AS SOON AS I tell Doug Marlette (b. 1949) I'm writing a book about the Baby Boom, he starts slamming Bill and Hillary Clinton. He's known them almost twenty years, both as a fellow southerner and as a Pulitzer Prize-winning political cartoonist. "Reptilian," he calls them. "Calculating. Cold-blooded. Astonishing."

Like Garry Trudeau (b. 1948), the Yale graduate who introduced "Doonesbury" in 1970, Marlette brought liberal Baby Boom politics into the funny pages—first as an editorial cartoonist, then through his "Kudzu" comic strip. But unlike Trudeau, a native New Yorker and a full-fledged member of the media elite, Marlette was born southern Baptist and raised to be a racist. He began his career in the Deep South and stayed there after attaining professional prominence, commuting between North Carolina, where he lives with his family in an 1833 farmhouse, and New York, where he's a syndicated editorial cartoonist for *Newsday.*

Marlette is surprised by his own ambivalence about his generation and its first American president. "I'm embarrassed by my younger self," he says that first time we talk. "I'm appalled by the glib, facile narcissism of Bill and Hillary. I've known, liked and identified with him, but what his self-absorption has done to this country is deeply depressing. He doesn't feel anyone's pain. He doesn't even feel his own."

Marlette was born in Greensboro, North Carolina, to a family of yellow-dog Democrats ("if a yellow dog ran as a Democrat, you voted for him"). His grandparents worked in the local cotton mills. "Lint was in the air," Marlette says. "So my people were called 'lintheads.' It's like 'nigger.' My father escaped the mill cycle by the grace of Adolf Hitler." A hospital corpsman in the Marines, Marlette's dad was among the first onshore in the invasions of Anzio and Salerno, carrying morphine instead of a rifle into the carnage and winding up with shrapnel in his forehead. Still he stayed in the Marines, "a lot better living than working in the mills," Marlette says. "So I was a military brat."

In his thirties Marlette learned his family's hidden history. His grandmother "Mama Gracie"—whom he remembers as an overpowering eccentric who chewed tobacco and carried a .38 in her purse—had been assaulted by a National Guardsman during the Uprising of 1934, when a half-million mill workers from Massachusetts to Alabama went on strike, their hopes raised by an early New Deal law granting them the right to unionize. Within three weeks they were defeated. Many went to prison, others were blacklisted. Though it led to the 1935 Wagner Act, which strengthened the right to organize, the uprising was a huge defeat for labor. "All across the South there was a mass amnesia about it," Marlette says.

As a child in Durham, he was taken to Burlington after church on Sundays to visit Mama Gracie and her husband, who lived in a back house and never spoke to his wife, mother of his eleven children— "Tennessee Williams stuff," Marlette says, laughing. On the hour-long drive home, the family would listen to the radio. "That had a huge impact, listening to Jack Benny and the Theater of the Mind," he remembers.

He first saw television at a neighbor's in 1953 and was captivated by Oswald Rabbit and *The Milton Berle Show, I Love Lucy* and Edward R. Murrow. Far less pleasurable was a broadcast he saw at age five, "something about the effects of nuclear war—everyone dying," he recalls. "I couldn't shake this thing; it was the first time I had the feeling things could spin out of control and the world could end and my parents couldn't do anything about it. But I was a sensitive lad."

As a first-grader he watched Mary Martin play Peter Pan on TV. "I remember sitting there weeping, weeping. My parents couldn't understand it. And I was too embarrassed to tell them: Wendy had grown up. I was devastated."

Television also gave him affirmation. "I remember, in '57, the University of North Carolina played Kansas in the national championship, Wilt Chamberlain played for Kansas, but we won in triple overtime, the beginning of the North Carolina legacy of great basketball. I remember the beginning of Andy Griffith's career, a North Carolina thing, too. It was the first time I heard someone who talked like us on national television."

Marlette had the foresight to preserve the cadences of his grandfather, interviewing him on tape when he was in his eighties and allowing him to give his southern-fried politics full vent. They talked about his birth in 1890, about his first vote—for Woodrow Wilson—and about his favorite President, F.D.R., "the only president who cared anything about the poor man," the old man told him, leaving Marlette "all dewy-eyed with sentimentality," he recalls. "And then he said, 'The only mistake he ever made, he should've let Hitler kill them Jews.'

"That's the contradiction that lies at the heart of the Southern Populist, the prideful need to feel that we may be bad off, but at least we're better off than somebody," Marlette says. "What was so interesting about that is that my grandfather was very kind to black people, to Jewish people. But he had these abstract notions that were obscene and had nothing to do with the reality of how he behaved, which was pretty decently, whereas in the North, people have all the correct ideals but behave horribly to other people."

Marlette's parents had the same inheritance; cultural segregationists, they were hostile toward the civil rights movement, quite active in largely black Durham under the leadership of Floyd McKissick, who would later head the Congress of Racial Equality (CORE). When the news broke about the 1954 Supreme Court decision *Brown* v. *Board of Education*, which mandated school desegregation, Marlette's family wasn't happy. And although the Marlettes voted for Kennedy in fall 1960, they weren't reconciled with that, either, Marlette recalls. "Catholics were like Jews. Other. Different. Foreign."

The Marlettes were devout Baptists. "Hellfire and brimstone, pulpit-thumping for Jesus: You'd go to church more than anybody on the face of the planet," he says—except for other Southern Baptists, that is, for whom it was a common experience. "Bill Clinton, Al Gore, we all know the same hymns."

Uncommon was Marlette's talent. As soon as he could hold a pencil, he started copying cartoon characters from ads for *The Mickey Mouse Club*. Once he traced a character, he could do it again and again; his visual memory was superb. By the time he started school, he could astonish friends by drawing Mickey Mouse and Donald Duck. "They would give me desserts and marbles to reward me," Marlette says. A teacher suggested his parents enroll him in a summer painting program. "But I wasn't serious. They said, 'Paint what you see out the window,' and I would paint Popeye." Every day, he'd read the "Peanuts" and "Steve Canyon" comic strips in the newspaper. Every week, he'd spend his allowance on Archie and Jughead, Batman, Superman and Caspar the Friendly Ghost comics. "I could get two comic books and a nickel's worth of gum, or a Cherry Coke and a comic book," he says. "I had my twenty-five cents figured out every week."

In 1962, Marlette was an eighth-grader. "I'd been doing well in school—I'd gone to my first dance and danced the Twist with a girl, was selected president of my class—and then we moved," he says with a sigh, to Laurel, Mississippi, a hotbed of racial unrest. A young man named James Meredith, the grandson of a slave, had sparked a riot when he became the first Black student at Ole Miss, the University of Mississippi, that November (with a little help from the Kennedy administration and the National Guard). A year after that, when Kennedy was killed two states away, Marlette walked home from school, listening to the reaction of his fellow Southerners. "I remember vividly kids cheering," he says. "The Kennedy brothers were Antichrists. It was much more interesting and complicated than the national media portrayed it. It's the Civil War, states' rights, and it's tainted with racism." Marlette headed to a field where he and his friends gathered. "It was a cold November day, gray and overcast, and I had that same feeling I had when I saw the nuclear war thing on television: *The adults are not in charge; you can't count on them.*"

The next February, Marlette, along with millions of others, watched The Beatles on *The Ed Sullivan Show.* "I was embarrassed by how much I liked it," he says. "I was not a hip kid. I was emotionally immature, because I'd started school early. I was behind my friends in going through puberty. They were dating and I was terrified. The next morning, in Algebra, I'm drawing John Lennon, I'm drawing Paul McCartney, and giving them to these cow-eyed adolescent girls who would pay me to draw one of the Beatles. It wasn't until I got older that I realized it was the first time we were all seeing the same things and listening to the same music." Late at night he and his older brother would sit in the car and tune in rock stations from Little Rock and Chicago. "I Want to Hold Your Hand" was number one. "She Loves You" was number two. "Please, Please Me" was number three. The Beatles—and the boomers—had taken over the charts, if not the world.

THE FIRST TIME Thomas J. Vallely (b. 1950) was in Vietnam, there was no such place as Ho Chi Minh City; it was called Saigon. A lance corporal in the U.S. Marines, Vallely won a Silver Star for conspicuous gallantry in combat. Thirty years later, he's finally succeeding at what he and his fellow soldiers so conspicuously failed to do all those years ago: He is making Vietnam a better place.

The bookshelves in Vallely's office off Harvard Square spill over onto tables stacked high with hardcovers about Vietnam, the war that defined the Baby Boom's youth as surely as World War II formed its parents'. As the Vietnam program director of the Harvard Institute for International Development, Vallely helps run the six-year-old Vietnam Fulbright program, which recruits Vietnamese students and professionals for scholarships and graduate study in the United States and offers a bilingual program in applied economics in Ho Chi Minh City for the all-American purpose of preparing Vietnamese managers for an open market economy.

Vallely was born in Boston and grew up in its suburbs, the fourth of eight children of a man who after World War II worked as a lawyer for James Michael Curley, the Boston mayor and political boss fictionalized in the novel *The Last Hurrah*. When Curley left office in 1950, Vallely's father lost his job. But a few years later, he became counsel to the state's then-governor, Foster Furcolo, and finally a judge.

"Someone in Vietnam once asked me, how did you get to know so much about communism?" Vallely says. "I said, 'It works almost the same as the party machine.'"

The Vallelys encouraged their children's curiosity. Their mother was a college graduate and a student of history. When Tom was a boy, the family lived in West Roxbury, an Irish Catholic community "where everyone was a bigot, in her mind," Vallely says. "And she was probably right. She was smart, worldly, and knowledgeable, so we did not get stuck thinking we were superior to other people." She wanted out of the neighborhood, and soon they were living beyond their means in a big, book-filled house in upper-middle-class Newton.

Like most boom-era parents, the Vallelys encouraged their children to follow current events and their own stars. "No one turned out particularly traditional," Vallely says of his siblings. Vallely thought himself the most normal among them. He played Little League baseball, loved electric trains, and wanted to be mayor of Boston. Politics suffused his childhood. Vallely remembers his father wearing Stevenson buttons and renting a television set at their summer house on Cape Cod to watch the 1960 Democratic Convention that nominated John F. Kennedy. "We were not a Kennedy family," he says. But when the president was shot three years later, "we watched the whole thing. I remember my dad crying. I had never seen my father have a tear in his eyes."

For Vallely, who had a bad stutter and undiagnosed dyslexia, school was a place of embarrassment. "I was a good observer but I was not a participant," he says. "Getting through school dominated my childhood." He was the worst student in the family, he adds, "which is basically how I got to Vietnam."

ARRANGING AN INTERVIEW with Marianne Williamson (b. 1952), the spiritual notable, is such an arduous process that at one point, *she* compares it to the Paris peace talks that ended the war in Vietnam. So when we finally begin, I say, "Le Duc Tho is at the table, is Mr. Kissinger ready?"

"Well, I don't know," she answers, "what shape is the table?" She laughs. "Are we dating ourselves, or what?"

The beautiful and celebrated Williamson has sometimes suffered from the side effects of fame, so her cat-and-mouse game, though annoying, is understandable. There are questions that may not be asked (I will ask them anyway) and nicknames that may not be repeated—a potential deal breaker I vow to forgo.

"Deal" language is appropriate. The distilled rap on Williamson is that she's a spiritual snake-oil salesman, more Hollywood than Kingdom of Heaven. She herself has said she wanted to be the Lenny Bruce or Aretha Franklin of the spiritual world.[4] And her agents and publicists do little to dispel the show-biz impression left by a career that began in a Houston New Age bookstore. Williamson's populist preaching, in lectures based on *A Course in Miracles*, a metaphysical tract that proposes belief in God as a sort of psychotherapeutic treatment for sickness, fear and other human failings, led inexorably to the *People–Vanity Fair* circuit, through which so many boomers had already planted roots in the shifting sands of celebrity. In a 1993 article that posited her as "a hustler of happy feelings and intellectual meringue," *Washington Post* sketched out Williamson's "sphere of influence": Barbra Streisand (b. 1942), Oprah Winfrey (b. 1954), Cher (b. 1946), Billy Crystal (b. 1948), and "Hollywood super-player" David Geffen (b. 1943).[5] Shortly thereafter, she added Bill and Hillary Clinton to her flock. In August 1998, she was part of an ad hoc spiritual healing team that ministered to the humiliated president.

Williamson was raised in Houston, where her father, Sam (née Vishnevetsky), a Russian Jewish Socialist, was a lawyer and her mother, Sophie Ann, a housewife. They were Depression-bred Conservative Jews who were also political progressives. A peripheral figure in the leftist Group Theater of the 1930s, Sam Williamson was kicked out of the American Communist Party for being too intellectual, his daughter says. He served as a major in the Philippines under General Douglas MacArthur, and afterward became a leading immigration lawyer, renowned as much for his longshoreman's mouth as his mentoring skills. "He was like a cross between William Kunstler and Zorba the Greek," Williamson says. "True characters are rare these days. Not as in a man with character but just a character. The modern world has become so homogenized that truly unique people—" She stops herself. "Let's just say that he was a very unique person."

Though the family lived in Eisenhower-era affluence, Sam Williamson didn't like the 1950s President, considering "gee" and "golly" the most profound things Ike ever said. His daughter has come to a more positive conclusion, recalling the former general's nobility, his warning against the military-industrial complex, and his admonition that politics should be the part-time profession of every American.

A Brownie and later a cheerleader, Williamson took piano, ballet and acting classes, idolized Eleanor Roosevelt, got good grades, and at her father's urging, read Marx, Lenin and Aquinas. But she had a self-esteem problem. "I shudder at the way children today are slapped so easily with labels of pathology like learning dysfunctions," she says, "because I'm sure if I were growing up now, I would be. The system of education under which I labored did not cater to my kind of intelligence." Williamson took an early interest in religion. "Go away, Mommy, I'm talking to God," she said at age three. But Hebrew school "was not one of the things that fired my religious imagination," she says. "Its superficiality did not make me reject God. But I, like millions of others in my generation, did not receive the spiritual sustenance we perhaps should have. If I had, I would probably be a rabbi today. The idea of being a religious facilitator was in my psyche." Instead, she thought it would be cool to be a priest.

Like so many her age, Williamson was wowed by John Kennedy's performance at his inauguration and, later, at televised press conferences in which he dazzled with his grace and wit. She was eleven and in sixth grade in November 1963. The day before Kennedy died, she'd been in the crowd at his speech at Rice University in Houston. When the news of his assassination came, she ran from classroom to classroom, telling all the other students and teachers.

Every summer, Williamson's father would take her away—to India, the Orient, even behind the Iron Curtain. "When you travel as a child, you become someone not easily susceptible to the illusion of differences," she says. "So when some spin machine tries to project guilt or blame or judgment or anything less than the full respect and honor due all children of God onto any group or nationality, I have a gut sense of rebellion. Because I learned very early we're all the same."

In summer 1965, she went to Vietnam because her father wanted "to show us what war was." Her social studies teacher had told the class that if Americans didn't fight in Vietnam, they would soon be fighting on the shores of Hawaii. Hearing that, her father stood up and pounded the table, roaring, "I'm going to sue the school board! Get the visas! We're going to Saigon!" In their hotel there, he showed her the telephone with buttons marked not A-B-C but Fire—Bomb Squad—Police. Then he took her outside and showed her bullet holes. "These are signs of war," he said. "Don't let anybody ever tell you it's okay."

Though their politics were liberal, her parents' cultural outlook was conservative. Her mother was controlling and frequently disapproving. "I was supposed to lead the revolution, but in white gloves and organza," she says. In tenth grade, she joined a sorority.[6] "I'm not someone who got it in 1965 or 1966. I was still a cute cheerleader, a student council type— but falling in love with the boys with long hair."

If mama didn't like it, so much the better.

I FIND STEVE Capps (b. 1955) in cyberspace. A friend tells me about him and sends me the e-mail address of his wife, Marie D'Amico, a lawyer specializing in intellectual property in cyberspace. She forwards it to Capps, who e-mails back to me. He tells me his office is thirty feet from his wife's at their home in Seattle, but they never speak during the day; they only e-mail.

Capps is a software architect for Microsoft, but because he's a star— working for Apple in the early 1980s, he co-authored the revolutionary Macintosh graphic user interface and still retains some fifty patents on which Apple products are based—he needn't report to the office. In the world of the wired, Capps rules. No mere hacker, he writes computer code for a very good living and is known among his peers as the fastest, most artistic coder on the planet, capable of designing everything from artwork to type fonts, willing to fight right down to the last pixel for what he believes consumers want.

It's best to e-mail Capps because his phone is usually lost under the mess on his desk. When he's in the coding zone, he doesn't answer it anyway. The focal point of the room is his computer, no longer an Apple but a Pentium PC. Around it chaos spills off the desk, off the monitor, off the windowsill, into piles on the floor. Atop the monitor are a screwdriver bit, the word *random* from a magnetic poetry kit, a toy ball that plays Spike Jones riffs when you jiggle it, a lead soldier crouched to fire a mortar, a stack of frequent-flier membership cards, 6 CDs without cases, and a thin layer of dust. His wife keeps a to-do list. Even though he is the spiritual father of the handheld computers known as Palm Pilots, Capps jots notes on scraps of paper. Apparently my phone number winds up on one of them, because eventually we get to talk.

Capps was born in Fort Wayne, Indiana. His mother, an artist, is the child of college professors. His father became an engineer for General Electric after serving stateside in the World War II army. "I was a GE brat," Capps says, moving every couple of years as his father rose from designing air conditioner motors into management. Finally, when Capps was in second grade, they landed in Schenectady, in upstate New York, where his father ended up running the company's turbine division. Filled with upper-middle-class scientists and engineers, Schenectady supported a school system so good that though he consistently scored in the top 10 percent of his class, "I didn't think I was anything special," Capps says.

Schenectady was special; it was home to the Knoll Atomic Research Power Lab, a government nuclear research facility run by GE. "There was a reservoir right near my house surrounded with high-security barbed wire, and so of course we all assumed it was a missile site. I'm sure it was a figment of our Cold War kids' imagination." Nonetheless, a friend's father, who headed the psychiatric department at a local hospital, kept a stock of the diet drink Metrecal in the basement. "That was their bomb shelter," Capps says. "My father didn't either fall for that, or he was right-wing enough that he didn't care." Capps's father was a Nixon Republican, "but it was never explicit," Capps says with what sounds like a sigh of a relief.

Though his family was well-to-do, Capps grew up without many of the modern conveniences most boomers took for granted. "We were a media-deprived family," he says. "We didn't have a color TV until my mother won one. We had a record player made of fiberboard." As a youngster, Capps "was essentially anti-social," he says. "I had one good friend and that was about it." He loved photography and film and would make movies with the family's super–8 camera. "We played music and we'd make tapes," he says. But he wasn't listening to the Beatles or the Stones. Inspired by Herb Alpert's Tijuana Brass, Capps formed a band in which he played snare drum and a homemade xylophone. "We were kind of weird," he says. "And we sucked, we absolutely sucked."

RUSSELL SIMMONS (B. 1957) is enduring some serious disrespect in the hallway of Rush Communications, the New York headquarters of his multimedia hip-hop empire. Simmons, a baby-faced mogul in oversize clothes, smiles fondly at a young producer telling him he's too old to have ears and too rich to be street anymore. With a string of curses and an endearing lisp, Simmons snaps that he was making hits when the whippersnapper was still sucking from a bottle. The producer backs off, but the curses continue, fading slowly as the young man wanders off and Simmons breaks into a proud smile. As long as his employees dis him, he's still one of them.

Russell Simmons is more often held in awe than derision. Though he didn't invent hip-hop, or its rap soundtrack, he is generally acknowledged as the man who brought urban entertainment into the mainstream, the baby boomer who killed off the boom's beloved rock and replaced it (on the charts, if not in their hearts) with a sound aging 1960s types regard with the same scorn their parents heaped on Bob Dylan's nasal twang and Mick Jagger's dirty desires. Rap, the latest voice of rebellious youth, beat of multicultural America, agent of change, has made Simmons a very wealthy man. He summers in the Hamptons, winters in St. Barthélèmy, dines at the best restaurants, trades in old Bentleys for new Mercedes, rubs elbows with Ronald O. Perelman and Donald Trump, and gets written up in business magazines. And though he hasn't made the *Forbes 400* yet, only a fool would bet against him. His curriculum vita barely contains his ambition.

Simmons was born in a lower-middle-class neighborhood in New York's borough of Queens, near the South Jamaica Houses, twenty-seven brick buildings built on the site of a squalid slum for "colored people" in the 1940s that became a model for public housing developments. Simmons's father was a war vet who supervised school district attendance for the board of education and went on to teach black history at Pace University. His mother, an artist, taught preschool classes as a social worker in the Department of Parks. But their son was not big on academics.

"Music and sports mattered, and that was it," he says. He cheered for the underdog New York Mets and listened to "all the stuff that didn't cross over into mainstream: the Delfonics and the Dramatics and the Moments, the Spinners and all that kind of shit was hot. Bobby Womack and Al Green." Motown, the first black music most white boomers heard, was too polished, too pop; of its acts, only the gritty Temptations were in Simmons's pantheon. "But James Brown was the hottest," he says. "Every fucking week he'd have eight records on the Soul Sixteen. I remember shit like that."

Simmons didn't idolize President Kennedy, but his parents did. "My father had this letter sent to him by Kennedy thanking him for his support, and being aware of his struggle." Years later, his parents would hang a picture of Kennedy and the martyred black leaders Malcolm X and Martin Luther King Jr. on their wall after all three were dead. "Every black household in America had that picture," Simmons says. "Those three people and a flag behind."

Simmons doesn't remember Kennedy's death, but has a clear recollection of Malcolm X, the fiery black nationalist, being shot early in 1965, just after Russell's family had moved to a better neighborhood. Simmons's father, a civil rights activist, often went to hear Malcolm speak. "My father was a fighter," Simmons says. "He organized picket lines in Jamaica where they'd sing, 'Can't let nobody turn me around, turn me around, glory'. . . Sing that shit and be on the line." Russell rode on his shoulders.

In America's ghettos, some were already haters. But Simmons's parents were integration-era exemplars. They'd taken some steps up the ladder, thanks to the war, the push for equality it inspired, and the opening of civil service jobs to minorities. And they gave their values to their son. "We were conscious of racism and conscious of what our duty was as individuals to rise above it," Simmons says.

WITH HER SPIKY, two-tone hair—blonde with a black diamond in the back—computer chip earrings, leggings and black jacket with badge-laden lapels, Kathryn Bond Stockton (b. 1958) looks nothing like an academic as she and her girlfriend enter the Marriott in Trumbull, Connecticut, near her parents' home. Yet the attire is perfectly appropriate for a hotel lounge or a lecture hall. Neither academics nor academia looks the way it did when boomers went to college, and Stockton personifies the change.

An English professor and director of graduate studies at the University of Utah in Salt Lake City, Stockton is also a leading light of the new academic specialty called Theory. This matrix of new thought, ignited in the questioning counterculture of the 1960s, was "a sudden illumination of how our unexamined habits of mind perpetuated an unjust status quo," the critic Richard Bernstein noted in his book *Dictatorship of Virtue*. "Out of the burning wish for betterment grew what has now become a kind of bureaucracy of the good."[7]

Theory combines comparative literature, the study of culture, and connected philosophical ideas like poststructuralism and deconstruction with innovative academic specialties like new historicism, Afrocentrism, and gender and ethnic studies. It challenges the preeminence of objective truth, rational discourse and logic, among other tentpoles of traditional Western thought, deriding them as oppressive constructs that oppress everyone but white heterosexual males. Though conceived by members of the preceding generation, Theory found a ready audience in students like Stockton, searching for a way to be gay in academe.

A descendent of Richard Stockton, a signer of the Declaration of Independence, Stockton hails from Columbus, Ohio, but grew up in Connecticut, where her family settled in 1961. Her father was born wealthy, but his family was impoverished by the 1929 stock market crash. He met his wife in college, where he studied to be an economist. A Socialist then, he was a strong believer in the civil rights movement, had political aspirations—he lost a race for the Ohio state legislature—and served stateside in the Air Force during the Korean War. Their daughter, a sickly child, spent most of her time with her mother, an early bonding experience she thinks might have encouraged her sexual orientation.

Stockton was three when the family moved to Bloomfield, Connecticut, an island of ethnicity surrounded by "lily-white, absolute Protestant towns," she says. Her father worked as an economist at United Technologies; her mother, who'd studied to be an artist, ran a nursery school. The Stocktons were Unitarians, but most of Kathryn's friends were from Jewish or Catholic families. Politics was a constant subject of dinner table conversation. Her father, a Kennedy supporter, "was very much a young Kennedy type, dashing, attractive, a charismatic presence," she says. "He and my mom went to Kennedy's inauguration, a very big deal for them." Among Stockton's earliest memories is watching the young president speak on television.

In awe of her brother, who is four years older, Stockton became a tomboy. She shared his enthusiasm for the space race. "Your parents would get you out of bed and you'd watch countdowns on TV," she recalls. She was also a sports fanatic. "That was the most important thing in my young life. Football, basketball, baseball, tennis, skiing."

In 1962 one of her neighbors built a backyard bomb shelter, and she and her friends would stage plays and mock weddings on its raised roof. "The bomb didn't seem very real to me," she says. "It was part of life. It just seemed like a remote possibility." She was in kindergarten the day Kennedy was assassinated. "They just dismissed us. I came home and my mother was watching TV and crying. I remember watching the funeral, and my parents bought books about it and saved all the clippings. The day Lee Harvey Oswald was killed, I remember Dad saying, 'The world is falling apart.' That seemed momentous," Stockton says. "If my parents were strongly moved by things, I felt it as a kind of second-order effect, never really feeling them forcefully."

What she did feel forcefully was that she had been born the wrong sex. "In my head, I thought I was a boy," she says. "I was the Dutiful Girl by day, a model straight-A student. I don't think I've ever gotten a B in my entire life." But as soon as recess was called, she says, "I would go out on the playground and play with the boys. Then, after school, I would immediately change out of those clothes and get into my tomboy clothes. For quite a long stretch in childhood, children really are allowed to be strange or different. I think that's what's interesting about being a proto-gay child. There is this problem, and you don't yet know what it means. "

Stockton was "interested in girls like other boys," and even perceived the Beatles through the lens of her sexual orientation. "I have very conscious memories of an attachment, watching them on Ed Sullivan. And then of course we played the Beatles in the neighborhood. Everybody was a Beatle. I was Paul, of course, trying to attract the girls."

IT'S THE DAY after Lincoln's Birthday, 1999, and David McIntosh (b. 1958), a Republican congressman from Indiana and chief ideologue of its Conservative Action Team, has just returned home to Muncie after one of the stranger episodes in American history—the impeachment of President William Jefferson Clinton.

Though McIntosh is a leader of House conservatives, his role in the process was limited. He'd made his position clear, both as an avowed Christian and a highly partisan Republican. "We have to send the message in everything we do that those . . . fundamental moral values that make a society work—honesty, integrity, keeping your word—are important to us," he'd said on *Meet the Press*, shortly after winning reelection in a season that saw many fellow House Republicans go down to defeat. Now, dandling his seventeen-month-old daughter, Ellie, on his knee, the boyish but gray-haired congressman returns to the subject that has consumed him and his colleagues for months. "A whole generation of people who have children have been forced to think about this because their kids have asked, 'What's going on?'" McIntosh says. This Christian conservative had been inspired to enter politics by a fellow Hoosier, George Bush's vice president, Dan Quayle (b. 1947), and by summer 1999 would announce a run for governor of Indiana. Though he is a fierce partisan, he admits partisanship probably isn't an effective means for reaching moral consensus. But he insists consensus must be found nonetheless.

"There have got to be some standards," McIntosh says. "And we have to find a way to establish them. The role of people who believe that the Bible is the source of moral values is to reach out to those who have never experienced it, or have done something that they feel ashamed of and so feel they have to reject it, and say that the ironic message Christ brought was that you have to love the sinner while you hate the sin. Yes, there are values, but above that, there's love, and whatever has happened in your life you're welcome.

"And that is very hard to do in a public discourse."

Public discourse has interested McIntosh for as far back as he can remember. Born in Oakland, California, he grew up in the suburbs of San Francisco, where his father opened a steak house with a partner in 1962. The restaurant was successful enough that the next year, just before McIntosh entered kindergarten, the family moved to a better house in a town closer to the city.

One of McIntosh's first memories is John Kennedy's death. "I remember my mom and dad crying," he says. His mother was a Kennedy Democrat. "Her views were shaped growing up in a small town, then moving to San Francisco, the big city. Before she met my dad, she lived in the Haight-Ashbury area and enjoyed being part of that culture and picked up a lot of postwar modern thought. She was a libertarian liberal. Very strong on equal rights. Racism was wrong, everybody was the same, the color of your skin didn't matter."

McIntosh doesn't know much about his father's politics because he died of stomach cancer in January 1964. At the end of that school year, the family moved to Kendallville, near his mother's hometown in northeast Indiana, where her brothers, both doctors, lived; one hired her as a nurse. Equidistant between Chicago and Detroit and surrounded by lakes, Kendallville, population 7,000, epitomized white, small-town America. First inhabited in 1832, it grew from a single log cabin into a blue-collar town named for a Civil War–era postmaster general and filled with Protestant churches. Many people worked at the Kraft caramel plant, a refrigerator factory, and several foundries that made auto parts. In the 1950s and 1960s, the foundries had recruited coal miners from Kentucky to come north for better pay, and the town filled with yellow-dog Democrats. Mostly, though, there were farmers. "If it was a bad year for farmers, everybody in town talked about it," McIntosh recalls.

Everybody knew everybody else's business in Kendallville, and nobody thought there was anything wrong with that. McIntosh walked the four blocks to school each day, "and if I strayed off the beaten path, immediately my mom knew because three or four neighbors would call," he recalls. "So it was a very sheltered place, a good place to raise a family, especially for a single mom. You didn't see a lot of the social turmoil that was happening in other parts of the country."

NINA HARTLEY'S HOTEL room is getting crowded. She's in Atlantic City for a videocassette dealer's convention that ended a few hours ago; as a superstar of pornographic films and producer of her own line of sex instruction videos, she was a featured attraction. Now she's bouncing around her room with two chirpy young women with unnatural breasts barely covered by T-shirts cropped to show their pierced belly buttons, and lips plumped so full of collagen they look ripe to pop. Their names are Shiloh and Tammi, and they've come with Dr. Phil Good, their boyfriend (the three live together), and a guy named Dave, who is setting up a camera to tape sex tips for something called *Sex Drive Video Magazine*.

Hartley (b. 1959), a petite, blue-eyed blonde, sits on one of the beds, shoeless, dressed in a black and red polka-dot flirt dress, a charm bracelet festooned with a gold vagina, a tiny crystal phallus, a crouching female figurine—a miniature of the Venus of Willendorf, a Paleolithic carving thought to be a prehistoric matriarchal goddess—and a pair of linked female symbols. On the other sits Bobby Lilly (b. 1942), a husky woman in aviator glasses with blonde hair streaked with gray, whom Hartley calls her wife; they share a husband named Dave (b. 1948).

They all talk about life in the three-way world ("Tripods are very stable," says Hartley) and Bill Clinton ("I'd push Bill out of the way to get to Hillary"), before Nina offers up impromptu sex tips for the camera ("A clitoris is not a doorbell; don't lean on it") for an hour. Then, as soon as the lights go off, she strips off all her clothes, poses for good-bye snapshots with her interviewers and, still in the nude, one hand plucking absently at her pubic hair, reveals that Nina Hartley is the nom de porn of a nice Jewish girl from Berkeley, California, a third-generation feminist and child of Communist Buddhists, a Jew-Bu, as she puts it, whose real name is Mitzi.

Mitzi is two years older than Nina. Her mother's family came from a small town in Alabama, where her great-grandfather built the synagogue. Mitzi's maternal grandparents were both professors at the University of Alabama until her grandfather read *Foundations of Leninism* by Joseph Stalin, declared himself a Communist, and promptly got fired. "He became a Jewish pinko nigger lover," Hartley says with a laugh, and went to work for an organization that defended political prisoners. Her grandmother quit her job, and joined him in the state of pariah.

Crosses burned on their front lawn, and her grandfather was beaten and left for dead by a mob that, family legend has it, included one T. Eugene "Bull" Connor, who would come to national attention years later as the chief of police and chief defender of racism in Birmingham, Alabama. By then, though, Mitzi's family was long gone. In the 1940s they moved to California, where Mitzi's mother earned a double degree in statistics and chemistry and tested airplanes during World War II. Her older sister, Mitzi's aunt, realized she was a lesbian and later came to family functions with her husband and their respective girlfriends.

Mitzi's father was Pennsylvania Dutch and German, the grandson of a turn-of-the-century art dealer who raised the boy in strict religious fashion in a mansion in Flushing, New York. A childhood visit to Germany, just as the Nazis began their rise, made him anti-fascist. A sensitive young man, he escaped an unhappy first marriage and moved to California to act. He tried but failed to enlist in the Army during the war, moved to Berkeley, joined the Communist party, and met his future wife when she auditioned for a part in a play a friend of his had written about the Spanish Civil War.

Kindred spirits—"not ideologues at all; they really wanted to make the world a better place," Hartley says, the pair married and quickly had three children. In 1949, Mitzi's dad began hosting a program called *This Is San Francisco* on local CBS radio as Jim Grady. Disillusioned by the 1956 Soviet invasion of Hungary, the couple abandoned communism, but that didn't help "Grady" when a process server from the House Un-American Activities Committee came calling the next year, said he never missed *This Is San Francisco*, and handed him a subpoena.

"He did the honorable thing, didn't name any names, and it ruined his career in[nbs]broadcasting," Hartley says. "And that severely affected my personal life, because it caused anger and resentment. My mother, whose father's politics were a burden on her, married a passionate, idealistic young man who ruined her life. You know he's doing something heroic, you hate him for it, but you can't get mad at him, and that gets buried for, oh, thirty years."

Grady got a series of low-paying jobs. But he'd get fired when, as Hartley says, "the guys in the suits come, knock-knock, 'It's about your employee.'" He was found guilty of contempt for refusing to say if he was a communist.[8] Desperately in need of an escape, the couple took a camping trip to the Samuel P. Taylor Regional Park in northern California in June 1958. "They made love under the moon and the trees and the tent, and Dad hadn't brought the condoms, and my mother's a Fertile Myrtle," Hartley says. "They took a chance, because I'm sure it was a romantic, wonderful moment." Nine months later, their youngest child, a daughter named Mary Louise, whom they called Mitzi, came along. "My mother calls me a purposeful accident," she says. "Which was a nice way of putting it. The emotional reality was, they really had no business having another child, and my mother had to go back to work when I was six weeks old, so I'm put in the care of a competent, caring stranger, but not a parent who really gives a shit." Seven years later, they could no longer afford help. Mitzi's father became a house husband while his wife worked at the California Department of Public Health.

Though she never cried between age six and twenty, Hartley hastens to add that Mitzi wasn't consciously unhappy. "I certainly have happy memories of childhood," she says, "but I was very shy, very malleable, terribly insecure about my worth as a person. I stayed to myself. I had a tree-house. I got lost in books very easily. I loved Prince Valiant and Captain America comics. I remember watching *The Love Boat*, Jackie Gleason, Lucy, *Gilligan's]Island* and *The Brady Bunch*. And I also remember I was one of those incessant talkers. My father called it radar. Keep blipping out until you find someone who'll respond."

CAMERON SEARS (B. 1960) arrives at a Mexican restaurant in Novato, California, near the Grateful Dead's office north of San Francisco, wearing a plain T-shirt over trekking shorts and climbing boots, his brown hair bowl-cut, his beard touched with gray, clutching a cell phone that rings several times as we dine on refried beans and burritos. The Dead is dead. Its days as an active band ended with the 1995 death of its front man, Jerry Garcia, but the Dead as an enterprise lives on. In 1998, Sears was president of Grateful Dead Productions.[9] He seems a little too clean-cut to be the man behind the band that inspired a generation of acid heads and three generations of Dead heads, but then, even the Dead grow up.

Sears was born in Boston, grandson of an Andover professor and the oldest of three children of a real estate executive and his wife, a classical musician. Well-educated and cultured, Sears's father, a sailor in the Korean War-era navy, was stationed in San Francisco when he met his wife, a University of Michigan graduate, waiting on line at the box office of the San Francisco Opera. After he earned his own degrees at the universities of Kansas and North Carolina, the couple moved to Boston. They summered in East Dennis, Massachusetts, on the elbow of Cape Cod, where Sears' ancestors, all seafarers, had built a house 200 years before. Sears' grandmother, who is in her mid–nineties, still lives in the beautiful bayside homestead that inspired her grandson's lifelong passion for the outdoors.

Sears moved to Washington, D.C., when he was an infant, and lived there until he was ten. His childhood was "very conventional," he says. What stands out was going backpacking with his father. And he can't forget the day his parents took him to a downtown office building to watch the cortege to John Kennedy's funeral. The slain president's flag-draped casket was carried out of the U.S. Capitol, loaded on a caisson drawn by six matched gray horses and a seventh mounted horseman and escorted by nine honorary military pallbearers and one riderless horse to St. Matthew's Roman Catholic Church, as an unprecedented gathering of world leaders followed behind. Though he was only three, says Sears, "it made a definite impression."

VICTORIA LEACOCK (B. 1963) keeps a bottle of fortified amber-colored wine called Leacock Madeira on a shelf in the living room of her townhouse apartment in the Chelsea section of New York City. Her family created the brand on the Portuguese island of Madeira, in the North Atlantic Ocean, in 1741. The label tells of her ancestor, Thomas Leacock, and his tenacity in overcoming a vine disease that wiped out many vineyards. Generations later, Victoria would play a small but crucial role in the battle against a disease that wiped out vast numbers of Baby Boomers.

Leacock was born on the fringe of America's celebrity culture. Her mother, Marilyn West, a Midwesterner, had been captivated by the Andrews Sisters when she was fourteen. After sitting in the front row through six straight concerts by the World War II-era harmony group in Chicago, she was invited backstage. With the encouragement of one of the sisters, Maxene, she interviewed them, sold the story to the *Chicago Tribune*, and then moved to California to become a fashion model. Years later, when Leacock learned that her red-haired, blue-eyed mother had been bisexual, she wondered if that explained the attraction. "I think Mom and Maxene were sort of enamored of each other," she says. "Whether it was requited, I never got a word out of either of them."

Back in New York after college, Leacock's mother continued to model (becoming the face of Toni Home Permanents) and had a love affair with France Burke, the daughter of Kenneth Burke, a philosophic and linguistic critic and niece of Catholic activist Dorothy Day. One of France's sisters was married to a filmmaker, Richard Leacock. Raised on a banana plantation in the Canary Islands and educated in English schools, Leacock came to America when the Spanish dictator Francisco Franco nationalized his family's business in 1937. He'd already made his first documentary, which caught the eye of a schoolmate's father, Robert Flaherty, director of *Nanook of the North*. Flaherty and such other family friends as Bertrand Russell wrote letters of recommendation that won Leacock admittance to Harvard.

War broke out in his third year there. Leacock got his American citizenship and enlisted in the U.S. Army, where he served for four years as a filmmaker. When he got out, Flaherty hired him to shoot a film called *Louisiana Story*, which promptly won a British Academy Award. By the late 1950s, Leacock was an unhappily married father of four when his sister-in-law's lover asked him to teach her how to use a darkroom. "Marilyn," he told her, "I am never going in a dark room with you."

In 1959, Leacock's wife left him for another man. Fortunately, his career as a documentarian was just taking off. He'd gone to work for Robert Drew of Drew Associates, home to many of the future stars of documentary filmmaking. In 1960, Leacock, Albert Maysles, and D. A. Pennebaker took off for Wisconsin, where Drew was making *Primary*, about the presidential campaigns of Democratic candidates John F. Kennedy and Hubert Humphrey. They had just developed a way to synchronize sound to motion pictures without cables, creating the raw, spontaneous films that became known as cinema verité.

In 1963, Leacock made *Crisis*, a film about Robert Kennedy's battle with Alabama Governor George Wallace over school desegregation. Between shoots in the South, he would return to New York where, early one evening, he ran into Marilyn West and Maxene Andrews at the Algonquin Hotel. "Who is that man?" Maxene demanded of Marilyn afterward. "You're all red. I've never seen you so flustered."

"That's the man I'm going to marry," she replied. Leacock was enjoying the sudden coincidence of bachelorhood and success. At the end of 1962, "Dad had three girlfriends tell him they were pregnant, all in one month," Victoria Leacock reports. "And my mom was apparently the only one telling the truth." She and Leacock both swore off other women and were married in February 1963. Victoria was born six months later. Maxene Andrews was her godmother. She was barely three months old when John F. Kennedy and an era of high hopes died.

IN JANUARY 1964, Bob Dylan released his third record, *The Times They Are A-Changin'*. Its title was prophetic. That month, Lyndon Johnson, the new president, declared a war on poverty and a military junta took over South Vietnam. The next, Cassius Clay (b. 1942) won the world heavyweight boxing crown and promptly changed his name to Muhammad Ali. Also in February, Dylan and his girlfriend Joan Baez played a concert together in Berkeley before heading to Europe, where legend has it he introduced the Beatles to marijuana.

That spring, crosses and churches burned across Mississippi as a warning to young white radicals from the North who were planning an action

called Freedom Summer, a series of civil rights protests and voter registration drives. Three of the Freedom Riders, James Chaney (b. 1943),
Andrew Goodman (b. 1944) and Michael Schwerner (b. 1940), were
murdered on their arrival in late June by the Ku Klux Klan. Six months
later and fifty miles north in Laurel, Mississippi, the father of one of
Doug Marlette's classmates was arrested in connection with those murders, just as the school year was ending. Laurel was also home to Sam
Bowers, Grand Dragon of the White Knights of the Ku Klux Klan and
one of Marlette's neighbors, who set up wiretaps on civil rights workers.

Marlette had been born in Greensboro, North Carolina, the city where
the modern civil rights movement began in 1960, when four black students sat down at a whites-only lunch counter. More than a dozen years
later Doug was still drinking from "Whites Only" fountains, going to segregated schools, attending racist rallies, and sitting up front in buses
where black people were forced to the back. "*This* is embarrassing," he
says. "My very first cartoon was anti-Martin Luther King." It questioned
how King could win the 1964 Nobel Peace Prize when so much violence
followed in his wake. "I wish I could say I'd had more insight and compassion," says Marlette, "but I sensed the party line. I was a good boy, a par-
ent-pleaser."

Marlette's mother was crippled; she'd contracted polio before the Salk
vaccine and walked with a stiff leg. "So I felt a great responsibility," he
says. "And part of my deal with my mother was to be her agent in the
world—emotionally. I was still in the thrall of my raising, expressing their
views, on the wrong side. But when I went with my dad downtown one
day when there was going to be a demonstration, I had that feeling in the
pit of my stomach again that the beast wasn't far from the surface."

From age nine, Marlette had been reading and collecting *Mad* magazine. Founded in 1952 by William M. Gaines (b. 1922), a diet-pill-gob-
bling grown-up child who'd inherited a company that published comic
books based on the Bible and begun churning out horror and war comics,
Mad was a profound influence on boomers. Parodying everything from
movies and films to its own staff ("the usual gang of idiots"), it fostered an
attitude of irreverence toward authority—any authority. In 1955, when
Mad introduced its gap-toothed mascot, Alfred E. ("What, me worry?")
Neuman, and switched from comic book to magazine format in order to
skirt the Comics Code, a law instituted to protect boomers from corrupting cartoon influences, its corrupting influence increased. By the time
Marlette bought his first issue in 1958, *Mad*'s satire was a well-planted
thorn in the side of mainstream culture.

Marlette perfected his drawing by copying caricatures and cartoons from *Mad*'s pages. In 1964, at fifteen, he wrote a letter to one of the cartoonists, including a satire he'd drawn of television's *The Man from U.N.C.L.E.* A form rejection letter promptly came back to Laurel. "My mother was furious," Marlette recalls. "She wrote them a three-page letter."

A mere year later, "Like a Rolling Stone," Bob Dylan's first rock single and the first six-minute song ever to top the charts, was played in a hamburger joint, where Marlette heard it and was stunned by Dylan's verbal fireworks. He worked his way backward through Dylan's oeuvre. Despite the way he'd been reared, he says, "Bob Dylan got under my skin." Dylan had been in Greenwood, Mississippi, not long before, singing for civil rights workers. "That had a huge impact on me. Because until then, they'd been the enemy."

LYNDON JOHNSON SIGNED the Civil Rights Act in the summer of 1964, as what were still called "Negro" neighborhoods seethed with protests and uprisings; in August the Democratic Convention in Atlantic City refused to seat delegates from the Mississippi Freedom Democratic Party, and America's troubles spanned the globe after U.S. forces attacked the North Vietnamese in the Gulf of Tonkin. Congress authorized escalation of the undeclared war in Southeast Asia, and America began drafting its young in numbers unheard of since the Korean War.

In the late 1950s, Beat culture—which gave America Jack Kerouac and Allen Ginsberg, and mass culture counterparts like Maynard G. Krebs, the bongo-batting beatnik on television's *The Dobie Gillis Show*—found a home in the cafes of the North Beach neighborhood of San Francisco. The Bay Area in general, and the University of California at Berkeley in particular, became magnets for progressive young people. A decade of protest began in May 1960, when students from Berkeley demonstrating against House Un-American Activities Committee hearings being held there were literally washed out of San Francisco's City Hall by police with fire hoses.

By 1963, students had begun emulating the civil rights activists of the South, picketing, committing acts of civil disobedience, and getting arrested at San Francisco car showrooms and hotels that discriminated against nonwhites. In July 1964, the Republican party held its convention in San Francisco's Cow Palace and nominated Arizona Senator Barry Goldwater, whose archconservative stance was summed up in his acceptance speech. "Extremism in the defense of liberty is no vice," he said.

"Moderation in the pursuit of justice is no virtue!" His call was soon to echo on the left.

That fall, Berkeley's dean of students announced that students could no longer use a stretch of sidewalk in front of the campus for political organizing. When students from across the political spectrum disobeyed, several were hauled before deans and suspended. In response, a coalition of student groups set up tables on the steps of Sproul Hall, the Berkeley administration building. Just before noon on October 1, university officials began citing them. One, a graduate student, Jack Weinberg of CORE, was arrested and tossed into a squad car. Before he could be carted off to jail, a crowd of students surrounded the car, launching an impromptu sit-in.

Returning home from a class in his varsity jacket and zebra-striped swim team sweater, John Gage caught sight of the 2,000 people who'd gathered in the plaza. "Everyone who had watched news coverage of the civil rights movement knew precisely what to do: sit down so the police car couldn't move," he says. Students began climbing on the car's roof and giving speeches, including Mario Savio, a twenty-one-year-old philosophy student Gage recognized from a math class. Savio, president of the Berkeley chapter of the Student Non-Violent Coordinating Committee (SNCC), had just returned from Freedom Summer.

Gage watched astonished as Savio, who stuttered, turned into a compelling orator. Even more surprising, the brainy jock found himself sympathetic. He believed universities should be free forums, and though he knew it wasn't rational, he realized, standing there, that he'd break the kneecaps of anyone who ever tried to stop him from speaking—or listening. At dusk, when a group of drunken students looking forward to a football weekend started pushing into Sproul Plaza to free the squad car, Gage was among the gang of crew men and football players who pushed back.

He didn't stick around that night—"It was dinnertime," he says with a laugh. By the next day, the university had dropped charges against Weinberg and the students dispersed, but the Free Speech Movement was just getting started. It was Weinberg who coined the phrase "Don't trust anyone over thirty" when the university appointed a man in his early thirties to negotiate with the students, thinking he'd be seen as a peer. When administrators still wanted to discipline the eight students cited in the plaza, Gage was among the growing number who decided the school wasn't playing fair.

In early November, students set up tables in the plaza again, and the university's position hardened. On November 20, about 3,000 students marched on a meeting of the university's regents. The school's policy on political activity was being debated, and the decision to suspend Savio and seven other students was upheld. When Gage returned home to conservative Orange County a few days later for Thanksgiving, family friends wondered if he wasn't turning Communist.

Back on campus, students announced a strike. Savio gave the speech that made him famous. "There comes a time when the operation of the machine becomes so odious . . . you can't even passively take part," he said. "And you've got to put your bodies on the gears . . . And you've got to indicate to the people who run it, to the people who own it, that unless you're free, the machine will be prevented from working at all."

When Savio finished, his audience of 800 occupied Sproul Hall again. This time, the police were ready. Beginning at 4:00 A.M. and for the next twelve hours, led by a deputy district attorney named Ed Meese—later Richard Nixon's Attorney General—they made 814 arrests. Television reports showed limp students being dragged down long flights of stairs to paddy wagons. Though faculty raised bail and the students were released from jail, Berkeley was paralyzed. Many began wearing IBM computer punch cards marked I AM A STUDENT. DO NOT FOLD, SPINDLE OR MUTILATE.

A compromise was worked out: amnesty for arrested students and a reversal of the ban on sidewalk tables. The school still insisted on the right to punish students for "illegal advocacy" on- or off-campus, a clear attempt to hobble civil disobedience. Four days after the mass arrest, 18,000 administrators, teachers and students gathered at Berkeley's Greek Theater for an "extraordinary" convocation. "There I was, wearing my striped zebra sweater again, and Mario sat down about two seats away in clogs and a long overcoat," Gage recalls. School president Clark Kerr announced the "compromise" couched with pointed remarks about reason and respect. Furious, Savio got up from his seat and moved toward the podium, where he was intercepted by university police and dragged off. Gage tried to follow, "yelling at various administration people," he says

In short order, Savio, released, was declaring victory at another rally as the school's chancellor was replaced. Still, Savio eventually was expelled and sentenced to four months in prison. His followers lost only a semester, but they—and the bulk of the Baby Boom just behind them—got the message. Having realized that authority could lie, Gage, like many others, now saw lies everywhere. Ironically, this seismic shift occurred just as *Time* magazine declared the boomers to be "a generation of conformists."

Gage quit the swim team and started doing things athletes didn't do. For middle-class, law-abiding, churchgoing kids like John Gage, marijuana had been the marker of the good child gone down the dope fiend path. Yet millions of them went to pot in one way or another during the next five years. A girlfriend gave Gage his first puff of the magic dragon. "It seemed like a good idea at the time," he says.

Suddenly, school seemed less interesting, even as student concerns increasingly set the national agenda. Lyndon Johnson had been elected to a full term as president in fall 1964, a peace candidate against the supposed warmonger Goldwater, but by spring 1965, the United States was sending ground troops into battle and bombing North Vietnam. Antiwar protests began. In May, Berkeley was the scene of a "teach-in"—a massive consciousness-raising symposium on the escalating war in Vietnam.

That summer, "Eve of Destruction," an anti-war song, topped the Top 40. In September Gage walked into the headquarters of an insurgent congressional campaign. Robert Scheer (b. 1936), an activist and journalist at a leftist magazine called *Ramparts*, was running in the Democratic primary against a Johnson-style pro-war liberal. Hired on to the campaign by its manager Alice Waters (b. 1944)—who went on to found the landmark Berkeley restaurant Chez Panisse—Gage took over two precincts and won them for Scheer. Unfortunately, the candidate lost almost everywhere else. His brand of radicalism had not yet entered the mainstream— even in Berkeley.

A Scheer win wouldn't have changed what happened next: Gage was drafted. And like most smart, white, privileged baby boomers, he promptly looked for a way out, joining a National Guard unit, then spending four months at Fort Ord Truck Driving School. He can still wax nostalgic about watching white, black, and Latin boys having their heads shaved and their identities and distinctions stripped away. "It's America at its best," says the self-described Jeffersonian Democrat. "You think I'm un-American? I'll show you who's American."

ACCEPTED AT BERKELEY, Tim Scully moved in with his grandparents again. In 1963, he wandered into and became a design consultant at Atomic Laboratories, a company nearby that made equipment to measure radiation. By 1964, he was doing so well he'd dropped out of school, bought a house of his own, and rented out rooms to fellow students. While many their age were marching for civil rights and disarmament, Scully was designing a fuel gauge for space rockets. "I had bottles of liquid Cobalt–60 in the attic," he says. Another chemical was about to set his future.

In 1943 Albert Hofmann, a biochemist at Switzerland's Sandoz Laboratories, accidentally ingested a minute amount of a material he'd first synthesized during medical research in 1938. He ate some more a few days later, on purpose. "I experienced fantastic images of an extraordinary plasticity," Hofmann would later say.[10] That compound, known as LSD or acid, after lysergic acid, its base material, soon became a subject of considerable interest in several separate but connected communities: the worlds of psychological research, the military, and espionage.

The foremost psychologist studying LSD was a Harvard lecturer named Timothy Leary (b. 1920). A roguish Irish Catholic, he was the son of West Point's dentist and went to the military academy himself. Accused of drunkenness by upperclassmen, he was asked to resign, but demanded a court martial instead. Though found not guilty, his bad form led to his being silenced—shunned—by his fellow cadets. He finally quit and continued his schooling in Alabama. During World War II, he served as an army psychologist in a veterans' hospital. After the war, he married, had two children, Susan (b. 1947) and Jack (b. 1949), earned a Ph.D. from Berkeley, and became a specialist in personality assessment and behavioral change.

Leary's own behavior changed profoundly after his wife asphyxiated herself in their garage on his thirty-fifth birthday. He quit his job, sailed to Spain, and returned to lecture at Harvard about a rebel movement then challenging behaviorism and psychoanalysis: existential-transactional psychology, which treated all behavior as a set of games. In August 1960, Leary rented a villa in Cuernavaca, Mexico, for the summer. Curious about the "divine mushrooms" of the Aztecs, just written up in *Life* magazine, he took some and was transformed.

Back at Harvard that fall, Leary learned that Sandoz had synthesized the active ingredient in psilocybin mushrooms. He started giving it to test subjects and graduate students as part of a psychological study. Leary quickly hooked up with Aldous Huxley (b. 1894), author of *Brave New World*, whose lifelong quest for higher awareness had led him to first take mescaline, another psychoactive drug, in 1953.[11] Huxley suggested it was Leary's responsibility to enlighten the elite about psychoactive drugs. Soon Allen Ginsberg arrived in Cambridge, where he took psilocybin and wandered Leary's house naked with his lover, Peter Orlovsky. Ginsberg then introduced Leary to Jack Kerouac, Robert Lowell, Dizzy Gillespie and William Burroughs, and psychedelics quickly became the secret vice of New York's hip elite. Leary began taking psilocybin every three days.[12]

Leary's closest colleague was Richard Alpert, the child of a great railroad fortune and a graduate of Tufts and Stanford. Alpert had tried marijuana in graduate school. While working for Harvard's Center for Research in Personality, he took psilocybin and signed on to Leary's project. Together, they started giving the drug to prisoners in a state penitentiary. The results were positive. Leary believed he'd found an agent that could alter consciousness and change people for the better.

His superiors weren't so sure. In February 1962, the Harvard *Crimson* began writing about Leary's mushroom experiments. The story broke nationally within a month.[13] Harvard asked Leary to turn over his psilocybin. Unknown to the school, he'd just tried LSD, provided by a Briton, Michael Hollingshead, who'd fallen in with a tiny circle of beats and psychedelic devotees in New York City and had convinced a friend who worked in a hospital to get some LSD from Sandoz's U.S. office.[14] After turning up at Leary's door with his stash in a mayonnaise jar, Hollingshead quickly turned Leary on and became Jack and Susan's babysitter.

That summer, Leary went to California. LSD research had been going on there since 1959. Several Hollywood psychiatrists and psychologists had experimented with the stuff, testing its effects on patients, including Henry and Clare Booth Luce (of the *Time* and *Life* Luces), Anaïs Nin, Cary Grant, James Coburn and Jack Nicholson.[15] LSD parties were becoming a phenomenon in Hollywood.[16] Beatniks, who had been "expanding their consciousness" with drugs for years, were also eager to try the new thrill.

Several hundred miles north, Tim Scully was still following his family's careful script. When Berkeley's Free Speech Movement began, he kept his distance. He'd read the riot act to a friend who'd smoked pot. But one of his tenants, a student of Oriental philosophy whom Scully knew from kindergarten, went to work on him after Tim showed interest in his talk of consciousness. "Don finally talked me into smoking marijuana while I was reading the *Tao Te Ching*. It certainly bends your thoughts in the right direction." The notion that marijuana and other drugs led to reefer madness was wafting out windows all over the world.

TIMOTHY LEARY WAS at Harvard during Leslie Crocker Snyder's senior year at Radcliffe. "Now, I never had anything to do with Timothy Leary," she says. "I heard that he was involved with some Radcliffe students and drug experiments, but I was a pretty straight kid. My crowd was fairly straight. Drugs were just not a part of our existence."

Still, Snyder felt the mood that encouraged drug use—even if she didn't go that far. By her junior year, "I was losing all interest in academia, unfortunately," she says. Aware of the student movement, Snyder admired civil rights workers, wanted to help, and knew she would one day. She also knew people in the thriving Cambridge folk music scene, but was more likely to be found on the banks of the Charles watching her boyfriend race crew. The day she broke out she found herself on the periphery of the Harvard Latin Diploma riot. When the school decided it would no longer issue diplomas in Latin, students gathered in Harvard Square, "and the police gassed us," she recalls. "I still remember the tears pouring down my face. And feeling outraged." Her fiancé, "a guy all the girls loved," was mean and unsympathetic. Luckily, just before they got married, she met someone she liked better, and she and the jock called it quits.

Snyder had lost direction. At huge Harvard, there was no one to turn to for advice. Both she and her fiancé had planned to go to law school, one at a time—he would have been first, of course. She was slated to enter a one-year program at Harvard Business School that would funnel her into a good, high-paying job in the interim. It was too late to change course.

Then there was the undeclared war in Vietnam. To most Harvard students, it was a vague, amorphous conflict, certainly no cause for concern. Snyder heard that a Harvard friend had been killed there, one of the first hundred American casualties. "And then," she says, "we started thinking and talking a lot more about Vietnam."

Snyder's first brush with discrimination came when she entered Harvard Business School. Radcliffe graduates were not considered full-fledged business students until their second year. Though they were taught by Business School professors, they were segregated into classes of their own. She decided to forgo a second year and, thanks to her fluency in French, got a job in Paris as an executive trainee. But her parents demanded she return home. "This is not a constructive thing to do," her mother told her. Snyder had desperately wanted to go to law school. But her parents wouldn't pay. Even if she could have gotten in—she'd been a B student at Radcliffe—loans for women law students were unheard of. Her father offered a deal: if she would come home, she could go to law school for free at Cleveland-based Case Western Reserve, where he was teaching.

"I was horrified because, god, to go to Cleveland for three years—and Case Western was a mediocre law school," Snyder says, but it did accept her and was, in essence, free. She agreed. First, unbeknownst to her parents, she hitchhiked across Europe with a young man. She even thought about staying. "I could have gone off course," she says, "but it just wasn't in me. I wanted to go to law school more than anything else."

In September 1963, Snyder moved in with her folks and enrolled as one of only two women in her law school class. If feminism was part and parcel of Radcliffe culture, it was nowhere to be found at Case Western. ("I hear you went to Radcliffe," a student said to her after her first class, "so obviously you believe in free love.")

Snyder was in class when she heard her idol Jack Kennedy had been killed. "I started weeping and went to find my father," she says. Like many around her, he was equivocal: "Well, he isn't that great a man or a president," he said.

Cleveland offered one consolation, the rock 'n' roll Snyder loved. She saw the Beatles play there on their first American tour, and she saw James Brown, too. This was still Middle America; it would be years before coastal craziness hit the banks of the Cuyahoga River. But it was coming. A neighbor's nephew, whom Snyder had a crush on, died of a heroin overdose. An unmarried couple she'd befriended who shared her taste for poetry got stoned when she wasn't around. "They were from New York," she says. "I had never heard of people smoking marijuana. That's how isolated I had been. I was never interested in drugs but was fascinated by people who were."

Fascination never led to experimentation, though. "I get upset if I'm not in control," says Snyder. She'd nearly made a wrong turn in Europe. Now on the right track, she was determined to stay there.

IN 1964, JIM Fouratt got a job as a page at New York's new Four Seasons restaurant. "I took people to their tables and got huge tips with little notes saying, 'We'll pick you up at eleven.' These gentlemen would pick me up in limousines. And I wouldn't put out. I didn't know that was the deal!"

He'd recently smoked pot for the first time, but hated the stuff. Fouratt preferred speed. Having first tried the bootleg Benzedrine pills known as white crosses that were sold in Washington Square Park, he graduated to pharmaceuticals when the poet Allen Ginsberg introduced him to one of New York's Doctor Feelgoods, renegades who gave "vitamin" shots laced with amphetamines to the elite (President Kennedy among them).

If Fouratt has trouble keeping his memories ordered, the breadth of his experience is a likelier reason than his drug use. For example, having met Brian Epstein when the Beatles manager, a closeted homosexual, had first come to New York, Fouratt was comped to see the band at Carnegie Hall, their second American concert, on February 12, 1964. Escorting the hottest girl he could find, Jill Haworth, an actress who'd just appeared in the movie *Exodus*, Fouratt went backstage afterward, met the Beatles, and took them to the Peppermint Lounge in Times Square to see the Ronettes, and then went back to the Plaza Hotel, where they were staying. "Jill wound up with Paul and I was pissed off," Fouratt remembers. "I didn't think she was going to leave me to go fuck a Beatle."[17]

Another example: On August 8, 1964, he met a fellow acting student in Duffy Square, to rehearse a scene. Instead, he got caught up in New York's second demonstration against the Vietnam War and wound up one of seventeen people arrested, in his case for breaking a window and resisting arrest. He was innocent, he says, but was convicted by a judge who solemnly informed him that police officers do not lie. "We'd all grown up in the fifties with everything nice on the surface, no one talking about what's underneath," Fouratt says. Some were, though. In summer 1965, Fouratt was there when Bob Dylan, inspired by the Beatles, strapped on an electric guitar and scandalized the Newport Folk Festival by playing "Like a Rolling Stone."

In December 1965, Mickey Ruskin opened a bar that became the Underground's clubhouse and Fouratt's new hangout, Max's Kansas City.[18] Fouratt had a $20-a-month duplex loft just off the Bowery near a neighborhood then becoming known as the East Village. Fouratt's new boyfriend was a Chilean poet and playwright named Claudio Badal who knew Andy Warhol, the Pop artist who'd emerged in 1962 and became the king of Max's, going there almost nightly in 1966. Max's was the place "where Pop Art and pop life came together," Warhol wrote, "Everybody went to Max's and everything got homogenized there."[19] It was also okay to be homosexual there—a matter of some import to Fouratt.

The fast lane finally caught up with Fouratt in early 1966. He came down with hepatitis—from Dr. Feelgood's speed shots, he thinks. Without insurance, he ended up in Bellevue, a public hospital. While there, his short hair grew longer, almost to his shoulders. By the time he got out, he had the latest look among the young: hippies had come onto the scene. The values the longhairs espoused (peace and free love), the drugs they took, which encouraged sexual experimentation, and the androgynous style they adopted were right up Fouratt's alley.

Never one to stay on the fringe of a fringe, compelled to propel himself right to the red-hot core, Fouratt began a noisy public career that has made him a figure of some controversy in boomer circles for three decades. Out of the hospital, he returned to San Francisco, where he met some of the leaders of the new hippie scene—members of the San Francisco Mime Troupe. The troupe, a politically progressive guerrilla band of actors that performed commedia dell'arte in the city's parks, had come to national attention the year before, when denied permission to perform a play San Francisco's parks commission considered obscene.

A few months later, several members of the mime troupe broke off to form a street theater and cultural action group called The Diggers, which became known for ladling free stew in Golden Gate Park's Panhandle. Fouratt was particularly taken with the Diggers' public information arm, the Communications Company, which published a stream of mimeographed communiqués and manifestos for the new community of hippies taking over the Haight-Ashbury section of San Francisco, a working-class neighborhood full of Victorian houses bordering Golden Gate Park. Ideas were free, too. When Fouratt returned east, he brought that one with him.

BARBARA LEDEEN'S SOCIAL consciousness was awakened in 1964 by the murders of Freedom Riders in Mississippi. She'd always had an inchoate sense of fairness. Her family situation was unfair. So was the curfew that got her expelled from school. Being a Jew instead of a Jackie Kennedy was unfair. So was being mistreated because you were a Jew. And now Jews were being killed for trying to cure the awful incivility Negroes faced in the South.

She burned to go South, but didn't. Still, she turned up the heat. She was seventeen, a junior in high school and president of her class, when she discovered the opposite sex. "I had a boyfriend, lovely guy," and so did her best friend. "We were the only four in the class who would have sex. Other people had more self-restraint. So the four of us would double date all the time." She played "bingo" with spermacides she bought herself.

When it came time for college, Ledeen wanted Barnard, but her parents vetoed her choice of a school in dangerous New York City. So she went to Syracuse University, close to home, where "everybody was Jewish except my roommate, the daughter of a Missouri Synod Lutheran minister who believed the Jews killed Jesus," she says. Ledeen took an instant dislike to Syracuse. She was horrified when she realized some of her fellow students didn't know how to use a library and cared more about football and sororities than poetry and philosophy. She'd escape when she could to visit her boyfriend at school in Wisconsin. By November, she had decided to transfer. The latest thing in college was work/study programs. Few colleges had them, but Beloit, an experimental school near her boyfriend's in Wisconsin, did. "It was me, because I didn't want to be in school anymore. I wanted to go do stuff."

AT COLUMBIA UNIVERSITY, Mark Rudd quickly hooked up with the campus radicals. "The guy who introduced me to what you might call an anti-imperialist analysis was John Jacobs," Rudd says. Jacobs (b. 1947), known as J.J., was a Russian revolution buff who'd worked for a leftist newspaper before entering the class of 1969 and joining the May 2nd Movement that summer. Named for the first antiwar demonstration in New York in 1964, May 2nd was a front for Progressive Labor, a breakaway faction of the Communist Party that followed the teachings of Chinese Communist leader Mao Tse-Tung. It had sponsored the Duffy Square protest in which Jim Fouratt had been arrested the year before.

J.J. was in thrall to revolutionary rhetoric. By the end of that school year, Rudd, in thrall of J.J., was organizing his first antiwar protest. Furious over the escalation of the war, he'd started seeing himself as an outsider in his own culture, and when he began smoking marijuana that year, it reinforced that feeling. "It's thirty-three years later, and I haven't stopped," he says. "The entire time, it's been illegal. That's made me an outlaw. I like that. Maybe if they made it legal, I'd stop."

In March 1966, Rudd and other members of the Columbia Independent Committee on Vietnam joined a crowd of about 40,000 people who marched down Fifth Avenue against the war. "We had snotty signs that read, 'READ BOOKS!,'" he says. That month, Buddhist monks in Vietnam kept the pressure on and demonstrators burned the U.S. Consulate in Hue before the new prime minister, Nguyen Cao Ky, used troops to end the rebellion. "I remember distinctly being moved by this," Rudd says.

After a summer spent hitchhiking solo through Europe, Rudd returned to school, where he first heard of Students for a Democratic Society. SDS was a descendent of the Intercollegiate Socialist Society founded in 1905 by Clarence Darrow and Jack London. It was reborn shortly after one of its leaders, Tom Hayden, visited San Francisco in the wake of the 1960 protest against HUAC, and made a Lourdes-like pilgrimage to the steps of City Hall.

In 1962, just after John Kennedy called for the nation to build fallout shelters, SDS was among the groups that drew several thousand anti-nuclear protesters to Washington. That June, Hayden wrote a document for the group's convention that would become known as the Port Huron Statement. "We are people of this generation, bred in at least modest comfort, housed now in universities, looking uncomfortably to the world we inherit," was the stirring start of the otherwise interminable manifesto. That December, Bob Dylan, whose antiwar song "Blowin' in the Wind," recorded by the folk trio Peter, Paul and Mary, had just hit the Top Ten, turned up at the annual SDS convention. Protest had gone pop.

Inspired by SNCC and Martin Luther King's stirring March on Washington, SDS devised an earnest program to organize the urban poor. The following summer, as hundreds of college students flooded rural Mississippi, SDS was operating in northern slums. Then, in April 1965, SDS drew 20,000 students to Washington, D.C., for the largest antiwar demonstration in U.S. history.

SDS began attracting more recruits, becoming a refuge for members of the May 2nd Movement, which disbanded early in 1966. That June, James Meredith returned to the headlines when he began a one-man voter registration march, and was shot and wounded just as he crossed the Tennessee-Mississippi border. In response, civil rights leaders like Martin Luther King Jr., Whitney Young of the Urban League, Roy Wilkins of the National Association for the Advancement of Colored People, and Stokely Carmichael (b. 1941), leader of SNCC, took over Meredith's march for him. When Carmichael was arrested in Greenwood, Mississippi, something changed. He emerged from jail with a new battle cry: Black Power. Carmichael and another SNCC leader, H. Rap Brown (b. 1943), picked up the torch of the slain black nationalist leader Malcolm X. So did the Black Panther Party, born in Oakland, California, after Bobby Seale (b. 1936) met Huey Newton (b. 1942) at junior college in 1966. With their fiery rhetoric and threats of violence, these new-guard black activists split the civil rights movement in half. White radicals in awe of the black radicals' authenticity, but expelled from their organizations, also found a new home in SDS. That fall, a group of them formed a chapter at Columbia. It would soon overshadow its parent—and outrage parents across America—by igniting a revolutionary impulse in the crowded, roiling ranks of the nation's young.

Adolescence

IN FALL 1962, with his Harvard teaching contract about to expire, Timothy Leary set up the International Foundation for Internal Freedom (IFF), a commune based on one of Aldous Huxley's novels, *Island*, about a druggy utopia. At IFF, LSD was being served far more than science. Trouble loomed. In spring 1963, the first adverse reactions to the stuff were reported. People never came down, had their personalities shattered. A new anti-amphetamine law had just given the FDA control of experimental drugs, and it began cutting off the supply of LSD. But Leary had his own supply and agenda: to turn on America.[1] On Good Friday 1963, he gave students LSD in Boston University's chapel. The publicity—in the Harvard *Crimson* and then in the national press—was explosively negative. Harvard fired Alpert on May 27, 1963. Leary was relieved of his duties.[2]

Leary's next project, the establishment of psychedelic communities in Mexico and Dominica, did not bear fruit. He was rescued by Peggy Hitchcock (b. 1933), a grandchild of the founder of Gulf Oil and a descendent of the Pittsburgh Mellons and Long Island's polo-playing Hitchcocks. She'd come into Leary's psychedelic orbit after hearing about Alpert's psilocybin experiments from a fashion model friend.[3] Hitchcock had introduced Alpert to one of her brothers, William Mellon Hitchcock (b. 1939), a broker at Lehman Brothers. "Billy," who was married to a Venezuelan fashion model, was a rising financial star who had recently become acquainted with numbered Swiss bank accounts.[4] Alpert gave him books by J. D. Salinger and Thomas Mann, his sister convinced him to try mescaline, and Leary gave him LSD. Fascinated by his psychedelic experiences, he rented Leary a sixty-four-room Bavarian house on his family's 2,500-acre private shooting reserve in horsey Millbrook, New York, for $500 a month.[5]

When, on the very day John F. Kennedy was killed, Aldous Huxley also died of cancer, high on acid, Leary took the King of Psychedelia's throne and moved his court to Millbrook. At the end of 1963, he dissolved IFF, started Castalia, named after a colony from a Herman Hesse novel, *The Glass Bead Game*, and began proselytizing. In a *Playboy* interview, he claimed LSD improved sex. Soon seekers filled Millbrook's many bedrooms. In summer 1964, the future arrived on a bus that proclaimed it was going FURTHUR in front and warned, CAUTION: WEIRD LOAD, in back.

The man behind the wheel, Ken Kesey (b. 1935), had lived in the late-1950s bohemian academic community of Palo Alto, California, in which drug experimentation was ritual. Kesey tried psilocybin and LSD at a veterans hospital where CIA-sponsored drug experiments were being done, went to work there, and was inspired to write his first novel, *One Flew Over the Cuckoo's Nest*, published to great acclaim in February 1962. That summer, Neal Cassidy turned up at Kesey's door. Cassidy, who'd grown up surrounded by pimps and hobos, was a car thief and a sex-and-drug-charged improvisational speaker who became a hero in the novels of Jack Kerouac. Just out of jail for marijuana smuggling, he helped inspire Kesey and his friends to form the Merry Pranksters—a band of on-the-road consciousness explorers based on Robert Heinlein's science fiction novel about a mystic cult, *Strangers in a Strange Land*.

When Kesey finished a new book, he bought his bus and decided to paint it psychedelic and drive it to New York for his publication party. Later, Tom Wolfe, a reporter from *New York* magazine, would write about it all, and *The Electric Kool-Aid Acid Test* would become one of the most influential books of the decade, captivating impressionable teenagers as late as 1969, when it was published in paperback, spreading the story of how LSD crossed the line from property of Apollo to plaything for Dionysis. "LSD, peyote, mescaline, morning-glory seeds were becoming the secret new *thing* in the hip life," Wolfe wrote. ". . . and in the heart of even the most unhip mamma in all the U.S. of A. instinctively goes up the adrenal shriek: beatniks, bums, spades—*dope.*"[6]

Millbrook proved too stodgy for The Merry Pranksters, who left quickly, declaring the East Coast acid academics constipated. As they drove away, they took the cutting edge of drug use with them.

In summer 1965, Kesey and the Pranksters held the first "Acid Test," a huge private party featuring LSD, Allen Ginsberg, strange sounds and a light show—a multimedia experience. Soon afterward, they did it again in San Jose, for the hip public, after a Rolling Stones concert. The band that night was the Warlocks, soon to be known as The Grateful Dead—led by Jerry Garcia (b. 1942), a guitar player who'd crashed Kesey's Palo Alto parties.[7] The Acid Test uncovered how many people were secretly taking drugs. Encouraged, Kesey decided to do it again and again—until these legal acid-rock parties made the papers. Then Stewart Brand (b. 1939), a post-Beat San Francisco biologist (who went on to found *The Whole Earth Catalog*), organized a commercial elaboration of the Acid Tests—the three-day Trips Festival, held at Longshoreman's Hall in January 1966. Three days before, Kesey, already arrested for marijuana possession in April 1965, was busted again, and forthwith jumped bail and disappeared. The Trips Festival made a nice profit, anyway, and *Time* magazine trumpeted the advent of the acidhead.

Kesey wasn't the only frontier scout in legal jeopardy. When Leary returned to Millbrook in spring 1965—a giddy marriage to a fashion model ended abruptly after a sobering honeymoon in India—things were a mess and the money was running out. That April, he and Alpert began commercializing their crusade, giving lectures with sound-and-light shows in a Greenwich Village theater he rented with Billy Hitchcock, selling LSD T-shirts and charging visitors for drug-free weekend "trips" to Millbrook.[8] He was becoming *too* visible. That Christmas, Leary, his kids and a new girlfriend took off for Mexico to meet Hitchcock. Leary was arrested at the border for a stash of drugs found in daughter Susan's underwear. Incensed, Hitchcock set up a legal defense fund to which he was the primary contributor.[9] Nonetheless, in March, Leary was sentenced to thirty years in Texas state prison. In April, while free on bail pending appeal, he was arrested again in a raid on Millbrook, led by a Duchess County district attorney named G. Gordon Liddy (who would later come to national attention as a Watergate burglar). Liddy was running for Congress "on a plank which was largely Throw Hitchcock Out of Millbrook," Billy later told a family biographer.[10]

The legal lashing was accompanied by a media campaign. Accounts of bad trips flooded the press, three congressional subcommittees announced hearings, and anti-LSD legislation was quickly drafted. That July, legal LSD research officially ended. A new Bureau of Drug Abuse Control began to root out underground supplies. By October, LSD was illegal in every state of the union.[11] All around the country, Baby Boom kids began to wonder, What was the fuss about?

The counterculture, the Youthquake, had overtaken America. Miniskirts were the new fashion. Ronald Reagan was elected governor of California in 1966, in part by running against the "insolent, ungrateful" students of Berkeley, but he couldn't hold back the tide. There was more and more crossover between radical culture and the rebel young. A writer in the *San Francisco Examiner* had coined the term "hippie" in September 1965 to describe the 15,000 long-haired young people who'd taken over Haight-Ashbury. Groups promoting marijuana and sexual freedom flourished in San Francisco. So did the new psychedelic rock culture. That summer and fall, groups like The Jefferson Airplane, The Great Society and Country Joe and The Fish emerged. In October, The Family Dog, a hippie collective, began promoting concerts at Longshoreman's Hall. Bill Graham, manager of the San Francisco Mime Troupe, promoted his first concert, starring The Jefferson Airplane, the Warlocks, Lawrence Ferlinghetti and the Fugs, in November 1965, as a benefit for the troupe featuring a tinfoil-lined garbage can full of LSD-infused Kool-Aid.[12] Astonished at the crowd, he promoted another the following month, starring the Airplane and the Grateful Dead, at the soon-to-be-famous Fillmore Auditorium. A month after that, Ken Kesey and the Merry Pranksters pulled into town for another of their Acid Tests.

The counterculture wasn't monolithic. While groups like the Diggers were giving away free food and clothes to the hippies, Graham was a prototype of the hip capitalist, promoting rock shows for profit. Despite the legal problems facing Leary and Kesey, their drug promotion schemes had also spawned commercial elaborations. In January 1966, The Psychedelic Shop opened on Haight Street and became the prototype for the head shops selling drug paraphernalia that sprouted like magic mushrooms nationwide.

That summer, as ghettos exploded again, the hip found common cause with political hotheads. Anger about a curfew on the Sunset Strip in West Hollywood boiled over into a riot, inspiring a hit song by a new band, Buffalo Springfield, that began, "There's something happening here/What it is ain't exactly clear." Increasingly clear was that a culture of opposition was rising—and it had a visual symbol. Despite a new ban on burning draft cards, they were going up in flames at demonstrations coast to coast.

IT WAS 1966. The Marlette family had just moved to a Navy air base in central Florida, where their younger son spent his last year in high school as his father prepared to ship out to Vietnam on the *U.S.S. Enterprise.* Doug Marlette had no idea there was a peace movement. He believed what he was told: we were winning and the undeclared war would be over soon.

The sudden move to Florida had stunted his social life again. He didn't date. Back in Laurel, he would have started on the basketball team. Instead, he drew for the high school paper and was taken with a hippie teacher who spoke of Bob Dylan and death-of-God theology. When Marlette went back to Mississippi to visit friends, he found he was "leaving them behind," he says. "I made them uneasy. I was asking questions about things nobody had thought about." In Florida, he started asking his father the same questions, just to get under his skin. He'd talk about a black person he'd met. "I smelled him, but I didn't smell anything," he'd say.

Marlette's mother had an emotional breakdown after her husband shipped out. With Doug's brother in college, at sixteen, he became the man of the house. He got a job at the local paper, the *Sanford Herald*, drawing cartoons of local sports figures for a couple bucks a pop. In short order, he graduated to the art department of the *Orlando Sentinel*. He enrolled at the local community college. Though he still sometimes fantasized about working for *Mad* or becoming a political cartoonist like Pat Oliphant, an Australian then making cartoon waves, Marlette's ambitions stayed small. Drawing decorations for church socials had given him the idea he might one day become a sign painter. He met his first girlfriend at church, the daughter of a local attorney whose family offered the stability his no longer had.

Marlette was simultaneously being pulled out of his cocoon by cartoons like those of Jules Feiffer, whose "Upper West Side, Jewish, intellectual sensibility spoke to a fifteen-year-old towheaded Mississippi Baptist," he says. In 1968, Doug discovered *Zap Comix*, R. Crumb's wildly outrageous sex-and-dope-filled underground comic books. "I felt woozy, like I'd entered someone else's dream," he says. People would try to get him to draw underground comics and he refused. "I considered it preaching to the converted. Hippies already knew. I wanted to sow seeds of sedition among the straight and comfortable."

AUGUSTUS OWSLEY STANLEY III (B. 1935), like his grandfather, a Kentucky governor and U.S. senator, felt called upon to serve his fellow Americans. Expelled from prep school for rum-running for his classmates in the ninth grade, he arrived at Berkeley in 1963 and got into the drug business by cooking up a batch of methedrine in his girlfriend's school lab. After a failed attempt to make LSD, Owsley moved to Los Angeles and embarked on a quest to make it with pharmaceutical purity. Though he produced less than half a kilo in his entire career, that was a substantial amount, and he knew how to share with others.

Acid was still legal, so Owsley was able to buy 460 grams of lysergic acid, the material LSD is made from, stored half of it in safe deposit boxes under false names, and whipped up the rest. Soon, people all over the West Coast were asking for Owsley and his acid. Moving to San Francisco, he became part of the Pranksters' scene, survived a serious acid freak-out, and spent what profits he made on equipment for the Grateful Dead.[13]

Across the Bay, Tim Scully and his tenant Don continued their quest for enlightenment. Scully read *Heaven and Hell* and *The Doors of Perception* by Huxley. Finally, the pair set out to find some LSD. "We were doing it in search of a mystical experience," Scully recalls. As they came down from their first trip, one of them said, "You know, we could make this stuff and give it away."

Scully's first trip, on April 15, 1965, was taken on acid Owsley had made in L.A. that spring. In the months that followed, as Scully failed to find a source of lysergic acid, he kept hearing about Bear, as Owsley was called by friends. Scully was looking for the chemist when the man himself turned up in Berkeley that fall, having met a girl at Kesey's who was renting a room from Scully. Owsley had gotten wind of Scully's interest in LSD manufacture and his appreciation for alchemy—now turning toward the transmutation of consciousness into cosmic gold. Owsley was also interested in Scully's knack for electronics, so Scully helped build sound equipment for the Dead, hoping to pass an acid test of his own and getting to make acid with the master. "Bear thought that we were almost certain to go to jail," Scully says. "He didn't want to end up feeling guilty for getting this naive kid sent away for a long time, so he tried to make it hard for me."

Midway through his junior year at Berkeley, Scully dropped out and moved to Los Angeles, where the Pranksters (minus Kesey, but with the addition of Hugh Romney, a Beat poet and comic who would later join a commune called the Hog Farm and take the name Wavy Gravy) were running Acid Tests. Scully built a mixing board for the Dead that would allow them to record their shows and practice sessions. Then he ran the board at the Pranksters' second L.A. event, the Watts Acid Test, which took place on Lincoln's Birthday, 1966, in a vacant warehouse in Compton, California, later the birthplace of gangsta rap.[14] At Romney's urging, two garbage cans full of Kool-Aid were placed on the floor, one pure, the other laced with LSD. Despite cryptic warnings, some attendees drank the drugged batch by accident. When one girl freaked out, several Pranksters filmed her and broadcast her wails. Behind his mixing board, Scully was upset by their callousness, but he stayed with the troupe through several more events in the next few months.

Scully wasn't *on the bus*, as Tom Wolfe famously put it; the band traveled and lived separate from the Acid Test crew. The fun of playing roadie for the Dead, renting a house and buying groceries for its extended family, setting up and tearing down equipment, not to mention losing his virginity and doing lots of acid and pot, more than made up for Scully's discomfort with the Pranksters' approach to psychedelia. "It felt a lot like running away to join the circus," he says. Meanwhile, Owsley pressed the last of his processed acid into 2,000 primitive tablets in the attic of the house Scully had rented for the band in East Los Angeles.

Scully wanted to make enough acid to turn on the world before the government's inevitable crackdown. "I had the fantasy that people who took psychedelics might produce a culture that was less likely to trash the planet, less likely to have wars," he says. That Owsley sold half his production and gave away the rest was a turn-on, as was the chemist's aim to make acid purer than that manufactured by Sandoz or Eli Lilly.

Finally, Owsley decided to set up a new lab and go back into production. He had to be more careful, since possession of LSD had become a misdemeanor in California that August, so he found a house in Port Richmond, near Berkeley, where emissions from an oil refinery would camouflage the smell of a lab. Though he had Eli Lilly's LSD formula, it didn't describe how to make a lot of acid in very pure form or how to stabilize the compound so it wouldn't decompose. Scully remembers countless conversations about purity and yield, and believes he contributed improvements to the process, which finally produced twenty grams of the purest LSD ever made. Scully had passed the acid test.[15]

Owsley was an instinctive marketer. They began naming their product—one batch of white tablets was called White Lightning. Then they made up five batches of 3,600 doses each and dyed them five different colors, hoping to confuse authorities as to the source. An unintended side effect: Buyers thought each color had different effects, and by and large preferred the pills they called Blue Cheer and Purple Haze.

AT UNION COLLEGE, Michael Fuchs was a political science major. As a freshman, he supported the war in Vietnam. By 1965, he'd grown skeptical. But Fuchs was no radical, politically or culturally. He remembers being unimpressed upon seeing the Beatles for the first time. "Their music was cutesy, they were foreign, a novelty. I didn't feel that they were taking me anywhere." Neither was basketball. He went out for the freshman team, but after realizing that "Union was not a great athletic power," he quit to play lacrosse. He couldn't commit to a fraternity, either. After living in a frat house his sophomore year, "I de-brothered," he says. "I have an enormously independent streak, and I didn't find any terrific benefits in fraternity life." Union was a party school, and he took advantage. "College in those days was alcohol; marijuana had just come in," Fuchs says. Skidmore, an all-girls college, was nearby, "so we were on the road a lot."

Despite his surface straightness, Fuchs embodied several clichés about the baby boom. Defiance was already his posture. He's been fired from every single job he's ever held, beginning with one at a summer camp in the early 1960s. "I was very outspoken," he says, "and it took me a while to understand I didn't deal with authority very well." He had no interest in SDS or in going to Mississippi, either. "I'm not a joiner," he says. He wasn't worried about making a living. "I wasn't anxious to get a job," he says. "I knew I was going to have to work the rest of my life. I thought this was the time to have fun."

EXCELLING IN SCHOOL, Leslie Crocker Snyder was named to Case Western's National Moot Court team and made an editor of the Law Review in 1965. She met a Cleveland criminal lawyer who let her work on cases. Then she applied for a summer job at one of the city's top firms. The interviewer didn't look at her when she walked in. "Sit down, Mr. Crocker," he said. Then he winced. "I'm sorry, but we don't hire women." Furious, she flew to New York and found work there, but the experience rankled.

In 1966, after graduating at the top of her class, Snyder returned to New York and became one of two new women hires at a large law firm that put her to work doing research and writing briefs. In the little spare time she had, she made some friends, visited the Village, went to Bill Graham's new Manhattan concert hall the Fillmore East, and sniffed around the New York scene. Briefly, she worked for Robert Kennedy, then a New York senator, in 1967. "I was still hung up on John Kennedy, Camelot and all that," she says.

A partner in her firm invited her into a contract conversation with one of the Rolling Stones, who then asked her to join him for a long weekend in London. "I was so straight, I said no," she reports. (And so unimpressed, she can't recall which Stone it was.) Snyder thinks skipping grades and always being two years younger than her peers put her at a social disadvantage that wound up a plus. "Because I was ahead of myself, I just missed it," she says wistfully of the 1960s. "It's like a train that's coming toward you; you're aware of it, but you're not hit by it."

Late in 1967, bored with her job, Snyder decided to apply for a new one as a criminal prosecutor with the United States Attorney's Office. But women weren't allowed in the federal prosecutor's criminal division. That same day, she applied for jobs with Legal Aid and the New York District Attorney, Frank Hogan. Though he was hardly a forward-thinker—he was the DA who prosecuted Lenny Bruce for obscenity—Hogan was willing to hire women. The interviewer at Legal Aid told her right up front how unhappy she'd be there; Hogan saw fit to ask repeatedly if she'd ever been married. "Mr. Hogan, I really think if I'd been married I'd remember that," she replied. He regarded her oddly and offered her a job working on legal appeals. She explained that if she was going to take a 50 percent pay cut, she wanted to do criminal work. He was offended. "I decide where my people will go," he huffed. "Women do very well in the Appeals Bureau." In that case, she told him she'd stay with her law firm. He asked her to sit outside for a few moments.

To this day, Snyder isn't sure what happened then. "He was a great DA, but he was a patriarchal moralist," she says. "Was he worried I was gay? Aberrant? Living in sin?" Hogan finally offered her a job trying misde-meanors—low-level criminal prosecutions. Snyder was a natural; she quickly blossomed in her job—and pleased Hogan by getting engaged.

WHILE DONALD TRUMP was in the military academy, "the world changed a lot," he says. "When I first went up there, the military was like God. In my last year, 1964, it was almost looked down on. It was the beginning of twenty years of turmoil."

Those changes stayed outside the walls of the school. Cadets were only allowed to see television on weekends. They weren't taught about *Brown v. Board of Education*, or the civil rights movement, or the Buddhist revolts in Vietnam. "They were teaching me how to march," Trump says. "You marched to meals, to class, to almost everything." Trump was march-ing when President Kennedy was shot.

He feels lucky to have been so sheltered. "Because it could be that I would have gone very strongly the other way, very, very strongly the other way. But you see, I didn't have a lot of exposure to it; I knew people who would just as soon shoot a beatnik as talk to him—literally. I mean, if they had the opportunity and were guaranteed not to get caught, they'd shoot as many as they could."

In 1964, Trump enrolled in Fordham University, a Jesuit school in New York City. After a year commuting from his parents' home, he got his first apartment in Manhattan, but he was still under close scrutiny. "The Jesuits had an almost militarylike grip over that school," Trump says. In 1966, rejecting the alternative of film school, he transferred to the Wharton School of Finance at the University of Pennsylvania. "Ultimately, I decided that real estate was a better business, and that maybe I could put show business into the real estate business," he says, "which I've done."

Trump noticed hippies, of course. "They were very idealistic, and I thought that was good. But I didn't look favorably upon them because they were always very dirty." He agreed with them on one point; he was opposed to the war in Vietnam. Trump "saw it as a terrible deal," he says. "The tremendous conflict at home, while well-intentioned, gave the other side an incentive to keep going, because they knew this country was being ripped apart from within."

Trump wasn't much for rock 'n' roll. "I was never somebody that liked watching the game; I liked to play the game," he says. Which partly explains why CBS founder William Paley's commencement speech at Wharton in spring 1968 made a bigger impression on him than the killings of Martin Luther King and Bobby Kennedy in the weeks just before. The next year, he would not be among the throngs at the Woodstock festival, either. "I thought they were crazy!"

Trump had fun, though. "I don't think anybody had more sex than I did," he boasts. "I didn't do drugs. I wasn't a drug guy. But there was a lot of sex. Sex was all over the fucking place. At Penn it was wild. And after I got out, it was even wilder."

He was already making deals, too, making money. While he was still at Wharton, he and his father bought a townhouse development in Cincinnati, fixed it up, got rid of old tenants, raised rents, and made a big profit.[16] He did the same with a series of small properties in Philadelphia, renovating and selling them. When he arrived back in Manhattan in summer 1968, his net worth was already $200,000. "I was always able to make a lot of money, for whatever reason," he says. "It's like a kid, three years old, sits down and he's playing Mozart. I was doing deals, and they were really cool deals."

Donald outshone his brother, nine years his senior and his father's designated heir. "Fred Jr. was a great guy, a nice guy, too nice," Donald says. "He had a great personality. He was very handsome. I learned a lot from him. But he wasn't somebody who enjoyed business. Which taught me one thing: if you're not into something, don't do it. Fred was a really good pilot. That's what he liked doing, and that's what he should have done. Instead, he went into the business, and he didn't like it. If you don't love it, you're not going to be good at it; he didn't, and it was very tough on him."

Fred Trump Jr., an alcoholic, died in 1980.

WHEN RUSSELL SIMMONS'S family moved to Hollis, Queens, it was a middle-class neighborhood of small businesses and homes with basements and neat front lawns. Simmons was in a fifth-grade class at P.S. 135—his parents had moved so he would be eligible to be bused to the better, integrated school—when Martin Luther King Jr. was killed.

Influence flowed to new leaders. In the fourth grade, Simmons saw his first speech by the separatist Nation of Islam's Louis Farrakhan (b. 1933). "I think everybody my age who is black and came from the lower middle class or any ghetto in America saw Minister Farrakhan speak." But Simmons was multicultural. At home in Hollis, he had black friends; at school he hung out with Jewish kids from nearby Queens Village.

Simmons played baseball with the Hilltop Little League. "It was all white except every team would have two or three black guys," he says. "They were mostly all Jewish, but the funny thing is, the All-Star Team was all niggers—except there was a great Italian pitcher, and Ricky Farina, who I'd always thought was white. I find out one day he's Puerto Rican."

Simmons gives thanks for busing "every fucking day," he says. "I had a lot of white friends, more than most people, because I was integrated, and it did affect my whole life. All of us got something out of being bused, because you learned to feel better about being in the white world. A lot of times I'm still the only black guy in the room. But I'm not aware of it, because I've been that a lot."

IN 1967, JOHN Gage was back in school, and running the math section at Cody's, a Berkeley bookstore. He smoked dope and drove a yellow Volkswagen convertible, but didn't get caught up in the new counterculture. His was not a Summer of Love. His girlfriend, a childhood polio victim, was an organizer for the rights of the disabled and was busy demanding wheelchair access to the Bay Area Rapid Transit subway system, then being built. They thought the hippie world was kid stuff. Local politics and poverty were more serious and had a grimmer edge. "I tried to keep a thin, continuous stream of hedonism, but not sink in it," Gage says.

There was more than enough to sink into. If the myriad events of 1967 and 1968 have been shorthanded to a Baby Boom mantra, consider how in any other time each one would have stood out as extraordinary.

At the First Human Be-In in San Francisco on January 14, 1967, Timothy Leary told the crowd to "tune in, turn on, and drop out"—facilitated by free Owsley acid. On March 26 another "be-in" was held in New York, and on April 15, 400,000 protesters marched on the United Nations, protesting the Vietnam War. Half a million marched in San Francisco.

On May 2, the Black Panthers gained national attention by invading the California Legislature, carrying M1 rifles. On May 20, the New York Diggers, a local version of San Francisco's free soup troupe, dropped dollar bills gathered from drug dealers, disco owners, and liberals from the spectator's gallery of the New York Stock Exchange (which was glassed in shortly thereafter).[17] Twelve days later, the Beatles released their psychedelic magnum opus, *Sergeant Pepper's Lonely Heart's Club Band*. On its heels, Paul McCartney told television viewers worldwide that the Beatles had taken LSD. Acid never got a better endorsement.

A race riot consumed Newark, New Jersey, that summer, leaving 20 dead and 1,500 injured, and another in Detroit lasted a week, resulting in 43 deaths and $400 million in property damage; there were more eruptions nationwide.

Congress ended draft deferments for graduate students on July 2. Then in short order and nearly the same breath the Beatles endorsed legalization of marijuana, and then promptly renounced the drugs and the hippie culture they'd helped create and took off on a pilgrimage (along with Mick Jagger and his girlfriend Marianne Faithfull) to hear transcendental meditation guru Maharishi Mahesh Yogi at a retreat in Wales. There word reached them of their manager Brian Epstein's death from an accidental overdose of sleeping pills. In October, the San Francisco Diggers sealed the coffin on the Summer of Love with a piece of street theater called "Death of Hippie, Loyal Son of Media, Birth of Free Man."

On October 22 national antiwar demonstrations culminated in the Exorcism of the Pentagon, a wacky attempt to levitate the building, which led to 647 arrests. Among those detained was author Norman Mailer, who parlayed the experience into a Pulitzer Prize with his book *The Armies of the Night*. On New Year's Eve, Berkeley activist Jerry Rubin joined with civil rights worker Abbie Hoffman, publisher Paul Krassner, acticvitst Robin Morgan and others to announce the formation of Yippie!, the Youth International Party. On Vietnamese New Year, January

30, 1968, the South Vietnamese liberation movement, known as the Viet Cong, launched the Tet Offensive—a mass attack on the South and American troops that snowballed American public opinion against the war. On March 8, students rioted in Warsaw. On March 12, antiwar senator Eugene McCarthy won 42 percent of the vote in the Democratic primary in New Hampshire. Four days later, Robert Kennedy announced that he, too, would run for president.

On March 31, a bitter, tired Lyndon Johnson announced a bombing halt in Vietnam and his decision not to seek reelection. Five days later, the Rev. Martin Luther King was shot and killed in Memphis, Tennessee, engendering riots nationwide.[18] On April 23, students occupied buildings at Columbia University in New York. May ushered in the Southern Christian Leadership Conference's Poor People's March on Washington, and student and worker uprisings in Paris, across Europe, and behind the Iron Curtain, where Prague Spring was under way.

Between mid-May and mid-June, H. Rap Brown, Catholic activist Phillip Berrigan, Baby Boom baby doctor Benjamin Spock and Yale University chaplain William Sloan Coffin were all sentenced and/or convicted for political activities. Andy Warhol was shot by Valerie Solanis, leader of a one-woman proto-feminist group she dubbed SCUM (The Society for Cutting Up Men). Two mornings later, on June 5, moments after he won the California primary, Bobby Kennedy was killed by a Palestinian named Sirhan Sirhan. In August, 10,000 demonstrators disrupted the Democratic Convention in Chicago, chanting "The whole world is watching," as it did—on television.

NEW YORK'S HIPPIE scene coalesced around Saint Mark's Place in the neighborhood newly dubbed the East Village, where rents were bottom-dollar. On October 6, 1966, the day California banned LSD, a group of young people held A Psychedelic Celebration in nearby Tompkins Square Park, burned incense and chanted "Hare Krishna" with a swami.[19] Swamis were suddenly everywhere, along with yogis, Buddhists,, and psychedelics, which were either illegal, like LSD, or too new to have attained that status, like DMT and STP. If people weren't taking drugs, they were likely still breaking some law or another. Ed Sanders, who ran a beat bookstore in the neighborhood, and Tuli Kupferberg were singing obscene songs at the Player's Theater with their ragged parody of a rock band, The Fugs. At the Dom, on Saint Mark's, Andy Warhol's Exploding Plastic Inevitable, starring the Velvet Underground and Nico, was a regular freak scene. Upstairs at the Balloon Farm, a New York version of the

Trips Festival briefly came down to earth. In February 1967, Timothy Leary's League for Spiritual Discovery opened a headquarters in the West Village attended by Leary, his Harvard colleague Alpert, and a batch of beats: Allen Ginsberg, Gregory Corso and William Burroughs.

Ginsberg felt New York needed its own Be-In. "Somebody has got to do it," he said. "I'm not going to."[20] Jim Fouratt and his boyfriend stepped into the breach, proposing an event on Easter Sunday. "I had learned that how you live your life is politics," Fouratt says. "You find similar people who share your values, and you conspire." Artist Peter Max, another prototype hippie entrepreneur whose psychedelic paintings became the Hallmark cards of the counterculture, agreed to create and pay for 40,000 Day-Glo notices, which a pack of private school kids plastered all over the city. The organizers had agreed the event would embody the hippie values of peace, love and ego transcendence, so when Max put his name on the notices, they made him reprint them—"the only time the proprietary yogi took his name off anything," Fouratt says, chuckling.

That spontaneous Sunday, Central Park played host to about 10,000 hippies, dressed in the finest thrift-shop regalia, faces painted, fists filled with kites, balloons and daisies. They danced in the meadows, climbed the trees, and cavorted with bemused refugees from the city's Easter Parade. "A lot of people think it was about LSD, but that was not the point, in my mind," says Fouratt, who now views it as the last completely uncorrupted moment of the era. The only time police threatened the action was when two men took off their clothes. A crowd quickly gathered, chanting, "We love cops," and the men in blue turned back.[21]

The Be-In gave Fouratt a sense of purpose—a way to stay in the spotlight and do good simultaneously. He quit the Actor's Studio. "The theater is in the streets," he says. "It's not on Broadway. I was really upset when I didn't get an Obie Award for it. I thought it was the most theatrical thing that happened that year."

More followed. They called them "goofs"—little pieces of street theater meant to befuddle the straights and attract new recruits to the hippie thing. They were often staged by New York's Group Image, a media-savvy Digger-like band specializing in cultural agitation and propaganda. Papers like the *Village Voice* spread the word, and Fouratt played his hand among the new media cropping up all around the movement: underground newspapers like the *East Village Other* and the *Berkeley Barb*; sexually explicit underground comics like *Zap*; "progressive" radio stations broadcasting on the FM band; the rock press, led by *Crawdaddy* and *Rolling Stone*; and mass-market magazines like *Cheetah* and Hearst's *Eye*, for which Fouratt wrote up happenings he would then create, so his New York column looked current when it ran three months.

Outside New York City and San Francisco, this new medium hit like bolts from the blue. Boomers poured into the hippie centers, the East Village and the Haight, to see for themselves, providing ready clientele for more long-haired capitalists, who opened countless psychedeli-catessens selling posters, black lights, hippie clothes and buttons bearing assorted slogans as well as random obscenity, beatnik books, rock records and drug paraphernalia—and often the drugs themselves.

Getting along just fine on extra work, odd jobs and unemployment insurance, Fouratt, armed with his trusty Gestetner mimeograph machine (donated by a *Voice* journalist prior to the Be-In), opened a Communication Company of his own, aimed at disseminating information the way the Diggers did in San Francisco. It got put to use fast when on Memorial Day seventy policemen and more than two hundred hippies clashed in Tompkins Square Park over the right to play music and sit on the grass. Within hours, Fouratt was printing out directions to the night court where beaded, barefoot kids were being arraigned. The next day, the Communications Company spread the news that a section of the park had been declared a troubadours' area. All charges were eventually dropped. "The Tompkins Square riot really galvanized the politicization of the hippie movement," Fouratt says.

He acknowledges that he had multiple agendas to fulfill—his progres-sive Catholic's need to do good, his ego's need to lead and his desire for sexual and cultural freedom. "I became a hippie leader," he says. "I mean, it was cloaked in all kinds of feel-good stuff, but I didn't play unless I could be in charge."

The New York hippies had ties to radical groups around the country, which were moving toward larger antiwar actions. In June 1967, a faction of SDS held a national meeting called "Back to the Drawing Boards" at a rustic camp in Michigan to rethink its agenda. Diggers and hippies crashed it, "trying to get them to take acid, essentially," says Fouratt, whose overt homosexuality didn't go over well with the self-serious macho men of SDS. He, on the other hand, admired them "because they really wanted to not adjust," he says. "They wanted to change the world." Fouratt also admired the butch Digger King Emmett Grogan and his out-rageous band of renegades, who had visited New York in March.

New alliances were forming all over, like the one linking Fouratt with civil rights activist turned hippie organizer Abbie Hoffman. Hoffman (b. 1936) was a graduate of Brandeis who'd worked as a pharmaceutical drug salesman until the early 1960s, when, inspired by both the civil rights movement and drugs, he became a full-time activist. Asked to leave SNCC along with other whites, he moved to the East Village and met Fouratt when both briefly worked as youth liaisons for New York's liberal Republican mayor, John Lindsay. "Abbie was trying to figure out how to co-opt the energy for his agenda," he says. "A lot of the hippie kids trusted me. They did not trust Abbie. And Abbie was smart enough to recognize that."

Suddenly, they were New York Diggers; emulating their San Francisco counterparts, they ladled out free stew and opened a store where everything was free. Fouratt renamed himself Jimmy Digger. Hoffman printed a guide to street survival called *Fuck the System*, using city Youth Board funds.

Homosexuality clearly put him off. Abbie wouldn't even acknowledge Fouratt's boyfriend. Though his lover warned him not to trust Hoffman, Abbie struck Fouratt as a cross between Lenny Bruce and Groucho Marx, and he got more involved with the older radical. "Abbie was always trying to fix me up with some hippie chick," Fouratt says, laughing. They began planning actions together. A huge disco, the Electric Circus, had just opened on Saint Mark's Place, with a big dance floor, bands, and a foam rubber room. George Plimpton attended the opening night party; the East Village and hippies were becoming chic.[22] The Diggers planted a tree in a mound of dirt out front.

That spring and summer, the Diggers tossed soot bombs outside the headquarters of Con Edison, New York's electric and gas company; formed the Committee of Concerned Honkies to deliver food to riot-torn Newark ("Diggersareniggers," Hoffman wrote under the pseudonym George Metesky; Fouratt was detained by police for refusing to specify his gender); shot off cap pistols at conferencing Socialists; and staged their invasion of the New York Stock Exchange. "War is profitable, and we wanted to show that," Fouratt says. "They stopped the clock, and people bent down and picked up the fucking dollars!" Hoffman and Fouratt were fired from their city jobs a few days later.

IN 1965, WHEN Cynthia Bowman was a rebellious sixteen, her father got her an apartment of her own and said that if she'd get a job, he'd pay for her to finish school at night. She started modeling at Bloomingdale's, the New York department store. "It really wasn't right," she says. "I was too young to be on my own." By summer 1967, her father had decided she was out of control and threatened to cut her off. Like the heroine of the Beatles song "She's Leaving Home," Bowman and thousands of others her age were hunting hard for freedom, fun, and "something inside that was always denied for so many years."

That and all the other songs on *Sergeant Pepper's Lonely Hearts Club Band* cast a mesmerizing spell on boomers. In the year since the Beatles' last LP, *Revolver*, the moptops had lost any lingering taint of cuteness when John Lennon told a reporter the band was more popular than Jesus—inspiring bonfires of their records in the Southern Bible Belt—and abruptly quit touring. Fueled by pot and acid, the twentysomething millionaires wrote and recorded their drug-soaked masterpiece.

Now it was out and had changed the world, immediately and indelibly. One day, as her father raged that he would no longer subsidize her lifestyle, Bowman nonchalantly flipped through *Time* magazine's new cover story, "The Hippies: Philosophy of a Subculture," while blithely inquiring how he expected her to pay for school. "If you're so smart" he yelled—she looked at a picture of the Grateful Dead, then of the Jefferson Airplane—"you figure it out!"

Bowman had an older girlfriend, Lexy, who'd "turned me on to pot and told me all about sex," she says. Lexy had just agreed to meet a guy in San Francisco. Cynthia took her to the airport in a taxi. At check-in, Lexy begged her, "Please, please come with me. What do you have to lose? You know you are going to die here by yourself." She didn't even have her purse. But tickets weren't expensive then. Late that night, she called her father from California. "I'm in a commune at Six-Thirty Lyon Street," she said, "and you need to go feed my dog and clear out my apartment. And could you send me my purse?"

"He was probably relieved," Bowman says now. "All he had to do was clean out an apartment and take a dog to the pound. Instead of having to deal with me anymore."

THE STUDENTS WHO joined SDS in the mid-1960s were different from the earnest radicals who'd started the organization. These new recruits saw radical students as the vanguard of a much larger movement. As an original SDS leader, Todd Gitlin, would later write, they were "breaking out of the postwar consensus . . . of complacency, good behavior and middle-class mores," allowing themselves to "break with adults, be done with compromises, *get on with it* . . ."[23]

In Mark Rudd's sophomore year, these impatient young radicals began confronting Columbia over its secret affiliation with the Institute for Defense Analyses (IDA) and its policy of allowing Marine Corps and

CIA recruitment on campus. Rudd spent the Summer of Love in an antidraft project in city summer schools. Stationed in a downtown SDS office, he planned rallies in front of high schools and offered draft counseling. And he started hanging out on the Lower East Side, "going to hear Country Joe and the Fish on Tompkins Square and dropping mescaline," he recalls.

That August, Rudd hitchhiked to California, stopping at the SDS National Office in Chicago, where the leadership gave him a book by Regis Debray about the Cuban revolution. The Americans were impressed by Debray's theory of the *foco*, a small vanguard band that could start a revolution when "their exemplary actions won over people ready to become radicalized," Rudd says. "You start doing it, you don't just talk about it, and that starts the revolution. We began to see ourselves as guerrillas within this country."

Rudd continued on to Haight-Ashbury at the tail end of the summer, when "the love had turned to hate on Haight, and there was a lot of drug-dealing and squalor." Then he went on to Los Angeles, where he stayed with SDS friends, and to San Diego, where he bunked in Herbert Marcuse's house, although the great man wasn't there at the time.

Back at school, Rudd skipped the Exorcism at the Pentagon, and was furious with himself afterward. A new friend, Jeff Jones from the SDS Regional Office, had gone and come back with wild stories. "I instantly realized that I had been on the wrong track; militancy and action was what was needed."

An argument began at Columbia that would split SDS there into two factions, dubbed the "praxis axis" and the "action faction." The former, led by the group's older founding chairman, was concerned with education and discussion, the latter with splatter. Like the Yippies and the Diggers, the action faction, younger students led by Rudd who'd seen the wisdom of Abbie Hoffman's ways, wanted to use street theater, massage the media, and turn on anyone who tuned in.

A month after the march on the Pentagon, Secretary of State Dean Rusk was set to give a speech to a Foreign Policy Association dinner at the Hilton Hotel. One of the peace groups had planned a legal picket, but the SDS Regional Office publicized a huge, unsanctioned street action— "Dine with the Warmakers"—and attracted a crowd of thousands. Deliberately provocative (they were armed with animal blood, red paint and eggs) and predictably provoked by charging police, they started a bloody riot that ended with forty-six arrests, Rudd's very first arrest among them.[24] Abbie Hoffman was one of his cellmates. "I don't think he paid any attention to me," Rudd admits. "I could see he had a lot of energy, but I also disagreed with him; I was more serious."

OWSLEY, THE ACID king, had finally decided to retire and train Tim Scully to take his place as the gourmet chef of LSD. Early in 1967, just after the San Francisco Be-In, Scully headed to Denver to find a lab of his own, where he expected to finish his training in the art of acid-making by processing the rest of Owsley's raw material. He also redesigned the lab equipment and tinkered with the Eli Lilly recipe so they could produce LSD on a grander scale. But when he came back to Berkeley for supplies, he discovered their success had a price. The authorities were on to them. Federal agents had been pressuring their suppliers for evidence against Owsley. "They didn't want to turn in their friend, so they turned me in," Scully says. When he came to pick up his order in the Sunshine Cookie truck he'd used as a Grateful Dead roadie, a Fed helped him load up and followed him.

He got away—and quickly learned evasive driving techniques. But the Feds always found him again. "It was terrifying until we realized they weren't about to swoop down and bust us, what they wanted to do was follow us," Scully says. "Every time I came back to California, they had my house staked out. So we had to lose them every time."

Then came another glitch: Owsley started playing cagey about the remaining raw materials. "I don't think it's the right time," he told Scully, handing him a 3-by-5 inch card with another recipe, for another psychedelic drug, a mescaline derivative with an amphetamine kick, that would soon be named after the automotive additive STP. Thinking this yet another test—making LSD was complex, STP easier—Scully worked months refining the recipe. "I spent a lot of time in the library," he says.[25]

While Scully made STP in Denver, Owsley took off for New York, where he visited Leary and *his* master chef: Nick Sand of Brooklyn, a teenage bathtub chemistry prodigy who'd made batches of DMT (a fifteen-minute hallucinogen) and synthetic mescaline. Owsley also met Billy Hitchcock, who gave him financial advice and provided contacts to help him set up an offshore account for the $225,000 he'd stashed in a safe deposit box.

Under government surveillance, too, Hitchcock, Leary and Sand left Millbrook one by one and headed west. Leary showed up in San Francisco spouting megalomaniacal nonsense about buying land with money he didn't have and setting up his own country, based on freedom of mind, body and drug ingestion.[26] Scully knew Leary and didn't think much of him. "Thinking you're doing something that's saving the world is totally addictive," Scully allows, "but he was strident and flamboyant in promoting acid, which felt wrong to me." Leary was a media personality hurtling headlong toward martyrdom—and taking a lot of people down with him.

AFTER THE SUMMER of Love, the bloom quickly came off Flower Power. Converts and tourists crammed the tiny enclaves of the Haight and Saint Mark's Place, driving crime rates up and the original colonists into the country, where they made news again by forming communes, most of which did not last very long. Panhandlers replaced street theater. "You no longer had middle- and upper-class kids being hippies," Jim Fouratt says. "You had all these kids coming in who had no safety net and no place to stay. Then the Mob took over LSD distribution, and started mixing it with speed. Amphetamine is a great street drug, because you don't have to go to sleep."

It wasn't only the Mob. Nick Sand had arrived in San Francisco in July 1967 and set up an STP lab. Owsley had been handing out Tim Scully's version, which he'd turned into high-dosage tablets. STP was sold as better, stronger acid, but even after they taste-tested it and cut the dosage in half, the market didn't like it. Luckily, just as word hit the streets that Scully's new product was too strong and causing lots of bad trips, Owsley finally came up with the second half of his stash of lysergic acid. It turned out that his girlfriend had locked the stuff in a safe deposit box, but forgotten the bank branch where the box was.

By fall 1967, the tide had turned, perceptibly. After the Diggers had declared hippiedom dead in San Francisco, New York Diggers including Fouratt and Hoffman appeared on *The David Susskind Show* flailing a toy duck Groucho Marx-style each time Susskind said the word *hippie*. On that show, Fouratt pulled off another first, announcing his homosexuality on national television. "I was all dressed in white, Indian cotton shirt, blond hair, the sweetest thing you could possibly find," Fouratt recalls. "I said things you weren't supposed to say on television—I might have been on acid; I don't remember. We were just trying to shock David, because he was the ultimate sort of liberal."

In New York that month, a wealthy blond art student from the New York suburbs, Linda Rae Fitzpatrick (b. 1949), and James "Groovy" Hutchinson, (b. 1946), two kids who'd lived in a crash pad commune on East 11th Street and loved amphetamines, were found with their skulls bashed in by bricks in the boiler room of a tenement on Avenue B. "The flower thing is dead," an East Village neighbor told the *New York Times*. In December, the New York Digger Free Store closed down after it turned up at the center of a mess of drugs, informants, violence, Puerto Rican gangs and hippie factionalism, and the police started busting apartments full of runaways. The hippie moment passed quickly in the places where it was born, but rippled out across the country for two more years.

Even among the hippie activists, the mood had changed. Tussles ensued between Fouratt and Hoffman, by then heavy into drugs, Fouratt says. Hoffman and Robin Morgan (b. 1941), a former child star who'd married a leftist poet and become a civil rights worker, appropriated the Communications Company's mimeograph machine. Hoffman also absconded with a bail fund Fouratt had raised, but Fouratt was undeterred. "There was a movement going, and I wasn't going to be left out of it," he says. Hoffman's magnetic energy had attracted the Bay Area antiwar activist Jerry Rubin, an organizer of Berkeley's first Vietnam Day who'd come in second in a run for mayor there. When Rubin came to New York in late summer 1967, he and Hoffman became fast allies and were photographed together burning money.

Rubin had been invited to New York to help plan a peace march in Washington. It was decided that the protesters should encircle the Pentagon, perform an exorcism, and attempt to levitate it. By injecting surreal fun into the serious work at hand, Hoffman, Rubin, and their fellows captured the imagination of America's young. They made national news, too, when Hoffman said that police use of Mace would be countered with demonstrators' use of "Lace," an LSD-infused skin-penetrating compound that when sprayed on cops and soldiers would cause them to rip off their clothes and start having sex. Unfortunately, Lace was a fiction, the Pentagon did not fly, and Hoffman and his new wife, Anita (whom he'd married in a Be-In–like media event in Central Park), were arrested. They gave their names as Mr. and Mrs. Digger.

CYNTHIA BOWMAN LANDED in San Francisco just after the Summer of Love ended. Her first day in town, she steered her friend Lexy to the Jefferson Airplane mansion, a Greek Revival house with seventeen rooms facing Golden Gate Park. The Airplane were already stars of the Haight-Ashbury scene. Marty Balin (b. 1942), Paul Kantner (b. 1941), Jack Casady (b. 1944) and Jorma Kaukonen (b. 1940) had been folk and bluegrass musicians, and Balin had opened a folk-rock nightclub called the Matrix in 1965, where many of the local bands played. Employing the name of a fictitious bluesman (Blind Thomas Jefferson

Airplane); a former fashion model and singer, Grace Slick (nicked from a competing band called the Great Society); and two of that band's songs ("Somebody to Love" and "White Rabbit," which were fast becoming psychedelic anthems), the band was among the first from the new San Francisco scene to score a record contract, signing with RCA for $25,000 in 1966. The next June, Kantner's band played songs from their second album, *Surrealistic Pillow*, at the Monterey Pop Festival, where they were filmed by Victoria Leacock's father. Monterey became the ideal for every rock festival that followed. Driven by the two Top 40 hits, *Pillow*, recorded for $8,000, grossed $8 million.[27]

"We spent the next year dropping LSD every other day and sitting across the street from the Airplane mansion, waiting for them to come out," Bowman remembers. "I would just sit there and stare at the big house, as high as I could get, watching them come and go. The only reason I didn't do it every day was because acid only works every other day." Meanwhile, the seventeen-year-old became involved in her first love affair, with one of her fellow communards, the boy Lexy had followed to San Francisco. "She lasted about a week and then I moved in and we were together for several years," Bowman says. "I would cook the same thing every night. Tuna fish, noodles, and cream of mushroom soup."

One afternoon, Bowman was tripping down Haight Street in her hippie jeans when a man began menacing her in front of the Haight Theater, where the San Francisco Hell's Angels parked their motorcycles. "One of the Angels saw this guy jump on me and he jumped on the guy and threw him onto the roof of a car," she says. "And within three minutes there had to be fifty Hell's Angels there, all knocking the shit out of this guy. And I was just horrified, crying, terrified—more of the Hell's Angels than the guy." But she was about to see their angelic side. "I started trying to get away, walking back to my house, and these Hell's Angels escorted me, pushing their motorcycles to my house, and I remember walking up the steps and all the hippies ran out the back door, thinking the Angels were going to kill us," Bowman says, laughing.

That fall she got a job wrapping Christmas gifts at a San Francisco department store. After work her first night, she walked out into the unfamiliar city, and promptly fell into an excavation for the new Bay Area Rapid Transit subway system. A steel beam almost severed her foot. She began a series of repair operations. Released from the hospital, she'd go out, walk on the foot, "screw it up again," and end up back in the hospital.

Like so many who rode the second hippie wave following the Summer of Love, Bowman didn't think the Haight scene had soured at all. "I guess if you'd been here a year before you might have thought of it as a death of an era, but for me it was all new," she says. "Everybody was smoking pot and taking acid, and there was free music on the street."

In 1968 she, her boyfriend and another of their roommates established a commune near Stanford University in Palo Alto. Bowman took classes there in exchange for work as a guinea pig in its psychic research lab. For the next few years, she shared an essentially irresponsible existence with her boyfriend. "But graduate students were not nearly as crazy as the people in San Francisco," she says. "It was a nice house. We all had our own rooms and we ate real food and made money one way or another." In pursuit of nirvana, they smoked pot all the time and took psychedelic drugs regularly. "My boyfriend and I would set the clock for four A.M., then pop acid, go back to bed, and wake up high as kites. We would go to the Zen center, looking for spirituality. Actually, he was searching for it; I just wanted to get high, to tell you the truth."

AT THE END of 1967, Owsley Stanley (who, no longer junior to anyone, had legally dropped the "Augustus" and accompanying roman numerals,) liberated his remaining lysergic acid from its safe deposit box and telephoned Tim Scully.

"Now is the right time," he said.

They promptly headed to Denver to whip up more acid. For weeks, they "worked in shifts," Scully says. "I worked while Bear slept." The first batch was called Monterey Purple in honor of the Monterey Pop Festival. The profits, earmarked for more raw material purchases, went into offshore accounts set up by Billy Hitchcock, who'd moved to Sausalito with a new girlfriend, formed a partnership with a Swiss bank, and gotten a job at a new brokerage house happy to collect commissions and not look at his transactions too closely.[28]

Police were still following Scully everywhere. He'd even photographed one drug agent and published the picture in the *Berkeley Barb*. He remained determined to turn on the world—even after federal agents raided Owsley's tableting operation in Orinda, California, in December and Owsley decided the time had come to quit for good. [29] Scully had to get himself a backer, a new source for lysergic acid, and a large-scale distribution network. Owsley had briefly used the Hell's Angels, but Scully preferred not to deal with them.

He approached Hitchcock, whom he'd met through Owsley, suggesting that the Eastern heir finance his grand plan for a mass acid giveaway. Hitchcock wouldn't go that far, but according to Scully, agreed to bankroll him with loans and provided the name of a chemical broker in London. Hitchcock denies bankrolling the purchases of raw materials. "He did get repaid, and of course, he got lots of free acid," Scully insists.[30]

With the new source of supply in place, Scully got back to work. He and Sand each went off to set up labs—Sand's in St. Louis, Scully's back in suburban Denver. Before the year was out, they'd both been shut down. Scully's landlord had gotten a whiff of the lab while its occupants were out of town, thought it was a body, and called the cops. When Scully's assistants returned two days later, they were arrested. Scully called shortly afterward, and when an unknown voice answered, "Scully residence," he hitched a ride to Eureka, Oregon. "I tried it for a few days and decided not to be a fugitive. I just went back to living my life. So later, when I was *really* indicted, I didn't try to dodge it, because I'd decided already I'd rather pay the dues and have it over with."

Scully headed to Billy Hitchcock's place in Sausalito to hunker down and figure out what to do. While there, he met John Griggs, founder of the Brotherhood of Eternal Love, a band of drug-dealing hippies, born when a motorcycle gang of petty thieves first encountered LSD and retired their bikes and guns to run Mystic Arts World, an elaborate head shop in Laguna Beach, and a marijuana-smuggling operation. Griggs was another quasi-mystic who'd seen the truth on acid and wanted to make a new world. He'd incorporated the Brotherhood ten days after LSD was banned.[31] By mid–1968, the Brotherhood had spread its operation around the world, smuggling hashish from Afghanistan in Volkswagen buses and surfboards.

Griggs had bought a ranch near Palm Springs on Tim Leary's advice and invited his mentor to stay. Leary introduced him to Hitchcock. Hitchcock, Sand, Scully and Griggs tripped together and decided to go into business. The Brotherhood would take over the distribution of Scully's and Sand's LSD. Scully felt he didn't have to fear the righteous brotherhood. "I was looking for psychedelic, visionary people to distribute the acid, and the Brotherhood seemed gentle and honest," he says. "They weren't college graduates; they were diamonds in the rough. I could front them half a million dollars' worth of acid, and they'd come back with the money later."

Unlike the street-smart Owsley and Sand, Scully had never banked any money—that's not why he was making acid. So Sand and Hitchcock had to provide the funds to pay for his new lab in Windsor, California, near Santa Rosa.[32] Hitchcock opened an offshore account for Sand, and the Windsor property was put in the name of a Liechtenstein corporation

Sand established as a blind for cash transactions. When raw materials arrived from England, Hitchcock stashed them in his local safe deposit boxes, helped Scully cart lab equipment to Windsor, and stuck around to help tablet the final product.[33] "That was the last lab I had, the one I ended up doing twenty years for," Scully says ruefully.

In Windsor, Scully made the best and most famous acid of the late 1960s, Orange Sunshine. The Brotherhood's marketing campaign began when 100,000 doses were given away free at rock concerts. They gave Scully a trip to their ranch as his reward. He wasn't rich, but he was thinking bigger. While there, he sketched out his Leary-esque fantasy of an offshore lab—a state with its own laws devoted to LSD.[34] The more practical Sand got a ranch of his own outside Cloverdale, California.

BARBARA LEDEEN ENTERED Beloit College in 1967 as a political science major, still the moderate Democrat she was raised to be. "Lyndon Johnson, he's my guy," she says. "Except there's this war in Vietnam which is not okay. I didn't know anybody who was for it except for my father. I was doing political science and reading about communism, and it didn't sound all terrible." Communists had been for civil rights, and that was Ledeen's political touchstone. Her library was full of books by Richard Wright and Langston Hughes.

A year later, she was given a list of work-study job options for poli-sci majors. Copy girl at *The Washington Post* sounded good. Armed with the name of a contact and a list of Beloit students in Washington, she packed her bags. "I thought I was pretty cosmopolitan," she says. "I wasn't a virgin, anyway—already very radical." But she wasn't ready for her hazing: a conversation with her male boss in a strip club. "I didn't know where to look," she says. "We didn't have concepts like hostile work environment, so it was cope, girl, just cope."

She rented a basement apartment. "I was looking for trouble, and it was easy to find. I had gazillions of boyfriends, married, unmarried, this and that." She wore short skirts and little boots. (*Post* owner Kay Graham's one comment to her was, "Get longer skirts.") Ledeen tried pot but didn't get high. She did mescaline once and "was messed up for a long time," she says, "so I knew if I did acid I would really be in trouble." Drugs were not her thing. Neither was Washington. "How can you go to their cocktail parties if you're a journalist?" she posits. "If you're part of that, how do you critique it? I'm thinking, 'This is beyond corrupt. This is an outrage, this is terrible.'" It wasn't all bad. "It's 1968, a crystallizing, catalytic year for everybody," she says. She remembers peace marches and protests; the last HUAC hearings; how Martin Luther King's successor at the Southern Christian Leadership Conference, the Rev. Ralph Abernathy, led a Poor People's March on Washington, in which 3,000 protesters lived in tents for fifteen days on the Mall. And she remembers getting the phone call telling the *Post* that Robert Kennedy had been shot. "It was me on the phone. And I was at the foreign desk the night the Russians invaded Czechoslovakia; all the bells started ringing on the wire service machines and I had to call [editor] Ben Bradlee at home—*stop the presses!*"

In the nation's capital, Ledeen saw—up close and personal—how politics affected everyday life. She was so bemused that she stayed a second trimester, and tacked on the vacation time she had coming, too, "just licking it up," she says, from "the hypocrisy and the dishonesty and the palsy-walsy Washington scene" to "people dying and putting themselves on the line to change an inherently corrupt system." Finally, at the end of the year, Bradlee called Ledeen into his office. "You are like a little mouse eating a big cheese," he said. "Time to go back to college."

IN JANUARY 1968, the SDS National Office started organizing a trip to Cuba—the first by Americans in four years. Mark Rudd cut five weeks of classes and went; he was on the rebel island when the Vietnamese launched the Tet Offensive. He toured a hospital and a collective farm, visited university students and intellectuals, ate tomato ice cream, and did "a lot of partying," Rudd says. "I come back and I'm ready. I'd been won over to the cult of Che Guevara. 'The duty of every revolutionary is to make the revolution.'" He didn't care that Eugene McCarthy was astonishing the country. "We mocked those 'clean for Gene' people," he says. But Lyndon Johnson's abdication made him sit up and notice. "That was the moment the government decided it couldn't win the war."

Between classes, the Columbia junior's involvement in political conflicts escalated. In October 1967, he'd been part of a polite SDS march on Grayson Kirk's office. The following February, SDS confronted napalm maker Dow Chemical Company's campus recruiters. Then in March, Rudd became chairman of SDS. When Colonel Paul Akst, who ran the draft in New York City, came to the campus a few days later to answer questions about the draft, a member of the action faction pushed a lemon meringue pie in his face.[35]

Rudd led another protest against Columbia's role in an IDA research project for the CIA. Demonstrators invaded the administrative office in the elegant, domed Low Memorial Library and angrily demanded a meeting with Kirk, a sixty-eight-year-old whose imperious attitude infuriated the students. A few days later, when Kirk refused to link arms with students for the singing of "We Shall Overcome" at a memorial service for Martin Luther King Jr., Rudd stood up and grabbed a mike—echoes of Mario Savio—called Columbia's hypocrisy "a moral outrage," and led a walkout. Kirk gave a speech calling America's young "nihilists." "I know of no time in our history when the gap between the generations has been wider or more potentially dangerous," he said.

"We *will* have to destroy at times, even violently," Rudd responded. "But that is a far cry from nihilism. . . . We the young people, whom you so rightly fear . . . use the words of [poet] LeRoi Jones, whom I'm sure you don't like a whole lot: 'Up against the wall, motherfucker, this is a stick-up.'"[36]

"So," Rudd adds now, "anybody could see there was a confrontation building."

In its first foray on the racial front, SDS decided to co-sponsor a rally against a gym Columbia was constructing on the site of a public park that separated the elite school from the black neighborhood it abutted. The demonstration was set to begin at midday at a large sundial in the middle of Columbia's campus.[37] The SDS organizers hoped the crowd would invade Low Library with a petition supporting six students, Rudd among them, put on disciplinary probation for their role in the IDA protest—while committing the same infraction in the process.

At noon on April 23, the Battle of Morningside Heights was joined. Cicero Wilson, the new head of the Students' Afro-American Society, till then a quiet, moderate group, spoke stirringly, inspiring the crowd to action. The mob roared off to the gym site, where it tore down a fence before police made an arrest. Rudd demanded the student's release. When an administrator ignored him, the crowd headed back to campus, where whites and blacks started arguing over who was in charge.[38]

"When somebody gets arrested, you're supposed to react," Rudd says. "So we thought, 'Let's take a building hostage for the guy who got arrested.' So everybody rushes into Hamilton Hall and we find the Dean of the College. So we decided to keep him hostage, and the whole thing escalated from there."

Demands were issued: that the gym project be halted, and that the university end its support of war research, lift the ban on demonstrations, settle disciplinary questions like Rudd's in open hearings, and dismiss charges against student demonstrators. Although the dean, Henry Coleman, was released the next day, students seized more buildings in his stead, "liberating" five altogether.

A Strike Coordinating Committee entreated students to support the occupation. Rudd's negotiating position only hardened when a dean told him that no matter what else happened, he would be expelled.[39] Though some students were annoyed that their education had been put on hold— a group calling itself Majority Coalition blockaded the protestors Low Library and vowed to cut off food supplies—the occupiers succeeded in halting work on the gymnasium on the second day of their revolt.

The Columbia takeover made national headlines. A now-famous photo of one student, sitting at Kirk's mahogany desk, puffing on one of his cigars, outraged as many Americans as it amused. For radicals, Columbia was the best show in town. Tom Hayden, Jim Fouratt, Stokely Carmichael, H. Rap Brown and Abbie Hoffman were among the spectators. Brown made the *New York Times* with his suggestion that if the gym got built, the people of Harlem should blow it up.

"Then, at a certain point, they call in the cops," Rudd says. In the wee hours of April 30, 1,000 police cleared the buildings. Final box score: 524 students removed, 692 people arrested, 103 injured (including a professor, a reporter and 20 police). And Kirk's office was totally trashed. The next day the Columbia undergraduate community went on strike and effectively shut down the school. Faculty, students and administrators met to try to end the impasse. Structures were created to let students finish the semester, although many simply left for the summer. A student strike committee created a "liberation school" with courses on Buddhism, Blake and the student movement in Spain. The Grateful Dead played a victory concert. Police were posted campus-wide. The question of disciplinary action against the students remained unresolved.[40] "This is where I learned a lot about the battlefield," says Rudd. "Basically, all the radical faculty sat on the wall."

Early one May evening, the strikers held another on-campus rally, at which a speaker announced a new front in the battle against Columbia. Local residents had occupied a nearby university-owned tenement. Students sat in the street outside the building. Again, in the middle of the night, the police moved in. Rudd was among the sixty-eight arrested for disorderly conduct. At the local precinct, cops congregated to stare at him.

The next day, Rudd and three other participants in the IDA protest were called before a dean to discuss the situation. Later on that day, another sundial rally declared the dean's authority illegitimate before moving en masse to seize Hamilton Hall. The administration gave the students an ultimatum—leave or be suspended—and called the police.

Their first two actions were to rip down a poster of Chairman Mao and to arrest Rudd, charging him with riot, trespassing and encouraging others to commit crimes.

Rudd—along with five dozen others—was immediately suspended, but Columbia's punishment didn't end there. The registrar informed his local draft board, so by December, he could expect to be drafted.[41] But, in many ways SDS had won: the gym wasn't built, the blanket ban on indoor demonstrations was rescinded, Columbia split from IDA, new disciplinary procedures were instituted, Grayson Kirk resigned after students walked out of his last commencement address, and all over the country, students were radicalized by watching their counterparts being beaten on TV, proving Regis Debray's *foco* theory—at least in the minds of Rudd and his Debray-esque band of revolutionary exemplars.

WHEN THE YOUTHQUAKE hit Boston in the middle 1960s, it missed Tommy Vallely. One of his younger brothers wanted to be a Beatle, but not Tommy, whose sense of solitude had evolved into an air of independence. He worked in a gas station and at a drugstore to make money, which he spent on clothes and having fun. "Friends, girlfriends, beer, football games—I was a very straight kid," he says.

Vallely's older sister was a leftist in college, and his mother, who had a EUGENE MCCARTHY FOR PRESIDENT bumper sticker on her car, went to antiwar demonstrations in Boston. He thought they were "wrong, but not to the point where I want to get in an argument," he says. "There was a debate in my high school, too, and I stayed on the sidelines and watched." He was already thinking about enlisting.

In spring 1968, as Vallely's high school graduation neared, he felt his options were few: "Go to Newton Junior College or get a job," he says. "I was certainly not going to Harvard." Yet he was ambitious. He stumbles for long minutes over his reasons for enlisting in the Marines. It wasn't as if he had a great desire to defeat communism, but for him, "America always did good, and I wanted to do good." He wanted to be as proud of himself as he was of his country, "like the people that went to World War Two," he says. "I would get to wear the uniform, do something other people would respect." He pauses. "I certainly changed my mind fairly quickly about a lot of those things."

Vallely spent the summer partying and planning his going-away party. Only as September approached, when he would enter boot camp at Parris Island, did he start to get scared, "a reflection of how little I knew," he says now. He took infantry training at Camp Lejeune in North

Carolina, then headed to Camp Pendelton in California, the jumping-off point for Vietnam.

"In fall 1968, the Marine Corps is not a place you want to be," Vallely says. "We were ten percent of the fighting force and were taking about sixty percent of the casualties. You go to Vietnam in the Marine Corps, you're crazy. So I do, at this point, get scared shitless. I begin to be aware I might get killed, and I regret it. I'm a middle-class kid from Newton; my father's a judge, I shouldn't have done this. I'd overstepped my desire to be different. But I've committed to it, I've taken an oath, and I want to keep my honor."

Suddenly, he saw thoughtfulness as a virtue, and what he was thinking about was getting home alive. His company, India Company, 3rd Battalion, 5th Marines, "had discipline, it had good people, it had good officers," he says. "And it gave you a certain amount of confidence that if you understood the rules, you'd do pretty well."

Rule Number 1 was to make friends who would watch your back. Looking around his base camp outside Da Nang, a region the Marines called the Arizona Territory, he fell in with a group from Massachusetts who'd been "in country" for some time. One of them was Tim "Salty" Vallely (no relation), a veteran of more than a few firefights. Salty's fatigues were clean, his backpack worked, and he had an air of confidence.

"I'm going to show you how to get out of here," Salty told him.

"I'm your best student," replied Vallely, who instantly became the scholar he'd never been in school. No one talked about "the fucking war," Vallely adds. "There's no 'war,' okay? We're talking survival."

Vallely's unit saw a lot of combat. "The first time I thought the world had ended," he says. "It was at night, a small ambush, not a big deal. All of a sudden, from over a hill you see bullets, tracer rounds, we're receiving. I have a shitty pack; I don't have one of the nice packs. I can't get it off to shoot. By the time I get my pack off, the thing is over with. Someone got wounded but nobody got killed. And that's my baptism of fire. I couldn't get my pack off. But I watched these other guys and they were firing back, seemingly not scared. A few of those and your fear starts to go away."

The next hurdle was walking point—being the first member of his company to enter new terrain. "Big honor, big problem," Vallely says. "You have to react quickly, you have to have confidence, you have to shoot first and think later because if you don't, you're dead. You've got to scare them as much as you're scared. Not everyone's good at it. And I, unfortunately, was good enough at it that if I'd kept doing it, my name would be on that fucking [Vietnam Memorial] wall."

He decided he wanted to be a radio operator. Despite his stutter, he knew how to talk, how to describe what was happening around him, even under fire. Radio operators "knew a ton," he says, because they had to write and dictate reports. They were aware of the big picture. They were vital links in the chain of command. The better he did it, the less the chance he'd have to walk point again. "That concentrated my mind," Vallely says. He soon became the number-two radio operator in India Company.

"That's the basic story of what happened to me in Vietnam," he says. "I went, I survived, I became quite skilled." Of course, that wasn't the whole story, because the longer he stayed in Vietnam, the more aware he became of the war's foolishness. "Having been in dozens of villages, I got a very clear sense that the villagers were with the other side," he says. "And what we were trying to do was not going to work."

Neither, he realized, were America's air power and artillery as effective as claimed. As a radio operator, Vallely could make the night day. He could light up the sky with illumination canisters, call in artillery strikes, Huey helicopter gunships, spotter planes, and B52s, and adjust the fire from off-shore naval battleships. "But I couldn't call anybody to tell them what we were doing wrong," he says.

"One time we bombed the shit out of this village and all the kids played soccer afterward," he says. He remembers thinking, "That's exactly what *we* want, we're not here to burn villages. We're here to survive."

The troops were disciplined, not gung-ho. They did what they had to do. They had their doubts, but Vallely believes those doubts did not affect performance. "When the Marines were engaged, they did a good job," he says. But evil abounded amid the camaraderie and valor, "war crimes that affected me deeply," says Vallely. When a Marine in his company set off a flare in a pregnant woman's vagina, he would have killed the guy had he not been stopped. "We had that type of a person," he allows. "But the good guys outnumbered the bad guys by a lot."

At home, politicians were claiming there was light at the end of the tunnel, and the tide of the war was turning in America's favor. In-country, Vallely and Co. didn't think so. "The Marine Corps never bought that bullshit," he says. Then, once Richard Nixon became president—a few months into Vallely's tour—American strategy shifted to disengagement. "We were just trying to get out of there," Vallely says. "But the Vietnamese weren't disengaging, they were trying to throw us out, trying to win the war. And if you get ambushed, you fight."

* * *

IMMEDIATELY AFTER LYNDON Johnson's near-loss in New Hampshire, the vaunted Kennedy campaign operation sprang into action and John Gage was among those called. Would he run as one of about a dozen students vying to be delegates for newly-annonced presidential candidate Robert F. Kennedy at the upcoming Chicago Democratic Convention? Gage flew to Los Angeles; met Jesse Unruh, speaker of California's assembly and head of the state's Kennedy campaign, in a smoke-filled room at an airport motel; and agreed not only to be a candidate but to help run the California primary campaign.

Working through the spring with Berkeley law students and political pros from Massachusetts, Gage won a vote at the convention. Kennedy beat McCarthy and was suddenly a strong contender to replace Johnson. But moments after he declared victory in Los Angeles, Robert Kennedy was shot dead. "There we are in Berkeley at my campaign headquarters," Gage says. "Everybody is in tears. No one can understand how this happened. The entire thing has absolutely ripped our hearts out. And we go on to Chicago."

MARIANNE WILLIAMSON WAS fifteen in April 1968, when Martin Luther King Jr. was killed in Memphis, Tennessee. Her father got home from work as the bulletin came over the television. "I saw a look on his face I had never seen before. His eyes seemed to focus on something impossibly far away and with an intensely pained expression, he spat out the words, 'Those bastards.' In that instant, I lost my innocence. That day changed history, and it certainly changed me. My father was signaling to me, This is the way things are. I took another road than my father—love for what could be is a much stronger dynamic than anger at what is—but I am looking for the same perfect world."

That is now. Then, the stunning succession of events in her last two years in high school pulled Williamson away from God and love and impelled her toward protests and picket lines. That June, the day after Bobby Kennedy was shot, she and her friends went to a nearby park to commemorate the event. Though she didn't realize it at the time, she preached her first sermon. "I stood up and gave this extemporaneous eulogy and we all sat there like 'Whoa!'—including me. I mean, clearly I was fired up."

It wasn't long until she and her friends were scared off public life. "The bullets that dropped the Kennedys and King struck all of us," she says. "We received a very loud unspoken message: You will now stop arguing with the prevailing authority or we just might kill you, too."

For any individual, any generation, maturing is a two-step process. The first is severance, the second, the forging of a unique role. "We went through phase one," says Williamson, "we took to the streets, we made it very clear that we were disconnecting from the way our parents had done it, but our politics were ultimately not as profound as we thought they were. Because when it came to establishing how we were going to do it, the heroes who articulated that vision were killed in front of our eyes and our whole generation became like the son of Bobby Kennedy who saw his father shot and never recovered. He basically just got stoned and died. At that very, very critical age, we were frozen."

Not only that, Williamson, like many of her peers, had unprecedented access to three numbing agents that "had never before been so accessible to so many so young: Sex, drugs, and rock 'n' roll," she says. "I was never *that* wild. I was never a drug addict. But I was very much a child of my age."

THE NEWLYWEDS, RICHARD and Marilyn Leacock, moved into a duplex apartment in Chelsea, upstairs from the art critic Lawrence Halloway, who'd just coined the term Pop Art. Briefly, they lived a charmed 1960s life, summering on Fire Island, partying with actors, artists and intellectuals. Leacock and Pennebaker formed a company, and in 1964, Pennebaker traveled to England with Bob Dylan to make a documentary called *Don't Look Back*, while Leacock pursued his own quite opposite interests and made films about Igor Stravinsky and Leonard Bernstein. In 1967, they collaborated on a film about the Monterey Pop Festival. Marilyn, meanwhile, worked as a fund-raiser for the NAACP.

It all seemed colorful to Victoria, who dressed as a flower child for a costume parade on Fire Island, accidentally ate a hashish brownie ("The babysitter was very upset"), and giggled when her mother took down their poster of Janis Joplin in the nude because other parents were coming to visit. Leacock's travels, and the temptations that came with them, took a toll on the marriage. By the time Victoria began school, the marriage was over. Leacock-Pennebaker went bankrupt after an abortive attempt to make a movie with the French director Jean-Luc Godard, and Leacock took a job several hundred miles away as the head of the film department at MIT. Victoria remembers visiting neighbors one Christmas because her mother didn't want to be alone. Instead, Marilyn smoked hashish while her daughter slept on the couch.

"It was very much the caftans, Valium, *Valley of the Dolls* sixties," Victoria says. "And my mom got in with a set of chi-chi women who were all getting divorced, and they got her a fancy lawyer, so instead of just being hurt and sorting things out, it became nasty." For weeks on end, her mother sat at home in the dark. "Mom wanted a family, you know?" Divorce papers were filed naming three women Leacock had had affairs with—a writer, a pianist and an Andy Warhol superstar. "I always joked that if my mom was going down, she was going down with a good crowd."

The next Christmas, her mother slipped, tore ligaments in her knee, underwent an unsuccessful operation, began taking cortisone and painkillers and, when taken off the medication, went into a coma for three days and ended up with rheumatoid arthritis for the rest of her life. She started abusing what the Rolling Stones called "Mother's Little Helpers"—"Librium and Demerol and Valiums and Percodans—an array of capsules," Victoria says. Though some were for pain, "that wasn't the only reason she was taking them,' she adds. "My dad was in a real struggle to get her to stop taking so many happy drugs. He went to see her in a hospital and she was high as a kite and they said she had hidden all her drugs in her Tampax box."

Victoria was with her mother the following June on the day Robert Kennedy was killed. "My mom went into a deep, deep, deep depression," she says. "We tried to go to the memorial at St. Patrick's Cathedral. It was very hot and people were passing out. And finally, Mom couldn't take it anymore."

That summer, on crutches, back on Fire Island, Marilyn Leacock sat down wrong one evening and crushed four vertebrae in her back. "I was supposed to go and see *101 Dalmations* that evening and my mom had been carted off to the hospital, and my grandmother wouldn't let me go and I was having a tantrum, and finally she said I could go and she sent me alone," Leacock remembers. "I went to the movie theater and there were all these hippies on line. And I got to the front of the line and I didn't see any kids. And they said you had to go in with a grown-up. And the hippies went, 'Yeah, man, we'll take her in.'" Onscreen was *M*A*S*H*, Robert Altman's antiwar film. "My mother had just been taken away by paramedics, and the opening scene is very graphic; it's all this blood in the hospital." She ran from the theater. "It was just one of those awful, traumatic things where you know everything's starting to go wrong," she says.

A FEW DAYS before the 1968 Democratic convention, Jim Fouratt ran into Allen Ginsberg in San Francisco. "Allen said he'd had this dream the night before—a sea of red blood in Chicago, and he came and parted the seas and shepherded the sheep through. Very Allen. He had to go to Chicago. Allen was always on the scene."

TO DELEGATES, CHICAGO was a Potemkin village, with a façade of normality imposed over chaos, just as the nomination of Hubert Humphrey had been imposed upon a party seething with dissension. Every morning John Gage and the California delegation were picked up at their hotel by bus and driven down corridors of chain-link fence to the heavily secured Chicago Amphitheater. At day's end, they were bused back to their hotel and then went out on the streets to try to find out more.

Only a handful of protesters had actually showed up, but with the unwitting cooperation of the Chicago police and the Democratic party, they mounted one of the most hypnotic pieces of street theater in history. "The McCarthy kids were the target of vilification by the Yippies, because they bought into the system," says Fouratt. But when the police entered McCarthy headquarters and beat his volunteers as the convention anointed Humphrey, it split the country in two. Seeing its children clubbed in the streets radicalized a great swath of Americans and polarized the rest from them. The second American Revolution had begun. It would not be as successful as the first.

In Berkeley after the convention, Gage joined a protest called Stop the Draft Week, a series of marches attempting to shut down the huge Oakland Induction Center—the hungry mouth of the draft. In a few days it morphed from protest to resistance to disruption. At a rally before the march, Ken Kesey gave an essentially apolitical yet prophetic speech. "Look at the war, and turn your backs and say Fuck it!" he announced.

"Like nitwits, we did nothing to help Humphrey get elected," Gage says. "This is the sad story about purity. Sometimes you lose track of what it is you want, and of what is effective. What matters, and why politics matters, is that decisions are made about who lives and dies, whether there will be an inoculation program for kids."

Like many, Gage dropped out of conventional politics after Chicago. A recruiter from Harvard Business School had convinced him to give it a try, and though he still hadn't graduated from Berkeley, that fall he entered the elite B-school, where he studied while America—and the world—continued to boil and burn.

Soviet tanks had crushed Prague Spring a few days before the Chicago convention. In September, Mexican troops moved on student demonstrators in that nation's capital. In America, white radicals began building up the Black Panthers. By 1968, the Panthers were pop stars who played to the media and were played up in return; they even had their own fan magazine—the radical journal *Ramparts*. Two days after Martin Luther King was killed, Panther leader Eldridge Cleaver (b. 1935) was wounded and another Panther was killed in another shootout with police. "Let there be war," Cleaver said. He got his wish, and the rout of the Panthers began. Huey Newton was soon convicted of killing a policeman, and Cleaver fled the country for Algeria.

On October 31, Johnson stopped bombing North Vietnam, five days before Richard Nixon, who claimed to have a secret plan to end the war, was elected president. During this brief honeymoon that spring, Nixon began secretly bombing Cambodia. Then, on March 20, his Justice Department indicted eight alleged organizers of the Chicago convention disturbances, including Tom Hayden, Abbie Hoffman and Jerry Rubin.[42] The whole counter-culture was going on trial.

WHILE TIM SCULLY was tabbing Orange Sunshine, Tim Leary was back in court. He'd been arrested again, along with his third wife and son, for possession of two marijuana cigarettes, in Laguna Beach on December 26, 1968. The following May he got some good news, winning an appeal on his 1965 Texas conviction. Reporters converged on the Brotherhood's ranch, and a jubilant Leary announced that he was going to run for governor of California against Ronald Reagan and Jesse Unruh.[43] His euphoria was premature. The government promptly filed new charges atop those pending in Laguna and Millbrook. Then, in July, a friend of seventeen-year-old Susan Leary was found dead on the Brotherhood ranch with traces of LSD in her blood, just before one of the brothers was busted with a hash-filled surfboard. A month later, John Griggs died from suffocation when he vomited while stoned on psilocybin. Then Leary was re-tried in Laredo, found guilty, and sent back to Laguna for his next trial, where he was found guilty again and promptly incarcerated. Then, on Christmas Day 1969, the Brotherhood's head shop mysteriously burned down.[44] It had become a vestigial organ of their empire—they were selling cocaine and hash oil now, buying Porsches and a yacht, and setting up shell companies.

THROUGH THE SUMMER of 1968, Mark Rudd, the newly minted radical celebrity, worked out of a rented fraternity house across the street from the Columbia campus, planning demonstrations at the Chicago convention and a renewed student strike in the fall. He attended the annual SDS convention that June, where Maoists who believed in organizing workers for "class struggle" and the cautious original SDS leaders were confronted by younger action types. The Motherfuckers, a politicized band of poets-turned-SDS street toughs, nominated a garbage can for one of the three SDS leadership positions, National Secretary, but it lost to Bernadine Dohrn (b. 1942).[45]

That fall and winter Rudd traveled the country, raising money, giving speeches to students about what had happened at Columbia, and recruiting for SDS. Between times, he stayed in Chicago at a house called the National Collective, shared by his ideological guru J.J. and J.J.'s new girlfriend, Dohrn. As the assistant executive secretary of the National Lawyer's Guild (which represented radicals and the Communist party) she'd advised Rudd when he was doing draft counseling. Dohrn's beauty, leather miniskirts, unbuttoned blouses and sexual adventurism made her an SDS face on a par with the mediagenic Rudd, who had just made the cover of *Newsweek*. "Bernadine is the most attractive person you will ever meet," says Rudd, who also slept with her. "She embodied the independent and strong woman, which was part of the revolutionary idea. Not all our ideas were bad."

Campuses were exploding all over the country in early 1969: at San Fernando State and San Francisco State and San Jose; at Berkeley, where Ronald Reagan declared a state of emergency; at Howard and the University of Massachusetts and Rice; at Penn State, and the universities of Wisconsin and Chicago. At Harvard, SDS seized a building and, after injuries, arrests and a student strike, won a black studies department. At Kent State, SDS was so militant, most of its members got kicked out of school. At Brown, graduating seniors turned their backs on commencement speaker Henry Kissinger. Rudd was right; revolution *was* in the air—at least among priviledged youth.

The National Collective included the head of the New York SDS office, Jeff Jones; Dave Gilbert, the son of a Republican mayor; Swarthmore grad Cathy Wilkerson, whose father owned radio stations; Terry Robbins, SDS's Midwest organizer; and a group from the University of Michigan that included Billy Ayers (son of the chairman of Chicago's power company), his girlfriend, Diana Oughton (great-granddaughter of the founder of the Boy Scouts), and her college roommate Kathy Boudin, whose father, Leonard, was a leading leftist lawyer.[46] In the course of several months, J.J. put their violent thoughts on paper.

The document aimed to out-Marx the Maoists; the oppressed were leading the way to world revolution, it said. "We took ourselves very seriously," notes Rudd dryly. Instead of recruiting bourgeois students with talk of the workers' struggle, or battering their heads against a working class they considered hopelessly reactionary, they proposed recruiting youth to a world revolution led by the international oppressed.

In a riff on the Bob Dylan lyric "You don't need a weatherman to know which way the wind blows," the group re-named themselves the Weather Bureau. The Weathermen, as they were generally known, became the most exciting thing in an overstimulated time: rock star revolutionaries. At the June SDS convention, when a Black Panther, invited to speak by the Weather Bureau, attacked the Maoist faction and then extolled feminism as "pussy power," the resulting fracas split—and then killed—SDS.[47] The Weathermen and their allies sided with the Panthers, expelled the Maoists, then walked out themselves, taking their star power (and the records and assets of SDS) with them.

The Weather Bureau's first action was called to coincide with the opening of the Chicago 8 trial that October.[48] "We did not call it the Days of Rage," says Rudd, whose influence in the organization peaked that season. "The media called it that. We called it the October National Action." They wanted to bring the war home, but the psychological corollary was a desire to shed their white-skin privilege and middle-class upbringings and, in essence, become the Panthers they worshipped—street-fighting men and women.

Rudd continued building the organization, working with local collectives and "occasionally running around in the street at local demonstrations," he says. Groups of Weathermen and -women (some with their breasts bared) would invade high schools and run through the halls screaming "Jailbreak!"[49] They leafleted rock concerts and gave speeches at movie theaters playing *Easy Rider*. Sometimes, though, the actions turned violent. There were clashes with Maoists and staged confrontations with police, planned to impress the street toughs they were trying to recruit.[50] Professors were beaten at Harvard, teachers bound and gagged in a Brooklyn high school. Cumulatively, these actions impressed no one but the Weatherrevolutionaries themselves.

IN 1967, MICHAEL Fuchs had decided that law school would be a good way to kill three more years. "I had no idea, really, what I wanted to do," he says, "and I had pretty good law boards," which got him into Georgetown Law. But show business nagged him. "When I was younger, I was always going to the movies, and as I got older I began to watch television in a kind of systematic way," he says. At Union, when a roommate asked him why he watched so much, he'd answered, "I'm doing my homework."

The summer before his first year in law school, Fuchs worked in the office of Senator Birch Bayh, a job he won through an uncle who supported many Democrats. Back at school, he marched on the Pentagon. The next summer, he decided he was going to work for Bobby Kennedy's presidential campaign, impressed by how the pugnacious former prosecutor had evolved into a champion of the oppressed. "I had seen Bobby on Capitol Hill when I worked there. I thought Bobby really felt for the disadvantaged. And I don't care how late it came to him. The fact that he changed as much as he did was a sign of terrific growth." But instead of joining the campaign in June, he attended Kennedy's funeral. "It just took a lot of wind out of my sails."

Fuchs had lost his draft deferment, so he joined the Army Reserves. "Almost all my friends got out; I don't know how," he says. "I didn't do any of that. Though I didn't want to go to Vietnam."

Just as his second year of law school was starting, Fuchs was activated and sent to boot camp at Fort Jackson, South Carolina. "I'd been going to school straight and I'd never taken a break. It was good to put your mind to sleep. I found it an enjoyable experience, although I had some very rough times because I stood up to the drill sergeant. I was like a barracks lawyer. I stood in their way. Because some of these guys are fucking sadists. And there were enough of us who were older, who were law students, who knew that they just couldn't do that."

He saw two men die in training—one in a hand grenade accident, the other while cleaning his gun. "And I saw young kids go to 'Nam, like volleyballs being kicked over to the side, they had absolutely no control over their lives," he says. Once, on the rifle range, he was "coupled with a guy who had been recycled several times, which meant he was a moron—he couldn't get through basic training," Fuchs says. "This kid kept pointing his weapon at me. And I remember saying to myself, 'I'm going to die on this fucking rifle range with this moron.' It was further forged in me that I would try to have control over my destiny."

When he could, he talked to returning combat veterans, who told him Vietnam was a "poor man's war," he says. "There was an unbelievably high percentage of blacks over there. And I could see who went in from my own company, young kids, seventeen, eighteen, who weren't educated; the kids who had more wherewithal and more resources were able to avoid it." Like Fuchs. He was never called to serve. "Reservists got called up. But it would turn out not to be us. We did get called up once, for about a day, in a postal strike."

SIDELINED IN THE Yippies, but determined not to be erased by Abbie Hoffman, Jim Fouratt joined the White Panther Party, founded by John Sinclair (b. 1941), a poet, jazz critic and proselytizer of the virtues of marijuana and LSD, with several drug arrests to his credit. Sinclair ran a performance space in Detroit called the Artist's Workshop and a commune called Trans-Love Energies and managed bands, including the MC5 and (with a partner) the Psychedelic Stooges, both of which played at the Chicago convention.

Fresh from the Yippies, Fouratt was sympathetic to the White Panther agenda, expressed in its slogan: "Rock 'n' roll, dope and fucking in the streets." "I really felt popular culture was a revolutionary tool, and that rock did have political meaning in that it mobilized kids and gave them something to do."

The cultural alliance between rock music and the youth revolution had its roots in Dylan's and other folk singers' involvement in the civil rights movement. By 1966, the relationship had been formalized, as record companies began seeking out street bands by means of a new kind of executive, the "house freak," who related better than the then-typical record man, often as not a besuited Sinatra fan. The first house freaks were older than the audience they were hired to connect with, but the industry's need for credibility in the new culture led to the hiring of younger folk. Danny Fields, born just weeks before the bombing of Pearl Harbor, was one of the first. A Harvard Law dropout, former teen magazine editor, and rock PR man who knew Fouratt from the Warhol scene at Max's Kansas City, he'd been hired by Elektra Records, a folk and blues music label expanding into rock. After receiving copious propaganda from the MC5, Fields went to Michigan and signed them to a record deal. On their advice, he also saw the Stooges and signed them to his roster.

Almost immediately, Columbia Records came calling on Fouratt, in the person of Al Kooper, pianist on Bob Dylan's "Like a Rolling Stone." Kooper, an in-house producer for Columbia, introduced Fouratt to its president, Clive Davis, who'd just boldly announced the label's ambitions in progressive rock by signing Big Brother and the Holding Company, a San Francisco blues band fronted by a powerful singer named Janis Joplin, for an unprecedented $250,000. Davis offered Fouratt a job as his house freak.

Columbia had lots of rules. You could have nothing on your walls in your office, and there was a suit-and-tie dress code. Fouratt began to decorate his office walls and every night the cleaning crew would take down the posters he'd put up. Human Resources threatened to fire him for not disclosing his draft status on his employment application. Human Resources was fighting a losing battle. When Joplin and Co. came to visit Davis, he brought Fouratt, who'd met the band previously in San Francisco, into the room to make them more comfortable. They all promptly stripped.

That fall, Columbia had stumbled badly in an attempt to position itself as hip when it began running ads with copy like, "If you won't listen to your parents, the Man or the Establishment, why should you listen to us?" and "The Man Can't Bust Our Music." "There was a lot of flack in the counterculture about Columbia and that campaign," Fouratt recalls. Davis asked him to lend a hand to the advertising effort.

Fouratt was trying to serve two masters—Columbia and the "revolution"—with one advertising budget. He convinced Davis to run ads in thirty underground newspapers, as well as music magazines, thereby subsidizing the alternative press, which had grown since its beginnings in the mid-1960s to a national force that was as anarchic (the Liberation News Service, founded in 1967, had just splintered into bitter factions; the Underground Press Service was being run by a secretive drug dealer named Tom Forcade) as it was influential. The campaign (toned down with the headline "Know who your friends are") continued into spring 1969. A few months earlier, an FBI memo accused Columbia of "giving active aid and comfort to enemies of the United States," and suggested that pressure be applied to stop it. Backlash against the counterculture was building now that it had burst out of the cities and spread across the country. Soon, conservative stockholders of the parent company, CBS, heard the FBI message, says Fouratt, "and all the ads were pulled."

IN SPRING 1968, prosecutor Leslie Crocker Snyder was in the courtroom when Mark Rudd was arraigned after the Columbia University takeover. "I come into court, and these kids are approximately my age," she says. They talked to her like she was one of them, asked her how she could possibly prosecute them. "And I'm feeling sympathy for them, I'm feeling very ambivalent," she says. "But not ambivalent enough not to do it." After all, they were mostly released with disorderly conduct violations—the equivalent of parking tickets.

Snyder kept a diary those first few months she was a baby DA, and was later shocked when she reread it. She'd never known a cop, and she'd bought into her generation's distrust of them. "All cops lie," she wrote. But as she worked with them—doing things she felt were worthwhile—and learned that they could be trusted and didn't always lie, her beliefs began to change. "I was getting to see what cops had to face," she says. "And they were good to me. I was a novelty, a sweet young thing, and they liked women. And when they see that you will take care of them and you're a hard worker and you will do a good job, then they become very protective of you. And then, I was seduced."

A few months later, Snyder attended various hearings and trials in what became known as the Panther 21 case—an alleged conspiracy to bomb department stores and police stations and kill police officers. "The prosecutor was horrible," she recalls. "They all got acquitted, and it was the biggest travesty, and it was the prosecution's fault. And in my view, they were criminals, and I think they should have been convicted. Peaceful revolution, that's okay. Once the violence started, any sympathy I had dissipated, because cops started getting killed. It was partly political, but it was largely criminal. I was totally turned off."

On May 4, 1970 (two days after students burned down the ROTC building there), National Guardsmen fired sixty-one shots, four fatal, into a group of Kent State University demonstrators protesting the April 30 American invasion of Cambodia. That invasion and the dramatic shooting that followed reenergized the dispirited peace movement and kicked off another spring of student strikes, ROTC burnings and bombings, and campus closings, leading Congress to grant eighteen-year-olds the vote. But Nixon's troop withdrawals, which had begun in 1969 and accelerated under cover of massive U.S. bombing, and the introduction of a draft lottery—coupled with factionalism and rising violence on the antiwar movement's fringe—compromised the protesters' resolve. Demonstrations would continue into 1972, but for many, the killings at Kent State put the lie to the idea of peaceful protest.

Though she was horrified by the repression of political dissent at Kent State, Leslie Snyder just couldn't accept people killing cops and burning buildings. Her transformation was complete. Finally, she'd escaped the eighteenth century. This was real life, real crime. And she knew whose side she was on.

IN SPRING 1969, Doug Marlette spotted a book called *LBJ Lampooned*, with a cover illustration by the *New York Review of Books* artist David Levine (satirizing Johnson's famous display of his surgical scar—replaced by a map of Vietnam), and an introduction about cartooning by Jules

Feiffer. Political cartoons were enjoying a renaissance. "Lyndon Johnson's lying legitimized questioning," Marlette says. "Establishment newspapers were starting to do cartoons that were really subversive and outrageous. Jules, in that essay, gave me an intellectual framework. I suddenly could see what my job was."

That fall, having earned an associate's degree at community college, Marlette joined the junior class at Florida State University in Tallahassee. He declared a philosophy major, and presented himself at the offices of the campus daily, where he promptly won a job drawing cartoons. Immediately, a war began for the nineteen-year-old's soul, pitting the good boy, who looked like a Southern Rotarian and was so overpowered by what was expected of him that he now married his churchgoing girlfriend, against another Doug who drew like a northern intellectual and couldn't help but note the disconnect between the way he'd been raised and what was happening in his world. "I was trying to salvage the values I'd been taught in civics classes and in Sunday school," he says. "But the things I'd been taught did not square with killing people and denying rights."

Two months after enrolling, Marlette joined a group of students he hardly knew in a Volkswagen bus painted camouflage green for the overnight trip to the Mobilization march in Washington, D.C. Outside Atlanta, a gas station attendant told them they should go home and study. Instead, they turned up the music and offered Marlette his first puff of marijuana. He didn't like it. "I had a natural ability to enter that stoned, free-associative state," he realized. "I do it in my work. I saw that, so dope didn't hold much allure for me. I never took acid and I'm glad I didn't, because I think I might not have wanted to come back. Something in me knew." In homage to his natural state of buzz and beatitude, his friends took to calling him "Drug" Marlette.

Though he grew his hair long and kept pumping out antiwar cartoons for the newspaper, Marlette didn't much like the radicals he met on that trip—or later. "It was the most activist school in the region," he says, "but I didn't feel like one of them. I marched on the draft board, I demonstrated, but I was never a joiner. I'm not quite there, but my cartoons are. When I think back, I had a sophisticated vision for someone that young. I saw through the bullshit, recognized the Stalinist stuff. I was drawing cartoons that were questioning the war, but also the Nazi tactics of SDS, the anti-free-speech stuff. I did not identify with groups; still don't. I do not link up with causes. SDS sounded like Baptists to me. It seemed like the same thing I had grown up with, those crazy dogmatists who would send you off to a gulag."

That summer, the first draft lottery was held and Marlette drew number 10—an almost certain ticket to Vietnam. Though he held a student deferment, it would only last another year. "I was already thinking about applying to be a conscientious objector, so I did," he says. It wasn't an easy choice by any means. "I took it seriously. I was reading Tolstoy, Bertrand Russell, conscientious objectors from the past. But there are other ways of looking at it. My father was a military man. It was a way of expressing resentment toward the military for all the uprooting and dislocations. I had already served my country."

Marlette rejects the notion that rejecting the war was an act of cowardice. "It was too painful to me to feel that I was getting out of something," he explains. "It would have been easier to go into the army; I would have probably been on *Stars and Stripes*. I thought the Selective Service system was wrong. I thought I was compromising by being a CO. To do the CO thing was going along with the system and with the draft. Canada was not an option. I believed that the 'correct' thing for me would have been to go to jail. I thought I was being a wuss by being a CO So it was torture. My mother was ill, and my dad's coming home from Vietnam, and we're arguing about it. He felt he was being rejected. It was not a good time in my family." But in the end, when Marlette submitted his CO application, his father wrote a letter supporting it, offering to go back to Vietnam in his son's place.

STEVE CAPPS ENTERED junior high school in 1967. But he didn't take much notice of the new youth culture barreling its way across the country, though he'd finally been introduced to rock music by his older brother, who would induce Capps to spend the money he earned mowing lawns on records that would immediately disappear into his brother's room.

They weren't all Capps missed, living in the sanctum of suburban Schenectady. "I remember drinking in eighth grade, but I did not smell a whiff of marijuana until I went to college," he says. "My best friend and his older brother were kind of literary types. They would hang around this chicken coop at the back of their property, with Oriental rugs from the Salvation Army. I remember it being weird in there. I'm sure they smoked dope all day. But I didn't know! I was such a nerd."

He was more interested in photography. "I was taking buses downtown by myself, walking around with my camera in neighborhoods I probably shouldn't have gone into, just completely naive but in that completely self-confident way." And that year, he found another interest. His new school had programmable calculators and a Moog synthesizer, which made computerized music, "so in seventh grade I was doing logic programming, and that had a very profound impact," Capps says. "But I never thought I was going to become a programmer. It was just fun."

In 1968, his older sister came home from college for Christmas vacation with a book about a computer language called FORTRAN. "I taught myself FORTRAN, even though I didn't have anything to run it on," he says.

The next summer, Capps's brother heard about the Woodstock music festival being held not far away, coaxed Steve to come along and take pictures, and "made a halfhearted, lame attempt" to talk their mother into letting them go. "I think he got two milliseconds worth of consideration before she said no," Capps recalls.

Capps didn't really care. He wasn't part of that culture and wasn't even sure it existed. Kids in his school were wannabe hippies, "because we were too young," he says. "When I look back at pictures, everybody is dressed absolutely identically. So we thought we were doing our own thing, but we were really being conformists. And the whole hippie thing was about privilege. So you'd talk about peace and love. You'd say, 'We love people of all colors,' but there didn't happen to be any in your school. And in my naiveté, I assumed I would never see prejudice."

DONALD TRUMP WENT to work for his father in fall 1968. He bought and built properties around the country, refinanced some of his father's properties, co-oped, and made tax-free swaps with others, learning the real estate ropes.[51] The Trump business was worth a respectable $40 million—minuscule compared to the real estate dynasties of Manhattan. Fred Trump had hidden strengths, though, and his son would exploit them—as he exploited tax shelters to build a nest egg in his first years in business. The elder Trump knew key figures in the Brooklyn Democratic machine, a feisty anachronism and the last vestige of the political powerhouse called Tammany Hall that once ruled all of New York City. As those politicians moved up in their careers and into Manhattan, Donald would continue to support them, leveraging his father's relationships into real money.

But Trump was still wet behind the ears. He wore maroon suits and matching shoes—a sure sign of an outer-borough boy. His father's business was headquartered in a six-story red brick building in Brooklyn. Donald had business cards made up with the address of his East Side Manhattan apartment. "It was embarrassing," he says. "I couldn't say I had a Brooklyn office and go out with a model. So I put a desk in my studio apartment." It looked out on a water tower.

Trump joined Le Club, a decades-old private club on Manhattan's East Side, where the last of the 1950s playboys held court, and New York's *ancien regime* waited out the cultural revolution that had usurped them. "It was hard to get in," Trump says. But not many young people wanted to; at the time, the children of New York's aristocracy preferred to downplay their privilege. Not Trump. He applied for and won a membership, "and I was far and away the youngest guy."

Manhattan became Trump's graduate school. He majored in making money. He minored in sex, though, taking full advantage of the times and the extraordinary opportunities they offered to indulge in consequence-free promiscuity, "my second business," Trump recalls. It wasn't the counterculture by any means. "Le Club was totally oblivious to it. You understand that? They didn't give a fuck." Yet recognizing that the elusive quality of "cool" meant almost as much as money, Trump studied men like Le Club founder and fashion designer Oleg Cassini, thirty-three years his senior and "a great playboy," Trump says, a little awed. "He was Establishment. He wasn't idealistic. He would flow with the tide."

Behind Le Club's locked doors, the tide was running as high and wild as in the streets outside. "I once saw the most beautiful woman in the world swinging nude from a chandelier at four o'clock in the morning!" Trump marvels. People also took drugs at Le Club, but not Trump. "I never had a drug in my life," he says. "Somehow, somewhere in my life, I was persuaded not to do the drugs and alcohol. It was available to me. But something told me not to do it."

THE WOMEN'S LIBERATION movement had roots deep in American history, but since the suffragettes, its visibility had waned until Betty Freidan published *The Feminine Mystique* in 1963. Simultaneously, women in SDS, who'd been considered no more than adjuncts to its men, began acting up. In December 1965, following its first big antiwar action, SDS held a conference at the University of Illinois, where Tom Hayden's wife, Casey, and another member, SNCC veteran Mary King, argued in a paper that women were an oppressed group, just like Negroes, even inside the radical movement. A discussion of their work turned into the first women's consciousness-raising session, after participants moved to a separate room away from the men.[52]

By 1966, women's issues were on the movement's front burner. The National Organization for Women was formed that year by women who realized they were not being protected by the Civil Rights Act. The next year, a women's liberation amendment was brought to the floor at the SDS convention. A few months later, the first women's liberation protest was held when a group called New York Radical Women led by Jim Fouratt's sometime colleague, Robin Morgan, picketed the Miss America pageant on the Atlantic City boardwalk and tossed bras, girdles and copies of *Cosmopolitan* and *Family Circle* into a "freedom trash can." They were denounced as "bra-burners" and the pageant proceeded regardless. Judith Ann Ford, a bleached-blond baby boomer from Illinois, won, but the protest would be remembered long after she was forgotten.

The Women's International Terrorist Conspiracy from Hell (WITCH), an organization Morgan then formed inspired by the Yippies, soon spearheaded another scandal when it plastered New York with stickers inviting women to "Confront the Whore-Makers at a Bridal Fair at New York's Madison Square Garden in 1969." WITCH invaded the event and called the attendees "whores" and "slaves," expecting them to jump up on chairs in response to five white mice released onto the show floor. They didn't, and the action floundered but the movement moved forward as radical women's groups continued to form. In January 1970, a band of feminists took over the bimonthly underground newspaper *Rat* and turned it into a militant feminist publication. In its first all-women's issue, *Rat* published "Goodbye to All That," a diatribe by Morgan (reprinted later that year in *Sisterhood Is Powerful*, her seminal feminist anthology), which trashed male movement leaders by name. Identity politics had crossed the gender line.

NINA HARTLEY, REMEMBERS being at a peace march while still in a stroller, her brother being arrested in a Berkeley demonstration, and dinner parties with radical friends of her lesbian aunt's husband, who was a member of the National Lawyers Guild. But she says her parents, "beaten and bruised by the political system, had retreated from politics by the time I came along." A return to political involvement would have disturbed the thick scar tissue that covered their wounded lives. "There was a great deal wrong, and they weren't talking about it," she says. "If they did anything 'wrong' in raising me, they did not give me an adequate sense of pride in their history. I see now that through my entire childhood, my mother was angry at my father for destroying himself, and for disrupting her life in the process."

In 1969, Mitzi's parents sent her to Scotland for the summer. The older kids were out of the house, too. When Mitzi returned in September, her mother's latent feminism had come to the fore, and she'd begun to explore her unhappiness and anger. Desperate to save their marriage, the couple began therapy-hopping. "It was, in no particular order, Zen, primal scream therapy, group therapy, biofeedback, guided mescaline trips, and Reichian therapy," Hartley says. None of it worked. By 1971, when Mitzi was twelve and women's liberation was gathering steam, things had deteriorated to the point that she believes her parents each fell in love with the same woman simultaneously.

"The abandonment of my needs for my parents' is a motif in my life," she says. "I protected them from my problems and tried to help them with theirs. And I realize now that really oppressed me. They never called me names; they never hit me; if I asked for something I got it. But I didn't think to ask for anything. I felt very responsible for their misery."

Things didn't improve for them until 1972, when Mitzi's mother took early retirement from her latest job and devoted herself to Buddhism full-time. She briefly became more accessible, but by then it was too late to alter the course of her youngest's life. A year earlier, Mitzi's only friend, a tomboy who lived across the street, had moved away. Devastated, she'd fallen into a deep depression her parents were too self-involved to notice. "Or if they did, they felt guilty and didn't know what to do," she says. The next year, they took off for a Zen monastery and placed Mitzi, thirteen, with a guardian.

DAVE McINTOSH'S WORLD got larger in 1968. "I remember watching Robert Kennedy's funeral and Martin Luther King's funeral," he says. It made an impression when his grandmother, riveted to the television, muttered, "Enough is enough."

The day Bobby Kennedy died, McIntosh was stunned when one of his classmates said he was glad, because it meant a Republican would be elected president. "I was very conscious that year that there was a change going on in the country," he says. Yet the culture of Kendallville sheltered him from it. Race riots and antiwar protests were roiling the country and the nearby cities, Detroit and Chicago, but those disturbances seemed remote alongside the presidential campaign.

McIntosh considered himself a Democrat like his mother, who'd remarried a man who ran a roofing company and spent the late 1960s having two more children. In fifth grade, when his teacher proposed that her students hold a mock election with students managing in-class campaigns for Hubert Humphrey and Richard Nixon, McIntosh was on the Humphrey team, and was outraged when students found a Nixon button in the teacher's desk. They decided she was secretly—*yuck!*—a Republican.

His mother got into politics in 1971. The local city judge was a Republican good old boy who didn't think women should be allowed to play golf and would hit balls at female foursomes on the links. "He did that one time to my mom and she got so mad," McIntosh recalls. She said, "He doesn't deserve to be judge." She had to run in a primary before she got to take on the mad golfer, but she won election by a two-to-one margin and was reelected unopposed in 1975. Whenever there was a parade in town, she would bring the kids to ride on the Democratic party's float.

JIM FOURATT WAS coming home late from work at Columbia Records on June 27, 1969—the day of homosexual icon Judy Garland's funeral—when he noticed a bunch of cops in front of the Stonewall, a gay bar on Sheridan Square in Greenwich Village. They were raiding the place, hauling the mourner-revelers within off to jail. Some of the arrested—drag queens and kings—kicked up a fuss, and suddenly a routine roust became a full-scale disturbance. Fouratt began calling his radical friends, a gay Paul Revere announcing "There's a riot going on"—but none responded.

Candlelight marches alternated with rioting for five nights. Then, on July 4, at a public meeting of the gay community, Fouratt, dressed in leather pants and cowboy boots, grew infuriated as he listened to "a heterosexual psychologist talk about how gay people were not assimilated and had to project a nice image." Leaping to his feet, he yelled "Bullshit!" and inveighed against the stereotype of soft, sweet homosexuals and the "pigs" who oppressed them.[53]

"We marched over to Alternate University, on Fourteenth Street and Sixth Avenue, where Living Theater used to be." Fouratt says. They were given a room by a rock critic who was teaching a course on Rock and Revolution. The suddenly self-aware gays discovered identity politics and formed the Gay Liberation Front (GLF). Like the women who kicked off the modern feminist movement in a closed-door session at an SDS conference, "We realized we had to deal with our own issues," Fouratt says. "We weren't going to be peaceful any more."

Later that year, Fouratt moved into one of several GLF-sponsored men's communes. GLF practiced coalition politics—it built bridges to the Black Panthers and to a new Hispanic group, the Young Lords—and Fouratt began attending radical conferences and meetings nationwide. "We formed consciousness-raising groups," he says. "We asked questions. What does it mean to be gay? Where does identity come from? Where does this behavior come from? How much of it is a reaction to oppression? How much is survival? How much is pathology because of oppression? We organized about fifty chapters on college campuses." The GLF later spawned Lavender Menace, a group of lesbians who demanded their right to be gay and proud within the women's movement. "It was about the inclusion of straight people in the gay community and the inclusion of gay and lesbian people in the revolutionary community," Fouratt says. "It was going to change everybody."

AS GLF WAS being born, so was the Woodstock Festival. The night before Stonewall, Fouratt had moderated a public meeting on behalf of the concert's promoters and publicists, who wanted to head off any "community" opposition to it. The idea was to discuss what Woodstock should symbolize. Rumor had it the concert was a profit-making venture backed, at least in part, by drug profits, which Fouratt believes. "Pot—that's where their money came from," he insists. Hundreds of members of the underground press, the rock industry and the local movement filled the Village Gate nightclub as street leaders hectored the festival promoters, demanding the event be politicized. Ultimately, the radicals agreed to take some tables in the concessions area, but have no other role at the festival. Later, though, Abbie Hoffman would attempt to extort $50,000 from the organizers—and finally got $10,000.[54] "Abbie invades Woodstock Ventures and says, 'There ain't gonna be a fuckin' festival unless . . . ,'" Fouratt recalls. "He never knew when to stop. Abbie was correct in his read of the bourgeois entrepreneurialism going on. Except Abbie was a part of that, too."

Fouratt attended Woodstock in August 1969, in his official capacity as house freak at Columbia Records, but he left after a single day on the site. The Motherfuckers had burned twelve of the festival's sixteen concession stands to the ground as a political protest.[55] Hoffman was there, too, furious that he'd been denied the chance to play master of ceremonies. Fouratt avoided him. Later, high on LSD, Hoffman would take to the stage in the middle of The Who's set to lecture the crowd for having fun while White Panther leader John Sinclair was serving nine years in jail for possession of two joints.

Fouratt was appalled. "It was a nightmare," he says. "It was raining, it was muddy, everybody was on fucking drugs. Grapes were being served backstage [despite Cesar Chavez's strike on behalf of California grape pickers], and Joan Baez was eating them. Janis was all fucked up. Jimi Hendrix was all fucked up. Everything was being played out against the contradiction between what they're pretending to be and what their real goal is. We got out of there and flew to a little island off of Italy. I'll never forget. We got on that plane, hating Woodstock, got off the plane and saw the Italian newspaper headlines, and immediately worked it, that we had come directly from Woodstock."

Back in New York that fall, Fouratt quit his job at Columbia after losing several arguments with executives. A new band called Chicago Transit Authority changed its name to Chicago over Fouratt's furious objection, and another lame ad campaign—"The Revolution Is on Columbia"—was about to begin. "I said, 'That's wrong,'" Fouratt recalls. "I would have joined them if I had stayed."

ON AUGUST 13, 1969, two days before Woodstock, India Company of the U.S. Marines was part of a massive regimental search-and-destroy mission five miles north of its camp at An Hoa in Quang Nam province when a large force of North Vietnamese Army regulars, hiding in trees, ambushed Tommy Vallely's unit. They opened fire on the point with small arms, automatics, a machine gun and a rocket-propelled grenade. "We were in the open," says Vallely. "You never want to be in the open. And they were kicking the shit out of us." It was a situation American commanders strived to avoid—one in which technological superiority was neutered—and he watched as several men, including his company commander, fell wounded. Realizing that his unit had been separated from the company, he radioed for reinforcements.

Instead of sitting tight, though, he worked his way to a wounded man, took his rifle, and charged the machine gun emplacement, single-handedly keeping the NVA soldiers occupied as more Americans took up positions near him. He then marked the machine gun with a smoke grenade and ran back and forth across an open field as bullets flew all around him, shuttling between the wounded commander and the other soldiers in his unit, relaying instructions and pinpointing the NVA troop locations.

"But we have so many casualties we got to get the hell out of there, and it's nighttime, and we don't know where we are," Vallely explains. Grabbing a map, he led the survivors out of harm's way to a place called China Beach—"not like the TV show," he notes. "It's where survivors, not the wounded, went for rest." Not only did he win the Silver Star, one of the highest military honors, but he was promoted to chief radio operator. He downplays his heroism. "You're going to react or you're going to be dead," he says. "Lots of people who should get Silver Stars don't; the company commander just liked me."

At nineteen, Vallely made the most of the opportunity. He encouraged positions of responsibility for a couple of black Marines, lessening racial tension in his unit. And he barred those under his command from harming prisoners, and made it clear to the South Vietnamese—or ARVN—soldiers they sometimes reluctantly fought alongside that he wouldn't let them act up, either. "I would not let them beat up prisoners or villagers for information. They were bullies."

Vallely never saw a Vietnamese city. He was at base camp for his entire thirteen-month tour of duty in Vietnam, aside from the rare rest-and-relaxation break in nearby Da Nang. Excluding the abuse of Vietnamese, he saw few of the other excesses later portrayed in Hollywood's version of the war. "We had a little marijuana, some alcohol in the rear," he says, "but in the field it was considered a violation if you had any dope. You would be in big trouble. You would endanger other people. You'd fall asleep, someone would cut your throat."

Mail call provided some amusement and comfort. His mother and leftist sister reported to him on the antiwar movement. "My sister didn't know what she was talking about, but it didn't bother me," he says. "I liked the demonstrators. I don't remember anybody in Vietnam hating demonstrators. I only knew a few people who took great pleasure in the war. Some of my company might have a different view, because part of my interpretation is what I've come to think."

Offered an officer's uniform, Vallely almost signed up for a second tour in Vietnam. He wanted to go home and get into politics, but he had to think about it because he'd "gotten to be attached to some of the people in the company and if I stayed things would go better for them."

But he'd turned against the war by then. He thought it was insanity. "I wanted to stop it but didn't know how; I certainly wasn't going to be a Trotskyite," he says. He spent his last few months of service back at Camp Pendleton in California, teaching radio operations to raw recruits, partying, and getting into barroom brawls. "We would go fight to have fun," he says. "We would drink and punch people and wake up in the morning and go back to work."

LIKE MANY LATE boomers, Kathryn Bond Stockton feels she missed the 1960s. In January 1965, her entire family attended Lyndon Johnson's inauguration. Aside from listening to songs from the "love rock" musical *Hair* and wearing bell bottoms, she recalls "see[ing] it off in the distance, but it's never happening to me."

Drugs were not an issue. After her parents let her smoke a cigarette at age eight, she decided smoking was dumb. "That was my parents' style, instead of trying to create forbidden domains." Two years later, in 1968, her fifth-grade class took mandatory drug education. "They would pound into your brain how terrible drugs are, and how marijuana is incredibly evil, right up there with heroin," she remembers. "So you had no ability to distinguish among these things, but I have to say, they had no appeal to me." In the rare instances when she heard about drugs at all, it was when someone her brother's age or older who'd left town died of an overdose.

She entered sixth grade in 1969. Two months later, her father was elected mayor of Bloomfield, Connecticut. As one of his first actions, he started school busing to achieve integration. "I remember when I saw black children for the first time," Stockton says. "They seemed more important than the rest of us, and I idolized them, and I thought, These are just amazing people, that they could come into this white school. I kept imagining what it would be like if it were reversed. And a lot of these kids were great athletes, and I admired athletic prowess."

Despite her political consciousness, Stockton didn't pay much attention to the Vietnam War. "And I don't remember my classmates giving a shit, either," she says. Her brother, who was more radical than she, worried about the draft and grew his hair long, "sort of an issue in the household," she says.

Stockton had more pressing concerns. As she neared puberty, sex became a threatening subject. She took sex education classes that year, and upon learning how her English teacher's wife had gotten pregnant, decided he had to be profoundly evil. "I refused to think of my parents that way," she adds. She became a devoted fan of Barnabas Collins, the vampire in the TV soap opera *Dark Shadows*. "He was this darkly tragic figure and he would have relationships with women and everything would be going perfectly fine, and then he couldn't help himself, he would have to bite them on the neck," she says. "I felt I was a vampire figure. I was basically admired and liked and could be attracted to people and have them attracted to me, but there would always come a point when my secret would come out, and then I would not be able to have the people I'd want to have. So I was determined no one will ever know. I used to think about how much torture I could stand before I would admit it. And I don't even know what words I had in my head. I'm not sure I knew the word *homosexual*."

The neighborhood girls surely didn't. They invited Stockton for a talk one day and gave her an ultimatum: give up her friendship with the local boys and they'd let her in their group. "It was like a tribunal," she recalls.

"I know they felt they were doing this pathetic creature a wonderful favor. I went home and cried and told my mother, and she said, 'You don't have to do anything you don't want to do.'" Yet she did: she had to wear dresses, so her mother bought her one that became her favorite. It had a sword dangling from its belt. "She said Robin Hood had worn something quite like it," says Stockton, who decided that made up for the humiliation of dressing like a girl.

That summer, preparing for her move to middle school, Stockton was stunned and fascinated by photographs of the Woodstock rock festival. "People were running around naked, and that was kind of interesting. I remember seeing this world explode and thinking, *What's that about?* But you're just slightly on the border of it. It's not quite your world."

AT THEIR NATIONAL Collective in Chicago, the Weathermen were trying to live by principles set down by the Soviet leader Lenin. In classic totalitarian double-talk, he'd called it Democratic Centralism. "The reason we lead this organization is that we're right more often than anyone else," Rudd said at the time.[56] Now he thinks it was something else. "People joined these things the way people join religious cults—the surrender. The idea was to build revolutionaries. There was also a weeding-out process called criticism and self-criticism, which was a kind of psychological group terror in which people had to criticize each other and criticize themselves for their lack of revolutionary will or zeal or whatever." Many dropped out. "The earlier you left, the saner you were," says Rudd, who came to believe that the war in Vietnam drove the Weather Bureaucrats insane. "It would be interesting if we could ever get together again to talk about who was sane and who was not," he adds, laughing.

Rudd didn't take many drugs—yet. "We were high on revolution," he says. And on violence. "I've got myself a gun—has anyone here got a gun?"[57] he asked during a recruiting speech at Columbia that fall. The antiwar movement, distanced itself from the Weather Bureau, condemning its adventurism. Chicago Panther leader Fred Hampton called Rudd "a motherfucking masochist" and knocked him to the ground.[58]

Just before the Weather Bureau's public debut—three days of violent demonstrations—a bomb went off in Chicago's Haymarket Square, destroying a statue of a policeman. Did the Weather Bureau do it? No one knew, but its members had begun discussing violence and stockpiling guns.[59] On October 8, 1969 the second anniversary of the death of Che Guevara, the action known as the Days of Rage opened with a rally in Lincoln Park, site of bloody clashes during the Democratic Convention the year before. All signs pointed to a debacle. Barely one thousand people showed up—armed with clubs, cans of oven cleaner, heavy boots, football helmets, gas masks, brass knuckles and Viet Cong flags—and they were surrounded by battle-ready police. After a brief rally, the crowd swarmed into the streets surrounding the park, committing random acts of violence, not only charging the police arrayed against them but also wrecking the automobiles of innocents. Many were arrested. Some were shot by police.

Two days later, demonstrators fought another brief but bloody battle in the heart of the city's shopping district. This time, a city lawyer was paralyzed, scores more were injured, and 103 were arrested, Rudd among them. He'd arrived at the base of the blown-up statue, where a march was to start, and was immediately "jumped by a gang of ten Red Squad cops," who hit him, maced him and stuck him in jail, he says. "That was the extent of my action: busted the second I arrive."

Though the Weather Bureau claimed victory ("that we are willing to fight the police is a victory," J.J. said), their idols, the Panthers, denounced them for "Custerism." Rudd was daunted by the experience, and by the low turnout. "It really undermined my confidence," he says.

If they'd been true believers before, now they were angry, frightened ones forming a vision of American apocalypse. "A new leadership within the leadership gets formed," Rudd says. "The issue is: Who wants the Revolution the most? It's an issue of will. I tended to be a doubting person. I would get my will buttressed by being slapped around in the Weather Bureau.

Will became even more important after Dohrn announced that the group had to go underground and engage in covert armed struggle against the state. She wasn't the only one to have the thought. In November, Jane Alpert and Sam Melville, a couple who lived in New York's East Village and had spent the preceding months with a collective that set off bombs in places like New York's military induction center, a United Fruit Company warehouse, and the headquarters of IBM, GTE, Chase Manhattan, General Motors, and Standard Oil, were arrested when Melville was caught placing time bombs on Army trucks at a Manhattan armory. Shortly thereafter, out on bail, Alpert took LSD and had sex with Rudd, whom she considered a movement celebrity.[60]

Weather held a War Council in December 1969. A cardboard machine gun, posters of Fidel Castro, Che Guevara, Eldridge Cleaver, Ho Chi Minh, Lenin, Mao and Malcolm X, and another featuring bullets etched with names of enemies of the people like Richard Nixon, Ronald Reagan and, curiously, the actress Sharon Tate (just murdered, along with several friends, by a band of hippie cultists led by a long-haired ex-convict, Charles Manson) decorated the hall in Flint, Michigan, during this revolutionary Woodstock for 400 hard-core radicals.[61] It was highlighted by evening *wargasm* sessions, speeches, singalongs (to rewritten classics like "Maria" from West Side Story, which now went, "The most beautiful sound I ever heard/Kim Il Sung, Kim Il Sung, Kim Il Sung"[62]), group exercise and group sex, Rudd enthusing about killing pigs and blowing up buildings, and Dohrn in a miniskirt, rhapsodizing about the Manson murders (". . . they even shoved a fork into pig Tate's stomach . . .") and holding up a four-finger salute to the fork. Manson was America's nightmare. Now the acid-taking revolutionaries aspired to be like the acid-taking murderer. One participant recalled it as "group psychosis."[63]

After the War Council, Rudd was demoted. The consensus was that he'd lost his nerve. The National Collective split into cells of the most trusted, directed by four Weather leaders Dohrn, J.J., Jones, and Robbins; the rest of the organization was simply cut loose. They destroyed the records of SDS as they left. "We were going to start armed struggle against the state, offensive armed struggle," Rudd says. "I could have affected the events. I could have blown the whistle. I could have stopped it."

In New York, Weather's Cathy Wilkerson, Kathy Boudin, former Columbia honor student Ted Gold, Diana Oughton, Terry Robbins and others began making bombs. On their first outing, in late February 1970, they ignited three gasoline bombs in front of the home of the judge in the Panther 21 case, causing minor damage. "Free the Panther 21" was scrawled in red on the sidewalk. About a week later, they bought a hundred pounds of dynamite and argued for days about how to use it. Four days after that, at noon, there was an explosion on West 11th Street in Greenwich Village, and the home of the vacationing Wilkerson family collapsed. Gold, Oughton, and Robbins were beneath it. Emerging half-naked from the wreckage, Wilkerson and Boudin borrowed clothes from a neighbor, and ran off. In the rubble was proof of a sharp change in the Weathermen's direction. The explosion occurred because they'd made a mistake while wiring an antipersonnel bomb, designed to kill people.

Mark Rudd went to the movies that night to establish an alibi and saw Michaelangelo Antonioni's *Zabriskie Point*, a pretentious film glamorizing radical violence, in which a house explodes—quite beautifully—at the climax, taking the gorgeous protagonists with it. When he got back to his collective house, his roommates shoved the next day's newspaper under his nose. "Isn't it an interesting irony, that instead of it being effective terror, we only killed ourselves?" Rudd asks today.

THREE DAYS AFTER the Days of Rage ended, John Gage helped organize the October 15, 1969, Moratorium demonstration that brought out two million people nationwide[64]—including the unprecedented 100,000 people who came to Gage's event on the Boston Commons, the day's biggest crowd.[65] That success earned him the job of running the Mobilization's Washington rally a month later.

Richard Nixon threw the movement a curve on November 3, when he announced his plan for Vietnamization—turning the war over to the Vietnamese—and launched an attack on the peace movement as an un-American vocal minority up against the silent majority. The peace movement was having problems of its own. Factionalism necessitated dividing the action in Washington, with separate entities in charge of separate events, beginning with a Death March from Arlington Memorial Bridge, concluding with the reading of the names of Americans killed in Vietnam at the White House, and including a march up Pennsylvania Avenue, a rally on the Mall, an ultraviolent Weatherman spree, and a Chicago 8 protest at the Justice Department.

Half a million people came to the rally. With its performances by Arlo Guthrie, Peter, Paul and Mary and the cast of *Hair*, and the calming presence of Hugh Romney, a/k/a Wavy Gravy, it reminded many of Woodstock. Many on the sound and lighting crew had previously done duty there. But it proved a logistical nightmare even before tear gas drifted over from a demonstration at the Vietnamese Embassy.

That didn't stop Gage. He moved a bus in front of the stage as a shield, in case some loony tried to shoot one of the speakers. By the end of the day, the backstage area was full of children who'd been separated from their parents. Exhausted, Gage was about to deal with them when he spied a wall of riot police moving slowly down the Mall toward him. A splinter group from the rally had unexpectedly marched on the Justice Department, and the police were clearing out all the lingering protesters.

"Wavy has one of these little boxes, when you pull a string, it starts to laugh," Gage recalls. "He'd walk up to some policeman and pull the string and the thing would start to laugh. It's really very funny." Only the police didn't get the joke. Bill Hanley, a ponytailed sound technician and son of a Boston policeman, went out next. He'd built the world's biggest sound system for Woodstock. He was sure he could get the cops to stop. Instead,

Gage watched as Hanley was maced and arrested. Finally Gage gathered all the lost children in the bus and planted himself in the door. When the police demanded entry, he refused. Miraculously, the cops backed off. "Then I had to get Hanley out of jail!" says Gage. "He had to get on the road down to the next event."

That was the last official show of the 1969 Rolling Stones tour, a two-day rock festival at a drag strip in West Palm Beach, Florida, that also featured Janis Joplin and Sly and the Family Stone. Fresh from jail, Hanley arrived and, faced with disorganization and chaos, called for the cavalry, in the form of John Gage.

The line between protest culture and counterculture was growing thinner. "I've got the governor of Florida showing up with state troopers, and troops stationed across the highway, and a tank with a water cannon on it coming to break in and arrest all the drug-crazed hippies, and two hundred thousand people, and canals and alligators—and mud, lots of good mud," Gage recalls. "Then the state policemen grab the first stoned kid they see and arrest him. Unfortunately for the governor, he turns out to be the son of the most prominent Protestant minister in Miami, who has some medical condition and is certifiably a non-druggie. Big publicity in the following weeks about this arbitrary exercise of police power."

Meanwhile, Gage was juggling phone calls from San Francisco. "The Stones are supposed to fly there next and do another concert, but nobody knows where. I'm supposed to airlift the entire operation: the world's biggest sound system plus six Super-Trooper lights on ninety-foot-tall stands from West Palm Beach out to California," Gage says. "And I'm tired." Luckily, he didn't follow the equipment. The concert was finally held in December in Altamont, California, where Hell's Angels hired to guard the stage jumped an apparently stoned man and stabbed him to death.

Extended Adolescence

CAMERON SEARS WAS eight years old when the Rev. Martin Luther King Jr. was killed. "That night is vividly etched in my mind," he says. His family lived in northwest Washington, and looking out the windows of his newborn sister's bedroom, he was awestruck by the orange glow of a city in flames. "We had National Guard driving around—it's martial law, basically—and my dad had commuted into the city that morning," Sears recalls. He was petrified—and not just for his father. Sears was attending public school at the time. "It was in a diplomatic area, so a lot of the students were affiliated with various embassies, some were even the sons and daughters of ambassadors, but a lot of the kids came from the ghetto, a very eclectic mix. And it really freaked me out, because a lot of my friends were black and lived in the part of town that was burning. I'd gone to birthday parties there, so that had a much bigger impression on me than Bobby Kennedy's assassination. Everybody was drawn to Martin Luther King in a very spiritual way, even if you were only eight years old."

The shocks kept on coming. Sears, whose parents had friends in the government, had a front-row seat, but only some of that summer's events made an impression on his preteen psyche. He does remember that a counselor at his day camp gave him a batch of blue-and-white McCarthy buttons and that he briefly became a supporter. "I gave them out," he says. "I thought it was a hoot. I was wearing tie-dye clothes; we made them at camp. I was totally into it."

Like many late boomers, though, Sears only got to live his generation's defining experiences secondhand. He never protested, but did dress up as a radical one Halloween. His third-grade teacher "had a fit," he says, and called his mother in for a chat. Sears was shocked; if radicals weren't acceptable, why were they always on TV? "I had a strong sense of Woodstock," he adds, even though he was only nine. "I knew it was a phenomenal happening. When my dad went out to San Francisco for work in the early seventies, I went with him, and I felt, 'Wow, San Francisco; this is it.'" Never mind that it wasn't anymore.

In 1970, the Sears family moved back to Massachusetts, to the Boston suburb of Lexington. Sears doesn't remember Earth Day, that spring's kickoff of what would become the environmental movement, but summers spent on Cape Cod placed him ahead of that curve. "We talked about conservation issues around the dinner table, because on Cape Cod, there was a lot of developmental pressure," he says. "The dredging of the harbor was an issue: Why was that good and why was that bad? What did that mean? So I had a very clear grasp of ecological concerns." The next year, he came upon his father's copy of *The Whole Earth Catalogue*.

First published in 1968, the oversize book purveyed tools aimed at communes, what *Whole Earth* author Stewart Brand describes as "intentional communities . . . bands of adventurous malcontents who were setting out to reinvent civilization, trying to get it right this time."[1] Most of its buyers were like Sears, who read it cover to cover, enjoying the running commentaries and cartoons in its margins that made the book much more than a mere catalogue. "I'm looking at solar energy and where to go get the hip backpack and how to go live an alternative lifestyle," he says.

Music played a big part in the Sears household. Since his grandfather had been the folksinging activist Pete Seeger's faculty adviser in high school, Sears would go backstage whenever Seeger played concerts in the Washington area. His mother transferred her love of classical music and the piano to her son—a soloist in his church choir—and his father loved jazz. Sears's own taste was diverse.

The lure of the waning counterculture was still strong. Both its attractions and dangers reached Sears through the media. He first smoked pot in seventh grade in 1971. He'd been curious ever since he saw a picture of a hippie smoking a joint on the cover of *Life* magazine, but he was scared off stronger drugs by *Go Ask Alice*, a 1972 made-for-television movie that portrayed a high school student's freakout. "At the same time, a friend's older brother committed suicide because he was having a bad trip," Sears says. "I had a cousin who became a speed freak. And because some of my friends' parents were teachers at Harvard and MIT, every once in a while we'd hear about a kid who went flying out a window, tripping his brains out. But that didn't prevent me from tripping a bunch."

Sears took his first LSD—Orange Sunshine—as a junior at boarding school. "And I remember doing a fair amount of windowpane," a later "brand" of acid. After experimentation and some proselytizing to friends, Sears "didn't trip so much anymore," he says. "It really wasn't my thing."

He'd turned into a teenage rebel, though. "I played soccer and hockey and I was a tennis player. But because I had long hair and I would smoke dope, the coach at this boarding school would fuck with me. I was the number-one singles player, but he would make me play number-two doubles. I got so fed up I quit." Instead, he'd go out backpacking. "I guess I didn't have a team consciousness," he says.

THE BARBARA LEDEEN who came back to Beloit College from the *Washington Post* was not the girl who'd left a year before. Her exposure to the power elite and the protesting masses had turned her into a Marxist. But the movement was moving faster than she was; back in the Midwest, she decided the new radicals didn't want her kind around. When her political theory class took a trip to the South Side of Chicago to hear Rev. Jesse Jackson (b. 1941) preach his doctrine of black self-empowerment, all Ledeen could hear was the civil rights movement rejecting whites, Jews, her. She was scared, too, by the Blackstone Rangers, a street gang from Chicago's South Side that briefly became the darlings of Midwest leftists.

"They're calling Jews honkies, so I'm out of there; I'm off the train, man." Within a year of finding her "team," she says, "you had no more team." Then came Nixon. "Poison gas," Ledeen says. "It reached the point where it was, pick up a gun or get out. All I could think about was getting out of this horrible country, because there was no corner of it that was not corrupt. Idealism had failed. The norm was the storm."

Her only refuge was literature. She'd saved two courses for her senior year: twentieth-century European literature—Hesse, Camus, Kafka and Brecht—and one on James Joyce. The existentialists gave her comfort. Not so the Joyce teacher, a married Irishman with whom Ledeen fell madly in love. "I was obsessed and he took advantage of my obsession," she says. At the end of that year, her parents expected her to go to law school, and in exchange for her reluctant agreement, her father gave her a round-trip ticket to Luxembourg, a Eurailpass, and $400. She had no intention of returning. Armed with a duffel bag and her nest egg, knowing no one and no languages other than English and Latin, Ledeen landed in Luxembourg in summer 1970, and hitchhiked through Paris to Barcelona, where she and a girl from San Francisco checked into a youth hostel in a little fishing village, on the Mediterranean coast. When they ran out of money, they hired out to work on fishing boats. "And not a single bad thing happened to us. We would leave around three A.M., come back in around seven at night. We'd throw out the nets, pull them in with the guys, have coffee with brandy in it in the morning, a big pot of fish stew for lunch. We did that for weeks. I was so stupid, it didn't occur to me what bad things could happen."

She hated America so much, she'd begun telling people she was Canadian. "Any anti-American demonstration in Europe I would go to," she says. From Spain, she moved on to Italy and Yugoslavia, where she came to rest again, selling paintings and explaining Bob Dylan lyrics to students in a Zagreb piazza. She finally called her parents and told them she wasn't coming home; they'd asked the State Department to find her, but she didn't want them to know where she was. Anyway, she was on the move again. "It was time to go, because I was not going to learn Serbo-Croatian."

There was another reason to leave Yugoslavia; her lover, the Joyce professor, was returning to Europe. They'd corresponded through the year, and now planned to meet, in spring 1971, on Elba, an island off Italy. But Ledeen had problems; her professor still had a wife. When she'd told her father she wasn't coming home for law school, he cut her off. She called him a corrupt capitalist and headed to Edinburgh. Why? The Scots were victims of British imperialism, and she'd heard students could rent dormitory rooms cheap at the University of Edinburgh.

"Then winter comes," she laughs, "and I have never been so cold in my entire life." So when she saw a want ad for an English tutor in Milan, she jumped. "Milan was close to Elba." She wrote her lover, met him at a hotel in southern Italy, and confirmed that he had no intention of leaving his wife. She lasted two more weeks in Milan, then begged her parents to take her back. "I had to admit defeat," she says. "It was awful." She moved home to Rochester, but soon returned to Washington, worked two jobs for several months, and socked away cash. "I buy another ticket," she sighs, "straight to Elba. But he was gone."

Forlorn, she was also resourceful and got a job organizing excursions for English visitors to a local resort. It paid well enough that she could rent a villa on a white sand beach, facing the Mediterranean. "All the fishermen, the housewives, the storekeepers know me. I can hitchhike around and nobody will bother me. My neighbors teach me Italian. It's idyllic. And then I get sick. And you don't want to be sick on Elba."

Ledeen ended up in a hospital in Rome, where she lost her appendix and made a friend, a fellow patient, the wife of the financial attaché to the Embassy of Sierra Leone, who rented her a room and helped her get a job at the Zambian embassy. "And we do black Africa," she laughs. "Fish heads and spicy bananas. And they have brought a niece of somebody in their family to be their household slave. She's not sent to school; they feed her the scraps; this is their culture; this is how they are. And I never even once say to them, 'Don't you think she should be in school?' "

The Zambian embassy made American corruption look benign. "Back home, they're starving to death, but these diplomats are living top of the line," Ledeen says. "They get shipments of caviar, champagne, the most incredible foie gras, they order suits from the finest tailors. And they never pay. Nobody speaks any known language, they speak what they think is English but really isn't, so I'm their communicator with the outside world. My job is to tell the grocers, the tailors, 'Sorry, he's not in today. And he won't be in tomorrow or next week, either.' "

THERE WERE CONTINGENCY plans in case the Weather Bureau's bombing at Fort Dix went awry, and Mark Rudd followed them in the hours after the West 11th Street townhouse exploded, helping the survivors regroup. As is the case with much of what followed, Rudd will still not go into detail. Briefly, he was listed among the presumed dead. He had an intermediary call his parents and assure them he was all right. They thought he was nuts and had told him as much, but they hadn't tried to stop him. The Weathermen had a vague plan to go underground, but the details hadn't been worked out. Now that was done on the fly. During the next two months, the Weather Bureau passed through a scrim of friends and supporters, communes and collectives, from Vermont to Oregon, and disappeared.

Still taking themselves seriously, they hunkered down and tied themselves in ideological knots trying to figure out what they'd done wrong, but they also had to deal with the logistics of being federal fugitives. A month after the townhouse bombing, the Nixon administration began planning a secret interagency crackdown on domestic terror—specifically targeting groups like the Weathermen and the Panthers. Rudd, Dohrn, Jones, Robbins, Boudin, J.J., Ayers and others were indicted in April for crossing state lines and inciting riots in Chicago. The case was assigned to Julius Hoffman, the infamous Chicago 8 judge. Four days later, a warrant was issued for Rudd's arrest when he failed to show up for trial on a riot charge stemming from the Columbia takeover.

Rudd was already underground, en route to San Francisco, where he was sent to an emergency meeting of the Weather Underground. He walked into a fierce argument.[2] J.J. was being blamed for what was termed the "military error" at the townhouse. "The problem with the organization was J.J.," Rudd recalls. "The error was armed struggle and going underground." Expelled, J.J. left the meeting and dropped out of sight.

Rudd was linked to J.J., so he fell farther down Weather's food chain. "I was already out of the Weathermen," he says. "The only reason I was at the meeting was because of who I used to be." He blamed himself. He was weak; he couldn't *do it*. And he couldn't go home. He was facing heavy felony charges and, he feared, the possibility of murder charges as well. Rudd was sent to San Francisco to join a collective and redeem himself. Dohrn, Ayers and Jones were nearby, living on a Sausalito houseboat. In May, Dohrn's voice was on a tape delivered to the underground press, declaring a state of war between the Weather Underground and "Amerika-with-a-K." A few days later the Associated Press and the *New York Times* got a note, signed Weathermen, threatening an attack against a "symbol or institution of American injustice." Two weeks later, a bomb exploded in New York's police headquarters, injuring seven people.

Beginning in summer 1970, and for months thereafter, Weather Underground bombings continued across the country. Early in 1971, Dohrn and Boudin blew up a women's bathroom in the U.S. Capitol building in response to the bombing of Laos. Following the shooting of black activist George Jackson in the yard at San Quentin Prison in August 1971, Weather blew up three offices of the California prison system.[3] After an uprising at New York's Attica Penitentiary, which resulted in the deaths of nine guards and thirty inmates, including Jane Alpert's lover Sam Melville, a bomb went off in the office of New York's corrections commissioner. The next year, shortly after America began bombing North Vietnam, Weather even hit the Pentagon—on Ho Chi Minh's birthday, no less.[4]

Rudd was blowing up buildings, too. He was working odd jobs, "trying to make a semblance of life, but more important, continuing with a political strategy which involved still more bombings," he admits. "But it was with a lot of caution, so nobody was hurt." Not all bombers were so scrupulous, but usually Weather approved of freelance copycats. "Part of the concept was exemplary actions that could be emulated," Rudd says. Even now, almost thirty years later, his is loathe to admit that he was engaged in terrorism. "We tended to differentiate between terror, or killing civilian people, and legitimate targets," he says. "You can blow up a bathroom in the Pentagon."

Rudd was told to make contact with the Youth Culture. This was Weather's new line—communicated in December 1970, in a manifesto named for Bob Dylan's song "New Morning." Rudd later said his comrades were a day late and a dollar short in discovering what they called Weather Nation, but he did his bit.[5] He grew his hair long, wore a disguise, lived in various apartments in San Francisco, hung out at Fisherman's Wharf, and hitchhiked up and down the California coast, making the hippie scene.

Weather Underground had an aboveground support network that helped with money, identification documents, and the difficult logistics of staying a step ahead of law enforcement. It also helped reconnect Rudd with a girl named Sue, his pre-strike Columbia girlfriend, in summer 1970; she stayed underground with him for the next seven years.

By that time, though, Rudd was suffering from depression. He'd gotten another woman pregnant. He and a dozen other Weathermen had been indicted again, in July in Detroit, for a conspiracy to bomb and kill. "There were moments of feeling suicidal," he says. "Was the rest of my life going to be this or prison? There was a lot of loneliness and fear and anxiety. A very tough time." But strangely, it all settled him down. Sue became his best friend and began to help him clarify what was happening and why. The next New Year's Eve, she and Rudd agreed they might strike out on their own. They bought a truck and began taking trips to Death Valley. They had to start a new life somewhere.

Early in 1971, Rudd told his comrades he was striking out on his own. No one argued. They thought him a shooting star, a creature of ego and publicity. "I was no longer functional as a true believer, as a soldier in that militant guerrilla organization," he says. "The logic of my leaving was obvious." Sue made arrangements to leave her job and disappear with him. They ended up in Santa Fe, New Mexico.

Rudd had many identities over the years. He was sometimes a greaser, sometimes a hippie, sometimes Tony Schwartz or Tony Goodman. His driver's license was in a different name, his car registered to a fourth. He was still trying to shed his white-skin privilege; now he understood the anxiety poor people live with every day. "Am I going to pay the rent, and will the FBI get me this week?" he says, laughing. Yet Santa Fe gave him peace. He settled on one identity, created a fictitious past, and worked construction. "We worked and we had friends, and we weren't obsessed with making the Revolution," Rudd says. "Well, Sue never was."

Things were fine until Rudd accidentally bumped into Jane Alpert, the New York bomber. Alpert had pleaded guilty on May 4, 1970, the day of the Kent State killings. Then, free on bail, she got on a train for the spring 1970 march on Washington and disappeared into the Underground. Still on the run in 1971, Alpert had a chance encounter with her ex-lover Rudd in Santa Fe. "Immediately after, Santa Fe was flooded with FBI agents looking for us," says Rudd. He packed and moved to Pennsylvania, where he and Sue lived for two years and had a son. They moved again in summer 1974, to a working-class neighborhood in New Rochelle, near New York City. Sue worked in stores and took care of children, while he kept doing construction work. The war in Vietnam ended when the Paris Peace Accords were signed in January 1973. Then the Nixon administration collapsed in the Watergate scandal.

Early in the Watergate investigation, it emerged that, galvanized by the 1970 townhouse explosion, the government had engaged in an illegal war against the New Left, accelerating a counterintelligence process begun after the Columbia uprising. An interdivisional intelligence unit was set up to cross-reference information gathered by the FBI, the military, the Secret Service, the Bureau of Narcotics and Dangerous Drugs, and other local and national police agencies, and a special litigation section was set up to pursue SDS, the Weathermen, the White Panther Party, and others.[6]

In June 1973, a federal judge ordered the government to disclose any evidence of burglary, sabotage, illegal surveillance, the use of agents provocateurs, or other espionage techniques used in the Weather investigation. Even though the Weather Underground was still bombing—in September 1973 it planted a bomb at ITT headquarters in New York to protest the coup that deposed Chile's elected Marxist leader, Salvadore Allende Gossens—the next month, the government dropped its case in Detroit; the following January, the Chicago charges were dropped as well. If they'd gone to trial, Rudd's lawyer Gerald Lefcourt claimed, he would have introduced evidence that, despite denials, the Nixon administration had drafted an illegal plan for centralized domestic counterespionage shortly after the Kent State killings, and put it into effect through a secret executive committee run by a Justice Department lawyer.

With charges dropped, Lefcourt called Rudd and told him he could come home. But he and Sue decided to stay underground. "I was in an ambivalent place," Rudd says. "I was detached from the organization, but I also was no less in opposition to U.S. imperialism." It took two more years of doing no more than not getting caught to finally change Rudd's mind.

By then, the Weather Underground was in disarray, having "evolved from terrorism to armed attacks that didn't hurt anybody, to becoming a publishing house," Rudd scoffs. They put out books and magazines (and even appeared in a documentary film) that reflected their latest ideology; under the influence of old-style communists, they were spouting "a standard, doctrinaire labor-workers line," and finally, Rudd says, had been seized by their own followers and "held hostage for their crimes." In a bizarre replay of the Stalinist show trials of 1930s Communists, they were purged from their own organization.

By 1976, Rudd was ready to surface. But after John Jacobs suddenly appeared, disrupting their plans, Rudd and Sue moved again and waited a year before finally emerging in September 1977.[7] "He's thirty years old," his father told *The New York Times*. "You get too old to be a revolutionary." Rudd unwittingly chose to surface on Rosh Hashanah, the Jewish New Year, a slow news day in New York; he made page one of the *Times* and swept past about 100 reporters as he entered the Manhattan district attorney's office. "I walked up from the subway a few blocks away, and there was this roar, and the cameras and everything," he recalls. "I thought there must be some event happening. So I walk into it, and it's me! I'm the event."

FIFTEEN DAYS AFTER the 1969 Moratorium, Jim Fouratt attended a regional conference of homosexual organizations, where a radical caucus called for support of the Panthers, the Chicago 8, the California grape pickers, and women's liberation—all of which outraged older gays, who wanted to live their lives in peace, and younger ones, who wanted to lead their sex lives in peace. Both disdained Goldilocks, as they called Fouratt, and his crowd of crazy revolutionaries.[8] In December 1969, the Gay Liberation Front splintered. Members of the new Gay Activist's Alliance rejected Fouratt's politics. Their attitude, he says, was: "Fuck the liberation and let's just deal with Gay."

Their rejection drove Fouratt even more firmly into the camp of the oppressed. He organized a group of gays and lesbians to go to Cuba to cut sugar cane with the Venceremos Brigade, which sent Americans to the communist island every year. "Two days before we were to leave, I was notified that I was not welcome, because I was openly gay." Homophobic Cuban officials feared he'd try to organize gay Cubans.

So Fouratt poured all his belongings into a VW van and drove to Austin, Texas, where there was going to be a gay liberation conference; he'd been invited to stay with a friend, the actor and screenwriter L. M. Kit Carson (b. 1947). But Fouratt was pulled over by police near Carson's house and charged with driving with an expired license. The police also found gay liberation and Black Panther literature, and copies of Mao Tse-Tung's famous little red book. "The next thing I knew, I was arrested for possession of heroin and guns, neither of which I had," he says.

Carson arranged for a wealthy friend to bail Fouratt out of jail. He was then confined to the man's property for a month, which wasn't bad; the man had an art collection and parties that attracted celebrities. Fouratt wasn't above singing for his supper. "I was the hippie," Fouratt says. "I hadn't really been around this kind of society."

Finally, Fouratt was allowed to plead guilty to possession of marijuana and leave Texas. When he went to a big antiwar demonstration in Boston in April 1970, he learned that in his absence, a rumor had started that he was an FBI informer. It could have been started by anyone, from his gay opponents to people jealous of his job at Columbia. He was also attracting government attention. He spoke at a May rally protesting the arrest of Bobby Seale for murder in New Haven and earned a statement in support of homosexuals from Black Panther leader Huey Newton in return. He attended a People's Revolutionary Constitutional Convention in Philadelphia that September. Having gotten to know Weatherman leaders before they went underground, he was helping them, too. The FBI, which had long ignored the New Left, now instituted the counterintelligence program that became known as COINTELPRO. Among its tactics were harassment and disinformation campaigns against radical leaders. Cops had even come to Fouratt's mother's door, saying he'd been involved in a bank robbery and asking for his picture.

Fouratt's parole officer in New York, who told him he couldn't associate with homosexuals, probably didn't like him gallivanting all over the country meeting fellow revolutionaries, either. But he took off for Seattle, for a meeting of the Weathermen support network, "something about moving people around the country," he says vaguely. Fouratt hadn't liked it when he heard that the Weathermen had been building anti-personnel bombs in that basement on West 11th Street, but that didn't stop him. "My allegiance was to struggle within that community tactically, but not to abandon them," he says. "And there's something very romantic about an underground. I knew where the safe houses were. All these groups had links to each other."

He was near the gay bars of Seattle's Triangle Square when he was nabbed for jaywalking by the police. That's when he found out his parole had been revoked. The marshals who flew him back to Dallas kept asking about Bernardine Dohrn. Finally, Fouratt got tired of it. "I'm Bernardine Dohrn," he said.

Again, friends in Texas set him up with a swell place to stay. His new hostess was five times married, with multiple Cadillac convertibles in a crayon box of colors. Through her, he met a gay minister and got involved in a group called the Purple Star Tribe, which took over a local alternative newspaper. Journalism was the bridge to his next stop, Washington, D.C., where he joined the Unicorn News Collective, which had started an alternative network by giving five-minute news summaries to college and noncommercial radio stations.

In 1972, Fouratt covered the Republican convention in Miami for Unicorn as Richard Nixon was nominated for a second term in office. Fouratt had an epiphany when he went to a rally in Flamingo Park, which had been given to the protesters in an attempt to obviate repeats of the Chicago riots. The event was sponsored by a breakaway faction of the Yippies, who considered Abbie Hoffman and Jerry Rubin sellouts. Led by Tom Forcade and Dana Beal, they called themselves Zippies. "I watched a mind-washing experiment," Fouratt says. Zippies were "giving acid to young people, and then taking them through classic brainwashing steps. They wanted to politicize these kids, who already were political because they were there, but for their own agenda, which was disruptive and nihilistic. Abbie was sort of stumbling around lost, because he was a leader but there was no movement anymore." Zippies tossed a pie in Rubin's face that week to remind him he was well over thirty.

All around them were the lost, the damaged, the chastened. The North Vietnamese were winning their war overseas, but the movement that helped them, drowning in its own narcissistic maximalism, was losing its war at home. Nixon won again. Politics no longer provided direction, and drugs rushed in to fill the void. Quaaludes had suddenly flooded the drug scene in 1972, numbing all who took them and inspiring a conspiracy theory that they were being distributed by the CIA to end the peace movement. For the committed, everything was falling apart.

"The middle seventies were dark times," Fouratt says. "I was trying to figure out what to do and how to be. You really had to decide what was important." He often stopped to reflect on his friends who'd died or gone underground, and he couldn't help feeling a profound sense of loss. "What doesn't ever get said is that these were smart, on-the-right-track kids who threw away everything," he notes. "These people no longer had any resources, any access, no longer could easily go back to careers. There's an incredible psychological price when you are a no-man or no-woman. When your dream is over, what do you fall back on?"

The Paris Peace Accords, signed January 27, 1973—the same day

Defense Secretary Melvin Laird announced the end of the draft—took whatever wind was left out of the antiwar movement's sails. Although the conviction of the Chicago 7 would shortly be overturned by a federal appeals court, the lives of several of the defendants had already spiraled out of control. Abbie Hoffman threw himself into drugs and promiscuity, and by mid-1973 was dealing cocaine. Arrested that August 28, he disappeared into the Underground. Rennie Davis renounced activism and swore allegiance to the guru Mahara Ji. Jerry Rubin spent 1971 to 1975 trying, as he wrote in a memoir, an even more extensive "smorgasbord course in New Consciousness" than that undergone just a year earlier by Nina Hartley's parents. Rubin's quest included est, gestalt therapy, bioenergetics, rolfing, massage, jogging, health food, tai chi, Esalen, hypnotism, modern dance, meditation, Silva Mind Control, Arica, acupuncture, sex therapy and Reichian therapy.[9] Hoffman and Rubin's friends, too, were in trouble. Tom Forcade, who'd continued to smuggle drugs after founding *High Times* magazine in 1974, fell prey to Quaaludes and committed suicide in 1979. John Lennon and Yoko Ono found a more old-fashioned way to deaden their pain: They took up heroin.

LESLIE CROCKER SNYDER wanted to prosecute felonies. Though her boss, New York's DA Frank Hogan, let her prosecute men caught masturbating in public toilets, he wouldn't let her near major crimes, let alone what she really wanted—murderers. "I was totally devastated," she recalls. Weenie-wagger detail just didn't cut it. "I'm not a moralist," she says. "If you want to live with someone, you should live with someone. If you want to be gay, be gay. If you want to smoke pot, smoke pot, as long as it's not going to affect your performance. I do believe in personal freedoms. I don't think anything is really aberrant as long as it doesn't affect others."

She'd decided to be a career prosecutor. "I wanted to go to the Homicide Bureau, which is considered the elite bureau," she says. It was also the ultimate bastion of testosterone. So she displayed some of her own, threatening to quit, and enlisting superiors in her cause. Finally, Hogan offered her a job prosecuting the least serious felony offenders, juvenile cases, which "a woman could only fuck up so much."

Snyder's sex was actually an asset; before the 1972 Supreme Court decision that made it far harder for women to avoid jury service, she typically argued in front of all-male juries. "I love men, they like me, and it was a great chemistry," she says. Not so with Hogan. After he finally let her try felonies, she asked for more—a place in the Homicide Bureau—as he tried to talk her into heading Consumer Frauds. "I've always seen you as a Betty Furness," he said, referring to the famous consumer advocate then considered a woman of the highest accomplishment. Finally, he came up with a foolproof plan to shut her up. "Bring me a letter of permission from your husband, and I'll consider allowing you in the Homicide Bureau," he told her with a gleam in his eye.

Homicide prosecutors were on call at all hours and often had to work in the city's worst neighborhoods, where there were few women police, no women detectives, and no women in the station houses where she'd have to take statements. "It was a very different time," Snyder says. "And Hogan's time was fifty years before that." Hogan was sure that Snyder, who'd recently married a pediatrician, would never get permission. He was wrong. Her husband acquiesced, several mentors went to bat for her, and she soon became the first woman to try homicides in New York City. Indeed, she was the only woman to make the bureau, which disbanded shortly thereafter. By then, Snyder had moved on.

In 1970, shortly before moving to Homicide, she'd tried a double rape-robbery, and learned how rape laws were skewed against women. Two women had been dragged at knifepoint into a Lower East Side tenement, where they were raped, sodomized and robbed. Sex crimes were typically tried before Hogan-esque male judges, who found the cases as confusing as they were distasteful. New York law then required corroboration of three separate elements of a rape: identification of the attacker, proof that force was used, and proof of penetration. The judge in this case insisted that although semen had been found in the women's underwear, that was insufficient proof of penetration—and set the rapist free. "I just thought it was outrageous, hypertechnical and unfair," Snyder says. "Women were just not worthy of belief."

Though she hadn't been involved with protests or the women's movement, the judge's remarks raised Snyder's consciousness—and snapped her experiences at Harvard, at Case Western, at the U.S. Attorney's Office, and in Hogan's office into sharp focus. "I had been able to do everything I wanted to do in my life. But all that stuff percolates, and suddenly you see it in its totally outrageous context," she says. The fact that more women were coming out of law schools, joining lonely pioneers like Snyder, made it seem ever more urgent that things change, and more possible that they might. "As women felt more free to do whatever they want in many ways, including sexually, they felt freer to speak out, to get laws changed, and to become more involved," Snyder says.

Snyder made contact with Hogan's Appeals Bureau, where prosecutors agreed that the rape laws were unfair and encouraged her to try to change them. In 1972, they did; henceforth, a rape victim's uncorroborated identification of an attacker was deemed sufficient evidence. Her victory did not go unnoticed.

Though other political movements had faltered, feminists were feeling their oats. Journalist Gloria Steinem had launched *Ms. magazine* in 1971. The Equal Rights Amendment passed the Senate the next year and was sent to the states for ratification. In 1973, the Supreme Court decision in *Roe* v. *Wade* legalized abortion, but Snyder, like many baby boom women, kept her distance from women's liberation, even as she worked with the Manhattan Women's Political Caucus, NOW, and New York Women Against Rape to revise rape laws further. The suspicion was mutual (she was a prosecutor, after all), but "clearly we all met on fervent common ground in these limited areas," Snyder says, "and it trumped the distrust. At that point, it kind of coalesced for me. What mattered was that women should be treated equally and have the same opportunities and legal rights."

The fight to change the rape laws went on for several years. Finally, in November 1973, a united front of women from all ends of the political spectrum testified at a New York legislative hearing, urging that *all* corroboration requirements be repealed. A year later, they were.

By then, Snyder was pregnant. The DA's office had no maternity leave policy, but she was granted one. When she returned to work six weeks later, she had a new boss. The aging Hogan had retired. The new DA pushed her to come back and take over the Consumer Frauds Bureau. She would do it part-time for a while, she agreed, but felt no passion for the work, and soon asked and was given permission to continue her rape work and form a Sex Crimes Bureau—the first in the country.

To prosecute rapists successfully, Snyder knew she needed more tools than the law gave her. "I'd witnessed any number of trials in which the defendant was forgotten," she says. "Most sex crimes offenders are recidivists, but you couldn't ask anything about the defendant's priors. But the victims had to take the witness stand, the cross-examination would go on for hours about every sex act they'd ever committed—nothing to do with the case, nothing to do with the defendant. Their morality, their prior sexual history became the focus of the trial. They became the defendant, basically. Women were utterly discouraged from testifying because of these antiquated laws."

In 1974, after a Women's Bar group asked Snyder to head its Criminal Law Section, she and another member researched and wrote a Rape Shield Law, a piece of legislation designed to ensure that rape victims not be put on trial themselves for their prior sexual history. Its passage in 1975 was the most exciting moment of her life.

Simultaneously, Snyder and three other assistant district attorneys were setting up their sex crimes bureau, concentrating on the most legally difficult cases from the moment they were reported, guiding, reassuring and shielding the victims. "So you had people who were interested in and knew about this crime, people who hand-held the victim, sent them to support groups, sent children to psychologists if needed," she says. "It was very exciting. Because you really felt you were helping."

Snyder continued to score legal firsts. She was named the first female bureau chief in the history of the New York DA's office. Then came Marvin Teicher, a New York dentist who was repeatedly accused of molesting his patients—rubbing them, exposing himself, even penetrating them—while they were under anesthesia. Because they were sedated when assaulted, their testimony was worthless in court. Teicher also chose his victims carefully—picking on disaffected hippie-ish girls less likely to be believed. For a year, Snyder tried to get him by conventional means, sending patients who thought they'd been molested back to see him again, wired for sound, but he was too cagey to get caught—even when faced with experienced undercover cops.

Finally, Snyder got a court order to plant a camera in his ceiling—video surveillance had never been requested before. Policemen posing as power company workers installed a camera focused on the dental chair, and set up a monitoring post in his basement. Then she sent in an undercover agent who looked like a hippie. The videotape was running as he knocked her out and felt her breasts. He would finally be convicted in 1977.

DOUG MARLETTE LEFT school in June 1971. He hadn't graduated because he'd failed to fulfill his six-hour foreign language requirement. But that didn't matter. He'd been accepted as a conscientious objector and to fulfill the requirements, he had to do two years of public service. He took a post with the nonprofit College Press Service. As the job didn't pay much and he had a wife to support, he also took a night job as a paste-up man in the art department of Florida's *St. Petersburg Times* and almost immediately got a promotion to a day job, replacing an artist who'd been busted for drug dealing. Six weeks later, he was fired as overqualified.

Through a friend back home in North Carolina he heard there were openings for editorial cartoonists at both the *Raleigh News and Observer* and the *Charlotte Observer*. He immediately flew north and applied. In the interim, the Supreme Court had declared that anyone who'd been drafted when Marlette was—a brief period when the Selective Service Act had expired and its future was being debated in Congress—had to be released. "So I took the job in Charlotte," Marlette says. "And the career begins."

His first cartoon for the *Charlotte Observer*, in January 1972, lampooned Richard Nixon's bombing of Cambodia. His first big local issue was school busing. He sided with the moderates who were for it and against "the concerned parents, who were really Segs"—or segregationists—he says. Their allies were doing things like burning crosses on the lawn of the federal judge presiding over the case. Archconservative Jesse Helms began serving as North Carolina's junior senator that year and became another target. "Within a few weeks I had petitions being sent in, demanding I be fired," Marlette says. After a year of Marlette, the publisher of the *Observer*—a member of the Knight family that owned the Knight-Ridder newspaper chain and "a racist and a reactionary of the extreme kind," according to Marlette—joined the chorus of detractors, complaining that their new pacifist cartoonist had come to town "both guns blazing." Knowing he was attracting national attention to their local paper, Marlette's superiors backed him up, but they moved his cartoons from the editorial page to the Op-Ed page just opposite, putting some distance between his work and the paper's masthead.

"The nation was polarized," Marlette says. "I got to learn my craft with these larger-than-life figures. I was drawing cartoons that were anti-segregation, antiwar, anti-Nixon, and anti-Helms in a place that was in favor of all those things. And doing it in a way that drove people crazy."

In 1974, he and his wife separated and divorced. That summer, Gerald Ford's ascension to the presidency marked the end of an ugly era. "It had been nasty, and that's one of the reasons my cartoons were so upsetting to people," Marlette says. "There was a certain gratitude for some kind of civility coming back. It got duller, though, professionally."

IT SUDDENLY SEEMED to Tim Scully as if there were cops everywhere. When Sand finished his Orange Sunshine production, Scully shut down the Windsor lab and spent his time learning to fly a plane, a Mooney M20E, which Billy Hitchcock had given him. Scully was en route out of

Napa County Airport when federal agents carrying a warrant from Denver converged on him. Accepting the inevitable, he waived extradition and spent the next year commuting to Denver, where his lawyers beat the charges by proving that the police should have had a search warrant before entering his lab. Legal ingenuity also overturned the convictions of Scully's accomplices.

Still, Scully decided to retire from the LSD trade. He'd done his time in the Underground Army, and it wasn't as if the world would be without acid. Scully had met a new backer/chemist who had access to raw lysergic acid, and brought him to Sand. Sand would still work at a lab in St. Louis and at a new one in Belgium.

Early in 1969, one of Hitchcock's associates had been caught at U.S. Customs with $100,000 in cash. Though the money belonged in large part to Sand and Owsley, the courier said it was Hitchcock's. In order to explain why no taxes had been paid, Hitchcock got his Swiss banker partner to say it was a loan.

Hitchcock, divorcing and afraid his wife might reveal his drug dealing, moved back to New York.[10] Scully headed to Albion, a little town in northern California. He'd grown scared of the consequences of his chemistry, and that played into a growing disenchantment with drugs, or at least with those who used them irresponsibly. He began building biofeedback instruments for use in drug rehabilitation programs—electronic measuring tools that help users alter consciousness without drugs. He'd been the subject of a biofeedback experiment in 1966, when he was in Los Angeles with the Dead, and a fascination with the idea of voluntary control of consciousness without drugs had lingered. Biofeedback helped Scully come down from the high "of doing something that we thought would save the world" and replaced it with "something considerably less dangerous while still making the world a better place," he says. He had dues to pay, and rehab programs were a good place to pay them. Most acidheads he met told him he'd changed their lives for the better, but "a small percentage had bad things happen," he says, and others went on to more dangerous drugs because they figured a government that lied about one must be lying about them all.

"I felt really bad about that," Scully says. "I still do. Knowing what I know, I would not have pushed so strongly to scatter acid to the four corners of the earth without any thought of channeling it to try to increase the likelihood that people who took it would use it responsibly. Producing tools to help people with drug problems was a step toward restitution." Ironically, the product of that mission—the $100 machines he made to help teach addicts and alcoholics to produce calming, meditative alpha brain waves—earned him more than LSD had. Which was lucky. Owsley's hidden drug profits had evaporated.[11]

In January 1970, with the stock market plunging from its 1960s highs, Billy Hitchcock's wife filed for divorce and included charges that she had seen him take Owsley's money, substantiated with documents from her husband's safe deposit boxes. Hitchcock flew to Switzerland, where he discovered that not only was all his money gone, he also owed the bank $1 million.[12] When negotiations broke down, the bank sued him and apparently sent its lawyers documents about his Swiss accounts—*and* those belonging to Owsley and Sand. The repercussions of these financial dealings would soon effect the entire counterculture.

In March 1970, Timothy Leary hired Michael Kennedy, the San Francisco radical lawyer, to handle a Supreme Court appeal of his Laguna Beach conviction. Kennedy had expanded his practice beyond radicals to include dealers and pornographers. Now he became the link between the drug underground and other clients in the Weather Underground. In September 1970, the Brotherhood paid the Weathermen $25,000 to break Leary out of prison. Leary later claimed that the middleman and mastermind of the plan was his lawyer, Michael Kennedy.[13] The Weather Underground picked Leary up outside the walls of a California prison. Mark Rudd helped set up an apartment for him. Others provided him with a disguise and false passport, and spirited him out of the country. "We are outlaws, we are free," the radicals boasted in a communiqué announcing the dramatic breakout.

Leary issued a letter a few days later saying he should be considered armed and dangerous, and eventually made his way to Algeria, where the exiled Black Panther Eldridge Cleaver double-crossed him by placing him under revolutionary house arrest. Finally freed from Cleaver's caress after an additional cash infusion from the Brotherhood, Leary abandoned his revolutionary pose and ended up in posh exile in Switzerland.

Just after Tim Scully beat his lab rap in Denver, he'd heard that a grand jury was investigating him again, this time for the Orange Sunshine lab in Windsor. Declaring that drug arrests of juveniles had risen 800 percent between 1960 and 1967, Richard Nixon's White House was cracking down even more. The problem was international and hardly limited to LSD. Marijuana smoking was epidemic, and by 1971, opiates were flooding America from Southeast Asia, where tribal warlords allied with the CIA's counterinsurgency efforts in Vietnam had launched a massive expansion of the heroin trade. That June, Nixon declared drug abuse "a national emergency."[14]

Gordon Liddy, Millbrook, New York's drug-busting DA, was now in the White House, coordinating the anti-drug effort. In May 1971, Laguna Beach police had busted a small-time dealer who'd given up the Brotherhood in return for leniency. Within a year, an intergovernmental task force uncovered what they called a major drug organization, a chain descending from the fugitive Tim Leary through Billy Hitchcock down to street dealers. In July 1972, a grand jury began considering conspiracy charges against the Brotherhood of Eternal Love. Fifty-seven people were arrested that August, huge stashes of hashish, LSD, cocaine, mescaline, and marijuana were confiscated, and two hashish oil labs were closed, but more important, the organization's unity was shattered. "Brothers" started ratting on one another.

Timothy Leary was indicted as the Brotherhood's godfather. Sand was arrested soon after, when someone left a sink running in the St. Louis mansion he was using as a lab and a concerned mail carrier saw the streaming water. The quality of LSD soon began to decline. Psilocybin and synthetic mescaline all but disappeared around the same time.[15] Drugs weren't over—marijuana would never go away and new kicks were just around the corner—but it was the end of the first acid era.

Sand was in jail for almost a year, fighting the St. Louis search. By the time his lawyers quashed it, he'd been indicted again, in April 1973—one of several indictments known collectively as the Brotherhood cases. The government's big break had come in March, when Billy Hitchcock turned state's evidence against his former friends. As part of its investigation of Nick Sand, the government had stumbled upon a lawyer named Peter Buchanan. Buchanan, Scully's lawyer, had aided in the laundering of the funds that purchased the Windsor lab property and Sand's Cloverdale ranch. When investigators contacted Buchanan, he volunteered to cooperate in exchange for immunity for himself, Scully and Hitchcock. Buchanan then called his clients and warned them that the government had obtained the bank records indicating Hitchcock's involvement.

In summer 1972, after grand jury subpoenas were issued to compel their testimony, Hitchcock and Scully went to Europe (separately, but at Hitchcock's expense) in order to avoid being compelled to testify. Just as the statute of limitations was about to expire, Hitchcock was indicted in federal court for tax evasion and securities violations. In February 1973, as he was turning himself in, he learned from a reporter that his wife had revealed details of his dealings with Owsley and his Swiss accounts. He decided he had no choice but to cut a deal. Scully thinks Hitchcock was also threatened by his family with the loss of his substantial inheritance.

As those cases moved inexorably toward the courtroom, Timothy Leary was arrested trying to enter Afghanistan from Switzerland and was sent back to California. Though he would long deny it, saying he only gave circumstantial evidence on the Weather Underground's foreign ties, it was widely thought that Leary made a deal with authorities and testified before a number grand juries in various cases and jurisdictions against groups like the Brotherhood and the Weather Underground.[16] Michael Kennedy, representing Nick Sand, dropped Leary as a client and branded him a rat. Leary was finally paroled in 1976 after thirty-two months in forty prisons. In 1978, he married a boomer born in 1947 and moved to Laurel Canyon, where he took drugs, wrote books on outer space and futurology, toured the country doing a standup philosophy/comedy act, debated Gordon Liddy, lived the celebrity life, and became an early advocate of cyberspace. Leary's daughter, Susan, hanged herself in prison in 1990, after being accused of shooting her boyfriend. Her father died at seventy-five in 1996. In April 1997, some of his ashes were shot into space aboard a satellite (along with those of Gene Roddenberry, the creator of the *Star Trek* TV series)—a fitting end for the Pied Piper of the Baby Boom.

HIS BRIEF SPELL of active duty in the reserves interrupted Michael Fuchs's education in the law. With a few months to kill before he could return to school at Georgetown, he spent the end of 1968 and the beginning of 1969 working odd jobs in Manhattan and traveling. He didn't demonstrate, go to Woodstock, or get lost in drugs. "I wasn't a hippie," he says. "Marching and stuff, I don't know what any of that accomplished. I stayed involved politically. I considered myself a liberal when it wasn't a dirty word. But I was marking time to get through school."

Inspired by his politically connected uncle, who in June 1967 flew to Washington to lobby for Lyndon Johnson's support for Israel's Six Day War, Fuchs was already looking beyond school. "You can do more good from a powerful position than you can as a social worker," he told a cousin entering that profession. Already, though, Fuchs was distancing himself from the power centers of Washington. "Washington at that time was a terrible fucking town, a desert," he says. "No Kennedy Center, there wasn't a restaurant open after nine o'clock at night." After six months in New York, he decided to stay and applied for a transfer to New York University. It wasn't what he hoped it would be, either.

"When I went to Georgetown, law school was very formal and disciplined, tie-and-jacket, *yes, sir,* stand up," he says. But things had changed"—students had run roughshod—"and at the end of that year, classes were suspended after the American invasion of Laos and Cambodia. "All grades and formalities went away. So those two years of law school became almost gradeless. I saw student power and attitude."

One positive manifestation of student power was the way law firms began to pander to promising law graduates. "The biggest issue in those days was pro bono," Fuchs recalls. "How much pro bono would your law firm allow you to do?" Using his pro bono allowance at the entertainment law firm that hired him when he graduated, Fuchs, who'd been a volunteer in Arthur J. Goldberg's failed campaign for governor of New York in 1970, went to New Hampshire in the early days of 1972 to work for Edmund Muskie "and became a part of history," he says. The Maine senator had run for vice-president in 1968 and become the front-runner for the 1972 Democratic presidential nomination, the moderate who would end the war.

As an advance man, Fuchs was part of the team that discussed what to do about a series of vicious editorials in the rabidly conservative *Manchester Union-Leader.* Its publisher, William Loeb, made great sport of liberals, and had not only pinioned "Moscow Muskie" for supposedly uttering a racial slur against French-Americans (who made up 40 percent of the state's Democratic vote) but also repeated gossip impugning Muskie's wife. Unaware that the purported racial slur was a Nixon dirty trick operation—a White House staffer had forged a letter containing the allegation—Fuchs advised Muskie to respond to Loeb in a speech outside the newspaper's offices.

Having moved on to the day's next stop, Fuchs wasn't there to witness the fruits of his labors, but as it turned out, his suggestion led inexorably to Muskie's Waterloo. Muskie stood hatless in a snowstorm defending his wife. "By attacking me, by attacking my wife," he thundered, Loeb had "proved himself to be a gutless coward." But then, he paused several times, his shoulders heaving, having seemingly lost his composure. The next day, the front page of *The Washington Post* and stories in other newspapers reported that he'd cried. Those reports—and their implication of instability—have long been blamed for his poor showing in the primary nine days later and for his eventual withdrawal from the race. Muskie would spend the rest of his life denying he'd cried, saying snow had melted on his face.

"My idea worked too well; it got too much publicity," Fuchs says. Like the press, Fuchs thought Muskie's melting snow story was "a very lame excuse," he says. "Reagan cried, Clinton cries every day, but in those days you couldn't cry."

Although Fuchs attended the Miami convention that summer, his days in politics were numbered. "I guess I got a little busier with my career," he says. He'd begun specializing in television law; his firm represented clients like sit-com star Dick van Dyke and talk show host Merv Griffin. Then, in 1974, Fuchs moved to a much smaller firm that worked in rock music and movies, and represented clients like Carly Simon and the producer Dino di Laurentiis.

Fuchs lasted nine months. "I was trying to find a career and some happiness," he says. "I didn't like being a lawyer. Law turned out to be not something fitting my personality. I mean, lawyers render a certain service, and I was probably not the best guy to be a service guy. I began to get restless and look around."

In 1975, he moved to the William Morris Agency as director of business affairs; in essence, he was the talent agency's in-house lawyer, but spent most of his time in the file room, studying contracts. "I lived in that file room," he says. "Because I was still of an age where I thought information was the key to everything. I even steamed open the Sonny and Cher divorce settlement."

KATHRYN BOND STOCKTON joined the girls' group in her neighborhood, only to see it split up as members headed off to parochial and private schools. Stockton stayed in public school. Her progressive parents wouldn't hear otherwise. Just after starting junior high school in fall 1970, she briefly decided she might be a feminist. "I remember a little period where I was arguing that girls should be able to play hockey," she says, but real feminism wouldn't enter her life for years. "I'd never met a feminist, never had a feminist class, never heard a feminist word in a classroom." Politics—feminist or not—didn't seem like a viable option; it required declaring who you were.

Religion became her safe escape. She sang in a Catholic church choir and went to mass in a Baptist church. She disdained Judaism because Jewish boys were no good at sports. "It's a weird form of homophobia," she observes. "You call people sissies because they can't do sports, and yet you've got this problem: you're gay." Finally, she settled on becoming an evangelical Christian. It was the time of Jesus freaks, blissed out instead of freaked out. Evangelicalism was a safe haven, thanks to its insistence on sex separation "because they're always so worried that anything sexual is going to take place," Stockton says. "*Perfect* for a gay child."

She became her group's resident intellectual, reading C. S. Lewis while they pored over their Bibles. "I was definitely cerebral. I had a lot of questions about the goofy stuff written by evangelicals." Because of her questioning nature, she stayed friends with a more secular crowd, too— "neighborhood friends, much more of their period. Definitely experimenting with sex, definitely doing drug stuff. And I'm in the swim with them, watching, but never participating." Though the drugs and sex part "didn't interest me so much," she says, "I wanted to be part of that cool scene."

Her parents were accepting, but she's sure that behind closed doors they were tearing their hair out. "I was, of course, constantly trying to convert them and all the Jews in the neighborhood, which was not cool at all." There was also a part of her troubled by the idea of telling anyone he'd go to hell if he didn't believe.

Always, in the background, was Stockton's secret. She was constantly falling in love with her girlfriends, connecting through their spiritual commitment. "But I was very anti-homosexual because of the religious stuff, and yet I knew that there was some disturbance here. I was some other kind of problem; I wasn't that problem," she told herself. Although her parents urged her to be tolerant of gays then coming out of the closet, she worried that if her mom and dad thought she was gay, it would kill them. "And I am dating boys at this time," she adds.

As a freshman in high school, Stockton started working in an outreach program at an Episcopal church in nearby Hartford, where she met her first boyfriend, a twenty-one-year-old working in a housing project her program targeted. He was from Texas, part Chicano, part Indian, dedicated to helping his neighbors. "I think he may have been gay, looking back on it," she says. "We had a very strong connection."

She liked him, but she was in love with a woman, a former wild-child hippie her little group had converted to Jesus. "I know my fascination with her had everything to do with the fact that she had had hippie experiences. I, in a sense, was her Christian mentor, and then we were mentoring each other. I felt like I had a girlfriend, even though she absolutely was not. She was very interested in boys."

Stockton's family were rabid Nixon-haters. Her father bought his first color TV just to watch the Watergate hearings. Her brother, who'd come down with mononucleosis, watched every moment of them "and I would sort of run in and out," she says. "I just loved the intrigue and piecing it all together, how Magruder fit in and what Haldeman was doing, and wanting him to be fried." She was a rare bird, left-wing evangelical. "I've never met another one," she says, laughing.

DAVID MCINTOSH WAS sixteen when Nixon was forced from office. He, too, followed the Watergate hearings intently, "fascinated," he says, by the drama. But if at the time he thought Nixon was evil "and got what he deserved," McIntosh was hardly a radical. He played tuba, had a job running a computer at a local plant that made sump pumps, and joined the speech and debate team, the Spanish club, the golf team, and the Eagle Scouts, which "reinforced those small-town values I didn't realize I was learning at the time," he says. He liked mainstream rock music: Three Dog Night, Stevie Wonder and Aerosmith were favorites. "Stairway to Heaven" was the theme at his prom, but rock was just music to him and his friends, not a soundtrack for rebellion. "There weren't a lot of problem kids in our school," he says, and there were no gangs or cliques or dropouts in Kendallville, Indiana.

McIntosh was typical, a good kid, an academic achiever, although not much of an athlete, which was unfortunate in a town where the year's biggest event is the high school basketball tournament. But he signed up as statistician for the basketball team, traveled to all the games, and got to "hang out with the team."

Drugs weren't an issue. "The drug at the time would have been alcohol," he says. "They'd drive to Michigan to get it and have drinking parties—if you were rebelling. I was one of those good kids that didn't."

THE SHOOTING OF students at Kent State University took place the day Steve Capps turned fifteen. Though protest "was in the air," Capps says ("We actually abolished our Student Council"), Kent State didn't have the meaning for him that it did for older boomers. "We cared about it. I'm sure we wore black armbands to school on Kent State Day. If you were a kid at that point, you were against the war. But it was a checkoff item, like asking a teenybopper today if she likes the Spice Girls."

Capps didn't indulge in typical teenage pursuits like television or drugs. "There was too much to do," he says, "and I already knew I had more ideas than I'd have time to pursue in a lifetime. I never wanted to check out mentally by watching TV or dropping acid because it was just too much fun to make things. Sorry to sound so Mr. Spock, but it's just illogical." So he spent his time with his best friend, making tapes imitating the comedy troupe Firesign Theater's Golden Days of Radio on LSD routines, or programming his school's computer.

An atypical ninth grader, Capps had quit the school's one computer class—reserved for seniors—because he already knew more than it covered. Then the school librarian asked him to automate the library, using a "donated 1959 computer that in its heyday was a million-dollar computer, but at that point was probably worth $5,000," Capps says. "I considered myself very lucky." And he was. He had a mainframe personal computer and got paid to program it. And no one dared pick on him because he was also co-captain of the school's football team. "So I was like King Nerd," he jokes.

TOMMY VALLELY RETURNED home to Newton, Massachusetts, in May 1970. Though Vietnam would linger long in his psyche, he adjusted fairly quickly, unlike fellow veterans unable to reintegrate in a society that wasn't exactly welcoming or interested in what had happened in combat. One friend who'd lost a leg in Vietnam and was still in the hospital would beg Vallely to smuggle drugs to him. Vallely did it once or twice, but finally refused, afraid of getting arrested. To his great regret, the friend later died of an overdose. "I'm not sure I would have survived if I lost a leg, but I never lost my bearings," says Vallely, who took a job as an asphalt inspector on the Massachusetts Turnpike.

Driving the highway every day, he'd listen to news of the war, trying to decide what, if anything, he could do about what he'd learned in Vietnam. "I was conflicted," he says. "I invested too much in this thing— I'm a fuckin' war hero—but I quit because I wanted to do something about the war." Finally, he found a way.

Father Robert F. Drinan, a Jesuit priest and official of Boston University Law School, had announced his antiwar candidacy in Vallely's congressional district that February. After winning a primary, he faced a long-time congressman who was a friend of President Nixon and head of the House Armed Services Committee in the general election. When the handsome Vietnam veteran volunteered to help the campaign, he was immediately sent out to accompany the candidate, so "wherever he went—fire stations, police stations, VFW halls—there would be a Marine with the peacenik," Vallely says. While working with Drinan, he met another, Vietnam veteran, John F. Kerry (b. 1943), another Silver Star hero who'd almost run in the same primary but dropped out of the race when Drinan won a local caucus vote. He and Vallely became fast friends.

After Drinan won election in November, Vallely got involved in the Vietnam Veterans movement. In late January 1971, his new friend Kerry was among a group of vets who met at a motel in Detroit for an ad hoc war crimes hearing, the Winter Soldier Investigation, named after the American revolutionary Thomas Paine's attack on "summer soldiers," sponsored by the four-year-old Vietnam Veterans Against the War and promoted by Jane Fonda. Attempting to show that the My Lai massacre—in which American soldiers killed hundreds of unarmed Vietnamese civilians in a South Vietnamese hamlet—was no aberration but a direct result of U.S. policy, they exposed everything from the murder of prisoners and civilians to illegal incursions into Laos. Although the testimony was read into the congressional record by Senators Mark Hatfield and George McGovern, the hearings attracted little attention, and much of that skeptical. So VVAW began planning a demonstration in Washington for April, as part of the peace movement's spring offensive.

Vallely was among the thousand veterans who kicked off the five-day demonstration the VVAW called Operation Dewey Canyon III (after the code names for the U.S. incursions into Laos) by marching to Arlington National Cemetery, many of them in fatigues and long hair, some in wheelchairs. The Nixon administration was ready for them; the cemetery gates were locked. Barred, too, from setting up tents on the mall or sleeping there as planned, the veterans vowed to stand up all night.[17] When a helicopter roared overhead as they returned to the Capitol for a rally, some vets raised their middle fingers, unaware that President Nixon was on board.

Later that day, the injunction against camping on the Mall was lifted by a federal court, but the next day, after they were allowed into the cemetery, the Justice Department won an appeal to force them off the Mall again. They stayed, without knowing that Nixon had decided arresting veterans would be bad image politics, but having heard from police and soldiers that orders to remove them would be disobeyed. The next day, the VVAW's spokesman, Kerry, gave eloquent testimony before the Senate Foreign Relations Committee. "How do you ask a man to be the last to die for a mistake?" the fatigue-clad Kerry said.

By the penultimate day of the demonstration, the vets were edgy and frustrated. Though they'd made an impact, they felt they were merely being tolerated. Their encampment had been infiltrated by Nixon spies, disinformation was being spread that many of them weren't veterans at all, and they assumed a fence that was being erected around the Capitol was meant to thwart their plans for a dramatic finale, a mass giveback of the medals they'd won, which they planned to leave on the building's steps. Despite the fence, this last piece of guerrilla theater proved a show-stopper. After the father of a boy killed in Vietnam played "Taps," his son's fatigue jacket over his shoulders, the vets stepped to the fence around the Capitol one by one and threw their medals, ribbons, canteens, discharge papers, citations and battle caps over. For hours afterward, tough, hard men stood there and cried.

Among the medals on the day's trash heap of history was Tommy Vallely's. "I was proud to get the Silver Star, and I was proud to throw it away," he says. "It was theater, good, big-time theater. I marched up, made some stupid statement, I don't know what I said; I'm embarrassed about how little I knew about the Vietnam War then. But my instincts knew something."

Back in Massachusetts that fall, he began college on the G.I. Bill, and, worked for Kerry in his 1972 race for Congress in Lowell, Massachusetts. Already a target of Nixonian dirty tricks for his work with VVAW—a Silver and Bronze Star-winner, he was painted as unpatriotic—Kerry's campaign was dramatic, and even had a mini-Watergate all its own. After hearing rumors that the candidate's phones would be sabotaged on election eve, Kerry's brother and Vallely overreacted, broke into the basement of his rival's campaign office, and got arrested. (Charges were later dropped.) Unfortunately, despite his matinee idol looks, auspicious initials (JFK), and the help of various Kennedys, Kerry lost the election.

Vallely, on the other hand, won a job. During the race, he'd hooked up with two political operatives-for-hire, John Marttila and Thomas Kiley, who incorporated in 1972. Based in Boston, Marttila, Payne, Kiley & Thorne helped write the rules for the modern political consulting business, offering a package of polling, strategy, advertising and operatives for then-young Democrats like Joseph Biden, Paul Sarbanes, Michael Dukakis and Thomas Eagleton. Vallely was one of a small team of political gunslingers who ran campaigns in the field. For the next four years, he alternated between studying and working races around the country, "writing papers on the road, trying to do my homework," he says. He really wanted to run for office himself, and hated "giving advice to people that didn't know shit," he says flatly.

Politics was more fun than school. In February 1974, for instance, Vallely worked as campaign coordinator for Richard VanderVeen, an obscure lawyer who ran for Gerald Ford's vacant congressional seat in Grand Rapids, Michigan, after the embattled Nixon named the genial

Ford his vice president. Though the district was solidly Republican, VanderVeen won by linking his opponent to Nixon. The victory was one in a series of upsets of Republicans that paved the way for Nixon's resignation that summer. Vallely went on to work for Morris Udall in his unsuccessful run against Georgia governor Jimmy Carter for the Democratic presidential nomination in 1976. But his life was on hold. "I'm just playing the game I'm in," he says.

JOHN GAGE, TOO, kept bouncing between education and activism. He still wasn't getting paid, but he had some money. He was in Harvard on scholarship, and his father had given him a few thousand dollars. That was all he needed. In 1970, he produced a benefit concert for peace candidates at Shea Stadium in New York, presenting twenty-two groups in eleven hours. In 1971, he co-produced several Washington demonstrations, including the May Day rally that followed the Vietnam Veterans march. Then he headed back to Harvard. Instead of finishing B-school, he switched to the Kennedy Public Policy School and started all over.

After a year, the siren song of politics drew Gage back when an organizer named Gary Hart came to Harvard to recruit for George McGovern's ill-fated 1972 peace campaign against Nixon. Gage had been on the East Coast since 1968. He was having girlfriend difficulties. So he agreed to pack his van, ship out, and work on the Arizona and California primaries for McGovern. He then shifted to McGovern's national campaign, where he was made a deputy press secretary.

Gage's job was logistical, neither political nor very glamorous. He was the engineer, the can-do guy—"We're going to land at two A.M. in Maine, and the vehicles have to be there, and ABC needs an extra truck, and on and on and on," he says. Meanwhile, events whizzed past at their usual pace. Nixon began to pull military units out of Vietnam. Third-party candidate George Wallace was shot and wounded by an assassin. National Security Adviser Henry Kissinger pulled his October Surprise on October 26, claiming that the Vietnam War would end within weeks. And a few days later, Nixon wiped the floor with McGovern.

Although Gage felt as if he'd headed an army that, wielding no more weapons than rustling branches, had managed to make the king open his fortress door and fight, he was still devastated. "You don't find out until later that public opposition actually caused people to change plans," he says. "I went back to school to try to pick up the pieces of my life."

Gage spent another half-dozen years at Berkeley in graduate limbo, teaching and working toward a doctorate in economics. "The beauty of mathematics was my primal therapeutic pathway," he says. After Nixon's resignation in 1974, Gage, married and about to become a father, learned he'd been on Nixon's famous enemies list. "And I'm studying math and econ," he says with a hearty laugh.

He still dabbled in politics, producing several rallies for Jimmy Carter's presidential campaign, but his community organizer days were over. "I wasn't doing very much," he admits. "I can't remember what I did."

WHILE LESLIE CROCKER Snyder was revolutionizing rape laws, zealous attempts were under way to root out police corruption in New York. From 1967 to 1970 Frank Serpico (b. 1936), an undercover detective who looked like a hippie, and several colleagues had collected evidence of corruption and payoffs in the city's police department. When he got no response from the city, he went to the *New York Times* and spurred the formation of the Knapp Commission, which held two years of hearings and alleged that half the police force was in some way corrupt. Though he was a cop, the ponytailed Serpico became a counterculture hero, especially after he was shot in the face during a drug bust and retired in 1972, later becoming the subject of a book and a hit movie. He moved to Europe for years, studied Eastern philosophy, treated the lingering pain and depression he suffered with alternative medicine, lived in a solar-powered cabin in the country, and neither voted nor read newspapers.

Though Serpico left the country, the mood he represented remained. At Richard Nixon's second inaugural, 100,000 people demonstrated, but the counterculture had mostly gone to ground. Patricia Hearst's kidnapping in February 1974, and her subsequent apparent transformation into Tanya, a bank-robbing revolutionary, was symbolic of the downright weird state of radical politics after a half-decade of Nixon. Jerry Brown's election as governor of California said much the same in the mainstream. Hemlines dropped along with the nation's birth rate. Perennial culture vulture Allen Ginsberg dropped out of politics altogether to co-found the Kerouac School of Disembodied Poetics in Colorado. And prophetically, streaking—a new form of self-exposure—and *People* magazine, a harbinger of the coming obsession with celebrity, both made their debut in 1974.

The 1973 Arab-Israeli war led to an Arab oil embargo and an energy crunch that kicked a hole in an economy defined by affluence and growth since 1945. Nixon imposed oil and price controls. For the rest of the decade, gasoline prices rose geometrically as supplies dwindled, the dollar was devalued, the stock market went into a long slow slide, jobs dried up, and inflation and unemployment multiplied dangerously.

In response, America read Alex Comfort's *The Joy of Sex* and Erica Jong's *Fear of Flying*, watched *American Graffiti* and *The Exorcist*, and gave up consciousness-enhancing drugs in favor of numbing Quaaludes and cocaine.

For those who didn't drop out but continued to engage in a public life, the new spirit of the times was either cleansing, vengeful or both. The minor robbery that turned into Watergate had repercussions that rippled throughout society. The Senate Select Committee on Intelligence and Rockefeller Commission hearings of 1975 opened new Pandora's boxes of illegal government plots, including assassinations and domestic spying.

In New York, Abraham Beame, a tiny, uncharismatic municipal accountant, succeeded the glamorous, patrician John Lindsay as mayor and immediately stumbled into a fiscal crisis of historic proportions as his city ran out of money and teetered on the brink of default on $8 billion in short-term municipal debt. At the end of 1977, Beame would lose his post after a single term to an insurgent Democrat, Ed Koch, running on a conservative platform of fiscal discipline, support of the death penalty, and opposition to unions. It was a political sea-change in a city that had long prided itself on a liberalism it could no longer afford—and a symbol of the national mood.

In 1976, John Keenan, Leslie Snyder's former boss in the Homicide Bureau, was appointed to oversee the criminal justice system and made Snyder his Chief of Trials, the number-three prosecutor in an office dedicated to prosecuting the sort of abuses the Knapp Commission had revealed. But for the next three years, every major case she was set to try was thrown out of court and she spent her time "prosecuting a lot of cops" for minor offenses Snyder says. She'd gone into her new job filled with optimism and excited by the challenge of weeding out corruption, but what she found was that the anti-corruption forces were corrupt themselves, that they'd distorted the law, browbeaten witnesses, and presented illegal evidence in their zeal to win indictments.

"My beloved cops were on the pad," she says. "I don't think I ever suspected the level of corruption that existed. Everyone hated us. But it was a great learning experience."

THOUGH HE CONTINUED managing properties in Brooklyn and Queens, in 1973—just around the time Abe Beame, of Brooklyn, was elected mayor—Donald Trump's father, Fred, gave his son a free hand in Manhattan. The twenty-seven-year-old went looking to buy. It was a propitious moment. With New York City in terrible financial trouble, the bottom had fallen out of the city's commercial real estate market.

Trump hired a Brooklyn PR man with a Manhattan real estate specialty, and made large donations to politicians in both parties. In 1973, when the government charged the Trumps with racial discrimination at its rental properties, Donald also hired Roy Cohn, the notorious, politically wired former counsel for Joseph McCarthy's Senate subcommittee, as his new lawyer. (He eventually signed a consent decree in that case, but kept Cohn on regardless.) And he hired Louise Sunshine, a fundraiser for New York's Governor Hugh L. Carey, as his political lobbyist.

In 1974 and 1975, Trump made the prescient deals that marked his emergence as a major figure in American business. In July 1974, the bankrupt Penn Central Transportation Company agreed to give Trump the option to develop two of its freight yards—vast tracts of land on the Hudson River.[18] Then, in 1975, Penn Central sold Trump the bankrupt Commodore Hotel on East 42nd Street, next to Grand Central Terminal, for $10 million.

New York was desperate in those years, and Trump knew it. Even so, his moves presaged the bravado baby boomers would bring to the financial markets in the next decade. Deal in hand, he convinced the Hyatt Hotel chain—then without a New York location—to join him in a partnership; he would renovate the Commodore, they would manage it. He then approached the Equitable Life Assurance Society and won seventy million dollars in mortgages. These deals were predicated on his ability to get a tax abatement on the property—something that had never been done for a private commercial developer. So Trump sold the hotel for one dollar to the Urban Development Corporation, and leased it back for ninety-nine years for a small fee in lieu of $56 million in taxes.[19]

Late in 1975, the city announced plans to build a new convention center at the southernmost tip of Manhattan. Trump called a press conference and unveiled a proposal to build it on one of the Penn Central yards, instead. Though it would take years to make it happen, the convention center was eventually built there, and Trump walked away with a hefty commission on the sale of the property to New York State.

Trump's next move proved crucial. From friends of Louise Sunshine, he learned in 1975 that a financially shaky conglomerate might be willing to sell the building that housed Bonwit Teller, a department store on the prestigious corner of 56th Street and 5th Avenue, as well as the lease for the land beneath it, which had twenty-nine years left to run. The deal, which included the $5 million purchase of air rights from Tiffany & Co. next door, allowing him to build a skyscraper on the lot, took years, but was completed in 1979. His timing was impeccable; transactions begun while the city was distressed were completed as the New York real estate business turned around, and zoning and tax concessions soon let him erect his name in brass letters over one of the best locations in the city.

"Every developer in the world was after this site, and I ended up getting it and it was a huge fuckin' coup," Trump crows. "And nobody really knew who I was. You have to understand, there was no Trump per se."

WHEN THE BROTHERHOOD of Eternal Love trial finally opened in November 1973, it focused on Nick Sand and Tim Scully. Both were charged with tax evasion and masterminding a worldwide scheme to sell LSD. Finally, Hitchcock, who'd agreed to pay tax liabilities and fraud penalties totaling nearly $850,000 and plead guilty to tax evasion and violating margin regulations, got immunity.[20] Before the trial, he loaned Scully $10,000 for legal fees and tried to get him to plead guilty, Scully thinks, so he would feel better about testifying himself. Scully was led to believe the government was really after Sand, but the prosecutors' best offer was four years in prison in exchange for Scully's testimony. "There was no way I was going to be a rat *and* go to prison," he says, laughing. "Going to prison was scary, but going to prison as a rat was even scarier. So I was able to maintain my high ethical standards."

Hitchcock, who'd moved to a Tucson cattle ranch, claimed Sand had been the financial backer of the scheme and portrayed himself as an errand boy. The defense said it was not Sand but Hitchcock, and claimed he'd invested hundreds of thousands of dollars in the scheme. Sand's lawyer, Kennedy, convinced Scully he should be the one to throw a Hail Mary pass for the defense. So Scully testified, that he'd had no profit motive but wanted to turn on the world, and argued, that Orange Sunshine wasn't LSD–25 at all but another of Albert Hofmann's discoveries, ALD–52, a slightly different, and therefore technically legal, chemical. "We wanted to stay one step ahead of the law," Scully testified. He says he'd found the new formula in his constant quest for purity, and had kept ALD's existence a secret until then because of the drug market's bad reaction to STP. Unfortunately, the ALD–52 Scully was foolish enough to introduce into evidence had decomposed—and turned into LSD!

Scully and Sand were found guilty, but Kennedy's tactic deflected the judge's wrath away from silent Sand onto the loquacious, dangerously idealistic loophole artist Scully. The judge accused him of "smirking" and "intellectual arrogance," and he ended up sentenced to twenty years, five more than Sand.[21] When Scully's lawyers then won an appeal of his $500,000 bail and he was released from the McNeil Island Federal Penitentiary on an island in Washington's Puget Sound where they'd briefly been jailed, Sand got out, too.

On September 11, 1976, their appeals were denied. Scully flew back to McNeil Island at his own expense, and presented himself at the gates. Sand snuck out the back of his houseboat in Sausalito and disappeared while his girlfriend held federal agents at bay, and continued making LSD and other drugs in Mexico and Canada until he was arrested in Vancouver an astonishing twenty years later. In January 1999, the same judge who'd first found him guilty sent Sand back to prison to serve his original fifteen-year sentence plus five more years for jumping bail.

BY THE TIME she left home for Pomona College in Claremont, California, in fall 1970, Marianne Williamson had begun her transition from good girl to, as she describes it, "a weird juxtaposition." In high school, she'd been attracted to drama. Once she got to college, though, she fell under the spell of philosophy, cast by an equally theatrical fellow student, Lynda Rosen Obst (b. 1950), who later became a Hollywood producer. Two of the few Jewish girls in school, they roomed together, discussed Kant, Kierkegaard and Sartre, and double-dated two philosophy professors during the next year and a half. "I looked up to her," Williamson says. "She taught me the *I Ching*."

Obst graduated from Pomona in 1972, and Williamson promptly dropped out. "I just couldn't find my niche, and I started unraveling," she says. In 1993, on the television show *20/20*, Williamson said her parents were alcoholics and she "was stoned for twenty, twenty-five years." Now she tempers both statements, saying, "We all come from dysfunctional families," and that while she was troubled—"Who in their mid–twenties isn't?—"she got high "no more, no less than anyone else I knew."

Williamson took to the domestic hippie trail, spending time in Berkeley, New Mexico and Austin, Texas. During those years, she revved up her metaphysical quest. "In the sixties, politics and spirituality and philosophy were married, however tenuously, and bound together by the music," she says. "But as we move into the seventies, spirituality and politics divorce. And many people said, Until we change our consciousness, nothing is really going to change anyway, so forget politics. I believed, as I still do, that an angry generation can't bring peace to the world, and I began to understand Gandhi's precept that we must be the change we want to see. The genuine mystical path is a search for the most real, not the least real."

Like her peers, Williamson was spoiled by the sense that high as she might fly, close as she might come to danger, she could always bail out and go home. Her mother never stopped asking what she was doing with her life, and she sometimes wondered, too. "I never stopped being a middle-class Jewish girl. I knew if things got too bad I could call Daddy. We were protected by our parents. In another generation I would not have been indulged." In time, her friend Lynda Obst began to worry about her, warning her to "stop bringing stray mystics home." But Williamson didn't see her men that way. "I always loved brilliant men," she says. "Still do."

In New Mexico, she lived with a designer of geodesic domes. Spherical dwellings made up of a network of triangular elements, domes were the homes of choice for the delightfully contradictory back-to-earth futurists who inhabited the communes of the early 1970s. Patented in 1951 by the visionary inventor and futurist R. Buckminster Fuller (b. 1895), who famously coined the expression Spaceship Earth, they became the physical expression of the New Age movement thanks to their "free," almost mystical design, said to impart a feeling of wholeness to those inhabiting them. Though Williamson practiced serial monogamy, not promiscuity, her parents still worried about her. "I think they were very concerned, frustrated, exasperated," she says. "I should have been in law school." Instead, she was waiting tables and temping.

Williamson sought what she believed was her birthright: happiness. For ten years, she hopped, skipped and jumped through fields of esoterica, ever more miserable at her inability to find what she was looking for. She cast the I Ching, read books by Carlos Castaneda, the mysterious author who wrote of Mexican shamans and their explorations of the frontiers of psychology and pharmacology, sat in on courses in Chinese philosophy at the University of New Mexico and on medieval philosophy at The University of Texas. "Religion and philosophy and spirituality were my all-consuming passion, but there was no way that I could get a Ph.D.; I was always in and out of places," she says.

Watching from a distance, her parents grew increasingly frustrated. "My mother would say, 'What are you going to do with that? What is that going to turn into?'" She knew couldn't "find the door," she says. "How could I have? The niche didn't exist then. What was anybody going to say? She's going to be a what I am now? What's the word for it, y'know? It didn't exist."

* * *

NINA HARTLEY'S SEXUAL education began with feminist literature her mother brought home that led Mitzi to examine her cervix when she was twelve. Around that time, her brother was the first to show her a copy of *Playboy*. On her thirteenth birthday, right about the time she began to menstruate, a male cousin gave her a copy of *Our Bodies, Our Selves*, the 1971 feminist classic about women's sexuality. "I had access to all sorts of tremendous information without it being awkward," she says, "and it was earth-shattering, it changed my life." She found she was fascinated with babies and bodies, and read anything she could get her hands on that described the mechanics of sexual behavior—"about menstruation, and ovulation and testicles and vas deferens and things like that," she says. She loved to look at classical art, particularly when breasts or penises were involved. "I was literally a voyeur."

At fourteen, she discovered pornography, which had been liberated from the strictures of American Puritan tradition in the mid-1960s by a handful of pioneer publishers and was openly available in liberal Berkeley. "Oooh, I would sit in a used bookstore for hours and read in my bib overalls and braids," she says. "My sex life was all in my head and in books, but I found out I had an immediate positive response to pornography. Then, around the corner was a swinging 1970s kind of couple I babysat for. I was looking in their closet and I found high heels and an Afro wig and Louis Comfort's book *The Joy of Sex*."

She read the breezy sex manual over and over, half a dozen times, and did the same with the famous madam Xaviera Hollander's memoir, *The Happy Hooker*, Betty Dodson's *Liberating Masturbation*, and David Reuben's *Everything You Always Wanted to Know About Sex (But Were Afraid to Ask)*. "Neglect allowed my mind to go where it wanted to, and sex was where it wanted to go," she says. "But I'm doing it with the tools my mother gave me. She brought those books in the house."

Though some of her neighbors were convinced she was already a sex fiend—"my girlfriends were sisters whose parents did not want them to play with me because they were afraid I was going to turn them into lesbians"—she'd still never even masturbated. "I remember being in the bedroom with them and getting naked and feeling breasts, and inserting things into vaginas, but it wasn't sensual," she says. "It was mechanical."

Her only heterosexual experience came when, at a Renaissance Fair in 1973, she allowed herself to be pulled into the kissing booth, untied her hair, pulled her blouse down below her shoulders and sold French kisses for a dollar. "I loved it," she says. "A public place with people around? Cool. Nothing bad gonna happen to me. But I didn't feel safe in private. I didn't know how to handle that energy. I didn't have sex for another four years. I didn't date at all. I hardly necked."

In 1974, when Mitzi and her parents moved to a Zen community near Carmel, her isolation grew. She has no memory of Watergate. She would sit in the town library poring through forty-year-old *Life* magazines or sit home listening to Broadway musicals. "I had no one to pull me out of myself," she says. "And I had no example. My parents were closing inward." When they moved again, to a Zen farm in Marin County, Mitzi asked if she could return to Berkeley, where the high school had a college-level theater department. She never lived with her parents again. In 1977 they both became ordained Zen priests. "If they'd insisted I live with them, everything would have been completely different."

In tenth grade, Mitzi finally found a social life. She joined the drama department as a costumer, and worked on several plays. She saw herself as terminally shy and unable to focus; others saw her as bright, sarcastic and sexy. Sex was all around her—it was Berkeley in the mid-1970s. Although she'd identified herself as bisexual by fourteen, she wasn't having any. She adopted the look of lesbian separatists. "Birkenstocks, overalls and flannel shirts, absolutely no glamour, no makeup at all, didn't start shaving my legs until I was twenty-one," she says. "Not because I hated men, but because I had such low self-esteem I didn't want anyone to notice me."

It was the same with drugs. "My friends did them," she says. "I didn't try pot till I was eighteen. And then they had to force me. I was a good girl, I think, still trying to get Mom's attention." Her only outlet was folk dancing, which allowed her the physical expression she craved without an accompanying emotional burden.

Mitzi—now living in her parents' house with an older brother, his wife, their infant child, and a succession of roommates—finished high school in 1977, got a job as a short-order cook in a hamburger joint, and promptly lost her virginity. Right before graduation, she'd had a near-sex experience with a boy from the drama department. "He was petting me all over and I was absolutely tingling and alive, and I knew that if he'd just do this to my clit I'd come, but I stopped myself," she recalls. "That summer, I thought, What was I scared of? I'd never been that turned on before. He'd been with a lot of girls, had a lot of sex, he was good at it." She smiles. "But I was that repressed, I could not let go." Finally, one afternoon, she did let go, and the result was "extremely not unpleasant," she says, "just not pleasurable" because, though she knew about birth control, she let him have sex with her without it. "And I'm worrying the whole time, 'How could I be so stupid as to allow this to happen?'"

Shortly afterward, Mitzi began dating her dance teacher—a man twice her age. "He had a savior complex, and I needed saving," she says. "I was desperately lonely, desperately confused, so I basically ended up going to high school for another four and a half years. I would help him teach folk dances. I really liked that dancing." He introduced her to jazz, theater, movies and LSD. They didn't have intercourse for months, and when they did, after she took him to see a film of the S&M novel *The Story of O*, he tied her up and blindfolded her, and she let him think it was her first time.

Her teacher boyfriend was a devotee of *est*, the movement driven by Jack Rosenberg, a car salesman in Philadelphia, who abandoned his wife and family in the 1960s to create a new identity, Werner Hans Erhard, and join the New Age craze in California. In 1971, melding aspects of Zen Buddhism, Scientology, the philosophies of Jacques Derrida and Martin Heidegger, and techniques he'd used in a previous job training door-to-door encyclopedia salesmen, he started Erhard Seminars Training (or *est*), promising followers he would increase their self-awareness and help their potential blossom through what was essentially instant therapy. Though thousands swore by it, and claimed it was better than therapy for helping them break habitual behavior patterns, detractors thought the training was fast food psychology and referred to devotees as *est*-holes.[22]

Mitzi's boyfriend used *est* to avoid emotional communication. He told her he wouldn't take responsibility for anything not directly communicated to him. "What an older woman would have known was, that was just an excuse not to have to pay attention and intuit his partner's emotional needs," Hartley says. After a while, the always tenuous relationship went sour, but Mitzi hung in. "I had to learn a lot of things, which is why I was there."

Throughout those years, San Francisco was a mecca for the business of pornography. The city's reputation as a modern sexual frontier state began with Gold Rush prostitutes who lent their names to some of the city's streets and continued in the famous topless bars of bohemian North Beach. In 1957, Beats were in the vanguard of sexual openness when Allen Ginsberg and Lawrence Ferlinghetti were acquitted on obscenity charges for publishing Ginsberg's poem "Howl." That same year, the Supreme Court redefined obscenity as material "utterly without redeeming social value."

The approval of a birth control pill by the Federal Drug Administration in May 1960 pushed the sexual vanguard toward the American norm. By the mid-1960s, millions of women around the world were taking the Pill. Its impact was best summed up by the writer, ambassador and LSD user Clare Booth Luce: "Modern woman is at last free as a man is free, to dispose of her own body, to earn her living, to pursue the improvement of her mind, to try a successful career."[23]

In 1969, sexual outlaws were in. *Oh, Calcutta!*, a sexually explicit revue, debuted on Broadway; swingers swapped spouses at California's Sandstone Ranch and Sexual Freedom League; Bob Guccione challenged the avatar of the early sexual revolution, *Playboy* magazine's Hugh Hefner, with *Penthouse*, which dared to show female pubic hair; Philip Roth published *Portnoy's Complaint*, his paean to masturbation; John Lennon and Yoko Ono appeared nude on the cover of a record called *Two Virgins;* and Jim Morrison of the Doors (b. 1943) was arrested for flashing his penis onstage in Miami. In 1970 a national Commission on Obscenity and Pornography declared that pornography had no significant effect on crime or delinquency. Rapidly, the porn film form evolved through displays of masturbation and physical contact between men and women to finally break the last taboo and show explicit sex.[24]

Among those pushing the envelope were several San Franciscans: Alex deRenzy, whose 1969 documentary, *Pornography in Denmark* (the Scandinavian country where depiction of sexual penetration was decriminalized that year), was the first widely seen porn movie; Jim and Artie Mitchell, better known as the Mitchell Brothers, who made films for their own theater, The O'Farrell,[25] and Gerald Damiano, whose 1972 film, *Deep Throat*, brought porn into the mainstream, selling fifty million dollars' worth of tickets.[26] By 1973, when Erica Jong extolled the "zipless fuck" in her novel *Fear of Flying*, hard-core was everyday and brothels were everywhere in the sexual supermarket of New York's Times Square. Soon, miniature equivalents sprang up across America.

That year, Mitzi's introduction to their world came when, still in high school, she'd snuck into her first hard-core movie, *Autobiography of a Flea*. A costume drama directed by a woman, it was based on an erotic classic she'd read. "I was astounded and transformed," she says, her voice going all gooey. "I wanna *do* that. I knew I was hung up about sex, and I hated it. I didn't like how uncomfortable and unsure of myself I felt. I didn't like not being good at it. I hated it that the culture said you couldn't get sexual skills without emotions. I had no emotional skill. I was scared to be alone with a guy. I did not know how to steer." Not long afterward, she induced her new boyfriend to take her to a strip club. "I was getting all juicy and wet," she says, and he fell asleep."

As the relationship stumbled along, Mitzi began to flirt with bisexuality. The same girlfriend from high school who'd made her smoke marijuana, an artistic bisexual, "basically seduced me," Hartley says. It wasn't hard. At twelve, she'd wondered what other girls' breasts felt like, and years later, the curiosity had only grown. "So, we end up in bed together and for me it was the most amazing—it was like, *Wow, smooooth!* No hair." Her boyfriend had a beard. "And I was going down on her, and didn't know what I was doing, didn't know if she came or not and that was the first time I realized, girls are complicated." But also appealing. "And I wanted to do more." So they tried three-way sex with her boyfriend, while taking LSD. "And that was as close as I ever came to a bad trip," Hartley says, "seeing him be tender and exploratory with her when he had not been that way with me. Freaked me out. He ended up having to take her home and he was very angry about that. He thought, I'd had her, why couldn't he?"

AS VICTORIA LEACOCK'S ailing mother's condition worsened and she was in and out of hospitals and rehabilitation clinics, Victoria was often alone. "I don't know where my brothers and sisters were when I was a kid," she says. Sometime in 1970, Victoria began to be sent to live with other families for months at a time. One had a son Victoria's age, Gordon Rogers, and they became close friends. "He'd bite me and we'd fight, and he'd copy my homework," she says. "So I got to have a sibling."

Victoria's father, who was teaching film at MIT, was a flitting presence. He would take her to the Caribbean once a year. Or show up in New York and take her to gloomy dinner parties and crazy restaurants, where they ate with her uncles, the other documentarians, "and I loved it when I saw him," she says. But mostly, she took care of her mother, who was completely bedridden by the time Victoria turned twelve. She could talk, though. "My friends loved staying over because we'd stay up and talk about adult things and she treated us as equals. We'd go grocery shopping and make dinner. I started signing her checks when I was around ten."

Leacock was at her grandmother's in Illinois during the Watergate hearings, when she was eleven. "My grandmother became obsessed with the hearings. I would beg to go over to other kids' houses and watch *Kung Fu.* Or *The Waltons.* Or anything. I hated Nixon because he was so fucking boring." Back home, she went to school about two days a week, and spent the rest playing nurse. She resented being responsible for an invalid, but she knew she had no choice.

* * *

THROUGH A SPANISH girlfriend, Barbara Ledeen met her first terrorist in 1972. He was an aboveground supporter of one of the dozen liberation groups then operating in Europe with Soviet assistance, Spain's ETA-Militar, a Basque nationalist group seeking independence from Spain. "He was a real Communist," she says. "This was not make-believe. And educated, articulate, multilingual and culturally sophisticated. I'm waiting for somebody like that." His name was Vincente. She moved into his apartment in Rome, a fifth-floor walkup, coldwater flat across the street from a prison.

They shoplifted food, bathed in freezing water, and attempted to live up to an abstract revolutionary ideal. But when Vincente told her she'd soon have to "lose" her Judaism and pick up a gun, she began to have her doubts about his business. Then Vincente came down with a kidney infection and returned to Madrid for treatment. While he was gone, Ledeen got distracted. She sometimes modeled for another friend, an Egyptian dress designer whom she'd met when she'd first arrived from Elba. One day, early in 1973, the designer called her at work and said, "There's an American I want you to meet."

"I don't talk to Americans," Ledeen replied. She hadn't spoken English in months; she was even dreaming in Italian. "He's got money," her friend said, and his wife had run off with his best friend a few weeks before. What the hell, Ledeen thought, she could rip off the ruling class for a meal at a good restaurant. So she and Michael Ledeen (b. 1941) went out to dinner. "I didn't weigh 100 pounds," she recalls. "I look at the menu and start ordering everything from beginning to end. And the bread that was left on the table and the sugar, I put in my pocketbook."

Michael Ledeen, a historian and author, was in Rome on a grant to write a book about the flamboyant Italian warrior-poet Gabrielle d'Annunzio. A student of Italian history, he'd arrived the year before from Washington University, where he was a professor of history and had campaigned for George McGovern. His allegiance was not to party, though, but to whoever stood against evil and mass movements.[27] He equated the totalitarianism of the fascists with that of the communists. To his dinner date, his passionate anti-fascism made up for the fact that he was anti-communist, American, Jewish, and altogether the sort of man her father might like.

After dinner, they walked back to his apartment—a glorious sublet compared to her hovel. "He offered me an Armagnac," she remembers. "And I'd never heard of Armagnac, but an American who lived in a great apartment, who knew from Armagnac, who spoke perfect Italian, who used the subjunctive? *Hmmm."* Then she asked to use the bathroom, "and there's a bathtub," she continues. "I hadn't seen a bathtub in I don't know how long. There's only so much you can suppress for the revolution. A long, hot soak in this bathtub was all of a sudden a very important thing." After he agreed that she could use it sometime, he took her home in a taxi, shook her hand, and asked if he could call the next day. "I hadn't been treated like that by a man in I can't tell you how long."

The two began an affair that was still going on a couple months later when Vincente returned from Madrid to collect his girlfriend for a jaunt to Cuba. He planned to hook up with the Palestine Liberation Organization, "which I could not do," Ledeen says. She wasn't even sure he'd been in Madrid. "He could have been at some terrorist training camp." She told him they'd reached the end of the road, "and off he went to do his revolutionary thing," she says. As his parting shot, he told her that if she gave up the cause, she'd end up a piece of Chippendale furniture.

Five months later, in July 1973, when Michael Ledeen's grant ran out and he had to return to Washington University, she agreed to accompany him. There was only one problem. "Michael had a ticket back to the United States that said Mrs. Ledeen, so I needed to be Mrs. Ledeen." They called their parents on a Friday and married that Monday in the Spanish chapel beneath the synagogue in Rome.

After Rome, St. Louis paled. Ledeen's former wife lived down the street. He had little reason to be there; he'd been denied tenure before leaving for Rome. That's when Barbara, who'd been told she couldn't conceive, got pregnant. At the end of the term, it was an easy decision. Back to Rome, where the Ledeens became part of a coterie of anti-fascist, anti-communist intellectuals. "They ratcheted up my intellectual curiosity," she says. One, Renzo De Felice, was a former communist who'd abandoned the party after it crushed a popular uprising in Hungary in 1956 and gone on to author a multivolume biography of Italy's fascist World War II leader, Benito Mussolini. Despite voluminous archival research, it outraged Italian communists by arguing that Mussolini was not only a popular leader but that his fascist philosophy grew out of the same dirt as communism. That became the subject of a book, *Interview on Fascism,* in which De Felice answered questions posed by Michael Ledeen.

As in America, these former leftists were finding their way toward the next political trend, a neoconservatism that rejected social engineering in favor of individual freedom. They weren't there yet. In summer 1974, the Ledeens cheered the fall of Richard Nixon. "We go out of our way to get a front page of the *New York Times* in Rome and frame it and put it on the wall," Barbara says. "My husband still has it in his office." Michael was changing, and Barbara was following, if a bit reluctantly. "We had knockdown dragouts about it," she says. "He'd say, 'Can you not understand that [leftists] are not who you believe them to be? Look at how many innocent people have suffered.'"

Their circumstances changed along with their politics. Michael won an appointment to teach at the University of Rome, which made Barbara, as she puts it, "the *signora* of the *professore.*" Using the proceeds of the De Felice book, the Ledeens abandoned their bohemian lifestyle and moved to an apartment near the Vatican. Barbara returned to America for the birth of her daughter in December 1974, then hurried back to Rome.

In 1975, Michael Ledeen was named Rome correspondent for *The New Republic.* After its purchase the year before by Martin Peretz (b. 1939), a former radical and Harvard social theory lecturer, and his wife, an heiress to the Singer sewing machine fortune, the formerly liberal opinion magazine began a slow drift to the pragmatic center. The next year, Michael Ledeen hooked up with Claire Sterling, another ex-communist who'd been a Rome-based journalist for many years, to pen an article for the magazine tracing the connections between Italian leftists and the Soviet Union.

"They upset the entire apple cart," Barbara says. "It was a huge deal." Ledeen had become quite controversial. His pariah status on the left was cemented when he was consulted by the Italian justice ministry on terrorism.

Terrorism was spreading, Americans were being targeted, and Ledeen was the only American teaching at a school where professors were being shot at on campus. Worried for their safety, Ledeen sent his documentary evidence on terrorist financing back to the States for safekeeping, and he and Barbara followed. In 1976, Walter Lacqueur, an author, historian and member of Georgetown University's foreign policy think tank, the Center for Strategic and International Studies (CSIS), hired Michael to join his staff and found a magazine, *The Washington Quarterly.* They returned to America just as Gerald Ford left the presidency, early in 1977. Michael moved into an office at CSIS, just down the hall from Richard Nixon's National Security Advisor, Henry Kissinger, who laughed at his framed *New York Times* page. Barbara promptly plunged into a deep depression.

IN THE EARLY 1970s, after years of goofing off and taking drugs in Palo Alto, Cynthia Bowman broke up with her boyfriend, moved out of her commune, went back to San Francisco, and got a job assisting one of the many orthopedic surgeons who'd operated on her over the years. Though still a beauty, she could no longer model, thanks to the scars on her leg. But she could party, especially after winning a $100,000 settlement in a lawsuit she'd filed over her accident. She bought a fur coat, moved into an apartment in one of San Francisco's best neighborhoods, and found a new boyfriend—a drug dealer associated with the Brotherhood of Eternal Love. He took her to Europe, where business mixed well with pleasure.

By 1974, her money and boyfriend gone, Bowman went looking for a job. Once again, she fell into a pot of honey, at *Rolling Stone*, the nation's leading rock magazine. Thanks to its founder Jann Wenner's riches and the Falstaffian excesses they paid for, Wenner's accomplishment has sometimes been overshadowed in the many accounts of his life and high times. A quintessential boomer, born in January 1946, he inspired his father to open a baby formula company the next year, and grew up in prosperous San Rafael, California.[28] Wenner attended Berkeley but avoided the Free Speech Movement, preferring to spend his time laying the groundwork for a media career, working as a gofer for NBC during the 1964 Republican Convention.[29] After taking his first LSD trip, Wenner sought out the *San Francisco Chronicle*'s music critic, Ralph J. Gleason, befriending the influential columnist and becoming something of a protégé. Wenner launched a column, "Something's Happening" (bylined "Mr. Jones"), in the Berkeley campus newspaper, then went to work for *Sunday Ramparts*, an offshoot of the radical magazine. When it went out of business in May 1967, Wenner took a civil service exam, hoping to win a job as a mailman.[30]

He got the idea to start a magazine from Chet Helms of the Family Dog, a concert-promoting commune, who wanted to do the same. There was already a magazine for new rock fans, *Crawdaddy*, founded in 1966, but it was full of serious essays. When he proposed to do something livelier to Gleason, the critic signed on, giving the venture ballast and the funds to pay for a prototype. His girlfriend's family kicked in more. To save money, he used the defunct *Sunday Ramparts* printer, paper and typeface, and to find readers, he spirited away a radio station's mailing list Helms had hoped to use for *his* magazine.[31] In late October, just a few days after the Death of Hippie rites, *Rolling Stone* hit the newsstands.

It was quickly established as the voice of the baby boom, and Wenner as its Henry Luce, its Hugh Hefner, the man who'd bottled an era's cultural lightning. Gleason was long gone, but had been replaced by a talented group that included Owsley Stanley's roommate Charles Perry,

Greil Marcus, Jerry Hopkins, who'd managed a drug paraphernalia store, and Ben Fong-Torres. When Bob Dylan, who'd been in hiding since a motorcycle accident in 1966, emerged from seclusion three years later, he gave his first interview to Wenner. When John Lennon did the same a year later—ripping into the Beatles and other sacred cows of the 1960s—*Stone*'s role was sanctified.

For years afterward, *Rolling Stone* ruled—despite the fact that it had no black writers and no more than knee-jerk coverage of black music, was less than innovative, and was hagiographic toward its editor's friends. It was also as inconsistent as its peripatetic readership. *Stone* vacillated between being a music magazine and something more ambitious. Briefly, in 1969 and 1970, it ran exposés of the Rolling Stones concert at Altamont and the Manson murders, and biting political articles, before retreating to the safety of music. Wenner, a rock groupie just like his readers, ping-ponged between his magazine labors and enjoying their fruits. Then, in the 1970s, *Rolling Stone* reengaged and became the last red-hot center of the New Journalism. Big bands like Grand Funk Railroad were drowned out by literary noisemakers like Hunter Thompson, Joe Eszterhas, Timothy Ferris and Howard Kohn. Their *Stone* was controversial, but it made money; between 1973 and 1975, when Bowman arrived as Fong-Torres's secretary, ad revenues doubled.

She still can't say how she got the job. "I didn't know how to type. I knew nothing about writing or grammar. I was highly unqualified. But I must have been endearing or something." Bowman soon graduated to a job she could do—music librarian.

About a year later, Bowman and a band of *Stone* staffers went to see Steve Martin (b. 1945), a comedian just gaining national stardom, in a San Francisco nightclub. When she ran into Bill Thompson, the manager of the Jefferson Airplane shared some of his cocaine and she won a job as the in-house publicist for the very band that had inspired her runaway scheme and filled her acid dreams. "He took me to meet the band the next night and I quit my job at *Rolling Stone*." Just in time, in fact, for the next year, Wenner moved the magazine to New York. The change of venue proved symbolic; Wenner was now a multimillionaire and his publication the very first pillar of what's now called the New Establishment. The punk rock revolt that began that year did as much to discredit the magazine as the Sex Pistols did to slime Queen Elizabeth and corporate rock. Though *Rolling Stone* put the Pistols on its cover, it downplayed punk and New Wave music, because Wenner, whose tastes ran to Loggins & Messina and Jackson Browne—and who was then running around New

York with the Kennedys, and Hollywood-on-the-Hudson types like Richard Gere—didn't quite get the art of punk noise.[32]

Bowman thinks she was running on looks and personality. "'Cause I certainly didn't have any skills," she says. But then, she wasn't exactly working at IBM. The Airplane was still fueled by sex and drugs and the revolutionary politics of its hit 1969 album, *Volunteers*. It had supported the Weather Underground. In April 1970, Grace Slick, a graduate of the New York finishing school Finch, had brought Abbie Hoffman as her "bodyguard" when she was invited to a White House tea for Finch alumnae with Nixon's daughter Tricia. Slick, who had powdered LSD in her pocket, planned to try and dose Nixon with it. White House guards wouldn't let Hoffman enter, and the pair gave up their plan, but the story got out and furthered both their legends.

In subsequent years, a dealer was in residence at the Airplane mansion, and jumbo nitrous oxide tanks were stored in the basement. Backstage, their road manager carried a clear plastic tray with divided sections for vitamins, methedrine, cocaine, LSD and aspirin.[33] "I'd walk in every day and there was a gram of cocaine on everybody's desk," Bowman says. "By lunchtime we would have identified somebody in the universe that was having a birthday, and [a secretary] would go out and buy four or five bottles of Dom Perignon and we'd be smashed by two in the afternoon. And then we'd take cocaine all afternoon to stay awake. Then Bill Thompson and I would go back to his house and play backgammon all night. And then we'd start all over again." Band members were constantly getting busted for drugs, obscenity, resisting arrest, drinking, driving under the influence—in short, for being themselves.

Grace Slick had been married when she joined the Airplane, but her husband was soon past history. In the meantime, Slick became part of the sexual roundelay of rock 'n' roll, sleeping with Airplane drummer Spencer Dryden (b. 1938) and Doors leader Jim Morrison, among others, before getting pregnant by Paul Kantner in 1970. That fall, with Slick sidelined by her pregnancy, the band splintered into several offshoots, including Hot Tuna and Kantner's Jefferson Starship, which was nominated for a Hugo Award for the science fiction of its first album (credited only to Kantner), *Blows Against the Empire*. With each such success, the cracks in the Airplane's fuselage widened. Born with the counterculture, the band was splintering along with its audience.

In January 1971, Slick gave birth to a daughter who was briefly named god—Slick was having a goof with a nurse—and then China. In February, Marty Balin quit the group, the first of a series of departures. In May, Slick was hospitalized after crashing her Mercedes into a wall while racing with Jorma Kaukonen, with whom she'd just had a one-night fling. Though the group would make several more records before formally breaking up in 1978, they played their last live show as Jefferson Airplane in September 1972.

By 1975, when Bowman arrived on the scene, the band she'd loved as a girl effectively no longer existed. Slick, Kantner and a constantly changing cast of others were still touring, but as Jefferson Starship, and the comings and goings were often more interesting than the music they made. Balin, who'd sworn he'd never play with them again, would parachute in, record a love ballad, and then leave as suddenly as he'd come.

Hedonism remained their watchword. Slick, alternating between alcohol and cocaine, fell in love with the Starship's twenty-four-year-old lighting director. By the end of 1975, Slick and Kantner had split, and he and Bowman hooked up. "Everybody was hoping Paul would find somebody to love," Bowman says, "because he was making Grace's life a nightmare."

Bowman moved into Kantner's house and into the fast lane with Jefferson Starship. In November 1976, Grace Slick married her lighting designer in Hawaii. Bowman was her maid of honor. Then in June 1978, Slick's drinking, combined with a stomach flu, disrupted a tour of Germany. When the band failed to take the stage at a rock festival there, local fans and American soldiers based nearby "burned a million dollars' worth of our equipment," Bowman says. "They burned our Mercedes. The cars were just melted. Our band was underneath the stage locked in a cage. Our Jewish band members were terrified. We had to be smuggled out in the dark in a bus." At their next show, in Frankfurt, Slick stuck her fingers up the nose of a fan in the front row. She left the band the next day, returned to America, and after several drink-related arrests, entered a rehabilitation program.

Slick wasn't the only problem. Back at home, Bowman and Kantner's relationship began to sour. At first, "it was flowers all the time and Dom Perignon," she says. "We were very attracted to each other. But after that, it was one long series of arguments and disagreements. We just didn't get along. He lives like Howard Hughes—stacks of newspapers and stuff everywhere. So as interesting as we thought each other was, we couldn't be in the same house, even if it was a thirty-room mansion."

GANGS RULED HOLLIS, Queens, when Russell Simmons was in junior high. "I was a warlord of the seventeenth division of the Seven Immortals when I was fourteen years old," he says. "But gangs back then was more hitting you with a pipe than shooting you with a gun. They were gangs like you read about, sometimes fighting each other, but mostly it was about wearing your colors on your back—a family thing, extra family."

As in white communities, drugs were all around as Simmons grew up. "My eighth-grade friends were shooting heroin," Simmons says. "Everybody was a heroin addict, my brother included. The number-one heroin corner was two blocks from me, and everybody would stand on the corner and sell heroin. A hundred people would be out there, so I was always aware of the drugs and the rest. I somehow got away from the shit, I don't really know how. You saw everybody else do it. Everybody was fucked up."

One force that stood against drugs was Islam, and its upright representatives, a constant presence in the neighborhood. "I remember Black Muslims on my corner," Simmons says. "On every black corner. And if you'd go to Steak-and-Take"—Philly cheese steak restaurants owned by the Muslims—"you'd straighten up. The effect of the Black Muslim movement in my community was unbelievable. Suddenly everybody's walking around with a suit and tie and they're selling magazines and they don't look like hell. You ain't gonna be a heroin addict in front of that."

Islam notwithstanding, Simmons started taking soft drugs in tenth grade. "All through high school I smoked a lot of pot. Most black kids were not into LSD, but we used to like LSD a lot." He bought it from his Jewish friends in Queens Village.

Simmons also sold pot. "Niggers had nothing but, 'Go to school and be a teacher.' That's why my father was a teacher. Own a store? No. Be a numbers runner, be a drug dealer, or be a teacher. That's what the black community teaches, still. No one is going to say, 'Start a business.' That's not part of the culture."

Dealing pot was part of the culture, and it was safer than selling heroin. "You'd still stand on a corner and everyone's selling heroin next to you," Simmons says. "But you go out and buy two pounds of weed, and a nickel bag costs you eighty-five cents and you sell it for five dollars, and you sell twenty nickel bags standing on Hollis Avenue in four hours, you know, you're a fuckin' hero! I had one thousand dollars on me one time, and I didn't have a job. I was a kid. And the idea of being fly and cold and fashion and all that was a big deal."

Simmons knew all about black separatism and identity politics, but didn't go that route. "I didn't feel any pressure," he says. "I was hanging out with my white friends, I was hanging out with my black friends."

Things were changing. The races were mixing, a little, at least among younger baby boomers. "Everybody was getting ready to change. There was a whole group of people who had that idea. Sometimes they'd come together, through me."

IN 1975, DAVE McIntosh left Kendallville, Indiana, to spend his senior year in Switzerland. He'd wanted to be a congressional page, but the local congressman, a Democrat, put his mother off with vague mutters that it was a bad idea. Years later, when a cocaine and sodomy scandal involving pages and congressmen broke open, McIntosh finally understood.

Having known several exchange students in his school, McIntosh hopped at the chance of a year abroad. He was placed with a stolid Swiss family in a town on the German border. "They were interested in America culture, but it was like Indiana—a few years behind the cutting edge." He spoke German and learned that in middle Europe, as in mid-America, American power was valued as the first line of defense for freedom. "That took me aback and opened my eyes," he says. "That sense of America's role in the world came through an older generation in Europe."

Back in Kendallville, a young congressional candidate named Dan Quayle, the grandson of a powerful Indiana publisher, came to speak at East Noble High School. "He was a young guy, longish hair, enthusiastic, talking to us about how, as a young person, he wanted to get involved in government and change things so we'd have more freedom." Quayle had been working for his father as an associate publisher when polls showed a fresh face could oust the Democratic congressman in his and McIntosh's district in 1976. Used to gray-haired local pols, the high-schooler found him "really exciting to listen to," despite the fact that Quayle was a Republican. "I didn't have my thoughts in order, so I'm sure it was his style and youth and energy that was attractive to me," McIntosh says. Not long afterward, he graduated second in his class and headed to Yale University to study politics and economics.

DOUG MARLETTE HAD only been drawing professionally for three years, but in 1975 he got his first syndication deal. Now his cartoons appeared all over the country and his earnings increased substantially. "I didn't really know what to do with it," he says. "I suddenly had more money than I ever expected to make." At the urging of a woman he was dating, he bought a blue Porsche 914.

Marlette disdained the quasi-religious movements ubiquitous in the mid-1970s. "It's like those old truths of Sunday school," he says. "When you drive one demon out of the Gadarene swine, ten thousand come in to replace it. If God is dead we find some other way in which we can feel special and elite and chosen. None of which are as time-tested or true as, say, Judaism or the Catholic faith. I've always had radar for phony, flaky stuff."

Marlette developed other obsessions. At twenty-seven, he threw himself full-time into learning to play the banjo, and within a year was playing in a band in clubs. The next year, disco hit Charlotte. He was one of the few single men in the paper's newsroom, and women started asking him to join them, taking dance lessons in clubs. "I learned how to dance and I spent a couple of years going out every night. I never knew how much women love to dance. But I became a snob. It didn't matter how great-looking a woman was if she couldn't dance." Years later, his friend Pat Conroy, the novelist, would kid him about that time. Whenever Conroy went on a book tour, he'd meet women who were disco "friends" of Marlette's.

"My twenties were an extended adolescence," he allows.

It was a good time to be funny; the children of *Mad* were everywhere. They'd been bred on the Jewish humor of Lenny Bruce and Bob Newhart; the black sass of Dick Gregory, Bill Cosby and Richard Pryor; the ensemble energies of Chicago's Second City comedy troupe and The Committee of San Francisco, which gave the world Woodstock's Wavy Gravy; the Smothers Brothers, those formerly All-American folkies whose prime-time comedy and music show was canceled by CBS in the early days of the Nixon administration because of their overt antiwar attitude; the surrealistic Firesign Theater; and George Carlin, arrested in 1972 for his routine about "seven words you can't say on television."

The *Mad* boomers who'd have the most impact of all were at a magazine called *National Lampoon*. The *Lampoon* was a descendent of the *Harvard Lampoon*, a preppy, upper-class product until the early 1960s, when it was taken over by a gang of mavericks who began producing biting parodies of national magazines. After a 1966 parody of *Playboy* and a 1968 take on *Life*, the *Lampoon*'s editors caught the attention of the publisher of *Cheetah*, an unsuccessful mass market psychedelic magazine. Henry Beard (b. 1947), Doug Kenney (b. 1947) and Rob Hoffman (b. 1947), and the team that gathered around them put together a comedy record, *National Lampoon's Radio Hour*, and a 1973 stage show, *Lemmings*, which parodied Woodstock as a symbol of a generation hurling itself off a cliff. The show opened that January at The Village Gate starring John Belushi (b. 1949) and Chevy Chase (b. 1943). A year later, those two became the heart and soul of the ultimate expression of generational self-satire.

On August 11, 1975, the last American soldiers left Vietnam. Two months later to the day, *Saturday Night Live* debuted on NBC, bringing impudent, cynical, often corrosively mocking comedy into the mainstream. The show's writers had a lot to work with. Reality had just offered up Charles Manson follower Lynette "Squeaky" Fromme taking a shot at Nixon's successor, the genial, undistinguished Gerald Ford, seventeen days before Sara Jane Moore, a political activist, shot at him again. In between, Patricia Hearst had been captured and put in jail.

Marlette listened to *National Lampoon's Radio Hour* once a week. "I still remember the first *Saturday Night Live*, when Michael O'Donoghue stuck long needles in the eyes of Tony Orlando and Dawn," he says, chuckling. In the depths of the Me Decade, this handful of comedians kept their generation's maverick spirit alive through laughter. "I feel a great affinity with and gratitude for what was going on there," Marlette says. "They were like a commune, being paid huge sums of money and getting famous by being subversive."

EIGHTEEN MONTHS AFTER arriving at William Morris, in 1976, Michael Fuchs was asked to join the fledgling pay cable network Home Box Office, known for broadcasting full-length theatrical movies uncut, uncensored, and commercial-free. When Fuchs learned that the job involved programming, making creative decisions and putting shows on the air, he jumped. "I thought I had good instincts," he said.

Four-year-old HBO had only 600,000 subscribers and was losing a fortune when Fuchs arrived. Launched in November 1972, its first broadcast, seen in 365 homes in Wilkes Barre, Pennsylvania, was a hockey game. The first movie it aired had an auspicious title, *Sometimes a Great Notion*. HBO aired its first original show a few months later: the Pennsylvania Polka Festival from the fairgrounds in Allentown. It also offered well-produced coverage of boxing matches and the Wimbledom tennis tournament.

HBO's owner, Time Inc., had long been a bastion of print journalism. After television was blamed for the demise of *Life*, Time Inc. had started investing in broadcasting. It bought and built cable TV franchises, including Manhattan Cable Television, and started HBO as a subscription programming service, transmitting its signal from microwave dishes strategically placed on rooftops. Cable systems were then isolated, local concerns offering no economies of scale, and these investments were losing millions. "Little did the print masters know," Richard M. Clurman wrote in his study of the company, *To the End of Time*, "that their wires in the ground and their dishes on stilts, which were draining so much capital and causing such executive anguish, would one day be half the company."[34] And little did they know that a "wired" world was a mere two decades away.

Not to say that the company was entirely clueless. In 1975 HBO's president, Gerald Levin (b. 1939), leased access to satellites allowing its signal to be beamed nationwide. Its first satellite broadcast that September was a heavyweight championship fight, "The Thrilla from Manila," pitting Muhammad Ali against Joe Frazier. The move to satellite caused worry at the broadcast networks and a bounce in Time's stock price, yet the division kept losing money. Nick Nicholas (b. 1939), a financial analyst who'd become president of Manhattan Cable, was moved to HBO in 1976 as president as Levin became chairman. Fuchs was one of several new executives who joined HBO that September; he was director of special programming, adding sports to his portfolio within a year.

The networks still ruled television, with 92 percent of the market. "HBO wasn't network television," Fuchs says. "It was countertelevision. Our job was to attack the Establishment. I wasn't joining any club, I was cutting against the grain. If there was ever a place that fit my personality, it was this. I would say to myself, 'Aren't you lucky that you found a place where you can succeed by being different?'" Cable had only two things going for it: good reception and HBO. "And HBO had an unbelievable inferiority complex," Fuchs says. "I coined a phrase we all laughed at, but it turned out to be true: 'We will change the face of broadcast television.' It was like a little kid with a slingshot saying, 'We will turn back the Nazis.'"

At first, HBO's original programming was limited to standup comedians like Robert Klein, broadcast live in concert. But Fuchs's superiors decided that in order to improve its negotiating position with the studios that licensed movies to HBO, the cable channel needed to produce more independent programming. "Network programming was so homogenized," Fuchs says, "so I bought in and helped create the philosophy that no one would buy this product if it wasn't different."

His first programming decision set the tone of the next eighteen years. In October 1976, Fuchs had to produce a comedy show, and the available talent boiled down to a choice between the Las Vegas comic Pat Henry and the boomer comic Steve Martin. Fuchs didn't know who Martin was and had to ask around. Then, the weekend before HBO's show was taped, Martin made his debut on the new *Saturday Night Live*. Not only was his one-man show a sensation, but all across the country, people started using his catchphrase, "Well, *excuuuuse* me!" Martin then went out on a tour pegged to HBO markets. "And by the time he came to New York," Fuchs boasts, "kids were doing his act with him."

As one-man shows starring Andy Kaufman (b. 1949), Richard Pryor (b. 1940) and Robin Williams (b. 1951) followed, HBO began to be seen as an experimental, permissive oasis in the television wasteland, and local cable operators made it their chief sales tool and their premium offering. "Network was homogenized," says Fuchs. "Everything was rehearsed, on a set, on video. It looked like shit. I was going to do a different style, a standup comedian in his natural habitat." HBO grew rich—it turned its first profit in fall 1977—because it started out too poor to buy established stars and lavish, empty network productions. And the comedians kept alive the spark of Fuchs's social conscience. "In those sleepy years, the comedians we specialized in were more socially relevant than the fucking politicians," he says.

Barbara Ledeen at
Beloit College, 1968.

Barbara Ledeen outside her Maryland
home, 1998.

(Courtesy of Marianne Williamson)

Marianne Williamson
performing her cabaret
show, 1978.

(Courtesy of Marianne Williamson)

Marianne Williamson in 1999.

(Both photos courtesy of David MacIntosh)

David McIntosh, high
school freshman, 1973.

David McIntosh on *Meet The Press*
following Newt Gingrich's resignation,
1998.

Tim Scully (right) building a linear accellerator, 1960.

Tim Scully in Albion, California, 1998.

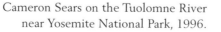

Cameron Sears, sixth grader, 1971.

Cameron Sears on the Tuolomne River near Yosemite National Park, 1996.

Cynthia Bowman at her desk
in the Airplane Mansion, 1976.

Cynthia Bowman in San Francisco, 1999.

Leslie Crocker Snyder
graduates law school,
1966.

HON.
LESLIE CROCKER SNYDER

Leslie Crocker Snyder at work in New York State
Supreme Court, 1996.

Steve Capps graduates
high school, 1973.

Steve Capps with his daughter,
Emma, 1998.

(Both photos courtesy of Steve Capps)

(Both photos courtesy of Michael Fuchs)

Michael Fuchs, Al Gore and Christopher Reeve
at the White House, 1995.

Michael Fuchs at his first public
performance, 1950.

Mark Rudd addressing students cut off from occupied Columbia University, April, 1968.

Mark Rudd at home in Albuquerque, 1995.

Kathryn Bond Stockton and date at a friend's wedding, 1974.

Kathryn Bond Stockton in 1994.

Doug Marlette in Charlotte,
North Carolina, 1974.

Doug Marlette in his office
at *Newsday*, 1998.

John Gage and farm workers organizer Cesar Chavez at the University of California at Berkeley's Sproul Hall, 1965.

John Gage at a software developer's conference, 1999.

"Mitzi" (a/k/a Nina Hartley), age 15, 1974.

Nina Hartley, sex star, 1998.

Thomas Vallely at his base camp in Vietnam, 1969.

Thomas Vallely and two North Vietnamese Army officers near Danang, 1985.

Donald Trump (with pointer) unveils his convention center, 1975.

Donald Trump on his helicopter, 1988.

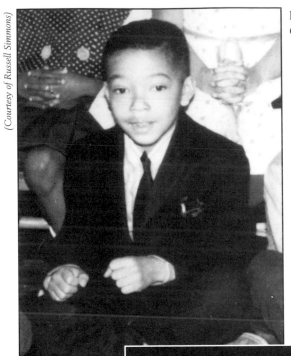

Russell Simmons in Hollis, Queens, 1965.

Russell Simmons and wife Kimora, 1999.

Jim Fouratt, house hippie at
Columbia Records, 1969.

Jim Fouratt, in his Danceteria II office, 1982.

Victoria Leacock and her father Ricky in New York's Central Park, 1965.

Victoria Leacock and *Rent* composer Jonathan Larson in New York, 1994.

Michael Gross at Max's Kansas City, New York, 1974.

Michael Gross in London, 1999.

Young Adulthood

STEVE CAPPS ENROLLED in the Rochester Institute of Technology in 1973. He could have gone anywhere. MIT tried to recruit him. "But I had thick glasses and zits on top of zits, and I was afraid if I went to MIT I would just be a nerd for the rest of my life, even though it turns out I have been."

Rochester had one of the best photography schools in the country. Its admissions officers promised he could study there and take a double major in computer science. But on arrival, he was forced to choose a single major, and since a favorite teacher had told him photography was a great hobby but a lousy profession, he chose computers. Only then did he discover that in those days before personal computers, he had to share the school's mainframe with others, who constantly crashed the big machine.

Though he hadn't lived with his parents since twelfth grade, staying in Schenectady to finish school while they moved to Connecticut ("I was squarer than a T-square and trustworthy enough to live alone," he says), he'd begun fighting with his father. "I didn't say fuck you, but I thought that. And we'd get into fifty-mile arguments about the right to wear no shoes." So when Capps returned for his second year at Rochester, a friend's new motorcycle suggested a solution to his dilemma. "I was a lost soul, definitely," he says. "I didn't know why I was in college. It was not challenging. Within a week, I'd dropped out."

He'd worked for General Electric Credit that summer ("if you're a son of GE, you get a great job at GE") and had made "a ton of money." So he went back, made some more, bought a motorcycle of his own, and within a month had taken off with his buddy to ride cross-country. He got as far as New Orleans, where his friend had an accident and "lost his gusto for traveling," Capps says. "It was just bad enough to deflate his Easy-Riderness."

His buddy crated his 350CC Honda and hitched home, but Capps decided to keep going. Though his father was furious and had vowed not to help him, he'd left a cache of funds with his mother, who sent money orders to post offices along the way. A hitchhiker they'd picked up was heading to Key West, and Capps decided to go, too. "I had discovered the *Whole Earth Catalogue*," he says. "Some kids became Jesus Freaks, I was definitely a Whole Earth Freak. So I lived in a landfill dump in Key West, great view. I scrounged a mattress—a vinyl one, so it wasn't too stinky. And I rigged up a desk because I like to draw and write. I had a whole little Hooverville setup."

Though he was the only permanent resident of his dump, other travelers would come and go. During spring break 1975, a whole pack of kids from Georgia moved in and soon discovered that flowers growing at Ernest Hemingway's house, a local attraction, contained the hallucinogen atropine. "They go eat these flowers, they're all hallucinating, and that's the night the cops do a sweep. Somehow, I round them all up and get them out of there." But he'd lost his home. "So I changed dumps," Capps says. "There was another landfill, next to a campground that you could sneak on to get a hot shower. I just kind of sat—and wrote nothing. It seemed profound at the time. My motorcycle wasn't working right. I finally said, 'Forget it. Going home.'"

The Rochester Institute of Technology had a work-study program, so when Capps got home from his aborted cross-country jaunt, he simply returned to his job and awaited a new semester. "I had a huge war chest at that point," he says. He also had his first girlfriend. When she suggested they build a log cabin on her family's land in the Adirondack Mountains, he dropped out again. "I still had aimless urges," Capps says of the bicentennial summer of '76.

Back at school that fall, he heard about a work-study job opening at Xerox, automating the technical library in one of its labs. Having already automated his high school library, he "walked in and blew away every other candidate," Capps says. Soon he was "making more money than you can imagine and learning ten thousand times more than I could in school." Here, not in the Whole Earth fantasy of his Key West Hooverville, was the real social revolution.

Capps met his first personal computer, the Alto, at Xerox. The Alto was conceived in the imagination of Alan C. Kay (b. 1940), a doctoral student at the University of Utah, where the Advanced Research and Projects Agency (ARPA) had established a tiny computer science department in 1966, run by a pioneer of computer graphics. In 1969, in a doctoral dissertation spiced with an epigraph from the hippies' favorite poet, Kahlil Gibran, Kay proposed the Dynabook, a personal computer small enough to tuck under your arm, complete with keyboard, screen, and enough memory to store a novel.

A few months later, New York-based Xerox opened the Palo Alto Research Center (a/k/a Xerox PARC); the copying company had seen the future—the paperless office—and decided to plan for it. PARC's engineers included several trained by the researcher who first proposed windows-based computing and the point-and-click device that came to be known as the mouse. In the next few years, PARC developed many of the innovations that would drive the PC industry, including laser printers; high-speed communication between devices (PARC's ETHERNET was essentially a traffic cop that kept data moving without collision); bit-mapped screens; and WYSIWYG (what-you-see-is-what-you-get) software that produced screen images identical to printed output.[1]

In September 1972, Alan Kay joined a PARC team working to build a PC. Completed the following spring, the Alto was the first fast, compact computer with a full-resolution screen. Xerox immediately ordered up several thousand and set to work making it consumer-friendly.

By 1974, PARC researchers had created the first word-processing software. A year later, its engineers demonstrated easy-to-understand graphic user interfaces (GUIs) with icons and pop-up and drop-down menus obviating hard-to-learn commands. But inexplicably, Xerox never capitalized on its collection of computing innovations, choosing instead to put its marketing muscle behind a dedicated word processor—in essence a typewriter with enough memory to store a page or two. The Alto effectively died.

Just a few months afterward, Capps found one of the discarded machines stuck away in a closet at Xerox's lab in Rochester. For the next year, Capps worked on the library automation project by day and played with the Alto at night. Then, just as he decided to cast his lot with the University of Utah's pioneering computer graphics department, Xerox offered him a full-time job at its nearby Webster Research Center if he'd agree to finish his degree at Rochester, tuition paid—a lucky thing, because most of the pioneers had long since left Utah. With the money he'd saved, he bought a house near his office and became a full-time hacker, writing programs for a combination laser printer/copier.

"What better life could you have?" he asks. "If you wake up at two in the morning with an idea for a program, you walk to work and code it all night! As long as you did your job, which was pretty ill-defined anyway, you could use a computer all you wanted. And you were given one day a week to do anything." He was having so much fun, he doesn't even remember when he graduated from college. "I have a degree," he says, vaguely. "Somewhere."

As part of his job, Capps would regularly visit Xerox PARC in California. "In typical twenty-one-year-old style, I assumed I was an equal to all these demigods who had created the whole thing at PARC," he says. At Rochester, engineers spent their entire careers developing copier toner, and one mathematician's lifework was to stop paper from curling when it passed through Xerox machines. The atmosphere at PARC was infinitely preferable. But how to get there?

JIM FOURATT RETURNED to a New York City reveling in decadence in 1974. It was in many ways the swan song of the 1960s—drugs were everywhere, sex was as free as it would ever be. In the straight community, glam rock and androgyny were the new styles. The gay world had turned to single-issue politics—putting sex above all, "sex for sex's sake," sprinkled with drugs, Fouratt says. In the wake of Stonewall, gay discos, run by the Mob, flourished, providing havens for all sorts of sexual and pharmaceutical excess. "Everybody is taking drugs," says Fouratt. "Quaaludes, speed, some cocaine, a lot of pot." He smirks. "A vibrant underground culture."

Fouratt thinks that in the wake of Stonewall, the powers of the city decided to decriminalize gay sex by unwittingly adapting Wilhelm Reich's dictum that a population kept in an orgasmic state will not be political and creating a "hands-off zone where every sort of oppressed desire got manifested: anonymous sex, compulsive sex." The new license didn't just apply to gays; throughout the mid-1970s, massage parlors, brothels and sex clubs for all sorts burgeoned. But after a decade spent in the closet while straight people had frolicked and enjoyed *their* sexual revolution, the city's gay population embraced their new freedom with special fervor.

Open trucks parked overnight along the Manhattan waterfront became "the trucks," a destination for anonymous male sex. Backroom bars, designed for furtive sexual encounters, were the latest thing. At the Anvil and other bars, performers and patrons practiced "fist-fucking," the insertion of forearms into lubricated anuses for sexual gratification, while trend-hounds from the fashion and entertainment industries clamored to get inside and watch. Clone culture—a new super-butch style among gays featuring short haircuts, buff bodies, jeans, flannel shirts and heavy boots—even included a set of handkerchief codes that advertised one's sexual preferences.

Everything was defined by sex. "As much sex as you could have—not my vision of gay liberation," Fouratt says. "Which probably saved my life." Seeking distance Fouratt decided the time had come to reinvent his career. He moved to Hollywood with his latest boyfriend and started looking for acting work again. He kept his radical ties, which both diverted him and held him back. He became an outspoken member of the Actor's Guild, attempting to organize its members for various causes, got involved in a strike at the local Gay and Lesbian Community Center, and joined the Socialist Media Group, which adopted the slogan "Everybody Is a Star" and attracted a handful of Hollywood leftists.

Like Fouratt, many political people had decided to infiltrate the culture industry. "And the Socialist Media Group was set up to be a conscience, so people didn't get bought out," Fouratt says. "Of course, they all did." Fouratt, on the other hand, believes his activities landed him on an informal blacklist. "It's a town where you don't make trouble," he observes. "You don't make trouble if you're a fuckin' star; you certainly don't make trouble if you're a nobody."

Fouratt lasted three years in Los Angeles, most of it on a downward slide, drinking and surrounded by what he calls Organic Junkies, who exercised and drank carrot juice by their pools all day and, like their East Coast disco brethren, drugged and danced all night. He woke up one afternoon surrounded by empty pints of vodka. "I walked out of that house with thirty dollars in my pocket, got on a plane, and came back to New York."

There a new music called disco had become the pulsing beat of gay culture. Fouratt never much liked disco. For all the behavioral liberty it brought about, its machine-like beat and hedonistic culture struck him as retrograde. The 1970s phenomenon was quickly embraced by many Boomers, though, among them those who hadn't succumbed to the lures of the 1960s and, having gone to work and made names for themselves instead in businesses like fashion, entertainment and the media, could suddenly buy the adolescent pleasures they'd missed.

The king of disco was Steve Rubell, born in Canarsie, New York, in 1943, the son of a postman and a teacher. During college at Syracuse

University, he enlisted in the National Guard to avoid going to Vietnam. When his unit was rumored to be heading there anyway, he transferred into military intelligence. From there, it was on to a brokerage house, where Rubell made some money in penny stocks. Then he opened a chain of steak restaurants. In 1974, Rubell hired Ian Schrager (b. 1946), a friend from college, as his lawyer. Together, the two bounced around New York, landing one night in a disco called Le Jardin, and decided they wanted one of their own. On the day after Christmas 1975, they opened the Enchanted Garden in unfashionable Douglaston, Queens. In 1977 the pair crossed the river, connected with Manhattan's gay-fashion-entertainment axis, and found themselves the center of things.

Rubell, a nebbish with a nasal voice and ingratiating manner, turned their new club, Studio 54, into fame's temple and the apotheosis of disco society. He coddled celebrities. Beginning with a birthday party for Bianca Jagger a few weeks after the club opened in 1977, Schrager and Rubell would finance regular fêtes for the bold-faced set. Those parties were the bait that lured lesser-knowns to line up outside Studio's doors. At a red, white, and black party for Paloma Picasso, they served $40,000 worth of salmon, caviar and champagne. For Valentino, they imported a circus, and for Giorgio Armani they hired twenty violinists in white tails to play in the lobby and the Ballet Trocadero de Monte Carlo to perform onstage.

Cocaine—pharmacology's analogue to the era's narcissism—was Studio 54's holy sacrament. Rubell even created private places where his precious celebrity set could indulge. It was the Roaring Twenties all over again. A strict entry policy permitted the rich, the powerful and the young and beautiful to indulge in every mode of sexual and pharmaceutical experimentation. Even reigning progressives were drawn to Studio's brief, bright flame. Carter administration aides and Kennedy family progeny were sometimes among those dancing or drugging the night away.

In summer 1978, Fouratt had set his sights on the music business. He'd begun managing a rock band, one of the groups creating an underground alternative to disco and corporate rock in the era of *Saturday Night Fever* and *Frampton Comes Alive*, and was steeping himself in the post-punk music then emerging from England, when a friend took him to a once-successful disco called Hurrah. Hurrah's decline had been driven by the raging popularity of Studio 54. Fouratt went to Studio 54 too, and was simultaneously fascinated and appalled. "Their value system was to get ahead and to use whatever and whoever they could to do it," he says. "It wasn't about young people, except as props and lures. You could be bought and sold and cocktailed and fucked. That's the truth."

Fouratt knew just how Hurrah could compete.

YOU REALLY DIDN'T need a weatherman to know which way the wind had blown. *Saturday Night Live* ruled television, Steven Spielberg (b. 1947) and George Lucas (b. 1944) were beginning to make waves in Hollywood, and cartoonists like Doug Marlette and Garry Trudeau were doing the same in the nation's newspapers. The former fringe had begun its move to the American center, when a presidential candidate who quoted Bob Dylan came roaring out of the South like a fresh wind.

Jimmy Carter, a born-again Christian, nuclear engineer and peanut farmer from Georgia, took office promising "a world order more responsive to human aspiration." Immediately he granted unconditional amnesty to all Vietnam-era draft resisters, inviting those who'd left the country or gone underground to come home. He followed that with more startling, progressive actions that seemed inspired by 1960s activism: announcing that American foreign aid would be cut to countries that violated human rights, opening talks with Vietnam to normalize relations, signing a treaty to return the Panama Canal to local control, postponing production of the neutron bomb, and mediating secret talks between Arabs and Israelis that ended in peace between Egypt and Israel.

The rise of Carter allowed Southerners to indulge in identity politics and group pride—to find the good in their redneck version of *Roots*. For Marlette, who'd looked north for education and enlightenment only to find more narrow-minded bigotry and provincialism, the late 1970s were a time of rediscovery. "The narcissism of the Me Decade wasn't only manifested in a shallow jogging-disco-do-your-own-thing-whatever, but also a healthy delving into tradition, history and self," he says.

Marlette began studying the Civil War as the source of his own rebel streak, reading William Faulkner and traveling to Nashville's Grand Old Opry and to the music clubs of Austin, Texas, where he immersed himself in the outlaw music of Willie Nelson and Waylon Jennings, "finding resonances and beginning to appreciate the authenticity," he says. Again, he saw himself reflected in the music of Bob Dylan, who by 1978 had declared himself a born-again Christian and recorded an album of religious songs. "That did not bother me a whit," Marlette says. "What was interesting was his instinct for the truth of the Jewish tradition. It's radical, rooted. That was the beginning of this generation rediscovering what we had rejected."

It was also the moment when Marlette was "discovered," singled out in a *Time* magazine article on Jimmy Carter's New South. "It was kind of hip to be a Southerner," he says. "Carter legitimized that." Unfortunately, the new president also had what Marlette calls the Southern Disease. "It's a love affair with defeat, a kind of self-destructiveness masked by a virtuous, arrogant, pious knowing what's best," Marlette says. "You think you can snap your fingers and have things be the way you want them. The Clintons have some of that, too. Hillary thinks she knows better. There's a kind of self-righteousness Hillary has that Carter had. But it's not enough to be right. You've got to be able to work with other human beings. That takes another kind of a genius."

Carter's years in office did offer ripe targets for a political cartoonist: the energy crisis (Marlette's cartoon showed a driver trading his firstborn for a fill-up), nuclear power (a plant shaped like a pair of dice), the Equal Rights Amendment (as pigs are led to a slaughterhouse, sows demand equal rights), abortion (a Supreme Court justice in the door of a clinic telling a poor woman, "If you have to ask how much, you can't afford one"), and the rise of fundamentalism in Iran (Carter slamming his head against a stone wall shaped like the Ayatollah Khomeini) and in America (Christ crucified on a TV antenna).

Jimmy Carter's cleansing of American society was overshadowed by the nation's continuing economic distress and by an event that happened in California in the summer of 1978, at least partly in response to those troubles. The passage there, by a vote of almost two to one, of a ballot item known as Proposition 13, which cut property taxes and the social programs they paid for in half, spelled the end of New Deal-era optimism, symbolized by an active, paternal government, and the beginning of what some called a new realism and others a new mean-spiritedness. Although it took the seizure of hostages by fundamentalists in Iran and Carter's failure to free them to finally kick the legs out from under his presidency, there was already a sense that Carter wasn't the answer.

AFTER HIS FAMILY moved to Sacramento, California, Cameron Sears's last year of high school was quite different from what it might have been at his tiny boarding school in Maine. "I'd had long hair and ridden a bike to school, but that just wasn't done," he says. "Kids were driving fancy cars, and the people were really flaky, in my opinion."

A year later, Sears was ready to escape. "I didn't go to college right away," he says. "I needed some time to sort it out." He enrolled in a three-month mountaineering course in Wyoming with the National Outdoor Leadership School, and spent weeks at a time in the American outback.

On his return, Sears enrolled in the University of California at Santa Cruz and spent the next five years earning an undergraduate degree. "Nobody was doing it in four years any more," he says. With the job market clogged with earlier boomers, it was just as well to extend your adolescence.

Santa Cruz was a highly progressive university. Many of his friends worked on the school's organic farm. There were no grades, although concern about the viability of that policy set in while Sears was there. Sears was well aware that there was a recession going on. Gasoline prices were skyrocketing, and Ph.D.s were driving taxis. He felt sure it wouldn't affect him. "Somewhat naively, I thought I was always going to be a soldier in the environmental movement," he says. "Not necessarily as an activist chaining myself to trees—although I was certainly willing to do that. But I wanted to operate on a higher level. I wanted to affect policy. That was my goal."

JOHN GAGE MADE his last foray into politics in 1980, when Ted Kennedy made an abortive run for the presidency. "I thought it was time to push for a change that would emphasize people who really were suffering, and so I said, 'I'll do it.'" Then he watched a videotaped interview with Kennedy. "They asked him, 'Why are you running?' Essentially he didn't have an answer. My heart sank." But he did his job—"get the plane into the air and into a five-media-stops-per-day campaign"—straight through the convention, where Kennedy lost to Carter, who then lost to Ronald Reagan. "So I went back to academic life," Gage says.

But he wasn't content. The abstractions of math and statistical physics couldn't explain human behavior. That's when he discovered something infinitely more satisfying: computing. A few years before, Gage had come upon Berkeley's mini-computers when a university computer system administrator and fellow grad student named Bill Joy (b. 1954) introduced him to software that did mathematical typesetting. "I discovered the populism of a system that allows anyone to create beautiful mathematics on a page," Gage says.

The computer revolution had begun in the late 1950s. At that time, there was only one paradigm for computer use. Manufacturers like IBM, Digital Equipment Corporation, Wang and Data General sold black boxes—huge mainframe computers with magic inside. "We're the priests with the keys to the temple; you've got to come to the priests," Gage says, satirizing the prevailing proprietary attitude. At MIT, computer aficionados (for there was no computer science department yet) began attempting to improve the software that ran the school's multimillion-dollar IBM mainframe computer. They called themselves "hackers,"[2] and though they seemed worlds away from the dope-smoking, anti-logic radicals then coming of age on less technocratic campuses, they had the equally radical idea that the keys to the temple of computing should be freely available to anyone, not only those approved by the priests. Indeed, they felt that all information should be free, so it might be shared and bettered.

In the early 1960s, the hackers got their hands on the tool that would wrest computing from the priests forever—the minicomputer. Though they were as big as refrigerators at first, these machines were revolutionary: unlike huge room-size mainframes, they were accessible, nimble and inspiring to those who didn't want to put on white shirts and ties and join IBM's army of bureaucrats.[3] By the 1970s, computer science and the hacker ethic had spread across the country. Computers offered a safe haven of logic in an increasingly illogical world. For students on the run from the collapsing 1960s youth culture, computer culture was a godsend. Here was something they could control.[4]

In the Bay Area, schools like Stanford and Berkeley formed the vanguard of the cyberrevolution. Beginning in 1969, they were all hooked up to a Defense Department-funded network called ARPAnet. ARPA, the Advanced Research Projects Agency, had been funding computer research since the end of World War II, investing about a billion dollars on advanced projects to make a better military. To kill people efficiently, you need to find them, so ARPA put money into radar and acoustic detection systems that would listen for the propeller beat of Russian submarines, and into computers to analyze those signals. It put money into materials, chip technology and university computer departments that could help airplanes fly faster and higher. But ARPA also funded pure computer research, allowing hackers to take its money without the slightest guilt.[5] At MIT and Stanford, some ARPA money was even spent developing early computer games like Spacewar and Adventure.

The ARPAnet was developed to make the most of scarce computing resources by connecting users and resources, even at a great distance, but it soon turned into a communications medium as academics, technical types and an avant-garde of ex-hippies, science fiction aficionados and anarchists began connecting through a new technology called electronic mail.[6] ARPAnet was based in "the belief that systems should be decentralized, encourage exploration, and urge a free flow of information," Steven Levy wrote in *Hackers*, a history of the computer revolution.[7] Similar values had driven the now-waning youth movement.

Key computer research was also taking place at Bell Labs, the phone company's scientific arm, which developed a computer operating system called Bell UNIX. Bell Labs was part of AT&T, which, as a government-sanctioned monopoly, was not allowed to market its creation commercially. Instead, it licensed the system to universities, the military and corporate researchers for a small fee, along with the right to alter the source code, its programming foundation and the hacker-esque obligation to share improvements with other users.

Bill Joy was one of the student programmers who dug into the program, creating a version known as Berkeley UNIX. In 1980, Joy rewrote a set of standards (computer instructions written in code) known as TCP/IP networking protocols, which systematized communication between computers on the ARPAnet. Without TCP/IP, "you could be getting it all but not understanding a word I'm saying," explains Gage, who by 1982 was working with Joy on Berkeley's computing strategy. "Bill put the new protocols out free on the Internet—very Berkeley—and everybody took his code and made their computers work. He became the God of Internet-distributed computing. Anybody in the world could now be in the conversation." A year later, the Domain Name Service came into being, a sort of cyberspace city planning agency, and the word *Internet* started being used in place of ARPAnet.[8]

As the Internet was being born, a separate group of computer boomers was creating the computer revolution's other essential component: cheap hardware. While Gage was working on the McGovern campaign, a group called Community Memory was installing a public computer terminal, open to anyone, near a record store in Berkeley. In 1971 a science fiction fan named Lee Felsenstein (b. 1945), who'd been arrested at Sproul Hall on December 2, 1964, and then joined the staff of the underground newspaper *Berkeley Barb*, gained access to his first computer.

Felsenstein was one of the pioneers—many of them former activists—of what would soon coalesce into a populist movement to bring computing power to the people. All over the Bay Area, others were having the same idea, and by 1975, the first commercially available PC, a bare-bones affair called Altair 8800, based on a new microprocessor chip made by a Santa Clara company, Intel, was made available in hobby kit form (although without any programs or input devices like keyboards or mice). On March 5, 1975, two computer kit enthusiasts held the first meeting of the Homebrew Computer Club at one of their homes in Menlo Park. Within four months, the meetings had grown so large, they had to be held in an auditorium at Stanford. In June, Felsenstein started chairing those meetings.[9]

Among those frequenting Homebrew—sharing information, advances, and even code, as required by the tenets of hackerism—were engineers from Hewlett-Packard, including shaggy-haired Steve Wozniak (b. 1940), often accompanied by a high school friend just back from a hippie trek to India and a spell in an Oregon commune, Steve Jobs (b. 1945). Jobs was working for Atari, which was then developing a computerized game called Pong. In college, Jobs and Woz, as he was known, had built and sold blue boxes, illegal devices that let users make free long distance calls. Now, inspired by Homebrew, Wozniak set out to build his own computer. By that winter, it was done, and Jobs, dazzled by his friend's invention, insisted they build and sell them. Financed by the sale of Jobs's Volkswagen bus, they incorporated in spring 1976. Jobs, who was proud of his hippie roots and often went barefoot, named the company Apple after the Beatles' record label.[10] Meanwhile, Wozniak created a new machine, the Apple II, which would include a color terminal. It wasn't as advanced as the Xerox Alto, but at least you could buy an Apple.

TIM SCULLY HAD a plan to use his time in prison to earn a doctoral degree and continue the psycho-electronic explorations he'd started while out on bail. In 1974, just after his release on appeal bond, Intel had introduced its 8008 chip, the key component in microcomputers. Scully built a physiological monitoring system around one for use in drug and alcohol rehabilitation programs. Then, when Intel's 8080 chip followed in 1975, he built a computer to detect and record changes in consciousness in biofeedback sessions.

He'd introduced himself to the prison's psychological services staff at McNeil Island during his first sojourn there and corresponded with them while he was out on bail, in the hope they'd allow him to set up a biofeedback program when he returned. He was afraid prison would be full of the sort of guys who'd beaten him up in high school. Instead, he arrived with a rep as a drug czar who didn't rat, and his worst problem was convincing inmates he couldn't sell them acid. But after he got an inmate job as an assistant to one of the resident psychologists, he *could* get them high, help them relax, and combat stress—with biofeedback.

While out on bail, Scully had met a woman suffering from cerebral palsy who could only communicate by laboriously pointing out letters one at a time to her parents with a telegraph key attached to her knee. After he'd been at McNeil a year, Scully got permission to build her a microcomputer and program it using principles of cryptography, allowing the young woman to communicate up to thirty times faster, and later, to write and print out notes and essays. It was so successful, he began building them for other disabled people, adding extensions that controlled devices from page-turners to light switches. When inexpensive speech synthesizers came on the market, he added those, too, so users could have their messages read out loud. Federal Prison Industries took note and began a program to build the machines and offer them to speech-impaired veterans. Though the costs of customizing the device and gaining necessary approvals made the project unfeasible, years later, Scully rewrote the program for PCs and distributed it free on the Internet. The project won him an award as 1979's Outstanding Young Man of the Year from the Washington Jaycees, which had a chapter inside the prison.

Scully was indeed an outstanding prisoner. "My first priority was to stay out of trouble with the inmate population, because the penalty could be death," he says. "Second was to stay out of trouble with the staff. After that, I just wanted not to rot away." He taught classes in computer design, programming and tai chi to fellow inmates, and wrote a dissertation on his biofeedback experiments, earning a Ph.D. He also won a sentence reduction. In August 1979, he was released to a halfway house in San Francisco.

JUST AS NEW YORK began to rise from ruin, Donald Trump got married. Ivana Zelnickova was one of a group of models who came to New York to promote the 1976 Olympic Games in Montreal. Trump spotted her across the room at the singles bar Maxwell's Plum and used his pull to get her a table. She proved to have more character than the Le Club cuties he was used to. In 1977, they were married by Norman Vincent Peale, the high priest of positive thinking.

"Which is probably a good thing, because it kept me out of trouble" during the hedonistic glory days of the disco era, Trump says. "If I hadn't got married, who knows what would have happened? You had drugs, women and booze all over the fuckin' place."

That summer, the couple rented a guest house in Long Island's exclusive Georgica Association; the beachfront property belonged to radical lawyer Michael Kennedy. After being lauded in a *High Times* survey of top drug lawyers, he had begun to represent its publisher, the former Yippie and Zippie Tom Forcade. When Forcade committed suicide in

1978, Kennedy—who'd been named a head of the charitable trust in which Forcade put his assets—took over the drug magazine. His path would keep crossing his clients' and tenants' as he followed the evolving Baby Boom in search of fresh legal fees.

AFTER HE CAME home in 1977, Mark Rudd decided to say nothing about his years underground, "because what could I have said?" he asks. "The Revolution is still strong? I'm sorry for what I'd done? It was a no-win situation. So I just shut up." Though all federal felony charges against him had been dropped, Rudd still worried that he would be hauled before a grand jury on the Weather Underground, even that he might face murder charges from the townhouse explosion. "But there was nothing from the townhouse, nothing stemming from subsequent bombings, nothing from the bombing of the Pentagon, breaking Tim Leary out," he marvels. "Nothing."

Instead, he was arraigned for several misdemeanors and released on modest bail. The next day, he flew to Chicago, surrendered again, and was given permission to return to New York. "*WSP*," he whispered to lawyer Gerald Lefcourt after the proceedings. "White-skin privilege prevailed," he explains. "I felt somewhat ashamed of the tremendous ease with which I reentered society." Ultimately, he would plead guilty to criminal trespass in New York and receive an unconditional discharge. A second guilty plea in Chicago cost him a $2,000 fine and two years' probation.

While he awaited the disposition of those cases, Rudd and Sue married and moved into an apartment in Brooklyn. Sue was pregnant and gave birth to their second child, a daughter, the following May. During the pregnancy, Rudd reestablished contacts in the pacifist community, but discovered he was a pariah to some former radicals. When he ran into two members of the faction that had taken over Weather, they were openly hostile. But for every bad experience, there was a good one. When he attended a celebration of Vietnam's admittance to the United Nations in 1977, an official of the government thanked him for helping liberate his country.

When he moved back to New Mexico in 1978, Rudd discovered that most people were willing to live and let live. He's glad he goes unrecognized. "I had more than fifteen minutes of fame and don't even want thirty seconds anymore," Rudd says. "I prefer to be a real person in a real community."

As Rudd settled into his new life, others came up from the underground. Cathy Wilkerson surfaced in 1980, was sentenced to three years, and served less than one. Billy Ayers and Bernadine Dohrn emerged, too; remarkably, Dohrn had been in New York, waitressing in an Upper East Side restaurant called Jim McMullen, a favored haunt of the city's ruling class. Charges against Ayers had been dropped. Dohrn was fined and sentenced to probation.

The saga of the Weathermen finally came to an ignominious close in October 1981, when Kathy Boudin, Dave Gilbert and Judy Clark were arrested following the botched holdup of a Brinks armored truck in Nyack, New York. After the purge of 1976, the trio had formed the May 19 Organization, named in honor of Ho Chi Minh and Malcolm X's birthday. It functioned as a support group for the Black Liberation Army, a gang of terrorists or gangsters (depending on your point of view), itself an offshoot of the Black Panther Party.

After Nyack, Jeff Jones and several lesser Weatherevolutionaries were busted, too. Jones was let off with a fine and probation. The May 19 group wasn't so lucky; Boudin was sentenced to twenty years in jail and Gilbert and Clark seventy-five for their part in the robbery and murder of two policemen. "They're still there, and they're still writing," says Rudd. "If you look on the Internet, you will probably find shit of theirs." He dismisses the tract he found there by a May 19 survivor as "long, unreadable." But then, when Rudd gave a speech at a rally on the anniversary of the shootings at Kent State University in 1989, Bernadine Dohrn got up and walked out. Though he's in touch with some of his former comrades-in-arms, "few of them figure into my life intimately," he says. Yet Rudd still admires Dohrn, who spent seven months in prison for refusing to testify to a Brinks-case grand jury.

WITH HER SEMI-FAMOUS father off in Boston and her model mother bedridden, celebrity culture became Victoria Leacock's touchstone. Her fascination with fame was fed by the television, which was always on. "Mom would have it on from 7:00 A.M. to 3:00 A.M. I was watching a *lot* of TV." Leacock's other cultural reference point was Judy Garland, a favorite of her mother's and the tragic heroine of so many gay men in the Village. "I was a gay man," she jokes. She and her friend Gordon—soon to realize he was gay—would put on dresses and tease their hair. Her mother recognized the need for escape. Her eighth-grade graduation gift to Victoria was a single ticket to the 1976 Lincoln Center premiere of Martin Scorcese's *New York, New York*, starring Garland's daughter, Liza Minnelli.

Leacock became obsessed with Minnelli and tried to emulate her. She sold Avon cosmetics to her friends to earn money to take acting and dance lessons. When her idol opened in a one-woman Broadway musical, *The Act*, in fall 1977, she waited backstage every Saturday with home-made presents and cards. Soon enough, she became Minnelli's pet fan, with full backstage access. She met the first boy she ever kissed there: Blake, director Gower Champion's son. She also met Diana Barrows, who played Annie in the eponymous musical, who was equally obsessed with celebrities. The girls' moms enjoyed each other as well, so they all became the best of friends, lightening young Leacock's burden.

The girls started sneaking into concerts, benefits, premiere parties and the second acts of Broadway shows together. They also went to Studio 54. Old enough to be baby celebrities, but too young for much else, they just watched. Victoria's mother always wanted a full report. "I'd come home and tell my mom we danced with the guy from *Murder by Death*, because that's who Truman Capote was to me. Who knew? We'd come home at midnight or one in the morning, stay up talking until three, then skip school the next day because we were tired." Her grades suffered, but she didn't care.

Victoria was on line to get into Tavern on the Green for a tribute to director George Cukor in spring 1978 when she met Andy Warhol. A reporter asked if she was Bianca Jagger, Warhol's date. Leacock was four-teen, wearing a ten-year-old dress of her mother's, hair in a ponytail. Warhol laughed and told the reporter that Jagger was in the lady's room. Leacock told Warhol that she'd gotten an A in art class by emulating his famous Campbell's Soup paintings, done the year before Victoria was born. "And I'm gonna be an actress and I want to be a filmmaker and I love *Interview* magazine and by the time we got through the buffet line, he looked at me and said, 'Why don't you come visit me at The Factory on Friday after school?'" She did so, and the visits continued every Friday until she graduated from high school.

"I just thought celebrities and artists and writers were the most amaz-ing, God-sent creatures, because my father was one," she says. Since her father was absent, Warhol became a surrogate. He was so nice, she refused to believe people who told her he could be a social vampire.

"How was your science test?" he'd ask. "Did the boy you like in math class look at you?"

DESPITE A FEW "little iffy periods" involving gangs and drugs, Russell Simmons was a fairly good student in high school. Graduating in 1976 and thinking to become a sociology teacher, he enrolled in City College of New York and moved near its campus in Harlem, the uptown Manhattan neighborhood long the center of black urban culture. After he was fired from an Orange Julius hot dog stand for throwing rinds in the street outside, he began selling ersatz cocaine—it was actually a commercial incense called Coco Leaf, made from the same plant. Though its pharmaceutical properties had been deactivated, it still caused a telltale "freeze" or numbing, just like cocaine, when it touched mucus membranes.

Decimated by heroin, black culture wasn't what it had been. Sports and music were still outs for black youth, but the music had changed. "Fucking disco was being forced on the black community," Simmons says. "Somebody decided that the music industry should invent a pop music out of black music," just like the spineless, preening, corporate rock that had formularized rock 'n' roll. Record companies "were competing for crossover," sales of black music to whites, "and disco was their vehicle. It was corporate black music." Simmons thought of it as music that made it easy for white folks to dance.

Not unlike the white rockers creating "new wave" in answer to corporate rock, Simmons and several like-minded young men began ferreting out a new music. Together with Curtis Walker (b. 1959), who sold so much Coco Leaf incense he was nicknamed Kurtis Blow,[11] Simmons went to cavernous gay clubs like the Loft and the Gallery, "because that was the hip thing to do in Harlem," he says. "We used to take tons of hallucinogenic drugs and go there, straight guys standing with their arms crossed. That was the hip place for music and we all wanted to be in the music business."

Just after his sophomore year at CCNY, Simmons got arrested carrying "six bags of weed," he says. "My parents were furious. I got in a lot of trouble. I had a whole year's worth of reporting to a parole officer. I'm two steps away from living in jail. But that gave me the energy to start my own shit; it made me become a club promoter."

He and his friends formed The Force, promoting rap parties for collegians like themselves in clubs like Harlem's venerable Small's Paradise. Rap, the music that would make him famous, was springing up all over uptown New York in the mid-1970s. It grew out of black American preaching; the mid-1960s rhymes of Cassius Clay; the black power poetry of 1960s artists like The Last Poets (who'd been introduced to the Baby Boom via the soundtrack of Mick Jagger's movie debut in the decadent film *Performance)*; jazz fusion pioneers like Gil Scott-Heron (b. 1949), who recorded the proto-rap "The Revolution Will Not Be

Televised" in 1969; boastful black radio deejays like Frankie Crocker and Pete "DJ" Jones; and "toasting," a marriage of West African praise singing with Jamaican reggae. In the early 1970s, toasters like Big Youth and U-Roy would rhyme over "dub"—instrumental—reggae recordings played on massive sound systems at outdoor dances in Jamaica; by 1973, recordings of their toasts made it to America.

Jamaican-born Clive Campbell (b. 1954), who'd come to the Bronx in 1967, began playing deejay at dance parties in a housing project's rec room. One night, he noticed he could isolate sections where the funk records he played broke into percussion. Experimenting, he discovered that by using two turntables, he could continuously hip-hop between those percussion tracks—which he'd name "the breaks"—driving dancers to distraction. He'd also "toast" his friends over the sound system, chanting rhymes about them. When he began playing regularly at a club called Twilight Zone, proving that his raps could fill a club more cheaply than bands could, his solo experiment turned into a social scene.[12]

Other deejays like Joseph "Grandmaster Flash" Saddler (b. 1958) and Afrika Bambaata (b. Kevin Donovan, 1960), a former street gang member dedicated to ending gang violence, were attracting crowds of their own, at parties on basketball courts and in parks, schools and clubs all over the Bronx and Queens. The deejays were constantly trying to top each other. Grand Wizard Theodore accidentally invented scratching in 1975, moving a record back and forth in syncopated rhythm beneath a turntable's needle. Renamed Kool DJ Herc, Campbell added dancers, the Nigger Twins, who inspired a new dance style called breaking, a series of lighting-fast moves and acrobatics performed during the breaks by competitive dancers Herc called b-boys.[13] Bambaata formed a troupe called Zulu Nation; Grandmaster Flash had the Furious Five.

Dancers flocked to their parties. As rap spread, the art evolved through rapping battles between the musical gangs. Graffiti artists were fellow outsiders, so these new ghetto prophets, inspired by a messenger named Taki who wrote his name, or "tag," on every surface he passed, painted ever more elaborate pieces of art on tenement and subway walls. Some of them allied with the rappers and began papering black neighborhoods with leaflets for shows. Bootleg tapes started circulating. And the cultural collision of art, movement, and music soon had a name: hip-hop. Simmons and his friends, relatively new to the scene, were determined to be part of it. Wearing a big gold medallion spelling out his nickname, Rush, Simmons promoted his first hip-hop party in 1977. Worried about debuting in the hothouse of Harlem, he started in Queens with his school friend Kurtis Blow as the entertainment. Under the slogan "Rush: The Force in College Parties," they promoted dances starring Blow, Eddie Cheba, DJ Hollywood and Grandmaster Flash, and their business grew so fast that within months, they were filling the ballroom at the Hotel Diplomat in Manhattan with up to 4,000 paying customers.

Rappers "were bigger than music stars, and they didn't have records!" Simmons exults. But they didn't draw quite the same crowd as the one pressed against the velvet ropes of Xenon, the Studio 54-like disco just up the block. Street kids and, very soon, suburban wannabes, they could get rowdy. Simmons admitted to *Village Voice* journalist Nelson George that there were often security problems; he and Blow would sometimes take refuge in the Diplomat's bulletproof box office.[14]

Rap was "totally from the streets," Simmons says. "A rebellion."

STEVE WOZNIAK WAS a believer in the hacker ideal. While he was working on the Apple, a competing idea entered the PC Garden of Eden and was quickly condemned as an unmitigated evil. Initially, the first small computer, the Altair, was shipped without an operating system. Then two computer-savvy friends from Seattle, Paul Allen (b. 1953) and Bill Gates (b. 1955), co-founders of what would become the software behemoth Microsoft, heard about the Altair and offered to create a basic program to run it. It was called Altair BASIC, modeled on the clunky but easy-to-use BASIC programming language developed at Dartmouth in the 1960s, and subsequently championed by the People's Computer Company in Berkeley and its founder, Bob Albrecht. Albrecht, a *Whole Earth Catalog*-type character, was the Johnny Appleseed of West Coast computing, and BASIC was his seed.

After Allen successfully sold the program to Altair, Gates dropped out of Harvard and began to debug—or perfect—it. Unfortunately, Altair's manufacturer had already started shipping machines without BASIC, so members of Homebrew, who'd gotten hold of an earlier version, started copying it and giving it away for free, as hackers had done since the 1960s. Gates, already working on versions for other microcomputer brands, was furious. His dream was "a computer on every desk and in every home, (all) running Microsoft software." This copying was a bad start. In an act that would reverberate for decades to come, Gates, then nineteen, wrote a widely circulated "Open Letter to Hobbyists," pleading with them to stop stealing his software. "Who can afford to do professional work for nothing?" Gates wrote. The Homebrew hackers dismissed him as a whiner.

From then on, the computing world broke down into two competing (if sometimes overlapping) camps, a war between two Baby Boom paradigms. On one side were post-hippies like Wozniak, Gage, Felsenstein and Joy, still openly idealistic. On the other were the new vanguard, folks like the software tycoon Gates, who believed in profit-making, proprietary, closed-model computing. Somewhere in the middle were the Apple crew, who played both ends against the middle, acting tastefully hip while they sold a proprietary hardware system (Jobs won out over Wozniak on that score).

At first, the big computer companies couldn't have cared less. Hewlett-Packard, for instance, had turned down Wozniak when he brought his Apple design to them. In 1977, major corporations like Commodore and Radio Shack began marketing microcomputers. It wasn't until fall 1979, though, that the still-quixotic microcomputer met its Sancho Panza, when VisiCalc, a spreadsheet or accounting program written for the Apple II by a Harvard Business School student named Dan Bricklin (b. 1951), went on the market. It was the so-called "killer app" that introduced first thousands, then millions of people to computing. The spreadsheet was followed by word processors. "With that combination," Gage says, "the little ugly box on your desk became useful."

By 1980, Apple was earning more than $100 million a year and poised to go public.

The next year, the giant IBM finally admitted it had been humbled by microcomputers and introduced its PC, but it, too, needed an operating system. Every consumer computer had one. Operating systems were necessary buffers between normal folk and the arcane language of machines. Apple had its own. Most others microcomputers used CP/M, for "Control Program/Monitor." IBM wanted CP/M, but a series of mishaps kept its executives from buying it before they met with Bill Gates about his BASIC program. When Gates learned IBM had no operating system, he sprang into action. A nearby company had one called QDOS ("quick and dirty operating system).[15] As John Gage tells the story: "Gates went out the back door, bought QDOS for some tiny amount of money, ran back to the IBM guys and said, 'I've got it for you! When do you want it? And by the way, we need an exclusive contract because you have to get to a volume that will make it worth my time. I just want a little part, but I want that little part.'"

Gates named the program MS-DOS. "He got a monopoly contract with IBM," Gage relates, "and off he goes."

* * *

UNDER JIM FOURATT'S direction, Hurrah was an instant success—a rock disco, an artistic anti-Studio, and an early cauldron of what would later become known as alternative culture—the Caucasian analogue to hip-hop's revolt against disco. What Hurrah's clientele lacked in money and power was more than made up for in independent creativity. "They all came to New York to be downtown artists," Fouratt says. "I wanted to bring the downtown culture uptown." Roy Cohn, the right-wing icon, a closet homosexual and lawyer for and constant presence at Studio 54, "would never have gotten into Hurrah," says Fouratt.

In place of disco, Hurrah hosted bands like Gang of Four, the Contortions, the Dead Kennedys, and the Feelies—and paid them a large portion of the door receipts. After nine months of his socialism, capitalism reared its ugly head when the club's owners demanded Fouratt pay *them* more and the bands less, and he walked out in a huff. Fouratt's next collaboration, with a German émigré named Rudolf Pieper (b. 1946), started badly. In October 1979, their first club, Pravda, opened the day American hostages were seized in Iran and folded after only two nights. Their next venture, which opened in spring 1980, was a raging success.

In part, that was because Studio 54's Steve Rubell and Ian Schrager had gone to jail that February. Rubell's brazenness ("The profits are astronomical," he would boast. "Only the Mafia does better") and his and Schrager's visibility had brought the law down on the duo. It turned out they'd stuffed bags of cash in the ceiling and tucked cocaine into one of their two sets of books. Their conviction for income tax evasion was a sign of the times. The 1980s were definitely going to be different.

MARIANNE WILLIAMSON'S WANDERINGS brought her to New York City, still intensely unhappy, drugging, drinking and overeating. Linda Obst, who'd moved to New York, introduced Williamson to Albert Goldman, a one-time Columbia University English professor who'd just completed a biography of Lenny Bruce. She became his Girl Friday. When she went through a painful break up with a boyfriend, he fired her, later recalling her as "profoundly confused" and constantly crying. "He certainly did not have eyes to see the likes of me," says Williamson, who nonetheless considered him a mentor.

Soon she was on the road again, ending up with a musician boyfriend in San Francisco, where she practiced Zen Buddhism, read the existentialists, and lingered over a Ouija board. "Most people are afraid of change," she says. "I'm afraid of not changing. I think that's what God does with people in their twenties. I wasn't on the straight path that my mother would have wanted me to be on, but hello, it turned out okay. I write books now based on what I learned then.

After she and her boyfriend returned to New York, she started appearing as a cabaret singer in small Manhattan clubs. Between songs she talked about the history of the music she was performing. "I would do long monologues about Gershwin, Kern and Harold Arlen and how so many of them were children of Jewish immigrants, the children of cantors, and how fascinating it was that they became lyricists because their parents couldn't speak the language very well. And how American popular music, torch songs and rock 'n' roll, grew out of gospel and Jewish music, out of a yearning for God." Williamson's patter often went over better than her singing.

Williamson first saw the 1,200-page, three-volume book called *A Course in Miracles* on a table in the apartment she and her boyfriend had borrowed. Later disavowed by its author, an emotionally disturbed, Jewish-born Columbia University psychology teacher named Helen Schucman, *A Course in Miracles* was supposedly dictated over a span of seven years by "a voice" the author decided was Jesus Christ. Billed as a correction to Christianity, stressing love and forgiveness, the course posits that poverty and illness, pain and suffering, materialism and negativity are all unreal, that only God is real, and that surrendering to God and doing good works will engender "miracles": good health and epiphanies of self-knowledge and self-worth. "God has established miracles as my right," the course proclaims, a gospel of divine entitlement likely to appeal to baby boomers. The course's lack of organization (its publishers encourage independent study) was another selling point to a generation turned off by the Judeo-Christian establishment. "Offering religion without rules, salvation without sacrifice," as one critic put it,[16] a cult sprang up around the book, which has sold about a million copies since it was published in 1975.

Williamson read the introduction and was intrigued. When she delved deeper, she was put off by the book's overt Christianity. The following winter, Williamson found herself reinspired to seek out a copy, but before she could—*miracle!*—her boyfriend brought one home.

"We had not talked about the book that whole year," she says. "I looked at him in surprise and he said, 'I thought it was time.'" Now she saw its use of Christian terminology as a metaphor for unconditional love and acceptance, and began to accept its message herself. A few weeks later, when she returned to the Foundation for Inner Peace, a non-profit organization that began as a group supporting parapsychological research, but eventually became best known as the publishers of the book, to buy a copy for a friend, she met a woman who was flying to Williamson's hometown of Houston that very day to give a talk about the book. Williamson, who'd decided the course was "spiritual psychotherapy,"[17] was intrigued to learn you could make a living doing such things. For the next year, she studied the course and worked at the foundation. Then, in 1979, she broke up with her boyfriend and abruptly went home to Houston. She's never said why.

"Did something horrible happen to you?" I ask her.

"Yes."

"Want to talk about it?"

"No. I can't comfortably do that. But it humbled me, and if you speak from a place of having been through something, people subconsciously know it."

Which may be why, at this point, when I ask if she feels the sexual behaviors of the 1970s would be possible today, her answer, referring to a novel and film about a woman who goes to bars looking for men and finds deadly trouble instead, seems portentous, even if it is also a bit of a non sequitur.

"If my daughter did what I did I'd be scared to death," she says. "Even before *Looking for Mr. Goodbar* came out."

The horrible thing, whatever it was, was followed by "what I think would today be termed a nervous breakdown—a highly underrated method of spiritual transformation," Williamson says. She lived with her mother in Houston for a few months before she took an apartment, worked more odd jobs, sang in more cabarets, turned thirty, and married a businessman in a big, traditional wedding.[18] The marriage lasted "a minute and a half," according to Williamson.[19] It's another moment in her life—"a wake-up call," she says—that she prefers to not discuss in anything but general terms. "In astrology, there's something called a Saturn return: the first significant trial period in a person's life," she says. "You become who you are between twenty-eight and thirty. Rarely does a person's life not take some radical turn."

Entering five-day-a-week therapy with a psychiatrist who coincidentally turned out to be another devotee of *A Course in Miracles*, Williamson slowly started getting better and had the notion that she could help herself by helping others. She opened the Heights Book Store, a homey place where she sold New Age books, ran a lecture series and arts club, sang torch songs on Sundays, and started a *Course in Miracles* study group.[20] She began remodeling the bookstore in 1983, but one night, after the carpenters left, she had the sudden premonition that she wouldn't be staying put.

A few weeks later, a girlfriend announced she was moving to Los Angeles, and suggested to Williamson that with her knowledge of books and metaphysics, she could get work there with the Philosophical Research Society. Founded in 1934, the PRS was led by an occultist and thirty-third-degree Freemason named Manley P. Hall (b. 1901), who authored books and pamphlets on what he called "esoteric teachings." His grand opus, *The Secret Teachings of All Ages*, encompassed Eastern religion, Masons, Druids, the Kabbala, Rosicrucianism, Gnosticism, Atlantis, the riddle of the Sphinx, parapsychology, astrology, the occult, mysticism, the controversy over who wrote William Shakespeare's plays, mystic Christianity and the Knights of the Round Table.

Though he came out of the tradition of American Transcendentalists, Williamson says, Hall's interests overlapped those of boomers on a quest for enlightenment and spiritual guidance. That phenomenon was reaching its peak of influence at the end of 1970s, just as Williamson hunkered down back in Houston. "The esoteric tradition says that in the last twenty-five years of every century there's a yearning for deeper understanding," she says.

Promising the dawn of a utopian Age of Aquarius, speaking of karma, auras, channeling, meditation and reincarnation, carrying crystals and Tarot cards and giving off a whiff of divine mystery, pantheistic New Age religionists were in synch with the counterculture's lingering distrust of science, logic and materialism. "Most of us came to see that a drug takes you to the top of the mountain but can't keep you there," says Williamson. "As a matter of fact, you will be hauled violently back to the bottom. Because ultimately everybody must do the climb themselves."

Williamson disagrees with those who say the human potential movements of the 1970s were a rejection of Judeo-Christian beliefs. "It was definitely an opening to the mystical elements of Christianity," she says. "And for Judaism, it wasn't so much escaping the confines of dogma. Rather, we were a generation that hadn't been taught our own religion. The great tradition of Eastern European Judaism was killed off by Hitler. So we were not taught the mystical roots of our own religion. The Eastern religions never lost their mystical roots. In twentieth-century America Judaism and Christianity played footsies under the table with the materialistic order. So the children said, If I can't get my mystical food here, I'll go wherever I can find it."

DAVID MCINTOSH VOTED for Jimmy Carter in the 1976 election, or rather, voted *against* Richard Nixon's appointee, Gerald Ford. He was, he says, "involved in the remnants of the left" at Yale, at least until he joined the Political Union, a campus group that brought speakers like George McGovern and William F. Buckley to campus. It was divided into factions ranging the political spectrum. "The progressive party on the far left was basically dead, defeated," he recalls. The liberals were "the big monolithic party," he says, "mouthing nostrums but not really that thoughtful. That's where I thought I was coming from."

But his politics had begun to evolve. While he was at Yale, the Political Union returned to its original role as a debating society, and he took part. One conservative got under his skin his junior year when she scolded him and told him his Christianity and belief in individual freedoms were anathema to liberalism. "She challenged me as a friend, as a philosophical adversary within the union. And I realized you don't want to guarantee equal results, you want to give people equal opportunity and let them make the most of it. And that was more a conservative than a liberal notion. The label I'd given myself wasn't in accord with the things I believed."

By 1980, the year he graduated from Yale, his conversion was complete. He'd begun to feel that Jimmy Carter couldn't do anything right, and the Democrats running against him—Jerry Brown and Ted Kennedy—weren't much better. Ronald Reagan, the former governor of California, who was running for the Republican nomination for President, was more appealing.

"At the beginning of the year, I was still clinging to the notion that I was some sort of progressive Democrat," he says. "But I remember watching Carter's malaise speech, and then watching Reagan harken back to the things Dan Quayle had expressed that I didn't really pick up on in high school, that you can change things from a conservative perspective." He announced he'd voted for Reagan at the family Thanksgiving a few weeks after the election. "Traitor," they called him.

"I've worked at gradually winning some of them over," he says.

CYNTHIA BOWMAN AND Paul Kantner's love affair was over, but their professional relationship continued. She was with the rock star when he had a cerebral hemorrhage in his room at the Chateau Marmont hotel that October, as the Jefferson Starship was recording an album in Los Angeles.

"We called an ambulance, and because he was Paul Kantner, everybody assumed it was a drug overdose," Bowman says. "I tried to explain it wasn't." When the city ambulance insisted on taking them to a city hospital, Bowman forced them to stop on the street as they passed Cedars Sinai, one of the city's best hospitals, and carried Kantner in through the emergency room door herself.

It looked as if he wasn't going to make it. "We were on the phone working out the details of his will, he was saying goodbye to his daughter; it was horrible," Bowman says. "They were just about to crack his head open when there was a miraculous recovery, the bleeding stopped; the doctors said the chances of that happening were one in a million." Two weeks later, Kantner was released from the hospital and returned to San Francisco to complete the record there. Then Grace Slick, who'd joined Alcoholics Anonymous in the interim, rejoined the band, and they all went back on the road together.

"I don't know how we managed to survive," Kantner told a reporter the following summer, backstage at a Starship show.[21] Bowman thinks she knows. The wife of a band member had just found religion, she says. "The whole band was in the chapel praying."

HAVING LOST HER professional momentum in the special anti-corruption office, Leslie Crocker Snyder decided to step off the career tread-mill in 1979 and spend more time with her family. "I can't conceive of a life without a career, but I can't conceive of a life without a family first." Snyder had always wanted to see criminal law from the defense side of the court-room. So she opened a midtown Manhattan office, and took private cases and court-appointed jobs for indigent defendants. There were so few women doing the latter in federal courts that she found herself much in demand. She handled sexual harassment lawsuits and defended a bank rob-ber and a vicious murderer. The latter was convicted, but Snyder took some pride in the fact that she kept the jury deliberating for three days and nights.

She enjoyed her three years as a part-time defense lawyer. "I realized that I really loved being in the courtroom," she says. And that she had a greater affinity for prosecution than for criminal defense. "But when you're in that courtroom, you are trying to win," she adds. "And it became absolutely clear to me that I am a total advocate. Yeah, I was viewed as aggressive and ballsy, but I think of myself that way."

So when her old boss John Keenan asked her to rejoin him as chief of New York's Arson Task Force in fall 1982, she jumped at the chance to supervise a staff of young lawyers and to write new arson legislation. She'd always planned to go back into public service, and her children were both in school. But years before, Keenan had also encouraged her to submit an application for a judgeship—and suddenly her name was in play.

Snyder didn't have a lot of respect for the judges in New York's criminal courts, a collection of barely competent political appointees and eccentrics. (One judge always wore sunglasses; another carried a gun.) Many got their jobs as so-called "midnight appointments" by departing officials, but Ed Koch, New York's new anti-machine mayor, had changed that, instituting a screening process and long-lasting judicial reforms.

After interviews with a number of screening committees, Snyder met Koch, who made the final appointments from a list of approved candidates. "I hear you're too aggressive; that's the only knock I've heard against you," Koch said. She bit her tongue and got the job. Years later, she reminded the famously aggressive Koch of his comment, and told him he'd had a lot of nerve to make it.

HER HIGH SCHOOL principal called Kathryn Bond Stockton to his office shortly before graduation to say that under no circumstances could she mention Christ in her valedictory speech, as a member of her evangelical group had before her. Her parents defended their daughter's rights, assuring him she would be tasteful and thoughtful. In her speech, she talked about transformation, "about how lives can take right-angle turns," she says. "The truth wasn't told why *my* right-angle turn was necessary, but I don't know if I was conscious of that."

Stockton enrolled at the University of Connecticut to study biochemistry in anticipation of becoming a medical missionary. "I'd basically been a math-science head all through high school, so I was very highly trained, I had won all the medals, but I started to get bored." Tired of calculus and chemistry, she tried classes in experimental psychology, philosophy and ancient languages her second year.

As time went by, her evangelical friends started getting boring, too. She'd joined a group called the Navigators that expected its members to "get up at this time of day and read your Bible in this way and I thought it all reeked of Republican militarism, which was striking me as bogus." So she joined a liberal Christian group, where at a meeting some gay Christians addressed the Bible's proscription against homosexuality and how they interpreted it. "I'd never met a person in college who said they were gay." At the time she was dating a boy, an older philosophy student who loved Gore Vidal and played piano.

Stockton wrote her senior thesis on the paradoxical nature of Christianity, how it puts together apparent opposites like God and man. "You have to embrace two things at once: Death is life," she says. "And that was enormously appealing to somebody who had been a contradiction throughout her life and needed to hold opposites together."

She thought about entering an evangelical seminary; her brother suggested Yale Divinity School. She snapped that Yale was godless, but then became intrigued. "Evangelicalism believes that you have God-ordained gender roles, and that men can be pastors and women can't," she says. "I really chafed against that." So she applied to Yale, won admission, and within a year discovered she preferred intellectual challenge to evangelical certainty. That year, she met her first feminists—"very powerful, interesting women"—in her dorm. Then she realized she was also surrounded by, "sexually experimental people trying to figure out what their gender is," she says. "And I'm beginning to think, 'You know what? God can love gay people.'"

By her second year at Yale, Stockton had been politicized. At a time when most protest was coming from the right—from anti-tax activists, right-to-life advocates and opponents of gay rights—the anti-nuclear movement, revived in the mid-1970s after "No Nukes" protests at the Seabrook nuclear power plant in New Hampshire, was ablaze following the March 1979 accident at the Three Mile Island power plant in Pennsylvania. A Washington demonstration that May felt like old times, thanks to the presence of comedian Dick Gregory, baby doctor Benjamin Spock, consumer advocate Ralph Nader, and Jane Fonda and her then-husband, Tom Hayden. Then, in September, a series of No Nukes concerts at New York's Madison Square Garden revived the rock-protest connection. President Carter's announcement the following February that he was reinstituting draft registration, followed hard by his abortive raid on Iran to free the U.S. hostages, gave the new "movement" a second front.

Stockton's political awakening followed a religious conversion. "I was no longer an evangelical; I was a political Christian," she says. "I'm writing papers on God as a person. To come down as this oppressed person and die destitute on a cross—what could be better than that?"

Election Night 1980 was meaningful in quite a different way. "I was just crushed," Stockton says. "I remember saying to my mother, 'It's so ironic. I go through all these years being an evangelical Christian when they have no political clout anywhere in the country, and just when I'm no longer an evangelical, here comes the right wing.'"

Stockton's Yale friends were intimately involved with the Plowshares movement, a loose group of about sixty religious activists that began on September 8, 1980, when the longtime antiwar Jesuit priests Daniel and Philip Berrigan and six others entered a General Electric plant in

Philadelphia, damaged missile nose cones and poured blood on documents. In Connecticut, their focus was the Electric Boat shipyard, maker of Trident nuclear submarines and a leading beneficiary of the new Reagan administration's massively increased defense spending. Stockton's new friends demonstrated at Electric Boat often. "They were passionately involved and I was extremely interested in their passion," she says.

Midway through her final year at Yale, Stockton befriended another "straight" woman in her dorm who also had a tendency to date gay men, and they became lovers. "I was thrilled," Stockton says. "Both of us having our first sexual relationship; she's having like not a shred of guilt, wants to tell everybody, I don't know what to do with that. I'm not in New York, not in San Francisco. Nobody is talking about gays outside of those places. I did not want to let my parents know, and I did not want to cease to be this person I had worked so hard to be, excellent student, scholar, athlete—I was imprisoned by that 'good' thing."

Stockton tried to quit the love affair. She left for graduate school at Brown in the fall, but ended up back at Yale most weekends. When her lover moved to nearby Providence to become a hospital chaplain, she finally decided to let her parents "see this relationship unfold before their eyes," hoping "they would just know what it was."

IN 1980, THE future Nina Hartley decided to go back to school. She began taking classes at a junior college and realized she wanted to become a nurse-midwife, "to help women, and also because I decided that was the only way I was going to learn to surrender. To really let go is to have to go through labor. You've got to let go; it's a natural force you cannot resist. My feminism came straight through the natural birth movement, out of the stirrups and the drugs and the strapping down. I'd known about my alienation and repression since I was twelve years old. I knew then how body-armored I was. I knew I needed to learn."

Her midwife was about to deliver her. He worked in the coffee shop where she'd gotten a job. "Hi," he said, "my name's Dave, and I'm non-monogamous." He was a thirty-one-year-old political activist from Detroit, a former member of SDS who'd moved to Berkeley for its politics and was disillusioned to find they'd become elitist, divisive and were on the wane. He lived—in a committed but nonexclusive relationship— with a woman named Bobby Lilly, and had long since learned to warn any woman he was attracted to right off the bat about his sexual preferences.

Dave became Mitzi's confidante. "He put words to what I was feeling," she says. "And he wasn't coming on to me sexually, because he had three other girlfriends." They'd hang out, give each other massages, and talk. She slept with a woman he was dating. Finally, she asked him to sleep with her.

Immediately, Mitzi found the sexual happiness that had eluded her. "He was the first competent lover I'd had," she says, "who could play and stop and go and give and take. He'd been dating asexually experienced, feminist co-eds who believed in their right to sexual pleasure. He took pride and delight in being good and passionate. The morning after our first time, we're in the shower together, and I reach up and take out my diaphragm and there was blood. My period had started, but the mess didn't faze him. I knew he was the guy for me."

Incredibly, Dave's lover Bobby Lilly approved. "She liked the way Dave acted when he saw me," Hartley says. "I remember thinking it was too good to be true that there was someone as cool as Bobby. But at first, I so wanted nonmonogamy to be possible that I didn't go meet her in case it was all a lie." Hartley grins ruefully.

Understandably, Mitzi's boyfriend, still on the scene, saw Dave as a rival. He'd found a new young girl to mentor, which had made Mitzi want to win him back; but once she did, she didn't want him anymore. About that point Dave, leaving town for six months, finally convinced Mitzi to meet Lilly, and though she was, as Hartley puts it, "ninety-five percent het," the two women became lovers during three-way sex with Dave. "She's my first regular pussy," Hartley says. "And she's so receptive, so femme, such a pillow queen, 'More, ooh, good, more, more.' It was like getting a Stradivarius your first time out."

Lilly started hanging out with Mitzi and ended up in bed with her and the soon-to-be-gone boyfriend. "She and I never fucked unless Dave was there," Hartley says, "because she needs dick. I mean girls are nice, but give her a penis, thank you. So we end up in bed together, and my boyfriend is transformed into a masterful lover. With me he never lasted more than five minutes, but Bobby's coming and coming, having one orgasm after another. After that, our sex problems were my fault. And that was the end." After a brief but futile spell of couples counseling, she and the boyfriend finally parted ways early in 1982. Mitzi was still living in the house in which she'd grown up. That September, Dave and Bobby moved in, and have been there ever since.

Dave was acquainted with the San Francisco adult entertainment scene, and would sometimes, take the bus across the bay to San Francisco, and visit the Mitchell brothers' O'Farrell Theater. At Mitzi's urging, he shared his favorite stops with her—she enjoyed peep shows where "loops," continuously cycling porno shorts, played in coin-operated booths—and they would often discuss her unrequited desire to be a stripper, to have that kind of confidence. For months they used it as a private fantasy. Mitzi would dance for him. He would teach her moves, tell her what he liked to see and what went on in an audience member's head.

Mitzi had begun to develop a sexual philosophy based on her decade-long pursuit of information in the Bay Area liberated zone. Exhibitionism, voyeurism and bisexuality were all normal, she'd decided, as long as they were consensual. It was all about "retaking, reclaiming, defining sexuality for yourself," she says. "I like looking at girls."

But should she—could she—become a sex worker herself? She, Dave and Bobby began a yearlong discussion of that question that resembled an SDS self-criticism session. Children (and beneficiaries) of the sexual revolution, they asked themselves whether it was possible to be in the sex industry without betraying their political beliefs. Could Mitzi fuck for money, even if she enjoyed it, and still be a feminist? Was it wrong to get pleasure from arousing men? Could she take money and not be an exploiter? Was her desire to exhibit herself defensible? What about her desire to bed other women? "Can this be done?" Hartley says. "Can we indulge this fantasy? Dave was a purist. It was important to him not to muddy his politics, but at the same time he was digging having a coed stripper girlfriend."

Once they decided she would try it, they invented a character, Nina Hartley, for her to play. "Now she's me," Hartley says. "Fifteen years ago, she was my idealized self—confident, sexy, comfortable with herself, all the things Mitzi wanted to be. We took my exhibitionist, bisexual, people-pleasing nature and gave it a backbone and a form as opposed to being strictly hedonist and narcissistic. We channeled Mitzi into a complete ideology. What would a feminist sex worker look like? What would she believe? How would she act? What would she do?" Later, when anyone charged that Dave was her Svengali, Nina would patiently explained that this was what she'd wanted long before she met him, and that acting that way was anathema to him.

Finally, one Tuesday night, they went together for her debut at the Sutter Street Cinema, a sex emporium. "He's in the audience and I'm in the dressing room with all the girls," Hartley says. "And I was the only amateur, the other girls were only there for the twenty-five dollars you get for showing up. And I'm terrified, they're all slapping on the bracelets, putting on the makeup. I was never cool, never hip, I disdained popularity contests and girls who would tilt their head over and brush their hair and toss it up. I'd had the lesbian hatred and distrust of women like that and men who liked them. Real superiority feelings. But then I'm doing a show, loving it, dancing, fucking myself with a vibrator on stage. It was so cool. The first time I was in a roomful of naked people I was immediately at home."

Mitzi, or rather Nina, had found her place in the world. "My first sex job after the kissing booth was exactly what I wanted—a live lesbian show in a peep booth," she says. "It was a round room, mirrored windows around it, chair, paper towels, wastebasket, revolving round bed, another girl. I loved it because I wasn't dancing for the guys, I was dancing for the mirrors, having sex with a girl, then we both went our separate ways. I got into the sex business because I was too chickenshit to be a whore, and I wanted easy, effortless access to pussy." She also got to indulge her own voyeurism. If they wanted to, the men in the booths around her could switch on a light so the performers could watch them masturbate. "That was the best," she says. "I got to look in a safe environment."

Six months later, she moved to the O'Farrell, the pinnacle of the live porn business, and added lap-dancing to her repertoire, gyrating on men's laps for a few dollars a minute. She did it every weekend for a year and a half while continuing nursing school. "I would take the bus over," she recalls. "Loved the lap dancing. Loved the actual contact with the guys, the casualness of it, the fact that there were rules and regulations and limits, but within that you were free to negotiate your own behavior. If I could have jerked them off, I would have. If I could have given blow jobs, I would have. And I was doing a dildo show, and every week I'd ask the girls, you want company onstage? So, sometimes once a week, sometimes twice a night, I got to be on the stage with the girl doing a hard-core sex show. It was sex without relationships, a supportive, safe context. None of that relationship shit. I didn't want to be in love with you to have sex with you."

She was an instant hit with audiences—and no wonder; her enthusiasm showed. "I love showing them my body and they'd look and they'd be enraptured," she recalls. "Absolutely attentive and respectful. And I realized that first year how much power there was in not hating them for looking at me. And I realized that talking dirty is not about giving the guy what you think he wants. Talking dirty is telling him what's real. My clit, my pussy, my breasts, what I like. And they never got tired of hearing it because it was sex talk by a half-naked girl sitting on their lap. And I realized how easy it was to make them profoundly happy. And I knew they weren't going to follow me home." That's because Dave would always show up at the end of her shift.

PRISON DIDN'T LESSEN Tim Scully's interest in consciousness expansion. While in a halfway house in 1979, he continued making biofeedback instruments. One institution interested in his work was the Stanford Research Institute, which was studying parapsychology—remote viewing, telepathy, precognition and telekinesis—funded by the military. "On odd-numbered days I believe that they're real, on even-numbered days I'm skeptical," Scully says. The researchers at SRI thought Scully's equipment—which allowed two test subjects to synchronize their brain waves—might increase parapsychological abilities.

"It's real stuff being done by real scientists," he says, "but when you get into parapsychology, the bar gets raised exponentially because the results are so hard to believe. You really-really-really have to prove it." In order to do so, Scully formed a company, Pacific Bionic Systems, to build non-vocal communication and biofeedback instruments (including electric trains that ran faster when burn victims learned to direct their blood flow to regions needing healing, and a Pong game that helped teach patients to control damaged muscles). He also manufactured a machine designed by a researcher to encourage extrasensory perception—and ended up teaching a course in designing equipment to measure ephemeral parapsychological phenomena.

In the worlds in which he operated, Scully found that his criminal record didn't hurt, and sometimes helped. "People in biofeedback or parapsychology or the computer industry all tended to have a pretty positive view of somebody who had been involved with psychedelics," he says. Still, denied a job at a Mendocino County community college because of his felony record, Scully became extra-cautious. "I didn't go to Grateful Dead concerts or hang out with people I had known before, because I didn't want to be in the wrong place at the wrong time and get in trouble again," he says.

He hadn't lost the business abilities that got him his own house in college. By the early 1980s, Scully's little biofeedback business had grown into a corporation selling and servicing microcomputer systems and running a psycho-physiological research lab. Scully also taught and lectured at a number of colleges, joined several professional organizations, and, after the FDA began regulating biofeedback instruments, adding expensive and complex approvals to the process, branched out into custom equipment design, making complete physiological monitoring systems and a microcomputer that monitored weather inside tornadoes.

He liked computers. "Programming gives you an opportunity to construct a world of your own where you're completely in control, and the outcome depends on how good a job you do," he says. "It's very attractive to introverts because it's less messy than dealing with real people, who are so much less predictable. On another level, as computers got less expensive and more powerful, there were tremendous possibilities for doing socially useful things with them. And on the more crass level the microcomputer era created really good opportunities for making a living. So it's been a wild ride."

Scully went to work for the Children's Television Workshop (albeit through a subcontractor) when it began planning an amusement park based on the PBS children's show *Sesame Street*. The park was originally going to feature biofeedback computer games. When budget cuts killed that project, Scully designed coin-box and keyboard interfaces, and then wrote educational games. Late in 1982, he wrote his first computer game, Honey Hunt, for Milton Bradley, the toy company. He went on to write more games for computers built by Atari, Apple, VIC, and Sony. Once again, he was changing the consciousness of children and through them, the world—only this time he was doing it completely legally.

BARBARA LEDEEN'S PERSONAL and political paralysis lasted through the Carter administration. To fight her way out of depression, she needed to "work out who has the truth," she says. "That was the only way that you could find something worth believing in." She was hardly alone.

Ledeen's conversion had begun even before she left Italy. Like many, she considered the revelations of Aleksandr Solzhenitsyn's *The Gulag Archipelago*, published in 1974, a turning point. Then came the communist takeover of Southeast Asia in 1976. Within a year, so-called "boat people" began to flee the new Marxist regimes in Vietnam, Laos, and Cambodia, as news came from those countries of killing, torture and mass suicides. Many gained a new perspective on the "liberation" movements they'd once supported without question. Ledeen was stunned, in 1979, when Joan Baez testified before Congress on the plight of the boat people and published an open letter—signed by eighty-five prominent activists—to the Socialist Republic of Vietnam charging that "the cruelty, violence and oppression practiced by foreign powers in your country for more than a century continue today under the present regime." Says Ledeen, "It took enormous devotion to the ideal of truth to look at the boat people and say, 'Omigod, I bear some responsibility.'"

In 1981, Michael Ledeen was hired as a special adviser to Alexander Haig, Ronald Reagan's Secretary of State, who'd spent several months at CSIS after leaving NATO. When Haig resigned in 1982, Ledeen became a consultant to National Security Advisor Robert McFarlane. Ever since, MIchael Ledeen has been shadowed by accusations of being, as the former journalist turned White House operative Sidney Blumenthal (b. 1948) once called him, "a mysterious ideological adventurer."

If that's true, this new career began when the Ledeens met a Russian dissident named Vladimir Bukovsky in 1976. Together he and Michael set up "a network of people in Europe, working to overthrow the Soviet Union by sending in computers and tapes and printers and fax machines," Barbara says. In 1981, they were part of the loose association of organizations that created Radio Free Kabul, broadcasting into Afghanistan, where Soviet troops were fighting anti-Communist *mujahadeen* guerrillas. In 1983, they formalized their operation, uniting groups from eleven totalitarian countries as Resistance International. It was funded, in part, by the National Endowment for Democracy, established by the U.S. Congress in 1983 to fight authoritarianism and promote democracy. Both Resistance International and a subsequent group begun by Bukovsky, the Center for Democracy, took a leading role in the ongoing—and eventually successful—effort to undermine the Soviets.

By 1982, Barbara Ledeen had given birth to a second child and was working as the assistant editor of *Biblical Archeology Review*, which ran an article on Jerusalem's Temple Mount, site of Solomon's ancient temple, where Abraham came to sacrifice his son Isaac; where Jesus taught and threw out the money-changers; and from which Mohammed ascended into the presence of Allah—an event commemorated by the Dome of the Rock, the Muslim mosque that now stands near the site. After fifteen years of research, an Israeli physicist had claimed to have found the foundation stone of the Temple, which held the Ark of the Covenant containing the tablets of the Ten Commandments—not under the mosque, as had long been assumed, but some 300 feet away. Ultranationalist Israelis demanded the Israeli government take over the Temple Mount, reserved for the Islamic faithful for fourteen centuries. Fundamentalist Christians, citing indications that the Second Coming was at hand, got into the fray.

Ledeen's teenage rejection of Judaism had wavered as the result of her marriage. She and her husband—who had strong pro-Israel sympathies and felt the Temple Mount had geopolitical implications—went to Israel to investigate. "I meet a bunch of Christians who are intelligent, erudite and articulate. I wouldn't call them a whole lot of fun, but these were not people to be contemptuous of. They're trying to live their life in accordance with what they believe to be true, trying to rise to a higher level of being." For Ledeen, this was a revelation on a par with meeting Bukovsky. "I was looking for something larger than myself to dedicate myself to," she says. "I now knew the world was not as narrow as I thought. I learned to look for the facts."

Ledeen's respect for facts continued to evolve, in large part, because of what she calls the disinformation campaign aimed at her husband. She says the smears were started by communists and repeated by American leftists to tarnish the Reagan regime and her husband, who has successfully pursued libel suits in Europe against some of them. [22] As the stories had it, he was supposedly in league with a secret lodge in Italy in the early 1980s. The lodge, the membership of which included leaders of Italy's intelligence service, to which Michael Ledeen had been a consultant, was said to have created a shadow regime within the Italian government. Ledeen had supposedly "set up" President Carter's brother, Billy, just before the 1980 election by revealing his business dealings with the Quadafi regime in Libya. In addition, he was supposed to have been responsible for fabricating the story of a "Bulgarian connection" in Mehmet Ali Agca's 1981 assassination attempt on Pope John Paul II, "framing the left for the crimes of the right," as leftist writer Alexander Cockburn put it. [23]

"The veil fell from my eyes as the attacks proceeded," Barbara says. She went to work for Reagan's Defense Department. She'd decided that "the [liberal] establishment had become completely anti-democratic, and we were the real revolutionaries."

BY MID-1978, MONEY had become a problem for the Leacock family. Victoria's parents were in an alimony fight. She left private school and entered New York's High School of Art and Design. Again, her attendance was sporadic. They had terrible luck with mother's helpers. One embezzled money, another quit by sticking a resignation note inside a sandwich she'd made for Victoria's lunch bag. "Glamour got me through," she says. "It was like my prize for being a nurse the other twenty-two hours a day."

Marilyn Leacock died on June 19, 1980. "I had a great mother until I was sixteen, and then I had my father," Victoria says. "He flew down that day." Coincidentally, the lease on the apartment where she'd lived was running out. He suggested she move to Tangiers and finish school at his alma mater, but she opted to live with the Rogers family, who'd offered her their spare room.

She still wanted to be an actress. She started a Xeroxed magazine called *Curtain Call*, and spent her spare time interviewing actors for it and then selling it in front of Broadway theaters. More important, she started dating. One of her first beaux was an artist who worked for the punk rock band The Ramones. He introduced her to a whole new world of nightclubs—the downtown equivalents to the uptown discos she'd frequented. "One night, five different people offered me cocaine," she says. "I said, 'No, no-no, no-no-no.' I went home. I was totally sober. It was midnight. And a woman's voice, perhaps it was my mother, said: 'Victoria, drugs will keep you sober, make you thin, you'll love them—and you'll die.' So that was why I've never tried drugs. It all made sense."

Though she didn't want drugs, she did want to lose her virginity. Unfortunately, many of the boys in her "theater-fashion-weirdo" clique in school were gay. She dated one for a year before realizing why he wasn't interested in having sex. "I was thrilled to find out," she exults. "It wasn't me!" She also learned that sex sometimes came with a high price. "I went to the abortion place many times with friends," she says.

She'd been apolitical most of her life. Nixon's resignation taught her that "everything was corrupt, you couldn't believe in anything," she says. She perceived Carter as a sincere failure. And Reagan scared the hell out of her. She'd visited Hiroshima when she was in Japan and had become obsessed with the idea of imminent nuclear obliteration. Reagan's militarism encouraged these fantasies, and his courting of the religious right "was really making us paranoid," she says. She found no solace in feminism, which suggests to her not Gloria Steinem or Simone de Beauvoir, but "feminist" commercials on TV, like the one featuring a woman singing, "I can bring home the bacon, fry it up in a pan, and never let you forget you're a man."

"Everything was media, I guess, in my neck of the woods," she says. The news the media carried in the 1980–81 school year was often scary. In December, Beatle John Lennon was shot and killed outside his home by a demented fan. Jodie Foster, child star of Martin Scorcese's *Taxi Driver*, was being stalked by another nut. Interest rates hovered at 16 percent. Children were being shot and killed in Atlanta. Blacks were rioting in England. Solidarity was striking in Gdansk, Poland. U.S. military advisers were heading to El Salvador, raising the specter of another Vietnam. And then Reagan was shot by John Hinkley a few months after his inauguration. Her friends walked around in a state of shock. "A lot of us wanted to escape, or we wanted to make things happen in theater or film to express our discontent," she says.

In spring 1981, Leacock accompanied friends to Adelphi University, a school in a nearby suburb, for auditions to enter its acting school. She hadn't given college a thought, but when she walked in, she announced that she wanted to try out, too. Though she hadn't even applied for admittance, she auditioned and to her amazement, she was accepted. That September, Leacock worked the lights in a school production of *Godspell*. "Of course, I fall in love with the person playing Christ," she says. His name was Jonathan Larson, and he was a senior and something of a prodigy. "I said to someone right then, 'He's the one.' After the rehearsal, I said something like, 'You're really talented and handsome,' and he went, 'You're really beautiful,' and that was the beginning."

Larson was different from anyone she'd ever met. Raised by intellectual Jewish parents in the suburbs, he wrote original cabaret productions for the drama department, many of them political. The first show Leacock worked on was *Sacrimoralimmorality*, an attack on the Moral Majority featuring Christian soldiers who gave Nazi salutes. Others were about abortion, women's rights, being gay. "There was a group anxiety that someone else's morals would take away our freedom," she says. But there was no feeling of solidarity with early boomers. "They fucked up and sold out everything they were fighting for," Leacock says. "They all got jobs and got married and got fat. That's what it looked like to us, at least. We grew up with people taking American hostages and hating our guts. We felt there was nothing we could do. Though we all changed our mind after we skipped our first vote and realized, we'd better get out there, someone's got to!"

Larson and Leacock started dating, "and I finally lost my virginity, which was a great triumph to me, because I was eighteen and desperately trying not to be the last person in New York who hadn't." Within a week they had a fight, broke up, and became best friends.

During Leacock's first year at Adelphi, Reagan began cutting spending, taxes and the federal budget. "There's enough fat in the government that if it was rendered and made into soap, it would wash the world," Reagan once said, and he intended to reverse the strongly interventionist governmental philosophy that had held sway since Franklin D. Roosevelt's New Deal. Although prices and interest rates began to drop, his promised "supply-side" economic rejuvenation didn't happen as fast as he claimed. The balanced budget would take years. "None of us really understands what's going on with all these numbers," said Reagan's budget director, David Stockman (b. 1946).

Some of the deepest cuts came in the budgets of the National Endowments for the Arts and Humanities, which funded museums, dance and theater companies, libraries and universities. After many of her favorite teachers lost their jobs, Leacock dropped out of Adelphi just before her third semester, at the end of 1982.

PAUL KANTNER OF the Jefferson Starship had begun to clean up his act after his daughter came along. "The day China was born, he stopped snorting cocaine," says Cynthia Bowman. "After his cerebral hemorrhage, he stopped drinking." Bowman still drank and smoked pot. "I was really pretty wrapped up in that whole road scene," she admits.

She was on the road with the band in spring 1981 when she discovered she was pregnant. Noticing that Bowman was out of sorts, Grace Slick, who was in an adjoining hotel room, administered a pregnancy test. Doing the math, Bowman figured out she'd probably conceived a few months before, on a night when she'd had a cocktail too many and gone home with Kantner. "Grace flew out the door and ran down the hall to tell their manager, he told Paul and then all of us were sitting around, trying to figure out what to do," Bowman recalls. "And there weren't really very many options because Paul was absolutely clear—he's a Catholic and abortion is just not an option. We'd broken up, the last thing on my mind was to have a baby with Paul Kantner. But after having a little pow-wow with Grace and Paul, we all decided I would go ahead and have the baby and we'd figure it out."

Though the pregnancy was unexpected, it was also serendipitous. "The day I found out I was pregnant I stopped smoking, drinking, everything," she says. "I'd been irresponsible for a long time and gotten away with it, but now I had a baby to take care of. That was my motivating factor. It had nothing to do with Reagan or politics or anything. I grew up when I got pregnant. That's what changed everything for me."

She and Kantner quickly decided they not only wanted the baby, but wanted to raise it together. Bowman moved back into Kantner's house, an assistant was hired to handle her Starship press work, and she went to exercise classes and "acted like a pregnant person," she says. Alexander Bowman Kantner was born on January 1, 1982, with Slick in attendance, and "turned out to be the best thing that ever happened to either one of us. He's an A student, an artist, a musician. He has no interest in drugs or alcohol. In fact, he came home last night from a party at which a bunch of adults were acting goofy because they'd had too much to drink, and he said it made him sick seeing people like that. And I thought to myself, 'Oh, thank God you weren't born twenty-five years ago.' He has no memories of his parents being like that."

Bowman and Kantner soon broke up again. "The reason we never got married was because we didn't get along and I'd moved in and out so many times I can't even count them," she says. "If we were going to raise a healthy kid, we couldn't fight constantly." She packed up and moved to Mill Valley. She was still the Jefferson Whatever's PR director, but her days there were numbered, too.

Paul Kantner was fed up with Jefferson Starship. He'd reorganized the band around a new singer (after Slick and Marty Balin left yet again), but commercial reality forced it to depend on outside writers, as 1980s bands needed middle-of-the-road hit songs to survive, and Kantner's songs, stuck in the 1960s, were no longer commercially viable. Even after Slick rejoined the group in 1984 they couldn't crack the Top Ten. The less well they did, the more Kantner resented the new reality. He couldn't adapt, couldn't tame his chaotic muse for life in the constricted universe of the three-minute pop song. And he hated himself for letting a pimple cream sponsor the Starship's tours, even though he understood that such arrangements were a necessary evil to cover the huge expenses of touring.

"He didn't want to play the songs," Bowman says. "He didn't need the money. He comes from a folk background and that was the antithesis of what he wanted to do. It got very unpleasant. Paul wanted to continue doing what he'd been doing, but Volunteers of America was not happening when Reagan was in office—absolutely not—and there were new people involved who really didn't appreciate the history of the band and just wanted to make money. Everybody had families to support and Grace decided to side with [the other band members]."

Increasingly associated with Kantner, Bowman was seen "as the enemy" and began to avoid the office. Finally, she and Slick had "what you might call an altercation," she says. "One version of the story is she fired me. The other version is I told her to kiss my ass. I can assure you that both things happened. And so I left and never went back and had to find other work. And that was the best thing they ever did for me, because forcing me out of that little spaceship got me onto my own."

IT WAS TIME for something new in clubland. A friend of Jim Fouratt's told him about a multilevel after-hours club on Manhattan's West 37th

Street that was about to go broke. He offered to fix it and they agreed. He called Rudolf Pieper, who signed on. The place was named Danceteria. With only a $25,000 budget to renovate it, they called on young artists like Keith Haring (b. 1958) and David Wojnarowicz (b. 1955) from the thriving downtown clubs that had filled the void left by Hurrah. Haring, who became a busboy, did one of his first installations in the club. "I walked in one day and Rudolf was tearing it down," Fouratt recalls. He started to protest and Rudolf replied, "It's the busboy, Jim; don't be so serious."[24]

The summer of Danceteria was the last moment of culturally sanc-tioned libertinism. Though uptowners clamored to get in, Fouratt only admitted a few of "the bodysuckers who would come in from jaded soci-ety to feed off our energy," he says. "It was a fabulous time, the last great pre-AIDS, pre-crack party. People still remember that summer, when they all got laid, they all got drugs." All but Fouratt, that is. He'd come down with hepatitis in the waning days of Hurrah, when he, too, went on a bit of a binge—drinking and doing cocaine—wound up in the hospital, and from there, a twelve-step program. He'd only been straight for a few months when Danceteria opened. "And everybody was on drugs!" he says. "It wasn't groovy, cool, hip. It was just nuts. All my friends were really fucked up."

Danceteria was closed after eight months for not having a liquor license. Rudolf and Fouratt moved to G.G. Barnum's—a drag queen bar with trapeze acts and gangsters"—not my idea of gay liberation," Fouratt says. But in the basement, he found the original decorations and candy-striped furniture from the Peppermint Lounge, where Fouratt had gone with the Beatles—and so they restored the name and revived the old club. Next, the duo went to work at the Underground, another cavernous disco. And an old friend turned up: Jerry Rubin, now married to Mimi Leonard, whose father co-founded the Esalen Institute and coined the term "Human Potential Movement." Leonard had gone to work on Wall Street in 1980, and Rubin followed, becoming marketing director for a brokerage house.[25] That July, he wrote a piece for the *New York Times* Op-Ed page about his conversion to capitalism. "I know that I can be more effective today wearing a suit and tie and working on Wall Street than I can be dancing outside the walls of power," he wrote. "I have learned that the individual who signs the check has the ultimate power. . . If I am going to have any effect on my society in the next forty years, I must develop the power that only control of money can bring."[26]

In April 1981, Rubin began giving parties in his apartment for stockbrokers to meet clients. The gatherings soon became quite successful among New York's young professionals—mostly boomers with a sudden need to get ahead in the world. When their brokerage house went out of business shortly thereafter, Rubin and Leonard accepted an invitation to move the parties to the Underground.[27]

Soon after that, Rudolf and Fouratt had moved on, as they were wont to do, working briefly for Steve Rubell and Ian Schrager, who were out of jail, then opening Danceteria 2 in February 1982, with art installations, a dance floor, a performance floor, a lounge floor and rooftop parties in summer. Once again, the deal descended into acrimony and litigation— only this time between Rudolf and Fouratt. Fouratt ended up broke and angry, but years later decided he'd been forced from club life at just the right moment. It was no longer the stage for artistic and cultural exploration it had once been. "MTV was starting," he says. "And it's what destroyed nightlife."

Of course, boomers were behind the new venture. Having grown up on rock and television, the cable station's president, Robert Pittman (b. 1954), boasted of having the attention span of a flea. A corporate comer ever since he became a teenage deejay in Jackson, Mississippi, in 1970, Pittman was named the program director of WNBC radio in New York in 1977. He was only twenty-three. Ten years later, the "Hippie from Mississippi" epitomized the late 1980s.

In 1979, Pittman married Sandy Hill (b. 1955), an editor at *Mademoiselle*. Bob had just moved from WNBC to the nascent Warner-Amex Satellite Entertainment Co., where he started out on The Movie Channel an HBO-like movie channel, then moved to MTV. On August 1, 1981, MTV, the all-music cable network, became a reality. But it wasn't a success yet. In 1982, MTV was reportedly losing $20 million a year. "All I worry about is winning," Pittman told the New York *Times* that year. By 1983, MTV was kicking out the boundaries of television. Ratings rose 20 percent, and by the fourth quarter the network was turning a profit. "MTV was a pet idea of mine," Pittman told the *Daily News* in 1986. But the true architect of MTV was John Lack (b. 1944), the man who'd hired him. Pittman was the general contractor who followed Lack's design. Still, he got the credit. In 1984, Pittman was runner-up to *Time* magazine's Man of the Year Pete Ubberoth. But it was the MTV mogul who was leading the culture.

Riding the zeitgeist became an obsession for both Pittmans. In 1986, Sandy would launch a daily fashion video show on cable TV and start running charity benefits in an attempt to enter New York's wealthy social set, and by the early 1990s, they became one of Manhattan's most promising young couples before they separated and divorced—a not atypical trajectory. After several overreaching attempts to go into business for himself, Bob went back to work for an old boss, Steve Ross of Warner Communications, eventually settling into a post running Six Flags Amusement Parks. For her part, Sandy got heavily into mountain climbing, trying some of the world's tallest mountains. Several people accompanying her on an expedition to Everest died in extreme conditions, inspiring books and articles that blamed their deaths on her insistence on reaching the top against all odds. That didn't stop her. Sandy Hill, as she's now called, still goes out with what passes for New York society. And after a brief exile at Century 21 real estate, Bob Pittman now rides the zeitgeist again as the president of America Online.

Pittman was hardly alone in turning the symbols of freedom and liberation into new sources of wealth and social position. Drug dealers had been doing it all along, as had purveyors of drug paraphernalia from pipes to posters; fashion designers like Yves Saint Laurent (b. 1936) and Calvin Klein (b. 1942), who made upscale versions of street styles; and the hip capitalists of the music business. "Their mentality said, 'I'm going to get as much as I can for me,'" a disapproving Fouratt says, "because that was the only thing that worked. The Nixon-Reagan years demonized social consciousness. The politics of greed replaced the politics of compassion."

WHILE STEVE RUBELL and Ian Schrager were still in jail, many former Studio 54 habitués, Victoria Leacock among them, stopped going to the club.[28] Following its brief renaissance when Rubell and Schrager reappeared, the club floundered again under the ownership of Mark Fleischmann. He quickly turned to a new breed of party promoters to fill the space and its till. A one-time booking agent for lecturers, Fleischmann called an old client, Jerry Rubin, after he'd held three of his "networking parties" at the Underground, and lured him to Studio 54 in March 1982.[29]

Rubin's events became so successful that a year later, they caught the eye of Bob Greene, the Chicago columnist who'd known him since the days of the Chicago 8. Greene had overheard someone joke that Rubin had gone from head of the Yippies to head of the Yuppies, Young Urban Professionals. When Greene wrote about the phenomenon in his nationally syndicated column, the word entered the vernacular, and became a self-definition for millions making the same transition as Rubin. The following January, Yuppies went mass market with the publication of *The Yuppie Handbook*.[30] And that October, Rubin and Abbie Hoffman—

who'd surfaced from the underground in 1980 and served time in jail on reduced charges—even went out on a lecture tour, billing themselves as Yippie versus Yuppie.[31]

In the mid-1980s, Rubin announced a plan to take his networking company public, but never managed to do it. He moved to Los Angeles in 1991. Still chasing the ever more health-conscious boomer market, he worked as a distributor for a company that sold powdered nutritional drink mixes until he died in 1994, hit by a car on Wilshire Boulevard.

THOUGH HE'S LOATHE to admit it, by 1981, HBO's Michael Fuchs had become a cocky, free-market Yuppie too, a major player in the entertainment business. HBO had just launched a second network, Cinemax. While less than a third of American homes were on cable, 300,000 new households were signing up a month. Studio attempts to horn in on HBO's action were being thwarted. When 20th Century-Fox, Columbia, Paramount, MCA and Getty Oil tried to launch a cable outlet, Premier, the Justice Department stopped them, but pay television and videocassettes were increasingly seen as Hollywood's salvation. For the first time, movie executives were calling their products "entertainment software."[32]

Fuchs, promoted to senior vice president the year before, was feeling feisty when a critical reporter from the *Christian Science Monitor* came calling that April, just after the announcement that HBO would become a twenty-four-hour-a-day service. Fuchs ticked off some of his achievements: a TV adaptation of Broadway's *Vanities;* one-man shows starring Diana Ross, George Carlin, Lily Tomlin, Bette Midler and Barry Manilow; and a *Consumer Reports* show that could only run on a network without advertising.

Fuchs says he was still a caring Kennedy Democrat, still committed to fulfilling his childhood vow to do good things, but Reagan's election that year had soured him on political activism. "I just felt like the world had ended," he says now, perhaps explaining why, not long after Reagan's inauguration, he waved off the *Monitor* reporter's suggestion that HBO wasn't doing enough public service programming. "There's no mandate here to do public service," he snapped.

Fuchs's goals clearly lay elsewhere. He predicted that cable would soon interact with computers and telephones. "The 1980s will be the period when all the amazing versatility of TV and cable is realized," he said. "To be part of this business is like holding on to the tail of a comet."[33] Convergence would remain a promise unfulfilled for twenty years, but that didn't stop Home Box Office.

"Great movies are just the beginning," was its new slogan. Its advertising budget had been increased 80 percent, and it was about to begin producing its own shows and films. "I found television getting more and more gutless and having less and less a point of view," Fuchs says. "I wanted to move in where they were vacating. I believed in reality-based programming. And to me, a comedian standing up, doing his thing uncensored, was real. The quickest way to get something on the air on HBO is say, 'The networks would never touch this.'"

HBO had turned the corner. Its competitors lagged far behind. Time's video group was producing almost half of all Time Inc. profits.[34] That year, Time Inc.'s CEO was replaced by the head of video, Dick Munro. "HBO looked like it was going to eat the universe, it was growing so fast," says Fuchs. Time's long-held devotion to the division between church, or the editorial side of the company, and state, the business side that sold advertising, was "one of the unsung reasons," Fuchs says. "They understood the First Amendment." When local governments attempted to stop him, legislating censorship of cable broadcasts in Utah and Miami, HBO fought and won crucial First Amendment court cases. Time even let him air George Carlin's "Seven Words You Can't Say on Television" *after* a court declared it obscene.

"We were for real," Fuchs says.

DOUG MARLETTE HAD begun six years of psychoanalysis in 1978. He'd spent years feeling guilty about his talent and the self-involvement it entailed. "If I thought of something quickly and easily, it could not be good," he explains. "I had to torment myself for hours. It took years to get spontaneous and direct and just do it. Therapy saved my life. I would have just blown apart otherwise. The self-destructive forces within me would have just had their way."

The next year, on the edge of the 1980s, he'd been the first cartoonist ever to win a Nieman Fellowship at Harvard, which allows journalists to take a year off and get paid to study. "I sat at B.B. King's feet and listened to him play the blues. I held the lamp for Robert Penn Warren as he read poetry. I heard John Updike, John Irving, William F. Buckley, Art Buchwald. I gave up my syndication, and then I started over, a risky thing to do, but it was worth it. I was ready for a change." He turned thirty and married again as well. "That was the beginning of learning about commitment and hard work and all that stuff," he says.

Marlette returned to Charlotte a full-fledged Yuppie with a Cutlass Ciera and a mortgage, "an emotional teabag—the zeitgeist just flows through me," he crows. "I don't see anything wrong with being young or upwardly mobile or professional. What are you supposed to be? Downwardly mobile? Amateurish? Old?" He started wearing a suit and tie even though nobody at the *Charlotte Observer* cared.

He gave up drinking and stopped being the "designated id" in his social set. He began getting up at 5:00 A.M. and going into the office early, before anyone was there, doing his daily cartoon and then working on a new comic strip he'd conceived. Double deadlines meant he'd never have time to torment himself again. "As Freud says, maturity is the ability to love and to work," Marlette says. "I was learning both those things. I needed to learn discipline. And it made me more creative."

Creating a comic strip wasn't easy. Eventually he gave birth to "Kudzu," set in Bypass, North Carolina, a sleepy Southern town (so named because the big state highway goes by without an exit), and its residents, Kudzu Dubose, a dreamy, awkward adolescent much like Marlette, who wants to go to the big city and be a writer; Maurice, his black best friend, a neo-gangsta wannabe; Kudzu's Uncle Dub at the filling station; his pet para-keet, Doris, and the preacher Will B. Dunn. The immediate success of the strip gave Marlette an instant six-figure income, but also taught him a les-son. "You look forward to seeing your comic strip on the Sunday pages; that's a big moment," he says. "The Sunday morning comes when my comic strip debuts and it's not in the *Charlotte Observer*. They 'forgot.'" His conclusion? "Not only was I taken for granted, but also punished for succeeding."

His experience at Harvard had invested his op-ed cartoons with new, mature shades of gray. His reactions were no longer knee-jerk. When John Belushi died of a drug overdose, Marlette drew a coke-snorting Blues Brother with a death's head, and his friends accused him of drawing a right-wing cartoon. "I think it's more important to feel than to feel good," he replied. "We live in a culture where the thing to do is gloss over symp-toms, or take it to Jesus or blame whoever. From cocaine to Prozac, it's all the same, and I began seeing that as the deadening of the human spirit.

"Believe it or not, wearing a coat and tie was how I began understand-ing my role as an artist," he says. "The great novelists see the whole pic-ture. Dostoyevsky, Tolstoy, Dickens, they empathize with the thief and with the saint. They feel the whole thing, and they show the whole thing. Ideologues don't." Even though he had a new appreciation of authority, he attacked Reagan relentlessly, because he saw no subtlety or empathy whatever in the president's conservative republicanism. "Have you ever been to a Republican convention?" Marlette hoots. "You can feel the assholes slamming shut! The answer is not imposing your thing on other people." Having grown up with fundamentalism, he was especially predisposed against it. "I know its wickedness," he says. "I know its arrogance. How it compromises and belies its own claims."

Since his beginnings in 1974, Marlette had been drawing Jim and Tammy Faye Bakker, the cheesy prom king and queen of televangelism and a local phenomenon in Charlotte long before they became a national embarrassment. In 1987, Bakker was exposed for committing adultery with a church secretary, Jessica Hahn, and in 1989 was sent to jail for defrauding thousands of contributors to his ministry.

Marlette's portrayals of Bakker's PTL television ministry lampooned its religious theme park, Heritage U.S.A., as a sort of Six Flags Over Jesus, a liquor-free, trailer-trash playground; and their ostentatious lifestyle as a perverted playing-out of the frustrated desires of the troubled souls in their flock. Bakker had built the five-acre water park for $8 million, calling it "pretty fancy bait" for a fisher of men. [35] "So I drew Jesus being baptized by John the Baptist with Jim Bakker coming down a huge water slide in a big rubber ducky," Marlette explains. Bakker held the cartoon up on his TV show and called Marlette a tool of Satan. He started getting complaints and crank calls from all over the country. He politely explained that the Charlotte *Observer* personnel department had a policy against hiring tools of Satan. "I understand those people," the cartoonist says. "I understand what they're doing. Turn over your autonomy to something else. But I can't do it."

IN 1980 IVANA Trump went to work as the Trump Organization's vice president for interior decoration. The Grand Hyatt—which opened that year—set the style for all followed it. One design critic described it as "overstated opulence."

Donald Trump admits that he strived to be the quintessential Yuppie, building glittering bronze, brass, glass and marble buildings full of luxury apartments and shops that offended architecture critics but had undeniable appeal to those reveling in Reagan-era wealth. Trump's cockiness was a piece of it. That year, when he began demolishing Bonwit Teller to make way for the glittering new edifice that would become Trump Tower, he ordered the demolition of two Art Deco bas-relief friezes and an intricate grillwork that had decorated the building, a piece of irreplaceable art he'd promised to the Metropolitan Museum of Art. He later claimed it would have cost $500,000 to fulfill that promise, and that the removal would have endangered passers-by. Those claims were mocked by preservationists and newspaper editorialists, but he brushed them off. The sculptures didn't really interest him; building did. "I really enjoyed what I was doing. I didn't do it to say, 'Fuck you' to the rest of the world," he says. "I didn't do it to say I'm better than this one or that one. I did it because I really liked it."

Trump Tower opened in 1982—and immediately became a business success and a tourist attraction. Everything about it was designed by Ivana in her inimitable style, from the doormen's Disney-ish uniforms to the eighty-foot-high atrium and waterfall lined in breccia pernice marble. She was pregnant with their second child during the Tower's construction. In October, Ivanka Trump was born. At age thirty-six, Donald Trump began telling reporters he'd already done everything he ever wanted to do. Now, there was nothing left but to become the glaring embodiment of his time.

RUSSELL SIMMONS ALMOST graduated from CCNY. "I went four years, I had one hundred and fourteen credits," he says. "And then I dropped out." He quit in winter 1979, when he had his first hit record after three years of promoting parties. All that time, he'd been circling the edges of the music business in dance clubs like Club 371 and Disco Fever in the South Bronx and the Harlem Renaissance, and, though he hated the music they featured, gay discos. "The gay disco deejays made the charts!" he says. "They made whatever the fuck chart they wanted. They decided. In New York, there was only gay disco radio."

Then Simmons heard his first near-rap record, "King Tim III," by the non-rap Fatback Band and thought, "We might really be in the record business one day." The same month, a black-owned label, Sugarhill Records, put a trio of non-rappers together in a studio and came up with "Rapper's Delight," by a group they dubbed the Sugar Hill Gang. Driven by the sampled bass line of Chic's disco hit "Good Times," the song sold two million copies and introduced America to rap.

"Rapper's Delight" was a novelty hit—and a watershed. Soon after hearing it, Simmons and Kurtis Blow wrote and recorded a rhyme about Santa Claus in Harlem. "The next thing you know, I had 'Christmas Rappin'" under my arms," Simmons says. "I was in the record business!" Some listeners weren't so sure.

Simmons would go to middle-class clubs for blacks, "begging them to play the records," he says. "But those niggers were never going to, because they're niggers in suits and ties and they don't want to hear that shit. They look at the world they live in. If they want to be rock-and-roll and take drugs, they're never going to get out of jail. They've got to have a strict attitude about life. That's why middle-class black people are so uppity and bourgie; it's to survive. Otherwise they'd be fuckin' crack-heads."

They weren't alone in hating rap. So did Frankie Crocker, a local radio monument. "I don't care how many records you sold, to Frankie Crocker, that's ghetto music. Frankie Crocker thought 'YMCA' by the Village People was hip. He's one of them niggers who didn't like niggers, or didn't like that cultural thing."

Then Kurtis Blow's Christmas record got played by deejay Larry Levan (b. 1954) at New York's best gay disco Paradise Garage and in April 1980, Blow played there live. In May, his second single, "The Breaks," came out and went gold with 800,000 copies sold. "Christmas Rappin'" soon matched those sales. Simmons started managing Blow, and signed him with a major record label. Simmons had given the record a false order number in the record company's ordering system. "We put it out, and it made a lot of noise in the street, and they were getting a lot of orders," he says. "That's how the Kurtis Blow deal got done." Rap was still a tiny subculture; Simmons had to fight for the right to make a full-length record. "Kurtis Blow had two gold singles before they let him make an album," he says. "That's unheard of." But finally he did; Blow's eponymous album was the first full-length hip-hop release. Rap was inching its way from street hustle to mainstream music.

For the next six years Simmons ran on overdrive, going to clubs ("Bentley's started at six o'clock in the afternoon, Danceteria started getting hot at nine o'clock, at four in the morning you can stop in the Garage or the Fever"), taking drugs (cocaine, angel dust), and working. "But I was more having fun," he admits. "I loved the music, the whole thing. It was now starting to evolve, to become respected and understood."

He was too busy for politics. "I was getting too high to give a fuck," he says. But he did notice what budget cuts in education did to Harlem, where he lived. "I felt bad; no one was going to school. Those opportunities were going away. But I wasn't a political activist, or even aware. Unfortunately."

Rap quickly infiltrated the hippest white clubs: the Mudd Club, the Peppermint Lounge, Danceteria. Simmons was an ambassador "wherever alternative clubs were starting to develop," he says. "I knew lots of people in every group at every club. I'd have friends in every world." So did Fred "Fab 5 Freddy" Braithwaite (b. 1959), an artist Simmons calls "the all-purpose Art

Nigger." Braithwaite, an artist and rapper, introduced the second-generation Warholites at Mudd to rap, and was soon honored by the new wave band Blondie, which released "Rapture," an homage to hip-hop, featuring lead singer Debbie Harry (b. 1945) rapping about her new friend.

Simmons got grief for border-crossing. "What do you want to go there for?" people said to him. "Bunch of faggots there." "Them niggers is ghetto; they'd murder us." "They're a bunch of drugged-out punk rockers."

"All the people were cool; it's not about color," Simmons says. "It's who's got the same interests, who's interesting and fun to be around, and that's the end of it." It was also good business. Simmons knew that cross- ing over, reaching white kids, was what he wanted. He never referred to the music he produced as rap; he called it black teenage music. In 1982, Simmons put Kurtis Blow on tour with the punk rock band The Clash, opening up a whole new record-buying audience.

Rush Productions, Simmons's management company, grew through the early 1980s. In 1982, he encouraged his younger brother, Joseph Simmons (b. 1964), and his friend Darryl McDaniel (b. 1964) to form a band, adopt- ing the nicknames Run and D.M.C. respectively. After graduating high school that spring, they added a friend, Jason "Jam Master Jay" Mizell (b. 1965), to scratch their turntables, and recorded their first single, which became a minor hit on the R&B charts in 1983. "Kurtis Blow, Fearless Four, Run-D.M.C., Whodini, Orange Crush—I managed all those bands, pro- duced records, oversaw management, helped develop their careers," Simmons says. Simmons dressed Run-D.M.C. in black hats and leather suits, giving them an indelible image.

In 1983, Simmons met Rick Rubin (b. 1963), a suburban white boy who was going to New York University but spending much of his time programming a drum machine and hanging out in rap clubs. "Every beat he plays is a smash," Simmons says. He'd produced "It's Yours," a single by T-La Rock and Jazzy Jay that caught Simmons's ear on the radio with its pop music-like structure. When they started hanging out together, Simmons began to incorporate Rubin's rock 'n' roll-bred attitude, trading in his sport jackets and penny loafers for jeans and Adidas sneakers. When the duo heard a demonstration tape by a sixteen-year-old from Simmons's Hollis neighborhood, they decided to start their own record company, Def Jam. They changed James Todd Smith's name to L.L. Cool J (b. 1968), dressed him up in a memorable uniform of sharp-creased Lee jeans and a Kangol hat, invested $4,000 each and in 1984, recorded his first single, "I Need a Beat," in Rubin's dormitory room for $700. It sold 100,000 copies.

That same year, Simmons met the Beastie Boys, a trio of well-to-do Generation X punk rockers: Adam "MCA" Rauch (b. 1965), Mike "Mike D" Diamond (b. 1966) and Adam "Ad-Rock" Horovitz (b. 1967). Their first rap single, "Cookie Puss," which sampled a prank phone call the group made to Carvel Ice Cream, bridged the gap between punk and hip-hop, and caught Rubin's ear. They soon signed to Def Jam.

By 1985, Rush Productions was managing twenty-two streetwise acts, and at age twenty-six, Simmons was about to make his move into the big time. That year, he made his first movie, *Krush Groove*, a fictionalized version of his and Rubin's story that included songs by many Def Jam acts; a $600,000 distribution, marketing, and promotion deal with CBS/Sony; and L.L. Cool J's first full-length album, *Radio*, as well as Run-D.M.C.'s *King of Rock* and the Beasties's *Licensed to Ill*.

Those records helped chart the course of rap into the mainstream. Under Rubin's influence, the Beasties and Run-D.M.C. both incorporated sampled rock guitar riffs into their sound. The Beasties, who toured as an opening act for Madonna that year, made the invitation to rock fans explicit with their metal riffs, parodic B-Boy patter, and anthemic single, "Fight For Your Right (to Party)". In a first since the 1960s, Simmons had also succeeded in institutionalizing a new sound that would outrage adults (older baby boomers primary among them) in direct proportion to how much it appealed to the young—the first successful update of the boomer era youth marketing paradigm.

The best was yet to come. In 1986, Run-D.M.C. recorded a rap version of the rock band Aerosmith's first hit song, "Walk This Way," with that band's singer, Steven Tyler (b. 1948), and guitarist, Joe Perry (b. 1950). Not only was the song a monster hit, the first rap single to break into the Top 5, it also broke the anti-rap rule on MTV—winning priceless exposure among white teenagers. Rap had crossed the color barrier. "It was alternative music," Simmons says. "Cool people across the country knew."

With CBS money behind it, Def Jam immediately became the world's leading rap label. Run-D.M.C.'s second album sold 2.5 million copies, L.L. Cool J's first sold 3.5 million (he'd eventually make four consecutive platinum albums), and the Beastie Boys' debut, the first rap album to hit #1 on *Billboard*'s pop record charts, sold a staggering 4.8 million copies.

There was still resistance from record companies, but Simmons doesn't think it was racism. "It was just new music," he says. "They had a nigger department, but the niggers didn't like this either. Niggers especially didn't like it. I was playing nigger to the niggers. They're afraid of change. You don't want to see records coming out you don't understand all over the place in your world. A forty-five-year-old record executive is not listening to that shit. So they put us behind their R&B records for radio play. But we just completely shit on R&B, killed it." Even then, they told him rap was a fad. "You know," Simmons says, chuckling, "they've said, 'It's just a fad' every year for twenty years now."

As early as 1980, Simmons had known better. That's when Polygram flew him and Kurtis Blow to Europe, where "Christmas Rappin'" had made the charts. "I'd never been out of the country," Simmons says. "I had my passport. Polygram put me on a plane. We sniffed all the coke in Amsterdam, we hit all the weed spots, and we partied and they treated us like we were rock stars, and I was rich from that day on."

THE COMPUTING GOLD rush was in full swing by 1982, fueled by two groups—creators, looking for powerful but versatile machines, and consumers, looking for the cyber version of a can opener. There were millions of them. So, "almost everywhere you turned there were millionaires," wrote Steven Levy in *Hackers*. "That smell of success was driving people batty."[36] Personal computing had long since passed hippies like Steve Wozniak by. In Silicon Valley, people snickered over how Woz had blown his fortune from the Apple stock offering producing massive rock concerts.

The arrival of ever-cheaper screens, computer memory, and microprocessors, essentially entire computers on a single chip, meant that graphics-capable computers once costing $300,000 could now be built for $20,000. They'd recognized the potential for this in the early 1970s at Xerox PARC. Now a group of graduate students at Stanford University, also in Palo Alto, California, turned another of the copier company's missed opportunities into a multibillion-dollar company. As part of his electrical engineering studies at Stanford, German science prodigy Andy Bechtolscheim (b. 1955) combined inexpensive off-the-shelf memory and microprocessors to create Stanford University Network—or Sun—workstations, linked into a cross-campus network. Xerox had built similar devices, but when the Defense Department's Advanced Research Projects Agency, the same group that put together the Internet, investigated buying them, it decided they were overpriced and approached Bechtolscheim. After failing to find a manufacturer, he enlisted two business students to write a business plan and find financing, and Sun Microsystems was incorporated to make the machines in February 1982.

There were many markets for Bechtolscheim's computing product, including the computer graphics division at Lucasfilm, the movie company making director George Lucas's *Star Wars* trilogy. Lucas's special effects magicians had been using Bill Joy's hopped-up UNIX operating system on Digital Equipment's VAX, a huge, expensive computer. The Sun workstation was a major improvement—"a little box that went as fast at one-tenth the cost," as John Gage puts it—so Lucasfilm suggested Bechtolscheim approach Joy about using his software on it. Joy introduced Bechtolscheim to Gage.

He was an immediate convert, and joined up as Sun's evangelist, the guy who knew how to explain things and how to turn wish lists into reality. "These workstations are an incredibly powerful tool you could use to build other tools, they're for serious computer people who are trying to build telescopes, design chips, design bridges, run battlefields and drilling rig platforms," Gage says. "None of them were the same people that your average computer VP would know. We represented a new rebel alliance."

Joy and Gage brought with them something as important as Berkeley UNIX: the idea that giving away software and unveiling its secrets, its source code, would be good business—and sell lots of Sun workstations—in the long run. "Free speech, open exchange; that's the ethic of the scientific community," Gage says. "More conversation rather than less. And more light, more light, more light. Allow communities to develop. A side effect of that, of course, is that dangerous communities will develop. But the health of the body politic depends on everyone being able to converse."

A year after their introduction, IBM-PCs, which were even smaller than Sun's mini-computers, had become a stiff challenge to the Apple II in the still-young personal computer market. Though Apple was still making huge profits, its market share plunged that year because unlike Apple, IBM let others use its PC architecture, increasing its market share. Sun's cyber neo-hippies would also take on those who clung to the proprietary standard.

Sun's customers "are people who have already decided what they need: networking, source code, openness, quick, communication Gage says. "They don't want to talk to a sales guy. They want to talk to Bill Joy or to somebody close to Bill, who could take them through what needs to be done at two in the morning when the cable shorts out and they can no longer control the telescope."

His customers were boomers just like him. They demanded instant gratification. "This was a social phenomenon," Gage says. "Open-systems guys are the hot-rodders who have to add their own thing. Looking at source code is like opening up an engine compartment. Because they could see inside it, they could be inventive in ways you could not be in the normal commercial world. They could hot-rod."

For Gage, it was all a great reminder of how he'd felt a decade earlier, when George McGovern won his nomination for the presidency. Maybe things really did work the way he'd once thought—and, lately, was thinking again. "You could make a serious change with one person. One smart kid could fundamentally alter a business or a political structure."

"I DON'T CARE to be a hero, ever," says Tommy Vallely. Indeed, throughout the years he worked as a political consultant, Vallely avoided Vietnam vets, particularly those who hadn't readapted to civilian life as well as he had. At least a little guilty that he had a support system at home—parents, money, political alliances—and they didn't, he resolved not to look back.

"It's hard," he says. "A lot of these people were in tough shape. Fucked up. I didn't want to deal with them. I've never been a member of a VFW, I'm never going to be. It's not that I dislike them, I just don't want to deal with that." Instead, he worked to build a life for himself. "I'm just playing the game I'm in, trying to get people elected," he says, "I work very, very hard at it." He learned about national politics, met members of the media, and married and had a daughter in 1979.

Vallely finally got a shot at elective office himself in 1982, when fate and politics arranged a seat for him in the state legislature, where he wound up serving for six years. "I was an insider, never gave a speech, couldn't give a speech," he says. "I learned how to be a public person. It was a very hard thing for me. And I was clumsy at first, so scared it would keep me awake at night." He realized he still wanted to run for Congress. So while serving, he started studying for a master's degree in public policy on scholarship at Harvard's John F. Kennedy School of Government. "And this time, I'm a pretty good student," he says. "I'm not a great student, but I can do it."

His friend, fellow vet John Kerry, became the Lieutenant Governor of Massachusetts under Michael Dukakis in 1982. Earlier that year, Vallely had sponsored legislation to create a Special Commission on the Concerns of Vietnam Veterans, and then become its vice-chairman. Shortly after the election, the commission revealed that the federal government had turned down the chance to investigate a big concern of vets, Agent Orange.

In January 1979, a federal class action lawsuit had been filed on behalf of 4.2 million Vietnam veterans against three manufacturers of an herbicide containing dioxin called Agent Orange used to defoliate vast swaths of Vietnam.[37] They alleged that Agent Orange caused cancer and other health problems—and Vallely was interested. Someone quite close to him had suffered from what he was sure were Agent Orange side effects. In December 1982, the commission ordered a study of the problem.

By the following June, Vallely was fed up. He told a reporter that most of the people who'd testified were from activist groups representing a troubled minority of veterans. He was angry that the Agent Orange study had been pushed aside by more political concerns like the issue of prisoners of war. Finally, Chris Gregory, a VVAW member and close friend of Kerry and Vallely, was appointed to head a Massachusetts Agent Orange program.

In 1984, when the state's senior senator, Paul Tsongas, retired, Kerry decided to run for his seat. Vallely, whose wife was wealthy, says he was hiding out on their 160-acre farm, studying John Deere catalogs at the time, "hoping Kerry doesn't call me 'cause I want to buy a tractor and I don't want to deal with him." After running a TV commercial showing him speaking in front of the Vietnam veterans memorial, Kerry was criticized by the same veterans who'd tried to usurp Vallely's hearings. Kerry was tarred as Ho Chi Minh's candidate. So Vallely helped organize the Dog Hunters, a group of about 100 Vietnam veterans, to support him.

"The Vietnam War started again with me during the Kerry election," Vallely says When Kerry was sworn in early to finish the ailing Tsongas's term in office, Vallely visited the Vietnam Veterans Memorial in Washington for the first time. Designed by Maya Lin (b. 1959) a student at Yale, the V-shaped polished granite wall, set into the earth like an outcropping of rock and carved with the names of 58,000 dead and missing soldiers, is a chastening, gut-wrenching place to visit for veteran and protester alike. "It had a fuckin' huge impact on me," says Vallely. He'd had a friend who died in Vietnam named James Coleman, a big strong Texan, and when he saw an elderly couple searching for their son's name on the wall, the father wearing cowboy boots, Vallely's internal dam broke and he sobbed.

Not long afterward, John Kerry, now a senator and just back from Nicaragua, where he'd been embarrassed by a misbegotten attempt at lone-wolf diplomacy, was invited to a performance of *Tracers*, a play about Vietnam written and performed by veterans. The Vietnamese ambassador to the United Nations was also invited, and Vallely joined them. As the senator and the ambassador chatted in French, a Vietnamese aide took Vallely aside and asked him if Kerry would visit Vietnam for the tenth anniversary of the fall of Saigon that April. "No, no, no, the senator's not going to Vietnam," Vallely thought. "He just got back from making a fool of himself in fuckin' Nicaragua." When he said he didn't think so, the Vietnamese diplomat asked if Vallely wanted to go instead—and something clicked.

Vallely did go to Vietnam, shortly after another party that included dozens of returning newsmen (among them Walter Cronkite, whose turn against the war following the 1968 Tet Offensive made broadcast—and American—history) and Arizona congressman John McCain (b. 1936) a former pilot who had been a POW and would later become a senator. Afterward, McCain would sum up the lesson of the war: "The American people and Congress now appreciate that we are neither omniscient nor omnipotent, and they are not prepared to commit U.S. troops to combat unless there is a clear U.S. national security interest involved," he said. "If we do become involved in combat, that involvement must be of relatively short duration and must be readily explained to the man in the street in one or two sentences."[38] The McCain Doctrine would be operative for years to come.

IN 1983, HIS last year at college, Cameron Sears joined Friends of the River, a decade-old environmental group in northern California. Since moving to the state, he'd been whitewater rafting for pleasure and business and first got involved in river-related protests in 1978 to protect the Stanislaus River, where the Army Corps of Engineers had commissioned the construction of a $100 million dam that would submerge the river under a reservoir. California fought for the state's right to limit the reservoir and keep the river open for rafting and fishing. After that right was granted, demonstrators converged on the state capitol to urge Governor Jerry Brown to request that the reservoir not be filled. He agreed, but despite the institutionalization of environmentalism in the Carter administration, which had even given Earth Day's founder an official job, the tide was running against "tree-huggers." After Ronald Reagan's election, environmental activism had grown more militant—at least on the fringes not co-opted by corporate America.

Continued threats to the river encouraged more overt activism among Sears and his friends, some of whom chained themselves to rocks in a vain attempt to stop the filling of the Stanislaus reservoir after Congress refused to add it to the National Wild & Scenic Rivers System in 1979. Four years later, the floodgates were opened and the river was drowned.[39] "It was a devastating blow to that community, and to date they still don't really use the water," Sears says. "It doesn't generate any power. And it just killed the river. It was one of those remarkable resources, up against one of the last really big dam projects in America."

That same year, Friends of the River sought to protect an even more pristine body of whitewater, the Tuolomne River, just outside Yosemite National Park, when it was threatened by a hydroelectric project. Though a bill had been drafted adding it to the wild rivers system, it hadn't been put into effect. "So in my senior year and a year after that, I was consumed with protecting this river," Sears says. He worked as an intern at Tuolomne River Preservation Trust, lobbying on Capitol Hill. And the following summer, he helped run a program of five dozen trips on the Tuolomne, taking "anybody who would go with us down that river to show them what was going on."

Sears was paid a pittance to run the program, recruit volunteers and guide trips, but he didn't mind. "I either lived at my parents' house or the river companies had little houses up in the foothills of California, and you'd just pull your sleeping bag out and that's where you stayed. My single vision was to work for the environment."

As part of that effort, Sears sought out rich folk willing to help, "all manner of people, from movie stars like Richard Chamberlain to congressmen—whoever we could get that had influence." Among them were his longtime heroes the Grateful Dead. In a letter to the band, he wrote: "Water politics are the issue of the day. Without water this state is no state." He'd just about given up on a response when, two months later, the Dead's manager called him. "I've got twenty people who want to go on this river with you," the man said.

"So I take them on a no-strings-attached kind of trip," Sears continues. "None of the band came. It was all the office workers and their kids, basically. And we all became fast friends. We do a few more trips, we're going gangbusters, getting along famously. And they give me a check for ten thousand dollars to give to Friends of the River."

Later that year, the battle for the Tuolomne was won, and Sears moved to San Francisco to start "groveling to find a job in an environmental community where everybody wants you to be an intern and work for free," he says. As in the wider world, all the good jobs were taken by people ten years older than Sears, "and they're entrenched, you know?" he says. "Because the people who got into the movement in 1970 were completely dedicated, and by 1985, they had only just achieved a level where they could eke out a living. Instead of making fifteen grand a year, maybe they were making thirty-five, big-banana wages at that time."

Finally, he accepted the idea that he'd have to get a real job. Luckily for Sears, the previous summer, he'd taken rock impresario Bill Graham on a river trip after one of his executives bought a business on the Tuolomne. "He was completely blown away," Sears remembers. "No phones, no nothing, just three days of bliss. We stayed up until seven in the morning. We took some Ecstasy, and we were just raving around the campfire. Now, granted, he was high, but he wanted me to be his personal guide. He wanted to buy a river company."

"This is just incredible; where else can we go?" Graham demanded. "You're my ticket."

Sears was boggled. "This guy is trying to set me up in business." It was a Yuppie's dream, but he didn't know how to play it. "Yuppies are anathema to me," he says. "So I'm like, 'Jesus Christ, what do I do?' I talk to my friends at Grateful Dead. They say, 'Be careful,' because they didn't really trust him. Wow. Bizarre." Sears trusted his Dead friends. He was by then dating the daughter of the woman to whom he'd handed his letter about the Tuolomne River. Instead of accepting Graham's backing, he proposed to create an adventure travel division inside Graham's company, to organize bimonthly, low-cost trips for his employees, based on a program Doug and Susie Tompkins (both b. 1943) had set up inside their fashion company, Esprit. "It was a way for people to connect and get real," Sears says. "We can go skiing in the winter, we can go biking up in Napa Valley, we can go sailing on the bay. I knew I could pull it off. And he bought it. So I start doing these trips. But it didn't really work as well as I'd hoped. It turns out people who work twelve hours a day don't really want to be with one another on the weekend."

IN 1980, ONE of Steve Capps's Xerox colleagues, a hardware hacker, had told him about the Apple II personal computer. Capps wasn't very interested, because his rescued Alto was far more sophisticated. But his friend's enthusiasm proved infectious. "He put in a requisition to buy an Apple II, and it shot up to VP level and we were told we couldn't buy it, it was against corporate policy because we were in the computer business." Xerox was only talking about computers, though; Apple was making them. So the frustrated hacker got a job at Apple through one of several former PARC-ites who'd moved there.

A year earlier, Apple chairman Steve Jobs and a team of his computer designers had toured Xerox PARC. Inspired by what they'd seen, Jobs had gone back to Apple and sketched out an idea for its next product, a computer called Lisa (named after a daughter he'd sired out of wedlock) that would incorporate most of PARC's best ideas. Capps's hacker friend was hired to join the Lisa hardware team.

Two months later, early in 1981, Capps paid him a visit. Within a few minutes, he knew he wanted to work at Apple. "When I'd dropped out my father said, 'You're not going to amount to nothin',' and I said, 'I'm going to be a millionaire before I'm thirty.' I had notebooks filled with ideas. I go out to Apple and there's a bunch of people who are like this, they're all just maniacs, trying to get something done."

They were trying to get rich, too, Apple's anti-Establishment image notwithstanding. Larry Tesler, the scientist who'd given Jobs the demonstration at PARC and joined Apple shortly thereafter, not only hired Capps to work on Lisa's laser printer, but convinced him to ask for a lot more money than he'd been making at Xerox. "There was a whole 'I'm gonna get mine' undercurrent," Capps says. Steve Wozniak, who'd represented Apple's altruistic side, was fading from the picture. Though he'd still stop by and play video games with his friends, he was no longer active.

Hired in September 1981, Capps moved to California with his girlfriend, another computer science student from Rochester. Briefly, he and several other ex-Xerox employees argued against borrowing the Alto's software. They soon realized that the Apple software designer who wrote the graphic interface (over a weekend, according to in-house legend) had actually done a better job than PARC had, perfecting aspects of the program that hadn't actually worked in Xerox's version. Now Capps was in the thick of it. Not only did he do his job, he also wrote several computer games for Lisa. It was the games that caught Steve Jobs's eye.

Though his selling skills were beyond question, the mercurial Jobs was somewhat less accomplished as a manager of people. After Apple went public, he'd given up day-to-day control of the company to a professional manager. Early in 1981, furious that that CEO had assigned Lisa's development to another executive and aware that Lisa was in trouble—during its gestation, Lisa's software had outgrown its hardware and it was effectively obsolete before it shipped—Jobs had looked for a way out. He found it in another executive's pet project; a team was trying to develop an easy-to-use, $600 personal computer called Macintosh. Jobs elbowed his underling out and converted Macintosh into a project to develop a smaller, cheaper, hacked version of Lisa, a Volkscomputer.[40] Just as he stole ideas from PARC and then Lisa, Jobs also stole people. He hand-picked a team of designers and engineers, and sequestered them in their own building, over which he sometimes flew a Jolly Roger flag; the Mac team were pirates, stealing whatever they needed.

They were on a mission. "Don't you want to make a dent in the world?" Jobs would demand. "This is going to be as revolutionary as the telephone." Convinced that they were doing something earth-shattering, they lived on soda and pizza, constantly pulled all-nighters, and worked like maniacs. "Steve would set unattainable goals, but he was a good enough salesman that he got people to believe in him, and he knew which strings to pull," Capps says. Sometimes the Mac team would compare Jobs to Jim Jones, the religious cult leader who'd induced some nine hundred of his followers to drink Kool-Aid laced with cyanide in a mass suicide in the jungles of Guyana in 1978. "You can't start asking questions, right?" says Capps. "You've just got to drink the purple Kool-Aid."

Capps joined the Mac effort late in the game—in 1983. The launch was set for a few months hence, but the burnt-out Mac team was at wits' end. Though the groundwork had been laid, they were unable to finish the software. Capps, already known as a demon code writer, was assigned to help another software designer, Bruce Horn, finish the Mac's most important piece of software. Finder was the first thing that appeared on the screen when a Mac was turned on. Before Windows, it was a window onto the little machine's many wonders. The philosophy behind Finder, like all Mac applications, was to make a computer fun, easy-to-use, intuitive, and above all, appealing to an artistic sensibility. Anyone who didn't find joy in its wonders could be dismissed as a Luddite or a cretin. It was meant to make the Mac the opposite of the clunky machines that used Microsoft's DOS operating system, like IBM's PC/XT, which had just been introduced.

While the rest of the Mac team gave prerelease promotional interviews, touting the Mac's wonders, Capps and Horn, hidden away in a conference room, spent eighteen-hour days trying to ensure the computer would live up to its hype. Sometimes Jobs would bring visitors around to show what the Mac team was up to. Once the visitor was the man whose software ran on PCs, Bill Gates. "You knew immediately who was the alpha male," Capps says, wryly. "Gates was just this software dink who didn't have a clue." Jobs, no dink, was dating Joan Baez. He'd bring her around, too, and the software designers would throw *Sesame Street* characters onto the screen so she could see that the Mac "didn't look like every other green-on-black computer."

Fact is, those demonstrations notwithstanding, the Mac didn't work.

"We were in trouble," says Capps. "It was pretty, but it was completely nonfunctional." Within a few months, though, Capps and Horn were able to build on the solid underpinnings written by another coder, Andy Hertzfeld, and make it function. Capps still had his doubts. The Alto he'd used at Xerox was far more sophisticated. "From a raw technical computing point of view, I was going way downhill," he says, but locked away under the Jolly Roger, even he became a believer. Even if Xerox *had* sold the Alto, it wouldn't have gone for $1,500, the price at which Jobs now said he planned to sell Macs. Even when Jobs and his latest CEO, John Sculley, formerly of Pepsi, suddenly raised its price to $2,495—rather expensive for a Volkscomputer—Capps didn't waver from his belief that they were after something special.

The Macintosh was formally announced in January 1984, with a $400,000 commercial shown only once, during that year's Super Bowl. Some forty-three million viewers watched as a woman dashed into a dingy room full of what Capps calls desk clones listening to an Orwellian Big Brother figure lecturing from a video screen. After she hurled a sledgehammer at the image, exploding the screen, a narrator intoned, "On January 24th, Apple Computer will introduce Macintosh. And you'll see why 1984 won't be like 1984."

The challenge to IBM was so startlingly direct that the commercial would be replayed over and over on news shows, implanting the Mac in the public's mind. A week later, at Apple's stockholder meeting, Jobs pulled the first Mac out of a bag. "Hello," said a synthesized voice. "I am Macintosh. It sure is great to get out of that bag." Jobs didn't mention that Capps and Horn had pulled three consecutive all-nighters, ending a mere two hours before Jobs took the stage, to get the machine to do that.

Though it could actually do very little, the Mac, *Time*'s Joshua Quittner would later write, "made mortals suddenly see the beauty and empowering potential of a desktop machine. . . . ordinary people could now make computers do extraordinary stuff."[41]

Unfortunately, the hype proved more extraordinary than the Mac's reality. "After the initial raft of Yuppies went out and plunked their twenty-five hundred dollars down, sales fell flat," says Capps. "And the reason was we didn't have spreadsheets, and corporate people would look at it and say, 'What can I do besides draw pictures of a shoe?' It was a toy. But that's why we worked so hard on it. Technology itself isn't all that interesting. How well we deliver that technology to humans is my focus."

Jobs was right. The Mac was "insanely great," and would soon find favor as the personal computer of choice for creative people, but it wasn't so great for Apple's business, which peaked the following year. Meantime, sales of the company's older Apple II computers, which sold to spreadsheet users—not artists—were slumping. Jobs began fighting boardroom battles with CEO Sculley. In 1985, the company reported its first quarterly loss and laid off 20 percent of its workforce. Plans for an improved Mac fizzled.

Capps, blissfully unaware of the political intrigues at Apple, paused long enough to marry his girlfriend and then busied himself improving Finder while waiting for his next assignment. "We were talking about a Mac phone, about a handwriting machine, we were all thinking revolutionary, but sales were in the toilet. The world was not exactly going along with our revolution."

That September, Jobs stormed out of the company. "It was surreal; we all go over to his house, and he's bemoaning his lot in life," Capps recalls. "I'm walking around going, 'This is a big house.'" Soon, Capps quit, too. "I was burnt out and all the cool people had left," he says. He wrote a little more software for Apple in exchange for a new computer, cashed out his stock—while the price was depressed; "a big mistake," he says now—and took off for Paris with his wife. He wanted to learn French. And he wanted to write software "for the good of the world," he says, laughing at himself. "I still had the extremely naïve idea that if you do something cool, the world will reward you."

Maturity

BORN AFTER THE draft expired and too old for it by 1980, when Jimmy Carter reinstituted Selective Service registration, David McIntosh regrets having missing out on military service, which he feels certain would have been a character-building experience. Law school at the University of Chicago was a philosophy-building experience, buttressing his new belief that government exists "to protect individuals and their rights, not to make decisions for them," he says.

Along with three friends he'd met at Yale, McIntosh founded the Federalist Society at the beginning of his second year in Chicago, inspired by the Reagan administration's proposal to decentralize what it considered the most pervasive, unmanageable, ineffective, costly and unaccountable government in American history—a radical vision that sought to transfer federal power to states and localities. The policy, a return to those propounded in *The Federalist Papers of 1788*, not coincidentally provided a counterweight to the liberal orthodoxy that dominated law schools.

"Liberalism and the counterculture had taken root both in style and in a lot of the legal teaching," McIntosh says. "Most conservatives didn't know there were others on campus. So we'd have lunch together and twenty students would show up and be surprised to find people who had similar views." They were encouraged by conservative professors Antonin Scalia at Chicago (who became their chief adviser, and later a Supreme Court Justice), and Robert Bork and Ralph Winter at Yale, who would also soon be appointed to the federal judiciary. Requests to form chapters poured in from all over the country. The back end of the Baby Boom ('til then better known as a breeding ground for criminals, suicides, druggies and other malcontents) was also giving birth to a very new kind of activist.

The summer before his final year of law school, McIntosh worked in a Chicago law firm that offered him a job in its Los Angeles office after graduation. He accepted, practicing real estate law there and sharing an apartment with a friend who helped run a local church youth group. McIntosh began taking their charges on ski trips, weeklong jaunts to Mexico to build housing for squatters, and side trips to Disneyland. "It was the blessing of the circumstances," he says, that he found wholesome activities even in Sodom-by-the-Sea, where some of the young lawyers in the firm lived a party-all-night lifestyle. "I'll go out dancing, but I'm not going to stay out all night, and no thank you to the marijuana-and-cocaine-type thing," he says.

McINTOSH'S PARTYING PEERS weren't the only cocktail shakers in the new club scene, or the only manifestation of the burgeoning conservatism of the Reagan era. In 1980, the publication of *The Official Preppy Handbook* signaled the return of inherited wealth and station as social signifiers. Around the same time that Jerry Rubin brought his networking parties to Studio 54, Gwynne Rivers, the beautiful, well-connected daughter of the painter Larry Rivers, went to work there too, as a party promoter, responsible for luring young clubgoers from her prep school set. Back in New York in 1982, Victoria Leacock joined that crowd while helping her friend Jonathan Larson find theaters to mount his first musicals. When Leacock realized she needed a paying job and an apartment of her own, Rivers introduced her to Mark Fleischmann, Studio 54's new owner, who hired her as his personal assistant in January 1983.

Her workday began at 10:00 A.M. in Fleischmann's office in a hotel he also owned, and ended at 1:00 A.M., when the club owner's limousine would take her home to a room she rented in another hotel. Life in Fleischmann's milieuwas a roller coaster of promoters, refined druggies and lowdown aristocrats. Leacock quickly learned who was who on the club scene, how to pronounce their names and keep them happy, how to design special invitations, and how to hand-address envelopes—social skills largely forgotten since the sloppy 1960s. "I also discovered power, because I made the guest list," she says.

She was no longer starstruck. "Whatever magic happened at the club came at such a high cost," she says. "By the time you got to the fucking party you knew all the horror it took to get there, and barely wanted to be there. And the hangovers in the morning. And I was having my own hangovers for the first time in my life." She was also having a torrid affair with a psychiatrist more than twice her age.

"It became very ugly," she says of the nights she saw people stick their noses in the rugs and sniff, hoping the dust contained cocaine. She started pouring Kahlúa into her morning coffee, and graduated to vodka and tequila as the day wore on. "I knew I had a problem, but I waited six years to do anything about it." In July 1983, Fleischmann and his partners sold their hotel to Steve Rubell and Ian Schrager, who'd decided to go into the lodging business.

Leacock had the sense to leave the club scene when Rubell and Schrager took over Fleischmann's office (and turned the place into Morgan's Hotel, foundation of the empire that is now Ian Schrager Hotels). She moved to London to go to theater school. Her last act at Studio 54 was to throw a party that would start a trend that would soon snowball. She and D. A. Pennebaker's son gave a "Second Generation" party for the children of Melvin van Peebles, Rip Torn and Geraldine Page, Anthony Quinn, Dustin Hoffman, Jerry Stiller and Anne Meara, Sidney Lumet and Gower Champion.

"We had a lot of similar character traits," Leacock says. "A feeling of being very in but for all the wrong reasons. And we all came out of this jaded period of time, and were trying to make some good out of it."

The party was a success, but Leacock's sojourn in England was a failure. Acting school sucked the desire to act right out of her. She returned to New York determined to become a producer or director but first, briefly, went back to work for Fleischmann organizing parties at a restaurant he'd bought when Studio 54 finally closed. New clubs had replaced it, of course. The latest was Area, the last gasp of urban boomer hedonism.[1] Leacock started going there. Though she didn't partake in the coke-sniffing and furtive sex in the unisex bathroom stalls, she was no model of decorum. "Looking for love became a much more random thing," she says. "And I started drinking a lot more."

AFTER SETTLING IN Albuquerque, Mark Rudd earned an education degree and got a job teaching remedial math to junior college students. Throughout the preceding decade, even when living under the most adverse circumstances, the tall, handsome, articulate Rudd had been a girl magnet. Groupies came with the territory. When times were tough, he had a tendency to indulge—which had become an issue with his Weather comrades. For a time, his girlfriend Sue had anchored him. "I survived those rough years because I had a partner," he says. "But after we hit

Albuquerque, the external constraints were off for both of us." They separated—he says the decision was mutual—after he got his degree.

For the next eighteen years, Rudd had "lots of relationships, good and bad." He stayed true to his general beliefs, at least, even if he engaged in as much issue-hopping as bed-hopping. "I have a tendency to involve myself in what's hot," he says. "I put huge amounts of effort into a movement, and then it dies down and I put it into another."

Ronald Reagan reenergized him. Reagan's initiatives against what he deemed the Evil Empire of communism inspired several large antinuclear demonstrations in New Mexico. Rudd threw himself into planning them. "I was not a general," he points out. "I did the work as much as anybody else." When the *Albuquerque Tribune* discovered the presence of the radical in its region, he ducked their offer of an interview, explaining that publicity "could do a number on me."

Rudd was seeking to balance the personal and the political. In 1982, he and his children and friends began building the house he now lives in, a solar adobe in a semirural, predominately Chicano barrio. "It heats and cools itself, and we did it ourselves," he says. "I've been living in it since 1984." Shortly after he moved in, Reagan was reelected.

One of Reagan's great concerns was Nicaragua, the Central American country that had been controlled by the Marxist-Leninist Sandinistas since their overthrow of the forty-five-year-old Somoza family dictatorship in 1979. Their opponents, the Contras, had been denied military aid by Congress in October 1984. Oliver North (b. 1943), an official of the National Security Agency (NSA), saw a way to raise clandestine funds to continue the Contras' war. The money came from Iran. Five years after fundamentalists deposed Iran's Shah, the Reagan administration placed the Islamic Republic on a list of countries that, because of their support of terrorism, were deemed untrustworthy and subject to strict export controls. Then, over the next eighteen months, twenty Americans, including the CIA's station chief in Lebanon, were kidnapped in Beirut.

Early in 1985, advisers to Israel's President Shimon Peres met with arms dealers from Israel and Iran—Manucher Ghorbanifar, a former officer of the Shah's secret police, among them—to discuss the possibility of a trade of weapons for the American hostages in Lebanon. That May, Barbara Ledeen's husband Michael, a consultant at the NSA, went to Israel and met with Peres to discuss Iran. On his return, Ledeen told Robert McFarlane, the head of NSA, that Ghorbanifar had a secret agenda: a plan to overthrow the fundamentalist Islamic regime.[2] Secretary of State George Schultz tried to cast doubt on Ledeen's statement, implying he was putting Israel's interests above those of the United States, but the plan had engaged the imagination of the White House. By late summer, U.S.-made missiles were en route to Iran via Israel, and the profits from the sales were routed back to the Nicaraguan Contras.

As the war in Nicaragua heated up, it became Rudd's new issue. "I saw it as Vietnam again, what I'd started out fighting," Rudd says. "I don't think I ever felt that the Sandinistas were that heroic, but I thought that they were doing their best to build a more just society."

Americans had been backing the Sandinistas since 1979, when the Nicaragua Network was formed to support what was then still a guerrilla army. By the mid-1980s, it had more than 100 chapters. "We were a check," Rudd says. "We prevented the United States from becoming directly involved, so the military had to use surrogate troops and covert warfare." In February 1986, Rudd spent four weeks building houses in Nicaragua with the New Mexico Construction Brigade.

That year, after Reagan announced his Strategic Defense Initiative, the space-based missile defense system better known as Star Wars, Rudd quit his teaching job and got a contract to write a revisionist history of the Vietnam-era antiwar movement. His publisher urged him to make it autobiographical. "It took a long time to write it, and I was very dissatisfied," he says. "There were many things I was ambivalent about. One is, why did I opt for violence? The second is my womanizing. The third is privilege and access to money. Even when I was underground and under a different name, I could easily get jobs, because I'm articulate." Unable to resolve these nagging issues, Rudd finally shelved the book.

HAVING SEX ONSTAGE snapped Nina Hartley's life into focus. She could have it all, career and family, even if both were a bit out of the ordinary. She could also embody the sex-positive message of *Our Bodies, Our Selves*. In 1984, she decided to dive in the deep end and start making porn movies. She answered a few ads for actresses, "but the people were just so icky," she says, definitely not the sort with which a feminist would associate. Then, one afternoon, her boyfriend Dave met a director, Juliet "Aunt Peg" Anderson (b. 1938), in the Berkeley Bowl supermarket.

Anderson, a Finnish feminist and former teacher, had been writing a master's thesis on porn when someone dared her to do a movie. By 1984, she was one of a small cadre of feminist sex workers beginning to make a mark, insisting that their lifestyle could be an acceptable choice for intelligent women, despite the claims of traditional feminists that pornography encouraged rape and was degrading to women.

Hartley's onscreen debut came in one of the first porn movies shot on video instead of film. As dramatized in the 1997 mainstream film *Boogie Nights*, within the world of X-rated movies, filmmakers had pretensions to art. Video was considered a lesser form, lacking even the modest production values and nods toward plot and character that supposedly elevated porn's golden age in the 1970s. Video producers were concerned with volume, not quality, and soon caused the bottom to drop out of the porn movie market. But by then Hartley was established as a star. After completing her nursing degree in 1985, she began cranking out movies. She's made four hundred and fifty in fifteen years. "It was almost impossible to get away from me," she boasts.

Hartley was savvy about marketing herself. "You could tell I was enjoying myself," she says. "It was important for me to showcase women enjoying sex, the role model of a happy, active, into-it female. I smiled at a penis, knowing people would notice. And I was consistent. I couldn't control the movie, but I could control my performance." Having married Dave, she insisted on his presence on sets, which kept things on an even keel. "Feminism told me I didn't have to do what I didn't want to do," she says. "I'm sure other girls who had VICTIM stamped on their forehead had more horrible experiences."

Until she began making films, Hartley managed to hide her work from her parents, telling them she was a cocktail waitress and a sportswear model. After "Nina" did an interview with the *San Francisco Chronicle*, though one of Mitzi's brothers called. "Do you know how upset Mom is?" he asked. It got worse when she learned about Nina's three-way marriage. "We're close, but estranged," Hartley says.

Politics had been anathema in the small world of pornography until the mid-1980s, when several separate groups of women in the industry began banding together, seeking a measure of control over their own destinies. In 1983, a group of late-1970s New York porn performers, all nearing the end of their onscreen careers, banded together in a consciousness-raising and support group.[3] Simultaneously, Nina Hartley and Bobby Lilly met Kat Sunlove (b. 1945), a former radical, at the premiere of Hartley's first movie. Sunlove, a Texan with a master's degree in political science, had been a union organizer, a wife and mother, and director of a Big Brothers program before moving to the Bay Area, where she changed her name and worked as a dominatrix, an adult performer, and a producer of workshops on sadism and masochism. She also wrote a sex advice column for *The Spectator*, a local sex newspaper descended from the 1960s underground newspaper *Berkeley Barb* (which had spun off its sex ads into the offshoot in an exercise in political correctness in 1978—and promptly died from loss of advertising income). Sunlove, who became *The Spectator's* publisher and president, brought Lilly and Hartley into the nascent pro-sex movement on the West Coast.

Sex-positive feminism was a reaction. It began in 1979 when, after *Roe v. Wade*, mainstream feminism veered into neo-Victorianism in search of its next issue. Inspired by the formation of Women Against Violence in Pornography and Media three years earlier, NOW began a campaign called Take Back the Night, tying sexual permissiveness to rape, and Andrea Dworkin (b. 1947), who'd begun reading porn in her first, abusive marriage to a Dutch radical, published *Pornography: Men Possessing Women*, an anti-porn polemic. Dworkin's extremism was such that she would later equate all sexual intercourse with rape, saying, "Sexual relations between a man and a woman are politically acceptable only when the man has a limp penis."[4] Along with Gloria Steinem, Susan Brownmiller and others, Dworkin was one of the founders of Women Against Pornography, which gave tours of New York's Times Square sex district.

Also in 1979, Catharine MacKinnon (b. 1946), a Yale-educated lawyer who'd opposed the Vietnam War and supported the Black Panthers and women's lib, published her landmark study, *Sexual Harassment of Working Women*. In it, the daughter of a Republican judge who'd once said sex in the workplace was only to be expected, argued that workplace sexual harassment was more than a private harm; it was discrimination. While that construct had merit, under MacKinnon's extreme interpretation, it led to situations such as the one in which a college teacher was forced to remove a photo of his wife in a bathing suit from his desk.[5]

In the early 1980s, sex permeated society. Public sex venues—gay bathhouses, movie theaters, and bookstores, S&M and fetish clubs like New York's Mine Shaft and Anvil, and swingers' spots like Plato's Retreat operated openly in major cities. Health clubs promised hard bodies, and we all knew what those were for. Even if you didn't have one, advertising promised that almost every product, whether a new car or a new pair of Jockey shorts, was a shortcut to whoopee. Sexual fruit was no longer forbidden, but a backlash was brewing.

Unlikely as it sounds, AIDS wasn't an issue in the porn world. Hartley says most performers who contracted HIV in the 1980s were known to have engaged in unprotected anal sex or to have used needles—and other porn people avoided them. They also felt safe because the conventions of porn limited the exchange of bodily fluids. They didn't discuss it; denial was a mental prophylactic. "Heterosexuals in the sex business were like heterosexuals everywhere 'Can't happen to us!'" Hartley says.

Concurrently, people nationwide who'd felt disenfranchised during the political and social upheavals of the preceding decades were finding their voice through newly resurgent conservative and religious fundamentalist groups. Millions, including many boomers—some who were always silently conservative, some who were becoming more so as they settled down and placed new emphasis on families, careers, and economic concerns—were redefining themselves. In 1981, the *New York Times* reported a sudden shift in political affiliation among people born between 1946 and 1955. "A year ago that group was 56 percent Democratic and 30 percent Republican," the paper said. "Today it is 44 percent Democratic and 43 percent Republican."[6]

Encouraged by the Reagan Republicans and by evangelical preachers who were reaching millions via satellite and cable TV broadcasts, they were leading a charge toward—or retreat to—old-fashioned ideas like commitment, romance and even the restoration of chastity and virginity as virtues. America wanted its hymen back.

Leading the way were groups like the National Federation for Decency, which declared advertiser boycotts and letter-writing campaigns against television shows, movies and musicians, and the Moral Majority, a coalition of conservative Christians and anti-abortion right-to-life groups that declared war on "filth" in 1985. The Moral Majority was founded by a right-wing journalist, Paul Weyrich (b. 1942), fronted by the evangelist Jerry Falwell, and supported by politicians like North Carolina Senator Jesse Helms, who summed up the new attitude when he said, "Surely it is not just coincidental that, at a time in our history when pornography and obscene materials are rampant, we are also experiencing record levels of promiscuity, venereal disease, herpes, AIDS, abortion, divorce, family breakdown, and related problems."[7] As early as 1982 a *New York* magazine cover had asked, "Is Sex Dead?" *Esquire* answered: "The Sexual Revolution: R.I.P." *Time* put herpes, a new, incurable venereal disease, on its cover, and reported that twenty million Americans had it.[8] Jimmy Carter's lustful heart had given way to Nancy Reagan telling us to just say no.

The fundamentalists and conservatives forged an unlikely alliance with feminism. Dworkin and MacKinnon had met when Dworkin put MacKinnon together with Linda Lovelace, the star of *Deep Throat*, following the publication of her memoir, *Ordeal*, in which she revealed she'd been coerced to make the movie under threat of death.

In 1983, Dworkin and MacKinnon taught a class on pornography

together at the University of Minnesota. After testifying at a zoning hearing on behalf of a local group trying to ban porn shops, the two were
asked to write a city ordinance defining porn as a violation of women's
civil rights. Lovelace testified at the hearings, and a law was signed in May
1984. Though immediately vetoed by the mayor of Minneapolis, it made
MacKinnon and Dworkin feminist superstars. At that year's NOW convention, Dworkin led a march against porn.

Soon a coalition arose to oppose the Dworkin/MacKinnon position on
First Amendment grounds, including the American Booksellers
Association, the ACLU, and the Feminist Anti-Censorship Task Force
(among the signatories were 50 prominent feminists, like Betty Friedan
and Kate Millett). The anti-porn movement wouldn't be stopped. In
1984 the Reagan administration set up an investigating commission
under Attorney General Meese, and the Justice Department launched a
simultaneous attack. Reagan had found a domestic equivalent to the
Soviet Evil Empire. Politicians clamored to bang the anti-porn drum. The
Parents' Music Resource Center was formed in 1985 by a group that
included the wives of Senators Gore, Packwood and Thurmond to promote hearings against salacious rock lyrics. In 1986, an official of the
Meese Commission threatened to boycott chains like 7-Eleven, Rite-Aid,
and KMart if they didn't stop selling *Playboy* and *Penthouse*.[9]

The underlying political assumption was that baby boomers, the great
beneficiaries of the sexual revolution, were feeling guilty about past pleasures and their unplanned side effects and were ready to renounce the
libidinous behaviors of their youth. But generalizing about the Baby
Boom will get you in trouble every time. Though there were certainly
boomers who felt that way—some in the forefront of the new fundamentalism—just as many treasured their sexual liberation despite the price
paid for it, and were ready to go to the barricades again to protect it.

San Francisco lesbians were just then supplanting gay men, whose
ranks were being decimated by AIDS and accompanying second
thoughts, at the forefront of the pro-sex movement. "Lesbians were
claiming the right to fuck without romance that gay men had claimed for
years," says Hartley, who joined a like-minded group to form Californians
Against Censorship Together in 1986, to defend the adult industry. The
Meese Commission reminded Hartley of "the Red Scares that fucked up
my father," she says. "It brought to mind people's attacks on [birth control
advocate] Margaret Sanger. Even if I hadn't been in the business, it would
have concerned me." The group lobbied for free speech in the state capi-

tal and against restrictions on pornography at the twentieth-anniversary meeting of NOW in Denver that year.

Hartley became their frontwoman "because no one else would speak out in public," she says. "It became imperative because the propaganda from the other side was so strong. Sexual control is the bedrock of social control. The 1960s were about discovering that. And the culture has been at war over that issue ever since. I agree with a lot of what feminists say about sex as commodity, but you don't get rid of that by getting rid of sex."

CORPORATE LIFE WAS good to the maverick Michael Fuchs. He was made chairman of the board and chief executive officer of Home Box Office in 1984, but he was also handed a huge problem. "Though the eighties were starting to boom, HBO's business was not," Fuchs says. The number of subscribers paying monthly fees had been growing by millions a year, and HBO had made plans based on that growth rate, despite Fuchs's warnings about the looming threat of videocassettes. When growth stopped dead thanks to increased competition from them and from new premium cable competitors, the company only stayed solvent because it had a deep-pocketed parent. HBO wasn't Time's only speed bump. A series of failures derailed the ambitions of several Time executives, leaving Gerry Levin and Nick Nicholas as heirs apparent to Time Inc.'s CEO Dick Munro—all cable guys.

Nothing was simple at Time, though, and executives constantly played musical chairs. Fuchs hired Frank Biondi in 1978, only to become his employee in 1983, when Biondi was named HBO's chairman. Within a year, Biondi was fired and Fuchs promoted to chairman in a shakeup that also saw Levin demoted and Nicholas positioned to take over the top spot at Time. Fuchs and Nicholas then teamed up to strengthen HBO. It was hardly a weakling; it had long made Hollywood dance to its tune. "The license deals were gigantic, and that created enormous tension," says Fuchs. When the studio tried to fight back, HBO started making end-runs around them to get rights to films, even financing them independently, becoming the largest backer of feature films in the world.[10] That infuriated the studios, and Fuchs didn't help matters by boasting, "I will bring Hollywood to its knees."[11]

"I've never had the respect for Hollywood so much of our society has because I know the emperor has no clothes," he explains. "And the movie studios felt angry and stupid, having missed this opportunity (to cash in on the new revenue stream of cable) being driven by their movies."

Though he was arrogant and on a roll, Fuchs didn't join in the money madness of nouvelle society. He says it disgusted him. "When I went to speak at colleges, they wanted to know how to get my job instead of hearing me talk about what they should believe in." Once, after a speech in Philadelphia, he and MTV's Robert Pittman was chased to the train station by students pushing their résumés on the pair. "I'd never seen anything like that. I'm not anti-capitalist. You participate, you try to earn money and invest. But I'm against the worship of the rich, of celebrity."

Still, he was in the entertainment and celebrity business. In 1986, Fuchs convinced Barbra Streisand to appear in her first full-length televised concert in two decades, and he cut a deal with boxing promoters Butch Lewis and Don King to present a heavyweight "world series" of boxing matches that produced the next world champion. And when a young boxer, Mike Tyson (b. 1966), won that title, he made a deal with Fuchs that would pay him more than $25 million dollars over the next two years and begin his transformation into a celebrity nightmare.

Many of the projects Fuchs greenlighted were about more than making money. "Good citizenship is good for business," he'd decided. A series of bio pics spotlit his personal heroes—Soviet dissident Andrei Sakharov in 1984, TV news pioneer Edward R. Murrow in 1986, South African anti-apartheid advocate Nelson Mandela in 1987, and Nazi hunter Simon Weisenthal in 1989. Only a tiny percentage of HBO viewers knew who any of them were, so Fuchs would educate them. "But this was not PBS," he says. "This was not an elite audience." Instead of making these movies with obscure English actors, he made them with stars and promoted them as events. "We were very good at spin," he says, better still at spinning product toward boomers with the money to buy both subscription cable services and the equipment to receive them.

Many boomers were belatedly starting families. "When you have kids and you can't go out as much, television becomes more important," Fuchs notes, and he knew how to reach them. "Although I'm single, I thought of myself as very much typical of the HBO audience," he says. He loved Robin Williams, Billy Crystal and Whoopi Goldberg. In 1986, he helped create Comic Relief, a four-hour live benefit comedy show starring the trio to finance health care for the homeless, a feel-good balm for boomers.

His issue-oriented programming decisions were carefully calibrated to be provocative yet beyond reproach. In 1987, HBO broadcast a special, *How to Raise a Street-Smart Child,* tied to a community outreach program to warn children about the dangers of victimization by adults. (The parents of boomers had called it talking to strangers.) Fuchs was also responsible for a documentary, *Down and Out in America*, that became the first pay-cable program to win an Academy Award. Then, in 1988, HBO won the cable industry's first primetime Emmy Awards.

Fuchs had long felt guilty that he'd served in the Reserves while poorer, less advantaged boomers went to Vietnam. One summer in the 1970s, he'd shared a beach house with a girl whose boyfriend was a veteran and "told stories of what it was like to come back to America, to veterans' hospitals where guys were paralyzed and rats would come in and chew on their toes and they wouldn't know it," Fuchs says. "They'd put him on Thorazine because he got so angry." Fuchs had joined the board of the Vietnam Veterans Ensemble Theater Company, or VetCo, the group that mounted the Vietnam play *Tracers*, and resolved to make a film that offered a positive portrayal of the once-maligned and too-often-ignored Vietnam vets. In the mid-1980s, a director brought him a book of eloquent letters written by soldiers in Vietnam called *Dear America: Letters Home from Vietnam*. Though some HBO officials were skeptical, Fuchs financed the project to the tune of more than a million dollars. Actors and veterans from VetCo provided the narration.

Fuchs couldn't have accomplished all he did alone; he not only had a major corporation behind him, but also the various wire-owners who'd financed the miles of coaxial cable carrying HBO across America. Still, he took pride in pointing out that competitors like Atlanta entrepreneur Ted Turner (b. 1938), who put his local station, TBS, onto satellite in 1976 and added CNN in 1980, Kay Koplovitz (b. 1945), who started USA Network in 1977, and John Lack, who'd conceived the flamboyant MTV, were relative latecomers compared to him. Fuchs is even prouder of having created a new template for entertainment marketing. Years later, Bob and Harvey Weinstein (b. 1954 and 1952 respectively), brothers who'd shown counterculture movies and produced rock concerts while in college, would pull off something similar at their Miramax Pictures—and be hailed for innovation. That brings out the combatant in Fuchs. "HBO had much more impact on America than Miramax has had," he says. "Miramax had a little impact on the motion picture business. It's a little oasis that occasionally makes a good movie. But HBO revolutionized television. And immodestly, I invented original programming on cable. And I started to pitch cable owners on promotion and public relations."

Slowly, HBO's business turned around, but just when Fuchs might have relaxed, in 1985, his father was diagnosed with cancer. "It had me totally discombobulated," he says. "It put me in a time of indecision and confusion." He dithered about buying an apartment and about marriage.

"I almost settled down," he says. "I felt that this shouldn't happen to you without a family, and really, the next woman who came along was the woman I decided to marry." That woman was the actress Brooke Adams. Fuchs ran into her one day, immediately cast her in an HBO movie, popped the question and announced their engagement. They broke up almost as abruptly. "Since then," the *New York Times* magazine reported in 1989, "his social life has included a range of companionship, from an heiress to an anchorwoman to a schoolteacher." (In the next few years he would add a celebrity activist, a world-class athlete, and at least one more actress to that list before proposing to a former actress in 1999. Though friends doubt he'll actually walk down the aisle, he insists, "It's about time.")

IN 1984, CYNTHIA Bowman became a single mother. "I had this infant," she says, "I'd left his father, we had no financial agreement, I was basically hoping he was going to do the right thing." Kantner did, and ever since, they've shared parental responsibility for their son. To pay her part, Bowman took freelance publicity work. One client, the singer/songwriter Boz Scaggs, had opened a restaurant, asked her to publicize it, and encouraged her to start her own business.

Bowman had a lot of catching up to do. The world had changed while she'd been ensconced in the narcotic cocoon of rock 'n' roll stardom. "My little world was pretty cool," she says. "I wasn't concerned about anything else." Now she had no choice.

In 1984 she opened Cynthia Bowman Public Relations. Soon, the San Francisco Symphony asked her to be their liaison to the local rock 'n' roll community, and recommended her to the San Francisco Opera as well. Rock stars had become accepted members of the mainstream community in the liberal Bay Area—and targets of opportunity for cultural fundraisers. Bowman, in the right place at the right time again, became the intermediary.

She couldn't entirely leave her past behind, though. In March 1985, Paul Kantner left Jefferson Starship, which promptly released three number one songs. Kantner descended into depression. "He was devastated," says Bowman. "People were worrying about him blowing his brains out." Just when she thought she'd gotten out, she moved back in to his house.

JUST AS KATHRYN Stockton arrived at Brown University in 1982, an academic trend from France took hold on American campuses, altering innumerable educational and political assumptions. Years later, its tenets would be derogated as political correctness. Stockton had already used the term at Yale Divinity School. "We used it to talk each other down," she says. "People would get so earnest, so self-serious. We even had T-shirts printed up: NUKE THE WHALES."

Stockton had given up her plans to study for a doctorate in either clinical psychology or philosophical theology, deciding that their generalizations were too easily challenged and that literature might be a better laboratory for applied philosophical and religious principles. When she heard about the new discipline, "Theory," which focused on historical and cultural context instead of just words, she didn't like the sound of it. Theory had its origins in the French philosophy of the 1960s called Structuralism, which argued that individuals were shaped by deep structures—social, psychological and linguistic—they don't control. It also said that Texts, sets of words and symbols, are not the product of an author but of the structures and the systems their authors inhabit. Structuralism was a profoundly different way of looking at human discourse and interaction—and proved to be tailor-made for a late-blooming lesbian.

Stockton explains it all with a metaphor. "Between you and your own skin, there is language," she says. "If I touch the back of my hand, one can say I'm touching the skin, but really it's language touching language. The direct contact we think we have with the world is massively mediated—by language and other things; we only communicate through this very complicated system of substitution. You have to understand the complex things that pass between people on the backs of words. There is something profound about that."

Structuralism was just a linguistic pit stop on the road to Theory. Poststructuralism added a new wrinkle: that language and society themselves can only be understood in their economic, political, and cultural context. Then came Deconstructionism, which held that all texts in Western culture were based on classic oppositions like light versus dark, good versus evil, and man versus woman, with the first always deemed superior. But since darkness, the absence of light, depends on light for its very existence, their opposition is open to interpretation—an attractive notion to someone on the wrong end of oppositions like male versus female and straight versus gay.

In Theory's world, certainty is impossible, identity is fluid, and there is no truth, no justice, only relationships of power. So when these ideas first crossed the Atlantic in translations in the late 1970s, they found a ready audience among academics who'd cut their teeth ten years earlier on opposition to systems and the not-so-absolute truths that propped those systems up. Having tasted victory—and subsequent defeats—in the era's various movements, these "tenured radicals," as the conservative writer Roger Kimball called them, banded together in self-promoting circles and sought to force change on campuses where nonwhites and non-males were now studying in unprecedented numbers.

In the Reagan era, ever more multicultural college campuses rediscovered their traditional role as bastions of opposition. Theory replaced Marxism and its homegrown offshoots as the basis of that opposition. The new academic activists wanted to make their theory manifest and, being typically impatient baby boomers, didn't want to wait for the process to play out. They began to question disciplines like literature, history, and in extreme cases, science, asking if supposed universals were not in fact bound to a set of liberal white male-driven assumptions about race, class, culture and gender. Though that humanist ethic had given them their voice, they still found it oppressive. Why not *our* tribal truths? they asked.

To a young gay woman who'd just realized where she fit in a society in which she'd never known a lesbian, Theory was a great gift. Stockton and a small group of feminist friends would study dense, jargon-laden books by French philosophers "to figure out what are they saying and then what do we think about what they're saying." They discovered that Poststructuralism was a window on "how the linguistic game has been fixed in ways that are obviously disadvantageous to women. Our linguistic system really puts Man and things Masculine at the center. So much of gender thinking in Western civilization is based on a notion that men and women are opposites, so that if man is rational, woman must be irrational, if man is human, woman must either be demonic or angelic." For suddenly deconstructive Stockton, here was proof that falsehoods propped up the patriarchy.

IN THE AFTERMATH of the Danceteria 2 debacle, people around Jim Fouratt began to get sick and die. An epidemic of pneumonia had started in the gay world, and was first made public by the Centers for Disease Control in June 1981.[12] A New York skin doctor named Alvin Friedman-Kien had found a cancer, Kaposi's sarcoma, in gay men who'd had frequent, multiple sexual encounters with as many as ten partners a night. Many of them were also drug users.[13]

By the end of that year, the demi-monde was buzzing with concern about something scientists called Gay-Related Immune Deficiency (GRID). Fouratt's oldest friend had fallen in love with a singer named

Michael Callen (b. 1955), who'd come down with it. Several Danceteria performers and a journalist who'd written about Fouratt had caught it, too. When Fouratt visited the journalist in the hospital, one of the performers, Klaus Nomi (b. 1945), was in a room down the hall. "That was the first time I faced this," Fouratt says with uncharacteristic brevity.

Looking for a way to help, Fouratt discovered an organization started in August 1981, Gay Men's Health Crisis (GMHC). A co-founder, a gay writer, Larry Kramer (b. 1935), had made himself a pariah in his community in 1977 by openly questioning the carnality of white, upper-middle-class, urban gay culture in a novel with the provocative title *Faggots*. "All we do is live in our ghetto and dance and drug and fuck," he wrote in his satiric plea for love and commitment. Late in 1981, Kramer again played Patrick Henry, with a series of articles on GRID in a gay newspaper the *New York Native*.

Few wanted to listen. The city's gay elite was closed to Kramer's warnings; it had institutionalized promiscuity as a cornerstone of gay identity and culture—and was now getting support in that view from academia. Just as Kathryn Bond Stockton found validation in Theory, gays claimed the same benefit from anonymous sex.[14] After attending a few of the initial GMHC dinners, Fouratt felt his fellow homosexuals would find it easier to accept the reality of their situation if GRID weren't seen as a *gay* disease. Others—including many gay doctors—were equally uncomfortable with the first word in GMHC's name. The disease had already crossed out of the gay population; hemophiliacs had begun to contract it through blood transfusions. That July, researchers coined a new name, AIDS, for Acquired Immune Deficiency Syndrome.

Fouratt quickly organized a new group, Wipe Out AIDS, in the hope that women and heterosexuals might join the fight. He put his hippie experience to work by sponsoring consciousness-raising sessions about how to avoid AIDS and whether it was possible to survive it. Others had also begun to raise the fine point that it was certain sexual practices, not homosexuality itself, that transmitted the disease. Late in 1982, Callen and a former gay prostitute and backroom bar habitué co-wrote an article decrying the notion that frank talk about responsible sexual behavior stigmatized the gay world. Though denounced as prudes and charged with encouraging homophobia, they collaborated the next year with Callen's doctor on the first safe sex instruction pamphlet, *How to Have Sex in an Epidemic*.

Though he kept a hand in the music business, managing several artists, Fouratt became a full-time AIDS activist. Wipe Out AIDS continued to sponsor informational meetings for the next two years. At one, as an expert discussed the health benefits of a macrobiotic diet, Fouratt found himself thinking, "What does macrobiotics really give to someone? A sense of discipline. What is the biggest problem gay men have with their lives? Lack of discipline, lack of self-control." He decided his group should advocate discipline, which meant championing an unpopular honesty. In 1984, Fouratt joined a Safer Sex Committee calling for doors to be taken off stalls in the gay bathhouses. That idea won him few friends.

Wipe Out AIDS was renamed HEAL (for Help Education AIDS Liaison) and began organizing 1960s-style agitprop actions to encourage sex education. HEAL members put out piles of safe sex literature in bathhouses and graffittied the walls of sex clubs with slogans like *AIDS Lives Here!* and *Sleaze Breeds Disease*, and were beaten by security men at one club in response. They researched who owned the gay establishments and discovered it was mostly gay people, not the Mafia, as in the sixties. "Gay entrepreneurs were worse," says Fouratt. "The only places willing to put up safe sex posters were the Mafia clubs."

Despite the insistence of the activists on their right to have sex, the public came to agree with Fouratt and his more careful fellows. By 1985, public sex of any kind—gay or straight—was no longer tolerated. Across the country, cities began to close down gay baths and straight sex clubs like New York's infamous Plato's Retreat, finally turning the page on 1960s-style promiscuity.

WHEN MARIANNE WILLIAMSON presented herself at the Philosophical Research Society in Los Angeles in 1983, her sketchy résumé proved a godsend. There was an opening for a lecturer on *A Course in Miracles*. Her first appearance, advertised with handbills, was enough of a success that the society offered her a yearlong lecture series, every Saturday morning.

Supporting herself with secretarial temp jobs, Williamson lived for those Saturdays. "When I started speaking in 1983, self-help yuppies were not my audience," she says. Addressing people in their fifties, the sort who might have come to hear Aimee Semple McPherson preach half a century before, Williamson combined her growing knowledge of the *Course* with her experiences as a seventh-grade debater and 1970s lounge singer and realized, "I am an orator; that's what I do."

After about a year, her audience began to change. "Gay people started trickling in," she says. "AIDS had hit Los Angeles. All of a sudden, you had a population in dire crisis and when they went to their churches, they were being told they were a bunch of sinners. Profound human crisis was the crucible out of which my career sprang."

Gay men could relate to Williamson. She was chic, charismatic and best of all, a former good-time girl who'd discovered being bad wasn't enough. She gave them hope and ginger ale and conducted heartfelt question-and-answer sessions after her talks, strolling through her audience like an afternoon TV talk show host. They called her a jazz philosopher and compared her to Janis Joplin, sharing her pain in order to succor others. "One night there were seventy-five people and I remember feeling scared," she says. "I shared that, and I got such a strong, strong feeling and message: Nobody here is thinking you're perfect, Miss Williamson. Your responsibility is to be honest." Soon she'd added Tuesday night lectures, then started renting out space in churches and halls so she could speak to even larger crowds. She professes not to know how word got out. "How does anybody find out anything?" she asks.

JUST BEFORE SHE'D gone to England in 1983, Victoria Leacock went to a fundraising dinner at the home of the head of the new American Foundation for AIDS Research. She didn't know anyone who had the disease then. Two years later, a half-dozen people she knew had gotten it, all gay. She continued to live dangerously. Her drinking escalated. She started blacking out and getting into romantic situations that were something less than romantic.

Change was indicated. But where to go? In the mid-1980s, New York rich and poor separated. On the club scene, yuppies stayed uptown and celebrated their money alongside Europeans who flooded the city looking to make some of their own, while those who would have once been in the counterculture went downtown and celebrated art and their artistic lifestyle.

Leacock got a job as the receptionist at *Details*, then a black-and-white journal of the downtown scene, published by a woman called Annie Flanders, who'd run a pop fashion boutique in the 1960's.[15] Downtown had replaced uptown as the source of the city's cultural heat, as surely as Area had replaced Studio 54. *Details* was the new bohemia's update on the underground newspaper, covering not revolution but fabulousness.

Leacock stayed two years, rising to advertising manager. She loved her new milieu, full of simultaneously entrepreneurial and artistic types fixated on a new paradigm of self-expression. "This was a group of talented people trying to be very individualistic," Leacock says. "It was, 'Let's celebrate us, let's celebrate our friends.' All of a sudden, fame was more accessible. I could be famous. You could be famous. We could all be famous."

* * *

IN MARCH 1983, Leslie Crocker Snyder became a judge in New York's criminal court, handling arraignments, bail and motion hearings, and a few misdemeanor trials. Her star rose quickly in troubled times. Crime in the city had exploded. By the 1980s, the municipal courts were overwhelmed. Snyder moved as many as 300 cases a day—offenses like low-level drug crime and shoplifting—through her courtroom.

The atmosphere worsened markedly in 1984 when a highly addictive, smokable form of cocaine called crack hit America's streets. Crack shattered the complacency of baby boomers, who'd long considered drugs a private matter, and only occasionally a problem. Despite years of negative reinforcement, even heroin had retained a certain glamour, perversely encouraged by the overdose deaths of troubled rock stars, comedians and actors. Into the early 1980s, many boomers were eager to try, or at least know about, the latest new drug. High prices gave them a strange exclusivity, even when the experience was downright seedy, but crack's price—as low as $1 a vial—allowed almost anyone to become a buyer or seller. Most of the defendants Snyder saw in court were black and Hispanic. "That doesn't mean I didn't see a few white Yuppie types come through," she says. "But yuppies were buying drugs inside, whereas the minorities were out on the street, much more subject to being arrested." Drug crime had left the relatively innocent days of the Brotherhood of Eternal Love behind.

Perhaps it was a coincidence, but post crack, the latest drug fashion among boomers was rehab. Age and abuse had taken their toll, and the drug scene suddenly lost any lingering allure and turned downright scary. "No codes, no rules, because crack, as we all now know, was not only highly addictive, but also had a total aspect of violence," Snyder says. "Dealers were taking over streets, shooting people from rooftops. There were wanton killings. Crack just overwhelmed everything."

AFTER TWO YEARS arranging adventure travel for Bill Graham Presents, Cameron Sears was ready for a change when his friends at Grateful Dead Productions called in 1987. Although they hadn't been in a recording studio in seven years, the Dead were still one of American rock's premier live attractions, playing to audiences from aging hippies to teenage flower-child wannabes wanting an alternative to the "no future" nihilism of Generation X.

It was a turning point for the Dead. A year earlier, while on the road with Bob Dylan, its leader, Jerry Garcia, had gone into a near-fatal five-day diabetic coma, brought on by years of debilitating drug use. Ironically, the experience echoed the Dead's first Top Ten single, "Touch of Grey," which, as its title implies, dealt with issues of age, if not infirmity. Even so, the single, which got regular exposure on MTV, vastly increased the band's audience, and changed the nature of its concerts. Suddenly the Dead's traditionally mellow audience had to share arenas with rowdier, new-breed fans whose reaction to the peace and love set was, all too often, to kick it in the face.

That was the atmosphere when Sears joined Grateful Dead Productions as an assistant to the group's manager. "So now I'm in the music business, which I know nothing about," he says. His first meeting with the band was more like a hazing. When he tried to get the Dead onstage, the drummer snapped, "Don't talk to me or any of my friends ever again." Then, at 4:00 A.M., he was awakened by the news that the keyboard player had trashed his room. Sears found him half-naked, sprawled in a mess of broken furniture, plate glass, and ketchup. The drummer, who'd been sleeping in the next room, appeared, yelled, "Clean him up and make him shut up," and slammed the door in Sears's face.

By mid-1990, Sears was managing a band that was still controversial, three decades after the Acid Tests. Sears's predecessor had quit after a year in which two fans died, one breaking his neck outside a show in New Jersey, and the other while in police custody in Los Angeles, high on LSD. Just as he took over, the Dead's keyboard player died of a drug overdose.[16] Traveling with a twenty-three-ton sound system and a similarly weighty entourage of family and friends (still sometimes including the august Acid King, Owsley), Sears was in charge of a high-tech New Age caravan that sometimes killed.

Nonetheless, he was in heaven. "I *still* have to pinch myself sometimes," he says. Not only was he working for his adolescent idols, but it was a multimillion-dollar business. Unfortunately, municipalities around America had long since lost their innocence about the side effects of rock and roll concerts. "So we were constantly having to deal with police chiefs and city bureaucrats," Sears says. "The kids of people who turned on to the Grateful Dead in 1968 were now coming to our shows, and there were those who resented the persistence of geezer rock 'n' roll." Now that rock's latest fashion, the alternative ethic, had crashed into the world of Deadheads, "we started having difficulty with our audience," Sears says. "The rebellion against authority espoused in the sixties reinvented itself in a way that is anti-everything. So we would have these kids, maybe as many as five hundred to a thousand, literally homeless, following us around with a very aggressive attitude. Their attitude was, Jerry Garcia would want me to take drugs and break into the venue. So we'd write impassioned, well-crafted statements to these kids, asking them to chill out. Jerry signed them in his own hand. But these guys were such jerks, there was absolutely no conversation with them."

Rock's tradition of rebellion had evolved, in its third next generation, into "an anger that's unchannelable," Sears says. "There's no resolution to it. They'd say, 'The world's a shithole, there's no prospect for me.'" And the Grateful Dead, who'd espoused the freedom that had now mutated into anarchy, weren't alone in failing to come up with answers.

DAVID McINTOSH WAS enjoying real estate law, but when his Federalist Society friends, who'd gone to work for the Reagan Justice Department, called and invited him to Washington in 1986, he jumped at the chance. In the intervening years, their creation had become influential on and off campus. All twelve of the Reagan administration's assistant attorneys general were members or friends of the society.[17] Co-founder Lee Lieberman was working as a clerk for justice Antonin Scalia at the Supreme Court. McIntosh got a job alongside another co-founder, Steven Calabrese, as a policymaking special assistant to Attorney General Meese, who'd prosecuted Berkeley Free Speech Movement protesters in 1964 and been made the nation's top law enforcer in 1985 after serving as Reagan's chief of staff.

Their influence was quickly felt throughout Washington as they sought to limit what they termed "judicial activism" by overturning liberal court decisions and screening nominees for the federal bench. "America was somewhat divided," McIntosh says. "Americans wanted to have it both ways, wanted to have bits of the sixties revolution of freer lifestyle *and* a traditional moral standard." He felt challenged to chart a course between them.

His boss tended toward tradition. In speeches, Meese railed against judges taking the law into their own hands, ignoring the Constitution, and usurping the rights of localities to set their own judicial standards, and spoke out against several landmark Supreme Court decisions, including Miranda, which mandated that police tell arrestees their rights, and Cooper v. Aaron, the 1958 case that desegregated schools in Little Rock, Arkansas.[18]

As Meese's whip, or manager, McIntosh ensured that the attorney general's directives were carried out, "a tremendous opportunity for somebody interested in Constitutional law," he says. "There were real intellectual debates going on inside the Justice Department, and we were filing briefs on abortion, on property rights. A lot of the career attorneys in the Solicitor General's office were on the opposite side of these issues."

MEESE'S TEAM DID not prevail in their controversial attempt to overturn *Roe* v. *Wade*, the 1973 Supreme Court decision that legalized abortion. McIntosh, who believes life begins in the womb and should be protected, had often argued about abortion with friends. "My view was we were talking about an intellectual issue and then I found out it had a real impact in someone's life," he says. A friend told him, "I had an abortion; does that mean you think I'm a bad person?" Wanting to stay consistent and true to his conscience, but not condemn those who held different views, McIntosh found safe refuge in federalism. "With one national standard, you've got people on all sides feeling unhappy," he says. "You'd have a better chance of consensus if you let communities or states decide whether they wanted to allow abortions. So Indiana could have a consensus where abortions are rare, and in New York, they'd be more readily available."

At twenty-nine, McIntosh moved to the Reagan White House as a domestic affairs aide under the new chief of staff, Howard Baker, and helped draft legislation "on everything from tax cuts to welfare reform to missile defense systems," he says. Just as important were the lessons he learned about politicking. "There's a lot at stake and staff people are all fairly ambitious," he says. "You don't leave your backside unattended."

DONALD TRUMP'S RARE ability to erect buildings on time and on budget dazzled bankers, who gave him unlimited credit. Trump was selling skill, without question; but he was also selling his obsessive bravado. That, and the compulsive spending that went with it, made him one of the tycoons of *Women's Wear Daily*'s nouvelle society, the latest insurgency against the stolid institutions of American power.

This new generation of wealth was the first to include baby boomers, whose wishes were now being fulfilled by a variety of economic factors ranging from the ever-growing federal debt to its private equivalent, the high-yield securities known as junk bonds touted by Michael Milken (b. 1946) of the investment house Drexel Burnham Lambert. In the hands of hostile-takeover artists and mergers-and-acquisition experts engaged in leveraged (i.e., financed with borrowed money) buyouts, junk bonds played a key role in retooling old companies for a new millennium and financing a new generation of American businesses like MCI, CNN and

Steve Wynn's casino empire. Their credo was simple: "Greed is good," as Gordon Gekko so memorably put it in the movie *Wall Street*, written and directed by Oliver Stone (b. 1946).

Corporate debt increased from $774 billion in 1979 to $2.1 trillion in 1989, growing 2.5 times as fast as the economy. Junk bonds represented about 28 percent of that amount. Called junk because they are the last to be repaid in the event of bankruptcy, the bonds were highly risky to investors. They were risky for issuers, too. Some, like fashion designer Calvin Klein, who expanded his business with Drexel bonds, were quickly driven to the brink of bankruptcy by high interest payments. But the stock market kept rising, as did real estate prices, speculation and the celebrity heaped on perceived leaders of the new pack of financial wolves, many of whom swept through the corridors of Wall Street and past the tables of museum benefits buzzed on cocaine. Counterpoints to the crack dealers of the crumbling ghettoes, they, too, were hunters looking for a kill. Who would control Getty Oil? RJR Nabisco? Who would head the Forbes 400? Who'd mount whose head on the wall?

They bought and sold junk, took over some companies, gutted some with downsizing, built others with deregulation, fought politicians one day and supported them the next. They lived in trophy houses with trophy wives, were barbarians in business but turned into lambs when they stormed the social barricades. Though many were older, Henry Kravis (b. 1944), Ronald O. Perelman (b. 1943), and Trump proved that baby boomers could do it, too. They also helped nudge their generation rightward on economic issues: against organized labor and big government and toward free trade, deregulation and tax cuts.

Between 1985 and 1990, Donald and Ivana Trump lived large, trading in their Hamptons rental for a forty-five-room Georgian weekend estate on five acres in tony Greenwich, Connecticut, and combining two triplex penthouses in Trump Tower into a Versailles-in-the-Sky. Trump bought cereal heiress Marjorie Merriweather Post's ocean-to-bay 118-room Palm Beach estate Mar-a-Lago (complete with private golf course and 400-foot beach), Saudi arms broker Adnan Khashoggi's 282-foot yacht, with its gold-plated bathroom and waterfall, a football team, two Atlantic City casinos, the Plaza Hotel, a Boeing 727, several helicopters, a small airline, and full-page ads in major newspapers criticizing American foreign policy, sparking rumors that he would run for President.

If that wasn't enough of a display of hubris, the Yuppie Icarus alienated his political allies in New York by demanding a billion-dollar, twenty-year tax abatement to build something he called Trump City, with 7,600 luxury apartments, a mall, a 9,000-car garage, a nine-acre riverfront park and twelve skyscrapers, one of which would top out at 150 stories—giving New York (and Trump) bragging rights to the world's tallest building. Unimpressed, New York's Mayor Koch called Trump "piggy, piggy, piggy," and the developer responded by dubbing the three-term Mayor an incompetent moron.

Trump admits that, sitting atop a personal fortune variously estimated at $1 billion to $3 billion, he looked to see if others were as impressed with him as he was with himself, but never once looked inward at his motives or at what he'd become. He was the ultimate solipsist. "I don't know if that was the ethic of the age," he says. "But it was my ethic. Everything I touched turned to gold. The Grand Hyatt wasn't supposed to work. The convention center wasn't supposed to work. Nothing was supposed to work. And they all worked. So you don't listen to anybody, because they're all idiots."

CYNTHIA BOWMAN HAD cut her ties to her adolescent rock idols in 1985. Unlike many of her former fellow freaks, she didn't go yuppie, though. "I maybe bought a couple of suits, so that when I went to a meeting at the symphony people could relate to me better, but I did not look like one of them. And I did not think like them, either."

She redressed her life, however. "I realized that if anything ever happened to me, my kid wouldn't have a mother," she says. "I really wanted to be somebody my kid could be proud of."

Drug casualties had long been a part of the rock scene. An original member of the Jefferson Airplane, Skip Spence (b. 1946), had exacerbated his paranoid schizophrenia with repeated applications of Owsley LSD and ended up institutionalized for years before his death at age fifty-two. Other musicians had been felled by overdose, liver failure, heart attack. "If you don't figure it out, you die or you go to jail; if you do, you survive," Bowman notes summarily. She didn't suddenly go straight—she's stayed friends with pot smokers—but she banned both marijuana and cigarettes from her house when her son caught a cold after being exposed to secondhand smoke.

Then there was AIDS. Like most boomers, Bowman had friends among its the early victims in the mid-1980s—and couldn't help being affected. "Since 1984, there have only been a few men in my life," she says. "When Alex was born, I decided I was eliminating all the riffraff and emotional turmoil that comes along with it."

* * *

IN JANUARY 1986, a group of six criminal court judges were promoted to New York's Supreme Court, to handle the explosion of felonies related to crack. "No one wanted to do those violent drug gang cases," Snyder recalls, "because they were perceived to be extremely dangerous. But they're important, they sounded interesting, they had to be done." Snyder's forte became multiple-defendant A–1 narcotics felonies—complex cases involving the sale or possession of large quantities of drugs and the violence that often accompanies them.

Once crack dealers started getting arrested, Snyder heard her first wiretap evidence of Colombians from the Cali cocaine cartel talking about wholesale distribution, and was shocked. "We're not talking junkies and nickel bags," she says. "We're talking greed, violence, they don't care who gets in the way. And I start feeling this is very serious stuff." Even more serious than the typical midlevel heroin dealer raking in $500,000 a week.

One early case involved a defendant who'd turned down a plea bargain of four years to life—a tiny sentence for major drug dealing. "But the problem with going to trial is that the judge hears and sees the evidence," she says. What Snyder heard—that the dealer was a member of organized crime, used his wife to take phone messages about drug deals, and took her and their infant on drug runs—convinced her to give him the maximum sentence allowable by law. "That was my first twenty-five years to life sentence, and I thought about it a lot," she says. She decided that in her courtroom, at least, a line would be drawn against mayhem.

Snyder thus became anathema to criminal lawyers. "Clearly, the Constitution tends to protect defendants, not victims," she says. "We have a job protecting defendants' rights, and I do it. But I'm also always aware that victims have rights, too." Early on, defense attorneys argued when Snyder cut off abusive or humiliating cross-examinations of victims. They don't anymore. "People know me now," she says with a smile. "I don't put up with a lot of crap in my courtroom." Defense attempts to overturn her decisions didn't dent her determination. In her first five years on the Supreme Court bench, her decisions were affirmed on appeal seventy-one times and reversed only three.

THROUGHOUT HER YEARS at *Details*, Victoria Leacock continued producing plays for Jonathan Larson. Aside from that, her life was spinning out of control. She started calling Alcoholics Anonymous, asking about meetings, then ran away to Europe "and exiled myself," she says. When she returned, heavy, unhappy, blacking out instead of falling asleep and waking up with shaking hands, she finally went to a meeting.

A few days later, in August 1988, she had dinner with and a lecture from a girlfriend named Ali Gertz. Two years younger than Leacock, Gertz had been one of the underage preppies who'd frequented Studio 54. "I was going out on a lot of first dates that wouldn't amount to anything, falling into the arms of the person I was with because I was not in a position to extract myself from those situations," Leacock says. Gertz decried her carelessness, then called it an early night. She wasn't feeling well. Two weeks later, she was in the hospital. A few days after that, Leacock got a phone call from a mutual friend.

"Ali has been diagnosed," she said.

"Oh my God," said Leacock, "It's cancer."

"No, Vicki, it's AIDS."

Leacock sank to the floor, clutching the phone. "I really had this crystal-clear knowledge that my entire life had changed at that moment, and that if Ali Gertz could get AIDS, anybody could." It took months before Gertz figured out how she'd contracted the virus. Her boyfriend of three years tested negative. She'd slept with perhaps six other men, and she managed to find and eliminate all but two of them. Finally, someone reminded her of a one-night stand she'd forgotten.

"Why?" she asked. "Is he sick?"

Came the reply, "Well, no, he's dead."

It turned out Gertz had caught the disease from the second man she ever slept with. She'd lost her virginity at sixteen to a summer romance, then spent the next year and a half flirting with one of Studio 54's bare-chested bartenders. "They finally made a date while her parents were out of town for the weekend, and he came over to her Park Avenue apartment and brought roses and champagne, and they slept together, and it was very good, and they decided to stay friends," Leacock reports. She'd asked him if he was gay; he'd lied and said no. Five years later, she'd come down with pneumonia. No one in the hospital thought to run a test for HIV, the virus that causes AIDS, until she'd been there for two weeks without improving.

Gertz asked around about the bartender, and learned that his family had refused to pick up his body from the morgue after he'd died. "That is when Ali became a political activist," Leacock says. "She was really appalled." She realized that before it spread further, someone had to tell the world that AIDS wasn't a gay disease—or a punishment for immoral behavior. "It's funny," says Leacock. "I took care of my mom for six years. She died. I was an alcoholic within a year. I finally stopped drinking, and that's when Ali was diagnosed. I had my calling and I was ready for the job."

In spring 1989, Gertz's mother called a *New York Times* reporter to ask why the paper never wrote about AIDS in the heterosexual community. He replied that no women with AIDS would come forward. Ali would. Her story ran on a Saturday when Gertz was away. When she came home, her answering machine had broken down after fielding 216 messages. Gertz gave interviews to *People* and television's *20/20*. *Esquire* named her its Woman of the Year. She began traveling the country, speaking about AIDS in schools. Her message was, "It can happen to you," Leacock says. "It's not Them anymore. It's our sister, our daughter, my best friend."

Leacock meanwhile, got a new job at the New York Shakespeare Festival, and kept pursuing her dream of producing Larson's musicals—and his of reinventing the American musical. Since they couldn't get financing for a full production of his rock opera, *Superbia*, Larson turned his attention to a one-man show about turning thirty and the collision of his own doubts and insecurities with the cruel fact that his best friend from childhood had been diagnosed as HIV-positive.

Cruel facts were accumulating in Leacock's life. Her surrogate brother, Gordon Rogers, with whom she was sharing an apartment, started limping, then slowly lost control of his appendages—a result of Guillaime-Barr disease. For three months he was on a respirator. Just as he began to recover, he learned that he, too, was HIV-positive. Then their roommate, Pam Shaw, came down with a yeast infection that wouldn't go away. She wasn't promiscuous, she never did IV drugs, and her gynecologist told her there was no need to be tested, Leacock says. But there was—she had AIDS. "She had no immune system," Leacock says.

BARBARA LEDEEN'S RÉSUMÉ lists her occupation from 1984 to 1988 as director of communications for Ronald Reagan's deputy undersecretary of defense for trade security policy, Stephen Bryen (b. 1942). A friend of her husband's, Bryen was a former congressional aide and protégé of the assistant defense secretary, Richard Perle (b. 1941), who oversaw "secure technology transfer policy in what became the final battle against the Soviet Union," she says.

Bryen hired Ledeen to promote their work in the press, to help explain their mission to technology companies whose foreign sales might be affected, and to fight opposition from government agencies that sometimes put business interests ahead of national security. Extraordinarily, despite her Marxist background, Ledeen was able to win top-secret security clearances. "If you told the truth, it was okay," she says. "The issue was blackmail; you couldn't blackmail me. So I went to work in the belly of the beast, at the Pentagon, where I had demonstrated. And to say that I felt like a piece of shit is not even close. I would think, How do I expiate my stupidity? Sometimes I would say it and they would say, Fine, let's go fight communism."

After her third child was born in 1986, Ledeen was embroiled in the biggest scandal of the Reagan era, the Iran-Contra affair. Shortly after the arms-for-hostages deal was first proposed to her husband, he'd been sidelined—kept out of the loop by his NSA colleague (and until then, friend) Oliver North, and Oliver Poindexter, who'd replaced Robert McFarlane at NSA. Only later did Ledeen found out why. North had not only pursued the Iran arms deal, but, in an apparent attempt to obscure his own diversion of the profits to Nicaragua's Contras, wrote an e-mail to Poindexter claiming that Ledeen was taking fifty dollars per missile from the Iranians.[19]

North's secret triangle trade continued until fall 1986. When it was revealed, Reagan was forced to fire him, Poindexter resigned, and a special commission began investigating the NSC. That November, shortly after Attorney General Meese disclosed the Iran-Contra connection and the FBI began a criminal probe, Ledeen was let go as an NSC consultant and asked to leave his think tank. An independent counsel, Lawrence Walsh, was appointed to investigate the deal and the Ledeens, the beginning of a long nightmare for the couple.

"They went through our phone records for seven years, they went through my children's bank account funds, my little Pentagon lunch money account," Barbara says. "The head of my twelve-year-old daughter's middle school said to her, 'Is your daddy guilty?' My son couldn't get into another school because his dad was controversial." Murky stories were recycled. "Michael was a sitting duck for this," Barbara says. In 1989 the Reagan administration ended, and she left the Pentagon. "The Bush people are the other Republican party, the moderates, and they got rid of every Reagan appointee," she says. "The fight we'd fought on tech transfers was no longer viable. But we had done the job." Though the Berlin Wall fell on November 9, 1989,[20] during Bush's presidency, it was Reagan and his team who properly got the credit. Though proud of the small part she'd played in it, Ledeen felt there was still much left undone by the Reagan Revolution.

Shortly after leaving the Pentagon, she met David Horowitz and Peter Collier, two former Berkeley radicals who'd undergone a similar conversion to neoconservatism. Horowitz asked what she was interested in. "I want blood," she said. "I am so pissed. I can't live my life until I get even." They made Ledeen executive director of the Second Thoughts Project, a sort of support group they'd started for former leftists who'd seen the error of their ways. Ledeen grudgingly acknowledges that the Left made good on some of its promises. "There was no opportunity before, you could not bust through the top, and that was worth fighting for," she says. "But why can't they declare victory and fucking go home?"

IN 1986, DOUG Marlette and his wife had a son. The day after the birth, Bill Kovach, a former Washington bureau chief of the *New York Times* who'd just been made the editor of the *Atlanta Journal-Constitution*, called Marlette. Atlanta was the great city of the South, and Kovach said he wanted to make a great national newspaper and wanted Marlette to join him. "I told my wife I was going to win the Pulitzer Prize there," he says. Two years later he did.

It was a good time for cartooning. When Colorado senator Gary Hart (b. 1936), a veteran of the 1960s anti-war movement, pitched his 1988 presidential campaign at baby boomers by promising new ideas, then stumbled in a sex scandal, Marlette skewered him relentlessly, outraged by Hart's taunting the press to find him out. One cartoon, bannered "Front Runner," showed Hart with his pants around his ankles.

"It was good material in terms of the issues of restriction and restraint and indulgence and entitlement," he says. "That sense of entitlement was one of the terrible things with our generation. We were so self-righteous, so pious. And then we get caught in our contradictions and we're stunned. We thought we were invincible! And we wanted to tell everybody else how to live!" Hart was forced out of the race.

The Bush administration wasn't as sexy and fun as the election that led to it. "You're kind of held hostage to the headlines," Marlette says. As a newspaper employee, he was also held hostage to forces larger than himself. Bill Kovach resigned in November 1988, following an argument with his bosses about the paper's take-no-prisoners reporting style. Kovach had angered business leaders by challenging Atlanta's reputation as the city too busy to hate with a Pulitzer Prize-winning series about local banks refusing to make loans to blacks. Marlette was vocal in his disapproval of the ouster. His support of Kovach—he gave interviews and spoke out at a rally protesting the editor's departure—made Marlette's situation untenable, so he, too, left Atlanta, in February 1989. *Newsday*, a local newspaper on Long Island, was opening an edition in New York City and needed a cartoonist.

The move to liberal New York didn't keep Marlette out of trouble in the South. He'd been picking on Jesse Helms for years. Wall-eyed behind his horn-rims, the rabid conservative was a cartoonist's dream. At first, Helms had demoralized Marlette by requesting the original art whenever the cartoonist drew him, but eventually, he began complaining. When Helms attacked the idea of Martin Luther King Day, Marlette drew a cartoon suggesting that April Fool's Day be renamed in Helms's honor. In 1984, when Helms won a vicious reelection campaign, Marlette drew him with *his* pants around his ankles, sticking his rear end out a window toward the U.S. Capitol over the caption "Carolina Moon Keeps Shining . . ." The next day, Helms's office stopped returning the *Charlotte Observer*'s phone calls.

"I understood Jesse," Marlette says. "I can be self-righteous like that. I am Jesse Helms. That's why I get under his skin, and why he gets under my skin." So six years later, with Helms running for reelection again, Marlette wrote him into "Kudzu." In response to Helms's attacks on the National Endowments for the Arts and the Humanities, he drew a cartoon Helms, suffering from Cold War Separation Anxiety, finding a new enemy in the evil International Artistic Conspiracy. Those strips earned "Kudzu" an election-cycle exile to the op-ed pages of some North Carolina papers, and banishment from the *Raleigh News & Observer*. Only after hundreds of complaints did the paper agree to reinstate "Kudzu" and run the Helms strips—the day *after* the election.

INEVITABLY, DONALD TRUMP'S luck changed. In April 1985, he'd installed Ivana as president of his second Atlantic City casino-hotel, Trump Castle. After three children, the sexual energy in the Trump marriage had faltered. For the first time, the pair were not side by side. Several times a week, Ivana made the hourlong run to Atlantic City in the couple's sleek black Puma helicopter. Arriving at 9:30, she spent her days entertaining 10,000 visitors, supervising 4,000 employees, reviewing books and purchasing and marketing, signing checks, and getting a crash course in casino and hotel operations before flying back to New York at 4:30. In her spare time she planned benefits for causes like cerebral palsy and cancer research and managed the couple's homes and the kids.

Trump's eye started wandering. Friends heard rumors about Donald and a professional ice skater, several actresses and nouvelle socialites, and finally, Marla Maples (b. 1963), a beautiful model from Georgia. By spring 1988, when Trump bought New York's Plaza Hotel and brought Ivana back from Atlantic City to run it, stories linking Maples with Trump were common coin in insider circles. Ivana set to work renovating the Plaza and got herself spruced up as well. Sometime in the spring of 1989, she visited a cosmetic surgeon. A few months later, Ivana visited another expert, a divorce lawyer.

Then came Aspen, Colorado. On December 30, 1989, the Trump family was outside a restaurant halfway down Ajax Mountain when Maples approached Ivana and they had words. The children kept going, but Donald Trump joined the two women and asked what was going on. A few seconds later, Ivana and Donald skied off grim-faced. She pulled ahead of Donald, skiing backward. A few more words were exchanged. Back in New York, Ivana called Michael Kennedy, who started an intensive but fruitless negotiation to save the marriage.

Early in February 1990, when Trump flew to Tokyo for a Mike Tyson fight and to meet with bankers, Ivana's team went into action, going public with her legal arguments. By the end of that month, there was more trouble in Trump's world. Rumors began to spread that he was in a financial bind. The rumors were true. Suddenly Ivana Trump's biggest concern was establishing her place in the line of Trump's creditors.

Midas had lost his touch, disempowered by an economy souring in the early days of the Bush presidency. Real estate values in the Northeast and Southwest flattened and declined, and savings and loan institutions that had invested in that real estate were failing. In February 1989, inflation showed its biggest jump in two years. The Resolution Trust Corporation, set up by Bush that month, drove real estate prices down further by dumping the assets of troubled S&Ls it had seized at fire-sale prices.

Prosecutors had been on the trail of financial high fliers since the Ivan Boesky insider trading scandal broke open in 1986. In March 1989, Michael Milken was indicted in Manhattan on ninety-eight counts of fraud and securities violations stemming from the Boesky case. Though he pleaded not guilty, Drexel Burnham Lambert put him on leave and settled its own disputes with the government, plunging the junk bond market into a deep slump. Milken finally agreed to plead guilty to six felonies, to go to jail, and to pay $600 million in penalties. Stocks hit a new high that October, but took their second-worst hit in history a few days later, just after a proposed buyout of United Airlines collapsed. Japan's stock market tanked, too.[21] The go-go 1980s were gone-gone.

At first, it seemed Trump hadn't noticed. He played hardball with his wife and opened his third casino in Atlantic City, the opulent Taj Mahal. Just before the opening, though, a gambling analyst said the casino couldn't cover its costs. A month later, *Forbes* cast doubt on both Trump's net worth and his financial stability, claiming his properties, worth $3.7 billion, were encumbered by $3.2 billion of debt. His bankers were paying attention. Attempts to refinance the Grand Hyatt and Trump Tower failed. So, too, did the plans for Trump City. Environmental activists tied it up in knots, costing him millions. And no one would lend him the $20 million he needed to build penthouses atop the Plaza Hotel.

In June, for his forty-forth birthday, Trump missed a deadline for a $42 million payment on the bonds that financed another of his casinos, Trump Castle, and a $30 million payment on a personally guaranteed loan, and Moody's Investor Services downgraded the ratings of bonds for the Taj and Trump Plaza casinos. "The 1990s sure aren't anything like the 1980s," he reportedly said. He'd just returned from promoting his second book, *Trump: Surviving at the Top*, when the *Wall Street Journal* revealed that he'd begun negotiations a month earlier to restructure his debt.[22] In the cold light of the new decade, some of his deal-making no longer looked so artful. He'd paid top dollar and more for properties that, in the mean new economy, were no longer performing. The slowdown hit his hotels, casinos and airline, and real estate sales were especially hard hit by the credit crunch and the disappearance of Japanese capital.

Trump's bankers were in as much trouble as he was, with credit tight as a noose around all their necks.[23] The "workout" of Trump's debt, begun when banks loaned him an additional twenty million dollars to make the missed payments and avoid personal bankruptcy, continued for a year and provoked an avalanche of bad publicity. It was gleefully repeated that in December 1990, Trump's father bought $3.5 million in casino chips to give his son interest-free cash to pay his bills.

"The 1990s are a decade of de-leveraging," Trump told *Time* that spring. "I'm doing it too." In exchange for $65 million in new loans and an easing of the terms on old ones, Trump gave up control of his personal and business finances; brought in a bank-approved chief financial officer; handed over land in Atlantic City and hundreds of New York condominiums; sold his yacht, the Trump shuttle, his half-interest in the Grand Hyatt, and other properties; limited his household spending (to $450,000 a month in 1990, dropping to $300,000 by 1992); and agreed to submit monthly itemized business plans for his bankers' approval.[24] He got to keep Trump Tower, the Plaza, the Penn Central yard, Mar-a-Lago, and half of his three casinos, though he was forced to reorganize the finances of the Taj Mahal under bankruptcy protection and eventually traded most of his equity in the Penn Central property for release of personal loan guarantees. "I was in really deep shit," Trump says. "You know, publicity is a funny thing. It does create value. But if things go bad, you get it."

One day during the workout, Trump was walking in front of Tiffany & Co. with Marla Maples when he saw a beggar. "Look at that man over there," he said. "Do you know he's worth more than I am?"

"But he's a beggar!" Maples argued. "He's worth nothing."

"Right," Trump replied. "And I'm worth *minus* nine hundred million dollars."

THE COLLAPSE OF the Soviet Union after George Bush's ascension to the presidency stunned Mark Rudd. "Socialism ceased to exist," he says. "It had really ceased to exist decades before, but my illusion was there was an alternative somewhere." In 1990, his beloved Sandinistas were defeated in an election, and the Nicaraguan civil war ended. Finally, the January 1991 Gulf War, in which American troops liberated Kuwait from Iraqi invaders, threw Rudd into a deep depression.

"The Gulf War was kind of like the end of the sixties," he says. "My disillusion was over the ease with which the United States military and propaganda machine was able to whip up support. They were mouthing ridiculous slogans about Saddam Hussein being Hitler and not looking at the real causes of the war, which were economic and geopolitical control! And the inevitable outcome of beating down the Islamic world was that now we are hated by hundreds of millions."

What made it all worse was the assent of Rudd's age peers, the very people who'd fought the same process in Vietnam twenty-five years earlier. It all sent Rudd into a six-year tailspin. He broke up with a girlfriend he'd been with for years, "started a series of disastrous relationships, and went into my forms of therapy and healing," he says. He tried massage therapy, homeopathy, acupressure, psychic healing, cranial sacral massage, and Reiki, "looking to heal myself from pain and hurt," he says. Through it all, he stuck to his political guns, only now, instead of trying to change the world, he worked on his little corner of it.

Having returned to teaching at the junior college in Albuquerque, Rudd got involved in his union and in a national movement to make math education more accessible to minorities and working women, the sort of students who filled his classroom. "They are people who never got what they needed in high school—the basics," he says. "People who've come out of prison, who are disabled and want to reenter the workforce.

Community college is the streets of education. No pretension. And a massive life transformation. It was the continuation of my investigation into how people learn, develop their critical capacity, change their lives, and transform their consciousness. Social change of any sort is going to require enormous changes in consciousness."

SHORTLY AFTER THE 1988 Republican Convention, David McIntosh quit his White House post to run a congressional campaign in Southern California's Orange County—the conservative enclave where John Gage was born—for a colleague from the White House Counsel's office, Christopher Cox (b. 1952). "I knew nothing about running a campaign," he admits, "but he had won a tough primary so he felt safe having a friend who knew nothing about politics being his campaign manager."

Cox had a political consultant who took McIntosh under his wing and taught him the art of campaigning. Briefly, he considered staying in California and building a political career there, but he decided it wasn't where he wanted to raise a family. "Children were under enormous pressure to try the latest things, whether it's drugs or clothes," he says. Though his family was still hypothetical, "I didn't want to subject them to that."

He moved back to Washington at the start of the Bush administration and spent three months unemployed, reading William Manchester's biography of Winston Churchill and taking comfort from the fact that the British leader had spent time in the political wilderness himself. "I was running up against the fact that the Bush people didn't want to hire former Reagan people," he says. Finally, his experience in regulatory law attracted the attention of his fellow Hoosier Dan Quayle, and he was offered a job on the new vice president's staff.

His Reaganite friends advised him against working for a man whose stumbling inexperience had made him a national joke. But McIntosh, remembering the impression Quayle had made on him in high school, said yes. "And I think because of that general view, he worked harder as vice president than other people have and was willing to take on some tough issues because he had to prove he could," McIntosh says.

In 1990, when McIntosh first considered returning to Indiana and making a run for Congress, Quayle kept him in Washington by naming him deputy director of the Competitiveness Council, formed to assess and recommend reforms of government regulations. He soon got another promotion, and headed the council for the remainder of the Bush administration. Though it wasn't glamorous, regulatory reform was a bedrock issue to conservatives. A mole among moderates, McIntosh dug in and bided his time.

IN FEBRUARY 1987, Steve Ross, the former funeral home executive who'd built Warner Communications into one of the world's most powerful entertainment companies, was looking for ways to make it even stronger. Meanwhile, HBO chairman Michael Fuchs was worriedly watching John Malone, a cable system owner from the west whose growing Tele-Communications, Inc. empire threatened Time's. Fuchs and his employers also worried that Time, the third-largest wire owner in America, might become the target of a takeover. Though it had a tradition of feuding with Warner, the sixth-biggest cable outfit, Fuchs proposed that the two companies should band together with several other Eastern competitors against Malone. Thinking Steve Ross would like that idea, he suggested to his boss, Nick Nicholas, that he give Ross a call.

Fuchs wasn't only ambitious for his company; he really wanted to run a movie studio. HBO had invested in the startup of Orion Pictures, and he had discussed succeeding Arthur Krim, its chairman and an old friend of the Fuchs family, but finally decided he'd invested so many years in Time, he'd be better off staying put. Even though a faction on Time's board was anti-entertainment, Levin and Nicholas agreed that Time could better control its destiny if it expanded into Hollywood. When Ross and Nicholas started talking merger, it looked as if they would all get what they wanted.

By summer, serious talks with Warner were under way. Levin, the company's strategist, was promoting the idea of a "transforming transaction"—a consolidation of Time, Warner, and perhaps Ted Turner's Turner Broadcasting System—that would turn Time into an entertainment-oriented communications behemoth.[25] In August, Fuchs met the heads of the Warner Brothers movie studio, Robert Daly and Terry Semel, at a sit-down with Ross and Nicholas and suggested HBO make four or five low-budget youth films a year for them, leveraging its relationships with comedians. Instead of synergy, there was a clash of titanic egos. The Warner executives shot Fuchs down. Fuchs, who insists Daly and Semel "felt the only guy at Time who could rain on their parade was me," says he hadn't expected an agreement—but why not try?

The Time-Warner merger, creating the world's largest media company and greatly enriching the top executives of both firms, was announced in

March 1989. By that time, the deal had been restructured as a cash- and stock-backed purchase of Warner by Time following Paramount Communications' hostile all-cash offer for Time. Though the final transaction was neither leveraged nor hostile, it was still a perfect symbol of the ego-driven dealmaking that began at the end of the Reagan era and has continued ever since. In order to assuage the powers atop both companies, it was agreed that after the merger, Nicholas and Ross would be co-chief executives, with the younger Nicholas taking over after five years. Nicholas presumably knew a secret: Ross had cancer, although it was in remission.

Fuchs made no secret of his unhappiness with the final terms of the merger. "The Warner people got bought out, paid out, and then got control," he says. "Our people sold out our people." Even after he'd decided to support the deal, he still worried that instead of running and expanding a well-regarded if small operation within a large corporation, he'd be lost in an immense enterprise in which he was proportionately less important. He suddenly had to be concerned about his place in the pecking order as well as HBO's in the public eye. Which audience would be more fickle—cable viewers or his superiors—was a toss-up.

Daly and Semel were not going to let him grow. Indeed, some thought they might even try to take over his fiefdom. Rumors flew that Warner boss Steve Ross's fair-haired boy, Bob Pittman, who'd returned to the company after his brief sojourn on his own, would take over HBO. Fuchs felt his position was unique and defensible. After the merger, even Time Inc., people who'd long disdained HBO saw him as an ally, "someone who kept the religion, but could function in that other world," Fuchs says.

He'd convinced himself that "Time's class and intellectual curiosity would rub off on Warner's, and Warner's aggressiveness would rub off on Time." It didn't quite work out that way. "After the merger, the consensus was that HBO suffered the most. We lost our identity, our ability to grow, because many of the things we would have grown into were already being done at Warner." Steve Ross "was going to have the upper hand," Fuchs says, "and Steve favored the movie studio." Officially, Time had taken over Warner, but its executives "began to be treated like household help," Fuchs continues. "They were walking around saying how well they were all getting together, when we all knew it was just a fucking shitstorm."

Even before the merger, Fuchs had begun a multifront effort to strengthen and expand his domain. "Funny is money," he'd always said, so in 1989 he launched the Comedy Channel, an advertiser-supported basic (i.e., free) cable service that would give HBO access to a much larger audience and a much-longed-for presence in the only area of the cable business still promising explosive growth potential. It didn't hurt that he'd be aiming it straight at the audience of the wildly successful MTV, a basic service owned by HBO's rival, Viacom.

Within days of the announcement, Viacom fired back. First, it filed a $2.4 billion lawsuit against Time and HBO, alleging that by favoring HBO over Viacom's Showtime and The Movie Channel on its cable systems, Time had engaged in anticompetitive practices. A few weeks later, Viacom president and CEO Frank Biondi, Fuchs's former employee-turned-employer, announced that MTV would be launching its own comedy subsidiary, HA! It did not go unnoticed that Biondi and other Viacom executives had worked at HBO when the alleged monopolistic practices began.

"I thought my manifest destiny was to run a comedy channel," Fuchs says. "HBO's early years were comedy. I was best known for that. I thought comedy would be the rock 'n' roll of the '90s. And I'm still convinced I could have done it." He pushed to get his channel on the air first, but Viacom's maneuvers, which included offering cable operators discounts on license fees for MTV and VH1, spoiled his plans. Faced with a choice, many cable operators refused to make a decision.[26] The Comedy Channel, featuring an MTV-ish comedy-clip format, went on the air that November. HA!, offering reruns of old situation comedies and funny films, launched the following April Fool's Day. Faced with losing fortunes in a war of attrition, the two cable giants quickly began talking about merging the startups. With Viacom's lawsuit and a Time countersuit hovering in the background, arguments over which team would run the new channel almost derailed the talks. Finally, in December 1990, a compromise was reached and the two channels agreed to merge under neutral management. Aware that the suit would be ruinous even if Time won, Fuchs then sought to settle it. In August 1992, he succeeded with a complicated deal encompassing concessions estimated to be worth a mere $170 million, far less than the $800 million in actual damages originally claimed. "Considering our exposure, I'd have to say we ducked a bullet," Fuchs says. In the next several years, driven by the programming he excelled at creating, HBO regained its momentum. In 1993 it added a million subscribers. The next year, it posted profits of $257 million, making it America's most profitable television channel.

Fuchs also raised his personal profile. In August 1990, he threw the first of a series of summer parties to promote HBO original movies in East Hampton, Long Island, a patrician resort that had lately begun attracting the powerful and the press. "I once asked Simon Wiesenthal why he lived in Austria," Fuchs recalls. "He said, 'If you want to study malaria, go where the mosquitoes are.' We understood you had to program to opinion-makers."

Fuchs understood more than that. A generation that had disdained logos in its youth had evolved into a logocentric herd that had to be the first with the latest, whether it was a Dolce & Gabbana dress or an opinion on the latest HBO movie. Money and success didn't give boomers security; in fact, quite the opposite was true. "Marketing, branding, high pressure, high level," Fuchs recites. "By branding you could raise the prices, you could create economic value without any real cost appreciation. That's what we did in the Hamptons. Now branding has become generic. Everyone talks about it. There is this incredible need to belong. T-shirts with names on them are an easy way. Maybe that's the Baby Boom's ultimate gift, this branded world. We perfected it."

WHILE STEVE CAPPS was in Europe in the mid-1980s, writing music-editing software for the Mac and sending his work to his co-authors over an early modem, the PC landscape changed drastically. Microsoft released Windows—its PARC-like, Mac-like operating system—and began its slow, steady rise to dominance. To Capps, this was inevitable. Steve Jobs *was* a revolutionary, selling the cyber-lifestyle, not a device. Once the Mac had hit the market, he was no longer interested in fine-tuning it and helping it live up to its potential. "The world is a better place because Steve Jobs isn't as smart as Bill Gates, and Bill Gates does not have the charisma of Steve Jobs," Capps says. "It takes somebody to jostle people's thinking, and then other people benefit. We mocked Gates, but he's so smart. He said, 'Steady as she goes. I'll get there later, but I'll get there.'"

While Gates played catch-up, Capps played with toys. He worked on an interactive version of his sound-editing program, created a drawing program, and developed a chip-driven interactive book for kids, all the while fending off the entreaties of Jobs, who wanted Capps at his new company, NeXT. Instead, he and his wife, who'd become a digital artist, moved to San Francisco in 1986, continuing to work on various software products and freelancing for Apple.

Capps finished his book project, but the company that backed it went out of business. SoundEdit and another program, Jam Session, which allowed users to play the Mac keyboard like an instrument against famous rock tracks, accompanied by animation, did make it to market and are still in use today, as is the Jaminator, an "air guitar" toy Capps later created using the chip from his interactive books and Jam Session software. But by the end of 1987, with no payoff from his work in France in sight, Capps had been lured back to Apple with the promise that he could develop what came to be called Newton, a pocket-size computer that could read handwriting and send and receive electronic messages.

He returned to Apple at the start of a decade of failure and mismanagement at the company. For the next two years, Capps and about ten others were paid to think. Just think. "We were clueless," he says now. "We were off by ourselves, in our own building, not doing anything. We played a lot of basketball. We had a lot of ideas. We built prototypes, and we'd go to the board of directors and plead with them, or at least I did, saying, 'You've got to start up five or six of these projects; you've got to let a thousand flowers bloom.'" They wouldn't. Finally, Capps went to see Apple's CEO, John Sculley, and pleaded for the funding to make the handwriting machine real. Capps had learned one thing from Jobs: he was selling potential, not reality. "So I spun this vision." Sculley liked it and sent him to the board again. Capps mocked up a screen he could write on, tethered to a Macintosh. "All the smarts were on the Mac," he admits, but it didn't matter; he won permission to proceed with Newton.

In 1990, a marketing manager named Michael Tchao joined the Newton team as it "flailed, trying to get it done," Capps says. Finally Tchao put into words what Capps had only thought: the technology of the day wouldn't support the Newton. Together, they brainstormed a new product, a mini-Newton they called Sputnik, a satellite to a desktop computer, a halfway measure, but one that could be realized. They still had to fight in-house battles against the team assigned to the larger Newton, but they'd eventually win as surely as the Mac beat out Lisa. "Lisa was real, and Mac was the toy," Capps observes. "I'm convinced, absolutely, that the renegade toy projects are the ones that always win."

By January 1992, Sculley was confident enough to refer to the Newton in a speech at an electronics show in Las Vegas, coining the term "personal digital assistant" and predicting PDAs would become a $3.5 billion industry within ten years. His optimism was understandable. Apple needed to be in the lead of a business like that. Windows 3.1 had been introduced that April, confirming what many had long known: Microsoft had become the undisputed heavyweight champion of personal computing.

Sculley had gotten his first inkling of that then-not-quite-inevitability in fall 1985, when he first learned about Windows and threatened to sue to stop it. At that point, Microsoft—via its word processor and spreadsheet application software—controlled more than half the Macintosh software market. Though he's denied it, Bill Gates allegedly threatened to stop making new programs for Macs if Apple followed through on Sculley's threat.[27] Undisputed is the fact that Apple then inexplicably agreed in writing to license the Mac software's look to Microsoft in present and future versions of Windows. By spring 1988, Windows had evolved from a clunky clone to a robust competitor. Apple finally saw the threat it represented and sued for copyright infringement.

Since Capps was the only high-level Mac developer left at Apple, he became a key player in the lawsuit. Blunt, funny and an almost stereotypical nerd with his long hair, beard and eccentric uniform of white button-down shirts, black shorts, wool socks and black-and-white-checked Vans sneakers, Capps proved an ideal witness. Microsoft contended that the operating system design was obvious, like the steering wheel on a car, and couldn't be protected. "I got up there and said I'd spent hundreds of hours working on this, tried three dozen different designs, and it wasn't intuitive at all," Capps says. Apple lost the suit, but Capps emerged a winner. One of the junior lawyers on Apple's side was Marie D'Amico, who shortly thereafter became his second wife. He'd split with his first when he realized he wanted children and she didn't. "Sometimes, when you fall in love and you're young, you don't ask the right questions," he says.

As they fought the lawsuit, work on Newton continued. Capps demonstrated it in May 1992, at another Consumer Electronics Show. The demonstration "was total bullshit," he admits. The Newton simply wasn't good enough. "It didn't have modem support, printer support. I look at videotapes of that show, and I think I'm a walking advertisement for heart attacks. I'd had no sleep, I demo this total hack, the press just eats it up and I remember going, 'Oh, fuck.'" Apple had made another promise it couldn't keep.

Capps spent the next year in hell, "ramping up production for this thing," he says, he and his team working eighteen-hour days, out of his and D'Amico's home rather than in the demoralized atmosphere at Apple. "One guy committed suicide, and work pressures I'm sure contributed to his lack of judgment," Capps says.

Newton's launch was postponed to August 1993. Days before its introduction, complete with MTV-style videos at a Macintosh trade show, Capps and Tchao—well aware that the $700 gadget's central feature, its ability to recognize handwriting, was limited—argued that its release should be limited, too. They were ignored. Despite interim upgrades that addressed some of its problems, by year's end, Newton had been effectively declared a failure. It was telling that the same month Newton was introduced, Microsoft reported that for the first time, it had $1 billion in sales in a quarter-year. John Sculley left a few months later.[28] Despite one critical success—its PowerBook laptop computers—Apple looked rotten.

BY 1989, RUSSELL SIMMONS and Def Jam were an established brand in the music business. Rap may not have been loved, but it was accepted. With every record he released going gold, people were comparing Simmons to Berry Gordy, who'd created the Motown empire in the 1960s. The year before, Rick Rubin had left Def Jam, but Simmons replaced him with another Jewish music entrepreneur, Lyor Cohen, and kept signing new acts like Slick Rick, Method Man, D.J. Jazzy Jeff, the Fresh Prince (a/k/a Will Smith) and Public Enemy. But after a restructuring demanded by its distributor, CBS (by then a division of Sony), Def Jam ended up $20 million in debt.

Rap had evolved. In the mainstream, ersatz pop raps by artists like M. C. Hammer (b. 1962) and the white rapper Vanilla Ice (b. 1968) were selling in unprecedented numbers for major labels. On the streets, rap was anything but ersatz. In 1982, Carlton Ridenhour (b. 1960), a graphic design student, had recorded a rap called "Public Enemy No. 1." When Rick Rubin heard it, he began courting Ridenhour, who eventually formed a group called Public Enemy. Its second album, *It Takes a Nation of Millions to Hold Us Back*, was a huge success in 1988, driven by dense production and an equally novel point of view, informed by Ridenhour's membership in the Nation of Islam. Chuck D, as Ridenhour styled himself, wrote overtly political, rage-filled rhymes that condemned racism and police brutality and extolled black consciousness. But after the band endorsed the controversial Muslim leader Louis Farrakhan and several group members made statements deemed anti-Semitic, Public Enemy's sales headed south.

In the meantime, a new hip-hop avant-garde had emerged on the West Coast. Building on Public Enemy's collage of sound, a former drug dealer who'd funded a record label with his profits put together a band called N.W.A. (an acronym for Niggaz with Attitude) and introduced a new, violent, misogynistic genre, gangsta rap. N.W.A.'s 1989 album, *Straight Outta Compton*, named for the group's suburban ghetto hometown, got little radio play or press but became a cult phenomenon thanks to songs like "Fuck Tha Police," which earned N.W.A. a warning from the FBI. It was an omen. In 1992 another gangsta rapper would be dropped by his record label after making a record called "Cop Killer." With gangsta rap, the music business had finally found a sound guaranteed to grate on the ears of formerly all-accepting baby boomers—turning them into their parents every time a speaker-equipped "boom" car or boom box passed them by. Every fresh outrage gained the music new enemies. Every sneer from an aging boomer made new fans. Gangstas would rule rap straight through the 1990s.

Simmons liked the gangsta rappers, and added several to the Def Jam roster. "They borrowed a lot of Run-D.M.C.'s energy and attitude, and I understood immediately it was great," he says. "I didn't know the culture and lifestyle, but the more I started to know what that lifestyle was, the more engaging it was. Because it was so good and so honest. Honesty is the killer. And people really can feel authenticity. You don't have to live in Compton to know that shit's real."

While gangsta rap was taking shape, Simmons was getting his troubled business back on its feet, and then extending his valuable brand. He established Rush Communications as an umbrella over Def Jam Recordings, its music publishing arm, and Def Pictures, his film production company. He joined forces with several Hollywood pros to create a talent management company and Russell Simmons Television, which began developing its first show, a showcase for black comedians called *Def Comedy Jam*, which debuted on HBO in 1992. The show was so successful, it helped pulled Def Jam out of its jam and would eventually lead to a second program, *Russell Simmons' Oneworld Music Beat*.

The more the critics howled that his comedy, like rap music, was hateful or filthy or racist, the more money he made. "People are saying something legitimate that's coming out of their hearts," Simmons says. "When their fathers tell them niggers shouldn't say fuck the police, they say, 'Fuck you, Dad; give me a rap record.'" By 1998, rap would be selling in excess of eighty million albums a year, more than any other music genre.

THE FIRST FIFTEEN key employees of Sun Microsystems all got stock in the company, which skyrocketed in value, with annual sales hitting $1 billion in 1988. John Gage, among the oldest of the fifteen, had two kids and almost immediately cashed out a huge block of stock to buy a new house. Sun stock has increased in value 100 times since then, but Gage doesn't seem to mind. "I have the most expensive kitchen in Berkeley," he jokes dryly.

All that money was made before the idea of the network crossed over into consumer culture. When Joy and Gage coined the phrase "the network is the computer," Sun's mantra, only university and military types and computer sophisticates were on the biggest network of all, the Internet. "You have a couple of hundred thousand people using it," Gage remembers, "it's not very well known, and it's ugly. There were only three things the Internet could do: e-mail, transfer a file, link directly into another computer. And you had to learn commands to make it work. But for our community, the Internet was the heartbeat. We lived and died by communications."

That all changed with the World Wide Web. Suddenly Gage's little community opened its gates. The Web's inventor, Tim Berners-Lee (b. 1956), built his first computer while studying at Oxford University's Queens College. In 1980, while working as a consultant at CERN, the European Particle Physics Laboratory in Geneva, Switzerland, he wrote an information storage program that allowed for the programming of random links—i.e., mouse-click jumps that could take you from any word in a computer network's virtual "filing cabinet" to any other. That led to his 1989 proposal for a global web of documents, linked by something called hypertext, designed to let people collaborate by combining and interconnecting knowledge. Backed by CERN, Berners-Lee began writing what he now called the World Wide Web programs in 1990, and put them on the Internet a year later. "It was all open," says Gage. "The protocol to do this, the rules to make it all work were completely open. Nobody owned it. Put your community intellectual property in here and share with everybody."

Berners-Lee wrote an early rudimentary browser, and others followed. Consumer Internet service providers began to appear. Marc Andreessen (b. 1971), a coder at the National Center for Supercomputing Applications at the University of Illinois, began distributing a highly compatible, easily installed image-reading browser called Mosaic and the Internet and the value of networking spread to the world at large. The web was the public's map to the hidden treasures of the network. Even Sun's jaded employees responded to it. At one point, their Internet usage rose so precipitously that a company accountant threatened to make them pay for access. Finally "the entire company rose up as one and sent him insulting e-mail saying, 'You idiot, this allows everybody to share across all departments for the first time!'" Gage recalls.

It was all great news for Gage and Sun, whose top code-writer, Bill Joy, had worked on many of the protocols. "No matter what computer you were on, you had a piece of Joy's code that he gave away for free," Gage says. "By the time Mark Andreessen's sitting down in '91-'92, he's on Bill Joy's shoulders." Mosaic and its Andreessen-designed commercial successor, the wildly successful Netscape, followed the pattern of ETHERNET and of TCP/IP. "Give it away for free, and suddenly it runs on every machine," Gage crows. "And people loved it, because it was completely opposite to what Bill Gates did. And that made Gates mad." After ignoring networking for years, Gates suddenly found himself playing catch-up on the unfamiliar field of the Internet.

Gage was among the first to demonstrate the Web to the wider world at PC Forum, a spring 1994 conference in Phoenix, Arizona. Gage compared it to air, "the first essence of freedom," he says. "I breathe air, I don't need to ask if it's French air or Russian air. I assume it's going to work. It's instantly understandable." The audience "had a degree of skepticism." Most of them had never experienced the Internet, let alone the heretofore unseen Web. "But it was so simple, and the linkage thing was suddenly so apparently powerful," says Gage, who began his demonstration by holding up a telephone wire, making a call to Sun, and going online. Then he said, "You can do this."

He didn't tell them about Java, a new Sun programming language, but it was on his mind. He and Joy had come up with the idea on a plane flight in 1992. Gage was reading *Lignes d'Horizon* (Fayard, Paris, 1990), a treatise on geopolitics by Jacques Attali, an adviser to French President Francois Mitterand who predicted the emergence of a new "nomadic man," living in a future of fax machines, cellular telephones, biological implants and all-purpose smart cards. Gage translated sections of the book aloud to Joy, who made a prediction of his own: before the end of the century, people would be able to communicate, compute and issue electronic commands by carrying four electronic devices weighing a total of less than five pounds. Java software and its successor, Jini, were invented to make that prediction manifest.

Java works with what Joy called "virtual machine" software implanted within every browser to allow the movement of programs, not just data, around the Internet; the more ambitious Jini allows even home appliances to connect instantly to and to communicate with networks; both programs bypass operating systems, carrying with them an implicit threat to the Microsoft Windows monopoly. Sun was jubilant about that, but slow and steady Microsoft fought back, developing a web browser of its own and integrating it into Windows 95, then more tightly into Windows 98. Microsoft also adapted Java without sharing their improvements, violating the hacker rule book. When congressional and antitrust investigators began looking into Microsoft, studying whether it had abused its monopoly position in consumer operating systems, Sun executives, among the few in the industry with no ties to Gates (for by then even struggling Apple had made a strategic alliance with Microsoft), were among the first to speak out against the Redmond, Washington-based giant. Then it sued over Microsoft's Java "improvements."

Gage, ever the maverick, feels free to poke sticks in Bill Gates's cage. "Joy tried to give the networking code to Microsoft, offered to help make it fit in these little tiny, uninteresting junk machines"—PCs—"but Gates was too dumb to understand what networking is," Gage says, adding a prediction that this oversight will eventually kill Microsoft, which would be found to be a predatory monopoly by a Federal judge late in 1999. "When technology changes rapidly, anything closed and proprietary will die," Gage vows. "That's how we see Microsoft. They have a niche. The niche will go away."

IN 1987, TIM SCULLY had begun consulting for the primary supplier of software for computer-assisted graphic design, Autodesk, writing programs that allowed the company's programs to speak to and command attached, and often incompatible, devices like printers and pointing tools. He eventually learned to program for DOS, UNIX, and Windows machines. In 1989, he was made chief engineer and put in charge of a half-dozen programmers. "Since I spent a lot of years designing hardware and writing software, the interface between hardware and software is the place where my skills were best applied," he says, dismissing his work as "low-level bit-banging."

Scully's superiors at Autodesk know all about his arrest record but care more about his record of achievement. "There have been times when people were taken aback," he admits. "But really, people have been very nice. I've been lucky, but I also think people respond to the fact that I have no ill will toward anyone."

In recent years, computer culture has helped him incorporate his past into his present. As many programmers and computer pioneers came out of the drug culture as out of radical politics. One of Scully's programmers is married to a psychologist who's spent a half a decade studying the Deadhead colony of fans. Scully was delighted when she told him many of them were programmers, too. She'd also met Owsley, who'd survived his own two-year stint in jail, moved to Australia in 1982, became a sculptor, and now sometimes returns to Dead-related shows, where he sells gold, silver and cloisonné artwork, medallions and belt buckles. "I am back in touch," Scully says.

Owsley is disappointed that his ex-apprentice won't take drugs anymore. Though Scully says he suffers no ill effects from his drug days, he adds, "It certainly can be hazardous to your freedom!" Nowadays he sticks to meditation, tai chi, and biofeedback, "doing various things to deliberately and consciously get into states that are in some ways similar to being high," he says. Owsley sometimes argues that since they've both "paid a lot of dues, we should be able to take all the acid we want," Scully says with an indulgent smile.

Owsley, he adds, is also convinced that a new Ice Age is coming.

"HOW DO YOU think David Geffen, Barry Diller and Sandy Gallin found out about this?" Marianne Williamson demands. "Through their caterers, masseuses, lovers." By 1987, those servants and lovers, many of them people getting sober, people with AIDS and people who loved them, had passed the word that Williamson was delivering a message worth hearing to Tinseltown boomers who'd lived their version of the 1960s in the discos and viper rooms of the 1970s and early 1980s. They weren't just AIDS victims; they were "the addicted, or the obsessed and compulsive," said *Time* magazine.[29] Williamson agrees. "You can't forget Alcoholics Anonymous and twelve-step programs in all this. People started getting sober. The party was over."

Many in Hollywood's power elite were looking for a reason to believe. "For some people, the eighties were a total materialistic orgy," Williamson says. "But most of those people finally got to the point where the rest of our generation is now: Okay, now that I have two Ferraris, a house in Vail and an apartment in Manhattan, now that I'm head of the studio, are you telling me this is all there is?"

Williamson added her own spin to *A Course in Miracles;* her nondenominational message combined Christ, Buddha, pop psychology, song and movie references, and the tenets of twelve-step in lectures about such hot-button topics as whether death exists, romantic delusions, fear of intimacy and forgiving your parents. It was just the thing for bummed-and burnt-out boomers who found the era's fundamentalist religious alternative too small-minded and mean. Not only that, Williamson was a performer in a town that had an insatiable appetite for them.

Four years after her first lecture, still barely supporting herself by selling audio- and videotapes and collecting a "suggested donation" of $5 dollars at her lectures, Williamson was coming into her own. News of her mystique had begun to spread. Not long after she began flying to New York in 1986 to lecture once a month, David Geffen, the music and movie mogul, heard her speak about her latest project, The Center for Living. The facility offered nonmedical, nonresidential support services (meals, housecleaning, discussion groups, yoga, massage and individual and group prayer) to the "life-challenged," as the politically correct lingo of the moment termed it. The center was inspired by a friend with breast cancer who'd asked Williamson why there was no place she could go to be healed, and failing that, to be helped to die with dignity. Williamson not only got it started, she also contributed much of its budget. "We were holding the hands of dying people, and we didn't have any money," she says. When Geffen called to offer her $50,000 in 1987, "it was like we had won the lottery." Two years later, she opened Project Angel Food in Los Angeles, to provide hot meals for AIDS patients, and a second Center for Living in New York, backed by another $50,000 from Geffen.

Flying back and forth to New York every week, surrounded, in the papers at least, by a celebrity coterie, Williamson became a spiritual celebrity herself in 1991, a year that began with her blessing Geffen's star-studded birthday party and ended with her presiding over the wedding of Hollywood legend Elizabeth Taylor to her eighth husband, construction worker Larry Fortensky, at Michael Jackson's Neverland Ranch as media helicopters buzzed overhead. Ever since, Williamson has been on the defensive, accused of selling a shallow version of salvation to the self-obsessed, the materialistic and the driven, and of being part of the very idol worship and cultural blight she inveighs against in her books and lectures.

"Contrary to some of those caricatures, I am not a starfucker," she says flatly. "The vast majority of people who came to my lectures—or come now—were not connected to any of that." The same goes for some of the stars identified as devotees after they supported her AIDS efforts at Project Angel Food. "These people feel manipulated and used and I don't blame them," she says. "It was very embarrassing and it continues to be. I was never the guru to the stars. I was tarred with that."

But she was something to some stars. They liked Williamson's idea that it was okay to be *somewhat* enlightened. And there was no getting around the Taylor-Fortensky wedding, "the stupidest career mistake of all time," Williamson calls it. "Anybody who thinks I did that for career purposes should know, if you want a serious career in America, don't marry Elizabeth Taylor."

It got worse. Just as her first book, *A Return to Love*, was being published (kicked off at a party hosted by television producer Norman Lear), a series of exposés painted her as an abrasive, egomaniacal, publicity-obsessed hysteric just out for a buck. In the harsh climate of celebrity culture, she'd gone from flavor of the moment to target of media opportunity in a nanosecond.

A year after she started a support and prayer group for four pregnant girlfriends, Williamson had also become an unwed mother.[30] In the papers, that and the fact that she refused to identify the father of her daughter, conceived in 1989 and born in 1990, was made to seem sad and sordid. Though she saw herself as a feminist living an only slightly alternative lifestyle, she allows that others considered her "a terrible role model." Even worse were the tales of self-promotion, bullying and micromanagement that emerged from her Centers for Living in 1992.

"We hear she yelled at a secretary when she was pregnant, so she must be the biggest bitch in the world," she repeats. "Yeah, I was pregnant and under unbelievable pressure and I'm not a perfect person." But still, this was juicy stuff. "I'm famous, I don't need this, damn it," she reportedly huffed at staffers after the *Los Angeles Times* reported that the Centers for Living were in turmoil.

Years later, Williamson is still wounded by the way a messy organizational conflict was used to diminish her. "You cross some line where your book is successful or you get a certain amount of press, you're the same person doing the same things, but the reaction turns from *Isn't she nice?* to *Who does she think she is?*" Williamson says. "Gay America gave me my career and opened the centers with me. Then a more glamorous element discovered AIDS as a cause and thought that they could take it from there. It's interesting. The myth about me is that I was horribly controlling. Having thought about this for many years, the problem was I was not controlling enough."

Yet she admits that for all the embellishment and distortion, the negative articles contained a grain of truth, and that she's since endeavored to take responsibility for her passions and her actions. "I'm real," she says. "I've never pretended to be anything I'm not, but I gave people the opportunity to imagine the worst. I've learned how dangerous attention is."

Prime Time

DOUG MARLETTE first met Bill Clinton at Renaissance Weekend, an event founded in 1981 by Philip Lader (b. 1946), a young college president (and later Clinton's ambassador to England) and his wife to bring accomplished baby boomers—especially Southern liberals—together with leaders of other generations. The touchy-feely invitation-only family get-togethers are held on Hilton Head Island, off South Carolina, each New Year's weekend.

Renaissance quickly became the power version of Jerry Rubin's networking salons, with a dash of New Age navel-gazing. ("Inward Bound," Marlette calls it.) Each year, personalities ranging from Supreme Court justices to folk singers would play golf, ride bicycles, and discuss everything from international policy to professional traumas and investment strategies. Seminars run the gamut from "Renaissance World Report: Commentaries on War Crimes, Human Rights and Refugees" to "Renaissance Quest: Stirring Waters of Belief" to "Renaissance Whispers: What My Spouse Is Wrong About."

Bill and Hillary Clinton and Marlette all attended their first Renaissance Weekend in 1984, when the guest list was still tiny. Arriving, Marlette spied a van with Arkansas plates pulling into the next parking space. Out popped the governor, his lawyer wife, and their young daughter, Chelsea. In an atmosphere at once democratic and elitist, Renaissance interwove all the dominant strains of baby boomerism: 1960s progressive politics, 1970s self-attuned spirituality, and the unchecked ambition of the 1980s, joined in a synergy that would define the 1990s. At one panel, Marlette's wife, Melinda, noted the disdain being heaped on newly named Yuppies and asked what was wrong with being young and ambitious. Clinton approached her afterward to say he agreed.

Another night, Clinton and Lader "tried to outdo each other with who would give the most moving and the most powerful speech," Marlette recalls. "They were doing this Yuppie Revivalism thing, these very successful people talking and bringing people to tears. Clinton talked about his brother being in prison. I'd been there before with the testimonies in Baptist church. This was in the service of political ambition, but it was the same thing as Youth for Christ." Driving home, Marlette said, "I would vote for him for President. I've never heard a politician that smart."

"Yeah," his wife said out of nowhere, "but he's a womanizer."

Marlette, who admits his cartoonist's instincts often run ahead of his consciousness, wasn't so sure. "He does it with everybody," he told Melinda. Over the years, the seduction continued. Clinton would write to compliment "Kudzu" strips. "I thought he was very likable," Marlette says. "I had an immediate affinity with him. His family was trailer trash, just like my family. So I got him from the get-go and thought he would do wonderful things." Something nagged, though, "something facile and glib. It's all there in your first encounters with people. He's doing that gaze and he's listening, he's holding my eyes, and talking, talking, talking, until there would come a moment at the end, when he saw he had me, the seduction had been successful, and the shades would go down, and he checked me off the list and moved on. You felt like Monica Lewinsky felt, and now the nation feels: used like a Kleenex and tossed aside."

Marlette felt it, but it didn't register yet. The enchantment of Clinton's attentive intelligence was overwhelming, and Marlette became one of a group of supporters known as Friends of Bill (FOB). "I'd tell friends, 'You've got to hear this guy Bill Clinton. This guy is the best speaker.'" When Clinton gave his famous, endless, awful speech at the 1988 Democratic Convention in Atlanta, introducing that year's presidential candidate, his fellow governor Michael Dukakis, "I had phone calls asking, 'What are you talking about! Are you crazy?'"

Marlette had moved to New York to work for *Newsday* that year and stayed two more before coming home to Hillsborough, North Carolina, where his father had been born. While in New York, other journalists, aware of his FOB status, asked him about Clinton, who'd gained a national profile. Marlette told them how profoundly he identified with the guy and how he was sure Clinton would do good things, especially on the issue of race, which continued to plague a nation that refused to address it.

By 1992, Reaganism had begun to infiltrate a Democratic Party desperate to move back to the political center after a dozen years out of power. That trend was embodied by Clinton, who'd established a base through the Democratic Leadership Council, a group formed in 1985 to revivify the party by selectively adopting conservative language and ideas. "The promise of America is equal opportunity, not equal outcomes," the group said in a declaration of principles at a March 1990 meeting at which Clinton was named its chairman. "The Democratic Party's fundamental mission is to expand opportunity, not government."

A few years later, Marlette didn't mind when Clinton, beginning his run for the presidency, claimed he had smoked marijuana but never inhaled. "I thought it was silly, but I understood. He was trying to win the election." It was different when Clinton began changing his story of how, out of college, he'd managed to avoid being drafted. At first, Clinton repeated the story he'd used since first running for governor of Arkansas in 1978: that he'd only been draft-eligible for a brief period in 1969 and had escaped the notice of the Selective Service. With a little help from the *Wall Street Journal*, it emerged that Clinton had received an induction notice, wangled himself an ROTC appointment to attend law school in Arkansas, and then reneged after pulling a draft lottery number high enough to eliminate worry about the draft. "I decided to accept the draft despite my political beliefs for one reason: to maintain my political viability within the system," Clinton had written to the head of the ROTC at the University of Arkansas. Then the twenty-three-year-old headed to law school—at Yale.

Marlette was incensed. "I give a lot of leeway. Those times were hideous. But when I think of anyone at that age writing and talking about his political viability, when people were dying and going to jail or Canada, that is so painful to me," Marlette says. "I can't imagine that calculation crossing my mind. It was a matter of how one lived and who one was. He was hollow and soulless, even then, and at such a young age."

Marlette smiles and adds, "I'm glad he was against the war."

BACK IN BOSTON after his trip to Ho Chi Minh City, early in 1985, Tommy Vallely declared himself a candidate for the Boston congressional seat occupied by the retiring Speaker of the House, Tip O'Neill. "I was a fairly popular legislator, I had my own money, I was going to play," says Vallely, who spent $200,000 on the run, which ended abruptly in December 1985, when Joseph P. Kennedy II, a son of Robert Kennedy, entered the Democratic primary. "I can't beat Joe Kennedy." Vallely decided not to seek reelection to the legislature, either. "I don't know what the fuck I'm going to do," he says. "My whole life just changed."

Having lost his seat to a Kennedy, he returned, appropriately enough, to Harvard's Kennedy School, as a researcher. He still dabbled in politics, playing a large role in Delaware Senator Joseph Biden's brief-lived presidential campaign in 1987. Biden (b. 1943) withdrew from the race following accusations that he'd plagiarized and inflated his academic credentials.

Back in Cambridge, Vallely, deciding to learn everything he could about the country he'd fought in two decades earlier, began reading about Vietnam and talking to experts at monthly discussions of Indochina sponsored by the Aspen Institute. At those meetings, he supported Arizona senator John McCain's proposal to set up an American diplomatic interest section in another government's embassy in Hanoi, and got to know the fellow vet in the process. Studying Vietnam, initially a hobby, became his raison d'être.

In Ho Chi Minh City four years earlier, Vallely had the idea of returning the funding he'd received to attend the Kennedy School in order to subsidize a scholarship for a Vietnamese student. In 1989, that fantasy came nearer to reality when he got a new job at the Harvard Institute for International Development as a research associate and director of a new Vietnam program. HIID, a think tank run by the university, is in effect a global management consulting service, working for governments and international organizations like the United Nations and the World Bank, running research and development projects around the world.

Vietnam was still a pariah nation to the America it defeated. Though the war had been over nearly fifteen years, remembering it—or at least its prisoners of war and soldiers missing in action—had become an American industry. Ronald Reagan had made POW politics a cornerstone of his presidential campaigns, but behind the scenes he'd begun the incremental process of reengagement with Vietnam.

Vallely didn't support Reagan ("I thought he was crazy") but has since changed his mind about the movie star president. "Reagan deserves credit for changing the way America thinks for the better," Vallely says. "I also think he did a very good job dealing with the dismantlement of the Soviet empire." In so doing, Reaganites changed the balance of power in the world and increased the geopolitical importance of Pacific Rim nations. As America's most knowledgeable behind-the-scenes proponent of a relationship with Vietnam, Vallely became an architect of policy toward the region. He argued that an opening to Vietnam would be good for U.S.

business and serve as a counterweight to Chinese influence. Even though three million Vietnamese had died in the war, shattering countless families, "they are very, very good at having relationships with people they were enemies with," Vallely notes. "That's how small countries survive."

The policy of resolving disputes and restoring ties to Vietnam, which was adopted by the Bush administration, got a boost following the 1991 Gulf War, when Senators McCain and Kerry went on a fact-finding mission to Kuwait and talked at length for the first time.[1] Shortly afterward, the two worked together on a newly created Senate Select Committee on POW/MIA Affairs—formed to investigate the fate of Americans unaccounted for since the war.

The Senate Select Committee built a relationship with the Vietnamese government. Kerry, the chairman, went there seven times in three years, and Vallely sometimes preceded or followed him. As the fact-finding mission proceeded, Bill Clinton's campaign against President Bush intruded. "I will always be a Democrat," says Vallely. "But I have voted for some Republicans." One was George Bush in 1992. Vallely just couldn't get past Clinton's draft antics. "He didn't want to go die," the ex-Marine says. "But some people got out of it by being honest. He got out by being himself, which is deceitful. I don't mind that he didn't go; I liked people that didn't go. But it's like his presidency. 'I can have everything I want.' Well, I don't think you can, Bill. He lacked character. And I voted for character, even though I didn't think George Bush understood America as well as Bill Clinton does."

The POW/MIA committee released a draft report a few days before Clinton's inauguration, concluding that while soldiers may have been left behind, there was no compelling evidence that any were still alive—or that the Vietnamese were holding any remains. Immediately, calls came to lift the eighteen-year-old U.S. trade embargo against Vietnam and to normalize relations.

Bill Clinton had a problem. His credibility on Vietnam-related issues had already been severely damaged—among vets like Vallely and beyond—by the draft revelations. On taking office, he'd stirred more bad feelings by immediately calling for an end to the ban on gays in the military. It was the first in a string of impolitic gaffes that by May 1993 had his poll numbers plunging. That month he began a campaign to repair his relationship with the military. On Memorial Day weekend, he gave a series of speeches setting the stage for reconciliation.

Clinton made a pitch for a strong military. In an interview before a speech at West Point, he said he'd secretly jogged by the Vietnam

Veteran's Memorial to look for the names of four friends from high school chiseled into it. On Memorial Day, he spoke at the wall after being introduced (and in effect inoculated) by the Chairman of the Joint Chiefs of Staff, Colin Powell. Though many jeered, the speech was a turning point, as pro- and antiwar forces alike realized the time had come to let old animosities go.

That happened fast. In June, several nations offered to refinance Vietnam's debts; a bipartisan delegation to Vietnam headed by former Secretary of State Edmund Muskie, issued a public call for normalization. Senator Kerry said it was time to stop spending $100 million annually in a futile search for POWs. To Vallely, it seemed silly to keep American companies from joining in the economic boom clearly beginning in Vietnam. Other countries were profiting by building hotels and golf courses. Six months later, when the President had yet to make a move, the odd couple of antiwar Kerry and pro-war McCain gave Clinton bipartisan cover with a Senate resolution to end the trade embargo. Finally, in February 1994, with the two heroes at his side, Clinton did so. In summer 1995, he restored diplomatic relations, "to bind up our own wounds," he said.

Some thought Vallely should be named the ambassador to Vietnam. Though Clinton passed him by, Vallely doesn't hold a grudge. "I was at the White House the day he normalized relations and I said, 'Mr. President, I apologize for underestimating you. I won't do it again.'" He could afford to be gracious. His dream was being realized.

Vallely had established a Fulbright exchange program to bring Vietnamese students to America in 1992 and quickly built it into the world's largest Fullbright program. He'd added an in-country teaching program in December 1994, after the trade embargo was lifted. In November 1995, he presided over the dedication of the Fulbright Center in Ho Chi Minh City. "Because of the war, the relationship between Vietnam and the United States remains tense, timid, and too often, bitter," he said that day. "But . . . it no longer matters what your position was during the war. We must think about the future . . . and reach out toward Vietnam in a peace of the brave."

BY 1991, WHEN her third child started school, Barbara Ledeen was ready for a new challenge. George Bush was beginning to campaign for a second term as President when Henry Hyde, a conservative congressman, came to dinner at the Ledeens' one night. She started badgering him about Bush's message to women. Though she knew she wouldn't vote for a Democrat, she still worried that the Republicans, in thrall to the Christian right and anti-abortion forces, had a problem. "What have you got for me?" she demanded of Hyde.

The answer came from another woman at the dinner. Ricky Silberman (b. 1937) had served as the vice chairman of Ronald Reagan's Economic Opportunity Commission under a younger conservative black lawyer named Clarence Thomas (b. 1948). Thomas had since been promoted first to the three-judge Federal Appeals Court—where he served with Silberman's husband, Laurence, and Douglas Ginsburg (b. 1946), whose nomination to the Supreme Court was derailed by his admission that he'd smoked marijuana—and then to the Supreme Court. But in his confirmation hearings that summer, Thomas had been accused of sexual harassment by a former protégé, Anita Hill (b. 1956). Hill's accusations caused a storm. The only counter was a group of 200 women Silberman organized to testify in Thomas's behalf. In doing so, they outraged the feminist establishment. Thomas's avowed opposition to affirmative action programs made him anathema to liberals.

After their evening with Hyde, Silberman and Ledeen sought out likeminded women. A former Pentagon co-worker, Lisa Schiffren (b. 1959)—who had gone on to write speeches for Dan Quayle, authoring his famous attack on television's Murphy Brown for having a child out of wedlock—asked Ledeen to lunch with "a nice bunch of Republican women who had not been radicalized," she says. Wendy Gramm, an economist, former head of the Commodity Futures Trading Commission, and wife of Senator Phil Gramm, liked Ledeen's idea of starting a conservative women's group. So did Anita Blair (b. 1959), a lawyer and member of The Federalist Society, who'd been politicized when she found herself afraid to admit she supported Quayle.

They all felt that traditional feminist organizations were too predictable, militant and concerned with divisive litmus-test issues, too interested in sustaining themselves, even if female equality was achieved, and too busy whining about how women were victimized to realize they didn't have to be anymore. Existing conservative women's organizations were too in thrall to the Christian right. "We could see there was an opening in the market," says Ledeen. An existing organization started by several Federalist Society lawyers was renamed IWF, the Independent Women's Forum, and Ledeen became executive director. She approached conservative foundations for seed money, and they were enthused at the prospect of a new women's group reflective of new times.[2]

Instead of building a grassroots organization, IWF's leaders decided to make its mark by providing the media with articulate women lawyers and writers, ready with cheeky quotes, provocative sound bites, op-ed pieces, congressional testimony, and *amicus* briefs on matters of law and public policy. The IWF program quickly attracted several hundred members and became a launchpad for conservative pundits like Danielle Crittenden (b. 1963), who edited IWF's cheeky magazine, *The Women's Quarterly;* Christina Hoff Sommers (b. 1950), a resident scholar at the American Enterprise Institute; and conservative sex symbol Laura Ingraham (b. 1964), the leopard-skirted lawyer and former Clarence Thomas clerk who gained fame by founding a conservative analogue to the liberal Renaissance Weekends. Demonstrating the new irreverence boomers brought to conservatism, she dubbed it the Dark Ages Weekend.

IN 1992, DAVID McIntosh decided that Bill Clinton had managed to pull off a neat trick, bridging the gap between the politics of the Baby Boom's youth and its middle-aged conservatism. "They liked Clinton and connected with him, and it's not because he protested the war or might have smoked pot," notes the congressman. "In the way he talked about things, he reached that stable American community, yet with a twinkle in his eye that said, 'I'm a rascal.' My brother-in-law, who went to Washington for antiwar protests, once said half the people were really there for free sex. And they saw Clinton, and thought, Yeah, here's somebody who's going to have fun."

Free sex had never been part of McIntosh's life. He was still a virgin at thirty-five. "I was always somewhat socially awkward and just had friends rather than steady girlfriends," he admits. But that summer, that all changed. He'd proposed marriage to a woman he'd met in the White House, Ruthie McManis, the director of First Lady Barbara Bush's Literacy Foundation. They married just after Clinton's 1993 inauguration. By then, McIntosh better understood the twinkle in Clinton's eye. "Ruthie was the first person I had been together with," he says.

At first, the newlyweds stayed in Washington; McIntosh worked with a group called Citizens for a Sound Economy, where he helped fight new taxes. When Dan Quayle settled into Indiana's conservative Hudson Institute, he offered McIntosh a job as an analyst there, and the McIntoshes moved back home. Meantime, Clinton's postelection leftward lurch hadn't gone unnoticed. In July 1993, McIntosh attended a town meeting with his local congressman, a moderate Democrat who'd been in office for years. "I'll never forget the union members, who had always been strong supporters of his, standing up and shouting, *Why did you vote for Bill Clinton's tax increase?"* Ruthie McIntosh whispered in his ear that since he'd fought that very tax increase, maybe he should run for Congress.

"I knew I wanted to," he says, "and that kind of clinched it." He announced his run before Thanksgiving. And again after. "I only had three or four people show up at each of the announcements," he says. "We did-n't have any organization; I was still working at Hudson at the time." When a woman who'd interned in Quayle's office approached him and asked for a job, he says, "That made it real, because you had to get on the phone and raise money to make a payroll."

Lucky breaks gave the newcomer the Republican nomination—the incumbent pulled out of the race, and another likely opponent missed her filing deadline—but the general election against Indiana's pro-labor secretary of state, a close friend of the popular governor Evan Bayh, was hard-fought. McIntosh had to spend a lot of money "to let people know who I was," he says, "let them know about working for Quayle and Reagan" and then fight the charge that he was a Washington insider. In response, he played the Clinton card. Yes, he wanted to go back to Washington—to fight the liberals.

In Indiana in the summer, every little town has a parade. McIntosh and his wife marched in as many as they could, wearing matching American flag shirts—coopting a symbol usurped by radicals a quarter-century before. "Occasionally you'd get some people who were older and conservative saying, 'I like everything you do, David, but don't wear the flag as an article of clothing,'" he recalls. "They were thinking back to when Abbie Hoffman wore one. But for the average person, it was a positive symbol. The culture had changed from the sixties."

Though the district's voters were mostly Democrats, they were also Bible Belt traditionalists with a strong libertarian streak. McIntosh appealed to union members angry about gun control. While he was working in the Justice Department, he'd learned to shoot and bought a gun. The same voters loved it when McIntosh disparaged Clinton's crime legislation as a "hug a thug" bill. "That kind of summed up the problem, wanting to coddle the criminals and then taking away innocent people's firearms."

Election night, he was stunned, and not just by his own win. "I had no idea of the magnitude of change until late that night when someone said, you know, not only are you going to be a Congressman, you're going to be in the majority." The next morning he showed up at a foundry at 5:00 A.M. to thank the union men who'd voted for him. Then he joined the famous 1995 freshman class in Congress.

Early in McIntosh's term, it seemed as if those freshmen and their leader, Georgia congressman Newt Gingrich (b. 1943), were taking over the political world. Gingrich had joined the House in 1979 but through the 1980s was considered a noisy troublemaker, when considered at all. He'd started his local career as a liberal Republican who admitted smoking pot in college, but by the time he arrived in Congress he was a disciple of New Right guru Paul Weyrich. Branded a kook, he'd toss off futuristic ideas like privatizing space launches. When he and several other congressional outcasts formed the Conservative Opportunity Society, they proved themselves ready-made for the Reagan Revolution.

In 1986, Gingrich took over a political action committee that helped him build support for and among Republicans across the country. He came to national prominence two years later when he spearheaded an ethics investigation that drove then-Speaker of the House Jim Wright from his job. His reward: election as minority whip, the Number 2 party post in the House.[3] A series of ethics charges against him didn't stop Gingrich, who, in 1994, created the Contract with America, a campaign document that promised to restore traditional values and limit government with a balanced budget, tax cuts, term limits and welfare reform, and led to the first Republican-controlled House in forty years. He'd come to embody a new political paradigm for a generation that still fancied itself activist even as it courted certainty and stability. Gingrich had a perverse appeal to a generation raised to distrust and challenge the establishment.

In its first few heady months in office, the House Class of '95 set about to make revolution. They helped elect Gingrich speaker, and he put an end to years of tradition, remaking Congress so that ideology, expertise and energy, not seniority, determined who'd be running things. The newcomer McIntosh was made one of the freshmen Republicans' liaisons with the House leadership, the head of a new subcommittee on regulatory reform, and assistant Republican whip. It was a heady moment. "It quickly became apparent to me that everybody in our class felt we should push for the Contract to show we had kept our word," he says. "There was a real sense that we were change agents in the political process."

At first, the Republican-controlled House seemed unstoppable. It voted to cut taxes and institute regulatory reform, while Democrats fumbled a crime bill and health care reform. McIntosh's collegiate vision was becoming reality; conservatives were the new activists. "These guys are controlling the Republican Party, and the old-style Republicans who have been here for years have no voice," James Carville, the Clinton campaign strategist, complained. "They're true revolutionaries. They're serious."[4]

McIntosh epitomized their take-no-prisoners style. He quickly made his positions clear; he opposed retroactive liability on environmental protection, calling it "immoral,"[5] and was against national health care and lobbying by federal grant recipients. "In government, the people we hear from the most, the people asking for grants, are living off the taxpayer, using public funds for elaborate lobbying efforts to keep the programs going," he charged.

Though many of McIntosh's bills passed the House only to go down in defeat in the Senate, the 104th Congress was seen as a watershed in American politics. But just at the moment of their triumph, when Gingrich was named *Time* magazine's Man of the Year, he and his conservative cadre stumbled. In fall 1995, after Senate Majority Leader Bob Dole suggested that proposed Republican tax cuts be scaled back, McIntosh urged his fellow freshmen to oppose *any* decrease. He also favored a tactic that proved a Christmas present to Bill Clinton. At the end of 1995, the House freshmen shut down the federal government for weeks in what appeared to be a fit of partisan pique, refusing to pass a stopgap spending measure until the White House agreed to their plan to balance the federal budget.

"Closing down parts of the government isn't that much of a problem," McIntosh had predicted, incorrectly.[6] The public was outraged. When Gingrich eventually compromised and agreed to reopen the government, a handful of the conservatives, McIntosh among them, briefly revolted. McIntosh finally came around, voting to reopen the government. "Newt said, 'Look, you're part of my leadership team; I'm making the judgment call; fall in line,'" he explains. "I disagreed but chose to do that."

Ironically, right around then Clinton fell in line, too, lurching right as suddenly as he'd moved left after taking office. Clinton adopted the Republican budget, signed appropriations bills that cut government spending for the first time in a quarter-century, and embraced the conservatives' desire to end the welfare state. Meanwhile, Gingrich and the House freshmen alienated many supporters by guarding their right flank, refusing to compromise and pushing radical social measures far less popular than their economic fixes. By the end of 1996, Clinton was able to win reelection handily by running against an aged symbol of the Silent Generation, Dole, and against Gingrich, the unruly representative of the Baby Boom present. In May 1997, Clinton and the Republicans reached agreement on one of the key ideas of the Contract for America: a plan to enforce strict spending caps to balance the budget.

McIntosh had won reelection in 1996, too, by a wide margin, running campaign ads that personalized his fight against government regulation. He'd intervened on behalf of one five-year-old constituent to gain FDA approval for a life-saving drug, and had deleted funding for a regulation that required asphalt-layers to wear long pants during summer months. "The purpose was to show that the theoretical things I was working for had real consequences for people," he says.

Back in Washington, McIntosh played a leading role when the House Government Reform Oversight Committee started investigating fundraising illegalities in the 1996 election. More significantly, he played a leading role in an attempted coup d'etat in summer 1997, when eleven confrontational conservatives sought to topple Speaker Gingrich. The group, which eventually doubled in size, considered Gingrich too weakened by ethics charges, too willing to compromise with the Democrats, too unpopular, and too often outmaneuvered by the White House. They drafted a document to oust him, began collecting signatures, and approached the Republican leadership, but their brash move ended when those leaders tipped off Gingrich.

The Speaker survived. McIntosh, though chastened, was also disillusioned and continued to skirmish with Gingrich in the House and in the press over government spending and tax cuts. "I'm not sure Newt quite understood what he had accomplished," McIntosh says. "I think that's why his numbers inverted fairly quickly. He could have been a Reaganesque character had he had some core philosophy. Fundamental principles—individual freedom, smaller government, strengthening the family—are why I'm in politics. He ended up somebody who used positions to acquire power, when people wanted him to use power to forward ideas."

THOUGH SHE WAS lecturing to thousands every week, Marianne Williamson's life didn't go into overdrive until her first book, *A Return to Love*, topped the self-help bestseller list and stayed there for months following Oprah Winfrey's endorsement. "I have never been as moved by a book," the talk-show host said on the air. Williamson had been talked into writing it by a literary agent who went to one of her lectures in 1988 at a low point in his life. That serendipity changed her life as much as her mix of mysticism and self-help psychologizing changed his. Royalties from the tome and a multimillion-dollar deal for several more let her move with daughter, Emma, from a small West Hollywood condo into a house with a pool in the Hollywood Hills, and to trade in her nine-year-old Peugeot for a new Infiniti sedan.[7]

Although Williamson had stepped down as president of the board of the Center for Living, waves of bad press kept rolling in and "totally kept me off balance," she says. "I was profoundly hurt and left L.A." for Santa Barbara, where she lowered her profile, cut back her lecture schedule, and churned out more books. Her second, *A Woman's Worth*, earned nineteen weeks on the bestseller list with its advice that women should examine their inner selves, overcome damage done to them by their parents, give more value to their intuition, passion, receptivity, and nonviolence, and find the goddess, the Amazon, the mystical princess within, before trying to conquer the outer world. A third book, *Illuminata*, filled with Williamson-penned prayers (including pleas for forgiveness aimed at African-Americans and Native Americans), followed.

In the meantime, Williamson had come to the attention of Bill and Hillary Clinton. There was a natural bond with Hillary, who'd tried to do as an adult what Williamson had (somewhat more appropriately) claimed to have done as a child: channel Eleanor Roosevelt. At the end of 1994, Williamson was invited, along with the motivational author and hot-coal walker Tony Robbins and Stephen R. Covey, author of *Seven Habits of Highly Effective People*, to visit with the First Couple at Camp David. They seemed ready to anoint Williamson the Baby Boom's Billy Graham. "New Age guru-ism is mostly alien to Washington's practical political culture," the *Washington Post* observed archly, but it added that Williamson's writings on bucking the patriarchy probably appealed to the feminist First Lady.[8]

Williamson's politics certainly did. Like her father before her, she is "quite progressive," she says, although "the left is quicker to mock me than the right, because I have the audacity to talk in spiritual terms. The only reason a fear-based perspective has such power in this country is because a love-based perspective is not expressed so loudly. The Reaganites and born-again Christians had more chutzpah than we did. They don't have any problem stating their worldview. We talk too much, but we talk too little about things that matter. The problem is that the most narrow-minded people are the most organized, enthusiastic and efficient."

Williamson won't reveal what she told the Clintons at Camp David or subsequently, when she stayed overnight—"alone," she stresses—in the White House's Lincoln Bedroom, but she did have strong political opinions and an eagerness to share them. "There is no dearth of genius in this country," she says. "There are people in every area—mainly baby boomers—who have elucidated principles, theories and ideas that would make society work and are applying those ideas. However, at this particular moment the political dynamic is actually an obstruction, because the goal of the American government is not to make the country a better place. In the absence of campaign finance reform, our government is little more than a puppet whose strings are being pulled by corporate interests."

Clinton's strings, presumably, included.

Williamson has often said that after 1968, most of her fellow boomers moved upstairs in the house of American life, leaving the service floor—government—to people like Clinton who could stomach the compromises of politics. "Many of us were fine with that," she says. "We were looking at the stars, having a great time. But now we're looking down and saying, 'Shit, they're burning down the house.' All of a sudden it's not funny. The grace period for our generation is over. The universe is demanding that we state what we stand for. And not engaging in the democratic process out of disgust or some pseudo-rebellion is exactly what the most reactionary forces in America would have us do."

IN 1989, A DRUG gang called the Wild Cowboys had effectively taken over a neighborhood in northern Manhattan where they sold vials of crack with tiny red stoppers—their trademark. One night, when the gang engaged in a shootout with competitors selling yellow-topped crack vials, more than 200 rounds of ammunition were fired, but no one called the police. The Cowboys made an estimated $16 million a year, used juveniles as couriers, were known for their motto "Snitches get stitches," and slashed potential witnesses with knives.

Eventually, the police traced eleven murders during more than a half a decade to the Cowboys (many to the gang's hitman, who called himself Freddie Krueger, after the horror film *Nightmare on Elm Street*) and arrested forty-two members of the gang, most of whom testified for the prosecution. Finally, in May 1995, nine Wild Cowboys leaders were found guilty of conspiracy, murder, assault and drug and weapons charges. Though they maintained their innocence, Leslie Crocker Snyder sentenced the smirking drug dealers to a total of 868 1/3 years to life. They were put in holding pens where letters from the parole board are posted like big-game trophies, testifying to urban jackals Snyder has put away: a hit man for John Gotti's Mafia family, a drug dealer who lost a shootout with ten cops, the murderer of an elderly couple.

Snyder received death threats during the eight-month trial, and has lived with a twenty-four-hour police guard ever since. She neither downplays the danger nor dwells on it. "Judges get more threats than people realize," she says. "Most of the time you don't take them seriously. But when you're talking about the Mob, or a gang, they may have abilities individuals don't."

Though Snyder insists politics doesn't enter her courtroom, she makes hers clear in her sentences. She is a registered Democrat, but she admired the maverick mayor Ed Koch, who appointed her, more than she did his successor, the doctrinaire liberal David Dinkins. Dinkins became New York's first African-American mayor in 1989 in large part because he represented a last fling with the 1960s ethic of optimism about social change. His laissez-faire approach to public order caused many to rethink their political positions. Primary among them were boomers who, in New York, at least, were now comfortable if not wealthy, and beginning to live the cliché that links increasing age with growing conservatism. Storefronts closed with security glass, blaring car alarms, crack vials on the sidewalks, an epidemic of petty urban pathologies, and a record number of murders—2,245 in 1990—fueled their rightward turn.

"Many people were utterly disgusted with Dinkins," Snyder says. The prevailing attitude was that the city was ungovernable, "and he had no control over it. In terms of appointing judges, his criteria were ludicrous. All he was interested in was: Were you a minority? If you were a prosecutor, you couldn't possibly understand defendants."

To the New Deal-style progressives who supported Dinkins, Snyder probably seemed like some kind of throwback. But she was actually the near future in black robes and pearls—balancing the Bill of Rights against a culture of violence grown so extreme, some were calling for martial law. Faced with cases where witnesses were being threatened against testifying at preliminary hearings, she pioneered a new technique to conceal their identities from defendants *and* defense lawyers until trial, while revealing the gist of their testimony and their prior records. "This drove the defense bar crazy," she admits. "It's a very dramatic departure. I don't like doing this, I don't want to do this, but I don't see an alternative." Seeking a reversal, defense attorneys appealed all the way to the U.S. Supreme Court, expecting her to be overturned. She wasn't.

Snyder thinks that if Dinkins had won a second term as New York's mayor, she would not have been reappointed to the Court. But he was defeated in 1993 by a law-and-order candidate, the former U.S. Attorney and Justice Department official Rudolph Giuliani (b. 1944), who did reappoint her to a ten-year term in 1995. Giuliani's election, in the most liberal of American cities, symbolized a sea-change in American politics. He adopted the "broken-window theory" of policing, which argued that if police addressed petty but seemingly intractable problems like vandalism and panhandling, they would send a message that could alter civic society and halt chronic increases in crime. During his first two years in office, there was a nearly 30 percent drop in major felonies in New York.[9] The same trend was seen nationally. In 1998, violent and property crimes dropped by 7 percent, the largest annual decrease since those numbers had peaked in 1992.

Snyder is quick to point out that Giuliani benefited from programs begun under his predecessor, and from demographic changes. As the Baby Boom aged, its members were less likely to be aggressive or criminal. She does agree that his initiatives also had a great effect—practical and psychological. "He's a total control freak," she says. "I can relate to that."

Giuliani's programs failed to address one underlying problem: the pernicious effects of racism, festering throughout the 1990s and in no way limited to New York. The arrest and trial of O.J. Simpson (b. 1947), the black football star and celebrity, for the murder of his white wife reminded the country of the gaping chasm between white and black Americans when a mostly African-American jury acquitted the African-American defendant, and most whites considered it jury nullification—a decision based on emotion instead of facts.

Snyder had recently presided over a case with a similar dynamic, the shooting of an African-American undercover police officer by three African-American men. The predominately black jury acquitted the defendants after some of them were heard shouting *"Cops are all racist pigs!"* from behind the closed doors of the jury room. "I was shocked," Snyder says. "Your temptation is to excoriate them because it's such a ludicrous result. I didn't because I felt that (a) it's not going to accomplish anything, and (b) I would say something I would regret, and it would be on the record."

She would remember that verdict, though, when not long afterward a racially mixed group of third and fourth graders she mentors started telling her cops couldn't be trusted—the same sentiment she'd written in her diary years before. "Of course some cops are bad. But they were so young to be so negative," she says. "And that does go back to our failure as a society to address things on a longer-term basis." Suddenly, this modern Draco begins to sound like someone else, decrying the erosion of the family unit, and the way the problems of the 1960s, when many poor children lived with only one parent or grandparent, became pathology in the mid-1980s, when the parents discovered crack, the grandparents grew too old, and the children went wild. "Education is the key to everything," Snyder says. "We haven't addressed homelessness, joblessness, lack of equal opportunities, lack of adequate education for the under- or even middle-class. But that's not a popular political quick fix."

By 1999, despite continuing drastic drops in crime, many in New York had tired of Rudolph Giuliani, and his troubles, like his successes, became a national news story. When the aggressive police tactics of the city's Street Crime Unit led to the killing of an innocent black immigrant early in 1999, a small but significant protest movement rose up, modeled by the Reverend Al Sharpton (b. 1954) on the nonviolent civil rights protests of the early 1960s and aimed at Giuliani. The mayor's popularity sank just as he began maneuvering toward a run for the U.S. Senate. Snyder, too, has her detractors. Defense attorneys charged that Manhattan District Attorney Robert Morgenthau (b. 1921) was steering high-profile cases to her, avoiding the standard random selection process for judges. One reason for the vehemence may be that the judge makes no secret of her desire to run for District Attorney, the top law enforcement job in New York, when Morgenthau retires, perhaps as early as the end of his term in 2002.

When and if she does run for elected office, Snyder's first priority will be setting out a philosophy "not as one-dimensional as some members of the defense bar would like to make out," she says. "If you witness the kind of viciousness for which I give out what appear to be draconian sentences, you wouldn't think they were draconian. On the other hand, there are dozens of young people I've put on probation, into programs, on deferred sentence, to see if they'll do well. I believe in the concept of rehabilitation, and I think we've failed miserably at that, too. But take the top members of a drug gang who have killed people. Who cares what the root causes are at that point? Who cares whether they are rehabilitated?"

Snyder's judgment of Bill Clinton aptly demonstrates her ability to parse legal complexities—and oddly parallel comments made by the president's wife in summer 1999, as she positioned herself for a Senate run against Giuliani. Bill Clinton's "background is relevant," Snyder says. "His family was dysfunctional." Just like those she so often sees in her courtroom.

"I can look at him as representing the worst of baby boomer values or lack of values," she continues. "But I don't think being a baby boomer means that you turn out like Clinton, that you take an oath as lightly, that you feel entitled to whatever you wish. A whole lot of baby boomers are egomaniacal and feel they should make as much money as they want and buy everything they want, but they would hesitate at doing things he's done. You can't take some individual and say he represents a generation. You can say he represents the worst of a generation."

WHEN KATHRYN BOND Stockton left Brown University, she figured she and her fellow Theory followers would end up teaching in community colleges or even driving taxis. "But on the job market we are incredibly salable, because we know stuff most of our professors didn't know," she says. After considering several offers, she took a teaching post at the University of Utah.

All over the country, humanities and literature departments were racing to catch up with cutting-edge Theory. Adherents would soon be promoted into positions of prominence throughout academia, and put on the fast tenure track as they shaped a new canon. Initially, professors with "strong and precise political views" saw its promotion of multiple meaning as a threat to their agendas. But as they came to understand Theory, they grew to like it. "The political benefit of believing things are socially constructed, whether you're a sixties radical or a nineties feminist, is to believe that then things could be otherwise," Stockton says.

Since the early 1970s, many colleges had established multidisciplinary departments that taught through the lenses of Afrocentrism or gender. Now, as Theory became practice on campuses, they turned into cultural war zones. At Smith College in Massachusetts, for instance, the Office of Student Affairs prepared fliers to make students aware of such "manifestations of oppression" as ableism (discrimination against the "differently abled"); ageism; and lookism, the tyranny of beauty.[10] "Grievance," wrote the critic Robert Hughes, had been "elevated into automatic sanctity."[11]

These ideas weren't confined to colleges. In many urban areas, community activists forced political changes in elementary and secondary curriculums. And outside the education system, a parallel culture of victimization and entitlement rose up among those who defined themselves as dispossessed. Bans on the use of demeaning language spread across the country—except when those being demeaned were white males.

Though they sprang from the same impulse, Theory and political correctness weren't identical. Academic deconstructionists focused purely on language. Their real-world counterparts saw the deconstruction of language as a sociopolitical tool for the reconstruction of culture. It was no surprise, then, that conservative critics would soon equate academic deconstructionists with radical Afrocentrists claiming quantum physics had been invented in ancient Egypt, superfeminists like Andrea Dworkin claiming that all sex is rape, and the rising cadre of campus mind police out looking for speech code infractions and felonious flirting. (A professor was charged with sexual harassment after he explained simile by comparing belly-dancing to Jell-O on a plate with a vibrator beneath it; traffic signs reading SLOW CHILDREN were suddenly deemed insensitive to the mentally handicapped.[12])

At first, academic leftists were opposed only by Moral Majority leaders and populist demagogues like Senator Jesse Helms. But by the late 1980s, a more broad-based reaction had set in. The "oppressors" began standing up to this new mode of thought, belittling all pressure for change from below or outside mainstream culture, and ridiculing what they called the "P.C. crowd's" frequent excesses. Wielding anecdotes like swords, conservatives accused the politically correct of being closet authoritarians, attempting to reconstruct society into conformance with their vision, and Theory-heads of being closet careerists creating new disciplines, duchies and opportunities for themselves and like-minded friends.

The critics weren't entirely wrong. "There are massive differences between these people," Stockton says, though she adds they "are not necessarily antithetical." They fit under the same umbrella, albeit a large one. Proponents of change and Theory mavens could agree on one thing: there is no such thing as normality. "Look up *queer* in the dictionary, you get two different definitions," Stockton says. "The first is strange; anything strange. And the second is slang for homosexual. Now, take the most 'normal' people out there. Go into their lives in enough detail, and they will deconstruct themselves, in the sense that they will cease to be coherent and normal. So now, obviously, everybody is Queer. Because everyone is strange."

Stockton thinks Theory's critics went too far. Political correctness "did not stop people from being sexist," she says. "It did not stop men from raping women at fraternities. It just meant there was another discourse in play." A First Amendment absolutist, she thinks everything should be expressed—even hateful opinions, even kiddie porn. "It strikes me as a bad idea to censor anything. As a Queer, I will always and forever be against censorship of any form. No learning will take place where people do not say what they believe. I am a professor of literature; my work is words, pleasuring words, empowering words, dangerous words. To keep people from speaking is an incredibly bad idea."

More than a professor, Stockton is also a provocative writer. In her first book, *God Between Their Lips*, published after five years at Utah, she dips into psychology, intellectual history, philosophy and theology to find an unseen erotic dimension in a novel by Charlotte Brontë. In her reading, the spiritual autobiography of the central character—an older woman looking back at her life and an unrequited love—becomes a means for the Victorian-era writer to talk about taboo subjects like sexuality, auto-eroticism and desire between women. "Spiritual autobiography is a perfect form for speaking about women's desire, because you have a fall, and then you wander in sin and suffering and look for Christ to come again. So it's all about desire. It has to end in a state of desire, because this pleasure, Christ, has not yet come."

Though far less *outré* than a fellow Theorist's discovery of hidden references to fist-fucking in the notebooks of Henry James, Stockton's imposition on Brontë might be shocking to some. "Whatever you think about Theory's excesses," she says, "its power is that it has trained us to ask a different set of smart and crucial questions."

IN THE LATE 1980s, corporate America discovered gays as a niche market. Ironically, instead of making homosexuality untouchable, AIDS had made it more visible and, curiously, more acceptable to the American mainstream. People were sympathetic. Business saw an opportunity. AIDS focused a market. It also revitalized the gay movement and gave it a cause to organize around. "The downside was that everything became about AIDS," Jim Fouratt says. "But I remember going to an ACT-Up meeting very early on and being absolutely amazed that all these young people were out. I had this moment of joy, realizing that these were my children."

ACT-Up formed out of anger and need—yet by accident. In March 1987, Larry Kramer was called on as a last-minute replacement for the director Nora Ephron, who'd canceled a speech at the Gay & Lesbian Community Center in New York. Four years before, increasingly exasperated, not just with the press and politicians, but with colleagues who disagreed with his screeds against promiscuous sex, Kramer had quit GMHC's board, but continued his attacks on anyone he felt was impeding AIDS research and care. Now he was even angrier, and his speech was a call to arms that led to the instant formation of the AIDS Coalition to Unleash Power. The group's backbone was late-model boomers. "You had a lot of young men, people who would have been Club Kids, art students—very sexy and not political, just angry," says Fouratt. "And they were going to use any fuckin' tool that they had to make their point." They became the Yippies of the 1990s, even staging an action at the Stock Exchange.

ACT-Up was well-marketed, like all brands created by and for boomers. And ACT-Up gave gay and bisexual men and women a new form of social life, just like the peace movement before it. Gays had been scared out of clubs. "Drugs were really back and they were taking young gay men and other young people and destroying them," says Fouratt. "The decadence of nightlife was upon us." ACT-Up meetings became a replacement. "A lot of what motivates people to do things is the desire to have intercourse," Fouratt says. "And not necessarily sexual intercourse. Just intercourse with other human beings. In New York City, everyone lives in tiny apartments. So people go out."

Fouratt thinks ACT-Up's activism inspired the next gesture of gay anger, a controversial attempt to "out" closeted prominent gays. The leader of the outing movement was Michaelangelo Signorile (b. 1962), who headed ACT-Up's media committee and wrote a gossip column for *Outweek*, a gay magazine that regularly named names. "I don't think [back-end boomers] understood what coming out had meant," Fouratt says. "For most of us who came out in the sixties and seventies, we gave up power, access, the ability to do things we could have if we had stayed closeted." Though Fouratt approved of outing dead people, like Steve Rubell, whose death from AIDS-related causes in 1989 was covered up,[13] he thought the living should have the right to decide for themselves. "You don't punish people for being gay, which is essentially what they were doing," Fouratt says. "The process of coming out is painful and scary, and to force someone out is really self-centered."

Fouratt increasingly found himself out of step with his fellow activists. He moved out of the leadership of HEAL after the cause of AIDS, the HIV virus, was isolated, because he thought it was important to continue to talk about other factors—including lifestyle and genetics—that contributed to the collapse of people's immune systems. "The multifactorial position, which said you have to look at a lot of different things, was very unpopular in the late eighties," he says. "What if we get something that cures HIV and gay men go back to the same lifestyle? I was accused of being sex-phobic, but you have to be responsible. The victim mentality is wrong. We didn't cause AIDS. But if you say someone else did, it's wrong too. You have to look at your life."

Fouratt looked at his own. He'd already done a lot of self-examination in twelve-step programs, and he'd started therapy. "All that gave me some self-awareness so I could change certain things that made me sexy but didn't really help meacting out, being dramatic, confrontational," he says. "I made a decision I wasn't going to fight in ACT-Up with people who were dying. It wasn't worth being right."

* * *

IN 1989 A playwright named Billy Aronson had the idea of updating Puccini's opera *La Bohème*, moving it to the modern day, and replacing tuberculosis with AIDS. Seeking a composer with whom to work, he met Jonathan Larson, and they quickly wrote three songs together. Larson, who'd been waiting tables for years while waiting for a break, and volunteering at Marianne Williamson's Manhattan Center for Living, suggested an East Village milieu and the multiple-meaninged title *Rent*. He felt it could be a modern version of *Hair*, incorporating aspects—good and bad—of the new bohemian scene: heroin addiction and HIV, fashion and fame, performance art and the mainstreaming of what had once been considered sexual perversity in unconventional venues like artists' spaces and drag bars.

Two years later, in 1991, surrounded by friends all suffering with AIDS, Larson called Aronson and asked if he could take over the idea and pursue it on his own.[14] Larson was attending meetings at Friends in Deed, which spun off from the Manhattan Center after Williamson's fight with her board. The philosophy of both groups—that one can learn to live with terminal disease and still have a fulfilling life—had spurred Larson to return to *Rent*. That year, too, Victoria Leacock and Ali Gertz decided to form an organization to educate young people about HIV. After rejecting the names Rough Hope and Love Cures (because, unfortunately, it doesn't), they settled on Love Heals.

In the meantime, Leacock had decided to become a filmmaker like her father. Supporting herself by working for artists as a personal assistant, she began making videotapes and small films, including one that aired on MTV about Blondie, the Tom-Tom Club and the Ramones. After that, she got a job as the cinematographer on an AIDS documentary produced by director Jonathan Demme. Demme had been partly inspired to make a movie about AIDS, *Philadelphia*, by the story of Juan Botas, an artist friend of his wife who'd contracted HIV. Botas convinced Demme a movie could be made about a Greenwich Village clinic where groups of gay men living with AIDS received two-hour intravenous infusions of drugs. When Botas realized he couldn't film their conversations and take part in them, he brought in Leacock, who'd impressed Demme's assistant when she videotaped a charity function the director had organized.

She and Botas were busy filming when Ali Gertz died in August 1992. Botas died three weeks later. "I kept filming because I didn't know what else to do," says Leacock, who finally stopped three months after that when her grandmother died as well.[15] Leacock turned her attention to Love Heals, and along with several friends, got it up and running. They felt that the AIDS community, so tied up in gay issues, could benefit from an organization formed to tell the story of a girl who contracted HIV through heterosexual sex. Their experiences became part of the development of *Rent*. Larson and Leacock videotaped Gertz's memorial, inspiring the opening of the musical.

As Larson continued struggling with *Rent*, Leacock helped mount readings, workshops and backers' auditions. After she sold a house she'd inherited from her grandmother, she also financed and helped produce a recording session of songs he'd written. And she helped Larson earn money, getting him work scoring music for home movies she edited for *Rolling Stone* founder Jann Wenner.

In the early 1990s, Leacock's life was still consumed with illness. Her roommates, Gordon Rogers and Pam Shaw, kept getting sicker. There was one bright spot. In spring 1994, Larson got a grant to stage *Rent*. The ten performances that fall were sellouts. More important, they attracted backers. With a production now likely, Larson began adding songs and tightening the concept. Among many other changes, he incorporated ideas that came from Rogers, whose reaction to his illness was rage—not acceptance.

BY THE MID-1990S, yuppies were no longer scum, and ambition, for so long a quasi-dirty word, had become a given for most baby boomers. Those who had wanted more, and those who didn't wanted in. There were baby boomer billionaires out there! "Doing good" had taken on a whole new meaning.

For Michael Fuchs, the Time-Warner merger no longer seemed like a mess of broken eggs but an opportunity to make a golden corporate omelet. Even before the deal was concluded, Fuchs was operating behind the scenes. Feeling that Nick Nicholas had turned his back on his Time Inc. colleagues, Fuchs switched sides in what was still a secret corporate joust and began promoting Gerald Levin's ambition to take over the company. They talked a lot. Levin involved him at the boardroom level. Fuchs just didn't think Nicholas would be as effective.

In 1991, when Warner chairman Steve Ross began chemotherapy following a relapse of cancer, the maneuvering in the ranks grew fierce. Fuchs went to Levin and renegotiated his contract to become one of Time-Warner's three highest-paid executives, along with studio chiefs Bob Daly and Terry Semel—a fact soon trumpeted by a press corps that had turned corporate warriors into latter-day rock stars by chronicling their lives as intensely as it once had Keith Richards's drug use.

Fuchs wanted a bigger job, believing he deserved and had been promised one. In January 1992, Time-Warner's board fired Nicholas and made Levin co-CEO. When Ross died that December and Gerald Levin—the chief of Fuchs's tribe—took over, Fuchs expected a promotion, but it never happened. He was agitated, to say the least, and sometimes his feelings showed. Three years, another Oscar, and seventeen Emmys later, Fuchs let it be known he wanted out. "I was restless and bored, which is dangerous for me." In May 1995, Levin responded by asking him to take over Warner's music operation—the largest in the world, encompassing Warner Brothers, Elektra, and Atlantic Records.

Fuchs accepted. "I was clear in my own head that I would like to run Time-Warner some day," he says. "So when they handed me music, I thought, Maybe this is a step in the right direction. And I was enormously excited to do something new." Fuchs got rid of several executives. Before he got the chance to start rebuilding, though he sensed that the knives were out for him. He'd let Levin announce his new position before they settled on a contract. By summer, Levin was asking him to give up all his responsibilities at HBO. But Fuchs loved TV and movies. He didn't want to throw away twenty years of equity in those businesses. And that didn't please his rivals, Daly and Semel, who denied they had anything to do with his difficulties but were reported to be fretting over Fuchs's new job and unhappy with reports he was being positioned to take over post-Levin.[16] "All that mattered for those guys was the perception that that they were the most powerful people in the company," Fuchs says.

Daly and Semel may not have been the problem. When Levin started hearing the heir apparent talk, he apparently got nervous, too. In September, just after Time-Warner's $7.4 billion merger with TBS was announced, Fuchs was fired and his music job handed to Daly and Semel. A press report said his "blunt ambition" for Levin's job was a factor in his sudden skid from grace.[17] Although Levin had paid out millions to rid himself of a number of executives, the market applauded him. Time-Warner's stock price rose with the news of Fuchs's firing.

Fuchs won't comment on Levin's role in his dismissal, or speculate on whether his canny boss maneuvered him into a no-win situation. But in a speech not long afterward, he said, "There is such a thing as being too good and wanting to excel too much and having politics overwhelm performance." And he seems neither surprised nor sorry that in 1999, Gerald Levin skillfully eased Daly and Semel out of Time-Warner, too.

ON AUGUST 9, 1995, workers at a drug abuse treatment clinic in California discovered the body of Jerry Garcia in the room where he'd been staying while trying to kick his drug habit. The immediate cause of Garcia's death was a heart attack. But many blamed his death on thirty years of drug abuse. "Everybody I work with had a drug habit at some point—myself included," says Cameron Sears. "I'd smoke dope with the best of them. When I started working for the Grateful Dead, I had to stop, because I was the responsible adult."

Sears believes that while Garcia was hero to millions, he didn't want to be. "He just wanted to play guitar. He accepted his celebrity as a function of what he did, but as it got bigger and bigger, it got more difficult for him. He led a relatively insulated life. That connection with people was a very important thing to him, but it had gotten to the point where he didn't have it anymore. So he numbed out."

Garcia's death reawakened the activist impulses Sears had put on hold when he went to work for the band. In its wake, he redoubled efforts to communicate to grieving fans that drugs and decadence were not what the Dead had been about. Within the Dead community, Garcia's death was a wake-up call, too. "There was a deep regret at allowing it to get as out-of-hand as it did," Sears says. "That free spirit the band represented musically came back to haunt us."

STEVE CAPPS REFUSED to let go of the handheld computer called Newton. In September 1995, it was reintroduced and redeemed, at least among the cognoscenti. (When Steve Jobs returned to Apple in December 1996 and killed it, its fans let out a collective howl, but their numbers were so small they could be easily ignored.)

Meanwhile, the Internet had profoundly altered the world of computing. Capps, who'd been watching it out of the corner of his eye, was concerned. He saw it as a sprawling frontier ready to be tamed. And he feared that Microsoft-style capitalists, not Apple-style idealists, would get there first.

Capps had almost quit Apple in 1994, thinking to create an Internet company after having seen his first Web browser. To keep him, the company made him its fifth Apple Fellow, and gave him a substantial raise. Apple Fellows were the company's pie-in-the-sky types. "They basically sit around and pull lint out of their navels," Capps says. "I like to ship products. I don't like to sit around and think. I'd much rather be a shark and keep moving."

After Newton 2.0 shipped, Capps was given a sabbatical. He spent it playing basketball, trying to have a baby with wife Marie D'Amico (their daughter, Emma, was born in 1997), and thinking about his future. "Apple is in the doldrums," he says. Yet another CEO had been hired that February to turn the company around. "And I'm sitting there looking at the business and looking at browsers and asking myself what we should do to save the Macintosh."

In December 1995, Bill Gates had admitted he'd been wrong to dismiss the Internet and put the considerable resources of Microsoft behind a catchup strategy. Capps told management "that if Gates could admit he was wrong, so should they." He urged Apple to scrap a long-delayed new operating system, join forces with a network-based company like Sun, and "make Apple the 'Net cruiser of the nineties." When they wouldn't listen, he and two of his Newton colleagues went looking for a way out.[18]

As usual, Capps was bursting with ideas, but the venture capitalists he went to see wanted him to have one, not a dozen. "I don't understand their logic," Capps says, "but they're successful at making their money grow by a factor of ten, so I shouldn't question them too much." When one of his team accepted a corporate job, Capps and his remaining teammate began interviewing, too. "They're all kind of hankering for us, because there's very few people who really understand user interfaces," Capps says. Capps's Apple-bred idealism proved a tough fit, even at forward-thinking places like Netscape and Sun. For Capps, Sun's UNIX-based mentality—and its feeling that personal computers were junky, uninteresting little boxes—was too big a hurdle to get over. "UNIX people think software is a necessary evil to sell hardware," Capps says. "They think they're making this big locomotive and we're the guys that polish and wax it just before it leaves the factory. Whereas at Apple, the user experience was the way you thought about the world."

Microsoft, meanwhile, was looking at the Internet and thinking hard about how users experienced it. Capps got a warm welcome when he called an Apple executive from the Macintosh days who'd moved to Microsoft and recently been put in charge of its Internet strategy. "I told him the story about my ten ideas and he goes, 'If you have ten good ideas, we'll fund them all,'" says Capps. Having recently bought his first Windows machine, he threw down a gauntlet, telling the executive he thought Microsoft's Internet Explorer browser (which, mirroring the relationship of Macintosh and Windows, was based on the pioneering Netscape) was badly designed. When the executive asked him to explain instead of hanging up, Capps was intrigued. He flew to Redmond, Washington.

"What do you want to do?" a Microsoft vice president asked.

"I want to work real hard for another five years and then retire," Capps replied. The executive asked him to name his price. Capps did.

"We can do that," he said.

AFTER BILL CLINTON'S election, Doug Marlette had put together a book of cartoons on the First Couple and soon enough was summoned to the White House to present Clinton with a copy. Still hopeful about Clinton, he accepted, and watched proudly as the President leafed through it, laughing so loudly that Colin Powell, Secretary of Defense Les Aspin, and Clinton's secretary, Betty Currie, all rushed in to see what the ruckus was about. Looking at a cartoon of himself as a Bubba Yuppie schoolboy, crafting a crude Rolodex in wood shop, Clinton muttered, "Boy, that's really close to the bone."

Back then, Marlette was gentle with Clinton, but by mid-1993 he'd grown skeptical. He wrote a cover story for *Esquire* that summer called "Never Trust a Weeping Man," which described the Clintons as the "First Bacilli of the disease of our age . . . where narcissism meets obsessive compulsion." He compared the president to "the anchorman, the televangelist, the actor, the carnival sideshow snake-oil salesman," saying Clinton appealed to boomers because they'd lost the ability to feel.[19]

Shortly after writing that piece, Marlette became *Esquire*'s "Good Behavior" columnist, writing on topics like corporate backstabbing, commuter marriage, and staying friends with a former spouse. He took on the national impulse to share. "Why can't we all take our pain and suffering and our gotta-be-me-ness back into the closet? Closets are where we store valuable things." And most revealing of all, he wrote of his torment over what he would tell his son when the boy asked, inevitably, if his father ever took drugs. "For a generation so long defined by the media as 'the kids,' becoming parents, however long postponed, finally makes us put lives where our mouths were, raising all the questions we had successfully ignored, rubbing our noses in the shallowness of our cherished assumptions. We are responsible. We are accountable. And they are mirrors."

Marlette's new mood showed in his cartoons of the Clintons, too. Now, Clinton paddled in a canoe called Whitewater; his policy advisors stuck *Playboy* centerfolds in his briefing books; chameleons in the trees outside the Oval Office envied Clinton's ability to change his policies to fit his surroundings; and Hillary and Bill were perfecting their Nixon impressions. "We are not a crook," read that caption.

After Clinton's election, the Renaissance weekends had changed for

Marlette. They were studied and parsed and relentlessly publicized. One year, there were "huge crowds, huge panels, overorganized, a gazillion people, and all of a sudden, the program had gotten so big, every speaker's time was limited, and there was a lot of talk of people not being invited back," Marlette recalls. "The final night, Bill and Hillary talked off the record to the group. And I noticed—this is my gimlet eye—when Hillary introduced the President, she was sort of chilly. And then she gave a canned speech." The next morning, Marlette spoke at one of the last events of the weekend and made a crack about Hillary's boring speech and how someone had held up a two-minute warning sign to limit her— when he looked again, he continued, it turned out to be the President. The audience roared, and Marlette recalls that the person laughing loudest was the President. Later on, Kathleen Kennedy Townsend (b. 1951), the Lt. Governor of Maryland, asked him, "Did you realize they'd been fighting?"

At that same December 1997 event, in a panel discussing the Clinton legacy, Marlette told the crowd that he always applies a favorite Beatle test before judging anyone. "And it's been documented that the President's favorite Beatle was Paul McCartney, and we all wish that it was John Lennon." He paused for the laugh. "Hillary's favorite Beatle was Yoko Ono." The laughter wavered a bit; Hillary was in the room. He then described his cartoonist's vision of Clinton's legacy: a national monument portraying a giant zipper. "On the entire panel no one had mentioned anything about his problems in that area," Marlette says.

The next day, before leaving, Marlette thanked Clinton for some kind words he'd offered to Marlette's son. "He's usually very warm," Marlette says. "He's usually hugging. He turned and looked at me and hummingbirds would have frozen in midflight. It was nuclear winter. I could feel that Hillary had talked to him. There's not been any contact since then."

Less than a month later, Clinton had bigger problems than Marlette. They were named Monica Lewinsky and Kenneth Starr, the intern and the independent counsel. And they gave Marlette the best gift you can give to a cartoonist: a million opportunities for political incorrectness. "Hail to the Creep," said one Marlette cartoon. Another showed the White House as a trailer, decorated with a satellite dish, a lawn flamingo, and the legend *White Trash Legacy*. In the mailbox out in front are the November 1998 congressional election results. "Yeeehiiii, Hillary, we been vindicated!" read the caption. Standards had changed. When Marlette drew Saddam Hussein mooning Clinton while an aide observes,

"It's another stalker in a beret who wants to show you his thong," nobody tried to censor it.

Marlette regards his generation's post-scandal support of Bill and Hillary Clinton as deep mass denial. "There's something that's going on that we don't want to think about and that's why we focus on Ken Starr," he says. "I was feeling this before the speech and the confession. You cannot have the President, the nation's putative father, behave as an infant. It turns everything upside-down. And Hillary is practically his procurer. She never looks better than when he is screwing up. We cannot look too closely at Bill and Hillary, because they're us.

"The President of the United States, the Chief Executive Officer, is teaching my son—and a generation—that if he is caught with his hand in the cookie jar, he should say, 'Define hand,' 'define cookies.' This is where I will take it to the hoop with Bill and Hillary. I know they've read Orwell's essay on language. Nixon and Kissinger talked about 'pacification' when they were destroying villages, and about 'incursions' instead of invasions. Bill and Hillary, for the sake of his survival, have engaged in the same debasement and devaluation and weasel-wording. And then they waged war as distraction." Marlette shows me a cartoon of the President and First Lady looking at a chart of a cruise missile, smiling, over the caption, "It takes out a village."

"It's a long way from 1968, isn't it?" he says.

It all brings to mind another Southern leader. "Robert E. Lee took responsibility for Gettysburg," Marlette says. "He did not 'spin'; he was accountable. But we live in a time of polls and focus groups." Marlette hopes the Baby Boom will eventually tire of being spun and finally find itself desperate for authenticity. "It has been polled and market-researched to near-death," he says. "It is beating the life out of everything. All of it is the same—Clinton, Hollywood, market research, the Disneyfication of America—it is pushing things down people's throats, and there is a gag reflex. I embody the gag reflex. I am always throwing up."

ON A FREEZING cold morning early in 1997, as the Supreme Court began hearing arguments over whether Paula Corbin Jones should be allowed to pursue a sexual harassment lawsuit against President Clinton, a reporter approached a parka-clad demonstrator holding a sign supporting Jones's right to sue outside the courthouse.

"Do this often?" he asked

"Not in years," she replied.

"When was the last time you demonstrated?"

"Many years ago, in front of the Pentagon. I was doing the same thing I am now, exposing hypocrisy."

"You demonstrated during the war in Vietnam?"

She said she had. The reporter looked confused. Finally, he asked, "Which side were you on?"

The parka'ed picketer was Barbara Ledeen. In its brief existence, her organization, the Independent Women's Forum, had never shied away from controversy, but nothing prepared her for what would happen when the Jones sexual harassment lawsuit metastasized into 1998's consuming scandal. Initially, IWF's involvement was peripheral. Still when Bill Clinton's partisans launched their scorched-earth defense of the First Boomer, the flames licked Ledeen—and kicked off a bizarre volley of charge and countercharge.

On August 11, 1994, the Associated Press had reported that the IWF had approached Kenneth Starr to write a friend-of-the-court brief opposing President Clinton's claim of immunity from Jones's charge, and that Starr had agreed. A few days later, he was named independent counsel in the Whitewater investigation. For the next four years, the charge that Starr had worked for the IWF on behalf of Jones followed him, repeated everywhere from the *New York Times* editorial page to the floor of the U.S. Senate.

Starr hadn't actually crossed that line. He'd been approached, but was never hired, at least in part because the IWF's leaders were put off by Jones's belated claim. "We don't support the idea that years after the fact, somebody can whine and moan" about harassment, says Ledeen. Regardless, the ensuing controversy put IWF on the political map and gave the tiny group influence far beyond its size.

Barbara and Michael Ledeen were simultaneously embroiled in an explosive lawsuit brought by one of Michael's longtime ideological adversaries. On August 11, 1997, Sidney Blumenthal, once a journalist for the *New Republic* and *The New Yorker,* had gone to work at the White House as an assistant to the president. The day before, Matt Drudge (b. 1967), the World Wide Web gossip columnist and Clinton-antagonist, had printed an anonymously sourced item alleging that Blumenthal had committed acts of violence against his wife, who also worked in the White House. Two days later, in response to a letter from the Blumenthals' lawyer, Drudge apologized, issued a retraction, and admitted to reporters that he believed he'd been used by a politically motivated source.

Unsatisfied, the Blumenthals sued Drudge and America Online, which carried his reports, for $30 million.[20]

At first, the Ledeens were amused, since Blumenthal was among those who'd reprinted the old charges about Michael Ledeen when his name surfaced in the Iran-Contra investigation. "We're hysterical laughing; it's lovely to see that he who gives, gets," Barbara says. Two days later, she got a call from Drudge, who wondered if she could help confirm his story. She and her husband suggested instead that he apologize, even grovel, but they also helped him find a lawyer.

On January 27, 1998, in the wake of Drudge's biggest scoop yet, the exposure of the president's affair with a White House intern, Hillary Clinton appeared on the *Today* show and claimed there was a "vast right-wing conspiracy" dedicated to sliming her husband. A month later, White House aide Blumenthal—nicknamed Grassy Knoll for what the *New York Times* referred to as his "dark tales of right-wing cabals intent on bringing down President Clinton and Hillary Rodham Clinton"—was summoned to a grand jury Ken Starr had convened in his latest investigation, into Clinton's relationship with Monica Lewinsky.

Afterward, Blumenthal sputtered in his outrage at being "hauled before a federal grand jury to answer questions about my conversations with members of the media."[21] Yet that July, Ledeen and her husband were subpoenaed in the lawsuit by the Blumenthals, to testify about their conversations with various members of the media. Conservatives erupted over the subpoenas—and the hypocrisy they seemed to represent. The *National Review* even dug up an appropriate quote from Blumenthal, who'd once said, "I play by Chicago rules. You come after me with a knife, I come after you with a gun. You come after me with a gun, I come after you with a howitzer."[22] The White House had begun a battalion-strength counterattack against its perceived enemies, and Blumenthal's subpoenas were only a small part of it. IWF's links to the *American Spectator*—the conservative magazine that dragged Paula Jones into the spotlight—and to their conservative benefactor Richard Mellon Scaife were relentlessly publicized in following months. The attacks galvanized Ledeen's fury at Bill and Hillary Clinton.

Baby Boom voters who supported the Clintons in their dark hour in the November 1998 election were, says Ledeen, destructive "suckers" who are afraid to question the President's behavior because to do so would require taking a close look at their own. In Ledeen's eyes, Clinton's supporters thought 1960s protest was a party and couldn't "see past the entertainment value of the demonstrations to what they were really about." Their minds are clouded, too, she continues, only today their drug is prosperity instead of pot. Deeply defensive, they cling to the Clintons as life preservers, rare examples of boomers who appear to have held to their beliefs.

To Ledeen, the Clintons are dangerous authoritarians and Hillary Clinton's Senate run is the latest attempt to impose their program on America. "They *have* to make the world better," Ledeen says. "They have a utopian vision of improving mankind." The President is Hillary's stalking horse, "but he's not the one with the power right now," Ledeen says. "Hillary is the policy driver. She's known about his women for years but she always had some other deal in mind."

Ledeen snorts with derision when she recalls how the President wagged his finger at the public and said he'd never had sex with Monica Lewinsky. He did that while endorsing a $22 billion proposal for a national child care initiative—a pet program of the First Lady's—at a White House event held just hours after Hillary's "right-wing conspiracy" interview. "That was Hillary's payoff," Ledeen says flatly.

If the First Lady drops out of or loses her Senate race, Ledeen predicts the President will reward her with a lame-duck appointment to the World Bank. "The vision I have is of the moving trucks pulling up to the White House and Hillary grabbing onto the upholstery with her fingernails and not letting go."

THOUGH HE CAME into Congress as a firebrand, by 1998 David McIntosh was an established congressional leader. That February, he was elected chairman of the Conservative Action Team, a caucus of conservative congressmen who earned the nickname CATs because of their sharp claws. Though he vowed he would work with Republican leaders, in an attempt to tone down the CATs' image as confrontational reactionaries, he also warned the leaders that they would ignore the CAT agenda at their own peril.[23] Speculation arose that it was only a matter of time before McIntosh tried to replace House Speaker Gingrich or another member of the party leadership.

Within a month, he had set out a new CAT agenda calling for a balanced budget, tight controls on government spending, increased tax exemptions for dependent children, an eventual overhaul of the entire tax code, and parental oversight of educational curriculums as well as of medical, psychiatric and psychological testing or treatment of children. He also stood against the income tax marriage penalty, funding of the

National Endowment for the Arts, and the use of tax revenues to subsidize abortion.

Quietly, the CATs were positioning themselves for increased influence in the Republican leadership and maneuvering to push a tax cut through Congress to increase defense spending and find more budget cuts. McIntosh was, he says, consciously seeking to strike a reasonable balance and define issues that both social and economic conservatives could support, without venturing into territory like an abortion ban, where a broader consensus is difficult if not impossible to find.

As an example, McIntosh points to the Supreme Court's ban on prayer in schools. Though reversing that ban has been a conservative touchstone for years, McIntosh prefers to get around it. "Society will find its social moorings if we allow religious activities to occur in ways everybody in the community agrees with," he says. "You won't have the Bible being taught in schools, because very few communities actually want that. But you won't have ridiculous prohibitions on students saying a prayer at a graduation. Freedom is not only the key to economic success and individual happiness, but also to allowing moral values to be taught—outside of government—in the community, whether it's in the church or the Boy Scouts or community organizations."

As McIntosh was establishing that agenda, Bill Clinton became the nation's biggest issue. For McIntosh, the link between the President's new problems and previous ones, such as the fundraising abuses he'd investigated, were clear. "Clinton and Gore bent the rules," he says. "They used government resources to woo donors. And that approach applied across the board. The place Clinton ended up getting caught was in his personal life. He cheated on his wife, who obviously knew he had been doing this and was reconciled to it because she enjoyed the power of being First Lady." To McIntosh's credit, he kept his eye on the big picture, and let others wallow in the dirty laundry.

In the wake of the Lewinsky revelations, House conservatives started getting uppity again. McIntosh even threatened to force another government shutdown if the President didn't negotiate in good faith over how to prioritize federal spending. House leaders and Republican moderates immediately voiced their fear that the politically adept Clinton would use the conservatives' threats to divert attention from the sex scandal. The CATs then issued assurances that they'd be willing to negotiate, and even lose on some issues, as long as their suggestions were considered.

In an interview that September, just after the President admitted he'd been lying about his affair, McIntosh disputed Clinton's contention that it was a private matter ("It happened in the Oval Office," the congressman said bluntly), but nonetheless issued a warning to the special prosecutor investigating the President that would prove to be prophetic. Focus on law, not sex, McIntosh told Ken Starr, noting that at a recent Rotary Club meeting in his district, only a quarter of those attending raised their hands when asked if the president should be impeached.[24]

Unfortunately for moderate Republicans in Congress, they didn't heed the young politician's warnings, and instead angered the CATs by delaying discussions of spending in hope that the President would be further weakened by Starr, which caused them to be outmaneuvered and forced to compromise on the budget. Though the Republicans still held a majority in Congress and the President was wounded, the $580 billion spending bill that passed that October allowed surplus funds intended to shore up Social Security to be used for other spending measures, failed to limit abortion, and offered no tax relief. McIntosh sneered afterward that it was "a terrible bill . . . a Great Society bill" and faulted Republican leaders for a distressing lack of vision.

A month before the November 1998 election, the House voted to hold an impeachment inquiry. McIntosh voted with the majority because he felt he had no choice. "It was a classic replay of what got Nixon—the coverup," he says. "And I was surprised as I was watching this, because Hillary was there during Watergate. Why didn't Clinton just say 'Yes, I did it, but Hillary's forgiven me?'

"Ultimately," he continues, "they made that appeal to the American public," but by dodging that admission for months, the Clintons "left everybody else in government with a choice: Do we pretend it didn't happen? Do we seem to condone it? And this is where my legal training really set my antennae going, realizing that that would totally undermine the judicial branch of government."

At home in Indiana, they must have liked what they saw. Though Republican losses in the congressional election that November were significant, and the election was seen as a punishment to the party trying to impeach the President over his Oval Office peccadilloes, McIntosh won reelection easily. During the next few days, he moved against Gingrich, briefly seeking a leadership job himself, then backing off slightly in order to achieve the larger goal of getting rid of the Speaker. Gingrich (who, it was later revealed, was having an extramarital affair of his own at the time) made that easy by resigning. McIntosh suffered a setback when another man he considered an appeaser, Robert Livingston, was made Speaker. Soon he, too, admitted he'd committed adultery and quit the House.

Despite his brashness and obvious ambition, the upright McIntosh remained standing, with a higher national profile than he'd ever had before. Although he knew it wouldn't be popular, he voted in Washington that December to send three of four impeachment charges to the Senate for trial. "I concluded we had to, even knowing it was very unlikely the Senate would actually impeach," he says. He doesn't regret doing so. "Watching what went on in the Senate, I had the sense that the Republicans were uncomfortable because the polls were against them. But the Democrats were also very uncomfortable because although the polls were with Clinton, so politically they to stand with him, they *knew* something was wrong."

IN 1994 RUSSELL Simmons bought back the distribution rights to his Def Jam record label and sold them (and a stake in the company) to the Dutch conglomerate Polygram for $33 million. Soon afterward, he turned Def Jam's music operation over to his partner Lyor Cohen and began living in Hollywood, where he produced several films. But movies weren't enough to occupy the ambitious entrepreneur. Simmons founded a charity, Rush Philanthropic Arts Foundation, focusing on the career needs of inner-city youth; started a magazine, *Oneworld*, to promote his vision of a new multiracial youth culture; and opened an advertising and promotion agency specializing in urban markets. After two years in Los Angeles, he returned to New York in 1998, determined to expand Phat Farm, a line of clothing he'd begun as a hobby in 1992.

For many boomers, fashion had come to fill the slot in their lives once occupied by drugs and rock music. Just as those enthusiasms made promises they couldn't quite keep, so fashion's trappings seemed to carry with them the aura of affluence. To understand the boom's fashion fascination, you have to return to when it was young, and anti-fashion was the fashion.

It all began with blue jeans. Denim's progress from totem of rebellion to status symbol charted the generation's progression. In the early 1970s, fashionable hippies were showing the first signs of premature yuppiedom. New York's Serendipity boutique offered "Lifestyle" jeans for $45 to $500, depending upon their level of "distress," a sort of prefabricated personalization meant to evoke walking (if ghost-written) autobiographies. And in the mid-seventies, Sasson introduced the status jeans, engendering back pockets bearing the *haute* signatures of baby boomer Diane von Furstenberg (b. 1946) and the older American aristocrats Charlotte Ford and Gloria Vanderbilt. The latter, backed by an Indian apparel manufacturer who owned garment factories in Hong Kong, can be credited with the unlikely synthesis of mass market designer fashion.

For the first time, fashion manufacturers were approaching the public directly, without the mediation of the previously dominant conduits, stores and fashion magazines. A whole new phenomenon of mass expansion and diffusion of high-fashion followed. Here were "name" designer goods one could buy for as little as 30 dollars. The status that attached to a signature brand was now available to all comers, never mind the fact that their status was diluted since everyone was wearing them.

It wasn't so much the jeans as the way they were sold that made designers rock star replacements. They began plowing jean profits into advertising featuring their own faces. "I've made a lot of money because people are fascinated with designers," Calvin Klein told a reporter. "I never would have run a portrait if people hadn't wanted to know who Calvin Klein was." The next step was television. Klein's multimillion-dollar TV campaign introduced in 1980 and starring Brooke Shields (b. 1965) and a group of other models mewling about their prolonged adolescence—was influential and copied far beyond the fashion business.

In exchange for their fame, designers offered concrete expressions of fantasy and dreams to people yearning for clues about how to live. They preyed on the baby boom's vulnerabilities, its desire for more, whether that was Ralph Lauren's forward-looking desire for money and status or Klein's nostalgic clinging to sex and irresponsible fun. Image manipulation, as much as any particular talent for design, put Lauren (b. 1939) into *Forbes* magazine's listing of the richest Americans, and paid Klein's 1987 take-home check of some $12 million a year.

Eventually, jean sales started slipping, but boomers were by then used to wanting and paying for labels. Designers were, in the words of art critic John Russell, mining a "vein of understated democratic poetry." Their clothes, beauty products and accessories became the tools of a participatory art. Now anyone could play at visual expression through appearance, expressing parallel yearnings for definition and status.

As wealth crept out of the closet in the anti-egalitarian Reagan years, hedonism, luxury and self-display became permissible again; indeed, they seemed to be encouraged by the new politics of self-indulgence. Baby boomers finally accepted the idea that the world was competitive and that in order to live in it, they had to worry about standing out for the right reasons. Fashion was there to serve. By the mid-1980s, when inflation was checked, affluence was on the rise, and a new sense of economic optimism set in, it was natural for fashion's stars to extend their lines—

first into image-management clothing, then into more permanent signifiers of style—designer "home" collections.

What might be called the fashion decade lasted from 1977, when designer jeans first became popular, to late 1987, when the stock market crash threw most high-end garment makers into a tizzy that lasted well into the next decade. Some, like Calvin Klein, went into personal tailspins. Other just suffered through business reverses. But the genie of democratized style would not be put back in the bottle. In the early 1990s, when a new generation of fashion consumers reached free-spending age, older designers scrambled to adapt (often selling the looks of their youths back to their children via 1960s and 1970s revivals promoted by boomer magazine editors and photographers), while new designers carved out new markets.

Primary among them was Tommy Hilfiger (b. 1952), the second of nine children born into a suburban family in Elmira, a small city in upstate New York. A frustrated athlete, he was a ripe candidate for the counterculture when he encountered it in summer 1969. That's when Tommy got a job in a boutique selling posters, candles and incense, grew his hair, and started wearing bell bottoms and sandals, which promptly got him thrown out of high school. So he and a partner invested $150 each, bought a batch of earrings, candles and jeans, and set up shop in a fifty dollar-a-month storefront they painted black, curtained in burlap, and called The People's Place. Soon he owned eight branches and had started designing clothes. By the early 1990s, backed by the same financier who'd put Gloria Vanderbilt in the jeans business, Hilfiger's sales had hit $50 million in a year. In 1992, Tommy Hilfiger went public, offering shares on the stock exchange.

Then, in 1994, came the accident that made Hilfiger truly famous. One of his partners was a Formula One racing fanatic and convinced Hilfiger to sponsor a race car and design uniforms for its team. After he saw how people reacted to the logo-splattered shirts he created, Hilfiger designed a nautical line, oversized as was his fashion, but with one added attraction: huge logos. Urban youth began buying them in job lots. Those in-your-face logos carried a big message; they said, "I can afford anything you have."

One day shortly thereafter, Hilfiger's brother spied a rapper, Grand Puba, in a Hilfiger shirt and dragged Tommy over the racial divide, introducing the ultra-white designer to the ultra-black hip-hop star. Now, he was "my nigga, Hilfiger," and designers like Ralph Lauren and Donna Karan soon followed suit, making clothes for the rising urban elite. The inheritors of integration were coming into their own and wanted to wave their success, just as their parents and grandparents had waved picket signs. More rappers soon came into Hilfiger's orbit, among them Russell Simmons, who offered Hilfiger his knowledge of the urban street scene and access to more rap artists in return for advice on his own clothing line. The cross-marketing of music and clothing proved an astonishing success. Hilfiger now sells nearly a billion dollars in clothes a year. Soon, to the distress of some admirers, Simmons looked to be more interested in clothes than in music.

In fact, it wasn't clothes that caught his attention—at first. "It was models, to be real honest," he admits. Although he'd given up drugs in 1989 (and, after taking up yoga and vegetarianism, would forswear cigarettes and alcohol for nine months every year), he never gave up his habit of going out until all hours with beautiful women. Only now he fished in a bigger pond. "I started to have an interest in people other than Alternative Outlaws," he says. "It was a more affluent, different world. I really didn't get to know the mainstream. But I wanted to know people who moved things, people who were about culture and change and were either powerful in some way or interesting." He laughs. "I always thought I'd know everybody."

First among these new faces were young fashion models, who flocked to the latest clubs and loved clothes and music. The hip young fashion crowd "brought me to fashion shows, and fashion shows brought me to a different world," Simmons says.

Simmons was still deeply involved with rap—even helping organize a rappers' summit meeting at the Chicago home of Louis Farrakhan, when disputes between rival factions of East and West Coast rappers led to murder and mayhem, culminating in the 1997 shootings of rappers Tupac Shakur (b. 1971), whose mother, Afeni, was one of the Panther 21, and The Notorious B.I.G. (b. 1972).[25] Simmons's vision of a multicultural universe had grown beyond the confines of rap's corner of the world.

In 1998, Def Jam grossed almost $200 million, making it the second-largest black-owned entertainment company after the cable channel Black Entertainment Television. When Seagram Co.'s CEO Edgar Bronfman Jr. (b. 1955) bought Def Jam's parent, Polygram Records the following year, Simmons's 40 percent stake in Def Jam was said to be worth in excess of $100 million. Phat Farm made only $17 million that year. Determined to build the business, Simmons vowed to triple that in 1999, and he has no intention of stopping there. He'll tell anyone who'll listen that he wants to make the kind of money Klein, Lauren and Hilfiger do. "They can't out-market me in my own market," he told USA Today.[26]

What makes Russell Simmons run? The same desires that have motivated upward mobility since time immemorial, multiplied by the power of modern media to communicate all there is in the world to want. "It's not rebellion for the sake of it," he says. "I've been watching TV, and I want every fucking thing on the screen. Rap is about getting money. Rap is about 'I don't give a fuck. I'm takin' it. If you don't have it for me, I'm gon' rob you.' Niggers have a different agenda because they come from the ghetto. This is not rock 'n' roll for the fun of it. The idea is, get yours and *don't* be angry. Even though you can't get a cab, you can get a Rolls-Royce."

Simmons had crossed a great divide and become a celebrity himself. He'd undergone another change, too, when he married a model, Kimora Lee, late in 1998, on the celebrity isle of St. Barth. "I think I'm growing up a little bit," he says. "I can't do all the things I used to do. It's not as much fun. I'm an adult." He settled down a bit; after years of play, he was ready to climb mountains again. "Now I feel very much motivated to work. I think that now we can do some more legitimate things from a business standpoint with the culture and how it's evolving. The ball is in our court to do a lot of things we want to do, including the clothing and more films. The television arena is becoming really open. I always looked ahead one day—to get the record finished, get it out on time, get the spring collection done. Now I'm thinking about the overall plan, which I never thought about before."

That plan is based on the simple fact of society's homogenization. "The backdrop of urban culture is black music," Simmons says. "But the rest of it is a free-for-all." He hoists a copy of *Oneworld* magazine. Lauryn Hill, the singer whose rap-R&B fusion won multiple Grammy Awards in 1998, is on the cover. But Leonardo DiCaprio, the star of *Titanic*, is profiled inside. "He's a star," says Simmons. "Black girls want to fuck him. Oneworld exists."

There are still battles to be fought against the old way of thinking that tries to minimize urban culture. "They'll stick you in a hole today," Simmons says. "I'm dealing with it everywhere." His ad agency does work for Coca-Cola. "My commercials are the number-one testing in the mainstream, but they still got me on a nigger budget," he complains. "You're told, 'This is what your space is.' The ethnic clothing business; I don't want to be in the ethnic clothing business. Fuck you. You don't get my clothes. It's not about color. It's who's got the same interests as you, who's interesting and fun to be around, and that's the end of it."

* * *

THERE IS A vague sense of sadness about Cynthia Bowman as she talks about recent times. When you've flown with Jefferson Starship, it's hard to come down. With rock, drugs and sex eliminated from her life, Bowman was left with her somewhat unconventional family—she, Grace Slick, Paul Kantner, their children and assorted significant others—and a thriving career. "I got lucky again," Bowman says. She began with people she knew—Bill Graham, whose company gave her a number of projects to publicize, including several Vietnam veterans' benefits and a concert for Earthquake relief; Boz Scaggs, whose restaurant account led to others; the symphony. "What I did I did well," she says. "And I made enough money to sustain myself and keep a decent lifestyle, and I kept moving forward."

Though she still worked with celebrities—particularly when their presence could attract attention to such good causes as afterschool programs for children—she disdained the burgeoning field of "suppress agentry," which sprang up in the mid-1970s, when rock stars needed protection from themselves, and by the celebrity-centric 1990s had PR people dictating content to editors of glossy magazines desperate to get stars on their covers and at their promotional parties. "I'm way too old for the celebrity crap that goes along with working with 'stars,'" Bowman says. "So unless there's a ton of money involved, I stay clear of them."

By the mid-1990s, her accounts ranged from established radicals like Bread and Roses, which produces performances in prisons, hospitals and other institutions, and the Haight-Ashbury Free Clinic to mainline institutions like the Fairmont Hotel and the San Francisco Museum of Art. She handled Willie L. Brown's mayoral inauguration in 1996 and in 1998 got a contract to publicize Sony's Metreon, a massive entertainment complex in downtown San Francisco—a deal that helped pay for her house, the first property she's ever owned. "My piece of the planet," she says. "I'd started realizing, wait a minute, where are you going to be in fifteen years? You don't have a husband, a retirement plan, a Keogh plan. Here's God's way of letting you secure your future. I'm not going to blow it again."

She's feeling her age. "I'm entering my twilight years here," she says. "There's no going back now. I'm in the second half of my life. I still don't feel grown up. I see that reflection of myself and I think, My god, that's me? I'm going to be fifty years old: that is hard to fathom, but that's reality. What's the alternative?"

Bowman's son is going to college in fall 2000. She plans to keep working until he's graduated and then to reinvent herself. "I am going to devote the second half of my life to something else," she vows. "Maybe go back to school and become a nurse. I haven't identified what it's going to be, but it's going to be community service. I have a little bit of power in this city because I've been here for so long, and I can refocus my power and use it in a different way. I'm tired of making everybody in the world look good when they're not."

Bill Clinton's impeachment made Bowman see that the world of image, privilege and self-indulgence is not where she wants to live anymore. "We thought he was the figurehead for our generation," she says. "Well, it turned out that like the rest of us, he's got a tarnished record. Only most of us weren't that bad. Clinton was hurting his wife and his daughter. We weren't hurting anybody. We were smoking pot. The only people we hurt were ourselves. It impacted our health, probably our productivity. But we weren't lying. I don't lie. I get in a lot of trouble because I *don't* lie. There's something wrong with a country where everybody is lying all the time. I don't even think a rock star would have done it in the Oval Office. That part of it really offends me. The kind of crap that goes on backstage or on a tour bus shouldn't go on in the White House."

A DECADE AFTER arriving in Salt Lake City, Kathryn Bond Stockton was named the University of Utah's director of graduate studies in English. Though it sounds strange that a lesbian feminist would find a warm welcome in the heart of Mormon country, she thinks it makes a queer kind of sense. "What you realize living in this environment, where there truly are guys called Patriarchs and they live downtown, is that you don't have to prove to anybody that there is a patriarchy. The very people who started being persecuted as sexual queers because of their polygamy now stand for family values and American normativity."

Even in Utah, there are people "who are hungry to hear something other than that message," Stockton continues. "Obviously, there are Mormon colleges, so if a student is devoutly Mormon they tend not to go to the University of Utah; it's considered to be the radical bastion. So we get students who have grown up in Mormon families and yet they may be gay, they may be feminists, and they are desperate to take classes called Feminist Theory, Deconstruction, the whole shebang. And you still have Shakespeare and Milton being taught, so I would hardly say that Theory rules the day."

As her appointment attests, it has become the latest thing. In the 1990s, a new offshoot, Queer Theory, stormed many campuses, examining marginalized, "transgressive" sexualities, and lauding them precisely because they disrupt the traditions and norms of the patriarchy. "I think we are seen as fashion hounds," Stockton admits, "but just remember, fashion is not necessarily a bad thing." Often, it's a mirror on society.

The baby boom specialized in raising the bar of outrage, so it was no surprise that the advent of Queer Theory caused shrill, anguished howls. The phrase first appeared in the press in 1992, in a report on the first semester of the University of Buffalo's Queer Theory Study Group.[27] Rutgers also introduced a "queer" specialization in its English department that year, and it attracted more students than Marxism and deconstruction combined. Queer Theory—propelled by off-campus movements like AIDS activism and its politicization of sexuality, Queer Nation (formed in 1990 to combat anti-gay violence), and pro-sex feminism and its sexualization of politics—took off like wildfire, just as gay people were gaining a measure of acceptance at the movies (*Philadelphia*), on Broadway (*Angels in America*), in medicine (the AMA finally gave up the idea of curing homosexuality), and in public education (Massachusetts passed a law to protect gay students, and a Los Angeles school held the first gay prom).

In spring 1994, the twenty-fifth anniversary of Hillary Rodham's graduation from Wellesley College, the *Boston Herald* reported on the latest trends at her alma mater, where orientation week now began with "intercultural awareness" sessions featuring readings from a tract called *Unpacking the White Privileged Backpack*; white students who showed insufficient sensitivity were urged to take African studies courses, such as one where students were assigned a book on the slave trade asserting that Simon Legree, the wicked slave owner of *Uncle Tom's Cabin*, was really named Seymour Saperstein; and dormitory resident assistants were given a masturbation orientation, including a demonstration of a vibrator, in order to help students overcome sexual repression.[28]

By 1997, the year lesbian comedian Ellen DeGeneres (b. 1958) "came out" on her television sitcom, the cutting edge had already sliced far past her. That fall, the State University of New York at New Paltz came under fire after it hosted a women's studies conference titled "Revolting Behavior: The Challenges of Women's Sexual Freedom" that included (among more conventional offerings) a sex toy demonstration; a workshop on "safe, sane and consensual" sadism and masochism; a performance in which an ex-stripper mounted and whipped a colleague dressed as a Hasidic Jew; the distribution of instructions on how to dispose of razor blades following "bloodletting sexual activities"; and, for lesbians, a step-by-step guide to using "a slippery, lubed-up latex glove" to "safely rock [their partners] into a frenzy."

Stockton is not shocked by any of this, but is herself shocking when she claims it's not political. "I don't really think our job is politics," she says. "I honestly believe our job is pleasure. What we're really trying to do is have pleasure with something that calls itself a literary text, and that is a luxury. Politics will be involved in that, because to read them we have to make interpretations, we have to make certain decisions that are full of bias and assumption. And what we need to realize is that the very luxuries that we pursue will end up puncturing our politics."

Pleasure? Luxuries? Though she's been good about avoiding the impenetrable jargon most Theorists hide behind, she's lost me there. It turns out she's arguing for instant gratification, for Peter Pan, for all those things the Baby Boom has supposedly left behind. "We learned from the fall of communism that nothing is more necessary than luxuries," she says. "Nobody needs literature, but nobody wants to live without it. Communism fell because it had no answer to pleasure. This is what makes queer politics different than African-American politics and a lot of the other identity formations. Queers are problems because of their pleasures."

Although many people say they don't like gays because they believe the gay lifestyle is unnatural, "I don't think anybody in their heart of hearts really believes that," Stockton continues. "I think what they're saying is, 'It's unfair. We cannot allow that form of pleasure to take place. If I am disciplining myself, I don't want to see you indulging yourself.' The heart of that argument is that queer pleasure is not about productive use. We bow to the god of productive use. We cannot allow for reckless expenditure. And that's what gay life is seen as."

The pathological view of homosexuality considered it a symptom of arrested development. "You don't grow up," Stockton explains. Growing up is a vertical concept, and vertical, logical, goal-attaining reason is another of those patriarchal apple carts Queer Theory seeks to upset. Horizontal thinking is feminine, sensitive, intuitive and a perfect fit for a postmodern baby boomer. "'Growing up' presumes I was this and now I have changed," says Stockton. "Yes, time is upon my body, my life has extended in these many ways. But that's very different than growing up, which presumes leaving certain things behind that are of childhood, and taking responsibility, and finding my place in a vertical chain."

That brings her back to her politics of luxury, which she holds up in opposition to the ticking of the career clock, the ticking of her biological clock. "Show me the person who does not have as their goal to waste time," she commands. "The evangelical is about deferred pleasure. You are waiting for the day when the true story begins, the Book of Revelations, the wedding banquet in Heaven, the streets paved with jewels. The most disciplined Marxists will not allow themselves any pleasure until the Revolution has begun, and all people drink good wine. Still, the goal is to bring pleasure to people. That's the story of the twentieth century. It's all about pleasure in the end."

So it fits that Stockton thinks that somehow, Bill and Hillary Clinton are queer. "Bill Clinton must be profoundly propelled in many directions," Stockton says. "He is probably deeply concerned about people. He needs to be popular in such a lethal way that that's his greatest fault as a human being. He got into politics to get things done and to be popular. And sexuality is very much a part of his person, one he never found a way to put a brake on. A queer reading sees the bind that he's in." But "the official discourse of the day is still the discourse of heteronormativity," Stockton continues. "In other words, you have to be normal. It doesn't matter who you are. You're going to have to talk about family values."

Baby boomers have created a society where monogamy is not what it once was, if it ever was, where divorce is a norm, where families are redefined daily. "Who knows what goes on in private relationships?" Stockton asks. "There is no normative pattern of pleasure-taking. So whatever arrangement the Clintons had strikes me as a very intricate one. I don't think Hillary was a person who, in some straightforward way, closed her eyes and stood by her man. Whatever he was doing in the White House, that's just the tip of the iceberg. So they have some understanding, some deal we cannot be told as a country, because that would be far more troubling to people."

Daughter Chelsea gives Stockton a bit more trouble. "But maybe she knows of her parents' agreement. Until we know that part, I don't see what we could possibly hold against him. What did he do that the country should be concerned about? Nothing. If he's sexually harassing people, which he may have along the way, that's a bad thing. But that didn't come into the Monica Lewinsky stuff. The story he was impeached over is just profound and utter nonsense."

NINA HARTLEY'S CAREER in porn hit a slump in the late 1980s. Luckily, a revival of burlesque in upscale strip clubs, where porn stars appear as featured attractions, allowed her to raise her income just as her onscreen activity dropped off. There were also social changes in the wind. Although aging baby boomers were behaving less promiscuously, it soon turned out they were not, as some claimed, turned off to sex. They were simply finding new outlets for their urges. Even as political correctness was being promoted by unreconstructed 1960s radicals grown up into tenured New Puritans on college campuses, their younger brothers and sisters from the back end of the baby boom were finding new ways to outrage the uptight and rebel against the prevailing repression.

By the time of Bill Clinton's election in 1992, sex was back in a big way. "The anti-pornography push eased considerably," Hartley says. "We started going mainstream." MTV was offering sexual suggestion twenty-four hours a day, and "people had gotten desensitized," says Hartley. So the latest wrinkle in porn was called gonzo, "sweat flying, makeup running, in your face, stripped of all pretense, anything to get a rise out of people." Mainstream sexuality wasn't so extreme, but it, too, was pushing the boundaries. Chastity had proved untenable; the sex drive couldn't be rebottled. With gay men leading the way, sex was passing through the valley of death to make real if tentative inroads into a brave new AIDS-aware world. "AIDS was a boon on one level," Hartley says. "Now we *have* to talk about this. I don't care if your mama don't like it."

Jesse Helms and the Moral Majority notwithstanding, sex had come back out in the open, forced there by discussions of the disease. Even kids knew all about *it*, and they were not only learning it in school, but from Clarence Thomas, whose Supreme Court confirmation hearings—with their talk of harassment by pubic hair and Long Dong Silver—exposed how extremes had become mainstream long before Bill and Monica.

Sexual freedom wasn't absolute. In 1993 Hartley and ten other women were arrested at a lingerie show in an adult video store in Las Vegas benefiting the Free Speech Coalition, the adult film industry's anti-censorship group. But Hartley has had the last laugh, as her brand of sexual liberation becomes increasingly mainstream. Porn is now estimated to be an $8 billion industry; video porn represents 25 percent of the home video market. Hard core is celebrated and emulated on the airwaves by Howard Stern and Jerry Springer, hard-core performers are crossing into the mainstream, and mainstream stars are doing porn, apparently without shame. Tommy Lee and Pamela Anderson appear in the best-selling porn tape of all time. In 1999, Paul Weyrich wrote a letter admitting that the Moral Majority had lost its crusade to de-liberate America.

Two years before that, Hartley appeared in *Boogie Nights*, a film made by a director who'd watched her videos as a high school student. Then, in 1998, she spoke at the World Pornography Conference in Los Angeles, sponsored by California State University, alongside college professors and the president of the ACLU. Andrea Dworkin and Catharine MacKinnon were invited but declined to participate, dissing the conference in print instead. "People . . . don't seem to care," Dworkin told *Time* magazine. "It makes me ill." MacKinnon agreed: "Society has made the decision they want the abuse to continue."[29]

"Give it up, girls," Hartley responds. "The truth has come out. You can read what Dworkin and MacKinnon have to say and what I have to say and make your own decisions based on your own experience. I won't say we've won. We've made significant strides. There is porn by women out there. Young women have more of a sense of themselves as sexual creatures. Younger folk are making their own families and their own tribes that cross gender and racial boundaries. Baby boomers set the example."

Hartley now hopes she'll be able to live out her dream of growing old as a sex educator, doing for the young what the authors of *Our Bodies, Our Selves* did for her. "Of course you can get old in this business," she insists. "I'm at the top of my game. I pretty much still have my looks. I don't know how I'll feel the first time a boy in his twenties looks at me and doesn't think I'm sexy. But the Baby Boom needs to see women getting older, it needs to see older women with younger men, so I think I have a glorious future. You have to be a certain age to be a healer. That's what I wanted to be from the first."

THE FALL OF 1995 was a series of crises for Victoria Leacock. Her best friend, Gordon Rogers, died of AIDS that September, her latest boyfriend broke up with her, she was evicted from the borrowed apartment in which she was living, her godmother Maxene Andrews died, and then her roommate, Pam Shaw, died of AIDS, all within ten weeks. Though Jonathan Larson was in the midst of rewriting *Rent*, he stopped work to speak at the two AIDS memorials, videotaped the memorial for Andrews, helped Leacock move out, and did his best to convince her that her ex was a jerk.

Rehearsals of *Rent* began in December. Larson wanted Leacock to be there with him, but without a role to play, she was unwilling. Previews of *Rent* were to begin a few days before an apartment she'd rented would be available to her, so Leacock decided to leave town until then. After videotaping Larson's last day as a waiter (he'd finally quit his job after nine years), she spent December with family in Barbados. "Eight years of my life had been devoted to people with AIDS, one after the other, and they'd all died horrible, agonizing deaths," she said. "The sun was so good for me. And I remember someone made me laugh, and I felt I hadn't laughed in years."

In January, Leacock's father invited her to join him in Siberia, where he was making a movie. She called Larson to apologize that she was going to miss his first preview, but said she'd be home for his thirty-sixth birthday a week later. He lied and told her things were fantastic—in fact, he was fighting with his director and the producers, plus he was broke and stressed to the breaking point. Unaware, Leacock flew to Siberia as *Rent* went into final rehearsals.

Four days before the previews began, Larson felt a pain in his chest. Taken to the hospital, he was diagnosed with food poisoning and sent home. On January 23, he went back to the hospital. This time he was told he had the flu. The next night, Larson attended the final dress rehearsal, which got a standing ovation. A reporter from the *New York Times* was there. Larson gave a brief interview, saying the show was inspired by friends who'd died of AIDS, and that its message was that what matters isn't how long you live, but what you do. Afterward, Larson went home and before going to bed, put water on the stove to make a cup of tea.[30]

In Siberia, Leacock and her father were "staying in a rathole, which is a nice apartment in Siberia," she says. They'd been unable to get the phone to work, but suddenly it started ringing. Richard Leacock answered. When he said the name Jonathan Larson aloud, Victoria knew something was wrong. "I thought, 'Oh my god, his show's been canceled.' That was the worst thing I could think of," she says. "I looked at Dad and said, 'Did Jonathan die?' so when I found out his show was canceled, it wouldn't be as awful." It was just that awful. Larson's chest pains had been a unheeded warning sign. On the evening of January 24, 1996, the young playwright/composer died of an aortic aneurysm while boiling water for tea.[31]

Leacock was bereft. She changed her flight plans in order to get home in time for Larson's memorial service, the day before his birthday, but weather caused delays. By the time she got to the theater, 400 of Larson's friends had already gathered. "In a way, the saddest part and the end of the story is, Pam Shaw's family was there and the Rogers were there," Leacock says. "All the parents felt like they'd lost another child. And then I went home, and I had sacks of mail. There were two things from Jonathan—the invitation to opening night and his Christmas card. I opened the Christmas card and it said, 'Dearest Vic: May '96 be our year. (And no more funerals.) Love, Jon.'"

Two days before the show's official opening, the *New York Times* ran its article featuring Larson's last interview. Then, on Valentine's Day, a *Times* review compared *Rent* to *Hair* for giving "a pulsing, unexpectedly catchy voice to one generation's confusion, anger and anarchic, pleasure-seeking vitality." The show sold out the next day, was extended, sold out again, and moved to Broadway in a matter of weeks.[32] Leacock was featured in many of the articles about Larson, she thinks, "because he'd died at a young age unexpectedly, and so a tremendous amount of people assumed he really died of AIDS—which he didn't. They were interviewing me so they could say 'his ex-girlfriend' and identify him as a heterosexual."

Leacock's connection to Larson and *Rent* continued. She became part of the small group that dealt with his property and archived the music and plays he'd left behind—a few of which she still hopes to produce. She'd given the composer close to $8,000 during his lean years, and he'd promised her a cut of *Rent* royalties in return. When his parents learned that, they told her they'd always suspected there had been "another bank," and soon weekly checks started to arrive. "My job became Jonathan Larson," she says. "And it was a good thing because I needed something to do, but it was also a bad thing because it kept me in permanent grief for a long time, and having the money to support me also meant I didn't have to get my head together." But the money also paid for her next short film, which has won awards, been shown at several film festivals, and raised her hopes that she has a future as a filmmaker.

DONALD TRUMP CALLS the years 1990 to 1994 the most interesting of his life. "Not necessarily the best time of my life, because it certainly wasn't, but I learned more about myself during those years than any other time," he says. "I had never had adversity, and all of a sudden, I am being fuckin' creamed. It was a bad time, obviously, for the country. It was a bad time for New York. And I was the symbol. So they wouldn't do a story that real estate in New York was doing terribly. They'd do a story that Trump is doing terribly."

In fact, as the same people who'd cheered his noisy rise jeered at his fall, he was setting the stage for a comeback. In March 1991, he settled with his ex-wife Ivana. Though she and her lawyer, Michael Kennedy, had sought as much as $2.5 billion—half of Trump's presumed assets—she eventually settled for exactly what her several ante-nuptial agreements promised her, about $14 million, child support, and their Connecticut mansion.

A year later, Trump filed prepackaged bankruptcy plans, approved by most of his bondholders, for the Trump Castle and Trump Plaza casinos, relinquishing half-ownership of one in exchange for lower interest rates.[33] If he met specified financial performance goals and made interest payments on time, his stake could rise again—up to 80 percent. Nine days later, he agreed to give his bankers 49 percent of the Plaza Hotel (which had gone into bankruptcy at the beginning of 1992), canceling $125 million in debt and gaining more favorable terms on a $300 million mortgage. At the same time, Trump finally won a crucial approval to develop his remaining Penn Central yard. By the end of 1992, the *New York Times* was reporting: "Wall Street clearly sees Mr. Trump in a new light."[34]

Trump kept fine-tuning his various deals, restructuring his debts, reducing interest payments, and reclaiming his equity. He was regaining his bravado. That spring, he sued the federal government, claiming that allowing Native Americans to run casinos without paying taxes discriminated against casino owners. The suit went nowhere, but indicated that his brief spell of uncharacteristic humility was over. On firmer financial footing, he finally married Marla Maples, two years after announcing their engagement, and two months after she gave birth to a daughter they named Tiffany. The ceremony was held at the Plaza Hotel in the presence of guests like radio shock jock Howard Stern and boxer Evander Holyfield.

In 1994, Trump tried to take his casinos public, but failed when he found he couldn't refinance and regain control of the Taj Mahal. A little more than a year later, Trump put together an initial public offering to sell stock in the holding company that owned the Trump Plaza, his least debt-ridden Atlantic City property. He used the proceeds to enlarge its casino, buy back two properties he'd lost to banks, get into riverboat gambling in Indiana, and reduce his personal loan guarantees. By October 1995, he was being hailed by politicians and businessmen at a luncheon in New York for pulling off "the comeback of the decade."

Trump's trick wasn't easy, but it was clever. "I now have an advantage I didn't have then—experience," he says. "I never saw a crash before." Now he is more cautious. He began selling his services and his name to others, forming partnerships in which he worked as pitchman, negotiator and construction manager. He made a deal that paid him $50 million to oversee the renovation and sale of apartments in the former Gulf & Western Building overlooking New York's Columbus Circle and Central Park. The building was renamed Trump International Hotel and Tower, even though others owned the building and paid the redevelopment bills. When apartments there went on sale in 1997, they included eight of the city's ten top apartment sale prices. Then, backed by a Hong Kong holding company, Trump began to build a scaled-down and environmentally friendly version of Trump City—first renamed Riverside South, then Trump Place—with 5,700 apartments in sixteen high-rise buildings and 1.8 million square feet of commercial space. Trump retained a 30 percent share of the seventy-five-acre site. Finally, after more negotiations and restructurings, Trump folded all of his casinos into Trump Hotels and Casino Resorts and ended up with 37 percent of its stock.

In summer 1998, just turned fifty-two, Trump was back. In partnership with an insurance company, he bought the General Motors building, a landmark overlooking Central Park, a few blocks from Trump Tower; his Trump Place apartments were selling rapidly, and he was refurbishing 40 Wall Street, which he bought for $5 million and subsequently mortgaged for $125 million. "I didn't appreciate my success in the eighties," he says, "because it just seemed natural. Now I appreciate it because I know the perils."

Unfortunately, his refound sense of security spelled the end of his brief second marriage. After months of rumors, Trump and wife Marla announced their separation that spring. "I don't know if I'd call it a midlife crisis," he says. Then he adds, "It could be. Certainly I'm having a good time with it." He felt he'd never had the chance to enjoy the fruits of his success. "I went from one marriage to another, which was a mistake. Marla's a good girl, and I had a good marriage with her, but it's just that I get fuckin' bored. One of those little things. Work to me is going on a vacation and sitting around going nuts, because there's no telephone. So I'm still young enough, and I want to have a good time for a while. I deserve it." Asked if he regrets not playing more when he was younger, he quotes John Paul Getty: "A lot of people have a happy marriage, but there's only one John Paul Getty."

Trump says he feels a closer bond to Getty than he does to his own generation. "I have absolutely no consciousness of my generation," he says, but he admits that like many his age, he doesn't want to get old. "I think you always want to fight it," he says. "I'm not a huge fan of the aging process. And I can't believe that too many people are. But I've seen people who fight it, and it doesn't work. People with facelifts look like they have facelifts. In many cases, they look a helluva lot worse."

Asked what he's proudest of, Trump points to photos of his four children lined up in ranks near his desk. "I wouldn't be happy not having children," he says. "There's something nice when a kid calls up and starts blabbing. Having children is a little bit of a hedge against age. A lot of my friends don't, and they regret it more now than they did when they were thirty and forty. But you can't beat the clock."

Trump keeps trying. After leaving his second wife, he's dated a series of beauties and opened a modeling agency, but he admits that can't go on forever. "I used to hate it, at Le Club, when I'd see a seventy-five-year-old guy walk in with two twenty-year-old girls," he says. "I'm conscious of that. And if you look at most of the girls I'm seeing, they're in their thirties, I'm very proud to tell you. This is a positive thing, okay? Is it a hedge, though?" Trump pauses and gestures at a copy of the *National Enquirer* sitting on his desk, open to a poll of young women, who'd been asked which billionaire they'd most like to date. As he reads the headline—TRUMP'S NEW JACKPOT: HE WINS SEXIEST DREAM MAN TITLE—he smiles to himself. "I think it's just like buildings," he says. "If I didn't like it, I wouldn't do it."

In fall 1999, as dot.com mania swept the country and instant Internet millionaires became common coin, rendering the 1980s the garish displays of wealth small-time in comparison, this baby boom P. T. Barnum took his show on the road again, this time with his girlfriend du jour, a 26-year-old Slovenian lingerie model, by his side, in order to seek the presidential nomination of the insurgent Reform Party, founded earlier in the decade by fellow billionaire, Ross Perot, and headed by wrestler-turned-governor Jesse Ventura (b. 1951).

Although that put him up against seasoned politicians Al Gore (b. 1941), Bill Bradley (b. 1943) and George W. Bush (b. 1946), and despite his warning that he wouldn't run if—as seemed inevitable—he didn't think he could win, some in both the public and press actually took Trump's posturing as something more than mere publicity-seeking. If it was, then his egocentric grandiosity likely served as a stand-in for the sort of self-indulgence his fellow boomers no longer allow themselves.

AT FIFTY-TWO, Mark Rudd is no longer a firebrand. "Political change takes much longer than I thought," he says. "I've developed a kind of existential point of view; you just keep plugging away and over time it accretes." In 1997, he met Marla Painter, an anti-military activist and environmental educator who advises philanthropists working with community organizers. When they married in June 1998, Rudd got a conciliatory note from his old comrade-adversary, Bernadine Dohrn.

"My view of my youthful idealism is bittersweet," he says, "but the basic analysis is still right. U.S. imperialism sucks bad. We've created a militarized world, and now it and global capital, which goes along with it, have created a world of haves and slaves. We are the haves and the Third World are the slaves.

"It's comforting to think it's human nature—then you can't do anything about it, you might as well just go enjoy your sport utility vehicle. I'm not saying I don't enjoy my pickup; I don't have a sport utility vehicle yet, but if I needed one, I'd probably go get one. But the world can't keep going at this level of imbalance. We live in a town in which five percent of the people live up on the hill and eat really well, and ninety-five percent are down below, inundated with toxins, eating next to nothing, slaving away twelve hours a day. It's an unstable situation, and there has to be some reaction, either disaster or rebellion or both."

Rudd's kids, both college-age now, know his stories and his worldview. "They think we tried to do too much, and failed," he says. "I don't think they have a clear sense of the euphoria and feeling of power you get when you're in a true mass movement."

The absence of young people in politics depresses him. The foot troops are "by and large people our age," Rudd says. "I kind of wish more of us had committed suicide politically so young people wouldn't be burdened by the heavy hand of the past. Youth energy is the sine qua non. The New Left got as far as it did because we rejected our elders. And we did accomplish something: the antiwar movement, the rise of the women's movement, the gay movement. When else has a foreign military adventure been successfully opposed by a movement in this country? But young people have got to just forget about it. They are constantly having to compare themselves to us."

Rudd, too, is condemned to keep comparing himself to the myth of Media Mark, which almost overwhelmed him, and the reality of who he was, which, try as he might, he can't push away. Toward the end of our talk he says something about the 1960s, but I get the sense he's really talking about himself. "I just want the thing to die so that nobody has to live up to it anymore," Mark Rudd pleads.

FOR MANY, THE Internet represents the best of everything the Baby Boom stood for in its youth. It's a place where artists, scientists, and just plain folks share wisdom, humor, sorrows and joys inexpensively and instantaneously. It expedites instant communication, not just with family and friends but with cultures around the world. It is nibbling away at the sense of the Other, which has caused racial, national and religious strife since time began. It embodies the values of grass-roots empowerment, speeding the decentralization of power. John Gage created Net Day in 1995, a national volunteer project to wire every classroom and library in America, and then the world, to the Internet so that "the same conversation reaches everybody and you can't exclude anyone," he exults. "The boundaries of the village encompass the world. And the kids think it's normal! They have not learned that this is not the way human history has been."

The rage of the 1960s was directed against centralized, indifferent power. "The Internet is the antithesis," Gage continues. "I can e-mail Bill Clinton. I can touch the levers of the machinery he also touches. The Internet allows all of us to reach hundreds of millions of people with no investment in machinery. The idea is loose and can never be controlled again."

The boomers were privileged kids and "much of what we were able to do was because we were privileged," Gage says. "Out of privilege came our sense of entitlement and freedom. That has now found expression in the Internet. And I think most of the people of our generation are deeply committed to extending this entitlement to every kid everywhere. The Internet will become a chaos of languages and cults, a means of community conversation. In the past, cinema opened a window. Now the windows are being opened everywhere and the people opening them are six, seven, eight years old. A natural justice will emerge from the great deal of human experience visible for the first time. We've put windows in walls. And we should be proud of it."

TIM SCULLY HAS some regrets about his role in opening windows of consciousness with LSD, but they don't color his forward vision, whether looking in or outward. "In the psychedelic years we had the fantasy of a commune where craftspeople and scientists and engineers would get together and have really good facilities and tools and raw materials so if you had an idea, you could materialize it quickly and be able to share it," he says. "We had a fantasy of being able to access the world's knowledge base by computer. And those fantasies have materialized on the Internet."

Having applied for a presidential pardon in 1994, Scully is understandably reluctant to talk about the politician who didn't inhale. He'd rather discuss his work with the Mendocino government, with his local airport's advisory committee (he still flies the plane Billy Hitchcock gave him), and with the local Grange, where he's assistant steward and where members well into their eighties "still feel very much the way they did when they were young," he says. "I don't think we lose that sense of who we were when we were fifteen or twenty."

Scully thinks the people we were have helped make a better world. "Women's rights, racial issues, and environmental issues are being worked on much more consciously," he says. "Those were special-interest issues that have now become central to our culture. Our attitudes about starting wars have changed quite a bit, too. There's a lot more tendency to question and be cautious. We may not be doing perfectly, but we're sure doing a heck of a lot better than we were thirty or forty years ago."

Scully won't condemn drug use, even if he no longer promotes it. "The goals of being more conscious and of becoming more integrated with the universe are valid and always have been," he says. "There are lots of traditions—meditation, yoga, religious disciplines—for pursuing those goals. Most people who follow those disciplines see taking drugs as cheating. But I think it's useful to be able to go to the back of the book, see what the experience is like, and know it's worth putting some real work into learning how to get there on your own."

He, for one, is happy to admit what he did and where it got him. "That time is still part of who I am," he says. "Pretty frequently I'll stop and remember there's more to life than just work, remember to be conscious and gentle, and remember how it felt to be really connected to everyone else. Every year or two, and sometimes a lot more often, I see a gleam in people's eye when they tell me that they tried acid. I think that everybody was changed in some way by the experience. Fortunately, most people feel that they were changed in a positive way." He gives me one last twinkling smile. "That, of course, was what we had in mind."

JONATHAN LARSON WROTE one character into *Rent* who reminds Victoria Leacock of herself. Mark, the narrator, is always filming things, and bemoaning that he's the one who survives while all around him die. "I think Jonathan was concerned that I couldn't get my eyes out of the grave," she says. She wonders if he wasn't trying to warn her not to be consumed by the sadness around her.

"To me everything was tainted by AIDS," she says. "And you know what, baby? It ain't over yet. Two weeks ago, for the first time in a long time, I had a friend tell me that he'd just found out he's HIV-positive."

Leacock, who still lectures to thousands of students each year about AIDS, has continued working on Larson's behalf, serving on the board of the foundation set up to give away the money he earned with *Rent* to, as she puts it, "encourage future Jonathan Larsons." She's followed his advice: taking the overwhelming sadness that has burdened her—and many of her peers at the tail end of the Baby Boom—and trying to turn it into something constructive. In 1998, she published a book of celebrity drawings, *Signature Flowers*, with 30 percent of the proceeds going to AIDS charities. And she still hopes one day to make films as good as her father's.

Where does she go from here? She's thirty-five and single. "I want to take one step at a time," she says carefully. Despite it all, she's cautiously optimistic. "I ask myself, What can I leave on this planet? I can hopefully fall in love, have some children, and learn to be happy. I still speak to kids because I figure if one person doesn't get infected, the world is changed forever. You know, everyone who lives changes the world."

BY 1999, DAVID McIntosh was chafing in Congress. He was still having fun, being a rabid partisan, mocking vice president Al Gore on the floor of the house for predicting that internal combustion engines would disappear by 2025, and knocking $32 million out of a spending bill to pay for a pet Gore project: a live Internet image of the earth spinning in space. It didn't pass unnoticed that in the process, he was getting revenge for the ruthless mockery of his sometime mentor Dan Quayle.

That spring, he acknowledged year-old reports that he was considering a run for the governorship of Indiana in the November 2000 election. In fact, since 1997, he'd been campaigning and raising political action committee funds for Republicans in state legislative races, building a base for a statewide run. He said he wanted influence over matters that have been transferred to localities, like welfare, education and health care. It may well have been the failed effort to impeach Bill Clinton, and its fallout in Congress, that finally made the choice for him.

Though the Republicans lost the political battle, McIntosh thinks the aftermath of impeachment will include self-examination and remorse on the part of those who backed Clinton and a strengthening of the base of support for conservative politicians. "The people who wanted us to stand up for conservative principles are happy," he says. "We've now got to show that our agenda is good for everybody else." That may not include the baby boom. "Boomers tried to fashion new moral standards," says McIntosh. "This whole episode made it harder for the generation to be the guardians of a new morality." It's Monica Lewinsky's generation that gives *him* hope. "The next generation is what the battle is all about." In retreating to Indiana, McIntosh is cleaving to fellow believers, with whom he can safely wait to see if the rest of the country will come around. "What will tell is what happens in the next two to ten years. Do people run away and say the lesson of Clinton is, 'Don't talk about it and don't ask'? Or do they tell their children, 'It's wrong to cheat on your wife'?"

In July 1999, McIntosh announced his decision to quit Congress and run for governor of Indiana, promising to concentrate his efforts on education, tax-cutting and attracting high-tech jobs to the Hoosier state. Though he faces both a primary and a fierce battle against an incumbent who is likely to portray him as a dangerous extremist, his rock-solid Midwestern virtues are a significant strength. And McIntosh's decision, implicitly criticizing a Congress mired in minutiae and partisan spitballing, may reflect more than a local mood. Intelligent, lucky, fearless and thus far undefeated, McIntosh is reaching for a political synthesis from the right like the one on the left that gave Bill Clinton his weightless approval ratings. "We have to think about moral values," he says. "We have to wake people up."

DAVE McINTOSH THINKS the way to the future lies within; Tommy Vallely thinks we need to look outward. "This country is not challenged enough, and when you're not challenged, you don't know what you have to give up," he says. "After the Second World War, America didn't get strong by making Idaho strong. It got strong by making Japan strong, by rebuilding Europe."

Vallely's involvement in Vietnam today is not a matter of making reparations, but of understanding the larger lessons of that divisive conflict. "What the United States got from Vietnam is what I got: self-knowledge," he says. "And self-knowledge is worth a lot. I certainly didn't go to Vietnam to get it. I went to Vietnam as a curious kid who felt, somewhat ideologically, that when America went somewhere, it did good."

That was the legacy of the boom's parents—the World War II generation—which, at the end of the 20th century, was hailed by many as the "greatest" generation in history. Vallely doesn't agree. "I don't think that generation has the self-knowledge my generation has," he says. "This generation knows more about humanity than that one did. Because that generation created Vietnam. D-Day—that's the day America went to Vietnam. That's the mentality. They landed in Normandy to do good. They wanted to defeat the Nazis. But when it's over, you think that all your actions create good. And what Vietnam teaches you is that sometimes when you think you're doing good, you do evil. Vietnam is not the first war that was the wrong war. It's much more than that. It's the maturing of America."

With a mindset forged by that war, Valley knows the new challenge facing America is how to get along with the rest of the world. Unlike many, he's come to respect Bill Clinton. "He's not somebody that I think the generation should be ashamed of. He does understand race. And he did change the Democratic Party. He eliminated a lot of the domination of the special-interest groups, because he's comfortable with black people, he's not afraid of them." But, Vallely adds, Clinton "doesn't understand the future, he's a short-term guy" who learned the wrong lesson from Vietnam.

"We can do good everywhere in the world?" Vallely scoffs, irony on full. "We're the most powerful country in the world with the best economy, the best military, but we haven't figured out a way to turn military and economic power into influence. We want influence on the cheap. Openness is our new value. Let's go to Russia and have democracy. Let's go to Cambodia and have democracy. But it's not working. And that's what America has to figure out, how to take the power it has and keep humanity from killing itself."

Vietnam is his model. "My relationship to Vietnam is clearly related to the future," he says. "I became interested in Vietnam, because I learned something there—that humankind can do really bad things to each other, and you need a certain amount of civilization to prevent it. That's the issue that I care about. How is humanity going to govern itself?" To answer that, Vallely has developed his own global philosophy, "which is," he says, "that there's not a big difference between Western values and Eastern values. I have as many Vietnamese friends as American. They want their kids to obey their parents, to have the identical value system we have, to go to Harvard. If we knew more about the world, it wouldn't seem as complicated."

To Vallely, hope lies with the Vietnam veterans in politics who've spent the years since the war trying to figure out what happened and how to prevent it happening again. "Their self-doubt, their conflicts, make them interesting and more understanding of other people and other ideas," says Vallely. "Americans are still the richest people in the world, but we can't live in this world unless poor countries do better."

It's an uphill battle, but the Silver Star winner believes it must be won. Surveying the field from age forty-nine, he hopes he'll be part of it. He's a little bit bored, he says, and he wonders whether any contenders for the presidency in 2000 will put him to work. He grins when asked what he'll do if they don't. "Retirement?" he says. "Golf?" Then he shakes his head and admits he may not be ready to give up just yet. "If you're not conflicted," Vallely says with a laugh, "you just don't know shit."

THOUGH IT RETAINED its hippie image, by 1995 the Grateful Dead had become a moveable corporation, traveling in rented Boeing 727 jets, crashing in luxury hotels. After Jerry Garcia died that summer, Cameron Sears had to help supervise the retrenchment and restructuring of Grateful Dead Productions.

Its small record label and large merchandising operation kept the business going, but its collective wisdom was that the band could no longer tour under its old name. Some members had gotten out of the rock business altogether. Two, Bob Weir and Mickey Hart, formed bands of their own, and toured the next two summers with like-minded musicians under the banner of the Furthur Festival, named for Ken Kesey's magic bus, "in an effort to keep the Dead community and spirit together," Sears says. In summer 1998, most of the surviving Dead members toured again as The Other Ones. "Life without Jerry was a daunting prospect, but it was important they be able to perform," Sears says. They toured in buses and stayed at Radissons. "On a comfort level, it was a sacrifice," Sears says. "But at the same time, it reconnected them with their audience in a very tactile way. We were all traveling the same roads."

Where once the Dead might have spent its off-hours tripping, now they arranged private trips to art museums and the White House and dinners with fans like Al Gore. They didn't miss their old life. "When you've been up the mountain a hundred times, it doesn't have the same fascination," Sears says. "And thanks to their wives and families, they finally began experiencing things most people take for granted." They'd also begun to think of their legacy, announcing plans to build Terrapin Station, a $60 million multimedia concert hall, museum and counterculture complex in San Francisco.

Unregenerate Deadheads quickly denounced the place as an attempt by the band to erect a monument to itself and, as a writer in the *San Francisco Chronicle* put it, "cash in on the Golden Age of Greed."[35] Sears mounted their defense. "People wanted to think of it as some sort of Planet Hollywood, but I explained that the intent is completely the opposite," he says. "Terrapin will show how the tradition that gave the Dead life has evolved as well as where it came from. We want to go back and celebrate the Beats, the Free Speech Movement, the social awareness movements that evolved out of that, and the music that was their backdrop."

Despite its influence and wealth, the Dead remains a lively part of a renegade movement survives lives thirty years after its moment. In that time, the band contributed in many extra-musical ways, often focusing on the environmental concerns that led Sears to them in the first place. It biggest splash was made in 1988, when the Dead played a benefit in New York for groups like Rainforest Action Network and Greenpeace. Afterward, it set up its own philanthropic organization, the Rex Foundation, to "look for and fund organizations that might otherwise fall through the cracks," says Sears, "not the big Sierra Clubs, but grassroots groups" like Friends of the River, organic farming groups, a coalition working to save California's last remaining old-growth virgin redwood groves from timber companies, a monitoring group that operates emission-monitoring sensors downwind of Pennsylvania's still-operating Three Mile

Island nuclear power plant, and a solo activist who spends his time sniffing out pollution in San Francisco Bay.

The idealistic fervor that turned Earth Day into a mass movement in the 1970s is a thing of the past, a luxury most boomers say they can no longer afford, even as they accumulate luxury cars, computers, cell phones and summer houses. "Everyone's gotten too comfortable and they've stopped paying attention," admits Sears, who himself drives a BMW. "We're all working more, and we want to spend what time is left with our families. I have not been on the front line like I was, but a lot of very dedicated people are still fighting the good fight."

Even activists have come to see the shades of gray in what were once deemed black-or-white conflicts. "The debate pitting jobs against the environment is very divisive," Sears says. "You've got vocal young hippie kids arguing with hard-working guys, basically. And the environmental movement has also always suffered from the fact that the places most at risk are extremely remote. But though we may never see them, we still take solace from their existence."

Sears isn't surprised that many dismiss the staged calls to arms issued by environmentally conscious politicians like Al Gore. "He has conviction; you can't quibble with his motivations," Sears insists. "But the fact is, people are less concerned about the environment than whether they're going to get in on next week's IPO."

It's enough to send any right-thinking boomer into paroxysms of guilt. Sears knows that running benefits and writing checks isn't enough. "The status quo won't suffice in the long run. We have the knowledge, technology, information and wealth to make things better. Take San Francisco. People can't eat fish out of the Bay. The wetlands are disappearing, and yet they're debating building a new airport runway through them. We're all driving around in gas-guzzling SUVs; it's like nobody remembers the gas crisis. But the challenge is to do something about it, to maintain the idealism we had at nineteen. I'm just afraid that until we get a radical wake-up call, the vast majority won't be motivated."

Sears sees a glimmer of hope in the scattered victories environmentalists still win. With contributions from thousands paying for the work of a highly motivated handful, he says, redwoods do get saved, organic farms stay in business, and endangered species are restored to viability. "None of us can afford to lose the roof over our heads to protect the coho salmon, but we can all do a little bit to spread the gospel and reaffirm our commitment to things that are important," he says. "You can be comfortable without forgetting who you were."

Sears wants to emulate boomer-led companies like Patagonia, the out-doors supplier, and Ben & Jerry's Ice Cream. "A percentage of their profits go back to the community," he says, "and lots of us can do that now. There's a reason the church got so powerful. People gave a percentage of their income to it. Why can't we do that for the environmental move-ment? The problem is, it doesn't have a product to sell. What value do we place on the air we breathe?"

WHILE ON TOUR for *A Return to Love* in 1992, Marianne Williamson conceived what would become her fourth book, *The Healing of America*. She said she'd sensed a collective despair in the country and wanted to suggest a radical, spiritual cure for what ailed the body politic. In the mid-1990s, she returned to that book, a call to spiritually motivated, non-denominational civic activism. Williamson describes the book as a last-ditch attempt to win her father's approval. He died in 1995.

Williamson found her political roots in a nineteenth-century philoso-phy propounded by Ralph Waldo Emerson and Henry Thoreau. Transcendentalism says that there are ideas, ideals and spiritual truths that exist apart from experience, and that they are where the individual and the universal meet and resolve their contradictions. Transcendentalism val-ues the reality of the spirit over the illusion of the material. Williamson, who sees democracy as transcendental, urges her readers to use the power of love to better the world. Like the boomer rock stars who said war would end if we all woke up one morning and declared it obsolete, her prescrip-tion for social injustice is, "Think the following thought: This should not be happening in America." Though it was hardly an earth-shattering notion, at least she was asking her followers to go beyond *me*-ism, to think and care about something bigger than themselves.

The response was predictable. She was accused of being a typical spoiled boomer, putting her self and its spiritual needs above even rational discourse. Decrying her "ersatz universalism," her tenuous grasp of history and her obsession with thinness and dieting, the *New Republic*'s Margaret Talbot denounced the "pious book" as a "delegitimation of judgment and a delegitimation of conflict; a promiscuous intermingling of the personal and spiritual realms with the public and political realms; a dalliance with conspiracy theories; and a distrust of rationality and the intellect that would make democratic deliberation meaningless." Finally, Talbot warned that Williamson's proposal to incorporate magical thinking into politics smacked of "fascist government, which always prefers charisma to law, and ecstasy to decency."[36]

Williamson is no proto-fascist. Her political views are decent, if naive. Though she's not a knee-jerk progressive (she allows that dismantling the welfare system was "not the worst thing in the world"), neither is she terribly practical. She is given to grand statements, both sweeping ("We have the information right now if we wanted to solve the problems of the world") and empty ("A young child in the inner city of the United States is an American citizen with the same rights and opportunities as a corporate CEO"). She is adamant in her dedication to inclusion, social justice, putting people before profit. She believes in the power of government to ameliorate social ills. "We'll spend billions of dollars on a war against drugs when, for a fraction of that, we could provide sustenance that would drastically reduce crime because people would not be in such despair," she says. "Do you know building prisons is our single largest urban industry? We've made big business out of misery."

To Williamson, the answer to America's dilemma won't be found until the new ruling class of baby boomers "goes back to the moment we were wounded," she says. "That's going back to Martin Luther King and Bobby Kennedy. Those voices expressed a higher philosophical vision within the political domain. There's a huge group of Americans for whom the over-secularization of the left has left them feeling very dry." The tough-minded lack heart, she continues, while loving hearts "need to read a book or two" and toughen up.

For her part, in 1998, Williamson went back to Detroit, Michigan, the town where her father was born. That March, feeling the need "to have dirt under my fingernails," she took over the Church of Today, in a Detroit suburb. The congregation is associated with the Unity Church, a Christian Science-like group founded in 1889 by two faith healers, Charles and Myrtle Fillmore, who considered Jesus an exemplar of a divinity available to any believer. Williamson had spoken at the Detroit church and, after its founding minister died, proposed herself as a replacement. The racially mixed congregation gave her the chance to put into practice ideas she'd propounded in her books, such as having white people apologize to blacks for the way they've been treated in America. "Racial issues are the hippopotamus on America's coffee table that none of us are talking about," she says. "So Detroit is perfect for me. I'm real big on applying the principles of personal healing to the collective psyche. You have to atone for mistakes before you're freed from their consequences. I don't know where white America gets off thinking we don't owe anything to these people."

That same spring, Williamson co-founded a group called the Global

Renaissance Alliance and recruited a board of directors that includes New Age and self-help celebrities like Deepak Chopra (b. 1946), Wayne Dyer (b. 1946) and Jean Houston (b. 1939), an early advocate of LSD, who turned to nondrug exploration of the inner-self after the drug was banned.[37] The Alliance's goal is "to provide a context for people to reengage in the democratic process and promulgate compassion and sharing and reverence for life as dominant political values," Williamson says. Its World Wide Web site (www.renaissancealliance.org, which is linked to www.marianne.com, on which Williamson touts her books, videotapes and spiritual vacation tours to Bali) explains that the alliance is based on "citizens' circles" of two or more people who agree to meet regularly and meditate on bettering the world. "These are open, emotionally safe forums," the web site says, "in which people join together to not only expand their political awareness but to also take action to help make manifest the most compassionate society."

Although Williamson won't reveal what was discussed with the August 1998 "spirit healing team" that ministered to Bill Clinton after his admission of Oval Office adultery, she thinks that the protracted impeachment process opened new avenues of awareness for Clinton's fellow baby boomers. "We are reaching a climax of disgust and the eye-opening realization that politics as we now know it is a completely corrupt mental, spiritual and emotional environment. People are going to be open to new voices and possibilities in a way they haven't been in a long time," she says.

The Baby Boom has come to a fork in the road, rather as Clinton did. "We were a narcissistic generation, but when things get really tough and you're a grown-up, you remember who you are," Williamson says. "Despite everything, despite the mistakes of this country and despite our own mistakes, at the deepest level we have a cellular recognition that this country is one of the great radical experiments in ultimate good on this planet."

The challenge ahead is to "marry the material mastery we achieved in our yuppiedom to the idealism we had before we made it in the world," Williamson continues. "If we can pull off that synthesis, future generations will bless us. Either way, they will remember us. But will we be known as those who woke up before it was too late, or will we be remembered as those bastards who used up all the resources and left an unsustainable planet? The reason we haven't had meaningful answers in America is that we have not been asking meaningful questions. The most meaningful questions are not *How do I get laid?* and *How do I make more money?* What's happening to the baby boomers now is that they're realizing they have more yesterdays than tomorrows. When you start combining questions about your own mortality with questions like *What did I contribute in my life?*, then a major, major earthquake will take place.

"Our generation had the longest postadolescent period in the history of the world," Williamson notes. "Most people hit puberty, take ten years and then they're grown-ups. But because of the traumas we experienced, we got frozen and created a culture that claimed maturity was something to be averted at all costs. We're now at the point where we have to make a choice. Are we going to actually have an adulthood? The idea that we haven't gone for it is scarier than the thought that they might kill us if we do. This is the last window of opportunity for this generation."

Rejecting pessimism as immoral, Williamson thinks her generation "yearns to get it right before we die," she says. "The wall in front of us now is personal courage. We know about global warming. We know there's an environmental crisis. The only way we will move forward as a generation is if we have the courage to do what it takes to change things. Otherwise we will go down as a generation of great shame because we will go down as a generation that knew and didn't do."

IT'S BEEN SAID that Michael Fuchs earned $50 million getting fired by Time-Warner. "I wanted revenge," he admits.

For months afterward, he believed he was up for a job running Sony in America, "but they never contacted me," he says. He was briefly considered for a job at Universal. It went to Frank Biondi, who'd lost his job at Viacom. "Then comes the great test of no longer belonging, no longer having the vehicle, and having risen to a certain height where jobs are not so easily available—and also being considered one of the more aggressive and difficult-to-manage executives in the business, although smart and successful," Fuchs says. "I was afraid to think of what it would be like without a job. I found out it could be pretty good."

There were some adjustments. He'd been a CEO so long, he'd forgotten how much was done for him. He'd never used a cash machine; HBO had a cash window. "But quite honestly, I've been able to master the acquisition of cash," he says laughing.

In 1999, Fuchs was still looking for a job. Just not very hard. Between tennis games, race car lessons and plane trips, he sits on the boards of several small companies he's invested in and works for cultural institutions like the avant-garde Brooklyn Academy of Music and for charitable foundations.

Fuchs has always criticized his colleagues in entertainment, so the fact that he still does is no surprise. Coming from a man who dodged Vietnam if not the draft, who chose the law over protest, who climbed the corporate ladder while his peers were listening to "Stairway to Heaven," and who made millions in the cutthroat climate of the 1980s and 1990s, what he has to say is as radical as it is surprising. For here in his lavish penthouse, Fuchs is railing against empty entertainment and shortsighted greed, two things he knows something about.

"Big companies clearly make creative decisions for business reasons and the bigger these companies get, the more they have at stake, the more that's going to happen," Fuchs says. "I always liked to go against the stream. I feel the stream increasing in speed in the opposite direction from where I want to go. Hollywood is one of the most greedy places on earth. Look at what people get paid, and the accumulation of money, and the quality of the product that results from all of that."

Fuchs fumes that these days, your job is to keep your job, even if that means fitting in, acting safe, and not challenging your superiors. To his former colleagues, he offers a challenge: "You are so lucky to be in a position where you can communicate to tens of millions of people. Wouldn't it be nice if you said something a little smarter, more irreverent, relevant or enduring?"

If they don't, Fuchs might. "I'm not dying to get back into big corporations. I am excessively prideful and would never come back unless I had the kind of authority I feel I'm entitled to. So I've scaled down my ambitions." But starting a small movie company is "not out of the question," Fuchs says. "I don't think I would have trouble raising the money or attracting the talent." So retirement may be just a way station. "At fifty-two, I still feel like a kid," he says. "Maybe I am Peter Pan."

JIM FOURATT RETURNED to the music business in 1991. "It's nice to make money," he says. "I've been able to save money, which I never did before. And I made a deal with myself that no matter what the provocation was, I wasn't going to quit. I think that is being adult and self-preservationist."

Fouratt sounds curiously conservative as he decries the factionalism he believes has destroyed the commonality popular music gave his generation. Punk, once the last best hope of cultural activists, degenerated into style and a nihilism that "takes kids who want to be outside society into darkness," he says, adding that the same goes for gangsta rap. "They're marketing nihilism, and they're co-opting and sucking the vitality out of any of these movements, just so they can sell. Rap was about how black kids survive in this culture without killing each other, without becoming drug addicts. It was about finding poetry within yourself, and trying to get that message out and have some kind of dignity. But gangsta rap is materialistic. It completely denies there is any other way to be a black kid. And no matter what anybody says, two or three black entrepreneurs were allowed to become heads of companies but the profits were made by white industry people."

Fouratt still attends political rallies and gay protests, and still votes in every election. "I have opinions," he says. "I engage people. Most of my friends don't vote. I think this is crazy. This is why we have the governments that we have now. Do I believe in Clinton? I voted for Bill Clinton. I'd probably vote for him again. He's been an enormous disappointment to me. But I'm not devastated like some people are. I learned long ago not to be a true believer. I have no illusions about Clinton. He's not a hero, so therefore he doesn't fall from grace for me."

Early in 1999, Fouratt lost his job at Mercury Records after it was taken over by Universal, which had itself been bought by Seagram. He was given back the name of his record imprint, Beauty, but none of its records or musicians. Nowadays he spends his days writing record reviews and consulting for various musicians and record companies, and his nights on the Internet, where he's gathered old cronies onto a mailing list he uses to provoke discussion. "Most of them have not given up on what they believe in," he says. "I've gathered other like-minded people of my generation to talk about what we can do. I want to provoke. One of the patterns we deal with in the late nineties is lethargy. So I try to prick, scratch, do something to get someone to take some kind of personal action. Because I really believe personal action is what makes the difference. Doing something that matters, that helps make a better world, that helps another individual to understand that they are powerful and meaningful. My goal is to say we're all part of the human society. Identity politics was important: to know how you're different. But it's not an end in itself. The end is, now that I know how we're different, what do you and I have in common?"

Fouratt cringes when I ask about getting older. "Our culture does not endorse getting older. This is what I talk about with my friends of a certain age. If we can figure out how to be vital and share our experience and be creative whatever age we are, that's the way we combat it. Boomers are a huge population, and the AARP is going to be transformed by the influx of boomers who are not willing to be old.

"I don't want to be old," Fouratt adds, shaking his head sharply, then shooting me an arch smile. "Whatever 'old' means."

* * *

IN MAY 1996, when Steve Capps quit Apple for Microsoft, it was national news. People hissed at him on the streets of Silicon Valley. He'd gone over to the dark side. But it wasn't really that simple.

Twenty years after finding his first desktop computer in a Xerox closet, Capps remained an idealist. He'd identified a job that needed to be done—distilling the miasma of the World Wide Web to a home computer's desktop. When he tried to sell the idea, it was as if the fabled library of Alexandria was sitting on a barge just offshore, he'd offered to build a bridge to it, and the Pharaohs of Egypt had told him to scram. He'd offered his scheme to Apple, to Sun, and to Netscape, and had been shown the door. Yet the allegedly evil empire welcomed him.

Capps came to Microsoft with a vague idea of developing a new computing paradigm that would make the Internet and the home computer more consistent and reliable, less chaotic, and easier to use. In his first few months at the company, he played freelance troubleshooter and idea generator, suggesting refinements to make its web browser, Internet Explorer, more user-friendly. "Then my desire to ship products came back," he says, and he started work on what will eventually be the first version of Windows for the new millennium, not Windows 2000, which will have the same basic user interface as the 1995 and 1998 versions, but a total redesign that will provide the one thing computers—even the ultra-simple, toylike iMacs with which Steve Jobs restarted Apple in 1998—still lack.

"When you buy a cell phone, you're handed a functioning thing," Capps says. "You don't even need to know your phone number to make a call. Today, if you're not a nerd, you still need a friend to set your computer up for you and even then, it's way too hard. There's no reason a computer can't be much simpler. The technology is all there; it's nothing new. We'd like you to be able to buy your eighty-two-year-old mother a computer, have it configured for bad eyesight and loaded up with your e-mail address and her investments, so she can turn it on and check how they're doing, and then brag to you about it."

Microsoft has finally realized what Apple always knew. "We want to make customers smile," Capps says. He knows it won't be easy. "There's lofty goals and then there's the reality of markets," he says. "In this economy, it's easy to have high ideals." Too easy sometimes. Time and again, Capps comes back to the hypocrisy he finds rampant in Silicon Valley. Capps admires the founders of Sun Microsystems, for instance, but he condemns their attacks on Microsoft, which escalated after the Justice

Department sued the company for antitrust violations and continued when America Online bought Netscape in November 1998, simultaneously forming an alliance with Sun. "It's so easy for the guys at Sun to be purists and say they believe in open source," Capps says. "Then they get in their Porsches and drive home to their big houses. Meanwhile, the guys who haven't made it yet, the guys who are doing startups and mortgaging their houses, are the ones being innovative."

It's more than innovation driving cyber-business today; Capps compares the atmosphere in Silicon Valley—and beyond—to a riot. "All these nerds are looting," he says. "He got his. I gotta get mine. I'm susceptible to it also. In the old days we worked crazy hours for our salaries. Now it's more like, we deserve to get rich. I know people who are turning venture capital away. It's a mob scene, and if you don't take advantage, you're kind of stupid."

Capps chose security over startup roulette. With an eye toward planning a family, going to work for Microsoft, even under the shadow of an anti-trust lawsuit, struck him as a sure bet. And he has nothing but disdain for those who say he's gone to work for Satan's son. "Everyone thinks Bill Gates is the Wizard of Oz, controlling everything. But the conspiracy theory is a joke. Gates monitors and gives feedback, but people do what they want." Microsoft's great success was happenstance, he thinks. "The world had to settle on one operating system just like it had to have one phone system," Capps says. "Microsoft lucked out with the right products at the right time. Serendipity played a large part here."

With age, Capps has come to realize that every revolution gets coopted eventually. Though ideals are fundamental, they exist in the real world. "Go back to the *Whole Earth Catalogue*," he says. "The commune that started weaving rope hammocks got into the business of rope hammocks, and then it broke up when capitalism got involved." The Internet and the hacker-driven open-source movement, with its talk of idealism, sharing and free exchange of information, "is a rebound from the sixties," Capps says. "But people also like to have five million dollars in the bank. Money will change open-source. It will be commercialized."

Economic realism and his own accumulation of capital aside, Capps remains the closet liberal he was when he argued with his parents about Watergate. Not that he does much about it. He grew up in "dropout mode, not go-march mode," he admits. "I haven't been mugged yet, so I haven't turned Republican." But neither does he play the cyber-mogul game of gladhanding liberal politicians. "My cynicism is such, I'd know they were there for wrong reasons, and I would be, too," he says. "I was a big Clinton fan, and I still like him, even though his libido got the best of him. I know he's totally fake; he's just fake in a way that aligns with my beliefs, the same way Reagan aligned with my mother's."

Like many boomers, Capps thinks the Internet has the potential to change things, but only if it doesn't drown in the noise of millions of know-it-alls chattering about nothing. "In our lifetimes, the Internet will have a lot of impact," he says, "but over my daughter's lifetime, who knows. The Net is a revolution that isn't over. Our kids will still be inventing it. Where we are now is equivalent to the telephone in the nineteen-twenties."

Capps's daughter is two and a half—and her impact on him has been incalculable. "The first time you yell at kids in a playground to settle down, you feel bizarre," Capps says. "But then you realize you're a grown-up in their eyes." When he looks in the mirror, he's not so sure. "I've been very blessed. When you think about it, I've never had a real job, I've always been able to do what I wanted, I've looked forward to work. I'll look forward to it even more when I'm totally in control."

When will that be? When he retires, though he has no plans to stop working. He figures instead that in a couple of years, he'll be able to quit "worrying about money," he says. "I want freedom, basically. Everybody around here is rich, but I still can't walk up to Bill Gates and say, 'Fuck you.' There are people who've quit Microsoft with a million dollars and think they've got it made." He snickers. "Maybe if they moved back to Idaho." What does he plan to do? "I've never had a deficit of ideas," he says. "I've got a list ten pages long of things I've invented." When he does quit Microsoft, one thing is sure: whatever he does will be "completely altruistic; it will make somebody smile."

Capps doesn't mind if people think he wants to stay a child. "What's wrong with that?" he says. "I haven't gotten to the point where I'm taking fifty pills to increase my sexual power and brain power. Will I? Who knows."

From the way he talks, it seems as if Capps will be content when age finally gets the better of him. "Our grandchildren will then have to find the next revolution," he says. He's thrilled to have played a small role in the second one in his generation's lifetime. Once not long ago, in bed late at night, he told his wife how cool it is that he's been part of it all. Marie D'Amico started to laugh.

"Go to sleep," she said.

Hereafter

"ISN'T THIS . . . UNNATURAL?"

We are in a corridor of the Alexis Park, a hotel in Las Vegas that has not a single slot machine or craps table. That's unnatural enough, but it's not what the reporter facing down Ronald M. Klatz, D.O., at an impromptu press conference is so upset about. Dr. Klatz (b. 1955), a bearded, bespectacled osteopath with shoulder-length black hair and a sloping, almost simian forehead, dressed in a black windowpane suit and cowboy boots, is president of the American Academy of Anti-Aging Medicine, sponsor of this Sixth International Congress on Anti-Aging & Bio-Medical Technologies. A4M, as his group is known, was founded in 1993 with the mission of slowing and eventually eradicating what it deems the disorder of aging.

Klatz, his own best patient, plans to live to 150. Think that's unnatural? "So is electric lighting, so are glasses, cell phones, synthetic clothing," he says. "Our lives are so good because we control our environment. We've controlled polio, diphtheria, whooping cough, extending life expectancy to seventy-seven years. But hormone replacement that increases life expectancy from seventy-seven to one hundred and seven isn't okay? I'm not okay with that."

Klatz is on to something. A4M's prescription for aging includes old-fashioned exercise and nutrition, cutting-edge detection of degenerative diseases, preventive measures from simple antioxidants to complex hormone therapies, and neo-sci-fi stuff like genetic engineering and human cloning. "When these come out of lab and into the real world, all bets are off in terms of lifespan," Klatz says. "We believe that half the healthy baby boomers will live to one hundred and beyond."

He's talking to you. An A4M handout, "Facts About the Demographics of Aging," makes its target audience evident, stating that in 1996, baby boomers comprised 29 percent of the U.S. population and that every 7.7 seconds a boomer turns fifty. When the first boomers were born, the pamphlet says, most people in the world died before age fifty; by 2025, when the last boomers are closing in on sixty-five, life expectancy will pass 100. Americans over fifty eat out three times a week, own 77 percent of the nation's assets, purchase 43 percent of cars, account for 90 percent of all travel, and spend a total of about $1 trillion a year, claims A4M. The number of cosmetic surgery procedures in the U.S. increased 75 percent between 1993 and 1997, with boomers accounting for much of the increase. Between 1992 and 1998, sales of fitness equipment doubled to $3.1 billion. More than $20 billion per year is spent developing—and $1 billion marketing—new products for boomers, all told a $300 billion industry. In its first three months on the market, 2.9 million prescriptions were written for Viagra, representing almost $260 million in sales.

Marketers, start your engines. It's the same old song with a different beat now that we're getting on. Klatz and his crew are busy turning the ultimate rebellion—against death—into money.

This convocation divides neatly in half; realists, medical researchers, and doctors in $3,000 suits on one side, wild-eyed health zealots and wishful thinkers, even one turbaned like a swami, on the other. The Alexis Park's large auditorium is hosting medical and scientific presentations, many by scientists with strong credentials. The rest of the hotel's facilities are so laden with bizarre promises of youth, Ponce de Leon would think he'd found his fabled fountain.

In the auditorium, they're talking about advances in imaging diagnosis of cancer, glutathione as a naturally occurring anti-aging protectant, the role of exercise in retaining competence in old age, the treatment of Alzheimer's disease, and the effect of nutrition on brain function. A few feet away, though, they're talking lifestyle. "I've got proteins that are profound," a voice proclaims. "I'm selling libido," extols another.

A lot of this is standard stuff, alternative medicine to some, quackery to others: nutritional supplements to promote brain function and blood flow; vitamins, minerals, melatonin and echinacea; blackberry-flavored Siberian Ginseng, Fo-Ti and Ginkgo smartness-enhancing drinks; books singing the praises of garlic; booths touting Laetrile and other ostensibly nontoxic cancer therapies; pain-relieving magnetized bracelets; $129 pendants with copper coil antennae to neutralize electromagnetic fields and enhance the bioenergy the Chinese call *chi* and Indians, *prana;* and a doctor who claims he can restore your cellular pulse by sending current through your DNA in search of your second genetic code—the one that stores energy, not information. "The theory is larger than any particular medicine," he patiently explains.

Some of the offerings are familiar to readers of supermarket tabloids. The spirits of Peter Pan and Michael Jackson hover over the Hyperbaric Oxygen Therapy booth. "I'm gonna force so much oxygen into you, you're gonna feel like a spring chicken," promises salesman Roland Cordova. "They've proven all degenerative disease from cancer to retinitis pigmentosa *and* all premature aging starts with a low oxygen level in the body." Who is *they?* Cordova has a leafletful of quotes purportedly from Nobel Prize winners. "Oxygen is affordable," he says. "You can have it in your home!"

Keep moving, I think, past skin creams fortified with immune-system boosters, pituitary-stimulating amino acids, energy-enhancing crystals, Trim Patches for homeopathic weight loss, rectal rockets, nonsurgical body-sculptors, Libidoplex Virility Enhancing Formula for Men (a "recreational vitamin" with "guaranteed potency"), the Posture Pump Spine Trainer. Rheotherapy, a sort of oil filter for the blood, is proffered as a cure for macular degeneration. "This is real medicine," says Dr. Richard Davis. "Some of this other stuff is, uh . . ." At the booth for the O'Neil Center for Skin Rejuvenation, the magic is "a chemical, kind of like a peel; it's a secret," explains Clara Asimakopoulos, who adds that in the last few years the average age of its customers has plummeted by twenty years. "You have to look younger to compete," she says, "even if you're experienced and knowledgeable."

Life Enhancement representative Will Block is touting smart drugs, "the zenith of the scientific aspect of the drug culture," he says. "It's not kids whipping up batches on street corners." Nearby, David Butler is defending an illegal substance called GHB, which induces sleep; he sells a legal precursor. Seems GHB is so effective it's been used for date rape. "It has been demonized," he complains. "It's dose-sensitive." He leans forward to confide, "This would put sleeping drug companies out of business, it's so powerful."

Theories of aging abound. "Tension makes you older," says Buddy Macy, who's touting a magnetic massager. "I'm not a doctor," he adds thoughtfully. "Medicine tells you disease and aging is from an imbalance and lack of enzymes," thinks Dr. Dic Qie Fuller, explaining his system of advanced enzyme formula nutritional support. "When people age it's because they don't make the right enzymes to digest their food. Our experience is, you have to balance the gut before you can do anything for the immune system or anti-aging."

Once you understand why you don't *need* to age, you can explore why you don't want to. John G. Scott, forty-nine, marketing director for three cosmetic surgery concerns, shows me plastic sleeves with before-and-after photos of his own face and torso surgery—he had liposuction to get rid of his potbelly and flanks, pseudo-gynocomastia on his breasts, an endoscopic brow lift, in which muscles are removed from the forehead, and an upper and lower blepharoplasty—to rid the face of drooping eyelids. "We can make you look better than you feel," he says. "Most people say they don't feel fifty. Well, they sure *look* fifty. The baby boomers aren't reluctant to indulge their vanity. It's no longer one of the seven sins; it's one of the keys to health. Youthfulness is intrinsic to their identity. They feel depersonalized growing older, being someone else—being their parents—and they're not comfortable with that."

"Baby boomers look at their parents and grandparents and don't want to go down that road," agrees Frank Scaraggi, president and CEO of Longevity Institute International, which trains doctors to manage the aging process using the company's Internet-ready Bio-Marker Matrix software, which helps diagnose the disease of aging and produces a multipage personalized aging blueprint for prostate, mood, bone, joint, brain, memory and sleep support. ("Our goal is to help you die fast; no slow, lingering diseases," Bio-Marker Matrix promises.)

"They do not want to end up in a nursing home," Scaraggi says. "They do not want to be a burden to their kids. They want to contract for eighty good years, grow old gracefully, and then see Dr. Kevorkian. The problem is, they'd feel good at seventy-nine and want to break that contract. I'm forty-eight, I've invested well; I have ten to fifteen million dollars; I don't have to work anymore. Now it's time to live, and I don't want my money to outlive me. That's the pot of gold. That's our market segment."

How far will boomers go? At a large stand in the corner of one of the showrooms, I meet Dr. Barbara Brewitt, founder and chief scientific officer of Biomed Comm, Inc., which sells recombinant Human Growth Hormone, or hGH. Natural hGH is produced in and secreted by the pituitary gland, but production declines with age. Its proponents say hGH replacement slows the aging process at a cellular level, promotes muscle tissue, decreases body fat, strengthens bones, skin and the immune system, optimizes mental and physical well-being, strength, endurance, libido, appetite and quality of sleep, and even increases penis size.

Unfortunately, the only way to get the stuff is by prescription, which can cost more than $1,000 monthly, or via a black market that may have harvested it from human cadavers frequently contaminated with tiny particles that can cause neural degenerative disease.

Brewitt says her lab-made, recombinant, reformulated, homeopathic versions, created using technology that inserts the DNA codes for hGH into natural organisms like yeast and bacteria, cost only $49 a month. This over-the-counter version is "the same stuff," she assures me, pointing to the results of double-blind placebo-controlled studies that show many of the same results as the prescription hormone. "I'm not saying it does the same thing," she adds carefully. So how do you tell the difference? "Buyer beware," she says. "Your desires may lead you astray."

Kathleen Slaven of the Pharmaceutical Corporation of America knows whereof Brewitt speaks. She shows me her gray hairs and says the hGH precursors she's selling for a mere $10 a dose have raised her energy level—a little too much. "Unfortunately, my libido increased, too," she complains. "I'm single, but I won't jump around with just anybody."

THE BABY BOOM'S interest in health may well have begun in the days when boomers *did* jump around with anybody. For many if not most, sex was intimately tied to pharmacology. One of the baby boom's bibles was the *Physicians Desk Reference*, an encyclopedic directory of drugs, more often consulted for illicit reasons than licit ones. Though many scoffed at the domino theory of drug use—which held that one puff of pot led straight to heroin addiction—a well-trodden path emerged from illegal substances to prescription pharmaceuticals like Quaaludes to ever-harder and more exotic drugs, like cocaine and the synthetic opiate Dilaudid. Often, when a boomer died of a drug overdose, autopsies would reveal they'd treated their bodies like experiments in recreational polypharmacy.

Drug use led to indiscriminate sex, too, which led in turn to venereal disease and the doctor's office. For many, too much fun turned sour and caused breakdowns, mental and physical. Younger boomers gained a rare advantage in that arena; they could see the bad examples set by their older brothers and sisters. It was someone even older, boomer role model Jane Fonda, who first propelled the generation toward healthier pursuits.

The daughter of actor Henry and sister of *Easy Rider* auteur Peter, Jane began her career as a fashion model, but by 1968 had gained fame as a sex kitten via the films of her then-husband, Roger Vadim. Uncomfortable in her objectification, she set about reinventing herself as the personification of the antiwar movement, championing the Black Panthers and Native Americans, and visiting Hanoi, the capital of North Vietnam, where she made antiwar broadcasts in 1972, earning herself the eternal enmity of American conservatives and the nickname Hanoi Jane. The following year, divorced from Vadim, she married the former SDS leader Tom Hayden.

After two decades of bingeing, dieting and amphetamine use, Fonda became concerned about her health after giving birth to a daughter in 1968. In 1974, she founded her own movie company with Hayden, I.P.C. (for Indo-China Peace Campaign), which produced movies with progressive themes to raise money for the couple's political campaigns. Five years later, after proving that a woman in her forties could still look buff by baring almost all in bikinis in her films *California Suite* and *On Golden Pond*, Fonda went into the aerobic exercise business, founding a company called Workout Inc. and opening her first aerobic studio, with all profits being funneled into Hayden's political action group, Campaign for Economic Democracy. By 1983, Workout Inc. was minting money from *Jane Fonda's Workout*, the videocassette industry's all-time bestseller, books, records and a line of clothing. Urging her followers to "feel the burn," Fonda helped the baby boom find a new kind of healthy high.

That year, working out got the Counterculture Seal of Approval when Jann Wenner's *Rolling Stone* put the health club craze on its cover in a story that called the fitness clubs the latest thing on the singles scene. With drugs fading fast as a tool of seduction and the baby boom's youth slipping away, too, exercise proved an apt Rx.

Around the same time, another healthy hippie offshoot sprang up. The alternative health movement, a conglomeration of New Age therapies and traditional medicines, "goes back to Watergate," says Ron Tepper, editor of the *Journal of Longevity*. "Watergate was the turning point when they questioned all the traditional things. You didn't do what the doctor said anymore."

Allopathic, or conventional, crisis-oriented medicine seemed like a branch of the same establishment that believed the war in Vietnam was necessary and smoking pot led to addiction. Facing the inevitability of middle age, the baby boom wanted more than a ten-minute consultation with a man in a white coat offering a fistful of prescriptions. Wanting what they presumed was the due of Dr. Spock-coddled babies—attentive, politically correct care—they were inevitably dissatisfied with a medical establishment just beginning to feel the pinch of spiraling costs and declining profitability, and went out to find an alternative. The advent of AIDS in the mid-eighties, and the long failure of traditional medicine to address it, supercharged that sometimes-desperate search.

As it turned out, Holy Grails were easy to come by. All over America, 1960s types had spent their adult lives becoming expert in a bouillabaisse of unconventional therapies, quackeries, and ancient disciplines: acupuncture, biofeedback, aromatherapy, homeopathy, craniosacral therapy, chelation therapy, relaxation-response therapy, mind-body medicine, mental imagery, naturopathy, energy healing, crystal healing, reflexology, guided imagery, hands-on healing, hypnosis, Chinese herbs, qi gong and tai chi, therapeutic detoxification, deep tissue massage, meditation, group support and stress reduction.

The New Age movement had grown in tandem with the baby boom ever since its precursor, the Age of Aquarius, dawned. The same phenomena that characterized the fabled apotheosis of Aquarius at Woodstock '69 wound their way through all the "isms" of the 1970s to find a new host in the yearning for health and wellness among aging boomers in the 1990s. Even if they weren't all they were cracked up to be, they offered things boomers had long felt entitled to: instant gratification, escapism, empowerment, self-indulgence, empathy, pleasure, vanity and even the sense of still being subversive.

Most of the superstars of alternative health come from the boom generation. Several spring out of its very core. Andrew Weil, M.D. (b. 1942), whose books on natural medicine and optimizing health typically top bestseller lists, was the reporter at the *Harvard Crimson* whose exposés of Timothy Leary and Richard Alpert's experiments with LSD led to their ouster from the university. Oddly, Weil ended up following their path and becoming friendly with both.

After earning a B.A. in botany, Weil, the son of millinery retailers, entered Harvard Medical School in 1964 with the express purpose of avoiding the draft. In his second year there, he led a student revolt against attending classes. In 1968, he won permission and funding for the first double-blind human study of the effects of pot-smoking. He concluded that the weed was a mild intoxicant with few side effects. The next year, he worked at Haight-Ashbury's infamous Free Clinic. Then he traveled through South America and Africa, studying shamanism, natural healing and the effects of medicinal plants, eventually founding a group to study "beneficial plants" and an annual symposium on the medical and psychoactive effects of mushrooms. His first book, *The Natural Mind*, argued against outlawing drugs, and a later one, *From Chocolate to Morphine*, was a controversial and oft-banned consumer guide to getting high.[1] A dozen years later, Weil had reinvented himself as the multimedia guru of natural healing, a field he's dubbed "integrative medicine," and teaches in a post-doctoral program at the University of Arizona.

As Weil rose up out of the boomer drug culture, Deepak Chopra, M.D., emerged from the post-drug mind-expansion fashion of transcendental meditation. Born in New Delhi, the son of a cardiologist, Chopra was a doctor in India, where he was introduced to the subcontinent's ancient healing tradition, ayurveda, which blends diet, herbs, yoga, breathing exercises, meditation, massages, purges, enemas and aromatherapy. After moving to America in 1970, Chopra studied endocrinology and eventually became chief of staff at a Massachusetts hospital where, stressed out, smoking, and drinking, he turned to TM for help. In 1985, after meeting the Beatles' old guru, Maharishi Mahesh Yogi, he was named head of the Maharishi's ayurvedic clinic and helped establish Ayurveda Products, to make and sell medicines. Lectures and articles raised Chopra's profile and, in 1991, immersed him in a scandal, when he was accused of deception after his commercial ties to the products he'd extolled in a medical journal were revealed. As with Weil, controversy propelled his career. By the end of the 1990s, he'd become an acclaimed spiritual leader, bestselling writer, television personality and, along with Marianne Williamson, counselor to President Clinton.

As Weil and Chopra have raised the popular profile of alternative medicine, Dr. Dean Ornish (b. 1953) has given it scientific credibility. The Sausalito, California-based cardiac specialist and nutrition expert, funded by private contributions from real estate and oil tycoons, amassed scientific evidence indicating that mental attitude adjustments, meditation and support groups, combined with more basic techniques like a low-fat diet and exercise, not only stop heart disease but can reverse damage caused by it.[2]

Thanks to his research—carried out despite initial opposition from the American Heart Institute—health insurance companies around the country began to cover "alternative" providers. By the mid–1990s, the work of Weil, Chopra, Ornish and others like them brought about a paradigm shift in the medical establishment. In 1992, the National Institutes of Health opened an Office of Alternative Medicine. And after a 1993 study published in the *New England Journal of Medicine* showed that millions of American were spending billions of dollars on unconventional treatments, doctors began to incorporate alternative techniques in their practices, and top medical schools rushed to study and teach them.

* * *

AGE IS THE Baby Boom's last new frontier, but will the fight to conquer it be the generation's last tilt at a windmill? Even though anti-authoritarians like Andrew Weil disdain it ("I take a dim view of anti-aging medicine," he says. "The goal is to accept aging and adapt to it, not try to reverse or defeat it, which is impossible."), boomers seem willing to spend fortunes in a hedge against the ultimate authority, mortality. More than a few of their fellows are eager to pander to them.

The most impressive exhibit at the A4M conference belongs to a company called Cenegenics, which bills itself as "the medical life-enhancement company." Open since 1997, Cenegenics claims to have signed up about 150 patients in its first year of operation. Cenegenics sells its services with stylish ads that could be peddling polo shirts as easily as Human Growth Hormone therapy. The headline "Coming of Age" appears next to the ever-so-slightly wrinkled-with-worry foreheads of beautiful youngish boomers with $150 haircuts in the company's pair of print ads, one aimed at each sex. "It comes as a sense of disbelief and subtle betrayal," the copy reads. "The knowledge that the hands of time have turned against you, silently stealing your thunder and slowly weakening your grasp on the good life. Will you accept this news?"

Hell no, we won't go!

In keeping with the baby boom's addiction to image, everything about Cenegenics ("dedicated to the science of youthful aging") is cloaked in studied style. Its convention booth staff wears black suits that match the company's furniture and violet T-shirts the same shade as the clinic's wall-to-wall carpet. Clutching a bottle of water, bodybuilder's arms nearly exploding the sleeves of his black Italian suit, John E. Adams, the company's president, separates himself from a pack of similarly clad bruisers and describes a comprehensive program of exercise physiology, hormone management and nutrition, before issuing an invitation for a shuttle bus tour to the company's nearby $5 million headquarters.

Two patients a day fly into the Cenegenics facility in a neoclassical office complex, set behind a golf course and surrounded by developments of $90,000 condominiums, a half-hour's drive northwest of the Las Vegas Strip. Though hardly homey, the clinic is a family affair. Alan P. Mintz, a six-tyish Chicago radiologist, created Cenegenics; paintings by a relative decorate the walls, and one office sports a photo of his mother running a marathon on her eightieth birthday. After touring the facility, customers fill in a 480-item multiple-choice questionnaire before undergoing a six-hour evaluation that gauges what Mintz calls age bio-markers: measurements of bone density, body fat, skin thickness, lung capacity, sight, hearing, strength, mental and physical response time, flexibility, speed, stability and memory, to document the subject's current status and biological, as opposed to actual, age. With its mauve examination tables, Cybex and video-game-style testing equipment and computerized gadgetry spitting out multicolored charts, Cenegenics is MTV medicine.

Results in, company doctors design a personalized program of exercise, neutraceuticals, and hormone management. In exchange for a monthly charge, patients get automatic vitamin and supplement refills, regular lab follow-ups conducted by physician partners near their homes, and telephone tracking of results. The Cenegenics program seeks to increase muscle and bone density, decrease fat, ameliorate sleep disorders, and elevate sexual performance. Such improvements don't come cheap—and they're not covered by medical insurance. Patients pay $1,300 for their initial visit. Follow-up charges are determined by age. The youngest boomers are charged about $200 per month. The older you get, the more you pay. And if you include Federal Express deliveries of injectible Human Growth Hormone—which come with self-injection kits complete with tiny needles "you just pop in your leg," Adams says—the cost escalates rapidly to as much as $1,800 a month. "It's an affluent demographic—business executives and entertainers born between 1946 and 1964—that can afford the program," Adams says.

The incentive to stay with the program is obvious. As someone on my tour mutters as we drive back into Vegas, "Once you stop, it's Dorian Gray time." An A4M panel on the ethics of anti-aging medicine, held just after we get back, raises the ghosts of more pertinent literary characters. The panel includes Fred Chamberlain, president of a company engaged in cryopreservation, the freezing technique he contends will "change death from near-term certainty to profound long-term uncertainty" (before admitting that currently, freezing the recently deceased causes irreparable damage to the corpse); and Richard Seed, Ph.D., a bearded, bombastic Old Testament type who insists, to many snickers, that by decade's end he will have cloned himself.

Other, calmer voices offer a reality check. Vernon Howard, co-director of Harvard's Philosophy of Education Research Center, reads a paper entitled "Body Parts and Tainted Blood," a look at medical ethics through the lens of Mary Shelley's *Frankenstein* and Bram Stoker's *Dracula*. Howard contends that the first, concerned with "creation and regeneration," and the second, immersed in "sex and contagion," have much to say to modern times. In Howard's reading, the story of Count Dracula and the undead becomes a poignant metaphor for AIDS. But it is Dr.

Frankenstein, defined by his overweening ambition, awful self-absorption and utter irresponsibility who speaks to the Baby Boom.

Victor Frankenstein represents the "threat of a medical technology whose reach has exceeded its moral grasp," Howard says. "This is perhaps a philosophical diagnosis one doesn't want to hear. But can we afford to ignore it when the market in pirated organs, often from underdeveloped countries, for recipients who can afford them, is now a fact? Can we ignore it now that researchers in Scotland and Hawaii have cloned sheep and mice from adult animal's cells?" Railing against the "egotistical pretentiousness" of those who would posit cloning as an acceptable path to immortality, Howard condemns the quest for longevity as an end in itself. "That way lies self-deception."

Finally, Dr. Thomas Wesley Allen, dean of the College of Osteopathic Medicine at Oklahoma State University, steps to the podium and compares the assembled anti-aging advocates and their customers to Prometheus, the thief who stole fire and was punished by Zeus by being chained to a rock where vultures fed on his immortal liver afresh each day. "Wouldn't it be great if our wisdom doubled as frequently as our knowledge?" Allen asks. "Is it for the body or the spirit that we seek immortality? What is it we are prolonging? I simply suggest we heed the words of the preacher in Ecclesiastes, 'For God shall bring every work into judgment. . . .' I hope that we will see to it that all our work can be judged as good."

As the Baby Boom hits the far turn in its race through life, haunted by its youthful ideals and chastened by experience, we would do well to hope for the same.

Acknowledgments

THE ORIGINS OF this book are explained in the text. But it would not have happened without Ellen Levine, a model of support, belief and perseverance for more than two decades. She introduced me to my inspiring editor, Diane Reverand of Cliff Street Books, who took a bad idea for a different book and turned it into *My Generation*.

I relied on the sage advice of several trusted friends while trying to distill the story of the baby boom into a narrative that would reduce, if not entirely eliminate, the accompanying noise and chaos. My most profound thanks go to my colleagues and friends, Peter Herbst, Stephen Demorest, Alan Deutschman, and Eric Pooley. Lanny Jones, Killian Jordan, Camille Paglia, Todd Gitlin of New York University, Peter Collier of the Center for the Study of Popular Culture, David L. Schalk of Vassar College, and Richard Esposito also gave invaluable advice and encouragement.

Carrie Schneider's editorial surgery and Lazar Bloch's persistence in tracking down photos made my life much easier and this book much better. My transcribers, Ted Panken and Jean Brown, are both treasures. Thanks to David Bailey and his assistant Andrew Brooke for making me look good and Chip Kidd and Joseph Montebello for doing the same for this book. And I can't give enough praise to my interns, Ananda Chaudhuri, Catherine "Cat" Connell, and Stacy Lavin, or enough thanks to Nancy Hass of New York University, who helped me find them.

This book rests on the foundation of nineteen extraordinary lives. But a number of other people were interviewed and then not included for various reasons. I want to thank each of them, for they nonetheless helped shape everything I wrote. They are venture capitalist Ann Winblad of

Hummer-Winblad Associates, Senator Robert Torricelli of New Jersey, defense lawyer Gerald Lefcourt, hacker extraordinaire Richard Stallman, Robert Stiller and Burt Rubin, the co-inventors of EZ Wider rolling paper, psychologist and drug evangelist Bruce Ehrlich, entrepreneur Mark Rennie, and Dr. Ronald Klatz of the American Academy of Anti-Aging Medicine. I am immensely grateful to all of my interviewees for giving me so many hours of their time. Transcripts of the additional conversations— along with other material on the Baby Boom—can be found on the World Wide Web at www.talkinboutmygeneration.com.

At various points, dozens of individuals helped me find a stray fact, straighten out a historical tangle, reach out to a necessary source, or simply grow smarter. In no particular order, I would like to thank Vicki Joy; Marie D'Amico; Sam Magee; Peter Coyote; Molly Irani; John Markoff; Norma Foederer; Mary Hamilton; Jo Schuman; Roy Eisenhardt; Lee Felsenstein; Andy Hertzfeld; Bill Joy; Vinod Khosla; Arianna Huffington; Darryl Inaba; Joel Selvin; Barney Hoskyns; Simone Reyes and Cassandra Inlme at Rush Communications; Larry Kramer, Michael Ledeen; Lorraine Spurge; Chris Jones and Angie Orem of Rep. David McIntosh's staff; Lona Valmorro, Joy Howell and Linda Baruchi of Senator Torricelli's office; Theresa Matushaj at New York Supreme Court; Allison Kelley; Linda Gage; Marie Koenig; May Goh; Jeremy Barnish; Patricia Fitzgerald; Susanne Vagadori; Sandy Mendelsohn; Kate Coleman; Linnea Due; Dennis McNally; Susie Bright; Candida Royalle; Jon Maynard of CSPAN; Michael Tomasky; Ray Brown of Court TV; Karen Ames; Bruce Raben; Brian Rohan; Andrew Weil; Anne Doyle; Edward Harrington; Owsley Stanley; Peggy and Billy Hitchcock; Hillard Elkins; Vernon Howard; Bob Strang; Cynthia Robbins; Dale Kern; Carol Queen; Garry Trudeau; Bernadine Dohrn; Edwin Moise; Elyn Wollensky; Eric Foner; Fred Baker; George Emery; Richard Bernstein; Dr. Barbara Brewitt; Ivy McClure; David Talbot; Robert A. McCaughey; Paul Berman; William Frederic Starr; Jennifer Mertz; Terry Housholder; Judith C. Bailey; Kat Sunlove; Michelle Wallace; Kath Weston; Danny Fields; Lewis Cole; Mareev Zehavi; Bobby Lilly; Randall Rothenberg; Michael Parker; and Alex Perry.

At the Ellen Levine Literary Agency, my thanks to Diana Finch, Louise Quayle, Bob Simpson, Deborah Clifford, Jay Rogers, Claudia Mooser, Brigit Dermott and Tom Dickson. At Cliff Street Books, I am grateful to Janet Dery, Margaret Meacham, Pamela Pfeifer, Robin Artz and Matthew Guma. At News Corp., my thanks to Anthea Disney. At *New York* magazine, thanks to Caroline Miller, John Homans and Maer Roshan; and

Dany Levy; Brett Kelly, Sam Grobart, Ariel Levy, Deb Slater, Michael Steele and Nick Meyer, who were always helpful, even when I wasn't. At *Travel & Leisure*, thanks to Nancy Novogrod and Laura Begley. At GQ, I am grateful to Art Cooper, Martin Beiser and Merv Kaiser.

For tea, sympathy and shelter from various storms, thanks to Kee Tan; to Lori Levin-Hyams, Debbie Dar and Richard Branson of Virgin Group; to Holly Solomon; to Guy Garcia; to John Weitz; to Melissa Olds; to Anita Sarko; to Susan Blond; to Dan Carlinsky; to Andrew Stengel; to Patrick McMullen; to Victor Kerpel; to Jackie Lividini; to Jim Haynes and Jack Moore; to Christine Biddle; to Dr. Gerald Imber and Catherine Collins; to Janis Kaye; to Marla Maples; to Brian Saltzman; to Matthew Snyder of Creative Artists Agency; to Keith Fleer; to Ken Norwick; to Chuck Roven, Doug Segal and the late Dawn Steel of Atlas Entertainment; to Jaan Uhelszki and Matthew Kauffman; to cousins Jimmy and Pammie; to Matthew and Louise Evins; to Judy Green; to Randy and Maya Gurley; to Stèphane and Bernard; to Fran Curtis and Jami Farbstein at Rogers & Cowan; to Tony Cacace; to Mary Goggin; to Zachary Bregman; to Dale Rubin; to Sharyn Rosenblum; to Silvano Marchetto of Da Silvano, Patricia and Michel Jean of Provence, Michael McCarty of Michael's and Elaine Kaufman of Elaine's; to Drew Kerr; and to whoever I haven't remembered and will always regret not mentioning.

Jane Gross was the first baby boomer I ever met, and has always stood by me—even when she thought better of it. For her constant encouragement, my special gratitude also goes to Denise Hale.

And finally, all my love goes to Messalina and Barbara, who share their house with me, keep me sane, and remind me that every once in a while, a little insanity is good for the soul.

Source Notes

CONCEPTION

1. Readers interested in generational theory, demography and the origins of the Baby Boom—none of which are covered in any depth here—should seek out two previous books that focused on the generation. *Great Expectations* by Landon Y. Jones (Coward, McCann & Geoghegan, New York, 1980) is a landmark demographic study with a significant focus on the period before the generation came to consciousness, when America had to adjust itself to make room for the boom. *Generations* by William Strauss and Neil Howe (William Morrow, New York, 1991), is a profound retelling of the history of America through a generational lens. Jones uses the demographic definition of the Baby Boom. Strauss and Howe define a generation as "a cohort-group . . . whose boundaries are fixed by peer personalities," and set the boom's beginning in 1943 and its end in January 1961, on the day of John Kennedy's inaugural. *My Generation* accepts aspects of both definitions in order to paint the fullest possible portrait of the generation's life and times.

2. *Great Expectations*, p. 4. Jones calls this elite the main agent of social change.

3. Which is not to say that front-end African-American boomers have not had both the kind of symbolic experiences this book focuses on, and the achievements its structure demands. Two such individuals, Thomas Jones, who was a leader of the black student takeover at Cornell University in 1969 and is now a top executive at Citicorp, and Cicero Wilson, a student leader at Columbia University in 1968 and later a fellow at the Conservative American Enterprise Institute, were approached for interviews but, regrettably, declined to participate.

4. Bennet, James, "At 50, a Rock-and-roll President Acts His Age in a Cable Special." *New York Times*, March 3, 1997.

5. Morse, Rob, "It's Not My Fault, Ken Started It," *San Francisco Examiner*, August 18, 1998.

6. From *Remarks of Hillary D. Rodham*, President of the Wellesley College Government Association, at Wellesley's commencement ceremony on May 31, 1969. I requested an interview with the First Lady for this book in September 1998. Her press secretary, Marsha Berry, responded that there were certain "legal contraints"against the First Family's cooperation with "commercial projects." I asked how then Mrs. Clinton was able to apear at the premiere of a film produced by one of her husband's political contributors, and to pose for the cover of the fashion

magazine *Vogue*. Berry cited the difference between a "personal project"—i.e., a book by a sole author—and "the media." I suggested that movies, books and magazines were all products of a free press. Berry responded that, "the point of difference is personal profit." I asked under what legal principle an individual author's profits were deemed different from those of a privately owned magazine or a movie studio. Berry referred that question to the White House Counsel's office. Despite repeated requests for clarification, it has not, as of the publication date of this book, responded.

7. Wenner, Jann S. "The National Affair," *Rolling Stone*, November 12, 1998.

8. Dowd, Maureen, "Liberties: An American Tragedy," *New York Times*, July 29, 1998.

CHILDHOOD

1. Fouratt refuses to confirm his birthdate. "You can't ask a gay man his age!" he says.

2. Jackson, Kenneth T. (ed.), *The Encyclopedia of New York City*, Yale University Press, New Haven, Connecticut, 1995.

3. Belis, Gary, "Donald Trump Explained," *Fortune*, January 4, 1988.

4. Robinson, John, "Marianne Williamson: A New Age Oracle Comes Down to Earth," *Boston Globe*, May 20, 1993.

5. Mills, David, "The Vision Thing; New Age Guru Looks to Heal What Ails Us," *Washington Post*, July 7, 1993.

6. Oumano, Elena, *Marianne Williamson* (St. Martin's Paperbacks, 1992), p. 44.

7. Bernstein, Richard, *Dictatorship of Virtue* (Vintage Books, 1995), p. 7.

8. When the Supreme Court overturned the conviction in 1962, Grady was indicted again. When the new indictment was thrown out a year later, the government appealed. It finally dropped the case six years after it began.

9. Sears left his job in 1999 to manage the solo career of Bob Weir, a member of the Dead.

10. Stafford, P. G. and Golightly, B. H., *LSD: The Problem-Solving Psychedelic*, (Award, New York, 1967), p. 31.

11. Stevens, Jay, *Storming Heaven: LSD and the American Dream*, (Grove, New York, 1987), p. 45.

12. Ibid, p. 150–51.

13. Ibid, pp. 162–63.

14. Tendler, Stewart and May, David, *The Brotherhood of Eternal Love*, (Panther, 1984), p. 49.

15. Leary, Timothy, *Flashbacks*, (Jeremy P Tarcher, LA, 1990), p. 131.

16. Stevens, p. 182.

17. In a telephone interview with the author on July 12, 1999, Haworth confirmed the episode. "It's absolutely true," she said. "I'm quite proud of it." She remembers Fouratt less well, but confirmed that "somebody" took her to the concert.

18. Sewall-Ruskin, Yvonne, *High on Rebellion*, (Thunder's Mouth, NY, 1998), p. 19.

19. Warhol, Andy and Hackett, Pat, *Popism: The Warhol '60s*, (Harcourt Brace & Jovanocich, NY, 1980), p. 185.

ADOLESCENCE

1. Stevens, Jay, *Storming Heaven: LSD and The American Dream*, (Grove, NY, 1987), p. 192.

2. Ibid, p. 195.

3. Tendler, Steward and May, David, *The Brotherhood of Eternal Love*, (Granada, London, 1984), p. 58.

4. Hersh, Burton, *The Mellon Family: A Fortune in History*, (William Morrow, New York, 1978), p. 479.

5. Billy Hitchcock replied to various questions posed by the author in a fax dated April 19, 1999.

6. Wolfe, Tom, *The Electric Kool-Aid Acid Test* (Bantam, 1969), pp. 120–21.

7. Ibid, p. 210.

8. Hersh, p. 480.

9. Ibid, p. 484.

10. Ibid, p. 485.

11. Stevens, p. 273.

12. Anthony, Gene, *The Summer of Love*, (Celestial Arts, Berkeley, CA, 1980), p. 53.

13. E-mail to author from Owsley Stanley, May 16, 1999.

14. Wolfe, p. 243.

15. In e-mail to the author, Owsley dismisses Scully's claims of collaboration in the process as "nonsense." "I guess Bear doesn't think I contributed anything to the work and I think I did," Scully counters.

16. Trump, Donald J., with Tony Schwartz, *The Art of the Deal* (Random House, 1988), p. 58.

17. Raskin, Jonah, *For the Hell of It* (University of California Press, CA, 1996), p. 108; and *WIN*, September 15, 1967, pp. 8–10.

18. "We knew what the FBI had done to Martin Luther King," says Jim Fouratt. "We knew about the mistress. We had our own sources of information. So when King died, it had a profound effect on us. We thought the government killed him."

19. McNeil, Don, *Moving Through Here* (Knopf,1970), p. 23.

20. Ibid, p. 6

21. Ibid, pp. 8–10.

22. Ibid, p. 25.

23. Gitlin, Todd, The Sixties: Years of Hope, Days of Rage, (Bantam, New York, 1987), p. 192.

24. Wells, Tom, *The War Within*, (University of Chicago Press, Berkeley, CA, 1994) p. 214.

25. In his e-mail to the author, Owsley claimed he never intended to give Scully his remaining raw materials, but only to train him in acid manufacture.

26. Tendler, p. 353.

27. Slick, Grace, *Somebody to Love*, (Warner, New York, 1998), p. 103.

28. Hersh, pp. 486–87; in his April 19, 1999, fax, Hitchcock denied setting up offshore accounts for Sand and Owsley, but admitted he introduced the pair to a Swiss bank.

29. In his e-mail, Owsley alleges that 27 grams of the seized LSD disappeared from police custody before trial and were eventually sold on "the street, where it belonged."

30. Hersh, p. 489.

31. Tendler, pp. 90–91.

32. Hitchcock says the money was in the form of a loan to Scully.

33. Hersh, p. 489.

34. Tender, p. 152.

35. Avorn, Jerry, L., *Up Against the Ivy Wall: A History of the Columbia Crisis*, (H. Wollf, New York, 1968), p. 32.

36. Ibid, pp. 25–27.

37. Ibid, p. 35.

38. Avorn, pp. 42–48.

39. Ibid, p. 88.

40. Ibid, p. 227.

41. Threatened with immediate conscription by his draft board, Rudd sought—unsuccessfully—an occupational deferment as a revolutionary, and was finally deferred on medical grounds.

42. Although he didn't attend the convention, Jim Fouratt proudly notes that he was named an un-indicated co-conspirator.

43. Leary, Timothy, *Flashbacks*, (Jeremy P. Tarcher, LA, 1990), p. 278.

44. Tendler, p. 166.

45. Gitlin, p. 387; Sale, Kirkpatrick, *SDS*, (Random House, New York, 1973), p. 468.

46. Collier, Peter and Horowitz, David, *Destructive Generation*, (Summit, New York, 1989), pp. 74–76.

47. Gitlin, p. 388.

48. After one of the defendants Black Panther Bobby Seale, was ordered tried separately, the group became known as The Chicago Seven. The designations are interchangeable.

49. Wells, p. 336.

50. Sale, p. 587.

51. Bender, Marilyn, "The Empire and Ego of Donald Trump," *New York Times*, August 7, 1983.

52. Gitlin, p. 367.

53. Martin Duberman, *Stonewall*, (Plume, New York, 1994), pp. 211–12.

54. Spitz, Bob, *Barefoot in Babylon*, (Norton, New York, 1989), p. 168.

55. Ibid, p. 452.

56. Sale, p. 595.

57. Collier and Horowitz, pp. 85–86.

58. Wells, p. 337.

59. Ibid, p. 85.

60. Alpert, Jane, *Growing Up Underground*, (William Morrow, New York, 1981), pp. 240–45.

61. Sale, p. 627.

62. Ibid, p. 627n.

63. Gitlin, p. 400.

64. Wells, p. 371.

65. Ibid, p. 372.

EXTENDED ADOLESCENCE

1. www.wholeearthmag.com.

2. Collier, Peter and Horowitz, David, *Destructive Generation*, (Summit, New York, 1989), p. 102.

3. Jacobs, Ron, *The Way the Wind Blew: A History of the Weather Underground*, (London, Verso, 1997) p. 137.

4. Ibid, p. 142.

5. Collier and Horowitz, p. 106.

6. Sale, Kirkpatrick, *SDS*, (Random House, New York, 1973) p. 644–45.

7. Kevin Gillies, "The Last Radical." In *Vancouver*, November 1998. J. J. wandered the West Coast for years and ended up in Vancouver, where he worked as a gardener, day laborer, and marijuana dealer, and never gave up his political beliefs or fugitive status. "The last Weatherman," as Rudd called him, died of cancer in 1977.

8. Duberman, Martin, *Stonewall*, (Plume, New York, 1994), pp. 226–32.

9. Rubin, Jerry, *Growing (Up) at 37*, (M. Evans, New York, 1976), p. 20.

10. Hersh, Burton, The Mellon Family: A Fortune in History, (William Morrow, New York, 1978), p. 490.

11. In an e-mail to the author, Owsley says the money belonged "to the community I was serving." He claims that Hitchcock ignored his instruction to invest those funds in gold and put them in speculative stocks instead. "The stocks which went up were put into Billy's accounts, the ones which fell were put into Tim's, Nick's and my accounts. Pretty soon there was no money in our accounts and one of Billy's schemes took down the little Swiss bank," Owsley writes.

12. In a fax to the author, Hitchcock says the Swiss bank invested Owsley's funds and "may have lost some but not all of it." Despite repeated requests, he declined to elaborate.

13. Interview with Timothy Leary by the author, January 1991.

14. Jonnes, Jill, *Hep-Cats, Narcs and Pipe Dreams*, (Scribner, New York, 1996), p. 261.

15. Eisner, Bruce, "LSD Purity," *High Times*, January 1977.

16. Leary testified against Mark Rudd, among others. "But he was Leary, so his evidence was worthless," Rudd says.

17. Wells, p. 491.

18. Trump bought the two yards for a small option payment against an ultimate purchase price variously reported as $62 to $100 million. The money came from his tax shelter proceeds.

19. Blum, Howard, "Trump: Development of a Manhattan Developer," *New York Times*, August 26, 1980; Bender, Marilyn, "The Empire and Ego of Donald Trump," *New York Times*, August 7, 1983.

20. According to Burton Hersh's *The Mellon Family*, Hitchcock would later be given a suspended sentence of five years with probation and be ordered to consult a psychotherapist. At the sentencing, Judge Morris Lasker commented on the irony that being rich is sometimes as much a burden as being poor. Hitchcock blamed his misbehavior on the death of his father in a military plane crash in 1944, and "the insane fucking war."

21. Scully was also fined and hit with a back tax bill. He later negotiated those down to $10,000 in taxes and penalties, and the IRS agreed that his bail and legal fees were deductible business expenses. He made time payments to the IRS for many years until the bill was paid.

22. In 1985, with enrollment declining, *est* morphed into the Forum, a less authoritarian training, and in 1991, plagued by controversy, and charges he was leading a cult, Erhard sold it and dropped from view. But *est*'s ideas ("Master the possibilities," "Be all that you can be") lived on.

23. Heidenry, John, *What Wild Ecstasy: The Rise and Fall of the Sexual Revolution*, (Simon & Schuster, New York, 1997), p. 32.

24. Hubner, John, *Bottom Feeders*, (Doubleday, New York, 1993), p. 99.

25. Often busted, they shared a lawyer, Michael Kennedy, with Timothy Leary and the Weather Bureau.

26. Kristof, Nicholas, D., "X-Rated Industry in a Slump," *New York Times*, October 5, 1986.

27. Michael Ledeen to author in telephone call, June 11, 1999.

28. Draper, Robert, *Rolling Stone: The Uncensored History*, (Doubleday, New York, 1990), p. 34.

29. Ibid, p. 44.

30. Ibid, p. 52.

31. Ibid, p. 67.

32. Say what you will about Wenner, no matter how classy the crowd he ran

with, there was nothing traditional about him. For the next decade, he swanned with the swells, while *Rolling Stone* lurched among caretaker editors, and finally started gathering moss as an advertising vehicle for youth marketers. Into the breach stole Bob Guccione Jr., the first credible threat to Wenner's place at the top of the pops. The son of *Penthouse* publisher Bob Guccione, Bobby Jr. conceived of *Spin* in 1983, counterprogramming against Wenner the same way his dad had done in 1969 when he pitted *Penthouse* (and the pubic hair of its Pets) against *Playboy's* airbrushed-to-perfection Playmates. Branding Wenner an aging, atrophied sellout, "the Dr. Faustus of the yuppie generation," he promised to "kick *Rolling Stone's* ass." Guccione had presciently identified the emerging market that would come to be called Gen X—and set out to serve it with a magazine modeled on—what else?— *Rolling Stone*, which suddenly found itself fighting to retain its prominence in a market that called boomers Mom and Dad. But Wenner's flagship took the hits and kept sailing; by the late 1990s, it was *Spin* that was flailing in the face of the rap revolution, while *Rolling Stone* had found stability as the magazine equivalent of a national monument, an integral, if oft-underestimated, part of the landscape.

33. Slick, Grace, *Somebody to Love*, (Warner, New York, 1998), p. 169.
34. Clurman, Richard M., *To the End of Time* (Simon & Schuster, 1992), p. 39.

YOUNG ADULTHOOD

1. Cringley, Robert X., *Accidental Empires*, (HarperBusiness, New York, 1996), pp. 82–84.
2. Levy, Steven, *Hackers: Heroes of the Computer Revolution*, (Delta, New York, 1994), p. 23.
3. Ibid, p. 52.
4. Ibid, p. 71.
5. Ibid, p. 131.
6. Available at various places on the Internet, The Jargon File, v. 4.0.0. A "comprehensive compendium of hacker slang," it is also an invaluable resource concerning the history of computing.
7. Levy, p. 143.
8. The National Science Foundation's NSFnet, a separate "pipeline," eventually replaced ARPAnet, which was shut down in 1990. By 1994, NSFnet had been broken up and sold to commercial concerns.
9. Levy, pp. 213–14.
10. Carlton, Jim, *Apple: The Inside Story of Intrigue, Egomania and Business Blunders*, (Times Business, New York, 1997), pp. 8–9.
11. Cooker, Chet H., "What a Rush," *Vibe*, December 1995.
12. Simmons, Sheila, "Pioneer Herc as Big as His Music Reputation," *The Plain-Dealer*, August 13, 1995.
13. Leland, John, "When Rap Meets Reggae," *Newsweek*, September 7, 1992.
14. Ibid.
15. Cringley, Robert X., pp. 132–33.
16. Gorov, Lynda, "Faith, Marianne Williamson is Full of It," *Mother Jones*, November 1997.
17. Servin, James, "Prophet of Love has the Timing of a Comedian," *New York Times*, February 19, 1992.
18. Oumano, Elena, *Marianne Williamson*, (St. Martin's Paperbacks, New York, 1992), p. 78.
19. The marriage lasted three months, according to Oumano.
20. Oumano, p. 84.
21. Author unknown, "Slick and Surviving," *Washington Post*, July 3, 1981.
22. The first mention of Ledeen as "a long time agent and disinformant for the

CIA" in the Nexis database of international news articles is in a BBC Summary of World Broadcasts on September 27, 1984, repeating charges made two days earlier in a Bulgarian publication, *Rabotnichesko Delo.*

23. Cockburn, Andrew, "Beat the Devil: the History of Hot Air," *The Nation,* August 17, 1985.

24. In a telephone interview on June 25, 1999, Rudolf confirmed that he'd taken down the Haring. "I took down a Basquiat, too, to put up other artists," he says.

25. Haden-Guest, Anthony, *The Last Party,* (William Morrow, New York, 1997), p. 224.

26. Rubin, Jerry, "Guess Who's Coming to Wall Street?" *New York Times,* July 30, 1980.

27. Haden-Guest, p. 226.

28. Studio 54 was rented out to a series of independent promoters. One night, when it was transformed into a black after-hours club, Jim Fouratt showed up with a man named Barry Freed, actually the fugitive Abbie Hoffman, who'd become an environmental activist under his new name, but was still curious about the cultural cutting edge.

29. Haden-Guest, p. 226.

30. Adler, Jerry, et al., "The Year of the Yuppie," *Newsweek,* December 31, 1984.

31. Hoffman returned to his career as a radical, community organizer, writer and counterculture comedian after he was released from jail. He was arrested, along with President Carter's daughter, Amy, at a protest against the Central Intelligence Agency in 1987. A chronic manic-depressive, he committed suicide with barbiturates and alcohol in April 1989.

32. Taylor, Alexander, "Bad Days at the Box Office," *Time,* June 1, 1981.

33. *The Christian Science Monitor,* July 3, 1981.

34. Bruck, Connie, *Master of the Game* (Simon & Schuster, New York, 1994), p. 252.

35. Smothers, Ronald, "Ex-Television Evangelist Bakker Ends Prison Sentence for Fraud," *New York Times,* December 2, 1994.

36. Levy, p. 384.

37. It would be settled in 1984 for $180 million.

38. Kempster, Norman, "Vietnam War Leaves Legacy of Anguish," *Los Angeles Times,* April 28, 1985.

39. www.friendsoftheriver.org.

40. Cringley, p. 190.

41. Quittner, Joshua, "A Crisis of Faith," *Time,* March 17, 1997.

<u>MATURITY</u>

1. Area, the "downtown"-style megaclub for big-spending uptown types, inspired the most mega club of them all, Palladium, the last disco created by Steve Rubell and Ian Schrager, along with the post-Fouratt Rudolf Pieper. Palladium opened in 1985, incorporating and commercializing many of the ideas that had been floating around bohemia during the preceding half-decade; it was the quintessential Postmodern nightclub. Jim Fouratt hated it. "They took a little, special thing and blew it up too big," he says.

2. Although the possibility of a coup was not mentioned in press reports at the time, Michael Ledeen confirmed his wife's account in a telephone interview with the author on June 11, 1999.

3. Chapple, Steve and Talbot, David, "The Changing of the Feminist Guard; Burning Desires," *Playboy,* June 1989.

4. Peterson, James R., "Politically Correct Sex," *Playboy,* November, 1986.

5. Bennett, Catherine, "Portrait: A Prophet and Porn," *The Guardian* (London), May 27, 1994.

6. Clymer, Adam, "Poll Finds Nation is Becoming Increasingly Republican," *New York Times*, May 3, 1981.

7. Dugggan, Lisa, "Pornography Makes Strange Bedfellows," *Bergen Record*, September 15, 1985.

8. Leo, John, "The New Scarlet Letter," *Time*, August 2, 1982.

9. Heidenry, *John, What Wild Ecstasy: The Rise and Fall of the Sexual Revolution*, (Simon & Schuster, New York, 1997), p. 330.

10. Haley, Kathy, "On Top of the Mountain," *Multichannel News*, July 28, 1997.

11. Carter, Bill, "No Laughing Matter," *New York Times Magazine*, November 5, 1989.

12. Shilts, Randy, *And the Band Played On*, (St. Martin's, New York, 1987), p. 68.

13. Altman, Lawrence K., "Rare Cancer Seen in 41 Homosexuals," *New York Times*, July 3, 1981.

14. In an unhappy irony, Poststructuralism's leading voice, Michel Foucault, would succumb to the new disease in 1984, and his death would be followed by rumors that he'd continued to have unprotected anonymous sex in bathhouses after his diagnosis.

15. Flanders's brother Howard Weintraub had once been Jim Fouratt's boyfriend.

16. www.allmusic.com: from the site's Grateful Dead biography page.

17. No Byline, "Judge Scalia's Cheerleaders," *New York Times*, July 23, 1986.

18. Moss, Debra Cassens, "The Policy and the Rhetoric of Ed Meese," *ABA Journal*, February 1, 1987.

19. Under threat of libel,North's source for that allegation—an Israeli—later admitted it wasn't true, according to and article in the *New York Times*, "On the Ledeen Case," March 23, 1987, no byline.

20. Exactly 51 years after Kristallnacht.

21. No Byline, "The Morning After," *Institutional Investor*, July 1992, p. 171.

22. Reibstein, Larry, et al., "Trump: The Fall," *Newsweek*, June 18, 1990.

23. Sherman, Stratford P., "Donald Trump Just Won't Die," *Fortune*, August 13, 1990, and Castro, Janice, "Trump Trips Up," *Time*, May 6, 1991.

24. Ibid, and Hylton, Richard D., "Banks Approve Loans for Trump But Take Control of His Finances," *New York Times*, June 27, 1990.

25. Clurman, Richard M., *The End of Time*, (Simon & Schuster, New York, 1992), p. 147.

26. Carter, Bill, "No Laughing Matter," *New York Times Magazine*, November 5, 1989.

27. Carlton, Jim, *Apple: The Inside Story of Intrigue, Egomania and Business Blunders*," (Times Business, New York, 1997), p. 54.

28. No Byline, "Timeline," *Infoworld*, January 31, 1994.

29. Smileis, Martha, "Mother Teresa for the '90s?," *Time*, July 29, 1991.

30. Oumano, Elena, *Marianne Williamson*, (St. Martin's Paperbacks, New York, 1992), p. 201.

PRIME TIME

1. Carroll, James, "The Friendship that Ended the Wark, *The New Yorker*, October 21, 1996.

2. One IWF backer is a foundation run by Richard Mellon Scaife, whose funds, curiously, come from the same Mellon fortune as those of Tim Scully's benefactor, Billy Hitchcock.

3. Morrow, Lance, "Newt's World," *Time*, December 25, 1995.

4. Shribman, David M., "The People to See," *Boston Globe*, January 28, 1996.

5. Browning, Graeme, "The Fire Brand," *National Journal*, January 27, 1996.

6. Ibid.

7. Robinson, Hohn, "Marianne Williamson: A New Age Oracle Comes Down to Earth," *Boston Globe*, May 20, 1993.

8. Devroy, Ann, "New Age 'Guru to the Glitterati' Advised Clintons," *Washington Post*, January 11, 1995.

9. Krauss, Clifford, "New York Crime Rate Plummets to Levels Not Seen in 30 Years," *New York Times*, December 20, 1996.

10. Taylor, John, "Are You Politically Correct?" *New York*, January 21, 1991.

11. Hughes, Robert, "The Fraying of America," *Time*, February 3, 1992.

12. Leo, John, "Looking Back at a PC Extravaganza," *U.S. News & World Report*, January 31, 1994.

13. Rubell's aged parents were alive and unaware that he was gay.

14. Larson, Jonathon, *Rent* (Morrow, New York, 1997), pp. 19–20.

15. The clinic film, titled *One Foot on a Banana Peel, The Other Foot in the Grave: Secrets From the Dolly Madison Room*, was completed by another director and eventually played on the documentary circuit.

16. Eller, Claudia, "Masters at Expressing Brotherly Love," *Los Angeles Times*, June 27, 1995.

17. Roberts, Johnnie L., "One More Stab At It," *Newsweek*, November 27, 1995.

18. Quittner, Joshua, "A Crisis of Faith," *Time*, March 17, 1997.

19. Marlette, Doug, "Never Trust a Weeping Man," *Esquire*, October, 1993.

20. AOL was eventually severed from the suit, after claiming that although it provides "media content," it is not a "publisher."

21. Broader, John M., "A Clinton Adviser Details Testimony," *New York Times*, February 27, 1998.

22. Lowry, Richard, "Sins of Sid," *National Review*, August 17, 1998.

23. VandeHei, Jim, "McIntosh Now Leader of House GOP Rebels," *Roll Call*, February 12, 1998.

24. Ferguson, Ellyn, "McIntosh Hopes Lawmakers focus on Budget, Tax Cuts," *Gannett* News Service, September 3, 1998.

25. "He called them to his house," Simmons says. "You think anybody else could make them go? No one else could make them go. No one in the world could call them niggers and have them go to his house. And it changed everything. People who had a problem with each other listened and talked, and everybody hugged — and that was it."

26. Wells, Melanie, "Urban Outfitter Picks Up the Tempo," *USA Today*, October 5, 1998.

27. Montgomery, David, "The 'Queer Theory' Connection," *Buffalo News*, December 6, 1992.

28. Feder, Don, "Many Faces of PC at Dear Wellesley," *Boston Herald*, May 26, 1994.

29. Stein, Joel, "Porn Goes Mainstream," *Time*, September 7, 1998.

30. Larson, pp. 49–50.

31. Ibid, pp. 51–52, 56.

32. Brantley, Ben, "Rock Opera à la 'Boheme' and 'Hair,'" *New York Times*, February 14, 1996.

33. Hylton, Richard D. "Trumps Settle; She Gets $14 Million Plus," *New York Times*, March 21, 1991, Associated Press, "Two Trump Bankruptcies," March 10, 1992.

34. Henriques, Diana B., "Trump's Back and May Be Bankable," *New York Times*, December 16, 1992.

35. Garcia, Ken, "The Dead's Unseemly Greedy Grab," *San Francisco Chronicle*, January 17, 1998.

36. Talbot, Margaret, "The Healing of America," *New Republic*, December 8, 1997.

37. Gardiner, Marin, "Jean Houston: Guru of Human Potential," *Skeptical Inquirer*, January 1997.

HEREAFTER
1. Weil, Andrew and Betzold, Michael, *Newsmakers 1997* (Gale Research, 1997).
2. Wallis, Claudia, "Why New Age Medicine is Catching On," *Time*, November 4, 1991.

Bibliography

Acton, Jay, Alan LeMond, and Parker Hodges. *Mug Shots: Who's Who in the New Earth*. New York: World, 1972.

Anderson, Patrick. *High in America*. New York: Viking, 1981.

Anthony, Gene. *The Summer of Love*. Berkeley: Celestial Arts, 1980.

Avorn, Jerry L. *Up Against the Ivy Wall: A History of the Columbia Crisis*. New York: H. Wolff, 1968.

Barr, Ann and Peter York. *The Official Sloane Ranger Handbook*. London: Ebury Press, 1982.

Bernstein, Richard. *Dictatorship of Virtue*. New York: Vintage, 1995.

Birnbach, Lisa (ed.). *The Preppy Handbook*. New York, Workman, 1980.

Bruck, Connie. *Master of the Game*. New York, Simon & Schuster, 1994.

Burkett, Elinor. *The Right Women*. New York, Scribner, 1998.

Carlton, Jim. *Apple: The Inside Story of Intrigue, Egomania and Business Blunders*. New York: Times Business, 1997.

Casale, Anthony M. and Philip Lerman., *Where Have All The Flowers Gone?* Kansas City: Andrews and McMeel, 1989.

Charters, Ann (ed.). *The Portable Beat Reader*. New York: Penguin, 1992.

Clurman, Richard M. *To the End of Time*. New York: Simon & Schuster, 1992.

Collier, Peter, and David Horowitz. *Destructive Generation*. New York: Summit, 1989.

Coyote, Peter. *Sleeping Where I Fall*. Washington: Counterpoint, 1998.

Cringely, Robert X. *Accidental Empires*. New York: HarperBusiness, 1996.

Crouse, Timothy. *The Boys on the Bus*. New York: Ballantine, 1973.

Davies, Hunter. *The Beatles: The Authorized Biography*. New York: McGraw Hill, 1968.

Delacoste, Frédérique, and Priscilla Alexander (eds.). *Sex Work*. Pittsburgh: Cleis Press, 1987.

Dickstein, Morris. *Gates of Eden*. New York: Basic, 1977.

Draper, Robert. *Rolling Stone Magazine: The Uncensored History*. New York: Doubleday, 1990.

Duberman, Martin. *Stonewall*. New York: Plume, 1994.

Gitlin, Todd. *The Sixties: Years of Hope, Days of Rage*. New York: Bantam, 1987.

Goldsmith, Judith. *A Biased Timeline of the Counterculture*, (unfinished project);

posted on the *well.com* gopher site and available via ftp (file transfer protocol).

Goodman, Fred. *The Mansion on the Hill*. New York: Vintage, 1998.

Gottlieb, Annie. *Do You Believe in Magic?* New York: Times Books, 1987.

Grathwold, Larry, as told to Frank Reagan, *Bringing Down America: An FBI Informer with the Weathermen*. New Rochelle, N.Y.: Arlington House, 1976.

Grogan, Emmet. *Ringolevio: A Life Played for Keeps*. Boston: Little Brown, 1972.

Haden-Guest, Anthony. *The Last Party*. New York: William Morrow, 1997.

Heidenry, John. *What Wild Ecstasy: The Rise and Fall of the Sexual Revolution*. New York: Simon & Schuster, 1997.

Henke, James, with Parke Puterbaugh (eds.). *I Want to Take You Higher*. San Francisco: Chronicle, 1997.

Hersh, Burton. *The Mellon Family: A Fortune in History*. New York: William Morrow, 1978.

Hiltzik, Michael. *Dealers of Lightning*. New York: HarperBusiness, 1999.

Hoffman, Abbie (as Free). *Revolution for the Hell of It*. New York: Dial Press, 1968.

———. *Steal This Book*. New York: Pirate Editions, 1971.

Hoffman, Jack, and Daniel Simon. *Run Run Run: The Lives of Abbie Hoffman*. New York: Tarcher/Putnam, 1996.

Hoskyns, Barney. *Beneath the Diamond Sky*. New York: Simon & Schuster, 1997.

Hubner, John. *Bottom Feeders*. New York: Doubleday, 1993.

Jacobs, Ron. *The Way the Wind Blew: A History of the Weather Underground*. London: Verso, 1997.

Jay, Karla. *Tales of the Lavender Menace*. New York: Basic, 1999.

Jones, Landon Y. *Great Expectations*. New York: Coward, McCann & Geoghegan, 1980.

Jonnes, Jill. *Hep-Cats, Narcs and Pipe Dreams*. New York: Scribner, 1996.

Kaiser, Charles. *1968*. New York: Weidenfeld and Nicholson, 1988.

———. *The Gay Metropolis*. New York: Harcourt Brace, 1997.

Klatz, Ronald, and Robert Goldman. *Stopping the Clock*. New Canaan, Connecticut: Keats, 1996.

Larson, Jonathan. *Rent*. New York: William Morrow, 1997.

Leacock, Victoria. *Signature Flowers*. New York: Melcher Media, 1998.

Leary, Timothy. *Flashbacks*. Los Angeles: Jeremy P. Tarcher, 1990.

Levy, Steven. *Hackers: Heroes of the Computer Revolution*. New York: Delta, 1994.

Marlette, Doug. *Drawing Blood*. Washington D.C.: Graphic Press, 1980.

———. *In Your Face*. Boston: Houghton Mifflin, 1991.

McNeil, Don. *Moving Through Here*. New York: Knopf, 1970.

Miller, James. *"Democracy Is in the Streets."* New York: Simon & Schuster, 1987.

Mills, D. Quinn. *Not Like Our Parents*. New York: William Morrow, 1987.

Mungo, Raymond. *Famous Long Ago*. Boston: Beacon Press, 1970.

Musto, Michael. *Downtown*. New York: Vintage, 1986.

Nagle, Jill (ed.). *Whores and Other Feminists*. New York: Routledge, 1997.

Oumano, Elena. *Marianne Williamson*. New York: St. Martin's Paperbacks, 1992.

Patterson, James T. *Grand Expectations*. New York: Oxford, 1996.

Pressman, Steven. *Outrageous Betrayal: The Dark Journey of Werner Erhard from est to Exile*. New York: St. Martin's Press, 1993.

Raskin, Jonah. *For the Hell of It*. Berkeley: University of California Press, 1996.

Rubin, Jerry. *Do It!* New York: Simon & Schuster, 1970.

———. *Growing Up at 37*. New York: M. Evans, 1976.

Sale, Kirkpatrick. *SDS*. New York: Random House, 1973.

Sann, Paul. *The Angry Decade: The Sixties*. New York: Crown, 1979.

Schlesinger, Arthur M., Jr. *The Almanac of American History*. New York: Putnam, 1983.

Sedgwick, Eve Kosofsky. *Novel Gazing.* Durham, N.C.: Duke University Press, 1997.

Sewall-Ruskin, Yvonne. *High on Rebellion.* New York: Thunder's Mouth, 1998.

Sheehy, Gail. *New Passages.* New York: Ballantine, 1996.

Shilts, Randy. *And the Band Played On.* New York: St. Martin's Press, 1987.

Slick, Grace. *Somebody to Love.* New York: Warner, 1998.

Sloman, Larry. *Steal This Dream.* New York: Doubleday, 1998.

Solomon, David (ed.). *The Marihuana Papers.* New York: Signet, 1966.

Spitz, Bob. *Barefoot in Babylon.* New York: Norton, 1989.

Stafford, P.G., and B.H. Golightly. *LSD: The Problem-Solving Psychedelic.* New York: Award, 1967.

Stevens, Jay. *Storming Heaven: LSD and the American Dream.* New York: Grove, 1987.

Stockton, Kathryn Bond. *God Between Their Lips.* Stanford, Calif.: Stanford University Press, 1994.

Strauss, William and Neil Howe. *Generations.* New York: William Morrow, 1991.

Tendler, Stewart, and David May. *The Brotherhood of Eternal Love.* London: Granada, 1984.

Wells, Tom. *The War Within.* Berkeley, Calif.: University of California Press, 1994.

Williamson, Marianne. *A Return To Love.* New York: HarperCollins, 1992.

——. *A Woman's Worth.* New York: Random House, 1993.

——. *The Healing of America.* New York: Simon & Schuster, 1997.

Index

Mastered By Love

Enter the World of Stephanie Laurens

The Bastion Club Novels*
See members list on pages vi-vii

#1 THE LADY CHOSEN • #2 A GENTLEMAN'S HONOR
#3 A LADY OF HIS OWN • #4 A FINE PASSION
#5 TO DISTRACTION • #6 BEYOND SEDUCTION
#7 THE EDGE OF DESIRE
CAPTAIN JACK'S WOMAN (*prequel*)

The Cynster Novels

TEMPTATION AND SURRENDER • WHERE THE HEART LEADS
THE TASTE OF INNOCENCE • WHAT PRICE LOVE?
THE TRUTH ABOUT LOVE • THE IDEAL BRIDE
THE PERFECT LOVER • THE PROMISE IN A KISS
ON A WICKED DAWN • ON A WILD NIGHT
ALL ABOUT PASSION • ALL ABOUT LOVE
A SECRET LOVE • A ROGUE'S PROPOSAL
SCANDAL'S BRIDE • A RAKE'S VOW • DEVIL'S BRIDE

Coming Soon

THE UNTAMED BRIDE

Also Available the Anthologies

IT HAPPENED ONE NIGHT • HERO, COME BACK
SECRETS OF A PERFECT NIGHT • SCOTTISH BRIDES

For information on Stephanie's books,
visit Stephanie's website at *www.stephanielaurens.com.*

Stephanie Laurens

Mastered By Love

A BASTION CLUB NOVEL

AVON

An Imprint of HarperCollinsPublishers

AVON BOOKS
An Imprint of HarperCollins*Publishers*
10 East 53rd Street
New York, New York 10022-5299

Mastered By Love

The Bastion Club

"a last bastion against the matchmakers of the ton"

MEMBERS

#7 ~~Christian Allardyce,~~ *Lady*
~~Marquess of Dearne~~ *Letitia*
Randall

#2 ~~Anthony Blake,~~ *Alicia*
~~Viscount Torrington~~ *"Carrington"*
Pevensey

#5 ~~Jocelyn Deverell,~~ *Phoebe*
~~Viscount Paignton~~ *Malleson*

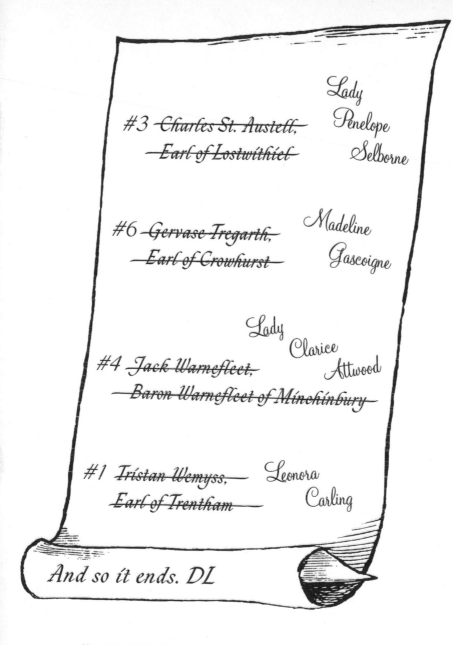

#3 ~~Charles St. Austell,~~ Lady
~~Earl of Lostwithiel~~ Penelope
Selborne

#6 ~~Gervase Tregarth,~~ Madeline
~~Earl of Crowhurst~~ Gascoigne

Lady
Clarice
#4 ~~Jack Warnefleet,~~ Attwood
~~Baron Warnefleet of Minchinbury~~

#1 ~~Tristan Wemyss,~~ Leonora
~~Earl of Trentham~~ Carling

And so it ends. DL

One

September 1816
Coquetdale, Northumbria

*I**t wasn't supposed to have been like this.*
Wrapped in his greatcoat, alone on the box seat of his excellently sprung curricle, Royce Henry Varisey, tenth Duke of Wolverstone, turned the latest in the succession of post-horses he'd raced up the highway from London onto the minor road leading to Sharperton and Harbottle. The gently rounded foothills of the Cheviot Hills gathered him in like a mother's arms; Wolverstone Castle, his childhood home and newly inherited principal estate, lay close by the village of Alwinton, beyond Harbottle.

One of the horses broke stride; Royce checked it, held the pair back until they were in step, then urged them on. They were flagging. His own high-bred blacks had carried him as far as St. Neots on Monday; thereafter he'd had a fresh pair put to every fifty or so miles.

It was now Wednesday morning, and he was a long way from London, once again—after sixteen long years—entering home territory. Ancestral territory. Rothbury and the dark glades of its forest lay behind him; ahead the rolling, largely treeless skirts of the Cheviots, dotted here and there with the inevitable sheep, spread around the even more barren hills themselves, their backbone the border with Scotland beyond.

The hills, and that border, had played a vital role in the evolution of the dukedom. Wolverstone had been created after the Conquest as a marcher lordship to protect England from the depredations of marauding Scots. Successive dukes, popularly known as the Wolves of the North, had for centuries enjoyed the privileges of royalty within their domains.

Many would argue they still did.

Certainly they'd remained a supremely powerful clan, their wealth augmented by their battlefield prowess, and protected by their success in convincing successive sovereigns that such wily, politically powerful ex-kingmakers were best left alone, left to hold the Middle March as they had since first setting their elegantly shod Norman feet on English soil.

Royce studied the terrain with an eye honed by absence. Reminded of his ancestry, he wondered anew if their traditional marcher independence—originally fought for and won, recognized by custom and granted by royal charter, then legally rescinded but never truly taken away, and even less truly given up—hadn't underpinned the rift between his father and him.

His father had belonged to the old school of lordship, one that had included the majority of his peers. According to their creed, loyalty to either country or sovereign was a commodity to be traded and bought, something both Crown and country had to place a suitable price upon before it was granted. More, to dukes and earls of his father's ilk, "country" had an ambiguous meaning; as kings in their own domains, those domains were their primary concern while the realm possessed a more nebulous and distant existence, certainly a lesser claim on their honor.

While Royce would allow that swearing fealty to the present monarchy—mad King George and his dissolute son, the Prince Regent—wasn't an attractive proposition, he held no equivocation over swearing allegiance, and service, to his country—to England.

As the only son of a powerful ducal family and thus barred by long custom from serving in the field, when, at the tender age of twenty-two, he'd been approached to create a network of English spies on foreign soil, he'd leapt at the chance. Not only had it offered the prospect of contributing to Napoleon's defeat, but with his extensive personal and family contacts combined with his inherent ability to inspire and command, the position was tailor-made; from the first it had fitted him like a glove.

But to his father the position had been a disgrace to the name and title, a blot on the family escutcheon; his old-fashioned views had labeled spying as without question dishonorable, even if one were spying on active military enemies. It was a view shared by many senior peers at the time.

Bad enough, but when Royce had refused to decline the commission, his father had organized an ambush. A public one, in White's, at a time of the evening when the club was always crowded. With his cronies at his back, his father had passed public judgment on Royce in strident and excoriating terms.

As his peroration, his father had triumphantly declared that if Royce refused to bow to his edict and instead served in the capacity for which he'd been recruited, then it would be as if he, the ninth duke, had no son.

Even in the white rage his father's attack had provoked, Royce had noted that "as if." He was his father's only legitimate son; no matter how furious, his father would not formally disinherit him. The interdict would, however, banish him from all family lands.

Facing his apoplectic sire over the crimson carpet of the exclusive club, surrounded by an army of fascinated aristocracy, he'd waited, unresponsive, until his father had finished his well-rehearsed speech. He'd waited until the expectant silence surrounding them had grown thick, then he'd uttered three words: *As you wish.*

Then he'd turned and walked from the club, and from that day forth had ceased to be his father's son. From that day he'd been known as Dalziel, a name taken from an obscure branch of his mother's family tree, fitting enough given it was his maternal grandfather—by then dead—who had taught him the creed by which he'd chosen to live. While the Variseys were marcher lords, the Debraighs were no less powerful, but their lands lay in the heart of England and they'd served king and country—principally country— selflessly for centuries. Debraighs had stood as both warriors and statesmen at the right hand of countless monarchs; duty to their people was bred deeply in them.

While deploring the rift with his father, the Debraighs had approved Royce's stance, yet, sensitive even then to the dynamics of power, he'd discouraged their active support. His uncle, the Earl of Catersham, had written, asking if there was anything he could do. Royce had replied in the negative, as he had to his mother's similar query; his fight was with his father and should involve no one else.

That had been his decision, one he'd adhered to throughout the subsequent sixteen years; none of them had expected vanquishing Napoleon to take so long.

But it had.

Through those years he'd recruited the best of his generation of Guards, organized them into a network of secret operatives, and successfully placed them throughout Napoleon's territories. Their success had become the stuff of legend; those who knew correctly credited his network with saving countless British lives, and contributing directly to Napoleon's downfall.

His success on that stage had been sweet. However, with Napoleon on his way to St. Helena, he'd disbanded his crew, releasing them to their civilian lives. And, as of Monday, he, too, had left his former life—Dalziel's life—behind.

He hadn't, however, expected to assume any title beyond

the courtesy one of Marquess of Winchelsea. Hadn't expected to immediately assume control of the dukedom and all it comprised.

His ongoing banishment—he'd never expected his father to back down any more than he himself had—had effectively estranged him from the dukedom's houses, lands, and people, and most especially from the one place that meant most to him—Wolverstone itself. The castle was far more than just a home; the stone walls and battlements held something—some magic—that resonated in his blood, in his heart, in his soul. His father had known that; it had been the same for him.

Despite the passage of sixteen years, as the horses raced on Royce still felt the pull, the visceral tug that only grew stronger as he rattled through Sharperton, drawing ever closer to Wolverstone. He felt faintly surprised that it should be so, that despite the years, the rift, his own less than susceptible temperament, he could still sense . . . home.

That home still meant what it always had.

That it still moved him to his soul.

He hadn't expected that, any more than he'd expected to be returning like this—alone, in a tearing rush, without even his longtime groom, Henry, another Wolverstone outcast, for company through the empty miles.

On Monday, while tidying the last of Dalziel's files from his desk, he'd been planning his return to Wolverstone. He'd imagined driving up from London by easy stages, arriving at the castle fresh and rested—in suitable state to walk into his father's presence . . . and see what came next.

He'd imagined an apology from his father might, just might, have featured in that scene; he'd been curious to see, yet hadn't been holding his breath.

But now he'd never know.

His father had died on Sunday.

Leaving the rift between them—vicious and deep, naturally enough given they were both Variseys—unhealed. Unaddressed. Unlaid to rest.

He hadn't known whether to curse his father or fate for leaving him to cauterize the wound.

Regardless, dealing with his past was no longer the most urgent matter on his plate. Picking up the reins of a far-flung and extensive dukedom after a sixteen-year absence was going to demand all his attention, command all of his abilities to the exclusion of all else. He would succeed—there was neither question nor option in that regard—but how long it would take, and what it would cost him . . . how the devil he was to do it, he didn't know.

It wasn't supposed to have been like this.

His father had been hale and healthy enough for a man in his sixties. He hadn't been ailing; Royce trusted that if he had, someone would have broken his father's prohibition and sent him word. Instead, he'd been blindsided.

In his version of his return, his father and he would have made their peace, their truce, whatever arrangement they would have made, then he would have started refreshing his knowledge of the estate, filling in the gap between when he'd been twenty-one, and last at Wolverstone, to his present thirty-seven.

Instead, his father was gone, leaving him to pick up the reins with a lag of sixteen years in knowledge hanging like a millstone around his neck.

While he had absolute confidence—Varisey confidence—that he would fill his father's shoes more than adequately, he wasn't looking forward to assuming emergency command over unfamiliar troops in terrain that would have shifted in unforeseen ways over the past sixteen years.

His temper, like that of all Variseys, especially the males, was formidable, an emotion that carried the same cutting edge as their broadswords of long ago. He'd learned to control it rather better than his father, to keep it reined, another weapon to be used to conquer and overcome; not even those who knew him well could detect the difference between mild irritation and a killing rage. Not unless he wished them to know. Control of his emotions had long become second nature.

Ever since he'd learned of his father's demise, his temper had been surging, restless, largely unreasoning, violently hungry for some release. Knowing the only release that would satisfy had, courtesy of fickle fate, been denied him forever.

Not having any enemy to lash out at, to exact vengeance from, left him walking a tightrope, his impulses and instincts tightly leashed.

Stony-faced, he swept through Harbottle. A woman walking along the street glanced curiously at him. While he was clearly heading for Wolverstone, there being no other destination along this road to which a gentleman of his ilk might be going, he had numerous male cousins, and they all shared more than a passing resemblance; even if the woman had heard of his father's death, it was unlikely she would realize it was he.

Since Sharperton the road had followed the banks of the Coquet; over the drumming of the horses' hooves, he'd heard the river burbling along its rocky bed. Now the road curved north; a stone bridge spanned the river. The curricle rattled across; he drew a tight breath as he crossed into Wolverstone lands.

Felt that indefinable connection grip and tighten.

Straightening on the seat, stretching the long muscles in his back, he eased the horses' pace, and looked around.

Drank in the familiar sights, each emblazoned in his memory. Most were as he'd expected—exactly as he recalled, only sixteen years older.

A ford lay ahead, spanning the River Alwin; he slowed the horses and let them pick their way across. As the wheels drew free of the water, he flicked the reins and set the pair up the slight rise, the road curving again, this time to the west.

The curricle topped the rise, and he slowed the horses to a walk.

The slate roofs of Alwinton lay directly ahead. Closer, on his left, between the road and the Coquet, sat the gray stone church with its vicarage and three cottages. He barely spared a glance for the church, his gaze drawn past it, across the river to the massive gray stone edifice that rose in majestic splendor beyond.

Wolverstone Castle.

The heavily fortified square Norman keep, added to and rebuilt by successive generations, remained the central and dominant feature, its crenellated battlements rising above the lower roofs of the early Tudor wings, both uniquely dog-legged, one running west, then north, the other east, then south. The keep faced north, looking directly up a narrow valley through which Clennell Street, one of the border crossings, descended from the hills. Neither raiders, nor traders, could cross the border by that route without passing under Wolverstone's ever-watchful eyes.

From this distance, he could make out little beyond the main buildings. The castle stood on gently sloping land above the gorge the Coquet had carved west of Alwinton village. The castle's park spread to east, south, and west, the land continuing to rise, eventually becoming hills that sheltered the castle on the south and west. The Cheviots themselves protected the castle from the north winds; only from the east, the direction from which the road approached, was the castle vulnerable to even the elements.

This had always been his first sight of home. Despite all, he felt the connection lock, felt the rising tide of affinity surge.

The reins tugged; he'd let the horses come to a halt. Flicking the ribbons, he set them trotting as he looked about even more keenly.

Fields, fences, crops, and cottages appeared in reasonable order. He went through the village—not much more than a hamlet—at a steady clip. The villagers would recognize him; some might even hail him, but he wasn't yet ready to trade greetings, to accept condolences on his father's death—not yet.

Another stone bridge spanned the deep, narrow gorge through which the river gushed and tumbled. The gorge was the reason no army had even attempted to take Wolverstone; the sole approach was via the stone bridge—easily defended. Because of the hills on all other sides, it was impossible to position mangonels or any type of siege engine anywhere that wasn't well within a decent archer's range from the battlements.

Royce swept over the bridge, the clatter of the horses' hooves drowned beneath the tumultuous roar of the waters rushing, turbulent and wild, below. Just like his temper. The closer he drew to the castle, to what awaited him there, the more powerful the surge of his emotions grew. The more unsettling and distracting.

The more hungry, vengeful, and demanding.

The huge wrought-iron gates lay ahead, set wide as they always were; the depiction of a snarling wolf's head in the center of each matched the bronze statues atop the stone columns from which the gates hung.

With a flick of the reins, he sent the horses racing through. As if sensing the end of their journey, they leaned into the harness; trees flashed past, massive ancient oaks bordering the lawns that rolled away on either side. He barely noticed, his attention—all his senses—locked on the building towering before him.

It was as massive and as anchored in the soil as the oaks. It had stood for so many centuries it had become part of the landscape.

He slowed the horses as they neared the forecourt, drinking in the gray stone, the heavy lintels, the deeply recessed windows, diamond paned and leaded, set into the thick walls. The front door lay within a high stone arch; it had originally been a portcullis, not a door, the front hall beyond, with its arched ceiling, originally a tunnel leading into the inner bailey. The front façade, three stories high, had been formed from the castle's inner bailey wall; the outer bailey wall had been dismantled long ago, while the keep itself lay deeper within the house.

Letting the horses walk along the façade, Royce gave himself the moment, let emotion reign for just that while. Yet the indescribable joy of being home again was deeply shadowed, caught up, tangled, in a web of darker feelings; being this close to his father—to where his father should have been, but no longer was—only whetted the already razor-sharp edge of his restless, unforgiving anger.

Irrational anger—anger with no object. Yet he still felt it.

Dragging in a breath, filling his lungs with the cool, crisp air, he set his jaw and sent the horses trotting on around the house.

As he rounded the north wing and the stables came into view, he reminded himself that he would find no convenient opponent at the castle with whom he could loose his temper, with whom he could release the deep, abiding anger.

Resigned himself to another night of a splitting head and no sleep.

His father was gone.

It wasn't supposed to have been like this.

Ten minutes later, he strode into the house via a side door, the one he'd always used. The few minutes in the stables hadn't helped his temper; the head stableman, Milbourne, hailed from long ago, and had offered his condolences and welcomed him back.

He'd acknowledged the well-meant words with a curt nod, left the post-horses to Milbourne's care, then remembered and paused to tell him that Henry—Milbourne's nephew—would be arriving shortly with Royce's own pair. He'd wanted to ask who else of the long-ago staff were still there, but hadn't; Milbourne had looked too understanding, leaving him feeling . . . exposed.

Not a feeling he liked.

His greatcoat swirling about his booted calves, he headed for the west stairs. Pulling off his driving gloves, he stuffed them into a pocket, then took the shallow steps three at a time.

He'd spent the last forty-eight hours alone, had just arrived—and now needed to be alone again, to absorb and in some way subdue the unexpectedly intense feelings returning like this had stirred. He needed to quiet his restless temper and leash it more firmly.

The first floor gallery lay ahead. He took the last stairs in a rush, stepped into the gallery, swung left toward the west tower—and collided with a woman.

He heard her gasp.

Sensed her stumbling and caught her—closed his hands about her shoulders and steadied her. Held her.

Even before he looked into her face, he didn't want to let her go.

His gaze locked on her eyes, wide and flaring, rich brown with gold flecks, framed by lush brown lashes. Her long hair was lustrous wheat-gold silk, wound and anchored high on her head. Her skin was creamy perfection, her nose patrician straight, her face heart-shaped, her chin neatly rounded. Itemizing those features in a glance, his gaze fixed on her lips. Rose-petal pink, parted in shocked surprise, the lower lushly tempting, the urge to crush them beneath his was nearly overpowering.

She'd taken him unawares; he hadn't had the slightest inkling she'd been there, gliding along, the thick runner muffling her footsteps. He'd patently shocked her; her wide eyes and parted lips said she hadn't heard him on the stairs, either—he'd probably been moving silently, as he habitually did.

She'd staggered back; an inch separated his hard body from her much softer one. He knew it was soft, had felt her ripe figure imprinted down the front of him, seared on his senses in that instant of fleeting contact.

On a rational level he wondered how a lady of her type

came to be wandering these halls, while on a more primitive plane he battled the urge to sweep her up, carry her into his room, and ease the sudden, shockingly intense ache in his groin—and distract his temper in the only possible way, one he hadn't even dreamed would be available.

That more primitive side of him saw it as only right that this female—whoever she was—should be walking just there, at just that time, and was just the right female to render him that singular service.

Anger, even rage, could convert into lust; he was familiar with the transformation, yet never had it struck with such speed or strength. Never before had the result threatened his control.

The consuming lust he felt for her in that instant was so intense it shocked even him.

Enough to have him slapping the urge down, clenching his jaw, tightening his grip, and bodily setting her aside.

He had to force his hands to release her.

"My apologies." His voice was close to a growl. With a curt nod in her direction, without again meeting her eyes, he strode on, swiftly putting distance between them.

Behind him he heard the hiss of an indrawn breath, heard the rustle of skirts as she swung and stared.

"Royce! Dalziel—whatever you call yourself these days—stop!"

He kept walking.

"Damn it, I am not going to—*refuse to*—scurry after you!"

He halted. Head rising, he considered the list of those who would dare address him in such words, in such a tone.

The list wasn't long.

Slowly, he half turned and looked back at the lady, who patently didn't know in what danger she stood. Scurry after him? She should be fleeing in the opposite direction. But . . .

Long-ago recollection finally connected with present fact. Those rich autumn eyes were the key. He frowned. "Minerva?"

Those fabulous eyes were no longer wide, but narrowed in irritation; her lush lips had compressed to a grim line.

"Indeed." She hesitated, then, clasping her hands before her, lifted her chin. "I gather you aren't aware of it, but I'm chatelaine here."

Contrary to Minerva's expectation, the information did not produce any softening in the stony face regarding her. No easing of the rigid line of his lips, no gleam of recognition in his dark eyes—no suggestion that he'd realized she was someone he needed to help him, even though, at last, he'd placed her: Minerva Miranda Chesterton, his mother's childhood friend's orphaned daughter. Subsequently his mother's amanuensis, companion, and confidante, more recently the same to his father, although that was something he most likely didn't know.

Of the pair of them, she knew precisely who she was, what she was, and what she had to do. He, in contrast, was probably uncertain of the first, even more uncertain of the second, and almost certainly had no clue as to the third.

That, however, she'd been prepared for. What she wasn't prepared for, what she hadn't foreseen, was the huge problem that now faced her. All six-plus feet of it, larger and infinitely more powerful in life than even her fanciful imagination had painted him.

His stylish greatcoat hung from shoulders that were broader and heavier than she recalled, but she'd last seen him when he'd been twenty-two. He was a touch taller, too, and there was a hardness in him that hadn't been there before, investing the austere planes of his face, his chiseled features, the rock-hard body that had nearly sent her flying.

Had sent her flying, more than physically.

His face was as she remembered it, yet not; gone was any hint of civilized guise. Broad forehead above striking slashes of black brows that tilted faintly, diabolically, upward at the outer ends, a blade of a nose, thin mobile lips guaranteed to dangerously fascinate any female, and well-set eyes of such a deep dark brown they were usually unreadable. The long black lashes that fringed those eyes had always made her envious.

His hair was still solidly sable, the thick locks fashionably cropped to fall in waves about his well-shaped head. His clothes, too, were fashionably elegant, restrained, understated, and expensive. Even though he'd been traveling hard, all but racing for two days, his cravat was a subtle work of art, and beneath the dust, his Hessians gleamed.

Regardless, no amount of fashion could screen his innate masculinity, could dim the dangerous aura any female with eyes could detect. The passing years had honed and polished him, revealing rather than concealing the sleekly powerful, infinitely predatory male he was.

If anything, that reality seemed enhanced.

He continued to stand twenty feet away, frowning as he studied her, making no move to come closer, giving her witless, swooning, drooling senses even more time to slaver over him.

She'd thought she'd outgrown her infatuation with him. Sixteen years of separation should surely have seen it dead.

Apparently not.

Her mission, as she viewed it, had just become immeasurably more complicated. If he learned of her ridiculous susceptibility—perhaps excusable in a girl of thirteen, but hideously embarrassing in a mature lady of twenty-nine— he'd use the knowledge, ruthlessly, to stop her from pressuring him into doing anything he didn't wish to do. At that moment, the only positive aspect to the situation was that she'd been able to disguise her reaction to him as understandable surprise.

Henceforth she would need to continue to hide that reaction from him.

Simple . . . was one thing that wasn't going to be.

Variseys as a breed were difficult, but she'd been surrounded by them from the age of six, and had learned how to manage them. All except *this* Varisey . . . oh, this was not good. Unfortunately not one, but two deathbed promises bound her to her path.

She cleared her throat, tried hard to clear her head of the disconcerting distraction of her still jangling senses. "I didn't expect you so early, but I'm glad you made such good time." Head high, eyes locked on his face, she walked forward. "There's a huge number of decisions to be made—"

He shifted, turning away, then restlessly turned back to her. "I daresay, but at present, I need to wash off the dust." His eyes—dark, fathomless, his gaze impossibly sharp— scanned her face. "I take it you're in charge?"

"Yes. And—"

He swung away, was off again, his long legs carrying him swiftly around the gallery. "I'll come and find you in an hour."

"Very well. But your room's not that way."

He halted. Once again stood facing away for the space of three heartbeats, then, slowly, he turned.

Again she felt the dark weight of his gaze, this time pinning her more definitely. This time, rather than converse over the yawning gap that once again separated them, a gap she now would have preferred to maintain, he walked, stalked, slowly back to her.

He kept walking until no more than a foot remained between them, which left him towering over her. Physical intimidation was second nature to male Variseys; they learned it from the cradle. She would have liked to say the ploy had no effect, and in truth it didn't have the effect he intended. The effect was something quite other, and more intense and powerful than she'd ever dreamed. Inside she quaked, trembled; outwardly she held his gaze and calmly waited.

First round.

He lowered his head slightly so he could look directly into her face. "The keep hasn't rotated in all the centuries since it was built." His voice had lowered, too, but his diction had lost nothing of its lethal edge. If anything that had sharpened. "Which means the west tower lies around the gallery."

She met his dark gaze, knew better than to nod. With Variseys one never conceded the slightest point; they were the sort that, if one surrendered an inch, took the whole county. "The west tower lies that way, but your room is no longer there."

Tension rippled through him; the muscle in the side of his jaw tightened. His voice, when he spoke, had lowered to a warning growl. "Where are my things?"

"In the ducal apartments." In the central part of the keep, facing south; she didn't bother telling him what he already knew.

She stepped back, just far enough to wave him to join her as, greatly daring, she turned her back on him and started strolling farther into the keep. "You're the duke now, and those are your rooms. The staff have slaved to have everything in readiness there, and the west tower room has been converted into a guest chamber. And before you ask"—she heard him reluctantly follow her, his longer legs closing the distance in a few strides—"*everything* that was in the west tower room is now in the duke's rooms—including, I might add, all your armillary spheres. I had to move every single one myself—the maids and even the footmen refuse to touch them for fear they'll fall apart in their hands."

He'd amassed an exquisite collection of the astrological spheres within spheres; she hoped mention of them would encourage him to accept the necessary relocation.

After a moment of pacing silently beside her, he said, "My sisters?"

"Your father passed away on Sunday, a little before noon. I dispatched the messenger to you immediately, but I wasn't sure what you wished, so I held back from informing your sisters for twenty-four hours." She glanced at him. "You were the farthest away, but we needed you here first. I expect they'll arrive tomorrow."

He glanced at her, met her eyes. "Thank you. I appreciate

the chance to find my feet before having to deal with them."

Which, of course, was why she'd done it. "I sent a letter with the messenger to you for Collier, Collier, and Whitticombe."

"I sent it on with a covering letter from me, asking them to attend me here, with the will, at the earliest opportunity."

"Which means they'll arrive tomorrow, too. Late afternoon, most likely."

"Indeed."

They turned a corner into a short hall just as a footman closed the massive oak door at the end. The footman saw them, bowed low, then retreated.

"Jeffers will have brought up your bags. If you need anything else—"

"I'll ring. Who's the butler here these days?"

She'd always wondered if he'd had anyone in the household feeding him information; obviously not. "Retford the younger—old Retford's nephew. He was the underbutler before."

He nodded. "I remember him."

The door to the duke's apartments neared. Clinging to her chatelaine's glamour, she halted beside it. "I'll join you in the study in an hour."

He looked at her. "Is the study in the same place?"

"It hasn't moved."

"That's something, I suppose."

She inclined her head, was about to turn away when she noticed that, although his hand had closed about the door-knob, he hadn't turned it.

He was standing staring at the door.

"If it makes any difference, it's been over a decade since your father used this room."

That got her a frowning look. "Which room did he use?"

"He moved to the east tower room. It's remained untouched since he died."

"When did he move there?" He looked at the door before him. "Out of here."

It wasn't her place to hide the truth. "Sixteen years ago." In case he failed to make the connection, she added, "When he returned from London after banishing you."

He frowned, as if the information made no sense.

Which made her wonder, but she held her tongue. She waited, but he asked no more.

Brusquely he nodded in dismissal, turned the knob, and opened the door. "I'll see you in the study in an hour."

With a serene inclination of her head, she turned and walked away.

And felt his dark gaze on her back, felt it slide down from her shoulders to her hips, eventually to her legs. Managed to hold back her inner shiver until she was out of his acutely observant sight.

Then she picked up her pace, walking swiftly and determinedly toward her own domain—the duchess's morning room; she had an hour to find armor sufficiently thick to protect her against the unexpected impact of the tenth Duke of Wolverstone.

Royce halted just inside the duke's apartments; shutting the door, he looked around.

Decades had passed since he'd last seen the room, but little had changed. The upholstery was new, but the furniture was the same, all heavy polished oak, glowing with a rich, golden patina, the edges rounded by age. He circled the sitting room, running his fingers over the polished tops of sideboards and the curved backs of chairs, then went into the bedroom—large and spacious with a glorious view south over the gardens and lake to the distant hills.

He was standing before the wide window drinking in that view when a tap on the outer door had him turning. He raised his voice. "Come."

The footman he'd seen earlier appeared in the doorway from the sitting room carrying a huge china urn. "Hot water, Your Grace."

He nodded, then watched as the man crossed the room

and went through the doorway into the dressing room and bathing chamber.

He'd turned back to the window when the footman reappeared. "Your pardon, Your Grace, but would you like me to unpack your things?"

"No." Royce looked at the man. He was average in everything—height, build, age, coloring. "There's not enough to bother with . . . Jeffers, is that right?"

"Indeed, Your Grace. I was the late duke's footman."

Royce wasn't sure he'd need a personal footman, but nodded. "My man, Trevor, will be arriving shortly—most likely tomorrow. He's a Londoner, but he's been with me for a long time. Although he has been here before, he'll need help to remember his way."

"I'll be happy to keep an eye out for him and assist in whatever way I can, Your Grace."

"Good." Royce turned back to the window. "You may go."

When he heard the outer door click shut, he quit the window and headed for the dressing room. He stripped, then washed; drying himself with the linen towel left ready on the washstand, he tried to think. He should be making mental lists of all he had to do, juggling the order in which to do them . . . but all he seemed able to do was feel.

His brain seemed obsessed with the inconsequential, with matters that were not of immediate importance. Such as why his father had moved out of the duke's apartments immediately after their confrontation.

The act smacked of abdication, yet . . . he couldn't see how such a proposition could mesh with reality; it didn't match his mental picture of his father.

His bag contained a complete set of fresh clothes—shirt, cravat, waistcoat, coat, trousers, stockings, shoes. He donned them, and immediately felt better able to deal with the challenges that waited beyond the door.

Before returning through the bedroom to the sitting room, he glanced around, assessing the amenities.

Minerva—his chatelaine—had been right. Not only were

these rooms appropriate given he was now the duke, the atmosphere felt right—and he had a sneaking suspicion his old room wouldn't have suited him, fitted him, anymore. He certainly appreciated the greater space, and the views.

Walking into the bedroom, his gaze fell on the bed. He felt certain he would appreciate that, too. The massive oak four-poster supporting a decadently thick mattress and silk covers, piled high with thick pillows, dominated the large room. It faced the window; the view would always be restful, yet interesting.

At present, however, restful yet interesting couldn't sate his need; as his gaze returned to the crimson-and-gold silk-brocade bedspread, took in the crimson silk sheets, his mind supplied a vision of his chatelaine reclining there.

Naked.

He considered the vision, deliberately indulged; his imagination was more than up to the task.

As unlooked-for developments went, his chatelaine took the prize. Little Minerva was no longer so little, yet . . .

Being his mother's protégée, and thus under his father's protection, too, would normally have placed her off-limits to him, except that both his father and mother were now dead, and she was still there, in his household, an established spinster of his class, and she was . . . what? Twenty-nine?

Within their circles, by anyone's assessment she was now fair game, *except* . . . while he'd developed an immediate and intense lust for her, she'd shown no sign whatever that she returned his interest; she'd appeared coolly, calmly unaffected throughout.

If she'd reacted to him as he had to her, she would have been in there now—more or less as he was imagining her, boneless and drowsy, a smile of satiation curving her lush lips as she lay sprawled, naked and utterly ravished, on his bed.

And he would be feeling a great deal better than he was. Sexual indulgence was the only distraction capable of taking the violent edge from his temper, capable of dulling it, dampening it, draining it.

Given his temper was so restlessly aroused, and desperately seeking an outlet, he wasn't surprised it had immediately fixed on the first attractive woman to cross his path, transmuting in a heartbeat to a driving lustful passion. What he was surprised by was the intensity, the incredible clarity with which his every sense, every fiber of his being, had locked on her.

Possessively and absolutely.

His arrogance knew few bounds, yet all the ladies who'd ever caught his eye . . . he'd always caught theirs first. That he wanted Minerva while she didn't want him had thrown him off-balance.

Unfortunately, her disinterest and his consequent unsettled state hadn't dampened his desire for her in the least.

He'd simply have to grin and bear it—continue to rein his temper in, denying it the release it sought, while putting as great a distance between him and her as possible. She might be his chatelaine, but once he learned who his steward, his agent, and the various others who were responsible for overseeing his interests were, he would be able to curtail his contact with her.

He glanced at the clock on the mantelpiece. Forty minutes had passed. Time to go to the study and settle in before she arrived to speak with him. He would need a few minutes to grow accustomed to occupying the chair behind his father's desk.

Walking into the sitting room, he looked up—and saw his armillary spheres lined up along the mantelpiece opposite, the mirror behind creating the perfect showcase. The sight drew him across the room. Scanning the collection, fingers idly stroking long-forgotten friends, he halted before one, his fingers stilling on a gold-plated curve as memories of his father presenting it to him on his eighteenth birthday slid through his mind.

After a moment, he shook free of the recollection and continued on, studying each sphere with its interlocking, polished metal curves . . .

The maids and even the footmen refuse to touch them for fear they'll fall apart in their hands.

Halting, he looked closer, but he'd been right. Each sphere hadn't just been dusted; every single one had been lovingly polished.

He glanced back along the line of spheres, then he turned and walked to the door.

Two

Armor of the sort she needed wasn't easy to find. Glancing at the clock in the duchess's morning room, Minerva told herself she'd simply have to manage. It was just over an hour since she'd left Royce; she couldn't hide forever.

Sighing, she stood, smoothing down her dull black skirts. She'd be wearing her mourning gowns for the next three months; luckily the color suited her well enough.

A small piece of reassurance to cling to.

Picking up the documents she'd prepared, she headed for the door. Royce should be in the study and settled by now; she stepped into the corridor, hoping she'd given him enough time. Courtesy of her infatuation and consequent close observation of him whenever they'd been in the same place—which covered all the time he'd spent at Wolverstone or in the London house from the age of fourteen, when she'd joined the household as a six-year-old and on setting eyes on him had been instantly smitten, to when he'd reached twenty-two—she knew him much better than he could possibly guess. And she'd known his father even better; the matters they had to discuss, the decisions Royce had to make that day and over those following, would not be easy, not without emotional cost.

She'd been in London with his mother at the time of the confrontation in White's; they'd heard enough reports to have a fairly clear idea of what had, beneath the words, really happened. Given Royce's puzzlement on hearing when his father had moved out of the ducal apartments, she wasn't at all sure he—Royce—had as clear a vision of that long-ago debacle as she. Aside from all else, he would have been in a shocking temper—nay, fury—at the time. While his intellect was formidable and his powers of observation normally disconcertingly acute, when in the grip of a Varisey rage she suspected his higher faculties didn't work all that well.

His father's certainly hadn't, as that long-ago day had proved.

Regardless, it was time to beard the lion in his den. Or in this case, prod the new wolf in his study.

The corridors of the huge house were often quiet, but today the staff crept even more silently; not even distant sounds disturbed the pall.

She walked calmly on through the unnatural stillness.

She'd spent the last hour assuring herself that her eruption of unwelcome awareness had been due to shock—because he'd come upon her unawares and nearly mown her down. That her reaction was due solely to the *unexpectedness* of feeling his hard hands curl over her shoulders—and then he'd lifted her, literally off her feet, and set her aside.

And then he'd walked on.

That was the key point she had to remember—that all she'd felt was in her head. As long as it stayed there, and he remained unaware of it, all would be well. Just because her long-ago—as she'd thought long-dead—infatuation had chosen this thoroughly inconvenient moment to surge back to life, didn't mean she had to indulge it. Twenty-nine was too old for infatuations. She was, absolutely and undeniably, too wise to obsess over a gentleman, let alone a nobleman—and she well knew the distinction—like him.

If he ever guessed her susceptibility, he would use it ruthlessly for his own ends, and then she and her mission would be in very deep trouble.

The study door appeared ahead, Jeffers standing dutifully alongside; eyeing the closed panel, she wasn't overly surprised to feel a certain wariness building. The truth was . . . if she'd considered herself free to do as she pleased, instead of acting as Royce's dutiful chatelaine and easing him into his new role, she would be spending the afternoon penning letters to her friends around the country inquiring if it would be convenient for her to visit. But she couldn't leave yet—wasn't free to flee yet.

She'd made a vow—two vows actually, but they were the same vow so it was really only one. First to his mother when she'd died three years ago, and she'd made the same vow last Sunday to his father. She found it interesting—indeed, revealing—that two people who hadn't shared much over the last twenty years should have had the same dying wish. Both had asked her to see Royce settled and properly established as the next Duke of Wolverstone. What they'd meant by "properly established" was, given the subject, plain enough; they'd wanted her to ensure that he was fully informed of all aspects of the dukedom, and that he understood and put in place all that was required to secure his position.

So on top of all else, she would need to see him wed.

That event would mark the end of her debt to the Variseys. She knew how much she owed them, how beholden to them she was. She'd been a six-year-old stray—no pauper, and as wellborn as they, but with no relatives to watch over her, and no claim on them—yet with negligent grace they'd taken her in, made her one of the family in all but name, included her in a way she'd had no right to expect. They hadn't done it expecting anything from her in return—which was one reason she was determined to carry out the late duke's and duchess's last wishes to the letter.

But once Royce's bride was established as his duchess and

was able to take over the reins she currently managed, her role here would end.

What she did next, what she would make of her life, was a prospect that, until last Sunday night, she'd spent no time dwelling on. She still had no idea what she would do when her time at Wolverstone came to a close, but she had more than sufficient funds to keep herself in the luxury to which, thanks to the Variseys, she was now accustomed, and there was a whole world beyond Coquetdale and London to explore. There were all sorts of exciting prospects to consider, but that was for later.

Right now she had a wolf—quite possibly bruised and inclined to be savage—to deal with.

Halting before the study door, she inclined her head to Jeffers, tapped once, and went in.

Royce was sitting behind the huge oak desk. The desktop was unnaturally neat and clear, devoid of the usual papers and documents commensurate with it being the administrative heart of a massive estate. Long-fingered hands, palms flat, on the desk, he glanced up as she entered; for a fleeting instant she thought he looked . . . lost.

Shutting the door, she glanced at the document uppermost in her hand as she walked across the rug—and spoke before he could. "You need to approve this." Halting before the desk, she held out the sheet. "It's a notice for the *Gazette*. We also have to inform the palace and the Lords."

Expression impassive, he looked at her, then lifted one hand and took the notice. While he read it, she sat in one of the chairs before the desk, settled her skirts, then arranged her prepared sheets in her lap.

He shifted and she looked up—watched as he reached for a pen, glanced at the nib, flipped open the ink pot, dipped, then applied the pen to her notice, slowly and deliberately crossing out one word.

After blotting it, he inspected the result, then reached across the desk and handed it back to her. "With that correction, that will do for the news sheets."

He'd crossed out the word "beloved" in the phrase "beloved father of." She suppressed the impulse to raise her brows; she should have anticipated that. Variseys, as she'd been told often enough and had seen demonstrated for decades, did not love. They might be seething cauldrons of emotion in all other respects, but not one of them had ever laid claim to love. She nodded. "Very well."

Putting that sheet at the bottom of her pile, she lifted the next, looked up—and saw him regarding her enigmatically. "What?"

"You're not 'Your Grace'-ing me."

"I didn't 'Your Grace' your father, either." She hesitated, then added, "And you wouldn't like it if I did."

The result was an almost inhuman purr, a sound that slid across her senses. "Do you know me that well, then?"

"That well, yes." Even though her heart was now in her throat, she kept firm control over her voice, her tone. She held out the next sheet. "Now, for the Lords." She had to keep him focused and not let him stray into disconcerting diversions; it was a tactic Variseys used to distract, and then filch the reins.

After a pregnant moment, he reached out and took the sheet. They thrashed out a notification for the Lords, and an acceptably worded communication for the palace.

While they worked, she was aware of him watching her, his dark gaze sharp, as if he were studying her—minutely.

She steadfastly ignored the effect on her senses—prayed it would wane soon. It had to, or she'd go mad.

Or she'd slip and he'd notice, and then she'd die of embarrassment.

"Now, assuming your sisters arrive tomorrow, and the people from Collier, etcetera, as well, given we expect your aunts and uncles to arrive on Friday morning, then if you're agreeable, we could have the will read on Friday, and that would be one thing out of the way." Looking up from tidying her documents, she arched a brow at him.

He'd slumped back, outwardly relaxed in the large admiral's chair; he regarded her impassively for several long moments, then said, "We could—if I was agreeable—have the funeral on Friday."

"No, we couldn't."

Both his brows slowly rose. "No?" There was a wealth, a positive surfeit of intimidation packed into the single, softly uttered word. In this case, on multiple counts, it was misplaced.

"No." She met his gaze, held it. "Think back to your mother's funeral—how many attended?"

His stillness was absolute; his gaze didn't shift from hers. After another long silence, he said, "I can't remember." His tone was even, but she detected a roughness, a slight weakness; he honestly couldn't recall, quite possibly didn't like thinking of that difficult day.

With him banished from his father's lands, but the church and graveyard at Alwinton enclosed within Wolverstone's boundaries, he'd literally driven around his father's edict; his groom had driven his curricle to the church's lych-gate, and he'd stepped directly onto hallowed ground.

Neither he nor his father had spoken to anyone—let alone exchanged so much as a glance—through the long service and the subsequent burial. That he couldn't remember how many had been in the church testified that he hadn't been looking around, unaffected; his normally extremely observant faculties hadn't been functioning.

Calmly, she recited, "There were over two hundred counting only family and members of the ton. For your father, that number will be more like three hundred. There'll be representatives of the king, and Parliament, quite aside from family and friends—let alone all those who will make a point of coming all the way up here simply to register their connection, however tenuous, with the dukedom."

He pulled a face, then in an explosion of movement sat up. "How soon can it be arranged?"

Relief slid through her veins. "The notice of death will run in the *Gazette* on Friday. Tomorrow, once your sisters are here to consult, we should send off a notice about the funeral—that will then run in the Saturday editions. Realistically, given so many will be coming from the south, the earliest we could hold the funeral would be the following Friday."

He nodded, reluctant but accepting. "Friday, then." He hesitated, then asked, "Where's the body being kept?"

"In the icehouse, as usual." She knew better than to suggest he should view his father's body; he either would of his own accord, or wouldn't. It would be better if he did, but there were some areas into which, with him, she wasn't prepared to stray; it was simply too dangerous.

Royce watched as she shuffled through the papers in her lap—eyed her hair, lustrous and gleaming. Wondered how it would look draped over her very white skin when said skin was bare and flushed with passion.

He shifted in the chair. He desperately needed distraction. He was about to ask for a list of staff—she was so damned efficient he would wager his sanity she would have one in her pile—when heavy footsteps approached the door. An instant later, it opened, admitting a majestic butler.

The butler's gaze fixed on him. Framed in the doorway, he bowed low. "Your Grace." Straightening, he bowed more shallowly to Minerva, who rose to her feet. "Ma'am."

Refocusing on Royce, who, as Minerva was standing, rose, too, the stately personage intoned, "I am Retford, Your Grace. I am the butler here. On behalf of the staff, I wish to convey our condolences on the death of your father, and extend our welcome to you on your return."

Royce inclined his head. "Thank you, Retford. I believe I recall you as underbutler. Your uncle always had you polishing the silver."

Retford perceptibly thawed. "Indeed, Your Grace." He glanced again at Minerva. "You wished me to inform you when luncheon was ready, ma'am."

Royce noted the meaningful look the pair exchanged before his chatelaine said, "Indeed, Retford. Thank you. We'll be down directly."

Retford bowed to them both, then with another "Your Grace," withdrew.

Still standing, Royce caught Minerva's eye. "Why are we going down directly?"

She blinked her eyes wide. "I was sure you'd be hungry." When he remained unmoving, patently waiting, her lips lifted fractionally. "And you need to allow the staff to formally greet you."

He summoned a not-entirely-feigned expression of horror. "Not the whole damned lot of them?"

She nodded and turned to the door. "Every last one. Names and positions—you know the drill. This is a ducal residence, after all." She watched as he came around the desk. "And if you're not hungry now, I can guarantee you'll be in dire need of sustenance by the time we're finished."

Moving past her, he opened the door, held it. "You're going to enjoy this, aren't you? Seeing me floundering."

As he followed her into the corridor, she shook her head. "You won't flounder—I'm your chatelaine. I'm not allowed to let you flounder at such moments—that's my job."

"I see." He quelled an urge to take her arm; she clearly didn't expect him to—she was already walking briskly toward the main stairs. Sinking his hands in his trouser pockets, he fixed his gaze on the floor before their feet. "So how, exactly, do you propose to do your job?"

By whispering in his ear.

She remained immediately on his left all the way down the long line of eager staff, murmuring their names and positions as he nodded to each one.

He could have done without the distraction. The temptation. The all but constant taunting, however unintentional, of his less civilized self.

The housekeeper, Mrs. Cranshaw—Cranny as he'd always called her—blushed rosily when he smiled and called her by that long-ago nickname. Other than Retford and Milbourne, there were no others who hailed from the last time he'd been there.

They finally reached the end of the long line. After the last scullery maid had blushed and bobbed, Retford, who had followed behind them radiating approval as much as a butler of his station ever did, stepped forward and bowed them into the smaller dining salon.

Royce would have gone to his customary chair halfway down the table, but Retford swept to the large carver at its head and held it . . . he smoothly continued up the table and sat in his father's place.

Now his—a fact he was going to have to get used to.

Jeffers sat Minerva on his left; from her and Jeffers's behavior, that was her customary position.

He remembered his need to create distance between them, remembered his question about the staff, but she'd left her papers upstairs.

Luckily, as soon as the platters had been set before them and the majority of footmen withdrew, she asked, "One thing we—Retford, Milbourne, Cranny, and I—need to know is what staff you have, and which household you wish them attached to."

A safe, sensible question. "I have a valet—Trevor. He was with me before."

Staring ahead, she narrowed her eyes. "He's younger than you, slightly tubby—at least he was."

A reasonable if brief description of Trevor.

She glanced at Retford, standing back on Royce's right; the butler nodded, indicating that he, too, remembered Trevor. "That's fortuitous, as I doubt Walter, your father's valet, would suit. However, that leaves us with the question of what to do with Walter—he won't want to leave Wolverstone, or the family's service."

"Leave that to me." Royce had long ago learned to value experience. "I have an idea for a position that might suit him."

"Oh?" She looked her question, but when he didn't reply,

but instead served himself from a platter of cold meats, she frowned, then asked, "Is Henry still your groom?"

He nodded. "I've already spoken with Milbourne—Henry should arrive tomorrow. He'll remain my personal groom. The only other to join the household here will be Handley." He met Minerva's gaze. "My secretary."

He'd wondered how she would take that news. Somewhat to his surprise, she beamed. "Excellent. That will absolve me of dealing with your correspondence."

"Indeed." A good first step in edging her out of his daily orbit. "Who dealt with my father's correspondence?"

"I did. But there are so many communications crossing a duke's desk, and so much I have to attend to as chatelaine, if we'd entertained more, there would have been problems. As it was, things often didn't get dealt with as expeditiously as I would have liked."

He was relieved she truly was prepared to let his correspondence pass out of her hands. "I'll tell Handley to check with you if he has any questions."

She nodded, absorbed with peeling a fig. He watched her take the first bite, saw her lips glisten—quickly looked down at the apple he was coring.

When next he glanced up, she was staring across the table, frowning in an abstracted way. As if sensing his gaze, she asked, still without looking at him, "Is there anyone else we should expect to accommodate?"

It took a moment for him to catch her meaning; it was the word "accommodate" that finally impinged, confirmed by the faint blush tinting her cheeks. "No." Just to ensure she— and Retford, too—were quite clear on the point, he stated, "I don't have a mistress. At present."

He'd tacked on the "at present" to make sure they believed him. Rapidly canvassing the possible eventualities, he added, "And unless I inform you otherwise, you should act on the assumption that that situation remains unchanged."

Mistresses, for him, constituted a certain danger, something he'd learned before he'd reached twenty. Because he'd been heir to one of the wealthiest dukedoms, his mistresses—due to his tastes, inevitably drawn from the ton—had shown a marked tendency to develop unrealistic ideas.

His declaration had tweaked Minerva's curiosity, but she merely nodded, still not meeting his eyes. She finished her fig, and laid down her fruit knife.

He pushed back from the table. "I need a list of the stewards and agents for each of the various properties."

She rose as Jeffers drew out her chair. "I have a list prepared—I left it on my desk. I'll bring it to the study."

"Where is your lair?"

She glanced at him as they headed for the stairs. "The duchess's morning room."

He didn't say anything, but walked by her side up the stairs and into the keep, to the room that, centuries ago, had been a solar. Its oriel window looked out over the rose garden to the south and west of the keep.

Following her into the room, he halted just over the threshold. While she went to a bureau against one wall, he scanned the room, searching for some sense of his mother. He saw the tapestry cushions she'd loved to make idly cast on the sofas, but other than that the room held few lingering hints of her. It was light, airy, distinctly feminine, with two vases of fresh flowers scenting the air.

Minerva turned and walked toward him, perusing a number of lists. She was so alive, so anchored in the here and now, he doubted any ghosts could linger near.

She looked up, saw him; a frown formed in her eyes. She glanced at the twin sofas, the only place they might sit, then faced him. "We'll do better going over these in the study."

She was uncomfortable having him in her domain. But she was right; the study was the more appropriate setting. Even more to the point, it had a desk behind which he could hide the worst of his reaction to her.

Stepping aside, he waved her through the door. He trailed

her around the gallery, but finding his gaze transfixed by her subtly swaying hips, he lengthened his stride to walk alongside her.

Once they were ensconced in the study—once more firmly in their roles of duke and chatelaine—he went through her list of his stewards and agents, extracting every detail he deemed useful—in addition to the names and positions, physical descriptions and her personal opinion of each man. At first she balked at voicing the latter, but when he insisted proved his point by providing a comprehensive and astute character study for each incumbent.

His memories of her from long ago weren't all that detailed; what he had was an impression of a no-nonsense female uninclined to histrionics or flights of fancy, a girl with her feet firmly planted on the ground. His mother had trusted her implicitly, and from all he was learning, so had his sire.

And his father had never trusted easily, no more than he.

By the time they reached the end of her lists, he was convinced that he, too, could trust her. Implicitly. Which was a huge relief. Even keeping her at a physical distance, he would need her help to get through the next days, possibly weeks. Possibly even months. Knowing that her loyalties lay firmly with the dukedom—and thus with him as the duke— was reassuring.

Almost as if he could trust her to protect his back.

Which was a distinctly odd notion for a man like him to have of a woman. Especially a lady like her.

Unknowingly underscoring his conclusion, having regathered her scattered papers, leaving those he'd appropriated, she hesitated. When he caught her eye and arched a brow, she said, "Your father's man of business is Collier— not the same Collier as Collier, Collier, and Whitticombe, but their cousin."

He could now read her tone. "Whom you don't trust."

"Not so much don't trust as have no confidence that he knows all that much about managing money. Heaven knows,

I don't, but I've seen the returns on the dukedom's investments, and they don't impress. I get significantly better returns on my funds, which are handled by another firm."

He nodded. "I have my own man of business—Montague, in the city. He does get impressive returns. I'll instruct him to contact Collier and go through the books, then assume control."

She smiled. "Excellent." She shifted, looked at the lists before him. "If you don't need me for anything else . . . ?"

He wished he didn't, but he had to know, and she was the only one he could ask. He focused on the pen in his hand—his father's. "How did my father die?"

She stilled. He didn't look up, but waited; he sensed she was ordering her thoughts. Then she said, "He had a seizure. He was perfectly well earlier—we met over breakfast—then he went into the library as he always did on Sunday mornings to read the news sheets. We don't know when he was struck down, but when he didn't ring for his elevenses, as he invariably did, the cook sent Jeffers to check. Jeffers found him lying on the floor behind his desk. He'd tried to reach the bellpull, but had collapsed."

She paused, then went on, "Retford summoned me. I stayed with your father while they sent for the doctor and made a stretcher to carry him to his room. But he didn't last that long."

Royce glanced up. Her gaze was far away, unfocused. "You were with him when he died?"

She nodded.

He looked down, turned the pen in his fingers. "Did he say anything?"

"He was unconscious until quite close to the end. Then he stirred, and asked for you."

"Me?" He looked up. "Not my sisters?"

"No—he'd forgotten. He thought you were here, at Wolverstone. I had to tell him you weren't." She refocused on him. "He passed away quite peacefully—if he had been in pain, it was before we found him."

He nodded, not quite meeting her eyes. "Thank you." After a moment, he asked, "Have you told the others?"

She knew to whom he was referring—his father's illegitimate children.

"The girls are on one or other of the estates, so I sent letters out yesterday. Other than O'Loughlin, to whom I sent word, the males are out of reach—I'll pen letters once we know the bequests, and you can sign them." She looked at him. "Or Handley could do it, if you wish."

"No. I'd appreciate it if you would handle that. You know them—Handley doesn't. But leave O'Loughlin to me. I don't want to start mysteriously losing sheep."

She rose. "He wouldn't, would he?"

"He would, if nothing else to gain my attention. I'll deal with him."

"Very well. If there's nothing more you need from me, I'll start planning the funeral, so once your sisters arrive we can proceed without delay."

He nodded curtly. "Please God."

He heard a soft chuckle as she glided to the door. Then she left, and he could, at last, focus on picking up the dukedom's reins.

He spent the next two hours going over her lists and the notes he'd made, then penning letters—short, to-the-point scrawls; he was already missing Handley.

Jeffers proved invaluable, knowing the fastest route to fly his communications to each of his holdings; it appeared he needed a personal footman after all. Through Jeffers he arranged to meet with Wolverstone's steward, Falwell, and Kelso, the agent, the following morning; both lived in Harbottle, so had to be summoned.

After that . . . once Jeffers had left with the last of his missives, Royce found himself standing at the window behind the desk, looking north toward the Cheviots and the border. The gorge through which the Coquet ran was visible here and there through the trees. A race had been cut into the steep bank some way north of the castle, channeling water to the castle mill; only the mill's slate roof was visible from the study. After the mill, the race widened into an ornamental stream, a series of pools and ponds slowing the pummeling torrent until it flowed peacefully into the large manmade lake south of the castle.

Royce followed the line of the stream, his gaze fixing on the last pool before the view was cut off by the castle's north wing. In his mind, he continued along the banks, to where the stream reached the lake, then farther around the western bank . . . to where the icehouse stood back from the shore in a grove of sheltering willows.

He stood for a while more, feeling rather than thinking. Then accepting the inevitable, he turned and walked to the door. Stepping out, he looked at Jeffers. "I'm going for a walk. If Miss Chesterton looks for me, tell her I'll see her at dinner."

"Yes, Your Grace."

He turned and started walking. He supposed he'd get used to the form of address, yet . . . it wasn't supposed to have been like this.

The evening, blissfully quiet though it was, felt like the lull before a storm; after dinner, sitting in the library watching Minerva embroider, Royce could sense the pressures building.

Viewing the body laid out in the icehouse hadn't changed anything. His father had aged, yet was recognizably the same man who'd banished him—his only son—for sixteen years, the same man from whom he'd inherited name, title and estate, his height and ruthless temperament, and not much else. Yet temper, temperament, made the man; looking down on his father's no longer animate face, harsh featured even in death, he'd wondered how different they truly were. His father had been a ruthless despot; at heart, so was he.

Sunk in the large armchair angled before the hearth wherein a small fire burned incongruously bright, he sipped the fine malt whisky Retford had poured him, and pretended that the ancient, luxurious yet comfortable surroundings had relaxed him.

Even if he hadn't sensed storms on his horizon, having his chatelaine in the same room guaranteed he wouldn't—couldn't—relax.

His eyes seemed incapable of shifting for any length of time away from her; his gaze again drawn to her as she sat on the chaise, eyes on her needlework, the firelight gilding her upswept hair and casting a rosy sheen over her cheeks, he wondered anew at the oddity—the inconvenient fact—that she wasn't attracted to him, that he apparently didn't impinge on her awareness while he—every sense he possessed—was increasingly fixated on her.

The arrogance of the thought occurred to him, yet in his case was nothing more than the truth. Most ladies found him attractive; he usually simply took his pick of those offering, crooked his finger, and that lady was his for however long he wanted her.

He wanted his chatelaine with an intensity that surprised him, yet her disinterest precluded him from having her. He'd never pursued a woman, actively seduced a woman, in his life, and at his age didn't intend to start.

After dressing for dinner—mentally thanking Trevor who had foreseen the necessity—he'd gone to the drawing room armed with a catechism designed to distract them both. She'd been happy to oblige, filling in the minutes before Retford had summoned them to the dining room, then continuing through the meal, reminding him of the local families, both ton and gentry, casting her net as far as Alnwick and the Percys, before segueing into describing the changes in local society—who were now the principal opinion makers, which families had faded into obscurity.

Not that much had changed; with minor adjustments, his previous view of this part of the world still prevailed.

Then Retford had drawn the covers and she'd risen, intending to leave him to a solitary glass of port. He'd opted instead to follow her to the library and the whisky his father had kept there.

Prolonging the torture of being in her presence, yet he hadn't wanted to be alone.

When he'd commented on her using the library instead of the drawing room, she'd told him that after his mother's death, his father had preferred her to sit with him there . . . suddenly recalling it was he, not his father, walking beside her, she'd halted. Before she could ask if he'd rather she repaired to the drawing room, he'd said he had further questions and waved her on.

On reaching the library, they'd sat; while Retford had fetched the whisky, he'd asked about the London house. That topic hadn't taken long to exhaust; other than having to rethink his notion of having his butler Hamilton take over as butler there, all else was as he'd supposed.

A strangely comfortable silence had ensued; she was, it seemed, one of those rare females who didn't need to fill every silence with chatter.

Then again, she'd spent the last three years' evenings sitting with his father; hardly surprising she'd grown used to long silences.

Unfortunately, while the silence normally would have suited him, tonight it left him prey to increasingly illicit thoughts of her; those currently prevailing involved stripping her slowly of her weeds, unwrapping her curves, her graceful limbs, and investigating her hollows.

All of which seemed guiltily wrong, almost dishonorable.

He inwardly frowned at her—a picture of ladylike decorum as, entirely oblivious of the pain she was causing him, needle flashing she worked on a piece of the same sort of embroidery his mother had favored, petit point he thought it was called. Technically, her living unchaperoned under his roof might be termed scandalous, yet given her position and how long she'd resided there . . . "How long have you been chatelaine here?"

She glanced up, then returned to her work. "Eleven years.

I took on the duties when I turned eighteen, but neither your mother nor your father would consent to me to being titled chatelaine, not until I turned twenty-five and they finally accepted I wouldn't wed."

"They'd expected you to marry." So had he. "Why didn't you?"

She glanced up, flashed a light smile. "Not for want of offers, but no suitor offered anything I valued enough to grant him my hand—enough to change the life I had."

"So you're satisfied being Wolverstone's chatelaine?"

Unsurprised by the bald question, Minerva shrugged. She would willingly answer any question he asked—anything to disrupt the effect that him sitting there, at his languid, long-legged ease in a sprawl that was so quintessentially masculine—broad shoulders against the high back of the chair, forearms resting along the padded arms, the long fingers of one hand cradling a cut-crystal tumbler, powerful thighs spread apart—was having on her benighted senses. Her nerves were so taut his presence made them flicker and twang like violin strings. "I won't be chatelaine forever—once you marry, your duchess will take up the reins, and then I plan to travel."

"Travel? Where to?"

Somewhere a long way from him. She studied the rose she must have just embroidered; she couldn't remember doing it. "Egypt, perhaps."

"Egypt?" He didn't sound impressed by her choice. "Why there?"

"Pyramids."

The darkly brooding look he'd had before he'd asked when she'd become chatelaine returned. "From all I've heard, the area around the pyramids is rife with Berber tribesmen, barbarians who wouldn't hesitate to kidnap a lady. You can't go there."

She imagined informing him that she'd long had a dream of being kidnapped by a barbarian, tossed over his shoulder, and carted into his tent, there to be dropped on a silk-draped pallet and thoroughly ravished—of course he'd been the barbarian in question—and then pointing out that he had no authority over where she went. Instead, she settled for a response he'd like even less. Smiling gently, she looked back at her work. "We'll see."

No, they wouldn't. She wasn't going anywhere near Egypt, or any other country seething with danger. Royce toyed with lecturing her that his parents hadn't raised her to have her throw her life away on some misguided adventure . . . but with his temper so uncertain, and her response guaranteed to only escalate the tension, he kept his lips shut and swallowed the words.

To his intense relief, she slipped her needle into her work, then rolled the piece up and placed it into a tapestry bag that apparently lived beneath one end of the chaise. Leaning down, she tucked the bag back into position, then straightened and looked at him. "I'm going to retire." She rose. "Don't stir—I'll see you tomorrow. Good night."

He managed a growled "good night" in reply. His eyes followed her to the door—while he fought to remain in the chair and let her go. Her idea about Egypt hadn't helped, stirring something primitive—even more primitive—within him. Sexual hunger was a tangible ache as the door shut softly behind her.

Her room would be in the keep, somewhere not far from his new rooms; despite the ever-increasing temptation, he wasn't going there.

She was his chatelaine, and he needed her.

Until he was solidly established as duke, the reins firmly in his hands, she was his best, most well-informed, reliable, and trustworthy source of information. He would avoid her as much as possible—Falwell and Kelso would help with that—but he would still need to see her, speak with her, on a daily basis.

He'd see her at meals, too; this was her home after all.

Both his parents had been committed to raising her; he had every intention of honoring that commitment even though they were gone. Although not formally a ward of the dukedom, she stood in much the same position . . . perhaps he could cast himself as *in loco parentis*?

That would excuse the protectiveness he felt—that he knew he would continue to feel.

Regardless, he would have to bear with her being always around, until, as she'd pointed out, he married.

That was something else he would have to arrange.

Marriage for him, as for all dukes of Wolverstone, indeed, for all Variseys, would be a cold-bloodedly nego-tiated affair. His parents' and sisters' marriages had been that, and had worked as such alliances were meant to; the men took lovers whenever they wished, and once heirs were produced, the women did the same, and the unions remained stable and their estates prospered.

His marriage would follow that course. Neither he nor any Varisey was likely to indulge in the recent fashion for love matches, not least because, as was recognized by all who knew them, Variseys, as a breed, did not love.

Not within marriage, and not, as far as anyone knew, in any other capacity, either.

Of course, once he was wed, he'd be free to take a mistress, a long-term one, one he could keep by his side . . .

The thought rewoke all the fantasies he'd spent the last hour trying to suppress.

With a disgusted grunt, he drained the amber liquid in his glass, then set it down, rose, adjusted his trousers, and headed off to his empty bed.

Three

*A*t nine the next morning, Royce sat at the head of the table in the breakfast parlor, and, alone, broke his fast. He'd slept better than he'd expected—deeply, if not dreamlessly—and his dreams hadn't been of his past, but rather fantasies that would never come to be.

All had featured his chatelaine.

If not always entirely naked, then at least less than clothed.

He'd woken to discover Trevor crossing the bedroom, ferrying hot water to the bathing chamber beyond. The keep had been built in an era when keeping doors to a minimum had been a wise defense; clearly knocking a door between the corridor and his dressing room and bathing chamber was an urgent necessity. He'd made a mental note to tell his chatelaine.

He'd wondered if she would ask why.

While he'd lain back and waited for the inevitable effect of his last dream to fade, he'd rehearsed various answers.

He'd walked into the breakfast parlor with a keen sense of anticipation, disappointingly doused when, despite the late hour, she hadn't been there.

Perhaps she was one of those females who breakfasted on tea and toast in her room.

Curbing his misplaced curiosity about his chatelaine's habits, he'd sat and allowed Retford to serve him, determinedly suppressing a query as to her whereabouts.

He was working his way through a plate of ham and sausages when the object of his obsession swept in—gowned in a gold velvet riding habit worn over a black silk blouse with a black ribbon tied above one elbow and a black riding hat perched atop her golden head.

Wisps of hair had escaped her chignon, creating a fine nimbus beneath the hat. Her cheeks glowed with sheer vitality.

She saw him and smiled, halting and briskly tugging off her gloves. A crop was tucked under one arm. "Two demon-bred black horses have arrived in the stables with Henry. I recognized him, amazingly enough. The entire stable staff are milling about, fighting to lend a hand to get your beasts settled." She arched a brow at him. "How many more horses should we expect?"

He chewed slowly, then swallowed. She enjoyed riding, he recalled; there was a taut litheness to her form as she stood poised just inside the door, as if her body were still thrumming to the beat of hooves, as if the energy stirred by the ride still coursed her veins.

The sight of her stirred him to an uncomfortable degree.

What had she asked? He raised his eyes to hers. "None."

"None?" She stared at him. "What did you ride in London? A hired hack?"

Her tone colored the last words as utterly unthinkable—which they were.

"The only activities one can indulge in on horseback in the capital don't, in my book, qualify as riding."

She wrinkled her nose. "That's true." She studied him for a moment.

He returned his attention to his plate. She was debating whether to tell him something; he'd already learned what that particular, assessing look meant.

"So you've no horse of your own. Well, except old Conqueror."

He looked up. "He's still alive?" Conqueror had been his horse at the time he'd been banished, a powerful gray stallion just two years old.

She nodded. "No one else could ride him, so he was put to stud. He's more gray than ever now, but he still plods around with his mares." Again she hesitated, then made up her mind. "There's one of Conqueror's offspring, another stallion. Sword's three years old now, but while he's broken to the bit, he refuses to be ridden—well, not for long." She met his eyes. "You might like to try."

With a brilliant smile—she knew she'd just delivered a challenge he wouldn't be able to resist—she swung around and left the room.

Leaving him thinking—yet again—of another ride he wouldn't mind attempting.

"So, Falwell, there's nothing urgently requiring attention on the estate?" Royce addressed the question to his steward, who after wrinkling his brow and dourly pondering, eventually nodded.

"I would say, Your Grace, that while there might be the usual minor details to be attended to here and there, there is nothing outstanding that leaps to mind as necessary to be done in the next few months." Falwell was sixty if he was a day; a quietly spoken, rather colorless individual, he bobbed his head all but constantly—making Royce wonder if he'd developed the habit in response to his sire's blustering aggression.

Seeming to always agree, even if he didn't.

Both steward and agent had responded to his summons, and were seated before the study desk while he attempted what was rapidly becoming a hostile interrogation. Not that they were hostile, but he was feeling increasingly so.

Suppressing his incipient frown, he attempted to tease

some better understanding from them. "It'll be winter in a few months, and then we won't be able to attend to anything of a structural nature until March, or more likely April." He found it difficult to believe that among all the buildings and outbuildings, nothing needed repairing. He turned his gaze on his agent. "And what of the holdings? Kelso?"

The agent was of similar vintage to Falwell, but a much harder, leaner, grizzled man. He was, however, equally dour.

"Nothing urgent that needs castle intervention, Y'r Grace."

They'd used the phrase "castle intervention" several times, apparently meaning assistance from the ducal coffers. But they were talking of barns, fences, and cottages on his lands that belonged to the estate and were provided to tenant farmers in exchange for their labor and the major portion of the crops. Royce allowed his frown to show. "What about situations that *don't* require 'castle intervention'? Are there any repairs or work of any kind urgently needed there?" His tone had grown more precise, his diction more clipped.

They exchanged glances—almost as if the question had confused them. He was getting a very bad feeling here. His father had been old-fashioned in a blanket sense, the quintessential marcher lord of yore; he had a growing suspicion he was about to step into a briar patch of old ways he was going to find it difficult to live within.

Not without being constantly pricked.

"Well," Kelso eventually said, "there's the matter of the cottages up Usway Burn, but your father was clear that that was for the tenants to fix. And if they didn't fix things by next spring, he was of a mind to demolish the cottages and plow the area under for more corn, corn prices being what they are."

"Actually," Falwell took up the tale, "your late father would have, indeed should have, reclaimed the land for corn this summer—both Kelso and I advised it. But I fear"—Falwell shook his head, primly condescending—"Miss Chesterton intervened. Her ideas are really *not* to be recommended—if the estate were to constantly step in in such matters we'd be forever fixing every little thing—but I believe your late father felt . . . constrained, given Miss Chesterton's position, to at least give the appearance of considering her views."

Kelso snorted. "Fond of her, he was. Only time in all the years I served him that he didn't do what was best for the estate."

"Your late father had a sound grasp of what was due the estate, and the tenants' obligations in that regard." Falwell smiled thinly. "I'm sure you won't wish to deviate from that successful, and indeed traditional, path."

Royce eyed the pair of them—and was perfectly sure he needed more information, and—damn it!—he'd need to consult his chatelaine to get it. "I can assure you that any decisions I make will be guided by what is best for the estate. As for these cottages"—he glanced from one man to the other—"I take it that's the only outstanding situation of that ilk?"

"As far as I'm aware, Y'r Grace." Kelso paused, then added, "If there are other matters requiring attention, they've yet to be brought to my notice."

Royce fought not to narrow his eyes; Kelso knew, or at least suspected, that there were other repairs or rectification needed, but the estate people weren't bringing them to him. He pushed back from the desk. "I won't be making any decisions until I've had time to acquaint myself with the details."

He rose; both men quickly came to their feet. "I'll send word when next I wish to see you."

There was enough steel in his tone to have both men murmur in acquiescence, bow low, and, without protest, head for the door, even though Falwell had earlier informed him that his father had met with them on the first Monday of every month. For Royce's money, that was far too infrequently. His father might not have needed more frequent meetings, but information was something he couldn't function, hated trying to function, without.

He stood staring at the door long after the pairs' retreating footsteps had faded. He'd hoped they would provide a bulwark between him and his chatelaine in all matters pertaining to the estate, yet after speaking with them for an hour, he wasn't prepared to accept their views as being the full story on any subject. Certainly not on the Usway Burn cottages.

He wondered what Minerva's views were—and why his father, who'd never doted on another in his life, much less changed his behavior to appease someone, had seen fit to, because of her ideas, stay his hand.

He'd have to ask her.

Seeing his plan to keep her at a distance crumble to dust, he couldn't hold back a growl. Swinging around the desk, he headed for the door. Jerking it open, he stepped out, startling Jeffers, who snapped to attention.

"If anyone should ask, I've gone riding."

"Yes, Your Grace."

Before eliciting his chatelaine's advice about the cottages, he'd test her advice about the horse.

She'd been right.

Incontestably right. Thundering over the gently rolling landscape, letting the gray stallion have his head, he felt the air rush past his face, felt an exhilaration he'd missed shooting down his veins, sensed all around him the hills and fields of home racing past at a madman's pace—and blessed her insightfulness.

His father had been an excellent horseman, but had never had the patience for a mount with a mind of its own. He, on the other hand, enjoyed the challenge of making a compact with a horse, persuading it that it was in its best interests to carry him—so that together they could fly before the wind.

Sword was now his. He would carry him whenever and wherever he wished simply for a chance to run like this. Without restriction, without restraint, flying over fences, leaping rocks and burns, careening between the hills on their way to the breeding fields.

On leaving the study, he'd stridden straight for the stables and asked Milbourne for the stallion. On hearing he intended to ride the recalcitrant beast, Milbourne and Henry had accompanied him to the paddock at the rear of the castle's holding fields. They'd watched him work the stallion, patient yet demanding; the pair had grinned delightedly when Sword had finally trotted all around the paddock with Royce on his back, then Royce had put the horse at the barred gate and sailed over to their cheers.

As he'd told Minerva, he hadn't kept a horse in London. When he'd visited friends in the country, he'd ridden mounts they'd provided, but none had been of the ilk of Sword—a heavy hunter fully up to his weight, strong, solid, yet fleet of foot. His thighs gripping the stallion's wide barrel, he rode primarily with hands and knees, the reins lying lax, there only if needed.

Despite his lack of experience, Sword had all but instantly picked up Royce's directions, almost certainly because Royce was strong enough to impress them on him clearly. But that took focused strength and concentration, an awareness of the horse and its inclination that few riders possessed; by the time the breeding fields came into view, Royce was no longer surprised that not even Milbourne had been able to ride the stallion.

Grasping the reins, he let Sword feel the bit, slowing him by degrees, until they were trotting.

He wanted to see Conqueror; he didn't know why. He wasn't a sentimental man, yet the memories stirred through riding his old mount's son had driven him there. Standing in his stirrups, he scanned the wide field, then heard a distant but soft trumpet; Sword answered with a snort and picked up his pace.

A group of horses emerged from a fold in the land, trotting, then galloping toward the fence.

Conqueror was in the lead. Much the same size as his son, yet heavier with age, the big gray slowed, ears flicking back and forth as he eyed Royce.

Halting Sword by the fence, Royce leaned over and held out his hand, a dried apple on his palm. "Here, boy."

Conqueror whinnied and came forward, lipped the apple from Royce's palm, chewed, then leaned over the rail and— ignoring his son—butted Royce.

He grinned, patting the great head. "Remember me, do you?"

Conqueror shook his head, mane dancing, then he noticed Sword's interest in the mares who'd followed him to the fence.

With a thunderous snort, Conqueror moved forward, pushing the mares away, herding them back.

Put in his place—second to Conqueror's harem—Royce sat and watched the small herd move away.

Settling back in the saddle, he patted Sword's sleek neck, then looked around. They were high on the rise of Castle Hill, north of the castle; looking down the valley, he could see the massive bulk of his home bathed in bright sunlight. It was barely noon.

Turning, he traced the valley northward, picking out the brown track of Clennell Street as it wound its way up through the hills. Temptation whispered.

He hadn't made any appointments for the afternoon.

The restlessness that had plagued him even from before he'd learned of his father's death, brought on, he suspected, by having to end Dalziel's reign while having no alternative life organized and waiting, then compounded by being thrust unprepared into the ducal harness, still roiled and churned inside, rising up at odd moments to distract and taunt him.

To unexpectedly undermine his natural Varisey confidence, and leave him uncertain.

Not a feeling he'd ever liked, and, at thirty-seven, one that irked. Mightily.

He glanced at Sword, then flicked the reins. "We've time enough to escape."

Urging the gray forward, he set course for the border and Scotland beyond.

* * *

He'd said he'd deal with O'Loughlin.

Royce found the farmhouse easily enough—the hills didn't change—but what had changed was the farmhouse itself. When last he'd seen it, it had been little more than a crofter's cottage with a lean-to barn alongside. Extended and refashioned, long and low, faced with rough-cut stone, thick timbers and with good slate on the roof, the house—now definitely a farmhouse—appeared warm and quietly prosperous, nestling back against a protecting rise, with a new, good-sized barn to one side.

A low stone wall circled the yard; as Royce walked the tiring Sword through the opening, a dog started barking.

Sword shifted, skittered.

The dog was chained inside the open barn door.

Drawing rein, Royce halted and sat patiently waiting for his calm, his lack of reaction, to sink in; once Sword had noticed and quieted, he dismounted.

Just as the farmhouse door opened and a mountain of a man strode out.

Royce met his half brother's blue eyes; other than their height and the width of their shoulders, the only physical resemblance lay in the set of their eyes, nose, and chin. Hamish's brown curls were starting to gray, but otherwise he seemed in his usual rude health. Royce smiled and stepped forward, holding out his hand. "Hamish."

His hand was engulfed, and then so was he, hauled into one of his half brother's bear hugs.

"Ro!" Hamish released him with a cuff to the back that—if he hadn't been expecting it—would have made Royce stagger. Grabbing his shoulders, Hamish searched his face. "Regardless of the reason, it's damned good to have you back."

"It's good to be back." Hamish released him and Royce glanced at the hills, at the view across their peaks to Windy Gyle. "I knew I missed it—I hadn't realized by how much."

"Och, well, you're back now, even if it took the old bastard dying to do it."

"The old bastard" was Hamish's way of referring to their father, not an insult, but a term of affection.

Royce's lips twisted. "Yes, well, he's gone, which is one reason I'm here. There are things—"

"To talk about—but after you've come in an' met Molly and the bairns." Hamish glanced at the barn, then pointed at a small face peeking out. "Hoi—Dickon! Come and see to this horse . . ." Hamish glanced at Sword, shifting nervously at the end of the rein.

Royce smiled. "I think I'd better help Dickon."

Hamish trailed alongside as Royce led Sword to the barn. "Isn't this the stallion that wouldn't let the old bastard ride him?"

"So I've heard. I didn't have a horse, so now he's mine."

"Aye, well, you always had the right touch with the head-strong ones."

Royce smiled at the boy waiting by the barn door; Hamish's blue eyes stared back at him. "This isn't one I've met before."

"Nah." Halting beside the lad, Hamish ruffled his hair. "This one came while you were away." He looked down at the boy, who was regarding Royce with wide eyes. "This here's the new duke, lad—you call him Wolverstone."

The boy's eyes switched to his father. "Not 'the old bastard'?"

Royce laughed. "No—but if there's no one else about but family, you can call me Uncle Ro."

While Royce and Dickon settled Sword in an empty stall, Hamish leaned on the wall and brought Royce up to date with the O'Loughlins. When Royce had last been at Wolverstone, Hamish, two years older than he, had had two young "bairns"; through the occasional letters they'd exchanged, Royce knew Hamish was now the proud father of four, Dickon at ten being the third.

Leaving the barn, they crossed the yard and entered the house; both Hamish and Royce had to duck beneath the low lintel.

"Hi, Moll!" Hamish led the way into a large parlor. "Come see who's here."

A short, rotund woman—more rotund than Royce remembered her—came bustling in from the kitchen beyond, wiping her hands on her apron. Bright blue eyes were set in a sweet round face beneath a shock of coppery red curls. "Really, Hamish, as if that's any way to summon me. Anyone would think you were a heathen—" Her eyes lit on Royce and she halted. Then she shrieked—making both men wince—and flung herself at Royce.

He caught her, laughed as she hugged him wildly.

"Royce, Royce!" She tried to shake him, an impossibility for her, then looked up into his face, beaming delightedly. "It's so *good* to see you back."

His own smile widened. "It's good to be back, Moll." He was increasingly realizing how true that was, how deep within him the feeling of coming home reached. Touched. "You're looking as fetching as ever. And you've expanded the family since last I was here."

"Och, aye." Molly sent a mock-glare Hamish's way. "Himself got busy, you might say." Face softening, she looked at Royce. "You'll stay to lunch, won't you?"

He did. There was thick soup, mutton stew, and bread, followed by cheese and ale. He sat at the long table in the warm kitchen, redolent with succulent aromas and filled with constant babble, and marveled at Hamish's children.

Heather, the eldest, a buxom seventeen, had been a tiny tot when he'd last seen her, while Robert, sixteen and bidding fair to be as large as Hamish, had been a babe in arms, with Molly barely recovered from the birthing. Dickon was next in age, then came Georgia, who at seven looked very like Molly and seemed equally feisty.

As they'd taken their seats, the four had regarded him with wide eyes, as if drinking him in with their confident candid gazes—a combination of Hamish's shrewdness and Molly's openheartedness—then Molly had set the soup on the table and their attention had shifted; they'd thereafter blithely treated him as family, as "Uncle Ro."

Listening to their chatter, to Robert reporting to Hamish on the sheep in some field, and Heather telling Molly about a chicken gone broody, Royce couldn't help but register how comfortable he felt with them. In contrast, he'd be hard-pressed to name his legitimate sisters' offspring.

When his father had banished him from all Wolverstone domains and banned all communication with him, his sisters had fallen in with his father's wishes. Even though all three had been married and mistresses of their own establishments, they'd made no move to stay in touch, not even by letter. If they had, he would have at least corresponded, because he'd always known this day would come—when he was the head of the family, and in charge of the dukedom's coffers, on which his sisters still drew, and, through them, their children did, too.

Like everyone else, his sisters had assumed the situation wouldn't last long. Certainly not for sixteen years.

He'd kept a list of his nephews and nieces culled from birth notices in the *Gazette*, but in the rush had left it in London; he hoped Handley would remember it.

"But when did you get to the castle?" Molly fixed her bright gaze on him.

"Yesterday morning."

"Aye, well, I'm sure Miss Chesterton will have everything in hand."

He noted Molly's approval. "You know her?"

"She comes up here to discuss things with Hamish now and then. Always takes tea with us—she's a proper lady in every way. I imagine she'll have everything running smoothly as usual." Molly fixed her eyes on his face. "Have you decided when the funeral will be?"

"Friday next week." He glanced at Hamish. "Given the ton's inevitable interest, that was the earliest." He paused, then asked, "Will you come?"

"Moll and I will come to the church." Hamish exchanged

a glance with Molly, who nodded, then he looked at Royce and grinned. "But you'll have to manage on your own at the wake."

Royce sighed. "I had hoped presenting them with a Scottish giant might distract them. Now I'll have to think of something else."

"Nah—I should think you yourself, the prodigal son returned, will be distraction enough."

"That," Royce said, "was my point."

Hamish chortled and they let the matter slide; Royce steered the conversation to local farming conditions and the upcoming harvest. Hamish had his pride, something Royce respected; his half brother had never set foot inside the castle.

As he'd expected, on the subject of farming he got more pertinent information from Hamish than from his own steward and agent; the farms in the area were scraping by, but were not exactly thriving.

Hamish himself was faring rather better. He held his lands freehold; his mother had been the only daughter of a freeholder. She'd married later in life, and Hamish had been her only child. He'd inherited the farm from her, and with the stipend his father had settled on him, had had the capital to expand and improve his stock; he was now a well-established sheep farmer.

At the end of the meal, Royce thanked Molly, bussed her cheek, then, following Hamish, snagged an apple from the bowl on the dresser, and they took their talk outside.

They sat on the stone wall, feet dangling, and looked across the hills. "Your stipend continues to your death, but you knew that." Royce took a bite of his apple; it crunched sharply.

"Aye." Hamish settled beside him. "So how did he die?"

"Minerva Chesterton was with him." Royce related what she'd told him.

"Have you managed to contact all the others?"

"Minerva's written to the girls—they're all on one or other

of the estates. That's eleven of the fifteen." His father had
sired fifteen illegitimate children on maids, tavern wenches,
farm and village lasses; for some reason he'd always drawn
his lovers from the local lower orders. "The other three men
are in the navy—I'll write to them. Not that his death materially changes anything."

"Aye, still, they'll need to know." Hamish eyed him for a
moment, then asked, "So, are you going to be like him?"

Tossing away his apple core, Royce slanted him a narrow-
eyed glance. "In what way?"

Unabashed, Hamish grinned. "In exactly the way you
thought I meant. Are you going to have every farmer in the
region locking up his daughters?"

Royce snorted. "Definitely not my style."

"Aye, well." Hamish tugged at one earlobe. "Never was
mine, either." For a moment they dwelled on their sire's
sexual proclivities, then Hamish went on, "It was almost as
if he saw himself as one of the old marcher lords, royal per-
quisites and all. Within his domains, he saw, he wanted, he
took—not, as I heard it, that any of the lasses resisted all that
much. M' mother certainly didn't. Told me she never regretted it—her time with him."

Royce smiled. "She was talking about you, you daft
beggar. If she hadn't spent that time with him, she wouldn't
have had you."

"P'rhaps. But even in her last years, she used to get a wist-
ful look in her eye whenever she spoke of him."

Another moment passed, then Royce said, "At least he
looked after them."

Hamish nodded.

They sat for a time, drinking in the ever-changing views,
the play of light over the hills and valleys, the shifting hues
as the sun edged to the west, then Hamish stirred and looked
at Royce. "So, will you be mostly at the castle, then, or will
London and the sassenach ladies lure you south?"

"No. In that respect I'll be following in his footsteps. I'll
live at the castle except when duty to the estate, family or

the Lords calls me south." He frowned. "Speaking of living here, what have you heard of the castle's agent, Kelso, or the steward, Falwell?"

Hamish shrugged. "They've been your father's eyes and ears for decades. Both are . . . well, not quite local anymore. They live in Harbottle, not on the estate, which causes some difficulty. Both were born on the estate, but moved to the town years ago, and for some reason your father didn't object—suspect he thought they'd still know the land. Not something you forget all that easily, after all."

"No, but things, conditions, change. Attitudes change, too."

"Och, well, you'll not get those two changing anything in a hurry. Right set in their ways—which I always supposed was why they suited the old bastard so well. Right set in his ways, he was."

"Indeed." After a moment of reflecting on his sire's resistance to change, and how deep that had gone, Royce admitted, "I might have to replace them—retire them—both, but I won't know until I've had a chance to get out and about and assess matters for myself."

"If it's information on the estate you need, your chatelaine can fill you in. Minerva's the one everyone goes to if there's a problem. Most have grown weary—in fact, *wary*—of going to Falwell or Kelso. Like as not, if they make a complaint, either nothing gets done, or the wrong thing—something worse that wasn't intended—happens."

Royce leveled a direct look at Hamish. "That doesn't sound good."

It was a question, one Hamish understood. "Aye, well, you'd written that you'd be giving up that commission of yours, and I knew you'd come home—didn't think there was any need to write and tell you how things were not going quite so well. I knew you'd see it once you got back, and Minerva Chesterton was doing well enough holding the fort." He shrugged his massive shoulders; they both looked south, over the peaks toward Wolverstone. "It might be not the done thing for me to say this, but perhaps it's as well that he's gone. Now you've got the reins, and it's more than time for a new broom."

Royce would have smiled at the mixed metaphor, but what they were discussing was too serious. He stared in the direction in which his responsibilities, growing weightier by the hour, lay, then he slid from the wall. "I should go."

Hamish paced alongside as he went to the barn and saddled Sword, then swung up to the saddle and walked the big gray into the yard.

Halting, he held out his hand.

Hamish clasped it. "We'll see you Friday at the church. If you get caught having to make a decision about something on the estate, you can rely on Minerva Chesterton's opinion. People trust her, and respect her judgment—whatever she advises will be accepted by your tenants and workers."

Royce nodded; inwardly he grimaced. "That's what I thought."

What he'd feared.

He saluted, then flicked the reins, and set Sword for Clennell Street and Wolverstone.

Home.

He'd torn himself away from the peace of the hills . . . only to discover when he rode into the castle stables that his sisters—all three of them, together with their husbands—had arrived.

Jaw set, he stalked toward the house; his sisters could wait—he needed to see Minerva.

Hamish's confirmation that she was, indeed, the current champion of the estate's well-being left him with little choice. He was going to have to rely on her, spend hours gleaning everything he could about the estate from her, ride out with her so she could show him what was going on—in short, spend far more time with her than he wished.

Than was wise.

Entering the house by the side door, he heard a commotion

ahead, filling the cavernous front hall, and steeled himself. Felt his temper ratchet up another notch.

His elder sisters, Margaret, Countess of Orkney, and Aurelia, Countess of Morpeth, had agreed, implicitly if not explicitly, with his father over his erstwhile occupation; they'd supported his banishment. But he'd never got on well with either of them; at best he tolerated them, and they ignored him.

He was, always had been, much closer to his younger sister, Susannah, Viscountess Darby. She hadn't agreed or disagreed with his banishment; no one had asked her, no one would have listened to her, so she'd wisely kept her mouth shut. He hadn't been surprised about that. What had surprised, even hurt a trifle, was that she'd never sought to contact him over the past sixteen years.

Then again, Susannah was fickle; he'd known that even when they'd been much younger.

Nearing the hall, he changed his stride, letting his boot heels strike the floor. The instant he stepped onto the marble tiles of the hall, his footsteps rang out, effectively silencing the clamor.

Silks swooshed as his sisters whirled to face him. They looked like birds of prey in their weeds, their veils thrown back over their dark hair.

He paused, studying them with an impersonal curiosity. They'd aged; Margaret was forty-two, a tall, commanding dark-haired despot with lines starting to score her cheeks and brow. Aurelia, forty-one, was shorter, fairer, brown-haired, and from the set of her lips looked to have grown even more severely disapproving with the years. Susannah . . . had made a better fist of growing older; she was thirty-three, four years younger than Royce, but her dark hair was up in a confection of curls, and her gown, although regulation black, was stylishly fashionable. From a distance, she might pass for an adult daughter of either of her elder sisters.

Imagining how well that thought would go down, he looked

back at the older two, and realized they were struggling with the fraught question of how to address him now he was the duke, and no longer simply their younger brother.

Margaret drew in a huge breath, breasts rising portentously, then swept forward. "There you are, Royce!" Her chiding tone made it clear he should have been dutifully awaiting their arrival. She raised a hand as she neared—intending to grip his arm and shake it, as had been her habit when trying to make him do something. "I—"

She broke off—because he'd caught her eye. Breath strangling in her throat, she halted, hand in the air, faintly shocked.

Aurelia bobbed a curtsy—a perfunctory one not nearly deep enough—and came forward more cautiously. "A dreadful business. It's been a very great shock."

No "How are you?" No "How have you been these last sixteen years?"

"Of course, it's been a shock." Susannah strolled up. She met his eyes. "And I daresay it was an even bigger shock for you, all things considered." Reaching him, she smiled, stretched up, and kissed his cheek. "Welcome home."

That, at least, had been genuine. He nodded to her. "Thank you."

From the corner of his eye, he saw the other two exchange an irritated glance. He scanned the sea of footmen sorting through the piles of boxes and trunks, preparing to cart them upstairs, saw Retford look his way, but he was searching for Minerva.

He found her in the center of the melee, talking to his brothers-in-law. She met his eyes; the men turned, saw him looking their way, and came to greet him.

With an easy smile, Peter, Earl of Orkney, held out his hand. "Royce. It's good to see you again."

Stepping forward, he grasped Peter's hand, responding equally smoothly, then stepped still farther from his sisters to shake hands with David, Aurelia's husband, and lastly to exchange a pleasant greeting with Hubert, Viscount Darby—

wondering, as he always did when faced with Hubert, why Susannah had married the faintly bumbling, ineffably good-natured fop. It could only have been for his fortune. That, and his willingness to allow Susannah to do whatever she pleased.

His maneuvering had brought him to Minerva's side. He caught her eye. "I take it everyone's rooms are organized?"

"Yes." She glanced at Retford, who nodded. "Everything's in hand."

"Excellent." He looked at his brothers-in-law. "If you'll excuse us, my chatelaine and I have estate business to attend to."

He nodded to them; they inclined their heads in reply, turning away.

But before he could turn and head up the stairs, Margaret stepped forward. "But we've only just got here!"

He met her gaze. "Indeed. No doubt you'll need to rest and refresh yourselves. I'll see you at dinner."

With that, he turned and climbed the stairs, ignoring Margaret's gasp of outrage. An instant later, he heard Minerva's slippers pattering up behind him and slowed; one glance at her face as she drew level was enough to tell him she disapproved of his brusqueness.

Wisely, she said nothing.

But on reaching the gallery, she halted a footman heading downstairs. "Tell Retford to offer afternoon tea to the ladies, and the gentlemen, too, if they wish, in the drawing room. Or if the gentlemen prefer, there are spirits in the library."

"Yes, ma'am." With a bow, the footman hurried on.

She turned to him, eyes narrow, lips compressed. "Your sisters are going to be trying enough as it is—you don't need to goad them."

"*Me?* Goad *them*?"

"I know they're irritating, but they always are. You used to be much better at ignoring them."

He reached the study door and opened it. "That was before I was Wolverstone."

Minerva frowned as she followed him into the study, leaving it to Jeffers, who'd trailed behind them upstairs, to close the door. "I suppose that's true. Margaret will undoubtedly try to manage you."

Dropping into the chair behind the desk, he flashed her a smile that was all teeth. "She's welcome to try. She won't succeed."

She sank into her usual chair. "I suspect she's guessed that."

"One can only hope." He fixed her with a gaze that, despite its distractingly rich darkness, was surprisingly sharp. "Tell me about the cottages up Usway Burn."

"Ah—your meeting with Falwell and Kelso. Did they tell you the cottages should be demolished?"

When he nodded, she drew breath, then hesitated.

His lips thinned. "Minerva, I don't need you to be polite, or politic, and certainly not self-effacing. I need you to tell me the truth, your conclusions, including your suspicions— and most especially your thoughts on how the estate people feel and think." He hesitated, then went on, "I've already realized I can't rely on Falwell or Kelso. I plan to retire them—pension them off with thanks—as soon as I can find suitable replacements."

She exhaled. "That's . . . welcome news. Even your father had realized their advice wasn't getting him the results he wanted."

"I assume that's why he held off doing as they suggested over these cottages?" When she nodded, he ordered, "Tell me—from the beginning."

"I'm not sure when the problems started—more than three years ago, at least. I didn't start working alongside your father until after your mother died, so my knowledge starts from then." She drew breath. "I suspect Kelso, backed by Falwell, had decided, more than three years ago, that old Macgregor and his sons—they hold the Usway Burn farm and live in the cottages—were more trouble than they're worth, and that letting the cottages fall down, then plowing them under, thus increasing the acreage, then letting that land to other tenants to farm, was a preferable option to repairing the cottages."

"You disagree." No question; he steepled his fingers before his face, his dark eyes never moving from hers.

She nodded. "The Macgregors have farmed that land since before the Conquest—as far as I can make out, literally. Evicting them will cause a lot of disquiet on the estate—along the lines of, if it could happen to them, who's safe? That's not something we need in these already uncertain times. In addition, the issues aren't as straightforward as Falwell makes out. Under the tenancy agreement, repair of damage from the wear and tear of use falls to the tenant, but structural work, repairs to the fabric needed to offset the effects of time and weather—that's arguably the responsibility of the estate.

"*However*, in one respect Falwell and Kelso are correct—the estate can't be seen to be repairing the first sort of damage, wear and tear. That would land us with requests from every tenant for the same consideration—but with the state the Usway Burn cottages are now in, you can't repair the fabric without simultaneously repairing the wear and tear."

"So what do you suggest?"

"The Macgregors and Kelso don't get on, never have, hence the present situation. But the Macgregors, if approached correctly, are neither unreasonable nor intractable. The situation, as it is now, is that the cottages urgently need wholesale repair, and the Macgregors want to keep farming that land. I'd suggest a compromise—some system whereby both the estate and the Macgregors contribute to the outcome, and subsequently reap the benefits."

He studied her in silence. She waited, not the least discomfited by his scrutiny. Rather more distracted by the allure that didn't decrease even when, as with his sisters, he was being difficult. She'd always found the underlying danger in him fascinating—the sense of dealing with some being who was not, quite, safe. Not domesticated, nowhere near as civilized as he appeared.

The real him lurked beneath his elegant exterior—there in

his eyes, in the set of his lips, in the disguised strength in his long-fingered hands.

"Correct me if I err"—his voice was a low, hypnotic purr—"but any such collaborative effort would step beyond the bounds of what I recall are the tenancy agreements used at Wolverstone."

She dragged in air past the constriction banding her lungs. "The agreements would need to be renegotiated and re-drawn. Frankly, they need to be, to better reflect the realities of today."

"Did my father agree?"

She wished she could lie. "No. He was, as you know, very set in his ways. More, he was inimical to change." After a moment, she added, "That was why he put off making any decision about the cottages. He knew that evicting the Macgregors and pulling down the cottages was the wrong thing to do, but he couldn't bring himself to resolve the issue by altering tradition."

One black brow quirked. "The tradition in question under-pins the estate's financial viability."

"Which would only be strengthened by getting more equi-table agreements in place, ones which encourage tenants to invest in their holdings, to make improvements themselves, rather than leaving everything to the landowner—which on large estates like Wolverstone usually means nothing gets done, and land and buildings slowly decay, as in this in-stance."

Another silence ensued, then he looked down. Absent-mindedly tapped one long finger on the blotter. "This is not a decision to be lightly made."

She hesitated, then said, "No, but it must be made soon."

Without raising his head, he glanced up at her. "You stopped my father from making a decision, didn't you?"

Holding his dark gaze, she debated what to say . . . but he knew the truth; his tone said as much. "I made sure he remembered the predictable outcomes of agreeing with Fal-well and Kelso."

Both his brows rose, leaving her wondering whether he'd been as sure as his tone had suggested, or whether she'd been led to reveal something he hadn't known.

He looked down at his hand, fingers now spread on the blotter. "I'll need to see these cottages—"

A tap on the door interrupted him. He frowned and looked up. "Come."

Retford entered. "Your Grace, Mr. Collier, from Collier, Collier, and Whitticombe, has arrived. He's awaiting your pleasure in the hall. He wished me to inform you he was entirely at your service."

Royce inwardly grimaced. He glanced at his chatelaine, who was revealing unexpected depths of strength and determination. She'd been able to, not manipulate, but influence his father . . . which left him uneasy. Not that he imagined she'd acted from any but the purest of motives; her arguments were driven by her views of what was best for Wolverstone and its people. But the fact she'd prevailed against his father's blustering, often bullying will—no matter how else he'd aged, that wouldn't have changed—combined with his own continuing, indeed escalating obsession with her, all compounded by his need to rely on her, to keep her near and interact with her daily . . .

His sisters, by comparison, were a minor irritation.

Minerva was . . . a serious problem.

Especially as everything she said, everything she urged, everything she was, appealed to him—not the cold, calm, calculating, and risk-averse duke, but the other side of him—the side that rode young stallions just broken to the saddle over hill and dale at a madman's pace.

The side that was neither cold, nor risk-averse.

He didn't know what to do with her, how he could safely manage her.

He glanced at the clock on a bureau by the wall, then looked at Retford. "Show Collier up."

Retford bowed and withdrew.

Royce looked at Minerva. "It's nearly time to dress for

dinner. I'll see Collier, and arrange for him to read the will after dinner. If you can organize with Jeffers to show him to a room, and to have him fed . . . ?"

"Yes, of course." She rose, met his gaze as he came to his feet. "I'll see you at dinner."

She turned and walked to the door; Royce watched while she opened it, then went out, then he exhaled and sank back into his chair.

Dinner was consumed in a civil but restrained atmosphere. Margaret and Aurelia had decided to be careful; both avoided subjects likely to irritate him, and, in the main, held their tongues.

Susannah made up for their silence by relating a number of the latest on-dits, censored in deference to their father's death. Nevertheless, she added a welcome touch of liveliness to which his brothers-in-law responded with easy good humor.

They dined in the family dining room. Although much smaller than the one in the main dining salon, the table still sat fourteen; with only eight of them spread along the board, there remained plenty of space between each place, further assisting Royce's hold on his temper.

The meal, the first he'd shared with his sisters for sixteen years, passed better than he'd hoped. As the covers were drawn, he announced that the reading of the will would take place in the library.

Margaret frowned. "The drawing room would be more convenient."

He raised his brows, set his napkin beside his plate. "If you wish you may repair to the drawing room. I, however, am going to the library."

She compressed her lips, but rose and followed.

Collier, a neat individual in his late fifties, bespectacled, brushed, and burnished, was waiting, a trifle nervous, but once they'd settled on the chaise and chairs, he cleared his throat, and started to read. His diction was clear and precise enough for everyone to hear as he read through clause after clause.

There were no surprises. The dukedom in its entirety, entailed and private property and all invested funds, was left to Royce; aside from minor bequests and annuities, some new, others already in place, it was his to do with as he pleased.

Margaret and Aurelia sat silently throughout. Their handsome annuities were confirmed, but not increased; Minerva doubted they'd expected anything else.

When Collier finished, and had asked if there were any questions, and received none, she rose from the straight-backed chair she'd occupied and asked Margaret if she would like to repair to the drawing room for tea.

Margaret thought, then shook her head. "No, thank you, dear. I think I'll retire . . ." She glanced at Aurelia. "Perhaps Aurelia and I could have tea in my room?"

Aurelia nodded. "What with the travel and this sad business, I'm greatly fatigued."

"Yes, of course. I'll have them send up a tray." Minerva turned to Susannah.

Who smiled lightly. "I believe I'll retire, too, but I don't want tea." She paused as her elder sisters rose, then, arm in arm, passed on their way to the door, then she turned back to Minerva. "When are the rest of the family arriving?"

"Your aunts and uncles are expected tomorrow, and the rest will no doubt follow."

"Good. If I'm to be trapped here with Margaret and Aurelia, I'm going to need company." Susannah glanced around, then sighed. "I'm off. I'll see you tomorrow."

Minerva spoke to Hubert, who asked for a tisane to be sent to his room, then retreated. Peter and David had helped themselves to whisky from the tantalus, while Royce was talking with Collier by the desk. Leaving them all to their own devices, she left to order the tea tray and the tisane.

That done, she headed back to the library.

Peter and David passed her in the corridor; they exchanged good nights and continued on.

She hesitated outside the library door. She hadn't seen Collier leave. She doubted Royce needed rescuing, yet she needed to ascertain if he required anything further from her that night. Turning the knob, she opened the door and stepped quietly inside.

The glow from the desk lamps and those by the chaise didn't reach as far as the door. She halted in the shadows. Royce was still speaking with Collier, both standing in the space between the big desk and the window behind it, looking out at the night as they conversed.

She drew nearer, quietly, not wishing to intrude.

And heard Royce ask Collier for his opinion on the leasing arrangements for tied cottages.

"The foundation of the nation, Your Grace. All the great estates rely on the system—it's been proven for generations, and is, legally speaking, solid and dependable."

"I have a situation," Royce said, "where it's been suggested that some modification of the traditional form of lease might prove beneficial to all concerned."

"Don't be tempted, Your Grace. There's much talk these days of altering traditional ways, but that's a dangerous, potentially destructive road."

"So your considered advice would be to leave matters as they are, and adhere to the standard, age-old form?"

Minerva stepped sideways into the shadows some way behind Royce's back. She wanted to hear this, preferably without calling attention to her presence.

"Indeed, Your Grace. If I may make so bold"—Collier puffed out his chest—"you could not do better than to follow your late father's lead in all such matters. He was a stickler for the legal straight and narrow, and preserved and grew the dukedom significantly over his tenure. He was shrewd and wise, and never one for tampering with what worked well. My counsel would be that whenever any such questions arise, your best tack would be to ask yourself what your sire would have done, and do precisely that. Model yourself upon him, and all will go well—it's what he would have wished."

Hands clasped behind his back, Royce inclined his head. "Thank you for your advice, Collier. I believe you've already been given a room—if you encounter any difficulty relocating it, do ask one of the footmen."

"Indeed, Your Grace." Collier bowed low. "I wish you a good night."

Royce nodded. He waited until Collier had closed the door behind him, before saying, "You heard?"

He knew she was there, behind him in the shadows. He'd known the instant she'd walked into the room.

"Yes, I heard."

"And?" He made no move to turn from the window and the view of the dark night outside.

Drifting closer to the desk, Minerva drew a tight breath, then stated, "He's wrong."

"Oh?"

"Your father didn't wish you to be like him."

He stilled, but didn't turn around. After a moment, he asked, voice quiet, yet intense, "What do you mean?"

"In his last moments, when I was with him here, in the library, he gave me a message for you. I've been waiting for the right moment to tell you, so you would understand what he meant."

"Tell me now." A harsh demand.

"He said: 'Tell Royce not to make the same mistakes I made.'"

A long silence ensued, then he asked, voice soft, quietly deadly, "And what, in your opinion, am I to understand by that?"

She swallowed. "He was speaking in the most general terms. The widest and broadest terms. He knew he was dying, and that was the one thing he felt he had to say to you."

"And you believe he wished me to use that as a guide in dealing with the cottages?"

"I can't say that—that's for you to decide, to interpret. I can only tell you what he said that day."

She waited. His fingers had clenched, each hand gripping

the other tightly. Even from where she stood, she could feel the dangerous energy of his temper, eddies swirling and lashing, a tempest coalescing around him.

She felt an insane urge to go closer, to raise a hand and lay it on his arm, on muscles that would be tight and tensed, more iron than steel beneath her palm. To try, if she could, to soothe, to drain some of that restless energy, to bring him some release, some peace, some surcease.

"Leave me." His tone was flat, almost grating.

Even though he couldn't see, she inclined her head, then turned and walked—calmly, steadily—to the door.

Her hand was on the knob when he asked, "Is that all he said?"

She glanced back. He hadn't moved from his stance before the window. "That was all he told me to tell you. 'Tell Royce not to make the same mistakes I made.' Those, exactly those, were his last words."

When he said nothing more, she opened the door, went out, and shut it behind her.

Four

oyce strode into the breakfast parlor early the next morning, and trapped his chatelaine just as she finished her tea.

Eyes widening, fixed on him, she lowered her cup; without taking her gaze from him, she set it back on its saucer.

Her instincts were excellent. He raked her with his gaze. "Good—you're dressed for riding." Retford had told him she would be when he'd breakfasted even earlier. "You can show me these cottages."

She raised her brows, considered him for a moment, then nodded. "All right." Dropping her napkin beside her plate, she rose, picked up her riding gloves and crop, and calmly joined him.

Accepting his challenge.

Loins girded, jaw clenched, he suffered while, with her gliding beside him, he stalked to the west courtyard. He'd known his sisters would breakfast in their rooms, while their husbands would come down fashionably later, allowing him to kidnap her without having to deal with any of them.

He'd ordered their horses to be saddled. He led the way out of the house; as they crossed the courtyard toward the stables, he glanced at Minerva as, apparently unperturbed, she walked alongside. He'd steeled himself to deflect any comment about their exchange last night, but she'd yet to make one. To press her point that he didn't have to be like his father in managing the dukedom.

That he should break with tradition and do what he felt was right.

Just as he had sixteen years ago.

Regardless of her silence, her opinion reached him clearly. He felt as if she were manipulating him.

They reached the stable yard and found Henry holding a dancing Sword while Milbourne waited with her horse, a bay gelding, by the mounting block.

On her way to Milbourne, she glanced at the restless gray. "I see you tamed him."

Taking the reins from Henry, Royce planted one boot in the stirrup and swung his leg over the broad back. "Yes."

Just as he'd like to tame her.

Teeth gritted, he gathered the reins, holding Sword in as he watched her settle in her sidesaddle. Then she nodded her thanks to Milbourne, lifted the reins, and trotted forward.

He met her eyes, tipped his head toward the hills. "Lead the way."

She did, at a pace that took some of the edge from his temper. She was an excellent horsewoman, with an excellent seat. Once he'd convinced himself she wasn't likely to come to grief, he found somewhere else to fix his gaze. She led him over the bridge, then across the fields, jumping low stone walls as they headed north of the village. Sword kept pace easily; he had to rein the gray in to keep him from taking the lead.

But once they reached the track that meandered along the banks of Usway Burn, a tributary of the Coquet, they slowed, letting the horses find their own pace along the rocky and uneven ground. Less experienced than the gelding, Sword seemed content to follow in his wake. The track was barely wide enough for a farm cart; they followed its ruts up into the hills.

The cottages stood halfway along the burn, where the valley widened into reasonable-sized meadows. It was a small but fertile holding. As Royce recalled, it had always been prosperous. It was one of the few acreages on the estate given over to corn. With the uncertainty in supply of that staple, and the consequent increase in price, he could understand Kelso's and Falwell's push to increase the acreage, but . . . the estate had always grown enough corn to feed its people; that hadn't changed. They didn't need to grow more.

What they did need was to keep farmers like the Macgregors, who knew the soil they tilled, on the estate, working the land.

Three cottages—one large, two smaller—had been built in the lee of a west-facing hill. They splashed across the burn at a rough ford. As they neared the buildings, the door of the largest opened; an old man, bent and weathered, came out. Leaning on a stout walking stick, he watched without expression as Royce drew rein and dismounted.

Kicking free of her stirrups, Minerva slid to the ground; reins in one hand, she saluted the old man. "Good morning, Macgregor. His Grace has come to take a look at the cottages."

Macgregor inclined his head politely to her. As she led her bay to a nearby fence, she reached for Royce's reins, and he handed them over.

He walked forward, halting before Macgregor. Old eyes the color of stormy skies held his gaze with a calmness, a rooted certainty, that only age could bring.

Royce knew his father would have waited, silent and intimidating, for an acknowledgment of his station, then possibly nodded curtly before demanding Macgregor show him the cottages.

He offered his hand. "Macgregor."

The old eyes blinked wide. Macgregor dropped his gaze to Royce's hand; after an instant's hesitation, he shifted his grip on the walking stick's knobbed head, and grasped the proffered hand in a surprisingly strong grip.

Macgregor looked up as their hands parted. "Welcome home, Y'r Grace. And it's right glad I am to see you."

"I remember you—frankly, I'm amazed you're still here."

"Aye, well, some of us grow older than others. And I remember you, too—used to see you riding wild over yon hills."

"I fear my days of wildness are past."

Macgregor made a sound denoting abject disbelief.

Royce glanced at the buildings. "I understand there's a problem with these cottages."

Minerva found herself trailing the pair, entirely redundant, as Macgregor, famed crustiness in abeyance, showed Royce around, pointing out the gaps in the walls, and where the rafters and roof beams no longer met.

Exiting the larger middle cottage, they were crossing to the smaller one to the left when she heard distant hoofbeats. She halted in the yard. Royce would have heard the horse approaching, but he didn't take his attention from Macgregor; the pair went into the smaller cottage. Raising a hand to shade her eyes, she waited in the yard.

Macgregor's oldest son, Sean, appeared, riding one of their workhorses. He slowed, halted just inside the yard, and dismounted, leaving the traces he'd used as reins dragging. He hurried to Minerva. "The rest of the lads and me are working the upper fields. We saw you come riding in." He looked at the smaller cottage. "Is that the new duke in there with Da?"

"Yes, but—" Before she could assure him that his father and his duke were managing perfectly well, Royce led the way out of the tiny cottage, ducking low to miss the lintel. He glanced back as Macgregor followed, then came on.

"This is Sean Macgregor, Macgregor's oldest son. Sean, Wolverstone." Minerva hid a grin at Sean's astonishment when Royce nodded and, apparently without thought, offered his hand.

After a stunned instant, Sean quickly gripped it and shook.

Releasing him, Royce turned to the last cottage. "I should look at them all while I'm here."

"Aye." Macgregor stumped past him. "Come along, then. Not much different to the others, but there's a crooked corner in this one."

He beckoned Royce to follow, and he did.

Sean stood, mouth a-cock, and watched as Royce ducked through the cottage door in his father's wake. After a moment, he said, "He's really looking."

"Indeed. And when he comes out, I suspect he'll want to discuss what can be done." Minerva looked at Sean. "Can you speak for your brothers?"

He shifted his gaze to her face, nodded. "Aye."

"In that case, I suggest we wait here."

Her prophecy proved correct. When Royce emerged from the dimness of the third cottage, his lips were set in a determined line. He met her gaze, then turned to Macgregor, who had followed him into the mild sunshine. "Let's talk."

They—Royce, Minerva, Macgregor, and Sean—sat at the deal table in the big cottage and thrashed out an arrangement that satisfied them all. While not condoning Kelso's and Falwell's tack, Royce made it clear that the precedent that would be set if the cottages were repaired under the current lease was not one he would countenance; instead, he offered to refashion the lease. It took them an hour to agree on the basic principles; deciding how to get the work done took mere minutes.

Somewhat to her surprise, Royce took charge. "Your lads need to give their time to the harvest first. Once that's in, they can help with the building. You"—he looked at Macgregor—"will supervise. It'll be up to you to make sure the work is done as it should be. I'll come up with Hancock"—he glanced at Minerva—"I assume he's still the castle builder?" When she nodded, he went on, "I'll bring him here, and show him what we need done. We have less than three months before the first snow—I want all three cottages leveled and three new ones completed before winter sets in."

Macgregor blinked; Sean still looked stunned.

When they left the cottage, Minerva was beaming. So, too,

were Macgregor and Sean. Royce, in contrast, had his inscrutable mask on.

She hurried to get her horse, Rangonel. There was a convenient log by the fence for a mounting block; scrambling into her saddle, she settled her skirts.

After shaking hands with the Macgregors, Royce cast her a glance, then retrieved Sword and mounted. She urged Rangonel alongside as he turned down the track.

At the last, she waved to the Macgregors. Still beaming, they waved back. Facing forward, she glanced at Royce. "Am I allowed to say I'm impressed?"

He grunted.

Smiling, she followed him back to the castle.

"Damn it!" With the sounds of a London evening—the rattle of wheels, the clop of hooves, the raucous cries of jarveys as they tacked down fashionable Jermyn Street—filling his ears, he read the short note again, then reached for the brandy his man had fortuitously just set on the table by his elbow.

He took a long swallow, read the note again, then tossed it on the table. "The duke's dead. I'll have to go north to attend his funeral."

There was no help for it; if he didn't appear, his absence would be noted. But he was far from thrilled by the prospect. Until that moment, his survival plan had revolved around total and complete avoidance, but a ducal funeral in the family eradicated that option.

The duke was dead. More to the point, his nemesis was now the tenth Duke of Wolverstone.

It would have happened sometime, but why the hell *now*? Royce had barely shaken the dust of Whitehall from his elegantly shod heels—he certainly wouldn't have forgotten the one traitor he'd failed to bring to justice.

He swore, let his head fall back against the chair. He'd always assumed time—the simple passage of it—would be his salvation. That it would dull Royce's memories, his drive, distract him with other things.

Then again . . .

Straightening, he took another sip of brandy. Perhaps having a dukedom to manage—one unexpectedly thrust upon him immediately following an exile of sixteen years—was precisely the distraction Royce needed to drag and hold his attention from his past.

Royce had always had power; his inheriting the title changed little in that regard.

Perhaps this really was for the best?

Time, as ever, would tell, but, unexpectedly, that time was here.

He thought, considered; in the end he had no choice.

"Smith! Pack my bags. I have to go to Wolverstone."

In the breakfast parlor the following morning, Royce was enjoying his second cup of coffee and idly scanning the latest news sheet when Margaret and Aurelia walked in.

They were gowned, coiffed. With vague smiles in his direction, they headed for the sideboard.

He glanced at the clock on the mantelpiece, confirming it was early, not precisely the crack of dawn, yet for them . . .

His cynicism grew as they came to the table, plates in hand. He was at the head of the table; leaving one place empty to either side of him, Margaret sat on his left, Aurelia on his right.

He took another sip of coffee, and kept his attention on the news sheet, certain he'd learn what they wanted sooner rather than later.

His father's four sisters and their husbands, and his mother's brothers and their wives, together with various cousins, had started arriving yesterday; the influx would continue for several days. And once the family was in residence, the connections and friends invited to stay at the castle for the funeral would start to roll in; his staff would be busy for the next week.

Luckily, the keep itself was reserved for immediate family; not even his paternal aunts had rooms in the central wing.

This breakfast parlor, too, on the ground floor of the keep, was family only, giving him a modicum of privacy, an area of relative calm in the center of the storm.

Margaret and Aurelia sipped their tea and nibbled slices of dry toast. They chatted about their children, their intention presumably to inform him of the existence of his nephews and nieces. He studiously kept his gaze on the news sheet. Eventually his sisters accepted that, after sixteen years of not knowing, he was unlikely to develop an interest in that direction overnight.

Even without looking, he sensed the glance they exchanged, heard Margaret draw in one of her portentous breaths.

His chatelaine breezed in. "Good morning, Margaret, Aurelia." Her tone suggested she was surprised to find them down so early.

Her entrance threw his sisters off-balance; they murmured good mornings, then fell silent.

With his eyes, he tracked Minerva to the sideboard, taking in her plain green gown. Trevor had reported that on Saturday mornings she eschewed riding in favor of taking a turn about the gardens with the head gardener in tow.

Royce returned his gaze to the news sheet, ignoring the part of him that whispered, "A pity." He wasn't entirely pleased with her; it was just as well that when he rode out shortly, he wouldn't come upon her riding his hills and dales, so he wouldn't be able to join her, her and him alone, private in the wild.

Such an encounter would do nothing to ease his all but constant pain.

As Minerva took her seat farther down the board, Margaret cleared her throat and turned to him. "We'd wondered, Royce, whether you had any particular thoughts about a lady who might fill the position of your duchess."

He held still for an instant, then lowered the news sheet, looked first at Margaret, then at Aurelia. He'd never gaped in his life, but . . . "Our father isn't even in the ground, and you're talking about my wedding?"

He glanced at his chatelaine. She had her head down, her gaze fixed on her plate.

"You'll have to think of the matter sooner rather than later." Margaret set down her fork. "The ton isn't going to let the most eligible duke in England simply"—she gestured—"be!"

"The ton won't have any choice. I have no immediate plans to marry."

Aurelia leaned closer. "But Royce—"

"If you'll excuse me"—he stood, tossing the news sheet and his napkin on the table—"I'm going riding." His tone made it clear there was no question involved.

He strode down the table, glanced at Minerva as he went past.

He halted; when she looked up, he caught her autumn eyes. His own narrow, he pointed at her. "I'll see you in the study when I get back."

When he'd ridden far enough, hard enough, to get the tempest of anger and lust roiling through him under control.

Striding out, he headed for the stables.

By lunchtime on Sunday he was ready to throttle his elder sisters, his aunts, and his aunts-by-marriage, all of whom had, it seemed, not a thought with which to occupy their heads other than who—which lady—would be most suitable as his bride.

As the next Duchess of Wolverstone.

He'd breakfasted at dawn to avoid them. Now, in the wake of the ruthlessly cutting comments he'd made the previous night, silencing all such talk about the dinner table, they'd conceived the happy notion of discussing ladies, who all just happened to be young, well-bred, and eligible, comparing their attributes, weighing their fortunes and connections, apparently in the misguided belief that by omitting the words "Royce," "marriage," and "duchess" from their comments, they would avoid baiting his temper.

He was very, very close to losing it—and inching ever closer by the second.

What were they thinking? Minerva couldn't conceive what Margaret, Aurelia, and Royce's aunts hoped to achieve—other than a blistering set-down which looked set to be delivered in a thunderous roar at any minute.

If one were possessed of half a brain, one did not provoke male Variseys. Not beyond the point where they grew totally silent, and their faces set like stone, and—the final warning—their fingers tightened on whatever they were holding until their knuckles went white.

Royce's right hand was clenched about his knife so tightly all four knuckles gleamed.

She had to do something—not that his female relatives deserved saving. If it were up to her, she'd let him savage them, but . . . she had two deathbed vows to honor, which meant she had to see him wed—and his misbegotten relatives were turning the subject of his marriage into one he was on the very brink of declaring unmentionable in his hearing.

He could do that—and would—and would expect and insist and ensure he was obeyed.

Which would make her task all the harder.

They seemed to have forgotten who he was—that he was Wolverstone.

She glanced around; she needed help to derail the conversation.

There wasn't much help to be had. Most of the men had escaped, taking guns and dogs and heading out for some early shooting. Susannah was there; seated on Royce's right, she was wisely holding her tongue and not contributing to her brother's ire in any way.

Unfortunately, she was too far from Minerva's position halfway down the board to be easily enlisted; Minerva couldn't catch her eye.

The only other potential conspirator was Hubert, seated opposite Minerva. She had no high opinion of Hubert's intelligence, but she was desperate. Leaning forward, she caught his eye. "Did you say you'd seen Princess Charlotte and Prince Leopold in London?"

The princess was the darling of England; her recent marriage to Prince Leopold was the only topic Minerva could think of that might trump the subject of Royce's bride. She'd imbued her question with every ounce of breathless interest she could muster—and was rewarded with instant silence.

Every head swung to the middle of the table, every female pair of eyes followed her gaze to Hubert.

He stared at her, eyes showing the surprise of a startled rabbit. Silently she willed him to reply in the affirmative; he blinked, then smiled. "I did, as a matter of fact."

"Where?" He was lying—she could see he was—but he was willing to dance to her tune.

"In Bond Street."

"At one of the jewelers?"

Slowly, he nodded. "Aspreys."

Royce's aunt Emma, seated next to Minerva, leaned forward. "Did you see what they were looking at?"

"They spent quite a bit of time looking at brooches. I saw the attendant bring out a tray—on it were—"

Minerva sat back, a vacuous smile on her face, and let Hubert run on. He was well-launched, and with a wife like Susannah, his knowledge of the jewelry to be found in Aspreys was extensive.

All attention had swung to him.

Leaving Royce to finish his meal without further aggravation; he needed no encouragement to apply himself to the task.

Hubert had only just passed on to the necklaces the royal couple had supposedly examined when Royce pushed away his plate, waved Retford's offer of the fruit bowl aside, dropped his napkin beside his plate, and stood.

The movement broke Hubert's spell. All attention swung to Royce.

He didn't bother to smile. "If you'll excuse me, ladies, I have a dukedom to run." He started striding down the room on his way to the door. Over the heads, he nodded to Hubert. "Do carry on."

Drawing level, his gaze pinned Minerva. "I'll see you in the study when you're free."

She was free now. As Royce strode from the room, she patted her lips, edged back her chair, waited for the footman to draw it out for her. She smiled at Hubert as she stood. "I know I'll regret not hearing the rest of your news—it's like a fairy tale."

He grinned. "Never mind. There's not much more to tell."

She swallowed a laugh, fought to look suitably disappointed as she hurried from the room in Royce's wake.

He'd already disappeared up the stairs; she climbed them, then walked quickly to the study, wondering which part of the estate he'd choose to interrogate her on today.

Since their visit to Usway Burn on Friday, he'd had her sitting before his desk for a few hours each day, telling him about the estate's tenant farms and the families who held them. He didn't ask about profits, crops, or yields, none of the things Kelso or Falwell were responsible for, but about the farms themselves, the land, the farmers and their wives, their children. Who interacted with whom, the human dynamics of the estate; that was what he questioned her on.

When she'd passed on his father's dying message, she hadn't known whether he'd actually had it in him to be different; Variseys tended to breed true, and along with their other principal traits, their stubbornness was legendary.

That was why she hadn't delivered the message immediately. She'd wanted Royce to see and know what his father had meant, rather than just hear the words. Words out of context were too easy to dismiss, to forget, to ignore.

But now he'd heard them, absorbed them, and made the effort, responded to the need, and scripted a new way forward with the Macgregors. She was too wise to comment, not even to encourage; he'd waited for her to say something, but she'd stepped back and left him to define his own way.

With skill and luck, one could steer Variseys; one couldn't lead them.

Jeffers was on duty outside the study. He opened the door and she walked in.

Royce was pacing back and forth before the window behind the desk, looking out at his lands, his every stride invested with the lethal grace of a caged jungle cat, muscles sleekly taut, shifting beneath the fine weave of his coat and his thigh-hugging buckskin breeches.

She simply stood, unable to look away; instinct wouldn't allow her to take her eyes from such a predatory sight.

And looking was no hardship.

She could sense his whipping temper, knew he could lash out, yet was utterly sure he would never hurt her. Or any woman. Yet the turbulent emotions seething within him, swirling in powerful currents all around him, would have most women, most men, edging away.

Not her. She was attracted to the energy, to the wild and compelling power that was so intrinsic a part of him.

Her dangerous secret.

She waited. The door had closed; he knew she was there. When he gave no sign, she advanced and sat in the chair.

Abruptly, he halted. He hauled in a huge breath, then swung around, and dropped into his chair. "The farm at Linshields. Who holds it these days—is it still the Carews?"

"Yes, but I think you probably remember Carew senior. It's his son who runs the farm now."

He kept her talking for the next hour, pressing her, questions flying at a cracking pace.

Royce tried to keep his mind wholly focused on business—on the information he drew from her—yet her answers flowed so freely he had time to truly listen, not just to what she was saying but to her voice, the timbre, the faint huskiness, the rise and fall of emotions as she let them color her words.

She had no reticence, no shields, not on this subject, not any longer. He didn't need to watch for hints of prevarication, or of reserve.

So his wider senses had time to dwell on the rise and fall

of her breasts, the way one errant curl fell across her fore-head, time to note the gold flecks that came alive in her eyes when she smiled over some recounted incident.

Eventually, his questions ended, died. His temper dissi-pated, he sat back in his chair. Physically relaxed, inwardly brooding. His gaze on her.

"I didn't thank you for saving me at luncheon."

Minerva smiled. "Hubert was a surprise. And it was your relatives we saved, not you."

He grimaced, reached out to reposition a pencil that had rolled across the blotter. "They're right in that I will need to marry, but I can't see why they're so intent on pushing the subject at this time." He glanced at her, a question in his eyes.

"I've no idea why, either. I'd expected them to leave that topic for at least a few months, mourning and all. Although I suppose no eyebrows would be raised if you became be-trothed within the year."

The fingers of one hand tapping the blotter, his gaze sharp-ened. "I'm not of a mind to let them dictate, or even dabble in, my future. It might, therefore, be wise to get some idea of the potential . . . candidates."

She hesitated, then asked, "What style of candidate are you thinking of?"

He gave her a look that said she knew better than to ask. "The usual style—a typical Varisey bride. How does it go? Suitable breeding, position, connections and fortune, pass-able beauty, intelligence optional." He frowned. "Did I forget anything?"

She fought to keep her lips straight. "No. That's more or less the full description."

No matter that he might differ from his father in manag-ing people and the estate, he wouldn't differ in his require-ments of a bride. The tradition of Varisey marriages predated the dukedom by untold generations, and, even more telling, suited their temperament.

She saw no reason to disagree with his assessment. The new fashion of love matches within the nobility had little to offer the Variseys. They did not love. She'd spent more than twenty years among them, and had never seen any evidence to the contrary. It was simply the way they were; love had been bred out of them centuries ago—if it had ever been in their mix at all. "If you wish, I could make a list of the candidates your relatives—and no doubt the grandes dames who come up for the funeral—mention."

He nodded. "Their gossip may as well be useful for something. Add anything relevant you know, or hear from reliable sources." He met her eyes. "And, no doubt, you'll add your opinion, as well."

She smiled sweetly. "No, I won't. As far as I'm concerned, choosing your bride is entirely your affair. I won't be living with her."

He gave her another of his bland, you-should-know-better looks. "Neither will I."

She inclined her head, acknowledging that fact. "Regardless, your bride is not a subject on which I would seek to influence you."

"I don't suppose you'd like to promulgate that view to my sisters?"

"Sadly, I must decline—it would be a waste of breath."

He grunted.

"If there's nothing else, I should go and see who else has arrived. Cranny, bless her, needs to know how many will sit down to dine."

When he nodded, she rose and headed for the door. Reaching it, she glanced back, and saw him sprawled in his chair, that brooding look on his face. "If you have time, you might like to look at the tithing from the smaller crofts. At present, it's stated as an absolute amount, but a percentage of profit might suit everyone better."

He arched a brow. "Another radical notion?"

She shrugged and opened the door. "Just a suggestion."

* * *

So here he was at Wolverstone, under his nemesis's roof. His very large roof, in this far distant corner of Northumberland, which was a point, he now realized, that worked in his favor.

The estate was so very far from London that many of the visitors, especially those who were family, would stay for a time; the castle was so huge it could accommodate a small army. So there was, and would continue to be, plenty of cover; he would be safe enough.

He stood at the window of the pleasant room he'd been given in the east wing, looking down on the castle gardens, beautifully presented and bursting with colorful life in the last gasp of the short northern summer.

He had an appreciation for beautiful things, an eye that had guided him in amassing an exquisite collection of the most priceless items the French had had to offer. In exchange he'd given them information, information that, whenever he'd been able, had run directly counter to Royce's commission.

Whenever possible, he'd tried to harm Royce—not directly, but through the men he'd commanded.

From all he'd been able to glean, he'd failed, dismally. Just as he'd failed, over the years, over all the times he'd been held up against Royce, measured against his glorious cousin and found wanting. By his father, his uncle, most of all by his grandfather.

His lips curled; his handsome features distorted in a snarl.

Worst of all, Royce had seized his prize, his carefully hoarded treasure. He'd stolen it from him, denying him even that. For all his years of serving the French, he'd received precisely nothing—not even the satisfaction of knowing he'd caused Royce pain.

In the world of men, and all through the ton, Royce was a celebrated success. And now Royce was Wolverstone to boot.

While he . . . was an unimportant sprig on a family tree.

It shouldn't be so.

Dragging in a breath, he slowly exhaled, willing his features back into the handsome mask he showed the world. Turning, he looked around the room.

His eye fell on a small bowl sitting on the mantelpiece. Not Sevres, but Chinese, quite delicate.

He walked across the room, picked up the bowl, felt its lightness, examined its beauty.

Then he opened his fingers and let it fall.

It smashed to smithereens on the floor.

By late Wednesday afternoon, all the family were in residence, and the first of the guests invited to stay at the castle had begun to arrive.

Royce had been instructed by his chatelaine to be on hand to greet the more important; summoned by Jeffers, he gritted his teeth and descended to the hall to welcome the Duchess of St. Ives, Lady Horatia Cynster, and Lord George Cynster. Although St. Ives's estates lay in the south, the two dukedoms shared a similar history, and the families had supported each other through the centuries.

"Royce!" Her Grace, Helena, Duchess of St. Ives—or the Dowager Duchess, as he'd heard she preferred to style herself—spotted him. She glided to meet him as he stepped off the stairs. "*Mon ami*, such a sad time."

He took her hand, bowed, and brushed a kiss over her knuckles—only to have her swear in French, tug him lower, stretch up on her toes, and press a kiss first to one cheek, then to the other. He permitted it, then straightened, smiled. "Welcome to Wolverstone, Your Grace. You grow lovelier with the years."

Huge, pale green eyes looked up at him. "Yes, I do." She smiled, a glorious expression that lit her whole face, then she let her gaze skate appreciatively down him. "And you . . ." She muttered something in colloquial French he didn't catch, then reverted to English to say, "We had expected to have you return to our salons—instead, you are now here, and no doubt plan to hide yourself away." She wagged a delicate finger at him. "It will not do. You are older than my recalcitrant son, and must marry soon."

She turned to include the lady beside her. "Horatia—tell him he must let us help him choose his bride *tout de suite.*"

"And he'll pay as much attention to me as he will you." Lady Horatia Cynster, tall, dark-haired, and commanding, smiled at him. "Condolences, Royce—or should I say Wolverstone?" She gave him her hand, and like Helena, pulled him nearer to touch cheeks. "Regardless of what you might wish, your father's funeral is going to focus even more attention on your urgent need of a bride."

"Let the poor boy find his feet." Lord George Cynster, Horatia's husband, offered Royce his hand. After a firm handshake, he shooed his wife and sister-in-law away. "There's Minerva looking harassed trying to sort out your boxes—you might help her, or you might end with each other's gowns."

The mention of gowns had both grandes dames' attention shifting. As they moved to where Minerva stood surrounded by a bewildering array of boxes and trunks, George sighed. "They mean well, but it's only fair to warn you you're in for a time of it."

Royce raised his brows. "St. Ives didn't come up with you?"

"He's following in his curricle. Given what you just experienced, you can understand why he'd take rain, sleet, and even snow over spending days in the same carriage as his mother."

Royce laughed. "True." Beyond the open doors, he saw a procession of three carriages draw up. "If you'll excuse me, some others have arrived."

"Of course, m'boy." George clapped him on the back. "Escape while you can."

Royce did, going out through the massive doors propped open in welcome and down the shallow steps to where the three carriages were disgorging their passengers and baggage amid a chaos of footmen and grooms.

A pretty blond in a fashionable pelisse was directing a footman to take care of her boxes, unaware of Royce's approach. "Alice—welcome."

Alice Carlisle, Viscountess Middlethorpe, turned, wide-eyed. "Royce!" She embraced him, tugging him down to plant a kiss on his cheek. "What an unexpected event—and before you'd even returned."

Gerald, her husband, heir to the earldom of Fyfe, stepped down from the carriage, Alice's shawl in one hand. "Royce." He held out his other hand. "Commiserations, old man."

The others had heard, and quickly gathered, offering condolences along with strong hands, or scented cheeks and warm embraces—Miles Ffolliot, Baron Sedgewick, heir to the earldom of Wrexham, and his wife, Eleanor, and the Honorable Rupert Trelawny, heir to the Marquess of Riddlesdale, and his wife, Rose.

They were Royce's closest friends; the three men had been at Eton with him, and the four had remained close through the subsequent years. Throughout his self-imposed social exile, theirs had been the only events—dinners, select soirees—that he'd attended. Over the last decade, he'd first encountered each of his many lovers at one or other of these three ladies' houses, a fact of which he was sure they were aware.

These six made up his inner circle, the people he trusted, those he'd known the longest. There were others—the members of the Bastion Club and now their wives—whom he would likewise trust with his life, but these three couples were the people he shared closest connection with; they were of his circle, and understood the pressures he faced, his temperament, understood him.

Minerva was one he could now add to that circle; she, too, understood him. Unfortunately, as he was reminded every time he saw her, he needed to keep her at a distance.

With Miles, Rupert, and Gerald there, he felt much more . . . himself. Much more certain of who he really was, what he really was. Of what was important to him.

For the next several minutes, he let himself slide into the usual cacophony that resulted whenever all three couples and he were together. He led them inside and introduced them to his chatelaine, relieved when it became obvious that Minerva, and Alice, Eleanor, and Rose, would get on. He would ensure that his three friends were entertained, but given the way the next days looked set to go, he was planning on avoiding all gatherings of ladies; knowing Minerva would watch over his friends' wives meant their entertainment would likewise be assured, and their stay at Wolverstone as comfortable as circumstances permitted.

He was about to accompany them up the main stairs when the rattle of carriage wheels had him glancing into the forecourt. Slowing, a carriage rolled into view, then halted; he recognized the crest on its door.

He nudged Miles's arm. "Do you remember the billiard room?"

Miles, Gerald, and Rupert had visited before, long ago. Miles arched a brow. "You can't imagine I'd forget the place of so many of your defeats?"

"Your memory's faulty—they were your defeats." Royce saw Gerald and Rupert looking down at him, questions in their eyes. "I'll meet you there once you've settled in. Some others have arrived who I need to greet."

With nods and waves, the men followed their wives up the stairs. Royce turned back into the front hall. More guests were arriving; Minerva had her hands full. The hall was continually awash with trunks and boxes even though a company of footmen were constantly ferrying loads upstairs.

Leaving them to it, Royce walked outside. He'd last seen the couple descending from the latest carriage mere weeks ago; he'd missed their wedding, deliberately, but he'd known they would come north to support him.

The lady turned and saw him. He held out a hand. "Letitia."

"Royce." Lady Letitia Allardyce, Marchioness of Dearne, took his hand and stretched up to kiss his cheek; she was tall enough to do so without tugging him down. "The news was a shock."

She stepped back while he exchanged greetings with her husband, Christian, one of his ex-colleagues, a man of similar propensities as he, one who had dealt in secrets, violence, and death in their country's defense.

The three turned toward the castle steps, the men flanking Letitia. She looked into Royce's face. "You weren't expecting to have the dukedom thrust upon you like this. How's your temper holding up?"

She was one of the few who would dare ask him that. He slanted her an unencouraging look.

She grinned and patted his arm. "If you want any advice on restraining temper, just ask the expert."

He shook his head. "Your temper's dramatic. Mine's . . . not."

His temper was destructive, and much more powerful.

"Yes, well." She fixed her gaze on the door, fast drawing near. "I know this isn't something you want to hear, but the next days are going to be much worse than you imagine. You'll learn why soon enough, if you haven't already. And for what it's worth, my advice, dear Royce, is to grit your teeth and reinforce the reins on your temper, because they're about to be tested as never before."

Expressionless, he stared at her.

She smiled brightly back. "Shall we go in?"

Minerva saw the trio enter, and walked over to greet the newcomers. She and Letitia knew each other well, which, she realized, surprised Royce. She hadn't met Dearne before, but approved of his presence, and especially his statement that he was there in part representing Royce's closest ex-colleagues from his years in Whitehall.

He added to Royce, "The others asked us to convey their regards."

Royce nodded in acknowledgment; despite his perpetual mask, she sensed he was . . . touched. That he appreciated the support.

She'd already assigned rooms to all those expected; handing Letitia and Dearne over to Retford to magisterially guide upstairs, she watched them ascend. Felt Royce's gaze on her face. "I know Letitia from all the years I spent with your mother in London."

He gave an almost imperceptible nod; that was what he'd wanted to know.

She'd met Miles, Rupert, and Gerald when they'd visited years ago, had met them and their wives in more recent times, too, although only in passing at ton entertainments. She'd been intrigued to learn—relieved to learn—that they'd stood by Royce over the years. She'd often wondered just how alone he'd been. Not completely, thank heaven, yet she was starting to suspect, his friends aside, that he wasn't as socially adept as he was going to need to be.

The next days were going to be a strain on him, in more ways than she thought he realized.

Turning from the stairs, she surveyed the hall, still a bustling hive of activity. At least there were no guests waiting to be greeted; for the moment, she and Royce were alone amid the sea of luggage.

"You should know," she murmured, "that there's something afoot regarding your wedding. I haven't yet learned exactly what—and your friends' wives don't know, either, but they'll keep their ears open. I'm sure Letitia will." She glanced at his face. "If I hear anything definite, I'll let you know."

His lips twisted in a partially suppressed grimace. "Letitia warned me that something I wouldn't like was coming—she didn't specify what. It sounded as if she, too, wasn't entirely sure."

Minerva nodded. "I'll speak with her later. Perhaps, together, we can work it out."

Another carriage rolled to a halt beyond the steps; she cast him a glance, then went out to greet his guests.

* * *

Late that evening, on returning to his rooms after soundly thrashing Miles at billiards, Royce stripped off his coat and tossed it to Trevor. "I want you to keep your ears open on the subject of my marriage."

Trevor raised his brows, then took his waistcoat from him.

"Specifically"—Royce gave his attention to unraveling his cravat—"my bride." He met Trevor's gaze in the mirror above the tallboy. "See what you can learn—tonight if possible."

"Naturally, Your Grace." Trevor grinned. "I'll bring the pertinent information with your shaving water in the morning."

The next day was the day before the funeral. Royce spent the morning riding with his friends; on returning to the stables, he stopped to speak with Milbourne while the others went ahead. A few minutes later, he followed them back into the castle, seizing the moment alone to review the scant information Trevor had relayed that morning.

The grandes dames were fixated on the necessity of him marrying and getting an heir. What neither Trevor nor his chatelaine, whom he'd seen over breakfast, had as yet ascertained was why there was such intensity, well beyond the merely prurient, almost an air of urgency behind the older ladies' stance.

Something definitely was afoot; his instincts, honed by years of military plotting, ducking, and weaving, were more than pricking.

He strode into the front hall, the necessity of gathering better intelligence high in his mind.

"Good morning, Wolverstone."

The commanding female tones jerked him out of his thoughts. His gaze met a pair of striking hazel eyes. It took him an instant to place them—a fact the lady noted with something akin to exasperation.

"Lady Augusta." He went forward, took the hand she offered him, half bowed.

To the gentleman beside her, he offered his hand. "My lord."

The Marquess of Huntly smiled benignly. "It's been a long time, Royce. Sad that we have to meet again in such circumstances."

"Indeed." Lady Augusta, Marchioness of Huntly, one of the most influential ladies of the ton, eyed him measuringly. "But circumstances aside, we'll need to talk, my lad, about your bride. You must marry, and soon—you've been dragging your heels for the past decade, but now the time has come, and you'll have to choose."

"We're here to bury my father." Royce's accent made the statement a none-too-subtle rebuke.

Lady Augusta snorted. "Indeed." She jabbed a finger at his chest. "Which is precisely my point. No mourning for you—in the circumstances the ton will excuse you, and gladly."

"Lady Augusta!" Minerva hurried down the main stairs, all but tripping in her haste to rescue them all. "We were expecting you yesterday and wondered what had happened."

"Hubert happened, or rather Westminster called, and he was delayed, so we set out rather later than I'd wished." Augusta turned to envelop her in a warm embrace. "And how are you, child? Managing with the son as well as you did with the father, heh?"

Minerva shot Royce a look, prayed he'd keep his mouth shut. "I'm not sure about that, but do come upstairs, both of you." She linked her arm with Augusta's, then did the same with Hubert on her other side. "Helena and Horatia are already here. They're in the upstairs salon in the west wing."

Chatting easily, she determinedly towed the pair up the stairs. As she turned them along the gallery, she glanced down and saw Royce standing where they'd left him, an expression like a thundercloud on his usually impassive face.

Meeting his eyes, she fleetingly shrugged, brows high; she

had yet to learn what was fueling the grandes dames' avid interest in the matter of his bride.

Correctly interpreting her look, Royce watched her guide the pair out of his sight, even more certain that Letitia had been right.

Whatever was coming, he wasn't going to like it.

Five

That evening, *Royce walked into the great drawing room* in no good mood; neither he, Minerva, nor Trevor had yet managed to learn exactly what was going on. The large room was crowded, not just with family but also with the elite of the ton, including representatives of the Crown and the Lords, all gathered for the funeral tomorrow, and talking in hushed tones as they waited for the summons to dine.

Halting just over the threshold, Royce surveyed the assembly—and instantly perceived the answer to his most pressing need. The most powerful grande dame of them all, Lady Therese Osbaldestone, was seated between Helena and Horatia on the chaise before the fireplace. She might have been a mere baroness in the company of duchesses, marchionesses, and countesses, yet she wielded more power, political and social, than any other lady of the ton.

More, she was on excellent terms with said duchesses, marchionesses, and countesses; whatever she decreed, they would support. Therein lay much of her power, especially over the male half of society.

Royce had always treated her with respect. Power, the amassing and wielding of it, was something he understood;

it was bred in his marrow—something her ladyship appreciated.

She must have arrived while he was out riding.

He walked to the chaise, inclined his head to her companions, then to her. "Lady Osbaldestone."

Intensely black eyes—true obsidian—fixed on his face. She nodded, trying to read him, and failing. "Wolverstone."

It was the first time she'd called him that—the first time he'd felt the weight of the mantle on his shoulders. Taking the hand she offered, he bowed, careful not to overdo the observance; she respected those who knew their place, knew what was due to them.

"My condolences on your father's death. Sadly, it comes to us all, although in his case the timing could have been better."

He inclined his head, declined to rise to the lure.

She uttered a soft "humph." "We need to talk—later."

He acquiesced with a half bow. "Later."

Swallowing his impatience, he moved away, letting those of his relatives and connections he'd thus far avoided have at him. Weathering their greetings and accepting their condolences grated on his nerves; he was relieved when Minerva joined the circle about him and set about distracting those he'd already spoken with, subtly but effectively moving them on.

Then Retford announced that dinner was served. Minerva caught his eye, whispered as she passed close, "Lady Augusta."

He assumed that was who he was to lead in to dinner; he located the marchioness—yet his senses, ensorcelled simply by Minerva passing so close, continued to track her.

She wasn't doing anything to attract his notice. In her weeds, she should have faded into the sea of black surrounding him; instead she—just she—seemed to shine in his awareness. The dull black suited her golden loveliness. With an effort hauling his mind from slaveringly dwelling on the loveliness inside the dull black, he surrendered to duty and strolled to Lady Augusta, while trying to push the lingering, elusive, wantonly feminine scent of his chatelaine from his brain.

The conversations in the drawing room had been muted. Continuing the trend, dinner proved an unexpectedly somber meal, as if everyone had suddenly recalled why they were there—and who no longer was. For the first time since he'd viewed the body, he felt touched by his father's absence, sitting in the great carver where his sire used to sit, looking down the long table, lined by more than sixty others, to Margaret sitting at the other end.

A different perspective, one not previously his.

His gaze tracked back to Minerva, seated toward the table's center, opposite Susannah, and surrounded by his cousins. There were nine male cousins present from both sides of his family, Variseys and Debraighs; given the numbers attending, his younger female cousins weren't expected.

His maternal uncle, the Earl of Catersham, was seated on Margaret's right, while the eldest of his paternal aunts, Winifred, Countess Barraclough, sat on Royce's left. Beyond her sat his heir, Lord Edwin Varisey, the third brother of his grandfather's generation, while on his right, next to Lady Augusta and facing Edwin, was his cousin several times removed, Gordon Varisey, eldest son of the late Cameron Varisey, Edwin's younger brother; after the childless Edwin, Gordon stood next in line for the ducal crown.

Edwin was an ancient fop. Gordon was dark and dour, but underneath a sound man. Neither expected to inherit the dukedom, which was just as well; despite his resistance to discussing the subject with all and sundry, Royce had every intention of marrying and siring an heir to whom he would pass the title. What he failed to comprehend was why he needed the help of the grandes dames to achieve that goal, and why it had to be achieved so urgently.

Luckily, the mood of the dinner, with the ladies in dull black, gray, or deep purple, with no jewels beyond jet and no fans or furbelows, and the gentlemen in black coats, many sporting black cravats, had suppressed all talk of his nuptials. Conversations continued to be low-voiced, constant, yet no one laughed, or smiled other than wistfully; across him, Augusta, Winifred, and Edwin swapped tales of his father, to which he pretended to pay attention.

Then the covers were drawn, and Margaret rose and led the ladies back to the drawing room, leaving the men to enjoy port and brandy in relative peace. Some of the formality eased as gentlemen moved to form groups along the table. Royce's cousins congregated in the center, while the older men gravitated to flank his uncle Catersham at the far end.

His friends came to join him, filling the chairs the ladies and Edwin and Gordon had vacated. Joining them, Devil Cynster, Duke of St. Ives, passing behind his chair, briefly clasped his shoulder. His pale green eyes met Royce's as he glanced up. Devil had lost his father and succeeded to his dukedom when he'd been fifteen. With a nod, Devil moved on, leaving Royce reflecting that at least he was shouldering the burden at a significantly older age; then again, Devil had had his uncle, George, to rely on, and George Cynster was a wise, knowledgeable, and capable man.

Devil took the seat next to Christian, easily sliding into the camaraderie of the group; they all opted for whisky, and sat savoring the smoky liquor, lazily exchanging the latest sporting news, and a few salaciously risqué on-dits.

With his impatience to learn what Lady Osbaldestone would tell him steadily mounting, as soon as it was reasonable he led the gentlemen back to the drawing room. Devil ambled beside him; they stopped shoulder to shoulder just inside the room, letting the other men pass by.

Royce surveyed the gathering; from the glances that came his way, many conversations had reverted to the subject of his bride. "At least no one's expecting you to marry tomorrow."

Devil's black brows rose. "You obviously haven't spoken to my mother on that subject."

"She called you recalcitrant."

"Indeed. And you have to remember she's French, which

is the excuse she uses to be as outrageous as she pleases in pursuit of her goal."

"You're hardly in your dotage," Royce returned. Devil was six years younger than he. "And you've a string of acceptable heirs. What's the rush?"

"Precisely my question," Devil purred, his green eyes fixed on someone in the crowd. Then he slanted a glance at Royce, one brow arching. "Your chatelaine . . . ?"

A fist clamped about his heart. The effort not to react—not to snarl and show his teeth—almost stole his breath. He waited a heartbeat, his eyes locked with Devil's, then quietly murmured, "No." After an instant, he added, "I believe she's spoken for."

"Is she?" Devil held his gaze for an instant longer, then he glanced across the room—at Minerva. "Earlier, she just frowned and told me to go away."

"Unlike most ladies, she probably meant it." Royce couldn't stop himself from adding, "If I were you, I'd take her at her word. Heaven knows, I do." He imbued the last words with sufficient masculine long-suffering to have Devil grin once more.

"Ah, well—I won't be here that long."

"Abstinence, they say, is good for the soul."

Devil shot him a look as if asking who he thought he was fooling, then wandered off into the crowd.

Royce watched him go, and muttered to himself, "However, abstinence is hell on the temper." And his was worse that most to begin with.

In search of relief, he located Lady Osbaldestone and would have immediately gone to her side, except for the numerous guests who lined up to waylay him.

Not family, but the ton's elite, including Lord Haworth, representing the Crown, and Lord Hastings, representing the Lords. None were people he could dismiss with just a word, not even a word and a smile; he had to interact, engage in social exchanges all too often layered with multiple meanings . . . he was reaching, had come close to socially stumbling, when Minerva appeared beside him, serenely calm, a stately smile on her lips, and the hints he needed ready on her tongue.

After just a few words, he realized she was an adept in this sphere, and gratefully, if reluctantly, attached himself to her apron strings. The alternative was too damning to permit him to indulge in any pretense.

He needed her. So he had to metaphorically grit his teeth and bear the sexual abrasion of her nearness—it was that or come to social grief, and he'd be damned if he did that. Failure in anything had never been an option, yet this arena was not one in which he'd had any real experience. Yet now he was Wolverstone, people expected him to simply take on the mantle; they seemed to have forgotten the sixteen years he'd spent outside their pale.

For the next half hour, Minerva was his anchor, his guide, his savior.

Courtesy of her vows, she had to be, or, damn him, he'd founder on the social shoals, or come to grief on the jagged rocks of political repartee.

She managed the glib exchanges with half her brain—the other half was entirely consumed by something akin to panic. A frenzied awareness of what would happen if he brushed her shoulder with his arm, if, for some benighted reason, he thought to take her hand. Beneath her smiles, underneath her ready replies, ran an expectation of disaster that clenched her lungs tight, leaving her nearly breathless, every nerve taut, ready to leap with hypersensitive reaction.

At one point, after she'd excused them from a group where the exchanges had looked set to grow too pointed for his—or her—good, he seized the moment of fleeting privacy to lower his head, lower his voice, and ask, "Was my father any good at this?"

Ruthlessly suppressing the effect of the subtle caress of his breath over her ear, she shot him a glance. "Yes, he was."

His lips twisted in a grimace. "So I'm going to have to learn how to manage this, too."

It was the look in his eyes as he glanced around, more than his words, that had her feeling sorry for him; he'd had to take on the business of the dukedom unprepared, and he had made and was making a huge effort in that regard, and succeeding. But this arena of high-level political and social games was one in which he also had to perform, and for that his exile—from the age of twenty-two to thirty-seven—had left him even less well prepared.

"You're Wolverstone now, so yes, you'll have to learn." She had every confidence that, if he applied himself—his incredible intellect, his excellent memory, and his well-honed will—he would succeed. To ensure he accepted the challenge, she added, "And I won't be forever by your side."

He met her gaze at that, his eyes so dark she couldn't read anything in them. Then he nodded and looked ahead as the next wave of guests approached.

The next time they moved on, Royce murmured, "I've been commanded to attend Lady Osbaldestone." Her ladyship was conversing with one of his cousins at the side of the room just ahead of them. "I can manage her if you'll keep the rest at bay. I need to speak with her alone."

Minerva caught his eye. "About this bride business?"

He nodded. "She knows the reason—and once I prostrate myself before her, will take great delight in informing me of it, no doubt."

"In that case, go." She smoothly stepped forward to intercept the next couple seeking an audience with him.

Lady Osbaldestone saw him approaching, and with a few words dismissed his cousin Rohan; hands folded over the head of the cane she didn't really need, she waited before one of the long windows for him to join her.

She arched a brow as he halted before her. "I take it you have, by now, been informed of the need for you to wed with all speed."

"Indeed. In various ways, by a number of your cronies." He fixed his eyes on hers. "What I don't understand is the reason behind the supreme urgency."

She stared at him for a moment, then blinked. She regarded him for an instant more, then murmured, "I suppose, having been in social exile . . . then you were summoned back here before . . ." Lips compressing, she narrowed her eyes. "I suppose it's conceivable that, omniscient though you are rumored to be, you might not have been alerted to the recent developments."

"Obviously not. I will be eternally grateful if you would enlighten me."

She snorted. "You won't be grateful, but clearly someone must. Consider these facts. One, Wolverstone is one of the wealthiest duchies in England. Two, it was created as a marcher lordship. Three, your heir is Edwin, already one step away from senile, and after him, Gordon, who while arguably a legally entitled heir, is nevertheless sufficiently distant to be challenged."

He frowned. "By whom?"

"Indeed." Lady Osbaldestone nodded. "The source of the threat." She held his gaze. "The Crown."

His eyes narrowed. "Prinny?" His voice was flat, his tone disbelieving.

"He's neck-deep in debt, and sinking ever faster. I won't bore you with the details, but I and others have heard from reliable sources close to our dear prince that the search for plunderable funds is on in earnest, and Wolverstone has been mentioned, specifically along the lines of, if anything should, heaven forbid, happen to you, then as matters stand it might be possible to press for the title, and all its entailed wealth, to revert to the Crown in escheat."

He could understand the reasoning, but . . . "There's a significant difference between Prinny, or more likely one of those panderers close to him, making such a suggestion, and it actually being acted upon, even were something to mysteriously happen to me."

Lady Osbaldestone frowned; something like exasperated alarm showed briefly in her eyes. "Don't shrug this off. If you were married, Prinny and his vultures would lose interest and look elsewhere, but while you aren't . . ." She closed a clawlike hand about his arm. "Royce, accidents happen— you of all people know how easily. And there are those around the Regent who are already looking to the day he'll be king, and how he might reward those who can put him in their debt."

When he continued to regard her impassively, she released him and arched a brow. "Did Haworth say anything beyond the expected comments on your father's demise?"

He frowned. "He asked if I had suffered any injury during my service to the Crown."

"I thought you served from behind a desk in Whitehall."

"Not always."

Her brows rose. "Indeed? And who knew that?"

Only Prinny and his closest advisors.

She knew the answer without him saying. She nodded. "Precisely. 'Ware, Wolverstone. That's who you now are, and your duty is clear. You have to marry without delay."

He studied her eyes, her face, for several heartbeats, then inclined his head. "Thank you for telling me."

He turned and walked away.

The actual funeral—the event he and the castle's household had spent the last week and more preparing for, that a good portion of the ton had traveled into Northumbria for—was something of an anticlimax.

Everything went smoothly. Royce had arranged for Hamish and Molly to be given seats at the front of the side chapel, ahead of those reserved for the senior household staff and various local dignitaries. He saw them there, exchanged nods across the church. The nave was filled with the nobility and aristocracy; even using the side aisles, there was barely room enough for all the visitors.

The family spread over the front pews to both sides of the central aisle. Royce stood at the center end of the first pew, conscious of his sisters and their husbands ranged beside him, of his father's sisters and Edwin in the pew across the aisle. Even though the ladies were veiled, there was not a single tear to be found among them; Variseys all, they stood stone-faced, unmoved.

Minerva also wore a fine black veil. She was at the center end of the pew one row back and opposite his. He could see her, watch her, from the corner of his eye. His uncle Catersham and his wife were beside her; his uncle had given Minerva his other arm into the church and up the aisle.

As the service rolled on, he noted that her head remained bowed, that her hand remained clenched tight about a handkerchief—putting sharp creases in the limp, damp square of lace-edged linen. His father had been a martinet, an arrogant despot, a tyrant with a lethal temper. Of all those here, she had lived most closely with him, been most frequently exposed to his flaws, yet she was the only one who truly mourned him, the only one whose grief was deeply felt and sincere.

Except, perhaps, for him, but males of his ilk never cried.

As was customary, only the gentlemen attended the burial in the churchyard while a procession of carriages ferried the ladies back to the castle for the wake.

Royce was among the last to arrive back; with Miles beside him, he walked into the drawing room, and found all proceeding as smoothly as the funeral itself. Retford and the staff had all in hand. He looked around for Minerva, and found her arm-in-arm with Letitia, looking out of one window, their heads bent close.

He hesitated, then Lady Augusta beckoned and he went to hear what she wished to say. Whether the grandes dames had issued a directive he didn't know, but not one lady had mentioned marriage, not even any eligible candidate, at least not within his hearing, at any time that day.

Grateful, he circulated, imagining his chatelaine would say he ought to . . . he missed hearing her words, missed having her beside him, subtly, and if he didn't respond not so subtly, steering him.

The wake didn't end so much as dissolve. Some guests, including all those who had to hasten back to political life, had arranged to depart at its close; they left as their carriages were announced. He shook their hands, bade them Godspeed, and watched their coaches dwindle with relief.

Those who intended to remain—a core of the ton including most of the grandes dames as well as many of the family— drifted off in twos and threes, going out to stroll the lawns, or to sit in groups and slowly, gradually, let their customary lives, their usual interests, reclaim them.

After waving the last carriage away, then seeing Minerva step onto the terrace with Letitia and Rupert's Rose, Royce escaped to the billiard room, unsurprised to find his friends, and Christian and Devil, already there.

They played a few sets, but their hearts weren't in it.

As the sun slowly sank, streaking the sky with streamers of red and purple, they lounged in the comfortable chairs about the fireplace, punctuating the silence with the occasional comment about this or that.

It was into that enfolding, lengthening silence that Devil eventually murmured, "About your wedding . . ."

Slumped in a wing chair, Royce slowly turned his head to regard Devil with an unblinking stare.

Devil sighed. "Yes, I know—I'm the last one to talk. But George and Catersham both had to leave—and *both* apparently had been asked to bring the matter to your attention. Both tapped me on the shoulder to stand in their stead. Odd, but there you have it."

Royce glanced at the five men slumped in various poses around him; there wasn't one he wouldn't trust with his life. Letting his head fall back, he fixed his gaze on the ceiling. "Lady Osbaldestone spun me a tale of a hypothetical threat to the title that the grandes dames have taken it into their heads to treat seriously—hence they believe I should marry with all speed."

"Wise money says the threat isn't entirely hypothetical."

It was Christian who spoke; Royce felt a chill touch his

spine. Of those present, Christian would best appreciate how Royce would feel about such a threat. He also had the best intelligence of dark deeds plotted in the capital.

Keeping his gaze on the ceiling, Royce asked, "Has anyone else heard anything of this?"

They all had. Each had been waiting for a moment to speak with him privately, not realizing the others had similar warnings to deliver.

Then Devil pulled a letter from his pocket. "I have no idea what's in this. Montague knew I was coming north and asked me to give this to you—into your hand—after the funeral. Specifically after, which seems to be now."

Royce took the letter and broke the seal. The others were silent while he read the two sheets it contained. Reaching the end, he slowly folded the sheets; his gaze on them, he reported, "According to Montague, Prinny and his merry men have been making inquiries over how to effect the return of a marcher lord title and estate in escheat. The good news is that such a maneuver, even if successfully executed, would take a number of years to effect, given the claim would be resisted at every turn, and the escheat challenged in the Lords. And as we all know, Prinny's need is urgent and his vision short-term. However, invoking all due deference, Montague suggests that it would be wise were my nuptials to occur within the next few months, because some of Prinny's men are not so shortsighted as their master."

Lifting his head, Royce looked at Christian. "In your professional opinion, do I stand in any danger of being assassinated to bolster Prinny's coffers?"

Christian grinned. "No. Realistically, for Prinny to claim the estate your death would need to look like an accident, and while you're at Wolverstone, that would be all but impossible to arrange." He met Royce's gaze. "Especially not with you."

Only Christian and the other members of the Bastion Club knew that one of Royce's less well-known roles over the past sixteen years had been as secret executioner for the government; given his particular skills, killing him would not be easy.

Royce nodded. "Very well—so it seems the threat is potentially real, but the degree of urgency is perhaps not as great as the grandes dames think."

"True." Miles caught Royce's eyes. "But that's not going to make all that much difference, is it? Not to the grandes dames."

The day had finally come to an end. Minerva had one last duty to perform before she retired to her bed; she felt wrung out, more emotionally exhausted than she'd expected, yet once everyone else had retired to their rooms, she forced herself to go to the duchess's morning room, retrieve the folio, then walk through the darkened corridors of the keep to the study.

She was reaching for the doorknob when she realized someone was inside. There was no lamplight showing beneath the door, but the faint line of moonlight was broken by a shadow, one that moved repetitively back and forth . . .

Royce was there. Pacing again.

Angry.

She looked at the door—and simply knew, as if she could somehow sense his mood even through the oak panel. She wondered, felt the weight of the folio in her hand . . . raising her free hand, she rapped once, then gripped the knob, opened the door, and went in.

He was a dense, dark shadow before the uncurtained window. He whirled as she entered. "Leave—"

His gaze struck her. She felt its impact, felt the dark intensity as his eyes locked on her. Realized that, courtesy of the faint moonlight coming through the window, he could see her, her movements, her expression, far better than she could his.

Moving slowly, deliberately, she closed the door behind her.

He'd stilled. "What is it?" His tone was all lethal, cutting fury, barely leashed.

Cradling the folio in her arms, resisting the urge to clutch it to her chest, she said, "Lady Osbaldestone told me the reason the grandes dames believe you need to wed as soon as practicable. She said she'd told you."

He nodded tersely. "She did."

Minerva could sense the depth of the anger he was, temporarily, suppressing; to her, expert in Varisey temper that she was, it seemed more than the situation should have provoked. "I know this has to be the last thing you expected to face, to have forced on you at this time, but . . ." She narrowed her eyes, trying to see his expression through the wreathing shadows. "You'd expected to marry—most likely in a year's time. This brings the issue forward, but doesn't materially change all that much . . . does it?"

Royce watched her trying to understand—to comprehend his fury. She stood there, not the least afraid when most men he knew would be edging out of the door—indeed, wouldn't have come in in the first place.

And of all those he considered friend, she was the only one who might understand, probably would understand . . .

"It's not that." He swung back to stare out of the window— at the lands it was his duty to protect. To hold. "Consider this." He heard the harshness in his voice, the bitterness, felt all his pent-up, frustrated anger surge; he gripped the windowsill tightly. "I spent the last sixteen years of my life essentially in exile—a social exile I accepted as necessary so that I could serve the Crown, as the Crown requested, and as the country needed. And now . . . the instant I resign my commission, and unexpectedly inherit the title, I discover I have to marry immediately to protect that title and my estate . . . from the Crown."

He paused, dragged in a huge breath, let it out with "Could it be any more ironic?" He had to move; he paced, then turned, viciously dragged a hand through his hair. "How *dare* they? *How* . . ." Words failed him; he gestured wildly.

"Ungrateful?" she supplied.

"*Yes!*" That was it, the core fueling his fury. He'd served loyally and well, and this was how they repaid him? He halted, stared out again.

Silence descended.

But not the cold, uncaring, empty silence he was used to.

She was there with him; this silence held a warmth, an enfolding comfort he'd never before known.

She hadn't moved; she was a good ten and more feet away, safely separated from him by the bulk of the desk, yet he could still feel her, sense her . . . feel an effect. As if her just being there, listening and understanding, was providing some balm to his excoriated soul.

He waited, but she said nothing, didn't try to make light of what he'd said—didn't make any comment that would provoke him to turn his temper—currently a raging, snarling beast—on her.

She really did know what not to do—and to do. And when.

He was about to tell her to go, leaving him to his now muted, less anguished thoughts, when she spoke, her tone matter-of-fact.

"Tomorrow I'll start making a list of likely candidates. While the grandes dames are here, and inclined to be helpful, we may as well make use of their knowledge and pick their brains."

It was the sort of comment he might have made, uttered with the same cynical inflection. He inclined his head.

He expected her to leave, but she hesitated . . . He remembered the book she'd held in her hands just as she said, "I came here to leave you this."

Turning his head, he watched her walk forward and lay the book—a folio—on his blotter. Stepping back, she clasped her hands before her. "I thought you should have it."

He frowned; leaving the window, he pushed his chair aside and stood looking down at the black folio. "What is it?" Reaching out, he opened the front cover, then shifted so the moonlight fell on the page revealed. The sheet was inscribed with his full name, and the courtesy title he'd previously used. Turning that page, he found the next covered with sections cut from news sheets, neatly stuck, with dates written beneath in a hand he recognized.

Minerva drew breath, said, "Your mother started it. She used to read the news sheets after your father had finished with them. She collected any piece that mentioned you."

Although the details of his command had been secret, the fact of it hadn't been, and he'd never been backward in claiming recognition for the men who'd served under him. Wellington, in particular, had been assiduous in mentioning the value of the intelligence provided, and the aid rendered, by Dalziel's command; notices of commendations littered the folio's pages.

He turned more leaves. After a moment, he said, "This is your writing."

"I was her amanuensis—I stuck the pieces in and noted the dates."

He did as she'd thought he would, and flipped forward to where the entries ended. Paused. "This is the notice from the *Gazette* announcing the end of my commission. It ran . . ." His finger tapped the date. "Two weeks ago." He glanced at her. "You continued after my mother died?"

Her eyes had adjusted; she held his gaze. This was the difficult part. "Your father knew." His face turned to stone, but . . . he kept listening. "I think he'd always known, at least for many years. I kept the folio, so I knew when it moved. Someone was leafing through it—not the staff. It always happened late at night. So I kept watch, and saw him. Every now and then he'd go to the morning room very late, and sit and go through it, reading the latest about you."

He looked down, and she went on, "After your mother died, he insisted I kept it up. He'd circle any mention as he went through the news sheets, so I wouldn't miss any relevant article."

A long silence ensued; she was about to step back, and

leave him with his parents' memento of his last sixteen years, when he said, his voice low, soft, "He knew I was coming home."

He was still looking down. She couldn't see his face. "Yes. He was . . . waiting." She paused, trying to find the right words. "He didn't know how you would feel, but he . . . wanted to see you. He was . . . eager. I think that's why he got confused, thinking you were here, that you'd already come, because he'd been seeing you here again in his mind."

Her throat closed up. There wasn't anything more she had to say.

She forced herself to murmur, "Tomorrow I'll bring you that list once I've made it."

Turning, she walked to the door, went through without looking back, and left him to his parents' memories.

Royce heard her go, despite the sorrow pouring through him, wished she'd stayed. Yet if she had . . .

She could make her list, but there was only one lady he wanted in his bed.

Reaching out blindly, he found his chair, drew it closer, then sat and stared at the folio. In the quiet darkness, no one could see if he cried.

By eleven the next morning, Minerva had made an excellent start on a list of potential candidates for the position of Duchess of Wolverstone.

Sitting in the duchess's morning room, she wrote down all she'd thus far gleaned of the young ladies and why each in particular had been suggested.

She felt driven, after last night even more so, to see the matter of Royce's wedding dealt with as expeditiously as possible. What she felt for him . . . it was ridiculous—she knew it was—yet her infatuation-obsession was only growing and deepening. The physical manifestations—and the consequent difficulties—were bad enough, but the tightness in her chest, around her heart, the sheer sorrow she'd felt last night, not for his dead father but for him, the nearly overwhelming urge to round his damned desk and lay a hand on his arm, to comfort him—even in the dangerous state he'd been in to recklessly offer comfort . . .

"No, no, no, and *no!*" Lips set, she added the latest name Lady Augusta had suggested to her neat list.

He was a Varisey, and she, better than anyone, knew what that meant.

A tap sounded on the door.

"Come!" She glanced up as Jeffers looked in.

He smiled. "His Grace asked if you could attend him, ma'am. In his study."

She looked down at her list; it was complete to this moment. "Yes." She rose and picked it up. "I'll come right away."

Jeffers accompanied her across the keep and held open the study door. She walked in to find Royce sitting behind his desk, frowning at the uncluttered expanse.

"I spoke with Handley this morning—he said that as far as he knew there were no estate matters pending." He fixed her with an incipient glare. "That can't be right."

Handley, his secretary, had arrived earlier in the week, and to her immense relief had proved to be a thoroughly dependable, extremely efficient, exemplarily loyal man in his early thirties; he'd been a huge help through the preparations and the funeral itself. "Handley's correct." She sat in the chair before the wide desk. "We dealt with all matters likely to arise last week. Given we were going to have so many visitors at the castle, it seemed wise to clear your desk." She looked at the expanse in question. "There's nothing likely to land on it before next week."

She looked at the list in her hand. "Except, of course, for this." She held it out to him.

He hesitated, then, reluctantly, reached out and took it. "What is it?"

"A list of potential candidates for the position you need to fill." She gave him a moment to cast his eyes over the page. "It's only a partial list at present—I haven't had a chance to check with Helena and Horatia yet—but you could start considering these ladies, if there's any one that stands out . . ."

He tossed the list on his blotter. "I don't wish to consider this subject now."

"You're going to have to." She had to get him married so she could escape. "Aside from all else, the grandes dames are staying until Monday, and I have a strong suspicion they expect to hear a declaration from you before they leave."

"They can go to the devil."

"The devil wouldn't have them, as you well know." She dragged in a breath, reached for patience. "Royce, you know you have to decide on your bride. In the next few days. You know why." She let her gaze fall to the list before him. "You need to make a start."

"*Not* today." Royce fixed her with a glare, one powerful enough to have her pressing her lips tight against the words he sensed were on her tongue.

The situation . . . was insupportable. Literally. He felt tense, edgy; his restlessness had developed an undercurrent with which he was familiar—he'd been without a woman too long.

Except he hadn't. That wasn't, exactly, the problem. His problem was sitting across his desk wanting to lecture him about the necessity of choosing some mindless ninnyhammer as his bride. As the lady who would share his bed.

Instead of her.

He needed . . . to get away from her before his temper—or his restlessness, both were equally dangerous—slipped its leash. Before she succeeded in prodding him to that extent. Unfortunately, his friends and their wives had left that morning; he'd wanted to beg them to stay, but hadn't—they all had young families awaiting them at home, and had been eager to get back.

Devil had left, as well, driving himself down the Great North Road. He wished he could have gone, too; they could have raced each other back to London . . . except all he wanted, all he now needed, was here, at Wolverstone.

A good part of what he wanted sat across the desk, waiting to see what he was going to do, ready to counter it, to pressure him into making his choice . . .

He narrowed his eyes on her face. "Why are you so keen to assist the grandes dames in this matter"—he let his voice soften, grow quieter—"even against my wishes?" Eyes locked on hers, he raised his brows. "You're *my* chatelaine, are you not?"

She held his gaze, then fractionally, instinctively, raised her chin. "I'm *Wolverstone's* chatelaine."

He was a master interrogator; he knew when he hit a vein. He considered her for a moment, then evenly said, "I am Wolverstone, a fact you haven't forgotten, so what exactly do you mean?"

Her debating-whether-to-tell-him expression surfaced; he waited, outwardly patient, knowing she'd conclude that she had to.

Eventually, she dragged in a breath. "I made a vow—two vows. Or rather, the same vow twice. Once to your mother before she died, and then before he died, you father asked me for the same promise, which I gave." Her eyes, a medley of autumn browns, held his. "I promised them I'd see you settled and properly established as the tenth Duke of Wolverstone."

Minerva waited to hear his response to that—her unarguable excuse for pressing him to follow the grandes dames' advice and choose a bride forthwith.

From the instant he'd started questioning her, his face—never all that informative—had become impossible to read. His expression was all stone, revealing no hint of his thoughts, much less his feelings.

Abruptly he pushed away from the desk.

Startled, she blinked, surprised when he stood. She got to her feet as he rounded the desk.

"I'm going riding."

The growled words froze her where she stood.

For one instant, his eyes, full of dark fire and unreadable

emotion, pinned her, then he stalked past her, flung open the door, and was gone.

Utterly stunned, she stared at the open doorway. And listened to his footsteps, angry and quick, fade away.

Hamish laughed so hard he fell off the wall.

Disgusted, when his half brother continued to chortle, Royce nudged his shoulder with his boot. "If you don't stop, I'll have to get down and thrash you to within an inch of your life."

"Och, aye." Hamish hauled in a breath and wiped tears from his eyes. "You and which sassenach army?"

Royce looked down at him. "We always won."

"True." Hamish struggled to tamp down his mirth. "You won the wars, but not every battle." Staggering to his feet, he wheezed; one hand held to his side, he hoisted himself back up beside Royce.

They both looked out across the hills.

Hamish shook his curly head. "I still keep wanting to laugh—oh, not about *why* you need to bed your bride with all urgency—that's the sort of thing our ancestors went to war over—but the notion of you—*you*—being hounded by these great ladies, all waving lists and wanting you to choose . . . heh, lad, you have to admit it's funny."

"Not from where I sit—and as yet it's only Minerva waving a list." Royce looked at his hands, loosely clasped between his knees. "But that's not the worst of it. Choosing a bride, having a wedding—doing it all *now*—that's merely an irritation. But . . . I'm not sure I can manage the estate, and everything that's bound up in that—the social, the political, the business, the people—without Minerva, but she's not going to stay once I marry."

Hamish frowned. "That would be a loss." A moment passed, then he said, "Nay—I can't see it. She's more Wolverstonc than you. She's lived here, what? Twenty years? I can't see her leaving, not unless you want her to."

Royce nodded. "So I thought, but I've since learned

better. When I first returned, she told me she wouldn't be my chatelaine forever, that when I married and she could pass the keys to my wife, she'd leave. That sounded reasonable at the time, but since then I've learned how important she is to the estate, how much she contributes to its management even outside the castle, and how vital she is to *me*—I honestly couldn't have survived the last days without her, not socially. I'd have fallen on my face more than once if she hadn't been there, literally by my side, to get me over the hurdles." He'd already explained about the social handicap his exile had saddled him with.

He looked out across the hills toward those that were his. "This morning she told me of the deathbed vows she'd made to my parents—to see me established as duke, which includes seeing me appropriately wed. *They* are what's holding her here. I'd assumed she . . . wasn't averse to being my chatelaine, that if I asked, she would stay."

He'd thought she liked being *his* chatelaine, that she *enjoyed* the challenge he posed to her management skills, but . . . after hearing of her vows, he no longer felt he had any claim at all on her, on her loyalty, her . . . affection.

Given his continued desire for her, and her continued lack of desire for him, the news of those vows had shaken him—and he wasn't accustomed to that sort of shaking. Never had he felt such a hollow, desolate feeling in the pit of his stomach.

"I don't suppose," Hamish suggested, looking toward Wolverstone, too, "that there's an easy way out of this?"

"What easy way?"

"Mayhap Minerva's name could find its way onto your list?"

"Would that it could, but neither she nor anyone else will put it there. This morning's list named six young ladies, all of whom have significant fortunes and hail from the senior noble families in the realm. Minerva's well-bred, but not in that league, and her fortune can't compare. Not that any of that matters to *me*, but it does to society, and therefore to her because of her damned vows." He drew breath, held it. "But aside from all that—and I swear if you laugh at this I *will* hit you—she's one of those rare females who have absolutely no interest in me."

From the corner of his eye, he saw Hamish suck in his lips, trying manfully not to be hit. A very long pregnant moment passed, then Hamish dragged in a huge breath, and managed to get out, "Mayhap she's grown hardened to the Varisey charm, seeing as she's lived among you so long."

His voice had quavered only a little, not enough for Royce to retaliate. It had been decades since he'd felt that going a few rounds with Hamish—one of the few men he'd have to work to fight—might make him feel better. Might let him release some of the tension inside.

That tension sang in his voice as he replied, "Presumably. Regardless, all those facts rule out the easy way—I want no reluctant, sacrificial bride. She's not attracted to me, she wants me to marry appropriately so she can leave, yet if I offer for her, in the circumstances she might feel she has to, against all her expectations and inclinations, agree. I couldn't stomach that."

"Och, no." Hamish's expression suggested he couldn't stomach it, either.

"Unfortunately, her resistance to the Varisey charm rules out the not-quite-so-easy way, too."

Hamish frowned. "What's that?"

"Once I fill the position of my duchess, I'll be free to take a mistress, a long-term lover I can keep by my side."

"You'd think to make Minerva your lover?"

Royce nodded. "Yes."

He wasn't surprised by the silence that followed, but when it lengthened, he frowned and glanced at Hamish. "You were supposed to clout me over the ear and tell me I shouldn't have such lecherous thoughts about a lady like Minerva Chesterton."

Hamish glanced at him, then shrugged. "In that depart-ment, who am I to judge? I'm me, you're you, and our father was something else again. But"—tilting his head, he stared toward Wolverstone—"strange to say, I could see it might work—you marrying one of those hoity ton misses, and having Minerva as your lover-cum-chatelaine."

Royce grunted. "It *would* work, if she wasn't unresponsive to me."

Hamish frowned. "About that . . . have you tried?"

"To seduce her? *No*. Just think—I have to work closely with her, need to interact with her on a daily basis. If I made an advance and she rejected me, it would make life hellishly awkward for us both. And what if, after that, she decided to leave immediately despite her vows? I can't go that route."

He shifted on the wall. "Besides, if you want the honest truth, I've never seduced a woman in my life—I wouldn't have the first clue how to go about it."

Hamish overbalanced and fell off the wall again.

Where was Royce? What was his nemesis up to?

Although the bulk of the guests had left, Allardyce, thank heaven, among them, enough remained for him to feel confident he still had sufficient cover, but the thinning crowd should have made his cousin easier to see, to keep track of.

In the billiard room with his male cousins, he played, laughed, and joked, and inwardly obsessed over what Royce might be doing. He wasn't with Minerva, who was sitting with the grandes dames, and he wasn't in his study because his footman wasn't standing outside the door.

He hadn't wanted to come to Wolverstone, but now he was there, the opportunity to linger, mingling with his other cousins who, together with Royce's sisters, were planning what would amount to a highly select house party to capitalize on the fact they were there, together and out of sight of the ton, and, more importantly, their spouses, was tempting.

Yet his long-standing fear—that if Royce were to see him, were to look at him often enough, those all-seeing dark eyes would strike through his mask and Royce would see the truth, would know and act—remained, the nearness to his nemesis keeping it forever fermenting in one part of his brain.

From the first step he'd taken down the long road to becoming the successful—still living—traitorous spy he was, he'd known that the one being above all others he had to fear was Royce. Because once Royce knew, Royce would kill him without remorse. Not because he was an enemy, a traitor, not because he'd struck at Royce, but because he was family. Royce would not hesitate to erase such a blot on the family's escutcheon.

Royce was far more like his father than he believed.

For years he'd carried his fear inside him, held close, a smoldering, cankerous coal forever burning a hole in his gut.

Yet now temptation whispered. While so many of his cousins remained at Wolverstone, he, too, could stay.

And over the years of living with his fear, of coming to know it so intimately, he'd realized there was, in fact, one way to make the living torment end.

For years he'd thought it could only end with his death.

Recently he'd realized it could end with Royce's.

Six

oyce walked into the drawing room that evening more uncertain about a woman than he'd ever been in his life.

After Hamish had staggered to his feet a second time, he'd made a number of suggestions, not all of which had been in jest. Yet the instant Royce's gaze landed on Minerva, he rejected Hamish's principal thesis—that his chatelaine was no more immune to him than the average lady, but was concealing her reactions.

From him? Gauging others was one of his strengths, one he'd exercised daily over the past sixteen years; she'd have to possess the most amazing control to hide such an awareness of him, from him.

As if sensing his regard, she turned and saw him; leaving the group with whom she'd been conversing, she glided to him. "Did you find the more detailed list of candidates I left on your desk?"

Her voice was cool, serene. She was annoyed with his treatment of her initial list.

"Yes." There was nothing subtle about his tone.

Her eyes locked with his. "Have you read it?"

"No."

Her lips tightened, but she didn't press her luck. The drawing room was still comfortably well-populated; he'd thought more people would have left.

For an instant, she stood looking into his eyes, then she glanced around.

Backing down, thank God. He hadn't realized before how arousing it was to have a lady cross swords with him; no other ever had.

For a moment he stood looking down at her, letting his eyes, his senses, feast, then silently cleared his throat and followed her gaze . . . "Bloody hell!" he muttered. "They're *all* still here."

"The grandes dames? I did tell you they were staying until Monday."

"I thought you meant Therese Osbaldestone and maybe Helena and Horatia, not the whole damned pack."

She glanced at him, then past him. "Regardless, here's Retford." She met his eyes briefly. "You have Lady Augusta again, of course."

"Of. Course." He bit back the acid comments burning the tip of his tongue; no point expending energy over what he couldn't change. Besides, while the grandes dames might have stayed on, so, too, had many of his cousins, and some of his sisters' friends. Two of his uncles and their wives were still there; they'd mentioned they'd be leaving tomorrow.

There were enough gentlemen still present for him to escape with after dinner. Until then, he would deploy his considerable skills in deflecting all inquisition on the subject of his bride.

Locating Lady Augusta, he went to claim her hand.

Royce practiced the art of avoidance throughout the following day. He didn't disappear, but hid in plain sight.

In the morning, he confounded everyone by joining the group going to church; not one of the grandes dames was devoted to religion. He dallied after the service, chatting to the vicar and various locals, timing his return so that he walked into the castle as the luncheon gong rang.

He played the genial host throughout the informal meal, chatting easily about country pursuits. Considerate host that he was, the instant the platters were cleared he suggested a ride to a local waterfall.

His chatelaine looked at him, but said nothing.

They returned in the late afternoon. He'd managed to keep largely to himself; the others all thought that when he grew quiet, he was brooding over his father's death. Not grieving— for that, one had to love—but angry over being denied his long-awaited confrontation with his sire.

He walked with the others into the front hall. Seeing no sign of grandes dames—or his chatelaine—he parted from the rest and went up the main stairs, and into the keep.

He headed for his study. No one had mentioned the words "marriage," "bride," or "wedding" in his hearing all day; he was feeling sufficiently mellow to wonder if his chatelaine had left him another amended list. If she had, she would have found her second list sitting alongside the first by his blotter. He would read them, but in his own good time, not at the behest of a pack of ladies, even be they grandes dames.

His hand was on the study doorknob, opening the door, before he registered that Jeffers wasn't at his post. Not that he had to be when Royce wasn't in the study, but the man had an uncanny sense of when he would be coming to the room. Pushing the door wide, he walked in—

And halted. He'd walked into an ambush.

Seven grandes dames were seated in a semicircle before his desk, the chairs carefully arranged so he hadn't been able to see them, not until he'd walked too far in to retreat.

Only one lady—Therese Osbaldestone—turned her head to look at him. "Good afternoon, Wolverstone. We'd appreciate it if you would grant us a few minutes of your time."

No real question, and his title, not his name; stiffly, he inclined his head.

Therese glanced behind the door, to where Jeffers stood with his back to the wall. "You may go."

Jeffers looked at Royce. He endorsed the order with a curt nod.

As the door closed silently behind Jeffers, Royce walked forward. Slowly. Passing one end of the line of chairs, he rounded the desk, his gaze touching each determined face. Horatia, Helena, Therese, Augusta, Princess Esterhazy, Lady Holland, and Lady Melbourne. Behind the chairs to one side stood Letitia and Minerva.

Combining their various connections, with Letitia representing both the Vaux and Dearne, the group commanded the collective might of the upper echelons of the ton.

These were the ton's foremost female generals.

He inclined his head. "Ladies."

He sat, outwardly relaxed, and regarded them impassively.

Lady Osbaldestone was their elected speaker. "I've already discussed with you the reason you need to marry without delay." Her obsidian gaze lowered to the blotter, on which three sheets—a new and longer list—lay spread. "We have pooled our knowledge—we believe that list includes every gel you might consider for the position of your duchess, along with her antecedents, her expected fortune, and sundry information we thought helpful."

Her gaze rose from the list as Royce's did; she met and held his gaze. "You now have all the information you need to choose your bride, which, as we've all been at pains to impress on you, you need to do forthwith. *However*, what you may not yet perceive is what will occur if you do *not* act promptly. Should the ton not hear of your betrothal soon, then you and this castle are likely to be stormed by every even halfway eligible chit in Christendom." She rapped the floor with her cane. "And I can assure you they will be a great deal harder to repulse than any army!"

Spine straight, she looked him in the eye. "Is that what you want? Because if you fail to act, that is precisely what will happen."

The vision was enough to make him blanch, but . . . were they actually *threatening* him?

Lady Augusta shifted, drawing his attention. "That's *not* a threat—at least, not from us. It will, however, happen precisely as Therese says, regardless of anything *we* may do, or indeed, anything you can do short of announcing your betrothal."

She hesitated, then went on, her tone more conciliatory, "If your father had lived, matters would be different. But he died, and so you are now Wolverstone, unmarried and childless, and with no direct heir—your marriage is urgent regardless. But for the reasons you now know of, that urgency has become acute. The matter of you choosing your bride has now become critical. And while we, and those others who would know, already recognize the urgency, the entire ton will become aware of it—of your need of a bride—sooner rather than later."

"Indeed," Princess Esterhazy said, in her accented voice, "it is a wonder you have not yet had a rash of carriages breaking down outside your gates."

"One would hope," Lady Osbaldestone said, "that they'll wait for at least a week after the funeral."

Royce studied her face, checked those of the others; she wasn't being facetious.

Helena, her normally clear eyes shadowed by concern, leaned forward. "We should perhaps make clear—we are not urging you to anything you would not at some point do. It is merely the timing that has changed." She pulled an expressive face. "Your family have always approached marriage as a means of alliance, of furthering the dukedom. All know that Variseys do not indulge in love matches. And while that may not be to the liking of all, we are none of us suggesting you change your spots. No. All we are saying is that you must make your choice—exactly the same choice you would at some point have made, *n'est-ce pas?* It is simply that the choice needs to be made with greater speed than you expected, yes?" She spread her hands. "That is all."

All? Before he could respond, Therese waved at the lists.

"Minerva gave you our initial recommendations, but these are more extensive. We've racked our brains, and included every possible potential candidate." She caught his eye. "Not one young lady on that list would turn down the position of your duchess should you choose to favor her by offering it. I realize—we all realize—that this situation has been forced on you, and that these ladies are not present for you to meet. However, in terms of the decision you must make, neither of those facts is relevant."

She drew a deep breath, held his gaze, her own weighty with the power she wielded. "We suggest you make your choice from these ladies—any one will make you an entirely acceptable bride." She paused, then went on, "I see no point in lecturing you, of all people, on the concept of duty—I accept you might well know more than even I of that quality. Be that as it may, there is no justifiable reason for you to drag your heels in this respect." Her hands tightened on the head of her cane. "Just do it, and it will be done."

She rose, bringing all the others to their feet. Royce eyed them, then slowly, stiffly, stood.

None of them were blind; not one had ever been foolish. They all sensed his temper, all inclined their heads to him and on a chorus of "Your Graces," turned, and filed out.

He stood, his face like stone, utterly expressionless, every instinct, every reaction, rigidly suppressed, and watched them go.

Minerva kept glancing at him. She was last in line for the door; she tried to hang back, but Lady Augusta, ahead of her, stepped back, took her arm in a viselike grip, and bundled her out before her.

Jeffers, in his usual position in the corridor outside, reached back and pulled the door closed; glancing back, Minerva caught a last glimpse of Royce, still standing behind his desk, looking down at her neat list.

She saw his lips curl in a soundless snarl.

* * *

She'd advised against it—the grandes dames' ambush—firmly and quite definitely, but they hadn't listened.

And then she'd stopped arguing because, suddenly, she hadn't been sure of her reasons, her motives in not wanting them to push him, not like that.

Was she arguing because of her burgeoning feelings for him—was she trying to protect him, and if so, from what and why?—or was she right in thinking that them banding together in such a fashion and laying before him what he would certainly interpret—marcher lord that he was—as an ultimatum, was a very unwise, not to say outright bad, idea?

She now knew the answer. Very bad idea.

No one had seen him since that meeting in his study the previous afternoon. He hadn't come down to dinner, electing to dine alone in his apartments, and then this morning he'd—so she'd learned—got up at dawn, breakfasted in the kitchens, then gone to the stables, taken Sword, and disappeared.

He could be anywhere, including Scotland.

She stood in the front hall surrounded by the grandes dames' boxes and trunks, and took in the set, determined, positively mulish faces of those selfsame grandes dames as they perched on said trunks and boxes, having vowed not to stir a step further until Wolverstone—not one of them was calling him by his given name—gave them his decision.

They'd been sitting there for fully half an hour. Their carriages were lined up in the forecourt, ready to carry them away, but if they didn't leave soon, they wouldn't reach any major town before nightfall, so they would have to remain another night . . . she didn't know if their tempers or hers would stand it; she didn't want to think about Royce's.

Her hearing was more acute than theirs; she heard a distant creak, then a thump—the west courtyard door opening and closing. Quietly, she turned and slipped into the corridor behind her, the one leading to the west wing.

Once out of sight of the front hall, she picked up her skirts and hurried.

She rushed around a corner—and just managed not to collide with him again. His face still carved granite, he looked at her, then stepped around her and strode on.

Hauling in a breath, she whirled and hurried even more to catch up with him. "Royce—the grandes dames are waiting to leave."

His stride didn't falter. "So?"

"So you have to give them your decision."

"What decision?"

She mentally cursed; his tone was far too mild. "The name of which lady you've chosen as your bride."

The front hall loomed ahead. Voices carried in the corridors; the ladies had heard. They stirred, rising to their feet, looking at him expectantly.

He glanced back at her, then looked stonily at them. "No."

The word was an absolute, incontestable negative.

Without breaking his stride, he inclined his head coldly as he strode past the assembled female might of the ton. "I wish you Godspeed."

With that, he swung onto the main stairs, rapidly climbed them, and disappeared into the gallery above.

Leaving Minerva, and all the grandes dames, staring after him.

A moment of stunned silence ensued.

Dragging in a breath, she turned to the grandes dames—and discovered every eagle eye riveted on her.

Augusta gestured up the stairs. "Do you want to? Or should we?"

"No." She didn't want him saying something irretrievable and alienating any of them; they were, despite all, well disposed toward him, and their support would be invaluable—to him and even more to his chosen bride—in the years to come. She swung back to the stairs. "I'll talk to him."

Lifting her skirts, she climbed quickly up, then hurried after him into the keep. She needed to seize the moment, engage with him now, and get him to make some acceptable statement, or the grandes dames would stay. And stay. They were as determined as he was stubborn.

She assumed he would make for the study, but . . . "Damn!" She heard his footsteps change course for his apartments.

His *private* apartments; she recognized the implied warning, but had to ignore it. She'd failed to dissuade the grandes dames, so here she now was, chasing a snarling wolf into his lair.

No choice.

Royce swept into his sitting room, sending the door swinging wide. He fetched up in the middle of the Aubusson rug, listened intently, then cursed and left the door open; she was still coming on.

A very unwise decision.

All the turbulent emotions of the previous evening, barely calmed to manageable levels by his long, bruising ride, had roared back to furious, aggressive life at the sight of the grandes dames camped in his front hall—metaphorically at his gates—intent on forcing him to agree to marry one of the ciphers on their infernal list.

He'd studied the damned list. He had no idea in any personal sense of who any of the females were—they were all significantly younger than he—but how—*how?*—could the grandes dames imagine he could simply—so cold-bloodedly—just choose one, and then spend the rest of his life tied to her, condemning her to a life tied to him . . .

Condemning them both to living—no, existing—in exactly the same sort of married life his father and his mother had had.

Not the married life his friends enjoyed, not the supportive unions his ex-colleagues had forged, and nothing like the marriage Hamish had.

No. Because he was Wolverstone, he was to be denied any such comfort, condemned instead to the loveless union his family had traditionally engaged in, simply because of the name he bore.

Because they—all of them—thought they knew him, thought that, because of his name, they knew what sort of man he was.

He didn't know what sort of man he truly was—how could they?

Uncertainty had plagued him from the moment he'd stepped away from the created persona of Dalziel, then been compounded massively by his accession to the title so unexpectedly, so unprepared. At twenty-two he'd been entirely certain who Royce Henry Varisey was, but when he'd looked again sixteen years later . . . none of his previous certainties had fitted.

He no longer fitted the construct of the man, the duke, he'd thought he would be.

Duty, however, was one guiding light he'd always recognized, and still did. So he'd tried. He'd spent all night poring over their list, trying to force himself to toe the expected line.

He'd failed. He couldn't do it—couldn't force himself to choose a woman he didn't want.

And the prime reason he couldn't was about to enter the room behind him.

He hauled in a massive breath, then snarled and flung himself into one of the large armchairs set before the windows, facing the open doorway.

Just as she sailed in.

Minerva knew from long experience of Variseys that this was no time for caution, much less meekness. The sight that met her eyes as she came to a halt inside the ducal sitting room—the wall of fury that assailed her senses—confirmed that; he'd roll right over her, smother her, if she gave him half a chance.

She fixed him with an exasperated, aggravated gaze. "You have to make a choice, make it and declare it—or else give me something I can take downstairs that will satisfy the ladies, or they're not going to leave." She folded her arms and stared him down. "And you'll like that even less."

A long silence ensued. She knew he used silences to undermine; she didn't budge an inch, just waited him out.

His eyes narrowed. Eventually, one dark, diabolically winged brow rose. "Are you really that keen to explore Egypt?"

She frowned. "What?" Then she made the connection. Tightened her lips. "Don't try to change the subject. In case you've forgotten, it's your bride."

His gaze remained fixed on her face, on her eyes. "Why are you so keen to have me declare who I'll wed?" His voice had lowered, softened, his tone growing strangely, insidiously suggestive. "Are you so eager to escape from Wolverstone and your duties, and all those here?"

The implication pricked a spot she hadn't, until that instant, realized was sensitive. Her temper flared, so quickly and completely she had no chance to rein it back. "As you know damned well"—her voice dripped fury, her eyes, she knew, would be all golden scorn—"Wolverstone is the only home I've ever known. It *is* my home. While you might know every rock, every stone, I know every single man, woman, and child on this estate." Her voice deepened, vibrating with emotion. "I know the seasons, and how each affects us. I know every facet of the dynamics of the castle community and how it runs. Wolverstone has been my *life* for more than twenty years, and loyalty to—and love for—it and its people is what has kept me here so long."

She dragged in a tight breath. His eyes dropped briefly to her breasts, mounding above her neckline; uncaring, she trapped his gaze as it returned to her face. "So no, I'm *not* keen to leave—I would much rather stay—but leave I must."

"Why?"

She flung up her hands. "Because you *have to marry* one of the ladies on that damned list! And once you do, there'll be no place for me here."

If he was taken aback by her outburst, she saw no hint of it; his face remained set, the lines chiseled stone. The only sense she gained from him was one of implacable, immovable opposition.

His gaze shifted from her to the mantelpiece, following the long line of armillary spheres she'd kept dusted and polished. His dark gaze rested on them for a long moment, then he murmured, "You're always telling me to go my own road."

She frowned. "This *is* your own road, the one you would naturally take—it's only the timing that's changed."

He looked at her; she tried, but, as usual, could read nothing in his dark eyes. "What," he asked, his voice very soft, "if that's not the road I want to take?"

She sighed through her teeth. "Royce, stop being difficult for the sake of it. You know you're going to choose one of the ladies on that list. The list is extensive, indeed complete, so those are your choices. So just tell me the name and I'll take it downstairs, before the grandes dames decide to barge in here."

He studied her. "What about your alternative?"

It took her a moment to follow, then she held up her hands, conceding. "Fine—give me something to tell them that will satisfy them instead."

"All right."

She suppressed a frown. His gaze fixed on her, he looked like he was thinking, the wheels of his diabolical mind churning.

"You may announce to the ladies downstairs"—the words were slow, even, his tone dangerously mild—"that I've made up my mind which lady I'll wed. They can expect to see the announcement of our betrothal in a week or so, once the lady I've chosen agrees."

Her eyes locked with his, she replayed the declaration; it would, indeed, satisfy the grandes dames. It sounded sensible, rational—in fact, exactly what he should say.

But . . . she knew him far too well to accept the words at face value. He was up to something, but she couldn't think what.

Royce surged to his feet—before she could question him. Shrugging out of his hacking jacket, he walked toward his bedroom. "And now, if you'll excuse me, I must change."

She frowned, annoyed by his refusal to let her probe, but with no choice offering, she stiffly inclined her head, turned, and walked out, closing the door behind her.

Tugging loose his neckerchief, he watched the door shut, then strode into his bedroom. She would learn the answer to her question soon enough.

Seven

he next morning, garbed in her riding habit, Minerva sat in the private breakfast parlor and consumed her marmaladed toast as quickly as she daintily could; she was intent on getting out on Rangonel as soon as possible.

She hadn't seen Royce since he'd sent her off with his response to the grandes dames' demand. He hadn't joined the guests still remaining for dinner; she hadn't been surprised. But she wasn't in any hurry to meet him, not until she felt more like herself, hence her wariness as, toast finished, tea drunk, she rose and headed for the stables.

Retford had confirmed that His Grace had breakfasted earlier and gone riding; he was most likely far away by now, but she didn't want to run into him if he'd cut short his ride and was returning to the keep. Avoiding the west courtyard, his favored route, she exited via the castle's east wing, and set off through the gardens.

She'd spent an unsettled evening, and an even more restless night, going over in her mind the ladies on the list, trying to predict whom he'd chosen. She'd met some of them during the seasons she and his mother had spent in the capital; while she couldn't imagine any of them as his duchess, that lack of enthusiasm didn't explain the hollow, deadening feeling that had, over the last days, been growing inside her.

That had intensified markedly after she'd delivered his declaration to the grandes dames and waved them on their way.

Certainly, being forced to state out aloud her unhappiness over leaving Wolverstone, giving voice to what she truly felt, hadn't helped. By the time she'd retreated to her room last night, that unexpected, welling emotion was approaching desolation. As if something was going *horribly* wrong.

It was nonsensical. She'd done what she'd had to do—what her vows had committed her to do—and she'd *succeeded*. Yet her emotions had swung crazily in the opposite direction; she didn't feel as if she'd won, but as if she'd lost.

Lost something vital.

Which was silly. She'd always known the time would come when she'd have to leave Wolverstone.

It had to be some irrational twisting of her emotions caused by the increasingly fraught battle she constantly had to wage to keep her frustrating and irritating, infatuation-obsession-driven physical reactions to Royce completely hidden—hidden so completely not even he would see.

The stables loomed ahead. She walked into the courtyard, smiling when she saw Rangonel waiting, saddled and patient by the mounting block, a groom at his head. She went forward—a flash of gray and the steel tattoo of dancing hooves had her glancing around.

Sword pranced on the other side of the yard, saddled and . . . waiting. She tried to tell herself Royce must have just ridden in . . . but the stallion looked fresh, impatient to be off.

Then she saw Royce—pushing away from the wall against which he'd been leaning chatting to Milbourne and Henry.

Henry went to calm Sword and untie his reins.

Milbourne rose from the bench on which he'd been sitting.

And Royce walked toward her.

Quickening her pace, she clambered onto the mounting block and scrambled, breathless, into her sidesaddle.

Royce halted a few paces away and looked up at her. "I need to talk to you."

Doubtless about his bride. Her lungs constricted; she felt literally ill.

He didn't wait for any agreement, but took the reins Henry offered, and swung up to Sword's back.

"Ah . . . we should discuss the mill. There are decisions that need to be made—"

"We can talk when we stop to rest the horses." His dark gaze raked her, then he turned Sword to the archway. "Come on."

This time, he led.

She had no option but to follow. Given the pace he set, that took all her concentration; only when he slowed as they started up Lord's Seat did she have wits to spare to start wondering what, exactly, he was going to say.

He led her up to a sheltered lookout. A grassy shelf on the side of the hill where a remnant of woodland enclosed a semicircular clearing, it had one of the best views in the area, looking south down the gorge through which the Coquet tumbled, to the castle, bathed in sunlight, set against the backdrop of the hills beyond.

Royce had chosen the spot deliberately; it gave the best, most complete view of the estate, the fields as well as the castle.

He rode Sword to the trees, swung down from the stallion's back, and tied the reins to a branch. On her bay, Minerva followed more slowly. Allowing her time to slip down from her saddle and tie her horse, he crossed the lush grass to the rim of the clearing; looking out over his lands, he seized the moment to rehearse his arguments one more time.

She didn't want to leave Wolverstone, and, as the pristine condition of his armillary spheres testified, she felt *something* for him. It might not be the counterpart of his desire for her, and she hadn't seen enough of him to have developed an admiration and appreciation of his talents reciprocal to his for hers. But it was enough.

Enough for him to work with, enough for him to suggest as a basis for their marriage. It was a damned sight more than could possibly exist between him and any of the ladies on the grandes dames' list.

He'd come prepared to persuade.

She was twenty-nine, and had admitted no man had offered her anything she valued.

She valued Wolverstone, and he would offer her that.

Indeed, he was willing to offer her anything it was in his power to give, just as long as she agreed to be his duchess.

She might not be as well-connected or well-dowered as the candidates on the list, but her birth and fortune were more than sufficient that she needn't fear the ton would consider their union a mésalliance.

More, in marrying him herself, she would be satisfying her vows to his parents in unarguably the most effective way—she was the only female who had ever stood up to him, ever faced him down.

As she'd proved yesterday, she would tell him whatever she deemed he needed to hear regardless of him wanting to hear it. And she would do so knowing that he could rip up at her, knowing how violent his temper could be. She already knew, was demonstrably confident, that he would never lose it with—loose it on—her.

That she knew him that well spoke volumes. That she had the courage to act on her knowledge said even more.

He needed a duchess who would be more than a cipher, a social ornament for his arm. He needed a helpmate, and she was uniquely qualified.

Her caring for the estate, her connection with it, was the complement of his; together, they would give Wolverstone—castle, estate, title, and family—the best governance it could have.

And when it came to the critical issue of his heirs, having her in his bed was something he craved; he desired her—more than he would any of the grandes dames' ciphers, no matter how beautiful. Physical beauty was the most minor attractant to a man like him. There had to be more, and in that respect Minerva was supremely well-endowed.

Yesterday, while she'd been insisting he appease the grandes dames, he'd finally accepted that, if he wanted a marriage like his friends', then, regardless of what he had to do to make it happen, it was Minerva he needed as his wife. That if he wanted something more than a loveless marriage, he would have to strike out, and, as he had with her help in other respects, try to find a new road.

With her.

The certainty that had gripped him, infused him, hadn't waned; with the passing hours, it had grown more intense. He'd never felt more certain, more set on any course, more confident it was the right one for him.

No matter what he had to do—no matter the hurdles she might place in his path, no matter where the road led or how fraught the journey might be, no matter what she or the world might demand of him—it was she he had to have.

He couldn't sit back and wait for it to happen; if he waited any longer, he'd be wed to someone else. So he would do whatever it took, swallow whatever elements of his pride he had to, learn to persuade, to seduce, to entice—do whatever he needed to to convince her to be his.

Mind and senses returning to the here and now, poised to speak, he mentally reached for her—and realized she hadn't yet joined him.

Turning, he saw her still sitting her horse. She'd swung the big bay to face the view. Hands folded before her, she looked past him down the valley.

He shifted, caught her eye. Beckoned. "Come down. I want to talk to you."

She looked at him for a moment, then nudged her horse forward. Halting the big bay alongside, she looked down at him. "I'm comfortable here. What did you want to talk about?"

He looked up at her. Proposing while she was perched above him was beyond preposterous. "Nothing I can discuss while you're up there."

She'd eased her boots from the stirrups. He reached up and plucked her from her saddle.

Minerva gasped. He'd moved so fast she'd had no time to block him—to prevent him from closing his hands around her waist and lifting her . . .

Increasingly slowly, he lowered her to the ground.

The look on his face—utter, stunned disbelief—would have been priceless if she hadn't known what put it there.

She'd reacted to his touch. Decisively and definitely. She'd stiffened. Her lungs had seized; her breath had hitched in a wholly damning way. Focused on her, his hands tight about her waist, he hadn't missed any of the telltale signs.

Long before her feet got within a foot of the lush grass, he'd guessed her secret.

Knew it beyond question.

She read as much in the subtle shift of his features, in the suddenly intent—ruthlessly intent—look that flared in his eyes.

She panicked. The instant her feet touched earth, she forced in a breath, opened her lips—

He bent his head and kissed her.

Not gently.

Hard. Ravenously. Her lips had been parted; his tongue filled her mouth with no by-your-leave.

He marched in and laid claim. His lips commanded, demanded—rapaciously seized her wits. Captured her senses.

Desire rolled over her in a hot wave.

His, she realized on a mental gasp, not just hers.

The realization utterly dumbfounded her; since when had he desired her?

Yet the ability to think, to reason, to do anything other than feel and respond had flown.

She didn't at first realize she was kissing him back; once she did, she tried to stop—but couldn't. Couldn't drag her senses from their fascination, from their greedy excitement; this was better than she'd dreamed. Regardless of all wisdom, she wasn't able to disengage, not from him, not from this.

He made it harder yet when he angled his head, slanted his lips over hers, and deepened the kiss—not by degrees, but in one bold, senses-shattering leap.

Her hands had fallen to his shoulders; they gripped, clung as their mouths melded—as he relentlessly pressed his advantage, rolled over her defenses and drew her with him into the scorching, shatteringly intimate exchange. She couldn't comprehend how his rapacious kisses, his hard hungry lips, his bold thrusting tongue, caught her, trapped her, then delivered her up, captive to her own need to respond. It wasn't *his* will making her kiss him so damningly eagerly, as if despite all good sense, she couldn't get enough of his thinly veiled possession.

She'd always known he would be an aggressive lover; what she hadn't known, would never have guessed, was that she would respond so flagrantly, so invitingly—that she would welcome that aggression, seize it as her due and demand more.

Yet that was precisely what she was doing—and she couldn't stop.

Her experience with men was limited, but not nonexistent, yet this . . . was something entirely beyond her ken.

No other man had made her heart thud, made her blood sing, sent it racing through her body.

With his lips on hers, with just a kiss, he'd transformed her into a greedy wanton—and some part of her soul sang.

Royce knew. Sensed her response in every fiber of his being. He wanted more—of her, of her luscious mouth, of her blatantly inviting lips. Yet beyond his own hunger lay the wonder of hers, a temptation like no other, one every primitive instinct he possessed had fixed upon, unswervingly fastened on as the most direct and certain route to appeasing his own, already tumultuous needs.

Sunk in her mouth, he wasn't thinking. Only feelings registered—the spike of disbelief when he'd realized what she'd been hiding—that she did indeed respond to him vibrantly, instinctively, most importantly helplessly—that despite his experience, his skills, she'd pulled the wool thickly and completely over his eyes . . . and a wave of hard anger that the agonies he'd suffered over the past weeks while subduing his lust for her hadn't been necessary. That if he'd given in and kissed her, she'd have yielded.

As she was now.

She was helplessly in thrall to the desire, the passion, that had erupted between them, more powerful, more driven from having been denied.

Relief swam through him; he would no longer need to suppress his lust for her. Expectation flared at the prospect of giving it full rein. Of indulging it to the hilt. With her. In her.

In the instant before he'd kissed her, he'd looked into her face, into her gorgeous autumn-rich eyes—and had seen them widen. Not only with the realization that he'd learned what she'd been hiding, not just with apprehension over what he might do, but with sensual shock. That was what had sent her eyes flaring, all rich browns and welcoming golds; more than experienced enough to recognize it, he'd instantly taken advantage.

He'd seen her lips part, start to form some word; he hadn't been interested in listening. And now—now that she was trapped in the web of their desires—he was intent on only one thing. On possessing what he'd wanted to seize for the last too many days.

On possessing her.

She was clinging to his shoulders, as deeply ensnared in their kiss as he. Her knees had weakened; his hands locked about her waist, he held her upright.

He didn't even need to think to steer her back, shouldering her horse aside as he guided her back until her spine met the bole of the nearest useful tree.

She instinctively braced against it. He wedged his right knee between her thighs, the hard muscle of his thigh riding against hers, holding her in place as he released his grip about her waist, easing back from the kiss as, hard palms to the velvet of her habit, he skated his hands, slow and deliberate, up, over her ribs, and closed them possessively about her breasts.

He broke from the kiss, let their hungry lips part just enough to catch the shocked, delicious inward hiss of her breath as he eased his hands, then closed them again, then provocatively kneaded. Just enough to savor her half moan, half sob when he found her nipples and through the screening fabric circled the tight nubs with his thumbs.

Then he dove back into the kiss, reclaimed her mouth, sent her gathering wits spinning again while he set his hands to learn everything he needed to know to reduce her to the sensual wanton he had every intention of drawing forth.

She had it in her, he knew.

Even just from this kiss, he knew beyond question that she was not just more responsive than any woman he'd ever known, but specifically more responsive to him. If he managed her correctly, educated her properly, she would willingly cede him everything, anything and everything he wanted of her; he knew it to his bones.

There was nothing the marcher lord within him found more alluring than the prospect of absolute surrender.

He plundered her mouth, and reveled in the knowledge that, soon, she would be his. That, very soon, she would lie beneath him, heated and mindless as he sheathed himself in her.

As he took her, claimed her, and made her his.

He wouldn't even need to go slowly; she wouldn't be shocked by his demands. She knew him well, knew what to expect from him.

Closing his hands possessively about her breasts, squeezing her distended nipples between his fingers, he shifted his thigh so the long muscle rode more definitely against the soft flesh at the apex of hers, caught her muffled moan, and held her, with lips and tongue bound her ever more tightly to the increasingly explicit exchange.

Drew her ever more powerfully along the road to his goal.

Minerva knew his direction, felt it—ached for it—with every muscle, with every taut nerve, yet while most of her mind was deliriously following him, wantonly abandoned to his desire and hers, a small part remained lucid, detached, shrieking that this was more than dangerous, more than disastrous—that this was calamity about to strike.

It didn't matter; she couldn't break away. Her mind was overwhelmed, seduced in every way.

He, his kiss, was all power and passion, intertwined, entwined, inseparable.

The taste of him, of that senses-seducing combination, overrode all good sense, devastatingly easily. The edged desire in his kiss, dangerous and uncompromising, lured her on. He devoured, seized, claimed—and she kissed him back, wanting more, inviting more; his hands on her body, hard and possessive, set a fire burning within her she knew he could quench.

She needed to feel it, that fire, that life, needed to burn in its flames.

She knew that, craved it, even though she knew that with him, that fire would sear, scorch, and ultimately scar.

Yet the fact that he wanted her, and she knew enough to know that his want was as honest and real as hers, completely overset, overcame, overturned her carefully constructed defenses. His need, his raw hunger, was the most powerful weapon he could wield against her—as if he'd needed more.

She knew she was a fool for permitting the kiss to rage—although how she might have stopped him, stopped them, she had no clue. Yet even knowing how witless it was to so wantonly accept every potent caress, and mindless—abandoned to all good sense—yearn for more, she couldn't stop herself from seizing this, this moment, with both hands, and wringing from it all she could. Clinging to him, savoring every nuance, every evocative, provocative sweep of his tongue, of his bold fingers, seizing as much as she dared, surrendering whatever he asked. Taking from him, from the moment, as much as she possibly could.

It wasn't going to happen again.

It was he who broke the kiss, he who lifted his lips from hers. They were both breathing rapidly. After several breaths, her senses returned enough to inform her how heated, how pliant, how weak she'd become.

How helpless in his arms.

He glanced left, then right. Then he swore.

Grated, his voice a deep rumble, "Not here."

Her wits returned in a rush, and she realized what he meant. Felt panic rise as she looked where he had, and realized she owed her escape to the heavy dew that had left the lush grass sodden.

If not for that . . .

She quashed a telltale shuddery shiver as he stepped back.

Royce felt it—sensed it in his marrow—but clamped down hard on his inevitable reaction. The grass was too damned wet, and the trees all had rough, deeply etched bark, but quite aside from such logistical difficulties, ones he could yet have overcome, that part of him ruled by his more primitive self was insisting, dictatorially, that the first time he sank into his chatelaine she should be sprawled naked beneath him in his ducal bed—the massive four-poster in his room.

His mind could, and did, supply any number of pertinent benefits, and after his proven-to-be-unnecessary abstinence of the past weeks, he wasn't in any mood to stint himself.

Stepping back, he waited until she was steady on her feet, then towed her to her horse and lifted her to her saddle.

Blinking in surprise, Minerva desperately tried to reorder her senses and her wits. While he untied Sword's reins and swung up to the gray's back, she slid her boots into her stirrups, reclaimed her reins.

With just a look that said very clearly, "Follow me," he turned Sword and led the way down. Luckily, they had to go slowly down the hill; once they reached the flat and the horses stretched into a gallop, she'd recovered enough to cope.

Nevertheless, she was amazed she made it back to the castle without a stumble. By the time the stables rose before them, her mind had cleared, and her wits had reassembled. Her lips were still swollen, and her body still warm, and if she thought too much, remembered too much, she would blush, but she knew what she had to do.

They clattered into the stable yard and he fluidly dismounted. By the time she'd halted Rangonel and freed her feet from her stirrups, he was by her side; she surrendered to the inevitable and let him lift her down.

And discovered that, if she wasn't tensing, fighting to suppress her reaction, then the sensation of his hands gripping her waist, that instant of being completely in his power as he lifted her, held more delight than trauma.

She reminded herself that when it came to him, she no longer had anything to hide. Yet when he grasped her hand, engulfing it in his, she would have tugged it back—except he tightened his hold, threw her a look, and proceeded to hold her beside him as, with a curt nod to Milbourne, he stalked out of the yard.

Deciding that having a tug-of-war over her hand with His Grace of Wolverstone in his own stable yard, watched over by various of his and her staff, wasn't an endeavor she was likely to gain anything from, she held her tongue, and strove to keep up with his strides.

She had to pick her time, her moment. Her battleground.

He led her to the house via the west courtyard, but instead of taking his usual route to the front hall and the main stairs, he turned the other way; she realized he was making for the west turret stairs, a rarely used lesser staircase from which he could reach the gallery, not far from his rooms.

Until he'd headed that way, she hadn't been sure what he intended, but given his preference for the minor stairs . . . he was taking her to his rooms.

She chose the small hall at the foot of the turret stairs to make her stand. There were no servants about, no one else about to see, let alone interrupt. When he reached for the newel post, she halted. Held steady when he tried to draw her forward. He looked around, met her gaze—saw her determination. Arched one black brow.

"What you have in mind isn't going to happen." She made the statement clearly, evenly. Not a challenge, but a statement of fact. She wanted to draw her hand from his, to lose the sensation of his long, strong fingers locked about hers, but knew better than to trigger his reaction. Instead, she met his gaze with steadfast resolution. "You are not even going to kiss me again."

His eyes narrowed; turning to face her, he opened his mouth—

"No. You will not. You might lust after me, but that, as we both know, is merely a reaction to being forced to name your bride. It will last for all of a day or two, and then what? It's possible that the only reason your eye has fixed on me is that I'm one of the few ladies in the house not related to you. But I'm not going to tumble into your bed just because you've decided it suits you. I'm your chatelaine, not your lover, not your mistress." She drew in a breath, held his dark gaze. "So we're going to pretend, going to behave, as if what just happened on Lord's Seat . . . didn't."

That was the only way she could think of to survive, heart intact, to get through this time as his chatelaine, fulfill her vows to his parents, and then leave Wolverstone and start a new life.

Somewhere.

Somewhere a very long way from him, so she'd never have to meet him again, not even set eyes on him. Because after what had just happened on Lord's Seat, she was going to regret not letting matters take their course, to regret not letting him take her to his bed.

And that regret would last forever.

Royce watched her denial form on her lips—lips he'd just kissed, possessed, and now knew beyond question were his.

He heard her words, could even make sense of them, but the reactions they called forth left him inwardly reeling. As if she'd picked up a broadsword and clouted him over the head.

She couldn't be serious—yet he could see she was.

He'd stopped thinking rationally the instant he'd possessed her lips, the instant he'd swept into her mouth and tasted her. Claimed her. He'd spent the ride home anticipating claiming her in a more absolute, biblical way—and now she was refusing.

More, she was insisting that their incendiary kiss should be ignored, as if she hadn't welcomed him, kissed him back, and clung.

Worse, she'd accused him of seducing her out of lust— that he would take her to his bed with no feeling whatever, that she was merely a convenient female body to him . . . inwardly he frowned. He felt offended, yet . . .

He was a Varisey, until now in this sphere archetypically so—she had every reason to believe any female would do.

Except no other would. He knew that to his bones.

He held her gaze. "You want me as much as I want you."

She lifted her chin. "Perhaps. But remember the reason I haven't accepted any offers—of any sort—from any gentlemen? Because they didn't offer anything I wanted." She looked directly into his eyes. "In this case, anything I want *enough.*"

Her last word echoed in the stairwell, filling the silence that fell between them.

A clear, unequivocal challenge.

One that called to him on a level he couldn't deny, but he could see from her eyes, her calmly resolute mien, that she was unaware she'd issued it.

The marcher lord within him purred in anticipation. Inwardly he smiled; outwardly he maintained his impassive expression.

Desire, lust, and need still ran rampant through his veins, but he reined the unruly, tempestuous emotions in. He wanted her, and was determined to have her. He'd gone to the lookout already committed to doing whatever it took to convince her to be his—in all the relevant spheres, of which this was one. His first test, apparently, was to convince her that she wanted him *enough*—to wit, a great deal more than she knew.

The prospect of exerting himself over a woman felt alien, but he shook aside the niggle.

He'd been intending to offer her the dukedom, his duchess's coronet; he toyed with the idea of asking her if that would prove *enough*. But the challenge she'd issued had been based on the physical, not the material; he would answer her on the same plane. Time enough once she was gracing his bed to inform her of the permanent position he intended her to fill.

His gaze lowered to her hand, still resting in his. He needed to let her go—for now.

Forcing his fingers to ease, he let her hand, her fingers, slide from his grasp. Saw, because he was watching intently, her release the breath she'd been holding. She didn't step away; she lowered her arm, but otherwise remained still. Watching him.

Wise; his more primitive side wasn't happy about letting her go, and was just waiting for any excuse to override her wishes and the counsel of his wiser self.

Too conscious of that primitive self prowling just beneath his skin, he forced himself to turn away, to start up the stairs. He spoke without turning around. "I'll see you in the study in half an hour to discuss the mill."

That afternoon, Royce's last traitor lay naked on his back in Royce's younger sister's bed.

Equally naked, Susannah lolled on her stomach beside him. "I sent off that note with the post last evening—it should reach town later today."

"Good." Lifting an arm, he trailed his fingers over the

quite delectable curve of her derriere. "It'll be amusing to see if dear Helen avails herself of your kind invitation."

"Poor Royce, forced by the grandes dames to choose a bride—the least I can do is arrange a little diversion."

"With luck, the beautiful countess will be here by Sunday."

"Hmm." Susannah looked pensive. "I really can't see him rushing to announce his betrothal, not given it was forced on him. Once she arrives, he might put it off indefinitely."

"Or even change his mind. Have you really no idea who he's chosen?"

"No. No one does. Even Minerva has no clue, which, as you might expect, is bothering her greatly."

"Can't you wheedle it out of him? You're his favorite sister, after all."

Susannah snorted. "This is Royce *Varisey* we're talking about. He might look on me more kindly than he does Margaret and Aurelia—and really, who wouldn't?—but 'wheedling' anything out of him would literally be the equivalent of getting blood from a stone."

"Ah, well—it seems we'll have to wait with everyone else to hear. A week or so . . . not that long."

Susannah sat up. "Wait a minute. He said the week's delay was to get the lady's agreement." She turned to him. "If we knew which lady he contacted . . ."

It was his turn to snort derisively. "Not even *I* would suggest you might induce Retford to tell you who his new master is corresponding with."

Susannah slapped his chest with the back of her hand. "Not me, silly—Minerva. I bet she's already thought of it." She grinned, then slid sinuously, sensuously, into his arms. "I'll ask her . . . later."

He pulled her over him, licked her lips, and slid his hand between her thighs. "Indeed. Later."

Eight

oyce walked into the drawing room that evening, and calmly surveyed the remaining company. His sisters had stayed, although their husbands had departed; all three had, apparently, decided to indulge themselves with a few weeks' break, taking advantage of the, for them, freer, less restrictive structure of his essentially bachelor household.

All three were indulging in affairs under his roof—Aurelia and Susannah with two of his cousins, Margaret with the husband of one of her "friends," who was helpfully otherwise engaged with another of his cousins.

Luckily, he wasn't, wouldn't be held to be, responsible in any way for them, their sins, or their marriages. For the moment, at least, they could do as they pleased; they—his sisters, cousins, and their assorted friends—would provide cover for his pursuit of his chatelaine.

For that, he would tolerate them, at least for now. He was easy enough in their company; he could interact with them or ignore them as he chose.

Some had mentioned staying for the Alwinton Fair, a few weeks away. It was a highlight of the local year; their mother had often hosted house parties coinciding with the event. As he glanced around, noting bright eyes, flushed cheeks, and meaningful looks, it seemed his sisters and cousins were intent on recapturing those youthful, more carefree times.

He, in contrast, was intent on capturing Minerva. With luck, the fair and the company would distract his sisters from any further misplaced interest in *his* affairs.

Despite the frustration he'd recently endured having been to no real purpose, that frustration was still continuing. Not, however, for long. He'd forced himself to toe her line through a few hours of her company, discussing the mill and other estate matters—lulling her into a sense of safety.

Into believing she was safe with him. From him.

Nothing could be further from the truth, at least not with respect to their current point of contention. She was going to land in his bed—naked—sooner or later; he was intent on ensuring it was the former that applied.

He located her at the center of a group by the fireplace; she still wore her weeds, as did his sisters, but the other female guests had switched to gowns of lavender or gray. Minerva still shone like a beacon to him. He prowled through the guests, heading her way.

Minerva saw him coming; continuing to smile at Phillip Debraigh, who was entertaining the group with a tale, she forced herself to take slow, deep breaths, and a firmer grip on her composure. Royce had, without argument, behaved precisely as she'd stipulated for the rest of the morning and all the afternoon, adhering to both the letter and intent of her dictate. There was no reason to imagine he'd suddenly change tack . . .

Except that she couldn't bring herself to believe that he would meekly accept her dismissal and fall in with her specified line.

Which was why she tensed, lungs tightening, when he neared. Phillip ended his tale and excused himself, drifting off to join another group. The circle shuffled, adjusted, as Royce came to stand by her side.

He greeted the others with his customary, coolly urbane air; last of all, he looked at her—and smiled.

Pure wolf. That he planned something was patently clear from the expression in his dark eyes.

Lips lightly curved, she inclined her head serenely in reply.

One of the other ladies launched into the latest ton story.

Nerves flickering, her lungs too tight, Minerva seized the moment to murmur, "If you'll excuse me . . ." She stepped back—

Halted, nerves leaping, as long, hard fingers closed—gently, yet with underlying strength—about her elbow.

Royce turned with her, one dark brow arching. "Whither away?"

Away from him. She looked across the room. "I should see if Margaret needs anything."

"I thought, as my chatelaine, you're supposed to remain by my side."

"If you need me."

"I definitely need you."

She didn't dare look at his face. His tone was bad enough; the tenor of his deep voice sent a shivery tingle skating down her spine. "Well, then, you should probably speak with those cousins you've spent least time with. Henry and Arthur, for instance."

Releasing her, he waved her forward. "Lead on." He paced beside her as she glided through the guests toward the group with whom the two youngest Variseys present were standing. As they neared, he murmured, "Just don't try to slip away from me."

The undisguised warning had her plastering on a smile, engaging Henry and Arthur, and dutifully remaining beside Royce as they conversed.

She quickly realized why he'd appeared in the drawing room the full regulation half hour before dinner—so he could use the time to torture her with a thousand little touches. Nothing more than the polite, unremarkable, customary gestures a gentleman bestowed on a lady—his grip on her elbow, a touch on her arm, the sensation of his hand hovering at the back of her waist . . . then touching, lightly steering—*burning*.

Her pulse leapt every time; when Retford at last appeared to announce dinner, she was wishing she'd brought down her fan. Under cover of the butler's stentorian announcement, she glanced at Royce, narrowed her eyes. Although his impassive mien didn't soften, with his eyes he managed to convey an expression of supreme innocence.

She narrowed her eyes to slits. "You haven't been innocent since birth."

He smiled—a gesture that, for her, didn't bode well—and took her arm.

Desperately tamping down her reaction, she indicated a lady across the room. "You should lead Caroline Courtney in."

"Lady Courtney can find her own partner. This is not a formal dinner." He looked down at her, his dark gaze suggestive. "I'd much rather lead you."

He deliberately omitted the "in," leaving her to supply the context—something the less sensible part of her mind was only too happy to do. Damn it. Damn him.

Reaching the dining table at the head of the line, he sat her to the left of his great chair. As he took his seat, she grasped the chance provided by the scrape of other chairs to murmur, "This ploy of yours won't work." She caught his eye. "I'm not going to change my mind."

He held her gaze, let a heartbeat pass, then slowly raised one brow. "Oh?"

She looked away, inwardly berating herself. She knew better than to fling gauntlets his way.

Predictably, he picked hers up.

She'd thought she would be reasonably safe at the table—the numbers had reduced so they weren't sitting overly close—but she quickly learned that he didn't need to physically touch her to affect her.

All he needed to do was fix his gaze on her mouth as she supped her soup, or as she closed her lips about a delicate fish dumpling; how he could communicate lascivious thoughts with just a glance from his dark eyes she didn't know, but he could.

She sat back, cleared her throat, reached for her wineglass. Took a sip, felt his gaze on her lips, then felt it lower as she swallowed . . . as if he were tracking the liquid as it slid down her throat, traveled down inside her chest . . .

Desperate, she turned to the gentleman—Gordon Varisey—sitting on her other side, but he was engrossed in a discussion with Susannah. Across the table, Caroline, Lady Courtney, was more interested in making eyes at Phillip Debraigh than in distracting her host.

"Is my ploy working yet?"

The soft, taunting words slipped past her ear like a caress; turning to face Royce as he sat back in his chair, wineglass in hand, she fought to quell a reactive shiver, and didn't entirely succeed.

Her only consolation was that no one else seemed to have noticed the subtle battle being waged at the head of the table. That being so . . . she narrowed her eyes on his, succinctly stated, "Go to the devil."

His lips curved in an entirely genuine—devastatingly attractive—smile. His gaze locked with hers, he raised his wineglass, sipped. "I expect I will."

She looked away; she didn't need to see the sheen of red wine on the mobile lips she'd spent a good portion of her girlhood dreaming about. She reached for her wineglass.

Just as he added, "If nothing else for what I'm imagining doing to you."

Her fingers missed the glass bowl, bobbled the long stem; the wineglass tipped—

He caught it, his left hand reaching over hers, then curling over it as he pressed the stem into her all but nerveless fingers.

His hand rested, hard and strong, over hers, until she gripped the glass, then he withdrew his hand slowly, his fingers stroking over her hand and knuckles.

Her lungs had seized long ago.

He shifted, using the movement to lean closer and murmur, "Breathe, Minerva."

She did, hauling in a huge breath—refusing to notice that as he sat back, his gaze lowered to her breasts, half exposed by her evening gown.

She was ready to do murder by the time the meal ended. Rising with the other ladies, she followed Margaret to the drawing room.

Royce wasn't going to let her be. She'd been chased by gentlemen—even noblemen—before; any man but he and she would have simply stood her ground, confident of her ability to trump whatever move he made, but she knew her limits. She needed to escape while she could. He would lead the gentlemen back to rejoin the ladies all too soon.

Reaching the drawing room, the ladies filed in; she paused just inside the door, waiting until the others settled. She'd speak with Margaret, then—

"There you are." Susannah slipped her arm through hers and drew her toward the side of the room. "I wanted to ask"—Susannah leaned close—"whether you have any idea which lady Royce is corresponding with?"

She frowned. "Corresponding?"

"He said he'd make an announcement once the lady he'd chosen agreed." Halting, Susannah fixed her eyes—a lighter brown than her brother's—on Minerva's face. "So I presume he's asking her, and as she's not here, I assume he must have written to her."

"Ah, I see. I haven't seen him write any letter, but then he uses Handley for most of his correspondence, so I wouldn't necessarily know." Much to her relief, especially in this matter.

"Handley?" Susannah tapped her lips with one fingertip, then slanted a glance Minerva's way. "I haven't met him, but perhaps he might be persuaded to divulge what he knows?"

She shook her head. "I wouldn't bother trying. Aside

from all else, he'll tell Royce." She hesitated, then added, "In fact, all Royce's personal staff are utterly devoted. You won't find any who'll discuss his private affairs."

Including her.

Susannah sighed. "I suppose we'll learn the truth soon enough."

"Indeed." She patted Susannah's arm as she drew hers free. "I have to speak with Margaret."

Susannah nodded and strolled off to join some others while Minerva headed for Margaret, enthroned in state on the chaise facing the hearth.

Susannah was right; Royce must have sent some communication to the lady he'd chosen as his duchess—a point she shouldn't have forgotten. In typical Varisey fashion, while waiting for his bride to agree to be his, he was intent on bedding his chatelaine.

If she needed any reminder of the unwisdom of letting him seduce her, recalling that she would learn any day who would be his duchess should help bolster her resolution.

She really didn't want to know; the thought curdled her stomach.

Refocusing on her plans to stay out of his arms, and out of his bed, she paused beside Margaret. "I have a headache," she lied. "Can you do the honors with the tea tray?"

"Yes, of course." Looking more relaxed than when her husband had been there, Margaret waved her away. "You should tell Royce not to work you so hard, dear. You need time for some distraction."

Minerva smiled and headed for the door; she understood perfectly what "distraction" Margaret was recommending— precisely the sort her brother had in mind. *Variseys!*

She didn't dally; she didn't trust Royce not to cut the men's drinking short, and under some pretext return to the drawing room early. Slipping out of the room, she went into the front hall, then quickly climbed the main stairs.

There was no one about. She heard no rumble of male voices; the gentlemen must still be in the dining room. Relieved, she walked into the keep, hesitated, debating, then headed for the duchess's morning room. It was too early for sleep, and her embroidery frame was there.

The morning room had been the late duchess's personal domain; her daughters had only intruded when invited. Since her death, they hadn't set foot there. Variseys had little interest in the dead; they never clung to memories.

That had suited Minerva. Over the last three years, the room had become her own.

Presumably it would remain so—until the next duchess arrived.

Opening the door, she went in. The room lay in darkness, but she knew it well. She walked toward the table that stood along the back of the nearer sofa, paused, then returned to the door and locked it. No sense taking any chances.

Smiling to herself, she strolled to the sofa table, set her hand on the tinderbox, and lit the lamp. The wick flared; she waited until it burned steadily, then set the glass in place, adjusted the flame—and suddenly felt—*knew*—that she wasn't alone . . . raising her gaze from the lamp, she looked—

At Royce, sitting at his negligent ease on the sofa opposite. Watching her.

"What are you doing here?" The words left her lips as her panicking mind assessed her options.

"Waiting for you."

She'd locked the door. Looking into his eyes, so dark, his gaze intent and unwavering, she knew that despite him being on the farther sofa, if she tried to reach the door, he'd be there ahead of her. "Why?"

Keeping him talking seemed her only option.

Assuming, of course, that he would oblige.

He didn't. Instead, he slowly rose. "Helpful of you to lock the door."

"I wasn't trying to help you." She watched him walk toward her, tamped down her flaring panic, reminded herself it was pointless to run. One did not turn and flee from a predator.

He rounded the sofa, and she swung to face him. He halted before her, looked into her face—as if studying it, her features, as if memorizing the details. "What you said—about me not kissing you again?"

She tensed. "What about it?"

His lips lifted fractionally. "I didn't agree."

She waited, beyond tense, for him to reach for her, to kiss her again, but he didn't. He stood looking down at her, watching her, his dark gaze intent, as if this were some game and it was her move.

Trapped in his gaze, she sensed heat stirring, rising between them; desperate, she searched for some way to distract him. "What about your bride? You're supposed to be arranging an announcement as we speak."

"I'm negotiating. Meanwhile . . ." He stepped forward; instinctively she stepped back. "I'm going to kiss you again."

That was what she was afraid of. He took another step, and she backed again.

"In fact," he murmured, closing the distance between them, "I'm going to kiss you more than just once, or even twice. And not just now, but later—whenever I feel like it."

Another step forward from him, another back for her.

"I intend to make a habit of kissing you."

She quickly took another step back as he continued to advance.

His gaze lowered to her lips, then flicked up to her eyes. "I'm going to spend a great deal of time savoring your lips, your mouth. And then . . ."

Her back hit the wall. Startled, she raised her hands to hold him off.

Smoothly, he caught them, one in each of his, and took one last step. Pinning her hands to the wall on either side of her head, he lowered his and looked into her eyes. Held her gaze relentlessly from a distance of mere inches.

"After *that*"—his voice had lowered to a senses-caressing purr—"I'm going to spend even more time savoring the rest of you. All of you. Every inch of skin, every hollow, every curve. I'm going to know you infinitely better than you know yourself."

She couldn't speak, couldn't breathe—couldn't think.

"I'm going to know you intimately." He savored the word. "I intend to explore you until there's nothing left to learn—until I know what makes you gasp, what makes you moan, what makes you scream. Then I'll make you do all three. Frequently."

Her spine was plastered to the wall; he wasn't leaning into her—yet—but with his arms raised, his coat had fallen open; there was barely an inch separating his chest and her breasts—and she could feel his heat. All down the front of her, she could feel his nearness, the beckoning hardness.

Everything her wanton self needed for relief.

But . . . She swallowed, forced herself to hold his gaze, lifted her chin. "Why are you telling me this?"

His lips quirked. His gaze lowered, fastened on her lips. "Because I thought it only fair that you know."

She forced a laugh. A breathless one. "Variseys never play fair—I'm not sure you 'play' at all."

His lips twisted. "True." His gaze drifted back to her eyes.

She caught it. "So why did you tell me?"

One brow lifted devilishly. "Because I intend to seduce you, and I thought that might help. Is it working?"

"No."

He smiled then, slowly, his eyes locked on hers. He shifted one hand, turned it so, when she followed his sideways glance, she saw he had the tips of his long fingers clamped over the veins at her wrist.

"Your pulse says otherwise."

His absolute unshakable arrogance set spark to her temper. Swinging her gaze back to his face, she narrowed her eyes on his. "You are the most ruthless, conceited, diabolical—"

He cut her off, his lips closing on hers, drinking in her temper—diverting it with ruthless, diabolical efficiency into something even hotter.

Something that melted her bones, that she fought, but

couldn't contain; the molten heat erupted and flooded through her, consuming intentions, inhibitions, all reservations.

Eradicating all good sense.

Leaving only hunger—blatant, explicit, ruthlessly seeking succor—in its wake.

The hard thrust of his tongue, the heavy, steely weight of him as he shifted closer and at last leaned in and pinned her body to the wall, was everything and more her witless senses wanted. Her tongue met his in a flagrant mating; her body strained, not to push him away but, every sense alive, to press against him.

To meet his hunger with hers.

To feed his desire with hers.

To meld the two, entwine them, until the power became too much for either of them to withstand.

This, now, was her only option; the rational part of her surrendered, and set her free to grasp the moment, and take from it all she could.

Wring from it every iota of pleasure.

He gave her no choice.

She left him with even less.

For long moments, mentally cursing, Royce kept both his hands locked about hers, safely pressed to the wall on either side of her head, for the simple reason that he didn't trust himself. And with her as she was, all but drunk on passion, he trusted her even less.

Her body was a heated feminine cushion pressed the length of his, her breasts firm against his chest, her long limbs riding against his, tempting and luring, the soft tautness of her belly caressing his already engorged shaft as if to urge him on.

He hadn't known she would respond as she had—instantly plunging them both into the fire. He recognized the flames well enough, but with her the conflagration threatened to run amok, to cinder his control.

That realization had been shocking enough to snap the

hold combined lust and desire had gained—enough to allow him to reassert that essential element. Control, his control, was vital—not just for him, but even more for her.

So he held on, battled the temptation she wantonly lavished on him, until his mind rose above the fog of his wracked and wholly engaged senses.

Then, at last, he knew what he had to do.

He didn't abate the passion, the possessiveness, in his kisses—not in the least. He angled his head and deliberately pushed her harder, further. Gave no quarter, accepted no appeasement.

Wasn't entirely surprised when, instead of retreating to safety, she met him, took all his passion, absorbed it, and then turned it back on him.

This time he was ready. Shifting against her, he used his hips to trap her against the wall; releasing her hands, he lowered his arms, and set his fingers to the tiny jet buttons running from her scooped neckline to the raised waist of her black gown.

She was so engrossed in the kiss, in inciting and taunting him, she didn't notice as he opened her bodice, then eased the halves apart. A flick here, there, and the ribbon ties of her chemise were undone. He set both palms to her shoulders, pressing the bodice wide, pushing the fine fabric of her chemise down as he ran his hands down, over and around, then filled them with her breasts. She gasped, literally quaked as he blatantly possessed—as he took charge of the kiss again, filled her mouth again, then let his attention shift to the warm, firm mounds in his hands.

To doing as he willed with them, tactilely savoring the fine skin, using one blunt fingertip to trace the ring of each puckered aureola, arousing her even more.

Then he closed his hands again, felt her drag in a breath and hold it as he played, possessed, kneaded. She shifted, tentative, restless; he sensed something within her—in the tautness of her slender frame—ease, change. Her hands fluttered, one on either side of his head, then closed, settled, one sliding to his nape, fingers tangling in his hair, gripping convulsively as he closed finger and thumb about her nipples and squeezed. Her other hand gently touched, traced, then cradled his cheek, his jaw.

Gently holding him.

First surrender, but he wanted much more, even though, tonight, he wouldn't take all he wanted from her.

He broke the kiss. Before she could react, with his head he nudged hers to the side, set his lips to the sensitive spot beneath her ear, then traced down the long line of her throat, paused to lave the point at its base where her pulse thudded frantically, then swept lower, to with his lips and mouth, with tongue and teeth, claim what his hands already had.

Head back against the wall, eyes closed, Minerva gasped, shuddered, felt her mind and her senses fragment under the assault he waged upon them. The sweep of his hard lips over her skin, the wet heat of his mouth applied to her aching nipples, the rough rasp of his tongue, the hot torment when he suckled her, ripped what wits she'd retained away, scattered them far and wide, and effectively routed any will she might have summoned against him.

His teeth nipped; pain and pleasure briefly combined, flaring hotly.

She was panting, wanton and abandoned, unable to think, her senses awash in a flood of heat; need, desire and passion were a growling, gnawing hunger in her belly.

He drew back, raised his head. His hands reclaimed her breasts, his fingers replacing his lips, continuing to play, to distract her as through the heated dimness he studied her face, assessed . . .

She felt the weight of his gaze, sensed his command, but she didn't want to open her eyes . . . she raised the heavy lids just enough to, through the fringe of her lashes, see him looking at her.

His face was harder, harsher than she'd ever seen it, lust and desire etching the edges of the already sharp angles and planes.

He saw her looking, caught her gaze.

A heartbeat passed, then one of his hands left her breast and, palm pressed to her body, skated slowly down. He held her gaze as, hand splayed, he paused at her waist to press . . . then that questing hand slid lower, pressed again as if testing the tautness of her stomach, then slid lower still, the rustle of her gown an evocative warning as he pressed his long fingers into the hollow between her thighs.

She shuddered, bit her lip, had to close her eyes, would have swayed if he hadn't been holding her against the wall.

His fingers stroked, then pressed further, deeper; her skirts did little to mute the effect of the intimate caress. His hand at her breast continued to idly play, further ruffling her senses, yet most of her awareness had locked on the heat emanating from where he was caressing her between her thighs.

She released her lip, gulped in a desperate breath—felt his fingers probe, and clamped her teeth over her lower lip again as her senses literally spun.

He leaned closer, one hard hip anchoring her while his fingers continued to stroke her soft flesh. He lowered his head, whispered in her ear, "Moan for me, Minerva."

She was utterly sure she shouldn't, that that was one surrender he shouldn't win. Eyes still closed, she shook her head.

Even though she couldn't see it, she knew his lips curved as he said, "Just wait. You will."

He was right; she did. And not just once.

He knew far too much, was too expert, too experienced, for her to stand against him. His fingers stroked, teased, probed, languidly caressed until she was utterly and insensibly desperate, for what she didn't fully comprehend, not until, with her wanton acquiescence, he rucked up her skirts and set his hand, his fingers, skin to skin to her wet, swollen flesh.

Then she learned, then she knew. Then she discovered what could make her moan, what could make her senses stretch tight, taut, to the sensual limit, where, quivering, they waited for release.

He thrust his fingers, one, then another, boldly into her sheath, worked them deep, and gave her what she wanted.

More pleasure, more sensation, more delight; the intimate penetration, his hard fingers slick with her passion, repetitively thrusting deep, filled her, drove her, sent her soaring.

Beyond recall; her senses, her nerves, started to unravel.

He locked his lips over hers, took her breath, gave it back as his fingers stroked deeply inside her—and her world shattered. She came apart, nerves fracturing, heat and sensation fragmenting, flying through her body, rocketing down her veins like shards of molten glass, flaring hot and bright everywhere under her skin, before sinking in, ultimately pooling low in her belly.

Long moments passed before her senses returned. Her first thought was that, if he hadn't kissed her at the last, she would have screamed.

Then she realized he'd drawn back, withdrawn his hand from between her thighs, and let her skirts fall. He'd shifted so he was leaning on one shoulder, set beside hers against the wall. His other hand was still idly, languidly caressing her naked breast.

She forced open her lids, turned her head to look into his face. He was watching his hand on her breast, but he felt her gaze and raised his heavy lids to meet her eyes.

She looked into his, and saw . . . shivered.

Royce didn't try to hide his intentions; he let them live in his eyes, let her see.

A frown swam over her face. She moistened her swollen lips.

Before she could say anything, he pushed away from the wall, shifting to stand in front of her; drawing his hand from the bounty of her breast, he set his fingers to quickly doing up the buttons he'd earlier undone.

He felt her gaze on his face, but didn't meet it, knew without looking that her mind was working again—that she would conclude, correctly, that he was playing a long game.

He didn't just want her beneath him, didn't simply want to sheath his aching erection in the soft flesh he'd just explored and claimed. He wanted her in his bed, willing and eager. Not because he'd overwhelmed her senses to the point where she didn't know what she was doing. He wanted to see her sprawled naked on his sheets, wanted her to hold out her arms, spread her long legs and welcome him into her body.

Knowingly. With full knowledge of her actions, and their repercussions.

He wanted that—her complete, absolute, unequivocal, and willing surrender—more than he needed temporary relief. Taking her, storming her castle now, wouldn't yield him the greater prize.

He was a tactician, a man of strategy first and last, even in this arena.

Her bodice reclosed, he glanced at her face, noted her deepening frown. He felt sure that, come morning, she'd have worked out his tack—much good would it do her.

She'd been a part of this household from the age of six; she was now twenty-nine. There was no chance that, over recent years, she hadn't taken—indeed, been encouraged by his mother to take—a lover.

Which meant that the interlude they'd just shared should have reawakened her passions.

Women, even those with sexual needs as strong as his own, could go much longer than men without relief. Almost as if they could make their passions lie dormant, put them into hibernation.

But once reawakened, once sexual release was again dangled before their senses . . .

All he had to do was keep up the pressure and she would come to him of her own accord.

Scripting, planning the interlude that would follow, allowed him to step back, to escort her—still stunned and wondering—from the room and across the corridor to her bedroom door.

He set it swinging wide and stepped back.

Minerva halted, looked him in the eye. "You are not coming in."

His lips quirked, but he inclined his head. "As you wish. Far be it from me to force myself on you."

She felt her cheeks heat. In what had just passed, while he might have been the instigator she'd been an equal participant throughout. But she certainly wasn't going to argue with whatever chivalrous streak had possessed him. As haughtily as she could, she inclined her head. "Good night."

"Until next time."

The dark murmur reached her as she went through the door. Clutching the edge, she swung around and looked back. Stated definitively, "There won't be a next time."

His soft, dark laugh slid like sin over her flushed skin.

"Good night, Minerva." He met her eyes. "Sleep well."

With that, he walked away, toward his apartments.

She shut the door, and leaned back against it.

For just one minute let the sensations he'd sent sweeping through her replay in her mind.

Felt again their power.

Heaven help her—how could she stand against him?

More to the point, how was she going to stand against herself?

Nine

Despite the physical frustrations of the night, Royce was in an equable mood as, the next morning, he worked through his correspondence with Handley in the study.

While he had no experience seducing unwilling or uncertain ladies, his chatelaine, thank God, was neither. Convincing her to lie in his bed would require no sweet talk, cajoling, or longing looks, no playing to her sensitivities; last night, he'd simply been the man, the marcher lord, she already knew him to be, and had succeeded. Admirably.

She might not yet have lain in his bed, but he'd wager the dukedom that by now she'd thought of it. Considered it.

His way forward was now crystal clear, and once he'd bedded her thoroughly, once she knew she was his to the depths of her soul, he'd inform her that she was to be his duchess. He would couch his offer as a request for her hand, but he was adamant that by then there would be no real question, most especially not in her mind.

The more he dwelled on his plan, the more he liked it; with a female like her, the more strings he had linking her to him before he mentioned marriage, the better, the less likely she was to even quibble. The grandes dames might be certain that any of the ladies on their list would unhesitatingly accept his offer, but Minerva's name wasn't on that list, and—despite her comment to the contrary—he wasn't so conceited, so arrogant, that he was, even now, taking her agreement for granted.

But he had no intention of letting her refuse.

"That's all you have to deal with today." Handley, a quiet, determined man, an orphan recommended to Royce by the principal of Winchester Grammar School, who had subsequently proved to be entirely worthy of the considerable trust Royce placed in him, collected the various letters, notes, and documents they'd been dealing with. He glanced at Royce. "You wanted me to remind you about Hamilton and the Cleveland Row house."

"Ah, yes." He had to decide what to do with his town house now he'd inherited the family mansion in Grosvenor Square. "Tell Jeffers to fetch Miss Chesterton. And you'd better stay. There'll be letters and instructions to be sent south, no doubt."

After sending Jeffers for Minerva, Handley returned to the straight-backed chair he preferred, angled to one end of Royce's desk.

Minerva entered. Seeing Handley, she favored him with a smile, then looked at Royce.

No one else would have seen anything unusual in that look, but Royce knew she was wary, watching for any hint of sexual aggression from him.

He returned her look blandly, and waved her to her customary chair. "We need to discuss the Wolverstone House staff, and how best to merge the staff from my London house into the ducal households."

Minerva sat, noting that Handley, settled in his chair, a fresh sheet of paper on top of his pile, a pencil in his hand, was listening attentively. She switched her gaze to Royce. "You mentioned a butler."

He nodded. "Hamilton. He's been with me for sixteen years, and I wouldn't want to lose him."

"How old is he?"

Royce cocked a brow at Handley. "Forty-five?"

Handley nodded. "About that."

"In that case—"

She provided information on the existing Wolverstone households, while Royce, with Handley's additional observations, gave her an overview of the small staff he'd accumulated over his years of exile. Given he had no wish to keep the Cleveland Row house, she suggested that most of the staff be sent to Wolverstone House.

"Once you're married and take your seat in the Lords, you and your wife will entertain a great deal more there than has been the case in the last decade—you'll need the extra staff."

"Indeed." Royce's lips curved as if something amused him, but then he saw her noticing and glanced at his jottings. "That leaves only Hamilton's fate unresolved. I'm inclined to assign him to Wolverstone House in a supportive capacity to old Bridgethorpe. In time, Hamilton can take over there, but until Bridgethorpe is ready to retire, depending on how much I need to travel between the various estates, I may use Hamilton as a personal butler."

She raised her brows. "One who travels with you?"

"He knows my preferences better than anyone else."

She inclined her head. "True. And that will allow all the other butlers to remain in their roles without causing tension."

He nodded and looked at Handley. "Is there anything else?"

Handley shook his head and glanced at Minerva.

"Nothing more about the households," she said, "but I wondered if you'd thought further about the mill."

Royce frowned. "I'll have to speak with Falwell, and I suppose Kelso, too, before I make any decision." He glanced at Handley. "Send a message that I wish to see them tomorrow morning."

Handley nodded, making a note.

In the distance, a gong sounded.

"Luncheon." Minerva stood, surprised and relieved that she'd survived two full hours of Royce's company without blushing once. Then again, other than that initial assessing look, he'd been entirely neutral when interacting with her.

She smiled at Handley as he and Royce rose to their feet.

Handley smiled back. Gathering his papers, he nodded to Royce. "I'll have those letters ready for you to sign later this afternoon."

"Leave them on the desk—I'll be in and out." Royce looked at Minerva, waved her to the door. "Go ahead—I'll join you at the table."

She inclined her head and left—feeling very likc Little Red Riding Hood; avoiding walking alone through the keep's corridors with the big, bad wolf was obviously a wise idea.

She had to own to further surprise when Royce chose to sit between Lady Courtney and Susannah at the luncheon table. The meal was strictly informal, a cold collation laid out on a sideboard from which guests helped themselves, assisted by footmen and watched over by Retford, before taking what seats they wished at the long table.

Flanked by Gordon and Rohan Varisey, with the startlingly handsome Gregory Debraigh opposite, she had distraction enough without wondering about Royce and his machinations. Presumably during the day, while he was Wolverstone and she was his chatelaine, he intended to behave with circumspection.

The meal had ended, and she was strolling with the others through the front hall, when Royce walked up behind her. "Minerva."

When she halted and turned, brows rising, he said, "If you're free, I'd like to take a look at the mill. It would help if I have a better understanding of the problem before I see Falwell and Kelso tomorrow."

"Yes, of course." She was the one urging the matter be dealt with immediately. "Now?"

He nodded and waved her toward the west wing.

They walked through the corridors, the voices of the others fading as they turned into the north wing. A side hall at the north end led them to a door that gave onto the gardens beyond.

Lawns and shrub borders fell away to more rolling expanses hosting larger, mature trees. The ornamental stream burbled beside them as they followed the gravel path along its bank. Ahead, the mill sat built over the stream; partially screened by a stand of willows, it was far enough from the house to be unobtrusive, yet was within walking distance.

As they approached, Royce studied the building, part stone, part timber. It sat squarely across the deep race, at that point only a few yards wide, through which the diverted waters of the Coquet rushed with sufficient force to spin the heavy waterwheel that turned the massive grinding stone.

The ground sloped upward, away from the castle toward the hills to the northwest, so the west bank of the race was significantly higher than the east bank. Spanning the race, the mill therefore was built on two levels. The higher and larger western section contained the grinding stone and the beams, levers, and gears that connected it to the waterwheel in the race.

The narrower, lower, eastern side through which he and Minerva entered contained beams and pulleys that raised and lowered the huge waterwheel; because of the bores that surged down the Coquet when the snows melted, it was essential the wheel could be lifted entirely free of the race. The eastern section also contained bins and storage cupboards set against the wooden railing that ran along the edge of the race.

The first crop of corn had already been ground; the second crop was yet to be harvested. For the moment, the mill stood silent and empty, with the wheel raised and braced above the race on massive beams.

"The problem's not hard to see." Minerva led the way into the soft shadows. The building had no windows, but light streamed in through the three open doorways—the one through which they'd entered, as well as the two at either end of the upper, western section.

Royce followed her along the continuation of the path, now paved; bins and cupboards formed a row on his left, the wood-and-stone outer wall to his right. The noise of rushing water was amplified inside, filling his ears. The cupboards were shoulder-height; when he looked over their tops, his eyes were level with the timber floor of the western section.

Ahead, beyond where the cupboards ended, Minerva had paused at the foot of a slanting gangplank connecting the two sections of the mill.

He nodded at the gangplank. "That's new." There'd always been a plank, but the ones he remembered had been literally planks, not this substantial timber board with cleats and a sturdy rail on one side. Halting beside Minerva, he studied the hinges, ropes, and pulleys attached to the plank, connecting it to the western section's floor and railing. "And it even swings out of the way."

In order for the waterwheel to be lowered and raised, the plank used to have to be removed altogether.

"After he'd replaced the old plank three times—you know how frequently they drop it in the race when they try to lift it away—Hancock designed this." Minerva started across the narrow platform. "He hasn't had to even repair it since."

"An estimable improvement." Royce followed her.

"Which is what we could do with up here." Stepping off the gangplank's upper end, Minerva swept her arms wide, encompassing the whole timber-floored western section in the middle of which sat the massive circular grinding stone supported by a stone plinth; the plinth continued through the floor into the earth beneath.

Letting his gaze travel around the otherwise empty area, Royce walked to the millstone, then cocked a brow at her.

"As I explained," she continued, "because we have to keep the doors open all the time, summer and winter, it's impossible to store anything here. The corn is ground, collected, and bagged—and then, each day, has to be moved, either to the castle cellars or back to farmers' holdings. If we close the doors to keep the animals out, the corn starts to mold by the next day. Bad enough, but preserving the millstone through winter is a never-ending battle. No matter what we've tried, it takes weeks of preparation every spring before we can use it without risking the corn."

"Mold again?" He walked back to the railing along the race.

"Mold, fungus, mildew—we've even had mushrooms growing on it."

Running a hand along the wide top rail, he grimaced. "Too damp."

"If we shut the doors, it sometimes gets so bad it drips."

He looked at her. "So what's your solution?"

"Hancock agrees that if we put up a timber wall all along the race, we can tar it and make it waterproof. We'd also need to fill the gaps in the outer walls and roof, and around the plinth, and put extra strips on the doors, to stop damp air getting in. And Hancock strongly recommends, as do I, putting in glass panes above the southern doors, so sun can shine in and help keep what's inside warm and dry."

Royce glanced around. "Shut those doors." He waved at the pair at the north end of the building, then walked to the larger set at the southern end. He waited until Minerva, frowning, shut both north doors, cutting off the light from that direction.

Sunshine coming through the doors in the eastern section didn't reach the western side. Royce swung one of the southern doors closed, blocking off half the sunshine that had been streaming in, then, more slowly, closed the other door, watching as the band of sunshine narrowed until it was a thin beam.

Shutting the door completely, he walked back along the line the sunshine had traced to where it had ended just before the millstone. Halting, he turned to look back toward the doors, at the wall above them reaching to the roof.

Minerva came to stand beside him.

"How much glass was Hancock thinking of?"

Glass was expensive. "He was thinking of at least two panes, one above each door, at least half the width of each door."

She watched as Royce studied the wall, then turned and looked at the millstone. "We'd be better off glazing as much of that wall as possible."

She blinked.

He glanced at her, arched a brow.

Quickly, she nodded. "That would definitely be best." She hadn't suggested it because she hadn't thought he would agree.

A subtle curving of his lips suggested he'd guessed as much, but all he said was, "Good." Turning, he looked at the millstone, then prowled around her, examining the stone.

She looked up at the area above the door, estimating the size, then deciding she might as well reopen the north doors, swung around and walked—into Royce.

Into his arms.

She was surprised.

He wasn't.

That last registered—along with the wicked glint in his eyes, the subtly triumphant lift to his lips, and that they were alone in the mill, acres from the castle, and the doors were closed—

He kissed her. Despite her racing thoughts, she had less than an instant's warning. She tried to resist—the intention formed; she tried to make herself stiffen as his arms slid around her, tried to make her hands, instinctively splayed on his chest, push him away . . .

Nothing happened. Or rather, for long moments she simply stood there and let him kiss her—savored again the pressure of his lips on hers, the subtle heat of them, and of his body so near, hard, and fascinating as he gathered her in, closer to that beckoning heat . . . she almost couldn't believe it was happening again. That he was kissing her again.

In a burst of startling clarity, she realized she hadn't truly believed what had happened the previous night. She'd been cautious, wary and watchful today, but she hadn't truly let herself acknowledge, not consciously, all that had happened in the morning room last night.

So it was going to happen again.

Before panic could gather wit and will, grab them back from where they'd wandered enough to mount any effective resistance, his lips firmed, hard and commanding, and hers parted. In the instant he surged, conquerorlike, into her mouth, she sensed his full intention—realized with absolute certainty that she had no hope of stopping him when fully half of her didn't want to.

When too much of her wanted. Wanted to know, to experience, to savor him and all he would show her, to embrace the moment, and the pleasure and delight it might bring.

To open herself to that, and him, to explore the possibilities she'd sensed last night—to follow the lingering urging of her infatuation-obsession and all the fanciful dreams she'd ever had . . . of just such an illicit moment as this.

With him.

Even as the thought resonated through her, she felt the dark silk of his hair sliding over and under her fingers, realized that, once again, she was kissing him back—that he'd succeeded once again in luring her—the inner wanton only he had ever touched—into coming out and playing with him.

And it was a game. A sudden sense of exhilaration gripped her and she shifted against him, then, utterly blatant, stroked her tongue boldly along his.

She felt his deep chuckle, then he returned the favor, his mouth, lips, and tongue doing things to hers that she felt perfectly certain ought to be banned. His arms tightened, steely bands closing to bring her body flush against his, then his hands went wandering, tracing, then evocatively sculpting her curves, sweeping over her hips and down, then drawing her closer, molding her hips against his hard thighs, the rigid rod of his erection impressing itself on her much softer belly.

Already lost in the kiss, to his embrace, she felt her inner flames leap from a smolder to a crackling blaze. Felt herself heat, then melt into them, become part of them as they spread and consumed her.

She felt like a fey creature as she let herself spin, senses alert, attuned, as she let the fiery, gathering vortex he was orchestrating draw her in.

At some point, his arms eased from her; hands gripping her waist, he turned with her, then drew her down to the millstone.

The next thing she knew—the next moment her senses surfaced from the firestorm of pleasure he wrought enough to know—she was lying on her back, the rough stone beneath her shoulders, hips, and thighs, her bodice wide open, and he was feasting on her naked breasts even more evocatively—more intently and expertly—than he had the previous night.

It was only because he'd drawn back to look down on the flesh he'd so thoroughly possessed that she'd been able to rise above the pleasured haze he'd wrapped her in. Trapped her in—yet she couldn't deny she was a very willing prisoner.

She was panting, gasping; she knew she'd moaned. Her hands lay lax on his upper arms; they'd lost all strength, after all he'd wrung from her. His dark eyes were tracing; she could feel the heat of his gaze, so much hotter on her bare skin.

But it was his face that, in that moment, held her, the sharp angles and planes, the long hollows of his lean cheeks, the square chin and wide brow, the blade of his nose, the intent line of his lips—the expression that, for that one unchecked instant, screamed with possessive lust.

It was that, it had to be; recognition made her wantonly writhe inside. Beneath his hand, she shifted restlessly.

His gaze flicked up; his eyes met hers for an instant, then he looked back at her breasts, lowered his head—and with calculated intensity swept her back into the flames.

She was far beyond any protest when he drew her skirts and petticoats up—all the way up to her waist. The touch of air on her skin should have felt cool, but instead she was already burning.

Already yearning for the touch of his hand between her thighs; when it came, she sighed. But she couldn't relax, caught her breath on an urgent half sob, her fingers gripping his sleeve as her body arched, helplessly wantonly begged as he stroked, caressed, teased . . .

She wanted his fingers inside her again. That or . . . she'd always wondered why, how, women could be persuaded to accommodate the hard, heavy reality of a man's erection, what madness possessed them to permit, let alone invite, such a thing to penetrate them there . . . now she knew.

She definitely knew, definitely burned with a want she'd never thought to feel.

Breathless, her voice no longer hers to command, she was struggling to find a way to communicate that burning, increasingly urgent desire when he released the tortured nipple he'd been suckling, lifted his head, slid down alongside her, ducked his head below the ridge of her rucked skirts—she gasped, shivered, as she felt his hot lips caress her navel.

Then she felt his tongue touch, caress, probe, then settle to a languid thrust and retreat; she shuddered and, eyes tightly closed, sank one hand in his hair, clinging to her whirling senses as between her thighs his fingers stroked in the same, evocative rhythm.

She was so deeply ensnared in the web of hot delight, of heated pleasure he sent coursing down her veins, that she was only dimly aware of him drawing back, of him easing her thighs wider apart.

What broke through the haze was the touch of his gaze, when, sensing it, faintly disbelieving, she cracked open her eyes and from beneath her lashes watched him studying, examining, the wet, swollen flesh his fingertips were tracing.

Her eyes locked on his face, captured by what she saw, sensed in the harsh, arrogant lines—the absolute drive, the all-consuming intent to possess her, all of her, that was engraved so clearly on his features.

The sight stole what little breath she had left, locked her lungs, left her giddy.

"Are you ready to scream?"

He hadn't looked up, hadn't met her eyes. She frowned; she hadn't screamed yet, or only in her mind.

He glanced up, met her gaze for a fleeting instant, then lowered his head. And replaced his fingers with his lips.

She gasped, arched, would have jerked away but he had her well anchored, her hips held immobile so he could lap, lick, and savor.

And taste her. The realization brought a moan to her lips. Lids falling, head back, she tried to breathe, tried to cope, had no other option but to, fists clenching in his hair, ride the wave of sharp delight he sent surging through her.

That with an expert's skill he crafted into a powerful, thunderous force that swept her into a fierce tempest of pleasure.

She battled to stifle a shriek as the tip of his tongue circled and stroked the tight bud of her desire, only partially succeeded. Her thighs trembled as his tongue continued to stroke . . .

Her spine arched helplessly as he eased it into her.

She shrieked, then screamed as he thrust it deep, then again more deeply into her.

Came apart in shuddering, sobbing waves as his mouth worked at her, on her, over her.

As the storm passed on and through her, leaving her utterly wracked and spent, Royce continued to lap at the nectar he'd drawn forth, savoring the gradual easing of her muscles, the slow roll of release as it swept through her.

Eventually, he drew back, looked at her face—that of a madonna pleasured to her toes—and smiled.

He reached for the buttons of her bodice and carefully did them up. A flick of his hand sent her skirts rustling down, covering her long, lithe legs. There was no sense in tormenting himself; this wasn't his bed.

Tactics, strategy, and above all else, winning the war.

He rose, and opened the northern doors, then, once he'd

ensured her skirts were fully down, opened the big southern doors as well. The afternoon sun slanted in; he stood there for a moment, ignoring the persistent ache in his groin, and looked back at the castle. He could see the keep's battlements, private and out of bounds to all guests, but all the lower windows were screened by trees. Returning to the castle, they'd be safe from any even mildly interested eyes until they got much nearer the walls.

Given he wanted her to agree to their wedding solely because she desired him as much as he desired her, keeping their liaison a secret was imperative; he was determined that no social pressure of any stripe would work its way into their equation. Reassured, he returned to her.

The instant she blinked back to life, he took her hand and drew her to her feet, steadying her until, her arm tucked in his, she could walk beside him.

He led her out into the sunshine, heading back to the castle via the path along the western bank of the race.

Minerva felt . . . detached. Light, floating, glowing. Her limbs felt deliciously relaxed.

If nothing else, she now knew beyond question that Royce was expert at this game—which left her wondering why he hadn't taken advantage of what he had to have known was her acquiescence, and sought his own release in her wantonly willing body.

The body he'd reduced to wanton willingness with caresses that, for the rest of her life, would make her blush.

As heat rose in her cheeks, she inwardly frowned; her features were still too lax to manage the expression.

"Because I intend to have you naked—not a stitch on—in my ducal bed." He made the statement in an even, matter-of-fact voice as he strolled beside her, his gaze on the castle. "That's where I intend to sink into you, to fill you and have my fill of you, for the first time."

A spurt of irritation gave her strength enough to turn her head and narrow her eyes on his profile, until he, lips faintly curved, glanced her way.

She looked into his eyes, dark as sin and still far too molten, and discovered she had nothing to say. They'd reached a footbridge spanning the race, now a wider, burbling stream; drawing her arm from his, she reached for the railing and started across. She needed to put space between them.

"At the risk of sounding arrogantly smug, I got the impression you haven't been accustomed to . . . life's little subtleties."

His tone made it clear to what he was referring; life's little subtleties, indeed! "Of course not. I've been your mother's confidante and your father's chatelaine for the past eleven years. Why would I know of such things?"

She glanced his way, and saw a faintly puzzled, somewhat quizzical look on his face.

The same qualities resonated in his voice when he replied, "Strangely, those same criteria gave rise to my question."

She looked ahead, felt his gaze on her face.

"I take it your past lovers weren't . . . shall we say, imaginative?"

Her past lovers were nonexistent, but she wasn't going to tell him that—he who had known more women than he could count. Literally.

That he, expert that he was, hadn't detected her inexperience left her feeling faintly chuffed. She cast about in her mind for a suitable retort. As she stepped off the bridge and set off down the path, with every step closer to the castle feeling more like herself, she inclined her head in his direction. "I suspect few men are as imaginative as you."

She felt certain that was nothing more than the truth, and if it caused him to preen and think he'd advanced his cause, so much the better.

After the afternoon's debacle, she was going to have to give avoiding him much more serious thought.

He thought she'd had lovers.

Then again, Variseys were sneaky, underhanded, and utterly untrustworthy when it came to something they wanted; he was quite capable of paying her a roundabout compliment like that in the hopes of further softening her brain.

Which, where he was concerned, was already soft enough.

Late that night, so late the moon was riding an inky sky over the Cheviots, casting a pearlescent sheen over every tree and rock, Minerva stood at her bedroom window and, arms folded, stared unseeing at the evocative landscape.

The door was locked; she suspected Royce could pick locks, so she'd left the key in the hole and turned it fully, then wedged a handkerchief around it, just to be sure.

She'd spent the evening with the other ladies, metaphorically clinging to their skirts. Although her bedroom was in the keep proper, opposite the duchess's morning room, not all that far from the ducal apartments and Royce's ducal bed, by steering the guests up the main keep stairs, she'd been able to tag along, stopping at her door while the ladies with rooms in the east wing walked on.

Royce had noticed her strategy, but other than an appreciative quirk to his lips, had made nothing of it.

She, however, was clearly going to have to take a stand against him.

The speculation the assembled ladies had indulged in after dinner, in the drawing room before the men had rejoined them, had underscored what she shouldn't have needed to be reminded of; they were all waiting to learn who he'd chosen as his bride.

Any day now, they would hear.

And then where would she be?

"Damn all Variseys—especially *him!*" The muttered sentiment relieved a little of her ire, but the major part was self-directed. She'd known what he was like all along; what she hadn't known, hadn't realized, was that he could take her idiotic infatuation-obsession and with a few lustful kisses, a few illicit caresses, convert it into outright desire.

Flaming desire—the sort that burned.

She felt like she was smoldering, just waiting to ignite. If he touched her, kissed her, she would—and she knew where that would lead. He'd even told her—to his ducal bed.

"Humph!" Despite wanting—now, thanks to him and his expertise, wanting quite desperately—to experience in the flesh all that her fanciful imagination had ever dreamed, despite her smoldering desire to lie beneath him, there was one equally powerful consideration that, no matter that damning desire, had her holding adamantly, unwaveringly, to her original decision never to grace his bed.

If she did . . . would infatuation–obsession–smoldering desire convert to something more?

If it did . . .

If she ever did anything so foolish as to fall in love with a Varisey—and with him in particular—she would deserve every iota of the emotional devastation that was guaranteed to follow.

Variseys did not love. The entire ton knew that.

In Royce's case it was widely known that his lovers never lasted long, that he inevitably moved on to another, then another, with no lingering attachment of any kind. He was a Varisey to his toes, and he'd never pretended otherwise.

To fall in love with such a man would be unjustifiably stupid. She strongly suspected that, for her, it would be akin to emotional self-immolation.

So she wasn't going to—could not allow herself to—take the risk of falling in with his seduction, if it even could be called that—his highly charged sexual game.

And while she might be crossing swords with a master, she had a very good idea how to avoid his thrust—indeed, he'd told her himself.

Somewhat grimly, she considered ways and means. She wasn't, when she dwelled on it, as short of defenses as she'd thought.

Ten

*T*he next morning, she commenced her campaign to pro-tect her heart from the temptation of falling in love with Royce Varisey.

Her strategy was simple; she had to keep as far as possible from his ducal bed.

She knew him; he was stubborn, not to say muleheaded, to a fault. Given he'd declared that he would first have her in the huge four-poster—even to denying himself over the point—as long as she kept clear of his bedroom and that bed, she would be safe.

After breakfasting with the other guests rather than in the keep's private parlor, she sent a message to the stables for the gig, went down to the kitchens and filled a basket with a selection of preserves made from fruit from the castle's orchards, then strolled out to the stables.

She was waiting for the gig's harness to be tightened when Sword came thundering in, Royce on his back.

Bringing the stallion under control, he raked her with his gaze. "Wither away?"

"There are some crofter families I need to call on."

"Where?"

"Up Blindburn way."

His gaze lowered to Sword. He'd ridden the stallion hard, and would need another mount if he chose to come with her; the gig couldn't hold the basket and them both.

He glanced at her. "If you'll wait while they fetch my curricle, I'll drive us there. I should meet these crofters."

She considered, then nodded. "All right."

He dismounted, with a few orders dispatched Henry and two grooms to harness his blacks to his curricle, while others unharnessed the old cob from the gig.

When the curricle was ready, she let him take her basket and stow it beneath the seat, then hand her up; she'd remembered his demon-bred horses—with them between the shafts, he wouldn't be able to devote any attention to her.

To seducing her.

He climbed up beside her, and with a flick of his wrist, sent the blacks surging; the curricle rattled out of the stable yard and down the drive, then he headed the flighty pair up Clennell Street.

Twenty minutes later, they arrived at a group of low stone cottages huddled against a hillside. Royce was quietly relieved that his expensive pair had, once they'd accepted that he wasn't going to let them run, managed the less-than-even climb without breaking any legs.

He drew the horses to a halt at the edge of a flattened area between the three cottages. Children instantly appeared from every aperture, some literally tumbling out of windows. All were wide-eyed with wonder. They quickly gathered around, staring at the blacks.

"Coo—*oo!*" one boy reverently breathed. "Bet they go like the clappers."

Minerva climbed down, then reached in for her basket. She caught his eye. "I won't be too long."

A sudden feeling—it might have been panic—assailed him at the notion of being left at the mercy of a pack of children for hours. "How long is 'too long'?"

"Perhaps half an hour—no more." With a smile, she headed for the cottages. All the children chorused a polite "Good morning, Miss Chesterton," which Minerva answered with a smile, but the brats immediately returned their attention to him—or rather, his horses.

He eyed the motley crew gradually inching closer; they ranged from just walking to almost old enough to work in the fields—whatever ages those descriptions translated to. He'd had very little to do with children of any sort, not since he'd been one himself; he didn't know what to say, or do.

Their bright, eager gazes flicked from the horses to him, but the instant they saw him watching, they looked back at the horses. He revised his earlier conclusion; they were interested in him, but the horses were easier to approach.

He was their duke; they were his future workers.

Mentally girding his loins, moving slowly and deliberately, he tied off the reins, then stepped down and strolled to the horses' heads. Some of the children were quite small, and the blacks, although temporarily quiet, were completely untrustworthy.

The crowd drew back a step or two, the older boys and girls bobbing bows and curtsies. The younger ones weren't sure what to do or why. One girl hissed to her recalcitrant little brother, "He's the new dook, stoopid."

Royce pretended he hadn't heard. He nodded amiably—a general nod that included them all—then, catching his leader's bridle, reached up and smoothed a hand down the long arched neck.

An instant passed, then—

"Do you ride 'em, Y'r Grace? Or are they just for hauling th' carriage?"

"Have you won any races with 'em, Y'r Grace?"

"Is this here a curricle, or one of them phaetons, Y'r Grace?"

"How fast can they go, Y'r Grace?"

He very nearly told them to stop "Y'r Grace"-ing him, but realized it might sound like a reprimand. Instead, he set himself to answering their questions in a calm, unruffled manner.

Somewhat to his surprise, the approach he used with horses worked with children, too. They relaxed, and he had the chance to turn the tables enough to learn a little about the small settlement. Minerva had told him five families lived in the three cottages. The children confirmed that only the older women were at home; all the other adults and youths werc in the fields, or working in the forge a little way farther along the track. They themselves weren't at school because there was no school nearby; they learned their letters and numbers from the older women.

After a few such exchanges, the children clearly felt the ice had been broken and their bona fides sufficiently established to ask about him.

"We did hear tell," the lad he thought was the oldest said, "that you was working in London for the government—that you were a *spy!*"

That surprised him; he'd thought his father would have ensured his occupation had remained a dim, dark secret.

"No, silly!" The oldest girl blushed when Royce and the others looked her way, but gamely went on, "Ma said as you were the *chief* spy—the one in charge—and that you were responsible for bringing down Boney."

"Well . . . not by myself. The men I organized did very dangerous things, and yes, they contributed to Napoleon's downfall, but it took Wellington and the whole army, and Blucher and the others, too, to finally get the deed done."

Naturally, they took that as an invitation to pepper him with questions about his men's missions; borrowing freely from otherwise classified exploits, it was easy enough to keep the expectant horde satisfied, although they were rather put out to learn he hadn't actually seen Napoleon dragged away in chains.

After delivering the preserves she'd brought, and being introduced to the latest addition to the combined households by its grandmother, juggling the swaddled infant in her arms, cooing while it batted at her hair, Minerva went to the window the better to see the child's eyes, glanced out—and tensed to hand the babe back so she could rush out and rescue its siblings.

Or Royce, whichever applied . . . but after an instant of looking, taking in the tableau centered on the black horses, the curricle—and the most powerful duke in England, who appeared to be telling some tale—she relaxed and, smiling, turned back to the baby and cooed some more.

The baby's grandmother came to the window; she, too, took in the scene outside. Her brows rose. After a moment, she said, "Looking at that, if I couldn't see with my own eyes that he's the last lord's get, I'd be thinking some cuckoo had got into the ducal nest."

Minerva's smile deepened; the idea of Royce as a cuckoo . . . "He's definitely a Varisey, born and bred."

The old woman humphed. "Aye, we'll all be locking up our daughters, no doubt. Still . . ." She turned from the window and headed back to her work. "If that had been his father out there, he would have snarled at the brats and sent them scurrying—just because he could."

Minerva couldn't disagree, yet old Henry would never have even considered coming out with her on her rounds.

Nevertheless, she didn't tempt fate; handing the baby back to its grandmother, she collected her basket, and was saying her farewells when a large presence darkened the doorway. Royce had to duck low to enter.

The three women immediately bobbed curtsies; Minerva introduced them before he could make any abrupt demand that they leave.

He acknowledged the women smoothly, then his gaze flicked over her, taking in the empty basket in her hand. But again, before he could say anything, the matriarch, who'd seized the moment to size him up, came forward to show him her grandchild.

Minerva held her breath, sensed him tense to step back—

retreating from the baby—but then he stiffened and held his ground. He nodded formally at the matriarch's words, then, about to turn and leave, hesitated.

He reached out and touched the back of one long finger to the baby's downy cheek. The baby gurgled and batted with tiny fists. The grandmother's face was wreathed in smiles.

She saw Royce notice, saw him take in the way the other women softened, too. Then he glanced at her.

She gestured with her basket. "We should be going."

He nodded, inclined his head to the women. "Ladies." Turning, he ducked out of the cottage.

After exchanging impressed looks with the crofter women, Minerva followed. Crossing the yard to the curricle, she saw and heard enough to know that the children had lost all fear of their duke; their eyes now shone with a species of hero worship more personal than simple awe.

His father had had no real relationship, no personal interaction, with his people; he'd managed them from a distance, through Falwell and Kelso, and had spoken with any directly only when absolutely necessary. He'd therefore only spoken to the senior men.

Royce, it seemed, might be different. He certainly lacked his father's insistence on a proper distance being preserved between his ducal self and the masses.

Once again he took the basket, stowed it, then handed her up. Retrieving the reins from the oldest lad, he joined her. She held her tongue and let him direct the children back. Round-eyed, they complied, watched as he carefully turned the skittish pair, then waved wildly and sang their farewells as he guided the curricle down the lane.

As the cottages fell behind, the peace, serenity—and isolation—of the hills closed around them. Reminded of her goal, she thought quickly, then said, "Now we're out this way, there's a well over toward Shillmoor that's been giving trouble." She met his hard gaze as his head swung her way. "We should take a look."

He held her gaze for an instant, then had to look back to

his horses. The only reply he gave was a grunt, but when they reached the bottom of the lane, he turned the horses' heads west, toward Shillmoor.

Rather than, as she was perfectly certain he'd intended to, make for the nearest secluded lookout.

Sitting back, she hid a smile. As long as she avoided being alone with him in a setting he could use, she would be safe, and he wouldn't be able to advance his cause.

It was early evening when Royce stalked into his dressing room and started stripping off his clothes while Trevor poured the last of a succession of buckets of steaming water into the bath in the bathing chamber beyond.

His mood was distinctly grim. His chatelaine had successfully filled their entire day; they'd left the little hamlet near Shillmoor with barely enough time to drive back to the castle and bathe before dinner.

And after overseeing the final stages of reconstruction of the well's crumbling walls and sagging roof, then taking an active part in reassembling and correctly recommissioning the mechanism for pulling water up from the depths of the very deep well, he needed a bath.

The local men had taken the day off from working their fields and had gathered to repair the aging well, a necessity before winter; when he and Minerva had driven up, they'd been well advanced with the repairs to the walls. Their ideas for shoring up the roof, however, were a recipe for disaster; he'd stepped in and used his unquestioned authority to redesign and direct the construction of a structure that would have some hope of withstanding the weight of snow they commonly experienced in those parts.

Far from resenting his interference, the men, and the women, too, had been relieved and sincerely grateful. They'd shared their lunch—cider, thick slabs of cheese, and freshly baked rye bread, which he and Minerva had graciously accepted—then been even more amazed when, after watching the men scratch their heads and mutter over the mechanism they'd disassembled, he'd shrugged out of his hacking jacket, rolled up his sleeves, and got to work with them, sorting the various parts and helping reassemble, realign, and reposition the mechanism—he was taller and stronger than any of those there—finally resulting in a rejuvenated and properly functioning well.

There'd been cheers all around as one of the women had pulled up the first brimming pail.

He and Minerva had left with a cacophony of thanks ringing in their ears, but it hadn't escaped his notice how surprised and intrigued by him the villagers had been. Clearly, his way of dealing with them was vastly different from that of his sire.

Minerva had told him he didn't need to be like his father; it seemed he was proving her correct. She should be pleased . . . and she was. Her excursions had ensured she won the day—that she had triumphed in the battle of wills, and wits, he and she were engaged in.

To him, the outcome was a foregone conclusion; he did not doubt she would end in his bed. Why she was resisting so strongly remained a mystery—and an ongoing challenge.

Boots removed, he stood and peeled off his breeches and stockings. Naked, he walked into the bathing chamber, and stood looking down at the steam wreathing above the water's surface.

His chatelaine was the first woman he'd ever had to exert himself to win, to battle for in even the most minor sense. Despite the annoyance, the frequent irritations, the constant irk of sexual denial, he couldn't deny he found the challenge—the chase—intriguing.

He glanced down. It was equally impossible to deny he found her challenge, and her, arousing.

Stepping into the tub, he sank down, leaned back, and closed his eyes. The day might have been hers, but the night would be his.

* * *

He walked into the drawing room feeling very much a wolf anticipating his next meal. He located his chatelaine, standing before the hearth in her black gown with its modestly cut neckline, and amended the thought: a hunger-ravaged wolf slavering in expectation.

He started toward her. Within two steps, he registered that something was afoot; his sisters, his cousins, and those others still at the castle were abuzz and atwitter, the excitement of their conversations a hum all around him.

Suspicions had started forming before he reached Minerva. Margaret stood beside her; his elder sister turned as he neared, her face alight in a way he'd forgotten it could be. "Royce—Minerva's made the most *wonderful* suggestion."

Even before Margaret rattled on, he knew to his bones that he wasn't going to share her sentiment.

"Plays—Shakespeare's plays. There's more than enough of us who've decided to stay to be able to perform one play each night—to entertain us until the fair. Aurelia and I felt that, as it's now a week since the funeral, and given this is as private a party as could be, then there really could be no objections on the grounds of propriety." Margaret looked at him, dark eyes alive. "What do you think?"

He thought his chatelaine had been exceedingly clever. He looked at her; she returned his gaze levelly, no hint of gloating in her expression.

Margaret and Aurelia especially, and Susannah, too, were all but addicted to amateur theatricals; while he'd been in the south at Eton, then Oxford, they'd had to endure many long winters holed up in the castle—hence their passion. He'd forgotten that, but his chatelaine hadn't.

His respect for her as an opponent rose a definite notch.

He shifted his gaze to Margaret. "I see no objection."

He could see no alternative; if he objected, put his foot down and vetoed the plays, his sisters would sulk and poke and prod at him until he changed his mind. Expression mild, he arched a brow. "Which play will you start with?"

Margaret glowed. "*Romeo and Juliet.* We still have all the abridged scripts, and the costumes and bits and pieces from when we used to do these long ago." She laid a hand on Royce's arm—in gratitude, he realized—then released him. "I must go and tell Susannah—she's to be Juliet."

Royce watched her go; from the questions thrown at her and the expressions evoked by her answers, everyone else was keen and eager to indulge in the amusement.

Minerva had remained, the dutiful chatelaine, beside him. "I assume," he said, "that we're to be regaled with *Romeo and Juliet* tonight?"

"That's what they'd planned."

"Where?"

"The music room. It's where the plays were always held. The stage and even the curtain are still there."

"And"—the most telling question—"just when did you make this brilliant suggestion of yours?"

She hesitated, hearing the underlying displeasure in his voice. "This morning over breakfast. They were moaning about how bored they were growing."

He let a moment pass, then murmured, "If I might make a suggestion, the next time you consider how bored they might be, you might first like to consider how bored *I* might be."

Turning, he met her eyes, only to see her smile.

"You weren't bored today."

There was no point in lying. "Perhaps not, but I am going to be utterly bored tonight."

Her smile widened as she looked toward the door. "You can't have everything."

Retford's summons rolled out. With irresistible deliberation, Royce took her arm. Noted the sudden leap of her pulse. Lowered his head to murmur as he led her to the door, "But I do intend to have everything from you. Everything, and more."

Placing her beside him again at dinner, he took what revenge he could, his hand drifting over the back of her waist as he steered her to her chair, his fingers stroking over her hand as he released her.

Minerva weathered the moments with what fortitude she could muster; jangling nerves and skittish senses were a price she was prepared to pay to avoid his ducal bed.

Frustratingly, no one—not even Margaret—seemed to think Royce monopolizing her company at all odd. Then again, with him leaning back in his great carver, making her turn to face him, their conversation remained largely private; presumably the others thought they were discussing estate matters. Instead . . .

"I take it *Romeo and Juliet* was not your choice." He sat back, twirling his wineglass between his long fingers.

"No. It's Susannah's favorite—she was keen to play the part." She tried to keep her attention on her plate.

A moment passed. "How many of Shakespeare's plays involve lovers?"

Too many. She reached for her wineglass—slowed to make sure he wasn't going to say anything to make her jiggle it; when he kept silent, she gratefully grasped it and took a healthy sip.

"Do you intend to take part—to trip the stage in one of the roles?"

"That will depend on how many plays we do." She set her glass down, made a mental note to check which plays were safe to volunteer for.

By example, she tried to steer his attention to the conversations farther down the table; with the increasing informality, these were growing more general—and more rowdy.

Indeed, more salacious. Some of his male cousins were calling suggestions to Phillip—cast as Romeo—as to how best to sweep his Juliet into the lovers' bed.

To her consternation, Royce leaned forward, paying attention to the jocular repartee. Then he murmured, his voice so low only she could hear, "Perhaps I should make some suggestions?"

Her mind immediately conjured an all too evocative

memory of his last attempt to sweep her into his bed; when her intellect leapt to the fore and hauled her mind away, it merely skittered to the time before that, to his lips on hers, to the pleasure his long fingers had wrought while he'd pinned her to the wall in the lust-heavy dark . . .

It took effort to wrestle her wits free, to focus on his words. "But you haven't succeeded."

She would have called back the words the instant she uttered them; they sounded collected and calm—nothing like what she felt.

Slowly, he turned his head and met her eyes. Smiled—that curving of his lips that carried a promise of lethal reaction rather than any soothing reassurance. "Not. Yet."

He dropped the quiet words like stones into the air between them; she felt the tension pull, then quiver. Felt something within her inwardly tremble—not with apprehension but a damning anticipation. She forced herself to arch a brow, then deliberately turned her attention back down the table.

As soon as dessert was consumed, Margaret dispatched Susannah, Phillip, and the rest of the cast to the music room to prepare. Everyone else remained at the table, finishing their wine, chatting—until Margaret declared the players had had time enough, and the entire company adjourned to the music room.

The music room lay in the west wing, at the point where the north wing joined it. Part of both wings, the room was an odd shape, having two doors, one opening to the north wing and one to the west wing corridors, and only one window—a wide one angled between the two outer walls. The shallow dais that formed the stage filled the floor before the window, a trapezoid that extended well into the room. The stage itself was the rectangle directly in front of the window, while the triangular areas to either side had been paneled off, blocking them off from the audience sitting in the main part of the room, creating wings in which the players could don the finery that made up their costumes, and stage props and furniture could be stored.

Thick velvet curtains concealed the stage. Footmen had set up four rows of gilt-backed chairs across the room before it. The crowd filed in, chatting and laughing, noting the closed curtains, and the dimness created by having only three candelabra on pedestals lighting the large room; a chandelier, fully lit, cast its light down upon the presently screened stage.

Minerva didn't even attempt to slip from Royce's side as he guided her to a seat in the second row, to the right of the center aisle. She sat, grateful to have survived the trip from the dining room with nothing more discomposing than the sensation of his hand at her waist, and the curious aura he projected of hovering over and around her.

Both protectively and possessively.

She should take exception to the evolving habit, but her witless senses were intrigued and unhelpfully tantalized by the suggestive attention.

The rest of the group quickly took their seats. Someone peeked out through the curtains, then, slowly, the heavy curtains parted on the first scene.

The play began. In such situations, it was accepted practice for the audience to call comments, suggestions, and directions to the players—who might or might not respond. Whatever the true tone of the play, the result was always a comedy, something the abbreviated scripts were designed to enhance; the players were expected to overplay the parts to the top of their bent.

While most in the audience called their comments loud enough for all to hear, Royce made his to her alone. His observations, especially on Mercutio, played to the hilt and beyond by his cousin Rohan, were so dry, so acerbic and cuttingly witty, that he reduced her to helpless giggles in short order—something he observed with transparently genuine approval, and what looked very like self-congratulation.

When Susannah appeared as Juliet, waltzing through her family's ball, she returned the favor, making him smile, eventually surprising a laugh from him; she discovered she felt chuffed about that, too.

The balcony scene had them trying to outdo each other, just as Susannah and Phillip vied for the histrionic honors on stage.

When the curtain finally swished closed and the audience thundered their applause for a job well done, Royce discovered he had, entirely unexpectedly, enjoyed himself.

Unfortunately, as he looked around as footmen hurried in to light more candles, he realized the whole company had enjoyed themselves hugely—which augured very badly for him. They'd want to do a play every night until the fair; it took him only an instant to realize he'd have no hope of altering that.

He would have to find some way around his chatelaine's latest hurdle.

Both he and Minerva rose with the others, chatting and exchanging comments. Along with the other players, Susannah reappeared, stepping down from the stage to rejoin the company. Slowly, he made his way to her side.

She turned as he approached, arched one dark brow. "Did you enjoy my performance?"

He arched a brow back. "Was it all performance?"

Susannah opened her eyes wide.

Minerva had drifted from Royce's side. She'd been complimenting Rohan on his execution of Mercutio; she was standing only feet away from Susannah when Royce approached.

Close enough to see and hear as he complimented his sister, then more quietly said, "I take it Phillip is the latest to catch your eye. I wouldn't have thought him your type."

Susannah smiled archly and tapped his cheek. "Clearly, brother mine, you either don't know my type, or you don't know Phillip." She looked across to where Phillip was laughing with various others. "Indeed," Susannah continued, "we suit each other admirably well." She glanced up at Royce, smiled. "Well, at least for the moment."

Minerva inwardly frowned; she hadn't picked up any

connection between Phillip and Susannah—indeed, she'd thought Susannah's interest lay elsewhere.

With a widening smile, Susannah waggled her fingers at Royce, then left him.

Royce watched her go, and inwardly shrugged; after his years in social exile, she was right—he couldn't know her adult tastes that well.

He was about to look around for his chatelaine when Margaret raised her voice, directing everyone back to the drawing room. He would have preferred to adjourn elsewhere, but seeing Minerva go ahead on Rohan's arm, fell in at the rear of the crowd.

The gathering in the drawing room was as uneventful as usual; rather than remind his chatelaine of his intentions, he bided his time, chatted with his cousins, and kept an eye on her from across the room.

Unfortunately, she wasn't lulled. She clung to the group of females, Susannah included, who had rooms in the east wing; she left with them, deftly steering them up the wide main stairs he didn't bother following. He would have no chance of laying hands on her and diverting her to his room before she reached hers.

He retired soon after, considering his choices as he climbed the main stairs. He could join Minerva in her bed. She'd fuss, and try to order him out, shoo him away, but once he had her in his arms, all denial would be over.

There was a certain attraction in such a direct approach. However . . . he walked straight to his apartments, opened the door, went in, and closed it firmly behind him.

He walked into his bedroom, and looked at his bed.

And accepted that this time, she'd triumphed.

She'd won the battle, but it was hardly the war.

Walking into his dressing room, he shrugged out of his coat, and set it aside. Slowly undressing, he turned the reason he hadn't gone to her room over in his mind.

In London, he'd always gone to his lovers' beds. He'd

never brought any lady home to his. Minerva, however, he wanted in his bed and no other.

Naked, he walked back into the bedroom, looked again at the bed. Yes, that bed. Lifting the luxurious covers, he slid between the silken sheets, lay back on the plump pillows, and stared up at the canopied ceiling.

This was where he wanted her, lying beside him, sunk in the down mattress within easy reach.

That was his vision, his goal, his dream.

Despite lust, desire, and all such weaknesses of the flesh, he wasn't going to settle for anything less.

Eleven

y lunchtime the next day, Royce was hot, flushed, sweaty—and leaning against a railing with a group of men, all estate workers, in a field on one of his tenant farms, sharing ale, bread, and bits of crumbly local cheese.

The men around him had almost forgotten he was their duke; he'd almost forgotten, too. With his hacking jacket and neckerchief off, and his sleeves rolled up, his dark hair and all else covered in the inevitable detritus of cutting and baling hay, except for the quality of his clothes and his features, he could have been a farmer who'd stopped by to help.

Instead, he was the ducal landowner lured there by his chatelaine.

He'd wondered what she'd planned for the day—what her chosen path to avoid him would be. He'd missed her at breakfast, but while pacing before the study window dictating to Handley, he'd seen her riding off across his fields.

After finishing with Handley, he'd followed.

Of course, she hadn't expected him to turn up at the haymaking, let alone that their day would evolve as it had, due to the impulse that had prompted him to offer to help.

He'd cut hay before, long ago, sneaking out of the castle and, against his father's wishes, rubbing shoulders with the estate workers. His father had been a stickler for protocol and propriety, but he had never felt the need to adhere to and insist on every single privilege at every turn.

Some of the men remembered him from long ago, and hadn't been backward over accepting his help—tendered, he had to admit, more to see how Minerva would react than anything else.

She'd met his gaze, then turned and offered to help the women. They'd worked alongside those they normally directed for the past several hours, he swinging a scythe in line with the men, she following with the women, gathering the hay and deftly binding it into sheaves.

What had started out as an unvoiced contest had evolved into a day of exhausting but satisfying labor. He'd never worked so physically hard in his life, but he, and his body, felt unexpectedly relaxed.

From where the women had gathered, Minerva watched Royce leaning against the fence enclosing the field they'd almost finished cutting, watched his throat—the long column bare—work as he swallowed ale from a mug topped up from a jug the men were passing around—and quietly marveled.

He was so unlike his father on so many different counts.

He stood among the men, sharing the camaraderie induced by joint labor, not the least concerned that his shirt, damp with honest sweat, clung to his chest, outlining the powerful muscles of his torso, flexing and shifting with every movement. His dark hair was not just rumpled, but dusty, his skin faintly flushed from the sun. His long, lean legs, encased in boots his precious Trevor would no doubt screech over later, were stretched out before him; as she watched he shifted, cocking one hard thigh against the fence behind.

With no coat and his shirt sticking, she could see his body clearly—could better appreciate the broad shoulders, the wide, sleekly muscled chest tapering to narrow hips and those long, strong, rider's legs.

To any female this side of the grave, the view was mouthwatering; she wasn't the only one drinking it in. With all ducal trappings stripped away, leaving only the man beneath, he looked more overtly earthily sexual than she'd ever seen him.

She forced herself to look away, to give her attention to the women and keep it there, pretending to be absorbed in their conversation. The quick glances the younger women cast toward the fence broke her resolve—and she found herself looking his way again. Wondering when he'd learned to use a scythe; his effortless swing wasn't something anyone just picked up.

Their lunch consumed, the men were talking to him avidly; from their gestures and his, he was engaging in one of his disguised interrogations.

If anything, she'd increased her assessment of his intelligence, and his ability to garner and catalog facts—and that assessment had already been high. While both were attributes he'd always had, they'd developed significantly over the years.

In contrast, his ability with children was a skill she never would have guessed he possessed. He certainly hadn't inherited it; his parents had adhered to the maxim that children should be seen and not heard. Yet when they'd broken for refreshment earlier, Royce had noticed the workers' children eyeing Sword, not so patiently waiting tied to a nearby post; waving aside their mothers' recommendations not to let them pester him, he'd walked over and let the children do precisely that.

He'd answered their questions with a patience she found remarkable in him, then, to everyone's surprise, he'd mounted and, one by one, taken each child up before him for a short walk.

The children now thought him a god. Their parents' estimation wasn't far behind.

She knew he'd had little to nothing to do with children; even those of his friends were yet babes in arms. Where he'd learned how to deal with youngsters, let alone acquired the requisite patience, a trait he in the main possessed very little of, she couldn't imagine.

Realizing she was still staring, broodingly, at him, she forced her gaze back to the women surrounding her. But their talk couldn't hold her interest, couldn't draw her senses, or even her mind, from him.

All of which ran directly counter to her intentions; out of the castle and surrounded by his workers, she'd thought she'd be safe from his seduction.

Physically, she'd been correct, but in other ways her attraction to him was deepening and broadening in ways she hadn't—couldn't have—foreseen. Worse, the unexpected allure was unintentional, uncalculated. It wasn't in his nature to radically alter his behavior to impress.

"Ah, well." The oldest woman stood. "Time to get back to it if we're to get all those sheaves stacked before dusk."

The other women rose and brushed off their aprons; the men saw, and stowed their mugs and jug, hitched up their trousers, and headed back into the field. Royce went with a group to one of the large drays; seizing the moment, Minerva went to check on Rangonel.

Satisfied he was comfortable, she headed to where the others were readying an area for the first haystack. Rounding a dray piled with sheaves, she halted—faced with a fascinating sight.

Royce stood five paces ahead of her, his back to her, looking down at a small girl, no more than five years old, planted directly in his path, nearly tipping backward as she looked all the way up into his face.

Minerva watched as he smoothly crouched before the girl, and waited.

Entirely at ease, the girl studied his face with open inquisitiveness. "What's your name?" she eventually lisped.

Royce hesitated; Minerva could imagine him sorting through the various answers he could give. But eventually he said, "Royce."

The girl tilted her head, frowned as she studied him. "Ma said you were a wolf."

Minerva couldn't resist shifting sideways, trying to see his face. His profile confirmed he was fighting not to smile— wolfishly.

"My teeth aren't big enough."

The poppet eyed him measuringly, then nodded sagely. "Your snout isn't long enough, either, and you're not hairy."

Her own lips compressed, Minerva saw his jaw clench, holding back a laugh. After an instant, he nodded. "Very true."

The girl reached out, with one small hand clasped two of his fingers. "We should go and help now. You can walk with me. I know how the haystack's made—I'll show you."

She tugged, and Royce obediently rose.

Minerva watched as the most powerful duke in all of England allowed a five-year-old poppet to lead him to where his workers had gathered, and blithely instruct him in how to stack sheaves.

Days passed, and Royce advanced his cause not one whit. No matter what he did, Minerva evaded him at every turn, surrounding herself with either the estate people or the castle's guests.

The plays had proved a major success; they now filled the evenings, allowing her to use the company of the other ladies to elude him every night. He'd reached the point of questioning his not exactly rational but unquestionably honorable disinclination to follow her into her room, trampling on her privacy to press his seduction, his suit.

While playing a long game was his forte, inaction was another matter; lack of progress on any front had always irked.

Lack of progress on this front positively hurt.

And today, the entire company had decided to go to church, presumably to atone for the many sins they'd committed. Despite none of those sins being his, he'd felt obliged to attend, too, especially as Minerva had been going, so what else was he to do?

Wallowing in bed when that bed was otherwise empty—devoid of soft, warm, willing female—had never appealed.

Seated in the front pew, Minerva beside him, with his sisters beyond her, he let the sermon roll over him, freeing his mind to range where it would—the latest prod to his escalating frustration was its first stop.

They'd chosen *Midsummer Night's Dream* for their play last night—and Minerva had suggested he play Oberon, a chant promptly taken up by the rest of the company in full voice. The twist of fate that had seen her caught by the same company's brilliant notion that she play Titania, queen to his king, had been, in his opinion, nothing more than her due.

Given their natures, given the situation, even though their exchanges on stage had been oblique, the palpable tension between them had puzzled a number of their audience.

That tension, and its inevitable effects, had resulted in another near-sleepless night.

He slanted a glance to his right, to where she, his fixation, sat, her gaze dutifully trained on Mr. Cribthorn, the vicar, rambling from his pulpit about long-dead Corinthians.

She knew who and what he was; no one knew him better. Yet she'd deliberately set out to cross swords with him—and thus far she was winning.

Accepting defeat on any stage had never come easily; his only recent failure had been over bringing to justice the last traitor he and his men knew lurked somewhere in the government. There were some things fate didn't allow.

Be that as it may, accepting defeat with Minerva was . . . entirely beyond his scope. One way or another she was going to be his—his lover first, then his wife.

Her capitulation on both counts would happen—had to happen—soon. He'd told the grandes dames a week, and that week was nearly past. While he doubted they'd haul themselves all the way back to Northumbria if they didn't see a notice in the *Gazette* this coming week, he wouldn't put it past them to start sending candidates north—in carriages designed to break axles and wheels as they neared Wolverstone's gates.

The vicar called the congregation to their feet for the benediction; everyone rose. Subsequently, once the vicar had passed on his way up the aisle, Royce stepped out of the pew, stepped back to let Minerva go ahead of him, then followed, leaving his sisters trailing shawls and reticules in his wake.

As usual, they were the first out of the church, but he'd noticed one of his more affluent farmers among the worshippers; as they stepped down to the path, he bent his head close beside Minerva's. "I want to have a word with Cherry."

She glanced back and up at him.

And time stopped.

With Margaret and Aurelia distracting the vicar, they were the only two in the churchyard—and they were very close, their lips inches apart.

Her eyes, rich browns flecked with gold, widened; her breath caught, suspended. Her gaze lowered to his lips.

His dropped to hers . . .

He dragged in a breath and straightened.

She blinked, and stepped away. "Ah . . . I must speak with Mrs. Cribthorn, and some of the other ladies."

He nodded stiffly, forced himself to turn away. Just as the rest of the congregation came flooding down the steps.

Searching for Cherry, he set his jaw. *Soon.* She was going to lie beneath him very soon.

Minerva let a moment pass while her heart slowed and her breathing evened, then she drew a deep breath, plastered on a smile, and went to speak with the vicar's wife about the preparations for the fair.

She was turning from Mrs. Cribthorn when Susannah approached.

"There you are!" Susannah gestured to where the castle's guests were piling into various carriages. "We're heading back—do you want to come, or do you have to wait for Royce?"

Royce had taken her up in his curricle for the drive to the church. "I . . ." *Can't possibly leave yet.* Minerva swallowed the words. As a recognized representative of the castle, the largest and socially dominant house in the district, it simply wasn't done to leave without chatting with their neighbors; the locals would see that as a slight. Neither she nor Royce could yet leave, a fact Susannah should have known. "No. I'll wait."

Susannah shrugged, gathering her shawl. "Commendably dutiful—I hope Royce appreciates it, and that you aren't bored to tears." With a commiserating grimace, she headed for the carriages.

Her last comment had been entirely sincere; the late duke's daughters had adopted their father's social views. Old Henry had rarely come to church, leaving it to his wife, and later Minerva alone, to carry the castle flag.

More interesting to Minerva, Susannah's comments confirmed that, despite the near debacle of last night's play— she'd thought the lust that had burned in Royce's eyes, that had resonated beneath the smooth tenor of his voice, the breathlessness that had assailed her, the awareness that had invested her every action, would have utterly given them away—not a single guest had realized that his interest in her had any basis beyond castle business.

Admittedly, every single guest was distracted on his or her own account.

That, however, didn't explain the pervasive blindness. The truth was, regardless of his pursuit of her, Royce had unfailingly ensured that whenever they were not alone, their interaction projected the image of duke and dutiful chatelaine, and absolutely nothing more. All the guests, and even more his sisters, now had that image firmly fixed in their minds, and blithely ignored anything to the contrary.

Looking over the congregation, she located his dark head. He stood in a group of farmers, most but not all his tenants; as was becoming usual, they were talking and he was listening. Entirely approving, she surveyed the gathering, then went to do her own listening with a group of farmers' wives.

She left it to him to find her when he was ready to leave. He eventually did, and allowed her to introduce him to the wife of the local constable, and two other ladies. After suitable words had been exchanged, they made their farewells and he strolled beside her down the path to where Henry waited with the curricle and the by now restive blacks.

Curious, she glanced at his face. "You seem to be . . ." She waggled her head. "Unexpectedly amenable to the 'letting the locals get to know you' socializing."

He shrugged. "I intend to live here for the rest of my life. These are the people I'll see every day, the ones I'll be working with, and for. They might want to know more of me, but I definitely need to know more about them."

She let him hand her into the curricle. While she settled, she pondered his words. His father—

She broke off the thought. If there was one thing she should by now have realized it was that he wasn't like his father when it came to people. His temper, arrogance, and a great deal more, were very familiar, but his attitudes to others were almost universally different. On some aspects— for instance, children—even diametrically opposed.

They were on the road beyond the village when he said, "Kilworth told me there's no school in the district, not even at the most elementary level."

Timorous Mr. Kilworth, the deacon, would never have mentioned such a matter, not unless asked.

"I suppose I should have guessed," he continued, "but it never occurred to me before."

She regarded him with something close to fascination— safe enough with his attention focused on his horses as he steered them toward the bridge. "Are you thinking of starting a school here?"

He flicked her a glance. "I've heard talk among other

peers—there's an evolving notion that having better educated workers benefits everyone."

And he'd seen a lot of croft and farm children in recent days.

"I wouldn't disagree." His father had—vociferously—when she'd suggested it.

"Any school shouldn't be solely for the estate families—it needs to be for the district, so we'd need to recruit wider support, but . . ." He sent the blacks rocketing across the stone bridge. "I think it's worthwhile pursuing."

As the horses thundered through the big gates and the wheels rolled more smoothly on the drive, he glanced at her. "Write down any thoughts you have." His eyes rested on hers. "Once I have the matter of my bride settled, we'll be able to move forward with that."

She felt ecstatic on the one hand, unsettled and oddly cast down on the other.

Minerva was given no time to examine her contradictory feelings; she and Royce walked into the castle as the luncheon gong sounded, then during the meal the idea of a fishing expedition upstream along the Coquet was touted, and instantly found favor with all the men.

And all the women, although none had any intention of picking up a rod. But the day was fine, sunny with the barest breath of a breeze, and everyone agreed a walk would do them good.

She was tempted to cry off, to use her duties as an excuse to remain behind and try to untangle her emotions, but Royce paused beside her as the company rose from the table.

He spoke quietly, for her ears only. "Keep an eye on the ladies—make sure the more adventurous don't attempt to investigate the gorge."

Inwardly cursing, she nodded. It was just the sort of witless thing some of the ladies present might do, and the gorge was dangerous.

The fishing rods and tackle were stowed in the boathouse by the lake; Royce led the men down to make their choices while the ladies hurried to fetch bonnets, shawls, and parasols.

From the lake, rods over their shoulders, the men followed the path north along the stream. Feeling like a sheepdog, Minerva marshaled the ladies and herded them along the west and north wings and out along the route to the mill.

The men were a little way ahead; some ladies called, waved. The men glanced back, waved, but continued walking.

Among the ladies, Margaret and Caroline Courtney led the way, heads together as they shared secrets. The other ladies walked in twos and threes, chatting as they ambled in the sunshine.

Minerva kept to the rear, ensuring no stragglers got left behind. The men crossed the bridge over the race; the ladies followed.

After passing the mill, the twin parties reached the end of the race where it came off the gorge, and turned north along the gorge. Minerva did, indeed, have to dissuade three ladies from descending into the gorge to investigate the rock pools. "I know you can't tell from up here, but the rocks are terribly slippery, and the stretches of water are treacherously deep."

She pointed to where the river ran strongly, gushing and churning over its rocky bed. "There's been rain on the Cheviots over the last weeks—the currents will be surprisingly strong. That's the biggest danger if you fall in—that you'll be dashed to death on the rocks."

In her experience, it never hurt to be specific; the ladies "oh"-ed and readily walked on.

The men drew ahead; the ladies loitered, pointing to this, examining that, but nevertheless drifting in the right direction. Minerva fell back, ambling even more slowly in her shepherdess role. Finally she had a moment to think.

Not that her thoughts were all that clear.

She was thrilled Royce wanted to establish a school in the village; she would cheer him on in that. More, she felt strangely proud of him, that he—a Varisey in so many ways—had thought of it on his own. She felt distinctly vindicated over encouraging him to turn from his father's example and forge his own way, follow his own inclinations; they were proving very sound.

But she wouldn't be around to see the outcome—and that galled her. Disappointment, dejection, dragged her down, as if some prize she'd worked for and deserved was, by fate's fickle decree, to be denied her. More, was to be granted to another, who wouldn't appreciate it given she wouldn't know him.

His bride still remained unnamed, and therefore nebulous; she couldn't fix a face on the female, so couldn't direct her anger at her.

Couldn't resent her.

She halted at the thought.

Shocked by the unhappy emotion she'd just put a name to.

Nonsensical, she chided herself; she'd always known his bride would arrive one day—and that, soon after, she'd leave.

Leave the place she called home.

Lips firming, she thrust the thought away. The others had wandered far ahead; they'd reached the end of the gorge and were continuing on, following the river path into more open meadows. Lifting her head, drawing in a deep breath, she lengthened her stride and set out to catch them up.

No more thinking allowed.

North of the gorge, the river was wider, wending down from the hills through fertile meadowland. It was still deep in the middle, and there it ran swiftly, but the spreading edges flowed more gently.

There was a particular spot where the river rounded a curve, then spread in a wide pool that was especially good for fishing. The men had descended the sloping bank; spreading out in a line along the pool's edge, casting lures into the stream, they talked only in murmurs as they waited for a bite.

Royce and his male cousins—Gordon, Rohan, Phillip, Arthur, Gregory, and Henry—stood shoulder to shoulder.

All tall, dark-haired, and handsome, they were an arresting sight, reducing the other male guests to mere contrast.

The ladies gathered on the bank above. They knew enough to mute their voices; standing in a loose group, they enjoyed the sunshine and the light breeze, chatting quietly.

Minerva joined them. Susannah asked again whether she'd discovered whom Royce had chosen as his bride; Minerva shook her head, then stepped a little away from the group, her eye caught by a flash of color upriver.

From their position, the land rose gently; she could see another party enjoying a pleasant day by the banks two bends upstream.

One of the tenant farmers' families, plus their laborers' families as well; squinting, she saw a gaggle of children playing by the water's edge, laughing and shrieking, or so it seemed, as they played tag. The breeze was blowing northward, so no sound reached her, yet she had to wonder how many fish the men would catch with such a cacophony two hundred yards upstream.

She was about to look away when a girl standing by the stream's edge suddenly flailed her arms—and fell backward into the stream. The bank had crumbled beneath her heels; she fell with a splash—breath caught, Minerva watched, waiting to see . . .

The girl's white cap bobbed to the surface—in the middle of the stream. The current had caught her skirts; even as the adults rushed to the bank, she was whisked downriver, around the next curve.

Minerva looked down at the men. "Royce!"

He looked up, instantly alert.

She pointed upriver. "There's a girl in the water." She looked again, spotted the bobbing white cap. "Two bends upstream. She's in the center and coming down fast."

Before the last word had left her lips, Royce was giving orders. Rods were dropped; his cousins and the others gathered around him, then the whole group turned and ran downstream.

Royce paused only to call to Minerva, "Yell when she comes around that bend." He pointed at the last bend before the pool, then raced after the others.

From their vantage point, the ladies watched in horrified fascination. Minerva went as far down the bank as she could without losing sight of the girl. Susannah and two friends joined her, peering after thc men. "What are they doing?" Susannah asked.

Minerva spared a quick glance downriver, saw where the men were going—Royce on his own, just beyond the pool, the others still hurrying, leaping over rocks and slipping over wet patches on their way farther down—then looked back at the girl. "Royce is going out on the nearer spit—he'll catch her. But he's likely to lose his footing when he does—the current's running strongly—it'll take both of them. The others will form a human chain farther down. It'll be up to them to grab Royce and haul him and the girl in."

Susannah knew the river; she blanched.

One of her friends frowned. "Why are they trying to catch him? He's so strong—surely he'll be able to—"

"It's the *gorge*." Susannah cut her off, her voice harsh. "Oh, God. If they miss him . . ."

She grabbed up her skirts, climbed the bank, and started running downstream.

"What is it?" Margaret called.

Susannah turned and called something back. Minerva stopped listening. The girl, still weakly struggling, cleared the bend.

She turned and looked downriver. "Royce! She's coming!"

Standing in the shallows around the next bend, just visible from where she was, he raised a hand in acknowledgment; no longer wearing his coat, he waded deeper into the river.

Minerva hurried down the bank, then along the water's edge, where the men had stood. Susannah's other friend, Anne, held her tongue and went with her. Minerva ran, but the current whisked the girl along faster; long braids floating on either side of her small white face, the poor child was almost spent. "Hold on!" Minerva called, and prayed the girl could hear. "He'll catch you in a minute."

She slipped and nearly fell; Anne, on her heels, caught her and steadied her, then they both dashed on.

The bobbing rag doll the girl had become was swept around the bend, out of their sight. Gasping, Minerva ran faster; she and Anne rounded the bend in time to see Royce, sunk chest-deep even though he stood on a spit in the stream-bed, lean far to his right, then launch himself across, into the swiftly running current; it caught him in the same moment he caught the girl, hoisting her up onto his chest, then onto his right shoulder where her head was at least partly clear of the increasingly turbulent water.

Minerva slowed, her fingers rising to her lips as she took in what lay beyond the pair. The river started narrowing, funneling toward the gorge, the water tumbling and churning as it battered its way on.

There was only one spot, another spit, where the pair, whisked along, could be caught, one chance before the building pressure of the water swept them into the gorge and almost certain death. On the spit, Royce's Varisey and Debraigh cousins were linking arms, forming a human chain, anchored by Henry and Arthur, the lightest, together on the bank. Each held on to one of Gregory's arms. Gregory had his other arm linked with Rohan's, who in turn was waiting for Gordon to link his arm with his, leaving Phillip at the end.

Minerva halted, put her hands about her mouth. "*Quickly!*" she screamed. "They're almost there!"

Phillip looked, then shoved Gordon toward Rohan, grabbed one of Gordon's arms, and waded into the stream.

The current swung away, around the spit, carrying Royce and his burden along the other side of the riverbed. Rohan yelled and the men all stretched . . . Phillip yelled to Gordon to hang on to his coat. As soon as he had, Phillip lunged out, stretching as far as he could, reaching out.

Just as it seemed the pair would be lost, Royce's arm lashed out of the water—and connected with Phillip's. They both gripped.

"Hold hard!" Phillip yelled.

The dragging weight—not just of Royce and the girl, but now Phillip as well, all drenched and sodden—tested the other men. Muscles bunched, locked. Henry's and Arthur's feet shifted; they both leaned back, faces grim and set as they hauled their kinsmen in.

Then it was over. Royce and Phillip, swung downstream and in toward the bank, got their feet under them.

Royce stood, breathing hard, then, shaking his head like a dog, he hoisted the girl free of the water, and holding her to his chest, walked, slowly and carefully, across the rocky riverbed. Phillip staggered up, then followed alongside. He reached over and lifted the girl's hair from her face, tapped her cheek—and she coughed. Weakly at first, but when Royce reached the bank and laid her on her side, she retched, coughed hard, then started to cry.

Minerva fell to her knees beside her. "It's all right. Your mother and father are coming—they'll be here soon." She glanced at Royce; his chest was rising and falling like a bellows, and water ran off him in streams, but he was unharmed, unhurt. Alive.

She looked up at the other ladies, gathering in an anxious, exclaiming knot on the bank above. Anne had come to stand beside her. Minerva pointed at the shawls some of the others carried. "Shawls—the woolen ones."

"Yes, of course." Anne climbed the bank partway and reached up, beckoning.

Two ladies surrendered their shawls readily, but Aurelia sniffed. "Not mine."

Royce had bent over, hands braced on his knees. He didn't bother looking up. "Aurelia."

His voice cut like a whip; Aurelia all but flinched. She paled. Her face set in sour lines, but she shrugged off her shawl and tossed it at Anne—who caught it, turned, and hurried back to Minerva.

She'd stripped off the girl's hat and sodden pinafore, and had been chafing her small icy hands. She stopped to take one of the shawls—Aurelia's large warm one. Shaking it out, with Anne's help she wrapped the girl tightly, then wound the other shawls about her hands and feet.

Then the girls' parents and the rest of the farmer's party arrived; they'd had to backtrack to cross the river by a wooden bridge higher up.

"She's all right," Minerva called as soon as she saw the parents' distraught faces.

Both rushed down the riverbank, eyes only for their child.

"Mary!" The mother dropped to her knees opposite Minerva. She placed a gentle hand on the girl's cheek. "Sweetheart?"

The girl's lashes fluttered; she tried to move her hands. "Ma?"

"Oh, thank God." The mother swept the girl up against her bosom. She looked at Minerva, then up at Royce. "Thank you—*thank you*, Your Grace. I don't know how we can ever repay you."

Her husband laid a shaking hand on his daughter's dark head. "Nor I. I thought she were—" He cut himself off, blinked rapidly. Shook his head and looked at Royce. Gruffly said, "Can't thank you enough, Your Grace."

One of his cousins had fetched Royce's coat; he'd been using it to mop his face. "If you want to thank me, take her home and get her warm—after hauling her out, I don't want her to take a chill."

"Yes—yes, we will." The mother struggled to her feet, lifting the girl. Her husband quickly took the child.

"And you may be sure," the mother said, tugging her damp clothes straight, "that none of that lot will ever play too close to the riverbanks again." Her severe look directed their gazes to the gaggle of children, watching round-eyed from up along the bank, their parents and the other adults at their backs.

"You might like to remind them," Royce said, "that if they do, there's unlikely to be a group of us here, in the right spot at the right time, to pull them out."

"Aye. We'll tell them, you may be sure." The father ducked his head as low as he could. "With your permission, Your Grace, we'll get her home."

Royce waved him up the slope.

The mother sighed and shook her head. She exchanged a glance with Minerva. "You tell them and tell them, but they never listen, do they?" With that, she followed her husband up the bank.

Royce watched them go, watched as the other farmers and their wives gathered around, offering comfort and support as they closed around the couple and their nearly lost daughter.

Beside him, Minerva slowly got to her feet. He waited while she thanked Anne for her help, then asked, "Who were they?"

"The Honeymans. They hold the farm up around Green Side." She paused, then added, "They would have seen you at church, but I don't think you've met them before."

He hadn't. He nodded. "Let's get back." He was chilled to the bone, and there was no earthly way to get his coat—expertly fitted by Shultz—on over his wet clothes.

Anne had joined the others, but now she came back. She touched Minerva's arm. "Susannah and some of the other ladies have started back with Phillip—his teeth are chattering. I thought I'd run ahead and warn the household." Although in her thirties, Anne was slim, fit, and swift on her feet.

"Thank you." Minerva lightly grasped Anne's fingers. "If you could tell Retford we need hot baths for His Grace, and for Phillip, and hot water for the others, too."

"I'll do that." Anne glanced at Royce, inclined her head, then turned and climbed swiftly up the slope.

With Minerva beside him, Royce followed more slowly.

Minerva humphed. Looking ahead to where certain of the ladies were still milling inconsequentially, some, with hands clutched to their breasts, exclaiming as if the incident had overset their delicate nerves, she muttered, "At least some people keep their heads in a crisis."

She meant Anne. Royce looked at her, felt his lips curve. "Indeed."

Arthur and Henry, together with the other male guests not in some degree soaked, had gone back to fetch the discarded rods and tackle.

As Royce and Minerva crested the slope, the remaining ladies, apparently deciding that the excitement was now entirely over, regrouped and started back to the castle.

With Minerva walking alongside, Royce found himself nearing the rear of the group, and wished they'd walk faster. He needed to keep moving, or he'd start shivering as badly as Phillip. His skin was already icy, and the chill was sinking deeper into his bones.

Margaret looked back at him a few times; he presumed she was assuring herself he wasn't about to collapse.

He wasn't entirely surprised when she stepped sideways out of the group and waited until he and Minerva drew level.

But it was Minerva to whom Margaret spoke. "If I could have a word?"

"Yes. Of course." Minerva halted.

Royce walked on, but slowed. He didn't like the look in Margaret's eyes, or her expression, and even less her tone. Minerva was no servant, not even to the family. She wasn't a penniless relative, or anything of the sort.

She was his chatelaine, and rather more, even if Margaret didn't yet know it.

"Yes?"

That was Minerva prompting Margaret, who had thus far remained silent.

Margaret waited until he'd taken two more steps before saying—hissing—"How *dare* you?" There was a wealth of furious, frightened venom in her voice; it shook as she went on, "How *dare* you put the entire *dukedom* at risk for a crofter's brat!"

Royce halted.

"The Honeymans are your brother's tenants, but regardless, saving that girl was the right thing to do."

He turned.

Saw Margaret draw in a breath. Her color high, eyes locked on Minerva, she all but shrieked, "For some stupid, silly girl, you risked—"

"Margaret." Royce walked back toward her.

She spun to face him. "And *you*! You're no better! Did you spare so much as a thought for us—for me, Aurelia, and Susannah, your *sisters*!—before you—"

"Enough."

His tone was all cold steel; it had her clenching her fists and swallowing the rest of her tirade. He halted before her, close enough so she had to look up into his face—close enough that she was just a touch intimidated, as well she should be.

"No, I didn't think of you, Aurelia, or Susannah—you all have wealthy husbands to support you, regardless of my continuing health. I didn't put you in danger by saving that girl. Her *life* was in the balance, and I would have been greatly disappointed had Minerva not warned me. I was in a position to save her—a girl who was born on my lands."

He looked down into his sister's mulish face. "What Minerva did was right. What I did was right. What you appear to have forgotten is that my people—even silly young girls— are my responsibility."

Margaret drew in a long, tight breath. "Papa would never—"

"Indeed." This time his voice cut. "But I am not Papa."

For a moment, he held Margaret silent with his gaze, then, unhurriedly and deliberately, turned toward the castle. "Come, Minerva."

She quickly caught up to him, walking alongside.

He lengthened his stride; the other ladies were now far ahead. "I need to get out of these wet clothes." He spoke conversationally, signaling he intended to leave Margaret's little scene behind, metaphorically as well as physically.

Minerva nodded, tight-lipped. "Precisely." A heartbeat passed, then she went on, "I really don't know why Margaret couldn't have waited until later to rail at me—it's not as if I won't be around. If she was really worried about your health, she'd have done better not to delay us." She glanced sharply his way. "Can you go faster? Perhaps you ought to run?"

"Why?"

"So you'll warm up." They were nearing the mill. Raising a hand, she pushed his shoulder. "Go that way—through the mill and over the race. It's faster than going down to the bridge and across."

She usually avoided touching him, yet now she kept pushing, so he diverted onto the paved path leading into the mill. "Minerva—"

"We need to get you to the castle, out of those wet clothes and into a hot bath as soon as possible." She prodded him toward the gangplank. "So move!"

He almost saluted, but did as she ordered. From Margaret, who thought of no one but herself, to Minerva, who was totally focused . . . on him.

On his well-being.

It took an instant for that to fully sink in.

He glanced at her as, her hands now locked about one of his elbows, she hurried him out of the mill. Her focus was on the castle, on getting him—all but propelling him—as fast as possible inside. Her intensity wasn't just that of a chatelaine doing her duty; it was a great deal more.

"I'm not likely to take a fatal chill from a dip in the river." He tried to slow to a fast walk.

She set her jaw and all but hauled him on. "You're not a doctor—you can't know that. The prescribed treatment for immersion in an icy river is a hot bath, and that's what you have to have. Your mother would never forgive me if I let you expire because you wouldn't treat the risk with due seriousness."

His mother, who had never wasted a moment worrying about his health. Male Variseys were supposed to be tough, and, indeed, were. But he bowed to Minerva's tugging and resumed his faster pace. "I am taking this seriously."

Just not as seriously as she was.

Or, as it transpired, any of his staff were.

The instant Minerva pushed him through the door into the north wing, Trevor pounced.

"*No!*" His valet was literally aghast. "That's another pair of Hobys ruined—two pairs in three days. And, oh, my heavens! You're drenched!"

He refrained from saying he knew. "Is my bath ready?"

"It better be." Trevor exchanged a look with Minerva, still by Royce's side, still hurrying him along. "I'll go up and make sure." Trevor turned and all but fled before them, his footsteps clattering up the turret stairs.

Royce and Minerva followed, taking the shortcut to his rooms.

Minerva halted outside his sitting room door; he kept walking, to the useful new door into his dressing room and the bathing chamber beyond that Hancock, the castle carpenter, was just testing.

Hancock nodded. "Your new door as ordered, Your Grace. Just in time, it seems." Hancock swung the panel wide. "Your bath awaits."

Royce nodded. "Thank you." He looked over the door and its frame as he went through into the dressing room, then nodded again to Hancock. "That's exactly what I wanted."

Hancock saluted, picked up his toolbox, and walked off.

Minerva appeared in the doorway—mouth a-cock, staring at the door, then at its frame. Then she looked at Royce.

"So Trevor and the footmen don't need to come through the bedroom to reach these rooms."

"Oh." She stood there, digesting that, while he started the difficult task of unwinding his sodden cravat.

Trevor appeared in the open doorway opposite, from which steam eddied as a footman poured what had to be a last pail of steaming water into the large bath; if any more was put in, it would slosh out when Royce got in. He signaled to the footman to stop.

His valet, meanwhile, was frowning at two glass-stoppered bottles he was holding. "Which would be better? Mint or peppermint?"

"Menthol." Snapping out of her trance, Minerva bustled in to join Trevor. "Pennyroyal is what you want—it's the best for warding off chills." She stepped around Trevor, let the footman squeeze past, then pointed to a rack of similar bottles set on a wooden table. "There should be some there."

"Pennyroyal. Right." Trevor went to the rack. "Here it is. How many drops?" He squinted at the tiny label.

"About a teaspoon, even two. Enough so you can smell it strongly."

Trevor took out the stopper, tipped a bit of the oil into the water. Minerva and he sniffed the steam. Both frowned.

Walking into the bathing chamber, Royce dropped his sodden cravat, which he'd finally managed to untangle, onto the floor; it landed with a splat, but neither his valet nor his chatelaine reacted.

He looked longingly at the hot water, felt ice seeping into his marrow—heard the other two arguing the merits of adding peppermint as well.

Lips setting, he yanked his shirttails free of his waistband, loosened the cords at his wrists and neck, then looked at his chatelaine. "Minerva."

She looked up, met his eyes.

"Leave. Now." He reached for the bottom of his shirt.

"Oh, yes—of course."

He pulled the shirt up, heard the flurry of her footsteps, then the door to the bathing chamber click shut. Grimly smiled. But wrestling free of the drenched folds was an exercise and a half; Trevor had to help—with that, his boots, and his breeches, designed to cling to him even when dry.

Finally naked, he stepped into the tub, sat, and leaned back, then sank right down. Felt the heat from the water slowly melt the ice in his flesh. Felt the warmth sink in.

Felt warmth of a different kind slowly expand from his center out.

His gaze on the door through which his chatelaine had fled, he slowly thawed.

Late that night, lounging shoulder to the wall in the darkness of an embrasure in the keep's gallery, Royce broodingly stared at Minerva's bedroom door.

The only thought in his mind was whether her caring about him as she clearly did was sufficient excuse for what he was about to do.

He understood perfectly well why the need to bed her had suddenly escalated to a level significantly beyond his control. Dicing with death had that effect, made one only too aware of one's mortality, and commensurately fired the need to live, to prove one was vitally alive in the most fundamental way.

What he was feeling, how he was reacting, was all perfectly natural, normal, logical. To be expected.

He wasn't at all sure she'd see it that way.

But he needed her tonight.

And not solely for his selfish self.

While in the matter of the rescue, he and she had been in the right, so, too, had Margaret. He'd accepted the need to secure the succession; he couldn't continue to put off speaking and gaining Minerva's agreement to be his bride.

To be the mother of his son—the eleventh Duke of Wolverstone.

At this moment in time, all roads in his life led to this place, and compelled him to act, to take the next step.

The castle had grown quiet; all the guests were abed, whoever's bed they were gracing that night. Within the keep, only he and Minerva remained; all the staff had long retired.

There was no sense dallying any longer.

He was about to push away from the wall, had tensed to take the first fateful step toward her door, when it opened.

He froze, watched through the darkness as Minerva came out. She was still fully dressed; clutching a shawl about her shoulders, she glanced right, then left. She didn't notice him, standing perfectly still in the enveloping shadows.

Quietly closing her door, she set off down the corridor.

Silent as a wraith, he followed.

Twelve

A **full moon rode the sky; Minerva didn't need a candle** to slip down the main stairs and follow the west wing corridor to the music room. Once on the ground floor, she walked quickly, openly; all the guests were on the floor above.

She'd loaned Cicely, a distant Varisey cousin, her mother's pearl brooch to anchor the spangled shawl Cicely had worn as the Princess of France in that evening's performance of *Love's Labour's Lost*—and had forgotten to take it back. The brooch was valuable, but much more than that, it was one of the few mementos she had of her mother; she wasn't of a mind to risk leaving it jumbled with the other pieces of finery in the costume box, not even just until tomorrow.

Not that she imagined anyone would steal it, but . . . she wouldn't be able to sleep until she had the brooch back.

Reaching the music room, she opened the door and went in. Moonlight streamed through the wide window, flooding the stage, providing more than enough light. As she walked up the aisle between the rows of chairs, her mind drifted to Royce—and the sharp clutch of fear, almost paralyzing in strength, that had gripped her when she'd seen him in the river, with his burden sweeping wide around the spit where his would-be rescuers had waited . . .

For one crystal-clear instant in time, she'd thought she— they—would lose him. Even now . . . She slowed, closed her eyes, drew in a slow, steadying breath. All had turned out well—he was safe upstairs, and the girl was at her home, no doubt cosseted and warm in her bed.

Exhaling and opening her eyes, she continued on more briskly, stepping up onto the low stage. The trunk of costumes stood in the lee of the paneled left wing. Beside it sat a box full of shawls, scarves, kerchiefs, mixed with fake daggers, berets, a paste tiara and crown, all the smaller items that went with the costumes.

Crouching by the box, she started sorting through the materials, looking for the spangled shawl.

With hands and eyes engaged, her thoughts, prodded by Margaret's outburst, and by comments she'd subsequently heard, not just from the ladies but from some of the men as well, roamed, circling the question of whether she'd done the right thing in warning Royce of the girl's danger.

Not all who'd commented had assumed she'd expected him to rescue the girl, but she had. She'd expected him to act precisely as he had—not in the specifics, but in the sense that he would do all he could to save the child.

She *hadn't* expected him to risk his life, not to the point where his death had become a real possibility. She didn't think he'd foreseen that, either, but in such situations there never was time for cold-blooded calculations, weighing every chance.

When faced with life-and-death situations, one had to act—and trust that one's skills would see one through. As Royce's had. He'd given orders to his cousins and they'd instinctively obeyed; *now* they might question the wisdom of his act, but at the time they'd done as he'd asked.

Which was all that mattered. To her mind, the end result had been entirely satisfactory, yet of all those above stairs, only she, Royce, and a handful of others saw the matter in that light. The rest thought he, and she, had been wrong.

Of course, they wouldn't think so if the girl had been well-born.

Noblesse oblige; those dissenting others clearly interpreted the phrase in a different way from her and Royce.

The spangled shawl wasn't in the box. Frowning, she piled the other things back in, then lifted the lid of the trunk. "Aha."

She drew the soft folds out. As she'd suspected, Cicely had left the brooch pinned to the shawl; freeing it, she closed the clip, and slipped the brooch into her pocket. Dropping the shawl back into the trunk, she lowered the lid, and stood.

Just as footsteps sounded in the corridor beyond the open door.

Slow, steady, deliberate footsteps . . . Royce's.

They halted in the doorway.

Royce normally moved impossibly silently. Was he allowing his footsteps to be heard because he knew she was there? Or because he thought there was no one around to hear?

She edged deeper into the lee of the panel; the thick velvet curtain, currently drawn back, gave her extra cover, ensuring her outline wasn't etched in moonlight on the floor before the stage. Sliding her fingers between the curtain and the panel, she peeked out.

Royce stood in the doorway. He glanced around the room, then walked slowly in, leaving the door wide.

A great deal tenser than she had been, she watched as he paced down the center aisle. Halting halfway to the stage, he sat in a chair at the end of one row; the wooden legs scraped as he shifted, the small sound loud in the night. Thighs spread, he leaned his forearms along them, linked his hands between. Head angled down, he appeared to be studying his loosely interlocked fingers.

Royce thought—again—of what he intended to do, but need was a clamor filling his mind, drowning out, sweeping aside, all reservations.

Despite his nonchalance, he knew perfectly well he'd come within a whisker of dying that day. He'd waltzed close to Death before; he knew what the touch of her icy fingers felt like. What was different about this time was that—for the first time—he'd had regrets. Specific regrets that had leapt, sharp and clear, to the forefront of his mind in the moment when Phillip's hand had seemed just too far away.

His principal regret had been over her. That if he died, he'd miss knowing her. Not just biblically, but in a deeper, broader sense, something he could put his hand on his heart and swear he'd never wanted with any other woman.

Yet another reason it was just as well he was set on having her as his wife. He'd have years to learn of, to explore, all her different facets, her character, her body, her mind.

That afternoon, while warming up in his bath, he'd considered the odd impulse her hurrying him back to the castle had evoked. He'd wanted to put his arm around her and openly accept her help, to lean on her—not physically—but for some other reason, some other solace. Not just for him, but for her, too. Accepting her help, acknowledging it—showing he welcomed it, that he was pleased, felt honored, that she cared.

He hadn't done it—because men like him never showed such weakness. Throughout his childhood, his schooling, through social pressure, such views had shaped him; he knew it, but that didn't mean he could escape the effects, no matter how powerful a duke he might be.

Indeed, because he'd been destined to be just such a powerful duke, the conditioning had reached even deeper.

Which, in many ways, explained tonight.

Beneath the flow of his thoughts, he'd been evaluating, assessing, deciding. Drawing in a long breath, he lifted his head and looked to the left of the stage. "Come out. I know you're there."

Minerva frowned, and stepped out from her hiding place. Tried to feel irritated; instead . . . she discovered it was possible to feel exceedingly vulnerable and irresistibly fascinated simultaneously.

Stepping off the stage, she told herself, her unruly senses, to concentrate on the former and forget the latter. To focus on all the reasons she had to feel vulnerable about him. About getting too close to him in any way.

Predictably, as she walked with feigned calmness down the aisle, her senses, skittering in breathless expectation, gained the ascendancy. Being within four feet of him was not a wise idea. Yet . . .

The light from the window behind her fell on him, illuminated his face as, remaining seated, he looked up at her.

There was something in his expression, usually so utterly uninformative. Not tiredness, more like resignation—along with a sense of . . . emotional tension.

The observation puzzled, just as another puzzling fact occurred. She fixed her gaze on his dark eyes. "How did you know I was here?"

"I was in the corridor outside your room. I saw you come out, and followed."

She halted in the aisle beside him. "Why?"

The moonlight didn't reach his eyes; they searched her face, but she couldn't read them, any more than she could tell what he was thinking from the chiseled perfection of his features, yet they still held that certain tension, a need, perhaps, or a hunger; as the silence stretched she sensed it more clearly—honest, sincere, direct.

Real.

A lock of sable hair had fallen across his brow; entirely without thinking, she reached out and smoothed it back. Fingertips seduced by the rich softness, by the sensual tingle, she hesitated, then started to withdraw her hand.

He caught it, trapped it in one of his.

Eyes widening, she met his gaze. Fell into it.

He held her ensorcelled for a long moment, then, uncurling her fingers with his, he turned his head and, slowly, deliberately, pressed his lips to her palm.

The shocking heat leapt like a spark into her; the blatantly intimate touch made her shiver.

He shifted his head; his lips drifted to her wrist, there to bestow an equally intimate lover's caress.

"I'm sorry." The words reached her on a dark whisper as his lips left her skin. His fingers shifted over hers, locking her hand in his. "I didn't intend it to be like this, but . . . I can't wait for you any longer."

Before her brain could take in his meaning, let alone react, he surged to his feet—angling his shoulder into her waist, using his hold on her hand to pull her forward—in one smooth move hoisting her up over his shoulder.

"What . . . ?" Disoriented, she stared down his back.

He turned to the door.

She grabbed the back of his coat. "For God's sake, Royce— put me down!" She would have kicked, tried to lever herself off his hard shoulder, but he'd clamped a steely arm over the backs of her knees, locking her in position.

"I will. Just be quiet for a few minutes."

A few minutes? He'd already walked out into the corridor.

Clutching the back of his coat with both hands, she looked around, then braced as he started climbing; through the dimness she recognized the hall before the west turret stairs— watched it recede.

A scarifying thought formed. "Where are you taking me?"

"You already know. Do you want me to state it?"

"Yes!"

"To my bed."

"No!"

Silence. No response, no reply, no acknowledgment of any sort.

He reached the gallery and turned toward his rooms. Any doubt that he meant to do as he'd said evaporated. Realization of how helpless she was grew; she couldn't prevent what would follow because she simply wouldn't, not once he'd hauled her into his arms and kissed her.

Just the thought of his hands—his clever, wicked hands— on her skin again made her shiver with damning anticipation.

Desperate, she braced her hands on his back, struggled to

push up enough to drag air into her lungs. "Royce, *stop!*" She poured every ounce of command she could muster into her tone. When he didn't so much as pause, she quickly continued, "If you don't set me down this instant, I'll scream."

"A piece of advice from one who knows—never threaten what you're not prepared to deliver."

Incensed, she drew in a massive breath, held it . . . waited.

His strides didn't falter.

But then he halted.

Hope flared—only to be drowned by a wave of disappointment.

Before she could decide what she truly felt, he walked forward again, then swung around. Her gaze raked the line of his armillary spheres. They were in his sitting room. Her last chance of being saved, by any means, died as she heard the door shut.

She waited, breath bated, to be put down. Instead, he walked through the next door, kicked it shut behind them, and continued on across his bedroom.

All the way to the foot of his massive four-poster bed.

Halting, he gripped her waist; dipping his shoulder, he slid her slowly down, breasts to his chest, until her toes touched the floor.

Valiantly ignoring the sudden rush of her pulse and her swooningly eager senses, she fixed her eyes, narrowed, on his as he straightened. "You can't do this." She made the statement absolute. "You cannot simply carry me in here, and"—she gestured wildly—"*ravish* me!"

It was the only word she could think of that matched the intent she could now see in his eyes.

He studied her for an instant, then raised his hands, framed her face. Tipped it up as he shifted closer, so their bodies touched, brushed, settled, as, eyes locked with hers, he bent his head. "Yes. I can."

His statement trumped hers. It rang with innate conviction, with the overwhelming confidence that had been his from birth.

Lids falling, she braced for an assault.

It didn't come.

Instead, he supped at her lips, a gentle, tantalizing, tempting caress.

Her lips already hungered, her body thrumming with awakening need when he lifted his head just enough to catch her eyes. "I'm going to ravish you—thoroughly. And I guarantee you'll enjoy every minute."

She would; she knew she would. And she no longer knew of any way to avoid it—was fast losing sight of why she should. She searched his eyes, his face. Moistened her lips. Looked at his, and didn't know what to say.

What reply she wanted to convey.

As she stared at them, his lips curved. Thin, hard, yet mobile, the ends curved up just slightly, invitingly.

"You don't have to say anything. You just have to accept. Just have to stop resisting . . ." He breathed the last words as his lips lowered to hers. "And let what we both want, simply be."

His lips closed on hers again, still gentle, still persuasive, yet she felt the barely leashed hunger in the hands cradling her face. Lifting one hand, she closed it over the back of one of his—and knew to her bones his gentleness was a façade.

Ravish he'd said, and ravish he meant.

As if to prove her correct, his lips hardened, firmed; she felt his hunger, tasted his passion. She expected him to press her lips apart, with no further invitation claim her mouth, then her—but abruptly he reined in the passion about to break free.

Enough for him to lift his lips an inch from hers and demand, "If you don't want to know what it would be like to lie with me, say so now."

She'd dreamed of it, fantasized about it, spent long hours wondering . . . looking into the dark richness of his eyes, at the heat already burning in their depths, she knew she should deny it, grasp the chance and flee, yet the lie simply wouldn't come.

"If you don't want me, tell me now."

The harsh words grated, deep and low.

His lips hovered over hers, waiting for her answer.

One of her hands lay on his chest, spread over his heart; she could feel the heavy, urgent thud, could see in his eyes, behind all the heat, a simple need—one that pleaded, that touched her.

That needed her to be assuaged.

If you don't want me . . .

He wanted her.

Tipping up her face, she closed the distance, and kissed him.

Sensed a fleeting moment of surprise, then he accepted—seized—the implied permission.

His lips closed on hers—ravenously. Hers were parted; he surged in and laid claim. Laid waste to any vestige of resistance, laid siege to her wits and flattened her defenses.

He filled her mouth, captured her tongue and caressed, seized her senses, engaged them with his. Commanded, demanded; even as his hands slid from her face and his arms closed around her, steely bands pulling her into him, locking her uncompromisingly against his hard frame, he lured her into a heated exchange that rapidly escalated, eager and urgent, onto another plane.

He fed her fire and passion, and more. He gave her, pressed on her, a taste of raw possession, an undisguised, shockingly explicit portent of what was to come, of his unleashed hunger, of her own heady response.

Of her ultimate surrender.

Of that last there was never any doubt.

Her shawl slid from her shoulders to the floor. She could barely find her wits in the maelstrom of her senses, could do little more in that first turbulent wash of passion and desire than cling to the kiss, to his lips, wind her arms about his neck and hang on for dear life.

For this was much more than he'd shared with her before.

He'd let fall the reins he normally held, and let his desire loose to devour her.

That was how it felt when he closed one hand about her breast. There was nothing gentle in his touch; she gasped through the kiss, felt herself arch helplessly into the caress—all possessive passion, expertly wielded. His fingers closed and she shuddered, felt his palm burn even through the layers of fabric shielding her skin. Felt a hot wave of desire, as before his and hers combining, undeniably twining, rise up and fill her.

Take her. Compel her. Overwhelm her.

In that instant she set aside all restraint, gave herself up to the moment, and all it would bring. Set herself free to take all and everything he offered, to revel and seize whatever came her way. To seize the moment fate had granted her to live her dreams—even if only for one night.

The decision resonated within her.

This was what she'd wanted all her life.

She reached for it. Boldly slid her fingers into his hair, tightened them on his skull—and kissed him back. Let her own hunger rise up and answer his—let her own passion free to counter his. To balance the scales as much as she could.

As far as that was possible.

His response was so powerfully passionate it curled her toes. He angled his head, deepened the kiss, took complete and absolute possession of her mouth. The hand locked about her swollen breast eased, released; he sent it skating down, trailing fire wherever he touched, over her waist, her hip, around and down to close, flagrantly possessive, about one globe of her bottom.

He lifted her into him, drew her up against him so the hard ridge of his erection rode against her mons. Caught in the kiss, trapped in his arms, she was helpless to hold back the tide of sensation he sent crashing through her as with a deliberate, practiced roll of his hips, he thrust against her.

Barely able to breathe, she clung as, with that simple, explicitly repetitive action, he stoked her fire until it cindered her wits, then he continued to move deliberately against her with just the right amount of pressure to feed the flames . . . until she thought she would scream.

Royce wanted to be inside her, wanted to sink his throbbing staff deep into her luscious body, to feel her wet sheath close tightly about him and ease the fiery ache, then to possess her utterly; he needed that more than he'd needed anything in his life.

Hunger and need pounded through his veins, relentless and demanding; it would be so easy to lift her skirts, lift her, release his staff and impale her . . . but while he wanted with blinding urgency, some equally strong, equally violent instinct wanted to draw the moment out. Wanted to make it last—to stretch the anticipation until they were both mindless.

He'd nevcr been mindless, never had a woman who could reduce him to that state . . . the primitive side of him knew he had the one woman who could in his arms that night.

It wasn't control that allowed him to draw back, wasn't anything like thought that guided him as he lowered her to her feet, snaring her senses once more in their kiss—an increasingly hot, evocatively explicit mating of mouths—then steered her around the end of his bed.

He backed her along, then turned into the high side; using his hips and thighs to pin her there, he set his fingers to the laces of her gown.

A heartbeat later, her hands eased from his skull, slid down and out across his shoulders, then swept in, reaching between them to the buttons of his coat.

Curious over how direct she would be, how openly demanding, he let her slide the large buttons free; when she slid her hand up the inner edges and tried to push the coat off his shoulders, he obligingly released her and shrugged it off, let it fall where it would as he found her laces again and tugged them free.

At no stage did he let her break from the kiss—their hungry, greedy, devouring kiss. He drew her back into the heat and the flames, drew her against him again as he reached behind her and parted the gaping halves of her gown, slid one palm beneath, but found the fine silk of her chemise a last barrier, separating his hand from her skin.

Impulse goaded him to rip the garment away; he shackled it, but the notion acted like a spur. He wasted no time stripping the gown from her shoulders and down her arms, pushing it over her hips, letting it swish to the floor while he tugged the ribbon ties at the shoulders of her chemise undone, and sent it even more swiftly down.

Lifting his head, he dragged in a breath and stepped back.

Shocked—by her suddenly exposed state, but even more by the loss of his hard heat and the elemental hunger of his mouth—Minerva swayed back against the bed, managed to remain upright as her senses whirled.

They locked on him, tall, broad-shouldered, powerfully built, handsome as sin and twice as dangerous—standing a mere pace away.

One part of her mind told her to run; another felt she should tense, use her hands to cover herself, at least make some show of modesty—she was standing utterly naked before him—but the heat in his dark eyes as they roamed her body was hot enough to scorch, to burn away all inhibitions and leave her wantonly curious.

Wantonly fascinated.

She reached for the waistcoat she'd already opened, but he blocked her, brushing her hand aside with a gesture that said, "Wait."

His eyes hadn't left her body. His gaze continued to trace her curves, the indentation of her waist, the flare of her hips, the long, smooth lines of her thighs. It lingered, hot, assessing, blatantly possessive on the curls at the juncture of her thighs.

After a moment, his gaze lowered.

And she realized she wasn't entirely naked; she still had on her garters, stockings, and slippers.

He shrugged out of the waistcoat, let it fall as he went to his knees before her. He gripped one bare hip, bent and pressed his lips to the curls he'd studied. She felt her insides melt, reached back with her hands to lean on the bed, let her head loll back as the heat of his lips sank in, then he deftly tongued her—one artful sweep of his educated tongue over her most sensitive flesh.

She jerked, caught her breath—just managed to stifle a shriek. Hauling in a breath, she looked down as he drew back, reminded herself he thought she was experienced.

He didn't look up to gauge her reaction but, sitting back on his ankles, set his fingers to one garter and slowly rolled it and her stocking down. Bent his head as he did and with his lips traced a line of small, tantalizing kisses down the inner face of her leg, from high on her thigh to just below her knee.

By the time he finished removing her slippers and stockings, only her braced arms were holding her upright.

Her lids were heavy; from beneath her lashes she watched as he looked up at her, then he rocked back on his heels and smoothly rose.

Pulling the gold pin from his cravat, he tossed it onto the tallboy nearby, then unwound the folds, his movements tense, taut. Tugging the long strip from his neck, he dropped it, flicked the ties loose at his neck and wrists, then grabbed fistfuls of his shirt and hauled the fine linen up, and off.

Revealing his chest.

Her mouth watered. She'd caught only a glimpse in his bathing chamber earlier. Her eyes skated, drinking in the vision, then settled to a leisurely appreciation of each evocatively masculine element—the wide, well-defined muscles stretching across his upper chest, the sculpted ridges of his abdomen, the band of crinkly black hair that swept across the width, and the narrower stripe that arrowed down, disappearing beneath his waistband.

She watched the shift and play of muscles beneath his taut skin as he bent and pulled off his shoes, dispensed with his stockings.

Then he straightened, his fingers slipping the buttons at his waistband free.

She felt a panicky urge to wave a hand and tell him to stop. To at least slow down and give her time to prepare herself.

His eyes on her body, he stripped off his trousers, tossed them aside, straightened and walked toward her.

Her gaze locked on his phallus, long, thick, and very erect, rising from the nest of black hair at his groin; her mouth dried completely. Her heart thudded in her ears, but he didn't seem to hear.

Like most men, he seemed to have no concept of modesty . . . then again, with a body like a god, why would he feel shy?

She felt . . . overwhelmed.

He was all hard, heavy muscle and bone—and he was large. Definitely large.

She had every confidence that he knew what he—they— were doing, would be doing, but she couldn't imagine how he—that—was going to fit inside her.

Just the thought made her giddy.

He halted before her, as close as he could given she hadn't shifted her gaze. She didn't lift her head, didn't—couldn't— peel her eyes from that impressive display of male desire.

Desire she'd evoked.

She licked her lips, boldly reached for the solid rod and wrapped one palm and her fingers about it mid-length. Felt it harden at her touch.

Sensed his body tighten, harden, too, glanced up in time to see his eyes close. Her fingers didn't meet, but she slid her hand down, absorbing the contradictory textures of velvet over steel, traced down to the base, looked down to see her hand brushing against his hair, then she reversed direction, eager to explore the wide head. He hissed in pleasure when she reached it, then she released her grip and trailed her fingertips over the swollen contours, then around the rim.

He caught her hand—tightly; when she jerked her gaze

to his face he gentled his grip. "Later." His voice was a low growl.

She blinked.

His jaw set as he raised her hand to his shoulder. "You can touch and feel all you like later. Right now, I want to feel you."

His hands slid around her waist to her back. He brought her away from the bed—into him.

Nothing had prepared her for the tactile shock. For the jolt of pure sensation that streaked like lightning down every nerve, leaving their ends frazzled, leaving her gasping, struggling to get air into lungs locked tight.

He was so hot! His skin seared her, but enticingly—she couldn't get enough. Enough of his hard chest against her breasts, the crinkly hair lightly, unspeakably deliciously, abrading her furled nipples. Enough of the feel of the long length of his steely thighs against hers, enough of the promise of the rigid rod at his groin pressing into her belly.

The lack of air nearly made her swoon, but instinct pushed her into his embrace as his arms slid around her and locked, wanton instinct that had her squirming against him, instinctively seeking the best and closest fit, wanting the maximum contact, the absolute maximum of his masculine heat.

She wanted to bathe in it.

Royce bent his head and took her mouth again, filled it, claimed it, possessed the delectable softness just as he intended to possess her body—slowly, repetitively, and thoroughly.

At last, he had her where he wanted her, naked in his arms. The first small step to fulfillment. He didn't need to think to have the rest of his campaign blazoned in his brain; primitive instinct had already etched it there.

He wanted her naked, helplessly, shudderingly, sobbingly naked and begging for his touch.

He wanted her lying, utterly naked, sprawled on his silk sheets, her breasts swollen and peaked, with the marks of his possession clear on her flawless skin.

He wanted her panting, her white thighs spread wide, her folds pink and swollen, glistening with invitation as she begged him to fill her.

He wanted her writhing beneath him as he did.

He wanted her to climax, but not until he entered her—wanted her to fracture in the instant he sheathed himself within her. Wanted her to remember that moment, to have it engraved on her sensual memory—the time he first penetrated her, filled her, possessed her.

He was Wolverstone, unquestioned all-powerful lord of this domain.

What he wanted, he got.

He made sure of it.

Made sure that, using his hands, lips, and tongue, but lightly, he awakened every nerve ending she possessed, arousing her, feeding her hunger, stoking her desire, luring her passion, yet not satisfying those wants in the least.

Expertly he urged them to grow, to well, swell, and fill her.

Until, on a shuddering moan, she caught his hand and drew it to her breast. Pressed his fingers hard to her firm flesh. "Stop playing, you fiend."

He would have chuckled, but his throat was too tight with suppressed desire; instead, he did as ordered, and palmed her breast forcefully, kneading evocatively, then he backed her against the bed, propping her against it so he could use both hands on her at the same time.

Until she sobbed, and reached for his erection.

He caught her hand, held it as he swept the covers back and off the bed, then releasing her, he swept her up in his arms, and climbed onto the crimson silk sheets. Laying her down in the center of the bed, her head on the piled pillows, he stretched out beside her, set his lips and tongue to her breasts, and tortured himself by torturing her.

When she was moaning unrestrainedly, hands sunk in his hair, gripping tight as she writhed and held him to her, he slid lower in the bed, sampling her passion-damp skin as he would, spreading her thighs wide, settling between to lightly lave and lick, in between tracing her folds with his fingertips.

Until, panting, she lifted her head, looked down at him, and, eyes gleaming gold with unslaked desire, gasped, "For God's sake, touch me *properly*."

His features were granite, but he inwardly grinned as she flopped back. Then he gave her what she'd asked for, inserting first one, then two fingers into her tight sheath, working them deep, but carefully avoiding giving her release.

Minerva shuddered; simply breathing was a battle as she struggled to absorb each blatantly intimate caress, as her senses, totally focused, strained, greedily seizing all they could from each slow, heavy thrust of his fingers into her body—and discovering that it never was enough.

Not enough to spring the catch on her overwound senses, not enough—nowhere near enough—to fill the throbbing, empty void that had opened at her core.

All her skin felt flushed; passion's flames greedily, hungrily, licked all over her just beneath her skin, but no matter how she burned, the furnace within her merely smoldered red hot, molten and waiting.

Some distant part of her mind knew what he was doing— was even aware enough to be grateful; if he was—as she knew he was—going to thrust his engorged phallus into her, she wanted to be as ready as humanly possible.

But . . . she was already sopping wet—and desperate. Frantically desperate to feel and experience all the rest. She *wanted* him atop her, wanted to feel him join with her.

Finally comprehended what drove otherwise sane women to crave a lover like him.

Her body writhed under his hands. She could barely find air enough to gasp, "Royce . . ." A half sob, half moan carried the rest of her wordless plea.

One he understood; one she had a sudden comprehension he'd been waiting for. Leaving his fingers buried within her sheath, he rose up, his long body sliding over hers as, bracing on one elbow, he fitted his hips between her widespread thighs.

He withdrew his fingers from her slick sheath, set the broad head of his erection within her folds, literally at her entrance, then he settled over her, looking down into her face.

From beneath her lashes, she looked into his dark eyes.

"Do you want me inside you?" His voice was so gravelly, she could barely make out the words.

Releasing the sheets her hands had fisted in, she reached up, sank her fingers into his upper arms, and pulled him down to her—or tried to. "Yes," she hissed. "Now!"

His features, locked in passion, didn't shift, but she sensed his immense satisfaction. Then—to her immense satisfaction—he obliged her in both her requests.

He let his body down on hers, and her senses sang in delirious delight—all that heat, all that solid muscle, all that heavy body pinning her to the bed. But then he lowered his head, and took her mouth again, filled it again—something she hadn't been expecting that momentarily distracted her.

Then he flexed his hips, and nothing could distract her from the pressure as he entered her—slowly, inexorably—then he paused.

She almost screamed; she did moan, the sound muffled by their locked lips. Suddenly more desperate than she'd thought she could be, she sank her nails into his arms, writhed and lifted against him, tipped her hips, trying to lure him deeper, needing, begging—

He thrust heavily, powerfully, into her. Filled her completely with that single forceful thrust.

And she couldn't absorb it all at once. The brief flash of pain, the overwhelming shock of the sensation of him so solid and heavy within her, the realization that this had really happened . . . like an overwound skein, her senses started to unravel.

He held still for a long moment, then withdrew, almost to her entrance, then thrust powerfully into her again, even more deeply—and her senses fractured. She screamed as they shattered; he drank in the sound.

And she was swept high on a spiral of infinite ecstasy, senses expanding and expanding, bright, sharp, crystalline clear as waves of sensation, increasingly intense, rolled through her—as he filled her mouth and claimed her there, as his body moved heavily upon hers, and hers responded and danced under his, instinctively responding to the deep, driving rhythm as he possessed her utterly—ravished her thoroughly—and everything within her sang.

Then ecstasy sharpened, gripped her anew, and pushed her even higher—he growled in his throat, caught her tongue with his, stroked, then thrust deep into her mouth just as he thrust even more forcefully into her body.

And she came apart again.

All her senses, every particle of her awareness, imploded. Fragmented. Shards of pleasure so intense they felt like light speared down her veins, then melted and made her glow, made her soften beneath him, around him, made her clutch him and hold him as he thrust one last time, even more deeply, then he stiffened, groaned, shuddered as his release swept him, as deep and intense as hers, leaving him wracked, helpless in her arms.

All tension released, fell away, and they were floating in some blissful, bliss-filled void, surrounded by a golden glory she couldn't name.

It caught them, buoyed them, cushioned them as they spiraled slowly back to earth.

That golden rapture seeped into her, spread through her veins, through her body, sank deep into her heart, softly, slowly, infused her soul.

He'd lost himself in her.

That had never happened to him before; it left him wary.

Something had changed. He didn't know what, but she'd opened some door, led him down a new path, and his view of an activity he'd taken for granted for years had altered.

His experience of that activity had been rewritten, re-scripted.

He was very familiar with sexual satiation, but this was much more. The release he'd found in her, with her, was infinitely more sating; the satisfaction he'd found with her had reached his soul.

Or so it felt.

Royce stood at the uncurtained window of his bedroom and looked out at the moonlit night. Raising the glass of water he held, he sipped, and wished it could cool the still smoldering heat inside him.

But only one thing could do that.

He glanced back at his bed, where Minerva lay sleeping. Her hair was a golden wave breaking over his pillows, her face madonna-peaceful, one white arm gracefully draped atop the crimson-and-gold covers he'd pulled up so she wouldn't get cold.

He'd memorized the sight of her lying naked and sated, sprawled on his crimson sheets, before he'd covered her. She'd bled hardly at all, just a few streaks on the inside of her thighs, enough to confirm her previous untouched state, but not, he hoped, enough to make her hesitate over taking him inside her again.

His primitive side had gloated; he'd wanted her then, wanted to wake her again, but had decided to play civilized and give her a little time to recover. He hadn't been inside her all that long; her sheath had been so incredibly tight her release had brought on his. Control in abeyance, he hadn't held back, but that also meant he hadn't pounded into her for long; with luck she wouldn't be too sore to let him inside her again.

At least she was where she was supposed to be.

Keeping her there, ensuring she remained, was his next step. One he'd never attempted—wished to take—with any other woman.

But she was his. He intended to point that out—to propose and be accepted—once she stirred.

In considering that proposal, and how best to phrase it, his mind circled back to the surprise she'd had for him—the little secret she'd been hiding so amazingly well.

She'd never had any previous lover. Despite being so focused on her, despite his expertise, he hadn't detected her inexperience; instead, he'd assumed, and been wrong.

Sunk in her mouth, as physically linked with her as it was possible to be, he hadn't missed that instant of pain as he'd thrust deeply inside her for the first time; he was too experienced not to recognize when a woman beneath him tensed in pain, rather than from pleasure.

But even as he'd registered the stunning fact that she'd been a virgin, she'd started to climax. Just as he'd intended.

The unexpected surge of primitive feelings knowing he'd taken her virginity had evoked, combining with the intense satisfaction of knowing he'd succeeded to the last detail with his plan, had detached him from all control. From that point on, he'd had none; he'd operated on instinct alone—that same powerful, primitive instinct that was even now prowling just beneath his skin, satisfied to a point, yet still hungry for her.

He tore his eyes from the bed, tried to focus on the night-shrouded landscape instead. If he'd known she'd been a virgin . . . not that he'd had much experience bedding virgins—only two, both when he'd been sixteen—but he would at least have tried to be less forceful, less vigorous. God knew he wasn't the easiest man for even experienced women to accommodate, yet . . . He glanced again at the bed, then took another sip of water.

As she'd done with him in every other arena, in lying beneath him, she'd coped, too.

Coped rather well, in fact.

The thought brought to mind her earlier fascination with his erection—a fascination he now better understood; she'd wanted to touch, to examine . . . the memory of her small hand and delicate fingers wrapped about his shaft had the inevitable effect.

Jaw setting, he drained the glass. Later, he'd said; it was later now.

She stirred even before he reached the bed. Setting the empty glass on the bedside table, he met her eyes as he let the silk robe he'd donned fall from his shoulders; lifting the covers, he climbed into the bed and laid down. She slid helpfully toward him; expecting that, raising one arm, he drew her closer; she hesitated, then came, tentatively settling against him. He waited, assessing yet again the possible tacks he might take in the discussion he was about to initiate.

Minerva found his heat, the solidity of his body and the warmth that emanated from his muscled flesh, both comforting and luring. Nerves that had tensed slightly relaxed again. Greatly daring, she sank deeper into his light embrace; his arm tightened about her, and it seemed only natural to raise her head and settle it in the hollow just below his shoulder, letting her hand rest, palm down, on his chest.

She quashed an impulse to snuggle her cheek into the pillowing muscle; he wasn't hers, not really—she should strive to remember that.

He lifted a strand of her hair from her face, smoothed it back.

She was wondering if she was supposed to say something—comment on his performance, perhaps—when he spoke.

"You should have told me you were a virgin."

The instant the words left his lips, Royce knew they'd been the wrong thing to say. The wrong tack to take in introducing his proposal.

She tensed, gradually but definitely, then raised her head and narrowed her eyes on his face. "Understand this, Royce Varisey—I do not, absolutely *do not want to hear* a single word about marriage. If you so much as mention the word in relation to me, I'll consider it the most *inexcusable* insult. Just because I was your mother's protégée and just happened—through no fault of mine or yours—to still be a virgin, is no reason at all for you to feel obliged to offer for my hand."

Oh, Christ. "But—"

"No." Lips set, eyes snapping, she pointed at his nose. "Keep quiet and listen! There's no point in offering for my hand—in even thinking of it—because even if you do, I will refuse you. As you're very well aware, I enjoyed the"—she paused, then waved—"*interlude* immensely, and I'm more than adult enough to take responsibility for my own actions, even if our recent actions were more yours than mine. Regardless, contrary to popular misconception, the last, very last thing a lady such as I want to hear after lying with a man for the first time is a proposal prompted by said man's misplaced notion of honor!"

Her voice had steadily gained in intensity. She glared at him, lips tight. "So don't make that mistake."

The tension investing her body, lying half atop his, was of entirely the wrong sort. His features impassive, he searched her eyes; he'd made a tactical blunder, and had to beat a strategic retreat. He nodded. "All right. I won't."

She narrowed her eyes even more. "And you won't try to manipulate me into it?"

He raised both brows. "Manipulate you into marriage because I took your virginity?" He shook his head. "I can assure you—I'll even promise on my honor—that I won't do that."

Eyes locked with his, she hesitated, almost as if she could detect the prevarication in his words. He steadily returned her regard. Eventually she uttered a soft "humph," and swung away. "Good."

She pulled out of his arms, and started wrestling her way free of the covers.

He reached out and lightly clasped her wrist. "Where are you going?"

She glanced at him. "To my room, of course."

His fingers locked. "Why?"

She blinked at him. "Isn't that what I'm supposed to do?"

"No." His eyes on hers, he drew the hand he held back beneath the covers—down to where his erection stood at full attention. Curling her fingers about his rigid flesh, he watched her expression change to one of fascination. "This," he ground out, "is what you're supposed to do. What you're supposed to attend to."

Her gaze refocused on his face. She studied his eyes, then nodded. "All right." Swinging back to him, she switched her right hand for her left, smoothing her palm up his length before, as she leaned into him, closing her fingers. "If you insist."

He managed a grating "I do." Reaching up, he slid one hand behind her nape and pulled her lips down to his. "I insist you learn all you want to know."

She took him at his word, hands touching, caressing, squeezing, gliding, tracing as she would. The unconscious, unguarded sensuality in her face as, eyes closing as if to imprint the heft and weight, length and shape of him on her mind, she explored as she would, tried his control to its limit and beyond. To a chest-shuddering, muscle-quivering extent he'd never before had to endure.

He clung to his sanity by planning what came next. He favored sitting her astride him, impaling her, then teaching her to ride him, but discovered he lacked the strength to counter the urges her bold, innocently brazen caresses called forth. Then incited and ignited.

She connected with his more primitive side far more than any other woman ever had.

Reduced to the point where control was a thin and rapidly shredding veil, he brushed her hands aside, rolled her over, pinning her beneath him, spreading her thighs wide and cupping her, touching her, to find her wet once more. Hauling in a huge breath, he wedged his hips between her thighs and entered her—slowly, slowly, slowly, *slowly*—steady and inexorable so her breath strangled in her chest and she arched beneath him, a cry fracturing on her lips as with a final short thrust he sheathed himself fully within her.

Letting himself down on her, he anchored her hip with one hand, found her face with the other and, lowering his head, covered her lips with his, filled her mouth, and plundered to the same rhythm with which he settled to plunder her body.

A bare heartbeat passed, and then she was with him, her hands reaching around to spread on his back, holding him, clinging, her body undulating, caressing, her hips lifting to match his heavy driving rhythm. Releasing her hip, he reached down, found her knee, and lifted it over his hip.

Without further direction, she hooked that knee higher, then did the same with her other leg, opening herself to him so he could sink deeper into her, could without restraint drive them both even harder, even faster, to oblivion.

He did; when she shattered beneath him he intended to hold back, to extend the engagement and take more of her, but the temptation to fly with her was too great—he let go and followed close on her heels, into the senses-shattering glory of climax and on into the void.

Wrapped in her arms, with her wrapped in his, their hearts thundering, breaths sawing, then slowing, they gradually drifted back to reality.

As, all tension spent, she relaxed, boneless, beneath him, he saw a small, subtle smile curve her kiss-swollen lips. The sight warmed him, curiously touched him.

He watched until it faded as she slid into sated sleep.

Thirteen

He woke her sometime before dawn, time enough to indulge his senses and hers in one last, brief, intense engagement, then let her recover enough to don her gown and walk back to her room.

He rose and helped her dress, then saw her out of his sitting room door. He would have preferred to escort her to her room, but if any others were drifting back to their beds and saw her, it was better they didn't see her with him.

She was the castle's chatelaine; there were any number of reasons she might be about early.

After listening to her footsteps fade, he returned to the bedroom, and his bed. Settling beneath the covers, sensing her warmth lingering beside him, conscious of her subtle perfume wreathing all about him, he folded his arms behind his head and fixed his gaze on the window across the room.

So what now? He'd made progress, real and definite progress, but then she'd stymied him in a way he hadn't been quick enough to foresee. While henceforth he could, and would, have her in his bed, he could no longer simply *ask* her to be his bride. There was no argument that stood any chance of convincing her he'd wanted to marry her *before* he'd taken her virginity. That he hadn't known she was a virgin meant nothing, and no matter how long he waited, she would still view his proposal as the insult she'd warned him not to offer her.

And she'd refuse. Adamantly. And she'd only grow more stubborn the harder he pressed.

Admittedly he had, for one foolish moment, considered using the age-old argument based on virginity and honor as a possible supporting reason for their wedding. He should have guessed how she would react.

He lay staring into space as his household slowly awakened, juggling possibilities, assessing tacks. If he'd asked her to marry him when he'd first set out to, rather than letting her distract him with her challenge into seducing her first, he wouldn't now be facing this complication, yet there was no point dwelling on what couldn't be changed.

He could see only one way forward. He would have to keep silent over his intention to marry her, and instead do everything in his considerable power to lead her to conclude of her own accord that marrying him was her true and natural destiny. More, her greatly desired destiny.

Once she'd realized that, he could offer for her hand, and she would accept.

If he applied himself to the task, how long could it take? A week?

The grandes dames had accepted the week he'd originally stipulated readily enough. That week had now passed, but he doubted any of them would hie north to castigate him—not yet. If he dallied too long, someone would turn up to lecture him again and exhort him to action, but he probably had another week up his sleeve.

A week he would devote to convincing Minerva that she should be his duchess.

A week to make it clear she already was, but just hadn't realized.

His lips curved, just as Trevor looked in from the dressing room.

His valet saw his smile, saw the bed. Raised his brows inquiringly.

Royce saw no reason to keep him in the dark. "My chatelaine—who will shortly be your mistress." He fixed his gaze on Trevor's face. "A fact she doesn't yet know, so no one will tell her."

Trevor smiled. "Naturally not, Your Grace." His expression one of the utmost equanimity, he started to pick up Royce's clothes.

Royce studied him. "You don't seem all that surprised."

Straightening, Trevor shook out his coat. "You have to choose a lady, and all things considered I find it hard to imagine you could do better than Miss Chesterton." He shrugged. "Nothing to be surprised about."

Royce humphed, and got out of the bed. "I will, of course, wish to know anything and everything you learn that might be pertinent. I take it you know her maid?"

Folding Royce's waistcoat, Trevor smiled. "A young person by the name of Lucy, Your Grace."

Belting his robe, Royce narrowed his eyes on that smile. "A word to the wise. I might bed the mistress, but you'd be ill-advised to try the same with the maid. She'll have your balls on a stick—the mistress, not the maid. And in the circumstances, I'd have to let her."

Trevor's eyes opened wide. "I'll bear that in mind, Your Grace. Now, do you wish to shave?"

Minerva awoke when Lucy, her maid, came bustling into the room.

After leaving Royce, she'd slipped back to her room without seeing anyone; she'd undressed, put on her nightgown, brushed out her tangled hair, got into bed—and to her surprise had fallen deeply asleep.

She yawned, stretched—and felt twinges where she never had before. She watched Lucy open the curtains, then shake out her gown; when Lucy turned to the armoire, she surreptitiously peeked down the front of her nightgown.

She blinked, then looked across the room. "The black with the buttons up the front, Lucy. Just leave it over the chair. I'll get up shortly, but you don't need to wait. I can manage that gown by myself."

And innocent Lucy didn't need to see the telltale marks on her breasts. She didn't want to think what she might discover farther down.

"I've brought up your washing water. Do you need me for anything else, ma'am?"

"No, thank you, Lucy. You can go and have your breakfast."

"Thank you, miss." With a cheery smile and a bobbed curtsy, Lucy took herself off. The door closed behind her.

Minerva exhaled, sank deeper into the mattress, and let her thoughts range over the previous night, and its entirely unexpected events. That Royce would act so directly—and that she would respond so definitely—had never entered her head. But he had, and she had, so where were they now?

She'd always assumed he'd be a vigorous lover. In that, he'd exceeded her expectations; her untutored self had never even imagined much of what, at his hands, she had now experienced. Yet despite her inexperience, she knew him—she hadn't missed the hunger, the real need that had had him carting her off to his bed, that had driven him as he'd ravished her.

Possessed her.

Repeatedly.

When she'd woken before dawn, just as, from behind, he'd filled her, and proceeded to demonstrate yet another way he could possess her—her body, her senses, and her mind—utterly and completely, with his lips in the hollow below her ear rather than on hers, she, her senses, had been freer to absorb the nuances of his loving.

That he wanted her, desired her, she accepted without question.

That that want ran deep, she now understood.

She'd never imagined being the focus of that degree of

desire, having so much male passion concentrated on her; the recollection sent a delicious shiver through her. She couldn't deny she'd found it deeply satisfying; she'd be lying if she pretended she wouldn't be happy to lie with him again.

If he asked, which he would. He wasn't, she knew, finished with her; that had been explicit in their final moments that morning.

Thank God she'd had sufficient wit to seize the chance and make it plain that she neither expected nor wanted to receive an offer from him.

She hadn't forgotten that other offer he was due to make— to the lady he'd chosen as his duchess. Not knowing if he'd made a formal offer yet, she'd needed to ensure he wouldn't, in some Machiavellian moment, decide to use her virginity—the taking of it—as cause to marry her instead.

While he'd toed the grandes dames' line, he wasn't happy about it; he might well seize an opportunity to take a different tack. And to him, marrying her might be preferable to having to deal with some unknown young lady who would know very little about him.

She—Minerva—would be a more comfortable choice.

She didn't need to think to know her response to that. He would be a sound husband to any lady who accepted the loveless partnership he would offer; just as long as said lady didn't expect love or fidelity, all would be well.

For herself, love, real and abiding, was the only coin for which she would exchange her heart. Extensive experience of Varisey unions had bolstered her stance; their type of marriage was not for her. Avoiding, if necessary actively resisting, any suggestion of marrying Royce remained an unaltered, unalterable goal; nothing on that front had changed.

And, to her immense relief, spending the night in his bed hadn't seduced her heart into loving him; her feelings toward him hadn't changed all that much—or only on the lust side, not in terms of love.

Thinking of how she now felt about him . . . she frowned. Despite her resistance, she did feel something *more* for him—unexpected feelings that had developed since his return. Feelings that had driven her panic of yesterday, when she'd thought he would die.

Those new feelings had grown through seeing him with his people, from his attitudes and actions toward those he deemed in his care. From all the decisions and acts that distinguished him so definitively from his father. The physical pleasure he'd introduced her to hadn't influenced her as much as all those things.

Yet while he might differ from his father in many ways, when it came to his wife and his marriage, he would revert to type. He'd demonstrated as much in his approach to his prospective bride.

If she let herself be bullied into marrying him, she would risk falling in love with him—irrevocably, irretrievably— and then like Caro Lamb she would pine, wither, and eventually go mad when he, not at all in love with her, left her for another. As he inevitably would.

She wasn't so foolish as to believe that she might, through loving him, change him. No; if she married him, he, indeed everyone, would expect her to stand meekly by while he indulged as he wished with an endless succession of other ladies.

She snorted, threw back the covers, and swung her legs out of bed. "That's not going to happen."

No matter what she felt for him, regardless of what evolved from her infatuation-obsession, no matter *what* new aspects of attraction developed over the however many nights she might spend in his bed, she would not fall in love with him, ergo she wouldn't marry him.

At least they were both now very clear on that last point.

Standing, she crossed to the basin and pitcher on her dresser; pouring water into the basin, she let her thoughts range ahead. As matters now stood . . .

Setting down the pitcher, she stared at the settling water as the immediate future cleared in her mind.

Of necessity her liaison with Royce would be short-lived—

he would marry soon, and soon after, she would leave. A few days, a week. Two weeks at most.

Too short a time to fall in love.

Slipping her hands into the bowl, she splashed water on her face, feeling increasingly bright. More alert and expectant, almost intrigued over what the day might bring—reassured and confident that there was no reason she couldn't indulge with him again.

The risk wasn't significant. Her heart would be safe.

Safe enough so she could enjoy without a care.

By evening, expectation had turned to impatience. Minerva sat in the music room, ostensibly watching yet another of Shakespeare's plays while she brooded on the shortcomings of her day.

A perfectly ordinary day, filled with nothing more than the customary events—which was the problem. She'd thought . . . but she'd been wrong.

Royce had summoned her to his study for their usual morning meeting with Handley; other than a fleeting moment when she'd walked into the room and their eyes had met—and he and she had both paused, both, she suspected, suddenly reminded of how the other's skin had felt against theirs . . . but then he'd blinked, looked down, and she'd walked forward and sat, and he'd subsequently treated her exactly as he had the previous day.

She'd followed his lead, then and later, as they'd parted, then met again, throughout the day, confident that at some point they would meet privately . . . but she was no longer so sure that would happen. She'd never engaged in a liaison before; she didn't know the script.

He did, but he was seated two rows in front of her, chatting to Caroline Courtney, who had claimed the chair beside him.

Under cover of the dinner conversations, he'd asked her if Cranny still kept stocks of the chicken essence she'd used to administer to them when they'd suffered childhood chills. She hadn't been sure, but when he'd suggested they send a bottle to the Honeymans for their daughter, she'd detoured to see the housekeeper before joining the company in the music room, thus missing her chance to sit next to him.

Narrowing her eyes on the back of his head, she wished she could see inside. What was he thinking? Specifically, what was he thinking about her? *Was* he thinking about her?

Or had one night been enough?

The more confident part of her brazenly scoffed, but a more vulnerable part wondered.

At the end of the play, she clapped politely, caught Royce's eye for an instant, then excused herself and retired, leaving Margaret to manage the tea tray. She could do without spending the next half hour surrounded by the lascivious throng with him in the same room, aware of his gaze occasionally resting on her, fighting to keep hers from him—while every inch of her skin prickled with anticipation.

Reaching her room, willing her mind from the question of "Would he?" she stripped off her clothes, donned her nightgown, shrugged on her robe, then rang for Lucy.

She had a set of faint marks at the top of one thigh that was beyond her ability to explain.

Seated at her dressing table, she was brushing out her hair when Lucy breezed in.

"You're early tonight, ma'am." Lucy bent to pick up her gown. "Didn't you enjoy the play?"

She pulled a face. "They're becoming rather boring—just as well the fair's next week or I'd have to devise some other entertainment." She glanced at Lucy as the maid bustled to the armoire. "Did you learn anything?"

Opening the armoire, Lucy shook her dark head. "Mr. Handley's a quiet one—he's kind and smiles, but he's not one to talk. And of course he sits at the top end of the table. Trevor's closer to me, and he's a right chatterer, but although he natters on, he never really says anything, if you know what I mean."

"I can imagine." She hadn't really thought Royce would employ staff who didn't keep his secrets.

"The only thing any of us have got out of the pair of them is that His Grace is still negotiating with this lady he's chosen." Shutting the armoire, Lucy turned. "Not even a whisper and nary a hint of who the lady is. I suppose we'll just have to wait until we're told."

"Indeed." She inwardly grimaced.

Lucy turned down the bed, then returned and halted beside her. "Will there be anything else, ma'am?"

"No, thank you, Lucy—you may go."

"Thank you, ma'am. Good night."

Minerva murmured a "Good night," her mind once again running down the names on the grandes dames' list. Which one had Royce chosen? One of those she knew?

She was tempted to ask him outright—it would help if she knew how well-trained his duchess-to-be was so she would know how much she herself would need to impart before said duchess could manage on her own. The thought of handing her chatelaine's keys to some giggling ninnyhammer evoked a response very close to revulsion.

Rising, she snuffed the candelabra on the dressing table, leaving only the single candle burning by her bed. Drawing her robe closed, she belted it as she walked to the window.

If Royce wished to spend the night with her, he would come to her room; she might not have indulged in a liaison before, but she knew that much.

He would come. Or he wouldn't.

Perhaps he'd heard from the family of the lady for whom he'd offered.

Crossing her arms, she looked out at the night-shrouded landscape.

And waited.

And wondered.

"Royce!"

Halting under the archway leading into the keep's gallery, Royce let his head fall back, eyes closing in frustration.

That had been Margaret's voice; he could hear her rustling and puffing as she toiled up the main stairs behind him, along with some other lady.

Taking a firmer grip on his temper, he turned, and saw that Aurelia was Margaret's companion. "Wonderful."

The muttered sarcasm reached Margaret as she bustled up, but only confused her. He waved aside her puzzled look. "What is it?"

She halted a pace away, glanced at Aurelia as she joined her, then, hands gripped before her, looked at him. "We wanted to ask if you would be agreeable to us inviting some others up for the fair."

"It used to be one of the highlights of our year when we lived here." Aurelia lifted her chin, her cold eyes fixing on his face. "We would like your permission to hold a house party, like Mama used to."

He looked from one hard, arrogantly aristocratic face to the other; he knew what those simple words had cost them. To have to ask their little brother, of whom they'd always disapproved, for permission to hold a party in their childhood home.

His first impulse was to tell them he'd rather all the visitors left—freeing him to pursue Minerva through the day as well as the night. But no matter his view of his sisters, this was their childhood home and he didn't feel justified in barring them from it—which meant having others about was necessary for cover, and to distract them.

Neither Margaret nor Aurelia was at all observant, and while Susannah was more so, not even she had yet divined the nature of his interest in Minerva. She was his chatelaine; they assumed that was the reason behind every word he and she exchanged.

Aurelia had grown restless. "We'd thought to ask no more than ten extra—those already here will stay."

"If you allow it," Margaret hurriedly added.

Aurelia's thin lips pressed together; she inclined her head. "Indeed. We thought . . ."

Tempting as it was to let them do more violence to their

feelings, he'd much rather listen to Minerva gasping, sobbing, and moaning. He spoke over Aurelia. "Very well."

"You agree?" Margaret asked.

"Keep it within reason—nothing more than Mama used to do."

"Oh, we will." Aurelia's eyes lit, her face softening.

He didn't want to feel the spark of pity that flared as he looked at them; they were married, had position, houses, and families, yet still they were searching for . . . happiness. Nodding curtly, he turned on his heel. "Speak with Retford, then tell Minerva what you want to do. I'll warn her."

His sisters' thanks faded behind him as he strode into the keep proper.

Anticipation mounting, he headed for his rooms.

When, more than an hour later, he closed his hand about the knob of Minerva's door, frustration was riding him hard. He'd assumed she'd left the gathering early so she could slip into his rooms unseen; he'd expected to find her there, in his bed, waiting. As he'd walked through his sitting room, the image he'd expected to see had filled his mind . . .

Instead, for some misbegotten reason, she'd retired to *her* bed. Turning the knob, he stepped quickly inside and shut the door. She was leaning against the side of the window; arms folded, she'd been looking out at the night.

As he crossed the room, she pushed away from the window frame, with one hand pushed back the heavy fall of her hair, then delicately smothered a yawn. "I thought you'd be up earlier."

He halted before her; hands rising to his hips, he looked down at her. She appeared faintly tousled, her lids already heavy. He wanted nothing more than to haul her into his arms, but . . . "I *was* up earlier." He spoke quietly, but his tone made her blink. "I expected to find you gracing my bed. But you weren't there. Then I had to wait for all the others to go to their beds before I came here. I thought I'd made it plain *which* bed we'd be using."

She'd straightened; she narrowed her eyes on his. "That was last night. Correct me if I err"—her diction attained the same cutting precision as his—"but when engaged in an illicit liaison, it's customary for the gentleman to join the lady in her room. In *her* bed." She glanced at her bed, then looked pointedly at him.

Lips thinning, he held her gaze, then nodded curtly. "Perhaps. In this case, however—" He stepped smoothly around her and swept her up in his arms.

She gasped, clutched his coat, but didn't bother asking where he was taking her as he strode for the door.

He juggled her, reached for the knob.

"Wait! Someone might see."

"They're all in bed. Someone's bed." Enjoying themselves. "They won't be playing musical beds just yet." He grasped the knob.

"But I'll have to get back here in the morning! I never wander the corridors in just my robe."

He glanced around, and saw the coat stand in the corner. He carried her to it. "Get your cloak."

She did. Before she could raise any further objections he whisked her out of the door and strode across the wide gallery, then down the short corridor to his apartments. Deep shadows cloaked them all the way; he thought she sniffed as he heeled his sitting room door shut behind them, then carried her into his bedroom.

To his bed.

He dropped her on the crimson-and-gold counterpane, then looked down at her.

Narrow-eyed, she frowned at him. "Why is it so important we use your bed?"

"Because that's where I want you." Absolute truth—for once primitive instinct coincided with good strategy.

She heard his conviction. Opened her eyes wide. "*Why* for heaven's sake?"

Because she belonged there. As far as his primitive self was concerned, there was no question of that, and using his bed would subliminally underscore how he thought of her, what her true role vis-à-vis himself was—one front in his campaign to impress that true role on her. The usual events of castle life would further advance his cause, but the day had been unhelpfully quiet; he'd taken steps to ensure tomorrow would be different. Meanwhile . . .

Toeing off his shoes, he shrugged out of his coat and waistcoat, tossed both aside, then grasped her slender ankles and drew her toward him until her knees were at the edge of the bed. Leaving her calves and feet dangling, he caged her legs between his and leaned over her; setting his hands palms flat on either side of her shoulders, he trapped her widening eyes. "Because I want you here, naked in my bed, every night from now on. And I always get what I want."

She opened her mouth, but he had no interest in further discussion. He swooped and covered her lips with his, captured them, tasted them long and lingeringly, then dove into her waiting mouth.

Gloried in the welcome she was helpless to deny him; no matter what she thought, she was already his. Yet he found himself spending longer than he'd expected hotly wrestling for supremacy; despite her inexperience, she boldly challenged him, even though this was one battleground on which she could never hope to stand against him. Ruthlessly deploying skills he'd honed over decades, he drew forth her desire, lured her senses to him, then shackled them, subdued them, suborned them to his will.

So they were his to wield.

Only then did he ease back from the passion-laden exchange enough to shift his weight to one arm; with his other hand he grasped the tie of her robe.

Minerva couldn't believe how desperate she was—couldn't believe he'd so effortlessly reduced her to such a state of wanton yearning, where desire, hot and urgent, flowed swiftly down her veins, where passion spread beneath her skin, and smoldered more deeply within her.

Waiting to erupt, pour forth, and sweep her away.

She needed to feel his hands on her skin—needed to feel his body on hers.

Needed, with an urgent desperation she couldn't fathom, to feel him inside her, linked and joined with her.

And that need wasn't his; it was hers.

And it felt glorious.

Glorious to give herself up to the heat, to without reservation, or hesitation, wriggle and help him strip away her robe, help his clever hands divest her of her nightgown.

And then she lay naked on his brocaded bed—and she suddenly sensed one reason behind his insistence that he have her there.

She knew what sort of nobleman he really was—knew the impulses of a marcher lord still ran in his veins. Knew, sensed, had always on some level recognized the primitive sexual possessiveness and predatoriness that was an innate part of him. Unwrapped like a present, displayed naked on his bed, offered up for his delectation, his to use in whatever manner he wished . . . a subtle shiver wracked her—one part wholly feminine fear, the rest illicit excitement.

He sensed her awareness through the kiss, felt that evocative shiver; he closed one hand about her hip, anchoring her, his thumb cruising the sensitive skin of her stomach. His touch seared, branded; she knew he would brand her even more deeply before the night was out. That he intended just that.

Her breath hitched. Anticipation and a strange, unfamiliar need clashed, then washed, tumbling and jumbling, through her.

Leaning closer, he released her hip, coming down on one elbow to anchor her head between his large hands as he kissed her deeply, voraciously, ravenously, snaring her wits in a maelstrom of sensation. She had to engage with him; he gave her no option. Had to respond, to meet the challenge of his tongue, of his lips, of the hot wetness of his mouth.

Locked with her in the kiss, he speared his fingers into her hair, spread and drew them away from her head, letting the long tresses flow through his fingers, leaving them fanned to either side.

He seemed as fascinated with the silky texture of her locks as she was with his; instinctively she'd sunk her hands into his hair, feathering the dark silk with her fingers.

His body was close; hers sensed it and reacted, need swelling like a warm wave within, the rising tide a solid beat in her veins. His heat was near, yet muted by his clothes; he still had his shirt and trousers on.

She drew her hands from his hair, slid them down the long column of his throat, splayed her palms over his chest and ran them down until she could grip handfuls of his shirt and tug it free of his waistband. Succeeding, she ran her hands up under the loose fabric, palms and fingers greedy for the incomparable feel of his skin, hot and taut over the heavy ridges and planes of his magnificent chest.

All but purring, she let her senses feast; had she the time, she could have savored for hours, but that complex, complicated, increasingly urgent need pressed her on. Pressed her to run her hands down to his waistband, to find and release the buttons there.

She slipped only one free before he broke from the kiss, smoothly shifting to catch her hands, one in each of his.

"Later." He murmured the word against her throat, then set his lips to trace the arching line.

Hot, urgent, his mouth fired her senses. With nipping pecks, he captured her attention, effortlessly held it as with openmouthed kisses he branded her skin. Here, there, as he would.

She was heated and panting when he reached her breasts.

She was writhing and frantic when, after expertly claiming them, he moved on, his wicked lips trailing lower to explore her navel, then lower still, to the apex of her thighs.

By the time he drew back, grasped her knees and spread them wide, she was far beyond all modesty; she wanted nothing more than to feel him there, for him to take her, possess her, however he wished.

She felt his gaze on her face. Heated beyond measure, she sensed his command, hauled in a tight breath and cracked open her lids. Enough for him to catch her gaze, for her to see the dark promise in the depths of his eyes, then he looked down, at her body, displayed, wantonly wet and eager, slick and swollen, all but begging. For him.

Then he bent, set his mouth to her flesh and ripped every sense she possessed away, ruthlessly took all she offered, all she had in her—then demanded more.

She sobbed and helplessly gave; as the second wave of unimaginable glory crashed through her veins, she screamed his name.

Even through the heated clouds of her release, she sensed his satisfaction.

Felt it in the touch of his hands as he rose, grasped her hips, and rolled her onto her stomach. He half lifted, half drew her toward him until her hips rested on the edge of the high mattress.

Awash in sensation, her skin flushed and damp, her wits still in abeyance, she wondered what . . . how. . .

He slid into her from behind, deep, then he pressed even deeper. She shuddered, gasped, felt her fingers close in the rumpled brocade cover. He gripped her hips and shifted her, positioned her, then he drew back, almost free of her cling-ing sheath, and thrust in again.

Hard. More powerfully.

Her breath puffed out on a shallow pant; her fingers tight-ened in the rough counterpane. He withdrew and thrust in again; eyes closing, she moaned. She could feel him high inside her, almost as if he were touching her lungs.

Then he settled to possess her, ruthlessly, relentlessly, thrusting deep and hard into her utterly willing body. Her wholly surrendered body. She moved fractionally under the force of the steady pounding, the subtle roughness of the brocade quickly becoming an excruciating abrasion against the peaks of her breasts.

Until she couldn't take any more. His hands locked about

her hips, he held her captive for each forceful penetration. Her skin flaringly alive, she could feel his groin meet the globes of her bottom, feel his testes against the backs of her thighs as he pushed deep and deeper. The rough fabric of his trousers abraded her legs; the edge of his shirt drifted over her bare back.

A sudden vision of how they looked—her utterly naked, he mostly clothed—taking her like this, exploded in her mind.

Her senses let go. Unraveled, fragmented, flew apart in a shattering release of imploding heat and tension.

He continued to thrust into her, and the release went on and on . . . until she fell from the peak with one last smothered gasp, and the blessed void gathered her in.

Jaw clenched, Royce slowed. Eyes closed, head back, chest heaving, he clung to the last shreds of his will, of his control, and rode out the incredible ripples of sensation, the aftermath of her heightened release as her sheath contracted repetitively about him, and lured, begged, commanded him to lose himself in her.

He had other plans.

Deeper plans. Plans that came from that more primitive self that, when it came to her, he could no longer deny. Didn't want to deny.

When she finally slumped, her body utterly lax, he withdrew from her, shed his clothes in seconds, then lifted her. He stripped back the covers, then knelt on the bed and laid her down on her back, her head and shoulders cushioned by the plump pillows.

He seized the moment as he stretched alongside to drink in the sight—of her so utterly ravished, so surrendered, so possessed.

So his.

On the thought, he lifted over her, spread her thighs wide, and settled between. Covered her. Slid deeply into her, then lowered his head, captured her lips, and sank into her. Into her mouth, deep into her body, received within the silken embrace of her scalding sheath.

He started to ride her slowly, unhurriedly, senses wide, drinking in every iota of sensation. Of the inexpressible delight of her body cradling his, of her softness accepting his hardness, of the innumerable contrasts between their merging bodies.

His felt tight, nerves taut and flickering, seeking, wanting, needing. His mind was open, receptive, overwhelmingly aware of the breadth, depth, and incredible power of the need that swelled and welled inside him.

Then she joined him.

Her small hands found his face, framed it for a moment, then lowered to spread across his shoulders.

As the tempo of their joining inexorably rose, she gripped, clutched, her body undulating beneath his, dancing to a rhythm as old as time.

One he set, but she was with him, waltzing in the heat and the flames, in the scintillating fire of their shared passion.

And it was everything he'd wanted the moment to be—appeasement and acknowledgment, satiation and surrender, all in one.

She was everything he needed her to be—his lover, his bride, his wife.

His all.

In the moment when together they crested the last peak and found ecstasy waiting to claim them, he knew beyond question that he had all he needed of life in his arms. For this, she was the only woman for him, with him creating, then anchoring him in, this deeper, more heart-wrenching glory.

Submitting to him, surrendering to him.

Vanquishing him.

Now and forever.

The storm took them, and he surrendered, too, his fingers locked with hers as the fury of their joint passion wracked them, rocked them. Shattered and drained them, then left their senses to slowly fill again—with each other.

He'd never felt so close to any woman before, had never shared what he just had with any other.

When he finally summoned enough strength and will to move, he disengaged and lifted from her, then gathered her to him, into his arms, soothed when she came readily, snuggling close.

Through the darkness he touched his lips to her temple. "Sleep. I'll wake you in time to leave."

Her only reply was that her last lingering tension eased, then faded.

He closed his eyes and, utterly stated to the depths of his primitive soul, let sleep claim him.

Fourteen

Royce woke her before dawn in predictable fashion; Minerva reached her room with barely enough time to fall into her bed and recover before Lucy arrived to draw back the curtains.

After washing and dressing, once again eschewing Lucy's assistance, she set about her usual routine with far more confidence than the day before. If Royce wanted her enough to insist she grace *his* bed, then he wasn't about to lose interest in her just yet. Indeed, if last night was anything to judge by, his desire for her seemed to be escalating, not fading.

She pondered that, and how she felt about it, over breakfast, then, leaving his sisters and their guests to their own devices, retreated to the duchess's morning room to prepare for their usual meeting in the study—and to consider what she might request of him.

If he could demand and insist on her physical surrender, then, she felt, some reward was her due. Some token of his appreciation.

When Jeffers arrived to summon her, she knew for what she would ask; the request would test Royce's desire, but who knew how long his interest would last? She should ask now; with Variseys it paid to be bold.

Jeffers opened the study door. Entering, she saw that Falwell, as well as Handley, was present; the steward was sitting in the second chair before the desk.

Royce waved her to her usual seat. "Falwell has been describing the current state of the flocks and the clip. There appears to be some decline in quality."

"Nothing major, of course," Falwell quickly said, glancing, surprised, at Minerva. "Miss Chesterton has no doubt heard the farmers' rumblings—"

"Indeed." She cut off the rest of Falwell's justification for doing nothing over recent years. "I understand the problem lies in the breeding stock." Sitting, she met Royce's gaze.

"Be that as it may," Falwell said, "to get new breeding stock we'd have to go far south, and the expense—"

"Perhaps O'Loughlin could help?" She made the suggestion as innocently as she could. Royce had summoned her to join this discussion; presumably he wanted her opinions.

Falwell bridled; he didn't like Hamish, but then Hamish had no time for him.

He opened his mouth, but before he could speak, Royce did. "I'll speak to O'Loughlin next time I'm up that way. He might have some breeders we could buy."

Unsurprisingly, Falwell swallowed his words.

Royce glanced at the sheet on which he'd been making notes. "I need to speak with Miss Chesterton, Falwell, but if you would remain, once we've finished, you and I should look over the castle flocks."

Murmuring acquiescence, Falwell rose, and at Royce's direction retreated to a straight-backed chair against the wall.

Minerva inwardly cursed. She didn't want Falwell to hear her request.

"So what have we to deal with today?"

Royce's question refocused her attention. She looked down at her list, and swiftly went through Retford's warning that in the wake of the funeral they would need to replenish the cellar, and Cranny's request for new linens for the north wing bedrooms. "And while we're looking at fabrics, there are two rooms in the south wing that could use new curtains." Because of the castle's isolation, all such items were normally procured from London.

Royce looked at Handley as his secretary glanced up from his notes. "Hamilton can make himself useful—he knows what wines I prefer, and for the rest he could consult with my London housekeeper—" He glanced at Minerva.

"Mrs. Hardcastle," she supplied.

He looked at Handley. "Send a note to Hamilton about the wines and fabrics, and suggest he ask Mrs. Hardcastle to assist him with the latter. Regardless, he should purchase the materials subject to Miss Chesterton's and Mrs. Cranshaw's approval."

Handley nodded, swiftly scribbling.

"The curtains need to be damask, with apple-green the predominant color," Minerva said.

Handley nodded again.

Royce arched a brow at her. "Is there anything else?"

"Not about the household." She hesitated; she would have infinitely preferred not to have Falwell present, but she had to strike while this iron was hot. She drew breath. "However, there's a matter I've been meaning to bring to your attention."

Royce looked his invitation.

"There's a footbridge over the Coquet, further to the south, a little beyond Alwinton. It's been allowed to deteriorate and is now in very bad condition, a serious danger to all who have to use it—"

Falwell shot to his feet. "That's not on castle lands, Your Grace." He came forward. "It's Harbottle's responsibility, and if they choose to let it fall down, that's their decision, not ours."

Royce watched Falwell slant a glance at Minerva, sitting upright in her chair; her gaze was fixed on him, not the steward. Falwell tipped his head her way. "With all due respect to Miss Chesterton, Your Grace, we can't be fixing things beyond the estate, things that are in no way ours to fix."

Royce looked at Minerva. She met his eyes, and waited for his decision.

He knew why she'd asked. Other ladies coveted jewels; she asked for a footbridge. And if it had been on his lands, he would have happily bestowed it.

Unfortunately, Falwell was unquestionably correct. The last thing the dukedom needed was to become seen as a general savior of last resort. Especially not to the towns, who were supposed to manage their responsibilities from the taxes they collected.

"In this matter, I must agree with Falwell. However, I will raise the matter, personally, with the appropriate authorities." He glanced at Handley. "Find out who I need to see."

"Yes, Your Grace."

He looked again at Minerva, met her gaze. "Is there anything else?"

She held his gaze long enough to make him wonder what was going through her head, but then she answered, "No, Your Grace. That's all."

Looking down, she gathered her papers, then stood, inclined her head to him, turned, and walked to the door.

As it closed behind her, he was already considering how to use the footbridge to his best advantage.

There was more than one way to skin a cat—Minerva wondered what approach Royce was considering. With the luncheon gong echoing through the corridors, she headed for the dining room, hoping she'd read him aright.

She hadn't been surprised by Falwell's comments; his role was to manage the estate as a business, rather than care for its people. The latter was in part her role, and even more so the duke's. Royce's. He'd said he would take up the issue—presenting her request more clearly in people terms might help. As she neared the dining room, Royce walked out of the parlor opposite. He'd heard her footsteps; he'd been waiting for her. He paused, met her gaze; when she reached him, without a word he waved her ahead of him through the dining room door.

The rest of the company were already at table, engrossed in a discussion of Margaret's and Susannah's plans for the six days remaining before the fair. She and Royce went to the laden sideboard, helped themselves from the variety of cold meats, hams, and assorted delicacies displayed on the platters and dishes, then Royce steered her to the head of the table, to the chair beside his. Jeffers leapt to hold it for her.

By the time she'd sat and settled her skirts, Royce was seated in his great carver, by the angle of his shoulders, and the absolute focus of his attention on her, effectively cutting off the others—who read the signs and left them in peace.

They started eating, then he met her eyes. "Thank you for your help with the sheep."

"You knew Hamish was the best source for breeders—you didn't need me to tell you so."

"I needed you to tell Falwell so. If I'd suggested Hamish, he'd have tied himself in knots trying to acceptably say that my partiality for Hamish's stock was because of the connection." He took a sip from his wineglass. "But you aren't connected to Hamish."

"No, but Falwell knows I approve of Hamish."

"But not even Falwell would suggest that you—the farmers' champion—would urge me to get stock from anywhere that wasn't the best." Royce met her eyes, let his lips curve slightly. "Using you to suggest Hamish, having your reputation supporting the idea, saved time and a considerable amount of convoluted argument."

She smiled, pleased with the disguised compliment.

He let her preen for a moment, then followed up with, "Which raises a related issue—do you have any suggestions for a replacement for Falwell?"

She swallowed, nodded. "Evan Macgregor, Macgregor's third son."

"And why would he suit?"

She reached for her water glass. "He's young, but not too young, a gregarious soul who was born on the estate and knows—and is liked by—literally everyone on it. He was a scallywag when younger, but always good-hearted, and he's quick and clever—more than most. Now he's older, being the third son, and with Sean and Abel more than capable of taking on Macgregor's holding between them, Evan has too little to do." She sipped, then met his eyes. "He's in his late twenties, and is still helping on the farm, but I don't think he'll stay much longer unless he finds some better occupation."

"So at present he's wasted talent, and you think I should use him as steward."

"Yes. He'd work hard for you, and while he might make the odd mistake, he'll learn from them, and, most importantly, he'll never steer you wrongly over anything to do with the estate or its people." She set down her glass. "I haven't been able to say that of Falwell for more than a decade."

Royce nodded. "However, regardless of Falwell's short-comings, I meant what I said about the footbridge being something the dukedom can't simply step in and fix."

She met his eyes, studied them, then faintly raised her brows. "So . . . ?"

He let his lips curve in appreciation; she was starting to read him quite well. "So I need you to give me some urgent, preferably dramatic, reason to get on my ducal high horse and cow the aldermen of Harbottle into fixing it."

She held his gaze; her own grew distant, then she refocused—and smiled. "I can do that." When he arched a brow, she smoothly replied, "I believe we need to ride that way this afternoon."

He considered the logistics, then glanced at the others.

When he looked back at her, brows lifting, she nodded. "Leave them to me."

He sat back and watched with unfeigned appreciation as she leaned forward and, with a comment here, another there, slid smoothly into the discussions they had, until then, ignored. He hadn't noticed how she dealt with his sisters before; with an artful question followed by a vague suggestion, she deftly steered Susannah and Margaret—the ringleaders—into organizing the company to drive into Harbottle for the afternoon.

"Oh, before I forget, here's the guest list you wanted, Minerva." Seated along the table, Susannah waved a sheet; the others passed it to Minerva.

She scanned it, then looked at Margaret, at the table's foot. "We'll need to open up more rooms. I'll speak with Cranny."

Margaret glanced at him. "Of course, we don't know how many of those will attend."

He let his lips curve cynically. "Given the . . . entertainments you have on offer, I suspect all those invited will jump at the chance to join the party."

Because they'd be keen to learn firsthand whom he'd chosen as his bride. Comprehension filled Margaret's face; grimacing lightly, she inclined her head. "I'd forgotten, but no doubt you're right."

The reminder that he would soon make that announcement, thus signaling the end of his liaison with her, bolstered Minerva's determination to act, decisively, today. While his desire for her was still rampant she stood an excellent chance of securing her boon; once it waned, her ability to influence him would fade.

Susannah was still expounding on the delights of Harbottle. "We can wander around the shops, and then take tea at the Ivy Branch." She looked at Minerva. "It's still there, isn't it?"

She nodded. "They still serve excellent teas and pastries."

Margaret had been counting heads and carriages. "Good— we can all fit." She glanced at Minerva. "Are you coming?"

She waved the list of guests. "I need to attend to this, and a few other things. I'll ride down later and perhaps join you for tea."

"Very well." Margaret looked to the table's head. "And you, Wolverstone?" Ever since he'd agreed to their house party, Margaret and Aurelia had been making an effort to accord him all due deference.

Royce shook his head. "I, too, have matters to deal with. I'll see you at dinner."

With that settled, the company rose from the table. Conscious of Royce's dark gaze, Minerva hung back, letting the others go ahead; he and she left the dining room at the rear of the group.

They halted in the hall. He met her eyes. "How long will you take?"

She'd been swiftly reviewing her list of chores. "I have to see the timber merchant in Alwinton—it might be best if you meet me in the field beyond the church at . . ." She narrowed her eyes, estimating. "Just after three."

"On horseback, beyond the church, at just after three."

"Yes." Turning away, she flung him a smile. "And to make it, I'll have to rush. I'll see you there."

Suiting action to her words, she hurried to the stairs and went quickly up—before he asked how she planned to motivate him to browbeat the aldermen into submission. The sharp jab she had in mind would, she thought, work best if he wasn't prepared.

After speaking with Cranny about rooms for the latest expected guests, and with Retford about the cellar and the depredations likely during the house party, she checked with Hancock over his requirements for the mill, then rode into Alwinton and spoke with the timber merchant. She finished earlier than she'd expected, so dallied in the village until just after three before remounting Rangonel and heading south.

As she'd expected, Royce was waiting in the designated field, both horse and rider showing their customary impatience. He turned Sword toward Harbottle as she ranged alongside. "Are you really planning on joining the others in Harbottle later?"

Looking ahead, lips curving, she shrugged lightly. "There's an interesting jeweler I could visit."

He smiled and followed her gaze. "How far is it to this footbridge?"

She grinned. "About half a mile." With a flick of her reins, she set Rangonel cantering, the big gelding's gait steady and sure. Royce held Sword alongside despite the stallion's obvious wish to run.

A wish shared by his rider. "We could gallop."

She shook her head. "No. We shouldn't get there too early."

"Why?"

"You'll see." She caught his disgruntled snort, but he didn't press her. They crossed the Alwin at the ford, water foaming about the horses' knees, then cantered on, cutting across the pastures.

A flash of white ahead was the first sign that her timing was correct. Cresting a low rise, she saw two young girls, pinafores flapping, books tied in small bundles on their backs, laughing as they skipped along a track that led down a shallow gully disappearing behind the next rise to their left.

Royce saw them, too. He shot her a suspicious, incipiently frowning glance, then tracked the pair as he and she headed down the slope. The girls passed out of sight behind the next rise; minutes later, the horses reached it, taking the upward slope in their stride, eager to reach the crest.

When they did, Royce looked down and along the gully— and swore. He hauled Sword to a halt, and grimly stared down.

Expressionless, she drew rein beside him, and watched a bevy of children crossing the Coquet, swollen by the additional waters of the Alwin to a turbulent, tempestuous, swiftly flowing river, using the rickety remnants of the footbridge.

"I thought there was no school in the area." His clipped accents underscored the temper he held leashed.

"There isn't, so Mrs. Cribthorn does what she can to teach the children their letters. She uses one of the cottages near the church." It was the minister's wife who had brought the execrable state of the footbridge to her attention. "The children include some from certain of Wolverstone's crofter families where the women have to work the fields alongside their men. Their parents can't afford the time to bring the children to the church via the road, and on foot, there is no other viable route the children could take."

The young girls they'd seen earlier had joined the group at the nearer end of the bridge; the older children organized the younger ones in a line before, one by one, they inched their way along the single remaining beam, holding the last horizontal timber left from the bridge's original rails.

Someone had strung a rough rope along the rail, giving the children with smaller hands something they could cling to more tightly.

Royce growled another curse and lifted his reins.

"No." She caught his arm. "You'll distract them."

He didn't like it, but reined both himself and Sword in; drawing her hand from the rigid steel his arm had become, she knew how much it cost him.

Could sense how much, behind his stony face, he fumed and railed while being forced to watch the potential drama from a distance—a distance too great to help should one of the children slip and fall.

"What happened to the damned bridge, and when?"

"A bore last spring."

"And it's been like this ever since?"

"Yes. It's only used by the crofter children to get to the church, so . . ." She didn't need to tell him that the welfare of crofter children didn't rate highly with the aldermen of Harbottle.

The instant the last child stepped safely onto the opposite bank, Sword surged down the rise and thundered toward the bridge. The children heard; trudging over the field, they turned and looked, but after watching curiously for several minutes, continued homeward. By the time she and Rangonel reached the river, Royce was out of the saddle and clambering about the steep bank, studying the structure from below.

From Rangonel's back, she watched as he grabbed the remaining beam, using his weight to test it. It creaked; he swore and let go.

When he eventually climbed back up and came striding toward her, his expression was black.

The glare he bent on her was coldly furious. "Who are the aldermen of Harbottle?"

He knew she'd manipulated him; the instant he'd seen the two girls he'd known. Despite that, his irritation with her was relatively minor; he put it to one side and dealt with the issue of the rickety footbridge with a reined fury that brought vividly to mind ghosts from his ancestral past.

There was a wolf in the north again, and he was in a savage mood.

Even though she'd had high expectations, Minerva was impressed. Together they thundered into Harbottle; she introduced him to the senior alderman, who quickly saw the wisdom of summoning his peers. She'd stood back and watched Royce, with cutting exactitude, impress on those unwitting gentlemen first their shortcomings, then his expectations. Of the latter, he left them in absolutely no doubt.

They bowed and scraped, and swore they would attend to the footbridge expeditiously.

He eyed them coldly, then informed them he would be back in three days to view their progress.

Then he turned and stalked out; entirely satisfied, she followed.

Royce set a furious pace back to the castle. The dark look he cast her as he swung up to his saddle made it clear he hadn't forgotten her tweaking of his temper, but he'd wanted an urgent and dramatic reason to give him justification for browbeating the aldermen into fixing the footbridge, so she'd given him one. Her conscience was clear.

Something she suspected he realized, for even when they reached Wolverstone, left their horses with Milbourne, and started toward the castle, other than another of his piercing, dark looks, he said nothing.

By the time they reached the west wing and were approaching the turret stairs, she'd stopped expecting any reaction from him. She was deep in self-congratulation, pleased and eminently satisfied with her day's achievements, when his fingers locked about her elbow and he swung her into the shadowed hall at the bottom of the stairs. Her back met the paneled wall; he followed, pinning her.

Startled, her lips were parted when he crushed them beneath his and kissed her—filled her mouth, seized her wits, and stormed her senses.

It was a hard, bruising, conquering sort of kiss, one she responded to with damning ardor.

Her hands were sunk in the dark silk of his hair when he abruptly pulled back, leaving her gasping, her senses reeling.

From a distance of inches, his eyes bored into hers. "Next time, just *tell* me." A growled, direct order.

She hadn't yet regained breath enough to speak, managed to nod.

His eyes narrow, his lips grimly set, he drew back a little— as if realizing how hard it was for her to think with him so close. "Is there anything else that bad on my lands? Or not on my lands but affecting my people?"

He waited while she gathered her wits, and thought. "No."

He exhaled. "That's something, I suppose."

Stepping back, he drew her away from the wall, and urged her up the narrow stairs. She went, her heart beating just a little faster from knowing he was directly behind her and not in a predictable mood.

But when they reached the gallery, and she turned for her room, he let her go. He stepped up from the last stair, halted.

"Incidentally . . ." He waited until she paused and glanced

back at him; he caught her eyes. "Tomorrow morning I'll want you to ride with me to Usway Burn—we can check on progress and I want to speak with Evan Macgregor."

She felt her brightest smile dawn, felt it light her eyes. "Yes, all right."

With a nod, he turned to his rooms.

Thoroughly pleased with her day, she continued to hers.

They next met in the drawing room, surrounded by the others all full of their day and their plans for the morrow. Walking into the large room, Royce located Minerva chatting in a group with Susannah, Phillip, Arthur, and Gregory. He met her eyes as Retford appeared behind him to announce dinner; stepping aside, he let the others go ahead, waiting until she joined him to claim her.

He wanted her with him, but hadn't yet decided what he wanted to say—or rather, how to say it. He sat her beside him; as he took his own seat at the table's head, she regarded him calmly, then turned to Gordon on her left and asked him about something.

The party had relaxed even further, all the members entirely comfortable in each other's company. He felt comfortable ignoring them all; sitting back, his fingers crooked about the stem of his wineglass, as the endless chatter flowed over and around him he let his gaze rest on his chatelaine's golden head while their day replayed in his mind.

All in all it had been a distinct success, yet he hadn't been—still wasn't—pleased by the way she'd evoked—deliberately and knowingly provoked—his temper over the bridge. He'd asked her to in a way, but he hadn't imagined she'd succeed to anything like the extent she had.

She had effectively manipulated him, albeit with his implied consent. He couldn't recall the last time anyone had successfully done so; that she had, and so easily, left him feeling oddly vulnerable—not a feeling with which he was familiar, one the marcher lord he truly was didn't approve of in the least.

However, against that stood the successes of the day. First in dealing with Falwell, then in deciding the steward's replacement, and lastly over the bridge. He'd wanted to illustrate one point, to demonstrate it in a way she, rational female that she was, couldn't fail to see, and between them they'd succeeded brilliantly.

Regardless . . . he let his gaze grow more intent, until she felt it and glanced his way. He shifted toward her; she turned back and excused herself to Gordon, then faced him and raised her brows.

He locked his eyes on hers. "Why didn't you simply tell me about the children using the bridge?"

She held his gaze. "If I had, the effect would have been . . . distanced. You asked for something dramatic, to give you something urgent to take to the aldermen—if you hadn't seen the children, but simply been told of them, it wouldn't have been the same." She smiled. "*You* wouldn't have been the same."

He wouldn't have felt like handing the aldermen their heads. He hesitated, then, still holding her gaze, inclined his head. "True." Lifting his glass, he saluted her. "We make a good team."

Which was the point he'd been bent on illustrating.

He might tie her to him with passion, but to be sure of holding her he needed more. A lady like her needed occupation—an ability to achieve. As his wife, she'd be able to achieve even more than she currently could; when the time came, he wasn't going to be backward in pointing that out.

She smiled, lifted her glass, and touched the rim to his. "Indeed."

He watched her sip, then swallow, felt something in him tighten. "Incidentally . . ." He waited until her gaze returned to his eyes. "It's customary when a gentleman gives a lady a token of his appreciation, for that lady to show her appreciation in return."

Her brows rose, but she didn't look away. Instead, a

faint—distinctly arousing—smile flirted about the corners of her lips. "I'll bear that in mind."

"Do."

Their gazes touched, locked; the connection deepened. Around them the company was in full voice, the bustle of the footmen serving, the clink of cutlery and the clatter of china a cacophony of sound and a sea of colorful movement swirling all about them, yet it all faded, grew distant, while between them that indefinable connection grew taut, gripped and held.

Expectation and anticipation flickered and sparked.

Her breasts swelled as she drew in a breath, then she looked away.

He glanced down, at his fingers curved about the bowl of the wineglass; setting it down, he shifted in his chair.

At least the company had tired of amateur theatricals; he inwardly gave thanks. The meal ended and Minerva left his side; he kept the passing of the port to the barest minimum, then led the gentlemen to rejoin the ladies in the drawing room.

After exchanging one look, he made no attempt to join her; with heightened passion all but arcing between them, it was simply too dangerous—not even this company were that blind. Outwardly idly amiable, he chatted to some of his sisters' friends, yet he knew the instant Minerva slipped from the room.

She didn't return. He gave her half an hour, then left the garrulous gathering and followed her up the stairs into the keep. Slowing, he glanced at the shadows wreathing the corridor to her room, wondered, but then continued on. To his apartments, to his bedroom.

She was there, lying in his bed.

Halting in the doorway, he smiled, the gesture laden with every ounce of the predatory impulses coursing his veins.

She'd left no candles burning, but the moonlight streamed in, burnishing her hair as it rippled across his pillows, gilding the curves of her bare shoulders with a pearlescent sheen.

No nightgown, he noted.

She lay propped high amid the pillows; she'd been looking out at the moon-drenched night, but had turned her head to watch him. Through the dark, he felt her gaze slide over him—sensed anticipation heighten, tighten.

He remained where he was and let it build.

Let it grow and strengthen until, when he finally stirred and walked forward, it felt as if some invisible silken rope had looped around him and drew him on.

The sight of her lying there, a willing gift, a reward, racked the hunger within him up another notch, set a primitive thrum in his blood.

She was his for the taking. In whatever manner his ducal self decreed.

Her willing surrender was implicit in her silent waiting.

He walked to the tallboy by the wall. Shrugging off his coat, he tossed it on a nearby chair, unbuttoned his waistcoat as he planned how best to use the opportunity to further his aim.

To advance his campaign.

Undressing casually was an obvious first step; deliberately drawing out the moments before he joined her with an activity that underscored his intent would increase her already heightened awareness, of him and all he and she would shortly do.

Drawing the diamond pin from his cravat, he laid it on the tallboy, then unhurriedly unwound the linen band.

When he drew his shirt off, he heard her shift beneath the sheets.

When he tossed his trousers aside and turned, she stopped breathing.

His stride slow and deliberate, he walked to her side of the bed. For an instant, he stood looking down at her; her gaze slowly rose from his groin to his chest, then eventually to his face. Trapping her wide eyes, he reached for the covers, lifted them as he held out his hand. "Come. Get up."

Anticipation flashed through her, a sharp, fiery wave

spreading beneath her skin. Her mouth dry, Minerva searched his face, all hard angles and shadowed planes, the unyielding, uninformative expression that simply stated: primitive male. She licked her lips, saw his eyes follow the small movement. "Why?"

His eyes returned to hers. He didn't answer, simply held the covers up, implacably held out his hand, and waited.

Cool air slipped beneath the raised sheets and found her skin. He, she knew, would be radiating heat; all she had to do to quell the shivers threatening was to stand and let him draw her near.

And then what?

An even bigger shiver of anticipation—a telltale sign he wouldn't miss—threatened to overwhelm her. Lifting her hand, she placed her fingers in his, and let him draw her out of the bed, off it and onto her feet.

He walked backward, drawing her with him, until they both stood within the shaft of silvery moonlight, until they were both bathed by the pale glow. Her breath suspended, trapped in her chest, she couldn't drag her eyes from him—a magnificent male animal, powerful and strong, every muscled curve, every ridge and line, etched in molten silver.

His fingers tightening on hers, he tugged her to him, drew her inexorably, irresistibly, into his arms. Into an embrace that was both cool and heated; his hands slid knowingly over her skin, assessing, caressing, as his arms slowly closed and trapped her, then cinched further, easing her against him, against the hot hardness of his utterly male frame.

His hands spread on her back, molded her to him; his dark eyes watched, drank in her expression as their bodies met, bare breasts to naked chest, her hips to his thighs . . . she closed her eyes and shivered.

The hard ridge of his erection seared like a branding rod against her taut belly.

She sucked in a breath, opened her eyes, only to find him closing the distance. His lips found hers, covered them, possessed them, not with any conquering force but with a languid passion, one all the more evocative, all the more compelling, for being so unhurried—a statement of intent he had no reason to make more stridently; she would be his however he wished—they both knew it.

The knowledge seeped into her even as she gave him her lips, then her mouth, then engaged in a hot, but undriven duel of tongues; she'd come to his room with the thought of rewarding him high in her mind. Rewarding him required no active action from her; she could simply let him take all he wished, follow his lead, and he'd be satisfied.

But would she?

Passivity wasn't her style, and she wanted this, tonight, to be a gift from her—something she gave him, not something she surrendered.

Because he wasn't whipping them along, the reins fast in his grasp, opportunity was hers for the taking. So she took— slid one hand between them and closed it firmly about the rod of his erection. Felt certainty bloom when he stilled, as if her touch held the power to completely distract him.

Taking advantage of the momentary hiatus, she eased her other hand down to join the first, linking them about his rigid member in tactile homage—and through the fading kiss sensed every last particle of his awareness center on where she held him.

Slowly breaking from the kiss, she moved her palms— watched his face, confirming that her touch, her caresses, possessed the power to capture him. His arms eased as his attention shifted; his hold on her weakened enough for her to ease back.

Far enough to look down, so she could see what she was doing and better experiment.

He'd let her touch him before, but then she'd been all but overwhelmed—there'd been so much of him to explore. Now, more familiar with his body, more comfortable standing naked before him, less distracted by the wonder of his chest, the heavy muscles of his arms, the long powerful columns of his thighs, no longer held in thrall by his lips, she could extend her explorations to what she most wanted to learn—what pleased him.

She stroked, then let her fingers wander; his chest swelled as he drew in a tight breath.

Glancing at his face, she saw his eyes, dark desire burning, glinting from beneath the thick fringe of his lashes. Took in his clenched jaw, the muscles taut with a tension that was slowly spreading through his body.

Knew he wouldn't let her play for long.

In a flash of recollection, she remembered a long-ago afternoon in London, and the illicit secrets shared by her wilder peers.

She smiled—and saw his gaze sharpen on her lips. Felt the rod between her hands jerk faintly.

Looking into those dark eyes lit by smoldering passion, she knew exactly what he was thinking.

Knew exactly what she wanted to do, needed to do, to balance the scales of give and take between them.

She took half a step back, lowered her gaze from his eyes to his lips, then ran it down the column of his throat and the long length of his chest, all the way down to where her palms and fingers were firmly locked about him, one hand above the other, one thumb cruising the sensitive edge of the broad bulbous head.

Before he could stop her, she sank to her knees.

Sensed his shock—compounded it by angling the stiff rod to her face, parting her lips, and sliding them over the luscious, delicate flesh, slowly taking him into the warm welcome of her mouth.

She'd heard enough of the theory to know what she should do; the practice was a trifle harder—he was large, long, and thick, but she was determined.

Royce finally managed to get his lungs to work, to haul in a desperate breath, but he couldn't drag his eyes from her, from the sight of her golden head bent to his groin as she worked her mouth over his straining erection.

The ache in his loins, in his balls and his shaft, intensified with every sweet lap of her tongue, every long, slow suck.

He felt he should stop her, bring the moment to a swift halt. It wasn't that he didn't like what she was doing—he loved every second of tactile delight, loved the sight of her on her knees before him, his shaft buried between her luscious lips—but . . . he neither expected nor generally had ladies service him in this way.

They were usually too exhausted after he'd had his way with them—and his way always came first.

He should, but wasn't going to, stop her. Instead, he accepted—accepted the pleasure she lavished on him, let his hands—hovering about her head—close, let his fingers tunnel through her silky hair and grip, gently guide . . .

She eased him deeper, then deeper still, until his engorged head was in her throat. Her tongue wrapped around his length and slowly rasped.

Chest swelling, eyes closing, he let his head tip back, fought to stifle a groan—fought to let her go on, to let her have her way.

To let her have him.

But there was only so far he could go. Only so much of the wet heaven of her mouth he could endure.

Her hands about the base of his shaft, she'd found her rhythm; her confidence had grown, and with it her dedication. Lungs screaming, nerves beyond taut, he fought to give her one more moment—then he forced himself to slip a thumb between her lips and draw his throbbing length from her mouth.

She looked up, licked her lips—started to frown.

He bent, gripped her waist, and lifted her—up and to him. "Wrap your legs about my waist."

She already was. He slid his hands down to grip her hips, positioned her so the heated head of his erection parted the scalding slickness of her folds and pressed against her entrance.

He looked at her face, caught her wide, desire-darkened eyes—watched as he drew her down, as he steadily, inexorably, impaled her. Watched her features ease, then blank, as her awareness turned inward to where he stretched her and filled her. Her lids lowered and she quivered in his arms, caught on the knife edge of surrender. He gripped more firmly, ruthlessly pulled her hips into his, tilting her so he could thrust the last inch and fill her completely.

Possess her completely.

He saw, felt, heard the breath shudder from her lungs. Shifting his grip, he took her weight on one arm, lifted his other hand to her face, framed her jaw, and kissed her.

Hungrily.

She surrendered her mouth, opened to his onslaught, and gave him, ceded to him, all he desired. For long moments, sunk in her body, he simply devoured, then she tried to move, tried to ease up and use her body to satisfy the rampant demand of his—and discovered she couldn't.

That she couldn't move at all unless he permitted it, that impaled as she was, she was wholly in his power.

That the rest of this script was entirely his to write—and hers to experience, to endure.

He showed her—showed her how he could lift her as little or as much as he wished, then lower her, as slowly or as rapidly as he wanted. That the power and depth of his penetration of her body was wholly his to decree.

That their journey to the top of the peak would be at his command.

She'd given herself to him, now he intended to take—all and everything he could from her.

He lifted her, and brought her down, one hand still at her nape, that arm wrapped about her body, pressing it to his so the movement of their joining made her breasts ride against his chest. With one arm about her hips, that hand spread beneath her bottom, her legs wrapped, now tight, about his waist, her arms slung around his shoulders, her hands spread on his back, he could feel her all around him, and she was wholly locked within his embrace.

A naked, primitive embrace that suited him well. That

would deliver her to him—make her surrender to him—at an even deeper, more primal level.

Minerva drew back from the kiss on a gasping sob, head rising as, breasts swelling, she struggled to find breath.

He let her, then, hand firming at her nape, drew her back.

Kissed her again.

Took, seized, and devoured again.

His hands were suddenly much more demanding, their grip like fire, just this side of painful, elementally commanding as he moved her on him, against him, flayed her senses in every possible way inside and out until she wrenched back from the kiss, let her head fall back, and gave herself up to him.

To the fires that raged between them, building and growing, then erupting in molten passion so hot it seared and scalded, branded and marked.

Flames, hungry and greedy, rose up and washed over them, through them, spreading beneath their skins and consuming as the insistent, persistent, tempo of his possession escalated and claimed her anew.

Made her burn anew, made her fragment and scream, made her cling and sob as he joined her.

As, at the last, she felt him, hard and hot and undeniably real, undeniably him, buried deep within her, deeper than he'd ever been.

Deep enough to touch her heart.

Deep enough to lay claim to that, too.

The thought drifted through her mind, but she let it go, let it fade as he carried her to his bed, and collapsed with her across it.

Holding her against his heart.

At the very last, she heard him groan, "Especially in this, we make an *excellent* team."

Fifteen

Two nights later, Minerva slipped into Royce's rooms, and gave thanks that Trevor was never there waiting. As per her recent habit, she'd left Royce and the rest of the company downstairs and slipped away—to come here, to his rooms, to his bed.

Walking into the now familiar bedroom, she found herself quietly amazed at how easy their liaison had become, how comfortable she'd grown over such a short time with the daily and nightly rhythms.

The last days had passed in a whirl of preparations, both for the house party and for the fair itself. As the major house in the district, the castle was always first in donating and participating, an association the household staff maintained regardless of the interest of their masters.

She'd always made time for the fair. Run under the auspices of the local church, the fair raised funds both for the upkeep of the church as well as for numerous projects for the betterment of the local flock. A flock the castle would always have a vested interest in, a fact she used to justify the expenditure of time and goods involved.

Stripping off her gown, she was aware of an unexpected contentment. Given Margaret's, Aurelia's, and Susannah's involvement this year, matters might have been much worse, but all was progressing smoothly on both the house party and the fair fronts.

Naked, her hair down around her shoulders, she lifted the crimson sheets and slid beneath the cool silk. If she was honest, her contentment, the depth of it, had a nearer, deeper, more powerful source. She knew their liaison would last for only a short while—in reality her time with him had to be more than half over—but rather than making her wary and reticent, rather than making her draw back from their engagements, the knowledge that her chance to experience all she might with him was strictly limited had served to spur her on. She was determined to live, whole and complete, to embrace the moment and seize the chance to be all the woman she could be, for however long his interest lasted. For however long he gave her.

It wouldn't be long enough for her to fall in love with him, for her to get trapped by unrequited emotion, and if she felt an unwelcome pang because she would never have the chance to know love in all its glory, she could accept and live with that.

She heard the sitting room door open, and close, heard his step on the floor—then he was there, powerful and dominant, literally darkening the doorway in the unlit room. He met her gaze; she sensed rather than saw his smile, his liking for the sight of her lying naked in his bed.

He moved forward, heading for his tallboy to undress; she literally licked her lips and waited. It was one of many individual moments she savored, watching him disrobe, watching his powerful body be revealed element by element to her hungry gaze.

Offered up, for her delectation.

He knew. She knew he did. Although he never gave any overt sign—never made any too obvious gesture or glanced at her to see how she was reacting—he artfully drew the moments out until, by the time he was naked and joined her in the bed, she was beyond desperate to get her hands on him.

To feel him against her, all that glorious muscle, all those heavy bones, to sense and feel the power inherent in his large frame.

To have that possess her, shatter her, and bring her unbounded, unfettered delight. Unrestricted, unrestrained pleasure.

She knew that was what would come to her as, finally naked, he crossed the room and lifted the sheets. She waited, breath bated, nerves taut, for that moment when the mattress sagged beneath his weight, and he reached for her, gathered her in, and their bodies met.

Skin to skin, heat to heat, desire to passion, wanting to yearning.

She came to him, and Royce drew her to him, half beneath him as he leaned over her. Her hand touched the side of his face, welcoming, encouraging, mirroring the messages her body gave as she sank against him, her softness molding instinctively to his hardness, giving against his heavier weight, cushioning and beckoning with sirenlike allure.

Without hesitation, without thought, he dove into her mouth, and found her waiting there, too. Waiting to engage, to meet and satisfy his every demand—to challenge him, did she but know it, with the ease with which she so effortlessly sated him.

Even after having her for more times than he'd ever had any woman, he still couldn't get enough of her—any more than he could solve the riddle of how having her had become such a bliss-filled act.

Why it so soothed his soul, both that of the man and that of the beast, the primitive being that lurked deep within him.

She embraced him all, and gave him surcease; in her arms he found an earthly heaven.

In search of it again, he drew his hand from her breast, reached down, caught her knee, and lifted it. Angling his hips, he nudged into her, then thrust deep. Seated fully within her, he rolled and settled fully upon her; wrapped in her arms and the billows of his bed, he savored her mouth as he savored her body, rocking them both with slow, deep thrusts, taking them both on a slow ride to paradise.

At the last, she clutched, arched beneath him as his name ripped from her throat; he buried his head in the sweet curve of her shoulder and gave himself to her in a long, intense climax that rolled on and on.

Afterward, once he'd regained possession of sufficient wit to move, he lifted from her, settled beside her, and gathered her close, and she came, snuggling against him, her head on his shoulder, her hand on his chest, spread over his heart.

He didn't know if she knew she did that every night, that she slept with her hand just there. With her warmth against him and all tension released, he sank deeper into the mattress, and let the quiet joy he always found with her seep slowly to his bones. To his soul.

And wondered, again, why. Why what he found with her was so different. And why he felt as he now did about her.

She was the woman he wanted as his wife—so he'd let her close, closer than he'd ever let anyone else, and therefore she meant more than anyone else to him. He shouldn't be surprised that she awakened, called to, drew forth emotions no other ever had.

He'd never felt as possessive of any woman as he felt about her. Never felt as consumed by, as focused on, as connected to anyone as he did to her. She was rapidly becoming—had already become—someone he needed and wanted in his life forever . . .

What he felt for her, how he felt about her, mirrored how his friends felt about their wives.

Given he was a Varisey through and through—knew that to his bones—he didn't understand how that could be, yet it was. In his Varisey heart, he didn't approve of it—his feelings for her—any more than he approved of any other vulnerability; a vulnerability was a weakness, a chink in his armor—a sin for such as he. But . . . deep within was a yearning he'd only recently recognized.

His father's death had been the catalyst, the message he'd

left with Minerva an unintended revelation. If he didn't need to be like his father in running the dukedom, perhaps he didn't need to be like him in other ways. Then his friends had arrived to comfort him, and had reminded him of what they'd found, what they had. And he'd seen his sisters and their Varisey marriages—and that hadn't been what he'd wanted, not anymore.

He now wanted a marriage like his friends had. Like his ex-colleagues of the Bastion Club had forged. That want, that need, had burgeoned and grown over the past nights, even more over the past days, until it was an ache—like a stomach-ache—lodged in his chest.

And in the dark of his bed in the depths of the night, he could admit that that want scared him.

He didn't know if he could achieve it—that if he reached for what he wanted, he could in fact secure it.

There were few arenas in life in which he doubted himself, but this newfound battleground was one.

Yet the one thing he now yearned for above all else was for the woman in his arms to love him. He wanted what his friends had found—lusted after her gentle affection if anything more intensely than he lusted after her body.

But if he asked for her love, and she gave it, she would ask for, and expect, his love in return. That's how love worked; that much he knew.

But he didn't know if he could love.

He could see that far, but no further.

If somewhere deep in his Varisey soul, so deep no other Varisey had ever found it, love lurked, a nascent possibility . . .

His problem was he didn't believe that was so.

"Ma'am?"

Minerva looked up from her desk in the duchess's morning room. "Yes, Retford?" The butler had entered and stood just inside the door.

"The Countess Ashton has arrived, ma'am—one of Lady

Susannah's guests. Unfortunately, Lady Susannah is out riding."

Minerva inwardly grimaced. "I'll come down." Laying aside her pen, she rose. Royce had ridden over the border to visit Hamish, presumably to discuss sheep and the required breeders; she'd hoped to use the time to catch up with her correspondence, which she'd neglected of late.

But duty called.

She consulted the list lying on one side of her desk, then turned to the door. "We've put the countess in the west wing—I'm sure Cranny will have the room ready. Please ask her to send up a maid, or has the countess brought one?"

"No, ma'am." Retford retreated into the corridor. "I'll speak with Mrs. Cranshaw."

Retford followed at Minerva's heels as she went down the corridor and descended the main stairs. In the huge hall below, a lady, curvaceous and dark-haired, turned from examining her reflection in one of the large mirrors.

An extremely modish hat sat atop Lady Ashton's sleek head. Her carriage gown was the latest in fashionable luxury, beautifully cut from ivory silk twill with magenta silk trimming; the skirts swished as, an easy smile curving delicately tinted lips, her ladyship came forward to meet Minerva.

Stepping down from the last step, Minerva smiled. "Lady Ashton? I'm Miss Chesterton—I act as chatelaine here. Welcome to Wolverstone Castle."

"Thank you." Of similar height to Minerva, Lady Ashton possessed classical features, a porcelain complexion, and a pleasant, confident demeanor. "I gather Susannah is out gadding about, leaving me to impose on you."

Minerva's smile deepened. "It's no imposition, I assure you. It's been some years since the castle hosted a house party—the household is quite looking forward to the challenge."

The countess tilted her head. "House party?"

Minerva hesitated. "Yes—didn't Susannah mention it?"

A faint smile on her lips, the countess glanced down. "No, but there was no reason she should. She invited me to another end."

"Oh." Minerva wasn't sure what was going on. "I'm sure Susannah will tell you about the party when she returns. Meanwhile, if you'll come this way, I'll show you to your room."

The countess consented to climb the stairs beside her. Halfway up, she grew aware of Lady Ashton's sideways glance, and turned her head to meet it.

Her ladyship pulled a wry face. "I didn't like to ask the butler, but is Royce—I suppose I should call him Wolverstone, shouldn't I? Is he about?"

"I believe he's out riding at present."

"Ah." The countess looked ahead, then shrugged. "He'll have to cope with us meeting again with others about, then— or if you see him, you might mention I'm here. Susannah sent for me well over a week ago, but I wasn't in London, so it's taken a while for me to arrive."

Minerva wasn't sure what to make of that. She fastened on the most pertinent fact. "You know Royce."

The countess smiled, her face transforming into that of a stunning seductress. "Yes, indeed." Her voice lowered to a purr. "Royce and I know each other very well." She glanced at Minerva. "I'm sure that's no real surprise to you, my dear—you must know what he's like. And while it was Susannah who penned the invitation to me, she made it clear it was for Royce that she summoned me."

A cold, iron fist gripped Minerva's heart; her head spun. "I . . . see." The countess must be the lady Royce had chosen. Yet Susannah had asked if Minerva knew . . . but perhaps that was before he'd had Susannah write to the countess.

But why Susannah, rather than Handley?

And surely the countess was married . . . no, she wasn't; Minerva recalled hearing that the Earl of Ashton had died several years ago.

They'd strolled past the short corridor to the ducal apartments and into the west wing. Halting before the door of the room the countess had been assigned, Minerva dragged in a breath past the constriction banding her chest, and turned to her ladyship. "If you would like tea, I can have a tray brought up. Otherwise, the luncheon gong will ring in about an hour."

"I'll wait, I think. I take it Wolverstone will return for lunch?"

"I really can't say."

"No matter—I'll wait and see."

"The footmen will bring up your trunk. A maid will be with you shortly."

"Thank you." With an inclination of her head and a perfectly gracious smile, the countess opened the door and went inside.

Minerva turned away. Her head was spinning, but that was the least of it. She literally felt ill . . . because her heart was chilled and aching—and it wasn't supposed to be.

Neither Royce nor Susannah nor the rest of the company returned for luncheon, leaving Minerva to entertain the countess by herself.

Not that that was a difficult task; Lady Ashton—Helen as she asked to be called—was an extremely beautiful, sophisticated lady with an even temperament, gracious manners, and a ready smile.

No matter the circumstances, no matter the sudden agonies of her foolish, foolish heart, no matter her instinctive inclination, Minerva found it difficult to dislike Helen; she was, in the very essence of the word, charming.

Leaving the dining room, Helen smiled rather wistfully. "I wonder, Minerva, if I may truly impose on you and ask for a quick tour—or as quick a tour as can be—of this enormous pile?" She looked up at the vaulted ceiling of the front hall as it opened before them. "It's rather daunting to consider . . ."

She trailed off, shot a look at Minerva, then sighed. "I've never been much of a hand at subterfuge, so I may as well be plain. I have no idea where I stand with Royce, and I freely admit to a certain nervousness—which is really not my style."

Minerva frowned. "I thought . . ." She wasn't at all sure what to think. She led the way to the principal drawing room.

The countess strolled beside her. As they paused inside the long formal room, Helen continued, "I assume you know of his inviolable rule—that he never spends more than five nights with any lady?"

Expressionless, Minerva shook her head. "I hadn't heard."

"I assure you it's true—there are any number of ladies within the ton who can attest to his refusal to bend on that score, no matter the inducement. Five nights are all he allows any woman." The countess grimaced. "I suppose it was one way to ensure none of us ever got any ideas, as one might say, above our station."

Surreptitiously, Minerva counted on her fingers; last night had been her fifth—and therefore last—night. She hadn't even known. Inwardly reeling, she stepped back into the hall, then led the way toward the formal dining room.

Helen kept pace. "I was his lover before he left London— for just four nights. I hoped for a fifth, but then he disappeared from town. Later I heard about his father's death, and so believed our liaison was over—until I received Susannah's note. She seemed to think . . . and then I heard about the grandes dames and their decree, but no announcement came . . ." She glanced at Minerva. "Well, I did wonder." She shrugged. "So here I am, come to throw my hat in the ring, if there is a ring, that is. But he does have to marry, and we get along well enough . . . and I do want to marry again. Ashton and I weren't in love, but we liked each other. There's a great deal to be said for companionship I've discovered, now I no longer have it."

Helen gave a cynical laugh. "Of course, all depends on the whim of one Royce Varisey, but I thought he should know that he does have alternatives to the giddy young misses."

Thrusting her reeling emotions deep and slamming a

mental door on them, Minerva forced herself to consider Helen's words. And who was she to answer for Royce? For all she knew, he might feel some real connection to Helen; it wasn't hard to picture her on his arm, as his duchess.

Dragging in a breath, she held it, then managed a mild smile. "If you like, I can show you around the main areas of the castle." As Royce had to marry someone, she'd rather it was Helen than some witless miss.

Later that evening, Minerva sat midway down the long dining table, conversing blithely with those around her while surreptitiously watching Helen sparkle, effervesce, and charm from her position at Royce's left.

The lovely countess had usurped her place there, and, it seemed, had displaced her in other ways, too. Royce hadn't spared so much as a glance for her since he'd walked into the drawing room and laid eyes on Helen, a stunning vision in rose-pink silk.

Feeling dull and drab in her weeds, she'd stood by the wall and watched, no longer sure of where *she* stood with Royce, and utterly unsure what to do.

She'd started her tour with Helen imagining there was, in the matter of Royce's bride, no worse candidate than a giddy young miss. After an hour of listening to Helen's views on the castle and the estate, and most importantly its people, she'd revised that opinion.

Helen would never rule as Royce's duchess at Wolverstone. Quite aside from all else, she didn't want to. She'd assumed Royce would spend most of his time in London, but he'd already declared he would follow in his father's and grandfather's—and even great-grandfather's—footsteps. His home would be here, not in the capital.

When she'd mentioned that, Helen had shrugged, smiled, and said, "We'll see." Helen couldn't imagine she would change Royce's mind, which had left Minerva wondering just what sort of marriage Helen envisioned—quite possibly one that might well suit Royce.

Which would compound the more serious problem, namely that Helen had absolutely no feeling for, no empathy with, the estate in general, much less the people on it. She'd already hinted that she assumed Minerva would stay on as chatelaine. Minerva couldn't, wouldn't, but she'd always imagined handing her keys to some woman with a heart, with compassion and interest in her staff and the wider community of which the castle was the hub.

Glancing up the table again, she saw Royce, lips subtly curving, incline his head to the countess in response to some sally. Forcing her gaze to Rohan, seated opposite her, she smiled and nodded; she hadn't heard a word of his latest tale. She had to stop torturing herself; she had to be realistic—as realistic as the countess. But what did reality demand?

On a purely worldly level, she ought to step quietly aside and let Helen claim Royce, if he was willing. She'd already had her five nights with him, and, unlike her, Helen would make him an excellent wife within the parameters he'd set for his marriage.

On another level, however, one based on the emotional promptings of her witless heart, she'd like to haul Helen away and send her packing; she was wrong—all wrong—for the position of Royce's bride.

Yet when she rose and, with the other ladies, filed behind Margaret to the door, she let her senses open wide . . . and knew Royce didn't even glance at her. In the doorway, she glanced swiftly back, and saw the countess very prettily taking her leave of him; his dark eyes were all for her.

Minerva had had her five nights; he'd already forgotten her existence.

In that instant, she knew that no matter how much of a fool she would think him if he accepted Helen's transparent invitation and offered her his duchess's coronet, she wouldn't say a word against his decision.

On that subject, she could no longer claim to hold an unbiased opinion.

Turning away, she wondered how long she would have to endure in the drawing room until the tea tray arrived.

The answer was, a lot longer than she wanted. More than long enough to dwell on Royce's iniquities; from his continuing obliviousness, her time with him had come to an absolute end—he'd just forgotten to tell her. The fiend.

She was in no good mood, but clung to the knots of others as they chatted about this and that, and hid her reaction as best she could; there was no value in letting anyone else sense or suspect. She wished she didn't have to think about it herself, that she could somehow distance herself from the source of her distress, but she could hardly cut out her own heart. Contrary to her misguided hopes and beliefs, she could no longer pretend it had escaped involvement.

There was no other explanation for the deadening feeling deep in her chest, no other cause for the leaden lump that unruly organ had become.

Her own fault, of course, not that that made the dull twisting pain any less. She'd known from the start the dangers of falling in love—even a little bit in love—with him; she just hadn't thought it could happen so quickly, hadn't even realized it had.

"I say, Minerva."

She focused on Henry Varisey as he leaned conspiratorially close.

His gaze was fixed across the room. "Do you think the beautiful countess has any chance of learning what no one else yet has?"

It took a moment to realize he was alluding to the name of Royce's bride. She followed Henry's gaze to where Helen all but hung on Royce's arm. "I wish her luck—on that subject he's been as close-mouthed as an oyster."

Henry glanced at her, arched a brow. "You haven't heard anything?"

"Not a hint—no clue at all."

"Well." Straightening, Henry looked back across the room. "It appears our best hopes lie with Lady Ashton."

Assuming Lady Ashton's wasn't the name in question . . . Minerva frowned; Henry, at least, didn't see Helen as even a possibility as Royce's chosen bride.

Across the room, Royce forced himself to keep his gaze on Helen Ashton, or whoever else was near, and not allow his eyes to deflect to Minerva, as they constantly wanted to. He'd walked into the drawing room before dinner, anticipating another delightful evening of enjoying his chatelaine, only to find himself faced with Helen. The very last woman he'd expected to see.

He'd inwardly sworn, plastered on an unruffled expression, and battled not to seek help from the one person in the room he'd actually wanted to see. He had to deal with Helen first. An unwanted, uninvited irritation; he hadn't understood why the hell she was there until he'd heard her story.

Susannah. What the hell his sister had been thinking of he had no clue. He'd find out later. For that evening, however, he had to toe a fine line; Helen and too many others—all those who knew she'd been his recent mistress—expected him to pay attention to her now she was there.

Because as far as they knew, he hadn't had a woman in weeks. He didn't have a mistress at Wolverstone. True, and yet not.

With everyone watching him and Helen, if he so much as glanced at Minerva, someone would see—and someone would wonder. While he was working toward making their connection public through getting her to convince herself to accept his suit, he wasn't yet sure of success, and had no intention of risking his future with her because of his ex-mistress.

So he had to bide his time until he could confirm Helen's status directly with her. As she was the senior lady present, he'd had no choice but to escort her into dinner and seat her at his left—in some ways a boon, for that had kept Minerva at a distance.

He hoped—prayed—she would understand. At least once he explained . . .

He wasn't looking forward to that conversation, but then again, Minerva knew him very well. She would hardly be shocked to learn that Helen had been his mistress, and was now his *ex*-mistress. In their world, it was the *ex-* that counted.

Even with his outward attention elsewhere, he knew when Minerva left the room. A quick glance confirmed it, and sharpened the inner spur that impelled him to follow her.

But he had to settle matters with Helen first.

And Susannah. His sister swanned past beyond Helen; she caught his eye—no difficulty as it was fixed on her—and winked. Hiding his reaction behind an easy expression, he left Helen to her conversation with Caroline Courtney; reaching out he closed his fingers about Susannah's elbow and drew her with him as he strolled a few paces.

Once they were sufficiently apart to speak privately, he released her and looked down as she looked up at him.

She smiled with childlike—childish—delight. "Well, brother dear, are you happier now?"

He read her sincerity in her eyes. Inwardly sighed. "Actually, no. Helen and I parted when I left London."

Susannah's face fell almost comically. "Oh." She looked thoroughly disconcerted. "I had no idea." She glanced at Helen. "I thought . . ."

"If I might ask, what, exactly, did you tell her?"

"Well, that you were here and alone, and having to make this dreadful decision of who to wed, and that if she came up, perhaps she might make your life easier, and, well . . . *those* sort of things."

Royce inwardly groaned, then sighed through his teeth. "Never mind. I'll speak with her and straighten things out."

At least he now knew his instincts had been right; Helen wasn't there to share just a night of passion. Thanks to Susannah's poor phrasing, Helen now harbored higher aspirations.

He let Susannah, rather subdued, go and returned to Helen's side, but had to wait until everyone else finally decided to retire to take her to a place where they could speak privately.

Leaving the drawing room at the rear of the crowd, he touched Helen's arm, and indicated the corridor leading away from the hall. "This way."

He led her to the library.

She passed through the door he held open for her, and came to a momentary halt; she was too experienced not to realize the significance of the venue. But then her spine straightened, and she walked further into the room. He followed and closed the door.

A candelabra on the mantelpiece was alight; a small fire blazed cheerily in the hearth. He waved Helen to the wing-chair to one side of the hearth. She walked ahead of him to the fireplace, but then swung to face him, hands clasped before her, fingers twining.

She opened her mouth, but he held up a hand, staying her words.

"First, let me say that I was surprised to see you here—I had no idea Susannah had written to you." Halting on the other side of the hearth, he held Helen's blue gaze. "However, courtesy of what my sister wrote, I accept that you may be laboring under a misapprehension. To clarify matters—" He broke off, then let his lips twist cynically. "To be brutally frank, I'm currently negotiating for the hand of the lady I've chosen as my duchess, and am entirely uninterested in any dalliance."

And if she'd thought she had any chance at a more permanent connection, she now knew better.

To give her her due, and as he'd expected, Helen absorbed the reality well. She was a natural survivor in their world. Her eyes on his face, she drew a long breath as she digested his words, then she inclined her head, her lips twisting in a rueful grimace. "Good Lord—how very . . . awkward."

"Only as awkward as we wish to make it. No one will be surprised if we amicably part and move on."

She thought, then nodded. "True."

"I will, naturally, do everything within my power to ensure you're not made uncomfortable while here, and I hope, in the future, you will continue to regard me as a friend." He continued to hold her gaze, entirely confident she would understand the offer behind his words, and value it accordingly.

She didn't disappoint him. She was far from stupid, and if she couldn't have him as either lover or husband, then having him as a powerful, well-disposed acquaintance was the next best thing. Again she inclined her head, this time in a deeper obeisance. "Thank you, Your Grace." She hesitated, then lifted her head. "If it would not inconvenience you, I believe I'll remain for a few days—perhaps for the house party."

He knew about saving face. "By all means."

Their interview was at an end; he waved her to the door, falling in beside her as she walked down the room.

He halted before the door, waited until she looked at him. "If I might ask, was it purely distraction you came up to Northumberland to offer, or . . . ?"

She smiled. "Susannah apparently believed I had some chance of becoming your duchess." She met his eyes. "To be perfectly honest, I didn't think it likely."

"I apologize for Susannah—she's younger than I, and doesn't, in fact, know me as well as she thinks she does."

Helen laughed. "No one knows you as well as they think they do." She paused, then smiled—one of her gloriously charming smiles. "Good night, Royce. And good luck with your negotiations."

Opening the door, she went out.

Royce watched the door close behind her; he stood staring at the panels, his mind immediately refocusing on the one burning issue dominating his current existence—his negotiations with the lady he'd chosen as his duchess.

His campaign to ensure Minerva said yes.

* * *

Minerva lay alone in her bed—a perfectly good bed she'd slept comfortably in for years and years, but which now seemed entirely lacking.

She knew what was missing, what lack it was that somehow made it impossible to fall asleep, but why the simple presence of a male body over a handful of days should have made such a deep impression on her psyche to the extent she—her body—fretted at his absence, she simply could not comprehend.

If her body was restless, her mind was even more so. She had to stop thinking about all she'd learned—had to stop wondering if Helen had actually meant five interludes, or five intimacies; on both counts she and Royce had exceeded the limit. Yet perhaps he, being male, simply counted nights?

The deadening truth she had to accept was that according to his immutable rule—and she could see why he, heir to a massively wealthy and powerful dukedom, had instituted such a rule and stuck by it—her time with him had come to an end.

It was just as well Helen had arrived and explained; at least now she knew.

Sitting up, she pummeled her pillow, then slumped down and pulled the covers over her shoulders. She closed her eyes. She had to get some sleep.

She tried to compose her features, but they wouldn't relax. Her frown refused to smooth away.

In her heart, her gut, everything felt wrong. So utterly wrong.

The click of her door latch had her opening her eyes. The door swung inward—rather violently—then Royce was in the room, shutting the door forcefully, but silently.

He stalked to the bed. Halting beside it, he looked down at her; all she could see of his expression was that his lips were set in a grim line.

"I suppose I should have expected this." He shook his head, and reached for the covers.

He tugged. She clutched them tighter. "Wh—"

"Of course, I'd hoped my edict that you're supposed to be in *my* bed might have been strong enough to hold, but apparently not." His accents were clipped, a sure indication of strained temper. He jerked the covers from her grip and flung them off her.

He stopped and stared down at her. "Heaven preserve me, we're back to nightgowns."

The disgust in his voice would, in other circumstances, have made her laugh. She narrowed her eyes at him, then dove to scramble off the other side of the bed—but he was too fast.

He caught her, hauled her to him, then hoisted her in his arms.

He started for the door.

"Royce!"

"Shut up. I'm not in a good mood. First Susannah, then Helen, now you. Misogyny beckons."

She glanced at his face, at his adamantine expression, and shut her lips. As she couldn't prevent him from carrying her to his room, she would argue once they got there.

He paused by the coat rack. "Grab your cloak."

She did and quickly flicked the folds over her; at least he'd remembered that.

He juggled her, opened her door, softly shut it behind them, then carried her swiftly through the shadows to his apartments, and on into his bedroom. All the way to his bed.

She pinned him with a stony glare. "What about the countess?"

Halting beside the bed, he met her gaze, his own hard. "What about her?"

"She's your mistress."

"*Ex*-mistress. The *ex-* is important—it defines that relationship."

"Does she know that?"

"Yes, she does. She knew it before she came here, and I've just confirmed for her that the situation hasn't changed."

He'd held her gaze throughout. "Any more questions on that subject?"

She blinked. "No. Not at the moment."

"Good." He tossed her on the bed.

She bounced once. Before she could grab it, he whipped her cloak off and flung it across the room.

He paused, then stepped back. His hands going to his coat buttons, he toed off his shoes; his eyes on her, he shrugged out of his tight-fitting evening coat, then pointed at her nightgown. "Take that off. If I do, it won't survive."

She hesitated. If she was naked, and so was he, rational discussion wouldn't be high on his agenda. "First—"

"Minerva—take off the gown."

Sixteen

inerva—take off the gown.

The words resonated in the dimness between them. He'd packed them with more distilled power, more direct command, than he'd ever used with her before; his tone filled her female ears with primitive threat, and unstated promise.

A not-at-all subtle reminder that he was the sort of noble man no one even thought to deny. Certainly no woman. Of their own volition, her fingers shifted on the fine fabric draping her legs.

She realized and stilled them, then, hauling in a breath through lungs suddenly tight, sat up, curling her legs, faced him, and narrowed her eyes on his. "No." She set her jaw, if not as hard, then at least as belligerently as he. "You didn't so much as glance at me all evening, and now you want to see me naked?"

His implacability eased not one jot. He drew his cravat off, and dropped it. "Yes." A heartbeat passed. "I didn't glance at you—and I'm well aware it was for the whole damned evening—because everyone, literally everyone, was watching *me*, watching to see me and Helen, my recent mistress, interact, and if instead I'd looked at you, everyone else would have, too. And then they'd have wondered why—why instead of looking at my recent mistress I was looking at you. And not being entirely devoid of intelligence, they'd have guessed, correctly, that my distraction with you at such a moment was because *you're* sharing my bed."

He shrugged off his waistcoat. "I didn't look your way once the entire evening because I wanted to avoid the speculation I knew would ensue, and I know you won't like." He looked down as he dropped the waistcoat on top of his coat; he paused, then lifted his head and met her eyes. "I also didn't want my cousins getting any ideas about you—and they would if they knew you were sharing my bed."

Truth—all truth. She heard it ring in every clipped, precise vowel and consonant. And the thought of his cousins approaching her—all the males were as sexually aggressive as he—had been the prod that had affected him most powerfully.

Before she could consider what that might mean, with a barely restrained tug he pulled his shirttails from his waistband.

His gaze lowered to her body, to the offending nightgown. "Take that damned gown off. If it's still on you when I reach you, I'm going to shred it."

Not a warning, not a threat, not even a promise—just a pragmatic statement of fact.

He was barely two yards away. She mentally threw up her hands and turned to draw the covers down so she could slip beneath them.

"No. Stay where you are." His voice had lowered, deepened; his tone sent a primitive thrill racing up her spine. He spoke increasingly slowly. "Just take the gown off. Now."

She turned back to face him. Her lungs had constricted again. She drew in a tight breath, then reached for the hem of the fine lawn gown, and drew it up, exposing her calves, her knees, her thighs, then, still sitting, her eyes locked on him, she wriggled and tugged until the long gown was bunched around her waist.

The roughness of his brocade counterpane rasped the bare skin of her legs and bottom—and she suddenly had an inkling of why he might want her naked *on* the bed, rather than in it.

And she wasn't about to argue.

From the waist down, she was no longer sheathed in the gown, but the folds shielded her hips and stomach, and all the rest of her, from his gaze.

Her mouth suddenly dry, she swallowed, then said, "Take off the shirt, and I'll take off the gown."

His gaze lifted from her naked thighs, locked with hers for an instant, then he grabbed the hem of his shirt and hauled it up and over his head.

She seized the instant—the barest fleeting instant—to drink in the arresting, arousing sight of his heavily muscled chest. Then he tore his hands free of the sleeves, dropped the shirt. His fingers reaching for the buttons at his waist, he stepped toward the bed.

Grabbing the folds of her nightgown, she hauled it up and off.

He was on her before she could pull her hands free. In a surging, muscled wave, he flattened her back on the bed.

Before she could blink she was stretched naked on her back across the crimson-and-gold brocade, with him stretched over her, one heavy hand locked about her tangled ones, pinning them, leaving her with her arms stretched out above her head.

Lifting off her, he set his hip alongside hers; leaning on the arm holding her hands captive, he looked down on her body as she lay displayed, naked and helpless, for his delectation.

For his taking.

Raising his free hand, he set it to her flesh. Used it to quickly, efficiently, ruthlessly arouse her until she writhed, until her body lifted and arched helplessly into that too-knowing hand, seeking, wanting.

His hand cupped between her thighs, working the slick,

swollen folds, with two long fingers buried in her sheath stroking deeply, he lowered his head and set his mouth to one breast.

He licked, lipped, nipped, then drew her furled nipple deep into his mouth and suckled so fiercely, body bowing, she shrieked.

Releasing her tortured flesh, he glanced at her face, caught her gaze, and thrust his fingers deep inside her—watched as she gasped and instinctively lifted her hips, wanting to, straining to, reach completion.

Through the pounding of her heartbeat in her ears, she heard him mutter something deep, dark, and guttural—she couldn't make out the words.

Her skin was so flushed, so excruciatingly sensitive, she felt like she was burning—literally burning with unslaked desire. Bare minutes had passed since he'd spread her beneath him on the bed, yet he'd reduced her to this—to needing him inside her more than she needed to breathe.

His fingers withdrew from her. She opened eyes she hadn't known she'd closed as he moved over her.

She tugged, wanting her hands free, but his hold didn't ease.

"Later," he ground out.

Then his body came down on hers and her lungs seized.

He was naked to the waist—the hair on his chest abraded her breasts, keeping her nipples painfully erect—but he still had his trousers on. The woolen fabric, finest worsted though it was, rasped the bare skin of her legs, made her gasp as it scraped along her inner thighs as with his legs he spread hers wide and wedged his hips between.

The skin on her back had already come alive, teased by the roughly textured counterpane. Her senses reeled under the concerted impact of so much sensory stimulation—of his weight pinning her to the bed, of the anticipation that soared as she felt him reach between her thighs and release his erection.

He set the broad head at her entrance, then gripped her

hip, and thrust powerfully into her. Filled her with one long, forceful stroke, then withdrew and thrust in even more deeply.

He held her down and rode her, with long, powerful, pounding strokes; every thrust shifted her fractionally beneath him, every inch of her skin, every nerve, abraded each and every time.

Royce watched her, watched her body undulate beneath him, taking him in, wanting and accepting. He watched her face, saw passion overtake desire, saw it build and sweep her up, catch her in its heated coils, saw them tighten, gripping, driving.

He waited until she was nearing the peak. Releasing her hip, he closed his hand about her breast, lowered his head and took her mouth, claimed her, possessed her, there, too, as his body drove hers on.

She came apart beneath him more intensely than ever before.

Minerva gasped, sobbed as her world fractured, but the climax rolled on and on. He kept it going, thrusting deep within her, making her body shift slightly against the abrading fabrics, keeping her nerves flaring even as inner satiation swept through her.

It was like nothing they'd shared before. More blatant, more powerful.

More possessive.

She wasn't entirely surprised when, after she'd slumped, spent and done, yet with her nerves and senses still alive, still flickering, he slowed, then stopped and withdrew from her.

He left the bed, but she knew he wasn't done with her yet; he hadn't yet claimed his release. From the sounds that reached her, he was dispensing with his trousers.

Eyes closed, she lay sprawled, naked and ravished, across his bed and waited. She hadn't freed her hands from her nightgown, couldn't yet summon the energy.

And then he was back.

He knelt on the bed, grasped her hips, and flipped her over. She rolled bonelessly, wondering how . . . Straddling her legs, he slid one large hand down and around to splay over her lower belly, then he lifted her hips up and back so she was kneeling slumped forward before him.

Hands still tangled, she drew her arms in so she could lean on her forearms. He pressed close behind her, his knees outside hers, then she felt the engorged head of his erection nudge her entrance.

Then he was inside her.

Pressing deeper than he'd ever been. Her toes curled, then he withdrew and thrust in again, seating himself even more fully within her.

She struggled to catch her breath, lost all she'd gained as he again thrust into her hard and deep.

Holding her to him, open and helpless, he set up a steady, driving rhythm that had her fingers curling, sinking into and clutching the crimson-and-gold brocade as he pounded into her, then he varied the speed, then the depth, then rolling his hips, he somehow caressed her deep inside.

She could swear she could feel him at the back of her throat.

She wasn't sure she was going to survive this, not this degree of shuddering intimacy. This absolute degree of physical possession. She could feel the thunder in his blood, feel the wave of heated need and physical desperation rise and build.

When it crashed it would sweep them both away.

Gasping, frantic, she was clinging to reality when he leaned over her, one fist sinking into the bed alongside her shoulder. He still held her hips up, anchoring her, holding her captive for his relentless penetration

His belly curved over the back of her hips; she could feel the heat of his chest all across her back as he bowed his head. His breath sawed past her ear, then he nuzzled the curve of her neck.

"Just let go."

She heard the words from a long way away; they sounded like a plea.

"Just let it happen—let it come."

She heard his breath hitch, then he pressed deep inside her, shortened his thrusts so he was barely withdrawing at all, just moving deep within her, rolling his hips into hers, stroking her inside.

The climax hit her so hard, on so many levels, she screamed.

Her body seemed to pulse, and pulse, and pulse with successive waves of glory, each brighter, sharper, more glittering as sensation spiraled, erupted, splintered, then flashed down every overwrought nerve, sank and melted under every single inch of sensitized skin.

Completion had never been so absolute.

Royce held her through it. His erection sunk deep within her convulsing sheath, he felt every scalding ripple, every glorious moment of her release; eyes closed, he savored it, savored her, savored the fulfillment he found in her body, and in her.

His own release beckoned, tempted, lured, but while he'd wanted to take her like this, he also wanted more.

Greedy, but . . .

It took effort to rein his aroused and hungry body in, to gradually slow his deep but short thrusts until he held still within her. He took one last moment to drink in the sensation of her sheath gripping his erection all along its rigid length, the scalding velvet glove of all men's fantasies.

Only when he was sure he had his body under full control did he risk pulling back from her.

Bracing her body with one hand, with the other he wrestled the covers down, then scooped her up and laid her back down. High in his bed, her head and shoulders cushioned in the pile of pillows, her delicate, flushed skin soothed by the cool silk of his sheets.

He sat back on his ankles, and looked at her, some primitive part of his psyche gloating. He fixed the image in his mind—her hair a rumpled silken veil flung over his pillows, her lush body lax and sated, skin still flushed, nipples still peaked, her hips and breasts bearing the telltale marks of his possession.

Exactly as he always wanted to see her.

Her head tilted slightly on the pillows; from beneath her long lashes, her golden eyes glinted as she watched him studying her. Her gaze slowly trailed down his body.

Then she raised one arm, reached out, and closed her fingers about his aching erection. She stroked slowly down, then lightly up.

Then she released him, settled deeper into the pillows, held out her arms to him, and spread her legs wide.

He went to her, into her arms, settled between her widespread thighs, and sank, so easily, into her body, into her embrace.

Where he belonged.

He no longer doubted that; he buried his face in the hollow between her shoulder and throat, and with long, slow strokes, gave himself up to her.

Felt her accept him, her arms wrapping around his shoulders, her hands spread on his back, her legs rising to clasp his flanks as she tilted her hips and drew him yet deeper.

As she opened herself to him so he could even more deeply lose himself in her.

His release rolled over him in long shuddering waves.

Eyes closed, Minerva held him close, felt the golden joy of such passionate intimacy well and suffuse her. And knew in her heart, knew to her soul, that letting him go was going to slay her.

Devastate her.

She'd always known that would be the price for falling in love with him.

But she had.

She could swear and curse her own stupidity, but nothing could change reality. Their joint realities, which meant they would part.

Destinies weren't easily changed.

He'd slumped upon her, heavy beyond belief, yet she found his weight curiously comforting. As if her earlier physical surrender was balanced by his.

Their combined heat slowly dissipated and the night air wafted over their cooling bodies. Wriggling and reaching, she managed to snag the edge of the covers and, tugging and flicking, drew the sheet up over them both.

Closing her eyes, she let the familiar warmth enfold her, and drifted, but when he stirred and lifted from her, she came fully, determinedly awake.

He noticed. He met her gaze, then flopped back on the pillows alongside her, reaching to draw her to him, into his side, her head on his shoulder.

That was how they normally slept, but while she let him hold her within his arm, she came up so she could look at his face.

He met her eyes, a faint lift to his brows; she sensed a certain wariness, although, as usual, nothing showed in his face.

Reminding herself she was dealing with a Varisey— a naked male one—and that subtlety therefore would be wasted, she went straight to the question she wanted to ask. "What happened to your five-nights rule?"

He blinked. Twice. But he didn't look away. "That doesn't apply to you."

She opened her eyes wide. "Indeed? So what rule does apply to me? Ten nights?"

His eyes narrowed fractionally. "The only rule that applies to you is that my bed—wherever it is—is yours. There is no-where else I will allow you to sleep but with me." One dark brow arched, openly arrogant. "I trust that's clear?"

She stared into his dark eyes. He wasn't a fool; he had to marry—and she wouldn't stay; he knew that.

But had he accepted that?

After a long moment, she asked, "What aren't you telling me?"

It wasn't his face that gave him away; it was the faint but definite tension that infused the hard body beneath hers.

He half shrugged, then settled his shoulders deeper into the bed, urging her down again. "Earlier, when you weren't here, I thought you were sulking."

A change of subject, not an answer. "After learning about your five-nights rule, then having you ignore me all evening as if I didn't exist, I thought you were finished with me." Her tone stated very clearly how she'd felt about that.

Having relieved her lingering ire, she yielded to his importuning, slumped back into his arms and laid her head on his shoulder.

"No." His voice was low; his lips brushed her temple. "Never that."

The last words were soft, but definite—and that telltale tension hadn't left him.

Never?

What was he planning?

Given how she felt—how deeply he'd already unwittingly snared her—she had to know. Hands on his chest, she pushed up again. Tried to, but his arms didn't give. She wriggled, got nowhere, so she pinched him. Hard.

He flinched, muttered something distinctly uncomplimentary, but let her lift her shoulders enough to look into his face.

She searched his eyes, replayed all he'd said, and how he'd said it. His plan for her, whatever it was, revolved about one question. She narrowed her eyes on his. "Who have you decided to marry?"

If she could get him to declare that, she could accept it, know it for fact, and prepare herself to hand over her keys, relinquish her place in his bed to another, and leave Wolverstone. *That* was her destiny, but while he refused to name his bride, he could draw their liaison out indefinitely, and draw her ever deeper into love—so that when she did have to leave, leaving him would shatter her.

She had to make him define the end of their affair.

He held her gaze, utterly expressionless. Utterly implacable.

She refused to back down. "Lady Ashton confirmed that your failure to make the promised announcement has been widely noted. You're going to have to make it soon, or we'll have Lady Osbaldestone back up here, in a foul mood. And in case you're wondering, her foul mood will trump your temper. She will make you feel as small as a flea. So stop pretending you can change your destiny, and just tell me so we can announce it."

So she could organize to leave him.

Royce was too adept at reading between other people's lines to miss her underlying thoughts . . . but he had to tell her. She'd just handed him the perfect opening to break the news to her and propose, but . . . he didn't want to yet. Wasn't yet sure enough of her response. Of her.

Beneath the covers, she shifted, sliding one long leg over his waist, then easing across and sitting up, straddling him, the better to look into his face. Her eyes, the glorious autumn hues still darkened by recent passion, narrowed and bored into his, golden sparks of will and determination flaring in their depths. "*Have* you chosen your bride?"

That he could answer. "Yes."

"Have you contacted her?"

"I'm negotiating with her as we speak."

"Who is she? Do I know her?"

She wasn't going to let him slide around her again. Jaw setting, eyes locked on hers, he ground out, "Yes."

When he didn't say anything more, she clutched his upper arms as if to shake him—or hold him so he couldn't escape. "What's her name?"

Her eyes held his. He was going to have to speak now. Engage with her now. He was going to have to find some way—forge some path through the mire . . . He searched her eyes, desperate for some hint of a way forward.

Her fingers tightened, nails digging in, then she uttered a frustrated sound; releasing him, she raised her palms, along with her face, to the canopy. "*Why* are you being so damned difficult about this?"

Something within him snapped. "Because it *is* difficult."

Her head came down; she pinned him with her eyes. "*Why*, for heaven's sake? *Who* is she?"

Lips thin, he locked his gaze with hers. "You."

All expression fled from her face, from her eyes. "What?"

"*You.*" He poured every ounce of his certainty, his determination, into the words. "I've chosen you."

Her eyes flared wide; her expression wasn't one he could place—she wasn't afraid of him. She started to draw back, pull away; he locked his hands about her waist.

"No." The word was weak, her eyes still wide; her expression looked strangely bleak. Abruptly she dragged in a breath, and shook her head. "No, no, no. I told you—"

"Yes. I know." He made the words terse enough to cut her off. "But here's something—some things—*you* don't know." He caught her gaze. "I took you up to Lord's Seat lookout, but I never told you why. I took you there to ask you to marry me—but I got distracted. I let you distract me into getting you into my bed first—and *then* you turned your virginity, the fact I'd taken it, into an even bigger hurdle."

She blinked at him. "You wanted to ask me then?"

"I'd planned to—on Lord's Seat, and then here on that first night. But your declaration . . ." He paused.

Her eyes narrowed again; her lips thinned. "You didn't give up—you never give up. You set out to manipulate me—that's what all this"—she waved her arms, encompassing the huge bed—"has been about, hasn't it? You've been working to change my mind!"

With a disgusted snort, she tried to get off him. He tightened his grip on her waist, kept her exactly where she was, straddling him. She tried to fight loose, tried to pry his fingers away, wriggled and squirmed.

"No." He bit the word off with sufficient force to have her look at him again—and grow still. He trapped her gaze, held it. "It wasn't like that—it was *never* about manipulating you. I don't want you by stealth—I want your willing agreement. All *this* has been about *convincing* you. About showing you how well you fit the position of my duchess."

Through his hands, he sensed her quietening, sensed that he'd caught her attention, however unwilling. He dragged in a breath. "Now you've forced my hand, the least you can do is listen. Listen to why I think we'd suit—why I want you and only you as my wife."

Trapped in his dark eyes, Minerva didn't know what to think. She couldn't tell what she felt; emotions roiled and churned and tumbled through her. She knew he was telling the truth; veracity rang in his tone. He rarely lied, and he was speaking in terms that were utterly unambiguous.

He took her silence as acquiescence. Still holding her captive, still holding her gaze, he went on, "I want you as my wife because you—and only you—can give me everything I need, and want, in my duchess. The socially prescribed aspects are the most minor—your birth is more than adequate, as is your fortune. While an announcement of our betrothal might take many by surprise, it won't in any way be considered a mésalliance—from society's perspective, you're entirely suitable."

Pausing, he drew breath, but his eyes never left hers; she had never before felt so much the absolute focus of his attention, his will, his very being. "While there are many ladies who would be suitable on those counts, it's in all the other aspects that you excel. I need—demonstrably need—a lady by my side who understands the prevailing social and political responsibilities and dynamics of the dukedom as, courtesy of my exile, I do not. I need someone I can trust implicitly to guide me through the shoals—as you did at the funeral. I need a lady I can rely on to have the backbone to confront me when I'm wrong—someone who isn't afraid of my temper. Almost everyone is, but you never have been—among females that alone makes you unique."

Royce didn't dare take his eyes from hers. She was listening, following—understanding. "I also need—and want—a duchess who is attuned to and devoted to the dukedom's interests, and first and last to Wolverstone itself. To the estate, the people, the community. Wolverstone is not just a castle—it never has been. I need a lady who understands that, who will be as committed to it as I am. As you already are."

The next breath he dragged in shook; his lungs were tight, his chest felt compressed, but he had to say the rest—had to step off the beaten path and take a chance. "Lastly, I . . ." He searched her autumn eyes. "Need—and want—a lady I care about. *Not* the customary Varisey bride. I want . . . to try and have more of a marriage, a more complete marriage—one based on more than calculation and convenience. For that I need a lady I can spend my life with, one I can share my life with from now into the future. I don't want to occasionally visit my duchess's bed—I want her in my bed, this bed, every night for all the nights to come." He paused, then said, "For all those reasons, I need *you* as my bride. Of all the women I might have, no other will do. I can't imagine . . . feeling as I do about any other. There never has been any other I've slept beside through the night, no other I've ever wanted to keep with me through the dawn." He held her gaze. "I want you, I desire you—and only you will do."

Staring into his dark eyes, Minerva felt her emotions surge and swell; she was in very deep water, in danger of being swept away. Being pulled under; the tug of his words, of his lure, was that strong—strong enough to tempt her, even her, even though she knew the price . . . she frowned. "Are you saying that you'll remain faithful to your duchess?"

"Not to my duchess. But to you? Yes."

Oh, clever answer; her heart skipped a beat. She looked into his eyes, saw his implacable, immovable will looking back—and the room spun. She drew an unsteady breath; the planets had just realigned. A Varisey was promising fidelity. "What brought this on?"

What on earth had proved strong enough to bring him to this?

He didn't immediately answer, but his eyes remained steady on hers.

Eventually he said, "I've seen over the years what Rupert, Miles, and Gerald have found with Rose, Eleanor, and Alice. I've spent more time in their households than in this one—and what they have is what I want. I've more recently seen my ex-colleagues find their brides—and they, too, found wives and marriages that offered far more than convenience and dynastic advance."

He shifted slightly beneath her, for the first time glanced beyond her, but then he brought his gaze back to her face—forced it back. His jaw tightened. "Then the grandes dames came and made clear what they expected—and not one thought that I would want, much less deserved, anything better than the customary Varisey marriage." His voice hardened. "But they were wrong. I want *you*—and I want more."

She inwardly shivered. She would have sworn she didn't outwardly, but his hands, until then warm and strong about her waist, left her, and he reached for the counterpane, drew it up to drape around and over her shoulders. She caught the edges, drew them closer. She wasn't cold; she was emotionally shaken.

To her toes.

"I . . ." She refocused on him.

He was looking at his hands adjusting the counterpane around her. "Before you say anything . . . when I went to see Hamish today, I asked his advice about what I might say to you to convince you to accept my suit." His eyes lifted and met hers. "He told me I should tell you that I loved you."

She couldn't breathe; she was trapped in the unfathomable darkness of his eyes.

They remained locked with hers. "He told me that you would want me to say that—to claim I loved you." He drew breath, went on, "I will never lie to you—if I could tell you I loved you, I would. I will do *anything* I need to to make you mine, to have you as my duchess—*except* lie to you."

He seemed to have as much trouble breathing as she did;

the next breath he drew shuddered. He let it out as his eyes searched hers. "I care for you, in a way and to a depth that I care for no one else. But we both know I can't say I love you. We both know why. As a Varisey I don't know the first thing about love, much less how to make it happen. I don't even know if the emotion exists within me. But what I can— and will—promise, is that I will try. For *you*, I will try—I will give you everything I have in me, but I can't promise it'll be enough. I can promise to try, but I can't promise I'll succeed." He held her gaze unflinchingly. "I can't promise to love you because I don't know if I can."

Moments passed; she remained immersed in his eyes, seeing, hearing, knowing. Finally she drew in a long, slow breath, refocused on his face, looked again into those dark, tempestuous eyes. "*If* I agree to marry you, will you promise me that? Promise you'll remain faithful, and that you'll try?"

The answer was immediate, uncompromising. "Yes. For you, I'll promise that, in whatever way, whatever words, you wish."

She felt strung tight, emotionally tense—poised on a wire above an abyss. Assessing her tension made her aware of his; beneath her thighs, her bottom, his muscles were all steel—he otherwise hid it well, his uncertainty.

Gazes locked, they were both teetering. She drew breath, and pulled back. "I need to think." She swiftly replayed his words, arched a brow. "You haven't actually proposed."

He was silent for a moment, then succinctly stated, "I'll propose when you're ready to accept."

"I'm not ready yet."

"I know."

She studied him, sensed his uncertainty, but even more his unwavering determination. "You've surprised me." She'd thought of marrying him, fantasized and dreamed of it, but she'd never thought it might come to be—any more than she'd thought she would share his bed, let alone on a regular basis, yet here she was—a warning in itself. "A large part of me wants to say yes, please ask, but becoming your duchess isn't something I can decide on impulse."

He'd offered her everything her heart could desire—*short* of promising her his. In one arrogant sweep, he'd moved them into a landscape she'd never imagined might exist— and in which there were no familiar landmarks.

"You've thrown me into complete mental turmoil." Her thoughts were chaotic, her emotions more so; her mind was a seething cauldron in which well-known fears battled unexpected hopes, uncataloged desires, unsuspected needs.

Still he said nothing, too wise to press.

Indeed. She couldn't let him, or her wilder self, rush her into this—a marriage that, if it went wrong, guaranteed emotional obliteration. "You're going to have to give me time. I need to think."

He didn't protest.

She dragged in a breath, threw him a warning look, then slid off him, back to her side of the bed; turning onto her side, facing away from him, she pulled the covers up over her shoulders and snuggled down.

After a moment of regarding her through the dark, Royce turned and slid down in the bed, spooning his body around hers. Sliding his arm over her waist, he eased her back against him.

She humphed softly, but wriggled back, setting her hips against his abdomen. With a small sigh, she relaxed slightly.

He was still tense, his gut still churning. So much of his life, his future, was now riding on this, on her; he'd just placed his life in her hands—at least she hadn't handed it straight back.

Which, realistically, was all he could ask of her at that point.

Lifting her hair aside, he pressed a kiss to her nape. "Go to sleep. You can take whatever time you need to think."

After a moment, he murmured, "But when Lady Osbalde-stone comes back up here and demands who I've chosen as my bride, I'll have to tell her."

Minerva snorted. Her lips curved, then, against every last expectation, she did as he'd bid her and fell fast asleep.

Seventeen

Hamish O'Loughlin, you mangy Scot, how dare you tell Royce to tell me he loves me!"

"Huh?" Hamish looked up from the sheep he was examining.

Folding her arms, Minerva fell to pacing alongside the pen.

Hamish studied her face. "You didn't want to hear that he loves you?"

"Of *course* I would *love* to hear that he loves me—but how can he say such a thing? He's a Varisey, for heaven's sake."

"Hmm." Letting the sheep jump away, Hamish leaned against the railing. "Perhaps the same way I tell Moll that I love her."

"But that's *you*. You're not—" She broke off. Halting, head rising, she blinked at him.

He gave her a cynical smile. "Aye—think on it. I'm as much a Varisey as he is."

She frowned. "But you're not . . ." She waved south, over the hills.

"Castle-bred? True. But perhaps that just means I never believed I wouldn't love, not when the right woman came along." He studied her face. "He didn't tell you, did he?"

"No—he was honest. He says he'll try—that he wants more of his marriage, but"—she drew in a huge breath—"he can't promise to love me because he doesn't know if he can."

Hamish made a disgusted sound. "You're a right pair. You've been in love with him—or at least waiting to fall in love with him—for decades, and now you have—"

"You can't know that." She stared at him.

"Of course, I can. Not that he's said all that much, but I can read between his lines, and yours, well enough—and you're here, aren't you?"

She frowned harder.

"Aye—it's as I thought." Hamish let himself out of the pen, latching the gate behind him. Leaning back against it, he looked at her. "You both need to take a good long look at each other. What do you think has made him even consider having a different sort of marriage? A love match—isn't that what society calls them? Why do you imagine they're called that?"

She scowled at him. "You're making it sound simple and easy."

Hamish nodded his great head. "Aye—that's how love is. Simple, straightforward, and easy. It just happens. Where it gets complicated is when you try to think too much, to rationalize it, make sense of it, pick it apart—it's not like that." He pushed away from the gate, and started lumbering up the path; she fell in beside him. "But if you must keep thinking, think on this—love happens, just like a disease. And like any disease, the easiest way to tell someone's caught it is to look for the symptoms. I've known Royce longer than you have, and he's got every last symptom. He might not *know* he loves you, but he feels it—he acts on it."

They'd reached the yard where she'd left Rangonel. Hamish halted and looked down at her. "The truth is, lass, he might never be able to honestly, knowingly, tell you he loves you—but that doesn't mean he doesn't."

She grimaced, rubbed a gloved finger in the center of her forehead. "You've only given me *more* to think about."

Hamish grinned. "Aye, well, if you must think, the least you can do is think of the right things."

As Minerva rode south across the border and down through the hills, she had plenty of time to think of Royce and his symptoms. Plenty of time to ponder all Hamish had said; while helping her to her saddle, he'd reminded her that the late duchess had been unwaveringly faithful, not to her husband, but to her longtime lover, Sidney Camberwell.

The duchess and Camberwell had been together for over twenty years; remembering all she'd seen of the pair, thinking of "symptoms," she had to conclude they'd been very much in love.

Perhaps Hamish was right; Royce could and might love her.

Regardless, she had to make up her mind, and soon—he hadn't been joking when he'd mentioned Lady Osbaldestone—which was why she'd come out riding; Hamish's farm had seemed an obvious destination.

Take whatever time you need to think.

She knew Royce far too well not to know that he'd meant: Take whatever time you need to think *as long as you agree to be my wife.*

He would do everything in his power to ensure she did; henceforth he would feel completely justified in doing whatever it took to make her agree.

In his case, "whatever it took" covered a great deal—as he'd demonstrated that morning, with shattering results. She'd escaped only because the sun had risen. If it hadn't, she would be at his mercy still.

In public, however, over breakfast, and then later when they'd met for their usual meeting in his study with Handley in attendance and Jeffers by the door, he'd behaved with exemplary decorum; she couldn't fault him in that—while in private he might pressure her to decide quickly in his favor, he did nothing to raise speculation in others.

"For which," she assured the hills at large, "I'm duly grateful. The last thing I need is Margaret, Aurelia, and Susannah hectoring me. I don't even know which way they'd fall—for or against."

An interesting question, but beside the point. She didn't care what they thought, and Royce cared even less.

For the umpteenth time, she replayed his arguments. Most confirmed what she'd seen from the start; marrying her would be the best option for him, especially given his commitment to Wolverstone and to the dukedom as a whole. What didn't fit the mold of convenience and comfort was his desire for a different sort of marriage; she couldn't question the reality of that—he'd had to force himself to reveal it, and she'd felt his sincerity to her bones.

And he did care for her, in his own arrogant, high-handed way. There was an undeniably seductive triumph in being the only woman to have ever made a Varisey think of anything even approaching love. And especially Royce—to claim him as her own . . . but that was a piece of self-seduction.

If he did love her, would it last?

If he loved her as she loved him . . .

She frowned at Rangonel's ears. "Regardless of Hamish's opinion, I still have a *lot* to think through."

Royce was in his study working through his correspondence with Handley when Jeffers tapped and opened the door. He looked up, arched a brow.

"Three ladies and a gentleman have arrived, Your Grace. The ladies are insisting on seeing you immediately."

He inwardly frowned. "Their names?"

"The Marchioness of Dearne, the Countess of Lostwithiel, and Lady Clarice Warnefleet, Your Grace. The gentleman is Lord Warnefleet."

"The gentleman isn't asking to see me as well?"

"No, Your Grace. Just the ladies."

Which was Jack Warnefleet's way of warning him what

the subject his wife and her two cronies wished to discuss was. "Thank you, Jeffers. Show the ladies up. Tell Retford to make Lord Warnefleet comfortable in the library."

As the door closed, he glanced at Handley. "We'll have to continue this later. I'll ring when I'm free."

Handley nodded, gathered his papers, rose, and left. Royce stared at the closed door. There seemed little point in wondering what message Letitia, Penny, and Clarice had for him; he would know soon enough.

Less than a minute later, Jeffers opened the door, and the ladies—three of the seven wives of his ex-colleagues of the Bastion Club—swept in. Rising, he acknowledged their formal curtsies, then waved them to the chairs Jeffers angled before the desk.

He waited until they'd settled, then, dismissing Jeffers with a nod, resumed his seat. As the door closed, he let his gaze sweep the three striking faces before him. "Ladies. Permit me to guess—I owe this pleasure to Lady Osbaldestone."

"And all the others." Letitia, flanked by Penny and Clarice, flung her arms wide. "The entire pantheon of tonnish grandes dames."

He let his brows rise. "Why, if I might ask, you—more specifically, why all three of you?"

Letitia grimaced. "I was visiting Clarice and Jack in Gloucestershire while Christian dealt with business in London. Penny had come up to join us for a few days when Christian relayed a summons from Lady Osbaldestone insisting I attend her immediately in London on a matter of great urgency."

"Naturally," Clarice said, "Letitia had to go, and Penny and I decided we could do with a week in London, so we went, too."

"But," Penny took up the tale, "the instant Lady Osbaldestone laid eyes on us, she made us joint emissaries with Letitia to carry the collective message of the grandes dames to your ears."

"I suspect," Clarice said, "that she thought you might be able to avoid Letitia, but you wouldn't be able to slide around all three of us."

Clarice glanced at the other two, who returned her regard, then all three pairs of feminine eyes turned on him.

He raised his brows. "Your message?"

It was Letitia who answered. "You are hereby warned that unless you do as you intimated and announce your duchess-to-be forthwith, you will have to cope with a fleet of carriages turning up at your gates. And, of course, the occupants of those carriages won't be the sort you can easily turn away." She shrugged. "Their version was rather more formal, but that's the gist of it."

Penny frowned. "Actually, it seemed as if you have quite a few people in residence already—and more arriving."

"My sisters are hosting a house party coincident with the local parish fair. It used to be a family tradition, but lapsed after my mother died." He focused on Letitia. "Is there a time limit on the grandes dames' threat?"

Letitia glanced at Clarice.

"We got the impression the limit is now." Clarice widened her eyes at him. "Or more precisely, your period of grace expires at the time a missive from us confirming your noncompliance reaches Lady Osbaldestone."

He tapped a finger on his blotter, letting his gaze sweep their faces again. Lady Osbaldestone had chosen well; with these three, intimidation wouldn't work. And while he might have been able to divert—subvert—Letitia, with the three of them reinforcing each other, he stood not a chance.

Lips firming, he nodded. "You may report to the beldames that I have, indeed, chosen a bride—"

"Excellent!" Letitia beamed. "So you can draft an announcement, and we can take it back to London."

"However"—he continued as if she hadn't spoken—"the lady in question has yet to accept the position."

They stared at him.

Clarice recovered first. "What is she? Deaf, dumb, blind—or all three?"

That surprised a laugh from him, then he shook his head. "It's the reverse—she's too damned insightful for my good. And please do include that in your report—it will make her ladyship's day. Regardless, an announcement in the *Gazette* at this point could well prove inimical to our mutual goal."

All three ladies fixed intrigued gazes on him. He regarded them impassively. "Is there anything else?"

"Who is she?" Letitia demanded. "You can't just dangle a tale like that before us, and not give us her name."

"Actually, I can. You don't need to know." They'd guess very quickly; he had as much confidence in their intelligence—individually and collectively—as he had in their husbands'.

Three pairs of eyes narrowed; three expressions grew flinty.

Penny informed him, "We're under orders to remain here—under your feet—until you send a notice to the *Gazette*."

Their continued presence might well work in his favor. Their husbands weren't all that different from him—and Minerva had been starved of the companionship of females she could trust, confide in, and ask for advice. And these three might be disposed to help his cause.

Of course, they'd probably view it as assisting Cupid. Just as long as they succeeded, he didn't care. "You're very welcome to stay and join the festivities my sisters have planned." Rising, he crossed to the bellpull. "I believe my chatelaine, Minerva Chesterton, is presently out, but she should return shortly. Meanwhile I'm sure my staff will make you comfortable."

All three frowned.

Retford arrived, and he gave orders for their accommodation. They rose, distinctly haughty, and increasingly suspicious.

He ushered them to the door. "I'll leave you to get settled.

No doubt Minerva will look in on you as soon as she returns. I'll see you at dinner—until then, you must excuse me. Business calls."

They narrowed their eyes at him, but consented to follow Retford.

Letitia, the last to leave, looked him in the eye. "You know we'll hound you until you tell us this amazingly insightful lady's name."

Unperturbed, he bowed her out; they'd know his lady's name before he reached the drawing room that evening.

With an irritated "humph!" Letitia went.

Closing the door, he turned back to his desk.

And let his brows rise. Lady Osbaldestone and the other beldames might just have helped.

Returning from her ride, Minerva walked into the front hall to discover a handsome gentleman ambling about admiring the paintings.

He turned at the sound of her boot steps, and smiled charmingly.

"Good morning." Despite his country-elegant attire, and that smile, she sensed a familiar hardness behind his façade. "Can I help you?"

He bowed. "Jack Warnefleet, ma'am."

She glanced around, wondering where Retford was. "Have you just arrived?"

"No." He smiled again. "I was shown into the library, but I've studied all the paintings there. My wife and two of her friends are upstairs, bearding Dal—Wolverstone—in his den." Hazel eyes twinkled. "I thought I ought to come out here in case a precipitous retreat was in order."

He'd nearly said Dalziel, which meant he was an acquaintance from Whitehall. She held out her hand. "I'm Miss Chesterton. I act as chatelaine here."

He bowed over her hand. "Delighted, my dear. I have to admit I have no idea whether we'll be staying or—" He broke off and looked up the stairs. "Ah—here they are."

They both turned as three ladies preceded Retford down the stairs. Minerva recognized Letitia and smiled.

Beside her, Jack Warnefleet murmured, "And from their frowns, I suspect we're staying."

She didn't get a chance to ask what he meant; Letitia, seeing her, dispensed with her frown and came hurrying down to embrace her.

"Minerva—just who we need." Letitia turned as the other two ladies joined them. "I don't believe you've met Lady Clarice, for her sins Lady Warnefleet, wife of this reprobate." She flicked a hand at Jack, who merely grinned. "And this is Lady Penelope, Countess of Lostwithiel—her husband is Charles, another of Royce's ex-operatives, as is Jack here."

Minerva touched hands with the other two ladies. "Welcome to Wolverstone Castle. I gather you're staying." She glanced at Retford. "Rooms in the west wing, I think, Retford." The other guests were mostly in the south and east wings.

"Indeed, ma'am. I'll have the ladies' and gentleman's bags taken up immediately."

"Thank you." Linking arms, Letitia leaned close. "Is there somewhere we can talk privately?"

"Of course." Minerva glanced at Retford. "If you would bring tea to the duchess's morning room?"

"At once, ma'am."

She looked at Jack Warnefleet. "Sir?"

He smiled. "Jack. And I believe I'll follow the bags and find our room." He inclined his head to them all. "I'll catch up with you at luncheon."

"You'll hear the gong," she assured him.

With a salute, he started up the stairs in the wake of two footmen hefting a trunk.

Minerva waved the ladies up, too. "Come up, and we can be comfortable."

In the duchess's morning room, they sank onto the sofas, then Retford arrived with a tray. After pouring and handing around the cups and a plate of cakes, Minerva sat back, sipped, caught Letitia's eye, and raised her brows.

Letitia set down her cup. "The reason we're here is that the grandes dames have lost patience and are insisting Royce announce his betrothal forthwith." She grimaced. "Of course, he's now told us that the lady he's chosen has yet to accept his suit. Apparently she has reservations, but he refuses to tell us who she is." She fixed her brilliant hazel gaze on Minerva. "Do you know her name?"

She didn't know what to say. He'd said he would tell, but he hadn't. And she hadn't anticipated such a question, especially from a friend.

A frown started to form in Letitia's eyes, but it was Clarice who set her cup on her saucer and, staring at Minerva's face, said, "Aha! 'She' is *you*." Her brows rose. "Well, well."

Letitia's eyes flew wide. She read confirmation in Minerva's expression, and delight filled her face. "It *is* you! He's chosen you. Well! I would never have credited him with so much good sense."

Head tilted, Penny said, "We're not wrong, are we? He has asked you to be his bride?"

Minerva grimaced lightly. "Not exactly—not yet—but yes, he wants me to be his duchess."

Letitia's frown returned. "Pray excuse me if I'm wrong, but I always sensed that you . . . well, that you wouldn't reject his advances."

Minerva stared at her. "Please tell me I wasn't that obvious."

"No, you weren't—it was just something about the way you paid attention whenever he was mentioned." Letitia shrugged. "It was probably feeling the same way about Christian that made me notice."

Minerva felt mildly relieved.

"So," Clarice asked, "why are you hesitating over accepting his suit?"

Minerva looked from one face to the other. "He's a Varisey."

Letitia's face blanked. "Oh."

"Ah . . ." Penny grimaced.

Slowly, Clarice nodded. "I see. Not being a giddy miss

with more hair than wit, you want . . ." She glanced at the other two. "What we've all been lucky enough to find."

Minerva exhaled. "Precisely." They understood.

After a moment, Penny frowned. "But you haven't refused him."

Minerva met Penny's eyes, then set down her cup and rose; swinging around behind the sofa, she started to pace. "It's not that simple." No matter what Hamish thought.

The others watched her, waited.

She needed help; Letitia was an old friend, and they all had marriages based on love—and they'd immediately understood. She halted, briefly closed her eyes. "I didn't mean to fall in love with him."

"We rarely do," Clarice murmured. "It simply happens."

Opening her eyes, she inclined her head. "So I've realized." She resumed her pacing. "Since he returned, well, he wanted me, and I am twenty-nine. I thought I could be . . . close to him for just a little while without risking my heart. But I was wrong."

"*Wrong?*" Letitia pityingly shook her head. "You've been infatuated with Royce Varisey for decades, and you thought you could be with him—by which I assume you mean you're sharing his bed—and *not* fall in love with him? My dear Minerva, you weren't just *mistaken.*"

"No, I know. I was a fool. But falling in love with him wouldn't have mattered if he hadn't decided to make me his duchess."

Letitia frowned. "When did he decide that?"

"Weeks ago. After the grandes dames saw him in his study. But"—Minerva forced herself to go on—"that's not the whole of my problem."

She continued pacing, ordering the elements of her explanation in her mind. "I've always been set on a marriage based on love—I've had offers before, a good many, and never been tempted. My parents' marriage was based on love, and I've never wanted anything else. At first . . . I had no idea Royce had his eye on me. I thought I could hide my interest in him, be the dutiful chatelaine, and then leave once his wife took up the reins. Then . . . he wanted me, and I thought it would be safe enough, given his marriage was imminent. I thought love would need time to grow—but it didn't."

Letitia nodded. "It can strike in an instant."

"So I'd heard, but I never really believed . . . regardless, once I realized I'd fallen in love with him, I still thought, given his marriage had to occur soon, that I'd be able to leave, if not heart-whole, then at least with dignity. I've never been in love before, and if I never was again, no one would know but me."

Minerva paused in her pacing, and raised her head. "Then he told me I was the lady he wanted as his duchess."

"Of course he *told* you." Penny humphed.

Minerva nodded. "Indeed—but I'd always known that the last thing, the *very* last thing I should do if I wanted a marriage based on love, was to marry Royce, or any Varisey. No Varisey marriage in history has been based on love, or in any way included love." She drew a deep breath, her gaze fixed across the room. "Until last night, I believed that if I married Royce, ours would be a typical Varisey arrangement, and he, and everyone else—all the ton, in fact—would expect me to stand meekly by while he indulged as he wished with any lady who took his fancy."

Frowning, Letitia nodded. "The typical Varisey union."

Minerva inclined her head. "And I couldn't do that. Even before I fell in love with him, I knew I'd never be able to stand that—that knowing he didn't love me as I loved him, when he went to another's bed, and then another's, I'd wither, pine, and go mad like Caro Lamb."

Their expressions stated that they fully understood.

"So what happened last night?" Clarice asked.

That needed another deep breath. "Last night, Royce swore that if I agree to be his duchess, he'll be faithful."

Complete silence reigned for several minutes.

Eventually, Penny said, "I can see how that . . . changes things."

Clarice grimaced. "If it weren't Royce we were talking about, I'd ask if you believed him."

Letitia snorted. "If he says he will, let alone swears he will, he will."

Minerva nodded. "Exactly. And at first glance, that should make it easy for me to agree, but, as I realized once I managed to find time to think, while him being faithful clears away one problem, it creates another."

Gripping the back of the sofa, she focused on the tea tray on the low table between the sofas. "He says he will never lie to me, and that I accept. He says he cares for me as he cares for no other—and I accept that, too. But what happens when, if we wed, and a few years pass, and he no longer comes to my bed." She raised her gaze, and met Clarice's, then Penny's, then lastly Letitia's. "How am I going to feel then? Knowing he no longer desires me, but because of his vow, is simply . . ." She gestured. "*Existing*. Abstaining. Him, of all men."

They didn't rush to reassure her.

Eventually, Letitia sighed. "That's not a comforting—or comfortable—thought."

Clarice grimaced. Penny did, too.

"If he loved me," Minerva said, "the problem wouldn't exist. But he's been brutally honest—and I can't fault him in that. He will promise me all that's in his power to give, but he won't promise love. He can't. He admitted he doesn't know if he even has it in him to give."

Clarice humphed. "That's not so odd—they never do know."

"Which leads me to ask"—Letitia swung to look up at her—"are you *sure* he isn't in love with you, but doesn't know it?"

Penny leaned forward. "If you haven't been in love before . . . are you sure you would know if he was?"

Minerva was silent for a long moment. "Someone recently told me that love is like a disease, and the easiest way to know if someone's caught it is to look for the symptoms."

"Excellent advice," Clarice affirmed.

Penny nodded. "Love isn't a passive emotion—it makes you do things you wouldn't normally do."

"It makes you take risks you otherwise wouldn't." Letitia looked at Minerva. "So what do you think? Might Royce be in love with you, but not know?"

A catalog of minor incidents, comments, tiny revelations, all the little things about him that had surprised her, ran though her mind, but it was Hamish's comment echoing her own earlier thought that held most weight. What on earth had proved strong enough to move him, the man he was, to break with long tradition and actively seek—want enough to strive for—a different marriage, one that, if she'd understood him correctly, he hoped as much as she might come to encompass love?

"Yes." She slowly nodded. "He might."

If she accepted the position of Royce's duchess, from the instant she said "yes" there would be no turning back.

The luncheon gong had curtailed her discussion with the other ladies; neither Royce nor Jack Warnefleet had appeared, but the rest of the company had, making it impossible to further pursue their debate—at least not aloud.

She spent most of the meal mentally enumerating Royce's symptoms, but while indicative, neither singly nor collectively were they conclusive.

Retford waylaid her on her way back to the morning room; the others went ahead while she detoured to assess the spirits store. After conferring with Retford, Cranny, and Cook, on impulse she asked after Trevor.

Fate smiled, and she found him alone in the ironing room, busily ironing his master's cravats. He saw her as she entered, quickly set the iron down, and turned.

"No, no." She waved him back to the board. "Don't stop on my account."

Hesitantly, he picked up the iron from the stand perched above a fire in the small hearth. "Can I help you with something, ma'am?"

This could be supremely embarrassing, but she had to ask, had to know. She drew breath, and plunged in. "Trevor—you've been with His Grace for some time, have you not?"

"Over seventeen years, ma'am."

"Indeed. Just so. So you would know if there's anything in the way in which he behaves toward me that differs from how he's behaved in the past with other ladies."

The iron froze in midair. Trevor looked at her, and blinked.

Embarrassment clutched at her chest; she hurried to add, "Of course, I will understand completely if you feel your duty to His Grace precludes you from answering."

"No, no—I can answer." Trevor blinked again, and his expression eased. "My answer, ma'am, is that I really can't say."

"Oh." She deflated; all that whipping up her courage for nothing.

But Trevor hadn't finished. "I've never known about any other ladies, you see. He never brought any home."

"He didn't?"

His attention on the strip of linen he was carefully flattening, Trevor shook his head. "Never. Cardinal rule. Always their beds, never his."

Minerva stared at the valet for a long moment, then she nodded and turned away. "Thank you, Trevor."

"My pleasure, ma'am."

"*Well!* That's encouraging." Perched on the arm of one of the sofas, Clarice watched her pace. "Especially if he's been so adamant over using *his* bed, not yours."

Letitia and Penny, seated on the other sofa, nodded in agreement.

"Yes, *but*," Minerva said, "who's to say that it's not just him viewing me as his duchess. He'd made up his mind I should marry him before he seduced me, so it's entirely in character for him to insist on treating me as if I already were what he wants me to be—his wife."

Letitia made a rude sound. "If Royce decided to ignore your wishes and roll over you, horse, foot, and guns, he'd have simply sent a notice to the *Gazette*—and *then* informed you of your impending change in station. That really *would* be in character. No, this news is definitely encouraging, but"—she held up a hand to stay Minerva's protest—"I agree that, for your purpose, you need something more definite."

Penny nodded. "Something more cut and dried."

"Something," Minerva stated, "that's more than just indicative, or suggestive. Something that's not open to other interpretations." Halting, she threw up her hands. "At present, this is the equivalent of reading tea leaves. I need something he absolutely wouldn't do *unless* he loves me."

Clarice blew out a breath. "Well, there is one thing you might try. If you're game . . ."

Later that night, after a final consultation with her mentors, Minerva hurried back to her bedroom. The rest of the company had retired some time ago; she was late—Royce would be wondering where she was.

If he asked where she'd been, she could hardly tell him she'd been receiving instruction in the subtle art of how to lead a nobleman to reveal his heart.

Reaching her door, she opened it and rushed inside—and came up hard against his chest.

His hands closed on her shoulders and steadied her as the door swung shut behind her. He frowned down at her. "Where—"

She held up a hand. "If you must know, I've been dealing with your friends' wives." She whisked out of his hold and backed away, already unbuttoning her gown. "Go to your room—I'll follow as soon as I've changed."

He hesitated.

She got the impression he wanted to help her with her gown, but wasn't sure he trusted himself. She waved him off. "Go! I'll get there sooner if you do."

"All right." He turned to the door. "I'll be waiting."

The door shut soundlessly behind him just as she recalled she should have warned him not to undress.

"Damn!" Wrestling with her laces, she hurried even faster.

He was *not* happy. The last weeks had crawled by without any real satisfaction.

It had taken Lady Ashton longer than he'd expected to get here, and then, instead of creating any difficulty for Royce—not even the slightest scene—the damned woman had, so it appeared, accepted her congé without even a tantrum—not even a decent sulk!

That was one thing. Her rejection of *him* was quite another.

Seething, he stalked out of the west wing into the deeper shadows of the keep's gallery. He'd gone to her room assuming that, as Royce had declined to share her bed—a fact she'd made light of when, at his subtle prod, Susannah had asked—then the delectable Lady Ashton would be amenable to entertaining him. She had a mouth he'd fantasized about using ever since Royce's interest had focused his attention on her.

Instead, the lovely countess hadn't let him past her door. She'd pleaded a migraine and stated her intention of leaving the next day as necessitating a good night's sleep.

He ground his teeth. To be fobbed off with such transparent and paltry excuses made his blood boil. He'd intended to return to his room for a stiff brandy, but he needed something more potent than alcohol to burn away the memory of Lady Ashton's blank politeness.

She'd looked at him, and coolly dismissed him as unworthy to take Royce's place.

To rid himself of the vision, he needed something to replace it. Something like the image of Susannah—Royce's favorite sister—on her knees before him. With him looking down at her, first from the front, then from the rear, as she serviced him,

If he pushed her hard, she might just be able to make him forget the countess.

Imagining doing to Royce's sister what he'd planned to do to Royce's mistress, he crossed the gallery. Susannah's room was in the east wing.

He was passing one of the deep embrasures slotted into the keep's walls when the sound of a door hurriedly opening had him instinctively sidestepping into the deeper shadows and halting.

Silently he waited for whoever it was to pass.

Light footsteps came pattering along the runner—a woman, hurrying.

She passed the opening of the embrasure; a glint of moonlight tangled in her hair. Minerva.

Seeing her hurrying about wasn't surprising, even late at night. Seeing her rush off in her nightgown, swinging a light cloak about her shoulders, was.

He'd been walking back from the countess's rooms for some minutes; in the pervasive silence he would have heard if any of the staff had knocked on Minerva's door.

He slipped out of the embrasure and followed at a distance, stopped breathing when she turned down the short corridor that led to the ducal apartments. He reached the corner in time to peer around and see her open the door leading into Royce's sitting room.

It shut silently behind her.

Despite the obvious implications, he couldn't quite believe it. So he waited. Waited for her to emerge with Royce, having summoned him to deal with some emergency . . .

In her nightgown?

Barging into Royce's bedroom?

A clock somewhere tolled the quarter hour; he'd been standing there watching the door for over fifteen minutes. Minerva wasn't coming out.

She was the reason Royce had dismissed the countess.

"Well, well, well, well, well." Lips curving, he slowly turned and walked on to Susannah's room.

Eighteen

inerva paused just inside Royce's sitting room to drag in a breath and steady her nerves.

A shadow across the room shifted. Her senses flared.

He emerged from the dimness, the shadows sliding away; he'd dispensed with his coat, waistcoat, and cravat, and was barefoot, but still had his shirt and trousers on. He set down the empty glass he carried on a side table. He didn't actually growl, "About time," but the sentiment invested every stride as he stalked toward her.

"Ah . . ." She grabbed her sliding wits and hauled them back, raised her hands to ward him off.

He reached for her, but not as she expected. His hands clamped about her head, angled it as he swooped and captured her lips with his.

The searing kiss overwhelmed all thought, submerged every last vestige of rationality beneath a scorching tide of desire. Of passion unleashed; the flames licked about them, crackling and hungry.

She was, as always, drawn into the sheer wonder of being wanted so blatantly, in this way, to this degree. His hands locked about her head, with his mouth, lips, and tongue, he claimed, possessed—and poured so much raw need, unfettered passion, and unrestrained desire into her, through her, that, swamped, submerged, instantly aroused, she swayed.

Her hands flattened on his chest; through the fine linen of his shirt she felt his heat and hardness. Unrelenting, demanding, commanding—she felt all he was beckon and lure. Sensed through her touch and the grip of his hands that amazing though it seemed he wanted her with an even greater passion than he had the night before.

Far from waning, a hunger gradually sated, his appetite—and hers—only grew. Escalated, deepened.

Fingers curling in his shirt, she kissed him back—an equal participant in the outrageously explicit kiss. If he never seemed able to get enough of her, she felt the same about him.

The thought reminded her of what she needed from the night. What more she wanted of him. The others had given her directions, not instructions. She knew what she had to achieve, had known she would have to improvise.

So how?

Before she could think, he released her head and drew his hands outward, letting her hair flow through his long fingers. Her cloak slipped from her shoulders, sliding down to puddle in a heap behind her. He broke from the kiss, reached for her body—and she'd run out of planning time.

"No!" Stepping back, palm braced on his chest, she tried to hold him off.

He halted, looked at her.

"I want to lead. For this dance, I want you to let me lead."

That was the critical point—he had to let her. Had to accept the passive role instead of the dominant, had to willingly relinquish the reins and let her drive.

He'd never shared the reins—not truly. He'd allowed her to explore, but it had always been a permission granted, time and duration limited, all subject to his rule. He was a marcher lord, a king in his domains; she'd never expected anything else from him.

But tonight she was asking—demanding—that he not just share, but cede her his crown. For tonight, in his room, in his bed.

Royce understood very well what she was asking. Something he'd never granted to any other—and never would grant, not even to her, if he had a choice. But it wasn't hard to guess from whom she'd got the idea, nor what, in her mind and theirs, it meant. What they thought his capitulation would mean.

And they were right.

Which meant he had no choice. Not if he wanted her to wear his duchess's coronet.

Desire had already locked his features; he felt them grow harder, felt his jaw tighten as he held her gaze—and forced himself to nod. "All right."

She blinked—he had to stop himself from scooping her up anyway and carrying her to his bed. He could rip away her wits, and her determination, but that way lay failure. This was a test—one he had to take. Easing back, he stretched his arms to either side. "So what now?"

A more cerebral part of him was intrigued to see what she would do.

Sensing his underlying challenge, she narrowed her eyes, then grabbed one hand, swung on her heel, and towed him into his bedroom.

His gaze locked on her hips, swaying naked beneath the near translucent poplin of an amazingly prim white nightgown. None of her nightgowns rated as provocative, but this one, with its long, gathered sleeves and high collar, closed all the way up to her chin with tiny buttons, seemed extreme— and erotic.

Because he knew the body inside the gown so well, the nunlike outer casing only spurred his imagination in picturing what it concealed.

She led him to the foot of his bed.

Releasing him, wordlessly she pushed until he stood with his back to the bed, his thighs against the mattress's edge.

She positioned him in the center of the four-poster, then grasped one arm, raised and slapped his palm to the ornately carved post on that side.

"Hold that. Don't let go."

She did the same with his other arm, setting that hand, too, level with his shoulder, against the other carved post. The bed was wide, but his shoulders were broad, his arms long; he could reach both posts easily.

She stepped back, assessed, nodded. "Good. That will do."

For what? He was utterly intrigued over what she was planning. For all his experience, he'd never considered anything from a woman's perspective; it was a novel, and unexpectedly arousing experience, arousing in an unusual way.

He'd been aroused from the moment he'd closed his hands about her head, painfully so once his lips had found hers; he would have taken her against the door in his sitting room if she hadn't stopped him. Although she had, courtesy of her peculiar direction, the fire in his blood hadn't died.

She trapped his eyes. "Under no circumstance are you to let go of the posts—not until I give you leave."

Turning, she walked away from him, and the fires inside him burned brighter.

He tracked her across the room, aware of his hunger growing. Curiosity balanced it to some degree, let him wait with some semblance of patience.

Crossing to where he'd slung his clothes on a chair, she shifted things, then straightened; because of the sharp contrast between the shadows cloaking the room and the brilliance of the shaft of moonlight beaming like a searchlight on him, he couldn't make out what she held in her hands until she drew near.

His cravat. Two yards of white linen. Instinctively he shifted his weight to his toes, about to step away from the bed.

She halted, caught his eye—waited.

He eased back, gripped the posts more firmly.

She uttered a small "humph," and walked down the side of the bed. The covers rustled as she climbed up, then came silence. She was on the bed a little way behind him, doing something; her gaze wasn't on him. "I forgot to mention— you aren't allowed to speak. No words. This is my script, and there are no lines for you."

He inwardly snorted. He rarely used words in this arena; actions spoke louder.

Then she moved closer behind him. He sensed her rising high on her knees; her breath brushed his ear when she murmured, "I think this might be easier if you." He sensed her arms rising over his head. "Can't." His cravat, folded to a narrow band, appeared before his face. "See."

She settled the band over his eyes, then wound the long strip multiple times around his head before tying it off at the back.

A cravat made a damned fine blindfold. The material sank across his eyes; he couldn't lift his lids at all.

Effectively blind, his other senses instinctively expanded, heightened.

She spoke by his ear. "Remember—no speaking, and no releasing the posts."

Her scent. The brush of her breath across his earlobe. Inwardly he smiled cynically. How was she going to remove his shirt?

She slid from the bed, and came to stand before him. The subtle beckoning heat of her. Her light perfume. The more primitive, more evocative, infinitely more arousing fragrance of her—the one scent he hungered for most strongly, that of his woman aroused and ready for him.

He'd had that taste on his tongue; it was imprinted on his brain.

Every muscle hardened. His erection grew even more rigid.

She was two feet away. With his hands locked on the posts, she was out of his reach.

"Hmm. Where to start?"

At his waistband, then head down.

"Perhaps with the most obvious." She stepped into him,

plastered her body against his, drew his head down, and kissed him.

She hadn't told him he couldn't kiss her back. He ravaged her mouth, seized a first taste of what he ached for.

For one heady moment, she clung, caught, helpless, in the passion he'd unleashed, her body instinctively sinking against his, yielding, promising to ease the ache in his groin, offering pleasure and earthly delight . . .

He sensed her find her feet, digging in so she could stand against him. On a gasp, she wrenched back. Broke the kiss.

Unable to see, he couldn't follow and reinstate the exchange.

She was breathing rapidly. "You're hungry."

An indisputable fact.

He smothered a growl as her body left his, clenched his jaw to quell the impulse to seize her and haul her back.

From his shoulders, her hands trailed slowly down, over his chest, over his abdomen, provocatively assessing. One paused at his waist; the other continued on, to, through his trousers, outline his erection, fingers tracing across the broad head before her palm flattened, warm and supple, over the throbbing length.

"Impressive." She gripped, then removed her hand.

He bit back a hiss. His fingers sank into the posts' carving. "Wait."

She left him, got back on the bed behind him; her hands gripped the back of his shirt at his waist, yanked it free of his waistband. Without freeing the sides or front, she slid her hands under the fabric, pressed her palms to his back.

Ran them—slowly—over him.

Over his back, up and over his shoulders, around and across his chest. The peaks of her breasts rode against his shirt-clad back. Her knees bracketed his hips.

She was still fully covered. So was he, yet with his sight gone and his other senses alive, her blatantly possessive caresses seemed infinitely erotic.

He was a slave and she his mistress, intent on possessing him for the first time. He sucked in a deep breath, chest swelling under her hands. Splayed, one on either side, she ran them slowly down from upper chest to waist.

They hovered for a long moment.

She drew back, warm palms and fingers trailing back over his sensitized skin, withdrawing from under the fall of his shirt, now hanging loose all around him.

Blind, he turned his head the better to sense her.

Noting the movement, Minerva smiled; sinking back on her ankles, she picked at the side seam of his shirt. "Did you know that the best tailors always use weak thread in their shirt seams, so if the shirt catches or tugs, the seam gives rather than the material?"

He stilled. She gave an experimental tug; the seam gave with a satisfying sound. Tugging, she opened the side and sleeve seams to the laces at his cuffs. The laces undone, with a wrench she had one side of the shirt hanging free.

She repeated the exercise on the other side, then swung off the bed and sauntered up before him. She flicked the hanging ends of the shirt. "I wonder what Trevor will think when he sees this."

Decidedly pleased, she unknotted the loose laces at his throat. Excitement flashed through her as she lifted both hands, found the front center seam. "Now, let's see . . ." She ripped.

The shirt parted all the way down the front.

"Oh, yes." Eyes feasting on his bared chest, she let the ruined halves fall to frame the heavily muscled expanse. Bathed in silvery moonlight, every powerful ripple and curve sheened, every line of bone was gilt-edged.

He breathed in, muscles tensing. His hands gripped harder.

Slowly she circled and climbed up on the bed again. Close behind him on her knees, she caught the shirt at the shoulders, drew it back and off, tossed it on the floor.

Although his back was in shadow, there was light enough to see. The long muscles, the supple, powerful planes, the quintessentially male sculpture rendered in muscle and bone and hot taut skin. She traced each feature. His tension built. Pressing against his back, she touched her lips to his shoulder, trailed her fingers around and reached for his waistband.

His stomach pulled in, letting her fingers slide past the band as she slipped the buttons free.

Lips curving against his shoulder, she drew the halves of the front placket wide, releasing his erection; careful not to touch, she grasped his trousers, edged them over his hips, down his thighs until they fell to the floor.

Leaving his body displayed naked in the moonlight, arms wide, muscles bunched as he gripped the posts. The only thing he still wore was the blindfold.

Drawing breath through lungs suddenly tight, placing both palms on his shoulders, she stroked slowly down, following the long muscles bracketing his spine to the slope of his rear; pivoting her hands over the tight cheeks, she slid them still farther, pressing against the mattress to reach and caress as far as she could down his thighs.

His head tipped back; his breath shuddered.

Retrieving her hands, she gripped the sides of his waist, eased her thighs wide, fitted herself against his back. Her cheek to one shoulder blade, she sent her hands around, down; lids falling, she found his erection, closed her hand about the rigid length.

He breathed out, short, sharp, as she squeezed and released. With her other hand, she reached further, caressed his heavy testicles, cradled them, fondled.

Royce's lungs locked tight, his body as rigid as his erection as she worked him with one hand, with the other weighed his balls, assessed, played. The sense of possession escalated. Head back, he gritted his teeth against a curse.

He'd felt nothing like this. Ever before. Sight cut off, he was functioning on touch, and imagination. Her lascivious acts conjured the image of a sultry, sirenlike seductress who owned him. Who could make free with his body as she wished, with total impunity.

That it was he who granted that immunity, his hands so tightly locked on his carved bedposts his fingers felt fused with the wood, merely added another layer to the swelling sensuality.

Her hand closed firmly. His control shuddered. Jaw clenched, he fought the impulse to pump his hips, work his erection in her fist. He wanted, desperately, to turn to her, rip the prim nightgown away, exposing the siren before spreading her beneath him and sheathing himself in her.

He burned to possess her with the same calculated intensity with which she was possessing him.

Over recent nights she'd learned what strokes, what actions, most pleasured him. Now she applied the knowledge. Too well . . .

Head back, he fought . . . every muscle locked tight.

"*Minerva!*" The plea was wrenched from him.

Her grip eased, her strokes slowed. Her hand drifted from his balls and he could breathe again.

"No talking, remember. Well, not unless you want to beg."

He growled, "I'm begging."

Silence, then she laughed. Sultry, rich, a siren's laugh. "Oh, Royce—what a lie. You just want to take control— but not this time."

She shifted position; her grip changed. "Not tonight. Tonight, you've ceded control to me."

Head rising, she murmured beneath his ear, "Tonight, you're mine."

Her fingers closed around his erection. "Mine to take. Mine to sate." Her breath fanning his ear, she ran her thumb over the weeping head. "*All* mine."

Sensation lanced through him. He locked his knees, sucked in a breath. He'd agreed—now all he could do was endure.

Easing her grip, but without releasing his erection, she slipped under his braced arm and off the bed. Taking him firmly in hand again, she came to stand before him. The hem of her nightgown drifted over his feet.

Pressing herself to him, she reached up, drew his head

down for a long, sultry kiss. Locked between them, her hand solidly fisted his erection. He let her dictate, did nothing but follow. She laughed softly into his mouth, then, lips locking on his, moved.

Sinuously, flagrantly, blatantly erotic, her breasts, hips and thighs caressed him, flooding his senses with images of her writhing against him, wanton and abandoned—as hungry, as urgent, as desperate as he.

She released his lips and sank slowly down, lips trailing down . . . head back, jaw clenched tight, he waited, prayed, wanted—feared . . .

She slid her lips slowly over his erection, slowly, deliberately took him into her mouth. Deep, then deeper, until he was sunk to the balls in her wet heat.

Slowly, deliberately, she reduced him to quaking desperation.

And he couldn't stop her.

He wasn't in control. He was at her mercy, completely and absolutely.

Hands gripping the posts, unable to see, he had to surrender, cede his body and his senses to her, hers to do with as she pleased.

One heartbeat before the point of no return, she slowed her attentions, then drew back.

His chest heaved; the night air felt cool against his damp, heated skin. She released him, rocked back, rose.

Fingers loose around his straining erection, she reached up and drew his head down. Kissed him, but briefly; drawing back, with her teeth, she tugged his lower lip—refocusing his attention.

"You have a choice. You can have your sight, or your hands. Choose."

He wanted his hands on her, wanted to feel her skin, her curves, but if he couldn't see . . . "Take off the blindfold."

Minerva smiled. His gaze she could endure, but with his hands free, her remaining in control for much longer was unlikely.

And she wanted longer.

The air was heavy, thick, the scent of passion and desire a miasma about them. The salty taste of his arousal was fresh on her tongue; she'd wanted to lure him to completion, but the hollow ache between her thighs was too insistent. She needed him there as desperately as he wanted her sheath enclosing his erection.

They each needed the other to achieve their ultimate in completion.

She reached up as he lowered his head. She picked the knot free, unwound the folds, drew the long strip away and stepped back. He blinked, focused.

His dark gaze burned, scorching, piercing.

She caught it, refused to think about his strength, that it was *his* control that gave her any chance of controlling him. "Put the insides of your wrists together in front of you."

Slowly he eased his fingers from their death grips on the posts, flexed his arms, then set his wrists together as she'd asked.

She bound them with the linen band. Releasing the trailing ends, she placed her splayed fingertips on his chest, pushed. "Sit on the bed, then lie back."

He sat, then let himself fall back onto the crimson-and-gold brocade.

Grasping one bedpost, raising the nightgown, she clambered up, kneeling, looking down at him. "Put your hands on the bed above your head."

In seconds he was lying stretched out on the bed, hands above his head, calves and feet dangling over the edge.

He lay there, naked, delectable, heavily aroused, hers for the taking.

Trapping his gaze, she wrapped one hand about his erection, with the other raised her nightgown so she could swing her thigh over his hips. Sinking down on her knees, she released the gown; the folds fell to his belly, screening her actions as she guided the blunt head of his erection between her slick folds, then eased back.

Releasing him, she sank slowly back, down, smoothly taking his turgid length into her body.

She shifted, sank further still, until she'd taken him all. Until she sat across his hips, impaled, full of him. He stretched her, completed her; the length and strength of him at her core felt indisputably right.

Her gaze locked with his, she rose slowly up, then slowly sank down.

Fingers braced on his chest, she changed angle, pace, found the rhythm she wanted, one she could maintain, sliding him deeply in, then almost completely out. He clenched his jaw, clenched his fists. His muscles hardened, tightened, as she devoted herself to taking every iota of sensual pleasure she could.

It wasn't enough.

Wrapped in his gaze, acutely aware of all she could see blazing in the dark depths of his eyes as his body strained, fought his control—as he battled his own instincts to give her all she wanted . . .

In that moment, she knew. For her, with him, taking would never be enough. She had to give—give him, show him, all she was. All that with him, for him, she could be.

All she could gift him with.

All that blossomed inside her.

She reached down, grasped her nightgown, drew it up, off, flung it aside. His gaze instantly lowered to where they joined. She couldn't see what he could, imagining was enough; the heat between her thighs flared. Within her, he grew larger, harder; she felt the change in his body between her thighs, deep inside her.

He glanced briefly at her face, then looked down again. His hips undulated beneath hers.

She should have ordered him to stop, to lie still. She didn't. Breath sawing in her throat, she arched back; head up, arms crossed behind, her hair a wild cascade about her, eyes closed, she gave herself up to the bucking ride, to the overwhelming pleasure, and rode him hard, then harder.

It still wasn't enough; she needed him deeper.

She sobbed, slowed, desperate . . .

He swore. Surged up from the waist, his bound wrists passing over her head, trapping her within the circle of his arms. Turning his palms, setting them to her back, his gaze locked with hers, he shifted between her thighs, then thrust up harder, deeper, higher with her.

He settled to a solid, heavy rhythm. His gaze lowered to her lips, inches from his. "You're still in control." He glanced up, caught her gaze. "Tell me if you like this."

He bent, set his lips to her ruched nipple. She cried out. He suckled; she gasped. Sinking her hands in his hair, she held him to her. Held him while he rocked her, pleasured her, while they came together and the sounds and scents of their joining wreathed through her brain, filling, reassuring, exciting.

She wanted more.

More of him.

All of him.

She wanted what he did.

Catching his head between her hands, she urged him to look up.

When he did, dark eyes heavy-lidded, lips rich, fine, wicked, she caught his gaze. Gasped, "Enough. Take me. Finish this."

His steady thrusting between her thighs didn't ease. He looked deep. "Are you sure?"

"Yes." Surer than of anything in the world. Slowing her own rhythm, she lost herself in his eyes. "However you wish, however you want."

For one long moment, he held her gaze.

Then she was on her back, flung across his bed, clinging to sanity as with her thighs pressed wide, his bound hands beneath her head, palms cradling it, he thrust into her body, hard, deep—

Sanity fractured and she flew apart.

Royce gasped, fought to hold still so he could savor her

release, but the contractions were so strong they ruthlessly, relentlessly drew him on, until with a muffled roar he followed her into oblivion, his release, so long denied, rolling over and through him, powerfully raking him, wrecking him, leaving him drained, a husk buoyed on a welling emotional tide, coming back to life as glory seeped in, and filled him.

As his heart swelled, and he drew in a shuddering breath, through the haze in his brain, he felt her lips caress his temple.

"Thank you."

The words were a ghost of a whisper, but he heard, slowly smiled.

She had it arse over tit; it was he who should thank her.

A significant time later, he finally summoned sufficient strength to lift from her, roll onto his back, and with his teeth pick apart the knot at his wrists.

She lay slumped alongside him, but she wasn't asleep. Still smiling, he scooped her up, dragged down the covers, then collapsed on the pillows, arranged her in his arms, and tugged the covers over them.

Without a word, she snuggled against him, all but boneless.

Pleasure, of a depth and quality he'd never thought to feel, rolled over and through him. And sank to his bones.

Tilting his head, he looked into her face. "Did I pass your test?"

"Humph. Somewhere through all that"—she waved weakly toward the end of the bed—"I realized it was a test for me as much as you."

His lips curved more deeply; he'd wondered if she'd seen that.

Curiously clearheaded, he revisited the events, and even more the emotions—all they'd broached, drawn on, used, revealed, over the last hour.

She was still awake. Waiting to hear what he would say.

He touched his lips to her temple. "Know this." He kept

his voice low; she would hear all he wanted her to hear in his tone. "I will give you anything. Anything and everything I have to give. There is nothing you can ask for that I will not grant you—whatever I have, whatever I am, is yours."

Each word rang with absolute, unshakable commitment.

A long moment passed. "Do you believe me?"

"Yes." The answer came without hesitation.

"Good." Lips curving, settling his head on the pillow, he closed his arms about her. "Go to sleep."

He knew it was a command, didn't care. He felt her sigh, felt the last of her tension fade, felt sleep claim her. Taking his own advice, contented to his toes, he surrendered to his dreams.

Nineteen

At a smidgen before dawn, Minerva floated back to her room, flopped into her bed, and sighed. She couldn't stop smiling. Royce had more than passed her test with flying colors; even if he couldn't promise love, what he had promised had more than reassured. He'd given her everything she'd asked for.

So what now? What next?

She still had no assurance that at some point what presently flared so hotly between them wouldn't die . . . Could she risk accepting his offer?

Could she risk not?

She blinked, felt a cold chill wash through her. Frowned as, for the first time, the alternative to accepting—refusing him, turning her back on all that might be and walking away—formed in her mind.

The truth dawned.

"Damn that mangy Scot." She slumped back on her pillows. "He's right!" Why had it taken her so long to see it?

"Because I've been looking at Royce, not me. *I* love him." To the depths of her soul. "No matter how many symptoms of love he has, *my* heart won't change."

Infatuation-obsession had grown to something a great deal

more—more powerful, deeper, impossible to deny, and immutable, set in stone. Whatever trials she staged, even when he passed with flying colors, were no more than reassurance. Comforting, enlightening, and supportive, yes, but in the end, beside the point. *She* loved him, and as Penny had said, love was not a passive emotion.

Love would never allow her to turn her back on him and walk away, would never allow her to be so cowardly as not to risk her heart.

Love would—and did—demand her heart.

If she wanted love, she had to risk it. Had to give it. Had to surrender it.

Her way forward was suddenly crystal clear.

"Your Grace, I will be honored to accept your offer."

Her heart literally soared at the sound of the words—words she'd never thought to say. Her lips curved, and curved; she smiled gloriously.

The door opened; Lucy breezed in. "Good morning, ma'am. Ready for the big day? Everyone's already bustling below stairs."

"Oh. Yes." Her smile waned. She inwardly swore; it was the day before the fair. The one day of the year in which she would have not a moment to call her own.

Or Royce's.

She swore again, and got up.

And plunged into the day—into a whirlpool of frenetic activity and concerted organization.

Breakfast for her was rushed. Royce, wisely, had come down early, and already ridden out. All the guests had arrived; the parlor was a sea of chatter and greetings. Of course, her three mentors were agog to hear her news; given the company, the best she could do was reconjure her radiant smile.

They saw it, interpreted it accurately—and beamed back.

Letitia patted her arm. "That's wonderful! You can tell us the details later."

Later it would have to be. It had been too many years since

the staff had coped with a house party and the fair simultaneously; panic threatened on more than one front.

Tea and toast downed, Minerva rushed up to the morning room. She and Cranny spent a frantic hour making sure their days' schedules included all that needed doing. The housekeeper had just left when a tap on the door heralded Letitia, Penny, and Clarice.

"Oh." Meeting Letitia's bright gaze, Minerva tried to refocus her mind.

"No, no." Grinning, Letitia waved aside her efforts. "Much as we'd like to hear all—in salacious detail—now is clearly not the time. Apropos of which, we've come to offer our services."

Minerva blinked; as Letitia sat, she glanced at Penny and Clarice.

"There is nothing worse," Penny declared, "than idly waiting, kicking one's heels, with nothing to do."

"Especially," Clarice added, "when there's obvious employment in which our particular talents might assist— namely, your fair." She sank onto the sofa. "So share—what's on your list that we can help with?"

Minerva took in their patently eager expressions, then looked down at her lists. "There's the archery contests, and . . ."

They divided up the tasks, then she ordered the landau to be brought around. While the others fetched bonnets and shawls, she grabbed hers and rushed down to speak with Retford. He and she discussed entertainments for the castle's guests, most of whom would remain about the castle that day, then she hurried to join the others in the front hall.

On the way to the fairground—the field beyond the church—they went over the details of the tasks each would pursue. Reaching the field, already a sea of activity, they exchanged glances, and determinedly plunged in.

Even delegating as she had, getting through her list of activities to be checked, organized or discussed took hours. The Alwinton Fair was the largest in the region; crofters came from miles around, out of the hills and dales of the Borders, and travelers, tradesmen, and craftsmen came from as far afield as Edinburgh to sell their wares.

On top of that, the agricultural side was extensive. Although Penny was overseeing the preparations for the animal contests, Minerva had kept the produce section under her purview; there were too many locals involved, too many local rivalries to navigate.

And then there was the handfasting; the fair was one of the events at which the Border folk traditionally made their declarations before a priest, then jumped over a broomstick, signaling their intention of sharing an abode for the next year. She came upon Reverend Cribthorn in the melee.

"Nine couples this year." He beamed. "Always a delight to see the beginnings of new families. I regard it as one of my most pleasurable duties, even if the church pretends not to know."

After confirming time and place for the ceremonies, she turned away—and through a gap in the milling throng, spotted Royce. He was surrounded by a bevy of children, all chattering up at him.

He'd been about all day, directing and, to their astonishment, often assisting various groups of males engaged in setting up booths and tents, stages and holding pens. Although he and she had exchanged numerous glances, he'd refrained from approaching her—from distracting her.

She'd still felt his gaze, had known that at times he'd passed close by in the crowd.

Given he was absorbed, she allowed herself to stare, to drink in the sight of him dealing with what she'd come to realize he saw as his youngest responsibilities. He hadn't forgotten the footbridge, and therefore the aldermen of Harbottle hadn't forgotten, either. Hancock, the castle carpenter, had been dispatched to oversee the reconstruction, and reported daily to Royce.

Every local, on first setting eyes on him—a tall, commanding figure in his well-cut coat, buckskin breeches, and top boots—stopped and stared. As she watched, Mrs. Critchley from beyond Alwinton halted in her tracks, and all but gawped.

His father hadn't attended the fair in living memory, but even more telling, his father would never, ever have assisted—have counted himself as one of this community. He'd been their ruler, but never one of them.

Royce would rule as his ancestors had before him, but not distantly, aloofly; he was one with the noisy horde around him. She no longer needed to think to know his views; his sense of duty toward those he ruled—to his people—infused all he did. It was a fundamental part of who he was.

Confident, arrogant, assured to his toes, he was Wolverstone, marcher lord incarnate—and using that power that by birth was his to wield, he'd rescripted the role, far more thoroughly, more fundamentally and progressively, than she'd dared hope.

Watching him with the children, seeing him turn his head and exchange a laughing comment with Mr. Cribthorn, she felt her heart grow wings.

That was the man she loved.

He was who he was, he still had his flaws, but she loved him with all her heart.

She had to turn away, had to battle to suppress the emotion welling inside so she could smile and function and do what needed doing. Irrepressibly smiling, she lifted her head, drew breath, and plunged back into the crowd, immersed herself in all she'd come there to do.

Later.

Later she would speak with him, accept his offer—and offer him her heart, without reservation.

"It's entirely thanks to you three that I'm heading home before dusk, let alone in time for afternoon tea." At ease in the landau, Minerva smiled at Letitia, Clarice, and Penny, all, like her, exhausted, but satisfied with their day.

"It was our pleasure," Penny returned. "Indeed, I think I'll suggest Charles investigates getting some ewes from that breeder, O'Loughlin."

She grinned, but didn't get to mention Hamish's background, distracted instead by Clarice's account of what she'd discovered among the craft stalls. By the time they reached the castle, she'd been amply reassured that her friends hadn't found their assumed duties too onerous. Alighting, they went indoors to join the company for afternoon tea.

All the ladies were present, but only a handful of the gentlemen, most having taken out rods or guns and disappeared for the day.

"It seemed wise to encourage them," Margaret said. "Especially as we want them to dance attendance on us tomorrow at the fair."

Smiling to herself, Minerva quit the gathering and climbed the main stairs. She wasn't sure she'd dealt with everything within the castle itself; she'd left those lists in the morning room.

She was reaching for the knob of the morning room door when it opened.

Royce stood framed in the doorway. "There you are."

"I've just got back. Or rather"—she tipped her head downward—"just finished afternoon tea. Everything seems to be proceeding smoothly."

"As, under your guidance, things always do." Taking her arm, he moved her back, joining her and pulling the door closed behind him. "That being the case . . . come walk with me."

He wound her arm in his, setting his hand over hers. She glanced at his face—uninformative as ever—as she strolled beside him. "Where to?"

"I thought . . ." He'd led her back into the keep; now he turned down the short corridor to his apartments—not entirely to her surprise.

But he halted a few paces along, looked at the wall, then put out his hand, depressed a catch; the door to the keep's battlements sprang open. "I thought," he repeated, meeting her gaze as he held the door wide, "that the view from the battlements might entice."

She laughed, and readily went through. "Along with the peace up there, plus the fact it's entirely private?"

Perhaps she could tell him her decision up there?

"Indeed." Royce followed her into the stairway built into the keep's wall. Once she'd climbed to the top of the steep flight and pushed open the door, letting light flood down, he closed the corridor door, then took the stairs three at a time, emerging to join her on the open battlements.

They were the original battlements, the highest part of the castle. The view was spectacular, but by long tradition was enjoyed by only the family, more particularly those residing within the keep; guests had never been permitted up there, on the walks where, over the centuries, the family's most trusted guards had kept watch for their enemies.

The breeze was brisker than in the fields below; it tugged and flirted with Minerva's hair as she stood in one of the gaps in the crenellations, looking north, over the gardens, the bridge, the mill, and the gorge.

As he neared, she lifted her face, shook back her hair. "I'd forgotten how fresh it is up here."

"Are you cold?" He closed his hands about her shoulders.

She glanced into his face, smiled. "No, not really."

"Good. Nevertheless . . ." He slid his arms around her and drew her back against him, settling her back to his chest, enveloping her in his greater warmth. She sighed and relaxed into his embrace, leaning against him, crossing her arms, her hands curving over his as she looked out. His chin beside her topknot, he, too, gazed out over his fields.

The unfulfilled impulse that had prompted him to take her to Lord's Seat lookout weeks before had prodded him to bring her here—for the same reason.

"All you can see," he said, "as far as you can see, all the lands beneath your gaze are mine. All that lies beneath our feet—that, too, is mine. My heritage, under my rule, under my absolute authority. The people are mine, too—mine to protect, to watch over—their welfare my responsibility, all part of the same whole." He drew breath, then went on, "What you see before you is the greater part of what my life will be. What it will encompass. And you're already an integral part of it. The day I took you to Lord's Seat, this is what I wanted to show you—all that I want to share with you."

He glanced at her profile. "I want to share all of my life with you, not just the customary parts. Not just the social and familial arenas, but all this, too." Tightening his arms, laying his jaw against her hair, he found the words he'd been searching for. "I want you by my side in everything, not just my duchess, but my helpmate, my partner, my guide. I will welcome you gladly into whatever spheres of my life you wish to grace.

"If you consent to be my wife, I will willingly give to you not just my affection, not just my protection, but the right to stand beside me in everything I do. As my duchess, you will not be an adjunct, but an integral part of all that, together, we will be."

Minerva couldn't keep the smile from her face. He was who he was, manipulative to his toes; he'd eloquently laid before her what he knew to be the most potent inducement he could offer—but he was sincere. Totally, unquestionably, speaking from his heart.

If she'd needed further convincing that she could have faith and go forward, that she should accept his suit and become his duchess, he'd just supplied it; all he'd said was predicated on, based on, built upon an "affection" he believed was sound, solid, as unshakable as the foundations of his keep.

She already knew the counter to that emotion lived, strong and vital, in her. To have such a fate, such a challenge, such a destiny offered her so freely . . . that was more than she'd ever dared dream.

Turning in his arms, she looked into his face, met his dark eyes. They were as unreadable as ever, but his lips twisted wryly.

"I know I shouldn't push—shouldn't press." He held her

gaze. "I know you still need time to assimilate all I've said, all that's happened between us, but I wanted you to know how much you mean to me, so your deliberations will be . . . fully informed."

She smiled at his phrasing; despite his undoubted intelligence, he hadn't yet realized that love didn't need that much thought.

He smiled back. "And now I'm going to give you all the time you want to decide. I won't say more, not until you tell me I should."

Lowering his head, he brushed her lips lightly in an undemanding caress.

It wasn't something he meant to do, but there was enough in his tone to remind her that, from a man like him, granting her time was a gift.

Her declaration hovered in the forefront of her mind, yet his unstated boon—unneeded though it might be—deserved some acknowledgment; as their lips parted, she rose on her toes, pressed her lips to his, parted them—invited. They were alone, private; no one could see.

Lifting her arms, she wound them about his neck, pressed herself to him. His hands fastened about her waist, held her for an instant, then he laughed softly, angled his head, and took the kiss deeper.

Took her deeper, into the familiar richness of their mutual desire.

For long moments, they savored—each other, the warmth of the exchange, the inherent comfort.

Then the fire took hold.

Neither had summoned it; the flames were suddenly simply there, greedily licking all around them, tempting, luring . . .

Both hesitated, sensing, seeking the other's direction . . .

Both surrendered. Grasped. Seized.

His hands, spread, moved over her back, his touch possessive and sure. She sank her hands into his hair, held him to the suddenly rapacious kiss, and flagrantly demanded more.

Kneading her breasts, kissing her with slow, relentless

promise, he backed her against the ungiving stone of his battlements.

Mutual need fired their blood, had her reaching for his waistband, had him raising her skirts.

Mutual passion had them gasping, hungry and greedy as he lifted her, braced her against the stone, sank into her, then thrust deep.

Mutual pleasure caught them; panting, chests heaving, they froze, forehead to forehead, breaths mingling, heated gazes touching, and drank in the exquisite sensation of their joining. Let it sink to their respective bones.

Then he closed his eyes and groaned, she moaned, and each sought the others' lips.

And let mutual surrender have them, take them.

A click was all the warning they had.

"Oh, my *God!*"

The shrill exclamation fell like a bucket of icy water over them.

It was followed by a chorus of gasps, and more muted expressions of shock.

Head up, spine rigid, Royce thought faster than he ever had in his life.

Women, ladies, an untold number, stood clustered in the doorway five yards behind his back.

Someone had brought them up here, but who had wasn't his first concern.

Locked in his arms, supported by his hand beneath her bottom and braced by his body sunk deeply in hers, Minerva was rigid. Hands fisted in his lapels, she'd ducked her head to his chest.

He felt like he'd been clouted with a battle mace.

His shoulders were broad; the women behind him couldn't see her, at least not her face or body. They would be able to see her topknot, telltale wheat-gold, over his shoulder, and even more damningly her stocking-clad legs clasped about his hips.

There was not a hope in hell of disguising their occupation.

A kiss would have been bad enough, but this . . .

There was only one course of action open to him.

Easing Minerva from him, he withdrew from her; given his size, that necessitated a maneuver that even viewed from behind was impossible to mistake. Her knees slid from his hips, he lowered her until her feet touched the ground. Her skirts tumbled straight of their own accord.

"Don't move," he murmured, quickly doing up the placket of his breeches. "Don't say a word."

She looked at him through wide, utterly stunned eyes.

Uncaring of the crowd, he bent his head and kissed her, a swift, reassuring kiss, then he straightened and turned to face their fate.

His expression aloof and cold, his gaze pure ice, he regarded the knot of ladies, round-eyed, hands at their breasts, their expressions as stunned as Minerva's . . . except for Susannah's. She stood at the rear, peering past the others.

Refocusing on those in the front of the group—a cluster of his sisters' London friends—he drew breath, then said the words he had to say. "Ladies. Miss Chesterton has just done me the honor of agreeing to be my wife."

"Well! It's Miss Chesterton! Whoever would have thought!" Caroline Courtney, all agog, broke the news as he circled the billiard table. With the other men present, most Royce's cousins, he halted and listened as Caroline blurted out the juicy details of how Royce and his chatelaine had been caught *in flagrante delicto* on the battlements.

"There was absolutely no doubt about it," she assured them. "We all saw."

He frowned. "Was she who Royce intended to marry all along?"

Caroline shrugged. "Who can say? Regardless, she's the one he'll have to marry now."

Frowning, Gordon stated, "I can't imagine Royce letting himself be trapped like that." Then he realized what he'd said, and colored. "Not that Minerva won't make a perfectly acceptable duchess."

Inwardly smiling, he mentally thanked Susannah; outwardly calm, he turned back to the table, savoring his victory.

The news would reach London as fast as the mail coach could carry it; he wouldn't need to lift so much as a finger.

So Royce would now have to marry his chatelaine—be *forced* to marry her, and that he wouldn't like.

Even worse would be the whispers traded behind scented hands, the sniggers, the unsavory speculation directed at his duchess.

Unavoidable within the ton.

And Royce wouldn't like that *at all.*

Smiling, he leaned over the table and sent one ball neatly into a pocket, then he straightened and, slowly circling the table, surveyed the possibilities.

In the duchess's morning room, Letitia watched Minerva pace. "I appreciate that it's the *very* last thing you would have wished to happen, but believe me, in the circumstances, there was nothing else he could have done."

"I know." Her tone clipped, Minerva swung on her heel. "I was there. It was *awful.*"

"Here." Penny held out a glass containing at least three fingers of brandy. "Charles swears it always helps." She took a sip from her own glass. "And he's right."

Minerva seized the glass, took a healthy swallow, and felt the fiery liquid sear her throat, but then the warmth spread lower, loosening some of her icy rage. "I felt so damned *helpless!* I couldn't even think."

"Take it from a Vaux, that scene would have taxed my histrionic capabilities." Letitia, too, was sipping brandy. She shook her head. "There wasn't anything you could have done to change the outcome."

Rendered more furious than she'd ever been in her life,

Minerva could barely recall descending from the battlements. In a voice that dripped icicles, Royce had, entirely unsubtly, informed the importunate ladies that the battlements, like the keep itself, were private; they'd all but tripped over each other fleeing back down the stairs. Once they were gone, he'd turned, taken her hand, led her down, and brought her here.

She'd been trembling—with rage.

He'd been incandescent with fury, but, as usual, very little showed. He'd kissed her lightly, squeezed her hand, said, "Wait here." Then he'd left.

Minutes later, Letitia had arrived, fired with concern, ready to offer comfort and support; she'd lent a sympathetic ear while Minerva had ranted, literally raved over being denied her declaration, her supreme moment when she accepted Royce and pledged her love.

Penny had joined them a few minutes ago, bearing a tray with the brandy decanter and four glasses. She'd listened for a moment, then set down the tray and poured.

The door opened, and Clarice came in. Penny held out the fourth glass; Clarice thanked her with a nod as she took it, sipped, then sank down onto the sofa opposite Letitia. She met their gazes. "Between us—Royce, Penny, Jack, and me—and surprisingly enough, Susannah—I think we've got everything smoothed over. Our story is that the three of us knew of the engagement—which, given your state this morning and what would naturally have followed from that, is the truth. And, indeed, that's why we're here, to witness the announcement for the grandes dames."

Minerva scowled, sipped. "I vaguely recall Royce muttering something about wringing Susannah's neck. Wasn't she the one who brought the ladies up to the battlements? If she was, and he hasn't, I will."

"She was." Penny sat beside Clarice. "But believe it or not, she thought she was helping. Being Cupid's assistant, so to speak. She'd learned, somehow, that you were Royce's lover, and decided she much preferred you as her sister-in-law over any other, so . . ." Penny shrugged. "Of course, she thought it was Royce dragging his heels."

Minerva grimaced. "She and I were much closer when we were young—we've always been friendly, although recently, of course, the connection's been more distant." She sighed, and dropped onto the sofa beside Letitia. "I suppose that explains it."

Penny's Charles was right; the brandy helped, but anger still coursed her veins. Thanks to Susannah, she and even more Royce had lost what should have been a treasured moment. "Damn!" She took another sip.

Luckily, the incident on the battlements and its outcome had changed nothing beyond that; she literally thanked heaven that she'd already made up her mind. If she hadn't . . .

Letitia stood. "I must go and speak with Royce."

"You know," Clarice said, "I always thought our husbands treated him with a respect that was somewhat overstated—as if they credited him with more power, more ability, than he or any man could possibly have." She raised her brows. "After seeing him in action downstairs, I've revised my opinion."

"Was he diabolical?" Letitia asked.

Clarice considered. "Mildly so. It was more a case of everyone being suddenly reminded of the Wolverstone family emblem—that it has teeth."

"Well," Penny said, "for my money, he has every right to feel savage."

"Be that as it may," Letitia said, "I have to go and bait the wolf."

"He's shut up in his study," Clarice told her. "'Ware the snarls."

"He might snarl, but he won't bite. At least, not me." Letitia paused at the door. "I hope."

On that note, she left.

Minerva frowned into her glass, now less than half full—then set it aside. After a moment, she rose and tugged the bellpull; when a footman arrived, she said, "Please inform Lady Margaret, Lady Aurelia, and Lady Susannah that I wish to speak with them. Here. Immediately."

The footman bowed—lower than normal; clearly the household already knew of her impending change in station—and withdrew.

Meeting Clarice's inquiring glance, Minerva smiled—intently. "I believe it's time I clarified matters. Aside from all else, with a ducal wedding to organize, the house party ends tomorrow night."

Royce was standing at the window when Jeffers entered to announce Letitia; he turned as she came in. "How is she?"

Letitia arched a brow. "Upset, of course."

The fury he'd been holding at bay—clamped tight inside—rose up at the thought, the confirmation. He turned back to look blindly out at his fields. After a long moment, during which Letitia wisely remained silent and still, he bit off, "It wasn't supposed to be like this."

Every word was invested with cold, hard rage.

The same words that had rung in his head as he'd driven back to Wolverstone after so many years away.

When he'd driven home to bury his father.

This time, the rage was even greater. "I can't believe—can't understand why—Susannah would do such a thing, even if, as she claims, she was trying to help." That was the other element that was eating at him. He raked a hand through his hair. "What help is this—essentially forcing us into marriage?"

Letitia saw the tremble in his hand, didn't mistake it for weakness; it was pure rage distilled. But he wouldn't be so angry, so close to true rage, if he didn't care—deeply—about Minerva's feelings. If he didn't have deep feelings of his own.

She was a Vaux—an expert in emotional scenes, in reading the undercurrents, the real passions beneath. Yet if she told him how pleased she was to see him so distraught, he'd bite her head off.

Besides, she had another role to fill. Lifting her head, she imperiously asked, "The announcement—have you written it?"

She hoped her tone would refocus his attention.

He continued to stare out. A minute ticked by. She waited.

"No." After a moment, he added, "I will."

"Just do it." She softened her voice. "You know it has to be done, and urgently." Realizing that he was at sea—on a storm-tossed emotional ocean he, of all men, was poorly equipped to navigate—she went on, "Get your secretary to pen it, then show it to Minerva and get her consent. Regardless, it must be on the mail coach to London tonight."

He didn't immediately respond, but then he nodded. Curtly. "It will be."

"Good." She bobbed a curtsy, turned, and walked to the door.

He stirred, glanced at her. "Can you tell Margaret she's hostess tonight?"

Her hand on the doorknob, she looked at him. "Yes, of course."

His chest swelled; for the first time he met her eyes. "Tell Minerva I'll come and see her in a little while—once I've got the announcement drafted."

Once he had his temper in hand. As a Vaux, Letitia knew all about temper—and she could see his roiling in his eyes.

He went on, "We'll dine in my apartments."

"I'll keep her company until then. Clarice, Jack, and Penny are going to mingle, to make sure there's no . . . uninformed talk." She smiled, anticipating doing the same herself—and putting a not-so-tiny flea in Susannah's ear. "I'll join them once you come for Minerva."

"Thank you. All of you."

Turning to the door, she smiled rather more delightedly, knowing he couldn't see. "Believe me, it's our pleasure."

She paused, hand on the knob. "We can discuss the wedding tomorrow."

He grunted.

At least it wasn't a snarl. She let herself out, closing the door behind her. Glancing at Royce's footman standing utterly blank-faced along the wall, she smiled gloriously. "Despite all, this is going to work out very well."

With that, she hurried back to the morning room, to relate to Minerva all she'd seen, heard—and deduced.

Minerva had assuaged a great deal of her anger by the time Royce joined her in the morning room. Having successfully dealt first with his sisters, and then the assembled ladies, having ensured all knew precisely how unamused she was over Susannah's misplaced meddling, and having made her expectations, as the soon-to-be Duchess of Wolverstone, of their behavior over the matter abundantly plain, she was feeling much more settled as she stood looking out of the window, idly surveying his domain.

Royce's gaze locked on her the instant he opened the door, but she didn't turn around.

Seated on the sofa facing the door, Letitia rose. "I was about to go down." She glided forward.

Royce held the door open for her. She touched his arm, glanced back at Minerva. "I'll see you in the morning."

Without looking around, Minerva nodded—a tense, brief nod.

With a pat for him, Letitia left. He closed the door, hesitated—sent a prayer winging to any god that might be listening that Minerva wouldn't cry. Feminine tears usually left him unaffected, but her tears would shred his control, rupture his tenuous hold on his temper—and the gods alone knew who he'd strike out at, or how. Not her, of course, but . . .

Breathing in, mentally shoring up his defenses, emotional ones he rarely used, he walked to her side.

It was early evening; beyond the window, the shadows

were lengthening, laying a purple wash over his lands. Spine poker straight, arms crossed, she was looking out, but he'd swear not seeing.

Halting beside her, he angled his head the better to see her features. She turned her head and met his gaze.

Her expression was controlled, composed, more so than he'd expected; her eyes . . . were unusually hard, and more unreadable than he'd ever seen, but . . . he could detect not a hint of tears.

Chin firm, she tipped her head toward the door. "They're really quite remarkable—Letitia, Penny, Clarice, and Jack. I'm sure between them they'll have the entire company in well-rehearsed order come morning."

Her tone was crisp, briskly businesslike. Determined. Steady assurance shone through her composed façade.

Confusion swamped him. Didn't she feel . . . *betrayed*? By fate, by his sister, by circumstance? By him? He drew in a breath. "I'm sorry." He felt his jaw harden. "It wasn't supposed to have been like this."

Her eyes locked on his. "No, it wasn't, but what happened was neither my fault nor yours. Regardless, however much we may wish matters otherwise, we're faced with the situation as is, and we need to deal with it—to make the best of it. To take control and make it work for us, not against us."

He mentally blinked. She was behaving as if what had occurred was some minor hiccup along their road. A challenge they'd deal with, vanquish, and leave behind.

She couldn't be that understanding. She had to feel forced . . . had to resent the situation as much as he. He was missing something here; he didn't try to hide his frown. "You're a lot less upset than I expected."

The look she returned was all cold, hard steel. Her features tightened; her diction grew more precise. "I am *not* pleased—I'm angry, nay *furious, but* I am *not* of a mind to allow Susannah to play fast and loose with our lives." Strength of a kind he'd assumed was there but had never before encountered in her—the kind he associated with Lady Osbaldestone—

radiated from her. "I am *not* going to let Susannah steal from us what we, both you and I, deserve. I know you don't understand, but I'll explain later." Alight with purpose, her eyes lowered. "Is that our announcement?"

He glanced down at the sheet of paper he'd forgotten he held. "Yes."

She held out her hand, fingers wiggling.

He handed over the excruciatingly generically worded statement he and Handley had labored over.

Turning, she held it so light from the window washed over it. "Royce Henry Varisey, tenth Duke of Wolverstone, son of the late Henry Varisey, ninth Duke of Wolverstone and the late Lady Catherine Debraigh, daughter of the fourth Earl of Catersham, announces his betrothal to Miss Minerva Miranda Chesterton, daughter of the late Lieutenant Michael Chesterton and the late Marjorie Dalkeith."

She frowned. "A lot of lates, but . . ." Face clearing, she handed the announcement back, met his eyes. "That will do."

"So why, exactly, are you nothing more than 'not pleased'? What is it I don't understand?"

Halting before the wide window in Royce's bedroom, facing the night-shrouded hills, Minerva let her watchful tension ease. *Finally.*

Finally they were alone; finally she could tell him on her own terms, as she'd intended.

At his decree, they'd dined privately in his sitting room; she'd come into the bedroom to allow Jeffers to clear the table and set the room to rights. Royce had followed; closing the door on the clink of cutlery and plates, he'd prowled to halt just behind her.

She drew a deep breath. "I know you thought, by remaining apart, to spare me the ordeal of facing the undoubtedly avidly curious company downstairs—I agreed *not* because I felt fragile or distressed, but because *your* temper was so aroused that I had no faith whatever that your sisters or one of their friends wouldn't have said something to make you lash out—and that wouldn't have aided our cause." She swung to face him. "*Our* cause. From this morning on, it's been *our* cause."

She tilted her head, considered him. When he'd joined her in the morning room, his rage had been palpable, resonating in the words he'd ground out: *It wasn't supposed to have been like this.* "I understand why you were so angry. Being forced, trapped, into marriage shouldn't have mattered to you, but it did. Because you knew it mattered to me. You were enraged on my behalf—yours, too, but less directly."

The incident had delivered to him exactly what he'd wanted and had been working to gain—her agreement to their wedding. Yet instead of being pleased, he, a nobleman who rarely if ever apologized, had abjectly apologized for something that hadn't been his fault.

Because it was something she hadn't wanted, and so something the protector in him felt he should have prevented, but hadn't.

All day, in him, she'd been viewing love in action. Since that moment on the battlements, she'd watched love reduce a man accustomed to commanding all in his life to a wounded, potentially vicious beast.

While some intensely female part of her had gloated over such violent championing, she'd had to defuse his temper rather than encourage it. She'd been waiting for it to cool to have a better chance of him believing the truth of what she was about to say.

She locked her eyes on his, as always too dark to read. "I'd planned to speak now—this evening, once we were alone." She glanced around. "Here—in your room." She brought her gaze back to his face. "In your ducal apartments."

Stepping forward, eyes locked with his, she placed one hand over his heart. "I was going to tell you, just like this. Tell you that, as of this morning, I'd decided to accept your offer—when you make it. That you could feel free to offer, knowing I'll accept."

A long moment passed. He remained very still. "This morning?"

Hope warred with skepticism, but hope was winning. She smiled. "You can ask Letitia, Clarice, or Penny for confirmation—they knew. But that's why I'm not overwrought, distraught, unhappy. I'm none of those things—I'm *angry*, yes, but against that . . ." She let her smile deepen, let him see the depth of her understanding, and the sheer certainty and joy that was in her heart. "I'm thrilled, ecstatic, *delighted*. No matter Susannah's actions, no matter their outcome, in reality, between us, nothing has changed."

His hands slid about her waist. She raised hers, framed his face, looked deep into his fathomless eyes. "The only thing we might have lost was this moment, but I wasn't of a mind to let that go, to let it be taken from us. From this morning, for me, it's been *us*—*our* cause—and from this moment on, now that you know, there will be only one cause for us both—*ours*. It's the right cause for both of us to give our lives to—we both know that. From this moment on, we'll devote ourselves to it, work at it, if necessary fight for it—our joint life." Lost in his eyes, she let a heartbeat pass. "I wanted— needed—to tell you if that's what you want—if that's what your offer can and will encompass—then I'll accept. That's what I want, too."

A long moment passed, then his chest swelled as he drew in a huge breath. "You truly are happy to put this . . . hiccup behind us, consign it to history, and go forward?"

"Yes. Exactly as we would have."

He held her gaze for another long moment, then his lips, his features, eased. Her hands fell to his shoulders; he caught one of them, carried it to his lips. Eyes locked with hers, he kissed her fingertips.

Slowly.

In that instant he truly was mesmerizing; she couldn't have torn her gaze from his had flames leapt about them.

"Minerva, my lover. My lady. My heart. Will you marry me?"

She blinked once, twice, felt her heart literally swell. "Yes."

Such a little word, and although she'd poured every ounce of her certainty, resolution, and joy into it, there was more she had to say. Raising her other hand, she laid her fingers against his lean cheek, lightly traced the angular planes that gave so little away, even now.

Felt her heart overflow as she looked into his eyes, smiled. "I'll marry you, Royce Varisey, and fill the place by your side. I'll bear your children, and with my hand in yours, face whatever the future might bring, and make the most of it that, together, we can . . . for Wolverstone—and you."

He was Wolverstone, but that wasn't all he was. Underneath was a man who deserved her love. So she gave it, let him see it in her eyes.

Royce studied the autumn hues, the brilliant golds, the passionate browns, the mysterious agate-green, knew to his soul how much she meant to him—and knew he was the luckiest man alive. Slowly bending his head, he waited until she tipped her face up to his, then lowered his lips to hers.

And let a simple kiss seal their pact.

The loving that followed mirrored that kiss—simple, uncomplicated, undisguised. And she was right—nothing had changed. The passion, the heat, the fervor were the same. If anything deeper, broader, more intense, brought to burgeoning richness by acceptance, by the simple declarations that had committed them both, minds, bodies, hearts, and souls, to facing their future together.

That pledged them to the adventure of forging something new, something never before known in his family. To forging a marriage founded on, anchored in, held together by love.

Spread naked beneath him on his crimson silk sheets, she wrapped her arms about him and arched in welcome; poised above her, as heated and urgent as she, he slid into the haven of her body, and felt her clasp him tightly, embracing him, holding him. On a soundless gasp, head rising, he closed his eyes—held still, muscles bunched and quivering as he fought to give them that moment, that instant of indescribable sensation as their bodies locked, that instant of flagrant intimacy before the dance began.

Sensing the reins slipping, sliding from his grasp, he hauled in a breath and looked down. Saw her eyes glint gold from beneath her lashes.

I love you. He wanted to say the words, they hovered on his tongue, yet he didn't know, even now, if they were true. He wanted them to be, but . . .

Her lips curved as if she understood; reaching up with one hand, she cupped his nape, drew his lips to hers.

And kissed him—a blatant invitation to abandon.

He accepted and let go, let passion take and fuse them. Let their bodies surge, merge, surrendering to need, hunger, and wanting.

Opening his eyes, he looked down at her face, glowing with passion, rapturous in surrender, the face of his woman, his lady, soon his wife, utterly and unreservedly his.

Given to him.

He put aside the torment of the day, let their joint passion swamp it, drown it, wash it away. Let himself free and sealed their pact.

And gave himself unreservedly to her.

Twenty

The next morning, Minerva stood beside Royce as, with the cheers of the crowd for the nine handfasted couples gradually fading, he stepped to the front of the dais from which, earlier, he'd opened the fair.

Quietening, the crowd regarded him expectantly. He let his gaze roam the upturned faces, then said, "Wolverstone, too, has an announcement to make." He glanced at her, with his gaze drew her closer. His smile was all she would ever hope to see; the undisguised warmth in his eyes held her as, capturing her hand, he raised it to his lips, and in full view of the assembled company, pressed a kiss to her knuckles. "Miss Chesterton has done me the honor of agreeing to be my duchess."

He hadn't spoken loudly, yet his voice carried clearly over the hushed crowd . . .

The crowd erupted. Cheers, huzzahs, triumphant yells, whoops, and shrieks; noise rose in a wave of unalloyed happiness and washed over the scene. Minerva looked, and saw Hamish and Molly, who they'd found and told earlier, beaming up at them. The castle's staff were all there—Retford, Cranny, Cook, Jeffers, Milbourne, Lucy, Trevor, and all the rest—all looking fit to burst with pride and joy. Looking further, she saw the faces of many of Wolverstone's people, all delighted, all thrilled. Saw happy, joyous, pleased expressions, clapping hands, laughter, happy tears. Even those from the house party, scattered here and there among the throng, looked pleased to be part of the upwelling gladness.

Royce held up a hand; the cheers and whistles died. "Our wedding will be held in the church here, in just over three weeks' time. As many of you know, I returned only recently to take up the reins of the dukedom—in just a few weeks I've learned a great deal about what has changed, and what yet needs changing. Just as I'll make my vows to my duchess, and she to me, together we'll stand committed to you, to Wolverstone, to forging ahead into our joint future."

"Wolverstone!" With one voice, the crowd roared its approval. "Wolverstone! *Wolverstone!*"

Minerva surveyed the sea of happy faces, felt the warmth of their people reaching for them, embracing, buoying; turning her head, she met Royce's eyes, smiled.

His hand tightened about hers and he smiled back, openly, honestly, his customary shields lowered, for once set aside.

No! No, no, no, no—how could this have happened?

Deep in the crowd, surrounded by, jostled by, the raucous, gibbering throng, all transported with delight over the news of Royce's wedding, he stood stunned, unable to think—unable to drag his eyes from the picture of Royce and Minerva standing on the dais, lost in each other's eyes.

Royce was an excellent actor when he wanted to be—he knew that. Minerva could hold her own, too . . .

He shook his head, wished he could deny what his eyes were telling him. Neither was acting—what he was seeing, what the entire crowd about him was taking in and responding to, was *real.*

Royce wanted to marry Minerva.

And she wanted to marry him.

She was in love with him—nothing else could account for the softness in her face.

And while Royce couldn't possibly love her, he definitely cared for her— in a far warmer way than he'd ever have thought possible.

Minerva wasn't, had never been, just another of Royce's legion of lovers. She'd been the one, all along—the lady he'd wanted as his wife . . .

"It wasn't supposed to be like this." He ground the words out through clenched teeth, fighting to keep his face a mask of utter blankness.

Their marriage was supposed to be a farce, a travesty—it was supposed to be *painful*. Instead, all his maneuvering had done was hand Royce precisely what he'd wanted.

He, through Susannah, had been instrumental in giving Royce the last thing he needed to complete the tapestry of an already rich and satisfying existence. He'd been instrumental in giving Royce something he craved, something he treasured . . .

Suddenly, he knew. Suddenly, he saw.

His features eased.

Then, slowly, he smiled, too.

Increasingly delightedly. He laughed, and clapped Rohan on the back when he passed him in the crowd.

Yes, of course. Now he saw it.

Royce had been the motive, the cause in bringing him his treasure—only then to take it away.

So fitting, then, that he would be the one to give Royce his greatest treasure—so he could return the favor.

Royce had taken his treasure.

Now he would take Royce's.

That evening, Royce, Minerva, Letitia, Clarice, Penny, and Handley met in the duchess's morning room. In the wake of the hugely successful fair—made even more notable by the news they'd shared—dinner had been an informal affair.

After refreshing themselves, they'd left the relaxed and apparently pleasantly exhausted company downstairs, and retired to address the logistics of a ducal wedding.

While the others settled, Royce, subsiding beside Minerva on one of the sofas, considered his wife-to-be. "Did you say something to the others downstairs? They seem strangely unexercised by our betrothal."

"I simply explained that Susannah's intervention was misjudged, and that as your duchess, I would be severely displeased were anyone to paint our betrothal in anything other than the correct light."

Sinking onto the sofa opposite, Penny chuckled. "It was masterful. She made Susannah's action appear a childish prank—one of those occurrences that are so excruciatingly awkward that it would be a kindness to Susannah to pretend it never happened."

Joining Penny on the sofa, Letitia added, "She only had to speak to the ladies—Jack reported that as none of the men were on the battlements, they were very ready to pretend it never happened. But turning the event around so it reflected on Susannah was a master stroke. I would never have thought of it, but it served wonderfully well."

"No doubt," Clarice said, settling on the end of the sofa, "your facility comes from having to deal with Variseys for decades."

"Indeed." Minerva turned to Royce, met his eyes. "Now, for our wedding."

Very early that morning, he'd suggested as soon as possible, and been informed that wasn't in his cards. When he'd grumbled, he'd been further informed, at length, why. "Three weeks, I believe you said?"

Her eyes lit. "Indeed. Three weeks—and we'll need every minute from now until then." She looked at Handley, seated before her desk. "What date are we looking at?"

Resigned—and inwardly happier than he'd ever felt in his life—Royce sat back and let them organize; his only task was to approve when applied to, which he duly did. They were the experts. Letitia knew everything about staging events in the ton. Although in semiretirement, Clarice was renowned as a manipulator of ton sentiments. Penny, like Minerva, understood the dynamics of major estates, of country and county, while Minerva knew everything there was to know about Wolverstone and the Variseys.

Together, they made a formidable team. In short order, they had the framework settled.

"So"—Minerva caught Handley's eye—"the banns will be read over the next three Sundays, and we'll be married the following Thursday."

Handley nodded and made a note. "I'll ask Mr. Cribthorn to call tomorrow." He glanced at Royce.

"I'll be here all day. We've rather a lot to get into place." The marriage settlements, among other things. "You'd better summon Montague."

Handley furiously wrote. "And your solicitors?"

"Yes—them, too." Royce glanced at Minerva. "I've been racking my brains, but can't find the answer—who will give you away? And as you keep reminding me, this is a ducal union, so who do you want to act for you?"

She blinked. "I'll have to think about it." She glanced at Handley. "I'll give you the names and directions of my agent and solicitor so you can tell Royce's who to contact."

"Yes, ma'am."

Various other details were discussed and decided. The announcement for the news sheets completed, Handley left to ferry it to Retford for dispatch.

"The guest list," Clarice warned, "is going to be the biggest challenge."

"Just thinking of it makes the mind boggle." Letitia shook her head. "I thought my second wedding was big, but this . . ."

"We'll simply have to be highly selective," Minerva stated. "Which, to my mind, is no bad thing." She looked at Penny. "I'm inclined to set the number by the size of the church."

Penny considered, then shook her head. "You won't get

away with that—not if by that you mean after you've accommodated the locals?"

"I did mean that." Minerva sighed. "So how many do you think?"

She'd wrestled the number down to five hundred when Royce decided he'd heard enough. *Five hundred?* Rising, he inclined his head. "Ladies, I believe I can leave the details in your capable hands." He glanced at Minerva. "If you need me, I'll be in the study, and then later in my apartments."

Waiting for her.

She smiled. "Yes, of course."

Smiling himself, he left them.

Minerva watched him go, sensing his inner peace, then, inwardly glowing herself, refocused on her list. "All right—how many do we need to allow for Carlton House?"

An hour later, with the major groups of guests identified and estimated, they called a halt. Retford had already delivered a tea tray; as they sat sipping, Letitia listed the areas they'd covered. "I really don't think there's much else we can assist you with, at least not at this time." She met Minerva's eyes. "We were thinking of leaving tomorrow at first light."

"Earlier than all the others, so we won't get caught up in their chaos," Penny said.

Clarice studied Minerva. "But if you truly need us, you only have to say."

She smiled, shook her head. "You've been . . ." She included the other two in her glance. "Immensely helpful, incredibly supportive. I honestly don't know how I would have got through all this without your help."

Letitia grinned. "You'd have managed. Given you can—demonstrably—manage your soon-to-be husband, I find it difficult to believe there's any situation you won't be able to overcome."

"I have to ask," Clarice said. "How did you get him to accept the three weeks so readily? We came prepared with a list of arguments, but you already had him agreeing."

"He's very predictable in some ways. I simply pointed out that our marriage should, by rights, be a major local event, and how disappointed everyone on the estate would be to be shortchanged."

Letitia grinned. "Oh, yes—I can see that would work." She gave a delighted quiver. "Ooh! You've no idea how much good it does to see the master manipulator manipulated."

"But he knows I'm doing it," Minerva pointed out.

"Yes, indeed, and that makes it all the more delightful." Letitia set down her cup. "My dear, is there anything else, anything at all, that we can help you with before we leave?"

Minerva thought, then said, "If you will, answer me this: What moved your husbands to recognize they loved you?"

"You mean what wrung that word from their lips?" Letitia grimaced. "I was dangling from battlements, literally held from Death's jaws by his grip alone, before he thought to utter the word. I wouldn't recommend it."

Clarice frowned. "In my case, too, it was after a brush with death—with the iniquitous last traitor's henchman. Again, not an activity I'd recommend."

"As I recall," Penny said, "it was after we assisted Royce in apprehending a murderous French spy. There was a certain amount of life-threatening danger, none of which came to pass, but it opened *my* eyes, so I declared I would marry him—and then he was quite put out that I hadn't forced a grand declaration from him. He considered the point obvious, but had convinced himself that I'd claim my due." She smiled, sipped. "He gave it to me, anyway." Lowering her cup, she added, "Then again, he's half French."

Minerva frowned. "There seems to be a consistent trend with our sort of men."

Clarice nodded. "They seem to require a life-and-death situation to prod them into listening to their hearts."

Penny frowned. "But you already know Royce is head-over-ears in love with you, don't you? It really is rather blatantly obvious."

"Yes, *I* know." Minerva sighed. "I know, you know, even

his sisters are starting to see it. But the one person who doesn't yet know is the tenth Duke of Wolverstone himself. And I honestly don't know how to open his eyes."

Three full weeks had come and gone. Sitting in the keep's breakfast parlor, Royce was quietly amazed; he'd thought the time would drag, but instead, it had flown.

On his left, a sunbeam glinting in her hair, Minerva was engrossed in yet more lists; he smiled, savoring as he did countless times a day the warmth and enfolding comfort of what he mentally termed his new existence.

His life as the tenth Duke of Wolverstone; it would be radically different from that of his father's, and the cornerstone of that difference was his impending marriage.

Minerva humphed. "Thank heavens Prinny balked at the distance. Accommodating him and his toadies would have been a nightmare." She glanced up, smiled as Hamilton placed a fresh teapot before her. "We'll finalize the assignment of rooms this morning—Retford will need a list by noon."

"Indeed, ma'am. Retford and I have devised a plan of the castle, which will help."

"Excellent! If you come to the morning room once you're finished here, that should give me time to finish with Cranny, and check the mail to make sure we have no unexpected additions." She glanced at Royce. "Unless you need Hamilton?"

He shook his head. "I'll be finalizing matters with Killsythe this morning." His solicitors, Killsythe and Killsythe, had finally wrested control of the last legal matters pertaining to the dukedom from Collier, Collier, and Whitticombe, so at last such issues were proceeding smoothly. "Incidentally"—with his finger he tapped a missive he'd earlier read—"Montague sent word that all is in place. He was very complimentary about your previous agent's efforts, but believes he can do better."

Minerva smiled. "I have high expectations." Reaching for

the teapot, she surveyed the seven lists arrayed before her. "I can barely recall when I last had a chance to think of such mundane things as investments."

Royce raised his coffee cup, hid a smile. One thing he'd learned about his wife-to-be was that she thrived on challenge. As with his father's funeral, the principal guests would be accommodated at the castle, as would the majority of both sides of his family, virtually all of whom had sent word they would attend. While he'd been engulfed in legal and business matters, some still pending from his father's death but most part of the preparation necessary for the execution of the marriage settlements, Minerva's time had been swallowed up by preparations for the wedding itself.

Hamilton had proved a godsend; after discussions with Minerva and Retford, Royce had summoned him north to act as his personal butler, freeing Retford for the wider castle duties, increased dramatically because of the wedding. As Hamilton was younger and perfectly willing to defer to Retford, the arrangement was working well, to everyone's benefit.

Royce turned to the social page of yesterday's *Gazette*; he'd religiously perused every column inch devoted to their upcoming union ever since the news had broken. Far from being cast in any unflattering light, somewhat to his disgust their wedding was being touted as the romantic event of the year.

"What's today's effort like?" Minerva didn't take her eyes from her lists. When he'd first remarked on the slant all the news sheets had taken, she'd merely said, "I did wonder what they'd do." She'd been referring to the grandes dames.

Royce perused the five inches of column devoted to their event, then snorted. "This one goes even further. It reads like a fairy tale—wellborn but orphaned beauty slaves for decades as the chatelaine of a ducal castle, then on the death of the crusty old duke, catches the roving eye of said duke's mysterious exiled son, now her new lord, and a marcher lord at that, but instead of suffering the indignity of a slip on the shoulder, as one might expect, she succeeds in winning the hardened heart of her new duke and ends as his duchess."

With a sound very like "pshaw," he tossed the paper on the table. Regarded it with open disgust. "While that might contain elements of the truth, they've reduced it to the bizarre."

Minerva grinned. At one point she'd wondered whether he might realize the fundamental truth underlying the reports—that dissecting news sheet inanity might reveal to him what she and many others already knew of him—but it hadn't happened. As the days passed, it seemed increasingly likely that nothing less than long, frequent, and deepening exposure to his own emotions was likely to open his eyes.

Eyes that were so sharply observant when trained on anyone and anything else, but when it came to himself, to his inner self, simply did not see.

Sitting back, she considered her own efforts; ducal weddings in the country had to top the list of the most complicated events to manage. He rose to leave; she looked up, pinned him with a direct look. "You'll need to be available from noon today, and throughout tomorrow and the next day, to greet the more important guests as they arrive."

He held her gaze, then looked at Jeffers and Hamilton, standing by the wall behind her chair. "Send one of the footmen, one who can recognize crests, up to the battlements with a spyglass."

"Yes, Your Grace." Jeffers hesitated, then added, "If I might suggest, we could send one of the lads to the bridge with a list of those it would be helpful to know are approaching—he could wave a flag. That would be easily seen from the battlements."

"An excellent idea!" Seeing Royce's nod, Minerva turned to Hamilton. "Once we've done the rooms, you and Retford could make up a list. I'll check it, then Handley can make copies." She glanced at Royce, brows rising.

He nodded. "Handley will be with me in the study for most of the day, but he'll have time in the afternoon to do the lists."

Minerva smiled. Letitia had been right; there was very little she couldn't overcome—not with Royce, and the entire household, at her back. There was something intensely satisfying about being the general at the head of the troops; she'd always loved her chatelaine role, but she was going to enjoy being a duchess even more.

Royce's eyes held hers, then his lips kicked up at the ends. With a last glance, and a salute, he left her. Reaching for her cup, she returned to her lists.

The next morning they tumbled out of his bed early, and together rode up Usway Burn. Against everyone's but Royce's expectations, the cottages were nearing completion; after glancing over the improvements, Minerva sat on a bench against the front wall of the largest cottage while Royce made a more detailed inspection, old Macgregor at his elbow.

Of the major projects Royce had approved since he'd taken up the ducal reins, the footbridge over the Coquet had had first call on Hancock's time. The bridge was now a proper footbridge, raised higher to avoid bores, rebuilt, and properly braced. The cottages had come next, and they were nearly finished; another week would see them done. After that, Hancock and his team would start on the mill—not a moment too soon, but luckily the weather had held, and all the wood and even more importantly the glass had already been procured. The mill would be sealed before winter, which, aside from all the rest, was a great deal more than she'd thought to achieve before his father had died.

She looked up, watched as Royce and Macgregor, deep in discussion, paced slowly across to the cottage on the left. She smiled as they disappeared, then let her mind slide to its present preoccupation.

The first guests, all family, had arrived yesterday. Today, his friends and hers would drive up. He'd chosen Rupert, Miles, Gerald, and Christian as his groomsmen; against that, she'd chosen Letitia, Rose, an old friend Ellen, Lady Ambervale, and Susannah as her matrons-of-honor. She'd felt obliged to have one of his sisters, and despite Susannah's idiotic attempt at manipulation, she'd meant well, and Margaret or Aurelia would have been too grim.

All three of his sisters had arrived yesterday; all three were being very careful around her, aware that not only did she now have their all-powerful brother's ear, she also knew virtually all their secrets. Not that she was likely to do anything with the knowledge, but they didn't know that.

One part of the guest list that he'd supplied had pleased her enormously; he'd invited eight of his ex-colleagues. From Letitia, Penny, and Clarice she'd heard much about the group—the members of the Bastion Club plus Jack, Lord Hendon, and all their wives; she'd heard that Royce had declined to attend their weddings, and hadn't been the least surprised to receive instant acceptances from the respective ladies. She suspected they intended to make a point by dancing joyously at *his* wedding.

Regardless, she was looking forward to meeting them all, those who had been closest to Royce professionally over the last years.

Over the few hours they'd managed to steal for their own—those not spent in his bed—she'd encouraged him to tell her more of the activities that had filled his lost years, those years of his life that had been lost to her, and his parents. After an initial hesitation, he'd gradually relaxed his guard, speaking increasingly freely of various missions, and the numerous threads he'd woven into a net for gathering intelligence, both military and civilian.

He'd described it all well enough for her, knowing him, to see it, feel it, understand how and in what way the activity of those years had impacted on him. He'd admitted he'd killed, in cold blood, not on foreign soil, but here in England. He'd expected her to be shocked, had tensed, but had relaxed, relieved, when, after he'd confirmed such deaths had been essential for national safety, she'd merely blinked, and nodded.

He'd told her of the Bastion Club members' recent adventures. He'd also told her about the man they'd termed "the last traitor"—the fiend Clarice had mentioned—an Englishman, a gentleman of the ton, most likely someone with a connection to the War Office, who'd betrayed his country for French treasure, and had killed and killed again to escape Royce and his men.

After the war's end, Royce had lingered in London, pursuing every last avenue in an attempt to learn the last traitor's identity. He'd cited that as his only failure.

To her relief, he'd clearly put that unfulfilled chase behind him; he spoke of it as history, not a current activity. That he could accept such a failure was reassuring; she knew enough to appreciate that, in a man as powerful as he, knowing when to walk away was a strength, not a weakness.

That over the last weeks he'd talked to her so openly, and in return had elicited from her details of how she'd spent the same years, had left her feeling increasingly confident of the strength that would underpin their marriage—had left her ever more secure in the reality of his love.

A love he, still, could not see.

Emerging from the cottage, he exchanged farewells with Macgregor, shaking the old man's hand. Turning to her, he met her eyes, arched a brow. "Are you ready?"

She smiled, rose, and gave him her hand. "Yes. Lead on."

He was back at Wolverstone, under his nemesis's roof once more. Even though he had to share a room with Rohan, he didn't care. He was there, close, and invisible among the gathering throng. Everyone could see him, yet no one really could—not the real him. He was hidden, forever concealed.

No one would ever know.

His plans were well advanced, at least in theory. All he had to do now was find the right place to stage his ultimate victory.

It shouldn't be too hard; the castle was huge, and there

were various buildings people paid little attention to dotted through the gardens. He had two days to find the perfect place.

Two days before he would act.

And finally win free of the torment.

Of the black, corrosive fear.

By Wednesday afternoon, the castle was full, literally to the rafters. With so many members of the haut ton attending, the number of visiting servants had stretched the accommodations below stairs—or rather in the attics—to their limit.

"We've even put cots in the ironing room," Trevor told Minerva when she met him in the gallery reverently ferrying a stack of perfectly ironed cravats. "We've moved the ironing boards into the laundry—unlikely we'll be doing much washing over the next two days."

She grimaced. "At least this time everyone is leaving the next day."

"Just as well," Trevor grimly declared. "There's a limit to how much mayhem one household can withstand."

She laughed and turned away. In reality the household was managing well, even though the castle was as full as she'd ever known it. Every guest chamber was in use, even the rooms in the keep. The only rooms on that level that had been spared were her morning room, Royce's sitting room, and the study.

Her morning room. Royce had started calling it that a few weeks ago, and she'd fallen into the habit.

Smiling, she continued around the gallery; it was late afternoon, almost early evening, and the guests were either resting or conversing quietly somewhere before dressing for dinner. For the first time that day, she had the opportunity to draw an unhurried breath.

"Minerva."

She stopped, turned, a smile already on her lips. Royce stood before the corridor to his apartments; he held out his hand.

There was nothing she had to do at that moment. Or rather . . . smile deepening, she went to join him.

Her smile mirrored in his eyes, he grasped her hand, turned down the corridor, stopped before the door to the battlements. As before, he released the catch, then let her go up before following.

She walked to the battlements, spread her arms wide and breathed . . . then turned to face him as he neared. "Just what I needed—fresh and *uncrowded* air."

His lips quirked. "The castle's all but humming with humanity. It's a living, breathing hive."

She laughed, swung again to the view, set her hands on the ancient stone of the battlements—and felt as if through the touch they grounded her. She looked out—and saw. Familiar sights, a familiar landscape. "When you brought me up here, and showed me this, and told me that this is what you would share . . . even though I'd been chatelaine for over a decade, I . . . it feels different, somehow, now." His hands slid about her waist; she glanced up and back at his face. "Now I'm to be your duchess."

Royce nodded; as she looked back at the hills, he dropped a kiss below her ear. "Before you weren't ultimately responsible—you were still one step removed. But now you're starting to see the fields as I do." He lifted his head, looking out over his lands. "You're starting to feel what I feel when I stand here and look out at my domain—and sense what that really means."

She leaned back against him. He settled his arms about her, felt her arms, her hands, settle over his.

For a moment, they were silent, seeing, sensing, feeling, then he said, "The message my father left me—that I didn't need to be like him. You took it to mean the dukedom, and the way I dealt with that. But the more I realize how much like him I am—and therefore how much like me he was—I think—believe—that he meant the comment more widely."

She tilted her head, listening, but didn't interrupt.

"I think," he said, his arms tightening about her, feeling

her, a warm, vibrant presence anchoring him, "that in those last minutes, he tried to address the regrets of his life—and from all I've learned, how he managed the dukedom wasn't high on that list. How he lived, I think, was. I think he regretted, to his dying breath, not making the effort to make more of his life—he had chances, but didn't seize them. Didn't try to forge more than the usual Varisey life—a life that was handed to him on a silver platter.

"He didn't try to forge what I'm trying to forge with you. Every day that passes, every hour we spend together, whether alone and looking inward, or dealing with our people, our responsibilities, is like another brick, another section of our foundations solidly laid. We're building something together that wasn't here before . . . I think that's what he meant. That I didn't have to follow in his footsteps, didn't have to marry as he had, didn't have to turn my back on the chance to build something more, something stronger, more enduring."

"Something more supportive." She turned in his arms, looked up at his face, met his eyes. Considered, then nodded. "You might well be right. Thinking back . . . he'd been waiting to speak to you, rehearsing for weeks, and then . . . he knew he didn't have much time."

"So he said the most important thing."

She nodded. "He meant life, not just the dukedom." She hesitated, then said, "I know you never realized, but his breach with you . . . opened his eyes. You holding firm was the catalyst—that was when he started to change. When he started to think. Your mother noticed, and so did I. He'd never been introspective before."

His lips quirked, half grimace, half smile. "At least he should feel pleased that, at last, I've taken his advice."

Minerva smiled, warm and deep. "He'd be unbearable— and unbearably proud."

He raised his brows, deprecatingly skeptical.

The deep bong of a gong floated up from below.

He held her before him, looked down at her face. "I suppose we should go and dress for dinner."

She nodded. "Yes, we should."

He sighed, bent his head and kissed her. Lightly . . .

Their lips clung, parted reluctantly. He lifted his head just an inch, breathed against her lips, "I don't suppose we can be late?"

Her hand had remained, splayed against his chest. It firmed. "No. We can't."

His sigh as he straightened was a great deal more heartfelt. "At least they'll all be gone the day after tomorrow."

She laughed, took his hand, and led him back to the stairs.

"Incidentally, don't be late tonight."

Pausing at the head of the stairs, she met his eyes. "Actually, tradition dictates that the bride and groom should spend the night before the wedding apart."

"In case you haven't noticed, I'm not wedded to tradition— and there's something I want to give you. Unless you wish to be carried through the gallery again—this time with every room around it occupied—I suggest you find your way to my rooms early rather than late."

She held his gaze, narrowed her eyes, then, struggling not to smile, humphed and turned down the stairs. "In case you haven't noticed, there are some Varisey traits you're very definitely wedded to."

Inwardly smiling, Royce followed her down the stairs.

"So what was it you wished to give me?" Minerva flicked her hair out of her eyes, struggled to lift her head enough to squint at him. "Or have I just received it?"

Royce laughed. He hugged her briefly, then hauled himself up. "No—there really is something." He had to sit on the edge of the bed for a moment until blood found its way back to his head, then he rose and crossed to the nearer tallboy. Opening the top drawer, he withdrew the package that had been delivered by special courier earlier that day. Carrying it back to the bed, he laid it on the sheet before her. "From me, to you, on the occasion of our wedding."

Minerva looked up at him, then, ignoring her unclad state, sat up amid the rumpled covers and eagerly unwrapped the odd-shaped parcel; it was vaguely triangular on one side, falling away . . . "Oh. My." The last piece of tissue fell away, leaving her round-eyed. "It's . . . *fabulous*."

That in no way did justice to the diadem that nestled in the layers of soft paper. Gold filigree of a complexity and fineness she'd never before seen wound its way around the band, rising in the front to support a plethora of . . . "Diamonds?"

The jewels didn't wink and blink; they burned with white fire.

"I had the whole cleaned and the stones reset." Royce dropped back on the bed, looked into her face. "Do you like it?"

"Oh, *yes*." Minerva reverently placed her hands around the delicate crown, then lifted it, glanced at him. "Can I put it on?"

"It's yours."

Raising her hands, she carefully placed the circlet atop her head. It sank just slightly, fitting neatly above her ears. She moved her head. "It fits."

His smile deepened. "Perfectly. I thought it would."

Uncaring of her naked state, she scrambled off the bed, and walked to the other tallboy so she could admire the coronet. The gold was just one shade darker than her hair, presently down and streaming over her bare shoulders.

Turning, she removed the crown; holding it between her hands, she examined it as she returned to the bed. "This isn't new—the design's old. Very old." She glanced at him. "I know it's not the Wolverstone duchess's coronet, at least not the one your mother had. Where did you get it?"

He met her eyes. "Prinny."

"Prinny?" She stared anew at the diadem. "But . . . this must be worth a small fortune. I can't imagine him parting with such a thing willingly."

"He wasn't exactly willing, but . . . I consider it ironically fitting that having pressured me into finding my bride, he should provide her wedding crown."

She sank back on the bed, carefully settling the crown back in its paper nest. "Irony aside, cut line—how and why did he come to give you such a thing?"

Royce stretched out on his back, crossed his arms behind his head. "You remember I told you about the treasure the last traitor had acquired from the French authorities?"

She nodded. "His payment for spying."

"Exactly. Not all of it was recovered from the wreck of the smuggling ship bringing it to England, but some pieces were found—among them, that crown. When the authorities matched it to the list of antiquities the French were missing, they discovered it was, in fact, Varisey property." He met her startled gaze. "It was made for one Hugo Varisey in the fifteen hundreds. It remained in the hands of the principal line of the family in France, until it fell into the hands of the revolutionary authorities. Thereafter it was considered property of the French state—until it was given in exchange for information to our last traitor—who we know is an Englishman. Now the war is over, the French, of course, want the crown back, but the government in Whitehall see no reason to hand it over. However, to end any discussion, and as it was felt I was owed some recognition for my service, they had Prinny present it to me—the head of the only branch of the Varisey family still extant."

She smiled. "So Prinny really had no choice?"

"I daresay he protested, but no." Royce watched as she carefully lifted the crown in its papers. "That's now mine—the oldest piece of Varisey family jewelry—and I'm gifting it to you."

Minerva set crown and papers on the bedside table, then turned and crawled back to him, a smile of explicit promise curving her lips. Reaching him, she framed his face and kissed him—long, lingeringly—as she slowly slid one leg over him. When she lifted her head, she was straddling him.

"Thank you." Her smile deepened as she looked into his eyes. "And that's just the beginning of my thanks."

He looked back at her with open anticipation—and something very close to challenge. "I was hoping you'd say that." He settled back. "Feel free."

She did—free to thank him to the top of her bent.

Later, when she lay pleasantly exhausted beside him, pleasured to her toes, she murmured, "You know, if it hadn't been for Prinny and his machinations . . ."

Royce thought, then shook his head. "No. Even if I'd taken longer to realize, I would still have set my heart on you."

Everything was ready. He'd found the right spot, worked through every detail of his plan. Nothing would go wrong.

Tomorrow would be his triumph. Tomorrow would see him win.

Tomorrow he'd break Royce.

And then he'd kill him.

Twenty-one

he clamor was deafening.
Royce leaned forward and spoke to Henry. "Pull
up."

Bedecked in full livery, garlanded with white ribbon— as
was the open carriage—Henry eased the heavy horses to
a halt in the middle of the road leading through Alwinton
village.

The cheering crowd pressed closer, waving, calling.

Royce threw Minerva a glance, a smile, then rose, and
drew her up with him; her hand clasped in his, he raised it
high. "I give you your new duchess!"

The crowd roared its approval.

Minerva fought to contain the flood of emotion that welled
and swelled inside her; looking out, she saw so many familiar faces—all so pleased that she was Royce's bride.

His wife.

She stood by his side and waved; the beaming smile on her
face had taken up residence when he'd turned her from the
altar to walk back up the aisle, and hadn't yet waned.

The crowd satisfied, he drew her back down; once she sat,
he told Henry to drive on.

Still smiling, she relaxed against Royce's shoulder, her

mind reaching back to the ceremony, then ranging ahead to the wedding breakfast to come.

The same carriage, freshly painted with the Wolverstone crest blazing on the doors and with ribbons woven through the reins, had carried her, the Earl of Catersham, and her matrons-of-honor to the church. Her gown of finest Brussels lace softly shushing, the delicate veil anchored by the Varisey diadem, she'd walked down the aisle on the earl's arm oblivious to the horde packed into the church—held by a pair of intense dark eyes.

In an exquisitely cut morning coat, Royce had waited for her before the altar; even though she'd seen him mere hours before, it seemed as if something had changed. As if their worlds changed in the instant she placed her hand in his and together they turned to face Mr. Cribthorn.

The service had gone smoothly; at least, she thought it had. She could remember very little, caught up, swept along, on a tide of emotion.

A tide of happiness that had welled as they'd exchanged their vows, peaked when Royce had slipped the simple gold band on her finger, overflowed when she'd heard the words, "I now pronounce you man and wife."

Duke and duchess.

The same, yet more. A fact that had been amply illustrated from the instant Royce had released her from the utterly chaste kiss they'd shared. A kiss that had carried both acknowledgment and promise, acceptance and commitment, from them both.

Their eyes had touched, then, as one, they'd turned and faced their future. Faced first the assembled throng, all of whom had wanted to congratulate them personally. Luckily, the others—his friends and the Bastion Club couples—had formed something of a guard, and helped them move reasonably smoothly up the aisle.

The roar as they'd emerged from the church into the weak sunshine had echoed from the hills. Hamish and Molly had been waiting by the steps; she'd hugged Molly, then turned to Hamish to see him hesitating—awed by the delicacy of her gown and the brilliance of the diadem's diamonds. She'd hugged him; awkwardly, he'd patted her with his huge hands. "You were right," she'd whispered. "Love really is simple—no thinking required."

He'd chuckled, bussed her cheek, then released her to all the others waiting to press her hand, shake Royce's, and wish them well.

An hour had passed before they'd been able to leave the churchyard; the guests and the rest of the wedding party had gone ahead, to the wedding breakfast waiting in the castle's huge ballroom, a long-ago addition built out at the back of the keep.

The carriage rolled across the stone bridge; a minute later, they passed through the heavy gates with their snarling wolf's heads. The castle rose before them; it was as much home to her as it was to Royce. She glanced at him, found his gaze dwelling on the gray stone of the façade.

Retford, Hamilton, Cranny, and Handley were waiting to meet them just inside the front door; all were beaming, but trying to keep their delight within bounds. "Your Grace." Retford bowed low; it took her a moment to realize he was addressing her.

Hamilton, Cranny, and Handley, too, all greeted her formally. "Everything's in readiness, ma'am," Cranny assured her.

"I take it everyone is here?" Royce asked.

Handley nodded. "Lord Haworth and Lord Chesterfield will need to leave in a few hours—I'll make sure to remind them."

Royce glanced at Minerva. "Any others we need to pay early attention to?"

She mentioned five others, representatives of king, regent, and Parliament, all of whom had to leave for London later that day. "Other than that, we'd be wise to give the grandes dames their due."

He snorted. "It's always wise to give those beldames due

attention." Taking her arm, he led her toward the ballroom.

"I suspect I should mention, Your Grace, that as from today, *I* am classed among the grandes dames."

He grinned. "My own grande dame. If that means that from now on I'll only have to deal with you"—he met her gaze as they paused outside the ballroom door—"I have no complaints."

Jeffers, liveried, proud, and bursting with delight, was waiting to open the door. Royce held her autumn eyes—eyes that saw him, all of him, and understood. He raised her hand, pressed a kiss to her fingertips. "Are you ready?"

She smiled a touch mistily. "Indeed, Your Grace. Lead on."

He did, ceremonially leading her into the huge ballroom where the entire company rose and applauded. They paraded down the long room to the table at the end; a smile wreathing every face, the company clapped until he seated her in the center of the main table, and sat beside her, then everyone followed suit and the festivities began.

It was a day of unalloyed happiness. Of enfolding warmth as the breakfast rolled on—through the long meal, the customary speeches, the first waltz. After that, the company rose and mingled freely.

Returning from doing his duty with the representatives of Crown and government, Royce resumed his chair at the high table. Content, aware of a depth of inner peace he'd never before known, he looked over the crowd, smiling at the undisguised joy apparent on so many faces. A moment to savor, to fix in his memory. The only friends missing were Hamish and Molly; both he and Minerva had wanted them to attend, but hadn't pressed, understanding that, in this milieu, Hamish and Molly would feel awkward.

Instead, he and Minerva planned to ride over the border tomorrow.

He wondered how much longer it would be wise for her to ride, especially long distances. He slanted a glance at her, in her chair beside him; as she hadn't yet actually *told* him anything, he suspected he'd be wise to hold his tongue, at least until she did.

A frisson of uncertainty rippled through him; he had absolutely no experience of ladies in delicate conditions. However, he knew several men who did—several, indeed, who were in much the same straits as he. Leaning closer to Minerva, deep in conversation with Rose and Alice, he touched her wrist. "I'm going to mingle. I'll catch up with you later."

She glanced at him, smiled, then turned back to his friends' wives.

Rising, he went looking for his ex-colleagues.

He found them in a knot in one corner of the room. All had glasses in their hands; all were sipping while they chatted, their gazes, one and all, trained in various directions—resting on their ladies scattered about the hall.

Accepting a glass from one of his footmen, he joined them.

"Ah—just the man!" Jack Hendon beamed. "Finally, you're here to join us—about time."

"I often wondered," Tony mused, "whether it was *our* weddings you eschewed, or weddings per se."

"The latter." Royce sipped. "The excuse of not being Winchelsea was exceedingly convenient. I used it to avoid all wider ton gatherings."

They considered, then all grimaced. "Any of us," Tristan admitted, "would have done the same."

"But we always have a toast," Gervase said. "What's it to be today?" They all looked at Charles.

Who grinned. Irrepressibly. He'd clearly been waiting for the moment. He raised his glass to Royce; the others did the same. "To the end of Dalziel's reign," he began. "To the beginning of yours—and even more importantly, to the beginning of *hers*."

The others cheered and drank.

Royce grimaced, sipped, then eyed them. "You perceive me in the unusual position of seeking advice from your greater collective experience." They all looked intrigued. "How," he continued, "do you . . . corral and restrain, for want of better words, your spouses when they're in what is commonly termed 'a delicate condition'?"

The only one of their wives not yet obviously blooming— and he suspected it truly was not *yet*—was Letitia.

Somewhat to his surprise, all his men looked pained. He looked at Jack Hendon. "You're an old hand—any tips?"

Jack closed his eyes, shuddered, then opening them, shook his head. "Don't remind me—I never figured it out."

"The difficulty," Jack Warnefleet said, "is in being subtle when what you want to do is put your foot down and state categorically that they can't do that—whatever 'that' is at the time."

Deverell nodded. "No matter what you say, how tactfully you try to put it, they look at you as if you have the intelligence of a flea—and then just do whatever they were going to."

"Why is it," Christian asked, "that we, the other half of the equation as it were, are considered to have no valid opinions on such matters?"

"Probably because," Tony replied, "our opinions are ill-informed, being based on a woeful lack of intelligence."

"Not to mention," Gervase added, "us having no experience in the field."

Royce glanced at them. "Those sound like quotes."

Tony and Gervase answered as one. "They are."

"What worries me even more," Tristan said, "is what comes next."

They all looked at Jack Hendon.

He looked back at them, then slowly shook his head. "You really don't want to know."

All considered it, but none of them pressed.

Royce smiled wryly. "What cowards we are."

"When it comes to that . . . yes." Christian drained his glass, then turned the conversation to the recent developments surrounding the Corn Laws. They were all peers, all managed estates of various sizes, all had communities under their protection; Royce listened, learned, contributed what he knew, his gaze resting on Minerva as she stood chatting with Letitia and Rose halfway down the room.

Another lady approached—Ellen, Minerva's friend, one of her matrons-of-honor; Ellen joined the group, then spoke specifically to Minerva and indicated one of the side doors. Minerva nodded, then excused herself to Letitia and Rose and, alone, went to the door.

Royce wondered what household emergency she'd been summoned to deal with . . . but why would Cranny or Retford or any of the others use Ellen to ferry a message? The summons had to be about something else . . .

He told himself it was their recent discussion of delicate conditions and their primitive responses that was playing on his mind, but . . . with a nod he excused himself and started moving through the crowd.

He felt Christian glance at him, sensed his gaze following as he made his way to where Letitia and Rose were still talking. They looked up as he halted beside them.

"Where's Minerva?"

Letitia smiled at him. "She just stepped outside to meet someone."

"They had a message from your half brother, or something like that." Rose tipped her head toward the side door. "They were waiting out there."

Royce looked toward the door—and knew Minerva wasn't in the hallway beyond it. Every instinct he possessed was alive, pricking. Leaving the ladies without a word, he moved toward the door.

Christian drew near as he opened it.

The hallway beyond was empty.

He walked into the narrow space; to his right the hall led back into the house while to his left it ran along the ballroom a little way, then ended in a door to the gardens. Common sense suggested Minerva had gone into the house; he prowled left, drawn by a white clump on the floor before the door.

Christian followed.

Royce stooped to pick up a beribboned band covered with white silk flowers—Minerva's mother's wedding favor; Minerva had worn it on her wrist. Bent over, he froze, sniffed. Turning his head, he crouched, looked; from the base of the umbrella stand he teased out a scrap of linen . . . a handkerchief.

Without even raising it to their faces, both he and Christian, drawing near, recognized the smell. "Ether." Rising, he stared out of the glassed doors into the gardens, but all looked peaceful, serene.

"She's been *taken.*" He barely recognized his voice. His fist closed on the handkerchief. Lips curling in a snarl, he swung around—

Christian caught his arm. "Wait! *Think.* This was planned. Who are your enemies? Who are hers?"

He frowned. It was a huge effort to get his mind to function; he'd never felt such scalding rage—such icy terror. "We don't have any . . . not that I know of. Not here . . ."

"You do. You have one. And he *could* be here."

He met Christian's eyes. "The last traitor?"

"He's the one person who has most to fear from you."

He shook his head. "I'm no longer Dalziel—he won. He got away."

"Dalziel may be gone, but you're here—and *you* never, ever, give up. He's someone who knows that, so he'll never feel safe." Christian released him. "He's taken her, but it's you he wants."

That was undeniably true.

"She's the lure." Christian spoke quickly, urgently. "He'll keep her alive until you come. But if you alert everyone, send everyone searching . . . he might feel forced to kill her before you or any of us can get to her."

The thought helped him force the terror-driven rage down, caging it like a beast, deep inside, letting his mind, his well-honed faculties, rise above it and take command. "Yes.

You're right." Hauling in a tight breath, he lifted his head. "Yet we need to search."

Christian nodded. "But only with those capable of acting and rescuing her if they find her."

Royce glanced outside. "He couldn't have imagined we'd realize so soon."

"No. We've got time to do this properly, so we can get her back alive."

"You seven," he said. "Hendon, Cynster, Rupert, Miles, and Gerald—they were all in the Guards at one time."

"I'll fetch them." Christian caught his eyes. "While I do, you *have* to think. You're the only one who knows this terrain—and you're the one who knows this enemy best. You are the best at planning battles like this—so *think*, Royce. We need a plan, and you're the only one who can supply it."

Minerva's life—and that of their unborn child—depended on it. He nodded curtly.

Christian left him to it, and went quickly back into the ballroom.

Two minutes later, Royce returned to the ballroom. He saw Christian moving smoothly through the crowd, surreptitiously tapping shoulders. His plan was taking shape in his mind, but there was something he needed to know.

Last time he and the last traitor had crossed swords, the traitor had won. That wasn't going to happen this time, not with what was at risk; he wanted to learn everything he possibly could before he took the field.

Letitia, still standing with Rose, was already alerted, restive and restless, when he halted beside her. "Can you and Rose find Ellen, and bring her to me in the hallway beyond the side door?" Briefly he met her eyes. "Don't ask, but hurry—and don't alert anyone else bar the other Bastion Club wives." He glanced at Rose. "Or Alice and Eleanor. No one else."

Both wanted to ask why; neither did. Lips tightening, they nodded, exchanged glances, then separated and slipped through the crowd.

Searching. He searched, too, but, finding it harder and harder to keep his expression impassive, he went back into the hallway and left the hunt to the women.

Minutes later, Leonora slipped through the door. "They've found her, but she was conversing with others. Eleanor, Madeline, and Alicia are extracting her."

He nodded, pacing, too tense to remain still.

The other ladies joined them, one by one slipping into the hallway, all aware something was amiss. They threw him searching glances, but none asked. Last to join them were Eleanor, Alicia, and Madeline, shepherding Ellen, wide-eyed, before them.

She didn't know him; sensing the anger he was trying to contain, she was already skittish.

"Just ignore the growling," Letitia curtly advised her. "He won't bite."

Ellen's eyes widened even more.

"I don't have time to explain," Royce said, speaking to them all, "but I need to know who Minerva came out here to meet."

Ellen blinked. "One of your cousins asked me to tell her your half brother's children were here, asking to speak with her. Apparently they had a gift they'd made her. He said they were waiting in the garden." She nodded down the corridor. "Out there."

Royce felt a sudden sense of inevitability. "Which of my cousins?"

Ellen shook her head. "I'm sorry, I can't say. I don't know them, and you all look so alike."

Phoebe stirred. "How old?"

Ellen glanced at Royce. "Of similar age to His Grace."

Letitia looked at Royce. "How many is that?"

"Three." But he already knew which one it was, which one it had to be.

The door to the ballroom cracked open; Susannah peered around it. She took in the ladies, then focused on him. "What's going on?"

He didn't answer, instead said, "I need to know if Gordon, Phillip, and Gregory are in the ballroom. Don't speak to them, just go and check. Now."

She stared at him, then closed her mouth and went.

Clarice, Letitia, and Penny headed for the door. "We know them, too," Penny said as she passed him.

Bare minutes later, all four came back. "Gordon and Gregory are in there," Susannah reported. "Not Phillip."

Royce nodded, half turned away, his mind churning.

Alicia said, "That's not conclusive. Phillip might be any-where—the castle is huge."

Mystified, Susannah appealed to the others; Letitia explained they were trying to learn which of the cousins had lured Minerva away.

"It'll be Phillip." Susannah was definite. Royce looked at her; she went on, "I don't know what bee he's got in his bonnet about you, but for years he's always wanted to know every last thing about you and your doings—and recently . . . it was he who suggested I invite Helen Ashton. He who told me Minerva was your lover and . . . not suggested but led me to think that engineering a situation might be a good thing. Of course, he never dreamed you loved her—" She broke off, paled. "Oh, God—he's taken her, hasn't he?"

For a long moment, no one answered, then Royce slowly nodded. "Yes, he has."

He glanced at Alicia. "The last traitor we've been hunting over the last year? We concluded he had some connection with the War Office. Of all my cousins, of all those here, only Phillip qualifies."

He felt a certain sureness infuse him. It always helped to know who he was hunting.

Minerva struggled through clouds of unconsciousness. Her head felt woolly; thoughts half formed, then slipped away, sank into the murk. She couldn't think—couldn't concentrate, couldn't formulate a coherent wish, much less open her eyes. But inside, where a cold kernel of panicked helplessness clung to reality, she knew.

Someone had seized her and carried her away. She'd gone to the door, looking for Hamish's children—and someone, some man, had come up behind her. She'd sensed him an instant before he'd grabbed her, tried to turn her head, but he'd slapped a handkerchief over her nose and mouth . . .

It had smelled sickly sweet, cloying . . .

Reality inched closer, seeped into her mind. She breathed in, carefully, but that horrible, nauseating smell was gone.

Someone—the man—was talking, the sound distant, fading in and out.

Familiar. *He* was familiar.

She would have frowned, but her features were still not her own. She was lying on her back . . . on stone, its rough surface beneath her fingers, under one palm . . . she'd been here before, lain just like this not long ago . . .

The millstone. She was lying on the grinding stone in the mill.

The realization evoked an inpouring of awareness; the clouds dissipated; she came fully awake.

Just as the man halted beside her. She sensed him looking down at her; instinct kept her perfectly still.

"Damn you—wake *up!*"

He'd spoken through clenched teeth, yet she placed him. *Phillip.* What the devil was he up to?

With a muttered curse, he swung away. Her hearing focused, her mind followed; still too weak to move, she listened as he paced, talking to himself.

"It's all *right.* I have time. *Plenty* of time to set the stage— to rape her, and beat her, then kill her—perhaps slit her throat, let her blood flow artistically over the stone—yes!"

His shoes scraped on the floor as if he'd swung around. She sensed him looking at her; she didn't move a muscle.

"Damn!" he muttered. "I forgot to bring my knife." He

paused, then said, "No matter. I've ball and powder—I can shoot her as many times, in as many places, as I like."

Again she felt him studying her, then he started pacing again.

"Yes, that will do nicely. I'll rip her gown to shreds, shoot her in the head, then again in the belly, and place that damned crown in the blood." He laughed. "Oh, *yes*, that will work. He has to be shattered by the sight. Completely and utterly *broken*. He has to finally see that *I'm* more powerful. That because he took my treasure, I've taken something he valued from him—that in our game, *I'll* always win. That I'm the truly clever one. When he comes in here, and sees what I've done to her—his new duchess, the woman he today vowed to honor and protect—he'll know I've won. He'll know that *everyone* will know what a failure he is— that he wasn't even clever enough, strong enough, powerful enough, to protect *her*."

His long strides brought him to the millstone again; again she felt his gaze. Unlike Royce's, his made her skin crawl. She fought to remain lifeless, utterly lax—battled the compulsion to tense, to hold her breath, to raise her lids enough to see.

She nearly sighed with relief when he said, "Time's on my side." He moved away again. "I've got more than an hour before that valet gives Royce the note. Plenty of time to enjoy debauching and killing her, and then get ready to welcome him."

Facts fell into place with a suddenness that left her mentally reeling. *Treasure.* Phillip had said treasure. *He* was Royce's last traitor.

That's what this was all about. He thought to use her to break Royce.

The fight she had to wage to suppress her reaction—not to let her jaw, her features, set, *not* to let her hands curl into fists, not to reach for the knife she had, for an entirely different reason, strapped to her thigh—was immense.

She could kill him with that knife, but Phillip was

strong—he was like Royce in that. Yet while he believed her unconscious, it seemed she was safe. Just as long as he kept believing he had time, her best strategy was to simply lie there and let him rant.

And give Royce time to reach her.

She knew he would.

How long had she been unconscious? How long was it since she'd left the ballroom? Phillip's plan had a large hole in it, one he'd never see. He might not be a Varisey, yet he was just like Royce in not understanding what love actually was.

He didn't comprehend that Royce would simply know, that he was always aware of her—even in a crowded ballroom. He'd never wait an hour before checking where she'd gone. She seriously doubted he'd have waited ten minutes. Which meant rescue was afoot.

Phillip was now ranting about his father, and his grandfather, how they'd always lauded Royce and never him. How they would now see that Royce was nothing, powerless . . .

Royce's maternal grandfather was long dead.

Not that she needed any further proof of the state of Phillip's mind.

Nevertheless, she forced herself to listen so she could track his movements; when she was sure he was pacing away from her, she quickly cracked open her lids—immediately closed them again and heaved a mental sigh of relief. He'd closed the mill doors.

Resisting the urge to smile intently, she worked on keeping every muscle flaccid.

Not so easy when Phillip stopped talking, then halted beside the millstone. She was fully awake now, could sense his physical closeness. Like Royce, he was large, well-muscled, and radiated heat—and quelling her revulsion and lying quiescent with him near was the hardest thing she'd ever had to do.

Then she heard a rustle; his arms moved.

Then he leaned near. "Come on, damn you! Wake up."

And then she discovered there were harder things to quell than mere revulsion.

Instinct had her peeking through her lashes. She only had an instant's warning, only an instant to scream at herself to relax, relax, *for God's sake don't react!*—then he jabbed her in the arm with his cravat pin.

Royce waited in the hallway until all the men had gathered. The ladies remained, too—they were all too sober to go back into the ballroom; if they did, they'd cause comment.

Christian slipped through the door. "That's all of us."

Royce raked the ranks of deadly serious faces. "My cousin, Phillip Debraigh, has seized Minerva. He's our last traitor—the one I failed to apprehend. As far as I can judge, he's set on wreaking vengeance of a sort on me—the diadem she was wearing"—*that he, Royce, had given her*—"was part of his thirty pieces of silver. He's taken her somewhere outside. Although the castle is huge, with it packed with guests there are staff constantly scurrying everywhere—something he knows. He won't have risked staging anything indoors." He glanced outside. "But there are only so many places he could use outside—which gives us a chance to rescue Minerva, and capture him."

He brought his gaze back to the grave faces. "He took her less than fifteen minutes ago—he won't be expecting us to have even noticed her absence yet, so we have a small amount of time to plan."

Rupert, on his left, shifted, caught Royce's eyes when he glanced his way. "Whatever we do, secrecy is imperative. No matter he's a traitor, and deserves to be brought down, you can't bring down the Debraighs as a family. You, especially, can't do that."

Because the Debraighs, his mother's family, had always supported him. Because his Debraigh grandfather had been so much a part of his formative life. Jaw set, Royce nodded. "As far as possible, we'll try to keep this secret, but I won't risk Minerva's safety, not even for the Debraighs."

He looked at the grouped ladies, at Letitia, Clarice, Rose, and all the rest. "You ladies are going to have to give us cover. You're going to have to go back into the ballroom and spread some story—of how we've adjourned for a meeting on whatever topic your imaginations can devise. You're going to have to hide your apprehension—make it appear as irritation, annoyance, resignation—anything. But we'll never keep this concealed without you."

Clarice nodded. "We'll manage. Just go"—she waved them off—"do what you're so good at, and get Minerva back."

Her waspish tone was reinforced by the looks on the other ladies' faces. Royce nodded grimly, and looked at the men. "Come up to the battlements."

He led them up the battlement stairs in a thunder of heavy feet. Just in case he'd guessed wrongly and Phillip was somewhere in the house, Handley, Trevor, Jeffers, Retford, and Hamilton were alerted, and a quiet search was under way. But as he walked to the battlements, waited while the others joined him, he knew he was right. Phillip was outside—somewhere in the grounds, all the relevant parts of which were visible from this vantage point.

Bracing his hands on the stone, he looked out. "He'll have taken her to one of the structures. There's not that many. There's—" He broke off. He'd come to the same spot to which he'd brought Minerva, twice. The view was to the north, up the gorge to the Cheviots and Scotland beyond.

The mill was in the foreground.

He straightened, his gaze locked on the building. "He's taken her to the mill."

All the others crowded the battlements, looking.

Before any could ask, he went on, "There is no one on the entire estate who would close those doors—for excellent reasons, they're *always* left open."

Christian was assessing the terrain, as were the others. "Two levels."

"Can he get out along the stream?" Tony asked.

"Not easily—not safely."

"So." Devil Cynster straightened, cocked a brow his way. "How are we going to do this?"

In a few succinct phrases, he told them.

They weren't entirely happy, but no one argued.

Minutes later, they were streaming from the house, slipping into the gardens, a silent, deadly force intent on only one thing—ending the last traitor's reign.

Royce was at the head of the pack, saving Minerva his only real aim.

Twenty-two

Minerva had weathered the prick of the cravat pin—
more through sheer terror than anything else. She'd
managed not to flinch, but her muscles had tensed.
Phillip had noticed; he'd nudged her, slapped her cheeks, but
when she'd stirred, mumbled, then slumped as if comatose
again, he'd muttered a raw expletive and swung viciously
away.

He'd fallen to pacing again, but closer, watching her all
the while. "Damn you, wake *up*! I want you awake so you'll
know what I'm doing to you—I want you to fight me. I want
to hear you *scream* as I force my way inside you. I specifically
brought you here—far enough from the house and with the
noise of the water to cover all sounds—just so I could enjoy
your sobbing and pleading. And your screaming—above all,
your screaming. I want to see your eyes, I want to feel your
fear. I want you to know every little thing I'm going to do to
you before I do it—and for every second while I am."

He suddenly swooped close. "You won't be dying anytime
soon."

She jerked her head away from the hot waft of his croon-
ing breath, tried to disguise the instinctive flinch as restlessness.

He drew back, his gaze heavy on her face. Then, "You aren't *pretending* to still be asleep, are you, Minerva?"

His tone was taunting; he slapped her cheek again. Then he sneered. "Let's see if this will wake you up."

He roughly seized her breast, hard fingers searching for, then framing her nipple. Her breasts were tender; she cracked open her lids, looked up—

Saw him above her, one knee on the millstone beside her, his features distorted into a mask of pure evil, looking down to where his hand imprisoned her flesh. His eyes glittered; his other hand rose, holding his cravat pin.

Her hands came up; with all her strength, she pushed him off.

Releasing her breast, he rocked back—laughed in triumph. Before she could move, he swooped and seized her arm.

He dragged her half upright, shook her like a doll. "You *bitch!* Time for your punishment to begin."

She fought him; he shook her viciously, then slapped her hard.

The crack of his palm on her cheek echoed sharply through the mill.

Something fell to the ground.

Phillip froze. Standing with his knees against the side of the millstone, with her on the stone before him, her legs trapped in the lace froth of her wedding gown, one of her arms locked in a painful, unbreakable grip, he stopped breathing and stared across the race.

The sound had come from the east side—the lower side of the mill. There were no doors on that side of the building; if anyone was going to come in unremarked, they would have to come that way.

"Royce?" Phillip waited, but no answer came. No hint of movement. No further sound.

He glanced down at her, but immediately snapped his gaze up again, locked it on the gangplank, presently set over the race connecting the two levels; his eyes searched the clear space on the lower side beyond it.

Minerva felt him shift his weight from one foot to the other; he was uncertain—this wasn't what he'd planned. Her gaze fixed on him, her senses locked on him, she waited for her chance.

Royce was somewhere on the lower level; her senses told her he was there. But Phillip couldn't see him because of the cupboards lining the race, not unless—until—Royce wanted to be seen.

Apparently realizing, Phillip snarled, and grabbed her with both hands; hauling her off the millstone, he dragged her up against him, her back to his chest. With one arm, he locked her there; he held her so tightly she could barely breathe. With his other hand he fished in his pocket; turning her head to the side, she saw him pull out a pistol.

He held it down, at his side. His body at her back was unbelievably tense.

He was using her as a shield, and she couldn't do anything; her arms were trapped against her body. If she struggled he'd just lift her off her feet. All she could do was grasp her skirts in her hands, hold them as high as she could—at least enough for her feet to be free—and wait for an opening. Wait for the right moment.

Phillip was muttering beneath his breath; she forced herself to focus, to listen. He was talking to himself, reworking his plan; he was ignoring her as if she were some inanimate pawn—no threat whatsoever.

"He's down there somewhere, but that's all right. As long as he knows I've killed her, I still win. And then I'll kill him." He hauled her with him as he edged around the huge circular stone. "I'll get into position, shoot her, then I'll have to grab the gangplank and swing it to this side—he'll be shocked, he won't be expecting that, I can have it done by the time she hits the ground."

His whispered words tripped over themselves as he frantically rehearsed. "Then I'll reload—and shoot him when he comes for me . . ."

She felt him look up; she looked where he did—at the

big beams forming the heavy structure supporting the waterwheel.

"With the gangplank gone, he'll have to come that way. He might not love her, but he won't let me get away with killing his duchess. So he'll come for me—and I'll have more than enough time to reload and shoot him before he can reach me."

She sensed welling triumph in his tone.

"Yes! That's what I'll do. So first, I get in place." Renewed confidence infused him. He tightened his arm, lifted her from her feet, and walked forward—toward the upper end of the gangplank.

She'd run out of time, but with her arms locked to her body there was nothing she could do.

Above her head, Phillip muttered, so low she could barely hear him. "Close enough to the plank ropes, close enough to my powder and shot."

He moved her forward. And she saw the powder horn and shot canister he'd left on the flat top railing, a few feet left of the gangplank.

She couldn't use her arms, but could she possibly raise her feet high enough to kick powder or shot away? Either would do—then he'd have only one shot. Only one person he could kill.

If he shot her, he couldn't kill Royce. Phillip slowed as he maneuvered into position; she was gauging the distance, tensing to try to kick up—

Something flashed across in front of them, right to left—and hit the powder horn and canister, sending both spinning.

The powder horn spun off the railing and fell into the race.

Something clattered on the wooden floor. Both she and Phillip instinctively looked.

And saw a knife. Royce's knife.

Like most gentlemen, he always had one somewhere about him—but she'd only known him ever to have one.

A thump had their heads snapping around—

Royce had leapt onto the lower end of the gangplank.

He stood directly before them, his gaze locked on Phillip's face. "Let her go, Phillip—it's me you want."

Phillip snarled; backing quickly, he pressed the muzzle of the cocked pistol to Minerva's temple. "I'm going to kill her—and you're going to watch."

"You've only got one shot, Phillip—who are you going to kill? Her . . . or me?"

Phillip halted. He rocked back and forth, heels to toes, indecisive, undecided.

Then his chest swelled; with a roar, he flung Minerva to the side, and swung his pistol up to aim at Royce. "*You!*" he screamed. "I'm going to kill *you!*"

"*Run*, Minerva!" Royce didn't even glance at her. "Through the doors. The others are outside."

Then he charged up the gangplank.

Having landed on her side on the millstone, she was frantically hauling up her skirts.

She sat up—saw Phillip brace his pistol arm with his other hand. His face aglow with maniacal joy, laughing, he aimed for Royce's chest.

Her fingers closed about the hilt of her knife. She didn't think, didn't blink, just threw it.

The hilt appeared on the side of Phillip's neck.

He choked, pulled the trigger.

The shot rang out, filling the enclosed space.

Phillip started to crumple.

Minerva scrambled off the millstone. Her eyes locked on Royce as he halted before Phillip, looking down on his cousin as he slumped to the floor. Her gaze raced over Royce, seeking the wound . . . she nearly swooned with relief when she finally accepted that there wasn't one. Phillip's shot had gone wide.

Her gaze returned to Royce's face; behind his mask, he was stunned. In that instant she knew he hadn't expected to survive.

He could have run for cover, but he'd run toward Phillip to give her time to get away, to make sure Phillip shot at him, and not her.

Dragging in a deep breath, she went to join him.

Just as the doors at both ends of the mill swung open, and Christian and Miles appeared at the lower end of the gang-plank.

Reaching Royce, she laid a hand on his arm. He looked at her then, met her eyes, then he looked down at the knife in Phillip's throat, and didn't say anything.

The others gathered around; what expressions were discernable were unrelentingly grim. She glimpsed pistols being slipped back into pockets, the flash of knives being put away.

Royce drew in a breath—almost unable to believe he could. Almost unable to believe that Minerva stood, shaken but otherwise well, beside him—that he could sense her there, steady and sure, that he was still alive to feel her comforting warmth, her vital presence.

The emotions churning inside him were staggeringly strong, but he battened them down, left them for later. There was one more thing he had to do.

Something only he could.

The others had formed a rough circle about them. Phillip lay sprawled, twisted half on his back, his head not far from Royce's right shoe. The knife wound would eventually kill him, but he wasn't dead yet.

He shifted to his right, crouched down. "Phillip—can you hear me?"

Phillip's lips twisted. "Almost got you. Almost . . . did it."

The words were barely a whisper, but in the intent silence, they were audible enough.

"You were the traitor, weren't you, Phillip? The one in the War Office. The one who sent God knows how many Englishmen to their deaths, and who the French paid in a treasure most of which lies at the bottom of the Channel."

Although his eyes remained closed, Phillip's lips curved in

an unholy smile. "You'll never know how successful I was."

"No." Royce curved one hand about Phillip's chin, with his other hand grasped the top of his skull. "We won't."

He sensed Minerva draw close, from the corner of his eye glimpsed the ivory lace of her gown. He turned his head her way. "Look away."

Phillip dragged in a hissing breath. He frowned. "Hurts."

Royce looked down at him. "Sadly nowhere near as much as you deserve." With an abrupt twist, he snapped Phillip's neck.

He released him. The features so like his own eased, fell slack.

He reached for the knife hilt, jerked the blade free. With Phillip's heart already stopped, the wound bled only slightly. He wiped the blade on Phillip's lapel, then rose, sliding the knife into his pocket.

Minerva's hand slipped into his, her fingers twining, gripping.

Christian stepped forward; so did Miles and Devil Cynster. "Leave this to us," Christian said.

"You've tidied up after us often enough," Charles said. "Allow us to return the favor."

There was a growl of agreement from the other Bastion Club members.

"I hate to sound like a grande dame," Devil said, "but you need to get back to your wedding celebration."

Miles glanced at Rupert and Gerald. "Gerald and I will stay and help—we know the estate fairly well. Enough, at least, to help stage a fatal accident—I presume that's what we need?"

"Yes," Rupert, Devil, and Christian answered as one.

Rupert caught Royce eye. "You and Minerva need to get back."

They took over and, for once, Royce let them. Devil, Rupert, Christian, Tony, and both Jacks accompanied him and Minerva back to the house, leaving the others to stage Phillip's accident. Royce knew what they would do; the gorge was both close and convenient, and disguising the knife wound as a wound from a sharp stick wouldn't be hard—but he appreciated their tact in not discussing the details in front of Minerva.

She hurried beside him, her skirts looped over her arm so they could stride faster.

The instant they came within sight of the house, the ladies—who had been banned absolutely from setting foot in the gardens until their husbands returned, and who, for once, had obeyed—broke ranks and came pouring out of the north wing to meet them.

They had, it transpired, been operating in shifts—some on watch, while the others did duty in the ballroom. Letitia, Phoebe, Alice, Penny, Leonora, and Alicia had just resumed the watch—they flocked around Minerva, reporting that all was under control, that although the grandes dames were suspicious, none had yet demanded to be told what was going on, then they announced that Minerva's gown would no longer pass muster—she would have to change.

"And that," Leonora declared, "is our perfect excuse for where you've been. This gown looks so delicate, no one will be surprised that you've chosen to change, even in the middle of your wedding breakfast."

"But we'll have to make it quick." Alice beckoned them back into the house. "Let's go."

In a flurry of silks and satins, the ladies whisked Minerva up the west turret stairs.

Royce and the other men exchanged glances, drew in deep breaths, then headed back to the ballroom. Pausing before the door, they donned expressions of relaxed jocularity, then, with a nod, Royce led them back into the melee.

No one knew, no one guessed; gradually all those involved slipped back into the ballroom, the men returning in jovial groups of three or more, the ladies ferrying Minerva back, ready with their tale to explain her absence.

And if the grandes dames wondered why Royce thereafter kept Minerva so closely beside him, why he so often drew her within the circle of his arm, if they wondered why she showed no inclination to stray, but instead often touched a hand to his arm, none of them voiced so much as a vague query.

The wedding celebrations of the tenth Duke and Duchess of Wolverstone were widely reported to have passed joyously, and—sadly for the gossipmongers—entirely without incident.

About a third of the guests left late that afternoon. It was evening before Royce and Minerva could disappear, could close the door of his sitting room on the world—and finally take stock.

She halted in the middle of the room, stood for one moment, then drew in a huge breath, raised her head, whirled—and plowed her fist into his arm. "Don't you *dare* do such a thing again!"

As immovable as rock, and equally impassive, he merely looked down at her, arched an arrogant brow.

She wasn't having that. She narrowed her eyes on his, stepped close and pointed a finger at his nose. "Don't you *dare* pretend you don't know what I'm talking about. What sort of maniac *invites* a deranged killer to shoot him?"

For a long moment, he looked down at her, then, his eyes locked on hers, he caught her hand, raised it, and pressed a kiss to her palm. "A maniac who loves you. To the depths of his cold, hardened, uninformed heart."

Her lungs seized. She searched his eyes, replayed his words—savored the certainty that rang in them. Then she drew in a shaky breath, nodded. "I'm glad you've realized that. Phillip was useful for that much, at least."

His lips quirked, but then he sobered. "Phillip." He shook his head, his expression turning grim. "I suspected the last traitor was someone I knew, but . . ."

"You never imagined the traitor had become a traitor *because* of you, so you never suspected anyone so close." She stepped back, with the hand he still held drew him with her. "There's more—Phillip ranted a lot while he was waiting for me to recover. I already had, but was pretending to be unconscious, so I heard. Come and sit down, and I'll tell you. You need to hear."

He sank heavily into one of the armchairs, pulled her down onto his lap. "Tell me."

Leaning against his chest, his arms around her, she recounted as much as she could remember.

"So it was his father's and my grandfather's attention he craved?"

"Not just their attention—their appreciation and acknowledgment that he was your equal. He felt . . . impotent when it came to them—no matter what he did, what he achieved, they never noticed him."

Royce shook his head. "I never saw it." He grimaced. "At least not that they lauded me and not Phillip, but I was rarely there to hear either." He shook his head again. "My uncle and grandfather would be horrified to know they were the cause of such traitorous acts."

"The underlying cause," she sternly corrected him. "*They* were entirely unwitting—it was Phillip's mania, first to last. He twisted his mind—no one else can be blamed."

He cocked a brow at her. "Not even me?"

"Least of all you."

The fierceness in her tone, in her eyes as she turned her head to meet his, warmed him.

Then she frowned. "One thing I've been puzzling over—if Phillip wanted you dead, and he definitely did, more than anything else, then why did he help rescue you from the river? Surely it would have been easy to miss catching you, and then your death would have been a sad accident."

He sighed. "In hindsight, I think he did intend to let me drown. He couldn't not help in the rescue because all the others were there, but by being the last in the line . . ." He tightened his arms about her, as ever anchored by her warmth, her physical presence. "At the time, I thought I wouldn't be able to reach his hand. It was just out of my reach—or so I thought. In desperation I made a herculean effort—and managed to grab his wrist. And once I had, he couldn't easily have broken my hold—not without being obvious. So he had to pull me in—an opportunity he missed, by pure luck."

Her head shifted against his coat as she shook it. "No. You weren't meant to die—he was. His time for being the last traitor had run out."

He let her certainty seep into him, soothing, reassuring. Then he shifted. "Incidentally . . ." Reaching into his pocket, he withdrew her knife. Held it up where both of them could see it. "This, as I recall, was once mine."

She took it, turned it in her hands. "Yes, it was."

"What on earth made you wear it—today, of all days?"

He'd tipped his head so he could see her face. Her lips curved in pure affection. " 'Something old, something new, something borrowed, something blue.' I had the crown as something very old, my gown as the new, my mother's wedding favor as something borrowed, but I didn't have anything blue." She pointed to the cornflower-blue sapphire set in the dagger's hilt. "Except for this—and it seemed oddly fitting." Her smile deepened; slanting her eyes sideways, she caught his gaze. "I thought of you discovering it when we came back here to continue our celebrations."

He laughed; he hadn't thought it possible after all that had happened, but the look in her eyes—the pure suggestion—made him laugh. He refocused on the blade. "I gave it to you when you were what? Nine?"

"Eight. You were sixteen. You gave it to me that summer and taught me how to throw it."

"There was an element of blackmail involved, as I recall."

She snorted. "You were sixteen—there was a girl involved. Not me."

He remembered, smiled. "The blacksmith's daughter. It's coming back to me."

Minerva eyed his smile, waiting . . . he saw her looking, quirked an arrogantly amused brow. She smiled back—intently. "Keep remembering."

She watched as he did. His smile faltered, then disappeared.

Expression inscrutable, he met her eyes. "You never told me how much you actually saw."

It was her turn to smile in fond reminiscence. "Enough." She added, "Enough to know your technique has improved significantly since then."

"I should bloody well hope so. That was twenty-one years ago."

"And you haven't been living in a monastery."

He ignored that. Frowned. "Another thing I didn't think to ask all those years ago—did you often follow me?"

She shrugged. "Not when you rode—you would have seen me."

A short silence ensued, then he quietly asked, "How often did you spy on me?"

She glanced at his face, arched a brow. "You're starting to look as stunned as you did in the mill."

He met her eyes. "It's a reaction to the revelation that I was singlehandedly if unwittingly responsible for my wife's extensive sexual education at a precocious age."

She smiled. "You don't seem to have any objection to the outcome."

He hesitated, then said, "Just tell me one thing—it was singlehandedly, wasn't it?"

She laughed, leaned back in his arms. "I may have been precocious, but I was only interested in you."

He humphed, hugged her tight.

After a moment, he nuzzled her neck. "Perhaps it's time I reminded you of some of the technical improvements I've assimilated over the years."

"Hmm. Perhaps." She shifted sinuously against him, her derriere caressing his erection. "And perhaps you might include something new, something more novel and adventurous." Glancing over her shoulder, she caught his eye. "Perhaps you should extend my horizons."

Her tone made that last an imperious, definitely duchessy demand.

He laughed and rose, sweeping her up in his arms. He carried her into the bedroom; halting beside the bed with her cradled in his arms, he looked down. Met her eyes. Held them. "I love you—I really do." The words were low, heartfelt, resonating with feeling—with discovery, joy, and unfettered belief. "Even when you refuse to do as I say—perhaps even because you refused to look away, to not see the violent side of me."

Her words were as heartfelt as his. "I love all of you—your worst, your best, and everything in between." Laying a palm against his cheek, she smiled into his eyes. "I even love your temper."

He snorted. "I should have you put that in writing."

She laughed, reached further, and drew his head to hers. He kissed her, followed her down as he laid her on his bed, on the crimson-and-gold brocade.

His. His duchess.

His life. His all.

Later, much later, Minerva lolled naked on the crimson silk sheets, and watched the last of the light fade over the distant hills. Beside her, Royce lay slumped on his back, one arm crooked behind his head, the other draped loosely around her.

He was at peace, and so was she. She was precisely where she was meant to be.

His parents, she thought, would have been pleased; she'd fulfilled her vows to them—quite possibly in the way they'd always intended. They'd known her well, and, she'd come to realize, had understood Royce better than he'd known.

She stirred, shifting closer to his muscled body—a body she'd explored at length, claimed beyond question, and now considered uniquely hers. Eyes still on the far-reaching view, she murmured, "Hamish told me that love was a disease, and you could tell who'd caught it by looking for the symptoms."

Even though she couldn't see it, she knew his lips curved.

"Hamish is frequently a font of worldly wisdom. But don't tell him I said that."

"I love you." A statement, no longer any great revelation.

"I know."

"When did you know?" One thing she'd yet to discover. "I tried so hard to deny it, to hide it—to call it something else." She turned in his arms to look into his face. "What did I do that first made you suspect that I felt anything at all for you?"

"I knew . . ." He brought his gaze down to meet her eyes. "The afternoon that I arrived back here, when I realized you'd polished my armillary spheres."

She arched her brows, considered, then persisted, "And now I know that *you know* you love me."

"Hmm." The sound was full of purring content

"So confess—when did you first realize?"

His lips curved; drawing the arm from behind his head, he caught a stray lock of her hair, gently tucked it behind her ear. "I knew I felt *something*, more or less from that first night. It kept getting stronger, no matter what I did, but I didn't realize, didn't even imagine, for obvious reasons, that it might be love. I thought it was . . . lust at first, then caring, then a whole host of similar, connected emotions, most of which I wasn't in the habit of feeling. Yet I knew what they were, I could name them, but I didn't know it was love that made me feel them." He looked into her eyes. "Until today, I didn't know that I loved you—that I would, without thought or hesitation, lay down my life for you."

Through her happiness, she managed a frown. "Incidentally, I was serious. Don't ever, *ever* do that again—put your life before mine. Why would I want to live if you die?" She narrowed her eyes on his. "Much as I value the sentiment—and I do, nothing more highly—promise me you will never give up your life for mine."

He held her gaze steadily, as serious as she. "If you promise not to get caught by a murderous maniac."

She thought, then nodded. "I'll promise that, as far as I'm able."

"Then I'll promise what you ask, as far as *I'm* able."

She looked into his dark eyes, and knew that would never hold. "Humph!"

Royce grinned, bent, and kissed her nose. "Go to sleep."

That was one order he seemed always to get away with. As if she'd heard his thought, she humphed again, less forcefully, and snuggled down, within his arm, her head on his shoulder, her hand over his heart.

He felt her relax, felt the soothing warmth of her sink to his marrow, reassuring, almost stroking, the primitive being within.

Closing his eyes, he let sleep creep up, in, over him.

In the now peaceful stillness of his mind, the thought that had jarred and jangled as, weeks before, he'd raced back to Wolverstone to bury his father and assume the ducal mantle echoed, reminded him of the uncertainties, the loneliness, he'd left behind.

Since then, through Minerva, Fate had laid her hands on him. Now, at long last, he could surrender; at last he was at peace.

At last he could love, had found his love, and his love had found him.

It wasn't supposed to have been like this.

That's what he had thought, but now he knew better.

This was precisely how it *was* supposed to be.

The following is a preview of

Temptation and Surrender

The newest Cynster novel
from *New York Times* bestselling author

STEPHANIE
LAURENS

On sale in paperback September 29, 2009
from

Avon Books

Colyton, Devon
October 1825

I *feel like tearing my hair out—not that that would do* any good."

The dark hair in question fell in elegantly unruly locks about Jonas Tallent's handsome head. His brown eyes filled with disgusted irritation, he slumped back in the armchair behind the desk in the library of the Grange, the paternal home he would eventually inherit, a fact that accounted in multiple ways for his current, sorely frustrated state.

At ease in the chair facing the desk, Lucifer Cynster, Jonas's brother-in-law, smiled in wry commisseration. "Without intending to add to the burden weighing so heavily upon you, I feel I should mention that expectations are only rising with the passage of time."

Jonas humphed. "Hardly surprising—Juggs' demise, while being no loss whatsoever, has raised the specter of something better at the Red Bells. When Edgar found the old sot dead in a puddle of ale, I swear the entire village heaved a sigh of relief—and then immediately fell to speculating on what might be if the Red Bells had a *competent* innkeeper."

Juggs had been the innkeeper of the Red Bells for nearly a decade; he'd been found dead by the barman, Edgar Hills, two months ago.

Jonas settled deeper into his chair. "I have to admit I was first among the speculators, but that was before Uncle Martin expired of overwork and the pater went off to sort out Aunt Eliza and her horde, leaving the matter of the new incumbent at the Red Bells in my lap."

If truth be told, he'd welcomed the opportunity to return from London and assume full management of the estate. He'd been trained to the task throughout his youth, and while his father was still hale, he was becoming less robust; his unexpected and likely to be lengthy absence had seemed the perfect opportunity to step in and take up the reins.

That, however, hadn't been the principal reason he'd so readily kicked London's dust from his heels.

Over the last months he'd grown increasingly disaffected with the life he'd more or less fallen into in town. The clubs, the theaters, the dinners and balls, the soirees and select gatherings—the bucks and bloods, and the haughty matrons so many of whom were only too happy to welcome a handsome, independently wealthy, well bred gentleman into their beds.

When he'd first gone on the town, shortly after Phyllida, his twin sister, had married Lucifer, a life built around such diversions had been his goal. With his innate and inherited attributes—and, courtesy of his connection with Lucifer the imprimatur of the Cynsters—achieving all he'd desired hadn't been all that hard. However, having attained his goal and moved in tonnish circles for the past several years, he'd discovered that life on that gilded stage left him hollow, strangely empty.

Unsatisfied. Unfulfilled.

In reality, unengaged.

He'd been very ready to come home to Devon and assume control of the Grange and the estate while his father hied to Norfolk to support Eliza in her time of need.

He'd wondered whether life in Devon, too, would now feel empty, devoid of challenge. In the back of his mind had hovered the question of whether the deadening void within was entirely an effect of tonnish life or, far more worrying, was the symptom of some deeper inner malaise.

Within days of returning to the Grange he'd been reassured on that point at least. His life was suddenly overflowing with purpose. He hadn't had a moment when one challenge or another hadn't been front and center before him, clamoring for attention. Demanding action. Since returning home and seeing his father off, he'd barely had time to think.

That unsettling sense of disconnection and emptiness had evaporated, leaving only a novel restlessness beneath.

He no longer felt useless—clearly the life of a country gentleman, the life he'd been born and bred to, was his true calling—yet still there was something missing from his life.

Currently, however, it was the missing link at the Red Bells Inn that most severely exercised him. Replacing the unlamented Juggs had proved to be very far from a simple matter.

He shook his head in disgusted disbelief. "Whoever would have imagined finding a decent innkeeper would prove so damned difficult?"

"How far afield have you searched?"

"I've had notices posted throughout the shire and beyond—as far as Plymouth, Bristol, and Southampton." He pulled a face. "I could send to one of the London agencies, but we did that last time and they landed us with Juggs. If I had my choice, I'd have a local in the job, or at least a Westcountryman." Determination hardening his face, he sat up. "And if I can't have that, then at the very least I want to interview the applicant before I offer them the job. If we'd seen Juggs before the agency hired him, we'd never have contemplated foisting him on the village."

His long legs stretched before him, still very much the startlingly handsome, dark-haired devil who years before had made the ton's matrons swoon, Lucifer frowned. "It seems odd you've had no takers."

Jonas sighed. "It's the village—the smallness of

it—that makes all the good applicants shy away. The countering facts—that when you add the surrounding houses and estates we're a decent-sized community, and with no other inn or hostelry in the vicinity we're assured a good trade—aren't sufficient, it seems, to weigh against the drawbacks of no shops and a small population." With one long finger, he flicked a sheaf of papers. "Once they learn the truth of Colyton, all the decent applicants take flight."

He grimaced and met Lucifer's dark blue eyes. "If they're good candidates, they're ambitious, and Colyton, so they believe, has nothing to offer them by way of advancement."

Lucifer grimaced back. "It seems you're looking for a rare bird—someone capable of managing an inn who wants to live in a backwater like Colyton."

Jonas eyed him speculatively. "You live in this backwater—can I tempt you to try your hand at managing an inn?"

Lucifer's grin flashed. "Thank you, but no. I've an estate to manage, just like you."

"Quite aside from the fact neither you nor I know the first thing about the domestic side of running an inn."

Lucifer nodded. "Aside from that."

"Mind you, Phyllida could probably manage the inn with her eyes closed."

"Except she's already got her hands full."

"Thanks to you." Jonas bent a mock-censorious look on his brother-in-law. Lucifer and Phyllida already had two children—Aiden and Evan, two very active little boys—and Phyllida had recently deigned to confirm that she was carrying their third child. Despite numerous other hands always about to help, Phyllida's own hands were indeed full.

Lucifer grinned unrepentantly. "Given you thoroughly enjoy playing uncle, that condemnatory look lacks bite."

Lips twisting in a rueful smile, Jonas let his gaze fall to the small pile of letters that were all that had come of the notices with which he'd papered the shire. "It's a sad situation when the best applicant is an ex-inmate of Newgate."

Lucifer let out a bark of laughter. He rose, stretched, then smiled at Jonas. "Something—or someone—will turn up."

"I daresay," Jonas returned. "But *when*? As you pointed out, the expectations are only escalating. As the inn's owner and therefore the person everyone deems responsible for fulfilling said expectations, time is not on my side."

Lucifer's smile was understanding if unhelpful. "I'll have to leave you to it. I promised I'd be home in good time to play pirates with my sons."

Jonas noted that, as always, Lucifer took special delight in saying that last word, all but rolling it on his tongue, savoring all that it meant.

With a jaunty salute, his brother-in-law departed, leaving him staring at the pile of dire applications for the post of innkeeper at the Red Bells Inn.

He wished he could leave to play pirates, too.

The thought vividly brought to mind what he knew would be waiting for Lucifer at the end of his short trek along the woodland path linking the back of the Grange to the back of Colyton Manor, the house Lucifer had inherited and now shared with Phyllida—and Aidan and Evan and a small company of staff. The manor was perennially filled with warmth and life, an energy—something tangible—that grew from shared contentment and happiness and filled the soul.

Anchored it.

While Jonas was entirely comfortable at the Grange—it was home, and the staff were excellent and had known him all his life—he was conscious—perhaps more so after his recent introspections on the shortfalls of tonnish life—of a wish that a warmth, a glow of happiness similar to that at the Manor, would take root at the Grange, and embrace him.

Fill his soul and anchor him.

For long moments, he stared unseeing across the room, then he mentally shook himself and lowered his gaze once more to the pile of useless applications.

The people of Colyton deserved a good inn.

Heaving a sigh, he shifted the pile to the middle of the blotter, and forced himself to comb through it one last time.

Emily Ann Beauregard Colyton stood just beyond the last curve in the winding drive leading to the Grange on the southern outskirts of Colyton village, and peered at the house that sat in comfortable solidity fifty yards away.

Of worn red brick, it looked peaceful, serene, its roots sunk deep in the rich soil on which it sat. Unpretentious yet carrying a certain charm, the many-gabled slate roof sat over attic windows above two stories of wider, white-painted frames. Steps led up to the front porch. From where she hovered, Em could just see the front door, sitting back in shadowed majesty.

Neatly tended gardens spread to either side of the wide front façade. Beyond the lawns to her left, she spotted a rose garden, bright splashes of color, lush and inviting, bobbing against darker foliage.

She felt compelled to look again at the paper in her hand—a copy of the notice she'd spotted on the board in the posting inn at Axminster advertising the position of innkeeper-manager of the Red Bells Inn at Colyton. When she'd first set eyes on the notice, it had seemed expressly designed to be the answer to her prayers.

She and her brother and sisters had been wasting time waiting for the merchant who'd agreed to take them on his delivery dray when he made his round to Colyton. Over the previous week and a half, ever since her twenty-fifth birthday when, by virtue of her advanced age and her late father's farsighted will she'd assumed guardianship of her brother and three sisters, they'd traveled from her uncle's house in Leicestershire by way of London to eventually reach Axminster—and finally, via the merchant's dray, Colyton.

The journey had cost much more than she'd expected, eating all of her meager savings and nearly all of the funds—her portion of their father's estate—that their family's solicitor, Mr. Cunningham, had arranged for her to receive. He alone knew she and her siblings had upped stakes and relocated to the tiny village of Colyton, deep in rural Devon.

Their uncle, and all those he might compel or persuade to his cause—that of feathering his own nest by dint of their free labor—had not been informed of their destination.

Which meant they were once again very much on their own—or, to be more precise, that the welfare of Isobel, Henry and the twins, Gertrude and Beatrice, now rested firmly on Em's slight shoulders.

She didn't mind the burden, not in the least; she'd taken it up willingly. Continuing a day longer than absolutely necessary in their uncle's house had been beyond impossible; only the promise of eventual, and then imminent, departure had allowed any of the five Colytons to endure for so long under Harold Potheridge's exploitative thumb, but until Em had turned twenty-five, he—their late mother's brother—had been their co-guardian along with Mr. Cunningham.

On the day of her twenty-fifth birthday, Em had legally replaced her uncle. On that day, she and her siblings had taken their few worldly possessions—they'd packed days before—and departed Runcorn, their uncle's manor house. She'd steeled herself to face her uncle and explain their decision, but as matters had transpired Harold had gone to a race meeting that day and hadn't been there to witness their departure.

All well and good, but she knew he would come after

them, as far as he was able. They were worth quite a lot to him—his unpaid household staff. So travelling quickly down to London had been vital, and that had necessitated a coach and four, and that, as she'd discovered, had been expensive.

Then they'd had to cross London in hackneys, and stay two nights in a decent hotel, one in which they'd felt sufficiently safe to sleep. Although she'd thereafter economized and they'd traveled by mail-coach, what with five tickets and the necessary meals and nights at various inns, her funds had dwindled, then shrunk alarmingly.

By the time they'd reached Axminster, she'd known she, and perhaps even Issy, twenty-three years old, would need to find work, although what work they might find, daughters of the gentry that they were, she hadn't been able to imagine.

Until she'd seen the notice on the board.

She scanned her copy again, rehearsing, as she had for the past hours, the right phrases and assurances with which to convince the owner of the Grange—who was also the owner of the Red Bells Inn—that she, Emily Beauregard—no one needed to know they were Colytons, at least not yet—was precisely the right person to whom he should entrust the running of his inn.

When she'd shown her siblings the notice, and informed them of her intention to apply for the position, they had—as they always did, bless them—fallen in unquestioningly and enthusiastically with her scheme. She now had in her reticule three glowing references for

Emily Beauregard, written by the invented proprietors of inns they'd passed on their journey. She'd written one, Issy another, and Henry, fifteen and so painfully wanting to be helpful, had penned the third, all while they'd waited for the merchant and his dray.

The merchant had dropped them off outside the Red Bells. To her immense relief, there'd been a notice on the wall beside the door stating "Innkeeper Wanted" in bold black letters; the position hadn't yet been filled. She'd settled the others in a corner of the large common room, and given them coins enough to have glasses of lemonade. All the while she'd surveyed the inn, evaluating all she could see, noting that the shutters were in need of a coat of paint, and that the interior was sadly dusty and grimy, but there was nothing she could see amiss within doors that wouldn't yield to a cloth and a bit of determination.

She'd watched the somewhat dour man behind the bar. Although he was manning the tap, his demeanor had suggested he was thinking of other things in a rather desultory way. The notice had given an address for applications, not the inn but the Grange, Colyton, doubtless expecting said applications to come through the post. Girding her loins, hearing the crinkle of her "references" in her reticule, she'd taken the first step, walked up to the bar, and asked the man the way to the Grange.

Which was how she'd come to be there, dithering in the drive. She told herself she was only being sensible by trying to gauge the type of man the owner was by examining his house.

Older, she thought—and settled; there was something about the house that suggested as much. Comfortable. Married for many years, perhaps a widower, or at least with a wife as old and as comfortable as he. He would be gentry, certainly, very likely of the sort they called the backbone of the counties. Paternalistic—she could be absolutely sure he would be that—which would doubtless prove useful. She would have to remember to invoke that emotion if she needed help getting him to give her the position.

She wished she'd been able to ask the barman about the owner, but given she intended to apply for the position of his superior that might have proved awkward, and she hadn't wanted to call attention to herself in any way.

The truth was she needed this position. Needed it quite desperately. Quite aside from the issue of replenishing her funds, she and her siblings needed somewhere to stay. She'd assumed there would be various types of accommodation available in the village, only to discover that the only place in Colyton able to house all five of them was the inn. And she couldn't afford to stay at any inn longer than one night.

Bad enough, but in the absence of an innkeeper, the inn wasn't housing paying guests. Only the bar was operating; there hadn't even been food on offer. As an inn, the Red Bells was barely functioning—all for want of an innkeeper.

Her Grand Plan—the goal that had kept her going for the last eight years—had involved returning to

Colyton, to the home of their forebears, and finding the Colyton treasure. Family lore held that the treasure, expressly hidden against the need of future generations, was hidden there, at a location handed down in a cryptic rhyme.

Her grandmother had believed unswervingly in the treasure, and had taught Em and Issy the rhyme.

Her grandfather and father had laughed. They hadn't believed.

She'd held to her belief through thick and thin; for her and Issy, and later Henry and the twins, the promise of the treasure had held them together, held their spirits up, for the past eight years.

The treasure was there. She wouldn't—couldn't—believe otherwise.

She'd never kept an inn in her life, but having run her uncle's house from attics to cellars for eight years, including the numerous weeks he'd had his bachelor friends to stay for the hunting, she was, she felt sure, more than qualified to run a quiet inn in a sleepy little village like Colyton.

How difficult could it be?

There would no doubt be minor challenges, but with Issy's and Henry's support she'd overcome them. Even the twins, ten years old and mischievous, could be a real help.

She'd hovered long enough. She had to do this—had to march up to the front door, knock, and convince the old gentleman to hire her as the new innkeeper of the Red Bells.

She and her generation of Colytons had made it to the village. It was up to her to gain them the time, and the facility, to search for and find the treasure.

To search for and secure their futures.

Drawing in a deep breath, she held it and, putting one foot determinedly in front of the other, marched steadily on down the drive.

She climbed the front steps and without giving herself even a second to think again, she raised her hand and beat a sharp rat-a-tat-tat on the white-painted front door.

Lowering her hand, she noticed a bell pull. She debated whether to tug that, too, but then approaching footsteps fixed her attention on the door.

It was opened by a butler, one of the more imposing sort. Having moved within the upper circles of York society prior to her father's death, she recognized the species. His back was ramrod straight, his girth impressive. His gaze initially passed over her head, but then lowered.

He considered her with a steady, even gaze. "Yes, miss?"

She took heart from the man's kindly mein. "I wish to speak with the owner of the Red Bells Inn. I'm here to apply for the position of innkeeper."

Surprise flitted over the butler's face, followed by a slight frown. He hesitated, regarding her, then asked, "Is this a joke, miss?"

She felt her lips tighten, her eyes narrow. "No. I'm perfectly serious." Jaw firming, she took the bull by the horns. "Yes, I know what I look like." Soft light brown hair with a tendency to curl and a face everyone—simply everyone—saw as sweet, combined with a slight stature and a height on the short side of average didn't add up to the general notion of a forceful presence—the sort needed to run an inn. "Be that as it may, I have experience aplenty, and I understand the position is still vacant."

The butler looked taken aback by her fierceness. He studied her for a moment more, taking in her high-necked olive green walking dress—she'd tidied herself as best she could while at Axminster—then asked, "If you're sure. . . ?"

She frowned. "Well, of course I'm sure. I'm here, aren't I?"

He acknowledged that with a slight nod, yet still he hesitated.

She lifted her chin. "I have written references—three of them." She tapped her reticule. As she did so, memories of the inn, and the notices—and their curling edges—flashed through her mind. Fixing her gaze on the butler's face, she risked a deductive leap. "It's clear your master has had difficulty filling the position. I'm sure he wishes to have his inn operating again. Here I am, a perfectly worthy applicant. Are you sure you want to turn me away, rather than inform him I am here and wish to speak with him?"

The butler considered her with a more measuring eye; she wondered if the flash she'd seen in his eyes might have been respect.

Regardless, at long last he inclined his head. "I will inform Mr. Tallent that you are here, miss. What name shall I say?"

"Miss Emily Beauregard."

"Who?" Looking up from the depressing pile of applications, Jonas stared at Mortimer. "A young woman?"

"Well . . . a young female person, sir." Mortimer was clearly in two minds about the social standing of Miss Emily Beauregard, which in itself was remarkable. He'd been in his present position for decades, and was well-versed in identifying the various levels of persons who presented themselves at the local magistrate's door. "She seemed . . . very set on applying for the position. I thought, all things considered, that perhaps you should see her."

Sitting back in his chair, Jonas studied Mortimer, and wondered what had got into the man. Miss Emily Beauregard had clearly made an impression, enough to have Mortimer espouse her cause. But the idea of a female managing the Red Bells . . . then again, not even half an hour ago he himself had acknowledged that Phyllida could have run the inn with barely half her highly capable brain.

The position was for an innkeeper-*manager*, after all, and certain females were very good at managing.

He sat up. "Very well. Show her in." She had to be an improvement over the applicant from Newgate.

"Indeed, sir." Mortimer turned to the door. "She said she has written references—three of them."

Jonas raised his brows. Apparently Miss Beauregard had come well-prepared.

He looked at the sheaf of applications before him, then tapped them together and set the pile aside. Not that he had any great hopes of Miss Beauregard proving the answer to his prayers; he was simply sick of looking at the dismal outcome of his recent efforts.

A footstep in the doorway had him glancing up.

A young lady stepped into the room; Mortimer hovered behind her.

Instinct took hold, bringing Jonas to his feet.

Em's first thought on setting eyes on the gentleman behind the desk in the well-stocked library was: He's too young.

Far too young to feel paternalistic toward her.

Of quite the wrong sort to feel paternalistic at all.

Unexpected—unprecedented—panic tugged at her; this man—about thirty years old and as attractive as sin—was not the sort of man she'd expected to have to deal with.

Yet there was no one else in the room, and the butler had returned from this room to fetch her; presumably he knew who she was supposed to see.

Given the gentleman, now on his feet, was staring at her, she dragged in a breath, forced her wits to steady, and grasped the opportunity to study him.

He was over six feet tall, long limbed and rangy; broad shoulders stretched his well-cut coat. Dark, sable-brown hair fell in elegantly rumpled locks about a well-shaped head; his features bore the aquiline cast common among the aristocracy, reinforcing her increasing certainty that the owner of the Grange sat rather higher on the social scale than a mere squire.

His face was riveting. Dark brown eyes, more alive than soulful, well set under dark slashes of brows, commanded her attention even though he hadn't yet met her gaze. He was looking *at* her, at all of her; she saw his gaze travel down her frame, and had to suppress an unexpected shiver.

She drew in another breath, held it. Absorbed the implication of a broad forehead, a strong nose and an even stronger, squarish jaw, all suggesting strength of character, firmness, and resolution.

His lips . . . were utterly, comprehensively distracting. Narrowish, their lines hinted at a mobility that would soften the angular, almost austere planes of his face.

She dragged her gaze from them, lowering it to take in his subtle sartorial perfection. She'd seen London dandies before, and while he wasn't in any way overdressed, his clothes were of excellent quality, his cravat expertly tied in a deceptively simple knot.

Beneath the fine linen of his shirt, his chest was well-muscled, but he was all lean sleekness. As he came to life and slowly, smoothly, moved around the desk, he reminded her of a predatory animal, one that stalked with a dangerous, overtly athletic grace.

She blinked. Couldn't help asking, "You're the owner of the Red Bells Inn?"

He halted by the front corner of the desk and finally met her gaze.

She felt as if something hot had pierced her, making her breath hitch.

"I'm Mr. Tallent—Mr. Jonas Tallent." His voice was deep but clear, his accents the clipped speech of their class. "My father's Sir Jasper Tallent, owner of the inn. He's currently away and I'm managing the estate in his absence. Please—take a seat."

Jonas waved her to the chair before his desk. He had to stifle the urge to go forward and hold it while she sat.

If she'd been a man, he would have left her standing, but she wasn't a man. She was definitely female. The thought of having her standing before him while he sat and read her references and interrogated her about her background was simply unacceptable.

She subsided, with a practised hand tucking her olive green skirts beneath her. Over her head he met Mortimer's gaze. He now understood Mortimer's hesitation in labeling Miss Beauregard a "young woman." Whatever else Miss Emily Beauregard was, she was a lady.

Her antecedents were there in every line of her slight form, in every unconsciously graceful movement. She possessed a small-boned, almost delicate frame; her face was heart-stoppingly fine, with a pale, blush cream porcelain complexion and features that—if he'd had a poetic turn of mind—he would have described as being sculpted by a master.

Lush, pale rose lips were the least of them; perfectly

molded, they were presently set in an uncompromising line, one he felt compelled to make soften and curve. Her nose was small and straight, her lashes long and lush, a brown fringe framing large eyes of the most vibrant hazel he'd ever seen. Those arresting eyes sat beneath delicately arched brown brows, while her forehead was framed by soft curls of gleaming light brown; she'd attempted to force her hair into a severe bun at the nape of her neck, but the shining curls had a mind of their own, escaping to curl lovingly about her face.

Her chin, gently rounded, was the only element that gave any hint of underlying strength.

As he returned to his chair, the thought uppermost in his mind was: What the devil was she doing applying to be an innkeeper?

Dismissing Mortimer with a nod, he resumed his seat. As the door gently closed, he settled his gaze on the lady before him. "Miss Beauregard—"

"I have three references you'll want to read." She was already hunting in her reticule. Freeing three folded sheets, she leaned forward and held them out.

He had to take them. "Miss Beauregard—"

"If you read them"—folding her hands over the reticule in her lap, with a nod she indicated the references—"I believe you will see that I have experience aplenty, more than enough to qualify for the position of innkeeper of the Red Bells." She didn't give him time to respond, but fixed her vivid eyes on his and calmly stated, "I believe the position has been vacant for some time."

Pinned by that direct, surprisingly acute hazel gaze, he found his assumptions about Miss Emily Beauregard subtly altering. "Indeed."

She held his gaze calmly. Appearances aside, she was clearly no meek miss.

A pregnant moment passed, then her gaze flicked down to the references in his hands, then returned to his face. "I could read those for you, if you prefer?"

He mentally shook himself. Lips firming, he looked down—and dutifully smoothed open the first folded sheet.

While he read through the three neatly folded—identically folded—sheets, she filled his ears with a litany of her virtues—her experiences managing households as well as inns. Her voice was pleasant, soothing. He glanced up now and then, struck by a slight change in her tone; after the third instance he realized the change occurred when she was speaking of some event and calling on her memory.

Those aspects of her tale, he decided, were true; she had had experience running houses and catering for parties of guests.

When it came to her experience running inns, however . . .

"While at the Three Feathers in Hampstead, I . . ."

He looked down, again scanned the reference for her time at the Three Feathers. Her account mirrored what was written; she told him nothing more.

Glancing at her again, watching her face—an almost angelic vision—he toyed with the idea of telling her he knew her references were fake. While they were written in three different hands, he'd take an oath two were female—unlikely if they were, as stated, from the male owners of inns—and the third, while male, was not entirely consistent—a young male whose handwriting was still changing.

The most telling fact, however, was that all three references—supposedly from three geographically distant inns over a span of five years—were on the exact same paper, written in the same ink, with the same pen, one that had a slight scratch across the nib.

And they appeared the same age. Fresh and new.

Looking across his desk at Miss Emily Beauregard, he wondered why he didn't simply ring for Mortimer and have her shown out. He should—he knew it—yet he didn't.

He couldn't let her go without knowing the answer to his initial question. Why the devil was a lady of her ilk applying for a position as an innkeeper?

She eventually ended her recitation and looked at him, brows rising in faintly haughty query.

He tossed the three references on his blotter and met her bright eyes directly. "To be blunt, Miss Beauregard, I hadn't thought to give the position to a female, let alone one of your relative youth."

For a moment, she simply looked at him, then she drew in a breath and lifted her head a touch higher. Chin firming, she held his gaze. "If I may be blunt in return, Mr. Tallent, I took a quick look at the inn on my way here. The external shutters need painting, and the interior appears not to have been adequately cleaned for at least five years. No woman would sit in your common room by choice, yet it's the only public area you have. There is presently no food served at all, nor accommodation offered. In short, the inn is currently operating as no more than a bar-tavern. If you are indeed in charge of your father's estate, then you will have to admit that as an investment the Red Bells Inn is presently returning only a fraction of its true worth."

Her voice remained pleasant, her tones perfectly modulated; just like her face, it disguised the underlying strength—the underlying sharp edge.

She tilted her head, her eyes still locked with his. "I understand the inn has been without a manager for some months?"

Lips tightening, he conceded the point. "Several months."

Far too many months.

"I daresay you're keen to see it operating adequately as soon as may be, especially as I noted there is no other tavern or gathering place in the village. The locals, too, must be anxious to have their inn properly functioning again."

Why did he feel as if he were being herded?

It was plainly time to reassert control of the interview and find out what he wanted to know. "If you could enlighten me, Miss Beauregard, as to what brought you to Colyton?"

"I saw a copy of your notice at the inn in Axminster."

"And what brought you to Axminster?"

She shrugged lightly. "I was . . ." She paused, considering him, then amended, "*We*—my brother and sisters and I—were merely passing through." Her gaze flickered; she glanced down at her hands, lightly clasped on her reticule. "We've been traveling through the summer, but now it's time to get back to work."

And that, Jonas would swear, was a lie. They hadn't been traveling over summer . . . but, if he was reading her correctly, she did have a brother and sisters with her. She knew he would find out about them if she got the job, so had told the truth on that score.

A reason for her wanting the innkeeper's job flared in his mind, growing stronger as he swiftly assessed her gown—serviceable, good quality, but not of recent vintage. "*Younger* brother and sisters?"

Her head came up; she regarded him closely. "Indeed." She hesitated, then asked, "Would that be a problem? It's never been before. They're hardly babes. The youngest is . . . twelve."

That latter hesitation was so slight he only caught it because he was listening as closely as she was watching him. Not twelve—perhaps a precocious ten. "Your parents?"

"Both dead. They have been for many years."

Truth again. He was getting a clearer picture of why Emily Beauregard wanted the innkeeper's job. But . . .

He sighed and sat forward, leaning both forearms on the desk, loosely clasping his hands. "Miss Beauregard—"

"Mr. Tallent."

Struck by her crisp tone, he broke off and looked up, into her bright hazel eyes.

Once he had, she continued, "I believe we've wasted enough time in roundaboutation. The truth is you need an innkeeper quite desperately, and here I am, willing and very able to take on the job. Are you really going to turn me away just because I'm female and have younger family members in my train? My eldest sister is twenty-three, and assists me with whatever work I undertake. Likewise my brother is fifteen, and apart from the time given to his studies, works alongside us. My youngest sisters are twins, and even they lend a hand. If you hire me, you get their labor as well."

"So you and your family are a bargain?"

"Indeed, not that we work for nothing. I would expect a salary equal to a twentieth of the takings, or a tenth of the profits per month, and in addition to that, room and board supplied through the inn." She rattled on with barely a pause for breath. "I assume you wish the inn-keeper to live on site. I noticed that there's attic rooms above, which appear to be unoccupied and would do perfectly for me and my siblings. As we're here, I could take up the position immediately—"

"Miss Beauregard." This time he let steel infuse his voice, enough so that she stopped, and didn't try to speak over him. He caught her gaze, held it. "I haven't yet agreed to give you the position."

Her gaze didn't flinch, didn't waver. The desk may have been between them, yet it felt as if they were toe-to-toe. When she spoke, her voice was even, if tight.

"You're desperate to have someone take the inn in hand. I want the job. Are you really going to turn me away?"

The question hovered between them, all but blazoned in the air. Lips thinning, he held her gaze, equally unwaveringly. He *was* desperate for any capable innkeeper—she had that right—and she was there, offering. . . .

And if he turned her away, what would she do? She and her family, who she was supporting and protecting.

He didn't need to think to know she'd never turned to the petticoat line, which meant her younger sister hadn't either. What if he turned her away and she— they—were forced, at some point, to . . .

No! Taking such a risk was out of the question; he couldn't live with such a possibility on his conscience. Even if he never knew, just the thought, the chance, would drive him demented.

He narrowed his eyes on hers. It didn't sit well to be jockeyed into hiring her, which was what she'd effectively done. Regardless . . .

Breaking eye contact, he reached for a fresh sheet of paper. Setting it on the desk, he didn't glance at her as he picked up his pen, checked the nib, then flipped open the ink pot, dipped and rapidly scrawled.

No matter that her references were fake, she was better than no one, and she wanted the job. Lord knew she was a managing enough female to get it done. He'd simply keep a very close eye on her, make sure she correctly accounted for the takings and didn't otherwise do anything untoward. He doubted she'd drink down the cellar as Juggs had.

Finishing his brief note, he blotted it, then folded it. Only then did he look up and meet her wide, now curious, eyes. "This"—he held out the sheet—"is a note for Edgar Hills, the barman, introducing you as the new innkeeper. He and John Ostler are, at present, the only staff."

Her fingers closed about the other end of the note and her face softened. Not just her lips; her whole face softly glowed. He recalled he'd wanted to make that happen, wondered what her lips—now irresistibly appealing—would taste like . . .

She gently tugged the note, but he held on. "I'll hire you on trial for three months." He had to clear his throat before going on, "After that, if the outcome is satisfactory to all, we'll make it a permanent appointment."

He released the note. She took it, tucked it in her reticule, then looked up, met his eyes—and smiled.

Just like that, she scrambled his brains.

That's what it felt like as, still beaming, she rose—and he did, too, driven purely by instinct given none of his faculties were operating.

"Thank you." Her words were heartfelt. Her gaze—those bright hazel eyes—remained locked on his. "I swear you won't regret it. I'll transform the Red Bells into the inn Colyton village deserves."

With a polite nod, she turned and walked to the door.

Although he couldn't remember doing so, he must have tugged the bell pull because Mortimer materialized to see her out.

She left with her head high and a spring in her step, but didn't look back.

For long moments after she'd disappeared, Jonas stood staring at the empty doorway while his mind slowly reassembled.

His first coherent thought was a fervent thanks to the deity that she hadn't smiled at him when she'd first arrived.

SONG OF THE MEADOWLARK

SONG OF THE MEADOWLARK

The Story of an American Indian
and the Nez Perce War

JOHN A. SANFORD

1817
HARPER & ROW, PUBLISHERS, New York
Cambridge, Philadelphia, San Francisco,
London, Mexico City, São Paulo, Singapore, Sydney

3. Oregon - Fiction

FIRST EDITION

Designer: Jénine Holmes
Cartographer: George Colbert

Library of Congress Cataloging-in-Publication Data

Sanford, John A.
  Song of the meadowlark.

√1. Nez Perce Indians—Fiction. √2. Nez Perce Indians—Wars, 1877—Fiction. ⅃I. Title.
PS3569.A5263S6 1985   813'.54   85-45443
ISBN 0-06-015546-9

86 87 88 89 90 RRD 10 9 8 7 6 5 4 3 2 1

To my son, John Stuart Sanford

Contents

Preface

There really was a Nez Perce Indian named Teeto Hoonod. L. V. McWhorter, an early chronicler of the Nez Perce war, quotes from Yellow Wolf's account of the battle of Canyon Creek: "A single Indian, Teeto Hoonod, manned the mouth of the canyon toward the close of the skirmishing, and held back the whole line of troopers" (McWhorter, *Hear Me, My Chiefs! Nez Perce Legend and History*, Caxton Printers, 1952; p. 462). Other than this nothing is known about him. I hope he doesn't mind lending his name to my fictional character in this story.

Although my Teeto Hoonod is fictional, many of the other characters in this story actually lived. Chief Joseph is the best known of these, but Looking Glass, Too-hool-hool-Sote, White Bird, Lean Elk, Kapoochas, and many others are historical persons, too.

Sometimes I have used or paraphrased an actual speech from one of these characters. The surrender speech of Chief Joseph and the replies by Howard and Miles are taken from Merrill D. Beal's book *I Will Fight No More Forever: Chief Joseph and the Nez Perce War* (University of Washington Press, 1963) and are actual quotations.

Here and there I retell an old Nez Perce story. These are mostly taken from the book by Archie Phinney, himself a

Nez Perce, entitled *Nez Percé Texts* (AMS Press, repr. of 1934 edition). Indian names of people or places are derived from Phinney or various other Indian sources.

Nez Perce personal and place names are spelled differently by different authors. Usually, I have followed the spelling of L. V. McWhorter, and I have chosen to use Nez Perce instead of Nez Perces, Crow instead of Crows, and Blackfoot instead of Blackfeet, as these seem to be the generally preferred plural forms. Earlier in the century, some authors added an accent to the Nez Perce name; later, it was dropped. Most authors, from McWhorter in the fifties to *National Geographic* in the seventies, have not included the accent, and I have chosen to omit it also.

American Indians sometimes complain today that white men like myself become absorbed in the romanticized past of the Indians in the nineteenth century and are unconcerned with the plight of contemporary Indians, as though the history of the Indians ended with the Battle of Wounded Knee in 1890. I fear there is truth to this, but at least this book includes an epilogue that comments briefly on the life of the Nez Perce people today.

I want to thank my friend Robert Johnson, who read this manuscript for me while it was in its infancy and made many helpful suggestions; my helper Helen Macey, without whose assistance this manuscript could not have been prepared; and my wife, Linny, who listened to me patiently as I read the story to her, made many helpful comments, and traveled with me as we followed the route the Nez Perce took in the flight of 1877.

When the last Red Man shall have perished, and the memory of my tribe shall have become a myth among the white man, these shores will swarm with the invisible dead of my tribe, and when your children's children think themselves alone in the field, the store, the shop, or in the silence of the pathless woods, they will not be alone. . . . At night when the streets of your cities and villages are silent and you think them deserted, they will throng with the returning hosts that once filled them and still love this beautiful land. The White Man will never be alone.

Let him be just and deal kindly with my people, for the dead are not powerless. Dead—I say? There is no death. Only a change of worlds.
—Chief Seattle, 1855

The foreign country somehow gets under the skin of those born in it. . . . That would mean that the Spirit of the Indian gets at the American from within and without.
—C. G. Jung

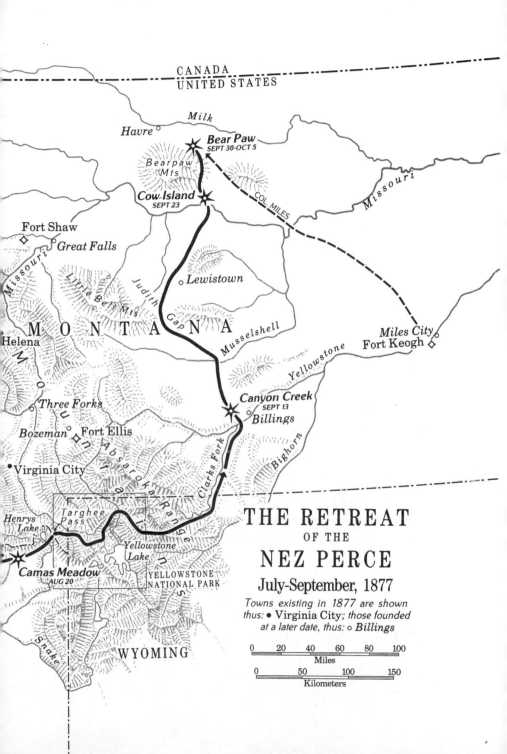

CANADA
UNITED STATES

Milk

Havre °

★ **Bear Paw**
SEPT 30-OCT 5

*Bearpaw
Mts*

COL. MILES

Cow Island ★
SEPT 23

Missouri

Fort Shaw
◇ ° Great Falls

Missouri

° *Lewistown*

Little Bell Mts

Judith Gap

M O N T A N A

Helena

Musselshell

Miles City °
Fort Keogh ◇

Yellowstone

° Three Forks

★ **Canyon Creek**
SEPT 13
° **Billings**

Bozeman ° Fort Ellis

Clarks Fork

Bighorn

• Virginia City

Absaroka Range

Henrys
Lake

*Targhee
Pass*

THE RETREAT
OF THE

*Yellowstone
Lake*

NEZ PERCE

July-September, 1877

★
Camas Meadow
AUG 20

YELLOWSTONE
NATIONAL PARK

*Towns existing in 1877 are shown
thus:* • Virginia City; *those founded
at a later date, thus:* ° Billings

Snake

WYOMING

| 0 | 20 | 40 | 60 | 80 | 100 |
Miles

| 0 | 50 | 100 | 150 |
Kilometers

SONG OF THE MEADOWLARK

CHAPTER ONE

Teeto Hoonod Begins His Story

The wind sighed and moaned like a lost soul, for though it was spring, winter would not let go of the land. The last light of day was fading fast, devoured by the dark clouds that had possessed the sky. The cold rain poured down my broad-brimmed hat, soaking the worn Indian blanket around my shoulders. I shivered with the cold as I tethered my horse outside the rough-hewn cabin. For a full minute I stood staring at it. Was this really the end of my long journey? Inside would I find the man for whom I had been searching these many months?

I drew closer and peered through the single small window. A fire glowed inside the one-room cabin. An oil lamp in a corner cast an eerie light into the cabin's darkness. Seated on a chair in front of the fire, cup in hand, staring into the flames, was a white man. He was middle-aged, of medium height, and sturdily built. His face was weather-beaten and grizzled from a long life in the outdoors. Yes, he looked like the man! But how would he receive me, a ragged, rain-soaked stranger and an Indian at that? A gust of the cold north wind pierced through me and dispelled my moment of hesitation. I went to the door and knocked.

I heard the man inside stir and walk toward the door. The footsteps stopped. Perhaps he was afraid. I could understand why. Montana was a rough country, full of desperate

1

people who came from who-knows-where. I heard more steps, and then the solid bolt on the inside of the door slid back and the heavy wooden door creaked partly open. The man stayed mostly behind it, but I found myself looking into the barrel of his rifle. I stood still and let him look me over; it was clear that I had no weapon. Then he emerged from behind the door and stared at me, his eyes seeming to go right through me, and I looked him over as well. Lean and lanky as I was, I stood a few inches taller than he did, but he was broader of shoulder and thick through the chest. I guess he must have been maybe fifteen, twenty years older than I was. One thing we shared in common: Both our faces showed signs of great strain and the effect of many years of sun and cold and wind. Perhaps, I thought to myself, he will shoot first and ask questions afterward, and this will be the end: of my journey, . . . of my quest, . . . of what hopes I had left. But to my surprise he put his rifle down.

"You're cold," he said matter-of-factly, as though it was the most ordinary thing in the world for a strange Indian to appear at his cabin door on a stormy night. "Better come inside."

I entered gratefully as the man leaned his rifle against the wall. "Why do you trust me?" I asked. "You know nothing about me. Have you no fear of strangers in these parts?"

"Certainly lots of reason not to trust strangers," he answered. "Can't say just why I trust you. Learned long ago, though, to trust my instincts. You don't look to me like you mean harm. You're hungry. You're cold. You want something, that's all. Here, I've coffee. I have some stew too, on the stove. I'll get it for you. Go on over by the fire. Then you can tell me why you're here."

I moved next to the fire. I stood with my back to it, then I faced it with hands outstretched. I let its warmth heal the coldness in me. I let the warmth penetrate my body, go down deep inside to the cold around my heart. Outside,

2

pellets of hail now came down and fell on the metal roof of the cabin as though giants lived in the black clouds overhead and were maliciously dropping ice on the world below. Cold lingered around the corners of the cabin as wolves linger around a herd of bison, but here by the fire it was warm.

The man returned with the stew. "Besides," he said, "I owe you people something."

"You do?" I answered in surprise.

"Sure. You're a Nez Perce, aren't you?"

A stab of fear went through me, for it wasn't healthy nowadays to be a Nez Perce around this part of the country. But there was no denying it. "How did you know?"

"Oh, I've been around. The way you wear your hair. Long like that. Even the way you carry yourself. The kind of blanket you've got. Am I right?"

"Yes, you're right."

"But you speak English?" His words were both a statement and a question.

"Yes, I speak English. I learned your language long ago, from the missionaries. That's part of my story."

"Good thing you do," he said, "because I don't know more'n a few words of your language. Tell me, what do I call you?"

"Teeto Hoonod. My name is Teeto Hoonod. And you, unless I am very wrong, are Henry Hunter. Until lately, Sergeant Henry Hunter."

It was his turn to be surprised. "Yes, indeed! Sergeant Henry Hunter. You know me, then?"

"You could say that," I answered with a smile.

"Then I'm right. You've come for a special reason."

"Yes," I answered. "I've come for a special reason. And if you're willing, I'll tell you my story and you'll understand why I'm here tonight. I've come a long, long way. Are you willing to hear what I have to say? Already you have made

3

me welcome with your food and drink and fire. Are you also willing to welcome me with attention to my tale? For I've a question to ask of you, but you will need to hear my story first."

"Why not?" he answered heartily. "I'm alone, I've nothing else to do, it's a long evening ahead, and I'm curious. Here's more coffee. We can both sit on this rug by the fire. I'll throw on more logs. See how the flames leap up! Now I'm ready. Go ahead and tell me what you have to say."

So I began my story.

CHAPTER TWO

❋

Early Life

Two great rivers pierced our land. The Pic-oon-nen—Big River—was known to the whites as the Snake, and the Heem-uh-keys-kous—Big Body of Water Moving—was known as the Clearwater. The Snake entered our land from the south, slicing abysmal canyons through the rocky hills as it worked its way to the northern extremity of our land, gaining in strength as waters from the Salmon and Grande Ronde rivers poured into it. The Clearwater started in the Eas-slum-eas-ne-ma, the great Bitterroot Mountains to the east. High up in these mountains hundreds of tiny rivulets, fed from springs that gurgled up magically from the earth or from the perennially melting snows, joined to form a stream that bounced over rocks and swirled through pools until it reached the broad, smooth valley below. Here the stream became a serene river, its hasty youth forgotten, that twisted and turned its way north like a sidewinder until it finally swerved west to join the Snake like old friends shaking hands.

A few miles before the Clearwater joins the Snake, a creek comes into it from the south. This is Lapwai Creek—the name means "place of the butterflies"—and this was my childhood home and the site of the Christian mission that was the center of my early life. North, across the Clearwater from the mission, were steep bluffs, but around the mission and along the creek the land was level and fertile. Here perhaps a hundred Nez Perce families made their homes, and among them, about a half mile from the mission, was the comfortable lodge that was home for my mother, father, older brother, and I.

Nez Perce was the white man's name for us. We called ourselves the Nee-me-poo, which simply means the "People," but since we have become known to others as the Nez Perce I will use that name as well as our native one.

A child doesn't remember forests but individual trees, not the whole sweep of a past life but just particular scenes. I remember as a small child sitting quietly between two women who were deep in conversation. One woman was stately in her bearing, slightly round, and with her dark skin and black eyes she seemed made from the earth. The other woman was slender, with light hair and blue eyes, and she was white. The first woman was my mother, Wayilatpu, and the second was Eliza Spalding, wife of Henry H. Spalding, who ran the Christian mission. My mother and Eliza would talk together for hours, my mother speaking our native tongue, and Eliza speaking English, so that each could learn the language of the other. The atmosphere between the two women was so warm that I, a restless child, would play on the floor beside them contentedly. And though I didn't realize it at the time, of course, I was in this way beginning to absorb the English language. In fact, later, playing with other Indian children, I would sometimes use a word that Eliza had taught my mother and my companions would look at me curiously.

I was three years younger than my brother, Hohots Illpilp, whose name means Red Grizzly Bear, and our natures were very different. I was a skinny boy, timid, shy, reflective, and often liked to be alone. He was tall and strong, active and outgoing, and a leader among the other boys. But in spite of our differences we were friends as well as brothers. I remember with affection how he taught me to handle a bow and arrow, showed me how to catch the elusive salmon and stalk deer, and especially how he defended me against the other boys, who often teased me because I was so skinny and timid. I told you that my brother's name was Hohots Illpilp, but this wasn't his childhood name. He received this name later in life, for reasons I will tell you soon.

What I can't remember is where my mother and Eliza talked. Was it in my mother's lodge or the house by the mission where the white people lived? I think I can't remember because the scene isn't one, but many; sometimes the talks were held in one place and sometimes in the other.

Eliza Spalding came to us like a blessing from the Great Spirit. She started a school where she taught us English, the white man's way of reckoning time, their sacred book, the Bible, and, perhaps most important, how to farm, for Eliza believed that the old Indian way of life was going to end soon and only if we learned to farm could we survive the change. But Eliza Spalding also learned from us. She became expert in our language and tried to understand as many of our native ways as she could. So she made many friends and loved us all, even those who disagreed with her about the need to change.

However, it was different with Henry Spalding. He never learned to speak our language. He took land from us and didn't pay us for it, and he made Indians work for him and gave them nothing in return. He thought he was always right and everyone else was wrong. He wasn't interested in our ways; we weren't people to him unless we had been won over to his way of thinking. He taught us that God would hate us unless we all agreed with what he said. He demanded obedience from us and even whipped some Indians who disobeyed him; it was a miracle he wasn't killed by some of the Nez Perce he mistreated. Eliza was beautiful

7

and flexible as a young willow tree, but Henry was rigid as an old oak, and in the end this was his undoing.

Because of Eliza Spalding my mother became a Christian, and my brother and I were sent to church and taught in the mission school. But it was different with my father, We-as-cus. He was twenty years older than my mother. He had been married before but his first wife had died, and perhaps this sadness injured him, for he seldom spoke and his spirit was so far away that I never felt close to him. He didn't ignore the needs of his family; we were given what we needed, and he provided for us as best he could, but he wasn't a man with whom you could talk.

My father wouldn't give up the old beliefs for the new beliefs of the white man, and he and my mother used to argue. My mother would say, "Why don't you ever come to the church and hear what the missionary has to say?"

"I don't want to hear a man who says my ways are evil."

"But it's important to learn the white man's ways. Eliza says in a few years the old ways will be gone."

"The old ways have always worked."

"They'll end soon. Eliza says the white people are many, and we are few. They are coming like snow comes in winter to cover the land. When that happens the game will be gone, and there will be no more land in which we can roam. Then those who have learned the white man's ways will live, and the others will die."

"Then I'll die," my father said grimly.

But because he wanted to live with my mother, he did live near the mission and did learn the white man's ways because if you lived near the mission this is what you did. But he wouldn't go to church, and he wouldn't accept the white man's beliefs, and he hated Henry Spalding, and from time to time he would mutter that he'd had enough. Then he would leave us for a few weeks and go to his ancestral lands in the Wallowa Valley to be with his own people, the Wall-waum-mah, who hadn't become Christians.

The Spaldings started their mission among us in 1836, four years before I was born. In the same year two other missionaries, Marcus and Narcissa Whitman, started a mission among the Cayuse Indians west of us on the Walla Walla River, at Wailatpu, "the place of the rye grass."

Henry Spalding often told why he came to the Nez Perce. According to him, five years before our mission was started four Nez Perce had traveled the long distance to the white man's city of St. Louis and asked to learn about the Bible and the white man's God. So touched were the Christians by this, Spalding said, that they raised the money to send him among us as our teacher.

But my father only snorted indignantly. "Those Nez Perce did go to St. Louis," he said, "but they didn't want the white man's Bible and salvation talk. They wanted his power. The white man knows things we don't know. They make knives and rifles of metal that are far better than our bows and arrows. We can use these things, but we can't make them, and we sent the four Indians to ask that we be taught about these things. But our people couldn't speak the white man's language. They were misunderstood, and they died soon after they reached the city anyway, so instead of sending us people to teach us about their power, we were sent this missionary to teach us that we are no good unless we think the way he tells us." This was a long speech for my father, but he spoke this way because he was so angry.

I guess it was because the Nez Perce thought Spalding had come to show them the way to the white man's secret power that the mission was a great success at first. Anxious to please, many Nez Perce helped Spalding build the mission and the house in which he and his wife lived, and many tried to believe what he taught them.

One of these was Tu-e-ka-kas. He was a leading chief of my father's people, and a noble and respected man. He was one of the first Nez Perce to be baptized by Spalding, who gave him a Christian name—Joseph. Spalding said God didn't like our names, so he named his converts after people in the Bible. Later Joseph became known as Old Joseph, to distinguish him from his son, Chief Joseph. Tu-e-ka-kas left his homeland in the Wallowa Valley and came to live near the mission, as all the Christian Nez Perce did, though from time to time, like my father, he would return to his own village for a while.

Unlike my father, my mother seldom traveled, for she did not want to go far from the mission. But each summer she would make the sixty-mile journey up the Clearwater River to Kamiah to visit friends, and when my brother and I were old enough we would go with her. Here by the banks of the Clearwater was another small mission, an offshoot of the one at Lapwai, and here I have another strong childhood memory.

One summer, when we were camped by the broad and silvery waters of the Clearwater River near Kamiah, my mother said to us, "Tomorrow we will go and see the Monster's heart." We pressed her eagerly for more information, but my mother only said, "Wait and see."

The next day we journeyed a few miles up the west side of the river, then went inland a short distance. My boyish mind was filled half with apprehension, half with excited curiosity, at the prospect of seeing a monster's heart. At last we came to it: a large, curious mound of stones. It stood three times as high as a tall man and took two hundred long steps to walk around. It lay there on the otherwise level and grassy land as though it had fallen from the sky.

"This," my mother said, "is the Monster's heart."

"Tell us the story," we begged.

She hesitated a moment. "No, we shouldn't have come to

10

see it. We listen to the Bible now. I shouldn't tell you one of the old stories."

I was bitterly disappointed: taken all that way, my curiosity teased, and then not to be told the tale? I filed the memory away, determined that one day I would find out who this monster was and how his heart came to be there at Kamiah.

The following winter I sensed the time had come to hear the story, for in winter our lives changed. During the long summer evenings there was much to do: working in the garden and playing with the other boys. But during the winter we huddled in our lodges like squirrels in their holes and drew our families and friends close around us for comfort.

One especially long and gloomy evening, when our lodge was cheered by the small but warming fire and my brother and I and other friends were gathered around my mother, I begged her to tell us the story of the Monster's heart.

"No," she said, but she hesitated again, and I thought I could see an ancient longing come into her eyes. I pressed her until at last she said coyly, "And what will you do for me if I tell you about Coyote and the Monster?" Eagerly we pledged ourselves to various chores, and eventually my mother began her tale. When she spoke of the Monster we trembled, and when she mimicked Coyote, saying his story words in his voice, we smiled because he was so pompous and foolish.

Once there was a terrible Monster, Itswa'wltsix was his name. And the Monster ate all the human beings, all the animals, devoured every living thing and swallowed them up in its stomach—except for Coyote. Now one day Coyote was going about his business fishing when someone shouted to him, 'Coyote! Why are you going about fishing when all the people are gone? The Monster has swallowed them.'

'Well,' Coyote said, 'there is no point in fishing if all the

11

people are gone, because I was doing this for them; no, I will just have to go along.'

But as Coyote was going along he happened upon Qotsqo'tsn—Meadowlark. And by accident he stepped on Meadowlark's leg and broke it.

In a furious temper Meadowlark scolded Coyote. 'What chance of finding the people do you have, just going along!'

Now Qotsqo'tsn knows what other people do not know. So Coyote said, 'My aunt, please inform me. Afterward I will make for you a leg of brushwood.'

So Meadowlark told Coyote all about how the Monster had swallowed the people, and where the Monster could be found. Then Coyote fixed Meadowlark a new leg out of brushwood, and took his five stone knives, and found Itswa'wltsix, and challenged him to an inhaling contest.

Now Coyote could not possibly win the inhaling contest because the Monster was so huge. His body covered the mountains, while Coyote was very small. But Coyote didn't want to win; he wanted to be sucked into the Monster and get into his belly where all the people were. And that is what happened. Coyote huffed and huffed, but he could not budge the Monster. And then the Monster drew in his breath and Coyote was drawn by the wind right into the Monster's mouth and then into his stomach.

So this was the way Coyote got inside of Itswa'wltsix, and when he got there he saw all the bones of the people scattered about, and he said to himself, 'It is clear that the people have been dying.'

Now while Coyote was looking around, Grizzly Bear came up to him and threatened him ferociously, but Coyote kicked him in the nose and that is why grizzly bears have such stubby noses even today. Then Rattlesnake came up and threatened to bite him, but Coyote just stepped on his head, and that is why rattlesnakes have flat heads.

When the Monster realized Coyote was inside of him he began to be afraid, and he tried to persuade Coyote to let him exhale him through his nose, or ears, or anus, but clever

12

Coyote refused to be tricked into leaving the Monster's belly. 'When I am the important man at the fishing feast,' Coyote said scornfully to Monster, 'do you want the people to say of me, "Oh, there goes old faeces officiating at the feast"?'

So instead of letting Monster exhale him, Coyote began to hunt for the Monster's heart, and finally some boys came up to help him. Then Coyote took out his five knives and started to cut away at the heart. He broke four of his knives, but finally, with the fifth knife, he had the heart almost cut out. Then he told the people inside the Monster to be ready to get out as soon as he killed him, and to take the bones of the dead people with them as they went. Then, when his last knife broke, he tugged at the heart with his bare hands until he tore it away from the Monster's body. And then, with a final *whoosh* of his breath, the Monster died, and when this happened all the orifices of his body were opened: the nose, the mouth, the ears, and the anus. As soon as they opened, the people escaped with the bones. All except Muskrat. Muskrat was always dallying, and he was slow in getting out. In fact he barely had time to get out through the Monster's anus when it closed over his tail and took off all his hair. And that is why muskrats do not have hair on their tails even today.

Once everybody was out, Coyote told the people, 'Gather up all the bones and put them in a pile.' When they had done this he said, 'Now we are going to cut the Monster's body into pieces.' Then Coyote smeared the Monster's blood on his hands, and whenever he touched any of the bones with the Monster's blood they sprang to life again. Then he took the pieces of the Monster's body and portioned them out to the various parts of the land all around, and the Monster's heart fell at Kamiah and was turned into the great pile of stones by the Heem-uh-keys-kous River.

Now wherever Coyote threw a piece of the Monster, there the people sprang up and lived: Coeur d'Alene, Cayuse, Pend Oreilles, Flathead, Blackfoot, Crow, Sioux. And this Coyote did until nothing remained of the Monster's body.

Then Fox came up to Coyote and said, 'Coyote, you have

thrown pieces of the Monster's body to faraway lands, and people have sprung up. But what about this place where we are? What does it mean that you have not brought people into being here?' Thus Fox scolded Coyote. 'Well,' Coyote retorted, 'why did you wait this long to tell me? Why did you not tell me this before it was too late? It is your fault for not telling me.'

Then Coyote washed his blood-smeared hands and sprinkled the bloody water in the region right where he was, and that is where the Nee-me-poo sprang up and lived. And Coyote said to them, 'You may never be a numerous people, but you will be strong. Even though I have deprived you by creating you last of all, nevertheless you will be very, very manly.'

So mother ended her story, and somewhere deep inside I sighed a great sigh, satisfied that I finally knew about Coyote, the pile of stones that were the heart of the Monster, and how it was that the Nee-me-poo were created. I could not put it into words then, but it was as though my mind and my soul had been separated, and the story put them together again.

For a while we all just sat there silently in the light of the fire, until at last I said, "Mother, tell us another story." But she answered, "Another time, another time."

And there were other times. It was as though ice had melted in my mother, and now the old stories of the People came pouring out. My mother was a born storyteller. She had kept from telling the stories because Henry Spalding said they were wrong, though when Eliza learned that mother was telling them she came and listened with us. So the stories were told, and my imagination became peopled with the characters: pompous Skunk; evil old Bear; Pa'yawit, the death spirit; dangerous Hummingbird and Mosquito; strange old Katydid Woman; Meadowlark with her uncanny knowledge; and always vain, arrogant, bum-

14

bling, comical, yet creative Coyote, the foolish hero of our tales. And as I listened to these stories during the long winter evenings, and then attended church services on Sunday mornings, I realized that my mother was not one woman but two: a Christian and a storyteller of the Nee-me-poo, whose roots lay in the far distant past.

Now and then some of my father's people from the Wallowa Valley—members of Joseph's band—would come to visit him. My mother made them feel welcome, and I recall talks between them and my parents, and much socializing during the summer evenings. They were splendid in their gay regalia, with their magnificent horses, which they rode bareback, scorning the white man's heavy saddles and riding as though they and their horses were one fantastic being.

From these visits and listening to the talk, I learned about these non-Christian Nez Perce. These were the ones who still wore the blanket, living in the old way. They worshiped Ah-cum-kin-i-ma-me-hut, the Great Spirit, and saw him in every living thing. They sought spiritual power for their lives through Wy-a-kin, the Power that came from contacting their spirit guide on their Vision Quest. When they were sick they might go to one of their holy people, or te-wats, men and women who were especially called by the spirits to be healers. They counted their wealth in their horses and their families and found their food by hunting wild game, catching and drying salmon in the early summer, and gathering camas bulbs and other edible foods from the prairies.

Henry Spalding told people what they should do and how they should live, but no one told my father's people what to do. Each person did as he or she saw fit. When they hunted they hunted hard, perhaps traveling to the k'usa'yna, the distant East Country beyond the Bitterroot Mountains to hunt the buffalo. When they played they played hard, racing horses, gambling, and playing games like the spear game in which each person would try to throw a spear through a

15

rolling hoop. When they did nothing they did that splendidly, too, and could be lazy all the day.

Eliza Spalding was friendly to these people and tried to get to know them, but Henry Spalding hated them. He hated their free ways, he hated their te-wats, he feared their young men who taunted his Christian young men and tried to entice them to go with them on adventurous trips to the East Country. And they hated Henry Spalding, resenting his high-handed ways and his rejection of their te-wats and religious beliefs and fearing him because they saw him as one of the stream of white people who were making their way past our country to settle in the West but who might, one day, try to settle in our land too.

As the early years of my childhood slipped past, the tension increased between the mission people and the non-Christian Nez Perce. Our way of life couldn't last, and it didn't, and I will always remember the day when the tension snapped like a breaking tendon.

I was seven years old, and it was Monday, December 6, 1847, by the white man's way of reckoning time. I was playing with my brother in front of our lodge. Father was working in the vegetable garden nearby. Mother had gone to be with Eliza Spalding for the morning so Eliza wouldn't be alone, for Henry had left for the mission at Wailatpu some days before to place his daughter in a school for white children. It was just like any other ordinary day until I saw mother running toward us as though she were pursued by an evil spirit and heard her call out to my father, "Come quickly, come quickly! We must help. Oh, We-as-cus, hurry!"

Father met her as she reached the lodge.

"Eliza is being threatened," mother said, all out of breath. "Her house is surrounded by Nez Perce who act crazy and are trying to kill her. She says Henry is already dead. The Cayuse have destroyed the mission at Wailatpu. They killed

16

the missionary there and all the other white people, and now some of our people are trying to kill Eliza and destroy our mission too."

Now father, as I have said, was no Christian, but he admired Eliza. He hurried inside for his gun, told us children and mother to stay at home, and set off for the Spaldings' house. Mother followed him anyway, and my brother and I followed her, full of dreadful curiosity and apprehension but careful not to be seen lest we be ordered back.

In a few minutes my brother and I reached the top of a small knoll that overlooked the Spaldings' place on the stream below. A crowd of Indians surrounded the house. There was much shouting and angry calling back and forth, and here and there we could see rifles and knives being waved. Then we saw that there were two groups of Nez Perce. An angry crowd was circled around a smaller group that stood at the door of the house preventing anyone from entering. Joseph stood in the center of the smaller group, holding the reins of a horse. Then I saw that my father was one of the Indians standing with Joseph and that my mother had wriggled her way through the angry crowd until she stood with them too.

Then the door of the house opened slowly and out came Eliza Spalding, pale and trembling and escorted by another group of her Nez Perce friends. She reached Joseph, who slowly and deliberately helped her mount the waiting horse. After she was securely in the saddle, Joseph began to lead the horse through the angry crowd while my mother and father and the others with them formed a bodyguard around her.

This caused more angry shouting and threats, and one man fired his rifle into the air, but Joseph and the others kept moving silently and steadily along. Finally a kind of hush came over the angry Indians as they fell back. Perhaps they had a guilty conscience, for they didn't attack but just watched sullenly as Joseph led Eliza to safety. Then, as Eliza disappeared around the bend in the road, the crowd suddenly let out wild yells and turned and fell upon the house, smashing the windows and beginning to plunder it. As I watched these Indians wild with rage and greed and out of their senses, I felt disgust that my own people would want to hurt a woman who had never been anything to them but a friend. Then my brother and I slipped unseen back to our lodge.

It was a long time before father and mother returned and told us what had happened. "They would have killed Eliza if Joseph and the others hadn't come in time," mother said. "We made a guard around her, and even though they were angry they wouldn't fight us because we are Nez Perce like they are. We led Eliza away to a place where she'll be safe, but she's half out of her mind because Henry is dead, and she doesn't know where her daughter is, and her home is destroyed."

As it turned out, Henry Spalding was not dead and their daughter was unharmed; the Cayuse had taken her as a hostage but later released her. Henry happened to be away at the time of the killings at Wailatpu. The Cayuse looked for him everywhere to kill him, and they almost did because he lost his horse and became exhausted. Somehow he found his way to the place where Eliza had been taken, his horse gone, his feet bleeding, and his clothes shredded as though by a grizzly bear. He wasn't hurt physically, but his spirit had been shattered like a tree split by lightning.

That was the end of the mission, for as soon as they were strong enough, Henry and Eliza Spalding left Lapwai with an escort of friendly Indians. I heard that Eliza died a few years after these sad events. Henry returned for a brief time many years later, long after I had gone, but he was like a crazy man then and could do no good work among us.

But this was not the end of the Christians. Led by Tu-e-ka-kas and other chiefs, and women like my mother, the Christian Nez Perce stayed where they were. They continued to farm, hold Christian services, teach the Bible to each other, remain friends with the white man, and learn to live as he lived.

Everyone was tense for quite a while after this, for we feared reprisal from the white people for the attack on the Spaldings' house. But the rescue of Eliza had also rescued our people from the kind of bad things that now fell upon the Cayuse who had killed the Whitmans. Even though I was only a boy, my mother took the time to explain to me what was happening, for my mother believed that Indians growing up in these times should know about events that would shape their lives in the future.

In this way I learned of the war that came upon the Cayuse, and how for the first time an American army fought against Indians in our part of the country. The Cayuse were defeated and scattered after two years of fighting. They wanted us to join them, but we refused. Too many of the Nez Perce believed the action of the Cayuse against the missionaries was rash, and we all feared the power of the American army. Besides, had not the Nez Perce always been the friends of the Long Knives, as we often called the Americans? And even though many Nez Perce resented the Americans, we would not break that tradition of friendship now.

Eight years later, two events happened that changed my life greatly. The first involved our whole nation; the second affected only myself and my family.

After the Cayuse war more and more settlers wanted Indian lands, and the American government put pressure upon the tribes of the region—the Umatillas, Walla Wallas, Palouse, those of the Cayuse who survived the war, and the Nez Perce—to make a treaty. In 1855 the government drew up a treaty that set aside a small portion of land for the tribes to the west of us and gave the rest of that land to the whites.

These tribes resented the treaty and many refused to agree to it, but the Nez Perce signed because the treaty reserved for us almost all of our ancestral land. We gave up only a small portion in the northwest, while the rest, from the Clearwater River in the north to the Wallowa Mountains in the south, and from the Blue Mountains in the west to the Bitterroots in the east, was to be ours forever. The white settlers came from the east, went south of us, and then settled west of us, bypassing our area. They did not want our land yet.

The tribes to the west of us were angry because of this treaty, and as a result another war started, which led to the destruction of all these tribes and their removal to reservations. Once again the Nez Perce did not join in the fight against the Americans, for had we not signed a favorable agreement with them?

But things *were* different. Some of our people who had always been loyal to the Americans were changed and became suspicious. The most important of these was Joseph, who now began to spend most of his time with his people in the Wallowa Valley instead of living at Lapwai. My father once told me that after the treaty had been signed Joseph had gone out to the western boundary of our land and set up a line of poles so no one could make any mistake about what land was ours.

The second event of that fateful year of 1855 began one dark, cold winter night. I had fallen asleep early that evening, feeling unusually tired, but woke in the night shivering. No matter how many robes I piled on myself I could not stop the chills that racked my body. Then I began to feel hot and developed a harsh, hacking cough. I threw the robes off, but still the heat raged within me until I felt I would be consumed. By morning I was too weak to get out of bed and was almost beside myself with the feverish poison that had come into me during the night. For a time my mother tried to help me with cool towels and water and soothing words, but by evening she too was ill, and my father and brother not long after that. We were violently ill for several days, and on the fourth day a rash broke out that soon covered our whole bodies.

For a week our family lay sick with the invisible poison that had gotten into us. For a while Christians from the church came and prayed with us, but still the fiery sickness burned on, and then no one came for they said that if they did they would get sick too. At long last I began to recover my strength, and my father and my brother also began to get better, until finally the burning heat left us and we were able to get up and walk about. But my mother remained weak. She would try to get up to prepare food and take care of her family, but, smiling wanly, she would have to lie down again. Now it was up to my brother and me to take care of my mother, for my father was no good at such things.

For days we cared for her. We brought her cool water to drink, and mopped her damp brow, and tried to get her to eat a little, and she would smile at us bravely but then lapse into a restless sleep. I was worried, and though occasionally I went out to play, my heart remained in the house beside her.

One evening she fell into a deeper sleep than usual. In the morning I was the first to awaken. I went to her bed and saw her lying there so still and peaceful. How quietly she is resting, I thought to myself. But as I looked at her it seemed that she was lying too quietly. I reached out and touched her, but she didn't open her eyes. I called to her, but she didn't respond. I called again so loudly that it wakened my brother and father, who came and stood beside me. But my mother lay still and silent, and we knew she was dead.

She was buried a few days later by the Christian Nez Perce. They made a grave for her in the Christian manner, and said prayers and sang songs, and we stood by and

21

watched. Even my father attended the service. But later te-wats from his own band at Wallowa arrived and my father had his own rituals for her with prayers in the old way for her spirit to journey to the spirit world. My brother and I poured out our grief in our tears, but my father only became more silent than ever.

A few days after the funeral, my father called the two of us to him. "We are leaving tomorrow for Wallowa," he said. "Gather your things and be ready to go." He would say no more, but my brother and I knew that it meant our life would be different forever. We would no longer live as Christians near the old mission; now we would live with Joseph's people in the old way by the blue waters of Wallowa Lake.

As I made the journey to my father's ancient homelands I felt a gaping hole in my life, for I knew my mother could never come back. It was not the Christian teaching about death that came to me now, but one of the old stories she had told us about Coyote and the Shadow People.

"This is how it happened that the dead can never return to the land of the living. It was Coyote who did it; because he is the inveterate doer of foolish things, we never see them again. One day Coyote's wife died and he grieved so deeply that Pa'yawit, the death spirit, came to him and offered to take him to see her. After a long journey they arrived at the land beyond the mountains, where the dead live, and here Coyote was joyfully reunited with his wife. For several days Coyote lived with the dead, and enjoyed his wife, and feasted and played. Then one day Pa'yawit said to him, 'Tomorrow you will go home. You will take your wife with you. And you must guard against your inclination to do foolish things. Do not yield to any queer notions. There are five mountains. You will travel for five days. Your wife will be with you but you must never, never touch her. Do not let any strange impulses possess you. You may talk to her but never touch her. Only after you have crossed and descended from the fifth mountain may you do whatever you like.'

"Full of hope, Coyote set out for home, with his wife following behind, and began to cross the five mountains which divided the land of the living from the land of the dead. But just before he crossed the last mountain he could contain himself no longer, and foolishly he turned and embraced his wife. At that moment she vanished, and Coyote stood there alone, and since that time no one from the land of the dead has ever returned to the land of the living."

And that's how I knew that I would never see my mother again.

CHAPTER THREE

※

The Wallowa Valley

Wallowa Lake was eighty miles south of Lapwai; burdened as we were with our belongings, it took us four days to make the journey. Out of Wallowa Lake flowed the Wallowa River, which made its way in a northwesterly direction and emptied into the Grande Ronde River, which in turn poured its waters into the mighty Snake. When the Snake was swollen in the spring and early summer with the waters of melting snow it could be a formidable obstacle to cross, but it was winter, so we were able to cross without difficulty.

My brother and I had never gone with my father on the trips to his ancestral homeland, so I was not prepared for the beauty of Wallowa Lake and Valley. Where I had grown up, near Lapwai, the country was flat; its chief beauty lay in the rivers that wound their way through the grassy lowlands. But the country we now were to call our home was far more varied and dramatic.

Its heart was Wallowa Lake, which lay like a turquoise stone cupped in the hand of mountains that came down to its edge on three sides. In summer its waters sparkled and shone in the bright sunlight, their deep blue reflecting back the lighter blue of the broad sky. It was constantly nourished by the many streams that danced down from the high, forested mountains and flowed into the lake like tears of joy streaming down a woman's face. This lake, and the Wallowa

River that flowed out of it, was sacred to us; it had been the heart of the life of our band, the Wall-waum-mah, for as long as anyone could remember.

South and southeast of the lake were the Wallowa Mountains, with trees reaching up to touch hands with the sky, and meadows offering their abundance to the deer and bears who browsed and foraged along the playful mountain streams. To the west were the richly forested Blue Mountains, their heights deep in snow in the winter, which formed the boundary between our land and the land that once had belonged to our cousins, the Cayuse and Umatillas, and now was being filled by the white settlers. To the east, a day's hard ride away, was the Snake River, which formed the eastern edge of that part of Nez Perce land that traditionally belonged to our band.

Near Lapwai the broad Snake flowed majestically through the level land, but here it was as though the Great Spirit had gashed the earth with a knife to make a narrow slice deep into the bowels of Mother Earth, and through this poured the river's turbulent waters. In between the Snake and Wallowa Lake were the highlands, rolling plateau country that stretched itself like a man waking up in the morning, flowing with grass in the summer and laced with many streams, each with its meadows lush with flowers in the spring and its line of cottonwoods and aspen.

This was our land. This is where the men hunted, where the young women gave birth to their babies, where our children grew up, and where we buried our old people when they died. Was it any wonder we believed that when Coyote divided the land he gave the best land of all to the Nee-me-poo and that the best of that land had been given to us, the Wall-waum-mah?

When my mother died it was as though my soul had been ripped away, and I felt an emptiness that my father's silent spirit could not fill. But when we reached Wallowa Lake and

25

were greeted by my father's friendly people, the empty place in me began to fill again. They were not many. No more than four hundred people ever made up the Wall-waum-mah, but perhaps for this very reason we were close, living together in many ways as one family. And always there was the wise guiding hand of Tu-e-ka-kas, still a Christian but now living with his own people because of his growing suspicion of the intentions of the Americans.

I was still a youth when I came to Wallowa Lake, and my memories of our days there are fresh with new life, like the dew is fresh on the grass in early morning. Strong among these memories stands the first journey I made with my people to Weippe Prairie, the summer after my brother and I came to live with the Wall-waum-mah.

Weippe Prairie was a hundred miles to the northeast, in the foothills of the Bitterroot Mountains. Here, nestled in the forest like eggs in a bird's nest, was a broad meadow that abounded in the early summer with the camas bulbs that we prized so highly for food. These bulbs were dug up by our women, who made cakes of them and dried them for food for the winter. Each year on this prairie the various bands of the Nez Perce gathered, and it was here that I saw for the first time the many different people who made up our nation. From the Salmon River country came the band led by Chief White Bird; White Bird was beginning to age, but he was still vigorous; he was both a chief and a te-wat and wore an eagle's feather as a symbol that he was a medicine person. From the highland country west of the Snake came another band, who in later years would be led by the formidable Chief Too-hool-hool-Sote. From the north, close by the boundary of the Christian Nez Perce, came Looking Glass's band. But I must call him Old Looking Glass, for he was soon to die and be replaced by his son, who bore the same name because, like his father, he wore a small mirror around his neck. And from the west some of the Christian

Nez Perce came also, casting aside their Christianity for this one time of the year because they wanted to join us in this great gathering.

Here the People were renewed, united in a common language, spirit, and worship of the Great Spirit. Here the young men raced and wrestled, hoping the girls would notice their prowess. Here the women dug camas bulbs and gossiped, and the men gambled and gathered to tell jokes and stories. Here the chiefs and leading warriors gathered in solemn council, and here we traded, danced, sang, and worked together as a common family. Here too we remembered the white man, for it was at this very spot many years ago that the Nez Perce met Lewis and Clark, the first Americans to visit our people, and helped them on their journey. Here William Clark had been given a young woman to be like a wife to him while he stayed with us, and from that union a son was born. This was long ago, but not so long ago that many of the old men and women did not remember the tall Americans they liked so much, and they still told anyone who would listen the stories of the first Long Knives, always concluding, "And for this reason we are friends of the Americans. Is it not so, even today?"

But even as day gives way to night, so happy times and unhappy times change places with each other. The same summer after my first trip to Weippe Prairie, my father announced one day that he would go and look for one of his horses that had strayed. As he rode off alone he called back to my brother and me, "Back before sundown." Then we watched him as he disappeared down the path, riding his big Appaloosa.

We continued our play, expecting him to return for dinner well before dark. The sun seemed to linger endlessly in the sky that day, as though it were reluctant to give up its place to night, until at last it sank beneath the Blue Mountains. But there was no sign of my father.

When the sun rose the next day and he had not returned, my brother and I sought help, and Joseph and other warriors rode out to look for him, taking us along. We had ridden for an hour, looking for a sign of him without success, when ambling along toward us came the big Appaloosa, and still strapped to him were the things my father had taken with him. We followed the tracks of the horse several miles and came upon my father's body lying lifeless on the ground.

Tu-e-ka-kas reached him first; he ran his hand expertly over my father's body searching for a sign of life or a wound. My brother and I leaped down to join him and the others gathered around. Tu-e-ka-kas placed his ear close by my father's mouth. "There is no sound," he said. "His soul has left his body. There is no wound to be found. He has been dead quite a while. Judging from how he lies here, he was dead before he fell to the ground. There is no sign of an enemy. He has died evidently as men do die sometimes: quickly, as though the Great Spirit suddenly calls the soul back home."

"Like land that ends suddenly as it reaches the edge of a canyon," I found myself saying. I was sad, but I didn't cry, for while my father had taken care of me, he had not won my soul as my mother had done.

We carried his body back to camp stretched across my brother's horse; Tu-e-ka-kas said that the older son should bear the body back to the village. Then my brother and I looked for a te-wat to sing prayers for my father's spirit, and an older man named Kapoochas agreed to chant for us. "He will need help," Kapoochas said, "for while his body lay unattended his soul must have been confused and didn't know where to go or what to do." So we made ceremony on behalf of my father's soul and then we buried the body.

I don't think my father ever recovered from the death of my mother, and I feel he yearned to be with her and that is why he died so quickly. For a time after his death my brother and I felt alone again, but quickly the warmth of the People closed around us once more and held us in a life-giving embrace. We were orphans now, but no one among the Wall-waum-mah lives alone, and a man who was somewhat older than my brother invited us to live in his lodge with him and his wife. Shuslum Hihhih was a warrior, a courageous man, and, like myself, he could speak English. Perhaps for this reason he was drawn to me and opened his home to us. So it was that the empty place soon filled again with the warmth of human fellowship.

A human being does not see life as the Great Spirit sees it. When my father died and I felt so alone again, I wondered why the Great Spirit had done this to me. But I soon realized that though I had lost my physical father I had gained a spiritual one. Kapoochas, who had sung the sacred songs on behalf of my father's soul, became such a father to me. Why Kapoochas chose to befriend a boy like me I don't know, though later he told me that he sensed something important in me that he wished to bring out. Whatever the reason, Kapoochas took me under his protection and nurtured my soul as a mother bird nurtures her young.

No one knew how old Kapoochas was, but he must have been nearing sixty, for he was one of those who remembered Lewis and Clark. Whatever his age, he had kept his strength in an amazing way. His slight, wiry body was as tough and strong as a mesquite bush. His black eyes were not dimmed. His mind was clear like the waters of Wallowa Lake. His hair was long and black like that of a young warrior. He covered the ground as swiftly and surely as a roadrunner.

We often talked together and spoke of many things. One day I said to him, "Old father"—this was my term of affection and respect for him, for among us it was honorable to be old—"how did you become a te-wat?"

"I did not choose it," he answered.

"Then how did it happen?"

"One becomes a te-wat when the spirits choose you for it."

"But how did you know?"

"I did not know all at once. Yet even when I was a boy I had suspicions that the spirits would call me to be a healer."

"Were you different from the other boys?"

"I played games like the others. I learned how to handle the bow and arrow, and how to ride a horse and race like everyone else. But from time to time I would feel a strange urge come over me. Then I would wander off alone into the forest and sit still on a craggy rock for hours and watch and listen. Then I could hear the voices of the spirits, as well as the sounds of the creatures of the woods and streams around me."

"Didn't your parents worry?"

"At first they did, but then someone told them, 'He is listening to the spirits; they have called him for some reason. Leave him alone.' Then they no longer interfered when I went out by myself."

"Did you know what the spirits wanted of you?"

"I didn't know. I only knew that I was close to them. It made me feel strange and different from other people, as though there was some special purpose in my life that I couldn't understand."

"When did you know you were to be a healer?"

"It was shown to me on my Vision Quest."

"I grew up in the Christian world; Christians don't believe in Vision Quests."

"No," Kapoochas replied, "and yet their own holy people went on Vision Quests. Moses talked with the burning bush, and Elijah went into the cave in the mountains to talk with the Great Spirit, just like one of our holy men. And Jesus went into the wilderness and there talked with spirits both good and evil."

I wondered how Kapoochas knew these biblical stories when he had never been a Christian, but Kapoochas seemed to know many things.

"Tell me about your Vision Quest," I begged.

"It was there I met my Wy-a-kin, my spirit being who gave me the Power and became my teacher."

"What being came to you?"

"This is not to be revealed. One does not talk lightly of one's Wy-a-kin to others lest it be lost."

I felt rebuked.

Then Kapoochas added, "Perhaps some other time I will be able to tell you. You're not ready, for you've not yet undergone your own Quest."

"But it was after your Vision Quest that you began to heal?" My curiosity seemed unsatiable. I wanted to know as much as I could about this old man.

"Not at once. At first I didn't want to believe my Wy-a-kin. To be a healer is to be different from others. I didn't want to be different. I didn't want to deal with sickness and with the dark things of the spirit world, for I knew it was a dangerous work. A healer risks the anger of his patients and their families if he does not succeed and can lose his own soul when he goes in search of the lost souls of others."

"Did this anger your Wy-a-kin?"

"You are perceptive, and you are right. Because I denied what my Wy-a-kin wanted of me I became ill, so ill that I seemed to lose consciousness and lay in my parents' lodge for days like one who was dead."

"Why do you say 'seemed to lose consciousness'?"

"Because all this time I was aware of what was going on. I had lost the power to talk and could not reach out to my parents, but I knew they were hovering anxiously over me. I could not talk to them because my soul had been taken by the spirits to be with them."

"Why did they do that?"

31

"To tell me that if I agreed to be a healer they would let me live, but if I refused they would keep my soul with them, and this would mean that my body would die. Then my parents would grieve, and my soul would not have a chance to live on this earth in the way the Great Spirit intended. So I said to them, 'Teach me what I need to know and let me live and I will be a healer.' "

"And what did they teach you?"

"First came the spirits of illness and death, and they taught me what makes people ill. Then came the spirits of healing, and they taught me how people become well again. From them I learned the art of binding a person's soul so closely to the body that the spirits of illness and death cannot enter."

"Tell me these things, old father."

Kapoochas looked at me sharply. "No, I cannot tell you these things. Such things can only be taught by the spirits themselves. Other things can be taught, but not these things."

I felt rebuked again but continued to press him for more. "Then what things can one healer teach another?"

"That is what I wanted to find out, so after I recovered my strength I sought out other healers and learned from them all I could. I found one man who was skilled in setting bones and knew how to make the flow of blood from wounds stop, and I learned from him. And I found one old woman who knew which plants had the power to cure, and I learned all I could from her. And after I had learned what I could from our own people I went on a journey to the East Country to talk to the healers among the Crow, the Sioux, and the Blackfoot and learn from them. This is where I spent the years of my early manhood."

"The Blackfoot are our enemies," I said doubtfully.

"Among te-wats there are no boundaries. Some are good, and some are evil. There are evil te-wats among our own people, and good te-wats among people who are supposed to be our enemies. I didn't want to learn the arts of evil, but wherever I went I found the holy people whom the Great Spirit loved, and whether these were Sioux or Blackfoot I was made welcome."

"What was the most important thing you learned from them?"

"From a wise woman among the Sioux I learned of the medicine wheel."

"Tell me," I begged.

Kapoochas smiled. "You want to know everything, don't you? I'm glad I can tell you about this. The medicine wheel is the way of the Great Spirit. It is the great round through which everyone must turn in his life. When each of us is born we are placed upon the medicine wheel at a particular place. This determines the kind of person we are and the special place in life we occupy. But as we live, so the great round slowly turns, and as it turns it takes us through different places. As we move through each place on the medicine wheel, we can learn something new and find a different way of seeing things. In this way something is always added to our original nature. But we have to be willing to learn and to change. We have to know that as the great round turns it will bring us new experiences, and that with each new experience there will be something to be learned. Finally we are brought back to the place on the wheel from which we started. We have completed the circle."

"And then?"

"Then we are ready to die, and if we do it is all right."

We were both quiet for a short while. "Help me undertake a Vision Quest, Kapoochas," I said.

"Soon. But you are not quite ready. You want to undertake a Vision Quest because you are curious. One day you will want to go because of a need. Then you will be ready."

And though I asked more questions, Kapoochas would

33

speak no further. I didn't understand all he had said, but my spirit felt satisfied within me, and for the moment my empty place was filled.

Though I didn't know it, my need was soon to be thrust upon me. It happened when I was with my brother. I have not told you much about him yet, but along with Kapoochas he was the most important person in my life. When the Great Spirit sent our souls to be born of the same mother, he meant for us to live so closely together that we were almost like one soul. And when our mother died, and then our father, the bond between us was drawn even more tightly. And yet we were different. I was timid, physically slighter than my brother, and was not a highly regarded person in our village. But my brother was a marvelous physical speci men, with smooth, powerful muscles, long black hair, eyes that were open and friendly, and a smile that welcomed everyone, but with a sense of power and confidence that let all people know this was not a man to trifle with.

As I have mentioned, my brother's name, Hohots Illpilp, was not his childhood name. I will tell you how he got this name, and then you will know how my need for a Vision Quest came about.

It was not long after my talk with Kapoochas. I was six-teen and my brother was nineteen when we went one day to hunt the deer that roamed the meadows along the streams of the lower mountain slopes behind Wallowa Lake. A third young man came with us. Wahlitits, whose name means "Shore Crossing," was from Chief White Bird's band, but he chanced to be with us at the time of the hunt and asked to go along. He was my brother's age and a match for him in strength and skill. Already Wahlitits had made a name for himself for his courage, his fighting power, and his great strength, and since he played a great part in the troubles to come his name should be remembered.

The three of us made our way to a small creek that meandered through a meadow bordered by the forest on either side. Here we knew deer would come at dusk or dawn to browse and drink. In order not to be seen, we approached the meadow through a woods. We had been hunting for some time and were beginning to be discouraged because we hadn't seen any deer, when I became separated from my brother and Wahlitits. They had stopped to study some tracks, and I, not realizing this, had gone ahead by myself. So it was that I was alone when, rounding a large rock, I found myself unexpectedly face to face with a great grizzly bear, a hohots. Of all the animals in our part of the country, the hohots was most feared. Coyote, who had destroyed most of the evil beings before the human race came, had somehow let the grizzly bear live among us. It is one of the few animals that, if wounded, provoked, or even just surprised, might charge a man.

For what seemed an endless time the bear and I stared at each other, and as I gazed into the yellow eyes of the great beast, fear began to seep through me like water through cracks in a rock and my limbs became paralyzed with a cold panic. I wanted to run but dared not, for then the beast would surely charge and I knew he could easily outrun me. In my fear I became as a little boy and dropped my bow and arrows on the ground, too frightened to act. At this point the hohots decided to attack and with a grunting roar came lumbering at me, shortening the distance between us with bewildering speed.

I thought death was certain, but just when the hohots was almost upon me I heard a *twang*, followed by a *thud*. An arrow had sped past me and struck the great bear just above the heart. It was my brother, who had come up from behind me, seen the danger, and let fly his arrow, driving it into the bear with all his strength. Red blood spurted out from the side of the hohots. The animal let out a bellow of rage and turned from me to his new tormentor, charging now at my brother, who was desperately trying to ready another arrow.

I was so frozen with fear I still couldn't move, but as I saw my brother facing the charging bear some of the fear melted. I reached for my knife and began to run toward the hohots, prepared to thrust the knife into its flank, when my brother let fly a second arrow that struck the great beast squarely in the heart. The hohots let out a roar of pain, staggered, and then fell to the ground as its red blood poured out upon the earth. Wahlitits now came up, and a third arrow struck the bear from his bow, but it was not necessary, for my brother's second shot had been enough.

My brother had acted with great courage, while I had shrunk with fear from the charging bear. Someone-in-me-who-is-afraid had taken over. True, another-one-in-me did at the last moment grasp my knife to run recklessly at the bear and protect my brother, but no one had seen me do this. My brother and Wahlitits only knew that I had been too afraid to move and had to be rescued.

I could see Wahlitits despised me for my cowardice, and was about to say something that would cut me in two, but my brother spoke first. "We'll say nothing about how Teeto Hoonod acted. He has never seen a hohots before, and he was taken by surprise. The next time he'll know what to do. It would shame him if we spoke of this matter to other people. We'll only tell how we met and killed the great animal."

As he said this he looked directly at Wahlitits as though to say, I will have my eye on you, and if you do anything to humiliate my brother I will be angry with you. And so great was the power of my brother that Wahlitits only nodded his head in agreement.

We carried the bear back to the village. It was the custom among the People that the meat of a bear belonged to everyone, so we gave a feast of bear meat for the whole village.

When they heard the story of how my brother's arrow had struck the bear directly in the heart so the red blood gushed out they gave him his name, Red Grizzly Bear.

Because of my brother I was not humiliated before the People, but I felt shame burning within me and heard sneering thoughts telling me that I was not a real man, but had a weak heart, and even that I might become a berdache.

A berdache is half man, half woman. It is said that when a boy is about my age the moon comes and holds out to him a bow in one hand and a woman's pack strap in the other. If he hesitates before he reaches for the bow, the moon hands him the pack strap and he becomes a berdache. Such a person is given a proper place in the life of our people, but he never lives the life of a warrior, and he prefers woman things to man things.

Now I had let my bow drop when the hohots charged me, and even though I knew the strong-one-in-me-who-wants-to-come-out had taken up my knife and that I was going to hurl myself on the hohots in another moment, no one had seen me do this, and if now I said to my brother and Wahlitits, "You know, I was about to attack the bear and thrust my knife into his side," it would have sounded weak and hollow, as though I were making up the story to cover my cowardice. So I had to keep this to myself, until even I was no longer sure that I had actually taken the steps toward the hohots. So while I loved my brother all the more after this event, I hated myself.

Yet the Great Spirit can bring good even out of evil if he so chooses, and perhaps this is what happened to me. It came about in this way. After the experience with the hohots I often went away from the village alone, as though in solitude I might find some healing for my tortured soul. One day as I sat by the side of a small stream whose gurgling waters laughed and played as they raced through sunken branches and over rocks, their merriment in strange contrast to my somber mood, I heard the sound of someone approaching. I looked up, ready to be resentful of the uninvited intrusion into my privacy, and saw Kapoochas approaching. Had it been anyone else I would have been angry, but Kapoochas I welcomed.

"Old father," I said, "what brings you here?"

The wiry old man sat down beside me. "The question is, what brings *you* here? I've come because of you."

I turned my face away. "I need to be alone."

"You come here hoping to feel better, but you don't. Your soul is sick. I have felt this in you for a long time."

"For a long time, Kapoochas? It has only been since the slaying of the hohots by my brother that this darkness has filled me."

"So it seems to you. You believe that you are sick because you behaved badly when the grizzly charged. But the sickness was there before. If it had not been so, you would have acted differently when the crisis came upon you."

"Kapoochas, how do you know these things? Did anyone speak to you about how I acted when the grizzly charged? And how can it be that I was already sick and yet didn't know it?"

"No one had to tell me anything. It was written all over your face what had happened. And it is in the nature of sickness to live for a long time in our souls and bodies before it finally comes to the surface where it can be seen. Now, if you are willing to tell me the story, we will see if I can help."

My shame was so great that I didn't wish to share it with anyone lest it overwhelm me again, but soon I found myself telling Kapoochas all that happened that day: how I came upon the bear, froze, dropped my weapon in fear, and had to be rescued by my brother. As I spoke my soul felt lighter, as though some of its burden was transferred to the old healer.

Kapoochas didn't interrupt, ask questions, or offer any

38

advice until I had finished. Then he said simply, "Teeto Hoonod, it is time now for you to go on your Vision Quest. You need to find your Wy-a-kin. If your Wy-a-kin had been with you when the bear charged, you would have had the courage to act. It is because you have no spiritual ally that your soul has been sick all this time. Make your Quest and find your Wy-a-kin, and your strength can be renewed."

I pondered what he said, then answered, "In order to make a Vision Quest a young man needs the help of an older man who is willing to be a guide and teacher along the way, for no one should go to the spirit world unprepared. I would like to go on my Vision Quest now. I can see that you're right and I need to find my Wy-a-kin, but I will need help. Will you be my helper?"

Kapoochas grinned broadly, sprang to his feet with remarkable agility, and extended his hand to me. "Come. We'll begin the preparations right away."

For three days Kapoochas talked with me about the Vision Quest. He explained to me about the spirit world and told me how to conduct myself properly if I was so fortunate that a Power from the spirit world came to me. He reminded me that if nothing came I must not lie about it but must be willing to try again, for the Powers do not like a lying spirit. Then he searched my heart to see if my intentions were pure, for it would be dangerous for me to meet any of the Powers if there was evil in me.

After he had instructed me, Kapoochas helped me prepare the sweat lodge. Together we heated stones until they were red hot. Then we placed them inside a lodge set aside especially for this purpose, and I then entered the lodge and took my place. Kapoochas poured water over the red-hot stones until steam filled the lodge and it became hotter than the hottest summer day. I sat in the steaming heat for many hours while the sweat poured out of my body, purging body and soul of any evil that was in me. Many times I almost left the lodge because I felt I could no longer endure the heat, but I remembered that Kapoochas had said this was a test of my spiritual strength and I must remain in the lodge until he came for me.

At last Kapoochas came and went with me to the banks of the Wallowa River, where I drank until I thought surely I had drained it. Then we prepared a meal together and ate, my last food until I would complete the Vision Quest. Now I was ready to start on my way.

Kapoochas led me along the shore of Wallowa Lake to the high, heavily forested mountains that bordered it on the far side. When we reached the other end of the lake, we went silently along a rushing stream that carved a deep gorge into the flank of the mountain. We walked for several hours, until we came to a place where the water plunged over a steep drop. Here it was necessary to find a way around the waterfall in order to get to the top, but when we finally reached it we found ourselves in a small clearing in the forest through which the stream meandered quietly, as though gathering its strength for the wild plunge that lay ahead of it.

The clearing was a meadow set in the midst of spruce trees, and here Kapoochas made a circle of stones and placed me inside the circle with instructions that I was not to leave it until the Quest was completed, which would be four days and four nights. Then he prayed and chanted to the Great Spirit, asking for protection for me and, above all, for a favorable response from the spirit world to my Quest. He made the prayer four times, once in each of the four sacred directions, and then twice more, once up to Father Sky and once below to Mother Earth. Then, having done all he could for me, he left me there alone, promising to return when the four-day vigil was completed.

As I watched Kapoochas disappear among the trees, loneliness settled over me like fog on a mountain. For sixteen years I had lived like a wolf cub, always surrounded by brothers and sisters and the warmth of the pack. I had never been alone for any period of time, and I felt a terrible longing to rush down the mountain after the old man and return with him to the comfort of the village.

But slowly, as awareness of my surroundings found its way through my fearful thoughts, I realized that I wasn't alone. Bright tiny flowers were strewn over the meadow— red and yellow and blue—and they danced and swayed as xa-epxalp, the gentle, playful summer breeze, stirred the meadow to life and made the limbs of the surrounding trees sway gently back and forth, like mothers rocking their babies in their arms. The air was filled with a chorus of songs from the birds and the complaining chatter of the squirrels. I remembered what Kapoochas had once told me: "No one is ever alone. Always the spirits are with us, watching. Always the Power of the Great Spirit is moving through everything that is on the face of the earth."

But as the loneliness eased, the gnawing emptiness in my stomach increased, for just as I had never been alone for that long, so I had never been without food. Even in winter, when food was scarce, my mother kept a pot of stew going, and anyone who was hungry needed only to dip into it and eat. Now, as my stomach began to complain, the small boy in me felt like whimpering and wishing that some woman would magically appear and feed me. But no one did, and when darkness began to descend I realized that for the first time in my life I would fall asleep hungry.

As night gradually covered the meadow and forest, the songs of the birds gave way to insect sounds, and the noise of the squirrels to the hooting of an owl and the muffled *whir* of a bat as it found its way by magic through the trees. Once, far away in the valley below, I heard the wild cacophony of the coyotes as though, like their namesake Coyote, they were laughing at some outlandish joke. I longed for sleep, sleep in which I could forget my fears and no longer have to feel the pain in my empty stomach, sleep in which, I hoped, my Wy-a-kin would appear in a dream.

At last sleep came, and though I woke often in the night I fell asleep again and again until finally the dawn began to find its way through the trees and the chill air began slowly to be warmed by the sun. I was grateful for the sleep, and grateful for the dawn, but no dream had come, no spirit being had spoken to me.

The second day continued much as the first, but my reactions began to change. As the sun climbed higher into the sky, I was less aware of my hunger and more aware of every little sound and movement around me. When a black beetle found its way into my circle it became a great event. I discovered that the beetle lived nearby, and as it wandered back and forth, on important missions that it alone understood, it became a friend to me and a source of consolation. And since I was sitting so very still now, the animals and birds became used to me and treated me as though I were a harmless rock. I distinguished the many different kinds of birds and the several types of squirrels, and once, to my surprise and delight, a bobcat emerged from the forest and stared at me for a long time with serious eyes until, satisfied at last that there was nothing within the little clearing of interest, he disappeared into the trees. For a moment I wondered: Was the bobcat to be my Wy-a-kin? But something told me no, I must wait for something else to come.

The second night passed as the first and I awoke still discouraged, for again no dreams had come to me. During that third day it was as though my mind was in a fog, and time seemed to pass in a blur until, when the sun stood directly overhead, thoughts began to torment me.

"You are not worthy," they said. "The spirit beings know how weak you are. They will not come to you. Give up. Return to the village. There at least you can eat and be warm again at night. There is no use staying here. You are not worthy of a Wy-a-kin."

I was so discouraged that I almost gave in, but when I thought of Kapoochas, and how he would look at me if I returned before the four days were over, and how disappointed he would be, I knew I could not go. Finally, tormented by the lying voice, I screamed into the empty air, "Away! No more lies! Don't speak to me like this. I won't listen."

The voice mocked me again: "No Wy-a-kin is to be yours, no spirit being will come."

I answered, "Then I will remain here anyway. I will stay here until the time is completed." Then the thoughts ceased to torment me, and I fell asleep.

The third night came and went uneventfully, and the fourth and last day was well under way, and still I sat there in my circle, my mind now numb with fatigue but determined to persevere. I had given up hope that my Quest would be rewarded by the gift of Wy-a-kin and expected to be rejected by the spirit world, but still I remained there, rooted to the ground, as though my body and soul had melted and I had become part of the trees and stones around me.

Then it began to happen. As I gazed vacantly over the meadow I saw a qotsqo'tsn, a meadowlark, perched on a low bush not more than three paces from me, handsome in yellow and black colors. The little bird was singing its vigorous song as though its heart would burst with pride and joy. And while I listened, the song seemed to grow and swell in intensity until it filled the forest. Never have I heard such singing! Though it looked right at me, the qotsqo'tsn was not afraid; it didn't fly away even when I moved slightly in order to see more clearly. Then the whole meadow and forest seemed to burst into intense, joyful song. It was not ordinary singing but spiritual singing. A chorus of birds

43

broke out all around me, as though they had been waiting for Meadowlark to lead them, and then an insect chorus added its joyful din to the sound of the birds. Soon it seemed as though everything about me was singing; flowers, grass, trees, the wind, all were alive with a joyous Power that expressed itself in the ecstatic chorus.

Then was revealed to me the secret of this holy place: that all things, though many, yet are one; that the world is alive with a joyous energy, and though the meadow and the forest are made up of many different things, each unique, they are all united in the One Great Source of life.

All this time the song of the Qotsqo'tsn was louder than any of the other songs, as though Meadowlark was the leader of this wild and gallant chorus, and as I listened to that bird sing it seemed as though our two souls were the same. My heart was lifted up as I felt the ecstatic Power surge within me; my very body joined in the unearthly melody bursting all around me.

I don't know how long I was immersed in the music of that forest and meadow. It seemed to last forever, and yet also to be over in a moment. Then suddenly Meadowlark stopped singing and took flight from the low-lying bush, and with his departure the forest fell back into its ordinary sounds, and the meadow became once more an ordinary meadow, and the magic of the place ceased and I was simply an ordinary boy sitting among ordinary trees and grass. But my soul was now at peace, for I knew my Wy-a-kin had come. Little Qotsqo'tsn, Meadowlark, was my spirit being and had shown me that what seemed ordinary was actually filled with a holy Power.

That night I had a dream in which Qotsqo'tsn appeared, again perched on the bush. He said nothing, but for the longest time his eyes looked directly into mine. If there was any doubt that Meadowlark was to be my Wy-a-kin, it vanished with that dream.

The next morning the sun was just beginning to warm the meadow when I heard a rustling sound in the forest, and in a moment Kapoochas emerged from the trees and strode into the clearing. Silently we embraced; it didn't yet seem right to speak. Then Kapoochas sang a sacred song over me, carefully put the stones that made the circle back in their original places in the meadow, and together we went down the mountain.

I began to tell Kapoochas my experiences, and the words flowed because I was happy to have a human companion again. When I came to the part of my story about the meadowlark, Kapoochas's eyes opened with delight and he said to me, "You're blessed. You should be happy that little Qotsqo'tsn has chosen you, for he has much Power."

But now that the memory of my experience was fading I had a doubt. "But Meadowlark is small among the animals. He has no great strength among them. Others hope they will be chosen by the elk spirit or the wolf spirit or the eagle. What would people say if they knew I had been chosen by Qotsqo'tsn?"

Kapoochas held up his hand as though to forbid such thoughts. "Don't doubt what has come to you. Remember the old stories of our people, the tales that tell how things were before the human race came? There you will see that Meadowlark is the one who knows; he is the one who has the vision and can instruct others. This is why he has chosen you. Your strength will not be in your arms or your legs but in your knowing. As for others, don't tell them what you have seen or heard. Important things like this must be kept to oneself or given only to those who can be trusted with them. Others, who do not understand, will be like vultures and make a dead thing of your experience and devour it."

And that is how I received my Wy-a-kin, that Power which, when I have been faithful to it, has always been faithful to me, but which I have also often forgotten.

CHAPTER FOUR

Mounting Tension

In the years that followed my Vision Quest, life for my people and myself slowly changed. It seemed there were fewer deer than there used to be and that the animals, once so fearless, were frightened now when we approached them. Hunters who returned from the East Country told us that white men with long-range rifles were killing the buffalo and the herds that once covered the earth like great, moving dark blankets were shrinking like a pool of water in summer. Travelers from the west told us that settlers were rapidly filling the land that once belonged to our cousins, the Cayuse, Umatillas, and Palouse, and were moving in our direction.

Still, most of my people, myself included, lived as we had always lived and made ourselves believe that our old ways would continue forever. Were there not still plenty of fish in the streams? Were the camas bulbs not still plentiful? Had any white people come to settle on our land? But when I spoke to Kapoochas of our future a cloud came over his eyes, and I could tell that he was worried.

One day in the summer of the year 1861, Kapoochas said to my brother and me, "Ride with me to the Snake River country north of us. I have been called by the Palouse to help a chief's son who is ill."

It was not unusual for Kapoochas to be asked for help by bands far away, for he was a famous healer, and often my brother and I would go with him for the sake of the adventure. So we agreed and began our journey.

Usually our travels with Kapoochas were festive occasions. The old man enjoyed his trips and was cheerful and full of wit, and my brother and I would laugh at his jokes and be flattered that he wanted us along. But this time he was quiet, and when we asked him about it he only replied, "Many things are on my mind."

When the Palouse Indians had been driven from their homeland, a small band of them had asked to settle on our land, west of Lapwai along the Snake River, not far from its confluence with the Columbia. It took two days of hard riding for us to reach their village, and Kapoochas spent two more days ministering to the sick young man. When he had done all he could and we were ready to leave, he said to us, "We will return home a different way. I have something to show you. It will not make you happy, but there is something you must know."

We begged him to tell us what it was, but he dismissed us with a wave of his hand, saying, "You will see."

For a day we rode along the trail that followed the Snake River. I realized that we were heading for the place where the Snake and the Clearwater joined; this would not be far from my childhood home at Lapwai. Kapoochas was pushing us hard, and our horses were tiring; we pleaded with him to stop and rest, but he rode along grimly, ignoring our pleas and putting us young men to shame with his endurance.

By midafternoon of the second day I knew where we were: We had reached the junction of the two great rivers. We had made our approach from the north, and on this side of the river is a high bluff that gives you a view in every direction. Here we dismounted, walked to the top of the cliffs, and looked down at the confluence of the rivers two hundred feet below us.

When I was a child I had sometimes climbed up to this spot. Then it had been a peaceful place, where a boy could sit for hours watching the silver of the Clearwater sweep along to join the blue of the Snake. But now the scene was different. A town of tents and crudely built shacks had sprung up at the junction of the rivers, and a wooden wharf protruded rudely into the water. By the side of the wharf was one of the great boats that sent black smoke into the air and carried the goods of the Long Knives. And everywhere were white people, hundreds of them: unloading the boat, carrying things here and there, nailing up new shacks.

"Kapoochas, what does this mean?" I cried out in horror. "What are these people doing here on our land?"

"This is as far up the river as their boats can go," Kapoochas replied. "They're building a town here so they can unload their supplies."

"But it's not allowed," my brother joined in.

"They call it Lewiston," Kapoochas added, as though lost in thought and hardly aware of us.

"But the treaty forbids it," I protested.

"They pay no attention to the treaty."

Hohots Illpilp spoke again. "But the treaty called for troops to enforce it and to expel any white people who tried to settle on our land."

"The troops aren't far away. They're stationed at Lapwai. But they choose to ignore what's going on."

"Why do they need supplies here?" I persisted.

"Gold. The yellow metal that white people crave was discovered on our land to the east, in the foothills of the Bitterroots. Already the land is filling up with Americans who are crazy to find it. It's like a disease with them, but their disease is going to affect us too. The men who are

48

looking for the gold need supplies, and this town has been built here to bring these supplies to them."

"I see," I said. "But how strange they should call it Lewiston. Meriwether Lewis was the first American our people saw. He became a friend to us and we were friends to him, as you yourself have told me. But these people here can't be our friends."

"They don't come to be either our friends or our enemies. That doesn't occur to them. They come only to get rich from the gold, or from selling supplies to men who look for the gold. These men are neither good nor bad, better nor worse than we are. But they're not aware of what they are doing, and that's what makes them dangerous. It's because they're not aware that they call their town after our great friend. Yes, Lewis and the great man Clark were our friends. I remember them well, though I was just a small boy when they came."

Hohots Illpilp spoke again. "Many years ago the white people came onto our land to trap the beaver. They came and hunted and went away again, leaving things as they were before. Won't it be the same with these men who come for the gold?"

"No, it will not be the same. The men who came to trap the beaver were few in number. We liked them, and they liked us. There was mutual respect, and it was easy to be friends. These men are many. They will swarm over our land looking for gold. They will not find much, but many of them will like this land and will stay here to settle. And these people who have built this town will not go. Having failed to get rich from the gold, they will stay to get rich from the land."

Kapoochas was right. The gold ran out, but the Americans stayed, and soon there were more white people in our country than Indians. He was also right that the gold that was the white man's disease turned out also to be our disease. For

49

many of the Nez Perce welcomed Lewiston and the Americans. They began to trade with them and grow rich by selling them supplies, and others craved the liquor the white men brought. The Christian Nez Perce, who lived closest to Lewiston, also accepted the situation. "This is the way we all knew it would be one day," they said with an air of resignation. But they could afford to talk that way. They lived now by farming, and it didn't threaten them as it did us when the white people who failed to find gold began pushing up the river valleys to settle the land, driving away the game and ruining the fishing.

During the next two years the tension between us and the Americans steadily increased, like a river swollen in spring with melting snow, until it threatened to overflow and bring murders and chaos and even war. It couldn't last, and finally in the year 1863 the American leaders called for a conference between them and the chiefs of all our bands in order to resolve the difficulties. Old Joseph was chosen to be the leader of the contingent that went from our band to Lapwai, where the conference was to be held. He was a natural choice, for not only was he highly respected by us for his wisdom and coolness of mind, but he was still a Christian and so closer to the spirit of the white people. He went full of hope, saying as he rode away, "At last they will listen. We will explain ourselves to them and peace will be made."

Two weeks later, early in the evening, Old Joseph returned. I will never forget the sight. Word passed through the village: "Tu-e-ka-kas and the others are back!" We gathered excitedly as Joseph rode into the village. He was frowning. His eyes stared fiercely straight ahead. He said nothing but went to the center of the village and signaled that a council fire be lit. When the fire was burning, all the people assembled around it, and then Tu-e-ka-kas spoke.

"We went to the white man's council full of hope. Surely,

we thought, the white man will now make an agreement with us so all can live in peace together. But the Americans did not come to make peace but to steal our land. They wanted us to sign a new treaty that would give our land away. What need do we have of a new treaty? Had we not signed a treaty with them already? We came to ask them to honor that treaty, not to make a new one. But they wouldn't listen. 'Sign a new treaty,' is all they would say. The new treaty would give this land on which we are now living to the white settlers. It would make us live with the Christians on the small land that is theirs. The other bands also would have to go. The Nez Perce country, this land the Great Spirit gave to us, would be gone forever. Here, I will show you!"

Tu-e-ka-kas took out his knife and called for a buffalo hide. He held up the hide and with his knife cut off a small corner and flung the rest into the fire. "Here," he cried. "This small piece of the robe is like the land that would be left to us!"

A groan of dismay came up from the people.

"But they didn't succeed because we wouldn't sign. None of us who live in the old way signed the treaty. I didn't sign, nor any of the other chiefs who still wear the blanket. We rode away. We left the conference because we saw it would not lead to good. But the Christian Nez Perce did sign. They signed because the small piece of land the treaty gives to the Nez Perce is the land they are on now. They had nothing to lose, but we would lose everything. So they signed, but we did not.

"Now," he continued, "it is over. The friendship between us and the Americans has melted away like snow in spring-time. From now on the white man is not to be trusted, and we are no longer one nation but two, for when the Christian Nez Perce signed they divided our people." And with this Tu-e-ka-kas took his knife, and slashed the small piece of buffalo hide he still held in his hand into two pieces, and held them up for everyone to see.

Then Tu-e-ka-kas went to his horse while all eyes were on him. He reached into his bag and took from it the Bible he had carried with him ever since he had become a Christian fifteen years earlier. Holding the Bible up before us, he tore the pages out of it in great thick clumps and threw them on the fire, where they made the flames leap up. We watched in silence while the Bible was completely destroyed.

After this, Tu-e-ka-kas changed. He became very quiet. He who had been the lifelong friend of the Americans was now filled with the spirit of distrust. He spent many hours riding along the borders of our land. He rebuilt the fence of posts he had put there years ago to separate our land from the land being filled by the white settlers to the west. He also became older very fast. His physical strength faded, and his eyesight began to fail until he could scarcely see. Yet his soul was not diminished, and his wisdom grew greater as his body grew weaker.

As Tu-e-ka-kas's strength waned, his oldest son became chief in his place. Hin-mah-too-yah-lat-kekht—the name means "thunder-traveling-to-loftier-mountain-heights"— was young to be a chief, especially since he had never gone to the East Country to make a name for himself as a warrior or hunter. Yet his influence among us was accepted without question because of certain inner qualities that radiated throughout his being. In spite of his youthfulness, Hin-mah-too-yah-lat-kekht was a man of wisdom, dignity, and eloquence, a man who never lost his head and always used his heart. He was tall and massively built, with the strong and stately bearing of a great oak tree, a man who laughed readily with his friends but was solemn and cautious in dealing with his enemies.

Old Joseph's oldest son was such an impressive person that he became known among the white people too. They called him "Young Joseph," after his father, and because he has become a famous person among whites as well as Indians I will use that name to refer to him, although among ourselves we always called him by his Indian name.

Young Joseph had a younger brother whose name was Ollokot, a Cayuse name that means "the frog." Ollokot was the most perfect athlete I have ever known, except perhaps Wahlitits. Graceful and supple in all his movements, he was full of fun and laughter and liked by all who knew him. Even the white people had good things to say about Ollokot. Unlike Joseph, Ollokot became a warrior and hunter on journeys to the East Country and won a big name for himself. Yet he never contested with his brother for power but was satisfied to be second chief to him. Joseph and Ollokot loved each other too much to quarrel and held the welfare of their people higher than their own. Both were married. Joseph's wife was Toma Alwawinmi, and Ollokot's wife was Wetatonmi—"Fair Land."

Eight years after the Christian Nez Perce signed the treaty with the Americans, it was clear that death was waiting outside the lodge of Tu-e-ka-kas, as winter lingers, waiting for the last leaf to fall from the trees before descending on the land. Then Tu-e-ka-kas called Young Joseph to his side and, with all the people watching, said to him, "My son, you will soon be the leader of your people. Do not forget that this land in which we live was never sold to the whites; your father never gave it to them. Whenever you are asked to sign a treaty giving away your home to the white people, you must close your eyes and not listen. You can be sure they have their eyes on this land and will try to get it away from you. But do not forget these words I tell you as I am dying. This country will hold my body. It holds the bodies of your ancestors. Never sell the bones of your ancestors, never trade away the land that is like a mother to us."

Young Joseph remembered Old Joseph's words. When his

53

father died he buried him near his favorite camping spot in his beloved Wallowa Valley. We built a fence around his grave and placed a bell on the fence that rang in the wind and signaled to all those who passed by that here lay the body of a great chief.

While these changes took place in the life of the People, changes also took place in the lives of my brother and me. Shortly before Old Joseph died, my brother married. Among the Nez Perce, every man and woman is expected to marry, for the survival of the People depends on our families, and our children and families were the center of our lives. So the fact that my brother married was not surprising. What was unusual was the young woman whom he chose for a wife.

Rising Moon was different from the other young women of our band. A young Indian woman is expected to be quiet and modest. She is taught to care for the children, to gather and prepare the food, to make the lodge or tipi ready for comfortable living. She is not to look boldly at men, and when she speaks to a man it is to be in a soft voice and with downcast eyes. To be sure, as she grows older these things change, but when she is young it is meant to be this way. And certainly she is never to do the things in life that a man does, unless she is called by the spirits to be a healer, for the spirits may choose a man or a woman to be a te-wat.

All the other young women conformed to these expectations, but Rising Moon had a different spirit. When she was a small girl she would often be seen playing with the boys. When she grew older she learned how to ride a horse like a man, how to handle a bow and arrow and, later, even a rifle. When she became a young woman she would speak openly and boldly with men when she chose to do so. She was fearless and would go off into the hills or forest to roam and be by herself and did not care that others said this was dangerous and not a good woman thing to do. When she felt strongly about something she expressed it, which sometimes made people uncomfortable. For this she was often criticized by the older women and looked at questioningly by the men.

Physically she was a lean woman, slightly taller than most, but her body was strong and agile, and she could run tirelessly. When you first looked at her face she didn't appear beautiful. But when her face was lighted by her spirit it changed and glowed; then her eyes flashed and sparkled like fireflies in the night, and she was wonderful to see.

Naturally others talked about her. It was rumored about by those women in the village who never seemed to have enough to do that she slept with the men with whom she spoke so freely. Yet we men knew this was not so. Others thought that maybe she was going to be crazy because she went off so often by herself, but the te-wats among us, like Kapoochas, said no, that she did this because the spirits called her and wanted her to be alone so they could talk with her.

Of course she was the despair of her parents. When asked about her independent ways her parents would shrug their shoulders and say, "Who can control her? She is like xa-lpxalp, Gusty Wind, which blows wherever it chooses and obeys no one."

So when Hohots Illpilp said he was going to marry Rising Moon everyone was surprised, for my brother was stronger and wiser than any other young man among us, and he could have had his pick of the modest young women in the village. Nevertheless, he chose Rising Moon as his bride and she accepted him at once.

I asked him about this. "Brother," I said to him, "why have you chosen Rising Moon to be your woman? She's headstrong and darts about here and there like a wild deer. She'll give you a lot of trouble and won't do as you say. There are many young girls among us whom I see watching you shyly as you walk past them, glancing at you when they think you're not looking. Why didn't you choose one of them instead of this young woman who wants to be free like a bird?"

My brother answered, "You're right that she's like a bird who doesn't want to be caged, or like a deer that darts here and there in the forest and can't be held. But I have looked into her dark and flashing eyes and have seen her spirit. It's a strong spirit, and she has a strong heart. I think she will give me strong children, and there is something about her woman-power that I love."

After that I looked at them closely when they were together and I could see the love light in my brother's eyes, and I could also see love and respect in the eyes of Rising Moon for my brother.

So they were married, which means that my brother brought some presents to Rising Moon's family, and her parents consented to the union, surprised and relieved that their willful and capricious daughter had made such a good match. Then, after Rising Moon and Hohots Illpilp had lived together for a short while, a wedding party was planned at which both families were to exchange gifts. However in this case, since my brother and I had no family, there were not many gifts offered back and forth. There was no ceremony. The fact that they now lived together publicly and the families had exchanged presents meant that they were man and wife.

After that my home changed, for Rising Moon and Hohots Illpilp made a place for me with them, and I no longer lived with my friend Shuslum Hihhih and his wife, though Shuslum Hihhih and I used to get together sometimes to speak the English language with each other, for we both thought that sometime this knowledge might be valuable to the People.

Since I now lived close to my brother and Rising Moon, often sharing meals with them, I also got to know Rising

Moon well, and we became friends. Because my brother and I were as one person, there was never any question of wrong coming between us because of Rising Moon, and even though she and I would sometimes walk and talk together my brother trusted us completely. Even if Rising Moon had wanted to express love with me I wouldn't have done so because of loyalty to Hohots Illpilp, but though Rising Moon talked with me she kept her lovemaking for her husband.

I married three winters after my brother did, but I chose a woman who was different from Rising Moon. Wali'ms was not a Nez Perce at all but a Shoshone who had been captured by one of our war parties on a foray into the Shoshone country. She had been brought back to the village, and the family of the man who captured her kept her as a servant. Her place among us was low, for she was not adopted into the tribe. Because of this, and because she couldn't talk our language at first, most of the young men ignored her.

Wali'ms was quiet and shy, average in height, with a slightly rounded body, gentle brown eyes, and soft features. At first I didn't think she was beautiful, but then I noticed that when she smiled her face lit up brightly and was full of fun and kindness, but this was rare, for her lot in life was hard. From the time that she first came to live among us I noticed that she would steal looks at me as I walked past, and I found myself glancing back at her as though I wished to see into her soul, intrigued by her woman-power. We spoke little together, of course, for although she gradually learned some of our language her circumstances in the village made talk difficult. Yet I knew that somehow we shared something of the same soul. Was it because each of us felt unacceptable—she because she was from a different people, and I because of my sense of shame?

Kapoochas said that when Wali'ms was born into this world and placed on the medicine wheel by the Great Spirit, she was given the place of the mouse. Now, whatever lies within range of the mouse's nose and whiskers it knows about; within that range it doesn't miss anything and can detect the tiniest seed. This is the way it was with Wali'ms, who noticed many small things in life that other people overlooked. She knew what plants had healing qualities and where to find them. She knew where the best grasses grew from which the tightest baskets could be made. She also knew how to make the most delicate and intricate designs on the baskets she made, intriguing patterns of circles, squares, and other shapes, each with its own color and its own special meaning. Her baskets were a marvel. It made you feel better just to hold one, and they were made so well they could hold water all day and never leak.

I can't tell you when I decided on the Shoshone girl as my wife, but one day I knew. Ordinarily if a young man wanted a young woman he would have to find a way to get to know her, to plan secret meetings away from the watchful eyes of her parents, and find remote places where he could persuade the girl to come and live with him. Then the matter would be negotiated with her parents and gifts exchanged, as I have said. All this time the girl might reject his advances, for that was always her right, and that would be a humiliation to him.

I was always afraid of being rejected like this, for unlike my brother, who was admired by women wherever he went, when I passed through the village the girls didn't seem to notice me. Not only did I not have the strength and agility of young men like Wahlitits, Hohots Illpilp, and Ollokot, I also lacked confidence in myself and so my man-spirit didn't show. For this reason I was afraid that no woman would want me.

But it was different with Wali'ms because she had no standing in our tribe, and when I finally knew I wanted her as my wife, I simply went to the family who owned her and gave them two horses to buy her from them. It was a high price for me to pay, as I was not wealthy. Since Wali'ms was a captive there was nothing else that had to be done, and since she was not a Nez Perce she had no choice but to accept me as her husband.

So I took Wali'ms with me to a lodge I had set up, and she came with me quietly and shyly. At first we didn't know what to do with each other. It was hard to talk because she didn't speak our language well, nor I hers. I wanted to make love to her, but I didn't want her to have to make love with me unless she wanted to. I wanted her to love me with her soul as well as with her body.

So we took walks together, and I taught her our language, and she taught me some of her Shoshone language. She was quick and learned rapidly. I could tell that she loved me, but I wondered if it was only because I had freed her from her slavery. So I decided to have her adopted into the tribe.

This was a bold step on my part. As an adopted member of the tribe, she would have the same rights as any other woman, which meant she would be free to leave me whenever she chose. So she was adopted, and received her Nez Perce name, and I wondered if she would leave me, but she didn't. And it was then that I made love to her, and she opened herself to me, and it became very beautiful that we were together.

One day I asked her, "Wali'ms, why is it that you love me? I'm not strong like my brother, I don't go to the East Country and come back as a famous warrior. I have no great standing among the People."

"Sometimes," she said, "a woman loves a man for what is within his mind and his soul. Out of your soul there came kindness to me, and out of your mind there came a bright light, and these are the things that make me love you."

It was true that my mind had a bright light, and I was increasingly valued among the People for a power with words that others didn't have. The English my mother

59

taught me gave me some standing now, for during these past winters we had more dealings with the white people, and these exchanges often required the presence of those who knew the white man's language. So I was increasingly called upon to speak when we met with the Long Knives to trade our furs and dried foods and baskets for the white man's guns, ammunition, and steel knives. In this way I became skilled in the things of the spoken word, and while sometimes other young men of the village would taunt me because I didn't go to the Buffalo Country, no one ever taunted me when someone was needed to make talk possible between us and the Americans.

All this time Hohots Illpilp and I remained close friends as well as brothers, and Rising Moon and Wali'ms likewise became friends, even though they were so different. We made our lodges close together in the village and often lived together as one family, and it was hard to say whether I loved my wife more or my brother. Rising Moon I regarded with respect, and she in turn treated me with concern and the kind of love a sister would have for a loved brother.

But once Wali'ms said, "Have you noticed the way Rising Moon looks at you sometimes? It's as though she loves you too."

I answered, "It's nonsense to say that. She's married to Hohots Illpilp. He is far more handsome than I am."

"And yet," Wali'ms replied, "while a woman admires a man for his strength, she sometimes loves him for his heart."

I didn't like what she was saying and wanted to put her words out of my mind, so I answered shortly, "Women are always making things up in matters of love. They like to talk about such things so much that when there's nothing to talk about they imagine something."

Wali'ms fell silent. I could see that I had hurt her. But I could also tell that she hadn't changed her mind.

A year after our marriage, Wali'ms gave birth to our daughter, and it was hard for me to know whom I loved the most. At the time of her birth five birds alighted nearby, so we named her Pahkatos Peopeo—Five Birds—until such time as she would have an adult name.

So this is the way it was with Hohots Illpilp and me and our young wives in those days. But all this time the tension between us and the Americans, which started with the discovery of the gold, increased and led to the great trouble that was soon to begin.

CHAPTER FIVE

> ❦

The Snake Must Be Crossed

It was the summer of 1874; Old Joseph had been dead for three years. We were preparing for our annual trip to Weippe Prairie, where we would play games, gamble, race horses, celebrate, and gather the camas bulbs as usual. Most important, this was the time we would renew our spirit as a nation, for all the bands who lived in the old way would be there: those of Chiefs Too-hool-hool-Sote, White Bird, and Looking Glass.

Too-hool-hool-Sote was a square, massively built man of great strength, with a gruff, rumbling voice and an indomitable and warlike spirit. He was an inveterate hater of the Americans and was the only chief who openly called for war.

White Bird was in his seventies now but was still strong and vigorous. He was cautious but not timid; not easily provoked, but courageous if a fight couldn't be avoided. He was a te-wat as well as a chief, as I have said, and wore an eagle feather to show it. He was a wise man, admired by all.

Looking Glass was named after his renowned father, who had died some years earlier but had been a major chief at the signing of the Treaty of 1855. Looking Glass was the most admired of all our leaders. A tall, strong man, he was physically impressive. His mind was quick; only Joseph matched him in intelligence. His prowess and reputation as a hunter and warrior gave him great standing. He did, however, have one failing: inordinate confidence in himself and a pride so great that he only paid attention to his own ideas. The day would come when we would pay dearly for this.

There were many other impressive warriors who would gather at Weippe this summer, but I will mention only two more: Wachumyus and Pahkatos Owyeen. Rainbow and Five Wounds spent most of their time in the East Country hunting buffalo. They were generally regarded as our best fighting men. They always fought together and had taken an oath that if one should die in battle the other would die also. If war ever came, what Rainbow and Five Wounds said would be listened to carefully.

But we would not all be there, for only a few of the Christian Nez Perce would join us at the prairie, those who had friends or relatives in the other bands they wished to see, or who were just homesick for a touch of the old ways.

We were happy as we prepared for the journey to Weippe, even though for the past several years white settlers had pressed farther up the Grande Ronde River, closer to our own Wallowa Valley. This disturbed us, but as long as they didn't enter the valley we told ourselves we had no cause for alarm. So in spite of this our spirits were high as the young men cut out the best horses, the women gathered the food and belongings we would need on the way, the children played around us in high excitement, and Joseph and Ollokot made plans. At last all was ready and we moved out— several hundred strong—for a leisurely journey of several days. We camped on the way, stopping early to enjoy ourselves in the warm, balmy summer air. By nature we are a happy people, and we put our troubles out of our minds as we anticipated the celebration and gaiety of the annual gathering at the prairie.

At last we wound our way through the low foothill country of the Bitterroots toward Weippe. Of all the bands we lived the farthest from the prairie, so we would be the last to arrive. We were used to this and looked forward to being greeted by the other bands, who would ride out to meet us singing songs and shouting greetings. But this summer no one came. As we marched along, the silence became oppressive and an ominous feeling took hold of us.

I rode beside my brother. "It's so quiet," I said to him in a low voice. "We should be hearing the shouts of the people ahead of us."

"It doesn't seem natural," he agreed.

"Perhaps the wind blows the other way and carries the sound to the mountains instead of to us." I said this to reassure him and myself when, in fact, I knew that the wind was blowing down from the mountains and into our faces as usual.

My brother and I were riding in the van of the procession; Joseph and Ollokot led the way. Suddenly Joseph held up his hand as a signal for us to halt. We looked ahead. Seated on their horses waiting for us was a band of Nez Perce. White Bird was the leader.

Joseph rode ahead. "Something is wrong?"

"Come and see," White Bird answered, and he and his companions turned their horses and started toward the nearby prairie.

We followed until we reached the edge of the prairie. White Bird pointed ahead with his lance as he looked back at us, anguish written across his face. The prairie, which usually at this time of year was strewn with flowers of every describable color, was cut and churned up as though by some violent force. The flowers were destroyed, and the camas bulbs, uprooted and torn, were rotting on the ground. The prairie was ruined, our food supply destroyed.

"What has done this?" Joseph asked.

"Pigs," White Bird replied.

"Pigs?" Joseph answered. "The Nez Perce have no pigs."

"Pigs from the white ranches nearby. The Long Knives turned their pigs loose here to feast on our camas bulbs. The animals have eaten some and ruined the others and, as you can see, have torn the skin of our Mother the Earth so that it lies here scarred and bleeding."

We stayed there for a while, but there was no celebration. And when we returned home downcast and angry, it was to discover that white settlers from the Grande Ronde River had come into the lower part of our own Wallowa Valley and were taking our land for their farms. What we had feared the most, but somehow thought would never happen, was happening now.

When we saw these settlers taking over our land, many people spoke of driving them out by force. But Joseph wanted to talk with them, and so a parley was arranged. Joseph, Ollokot, Kapoochas, and the other leading men of our band went to confer with the settlers, and I went along as an interpreter.

We met on the newly established ranch farthest up the river. Indians and whites gathered underneath the branches of a grove of great spreading live oak trees. Joseph insisted that all weapons be left behind. He greeted the white strangers courteously, and their leaders also greeted him with respect. Everyone relaxed a bit, and we began to hope that an agreement could be reached.

Joseph began by patiently explaining that there must be a mistake, that the land these people were settling had been Nez Perce land for longer than anyone could remember.

But a spokesman for the settlers answered, "No, Joseph, you gave up your land. You signed a treaty and the land has been opened to settlement. We didn't come to be your enemies, but we are told by our government that it's our right to have what land in this valley we want."

Joseph answered, "Lawyer and the Christian Nez Perce signed the treaty, but we did not. They may have given

65

away their land, but we didn't give away our land."

The white people looked mystified and uneasy at this statement from Joseph, but the man who was their chief spokesman answered him, "Joseph, we don't want to have any trouble, for we have been friends with the Nez Perce. But we were told that when Lawyer and the others signed the treaty in 1863 it was binding on all of you. Lawyer is the head chief of all your people, so when he signed, he signed on behalf of everyone. This is why we have a right to the land."

But Joseph, as always, knew what to say. "Lawyer is not our head chief. The Nez Perce have no head chief. You Americans have declared that he is our head chief, but we don't recognize him."

The spokesman pressed his point. "But there are so few of you, and there is so much land, and there are many of us, and we need land of our own on which to have farms and raise families. It isn't right for you to keep all the land for yourselves."

"Then we will make a new agreement. You can keep the lower part of the valley but agree that the upper part of the valley, and the land around our sacred Wallowa Lake, is to be ours."

This seemed to me, and to the other Nez Perce listening, like a generous and creative solution and we murmured approval, even though we would be surrendering land that had always belonged to us, but the spokesman insisted, "No, Joseph, you have already sold your land."

Joseph, standing tall and firm beside the greak oak tree, slowly moved his extended arm around him in all directions to indicate the land that was ours and answered, "Suppose a white man came to me and told me he wanted to buy my horses, and I replied that I would not sell them. Then suppose he went to my neighbor and told him that I had some good horses and would not sell them, and my neighbor said,

'Don't worry about it. I will sell you Joseph's horses. Just pay me.' Then the white man returns to me and says, 'Joseph, your horses have been sold to me; you must give them to me now.' If we sold our lands to the government, this is how it happened."

No one could argue with Joseph after this, and for a while it appeared that some good might come out of our talk. An effort was made to divide the Wallowa Valley into an upper and lower half, and we learned that the great white chief in Washington had signed an order to that effect. But a mistake was made. The order gave the upper part of the valley to the white people, and the lower part to the Nez Perce, which was just the reverse of the actual case. So the decree of the President was not enforced, and he soon withdrew it without signing another in its place.

Tension and clashes came inevitably with the Long Knives in the months that followed. Ever since the gold rush of 1860 there had been incidents, but now they multiplied in number and gravity. One of the most distressing was the murder of a crippled woman named Dakoopin. A white man's horse had gotten into her garden, and while she was removing it the man came upon her and killed her. Other problems arose when unscrupulous Americans sold liquor to the Indians. One of the worst of these offenders was a man named Sam Benedict, who owned a store along the Salmon River. He cheated Indians of their change and sold them the illegal firewater that made them act crazy.

The result was that more troops were stationed on our land, and a new general came to take charge of them: General Oliver O. Howard. I will have more to say about him later, for he was important to us. We were told that the soldiers came to keep the peace, but they acted as though they meant to protect the settlers from us, even though we were the ones who were suffering at the hands of the Americans.

67

One day Wahlitits came to visit us, the athletic and courageous young man who was with my brother and me on the day the grizzly bear charged. That night we lit a great campfire in the middle of the village and many of us gathered around, Joseph among them. Wahlitits held up his hand for silence, and when all eyes were on him he told us why he had come.

"Several suns ago I returned from a hunting trip to my father's home. Now some months earlier a white man named Larry Ott had moved next to my father. My father, Eagle Robe, whom many of you know, is a peaceful man, and he gave the white man part of his land. When I returned from my hunt I saw my father lying on the ground, dying from a bullet wound. I rushed to him and embraced him and tried to stem the flow of blood. 'Tell me, father, what happened?' I cried. He was so weak he could hardly speak, but he slowly told me his story. My father had left his land for a while. When he returned Ott had moved the fence so it took in all my father's land as well as his own. My father went to talk to him about it; there were words, and Ott drew his revolver and shot my father. When I heard this I cried out, 'I'll kill him!' But my father held me fast with his dying strength and said, 'Do not kill him, my son. Let the white man's law punish him. If you kill there will only be more bloodshed. Other white men will come for you. Give me your word that even though I die you will not take vengeance into your own hands.' What could I say? My father died, and I have not taken revenge. But the white man's law has not acted. Everyone knows who killed my father, but there Ott sits on my father's land, the land of the noble Eagle Robe whom he murdered."

A murmur of dismay and rage swept among us. The young men, and even some of the women, clamored for war. The agitation for vengeance became stronger and stronger among us until Joseph held up his hand. We fell silent, waiting for our wise chief's words.

"There must be no war. Many of the white settlers came among us honestly and want to be our friends. They were told by their government that the land is theirs to settle, and they don't understand why we object. With these people we can be friends. But others have come to do us harm. They want all the land for themselves, but they can't move us out without the help of the troops. These men are deliberately pillaging our land, breaking down our fences, and, as we now see, even murdering some of our people. But if we go to war we do just what they want, for if we fight, the army will come against us, and against the army we cannot possibly win, for we are like deer and they are like grizzly bears. Believe me, all you who listen tonight, to go to war is to fall into the hands of our enemies. No, we must be patient, and not strike back, and keep pressing the white man to enforce his own laws."

Joseph was right. We all knew it. The war talk died away, and even Wahlitits gave up his desire for revenge for the time being.

But not long after this something happened that tried even Joseph's patience to the limit. Late on a warm June afternoon in 1876 I heard a moaning cry, the wailing sound women make when someone has died in battle. Running into the center of the village, I saw Eskawus, one of our best hunters, an honest and humble man, riding slowly into camp with the body of a Nez Perce stretched over the front of his horse. When Joseph saw who the dead man was he broke into tears, for Wilhautyah was his close friend. Eskawus told his story to Joseph while we all listened.

"Eight of us were hunting. We made camp, and because there was no reason to fear anyone we stacked our rifles safely away. Then we saw two white men suddenly coming upon us. We recognized Wells McNall as one of them and Findlay as the other. We knew they were quarrelsome men who sold liquor to Indians, and since it looked like they wanted trouble seven of us moved away from the camp to avoid them. But Wilhautyah stayed. They accused him in a loud voice of stealing two horses. There were words, and McNall leaped from his horse onto Wilhautyah. They wrestled on the ground but Wilhautyah proved to be the stronger and was winning the fight when the other man killed him with a shot from his rifle. We could do nothing, for our arms were in the camp. Then the white men rode away, and we returned and rescued the body of our dead brother."

Later we learned that the white men found their two horses waiting for them when they returned to their homes. This murder enraged us more than any of the others. It was the first time a member of our own band had been killed, and Joseph was determined that this time justice must be done. He went to the agent and demanded that the two men be arrested and tried. No one denied that they were guilty; they had openly boasted of their crime. The agent told Joseph to keep our people quiet and assured him that the matter would be properly dealt with. But time went by and nothing happened. The two men were never punished, and since no Indian had any standing in the white man's court, there was nothing we could do.

Indirectly, this incident brought about the events that led to the tragedy that was to follow. Because of this killing the white authorities recognized that the situation in the Wallowa Valley had become intolerable. As a result, a series of commissions and smaller councils were held in the fall of the year following the death of Wilhautyah. Some of the white commissioners investigating the situation actually ruled in our favor, but more ruled against us.

It was about this time that news reached us of the defeat of the Sioux. The Sioux were the strongest of all the Indian nations. In June of 1876 they had annihilated the troops of the long-haired General Custer. But other troops were sent against them, which destroyed their villages and harassed them continually, until they were forced to give up their lands and enter a reservation. But about two thousand warriors led by Sitting Bull escaped to Canada, where the soldiers couldn't follow them.

At last a final council was planned for May of 1877, to be conducted by General Howard himself. Joseph, Too-hool-hool-Sote, Looking Glass, Kapoochas, White Bird—all our great chiefs and wisest people were there. And I was there too, to listen to the interpreter and tell Joseph if what he said was being reported correctly.

I must tell you more now about General Howard. Strong, energetic, physically large and robust, a man in late middle-age, he was a figure to command respect and a man of war. He had distinguished himself among his people in the recent war the whites had fought among themselves, losing an arm in the fighting. From this he earned from us the name "One-arm" Howard. When he first came among us we had liked him and believed him when he said he thought we should be allowed to retain our land. But at this conference he turned his back on us and would not listen; we felt that he had betrayed us and that he, more than anyone else, brought about the war.

The meeting was held at Lapwai, at the fort where the soldiers were stationed, not far from my childhood home. General Howard was spokesman for the Americans; his aides and other officials gathered around him. We arrived one day earlier than the other Nez Perce bands. Howard wanted to start the talks right away; his impatience seemed like a bad sign to us. Joseph succeeded in delaying him until the next day when the others arrived. He didn't want Howard to talk to the Nez Perce one group at a time because that way he could divide and weaken us. It was a tactic used by

71

the government when the Treaty of 1863 was signed, and it was not to be repeated.

All our bands arrived: sturdy old White Bird with his eagle feather; Looking Glass, tall, proud, imperious in his manner; Too-hool-hool-Sote, whom I didn't trust because his hatred for the white people obscured his powers to think straight. All our most renowned people were there except the warriors Wachumyus and Pahkatos Owyeen, who were away in the East Country.

Joseph spoke first. The white people, as well as the Nez Perce, were impressed by his dignity and calmness. Joseph had the ability to press his points without getting angry. He didn't blame the white people, he only wanted justice and a fair agreement. He carefully repeated our arguments: The Nez Perce land had been given to us by the Great Spirit. . . . We had never signed it away. . . . We could not move onto the reservation at Lapwai with the Christian group because it was too small. . . . The Indian spirit was free and could not live cooped up on small plots of ground. . . . The Treaty of 1855 had recognized our right to our homeland, and the Americans must now honor it. . . . There was no need for the Americans and the Indians to quarrel because we have one Father and one Mother, and the Great Spirit wants all of his children to treat each other fairly and prosper.

Now it was Howard's turn to speak, and at once the atmosphere became tense, like the air on a hot day when the lightning power lies heavy everywhere, about to strike out of dark clouds above. As soon as I heard his opening words it was clear that he was not there to try and make an agreement but, as a war chief, to make us do what he wanted. Unlike Joseph, who spoke calmly, Howard's voice was gruff.

"You deny my authority, do you? You want to dictate to me, do you? You may as well know at the outset that in any event the Indians must obey the orders of the government of the United States."

That was the spirit in which he replied to Joseph's friendly and conciliatory words! He didn't even answer the arguments Joseph had raised.

I saw a restless spirit move among the Nez Perce as they heard Howard's belligerent answer. The Long Knives also began to act in a nervous way, glancing at us uneasily as though wondering if we had weapons concealed beneath our blankets. However, except for our knives, we had no weapons. We had come in peace and left our rifles behind, although I observed as we entered the tent that Howard's soldiers, though waiting at a distance near their barracks, had their rifles with them.

I saw one man look suspiciously at the eagle feather Chief White Bird was wearing and heard him whisper to his companion, "See that old chief there, how he hides his face behind that feather so we will not see what he is thinking?" He didn't know I could understand what he was saying. I felt contempt for him that he was so ignorant of our ways that he mistook the eagle feather, a symbol of spiritual power, for an attempt at concealment.

That ended the first day of talking. When the meeting resumed the following day, our spokesman was not the thoughtful Joseph but the fiery Too-hool-hool-Sote. During the night the chiefs had decided the time had come for tough talk, and they chose Too-hool-hool-Sote to speak for us. I thought they made a mistake. Too-hool-hool-Sote was not the man Joseph was, and the hatred that came from him could only harden the hearts of the Americans. Nevertheless, he argued well as he tried to make Howard understand our view of the Great Spirit and our Mother the Earth, for on this rested our conviction that we belonged on our land.

"The Great Spirit," he began in his growly voice, "made

73

the world as it is and as he wanted it, and he made a part of it for us to live on. I do not see where you get authority to say that we shall not live as he placed us."

The stubborn chief's challenge angered One-arm Howard. "I don't want to hear any more of such talk! The law says you shall go to live on the reservation, and I want you to do so, but you persist in disobeying the law. If you do not move, I will take the matter into my own hands, and you will suffer from your disobedience."

At this point the Indian agent broke in. He spoke in a more pleasant voice, and I could tell he was trying to soften Howard's words. "The law is," he said, trying to smile, "that you must come to the reservation. The law is made in Washington; we don't make it."

Too-hool-hool-Sote answered, "We never have made a trade. Part of the Indians gave up their land. I never did. The earth is part of my body, and I never gave up the earth."

But Howard didn't understand; he was a Bible-quoting general, and to him all this talk of the sacredness of the earth was nonsense. Between him and Too-hool-hool-Sote was a spiritual chasm as deep as the canyon of the Snake River.

Howard tried to talk calmly, but he had no more control over his emotions than Too-hool-hool-Sote had, and he finally exploded angrily, "We do not want to interfere with your religion, but you must talk about practical things. Twenty times over you repeat that the earth is your mother, and about chieftainship of the earth. Let us hear it no more, but come to the practical matters."

Clearly, nothing more was to be accomplished that day, so it was agreed that the council would adjourn and meet again in four days. We supposed this was to give all of us, whites and Indians alike, time for further reflection, but the only change we could see when we reassembled was that additional troops had arrived.

When the council resumed I saw that there was going to

be another clash between Too-hool-hool-Sote and Howard. Too-hool-hool-Sote spoke as before, gruffly and angrily. I could see that Howard was provoked at the stubborn chief who was so unimpressed by talk of the law. Impatiently, Howard interrupted the chief and repeated his orders that the Nez Perce must move onto the reservation at once without any further talk of our Mother the Earth.

When Too-hool-hool-Sote heard this he answered, "Who are you, that you ask us to talk and then tell me I shan't talk? Are you the Great Spirit? Did you make the world? Did you make the sun? Did you make the rivers for us to drink from? Did you make the grass to grow? Did you make all these things, that you talk to us as though we were boys? If you did, *then* you have the right to talk as you do."

Howard's eyes blazed. "You know very well that the government has set apart a reservation, and that the Indians must go on it. If an Indian becomes a citizen he can have land like any other citizen, but he has to leave his tribe and take land precisely as a white man does. The government has set apart this large reservation for you and your children, that you may live in peace and prosper."

At this Too-hool-hool-Sote retorted disdainfully, "What person pretends to divide the land and put me on it?"

At this Howard shouted, "*I* am the man. I stand here for the President, and there is no spirit good or bad that will hinder me. My orders are plain and will be executed. I hoped the Indians had good sense enough to make me their friend, not their enemy." Then, when Too-hool-hool-Sote tried to continue, Howard declared, "You are an impudent fellow!" He motioned to some of his soldiers who were standing nearby, and they came over to Too-hool-hool-Sote and grasped him by his strong shoulders and started to lead him off toward the jail.

Too-hool-hool-Sote said, "Is this your order? I don't care. I have expressed my heart to you. I have nothing to take

75

back. I have spoken for my country. You can arrest me, but you cannot change me or make me take back what I said." And then he was led away.

When I saw this happen I was so angry that I wanted to hurl myself on the soldiers who were leading the chief away. The Indians around me were likewise extremely agitated at this insulting and treacherous action on the part of One-arm Howard, and I saw Hohots Illpilp reach for his knife. But first we looked to Joseph to see what he would do. He alone remained calm, and his eyes indicated that we should not make any move to free Too-hool-hool-Sote.

Later Joseph explained to us why he acted as he did. "I counseled you to submit, for I knew if we resisted all the white men present, including Howard, would be killed in a moment, and we would be blamed." As always, Joseph acted for peace and resisted war and had the presence of mind to think of the welfare of all the People. "As for Too-hool-hool-Sote," he continued, "I knew the white people would not dare to keep him as long as they were trying to persuade us to go onto the reservation." And that was the way it was, for in five days Howard released Too-hool-hool-Sote.

So once again Joseph spoke for peace, but Howard started forces in motion that no one, not even Joseph, could control; for in the eyes of our warriors and young men he had "shown us the rifle." So began the energy of war which, like a rock pushed over the side of a mountain, cannot be stopped once it is started.

Too-hool-hool-Sote's imprisonment ended the council, for we saw that there was no longer any point in talking; Howard and the others had made up their minds before the council even began. When we left, the young men wanted to form a war party and free Too-hool-hool-Sote, but Joseph, Looking Glass, and White Bird restrained them. Instead, the chiefs went with Howard to inspect the reservation at Lapwai and choose a portion of it, while the rest of us waited. The best land had all been taken by the Christians, but sadly each chief selected part of what was left for his band. As soon as they had done this, Howard informed them that they must now return at once to their homes and prepare to move, for he gave us only thirty days to gather our families, stock, and belongings and move onto the reservation.

"If you are not on the reservation within thirty days," were Howard's parting words to us, "I shall consider that you want to make war and my soldiers will come and drive you on."

His words were ringing in our ears as we rode back to our homes. When we left the Wallowa Valley for the conference at Lapwai we had a hopeful spirit, but now as we returned to our village our spirits crawled along on the ground like a snake. I found myself wondering, Will I ever see this valley again? Will Wallowa Lake no longer be ours? Will white men now catch the salmon in the rushing river that we and our ancestors have fished for as long as anyone can remember? Will the canyons no longer ring with our laughter and the hills no longer resound with the sound of the hooves of our charging horses? Will the grave of Tu-e-ka-kas be desecrated by strangers? My heart sank as a stone sinks to the bottom of a lake.

It was hard to break the news to Wali'ms and Rising Moon. Rising Moon's face clouded over with anger when we told of the council, but she showed no surprise; in her way she had known all along what the outcome would be. High-spirited Rising Moon! Had she been a warrior she might have gone by herself to avenge our wrongs. Wali'ms listened quietly. Then, always practical, always concerned over the welfare of her little family, she asked sadly, "How can we gather together all our belongings, bring in the horses and cattle that are scattered throughout the mountains, and be ready to move all within one moon's rising?"

Hohots Illpilp answered, "It can't be done. We will gather what we can, but many hundreds of our animals must be lost and much must be left behind."

Rising Moon broke in, "And the Snake River? We have to cross it to reach the reservation at Lapwai, but this is the season of the high waters that come rushing down the mountains from the melting winter snows. Men and horses can get across, but how about the old people and the children, the cattle and the foals?"

Hohots Illpilp, who was emerging as a leader in this time of crisis, reassured her. "We will take across the old people and children in boats we will make of skins. We will place as much of our goods as possible on the backs of our horses. We will swim across the river what other horses we can. Perhaps we can leave the cattle for a while on the other side until the waters subside."

A time of frantic activity now began. The women gathered the household things together. The men, I among them, roamed the hills and valleys and herded together as many of our half-wild animals as could be found. As we struggled with our impossible task I felt again how unfair it was of Howard to say that we must be on the reservation by the time the sun stays longest in the sky during the day.

It's a wonder that we all came, for no one among us had to do anything that the chiefs asked; any of us could have chosen to defy Howard's orders and stay. But not one of us left the band, for in good fortune or bad we were one People. We would rather belong to each other than hang on to our material possessions, and to be with each other was even more important than to remain on our land. Nor did any of our band yield to the talk of war that was still swirling about in the thoughts of many of the Nez Perce. Indeed, Too-hool-hool-Sote, who naturally was enraged at the way he had been treated, was openly talking of war in his band

and many of the young men might have joined him, but Joseph was again persuasive and his wiser head prevailed.

We worked for many suns until the day came when we had to move, and then, with Joseph and Ollokot organizing the march, we began the long trek away from our homeland. Loaded onto the animals and travois were our earthly belongings, and being driven alongside were our extra horses, with the cattle following under the protection of a small band of warriors. But many things had to be left behind: horses that could not be found, cattle that got away, lodges and tipis that were too heavy to be carried, countless household articles and caches of food that could not fit on the travois.

Slowly our long line of people and horses wound its way down the Wallowa Valley, until we reached the Grande Ronde River. Then we turned and followed this river past the settlements of the white ranchers, whose need and greed for our land was responsible for the loss of our homes, until at last we reached the Pic-oon-nen, the great Snake River.

As Rising Moon had predicted, it was a roaring torrent, and as I stood on its bank and watched its swirling, raging, foaming waves I wondered how we could cross it safely, encumbered as we were with our goods, our old people, our women, and our children. But there was no time to lose. Joseph and Ollokot set us to work building boats of skins stretched tightly across stout willow branches that we bent into circles and tied securely. In these boats we placed our children, old people, and belongings, and then the braves mounted their horses and rode out into the stream and with ropes attached to the boats guided them slowly and safely across that monster torrent.

But we didn't get across without loss. Many of the young foals and the older horses weakened and sank beneath the waves, to be seen no more. Because we knew the cattle would have great difficulty crossing the stream, we left most of them on the other side with a few braves to guard them until the waters subsided and it would be safe for them to cross. That was the last we ever saw of them, for two suns later the braves who had been left with the cattle rejoined us and told us that some white men had come, threatened them with guns, and driven off the cattle.

Once we had reached the other side of the river, our water-soaked column struggled on to a traditional camping place called Tepahlewam, which means "Split Rocks"; from here it was an easy two days' march to the reservation at Lapwai. Here we camped and were soon joined by the bands of White Bird and Too-hool-hool-Sote. Looking Glass's band didn't join us; he had already moved onto the reservation, since his band lived adjacent to it to the east.

Together our three bands numbered about six hundred persons. Our band was the largest, White Bird's was next, and Too-hool-hool-Sote's band was the smallest. There were about 140 men, but only about half of these were warriors. We had about three thousand horses.

When we reached Tepahlewam, the chiefs decided to stay for a short while; it would be easy now to reach the reservation, and we needed time for our souls to catch up with our bodies because we had been moving so fast. Wali'ms and I and our little daughter made our camp near Rising Moon and Hohots Illpilp.

While we made camp the chiefs and many of the warriors formed a council, which remained in session all during our stay at Tepahlewam, for Too-hool-hool-Sote was still talking and urging war, and many of the hotheaded young men were eager to follow him. Once again Joseph had to speak for peace. As I listened it seemed to me that he was weary of repeating his arguments, and yet again they seemed to carry the day. "Does the gray fox attack the wolverine? Does the meadowlark dive down upon the hawk? That is the way it would be if we were to attack the whites." And since no one could answer him the war talk died down, until at last I could see by the look in their eyes that Joseph and Ollokot were satisfied. In fact, Joseph now felt sufficiently sure that there would be peace that he and Ollokot left camp the next day and crossed to the other side of the nearby Salmon River to butcher some of the cattle that had wandered away so they would have meat for their families. One of Joseph's two wives, Toma Alwawinmi, was soon to give birth to a child, and the welfare of his family was much upon his mind.

Later Joseph was blamed by his enemies for the bad things that happened, but the fact is that he wasn't even at the camp when the fighting broke out, and he had always spoken for peace.

CHAPTER SIX

The Storm Breaks

The day after Joseph and Ollokot left the camp to prepare meat for their families I joined the council. I was listening to the usual arguments: Most people said talk of war was pointless and that we should move right away onto the reservation, but a number of people said we should wait until the warriors, Pahkatos Owyeen and Wachumyus, returned from the East Country. In the midst of this talk I became aware of a stir in the camp: the noise of people breaking into a clamor, a sound swelling like the sound of a flash flood as it comes ripping down the desert mountains. Suddenly someone broke into the council and shouted, "You people are talking for nothing! Three of the young men have killed a white man on the Salmon River, and one of them has ridden the white man's horse to the camp. It's war already!"

The council broke up, and we rushed out and joined the crowd of excited people gathered around a young man. He was Wetyetmas Wahyakt—Swan Necklace—a youth of only seventeen winters, and he was shouting excitedly, "They are dead! The white men are dead!"

"Who's dead?" I heard my brother call to him sternly. "And what have you done? Where did you get this horse that doesn't belong to you?"

Swan Necklace was agitated. "They're dead! The white man who killed Dakoopin, and the one who used to set his dogs on us when we walked by, and the other man who was with him."

We crowded around and excitement, fear, and wonder swept over us like rain sweeps over the prairie from a great storm as Swan Necklace's story tumbled out. This is what had happened: Two days before, Wahlitits and his cousin, Sarpsis Illpilp, paraded through the camp on their horses when the horses stepped on some camas roots set out to dry in front of the tipi belonging to a man named Heyoom Moxmox. Offended, Heyoom Moxmox shouted at Wahlitits, "Look what you are doing! Playing the brave, you ride over my woman's hard-worked food. If you're so brave, why don't you kill the man who killed Eagle Robe, your father?"

Wahlitits was furious. He called back, "You'll be sorry for your words!" Early the next morning Wahlitits set out with Sarpsis Illpilp to avenge his father's death, taking Swan Necklace along to hold their horses. They rode to the place where several white ranchers had their homes. They were looking for Larry Ott, who had killed Eagle Robe, but Ott had seen them coming and had fled. Determined not to return without shedding blood, they continued to the home of Richard Devine, the man who killed the cripple, Dakoopin. All night they hid near his home, and early in the morning, leaving Swan Necklace in charge of the horses, they pushed in the door of Devine's house and shot him dead.

Their hearts now infected with the fever of killing, they rode to the ranch of another Indian-hater named Henry Elfer and killed him too. They also took his roan stallion (the horse Swan Necklace rode into the camp) and helped themselves to his guns and ammunition. But they didn't injure Elfer's wife or some other women who were in the cabin.

Leaving Elfer's place they rode on and killed two other

white men known for their brutal treatment of the Indians. Then they went to the store owned by our archenemy, Sam Benedict, the one who had shot and killed a drunken Nez Perce to whom he had sold illegal whiskey, and who always cheated the Indians dealing at his store. They wounded Benedict and chased him into the brush, as well as two others with him who also were known to cheat the Nez Perce.

They also stopped at the home of a settler named Cone and purchased food. Cone had been friendly to the Indians and they did him no harm. Nor did they harm the family or store of friendly Charles B. Wood. In fact, later they returned to warn him that he and his family should leave so they wouldn't be hurt in the troubles to come.

Exhilarated by what they had done, Wahlitits and Sarpsis Illpilp, accompanied by Swan Necklace, raced back toward the Tepahlewam camp. But as they approached they realized that their actions could have serious consequences for everyone, so they stayed away and sent Swan Necklace to break the news to the People. They didn't want white people, who would certainly seek revenge, to hold everyone guilty for what they had done.

As I listened to Swan Necklace tell his story, I realized again how many reasons there were to justify these killings. Had we not suffered many indignities at the hands of these very white men who had been killed? Had not Howard insulted us with his overbearing attitude and showed us the rifle with his imprisonment of Too-hool-hool-Sote? Had not Howard placed an impossible burden on us when he gave us only thirty suns to gather all our belongings, round up all our horses, and bring all our cattle to the reservation? Did we not have twenty winters of injustices and murders burning within us? It was not surprising that a hot-blooded warrior like Wahlitits, stung by the remark of Heyoom Moxmox, decided to take matters into his own hands.

Nevertheless I wondered where all this would lead, and my anxiety grew as I saw the confusion that Swan Necklace's story created among us. The war spirit was beginning to roll through the young men like dark clouds preceding a summer storm. Two of the young men, Two Moons and Big Dawn, rode around the camp demanding to know who would join a war party to meet Wahlitits and Sarpsis Illpilp the next day. Others panicked and began to throw their belongings together in preparation for flight, certain that troops would soon be seeking revenge. The chiefs could not decide what to do, except to call upon everyone to be calm and wait until the morning. I wished Joseph and Ollokot were here, but though messengers were sent for them, they could not possibly arrive until tomorrow.

As the sun marched across the sky that dreadful day, it became clear that there was no stopping many of the young men from joining Wahlitits. I listened to Big Dawn and Two Moons.

"We're tired of the old men among us who tell us we should be afraid of the Long Knives. Haven't Wahlitits and Sarpsis Illpilp shown us how easy it is to kill them? Let the women and the children and the old men and those who are afraid run away, but as for us we're going to join Wahlitits and help him kill the other white men who deserve to die. Those of you who aren't afraid, join us. Wahlitits is waiting for us outside the camp. We meet him at dawn."

I was one of the young men, and I knew that soon I would be challenged to go on the war party with the others. Not all the young men were going. I heard Two Moons ask Hohots Illpilp if he would come with them, but my brother replied no, he would not go, it would be against Joseph's wishes. No one made fun of Hohots Illpilp for this; he was respected and didn't have to prove his courage. But I still had to prove I was a man. I was divided in my soul. Should I join the raiding party or not? Like many others I wanted revenge for the many wrongs done to the People, but I could also hear Joseph's words: War against the Americans will only lead to our destruction. I loved and respected Joseph and Hohots Illpilp and did not wish to offend them. But if I didn't go, wouldn't it look like I was afraid? So the different spirits fought each other; I was not of one mind but two, and it felt like a sickness inside of me.

Finally the moment that I knew would come fell upon me. Two Moons, with Big Dawn riding beside him, came up to me and called, "And you, Teeto Hoonod, are you coming with us or are you staying here like a timid grandmother?"

I was like a frightened rabbit as the coyote approaches; I couldn't speak because the two spirits had divided my soul. Finally it was the afraid part of me that answered; I heard the words come out of me, speaking themselves, not being directed by my mind. "But I haven't seen war, I know nothing of fighting." And as I heard these words I was ashamed, for I knew how weak they sounded, and I hated myself because I said them.

Two Moons laughed derisively. "You can learn soon enough," he said. And then he added, looking straight into my eyes, "That is, if you aren't afraid."

I couldn't let him see the fear in me. I couldn't let him see that the two spirits in me had made me weak. As stoutly as I could I answered, "Joseph says we shouldn't fight, that it will only bring disaster on all of us." This is what Hohots Illpilp had said; coming from him it had the ring of strength, but coming from me it sounded like weakness.

Then Big Dawn spoke, not to me but to Two Moons, but so I could clearly hear. "Well," he said mockingly, "what can anyone expect from the boy who ran away from the hohots?" Two Moons laughed, and Big Dawn joined him, and without a further word the two warriors rode away.

So they knew! Wahlitits had told, after all. They had known all this time about my shameful conduct at the time the hohots charged, and all this time they held me for a coward, but no one had spoken because Hohots Illpilp had forbidden them to mock me.

Big Dawn's words went through me like a knife, and now I knew I had to push away from me all the other spirits except the talk in me of going to war. I *would* go. I would not listen any more to Joseph. I would draw white blood and show Two Moons and Big Dawn and all the others that I wasn't afraid.

I found Two Moons and told him I would go. He looked at me incredulously but said only, "Don't be late. We meet Wahlitits as soon as the sun is over the hills."

I told no one what I was going to do, not Hohots Illpilp, Wali'ms, Kapoochas, or Rising Moon. Why didn't I want anyone to know? Was I afraid they would persuade me not to go? Was I ashamed of what I was going to do? I pushed these questions away and wouldn't look at them. As the day crept on, Wali'ms kept glancing at me strangely, but still I kept my plans to myself. That night I didn't sleep much, and when I did I was troubled with dark dreams. Finally it was time to leave and I stole out quietly, being careful not to waken Wali'ms or Pahkatos Peopeo. It was still gray outside, with only a trace of dawn in the east. I was almost on my way when I heard Wali'ms call out to me plaintively, "Teeto Hoonod, don't go."

I spun around and there was Wali'ms, standing in the door of the tipi. I was angry that she was interfering. "Why are you awake?" I retorted, "And where is it you think I'm going?" I said this because I didn't know how much she knew.

Wali'ms replied softly, "I've been awake for a long time, watching you, waiting to see if it's true what I've heard."

"And what have you heard?"

"That you told Two Moons you would go on the raiding party that is to join Wahlitits."

I saw there was no use pretending. Somehow word had reached her as to which young men were going on the warpath. It made me angry that she knew, and I said, "Yes, I'm going. It's no business of yours. This is man's business."

Wali'ms's eyes flashed fire. "It's woman's business too when her man goes out to kill and be killed."

I snapped back at her, "Then you're thinking only of yourself, wondering what you would do if I, your husband and provider, were killed!" As soon as these words escaped from me I was sorry, for I knew this was unjust, and I could see the hurt in her eyes, but I quickly shut out the feeling. I wanted to be angry; I didn't want to be sorry for her.

Wali'ms continued to plead with me. "You're not a warrior, Teeto Hoonod. You know nothing of fighting. Look, you don't even have a rifle, only your bow and arrow."

Wali'ms was right; I didn't own a rifle. I knew how to use one, but only the tested warriors had rifles because there weren't enough for everyone. But I didn't want to pay attention to anything that would keep me from my purpose, so I used my anger to drown out her argument and retorted, "You're talking like a woman. You're trying to make me soft. But it won't do you any good. I'm going now. Don't try to hold me back."

Little Pahkatos Peopeo, wakened by the talking, stole silently to her mother's side. Wali'ms picked her up and held her as she spoke to me one more time. "Joseph is against it. He counseled us to restrain our urge for revenge, to do things only for peace; he says war can only bring death to us."

"Joseph is a woman!" I was almost shouting now, talking big because I felt small. "He has never become a warrior himself and is afraid to fight and that's why he counsels peace." Even as I said these words I knew they weren't true, but my pride wouldn't let me take them back. I could see that I had hurt my gentle Wali'ms badly. I couldn't stand the

88

pain in her eyes, so I turned abruptly and left her standing in sorrow in the door of the tipi, holding our child.

I made my way through the still-slumbering camp, past the goods ready to be loaded onto the horses and travois for the flight that would take place this day, past the tipis where the People were sleeping, and past the dogs that came out to sniff at me to see if I was friend or foe. Only two people seemed to be awake. One was half-blind Natalekin, always the first person up in the camp. The other was Kapoochas. He called to me as I passed, as though he had been waiting for me, as though he knew I would come by; Kapoochas always seemed to have a mysterious way of knowing things. But for the first time in my life I paid no attention to him. I didn't want to listen to him for fear that if I did my soul would become divided again.

As I left Kapoochas and neared the outskirts of the camp I saw a qotsqo'tsn perched on the top twig of a bush singing its heart out to greet the dawn. My spirits rose as I heard the glorious trilling song, for was this not my Power, the source of my Wy-a-kin? But as I passed near, the bird fell silent, and when I looked again it had flown away. My heart sank, but I refused to ask myself the meaning of what I had seen.

On I went to the meadow where I had left my horse the night before. I owned only one horse but she was a strong Appaloosa and a fine runner. Though it was hard to see in the half-light, I knew exactly where I had left her. But when I reached the spot where I had tethered her, she wasn't there. I searched in a wider and wider arc for her, but she was nowhere to be seen. I began to get anxious. The light was increasing rapidly; already Two Moons and Big Dawn and the others would be assembling at the appointed spot. Then I saw a slim figure loom up in front of me in the gray dawn of that unearthly morning. I strained my eyes to see who was approaching, and suddenly there was Rising Moon standing before me as slender and straight as an arrow.

89

Astonished, I could only say, "Rising Moon! What are you doing here?!" There was no answer. Rising Moon stood silently before me. I asked the question a second time, and still she didn't reply. Slowly the suspicion found its way into my mind that my missing mare and Rising Moon's presence in this spot were connected. "Rising Moon," I asked incredulously, "do you know where my horse is?"

Finally Rising Moon spoke. "I've driven her away. When daylight comes you'll find her easily; she won't go far."

"When daylight comes!" I shouted. "Then it will be too late. They'll have gone. Two Moons and Big Dawn won't wait." Then I continued, in a voice made quieter now by an anger that was beginning to run from hot to cold, "What have you done, Rising Moon? You're trying to keep me from joining Two Moons. You're putting yourself in my way."

"Yes, I'm keeping you from going. It's not right that you should go, and for this reason I've driven off your horse. Already the sun is above the hills. Two Moons and Big Dawn will be riding off now, and you're not with them."

"And they will think me a woman and a coward. They'll think I was afraid and didn't come because I was weak. Why are you doing this to me?"

She wasn't afraid of my anger. "You hate me now, Teeto Hoonod, but one day you'll be thankful, for this will spare you from shedding white man's blood, and you'll be free of guilt for the tragedy this action will bring on the People, on Wali'ms, your own wife, and Pahkatos Peopeo, your own child."

"And who are you to think that you know what's best for me?"

For a moment Rising Moon was silent. Then she replied. "The Moon-power spoke to me last night and told me you were in great danger. The danger is not to your body but to your soul. I was bidden to act; I couldn't have gone against it."

"And who, then, is to avenge the death of our many brothers and sisters if we don't take matters into our own hands?"

Rising Moon continued almost as though I had not spoken. "I was told by the Power that if we fight against the evil that is in some of the white men, we too will become evil. Evil can possess all people, red and white alike. I don't want to see this happen to you, Teeto Hoonod. Your heart has been good until now. Don't stain it with this evil thing."

I argued, "It's not evil to avenge the wrongs done to one's own people!"

"It's not wrong if you have no choice, but you have a choice. To choose revenge is to become evil yourself. Revenge has a sweet taste at first, but in the end it is always bitter. It is not in you to do this, and if you keep on you will go against your own Wy-a-kin and perish. Did not even the meadowlark fly away from you as you left the camp?"

So she had seen the qotsqo'tsn fly away! But how could she have known, how could she have been there? She and Kapoochas—they both had ways of knowing things that other people couldn't know, of seeing things in ways other than with their eyes. Still I wasn't through. "Fighting is man's business," I said. "No other woman of the People would do what you are doing."

"But, Teeto Hoonod, I'm not all those other women. I am myself."

Because I couldn't think of any more arguments, I exploded with anger. "Rising Moon, you're a witch! Out of my way. I'll take another horse. I *will* do this thing!" And with this I pushed her roughly aside and began to run about frantically to catch another animal to ride.

I did find another horse and spurred it on to the appointed place, but Two Moons and Big Dawn were gone. I rode on to the place where we were to meet Wahlitits and Sarpsis Illpilp, but they had left. I followed their trail as far as I could, but lost it where they crossed the Salmon River. (They had evidently ridden up the stream quite a distance to hide their trail from those who might later seek to place the blame for the raid on those camped at Tepahlewam.) All day I wandered about aimlessly, not knowing what to do. I was afraid to return to the camp for fear I would be ridiculed, but I didn't know where else to go. Anger against Rising Moon turned into anger at myself as I felt my deep disgrace; I felt again as I had after the hohots had charged and I had stood still. Somewhere deep inside of me a small spirit seemed to say that what Rising Moon had done was good, but I quickly pushed it away.

Finally, as darkness fell, I rode slowly back to the camp at Tepahlewam. I saw at a glance that most of the people had left. Only a few tipis were still occupied. I went to the place where Wali'ms and I had camped, and there was our tipi still in place. I stole inside. Little Pahkatos Peopeo looked so tender as she lay in Mother Earth's deep embrace of sleep, and there was Wali'ms, lying on our bed of buffalo robes but awake. She watched me silently as I entered. I crept into the bed and lay beside her as she stretched out her arms to greet me. I realized that she knew what had happened, how Rising Moon had prevented me from joining the war party. Now I, who had tried to prove that I was a man, let myself be comforted by the woman I had hurt so much that very morning. I lay there for a long time before falling into a sleep born of exhaustion.

CHAPTER SEVEN

The First Shot Is Fired

The sun was high above the hills when I awoke the next morning; I could hear the sound of activity in the camp. Wali'ms wasn't there; no doubt she was getting things ready for the march. I was afraid to leave the comforting darkness of the tipi because I didn't know what to say to people. Did they know I left to join the raiding party? Did they know that a woman had kept me from going? And what had happened to Wahlitits, Two Moons, and the others? As I staggered to my feet I felt weak, as though my Wy-a-kin had left me. I thought of the qotsqo'tsn that had flown away from me the day before, as I walked out of the camp, and knew that I should search out the dark corners of my soul and try to recover my lost protective spirit, but I didn't want to face the confusion that was inside me.

More noise outside; the People were breaking camp. Then the flap of the tipi opened. For a moment bright sunlight poured into the dark interior as Wali'ms entered; then darkness as she let the flap close again.

"It's time to be up," she said simply. "We're leaving this place, to join the others at Sapachesap." This was a day's march away, on the way to White Bird Canyon.

But I was thinking of myself. "What do people know about me?"

"Some people know that you were planning to leave with Two Moons. If they ask me, I tell them you rode off to join the raiding party but returned early. That's all they know. Others know nothing and are not concerned; they have more important things to think about right now."

I was relieved. Wali'ms had protected me. Now I began to think of the others. "When I rode into camp last night I could see that most of the People had gone. Only our own band is left. Why are we here, and what about Joseph and Ollokot?"

"Yesterday morning, after Two Moons had left with his party to join Wahlitits, Joseph and Ollokot rode into camp. When they heard what had happened they were horrified. They found our camp in confusion, everyone milling about here and there, people packing to leave, everyone afraid that war would soon be upon us. Joseph and Ollokot rode about the camp trying to get people to stay. 'Don't run!' they said. 'If we run, Howard and the government will think we're all guilty. We must stay here until the troops come. Then we can talk.' But for once no one paid any attention to Joseph. The young men were too anxious for war and the old people were too afraid. So White Bird and Too-hool-hool-Sote got their people ready for the flight to Sapachesap. Joseph might have gone then too, but at that moment his wife began to have her child. Of course Joseph and Ollokot decided to remain here with her until the child was delivered, and some of the rest of us, including your brother and Kapoochas, remained also. All this time Joseph was still hopeful that if we stayed we could talk to the white soldiers and explain that only a few people, not all of us, were at fault. But during the night while you slept part of the camp was attacked. Out of the darkness bullets ripped through some of our tipis. Fortunately no one was hurt. Joseph and Ollokot raced outside to defend us, but the attackers fled. Now we're afraid to stay because we might be attacked again. Still, Joseph pondered what to do. He and Ollokot and Kapoochas met during the night to decide upon a plan. Of course Joseph had his newborn baby on his mind as well. Rumors circulated among us about what their decision would be. Some said Joseph would surrender, but we couldn't believe this would be so. Others said he would gather warriors and attack General Howard, but we knew Joseph was against all fighting.

"Finally Joseph reached his decision. 'The white man and our own rash young men have brought war upon us. I can see ahead only darkness, perhaps death itself. Yet now that the war I have opposed for so long has come I won't avoid it. We have decided to join the other bands. All who wish can follow us. Others can seek safety by turning themselves in to the white soldiers, or they can do as they please.' So Joseph spoke, and of course we all as one person decided to follow him. We are packing now and will move shortly."

So we joined the others on the march to Sapachesap. This meant that I would see Rising Moon. When we first met she stole a glance at me. I thought I could see anguish, concern —yes, even love in her eyes. But I wouldn't look at her and punished her by not speaking. I felt as though everyone was looking at me. Some of them must surely think I was one of the raiding party who had killed the white men and brought this war upon us. But others must know that I had returned early from the raids; perhaps they thought I had run away. Still others, I feared, must know how Rising Moon had humiliated me. So I couldn't look people in the eye, but worst of all I hated myself. "You let a woman keep you from being a man! You almost joined others in bringing disaster on the people you love! . . . People see into you and know what a coward you are! . . ." These thoughts whirled around inside of me until I thought it would be better if I were dead. Yet even as I longed for death, I also had the thought: "You must never surrender to the white people or let them capture you. They will think you are one of the murderers and hang you." In this way the spirit in me that longed for death and the spirit that clung to life fought with each other.

I also saw Hohots Illpilp not long after I emerged from the tipi. It was clear he had been waiting for me, and I knew from the look in his eyes that he knew what had happened. I felt as though I had disgraced him, first by wanting to join the marauders, then by being tricked into returning empty-handed to camp. But my brother smiled at me gently and said, "We won't speak of this matter. What's done is done. You acted from what was in your heart. Your return to the camp is no disgrace. You and I are still brothers, we still have one soul and one mind." Hohots Illpilp extended his hand to me, and I embraced him. For a moment I felt healed; a little strength flowed back into me, and I loved my brother more deeply than ever.

I saw Kapoochas too. He looked at me with his shrewd, piercing eyes. It was clear that he also knew what had happened and was waiting to see if I would speak to him about it. But I was not ready to talk with the old medicine man. Talking with Kapoochas was like talking with the Great Spirit; you couldn't speak with him and hide anything, and I still had too much to hide.

So it was that we made our way to Sapachesap, where we were given a welcome by the other bands, who had been afraid we might surrender rather than join them, and the next day all of us moved to another traditional camping spot we called Lahmotta, which was on the banks of tree-lined White Bird Creek near its junction with the Salmon River. Here, at the end of a long grassy draw that led down from the high open hills to the bank of the creek, we made our camp and awaited further developments, for the truth is that we didn't know what to do next.

We weren't here long before there was a great stir. Wali'ms and I raced out to join a throng of people who were surrounding a small group of men who had evidently just ridden into the camp. When I saw who they were I shrank back toward the outer edge of the milling crowd. They were Wahlitits, Sarpsis Illpilp, Two Moons, and the rest of the party that made the raids on the Salmon River. Of course everyone wanted to hear their story, and so did I, though I was afraid if they saw me they would say to me, "And where were you when we rode out to war?" Still, I stayed within earshot as they told the story of how they continued the killing that Wahlitits and Sarpsis Illpilp had begun.

Big Dawn, who had humiliated me with his reference to my cowardice on the day the hohots charged, began. "There were fourteen of us all told, and we met at dawn outside the camp at Tepahlewam. As soon as all of us were gathered we rode off to join Wahlitits and Sarpsis Illpilp, who were waiting for us some distance from the camp because they didn't want to bring guilt upon the People for what they had done. Our spirits were high. We were filled with confidence and were glad that finally the humiliations brought upon us by our enemies would be revenged. Wahlitits and Sarpsis Illpilp led us as we made our way over the White Bird Mountains and down to the valley of the Salmon River below."

Now the redoubtable Wahlitits took up the tale. "We were headed for the store of Sam Benedict, which Sarpsis Illpilp and I had visited the day before, but this time we were determined to catch Benedict and take revenge for all the wrongs he had done to us. But on the way we encountered by chance the one called Harry Mason." For the benefit of those who didn't know the full story, Wahlitits explained, "He's the man who only a few suns ago used a blacksnake whip on two unarmed Nez Perce. They couldn't resist him because he was armed and they weren't. They were doing nothing, only traveling along the road, when Mason came upon them and whipped them. He did this only because he hates all Indians. When we saw Mason we whipped our horses until we caught up with him and when he saw who

97

we were, and that he couldn't escape, he was really frightened. For a while we played with him like a bobcat plays with a mouse before he kills it. Then we ordered him to run for his life. That man, who had been so brave before, spurred his horse and took off. We gave him a fair chance, and then Strong Eagle drew his bow and let fly an arrow. It struck Mason squarely in the back and he dropped dead from his horse. Strong Eagle might have fired his rifle, but it was more sporting to use his bow and arrow. Who knows," he ended with a wry smile, "if Mason had been a bit faster he might have escaped. We gave him more of a chance than he would ever have given us."

It was Sarpsis Illpilp's turn to continue the narrative. "We went on to Benedict's store. We thought he might have fled for fear that we would return for him, but we suspected he was too greedy to abandon his store, his money, and his liquor, and that's the way it was. He heard us coming and hid in the back of his place, but we found him anyway. When he saw that he was discovered he tried to run, he and a companion, a man whose name we didn't know, but as they tried to cross the Salmon River our shots killed them both. Benedict fell into the river; the last we saw of him, his body was being carried away by the current. Before, Benedict had seemed like a big man, cheating our helpless women and making our men afraid with his guns, but he looked very small as he vanished under the water.

"After Benedict was dead we returned to his store and wrecked it and scattered his gold dust all over the ground. We also found his whiskey and drank some of it. It was good going down; it made us hot inside, but it also made us crazy. After we drank the whiskey we weren't the same. Some things happened then that we didn't intend."

For a while none of the party spoke; it was clear that they hesitated to speak of the things they did next. But at the urging of the chiefs, who said they must know everything, the narrative was resumed by Lahpeealoot, whose name means Goose-Three-Times-Lighting-on-Water and who was the only member of Chief Joseph's band who was with the war party. "We split up after this. Some of us went one way and some went another. My group went to a second store, but the white man had heard we were raiding and had left, so we could only wreck the place. Then we saw a white man mounted on a horse trying to get away, with a small child riding behind him. I put an arrow to my bow and let fly, but the arrow struck the child and not the man. The child cried out and this made me feel bad. It hurt me to think that I had hit the child, because he sounded so piteous. So I stopped chasing the white man and let him go. Later I learned that other members of our party raided the home of a man called Jack Manuel, another man who had a history of hating our people. They had killed him and chased away his wife, but the child had been let go. It was this child whom I hurt. Evidently another white man had found the child and was trying to get away with him."

Joseph interrupted to ask, "And what happened to the Manuel woman?" I knew Joseph wanted to know if women, as well as men, had been killed by the raiders.

The warriors were uncomfortable with this question, but finally one of them named Red Wolf replied. "I know what happened to the woman. I came upon her and decided to take her captive. So I put her on my horse behind me, but she snatched the knife from my belt and tried to stab me in the back. We were riding hard and when I struck her, to save myself, she fell to the ground. The force of the fall was great, and when I went back to her I saw that she was dead."

"It's not good," Joseph said, "that a woman was killed and a child was injured." I heard Joseph say this with my own ears, and this is important, for later some of the white men said that Joseph started the raids and that it was Joseph himself who killed the Manuel woman. Nothing could have

99

been less true than this. Joseph didn't have any of that kind of killing in his heart.

It was Whylimlex, Black Feather, who answered Joseph. "I am sorry too that the woman was killed. We hadn't meant that she should be. But the child didn't die. I know because we ran into that same child later in the day. There were several of us who stopped to make camp and rest, when a white man emerged from the woods carrying a child. He must have been the same one we had seen earlier fleeing on his horse. He didn't know we were there until suddenly there he was in the middle of the camp. This white man looked at me, for I was closest to him, and simply said, 'Will you kill me?' I liked him. He was not afraid. He wasn't an enemy but was only trying to save the child. So I answered, 'No.' But one of the warriors there had drunk the whiskey and he raised his rifle to shoot the man. The rest of us cried out, 'Hold there! Don't shoot! Can't you see the child in his arms?' I then put myself between the drunken Indian and the white man and told him to go; he gave me a look that spoke more than many words and disappeared into the forest with the child. I was angry at the drunken Indian who wanted to shoot and said to him, 'If you shoot the man, who can care for the child? Would you take care of it?' "

So the warriors who made up the raiding party told their story, and it was clear that because of the whiskey some innocent people were hurt. We learned later that one little girl had her tongue cut partially out, but no one would admit that he did it. However, white men who were known to be friends were spared. There was one man in particular, a surveyor named Briggs, whom we liked. Some of the warriors ran across him at night and caught him. A lighted match was thrust in his face, but when they saw who it was they let him go. "Hurry on," they said, "but be careful. You may meet Nez Perce who don't know you."

Altogether there were fourteen white people killed on that

raid. Almost all of them were men who had wronged us in the past. But it can't be denied that some innocent people were killed or injured too, and even though it was the whiskey drinking that brought this about, it still brought shame upon all of us, for killing innocent people, women and children, was not the Nez Perce way.

As I listened to the warriors tell their story and learned of the death of the woman and the injury to the child, I was aware of small thoughts darting through my mind like birds: Aren't you glad you weren't one of them? Would you want the blood of that woman and the pain of that child on your hands? But there was no time to dwell on these thoughts for very long because there were too many decisions to be made and many things to be done.

We were in great danger. By now the news of the raids would have reached General Howard. No doubt there was an uproar among the white people. Perhaps the troops were already on the way to us, and yet we didn't have any idea what to do. So the chiefs and warriors decided to hold a council. I was no longer so afraid of people because everyone was too excited or frightened to be thinking about me. Nor had Two Moons or any others mentioned the fact that I was not with them. I guess they had too much on their minds. So I joined the others at the council and listened to what was being said.

Too-hool-hool-Sote spoke first and as usual argued for war; his grudge against One-arm Howard made it impossible for him to think any other way. He proposed that instead of waiting for the troops to come to us we form a strong war party and go out to meet them. This way we might surprise them, and also we could keep the fighting away from the women and children.

Chief White Bird spoke next. The oldest of the chiefs, he was wiser than Too-hool-hool-Sote, and though he agreed that war was now going to happen, he was against going out

101

to meet the troops. He argued that we should send out scouts to watch the movements of the soldiers while we waited where we were. The one thing that must not happen, he urged, was that we be taken by surprise.

But it was Joseph whose words finally prevailed. "You may be right, White Bird," he said, "that war cannot now be avoided. For this reason we must be prepared for battle. You take charge and send scouts out far from our camp to watch the soldiers and bring us word of what they do. We must be as vigilant and watchful as the ground squirrel, who is surrounded everywhere by his enemies. But if the soldiers come we must try to talk with them first. We can explain what happened so they will not place the blame on all the People and we can still make peace. If that is not possible, we can fight if necessary. The Salmon River isn't far away and this is our protection, for if the soldiers are too many, we can cross the river and put it between them and us."

Joseph's words seemed good to the council, and it was decided to follow them. White Bird saw to it that scouts were sent as far away as Lapwai, where General Howard had stationed the major part of his troops, and he placed other scouts nearby on high places where they could see in every direction so that no one could approach us without being seen. Too-hool-hool-Sote circulated among the warriors, telling them how they could deploy themselves if the soldiers came to fight, while Joseph and Ollokot took charge of arranging the camp. Wali'ms and I set up our tipi alongside that of Hohots Illpilp and Rising Moon in the place assigned to our band.

These preparations were good, but a bad thing was also happening. The warriors who had been on the raids had brought liquor back with them, not only liquor from Benedict's store but also quantities of the fiery water from a wagon train they had overtaken. Now many of them were getting drunk. This is why, when the fighting started, only about half of our fighting men were ready for it.

It seemed as though our scouts had hardly reached their positions when they began sending back word to us of ominous movements by the soldiers. The scouts at Lapwai had the darkest news, which they sent back to us by warriors who ran the whole way from Lapwai to White Bird Creek, where we were camped.

"Soldiers are coming from all over to Lapwai," they reported. "Some from Walla Walla and others from more distant places. Howard is gathering a great army, but he's not waiting for all his soldiers to assemble. Already he has sent out a troop of over one hundred horse soldiers led by one of his sub-chiefs. These horse soldiers are coming fast. They will ride all night and will soon be upon us."

And come they did, accompanied by settler volunteers, but they did not come unnoticed. Unseen Indian eyes from a score of outposts on hilltops, in ravines and groves of trees watched them all the way and kept us informed of their approach. So we knew they were coming, but there was nothing we could do except wait for them and hope they would talk first before they began to fight.

The sun was not quite above the line of hills that overlooked our encampment two miles to the northeast when the sound of a coyote's eerie cry cut through the still black darkness of our camp. To untrained ears it was only another coyote, but to us it was the signal from one of our lookouts that troops were here and we might soon be attacked. Sure enough, with the first light of dawn the horse soldiers approached from the hills above the creek. They rode down in long single files, descending into the sweeping draws that led to our camp.

As soon as the troops were in sight, our men put their plan in motion. In the center Joseph assembled a small delegation of Indians with a white flag and rode out to talk with the soldiers. At the same time groups of warriors formed to our right and left and fanned out away from the camp toward the soldiers to be ready in case of an attack. First Joseph would try to talk; only then would we fight.

There were two buttes that lay above our camp, one on either side of the grassy draw down which the horse soldiers were moving. Whoever commanded these two buttes would also command the field of battle. The soldiers and volunteers were moving toward these buttes. The volunteer soldiers were making for the butte on our right, and the troopers were heading for the butte on our left. Our warriors were also heading for these two buttes; my brother with a group of men was heading for the same butte as the white volunteers.

I didn't know what to do. I wasn't a recognized warrior, yet I didn't want to remain in the camp if fighting broke out. I felt again the struggle within me between the one-who-is-afraid, and the one-who-wants-to-come-out. I tried to seize my weapon and make myself join my brother and the others, but suddenly the memory of the charging hohots came back to me and I felt like a small boy again, paralyzed with fear.

At this moment I heard Rising Moon's voice speaking loudly from close by: "Teeto Hoonod! Aren't you going to join your brother?" When I heard her words, suddenly the paralysis was over. Now I could act! I reached for my bow and arrow, only to find that Wali'ms was standing beside me to hand them to me. I found my horse and leaped astride her and was about to ride out after Hohots Illpilp when Shuslum Hihhih suddenly appeared and called, "Teeto Hoonod, come with me. Joseph goes to talk with the soldiers. You and I who speak the white man's language are to join him."

That is how I was with the small delegation of six Nez Perce who tried to talk with the soldiers. My blood was racing wildly with excitement and apprehension as I joined Joseph and we slowly rode out from the camp under a large white flag. Joseph turned to me and said in his quiet way, as though we were only going out on a simple hunting trip, "When I give the word, call out to the white soldiers. Ask them what they want, and tell them we wish to talk."

The tension was like the energy in the air when you are high on a mountain and the lightning power is so thick it crackles through your hair. Slowly we rode out. Slowly the army captain advanced, with a strong force of horse soldiers accompanying him. When they came closer they broke their single file and made a horizontal battle line; still they marched on. To my right I saw twelve of the civilian volunteers had almost reached the butte, and Hohots Illpilp and our warriors were approaching from the other side. On my left I saw the horse soldiers closing in on the other butte while our warriors on that side were moving in to challenge them if necessary.

At last the captain and his soldiers were within hailing distance, and Joseph gave me the signal to speak. I cupped my hands to my mouth and shouted as loudly as I could, "What do you people want?" For a moment there was no answer, only the slow *cloppity-clop* of the advancing horses. Then a white settler who was with the captain, a man named Ad Chapman whom we all knew because he had once bragged, "I could lick the whole Nez Perce nation single-handed," ignored our white flag and my call, raised his rifle, and fired a shot. And with that shot the war began.

CHAPTER EIGHT

Victory and Retreat

Events now happened with the speed of a snapping tendon. Our little band with the white flag quickly galloped out of rifle range of the troopers in front of us and then we divided, some going to the band of warriors on the right and some to the band on the left. On my left I saw Wahlitits and Sarpsis Illpilp, wearing full-length red blanket coats to draw the fire of the soldiers and show their contempt for them. In the center, other warriors were riding boldly forward; as they neared the enemy they hung onto the sides of their horses to shield themselves from the bullets. Then I heard the crack of a rifle fired by a warrior named Otstotpoo, and with that single shot the bugler, who was riding near his captain, dropped dead from his saddle. It was a tremendous shot, for we were a long way from the line of troopers, and was one of the many effective shots that would teach the soldiers that the Nez Perce were great marksmen.

After the remarkable shot by Otstotpoo I galloped ahead to join my brother, who with a band of other warriors was moving toward the butte on our right, which was now occupied by the volunteers. I joined Hohots Illpilp and then, as the hawk swoops down suddenly on his prey, we swooped upon those men on the butte.

We acted decisively in three ways. To understand the first action you must remember that when Indians fight, even

106

though the chiefs may have outlined a general plan of battle, each warrior is his own person fighting as he sees fit, but when the soldiers fight they don't know what to do without orders from their war chief, and he can only give instructions with the help of his bugler. One of the two buglers the white chief had with him had already been killed by Otstotpoo, and minutes later a shot from another of our sharpshooters—I never did find out whose shot it was—dropped the second one. The white war chief had been foolish to expose his buglers to our fire; now he had no way to give orders to his men, and his troops were soon confused. The killing of the buglers was the first decisive event in this battle.

I myself took part in the second decisive event, which took place on the butte the volunteers occupied and toward which Hohots Illpilp and the others were advancing. When I caught up with my brother, he called me to his side and said, as though this was something he did every day, "We're trying to drive those Long Knives from the butte. If we can do this we can fire down upon the whole line of troopers." We then moved forward with the others, skillfully utilizing the cover afforded by rocks and ravines. My brother was calm, but my heart was pounding with anxiety and excitement until I feared it would burst through my chest.

As we advanced I could see to my left the troopers who were in the center of the line. They were firing wildly, seemingly at random, but the Indians in front of them were making each shot count. Now one, now another of the troopers was hit. This forced the horse soldiers to dismount and seek shelter among the rocks. Meanwhile we moved steadily up the flank of the butte toward the volunteers. Forward, halt, and fire; each warrior advanced. I was angry that I was armed only with my bow and arrow, which was not effective at this distance, but beside me Hohots Illpilp fired his rifle and I saw a white settler fall with a crash among the rocks. Now we were close enough so I could make out the faces of the men above us, and my bow might soon be effective. The volunteers on the butte fired rapidly but wildly, their bullets careening harmlessly among the rocks, while our fire was precise and effective. Then suddenly they broke and ran! Those white settlers whose leader had said he could lick the whole Nez Perce nation single-handed fled like jackrabbits running from a coyote. In moments we reached the top of the butte, pouring fire down on the fleeing men. Our warriors were about to pursue them farther when Hohots Illpilp signaled them to halt and pointed instead to our left. Sure enough, there below, their left flank exposed to our fire, was the main line of horse soldiers. So while a few of our warriors continued to chase the fleeing volunteers, most of us remained on the butte and poured a deadly fire on the exposed soldiers below us. The capture of this butte so early in the fighting was the second decisive event.

The third event happened when Wahlitits, Sarpsis Illpilp, and Ollokot led their men to the top of the other butte, which commanded the soldiers' right flank, driving ahead of them the troopers that had been assigned to hold the butte against them. Now Ollokot and his men were also firing down on the soldiers, and we had the troopers caught in a cross fire.

It was too much for them; the soldiers broke and ran. Some scrambled away on foot, others struggled to find their horses. We pressed them closely and our accurate fire dropped now one, now another. Their captain tried desperately to rally them (he was a brave man, though foolish to have ridden toward us with such an exposed position), but his men were so frightened they ignored his orders; besides, without his buglers he couldn't give effective commands. Of course we tried to shoot the captain, but he must have had a strong power for none of our bullets hit him. Back the way they had come those soldiers fled, with us pursuing them relentlessly. Finally, near the head of the draw, a lieutenant rallied a group of soldiers and made a stand, but they couldn't survive our fire for long, and within minutes we had killed every one of them. Nevertheless, they delayed us long enough so the other soldiers managed to form a rear guard to cover their retreat. We continued to press them but they were more organized now, and their captain directed the rear guard to stop, fire, hold us back, and then hasten on to join the others. Time and again they repeated this maneuver, and although some of our warriors pursued and harassed them for twelve miles, we were not able to destroy them all.

I didn't join in further pursuit of the troops; it would have been futile, for my bow and arrow was not effective in such fighting. So I watched as Hohots Illpilp and the others drove the enemy back up the draw until finally he returned to meet me. Silently we greeted each other with a handshake and a glow of warmth in our eyes. Then we turned to examine the fallen troopers and make sure none of them were still alive, and as we did this we realized that these men had used fine rifles. Hohots Illpilp took one of them from a dead volunteer, handed it to me, and said, "Today you fought as a warrior. There will be more fights. Take this rifle. Keep it as your own and treat it carefully, as you would a good friend."

The weapon was a beautiful breech-loading rifle that had hardly been used. I was so deeply moved to receive it with the praise from Hohots Illpilp that I could say nothing, but he could tell that my heart was full of love for him, and gratitude that he had emerged unscathed from the battle. Jauntily we rode back to the camp, coming in together like si'kstiwain, comrades who are close together like birds that live in the same nest.

On our way we saw other warriors stripping the dead soldiers of their weapons. When the battle began only half

109

our warriors had good rifles; the rest had old muzzle-loading guns or bows and arrows. But from this time on we were well armed, for we gathered sixty-three breech-loading rifles, plus many pistols and knives.

The enemy had come into the battle with 110 men. Our three bands included 90 warriors, but only about half of these took the field that day because of the liquor in the camp. Although we had been outnumbered almost three to one, we defeated the soldiers completely, because their tactics were so bad and we were much better fighters, and because our Wy-a-kin was strong that day. We counted 33 enemy soldiers dead on the field and one enemy officer. We left the bodies where they fell and didn't scalp or mutilate them, for that is not the Nez Perce way. As for us, not one Nez Perce was killed and only two were wounded, and these but slightly. It was a great victory for us; if we had been able to send all our warriors into the battle, there would not have been a soldier left alive. We returned to the camp elated, and for a time there was much joyful shouting and praise of one another.

We also captured three Christian Nez Perce who had joined the cavalry as scouts. We spoke to them angrily and told them if we caught them again they would be whipped, but then we let them go. Although they had turned against us, still they were our brothers and so we didn't hurt them.

When Hohots Illpilp and I returned to the camp we were greeted by Wali'ms and Rising Moon. There were tears in gentle Wali'ms's eyes as she said to both of us, "I was so afraid all the time you were gone. I sang songs for you to the Great Spirit that you would be protected. Now you are safely back and my heart is alive again with joy." I embraced her and picked up little Pahkatos Peopeo and hugged her. From that day on I felt bigger inside. Although I still heard from the bad voice within me that I was a man with a timid spirit, it was no longer so strong.

I could see that Rising Moon also was deeply affected, and I couldn't help but notice that she seemed as moved by my safe return as by that of my brother. Later I spoke to her for the first time since she betrayed me: "Rising Moon, when I wanted to go with Wahlitits to avenge ourselves on the white men who had wronged us for so long you prevented me from going, but today, when the soldiers came, you urged me to go and fight. I don't understand how one day you can be one way, and another day another way."

Rising Moon replied, "Teeto Hoonod, if you had gone with Wahlitits you would have gone against your own soul; your Wy-a-kin would have turned against you, and the blood you would have taken would have been bad blood, making you bad too. Today you fought to protect your women and children; this was the only way to deal with the evil that was upon us, and so you fought, and though you would have killed if you had been able to, your soul would not have been hurt."

I wanted to object, for I was still angry at her for humiliating me, but I couldn't think of an argument, so I shrugged my shoulders disdainfully and walked off. I wouldn't give her the satisfaction of knowing that a part of me was beginning to acknowledge that she was right.

So ended the fight that became known as the Battle of White Bird Canyon. The soldiers had tried to take us by surprise. They ignored our white flag and disdained our attempt to make peace. They fired the first shot but were punished severely for it. I knew there would be much weeping that night in the lodges of those soldiers who had been killed.

For our part, there was a mood of elation among us. The victory had been so easy! Not even the most optimistic among us thought that the soldiers would be routed so speedily, without any casualties of our own. The soldiers fled even though they outnumbered us, and this left us with a disdainful opinion of the white horse soldiers that we were never to lose. The foot soldiers we came to respect, and the howitzers and Gatling guns we feared, but when it came to cavalry we knew we were superior.

Some were so carried away by the victory that they thought the war was over. Wali'ms asked hopefully, "Does this mean an end to the fighting?" And others who had clamored for war, like Too-hool-hool-Sote, strutted around the camp feeling that they were now vindicated in their stand. "Is it not as I told you?" Too-hool-hool-Sote declared to all who would listen. "Killing them was easy. We should have fought long ago."

For the time being Wahlitits and his band of marauders also seemed to be vindicated by the results of the battle, and many looked upon them as heroes. Since some people thought that I had been one of the raiders, I also received some of this approval. This made me feel uncomfortable, but it strengthened the part of me that had wanted to go on the raid and renewed my anger at Rising Moon. The words she had recently said to me were disparaged in my mind now, and I told her again of my anger. "You see, it was right that we start a war against the Americans, and you were wrong to hold me back." She didn't answer this time but looked at me silently with her piercing gaze until, strangely discomfited, I slunk away like a wolf that has come too near the fire.

But soon our elation began to fade as more thoughtful spirits among us reminded us that our plight still existed. Joseph said, "We fought well, and the white horse soldiers and volunteers were driven away like mosquitoes before the wind. But they will be back. We haven't yet seen One-arm Howard. He won't give up so easily, and when he comes there will be many more soldiers with him. We must not be caught here with our back to the river, for he will have an overwhelming force. The war is not over; it has only begun." Joseph was right, but no one knew what to do next.

Our dilemma was solved the day after the battle when our two most famous warriors rode into camp. Pahkatos Owyeen and Wachumyus had been hunting the buffalo for many moons and were on their way back to the People when runners found them and told them what had happened on Salmon Creek. They hurried but arrived too late to be part of the battle at White Bird Creek. With their arrival we felt stronger, for they were men of great power and they brought with them a hardy band of warriors.

Pahkatos Owyeen and Wachumyus immediately joined the council and soon came up with a plan. Speaking in his great deep voice, Wachumyus said, "Howard will be approaching us soon, and he will bring hundreds of troops with him. Joseph is correct that we can't remain here; we must put the Salmon River between us and Howard, and then we must let him see us on the opposite shore. The women and children will be safely hidden behind the hills, but the warriors will be seen. We will put on a great demonstration and hope that we can lure Howard into crossing the river. The stream is filled now with the waters of melting snow and he will find this difficult. While he is crossing we can slip away from him, travel to the north, recross the Salmon, and get in the rear of his army. Most of his troops will be with him, and we can then travel unopposed through the land while we make further plans."

All agreed that the plan was good, and it was immediately put into effect. Once again the women, children, and old people were taken across a roaring river in boats made of skin while the warriors rode the horses across, until all were safely on the other side. At the same time the scouts that were watching the movements of the enemy sent reports to us.

113

What we learned was ominous. General Howard was using the military post at Lapwai as a gathering point. A thousand soldiers were assembled there, and several of the guns that spoke with a big thunder, and the Gatling guns that could fire more bullets at one time than fifty of our warriors. Then we received word that Howard was marching toward us with a force of 500 foot soldiers and horse soldiers, leaving the rest of his soldiers behind to protect his rear.

By the time Howard arrived at the site of the White Bird battle we were on the other side of the Salmon, having crossed a few miles downstream at a place known as Horseshoe Bend. Since the country was open we had no difficulty in observing Howard's movements. For several suns he lingered at the battleground, burying his dead. Then he followed our tracks to the place where we had crossed the stream, so that our two forces were now opposing each other on either side of the Salmon River.

For a while it seemed as though he didn't know what to do, so to help him make up his mind we put on our demonstration. All the warriors mounted their best horses, decked themselves out in their finest war paint and most effective costumes, and made a rush down the grassy mountain slopes toward the troops on the other side of the stream, shouting their war cries as they raced their horses at full gallop. The soldiers were excited. Howard must have thought we were going to plunge into the stream and come right into his tent! They raced about wildly and soon began firing at us. Of course they were so far away their bullets caused no harm. When the warriors reached the bank of the stream they broke into two columns; one column raced downstream and the other upstream, and then both columns turned back into the bordering hills and vanished from the view of the troops. Then we had a good laugh. The soldiers thought it was an attack. They didn't know that

Indians love such hijinks and that we had done this in the spirit of Coyote.

Just as we had hoped, our little demonstration made up Howard's mind for him. He would come and get us! His troops made ready to cross the river. As soon as he committed himself to the crossing, the main body of our warriors and all of the People started northward, downstream, toward a crossing place known to the whites as Craig's Ferry, and near one of our favorite camping places known as Aidapass. This was a favorable spot to cross, about twenty miles to the north of Horseshoe Bend, where Howard was crossing. Only a small rear guard stayed to watch Howard from the west side of the stream and make him think we were still in force in that vicinity.

I remained with the rear guard because I wondered how the soldiers were going to cross the swollen river. It was about 200 yards wide, and the water was boiling and surging along over treacherous rocks, a madness of waves rushing to get to the faraway sea. Since his men didn't know how to make boats of skin, Howard sent them to find wooden boats, and they eventually came back with three small skiffs. The water was too swift to row these skiffs across so Howard strung a rope across the stream to use in pulling the boats, but much to our amusement Coyote saw to it that the rope broke, scattering boats, men, and equipment far down the stream. When that didn't work, Howard had his horses and mules swim the river while his men hung on to the animals precariously. A number of these animals were swept away, and perhaps some of the men drowned.

I wondered, as I watched his frantic efforts, if Howard remembered that only a short time ago he had made us cross the swollen Snake River with all our women and children, a river even larger and more dangerous than the Salmon. But if he remembered his orders to us, and how he refused to relent when Joseph pleaded with him that we be allowed to wait until summer when the stream would be easier to cross, we would never know. Those of us who made up the rear guard watched for a long time, until we were satisfied that Howard was firmly committed to moving his army across the stream; then we rode north to rejoin our people, who by that time had reached Craig's Ferry.

The day after Howard succeeded in crossing to the west side of the Salmon River, we recrossed the river twenty miles north of him and camped on the east side. We had escaped from Howard for the time being, and made a fool of him in the process, but we still had no plan, and of course it was only a matter of time before Howard figured out what we had done and came after us. So we decided to make our way across our country to the east, putting as much distance as possible between us and Howard's army.

We didn't want any more battles, and we didn't want to kill any people, but we knew there were soldiers in the area through which we had to travel. We didn't want them to surprise us or attack the flanks of the People as they marched, so warriors were sent out to find the troopers and keep them away. A number of sharp engagements took place when our men clashed with bands of troopers. We won them all, and forced the soldiers to keep holed up in their defenses, but one of our men was wounded and died later, the first Nez Perce casualty of the war. We also came across some bands of civilian volunteers. They came out to attack us but soon found they had run into a beehive, and after inflicting many casualties on them we drove them off.

After several days we reached the South Fork of the Clearwater River, which was at the foot of the Bitterroot Mountains and near the eastern boundary of our land. Here we camped on the west side of the stream where it is joined by Cottonwood Creek. We felt safe now and began to relax. The troops in the area had all been beaten, and Howard and his army were nowhere to be seen. But we still had no general plan and no idea what to expect next.

The sun was high in the sky the morning after we made our camp on the Clearwater when scouts we had posted on the nearby hills reported that Looking Glass was on the way to join us with his whole band. This made a great stir among us, for Looking Glass had said he wouldn't join in the war but would simply move his people onto the reservation at Lapwai because his band lived only a short distance from it. Now the great Looking Glass was bringing his people. Something had happened, and we all gathered to meet him and hear the news.

Into the camp they came. The men rode proudly on their best war horses, but fatigue, anger, and pain were in their faces. The women and children marched along with them, but they were carrying only a meager portion of their many possessions. Nor was there the usual herd of spare ponies that ordinarily would accompany a Nez Perce band on the march.

Soon Looking Glass spoke for all of them and told their story. "Two days ago," Looking Glass reported, "soldiers were seen approaching our camp. We didn't suspect there would be any trouble for we were within the boundaries of the reservation. So I sent Peopeo Tholekt to tell them they should go away and leave us alone. But the soldiers refused to go away and demanded that I be sent to them. I didn't go, for I was afraid of treachery, and so I sent Peopeo Tholekt again to talk with them. This time they treated Peopeo Tholekt roughly and would have killed him, but they wanted me so they had to send him back with another message that I should come. Now I was more determined than ever not to let the soldiers get hold of me, and I signaled to them again that they should go away and leave us alone. By now the soldiers were close to the village, but we still didn't think there would be a fight. Had we not decided for peace? Weren't we on the reservation? So our warriors were unprepared when one of their men started firing at us, and then the main body of soldiers charged. The women and children scattered like quail, while the warriors ran for their weapons and began to fight back. They held off the soldiers long enough to allow the people time to escape, but we had to retreat. We watched helplessly from a distance as the soldiers burned our village, destroyed our food and utensils, and ran off with most of our horses. Fortunately no one was killed, except one woman and her child who drowned crossing the stream."

We listened silently to this story, and Looking Glass sensed the warmth for him and his band.

"Now you are my people, and as long as I live I will not make peace with the Americans," he finally concluded. "Did I not do everything I knew to preserve their friendship? What more could I have done? The officer who ordered the attack may say it was a mistake, but that is a lie. He knew it was my camp, and he knew I was within the reservation. They came for war, and now I am ready for war."

Not long after this we were also joined by Hush-hush-Cute and his Palouse Indians. They too had gone onto the reservation, but when they heard what happened to Looking Glass they were afraid and decided to throw in their lot with us. They were only a small band, but they increased our total strength to about 650 people. Maybe 140 were able-bodied fighting men; we were at our peak strength.

The next day Looking Glass was revenged. Our scouts brought us word that a force of eighty white volunteers was approaching us. I guess these volunteers decided that if the soldiers were afraid to attack us, they would do it. Well, Ollokot didn't wait for them to attack. With the help of Pahkatos Owyeen and Wachumyus he formed a strong war party and rode out to meet the approaching volunteers.

Even though he was outnumbered, Ollokot succeeded in forcing the eighty men to take a defensive position on a rocky knoll. He kept them penned up there all day and all night and inflicted some casualties among them. None of the Indians were hurt, and Ollokot was able to run off with the settlers' horses. When he brought these back to camp, it was discovered that most of them were the horses stolen from Looking Glass two suns before! So Looking Glass got his horses back and made a great speech in praise of Ollokot and his men.

So far we had fought the soldiers and settlers in four major engagements. We had killed about fifty of them, defeated them each time, and had lost only one of our men. (We didn't count Looking Glass's engagement, since that was a treacherous surprise attack and not a real battle, and Looking Glass had only tried to escape.) But we couldn't afford to become overconfident for we had not yet fought One-arm Howard, who had the main body of troops with him. Where were these troops? We hadn't seen them since we left the Salmon River many suns ago.

It was because of our concern over Howard and his army that we didn't send out a strong war party to wipe out the volunteers Ollokot had penned up on their miserable hill. Why should we do this? Yes, we could have overrun them and killed them all, but we would have lost many of our own men. It was not our aim to kill white people for the sake of killing them, but only to escape from the troops until some kind of peace could be made. The volunteers couldn't hurt us. We had our eye on them, and they were frightened and hurt from our previous attack. But we had to look out for Howard, and so we had our scouts posted well to the west, from which direction we thought he must surely approach. We were especially anxious because we knew the volunteers had seen our camp and must have sent messengers to Howard. We had no one leader, of course, and decided all things in council. This made it hard to arrive at a definite plan of action. Insofar as we had any plan at all it was to wait until we saw Howard's troops approach and then select the best direction in which to take flight.

But as days slipped by and there was no sign of Howard approaching from the west, we began to relax. We knew we could deal with any soldiers or volunteers in the area, and it appeared that now we had left Howard far behind, struggling along after us in the wild and steep country on the other side of the Salmon River. So we began to enjoy ourselves, gather food, and race our horses along the valley of the river. Many of our scouts came back to camp, and in the relaxed atmosphere and the warmth of summer we allowed ourselves to let down our guard. We should have been like ground squirrels, who always have a sentry posted to look out for danger, but instead we became like foolish porcupines who amble along carelessly because they think they are safe.

That is how things were when, on a fine summer day just after the sun had reached its highest point in the sky, we were startled by a great *boom*, like thunder coming from a clear sky. Then came another *boom*, and another. The sounds were coming from the hills that looked down on our camp from the other side of the stream to the east. Then came a fourth *boom*, and this time a cannonball landed with a crash not far from the camp. There could be no doubt about it: We were being attacked by Howard's army, not from the west, where we expected it, but from the east.

CHAPTER NINE

❈

Tragedy

People scattered like flies when a horse swats them with his tail. Women scrambled to find their children; old men stumbled about after the horses. No one seemed to be in charge, and yet the chiefs and warriors acted decisively. I saw Too-hool-hool-Sote with twenty-four warriors cross the Clearwater River and snake rapidly up a ravine that led to the top of the bluffs from which the firing was coming. At the same time two other groups of warriors formed, one led by Ollokot and Pahkatos Owyeen, at the north end of the camp, and the other at the south end, but they weren't as swift as Too-hool-hool-Sote and his men, and the fighting chief and his twenty-four warriors were the first to engage the enemy.

Since I wasn't a warrior, I didn't go with the fighting men right away but looked around the camp until I found Wali'ms and our small daughter, and then I joined Joseph and the others, who were organizing the camp in case we had to make a sudden flight. But when I saw Hohots Illpilp leave with the band of warriors led by Ollokot I couldn't stay. I seized the rifle I had picked up from the dead volunteer at White Bird Canyon, leaped on my horse, and with a wave to Wali'ms and Rising Moon rode off to join my brother.

We crossed the river and made our way laboriously up the

steep hill. Hohots Illpilp nodded to me appreciatively. "Today," he said, "we will fight together. You will stay beside me, and I beside you. We will be si'kstiwain and fight as close comrades, and we will not be afraid, for it's a good day to die."

As we approached the top of the hill we realized that the howitzer had stopped firing, but there was the sound of rifle fire instead. Then we saw that above us and to our right Too-hool-hool-Sote and his men had come to the top of the wooded ravine and formed a firing line at the edge of the bluffs. It was their fire that had silenced the howitzer, but they were now engaged in a fight with the main body of advancing soldiers.

We reached the top of the slopes overlooking the river and found ourselves on the edge of a broad, rocky, treeless plateau. Even I, inexperienced as I was in matters of war, could see the situation that had developed. Howard's army had come up from the south and made its way east of us. Why they had not approached from the west as we had thought they would, I didn't know, but evidently they had been strung out in their line of march when someone riding on the flank spotted our camp far below in the river valley. Howard had sent the howitzer ahead to fire down upon us while the soldiers turned about and changed from a line of march to a line of attack; then they advanced toward the crest of the hill in support of the howitzer. This was not a wise tactic because the firing of the cannon had warned us of the approach of the army, which enabled Too-hool-hool-Sote and his men to gain the brim of the plateau before the soldiers did.

Our band of warriors had now reached the top of the slopes to the north of Too-hool-hool-Sote and his men, and the other band of warriors was coming up from the south. It was a good thing, for though Too-hool-hool-Sote's fire had halted the advancing soldiers, he couldn't hold them back for long, for they numbered hundreds and he had only twenty-four men. Already we could see that he was being forced off the edge of the plateau.

At this moment we came up, and Ollokot and Pahkatos Owyeen directed us to outflank the soldiers. Howard saw this maneuver on our part and rapidly extended his line so we couldn't position ourselves on his flank and catch him in a cross fire between us and the other warriors, who were now to the south trying the same tactic. But our swift action did force Howard to stop pursuing Too-hool-hool-Sote, and soon we had the soldiers pinned down by our rapid and effective rifle fire.

We had stopped the soldiers for the time being, but the odds were against us. For while we numbered less than a hundred, Howard had five times that many soldiers, plus settler volunteers and some Indian scouts as well. The firing now became intense and I could feel the fear spirit rising within me, but my brother had said we would fight together, and I wouldn't leave his side. I struggled against the one-in-me-who-is-afraid and told it I would not be frozen with fear, as I had been when I met the hohots, even if I had to die. So I stayed, and together we built a low wall from the rocks that were scattered about everywhere, as though long ago the Creator had been carrying them in his hand and then had spilled them out haphazardly on the ground just for us to use in this hour of our need.

The bullets whizzed around us but did little damage, because the soldiers were so afraid of our marksmen they kept at a safe distance. Slowly I became more confident as I lay prone on the ground behind the protective shield of rocks and together with Hohots Illpilp fired back at the troopers, not rapidly, carelessly, and at random as they were doing, but carefully, trying to make each shot count.

The battle at White Bird Canyon had been over in a few minutes, but it soon became clear that this battle would not

123

end so quickly. There were too many of the enemy troops and too few of us, and the white soldiers were not exposed as they had been at White Bird Canyon, but had halted their advance and were digging in. They also still had their thunder weapon that they kept safely behind the main line of their troops, in a depressed spot where our bullets couldn't reach it, and from there it continued to fire at us. This was frightening, even though the great gun didn't actually kill many of us because we were so well protected by our rocks. We could see that Howard was also using this depression behind their main lines as his headquarters and was directing the battle himself, and we knew he was a careful soldier, not reckless like the war chief we beat at White Bird Canyon.

So the fighting continued all that day. The troopers were afraid to advance, for whenever a soldier showed his head there would be the crack of one of our rifles and he would quickly fall back into his trench, often with a bullet through his skull. As the day wore on more of the troops became casualties, but not enough to make a decisive difference in the battle because they had so many.

But we did have one advantage: The soldiers had no water. It was dry up on the bluff, and the day was hot. There was one spring nearby, but it lay between us and the soldiers, and our rifle fire kept the soldiers from reaching it. Soon the soldiers began to get thirsty, but while they could see the cool waters of the spring they didn't dare go to it. As the battle wore on the thirst among the soldiers became a torment to them, especially to the wounded, for the thirst of a wounded man is like a raging fire in him.

And how about us? How did we get water? Later in the morning of the fight, after Hohots Illpilp and I had been fighting long and hard and thirst was beginning to weaken us, I heard Ollokot's voice behind me directing someone toward us. And there was Wali'ms! She had struggled up the

124

steep slope carrying water from the river far below in one of her tightly woven baskets. That is how we quenched our thirst: with the water our women brought us, struggling with it up that steep, rugged slope. Our need for water and support was part of the reason our camp did not break up immediately and escape.

On that first day we were winning. We had the white soldiers under virtual siege; pinned down by our fire, they couldn't move. Our camp below was protected, and while our casualties were few theirs were many. But it was wearisome. I felt my body ache from the cramped position I was in on the ground. The deafening noise of the thunder weapon began to weigh heavily on me. I wondered how Wali'ms and Pahkatos Peopeo were, far down below, and, to my surprise, I also found myself worrying over Rising Moon. Finally night came and it was cold. We had little protection against the chill that crept into us as soon as the hot disk of the sun sank below the horizon, for in our haste to join the battle we had not brought blankets.

It was the longest night of my life. Though the firing died down we had to sleep in shifts because we were afraid of being surprised, but it was hard to sleep in the chilly night and among the hard rocks. The next day, as the sun made its way over the distant hills with what seemed like agonizing slowness, I began to lose heart for the fighting. This wasn't the kind of warfare we liked. We preferred fast-moving battles on horseback in which we could fight as individuals and show our bravery. Howard must have been surprised that the Nez Perce could fight a siege battle like this at all. As usual, he underestimated us.

I complained to my brother, "How long will we stay here and fight the troops?"

"Until they've left us, or the women and children are gone and the chiefs have given us the word," Hohots Illpilp answered stoutly. So, grudgingly, I stayed where I was, not

125

because I wanted to but because I didn't want to be a coward, and I didn't want my brother to disapprove of me.

Others must have felt as I did, for as the day wore on I could see individual warriors quitting their place in line and making their way down to the camp. Some of them returned to the firing lines later, but most did not, even though their companions who stayed called them cowards. Yet they weren't cowards, only tired of the waiting and the desultory fighting. Clearly there was disagreement springing up among us about how we should proceed. Some thought we should stay and continue the fight; others thought it was foolish to do so and we should leave, for the women and children were packed and ready to move. Now I could see the advantage of the white man's army with its single commander who told everyone what to do, but we would not give up our belief that each person should do as he saw fit, so we had no single war chief leading us as Howard was leading the troopers.

Then a bad thing happened: The soldiers tried to gain control of the spring. They covered their advance with a barrage of rifle fire and great booms from the thunder weapon, and though we fired at them briskly we couldn't hold them back this time, for so many warriors had left the line that our firepower was greatly reduced. The soldiers now had water. They were heartened by this, but our fighting spirit sank.

By midmorning when I looked down into the valley I saw that the camp had been struck and the People were on the march to the northeast. Travois, loaded the day before, were hitched to the horses, and a long line of older men, women, and children were threading their way to a place where they would be safe. I thought I could spot Joseph leading the band, and once I thought I saw Kapoochas and half-blind old Natalekin. I became homesick for Wali'ms, but I couldn't pick her out from among the many women. Many young

126

men were with them, for the trickle of warriors deserting the battle had now become a stream. Of course this left the remaining line of defense very thin.

I asked Hohots Illpilp again, and perhaps this time there was something of a timid child in my voice. "The others are leaving. We are now almost alone in this place. Don't you think it's best if we leave also?"

He shrugged his shoulders carelessly. "It's true that others are leaving, but not all have left. See, Ollokot stays, and a few with him. Some of us must hold back the soldiers until the women and children are far away. I will remain and fight as long as there is a need to do so, but you can leave if you choose But stay until night. Then it will be safe to go."

I wanted to go then but was afraid my greathearted brother would think my own heart was small if I left. So I stayed for that reason, and then, as the day wore on, I stayed because suddenly Hohots Illpilp and I had no choice, for the soldiers had come close to us. They were so close now that if we rose to our feet we would surely have been shot. The fear spirit gripped me again as I realized the increasing peril we were in. I prayed hard to Qotsqo'tsn for protection, but Hohots Illpilp remained calm, and from time to time his rifle spoke out authoritatively.

I looked around again and saw that almost all those warriors who could leave had gone, which left only a few of us. At this point the soldiers rose up as one man and charged! In moments, the warriors withdrawing from the battle looked more like flight as they ran down the mountain to escape the fire of the charging soldiers.

I think the soldiers were surprised when they broke through our line so easily; they hadn't realized that so many of us had gone. Yet it didn't really matter, for the People were now safely on their way.

As the withdrawal of our men became a rout, even the bravest of the warriors left on the firing line began to retreat.

127

A little distance away I could see Pahkatos Owyeen looking at us and waving to us to come. All this time Hohots Illpilp and I kept firing at the advancing troopers, and so effective was our fire that right where we were the soldiers were pinned down and couldn't advance farther. Now my brother looked at me and smiled in the manner of a man who knows he has performed his job well. "All right," he said to me, "now we will go. Get ready to leap to your feet when I give the signal, and we will race for the camp." I could feel my breath tighten with tension until I thought I would choke. Hohots Illpilp beckoned with his hand and with a bound we were on our feet, like deer startled in the forest. And then it happened! I heard the crack of a rifle from close by. There was a thud of a bullet striking a human body, and my brother slumped to the ground beside me!

Turning in horror toward the sound of the rifle, I saw a soldier. He had evidently crept close to us without our knowing it. It was his bullet that had felled my greathearted brother, the noble and strong Hohots Illpilp. I don't know where the fear spirit went, but it was gone now and a great rage possessed me. I no longer felt as I did when the hohots was charging me; instead *I* was a hohots, a raging bear. I raised my rifle and aimed at that white soldier. I could see his face clearly. I could see his uniform and could tell that he was a minor officer. For an instant we gazed into each other's faces, and then I fired. I missed, for at the instant I shot, the soldier dropped to the ground for safety, and now I too was forced to the ground beside the body of my stricken brother. Was he dead? I crawled to where he lay on the ground. Blood streamed from a deep wound on his left side. "Hohots Illpilp, dear si'kstiwain," I cried, with tears streaming down my face. I silently implored his spirit not to leave his body, but to remain within it and keep it alive. For a moment there was no sign of life from him. Then he opened his eyes and gazed at me. A thin, beautiful smile crossed his strong face. He reached out one hand toward me and took my hand in his. "Teeto Hoonod, si'kstiwain, it's all right, it's all right." Then his eyes closed. A calm came over his face. He looked serene, like the water of a lake that has become smooth again after a violent storm. I knew he was dead.

I flung myself on his body and begged his soul to come back, but my brother lay still, for hadn't Coyote made it so the dead would never return when he embraced his wife before he crossed the fifth mountain range? Suddenly a rifle shot nearby jerked me away from my grief to a realization of my own perilous position. I had an impulse to run for my life, but if I ran what would happen to my brother's body? I wouldn't leave it! I crouched over it and watched, hidden, as the troopers ran past me, charging toward the camp below. They were between me and the camp now. I would stay where I was, guarding the body of my brother.

By some miracle I was not discovered. I waited and waited that hot afternoon beside the motionless body of Hohots Illpilp, still with the calm smile on his face. I waited as the chill of evening came and the cold began to creep into a body whose heart was already cold with the knowledge of death. I waited throughout that cold night, with a heart emptied from within by the tears that flowed from me like a heartsick woman. I was not ashamed of the tears but let them fall like rain. Then, slowly, as the night wore on and the first light of the new day began to cross the eastern sky with a faint glow, a new spirit came to me; a revenge spirit filled my heart. It was cold and dark, that revenge spirit. It was an evil spirit that came into me, but I welcomed it. It was a spirit that kept me from further tears, that made my heart hard like a stone. I would find and kill that soldier who had shot my brother! I would make that the meaning of my life. I had seen that soldier's face and I would never forget it. I made myself remember that soldier's face, the color of his hair, the shape of his nose. Wherever I met white soldiers I

129

would look for him until I found and killed him.

When the dawn finally came, all was silent around me. The soldiers were gone. I could see them far below in our abandoned camp, destroying what had been left, burning the tipis, ravaging the caches of food the women had made so painstakingly. Now I buried Hohots Illpilp. Silently I worked on that hard and rocky soil, digging for hours with my knife and bare hands until I made a safe grave. I would not let my brother's body be mutilated by the enemy or torn apart by animals. When finally I lowered him safely into the welcoming arms of his Mother, the Earth, long dark shadows had begun to cast themselves on the ground, heralds of the approaching night. I piled rocks on top of his grave to keep the coyotes from digging it up, and then I sat and sang our sacred songs for the departed. For hours I sang the prayer songs that would help the spirit of Hohots Illpilp leave this accursed spot and make its way to the spirit world beyond.

Finally it was time to go. When I had gone but a short distance I made two unexpected discoveries. First I found my brother's horse, which I thought surely had wandered away by now. I slit the throat of the uncomprehending animal, for in this way the horse became a spirit horse, and my brother could ride it on his way to the land of the departed; it would make his journey swifter and easier. The second discovery was a pistol, lying on the ground where the white soldier had stood who killed Hohots Illpilp. I picked it up. It was a beautifully made revolver and on its handle was carved a name. It must belong to my enemy! I tucked the pistol in my clothing and vowed to keep it until I had my revenge.

Now, when there was nothing else I could do for my brother, I walked away from that grim spot where Pa'yawit had robbed me of the man I loved as father and mother, friend and soul mate, that place where the cold spirit of revenge laid hold of me, that place where someone great and mighty had fallen. I made my way to the north, avoiding the camp area and river valley filled with soldiers. I traveled north many miles, in the direction taken by the People, and then crossed the Clearwater River far above the camp and turned east. I was exhausted but I scarcely rested, for the revenge spirit had given me a stubborn reason for living, and my soul was fed now with its new and strange food. On and on I traveled until, in the evening of the next day, I saw signs that the People were camped not far off. Not many minutes later I stumbled into the camp, almost out of my head with exhaustion and grief.

CHAPTER TEN

Over the Trail

The People were camped one sun's journey from Weippe Prairie, where in happier times the various bands came each year to celebrate and gather the camas bulbs. Ordinarily there would be joyful anticipation by the time we arrived this close to our old gathering spot, but now as I walked among the People, unrecognized in the gathering darkness, there was no joy, and signs of devastation were everywhere. It was as painful as the sting of the bee to see the little children, ordinarily so bright with laughter and life, gazing up at their elders out of solemn faces. The men, too, had worried looks, and here and there among the women was the sound of mourning for someone who had been killed or wounded. Materially, too, a great deal had been lost, for Joseph had been forced to leave much behind. Only the horse herd had been preserved intact; Joseph had seen to its safety, for our horses were essential.

I didn't want to make myself known to anyone until I found Wali'ms. Eventually I came upon the temporary shelter of poles and skins she had made for herself and Pahkatos Peopeo. I pushed aside the flap that served as a door and stood inside in the darkness. For a moment there was silence; then I heard a sobbing cry, and a greeting in Shoshone, the language Wali'ms spoke when experiencing great emotion, and she was in my arms. For many moments

132

we held each other while our child slept nearby. Then Wali'ms spoke. "Teeto Hoonod, you're alive. I was sure you were dead. When you didn't return I could only think you had died. The others also told me, 'He must have died in the fighting; the soldiers must have killed Hohots Illpilp and your man too.' "

I stroked her hair gently. "No, Wali'ms, I am not dead, nor am I hurt in my body, but my soul is hurt, and my heart is bleeding inside of me." I felt her hands run carefully over me as I spoke, as though she were not satisfied with my words but had to explore my body for herself to make sure there were no wounds. I continued my tale. "I stayed with Hohots Illpilp. Together we fought the advancing soldiers. We remained in our places too long and the soldiers overran our position. I remained behind during the long night and hid until the soldiers passed beyond me. Only then could I return in safety."

Suddenly another voice was heard in the tipi. It was Rising Moon. "And Hohots Illpilp, Teeto Hoonod, what of him? He has not come back with you."

I turned and there was Rising Moon standing in the doorway, her slim, lithe body silhouetted against the dying light of the late evening sky. How beautiful she looked, like a sparrow hawk perched on the limbs of a tree just before darkness falls. "No, Rising Moon, my brother, your husband, has not returned. He has gone to join his ancestors; he is on his way now to the land of the Great Spirit. He wouldn't leave his position in the battle. He told me he must remain where he was and hold back the soldiers as long as possible so the women and children could escape. Other warriors were retreating, but he wouldn't leave. I remained with him until finally it was right for us to go. But then, as we rose to depart, a soldier appeared, much closer to us than we realized. That soldier shot Hohots Illpilp. He fell to the ground and died quickly from the wound."

There was silence. Then Rising Moon asked softly, "And you, Teeto Hoonod?"

"I turned when I heard the shot. I saw the white soldier clearly. I fired at him, but the instant before I pulled my trigger he dropped to the ground. But I will never forget his face!" My voice was rising now because of my anger. "Wherever I go, wherever I see the white troops, I will look for that soldier, and when I see him I will kill him!" There was silence for a moment, and then I continued more quietly. "I remained there with the body of Hohots Illpilp all night. In the morning the soldiers were gone. I stayed until I had dug a grave for my brother and sung the right songs. Then I left and made my way back."

Now the women could no longer control their emotions; we wept together.

The news began to spread through the camp that Teeto Hoonod was safely back but Hohots Illpilp was not with him. People came to greet me and express their sorrow over the death of the strong-hearted one. Among them was Kapoochas. He held me firmly. He didn't need to say many words in order to convey to me what he felt. The old man's power was great, and I knew that he loved me, and his power and love renewed my strength.

Joseph also came to hear my story, and when I finished speaking he told me how brave my brother had been, how he had helped save the People, and how brave I had been too and how grateful he was for my safe return. These were not just words with Joseph; I could see in his eyes and in the lines in his face his deep suffering. Others suffered for themselves; Joseph suffered for everyone. It was the first of many times that I was to see that look on his face, the look of a man whose spirit runs deep and who feels pain whenever any of his people feel pain.

While we were camped, our scouts reported that Howard

was forming a group of cavalrymen and that evidently he had been told by some of the Christian Nez Perce of a secret place to cross the Clearwater that would enable his horse soldiers to reach the Weippe Prairie before us. Joseph acted quickly and sent a lone Indian, Zya Temoni, which means "No Heart," to make an appearance before Howard's camp and signal that he wanted a parley. It was a ruse, but it worked. The general must have thought, Now the Indians are going to surrender because I have beaten them so badly. So he sent some of his officers to talk to Zya Temoni, who was on the other side of the river from the troops. Zya Temoni talked with them, but when someone fired a shot—no one knows who it was—he rode away, after slapping his bare thigh at the soldiers to show his contempt for them.

This gave Joseph a chance to get the People safely to Weippe Prairie. That evening, after we made camp at Weippe, the chiefs met in a great council. This was to be an exceedingly important council for us and all the chiefs were there, as were most of the best warriors. I didn't speak at the council but I did sit in on it, for my part in the battle of Clearwater entitled me to this privilege. Because this was an important gathering, the chiefs passed the pipe. As the smoke from the pipe curled upward it carried our prayers to the Great Spirit, and as we passed the pipe around it meant that we were all united, one in spirit. So we gathered in council, while I, feeling like a man now and no longer like a boy, listened to what the important men of our tribe said. Each spoke in turn for as long as he liked and no one interrupted him until he was finished, for this was the Nez Perce way. When these men had finished, others of us could speak if we wished to, but we who were lesser persons mostly deferred to the older, wiser heads among us.

We had only a few choices. One was to surrender. "Better to surrender than to die, better to give up now than see all the women and children killed." This was the view of defeated spirits, but they said so in hushed voices, for they knew this was not a plan of brave men and they were afraid to stand up boldly and argue for it in front of the chiefs and warriors.

The greatest of our chiefs—Too-hool-hool-Sote, Looking Glass, White Bird, and Hush-hush-Cute—and the warriors Wachumyus, Pahkatos Owyeen, and Wahlitits would not even consider the idea of surrender, but no one could agree on another plan. Then Looking Glass argued that we should leave our land and retreat over the Lolo Trail, the ancient route through the Bitterroot Mountains, and then head for the Buffalo Country. This way, by marching fast, we could leave Howard and his war far behind. He spoke eloquently, and the others began to agree with him. Moreover, Looking Glass added, the Crow were in that country, and they were his friends and would become our allies.

Joseph alone disagreed. When all the others had spoken Joseph stood up, his massive body framed against the glowing light of the fire, and spoke with great dignity. "What are we fighting for? Is it our lives? No. It is for this fair land where the bones of our fathers are buried. I don't want to take my women among strangers. I don't want to die in a strange land. Some of you once said that I was afraid to fight. Stay here with me now and you will have plenty of fighting. We will put our women behind us in these mountains and die on our own land fighting for them. I would rather do that than run I know not where."

We were all surprised at Joseph's words, for we thought of him as a man of peace, not of war. Perhaps he remembered his father's dying plea not to give up the land. Now he alone was willing to stay where we were and fight to keep our country.

But Looking Glass won the council over to his plan. As tall and strong as Joseph, Looking Glass made an impressive figure as he stood up to rebut his fellow chief. "Listen to me,

136

my chiefs!" he called out, speaking in a loud voice (Joseph had spoken softly). "It is foolish to stay here and die fighting the soldiers. We can move tomorrow over the Lolo Trail and put the mountains between us and Howard's army. Then we will march to the Buffalo Country, a land I and many others know well. There will be plenty of food there for the winter, and my friends the Crow will be there too and will welcome us. We will make an alliance with them and together we will be too strong for the soldiers, who will have to leave us alone."

There was a murmur of approval at these words. Only Joseph objected. "Looking Glass, how do we know that the Crow will help us? How do we know that we will not leave our native land here, where we know every mountain and valley, for a strange land where we may be surrounded by all men as our enemies—whites and Indians alike? It is better to fight and die here."

Looking Glass spoke angrily; he always became angry when anyone insisted on having an opinion different from his. "The Crow as the same as my brothers! If you go there with me you will be safe!"

All the other chiefs agreed with Looking Glass: "All right, Looking Glass, you take us to the Crow country."

Because Joseph didn't want to leave his people he also agreed to go, but he had one final thing to say. "If we do this, then when we cross the great mountains into the Bitterroot Valley we must come in peace among the white people there. There must be no fighting, and no raiding, and if we take any goods we must pay for them. Otherwise we will take the war with us wherever we go. Later, when all the anger has died down, we must try again to talk with Howard and make an agreement with him so that we can return to our land, for though we may find safety in the Crow country, this is where we belong." Everyone agreed with Joseph on this point, as they had agreed with Looking Glass before, and even Looking Glass consented to Joseph's thought, though later he made it sound as though it had been his idea and not Joseph's. So the decision was made to go on the Lolo Trail and make the long trek to the Buffalo Country, and Looking Glass was chosen as our war leader (though Joseph remained in charge of the march and principal caretaker for the welfare of the women and children), a choice that was destined to have far-reaching consequences that none of us could foresee.

The next morning, with the first light of the sun, the criers rode through the camp telling the People of the plan and instructing everyone that when we reached the other side of the Bitterroot Mountains there was to be no more fighting, that we were not to injure or steal from any of the white people but were to travel in peace. Camp was then broken and our band, numbering over 700 men, women, and children, with our 3,000 horses and all of our belongings, began to wind its way toward the Lolo Trail. Looking Glass left behind a small detachment of warriors to watch for Howard and warn us if he pursued too closely, and an advance screen of warriors rode in front to make sure there was no danger ahead, while Joseph directed the march. The women were busy packing our belongings and food; the men in bringing up the horses; the little children, faces filled with mingled looks of trust and uncertainty, remained close by their parents. I joined the men who were rounding up the pony herd, while Wali'ms and Rising Moon secured our worldly possessions and Pahkatos Peopeo played as though this was just an ordinary day.

But it was not an ordinary day for the Nez Perce. As we left Weippe Prairie later that morning and began to wind our way into the mountains, I recalled that it was at this very Weippe Prairie where, some seventy-five winters earlier, the Nez Perce had first met the Long Knives, those starving men of the Lewis and Clark expedition whom our grandparents helped so much. It was then that our friendship with the Americans had started, a relationship of trust that we had never broken. But now we were leaving our lands in the hands of white settlers and riding off to an unknown future. To be sure, Looking Glass and others assured us that we would be back, but I knew it would never be the same for us again. How had it happened? How had it come about so quickly that we had lost and the white man had won our land?

All that day we traveled deeper into the mountains, our long line of men, women, children, horses, and dogs winding its way through the thick forest like a snake winds its way through the underbrush. The Bitterroot Mountains, which formed the eastern boundary of our ancestral lands up to the Eas-slum-eas-ne-ma, the Great Divide, were heavily forested and deeply slashed by streams and rivers that plummeted down from distant mountain heights. Through this country, following a knifelike ridge that separated two rivers, was the Lolo Trail.

No one was sure how the trail came to have this name, but the story told most often was that there was once a half-breed trapper named Lolo, a friend of the Indians, who had the misfortune to be killed by a huhots along this trail. After that people spoke of "the trail where Lolo was killed" and soon, simply, "the Lolo trail." However it received its name, it was a tangled path with many fallen trees across the way and deep underbrush on either side, and it threaded its way through a forest so thick it was often all we could do to force our reluctant horses over, under, or around the many obstacles, so that more than one horse had to be abandoned because it became too exhausted or bloodied to continue the journey. The trail had been used for many winters by hunters and warriors, but it was not a trail for a whole nation of people to move along, and the journey was a hardship for old people, like Natalekin, and the wounded. The little children, too, became weary, though they seldom complained, for Indian children do not often cry and are used to taking the hard times with the good. But even though the mountains seemed to resist our every step we made steady progress, for we were a proud and determined people.

The evening of our first camp along the trail I wandered away from the others to be alone with my thoughts. I was gazing into the forest when I heard a sound and, turning, saw Kapoochas standing beside me.

"Teeto Hoonod," the wiry old medicine man said to me, "I need to speak to you."

"Kapoochas," I said warmly, "you are always a friend to me. I will listen to you gladly."

Kapoochas hesitated; it was clear that the old man was going to have difficulty expressing himself. Finally he began. "Teeto Hoonod, Hohots Illpilp is dead. Ah-cum-kin-i-ma-me-hut has called him back and nothing can be done. There is a great hole in the hearts of those of us who loved him. This is the price that is paid by those who love and have to go to war. Now, Teeto Hoonod, I am worried about you. I don't want to lose you as well as your brother."

"Old man," I said with affectionate disrespect, "we're not fighting now. We are leaving the soldiers behind. There may be no more trouble, and, if there is, my Wy-a-kin is strong and I have nothing to fear."

"That is not what I mean. I am not worried about your body but about your spirit. Since the death of Hohots Illpilp you have allowed an evil power to enter your soul. There is danger that your guardian spirit may leave you and another spirit, an evil spirit, may enter."

I objected. "Qotsqo'tsn is my guardian spirit, Kapoochas. You know this, and he is not evil."

"But you also know, Teeto Hoonod, that if a person does not follow the bidding of his Wy-a-kin it may desert him and then another spirit may enter the empty space of that

140

person's soul. In your case it is the spirit of revenge that you have allowed to take hold of you that Qotsqo'tsn does not like. This may cause him to forsake you, turning you over to an evil power."

My face became like the sun when a dark cloud comes over it. I didn't like his talking to me this way, and I answered him roughly, "Kapoochas, it's not for you to talk with me about my soul. If I want to talk with you of spirit matters I will come to you. I am determined not to rest or die until I avenge my brother's death. It is this spirit, which you call evil, that nourishes my soul now and keeps me in this life. It's this that makes my Wy-a-kin strong."

Kapoochas would not be intimidated. "Your Wy-a-kin comes from Qotsqo'tsn, not from this spirit of revenge. Have you forgotten how, when you set out to join Wahlitits and his war party, the qotsqo'tsn that was singing on the tree flew away from you? It's not the dark spirit that keeps us in this life, Teeto Hoonod, for that is a spirit of destruction. It can live only to destroy, and when there is nothing left for it to destroy, it destroys itself. This spirit of evil will destroy you if you do not destroy it first."

I became angrier. "Do you see everything then, old man? Did you see even the meadowlark who flew away from me that morning at Tepahlewam? It was nothing. The bird was startled by something; it was only a chance event."

"There is no chance," Kapoochas replied. "Everything that happens does so for a purpose."

My suspicions were aroused. Why had Kapoochas approached me? How did he know so much about what I was thinking when we had not spoken together? "Kapoochas, how do you know these things about me? Has Rising Moon spoken to you?"

"Yes," he replied. "Rising Moon told me what was happening with you. She implored me to come and speak with you and beg you to lay aside the dark spirit that is in you.

But I would have known anyway. It's clear to all who have the inner vision that an evil power has laid hold of you."

I erupted angrily, "That woman has already interfered once in my life, and now she interferes again. She's a witch who tries to keep me from being a man. What right has she to send you to speak to me, to criticize what is in my heart?"

"And yet, Teeto Hoonod," Kapoochas replied, "is it not true that if it were not for Rising Moon your brother's blood would be on your hands? Be glad that she kept you from being part of an evil which, like Cannibal, will devour everything it can reach."

I couldn't answer Kapoochas, for it was true. If the warriors who had gone on the raiding party had heeded Joseph's words, my brother would still be alive; and my own thoughts had whispered to me already that if it had not been for Rising Moon's interference on that fateful day I would have been one of those whose blood lust brought this disaster on the People. And I also knew who Cannibal was, for my mother had told me his terrible story.

Many, many years ago, before the human race had come, there were five brothers who used to go hunting. One day the eldest brother did not come back. Coyote sent the second oldest brother to look for him, but he didn't return either. Neither did the third, or the fourth. Finally Coyote sent the youngest brother, but before he looked for the missing brothers he consulted Meadowlark. It was Qotsqo'tsn who told him that the eldest brother, while hunting, had accidentally cut himself and drunk some of his own blood. "Then," Meadowlark told the youngest brother, "somehow it made him crazy. He became mad and ate himself and became self-eaten. Now he has eaten up the other brothers. And here you are. He will do the same thing to you." The youngest brother escaped from the ravenous cannibal brother because Meadowlark told him what to do, but he couldn't destroy the brother who had become evil, who continued to haunt people, devouring everything he could reach. And, when Cannibal could eat nothing else he ate himself, until he was only a bare, horrible, ravenous skeleton.

That was Cannibal, and Kapoochas was telling me that this was the way it is with evil and I must not become part of it or it would devour me too. But I couldn't admit these things to myself. I wanted to live on my hatred and cling to the dark spirit of revenge that I had invited into my soul. So I stared at the kindly old man with anger in my eyes, even though he had come only with the intention of helping me, and then, because I had no real answer for him, I turned and walked away, leaving Kapoochas standing there alone.

Only one hostile action occurred during the eleven days it took us to cross the Bitterroot Mountains over the tortuous Lolo Trail, and since I was part of this minor battle I can give a first-hand report. Word reached us from our rear guard that a considerable force of cavalry, settlers, and treaty Indians was following us closely. The chiefs decided to send back a small force of warriors to discourage such close pursuit, and I volunteered to go with them. I did this partly to aid the People and turn back the pursuers, but mostly in the hope of catching a glimpse of my enemy and getting a shot at him. To this extent had my urge for revenge consumed me, for I now thought day and night of the face of that white man who had killed Hohots Illpilp, impressing it so firmly on my mind that I would be sure to recognize him and react to him even in the urgency of a battle.

So it happened that four suns after we started up the Lolo Trail I found myself hidden in a thick woods with a small group of other warriors under the leadership of Wachumyus, Two Moons, and Wahlitits. We were planning a little surprise for those soldiers when they entered the woods where we were hidden, and hoped to avenge ourselves for

143

our losses at the Battle of the Clearwater. To my disappointment, the white troopers didn't enter the woods but in a cowardly fashion sent the Christian Nez Perce scouts into danger ahead of them, with the settler volunteers not far behind.

I suppose we could have inflicted more damage on the enemy if we had let these Christian Nez Perce pass through the woods unmolested and waited for the troopers to follow. But when our men saw these Indians, our own blood and kin, helping the whites and turning against us, their blood was too much on fire and they couldn't wait. Shots rang out, and two of the Christian Nez Perce fell from their horses. The rest retreated hurriedly, taking one of the wounded men with them and leaving the other. We came up to him and saw that he was Hemene Istooptoopnin—Sheared Wolf—whom the white men called John Levi, and he was dead when we reached him. "Is this what it means to become a Christian?" we said about him among ourselves, "that you turn against your own people?"

As usual, the settlers had fled at the sound of the shots, and the troopers hurried back to their camp. They didn't even return to bury Sheared Wolf, though perhaps his friends came back later to do so. Even the Christian Nez Perce would not leave an Indian unburied if they could help it. If his body were mutilated by animals he would enter maimed into the next world, and the Christian Nez Perce somehow continued to believe this, though it was not the teaching of the church.

We didn't pursue the retreating troops because we were sure they wouldn't follow us so closely again for fear of another ambush. Our Wy-a-kin was strong and none of us were hurt, so we called our expedition a victory and rejoined the others. But I was disappointed because the white troopers didn't show up for the battle so I had no chance to find my enemy.

The People had not made much progress. I helped herd our ponies through the tangle of fallen trees and the clinging brush that blocked the trail, and at night I helped Wali'ms prepare our campsite. I also helped Rising Moon. We were speaking now, for since Hohots Illpilp had died it seemed foolish for me to hold her off in silence. Besides, now that Hohots Illpilp was dead she was alone in the world, with no family left except Wali'ms and me.

Rising Moon continued, even in her distress, to hold herself erect and walk with dignity. She didn't go about wailing and mourning, as was the custom for Nez Perce women who lost their husbands, and many criticized her for this and said she couldn't have loved Hohots Illpilp very much. But I knew this was her way: to show courage on the outside and grieve within. She was quiet and thoughtful these days, but when she spoke with me it was in a friendly way. She and Wali'ms became closer than ever in the kind of friendship women can have, and though Rising Moon kept her own camp she knew she was always welcome in ours.

I also spent a great deal of time alone during these days because my mind whirled with many thoughts and emotions. Sometimes, when I was herding the ponies and others were not around, I would find that I had stopped and was thinking and thinking as though staring into a deep pool of water hoping to see something. And in the evening, when the camp quieted down, I often stole away to the edge of the darkness and became lost in my own world.

The sun had risen and set five times on our march along the Lolo Trail when I found myself early one evening in such a state, drawn by unknown, compelling powers within me to seek solitude in a small clearing with the towering forest around me on every side. To the west, the sun was rapidly sinking into the distant line of hills. To the east, the fading light was stealing down mountain peaks, leaving them swallowed by the stealthy shadow of approaching night.

Now the katydids, stirred to wakefulness by the softness of the evening light, began their chorus all around me. How they sang! With a burst of vigor the katydid chorus would break into song, then suddenly fall silent, and then the silence would be broken by a single katydid singing a plaintive solo, as though trying to catch up with the others. Then abruptly the tremendous katydid chorus would begin again, and the voice of the solo singer would be drowned out no matter how loudly and desperately she tried to be heard. They repeated their evening rhythm over and over: the chorus, then the single song, then the ringing chorus breaking in again.

As I listened I remembered the story my mother used to tell of the katydid woman who lived in a warm lodge with her daughter and her daughter's husband. "Whatever you do," the daughter said to her husband, "never tell of the incidents of the day when the old woman might hear you." But the man forgot and one day mentioned that the time of year had come when the katydids made a great din in the forests and meadows. With that the old woman left the house forever and tried to rejoin the katydids, for she was a katydid woman. Piteously she sang, trying to catch up to the katydid chorus, but she could never succeed. And that, so the story goes, is why, when the katydids sing, there is always one singer who is left out. It's the katydid woman, no longer human, yet not able to become again one of her insect kind.

Memories of the poignant tale of the katydid woman transported my mind into a strange place where the reality of spirit things becomes greater than the reality of outer things. It seemed as though the forest became uncannily quiet, as though all life had come to a halt, and then I saw perched on a small bush not more than five strides ahead of me Qotsqo'tsn, Meadowlark.

I knew at once that this was a spirit bird, not an ordinary one. Then it seemed as though a voice called my name: "Teeto Hoonod! Teeto Hoonod! Teeto Hoonod!" I looked up and Qotsqo'tsn was speaking to me. "Why are you making a home in your heart for evil?"

Strangely enough, due to my unusual state of mind, the presence of the speaking bird seemed perfectly natural. I found myself answering, "I am not making a home for evil in my heart. I don't know what you mean."

The bird spoke again. "The revenge spirit in you is evil. Already this spirit has brought trouble and death among the People. Why are you making a home for this spirit within you?"

Testily I answered, "It's justice to take life when it is done to rectify evil. Only in this way can the score be evened."

The voice persisted. "You may call a wolverine whatever name you will, but it remains a wolverine. Call revenge what you like; it remains what it is."

I became angry. "It's only justice that this man should die for the death that he caused."

"It is not yours to decide what should die and what should live."

"Then whose right is it to decide?" I answered hotly. "Is it the Great Spirit's? He only looks the other way when evil is done." I found myself surprised at the anger within me toward the Great Spirit. It seemed a wrong thing to say, and yet it also made me feel good to have said it.

The bird voice persisted. "The only thing to fear from evil is if you become evil yourself. When blood begins to run, an evil spirit is never far away. If you long to extinguish the life of a person, you are in danger of being used by the evil power. So far you have been protected against this evil; the

147

woman who loves you saw the evil coming and kept you from it. But now you must fight and win your own battle. You are a boy no longer, but must become a man."

Angrily I replied, "Then you, too, take her side! You, too, don't care about the humiliation she brought on me!"

The voice of Qotsqo'tsn seemed to regard my comment as unworthy of a reply. It spoke only one more time: "Remember, if you directly oppose the evil power, you are in danger of becoming evil yourself. You must not oppose evil directly, but only seek to defend the good." And with that the meadowlark rose into the air and soared off into the fading light of the sun, and the katydid chorus erupted again in a furious cacophony of sound. The voice was gone, and I was alone.

When I returned to the camp, darkness had fallen and the shadows of the great trees engulfed the men and women and children who were huddled in the forest seeking comfort from each other. As I approached our camp I saw Wali'ms, with Kapoochas sitting beside her. Because I came out of the night they didn't see me at first, and I heard Wali'ms say to the old man, "See how he goes off alone into the forest? He's alone too much. Since his brother died his mind is not the same, and I'm afraid for him."

I heard Kapoochas reply, "I, too, fear for him, but don't be afraid that he goes alone into the forest. There the spirits can come to him and he can talk with them. Sometimes only in aloneness can a cure be found."

As I entered our camp their talk ceased. They greeted me as though nothing had been said, and I spoke to them as though the voice of Qotsqo'tsn had not spoken to me. But I couldn't forget the words of the meadowlark, even though I still wouldn't give up the dark spirit in me.

The Lolo Trail from the west side of the Bitterroot Mountains to lofty Lolo Pass took even hardy warriors many suns to travel, but once the trail reached the pass the way plunged down quickly on the sun-rising side of the mountains to the Bitterroot Valley below. This valley was lush and inviting. It was settled by both Indians and white people, but for as long as anyone could remember the Nez Perce had enjoyed friendly relations with both. The Indians were our long-standing friends, the Flatheads, who made their home in the northern part of the valley. Our hunters and warriors used the Bitterroot Valley for a road to the Buffalo Country to the east, and whenever they entered the valley they traded with the white people there, and in this way good relations had been built up because the relationship had been beneficial to everyone. The white people welcomed the Nez Perce because we bought goods from them and they always dealt with us honestly, and the Nez Perce respected the rights of the white people and were careful to pay for everything and never to steal. In fact, many Nez Perce liked this valley so well they had made it their home.

So the Bitterroot Valley seemed like a place of peace and refuge, and as we made our painful but steady progress toward the Lolo Pass our courage rose, for the Great Spirit had made us a happy and high-spirited people, quick to laugh and with a keen power to enjoy life. As we neared the pass, with no sign of Howard's troops in pursuit of us, most of the People believed the worst of our hardships was behind us. Surely, they thought, we are now leaving the war behind, and someday, when the heat of emotion has died down, Joseph and the other chiefs will be able to talk with Howard about returning to our own land.

This was the spirit the People were in as we moved closer to our destination, but I could not share in it, for whenever I closed my eyes to seek rest I heard again the sound of the rifle that killed my brother, the thud of his body as he slumped to the ground, and the look in his eyes when he died. Rising Moon shared my thoughtful mood. She was

149

quiet these days and, like myself, was often wrapped in the blanket of her own thoughts.

This was the way I found her one evening when, following my custom, I sought solitude once more in the forest away from the busy camp. As I approached an opening in the trees made by a small brook, I was startled to see her slim figure standing there as though she knew I would come and was expecting me. When she saw me approach she came over to me like a waft of air that comes into a lodge on a gentle spring day and spoke as though it was the most natural thing in the world that she should be there waiting for me.

"See how the moon rises? Already it can be seen shining through the trees. It's like the eye of our Mother the night, giving light to all her creatures who shun the fierce glare of the sun, but steal out of their homes and burrows as soon as the welcome darkness has fallen."

I hadn't noticed it before, so lost had I been within myself, but it was the full moon this evening, and it had appeared early, glowing orange, as the moon does when it still hovers near the horizon, newly emerged from the cave in which it dwells during the day, renewing its strength, and ready to make its ascent through the world of the stars.

Rising Moon continued, "The moon is round tonight like the tipis of the People are round, and like the nests of the birds are round, and like the seasons of the year that make a great round from summer to winter and back again."

"Yes," I answered her, mysteriously drawn into a conversation that would have seemed strange with anyone but Rising Moon, "and in that roundness is the wholeness of the People. For is it not said that the Great Spirit created us and the whole world to be round?"

"So it is said," Rising Moon replied quietly. "But in these days the roundness of the People is broken. Evil forces have penetrated our circle, and the round life that was ours is in danger."

I answered spiritedly. "Not if we are able to remain in the roundness ourselves, Rising Moon. Even though evil presses upon us from outside, we can still remain held in the roundness if we are correct within ourselves. The circle can be broken only by dangers within, not by dangers outside."

I said this because I had heard Kapoochas say it, but even as the words escaped me I felt uneasy about them, as though they were true but did not belong to me. Rising Moon looked keenly at me as I spoke, her gaze penetrating into the depths of my soul like the gaze of the great blue heron into the depths of the lake. Suddenly I felt ashamed. I knew what she was thinking: that my heart was not part of the roundness of the Great Spirit but was part of the power that would break the circle.

Brusquely I said, "And yet evil must be opposed. A man must fight against it and destroy it and avenge himself when he can."

Rising Moon's gaze softened. "I didn't come here tonight, Teeto Hoonod, to talk of the dark spirit you've been following. The death of Hohots Illpilp has been like a shaft into the hearts of both of us. I know how you loved him, and how his death has wounded you, and I don't blame you for wanting to avenge his death. But tonight I want to talk of other things, to talk of life, not of death."

My anger was beginning to fade. "I don't know what you mean, Rising Moon."

"The Moon goddess is a power of life," she continued. "She grows thin and then full again, like life grows thin and moves toward death and then swells up once more with the life power. When the moon grows fat and strong and round, all life increases with her power. Then it is that the plants grow the most, the seeds swell and burst, and the womb of

151

woman also swells with life that comes from the seed of man and the Moon-power that is in her. Yes, even though life must die, it must also increase again because of the power of the moon. That is why I am here."

For Rising Moon, the moon was her Power and she spoke of it as others spoke of the Great Spirit. I replied to her gently. "Rising Moon, why aren't you with the women getting ready for the night? Why do you come here and speak to me of these things?"

Rising Moon was silhouetted now against the moon's great orange disk. I saw her slim ankles, her gently rounded breasts, and the outline of her body, as though it had been sharply drawn by one of our master artists. She replied, "I come because my womb is crying out for life. It wants to be filled with the life power. It is ready to grow full and round like the moon. It hungers to serve the Moon-power and bring life into the world. But I need help, for Hohots Illpilp is dead."

I wasn't sure of the intention behind her words. "I don't understand, Rising Moon. What is it you're saying?"

She moved away slightly and sat on the edge of a fallen log, almost invisible now in the gathering darkness as the round disk of the moon rose above her and was hidden by the tops of the trees. "My womb craves to be round like the moon, but instead it is flat and empty. The Moon-power in me yearns for the seed that would enable it to grow."

The full impact of what Rising Moon meant struck me like lightning strikes and lights up the dark sky. "Rising Moon, you wish me to make love to you and help your womb to be full?"

I could tell by her silence that this was so.

"Why, Rising Moon? I'm the one you stopped from killing the white men because you disapproved of what I was going to do. I'm the one who you have said has evil in his heart for desiring to kill the man who shot Hohots Illpilp. We've been

152

angry with each other, and you've made no secret that you don't like what I do, or the thoughts that are within my mind. Why now do you wish me to be your lover?"

Rising Moon replied softly, "Do you think, Teeto Hoonod, that I stopped you from killing the settlers because I didn't care for you? I could also have tried to stop Wahlitits or the others, but I did not. Why do you suppose I risked your anger at me? Why do you suppose I interest myself in your thoughts? Do I go to others and tell them I think they are heading the way of evil?"

"I suppose that in your way you concern yourself with me because you have love for me. A woman shows love in a way a man does not."

"A woman's love is like the disk of the full moon. Those who are in her circle feel the power of her love, and those who are outside are not her concern. You must surely know, Teeto Hoonod, that you have long been within the circle of my love."

I was shocked by this revelation of her love for me and answered somewhat sternly. "Rising Moon, a woman should not love any man other than her husband. It's forbidden that you should love me. Where is your love for Hohots Illpilp?"

Rising Moon rose and walked about for a moment. "When Hohots Illpilp was alive I loved him first and foremost. My love for him was so strong that it almost filled my Moon-circle. But there was always a place within that circle for you as well. Now that Hohots Illpilp is dead my love for him is no less, but he himself speaks with me and tells me that you are the one whom he wishes to fill my womb."

Now if any other person, except perhaps Kapoochas, had told me the voice of a dead person was speaking to them, I might have thought them possessed by a ghost, but when Rising Moon spoke of Hohots Illpilp making known to her his will in this matter it seemed to me the most natural thing

153

in the world. But I also heard things within myself: the voices of all the ancestors who, for as long as any of the People could remember, told us how things should be done. So I found myself saying, "Rising Moon, now is the time you should be mourning for Hohots Illpilp, not thinking of love-making. Already you are talked about among the People because you don't adopt the proper attitude of mourning. And with Hohots Illpilp hardly on his journey to the spirit world you are talking of making love with another man. You are not like other women, Rising Moon, and I should not be here talking with you this way." I spoke these words to her in a strong way, but I was aware of other feelings too, of admiration that did not yet have words, and I could feel her body drawing my body to her like the bee is drawn to the sweetness and color of the flower.

"It's true that I'm not as other women are. I am myself, Teeto Hoonod, and I follow what the Moon-spirit tells me to do with my life. I have talked long and hard with my Power, and with the spirit of my husband as well, and I am not ashamed that I wish now to have you love me."

The ancestor voices in me were still strong. "For a year a woman mourns as a widow. Then, perhaps, she thinks of another man."

Rising Moon answered, "That is for ordinary times, but these are not ordinary times. We are a wounded people, Teeto Hoonod, and there is death all around us. There is no time now to wait for the passage of time, for the life spirit of the People must be renewed now lest the death spirit de-stroy us all."

"You mean our war with the whites, Rising Moon? Non-sense. We have left Howard far behind. Our war with him is over. Looking Glass leads us to the Buffalo Country, where we will make allies with the Crow and find a new life until Joseph can settle the matter with the government and we can return home."

"That's not so," she retorted. "The dark time is not over. More death is coming. I can see it with the eyes of my soul. Pa'yawit is hovering over the People. He is stalking us like the mountain lion stalks the unwitting deer. And you, Teeto Hoonod, you may be killed too."

"And if I were killed there would be others to fill your womb, Rising Moon," I answered, surprised at myself that I had no arguments against her assertion that the dark time was not over for us.

Rising Moon pursued her point. "But it is not other men that my womb wants; it is you. You are the one who is within the circle. You are the one whom Hohots Illpilp has said should take his place by my side. You spoke of customs among the People. It is also, you know, the custom that when a woman loses her husband her husband's brother shall take his place and give her a child. In this way some of the husband's spirit is reborn into this world."

Her powerful Moon-spirit and her arguments were overcoming my resistance. My doubtful thoughts were still not entirely gone, but my admiration for her was growing. She was bold, far bolder than a woman should be, but it belonged to her. It was her way of being true to her power. I realized with a start that though she made me angry I also loved her. And with this realization I suddenly remembered Wali'ms. "And what of Wali'ms?" I asked. "Wali'ms is my wife. I love her greatly. She would be injured to think that I had made love with another woman, even with you."

Rising Moon was prepared for this. "Among the People it is the custom for a man to take another wife."

"Perhaps," I replied, "but only with the proper passage of time, and only when the first wife agrees, or has become very old, or is unable to give him a child."

Rising Moon's eyes looked straight into my own; they were not downcast as a woman's eyes should be when such things are discussed. "What you say is true, and that is why I

155

ask that you fill my womb not out of love for me but because I ask it of you. I don't ask you to set Wali'ms aside and take me as your woman instead. If I become filled with child I will tell the People it is from Hohots Illpilp. I will carry the burden of the secret myself and not ask you to be my man. I will not interfere with you and Wali'ms and will not try to take you away from her, for I too love Wali'ms, and though I am being unfair to her in coming to you secretly like this, I don't wish to hurt her. The Moon-power has told me that I am to bring a child into this world to replace those who are dying, and this is not only for my happiness but also for the life of the People."

I had no more arguments and we spoke no more words. I drew near to her in the darkness that had cast its protective blanket around us. I drew her with me to the ground and removed her clothes and we lay there together naked. It was cold, but we warmed each other, and her body seemed to fit with mine as though it had been made for that purpose. We made love silently, to the music of the brook beside us, and I was as tender with her as I was with Wali'ms. Only our Mother the Earth beneath us, the moon climbing higher into the night sky above, and the scurrying creatures of the forest were witnesses to our lovemaking that night.

When we finished we dressed silently. I spoke again. "Rising Moon, it's true that the war may not be over for us. The old people tell us that a man shouldn't make love during war, that the woman-power weakens him and exposes him to danger. It's said that the warrior spirit and the love spirit can't mingle together without injuring each other. But I'm glad that I loved you tonight. You called me as a woman calls a man, and I responded."

Rising Moon squeezed my hand gratefully. "You risked yourself for me, Teeto Hoonod. I will say prayers for you to surround you with protection so that when the fighting starts again the bullets cannot find you."

I was startled that she said *"when* the fighting starts again," as though she had a way of knowing this would certainly happen. So we parted. At her request I returned to the camp first, leaving her with her own thoughts. When I found my way back to our fire Wali'ms said, "Teeto Hoonod, you're back. I'm glad. It's dark and I was afraid." I gave no explanation but embraced her silently. Soon she was asleep, but I lay awake for many hours.

CHAPTER ELEVEN

Death Strikes at Dawn

When the sun rose the next day my thoughts went quickly to the evening before, but there was no time to let them linger there. I heard the voice of the crier as he rode through the camp: "Is everyone awake? It's morning, and we are alive, so awake and give thanks! Look around you! See to the horses, lest one was hurt in the night. Give thanks for your children and for your friends, but remember also those who are sad and ill. I wonder who is awake, getting ready for the day's march!"

I stepped outside. Dogs were barking excitedly, horses were neighing at the edge of the encampment where the men would soon catch those they would use today, and the women were preparing our meager breakfast.

The soldiers following us had pack trains to carry their food, but we found food in the forest. We knew each plant and root that was good to eat, and each tree whose bark could be used for food when all else failed.

Wali'ms, who was more skilled than anyone else I knew in gathering the secret sources of food from the forest, soon had our breakfast ready. We ate quickly, while Pahkatos Peopeo played about happily, with the blissful unawareness of evil that children have when their world of father and mother is intact. Wali'ms and I didn't talk much because of the need to hurry, but I found myself more concerned than usual with her welfare and wondered if there was a hurt look in her eyes.

I dismissed these thoughts from my mind for this was to be a big day; today we would cross the Lolo Pass and begin the descent down the other side of the mountains. It wouldn't be long before we would be in Bitterroot Valley, where there was good food and plenty of forage for the horses, and One-arm Howard would surely be left far behind.

I saw Rising Moon that morning as she prepared to move on with the rest of us; we spoke pleasantly as though nothing had happened. However, I was surprised at the way my heart leaped within me when I saw her. My anger was gone and I felt warmth for her, as I did for Wali'ms. The new feeling confused me. If I cared for Wali'ms, how could I also love Rising Moon? It made me feel disloyal to Wali'ms to feel this way, and I tried to make up for it by being extra attentive to her. But as the day progressed I was aware that I had two women in my mind now, not one. Just as my man nature had at one time been divided between the fear spirit and the one-in-me-who-wanted-to-come-out, so now my love nature seemed divided between two women. My soul was not one; I had many part-souls, warring against each other.

Only in my determination to avenge the death of my brother did I feel undivided. The fire of revenge sent other thoughts away, like a campfire at night sends the animals into the black forest. For the sake of the People I hoped the war was over, but for the sake of revenge I hoped we would meet the soldiers once more.

Later that day our long line of men and women, children and old people, horses and dogs made its way down a long narrow canyon until we were less than a sun's march from the Bitterroot Valley. Then we came to a halt. The word spread along the line: Our scouts had found that soldiers

159

had erected a log barricade across a narrow section of the canyon flanked on either side by steep hills and were preventing our further progress. No one knew how many there were, but in addition to the soldiers there was a considerable force of settler volunteers and also a small number of Flathead Indians wearing white turbans.

Along with other men of fighting age I made my way to the front of our long caravan where the chiefs were consulting with each other. The barricade was only a short distance ahead, and Joseph and Looking Glass, with Shuslum Hihhih to interpret, marched out to exchange words with the white war chief while others reconnoitered the area. It seemed that there were not more than thirty soldiers, but a hundred settlers and twenty Flatheads. These last wouldn't fight. They had long been our friends and told our scouts they had come to please the whites, but if there was a battle they would fire harmlessly into the air. The white turbans they wore were to distinguish them from us so they wouldn't be shot by accident.

Joseph and Looking Glass soon returned. The white war chief had said we could not pass unless we gave up our weapons. A council was held to decide what to do. Some of the warriors pointed out that the soldiers weren't many and that the volunteers might break and run if shooting broke out, and they advocated that we charge the barricade and overrun it. But Looking Glass argued that while this was true we would lose many men in such a battle, and Joseph pointed out that if we fought the troops and settlers we would enter the Bitterroot Valley in a state of war. Firmly he reminded us all, "We do not want to turn the white people in this valley against us. We must make them know that our war is not with them but with Howard. We must enter the valley in peace, and no white blood must be shed. We must talk, not fight, and if the soldiers still won't let us pass we must find a way around them."

Thus Looking Glass and Joseph spoke and the rest finally agreed, so instead of fighting we asked for another talk, and Shuslum Hihhih and I went along to make sure the right words were being spoken. There was a small group of us, and for the whites an equal group, composed of both soldiers and settlers, and we met at a point midway between their barricade and our encampment. While we talked, our scouts fanned out onto the hills to the right and left, trying to find a way through the cliffs that we could use in case our parley failed.

Joseph, Looking Glass, and White Bird told the white people we had come in peace. They reminded them that the Nez Perce had traveled through the Bitterroot Valley to the Buffalo Country many times and there had never been any killing, stealing, or destruction, and this was the way we wanted to pass through the valley now. They reassured the soldiers and settlers that our war was not with them, but with Howard and the people in Idaho.

But the white chief would not change his demand that we surrender our arms. When an agreement was not reached he said we should talk again the next day, but it was clear that he only wanted to delay our progress, perhaps so Howard's soldiers would have time to come upon us from the rear. So we pretended to want to talk again, but in fact we had already planned to bypass them.

When the sun rose the next day we were on our way around the log barricade, for our scouts had found a narrow defile in the cliff that led to the top of the ridge. From the valley it seemed impossible that women, children, and horses could make their way up such steep cliffs, but our people went up through the rocks like mountain goats and went safely past the annoyed soldiers without a shot being fired. Looking down we saw the settler volunteers returning to their homes. That must have made the soldiers angry too, but it made sense to us. Many of these men knew us personally. They believed our word could be trusted and were now confident that we did not mean war. Besides, if war had broken out they knew the soldiers couldn't protect them, and they and their families would have to suffer. So it was only natural that they left the soldiers by themselves in a barricade that now served no purpose.

The soldiers were too few to attack us, and we assumed they would return to their post at Missoula, which was at the northern end of the Bitterroot Valley. As for General Howard, we didn't know where he was, but if he was still pursuing us he was far behind. He had already won from us the derisive name "General Day-After-Tomorrow" because he always seemed to be lagging two days behind. Now we practically forgot about him, because there was no sign of his soldiers anywhere.

So it was that we reached the valley safely and were not bothered by the whites, nor did we bother them, and no blood was shed. In fact, when two of the volunteers fell into our hands during our flanking movement they were released without harm and told to go home to their wives and children and spread the word that our intentions were peaceful.

Once we reached the valley we held another council to plan our next move. Looking Glass's plan had called for us to go to the Buffalo Country, but there were three routes we could take, so the chiefs discussed each one. The first would take us past Fort Missoula to the Blackfoot River, then up this river and across the pass to the Buffalo Country. This was the shortest route, but it was rejected because it would take us past several military posts and mining towns where there might be trouble. The second route, somewhat to the south, would take us along the Jefferson River and across Bozeman Pass to the Yellowstone River, which would lead us out to the Buffalo Country. But this would take us past settlements at Fort Ellis and Virginia City, and we were afraid of an attack by overanxious soldiers or settlers.

Then Chief White Bird came up with a novel idea, though it was different than the one Looking Glass had devised. White Bird, the oldest of our chiefs, wise and experienced, showed that he had an original mind. "We move down the Bitterroot Valley, north toward the star-that-stays-always-in-one-place. To avoid the soldiers at Fort Missoula we cross the Bitterroot River by night to the setting-sun side and put the river between us and the soldiers. Then we continue through the land set aside for the Flathead Indians. We send word ahead to Chief Charlo that we only wish to travel peacefully through his country. They will be friendly and will let us pass, but if they do not, we can fight them and they are no match for us. This route will lead us away from the white people and directly toward Canada, where there will be refuge for us, for the Great-grandmother from across the seas does not allow the American soldiers to come into her country."

There was a murmur of approval from many of us, but then Looking Glass spoke. As I have mentioned, Looking Glass was opinionated and didn't like any idea that he had not thought of first. Since he had been named war chief he had grown even more arrogant and sure of himself, so he pressed for his idea. "White Bird's plan is not good. You have made me your head war chief, and I know this country more than anyone else. It is my plan to go to the land of our friends the Crow and become allies with them. Then we will be too strong for anyone to attack. It is true that we must avoid contacts with the white towns and soldiers, so we will go south up the Bitterroot Valley, over the great pass that divides the mountains, and down into Big Hole. This is country we know well. From here we will go into the Yellowstone Country. This is a big swing to the south and will take the soldiers by surprise. Even if they pursue us they will not know where we have gone. We can then make our way down the passes into the Buffalo Country and the land of our friends the Crow. I have been with the Crow often and have led war parties that helped them in their fights with the Sioux. They are grateful to us and will receive us as friends and help us even as we helped them."

So Looking Glass spoke, and Pahkatos Owyeen and Wachumyus and other warriors who had gone on war parties with the Crow spoke in favor of his plan. But others were still doubtful, and Chief White Bird, looking for allies for his plan, asked Joseph what he thought.

"I have no words," Joseph replied. "You know the country; I do not. My plan was never to leave our own land. Now that we are here I have no knowledge of which way we should go."

Looking Glass, annoyed that his plan was not accepted at once, declared roughly, "Did you not make me your leader through this country because I know it and the people, and did you not promise that I should give the orders as I saw fit?"

Then everyone felt they had to agree with Looking Glass. "Yes, Looking Glass, we did make you head man. Go ahead and do what you feel is best, and we will follow."

By the time the birds were singing the next day the camp was awake. In the chill of the early morning hours men, women, and children milled about. Cooking fires were kindled, tipis were taken down, the children played, and the dogs skulked about hoping to find some unguarded food to snatch. After we had eaten, the men gathered the horses and the women packed our belongings. Soon, like a miracle, the camp that had been a scene of such confusion was ready to move. Older horses were used to carry our goods, and the better animals were ridden by the men and women. Bigger children might run along beside, and the little ones were tied firmly in the saddle of a dependable animal. So we moved through the morning hours, with nothing left behind to show we had camped there except the remains of our fires.

Our progress was leisurely. Women stopped to pick berries, and parties of men spread out to hunt in the nearby hills, while other men herded our extra horses. So we moved until the sun stood straight over our heads, and then a new camp was chosen, everything was dismantled, the tipis set up, food prepared, and the rest of the day was spent in talk, play, and sport.

When evening came the mood of the camp changed. We became quiet, and stories were told around the fires that lit up the darkness and kept our hearts and bodies warm against the gathering chill of the night. This was the way we had always traveled, and it was easy for us to believe that there was, as Looking Glass said, no cause for worry any more.

However, as we traveled on, there were some small dark clouds in our blue sky. One morning, after we had journeyed but a few miles up the valley, Wahlitits appeared with a gloomy look. "My heart tells me," he announced to all who would listen, "that Pa'yawit is not far away. I have been shown in my mind a scene of death among the People, and I have also seen myself as one of the dead."

Now Wahlitits was one of our bravest warriors, a man whose spirit was like that of the eagle that soars high above the hills. It was not like him to see things through dark eyes, but most of us paid no attention to him, except Kapoochas, who was greatly disturbed by what he said and tried unsuccessfully to get the chiefs to reconsider their plans.

Two suns later we camped near a tree known for its great medicine power. The tree was an ordinary yellow ponderosa pine, but in some manner a horn from a mountain sheep had become imbedded in it and the tree's inner power came out through this horn. For trees too are a people and have power, and if you know how to listen to them you can learn a great deal. Our hunters and warriors had often received help from this tree, and this is why we believed it to be Tematnepitpa, or holy.

The medicine tree tried to help us, for here we were joined by six tipis of Nez Perce who made their home in the Bitterroot Valley. The most important of these was Wahwookya Wasaaw, Lean Elk, a half-breed Nez Perce. Lean Elk was a small man but wiry and strong, and he proved to be a great warrior and leader for us later on. The tree also warned us of danger by sending a dream to Lone Bird, who rode about the camp crying out for all to hear: "Why do the chiefs have this idea we should travel slowly? Perhaps our enemies are even now coming up. We should keep moving, we should watch out everywhere. Every chief should see to it that his own warriors are ready! My dream says we should be ready for fighting at any time, we should keep going, we should move fast. Death may even now be following on our trail. I cannot hide what I see in my dreams. I must speak what the Great Spirit has revealed to me. Up! We must be gone to the Buffalo Country!"

Kapoochas and some of the others believed that Lone Bird knew these things from the medicine of the tree, so Kapoochas spoke to Looking Glass and Pahkatos Owyeen. "The Great Spirit is trying to warn us. He sent dreams and visions to Wahlitits and Lone Bird, because they are open to them, to tell us that evil is coming. Let's not continue to walk like the tortoise, but run like deer to the safety of the Buffalo Country."

But Looking Glass answered haughtily, "Lone Bird is a crazy man. He imagines things that are not so and is frightened by every falling twig and rustling leaf."

Now it was true that some people thought Lone Bird was crazy, though others, like Kapoochas, believed he was used by the Great Spirit, but Wahlitits had also received an evil omen, so Kapoochas replied, "And Wahlitits? Do you believe he too is a man who is frightened by every falling twig and rustling leaf?"

Looking Glass had no answer for that, so he simply replied stubbornly, "There will be no more war."

Kapoochas took his cause to Joseph, but Joseph replied, "Kapoochas, I have no power now among the chiefs. I don't know the country, nor do they regard me as knowing matters of war. My words go from me and fall to the ground like stones because no one receives them. I too do not believe that we should be here, though whether there will be more war or not I don't know."

So we continued to make leisurely progress up the Bitterroot Valley, eased into a sense of security by the peaceful trade with the settlers, the warmth of the midsummer sun, and the plentiful supply of food.

I too allowed myself to be lulled to sleep. If the chiefs, and especially Looking Glass, who was wise in war and knew this country, said there was no more danger, why should I be troubled? My only regret was that if we fought no more white troops there would be no opportunity for me to avenge the death of Hohots Illpilp. In my mind the face of that white man who shot him was as clear as ever, shining in my memory like the moon shines in the night. I even dreamed of this man, though my dreams were curious, for now he appeared one way and now another, sometimes he seemed to elude me, and sometimes to come up to me and even smile at me graciously and then disappear when I raised my rifle.

Perhaps I was so filled with my own problems that I didn't want to acknowledge that the problems of the People were not yet over, for while I thought often of my enemy I found myself even more preoccupied with thoughts of Wali'ms and Rising Moon. Since our night of love in the Bitterroot Mountains, Rising Moon and I spoke little to each other. I was afraid that if I talked with her Wali'ms would suspect our intimacy, and Rising Moon may have avoided talking with me out of deference to my feelings. But I could tell that she looked at me the way a woman looks at a man she loves, and I felt as tender and protective toward her as though she was my wife. Yet at the same time my love for Wali'ms was not diminished; if anything it grew stronger, and I saw her as more resourceful and beautiful than ever before. I didn't tell her of Rising Moon and myself. I told myself that I didn't want to hurt her, but if I had been completely honest I would have realized that I was trying to spare myself the pain of seeing the hurt in her eyes.

It seemed as though my conflicting feelings appeared in my sleep, for in my dreams there appeared now one woman and now the other, and sometimes both of them appeared together and I would waken troubled. These dreams distressed me so much that I decided to share them with Kapoochas. I was afraid to tell him about Rising Moon and myself, yet as I told him my dreams and he looked at me with those penetrating eyes, I suspected that he knew, so great was his ability to see into the soul of someone else.

Kapoochas listened carefully, his bony, wiry body squatting on the ground as though he wanted to absorb into himself the wisdom of Mother Earth as he listened to the soul talk of a troubled spirit. When I was through he answered, "Within each man is the image of a woman. The Great Spirit didn't make us to be all man or all woman, but gave to all of us both the sun-power and the moon-power. The women in your dreams are the moon side of you, and they appear to you as two because the moon-power within you pulls you in two directions. Until you can understand this you feel divided, as though two spirit beings call to you, each one beckoning you in a different direction."

I didn't like what Kapoochas told me. I wanted a simple answer. I wanted him to solve my problem for me. So I retorted, "Why then do not all men suffer the same way as I do with these things? I don't see Wahlitits or Looking Glass carrying these things in their hearts!"

Kapoochas ignored the ungrateful sharpness in my voice. "They don't carry these things within them because the moon-power within them isn't strong. They are not meant to serve the moon-spirit in life, but the sun-spirit, and that is why they are great warriors. But you are not a warrior. You are a man with a different kind of soul. For the Great Spirit has put a different soul into each one of us. We are not all alike, just as no two trees are alike, even trees of the same type. This is why you cannot compare yourself to Wahlitits and Looking Glass and say, 'Why am I not like them?' The Great Spirit has created you to be yourself. But there are others among us who are like you."

"And who might that be?" I responded.

"Joseph," Kapoochas answered. "Joseph can fight when he must, but his Wy-a-kin is not interested in fighting, only in the care of the women and children and wounded among us. He guards the People like the hohots guards her young. It is dangerous to attack her young when she is there, but she doesn't seek to do battle. This power in Joseph also comes from the moon-spirit, though his moon-spirit is different from yours."

We might have continued talking longer, for I felt my soul ready to pour out to him, but at this point Shuslum Hihhih came up with an urgent message about one of the People who had been wounded at the Battle of the Clearwater and was still suffering and needed the old medicine man's help. Kapoochas had to excuse himself, and I had to put my soul needs behind the needs of the wounded man.

Twelve suns after we had started up the Bitterroot Valley we reached Izhkumzizlakik Pah, the place of the squirrel, an old Nez Perce camping site that had been used since ancient times by our war and hunting parties as they traveled to the

Buffalo Country. It is located in what the white people called the Big Hole Basin. It was an exceptionally favored spot, located in a long valley not far from the mountains that separate the waters that flow to the east from those that flow to the west. The place was too high to be good for farming or pasture and so had been passed up by white settlers and allowed to remain much as it had always been. In the winter great snows gathered here, but now in the height of summer it was a perfect place to camp, warm in the daytime and cool at night.

We made camp by the side of the Big Hole River, a lovely and easily fordable stream that flows in a generally north-easterly direction, wandering here and there, this way and that way, in the flat bottomlands of the valley. Our camp was in a flower-strewn meadow along the east bank of the river. Joseph had us lay out the tipis in the shape of a V with the point of the V up the stream, and Wali'ms and I placed our tipi in the middle. For the first time in a long while we made an elaborate camp: We planned to stay here for some time so we could gather food and the women could cut new poles for tipis, because in the Buffalo Country there were no trees.

To the east of the camp was a broad open area, rising gradually as far as the eye could see, sprinkled with flowers of every imaginable color and lush with grass, but with no trees or rocks to provide cover. Westward, across the river, was a swampy area, with many shallow sloughs made by the river during its flood season, and heavily overgrown with dense stands of willows and bushes. This low area extended some two or three hundred yards until it reached the base of a hill. Part of this hill was open, like the country to the east of us, and was covered with good grass for the horses, but most of it was heavily forested. Our horses were let out to pasture in this open area on the hillside and in the meadowlands to the east of the camp.

The day after we made camp was a beautiful summer day. A mood of tranquillity and peace filled us as the children played, the horses foraged, the men hunted and fished, and the women talked together and gathered food. It's true that some of our women noticed a small party of white people looking down on our camp from the hillside, but we paid no attention to this for we were aware that we had been under surveillance all the time we had proceeded, tortoise fashion, up the Bitterroot Valley. Since we regarded ourselves at peace now, no move was made to intercept or injure these people, who, no doubt, didn't realize they had been seen.

Yet not all of us were at ease. Some of the more experienced warriors were distressed because we didn't know the whereabouts of Howard's troops and because of the bad dreams reported by Lone Bird and Wahlitits. So a council was called by Pahkatos Owyeen and Wachumyus. The chiefs and warriors attended, and I too listened to the discussion, along with Kapoochas. Pahkatos Owyeen and Wachumyus spoke first and expressed their anxiety, while Looking Glass, Lean Elk, Too-hool-hool-Sote, Joseph, and White Bird listened. The two famous warriors unfolded their plan: They would send a few select men back over the trail as scouts; if soldiers were seen approaching they could send some of their number back to warn us while the others remained to watch the approaching troopers. It seemed a good plan, and two of the young warriors, Sarpsis Illpilp and Seeyakoon Illpilp, volunteered to go. However, this plan would call for swift horses, and these warriors were too young to have such mounts, not having accumulated much wealth. So while Pahkatos Owyeen and Wachumyus were speaking, the young warriors sent their wives to ask a wealthy old man, Semu, to lend them two of his many swift ponies.

While the women went for the horses the plan was debated in the council, and it soon became clear that Looking

Glass was opposed to the idea. "The war is behind us," he said, repeating the opinion he had expressed before. "Howard is far away. The white people we have passed have been friendly and have traded with us. We are at peace with them, and there are no soldiers near, so we have no cause for fear. If we act as though we don't trust them, the white people won't trust us. We may provoke them into being hostile if we don't make clear to them our peaceful intentions. So we must not send scouts to the rear as though we were looking for trouble."

Meanwhile the women returned to their men and reported that Semu refused to let them use his horses. Probably Looking Glass had sent word privately to Semu telling him not to lend them. That is why the two young warriors didn't go back as scouts. If they had had good horses they probably would have gone scouting in spite of what Looking Glass said.

It was such a peaceful spot there by the Big Hole River that it was hard not to believe that Looking Glass was correct. Besides, he was head war chief, and the warriors and chiefs soon found themselves agreeing with him. Kapoochas did not, but he had already spoken his mind to Looking Glass and, not being a warrior himself, he had no influence in the council. So after a brief debate it was agreed that we would follow the advice of Looking Glass. Only the great warriors Pahkatos Owyeen and Wachumyus and the young men who had volunteered to scout were adamant in their disagreement. Pahkatos Owyeen ended the council with these words: "All right, Looking Glass. You are one of the chiefs! I have no wife, no children to be placed fronting the danger that I feel is coming to us. Whatever the gains, whatever the loss, it is yours."

And that is how it happened that when the camp fell asleep after a late evening of merrymaking, no scouts had been sent back on the trail, no sentries had been posted, and none of the boys or old men had been assigned to guard our herd of ponies. And I too, after spending the evening with Kapoochas and some others and making sure Rising Moon had what supplies she needed, joined my warm and tender wife, saw that my little girl was securely asleep, and crawled under the comfort of the buffalo robes that would keep us warm during the chill mountain night. Soon I was fast asleep, anxious about my own troubles, but with no worries about the People. For was not Looking Glass a great chief? And didn't he know the things of war?

Many hours later I was awakened by the sound of a single gunshot, followed almost immediately by the crashing fire of many rifles. Half asleep, but guided by the nape of the neck with its instinctive power, I leaped to my feet, then fell to the ground again as bullets tore through our fragile tipi. Wali'ms was struggling to her feet, but I grabbed her and pulled her down. "Keep down, Wali'ms," I cried. "Hug the ground. Put your arms around the earth, and keep Pahkatos Peopeo underneath you." I waited for what seemed like an eternity, though it could have been only a short time, for the rain of bullets to cease. Finally they stopped for a moment, and I crawled across the floor of our tipi toward my rifle. Seizing it and also the revolver I had taken from the soldier who killed Hohots Illpilp, I made for the tipi door. I was aware for a moment of the fear spirit within me holding me back, but the one who-wanted-to-come out was stronger now and I pushed through the flap of the tipi, calling to Wali'ms as I went, "Stay low. I will come back!" I had no idea how long it would be before I did so, nor what I would find when I did.

The first faint rays from the dawn were finding their way to the camp, and in this ghostly light I saw a lurid scene. All was confusion as women, children, and braves stumbled out of their tipis and into a rain of bullets, while, to the west, just across the river and advancing through the willows, barely

173

visible in the early morning light, soldiers were approaching, firing wildly as they came, looking like so many evil spirits.

Some people were dropping, hit by the bullets, and others ran for the river, whose banks and willow trees could provide some shelter from the bullets that were everywhere, like flies. The sound of exploding rifles was coming closer, and I too now plunged toward the river determined to put myself between the approaching enemy and the camp. Suddenly I became aware of someone beside me. It was Rising Moon, and in her hand I saw a belt of bullets. "Go back, Rising Moon," I shouted. "You'll get hit." But she shouted back, "I'll fight by your side, Teeto Hoonod." There was no time to argue, for soldiers were almost upon us. Together we ran and plunged like deer into the thicket of willows. At that very moment a soldier suddenly appeared in front of me. I thought, It is my enemy! But then I saw that it was not, and had no more time to think as the soldier raised his gun, but he was too late; my rifle exploded in his face and I could see that my bullet had shattered his head. The soldier fell to the ground, killed instantly. I had slain my first man, and I felt both a sickness come over me and a thrill, as though it came from some ancestor spirit.

Looking to my left, upstream, I could see that soldiers had now overrun the upper part of the camp. The firing there was intense and the warriors couldn't put up an effective resistance. Looking to my right, downstream, I saw that the soldiers had not yet reached the lower part of the camp and the warriors there, after their first surprise and panic, had returned to their tipis, grabbed their weapons, and were beginning to fight back. I could also spot a small group of warriors moving farther down the stream to try to outflank the approaching line of soldiers. In the center, where I was crouched in the willow trees, trying to get a soldier within the gunsight of my rifle, I saw that we were faring badly. Some of the soldiers had overrun my position and were within the camp, and men, women, and children, all alike, were being killed by them.

I saw one woman trying to flee with a baby in her arms, and a soldier ran up to her and fired at her point-blank. The bullet hit the child and what had been a little baby was now only blood and mangled flesh, and then I saw that the bullet had torn through the child into the mother and she fell to the ground. With a sickening realization I knew this was Toma Alwawinmi, Joseph's wife, and the baby daughter born to him only two moons ago at Tepahlewam. Then I saw soldiers running into tipis where families had been sleeping and I heard shots and cries. All were being killed! Children were as warriors to the soldiers! One woman thrust her child pleadingly toward the arms of a soldier, but he raised his rifle and with the butt end of it smashed in the child's head. I felt red-hot fury grow in me. My fear was gone. I didn't care if I died or not. The strength of the wolverine was in me and I fired at that soldier, but the bullet missed and he went on with his bloodthirsty rampage.

Soon another soldier loomed up just as a woman emerged from the cover of her tipi. She was Wetwhowees, a strong, sturdy woman. I saw the soldier fix his bayonet and charge at her, but she stepped aside, seized the gun, and twisted it so that he fell to the ground. The soldier sprang up and began to run, but Wetwhowees fired at him and the soldier dropped dead in his tracks.

But other women were not able to defend themselves as well as Wetwhowees. To my horror I saw a soldier and a woman meet almost face to face. I raised my rifle to shoot the soldier, but was too late, and he shot her through the side. I heard Rising Moon beside me gasp, "Wetatonmi is shot!" Wetatonmi was "Fair Land," the wife of Ollokot, and the mother of an infant son. I learned later that she was not killed immediately but lay among the wounded and was found and cared for by Joseph. The child was not injured. I knew if Ollokot, who was fighting in another part of the battle, knew his wife was hurt, he might lose heart for the fight, but if he learned about it he didn't let it destroy his fighting spirit, for he remained in the battle until the end.

Yet not all soldiers wanted to kill. I saw one soldier raise his gun at a woman, take careful aim, and then lower his gun and watch silently as she ran away. I saw another woman lose hold of her small child and drop him as a soldier approached. The soldier picked up the child and handed it back to her and didn't harm either of them. I saw a man and his wife run with their five-year-old child until both were cut down by rifle fire, but when another woman picked up the boy these same soldiers let her go.

Then I saw Wahlitits. He who had started the war was now in the middle of the raging battle! He ran for cover behind a log, his wife with him. Soldiers pursued them and Wahlitits dropped to one knee and fired and a soldier fell. But there were too many for him. A storm of bullets poured into him and the great warrior fell at last. Then his wife, wounded herself, seized her husband's rifle and sent a bullet crashing into the head of the nearest soldier before she too was riddled by enemy fire and joined her husband in death.

All this time that I watched and fired at the enemy my heart was aflame with rage, but even then an ice-cold voice spoke within me: Your enemy, is he here? I looked, but I couldn't see him.

The soldiers who had taken the upper end of the camp looted the tipis and tried to burn them but had difficulty because they were wet with dew. So they gave up trying to destroy the camp and began moving toward us in the center. There were many of them and few of us, so Rising Moon and I crawled through the underbrush on the river bottom toward the lower end of the camp, where some of the warriors had been trying to make a stand. Soon we were among them. Not far off to my right I could see Pahkatos Owyeen,

Wachumyus, and Ollokot. There were still many people panicking, and warriors not knowing what to do, but now voices began to be heard amid the din of the battle. "Why are we retreating?" I heard a strong voice call out. "Since the world began men have fought bravely for their families. Are we going to run away and let the white soldiers kill our women and children while we watch? It's better to stay here and die fighting. This is a good day to die. Now is the time to fight!" It was Chief White Bird calling out. He had lived seventy winters, but now in the midst of battle his spirit was as defiant as that of a young man. I felt strengthened by the spirit of this fine old man. I called upon my Wy-a-kin for help and joined Pahkatos Owyeen and Ollokot and the others, who were now making their way out of the camp toward the slightly higher ground across the river. From here we commanded a view of the whole campsite and could fire down upon the soldiers from their flank and rear. But I was now far away from the tipi where I had left Wali'ms, and I could see that the soldiers had overrun that part of the camp.

The soldiers evidently had crept up on us during the darkness and hidden all night in the willows not more than a hundred yards away. No one noticed them because we had posted no guards. Their plan was to stalk the camp with the first ray of light and then charge and fire into it. Their plan worked almost perfectly, but two important things had gone wrong.

The first mistake was made by the volunteers who were with the soldiers. It seems that half-blind old Natalekin had gone out early in the morning to see to the horses and had stumbled into the path of the soldiers. Some of the volunteers fired and killed the old man, but that shot started the soldiers firing too soon.

The second mistake was made by the soldiers who overran the upper part of the camp and tried to burn the tipis, but because the tipis were hard to burn the soldiers were delayed and didn't charge the rest of the camp at once as they should have. This gave us a chance to make a stand at the lower end of the camp, and now that our warriors had recovered from the shock we were taking good advantage of the extra time the soldiers gave us. Here and there our warriors found their way to well-chosen spots; some, like us, reached the high ground that overlooked the camp, and others were in well-concealed positions among the willows in the river bottom. Now it was the soldiers who were exposed to our fire, for they were in the camp and out in the open while we had found cover.

Meanwhile most of the women and children who had not been killed or wounded in the soldiers' charge had begun to find their way to safety. I saw that Joseph was gathering them in the open area to the east of the camp, and he had also sent the boys and older men to round up the horses and bring them where he was. I felt sure that Joseph didn't know yet what had happened to his wife and child, but even if he had known he would have continued to gather together the horses, women, and children and lead them to safety.

The tide of battle began to turn. We had the soldiers in a cross fire, and it was now the soldiers who were dropping to the ground from our bullets. Smoke filled the camp as our bullets whizzed and whined among the troopers. They were frightened, and their officers couldn't rally them, for whenever our sharpshooters spotted an officer they made a special effort to kill him. We had already killed the main officer who was supposed to have led the charge on the lower end of the camp, and that is one reason why the soldiers and volunteers who charged there failed in their attempt.

Then I saw a white war chief mounted on a great gray horse, and I could see that he was ordering his men to fall back through the willows, in the direction from which they had come, toward the pine-covered hills. One of our men took careful aim at this war chief, and the bullet smashed his leg and killed his horse, but the officer got to his feet, wounded but not killed. Afterward I learned that this man was Colonel Gibbon; the force we were fighting was his and not that of One-arm Howard, and that was why my enemy was not among these soldiers.

The fight became more organized. Our women and children and horses were safely away; our warriors had their places, and each one knew instinctively where to go to fight most effectively. We had the upper hand, and killing the soldiers was like swatting mosquitoes. Soon they retreated from the camp and moved back into the wooded hills; we followed them so closely they were forced to hole up on a low knoll among the trees and make shelters from fallen logs and rocks. We surrounded them, crept up close, and poured fire into the circle they defended. Whenever a soldier showed his head shots rang out, and so accurate were our marksmen that almost always the man was hit. I too shot, with Rising Moon, slender and strong as a young warrior, by my side. Whether I killed any of the soldiers or not I don't know, but others were better shots than I. One of our men climbed a tree above the soldiers' position, and from this perch he killed several of them before they spotted him and brought him down. Another of our warriors crept up behind a dead log within short range of the enemy and fired into their hastily dug entrenchment, killing four soldiers before he too was killed.

We also suffered. I saw Pahkatos Owyeen silently approach the enemy lines. He had a strange look on his face as he came near the entrenched soldiers, and he was singing as he came. Suddenly I realized with horror that Pahkatos Owyeen was going to throw himself single-handed upon the enemy! Other Indians saw this too and hands reached out to hold him back, but they were too late. Pahkatos Owyeen rushed upon the soldiers, and their fire felled him.

Like a tree struck by lightning, the mighty warrior fell to the ground and a groan went up from among us. For was not Pahkatos Owyeen the greatest of our fighters?

Later I remembered that he was a war mate with Wachumyus, and they had pledged to fight and die together. Wachumyus had been killed early in the battle. He had always said his Wy-a-kin was so strong that no bullets could touch him once the sun rose, but he was struck and killed in the beginning of the fight before the sun had made its way over the hills. When Pahkatos Owyeen saw this he grieved. "My brother has died," he wept, "and I will follow him into death." That is why he went deliberately toward the enemy, singing his death song as he walked into their fire.

So many of our best warriors were killed: Pahkatos Owyeen, Wachumyus, Wahlitits, and Sarpsis Illpilp all died in the fighting that day. Most of those who had started the war by their raid on the Salmon River were now dead.

But the soldiers suffered more. As the afternoon wore on we hemmed them in and kept them from water, and because they now seldom fired back we knew their ammunition was running out. We could hear their wounded crying, and the sound was so piteous that we even began to feel sorry for them, those same men who had tried to kill us and our women and children.

Then Too-hool-hool-Sote, who along with Ollokot had been our main fighting chief during this part of the battle, thought of a plan. The wind was blowing and we lit a fire in the grass, hoping the wind would drive the fire to the soldiers and force them out into the open where they could be shot more easily. We watched full of bloodthirsty hope as the flames neared the hapless soldiers, but at the last moment, when the fire was within a few paces of them, the wind turned back upon it and the fire died out. That was when we gave up trying to destroy them all for we knew then that their Wy-a-kin was too strong; that was why the wind had shifted in their favor. It is true that we could have rushed upon them and killed them all, but as Yellow Wolf, nephew to Joseph, reminded us, "If we kill all of them there will be a thousand more to take their place, but if we lose one warrior there will be no one to take his rifle." So we didn't rush upon them, but kept them penned up with our sharpshooting.

There was only one other time when we feared the soldiers might win the battle. Late in the afternoon we heard the great booming noise made by the soldiers' big thunder weapon. It fired twice, at some distance from us, and then there was silence. Huddled behind our rocks and trees we feared other soldiers were bringing the howitzer into the battle and might find a place from which they could fire down upon us, but as we waited there was only silence; we heard no more from the big gun.

Later I found out that some of our warriors, led by Peopeo Tholekt from Looking Glass's band, had scouted up the mountain trail down which the troopers had originally come and found the cannon as it was being marched toward us by a guard of six soldiers. The sounds we heard were made when the soldiers turned the cannon on Peopeo Tholekt and his men, but the Nez Perce had not been injured and had charged the soldiers successfully, killing one, driving the others away, and capturing the howitzer. Peopeo Tholekt had then taken it apart, rolled it down the mountain, and buried the pieces. Peopeo Tholekt also captured from the cannon soldiers a great many rounds of ammunition for our rifles. This additional ammunition helped us greatly in our later fights.

I remained with the warriors guarding the besieged soldiers until it was afternoon. Then I said to Rising Moon, "We are no longer needed here. Let's return to the camp and find Wali'ms and Pahkatos Peopeo and make sure they are safe." In the heat of the battle, I had been so filled with the fighting spirit I had not had time to think of Wali'ms and our daughter, but now, as the two of us made our way back to camp, I was filled with dread.

When I saw the camp I knew why. Everything was destroyed. Tipis were smashed and their contents strewn about on the ground as though a giant hand had reached down from the sky maliciously to spread destruction. Smoke rose aimlessly into the sad late-afternoon sky from a score of smoldering fires started by the soldiers. The corpses of horses and dogs that had had the misfortune to get in the way of the battle were strewn about the camp helter-skelter, and dark and ominous splotches of blood were here and there as though a dreadful monster had devoured human beings and spat out their life substance on the ground. Scattered among the destruction were the bodies of dead soldiers—many of them. Once our warriors had recovered from the shock of the surprise attack, they had done their job well and taken a dreadful toll from the enemy.

But where were the People? Only a few could be seen, stumbling about in the debris of the camp. Joseph had started them on their march to the south, and those who remained looked at me silently with dull, grief-stricken eyes. These were women and a few men, rambling through the camp looking for the scattered remains of household utensils they would need on the journey, or plunging about among the bushes and trees searching for a missing friend or relative. Here and there I heard the *clink, clink, clink* of tools digging in the soil, and I knew that a Nez Perce was digging a grave for the body of a friend or relative who had at last been found.

I searched until I found the tipi Wali'ms and I had shared the night before, but the tipi was now only a smoking ruin, and there was no sign of my family. Desperate, I searched the camp from south to north, working my way carefully through every ruin. At last I came upon a small group of people and there, moving among the wounded like the true medicine man he was, was old Kapoochas!

Like the sun breaks through dark clouds and suddenly sends rays of light and warmth down on the weary earth, so my heart was suddenly filled with light when I saw my old friend and healer. But then the dark clouds closed over the sunlight of my soul quickly and I felt a dark chill of fear, for Kapoochas's right arm was hanging uselessly from his side, and blood was still trickling from a wound in his skull. But Kapoochas, wounded himself, would not rest until he cared for the others.

Rising Moon and I hurried up, and when he saw us a smile lighted his face and he reached out to us with his one good arm. "Kapoochas," I cried out in a voice mingled with joy and grief, "you're alive—but you're hurt." I embraced him, paying no heed to the sticky red blood smeared on the old man's body.

Kapoochas tried to sound casual. "It's nothing," he said, as he looked me over with eyes weary with grief and exhaustion. "I will soon be well, for I see now that you are well, and Rising Moon is well, and this makes my heart strong and calls my spirit back into me."

Kapoochas and Rising Moon and I held each other closely, and the old man let himself go and allowed himself to be supported in my arms. Yet he remained strangely silent, as though he guarded some terrible secret.

At last I asked, "Wali'ms and Pahkatos Peopeo: have you seen them?" The old man said nothing but turned his gaze toward a place on the ground a little distance away. I followed his eyes and there, almost hidden in the grass, I saw a woman stretched out on the ground.

Fear-stricken I begged of Kapoochas, "Is she dead? Tell me she's not dead!"

Kapoochas replied, "She's not dead, but she barely clings

to life. Go to her. I think she has refused to die because she had to live to see that you are all right."

In a moment I was at her side, and as my body pressed upon hers, her eyes opened ever so slightly. Relief flooded over me like floods from the mountain storms in summer that come racing down the dry creek beds. Soon Rising Moon was at my side, and her hands were running tenderly, expertly over Wali'ms's body. "Here," she said. "Here is the wound, in her side."

Wali'ms smiled faintly and said in a thin voice, "It doesn't matter. Now that you both are here and well I will become strong again." But as I looked at the great gaping hole in her side where a bullet had gone through her body and left masses of torn and bleeding flesh I could not share her confidence.

Kapoochas, I could see, had done what could be done for the wound. "What happened, Wali'ms," I asked, "and where is Pahkatos Peopeo?" I asked this question fearfully, for there was no sign of our little girl.

Wali'ms's face contorted with pain, and Kapoochas started to gesture that she shouldn't speak, but she waved him away weakly but firmly with her hand. "When the soldiers came I remained in the tipi as long as I could, hoping to hide myself and Pahkatos Peopeo from them. When I saw they were in the camp, tearing open the tipis and shooting everyone, I took her in my arms and rushed to the river. Smoke was everywhere and I could hardly see in the dim light. Suddenly a soldier rose up before me. I turned away from him and put my body between him and our child. The soldier fired. As you can see, the bullet went through my side, but it also went through Pahkatos Peopeo. Even now she is on her way to the Great Spirit."

Her talk had exhausted her, and her eyes closed. I thought perhaps she was now dead, but Kapoochas told me, "It took all her strength to tell you the story. After she was shot she lost consciousness. The soldiers were everywhere. When I awoke at the sound of the firing I knew immediately what was happening, and I fled to the bushes in the river and hid there to be safe. I am old and have no weapon, and there was nothing I could do in defense of the People. But as soon as the soldiers were driven from the camp I came out of hiding to try to help the wounded. Joseph was soon with me, organizing the old men and women and children and wounded and getting them on the march. There were so many wounded! We made travois for them as quickly as we could to get them on the way to safety, for we feared other soldiers might soon be upon us. Joseph started the long column on its way, but he asked me to remain here with the few others who were still looking, and to care for any more of the wounded who might be found. It was while I was doing this that I came upon a wounded soldier. I went to do for him what I could, for though he was an enemy he now was only a man in need, but he thought I intended to harm him for he fired his revolver at me and that is how I got this wound in my arm."

Kapoochas told all of this simply, as though this act of heroism was his daily routine, but when he got to the part about his wound his voice faltered; he had been hurt badly. He continued, "When the man shot his revolver he also sealed his own death, because one of our warriors, returned from the battle, came racing over, and a shot from his rifle quickly dispatched the soldier. Now I had to care for my own wound, and then I continued to see if I could help the others. For a long time we didn't find Wali'ms. Then, as we were looking through the bushes along the river for dead bodies or survivors, we found her, lying wounded on the ground, with your little daughter dead beside her. Already a grave has been dug for her, and she lies in the ground. We brought Wali'ms here. I have done what I can for her. The wound is a bad one, and there has been much loss of blood."

185

We remained in the camp until we were sure there were no more wounded people. Then, as the sun began to set behind the hills, we went with the others who had remained behind to join Joseph. Wali'ms had to be carried on a travois. Kapoochas was exhausted from his wound and his efforts and rode precariously on his horse. I remained behind a little longer because I had one more task to do. Following Kapoochas's directions, I found the place where my little girl was buried. I took out my knife and dug into the shallow grave and found her body. I held the tiny body against my own and let my tears pour shamelessly down my face. Then, using the bayonet from a dead soldier's rifle, I dug a new grave. I dug it away from the river, so the spring floods wouldn't wash it away, and deep, very deep, and then I carefully laid the body of my only child within it. I filled it with stones and dirt and then, using a branch from a tree, erased any signs that a grave had been dug there. I noted the spot carefully in my mind. Should I ever return, I would visit the place where the world had seen the last of Pahkatos Peopeo. Finally I left her, with one last prayer in which I asked the Great Spirit to keep her soul near the earth so it could slip into the womb of another woman soon and be reborn without having to make the long journey back to the spirit world, for it was important that the soul of my child have her chance to live in this world. Then, hurrying, I caught up with the others. It wasn't hard to catch up with them because they moved so slowly.

Later I learned what happened when One-arm Howard arrived on the battle scene. Yes, Joseph was right. Howard was not far behind the troops who had attacked us, and soon he was camped near the place of the battle and he and his soldiers were inspecting the campsite, burying their dead, and examining the debris. Howard had a number of Bannock scouts with him, and he allowed these ferocious Indians to dig up the bodies of our dead and to scalp and mutilate them, while the soldiers stood by and watched. We couldn't understand why this was allowed. Wasn't it enough for Howard that Gibbon and his troops so treacherously attacked us? Was he so rapacious that he couldn't be content until the Bannocks defiled the dead bodies, so that our dead would have to enter the spirit world maimed?

At least they would not find the body of my little girl. I had hidden it well.

CHAPTER TWELVE

Kapoochas

The night after the battle, the People camped at a place called Takseen, but Kapoochas, Wali'ms, Rising Moon, and I didn't reach them until the end of the second day. When we made our way wearily into the camp we found a desolate scene.

One of the old stories my mother used to tell is about a youth who shot a maiden he loved with one of his arrows and killed her. Filled with remorse he tried to hide the hated arrow, but it followed him wherever he went. Desperate, the youth seized the arrow and shot it into a willow tree—and with that the twigs of the willow turned red with the maiden's blood, and the branches bowed down in grief.

Now, like the willow tree that weeps perpetually, so the People were bowed down with grief. Of the seven hundred persons who had camped that dreadful night by Big Hole at least ninety were casualties, and there was scarcely a person among us who didn't have a friend or relative who was killed or wounded. Most of the victims were our old people, women, and children, but we also lost fifteen of our best fighting men.

Not long after we arrived at Takseen, Ollokot and the others who had stayed behind to keep up the siege joined us. All night they had kept the soldiers bottled up; then in the morning they fired two final volleys in defiance and rode off on the horses that Joseph left behind for them. The return of Ollokot and his men lifted our spirits momentarily and reminded us that we had won the battle. In spite of the surprise attack we had repulsed them and killed or wounded over half the soldiers. The survivors were saved from destruction only by the wind that turned back the fire we set. Even then we could have starved them out or made them use up their ammunition if Howard's troops hadn't come to their relief.

When Joseph heard that Kapoochas and I had come into the camp, he came to visit us. "Teeto Hoonod," he greeted me warmly, "it is well. You are alive. You are greatly needed."

I was touched by Joseph's recognition of me and his concern. I felt proud that Joseph, who in my mind was, along with Kapoochas, the holiest man in our nation, would say that I was needed. But I felt awkward at being in his presence for such praise and could only ask lamely why, if we had defeated the soldiers, we were retreating.

Joseph smiled at the foolishness of my question. "We whipped those soldiers, but others will follow. Howard can't be far behind. We must get the women and children and wounded as far away as possible. This will be difficult, because we must travel so slowly."

Joseph was beautiful, almost like a woman, when he smiled. He used to smile often, but now he only smiled a little, and when he did it was just a brief smile, lighting up his face like the world is lit up when the sun breaks through on a cloudy day only to vanish again quickly. He was suffering dreadfully because of the death of his wife and child, but when he saw Kapoochas and Wali'ms he wept for them too. Suffering seemed to ooze through Joseph. He never tried to avoid it, but carried it as though he were carrying the burden of all his people, for to Joseph we were all his family and he cared for us all equally.

189

I had many things to do to be ready for the march, but when I could I visited Wali'ms. She looked at me with her great black eyes, smiled weakly, reached out her hand to mine, and spoke words of endearment to me in her native Shoshone. And I, to show I was one with her, answered her in her own language. When I told her I had reburied our daughter she listened carefully and I saw she was comforted, but I feared she felt the loss so much that her spirit was tempted to leave her body and go in search of our child's spirit in the next world.

As for Kapoochas, he seemed to be weaker; he had spent too much of his vital energy in caring for the wounded and now had little left for himself.

The next several days we traveled as rapidly as we could, for we feared pursuit by Howard and his soldiers, as well as by the remnants of Gibbon's troops, but it was difficult with the wounded. The journey was incredibly hard for them, and each day we buried several who died along the trail, hiding their graves so the Bannock Indians could not find them. Of course some of the wounded began to recover, for the life power renews itself whenever it has a chance, but not Kapoochas; his age was against him, and though I observed him carefully each day I didn't see that his power was coming back.

Joseph and Lean Elk were now our leaders, Joseph in charge of the march and Lean Elk our war leader, for Looking Glass was disgraced because he had not protected us at Big Hole, and even though he had fought bravely he was still held responsible for our great losses. No one spoke to him directly about this. It wasn't necessary, for he knew that he had misled us, and he accepted, at least for the moment, the new leadership offered by Lean Elk, even though Lean Elk was a half-breed, and not a full-blooded Nez Perce like himself.

Lean Elk was small in body, but he was large in spirit and

190

a good war leader. He knew the country well, and as long as he led us no calamity came upon us. It was he who now chose our route: through the open country beyond the Big Hole, over the wide Bannock Pass, down the other side of the mountains through the Lemhi Valley and toward Targhee Pass many miles away. The country was open, the mountains were high but not steep or heavily wooded, and except for the burden of the wounded our progress would have been rapid.

On the far side of Targhee Pass (which was named after a Shoshone chief, for this was Shoshone land) was the Yellowstone Country. For as long as anyone could remember this extraordinary high country of mountains and plains, rivers and gorges, had been a no man's-land among the Indian nations. Except for a small, peaceful, horseless Indian people who lived here all year long, surviving by trapping the mountain sheep, no Indian nation claimed these hunting grounds, though in the summer this land might be visited by many groups—Blackfoot, Crow, Shoshone, or Sioux—hunting moose and elk. Because it was so empty we hoped that even as large a group as ours could conceal its movements there and be free from prying eyes.

Beyond the Yellowstone land lay the open Buffalo Country. Here were the Crow, whom Looking Glass said would be our friends, and to the north lay Canada. Grandmother's Country, where Sitting Bull had taken refuge and which was our final destination.

So we traveled, but the spirit among us was different as we passed through this country from what it was when we traveled through the Bitterroot Valley. Then we had assumed that the white people were our friends, and so no one was molested. Now we believed that all white people were enemies and none of them could be trusted. For had not many of the settlers with whom we had made peace in the Bitterroot Valley, whom we had treated fairly when we

191

could have destroyed them, joined with Gibbon's soldiers to kill our women and children? Now our warriors took what we needed from the white settlers whom we passed.

It was Lean Elk's plan to strip the country of everything that would be useful to a pursuing military force, so we took not only food and ammunition but also horses from the ranches we passed. We didn't need the horses ourselves because we had escaped from Big Hole with our herd of ponies intact, but we took them so Howard's horse soldiers couldn't use them. Our herd of remount ponies was our one advantage over Howard's pursuing troops. We were burdened with the sick and wounded and he was able to move freely with only grown and healthy men, but he lacked extra horses. When his soldiers' horses tired, and when the mules that pulled his pack trains weakened, he had to slow down, but when our horses tired we simply rode fresh ones.

Sometimes when our warriors came for the white settlers' horses they were foolish enough to resist, and then our warriors, maddened by their grief and anger, were only too ready to kill them. I took no part in these slaughters but there were several; fifteen white men must have died as we traveled through that land. Yet even then we didn't attack the women and children, nor did we scalp or mutilate the dead bodies. As Joseph said to our warriors when they went on their raids, "Kill only the men if you must. To harm the women and children or scalp the dead is not the Nez Perce way." And the angriest brave among us respected his words.

We traveled for nine suns from the battle at the Big Hole, and each day Kapoochas grew weaker and Wali'ms lingered between life and death so no one could tell which spirit would claim her body. Rising Moon and I cared for her as tenderly as we could. She wanted very little, but we often brought her water to drink for her thirst was terrible because of the summer heat and the fire from her wound. During these days our souls became closer than ever before. Rising

192

Moon could see this, and she respected and honored it and joined with me sometimes in my prayer songs to the Great Spirit for Wali'ms's healing.

In spite of Lean Elk's plan to slow the soldiers down by keeping them from getting fresh horses, our scouts, who watched the movements of Howard's pursuing army closely, brought word that he was gaining on us every day. At the end of the tenth day's march from Big Hole we camped at a place called Camas Meadow, in open country about three suns' travel from Targhee Pass. The next day we moved to another campsite some miles beyond Camas Meadow. But that evening our scouts brought word that Howard was now so close to us that he had pitched his camp at the very place at Camas Meadow where we were the night before. This meant he was gaining on us rapidly.

A council was held to decide what to do. If we abandoned the oldest people and the wounded we could escape, but this idea was unthinkable and was discarded by the chiefs at once. A second plan was to send the families and wounded on ahead, while the warriors stayed behind to fight a battle with the soldiers, but this meant the women and children would march without protection, and even if we won the battle there would be more casualties, and we couldn't spare a single man after our great losses at Big Hole. Then one of our dreamers, a man called Black Hair, sent word that he wanted to speak to the chiefs. He was wounded and couldn't come by his own strength, so some of the warriors carried him to the council. While all listened carefully he told how the night before, as he slept at Camas Meadow, on the very ground where Howard was now camped, he had a dream, and in this dream he saw himself and other warriors escaping with Howard's horses.

That is how the chiefs decided on a daring plan: to take a select group of warriors, steal up to Howard's camp under cover of night, and make off with his horses. On foot the

193

soldiers would not be able to keep up with us, and we could widen the gap between us and Howard's army. It was a desperate idea, filled with many chances for failure, but encouraged by Black Hair's dream the chiefs were determined to make the attempt.

Volunteers were asked to make up this war party. Twenty-eight warriors were selected and I was one of them, for I was recognized now as a warrior. I went on this raid because I hoped to avenge the death of Pahkatos Peopeo and the wounding of Wali'ms, and because I hoped for a chance to kill the soldier who killed my brother. The fear spirit that had been with me for many years was gone. My desire for revenge was so strong there was no room for fear, and my grief so great that if death threatened I no longer wanted to cling to life.

When the night was black we rode out from the camp in a long file. We traveled slowly so we would make little noise, and Ollokot and Too-hool-hool-Sote, who were our main leaders on this raid, ordered, "No talking, no smoking, no lights." For a long time we rode in silence until we were near the soldiers' camp and could hear the sounds of their horses not far away. Now the chiefs debated in whispers what would be best: Should we go ahead on horseback, or dismount and proceed on foot? Some argued that we would do better on foot, leaving our horses behind in charge of a few warriors, but Indians don't like to be separated from their horses so finally we decided to approach the soldiers' camp on horseback.

It was two hours before dawn, and the tension was like the air in the mountains before the lightning storm hits, for we didn't know when we might stumble across soldier scouts or pickets posted by Howard to guard against just such a maneuver as the one we were attempting. But remarkably enough no such precautions had been taken. Perhaps we had been on the run so long, with Howard always attacking us, that he didn't consider the possibility that *we* might attack *him*.

Near the edge of the herd, a few of the warriors dismounted and stole in among the animals, setting them free from their hobbles and ropes, while the rest of us, including myself, remained on guard. I sat tensely on my horse, peering into the darkness for signs of an enemy stirring. I saw no soldiers but could make out the dim outline of scores of animals as they milled about restlessly, confused by the mysterious appearance among them of our warriors. Then suddenly a shot rang out! The shot was from an Indian rifle, but it had come too soon. Everyone had been told by Ollokot and Too hool-hool-Sote, "Do *not* shoot, do not give any alarm, until all the horses are freed." I learned later that it was Otskai who fired the shot, a man noted for doing foolish things and who could never hold himself back. For this foolishness of his, which almost spoiled our plan, he was much laughed at when we returned to our own camp.

As soon as the shot was fired the soldiers woke up. No time now to set more horses free! So we all plunged into the herd and began to whoop and holler and fire our guns and stampede the animals in the direction of our camp, while a few of us rode toward the sleeping soldiers, firing in their general direction in order to discourage them from pursuing too swiftly. I was among those who stayed to shoot at the soldiers, hoping for a glimpse of my enemy, but in the darkness I couldn't make out any faces.

Everything now was noise and confusion; it was like thunder crashing everywhere at once. Animals were rushing past us; Indians were riding among them shouting eerie cries and yelps to frighten them and urge them to their greatest speed. Shots were fired wildly by both sides, and the soldiers' angry cries could be heard above the din, while their confused officers barked out contradictory orders. It seemed forever, but it could only have been a few minutes before we were on our way, driving the herd ahead of us. All of us were safe. No one had been hit, and no one had been captured.

We drove the animals for several miles and then dawn began to break. As the pale light of the new day filtered through the early morning mist we could see for the first time the animals we had stolen. Almost all were mules! In the darkness we had missed their cavalry horses and had stolen their mules! We didn't know whether we should laugh at our silly mistake or weep because our plan had apparently failed.

We soon realized, however, that we had not failed. One-arm Howard was almost as helpless without his mules as he would have been without his horses, because now he had no way to bring along with him the great amount of supplies that seemed necessary to his troops before they could go anywhere. So our dismay at discovering that we had the mules turned to a joyful mood. Coyote had ridden along with us. Coyote had helped us trick the soldiers, then he had tricked us, but he was on our side that day, and while he had seriously hampered the soldiers he had only played a joke on us.

We drove those mules as fast as we could, but now that it was light the horse soldiers could make good time and we couldn't keep ahead of them, so we sent a few of the warriors on ahead with the mules and the rest of us formed a line of defense across the valley. There were many more of the soldiers than there were of us, but we were in carefully chosen positions and our fire soon forced the horse soldiers to dismount and seek cover.

For a while we traded shots with them at long distance. We were too far away to do any serious damage, but we made them afraid to move closer for fear of our marksmen. While we held them off in this fashion, a few of the most experienced warriors crept away and took up positions on the flank of the line of dismounted soldiers; this meant they could now pour shots down upon them from the side. Caught in this cross fire their officer gave his troops the order to retreat, which produced great confusion among them as they struggled to remount their horses amid our stream of bullets. Most of them finally made it safely to the rear, going back a mile or two, but one company couldn't get away. They moved off to the side rather than risk our bullets and took up a position behind some rocks at an outcrop of lava. We moved in upon them and, firing from behind rocks, made their lives miserable. I don't know how many we hit, but this is where the soldiers suffered their greatest losses. As for us, only two warriors had slight wounds; the soldiers were bad shots that day. I remained in the fight, still hoping to see my enemy in the light of day, but with no success. The herd of mules was now far away, safely out of reach. The troopers never did get back their animals except for a few broken-down strays that they picked up here and there.

We broke off the fight when One-arm Howard came with the rest of his army. He had expected the officer he sent against us to defeat us and get back the mules, but when that didn't happen Howard finally came up with the rest of his force. They were too many for us, so we left the field. We had achieved our purpose, and there was no point in risking our lives further. So we slipped away and Howard returned to his camp.

It was midafternoon when we rejoined the People, driving ahead of us our captured herd. We distributed the mules to those who needed them the most. I took a sturdy one to pull the travois for the ailing Wali'ms, and another for Kapoochas; also one of the few horses for Rising Moon, a splendid animal that she needed badly because until now she had only one aging mare to ride. Our return to camp was a joyous one. Not only was it a victory, but we regarded it as a great joke on Howard, and our merrymaking in celebration of our triumph was unclouded because none of us had been seriously hurt. That is why we just laughed at the foolish Otskai who fired the shot that warned the soldiers. I suppose General Howard would have tried him in court and had him punished, but we just made life miserable for him for a few days by poking fun at him.

Meanwhile, scouts kept a sharp watch on Howard, and Joseph had the camp ready to move at a moment's notice should they bring word that his troopers were showing signs of resuming the pursuit. But the soldiers seemed to be exhausted by their efforts to catch us and disoriented by the loss of their pack animals. Even though our scouts reported that the day following the raid Howard was joined by a couple of hundred additional foot soldiers, swelling his numbers to far more fighting men than we could muster, he still made no move.

The next day we were on the march again; that night we made camp at Henry's Lake, and the day after that we reached Targhee Pass. Joseph and Lean Elk thought we might encounter soldiers here, because it was a vital crossing point over the mountains. If there had been soldiers in our way we would have been caught between soldiers in front and Howard's army coming from behind and it would have gone badly with us. In fact, we did see signs that soldiers had been here recently, but for some unknown reason they had left. So we crossed the pass in safety, and now ahead of us lay the Yellowstone Country; we began to relax and feel more secure as we approached the shelter of its mountains and forests and the abundance of its game.

But I couldn't be glad because my wife wasn't getting well, and Kapoochas was very weak. One evening, having done all I could for Wali'ms, I received word that Kapoochas wanted to see me. When he saw me coming, he extended his bony hand to me and greeted me with a smile as thin as the new moon when it makes it first appearance in the night sky. His body looked so weak and frail that I wanted to cry out when I saw him, yet the warmth from his heart reached out to me as usual and warmed me like the rays of the sun warm the earth after the cold of the night.

Though Kapoochas's voice was weak his words were clear and distinct and his mind was strong. "Teeto Hoonod, I am glad you have come. Though you are young and I am an old man, you have been a good friend to me. Your soul and my soul have been brothers and have walked closely together on their journeys through this world. Now I, who in my lifetime have helped the Great Spirit heal many people, am not able to heal myself. I can feel the poison from my wound eating through my body. Each day I can tell that the life power in me becomes weaker; it runs out of me like water runs out of a broken bowl. I can hear my ancestor spirits calling to me. They are saying, 'Kapoochas! It is time to join us. You have lived your days on earth. You have become a burden to the People whom you have served for so long. We are waiting for you. Don't be afraid. Let your spirit go. Already it strains to leave your body. Let your spirit come where we are waiting for you.' "

I couldn't hold my tears back, and they flowed down upon the old man's wasted body. "Kapoochas," I cried, "you must not talk this way. You mustn't leave us. You have fought before against the evil of sickness. Now fight again. Regain your strength. Your wounds can heal and you can be strong again. Kapoochas, first Hohots Illpilp died and then Pahkatos Peopeo. Everything is being taken away from me. Must I lose you too?" As I spoke I knew I was being selfish, that I wanted to keep Kapoochas here for my sake and was trying to deny him the release he so greatly deserved.

Kapoochas answered gently, "No, Teeto Hoonod, it is not right for me to fight any longer against what must be. When a woman is with child she fights to keep the child within her womb until it is time for the child to be born. Then freely, joyfully, she lets the child leave her body. So it is with death. Until our lives have been lived we fight to keep the life spirit in this body and this world, but when the medicine wheel has made its full round and our life has been lived, then we give it back to the Great Spirit when he calls for it. This is the way of all living things, and you must not hold me back. My circle has turned all the way around, and the medicine wheel is completed within me. Help me to let my spirit go."

What could I say? I knew the old man was right. I was silent awhile and then answered, "Kapoochas, I am ready to do all I can to help you."

"Good!" he said with surprising alertness. "Then this evening go to Joseph. Tell him that the old te-wat Kapoochas is ready to go to the Great Spirit. Tell him I have become a burden to him and the People, and I don't wish to hold him back any longer. For this reason I go now to greet death, not as an enemy but as a friend, and when he and the People leave in the morning I will remain behind. Then, so that I do not fall into the hands of the enemy, you help me to get into the hills. Bring a little water with you, and a blanket to keep me warm should I live another night, but nothing else. There in the hills I will wait for death to come."

"I will stay with you!" I cried.

"No, Teeto Hoonod," Kapoochas answered severely. "That is not the Nez Perce way. You are needed here with the People. Wali'ms needs you. There is nothing you can do for me. Take me to the hills and leave me with your prayers. Don't be afraid, I will not be alone."

I found Joseph and told him what Kapoochas had asked me to say. Joseph listened carefully and then replied, "My heart is with the old healer. I understand what it is that he must do. He has worked all these years for us, and now, even in his death, he puts us before himself. He will always have our gratitude and will never be forgotten." Then Joseph went to find Kapoochas.

I don't know what the two men said to each other, but the next morning when I went to Kapoochas the first thing he said to me was, "Joseph came to see me last night." The old man's eyes were full of tears. Now, while the People got ready for the march, and Rising Moon cared for Wali'ms, I took Kapoochas far back into the mountains that lay on the north side of Targhee Pass. At first we went on horseback, Kapoochas tied securely to his mount, but then we went through a deep forest and over ground so rough that I carried him on my back. On we went until I found a flower-strewn meadow sheltered by great trees on all sides; a small stream ran through it from which he could drink. We rested here at Kapoochas's final camp. I made him as comfortable as I could, and sat beside him as he sang his death song. I think I would have stayed forever, but finally Kapoochas said, "Everything is done that needs to be done. Go now. Return to the People, Teeto Hoonod. Return to Wali'ms, who needs you. We part, but we are friends forever. Now go!"

So I left Kapoochas and never saw him alive again, but in my mind he still lives, and sometimes at night, when I am afraid, Kapoochas comes back to me and I feel strong again, and sometimes when I am disheartened I hear his voice saying to me, "Your Wy-a-kin, Teeto Hoonod, do not forget little Meadowlark; there is your strength." Then I feel life coming back into me.

CHAPTER THIRTEEN

Trapped

I rejoined Joseph as the People were going up the Madison River into the Yellowstone Country. The Madison River is a broad, cold, rushing stream, bordered by lush grasslands and open forests. Here there was plenty of forage for our horses, and fish that seemed anxious to be caught. For the first time in many days, our hunger was satisfied and we began to feel stronger. We spent one whole day traveling eastward along this life-giving stream to the point where it divided, one fork going northeast and the other fork going south. Here there was a trail that went northeast over the Gallatin Mountains and then through the north Yellowstone Country. It was known as the Great Bannock Trail because the Bannock Indians often traveled it, and if we took this trail we would know where we were and could make good progress. But this trail also was easy for the soldiers to follow and we were afraid we would run into parties of white people or hostile Indians, so the chiefs decided to find a new route by following the river to the south.

This meant that we were no longer sure exactly which way we should go. However, we did know that we must go south a short distance, so after about five miles, when we came to a stream coming in from the east, we turned and made our way up it. At this point we were lost, but fortunately two of our warriors, Yellow Wolf and the same Otskai who fired the foolish shot at Camas Meadow, happened upon an elderly prospector who knew the country well. We made a bargain with this old man: He would guide us through the Yellowstone Country and we would let him keep his life. The old man led us for several days until we knew where we were, and then he was allowed to escape unharmed.

Meanwhile, our spirits began to rise. As I said earlier, the Nez Perce by nature are a life-loving people, quick to laugh and with a spirit that finds its way through troubles like flowers push up from melting snow in the spring. Our recent disaster crushed this spirit, but Joseph urged that after the period of grieving was over no one was to mention the names of the dead. This freed us to go on living and to keep our spirits from being tempted to join the dead in the Beyond. So a slow healing of the People took place. Also, by this time most of those who were wounded had either succumbed to their wounds or recovered. As for the pursuing soldiers, we had tricked Howard badly at Camas Meadow and he was again far behind. More laughter was heard among us now, and once more we hoped that we would escape our enemies and make our way to safety with Sitting Bull, or, as Looking Glass kept saying, become allies with the Crow.

However, it was hard for me to be happy, for I missed Kapoochas, and Wali'ms continued to suffer dreadfully from the wound in her side. She alone among the wounded people had neither died nor begun to recover; she was among the few who still had to be carried in the travois, suffering greatly as a result, because her wound stubbornly refused to heal, and its poison still worked its way through her. Each day Rising Moon and I did what we could for her, and it was hard to say which of us was more attentive to her needs and tender with her in her suffering. And each time I was with Wali'ms and saw her great suffering my own pain came back to me, and the dark revenge spirit in me was renewed.

Now Joseph made it his custom to visit as many of the sick and wounded as he could, offering them strength and encouragement. As I was leaving Wali'ms one evening, having provided for her as well as I could, Joseph was standing nearby. I decided to speak to him of my despair over Wali'ms and my longing for revenge.

Joseph said nothing until I finished what I had to say. This was his custom. He never spoke his own thoughts until he was sure he had heard and understood the thoughts of the other person. Then he spoke to me as a father might speak to a troubled son. "Teeto Hoonod, I can understand your feelings. I also grieve for my wife and newborn daughter. The heel of the enemy crushed us both while the Great Spirit was looking another way. But let me tell you: Sometimes it happens that an animal is poisoned and its body is made evil by its sickness. When another animal comes along, it will leave it alone, for to eat the poisoned animal would spread the death. Those who pursue us have been poisoned by an evil power, even though they do not know it. If we feed off the evil that is in these people, we too will sicken and die. This is why you must quench your thirst for revenge. Don't hold it against the white man that he does these things; leave your revenge to the Great Spirit, who sees that justice is done in the end, for no one does evil without having it finally come back upon himself."

Affection welled up in me for Joseph, the same affection that was growing each day among the People, for Joseph was more than a war chief, he was a man who could lead the souls of others, as well as their bodies, but I couldn't bring myself to put out the revenge fire within me.

The next evening, as I wandered away from the camp to be alone with my thoughts, I became aware of another presence near me. For a moment I was afraid and stepped into the darkness of a great tree to see who was approaching. Then I saw Rising Moon step out into the clearing, lithe and graceful, as much a part of that forest as a deer that comes out from its daytime hiding to feed among the tender plants in the safety of the gathering darkness.

"Rising Moon," I said, my voice filled with surprise, "why are you not in the camp with the others? Night is coming fast. Here in these mountains the nights don't know it's summer. They think it's winter and chill us when we don't stay by the fires."

Rising Moon took my hand. "Teeto Hoonod," she said, ignoring my words of caution, "we have spoken little together since that evening in the mountains when you loved me. Since then you have been filled with war and concern for your wife; we have passed by each other speaking only of ordinary things, but keeping our real thoughts secret."

"That's so, Rising Moon," I replied. "And yet you were always in my thoughts. When I let my mind run back over the trail we have taken I remember you by my side at the Big Hole. When you come with me to the side of Wali'ms and are gentle and healing with her as though she were your own sister, I feel my heart become soft for you."

"Then you do not regret the love that we shared a moon ago? You are not sorry that you gave my womb hope that night?"

"I'm not sorry. Even though the love feelings in me were divided that night, I'm not sorry if it pleased you and gave you hope."

"Then I will tell you why I came here tonight to speak with you. The woman's way has not come to me this moon past. I waited for it to come many suns ago but it has not come. I have talked with my womb, and it tells me that a child is within me, that the Great Spirit has sent a soul into my womb, a child to replace the life of the child you lost."

I was stunned. Even though I had wanted to love and

205

please Rising Moon, it did not seem real to me that a child might come from our one night of love. "Rising Moon," I said at last, "I am glad when I think of a child being born to you. If the child comes, I will help and provide what is needed."

"That isn't why I have spoken to you tonight, Teeto Hoonod," Rising Moon answered quickly. "It's very soon. Only one moon has passed and eight more must come before any child born between us can enter into this world. Many things may happen between now and then, and usually I would have kept this to myself until the child's growth within me began to show in my body and I was sure. But I have spoken now because we live in great danger. There will be more trouble and more fighting before we reach a place of safety. It's important that we speak what is in our hearts now while we live, for tomorrow either you or I may die. That's why I have spoken to you, for I want you to know of the hope you gave me that night, and my gratitude to you."

It wasn't necessary to speak more words. We only needed a glance between us, exchanged now and then, firefly looks that flash between two people in the night, to know that there was a bond between us and that we were both strengthened by the hope for the birth of a new soul.

Yet this didn't lessen my concern for Wali'ms. My anguish remained for her, and my confusion that I could love two women, and as we traveled through that great, beautiful, terrible land of forests and mountains and streams I prayed each day that my wife might live.

The Great Spirit must have been especially happy when he created the land through which we were now traveling. Wherever the white man goes he feels he has to change the land. He plows the earth, builds fences, makes roads, and dams the rivers. But the Indian likes the land the way the Great Spirit made it; he changes nothing, but makes himself

206

a part of it. And here was land to my liking. The mountains, home to the agile mountain sheep, towered above an expanse of trees, their peaks ending in rock and snow; the Creator had spaced them in great rows like waves on a storm-tossed lake. Near their base the mountains swept down to form broad forests and grassy hills, flowing down to the streams that abounded in this land. Fed by the melting snows and the thunderstorms that came up almost every afternoon in the summer, these streams formed some valleys as deep and jagged as the valleys of our homeland many suns' travel away. One of our ancient stories tells how Eagle, in order to confuse his enemy, Coyote, had gashed the land with his wings, wherever his wing struck the ground a jagged canyon appeared. This, I thought to myself, must be where the two powerful mythical creatures contested with each other; these valleys must be the very ones Eagle made.

But elsewhere the streams were gentle, bounded by serene meadows, which at this time of year were bursting with brilliant flowers whose vivid colors seemed to celebrate the joy and vitality of life. Here in these meadows, and in the deep forests that bordered them, were the deer, elk, wolves, mountain lions, porcupines, coyotes, moose, buffalo, wolverines, and grizzly and brown bears that made this country their home. For the land was like a gigantic womb of Mother Earth that offered an abundance of food and life for all.

Some of these animals were strange to me; the moose, elk, mountain sheep, and buffalo I had never seen before. They were known only to those of us who made the trek to the East Country, for they didn't live in our homeland. The story is told that once these animals might have come across the mountains to inhabit our land too. East Country Boy, hero of the tale, had the chance to bring them back with him from an expedition to the Buffalo Country, but they would only follow him if he didn't look back on them as he crossed the mountains from east to west. Alas, East Country Boy couldn't resist. At the last moment he looked back, and the moose, elk, mountain sheep, and buffalo all went back to the land from which they came, and that is why the Nez Perce have to make the long journey to the East Country when they wish to hunt these animals.

Then, of course, there were the fish. Every rushing stream, great or small, was filled with them. You could stand by the side of the rock-strewn streams, watch the water pour endlessly by, and then train your eyes upon some rock-protected pool, and if you stood still and watched carefully you would soon see the fish lurking in the bottom, waiting for food to be swept down to them by the ever-rushing current of water. With a quick hand, a sharp spear, or a clever line you could catch them and make a feast of one of Mother Earth's great gifts to the Indian. But always, when you killed the fish or hunted the elk, you gave thanks to the animal for giving up its life for you. For while everything must eventually die so that something else can live, no creature should take the life of another without thanking that creature for the sacrifice it has made.

To the north of us were Indians who believed that each animal had a Master Spirit Animal who lived far away. When an animal died its spirit returned to the Master Spirit Animal, and it was this Master Spirit Animal that sent the spirit of the dead animal back again to the earth. Sometimes the Master Spirit Animal could be seen among the earth animals, in the herds of buffalo or elk, and then the hunter must never try to shoot it. It could not be killed, and if the hunter tried, the hunting would fail and the animals would disappear. If you wanted to hunt successfully you had to pay proper respect to the Master Spirit Animal; then your hunting would meet with success. When the white man hunted, he disregarded the Master Spirit Animal because he killed wantonly, and that is why the animals disappeared wherever the white man went. Then he would fill the empty places with his tame animals, cattle and sheep. But these northern Indians believed that these animals were not good to eat, for unlike the animals of the woods and meadows they had no Master Spirit Animal and so their flesh was bad for you. As I went with the People through this land so abundant with animal life, I thought of these beliefs. I liked them. They seemed right to me, and I made them my own.

Our way now took us eastward many miles up the small creek. Then we reached a prominent mountain with a lake nestled at its foot, the two standing together like man and wife, and from here we went through an open area that led to the greatest, broadest, deepest river of them all —the river of the Yellowstone. Here we turned south and followed the Yellowstone to the largest lake I had ever seen, as blue as our own Wallowa Lake but much bigger.

On the way through the broad, treeless valley that bordered the Yellowstone River I had a curious experience. I was with Shuslum Hihhih and two other warriors when we heard a strange noise. It didn't sound like an animal, or a human, or thunder, or an explosion, yet it partook of all of these sounds. "Whatever can that be?" we wondered, and leaving the main body of the People we cautiously approached the turbulent noise. Then we came upon a strange sight. In an open area, great masses of thick mud and steaming water were gurgling forth from the depths of the earth. "It's like looking into the anus of Monster," Shuslum Hihhih said, with characteristic Nez Perce wit. And then, here and there, the water would suddenly gush forth into the sky, sending a stream of vapor high above our heads, while all around us the heat was so intense we were driven back to a safe distance. I had never before, nor have I since, seen such strange sights as these gurgling, gushing, erupting holes from which Mother Earth poured forth her insides. Shuslum Hihhih commented as we left, "This is where the

209

earth farts." And we all laughed.

We stayed a short time by Yellowstone Lake but soon were on our way again for fear of close pursuit by the soldiers. Our route became more difficult. First we made our way up another creek that led east to its source in a range of mountains, then through thick forests, and over these mountains to a river on the other side. From here we went along the river to its junction with a creek that entered from the northeast. From here we followed the creek to a pass that led over the highest mountains in the region. This was the most difficult part of the journey, for there were only a few places where these mountains could be crossed, and it was essential that we get over the passes quickly lest the soldiers reach them before us. Then on the other side of the pass we met the head of another creek that led northeast, away from the mountains. We would follow this creek down to its junction with the Clarks Fork River and then down the precipitous canyon of this river until it poured out upon the broad prairie lands we were seeking. This would be the land of the Crow, who Looking Glass said would be our friends, and from here we hoped to reach the safety of Grandmother's Country, many suns' travel to the north.

You can imagine the extraordinary difficulty we had in getting Wali'ms through this land and the great suffering our journey caused her. But Wali'ms, even in her sickness, loved this land. She rejoiced in the flowers and had me bring her each tiny one. She exclaimed joyfully over those she recognized and wondered at those that were strange to her. Some of them she knew would be good for medicine, or for healing teas, and these she instructed us to keep for future need. So even though the journey tired her greatly, her spirit was fed by the land through which we passed, keeping alive my hopes that she might become strong again, even though her face, which once was nut-brown, was now as pale as the snow.

No one opposed us; there were no signs of Howard's army, although we suspected we were being followed by Bannock Indians acting as his scouts. But that doesn't mean that there was no action along the way, for many incidents took place as our warriors found several groups of white people who were camping in the region. One group of our scouts came across eleven campers, including two white women. They were taken prisoner and brought back to our camp and presented to the chiefs, for we were always looking for spies and since the Battle of Big Hole were suspicious of everyone. But after some debate the chiefs decided these white people were innocent and should be released without harm. It was wiry Lean Elk's words that decided the matter: "The soldiers killed many Nez Perce women and children on the Big Hole, but we do not hurt Montana people unless they are spies. You may go. Take these old horses and leave." He told them to take old horses so they would travel slowly and couldn't bring Howard word of where we were. Unfortunately for the white people, two of their party didn't believe we were letting them go unharmed and tried to run away. This gave some of our young warriors an excuse to turn ugly, and Swan Necklace, the only one of the three warriors who had gone on the first Salmon River raids who was still alive, shot one of these men and wounded him badly. He was left to die, but the others were saved by the timely arrival of Lean Elk, who put a stop to any more killing.

After this the rest of the party was taken back to camp for safekeeping, and the women spent the night by Joseph's campfire. No doubt they were frightened by the somber, meditative Joseph, and not knowing his thoughts must have feared for their lives, but in the morning they were released again and guided safely away from the angry young men who might have hurt them.

We came across other innocent travelers and none were

211

hurt, but some whites who might have been scouts or spies were killed by Nez Perce scouting and raiding parties that roamed over a wide distance looking for the enemy, and always with an eye out for fresh horses and supplies. But these white people who were killed were considered combatants and enemies, each one a potential spy.

That is the way it was until we began our descent down the high mountains on the east side of the Yellowstone Country toward the Clarks Fork River. Then our situation suddenly became desperate as ominous news reached us from several sources.

First, some of our scouts, who had been working in advance of the main body, brought us a frightening report: Many soldiers were lying in wait for us, some at the place where the Clarks Fork River emptied onto the prairie and others at the outlet of the other canyons that led out of the mountain area. When this news spread among us we felt like deer who have smelled the presence of the mountain lion lying in wait to strike.

Where was Howard's army? We hadn't seen signs of him for a long time, but we knew he must be somewhere in the Yellowstone Country behind us. Before, we suspected we were followed by Bannock scouts, but now there was no doubt about it, for these Indians, led by a white man who was known for his tenacity and skill in tracking, were so close upon our heels that some of our rear guard had engaged them in talk, hoping to dissuade them from their evil purpose, but to no avail. Beyond a doubt we were being carefully watched, and somewhere behind us, perhaps rapidly approaching by another route than the one we had taken, was One-arm Howard and his soldiers.

Then there was a gloomy report brought by Looking Glass. All this time Looking Glass never gave up his belief that the Crow would come to our aid, and as soon as we had crossed the high eastern mountains Looking Glass went ahead to the Crow country to talk with his friends. Now he returned, and we didn't need his talk to know that his mission had been a failure, for his face was as dark as a cloud filled with rain, and his eyes looked down porcupinelike as he walked. Poor Looking Glass! It was hard for him to admit that his great friends the Crow would not help us. They were afraid of the soldiers, it seems, and regarded our cause as lost. The best they would do was promise not to fight us as we passed through their country, although even this promise was broken by some of them who joined the army as scouts and tried to steal our horses.

To understand the difficulty we now faced you must remember the nature of the land through which we were traveling. As I have explained, we had crossed the high mountains that form the eastern boundary of the Yellowstone Country and were making our way down a small creek toward the Clarks Fork River, which was to be our route out of the mountains and onto the plains below. There were only three possible ways for us to leave the mountains and continue on our way. The Clarks Fork River was one, the Yellowstone River to the north was another, and the Stinking Water River to the south was the third. The Yellowstone River was out of the question because we would have to go west, back in the direction from which we had come, and would almost certainly encounter Howard's troops. Now we knew that soldiers were guarding both the Clarks Fork River exit and the Stinking Water canyon. We were trapped. No matter which way we went we were certain to run into the enemy, and with Howard coming up behind us we would be caught between the grizzly-bear jaws of the army and destroyed.

Or so it seemed. That night a council was held. Looking Glass sat silent and discredited because he had been so wrong about the Crow. But Lean Elk and Joseph came up with a plan, and Ollokot, White Bird, and Too-hool-hool-Sote agreed to it after much debate. This was one of the few times that Joseph actively shaped our military strategy. I think he took an active role this time because Lean Elk, who came up with the original idea, was only a half-breed Nez Perce, and there were those, such as Looking Glass, who resented this and said only a full-blood should lead the People in war. But when Joseph joined with Lean Elk in making a plan, it gave Lean Elk prestige. The plan was a gamble, but it was our only chance.

Lean Elk described it first: "We have one advantage in our favor. Howard, who is coming behind us somewhere from the west, cannot know of the location of the white war chief who has placed his troops across our line of march to the east. The two armies, one to the west, one to the east, are separated from each other by these mountains, and neither white chief can know what the other is doing. Because of this, there may be a way we can find to escape."

Chief White Bird nodded in agreement but had a question. "Lean Elk, you have forgotten the singing wire. The white people can talk long distances with each other by means of the singing wire."

Lean Elk answered the old chief with the respect which was his due. "You do well to think of this, White Bird, but the singing wire only works for the white people where the country is open. In this forest and among these mountains no singing-wire talk is possible. This means that the soldiers can talk with each other only by sending messengers between their armies. We have known this, and this is why our warriors have roamed the mountains in all directions. When they have come across a soldier, a prospector, or a trapper, they have been forced to kill that person lest that man become the eyes and ears of the enemy. We have reason to believe that no one has been able to get through, and by redoubling our efforts we can make extra sure that no talk flows between Howard to the west and the other generals to the east."

Now Joseph spoke. "Lean Elk's words are good. What we must do is persuade the troops in front of us to leave their position so we can go down the Clarks Fork River and onto the open prairie country without having to fight them. We must not fight them! For while we are fighting them, Howard will come from behind and fall upon us. There can be no victory in such a battle, even if we should prove a match for the soldiers lying in wait. So we must make some maneuver to deceive the enemy, to make them believe we are going to leave the mountains another way."

Joseph's words fired Lean Elk's enthusiasm. "Well spoken, Joseph, and I see now what we must do. We must continue down the Clarks Fork River far enough to be sure the scouts from the soldiers in front of us see us coming and observe our movements. To make sure we are seen, we must tell our own advance scouts to relax their efforts and not kill anyone they see in the immediate line of our advance, but only to range to the right and left to keep them from carrying word to Howard. Then, once we are sure we are being watched, we must leave the Clarks Fork River canyon, make our way to the canyon rim, and travel to the south and east as though we had changed our minds and were going to leave the mountains by way of the Stinking Water River. Then, after we have gone far enough from the Clarks Fork River to deceive the enemy about our intentions, we must double back, hiding our movements under the cover of the forest, and make our way to the Clarks Fork River again down below the place where we left it. In this way the soldier chief in front of us will be persuaded that we are going away from the Clarks Fork River and may quit his

215

position and march to the Stinking Water River, hoping to intercept us there."

Too-hool-hool-Sote had an objection. "But what if the Bannock scouts who have been following us watch these maneuvers and carry word to the enemy?"

Lean Elk answered. "Your point is a good one, Too-hool-hool-Sote, and we must take that into account. To throw them off, we will not leave the Clarks Fork River until we reach the place where it begins to become narrow. Here we will be able to post a rear guard to keep the Bannocks at a distance. And even if they should see our movements, we will have our warriors ranging the country on all sides to intercept any messengers they might try to send to the soldiers ahead of us."

Now Looking Glass, who had been listening carefully and, as usual, didn't like ideas that weren't his own, interjected his thought. "But if we do this, Lean Elk, we won't be able to return to the Clarks Fork River. For once the canyon narrows it soon becomes so steep that it would be impossible to reenter it farther down. Our women and horses and old people and wounded couldn't possibly descend the steep canyon walls. We would leave the canyon only to find we couldn't enter it again, and then we would be open game for our enemies."

Joseph joined in again. He was remarkably patient with Looking Glass, who would have done better to have remained silent and let someone else do the talking. "Looking Glass, you have shown strong thinking powers. But somewhere there must be a place where we can reenter the canyon. The Nez Perce who made their way over the Lolo Trail can surely find a way back down into this canyon. Such a place must be found!"

Lean Elk spoke again. "Yes, there must be such a place. You who have been scouts working in advance have seen the country. Have you seen a place where the canyon could be reentered once we left it?"

Now my friend Shuslum Hihhih spoke. "I have been one of these scouts. I have worked my way far down this river. The walls are steep, but there is one narrow defile, so narrow that only a single horse could pass through at a time. It is very steep, but not so steep that people couldn't pass through safely if they wanted badly enough to reach the canyon floor."

And this is the way it was. Down the river we went. Then up to the forest land above it. Then, when we reached a densely wooded place, we milled our horses round and round, making a great confusion of our tracks. This was so enemy scouts who might stumble upon our trail would not know which way we had gone. Then we doubled back to the Clarks Fork River, to a place down the river from where we had originally emerged. Here, just as Shuslum Hihhih had said, was a narrow opening in the canyon rim wall. How we made it through this place I don't know. Sometimes the horses could barely squeeze through. The old people and the sick people had to be helped lest they fall and slide. The passage was too narrow for Wali'ms's travois and I had to carry her on my back, which was exceedingly painful to her, but she didn't cry out. Somehow we made it. We regained the floor of the Clarks Fork River and then went swiftly to the place where the stream empties out of the mountains.

As we neared this place the tension rose. Had we deceived the white chief ahead of us, or was he waiting with his soldiers to block our way? If so we were lost. But at last Shuslum Hihhih and other scouts reported. "The way is clear! The troops are gone, vanished to the south, headed for the Stinking Water River without leaving behind so much as an outpost."

Lean Elk and Joseph gave the word. "Ahead! Go fast! No

one must spare himself, no one must linger. Speed is essential!"

Down we went, out of the canyon, onto the broad open country. Then, turning, we traveled along the river valley swiftly to the north. We had escaped the trap. We were on our way to Grandmother's Country!

CHAPTER FOURTEEN

❋

Death in the Canyon

At last we were in the Buffalo Country which the chiefs, with the exception of Joseph, who had wanted to remain in our own country for better or for worse, had selected as our objective. Originally we hoped to travel peacefully through this broad land, with the help and alliance of the Crow. As you know, when we entered the Bitterroot Valley we made peace with the settlers, injured no one, and paid for everything. But at the Big Hole all that changed, and we were forced to regard all white people as our potential enemies. Now as we entered this new country Joseph urged that once again we stop killing white people and move rapidly but peacefully through this region.

So we hoped to travel peacefully over the prairie, but we also knew that the troops we had tricked would soon be pressing upon us. For One-arm Howard had shown that he was determined to annihilate us, and now we knew that other soldiers from different parts of the country were with him. That is why Joseph and Lean Elk urged that we travel fast, for though we had not thrown Howard off our trail, no matter how we twisted and turned, we had shown that even though we traveled with the burden of our families we could leave his army in the dust.

Yet there were some who thought that now we had reached this land we need worry no more. They argued,

219

"We have left Howard behind us. He has many slow foot soldiers, and his horses are weary, and the other troops we fooled are dispirited. We can move more slowly and shoot game as we go and begin to enjoy ourselves."

"That's not so," Joseph argued. "The war chief we fooled will be angry and want to avenge himself upon us. Howard will send ahead the fastest troops he has, mounted on his best horses, hoping to catch up with us and make us fight. And while we are fighting them the Crow will be stealing our horses, and Howard's walking soldiers will also come upon us. We must move swiftly as does the great goose when winter is approaching and it seeks the warmer lands. There is no peace or safety for us, unless it be with Sitting Bull in Grandmother's land." And because we had learned to respect Joseph, we followed his advice and pressed on with all the speed that was possible.

The terrain over which we now traveled was easy and our horses went swiftly. But we knew that the horses of the enemy could travel with equal speed. What favored us also favored them.

However, the easier terrain was a blessing to those who still suffered from their wounds. There were only a few left who had to be pulled on the travois, and Wali'ms was one of these. The journey over the mountains had been incredibly hard on her. The cold nights had chilled her and lowered the strength of her body to fight the poison from her wound. One of her legs was now black with this poison, and her brow was fiery hot to my touch. As I walked by her side to steady the lurching travois I wondered how Wali'ms could still cling to life, but even as the spruce trees, high in barren and rocky mountains, cling tenaciously to life by sinking their roots deep down into cracks and crevices, so Wali'ms's life force clung stubbornly to this world.

Rising Moon was a great help: sisterlike, she tenderly took care of Wali'ms. Rising Moon and I spoke little together, and when we did it was mostly to discuss matters of the day or Wali'ms's condition. It was as though we didn't need to say much in order to know what was in each other's heart. But I found myself thinking often of the child Rising Moon might be carrying. Once I asked her, "Do you still believe the Great Spirit has sent a soul into your womb?" She answered me, with a certainty that would have sounded strange from anyone but Rising Moon, "When I speak to my womb it tells me that a new life grows within me."

I reflected. "It's good. Your child will come like new life to the People, and a new hope to us." And I held her close to me for a while, all the time wondering how I could love both Rising Moon and Wali'ms.

So it was that my mind continued to be filled with thoughts. Two women filled my imagination and my dreams; the picture of the child-still-to-be-born began to appear more often in my thoughts; yet at the same time my mind was often filled with terrible memories of the deaths of Pakhatos Peopeo, Kapoochas, and Hohots Illpilp and the dreadful events at Big Hole. Nor could I forget the soldier who had killed my brother.

This is how it was with the People, and how it was with me, when the soldiers came upon us again after we had crossed the Yellowstone River and were entering a place we called Tepahlewam Wakuspah, at the mouth of Canyon Creek. It was Lean Elk who chose this route, for not only did this creek provide a way through the rimrock that bordered the river, it also was a way that could be defended in case of attack. This time we were not taken by surprise. After crossing the Yellowstone River, we began to make our way up the wide mouth of the creek and into the narrow canyon that led northwards in the direction we wished to go, but we left scouts to watch for soldiers. As we made our way up the canyon the scouts signaled to us with smoke fires that horse soldiers were only a few miles behind us and were coming

221

up fast. Of course the warriors could easily have escaped them, but because of the women and children and wounded we couldn't go fast enough to get away without a fight. So Lean Elk formed a rear guard, led by himself, Looking Glass, Too-hool-hool-Sote, and Ollokot, while Joseph led the march and White Bird, with a band of warriors, guarded the flanks of the People. I joined the rear guard because I hoped to see my enemy.

The mouth of Canyon Creek as it empties into the Yellowstone River is broad and open; had we been caught here by the horse soldiers it would have gone badly with us. But after a mile of this open country the creek enters a canyon that becomes increasingly narrow as it makes its way through a rim of rocky cliffs, and this was a good place for us to make a stand. A number of us took up our positions behind rocks in the lower part of the narrowing canyon, while others scaled the cliffs on either side and took up positions on the rimrock so we could not be outflanked.

As soon as the horse soldiers had crossed the Yellowstone River they saw us. We heard the trumpeter blow his bugle for a charge, and soon the mounted men were racing toward us, shooting as they came. We waited until they were close and then opened fire, and even though we were still at some distance from them our good shooting caused a soldier here and there to fall to the ground. Perhaps because he feared our rifles, or perhaps because he thought we had decided to have a pitched battle with him, the white war chief now had his trumpeter blow the signal for his men to dismount and fight on foot.

Now this is just what we wanted, for dismounted the soldiers could only advance slowly, and while we were holding them back the People would have a chance to get far away. If they had continued their horse charge they would have lost many soldiers, but they might also have broken through our line of defense, rushed up the canyon, and either caught the People or forced us to fight a major battle. So we kept firing to keep the soldiers from advancing, and when they pressed too closely upon us, we moved back a little into the canyon and took up a new position, and each time we withdrew the canyon became narrower, which made it still easier to hold the soldiers back. While we lost no one from their bullets, we dropped more and more of them because as they advanced toward us they had to expose themselves to our fire.

We had an anxious moment when a group of the soldiers raced for the foot of the rimrock walls that overlooked the canyon where we were fighting. They were going to try to scale the walls, and if they had been able to do this they would have looked down on us and commanded the whole battlefield with their fire. But we had already thought of that and had posted warriors on top of the cliffs who repulsed the soldiers without difficulty.

So we continued to fire, hold the soldiers back, retreat a little farther, form a new line of defense, and fire again. And as the day wore on in this way the People, with Joseph and White Bird leading them, were getting farther away.

I wondered why Lean Elk left so many warriors with Joseph and White Bird, but later I learned this was a wise decision: As the People were retreating, some of the Crow tried to run off with our horses. The warriors who remained with the main band, with White Bird leading them, fought them in several small engagements, killing some and preventing them from stealing the horses. Although the Crow killed one of our warriors and two unarmed old men, they were not able to do any more damage, but if some warriors had not been left with the main band it would have gone hard on us that day. I wondered bitterly why those Crow did that. Why should Indians fight against Indians? It seemed that we were alone now in the world, with no one as our friend.

Still, I don't believe all the Crow wanted to attack us or steal from us, only some of them. For instance, once I saw a Crow scout with the advancing soldiers. He raised his gun and fired at us, but the bullet went high over our heads. He fired at us because he had joined the army as a scout and was expected to, but he shot into the air deliberately because he didn't want to hurt us.

Each time we withdrew from our position and went farther up the canyon, some of the warriors left the rear guard and joined the main band. As they went they rolled rocks and fallen timbers into the narrowing canyon bottom to slow down the soldiers and prevent them from mounting their horses and riding through. Later, when we had stopped fighting and the soldiers tried to come through the canyon and catch up with us, they came up against so many of our obstacles that they gave up the pursuit. So the People left the soldiers behind, and I knew that when they camped that night, after traveling long after dark, they would be safe.

As for me, while many of the warriors left the fighting to rejoin the main band, I remained behind, for I still hoped to see my enemy. Wherever I could see a soldier's face I looked to see if it was him; always I was disappointed. I fought hard that day, for the sake of revenge, for the sake of the People, and for the sake of Wali'ms. I didn't know fear any more, for I didn't care if I died, and I was angry at the soldiers and wanted to defend the People. So I said to myself, "This is a good day to die," sang my death song in case a soldier's bullet found me, and called on Qotsqo'tsn for strength and protection, and although bullets hit all around me I wasn't hurt. So the day moved on, and the sun began to lose strength and sink toward the canyon rim to the west, while the shadows devoured the eastern slopes, and still I stayed and fought. Then, as I was lying behind a great rock, peering out through a tiny gap, firing at any soldier who dared show his head, I became aware of the silence around me. Why were no other shots being fired than my own? Slowly I realized that I was the last warrior left. Nervously I looked to the rear. No one was there, only my horse, tethered behind me, waiting for me with animal patience. For a moment the thought occurred to me to leap on his back and make a run for safety, but I decided to remain where I was. I would not leave until darkness came. Then, sheltered by the night, I would lead my horse away and leave the deserted, barricaded canyon to the soldiers. They could have it then. The People would be far away.

The shadows cast by the rocky walls of the canyon grew longer, stretching out like great fingers to swallow the narrow creek bed in darkness, and finally it was night. Then I broke off the desultory fight and under the welcome mantle of darkness made my way up the creek to my horse. She was a fine animal in good condition, and a fast runner, but it was too dangerous to ride her in the darkness over such rough ground. So I led her up the dry creek bed, making my way with difficulty around the barricades of rocks and logs that the retreating warriors had strewn behind them. I walked this way for several hours until I felt it was safe to stop and make a lonely camp for myself. As I closed my eyes and gave myself over to Mother Earth for her healing sleep, a coyote uttered his eerie cry off in the distance, and then his companions answered with a wild cacophony of yelps and howls. It was Coyote laughing with me at the way we had fooled those troops! It was the last sound I heard before falling into an exhausted sleep.

I wakened when the first ray of light from the rising sun reached me and was soon on my way again. I was hungry now, for I hadn't eaten since sunrise of the preceding day, but I was strengthened by my confidence that I would soon find the People and by the hope that perhaps Wali'ms, now that we were out of the rough mountain country, would be stronger. It wasn't hard to follow the trail the People made, for several hundred Indians with two thousand horses and all their belongings can't help but leave a broad path behind them when they make their way across a rolling, grass-covered prairie. I could tell from the trail that the People were moving rapidly; Joseph was clearly urging them to great speed to keep them ahead of the soldiers and had not let them stop to rest on the way. Eventually I came upon the campsite they made the night before; they had camped after I fired my last shot at the soldiers and started to make my way back.

The sun now stood high in the sky. The place Joseph had camped was on a low hill. He selected it for defense, and I could tell that warriors had maintained a watch on top of some rocks that crowned the top. I decided to press on in the hope of catching up with Joseph by nightfall, but as I moved through the deserted campground I heard a voice cry out my name: "Teeto Hoonod, over here, we're over here!" Startled like a deer, I looked about. The voice was familiar. Yes, it was Rising Moon!

"Rising Moon," I called back, "why are you here? Are you all right? Where are the People? And Wali'ms?"

There was Rising Moon, standing on a rock, her slender form silhouetted against the yellow-green grass of the rolling prairie. She smiled wanly as she answered. "So many questions, Teeto Hoonod, and all at once. You always were an inquisitive fellow!" Then her face darkened. "I am all right and the People are all right. They are half a sun's travel ahead. But Wali'ms . . ." Her voice hesitated, then continued firmly, "Wali'ms is here with me. We have waited here for you. We knew that if you were still alive you would come through this place following our trail."

"And what if I was not alive?" I asked, as I made my way over to the place where Rising Moon was standing. "Would you have stayed here forever?" I was about to add, What a foolish thing that was to do, when I saw Wali'ms. How tired she looked! She smiled a thin smile at me as I approached, and held out her hand. Her life power seemed thin and weak, like the thin sliver of the new moon that barely has the strength to find a place in the night sky. I knew that she was dying, and I knew now why Rising Moon had waited here for me, taking the chance that I would still be alive. As I knelt by Wali'ms and took her hand in mine, Rising Moon told me their story.

"As you can see, Wali'ms is very weak. The poison in her has increased greatly since you last saw her. Her body is filled with pain, and traveling on the travois was like having knives thrust through her over and over. Joseph came to her and did all he could to help her, but it was very hard. We had to move fast to keep ahead of the soldiers, and also the Crow, who have attacked us and tried to steal our horses. Wali'ms saw that she was holding the People back, so when we reached this campsite she begged Joseph to let her stay here."

Now Wali'ms, summoning her strength, said in a thin voice, "I was a burden to the People. I was holding Joseph back. Because of me the soldiers might catch us. I wanted to stay here, to see you once more. . . ."

Wali'ms's voice trailed away, and Rising Moon continued. "So we rested here, hidden behind these rocks for fear of the Crow, waiting for you."

Wali'ms spoke again. "And you have come, Teeto Hoonod, you have come, and you are safe. Your Wy-a-kin has protected you and brought you to me one more time."

"Hush, Wali'ms," I found myself saying, "you must save your strength for the journey to rejoin the People."

Wali'ms held up her hand. "No, Teeto Hoonod," she said, "I'm not returning to the People. I am going to die. I see you this one last time and then I die, here on this spot. Don't try to hold me back."

"Wali'ms!" I cried. "You can't go! There is life in you yet. See, I have a strong horse. I will carry you on the horse and we will return to Joseph and you will be strong again." I buried my head on her breast in grief.

With what strength she had left, Wali'ms stroked my hair. "No, it is not good. I can feel my life emptying out, and soon the stream within me will be dry. But see, Rising Moon is here. She has loved you all this time. I have seen her love for you and have been jealous many moons. But now I die, and I give her to you. Take her, Teeto Hoonod, and let her be your woman now."

So Wali'ms had known of the love between us but had said nothing. What pain had this knowledge caused her? And now, because she knew Rising Moon truly loved me, she was saying we should be man and woman together. My love for Wali'ms was never greater; I could only express it by holding her close to me. But her death? I wasn't ready for that. I didn't want to solve the two-woman conflict in me in this way. I would fight for her life and somehow give her of my energy to fill her stream of life up again. But before I could reply, the crack of a rifle exploded from nearby, and a bullet passed within inches of my head, struck a rock, and ricocheted crazily among the rocks behind me. "Down!" I cried to Rising Moon. She fell to the ground beside me. I seized my rifle and, hugging the earth, crawled on my belly to the shelter of the rocks and peered between them in the direction from which the shot had come.

I saw forms flitting here and there among rocks some distance away. "Crow!" I said to Rising Moon and Wali'ms. "They've come for our horses. Don't show your head." I saw an Indian slowly rise from behind the rocks. Evidently they were not sure whether or not they had killed me. I didn't fire, but waited silently until he became overconfident and exposed himself. Then I fired, and my bullet struck him squarely in the chest. With a thud that Crow fell to the ground, a dead man. Immediately a rain of bullets struck the rocks that sheltered us. Their shots were fired in anger because I had killed one of their men, and their bullets did us no harm, but I knew now that there were several of them and wondered what hope there could be for us. For a moment, Wali'ms was forgotten as I fought for our lives.

Whenever a Crow showed his head I fired, but they were canny now and didn't give me a good target. As I fought I spoke with Rising Moon. "They want our horses, but if we stampede the horses out to them we will never be able to catch up with Joseph, and they would kill us anyway to get revenge for the warrior I have slain. They know we are few and they will try to surround us. While some hold our attention in front, others will try to gain our rear. We must make them believe that we have many rifles. You must take up a position in those rocks behind us. Use this revolver; it's the one I took from the soldier who killed Hohots Illpilp. If you see a Crow, shoot to kill; if not, shoot anyway from time to time to make them believe that there are many of us and we can't be taken from the rear. Wali'ms will be safe on the ground. We can hold them off this way until dark, for I see that you have food and drink with you and this will keep up our strength. Then we will see what we can do."

So we fought all during that long afternoon, and sometimes I shot and sometimes Rising Moon shot, handling that soldier's revolver as though she were a warrior. We killed no more Crow, but we made them respect our fire. They dared not charge us, but I knew they were waiting until night and then they would creep up under cover of the darkness to do away with us. So Rising Moon and I fought, the rifles cracked, and Wali'ms was very quiet.

As the day wore on I began to work out a desperate plan, and when evening came I shared it with Rising Moon. "Here is what we must do. As soon as it is dark I will not wait for them to attack us, but I will move out and attack them. I hope I will take them by surprise. They have divided their forces and only a few are in front of us; the rest are behind. You must wait with the horses ready. As soon as you hear firing in the direction I have gone, wait for my call. I will give the song of the qotsqo'tsn. This will mean that I am alive and you are to come ahead. Come at once with the horses and with Wali'ms on the travois, which somehow we must carry through the darkness. Make for where I am and then press on ahead of me, and I will remain behind to hold the others off. It's our only chance."

Rising Moon said quietly, "Your plan is good, Teeto Hoonod, but it's not necessary to take the travois for Wali'ms. The Crow can't hurt her. She is dead. The Great Spirit decided she has suffered enough and has taken her back. While we were fighting and didn't notice, her spirit slipped quietly away. See how still she lies. See how calm her face is now that Pa'yawit has come for her. Pa'yawit, the one she held off for so long as an enemy, has finally come to her as a friend."

I looked at Wali'ms. Her eyes were closed; all the pain was gone now, and across her face there was a smile, as though she had seen something beautiful that we couldn't see. It was too late now for tears, and I saw it was good she was gone where the pain could no longer reach her. I wouldn't try to hold back her spirit from its journey by my grief. I asked, "How long do you think she has been dead?"

Rising Moon answered, "Many hours."

"As you said, we will not need the travois, but the Crow must not get her body, Rising Moon. They would defile it and try to hinder her journey in the spirit world by mutilating her. We will leave the travois, but tie her body to her horse, and when we are away from the Crow we will give her a proper burial." And then I spoke to Wali'ms, holding her broken body as I chanted my song:

Go now, Wali'ms. Do not look back.
Those who love you do not hold you back from the journey
you must now take.
Go, and travel quickly, away from the earth and the pain,
Away to the land of the Great Spirit where the power of the
enemy
Can hurt you no more.

Darkness had now fallen. I finished my song. "Get the
horses ready, Rising Moon," I said, "We must move before
they move. Remember, listen for my sound. If you do not
hear the call of the qotsqo'tsn it means their bullets have
found me before I could find them. If that happens, mount
your horse and ride as fast as you can in the darkness."

She nodded her agreement. "When you call I will be
ready."

Slowly, my rifle clutched in my hand, I made my way past
our sheltering rocks toward the waiting Crow. Knowing I
could become confused in the darkness, I fixed my course by
the great dog star in the brilliant sky overhead. All odds
were against me except for one: The Crow would not be
expecting me to attack them. I inched my way along, crawl-
ing snakelike, stopping frequently to deaden the sound of
my approach, until I could hear voices. The Crow were
talking with each other in hushed tones; I knew they were
making their plans even though I could not understand their
words. I also knew that they didn't suspect my presence or
they would not be talking as they were. I inched ahead
again, only a short distance at a time. Once the voices
stopped suddenly, and I stopped too, knowing they had
heard my sounds, but when all was quiet again they began
to talk once more. From the different voices I knew there
were three of them.

At last, peering through a crack between two rocks, I
made out the shadowy forms of the warriors in the darkness

ahead of me. How would I attack? I waited to have a plan form in my mind, but then two of them rose and began to move off to the sides, each in a different direction. They were beginning their own attacking movement. There was no more time! I rose to my knees and blazed away with my rifle. The Crow in front of me saw me and reached for his rifle, but he was too late and my first shot split open his skull and scattered his brains on the ground. From the corner of my eye I could see the warrior on my left swing his rifle to his shoulder, but my second shot hit his rifle squarely and smashed it to pieces. Then from my right the third warrior fired, but my Wy-a-kin was strong and the bullet barely grazed my head. I turned and fired at him blindly, but he vanished into the darkness. I rushed after him, stumbling over rocks, but I heard him racing ahead of me. Now I turned back and found the dead warrior, and then the remains of the other warrior's rifle. He too had fled. I had won! But there was no time to lose.

Turning toward Rising Moon I called out the triumphant song of the qotsqo'tsn. Then I took shelter behind the rocks again, on guard lest those warriors return. Soon I heard the sound of the horses approaching and there was Rising Moon riding her mount, with the body of Wali'ms tied securely to another mount, and my mare ready for me to ride. "We go!" I shouted to Rising Moon as I leaped on the back of my horse. I threw her the rifle of the slain warrior. "Hand me back the revolver and use this instead if you need to," I said. We pressed on in the darkness, praying to the Great Spirit that our horses wouldn't stumble. Over the rough ground and rocks we clambered. I listened for sounds behind us, but those Crow were afraid and didn't follow us.

We rode all night, and when the sun finally began to rise over the distant hills we were many miles away. A short distance ahead of us I could see the green of some trees in the bottom of a stream. Here there would be shelter and water. We rode into the sandy stream bed, into the shade of the trees, and dismounted from our weary animals. But I couldn't rest yet. With my hands and the blade of my knife I dug a hole in the sand at a place where there grew a little stand of willows. Soon the hole filled with water, and Rising Moon and I, and then our water-crazed horses, slaked our thirst. Then I led the horse with Wali'ms's body on it up the stream a little way, and then onto the ridge that bordered it. Using my knife I began to dig into the hard ground. I dug and dug for hours until at last there was a secure grave for Wali'ms's body, and then I lowered her earthly remains into the waiting arms of her Mother the Earth, whom she had loved so much.

Memories of Wali'ms flooded back to me. I saw her as she was when she first was brought to our camp, a frightened Shoshone maiden. I saw her as she looked when I married her, shy, tender, fearful of the strange man who had come for her, yet also somehow confident. I saw her as she worked on her baskets, weaving by the hour the watertight marvels that everyone admired so much. My mind flashed back to the ridge high above the Clearwater River, where Hohots Illpilp had died, and I saw Wali'ms again, bravely struggling up that steep slope with water in one of her baskets; fearless of the bullets of the soldiers, she was looking for her men to bring them the water that might make for them the difference between life and death. I saw her again gathering the tiny medicinal plants of the forest, which only she knew how to find, and carefully naming each tender flower of the meadows as though it were her special friend. And I saw her, of course, with Pahkatos Peopeo, mother and child as one person. And now this was all there was left of her on this earth. Slowly I filled the grave with dirt and piled rocks on top to keep it safe from marauding animals. Finally, as was our ancient custom, I killed her horse and carried the carcass a safe distance away so it would not betray the location of the grave. It would become a spirit horse for her to ride on her spirit journey to the other world.

All this took time, and when we once more resumed our journey, following the broad trail the People had left, it was almost evening. Soon we had no choice but to make camp. We said little, but we felt close. It gave me strength to have Rising Moon by my side, and I knew that for her also my presence was like a warming fire. Only one thing did I say to her. "The child you are carrying, is it well with the child?"

Rising Moon answered, "It is well with the child. I think just today I felt the baby move. My womb is a safe place for it."

I smiled in relief and fell into a sleep born of exhaustion.

Two suns later, just as darkness began to fall again, we reached the Musselshell River and found the People camping for the night. Silently we rode into the camp on our weary horses. We had rejoined Joseph at last.

CHAPTER FIFTEEN

Surrounded

As soon as we crossed the Yellowstone River we were in country that was known to our buffalo hunters, and Lean Elk, Looking Glass, White Bird, and Too-hool-hool-Sote all claimed to know the best route to follow to reach Grandmother's Country, which was 200 miles to the north. Perhaps because he was so familiar with the country, Looking Glass's prestige began to rise again, and people no longer listened so attentively to Joseph, or even to Lean Elk, who had served so ably as war chief during the journey from Big Hole. Now that Looking Glass knows the country again, let him lead once more, was the attitude that many people took.

We found the Musselshell River no great obstacle, for at this time of year it was low enough to ford easily, and from here we made rapid progress through Judith Gap, which made a broad path through the Judith and Snowy mountain ranges and took us north toward the Missouri River, which we intended to cross at a place called Seloselo Wejanwais, known to the whites as Cow Island. As we traveled through Judith Gap some of our warriors came upon a band of Crow led by their chief, Dumb Bull. The Crow had been hunting and were cutting up and drying the animals they had killed. That day our young men got revenge on the Crow for their treatment of us, killing several of them and taking their horses. The fresh horses of the Crow were welcome, for many of our ponies were exhausted or injured by our arduous journey; these we abandoned as we went along, cutting one foot of each horse so it could not be used by our pursuers.

Ten suns after the battle at Canyon Creek we reached Cow Island, where the Long Knives often unloaded supplies for their northern forts and settlements. Their big river boats could make their way up the Missouri River this far but no farther, and that is why they established a landing place here for their goods. We needed many things, and the chiefs approached the white people at the Cow Island landing and asked to talk with them. There were twelve soldiers and three civilians at this place, but their officer refused to give us supplies, even though we offered to pay for the goods. Then the soldiers and civilians withdrew behind some earthworks they had prepared as a defense. We could easily have wiped them out, but what was the point? Killing twelve soldiers wouldn't make the Americans any weaker, for they had many soldiers, and we were certain to lose warriors we couldn't replace. Nor was it necessary to kill the soldiers in order to get what we needed, for the earthworks were not in a position to keep us from the supplies. So, since they wouldn't sell us what we needed, we simply helped ourselves. Food, knives, pots and pans—we replaced all the items we had lost at Big Hole, and we felt that this was not stealing, for was this not war? But except for some desultory shooting from both sides there was no fighting at Cow Island and we soon moved on, leaving the soldiers and civilians unmolested. Nor did we molest any other settlers in the area, though we did set fire to the supplies we didn't need for ourselves so the soldiers following us wouldn't have them.

There was one attack on white people in the area, however. Some of our rear guard came upon a wagon train and couldn't resist attacking it. Three of the teamsters were killed, though others were allowed to escape. While the warriors were helping themselves to the contents of the wagon train, a band of mounted civilian volunteers approached, led by an army officer, and began to fire. Our men stopped their looting and engaged the mounted men in long-range rifle fire. I guess we won because no one on our side was killed and one of the settlers was shot by a warrior who was an expert long-range marksman. Those white riders apparently had second thoughts about attacking us and withdrew from the field. We never saw them again.

The day after we raided the supplies at Cow Island a brief council was held that was to have bad results for us. As I have mentioned, Looking Glass was beginning to recover his lost prestige because of his knowledge of the country, and his old arrogance and confidence were coming back also. So he began to contest Lean Elk's leadership.

"I am tired of going so fast," he said. "The old people are weary, and it's because we are going so fast that they suffer so much. What's the point? Our scouts tell us the soldiers are far behind. They are at least two days' march to the rear and have not gained on us since we left the Yellowstone River. It's not good that the half-breed keeps us moving so fast." Of course he was referring to Lean Elk, implying that because he was not a full-blood Nez Perce he didn't have the interests of the People at heart.

People were tired, and many of them sided with Looking Glass. "All right, Looking Glass," Lean Elk finally shouted, throwing up his hands in despair. "You lead. I'm trying to save the People from the army by getting to Canada before the soldiers can catch up to us. But you think you know best. You take command, but I think we will all be caught and killed."

Joseph's opinion was not consulted in this matter. Although Joseph was almost the only one among us who had not made a bad mistake during our flight, he was disregarded this time because he didn't know the country. But he did raise a troublesome question. "Will the Sioux welcome us in Canada? We have fought them in years past when the Crow were our allies. When we arrive in Canada, winter will soon be coming. Sitting Bull may not be pleased to have so many more mouths to feed." But no one wanted to think such thoughts, and the matter Joseph raised was ignored.

Now we were under the direction of Looking Glass again and traveled slowly for four days. We rested often. The men hunted, and the women took time to prepare food, and our horses were allowed to forage. People began to relax, for our scouts told us that even though we had slowed our pace Howard also had slowed his pace and was still two suns' travel behind us. So we traveled like a tortoise, which moves slowly and fears no enemies, until finally we reached a small tributary of the Milk River known as Snake Creek, only forty miles from the border of Grandmother's Country.

"Here," said Looking Glass, "we will make camp." He said this even though it was only noon when we reached Snake Creek. It was a good spot for a camp, but not for defense because the country was so open around it, but the people wanted to rest again, and we didn't worry because the soldiers were so far behind.

Snake Creek was a shallow stream that wound its way in a generally northerly direction. There were no trees or large rocks for protection, but there were plentiful buffalo chips to burn, and soon fires protected us against a cold wind that was sweeping in ominously from the north, bringing with it a bone-chilling rain. The land on all sides was open and gently rolling and offered no protection, but there were ravines that emptied into the sandy creek bed and we could take refuge against the wind behind their six-foot-high walls. We made a fairly comfortable camp. We had enough food for the time being, and the water in the stream was good to drink. So we prepared to stay awhile and pastured our horses a half mile away on the other, northwestern side of the stream.

We hadn't been in camp long when Wottolen, one of our best warriors and a brave man, rode through the camp crying out, "We must be off! Away! I have had a dream in which I saw soldiers charging us. They will be upon us in the morning. Do not remain here. Quick! There is no time to lose!"

Those of us who heard Wottolen's warning were dismayed; it sounded much like the warning we had received from Lone Bird just before the battle at Big Hole. But now, as then, Looking Glass chose to scoff at the vision sent to Wottolen. "There are no soldiers near us," he said disdainfully. "Wottolen is a fool; like a ground squirrel he is scared by every little thing." Incredibly, everyone believed Looking Glass. When people are as tired as we were they don't think clearly, and all they wanted to do was rest.

When we woke the following morning the weather was still damp and cold, and we decided to break camp and resume our journey because it was so uncomfortable where we were. Our preparations were leisurely for there seemed to be no occasion to hurry. Not long after the sun came over the hills and was trying to struggle through the dark clouds, two of our scouts, who were returning to camp after spending the night with neighboring Assiniboin Indians, were seen on a distant hill. They were signaling us, and their smoke language said, "Soldiers coming!" Later I learned that they had seen a buffalo herd stampeding and surmised, correctly, that they had been panicked by approaching horsemen. But Looking Glass said to pay no attention. "If there are soldiers near us," he said, "it can only be a small band of scouts."

So we continued our leisurely preparations for the march. The women began to pack our gear and lash our belongings on the travois, and the men went out among the horses to cut out those that would be used on today's march. Soon some of the women were also among the horses, loading gear on them, until about sixty of the men and a hundred women and children were ready to go. Joseph was there among the horses too, and I was also there getting horses ready for Rising Moon and myself, while Rising Moon was at the main camp packing our belongings. All was peaceful until we suddenly saw another of our scouts, much closer than the first two, signaling to us frantically, "Many soldiers, coming fast, soon upon us!" I looked in the direction in which the scout was pointing and there I could see them: hundreds of horse soldiers sweeping down upon us in a full charge from about two miles away!

It was clear that we were in great danger, for the force of soldiers was overwhelming; we were like the antelope that the mountain lion has been stalking and is now charging at full speed. Moreover, behind the charging horse soldiers a long line of foot soldiers could be seen; if the horse soldiers broke through our lines, the foot soldiers would soon follow and wipe us out completely. It looked like it was going to be Big Hole all over again, only much worse for we were greatly outnumbered.

The soldiers were charging in two main groups. The larger group was coming straight for the camp by the creek, but another group was headed for our horses, and this group had a band of Cheyennes with them. We had only one thing in our favor: The land was so open that though we were totally surprised that soldiers were in the area, we had seen them while they were still at a distance. This gave us a chance to make a stand before they fell upon us.

By now everyone had seen the charging soldiers and all was confusion. The warriors who were in the main camp ran to find places among the ravines where they could defend themselves, and those warriors who were not too far away raced to join them. The women and children were making

240

for the banks of the creek to find shelter. A few warriors, too far away from the camp to get back to it in time, flung themselves on the ground, hiding behind what shelter they could find to meet the charge. But those of us who were among the horses and ready to go didn't know whether to return to the camp or try to escape. Then Joseph urged, "Away! Ride! Don't pause. Those of you who are ready, go!" Soon scores of people—men, women, and children—raced northward toward Grandmother's Country, including Joseph's daughter. But Joseph remained because he wouldn't leave the main group of people, and I remained because I wouldn't leave Rising Moon.

The soldiers who were charging the horses saw that many of us were escaping, and a large number of them swept around the herd and, whipping their mounts, went in pursuit of them, but the Nez Perce who were fleeing had a head start, and their horses were fresh, so I knew the Long Knives would never catch them. A feeling of relief mingled with my deep sense of fear: At least some of the People had gotten away! At least some of us would find the way to freedom.

But I didn't have long for such reflections, for now the horse soldiers who had been charging our herd of horses were upon us, and to my dismay I saw that many of them were now between Joseph and myself and the main camp. We were cut off, and the herd of horses was almost surrounded. This was my last chance to escape; it was still not too late for me to leap on one of the horses milling around and make my dash for freedom. Joseph called to me, "Teeto Hoonod, go quickly before it's too late." But I shouted back, "No, Joseph, we must find our way back to camp. Quickly, there may still be time."

So Joseph and I ran for the main camp, right through those soldiers who were between us and the creek. Why we weren't killed I don't know, although we had one advantage: surprise. For the soldiers had their backs to us, facing

241

the Nez Perce in the camp on the creek, and when we ran through their lines we came from their rear and they didn't expect this. Even then the bullets flew past us like bees. One of them made a hole through my leggings, another creased my scalp painfully. Yet they didn't hit either Joseph or me. Perhaps the soldiers were too startled to take good aim; perhaps our Wy-a-kin was too strong and turned the bullets away. So it happened that with prayers to the Great Spirit, and our death songs being sung in our hearts, we made our way through that rain of death and with a final burst of speed flung ourselves into the camp.

In a moment Rising Moon was by me, my rifle in her hand. "When the soldiers charged," she said breathlessly, "I looked to the horses to see you. I knew you would come. I waited and brought you your rifle."

I saw the rifle was smoking and knew that Rising Moon had fired at the soldiers in order to cover me. Then I heard Joseph's wife call to him, "Here's your gun! Fight!" Soon Joseph and I were behind the ravines with other warriors peering out anxiously at the horse soldiers from the south, who were sweeping rapidly closer.

I glanced around quickly. Ollokot was nearby. His arm was raised; this meant we were to hold our fire until he gave the signal and then fire as one man. Farther up the line I could see Too-hool-hool-Sote and some of his warriors defending the northern extremity of the camp. Shuslum Hih-hih was near my side, and White Bird, aged but still full of fight, was between Joseph and Too-hool-hool-Sote. I didn't see Lean Elk and knew that he must be outside the camp; I only hoped that he had found a spot where he could defend himself. There couldn't have been more than fifty warriors in the camp, and coming upon us were at least six hundred of the enemy. What chance did we have?

The sound of the charging horses was like rolling thunder; my finger ached to pull the trigger on my gun, but still

Ollokot kept his arm raised. It seemed forever before finally, with the charging soldiers only a hundred yards in front of us, he pulled down his arm. We fired now as one man, and it seemed as though every shot brought down a trooper. Their proud line was suddenly all confusion. Wounded and frightened horses were plunging and milling about, bodies were hurled to the ground, yet still they came on. Then we fired again, and again, and this time I could see that most of the officers had fallen; our marksmen were picking them off, until soon among all that charging mass of soldiers scarcely an officer could be seen. We were cutting those soldiers down; they were falling like leaves fall from a tree when the first winter storm hits.

But we suffered badly too. Hundreds of bullets raced through our lines. Here, there, an Indian fell. It sickened me to see my comrades struck one by one. Yet still we kept firing. There was no thought of surrender; we would fight to the death, and the women behind us kept us supplied with ammunition. Then that charging line of soldiers broke. Like a wave breaks on shore and then recedes, so that line of soldiers broke and began to retreat. Only a few made it into our camp, and these we grappled with hand to hand. I saw Shuslum Hihhih spring upon one soldier who, with his rifle up, was about to fire at a huddled group of women. The soldier turned to meet his charge. The two fell to the ground fighting. I raised my rifle to aid Shuslum Hihhih, but feared that I would kill him by mistake. No need. With a mighty swing of his arm my friend drove his knife deeply into that soldier's chest and I heard the life go out of him with a sickening gasp. In a few moments those soldiers who made their way into our lines were all dead, and the charging horse soldiers were falling back before our onslaught of bullets.

Now the foot soldiers found it was their turn to charge. There was no respite for us! But their heart wasn't in it. They had seen the damage we had done to their fellows, and they didn't want to die. So those foot soldiers soon retreated until they were almost out of range of our rifles. Then they dug trenches and hid in them, firing now and then.

The battle became a contest of marksmen. There were many more of them than there were of us, but we were the better shots and we kept those soldiers from showing their heads lest our bullets find their mark. All day we kept up the firing and those soldiers never had another chance to charge. But our plight was desperate, for the soldiers and Cheyennes had us surrounded, and all our horses had been run off except for a few within the main camp. Still, we could have escaped if we had all been warriors, because the soldiers' line around us was thin in places and with a determined charge, or a night attack, we could have broken through. Joseph knew this, and so did White Bird and Looking Glass. But there was no thought of it. "We cannot desert the women and children," Joseph said, and so we stayed and fought.

But Too-hool-hool-Sote said nothing, for he was dead. And Ollokot said nothing, for a bullet had found its way through his brave heart. And many other warriors said nothing, for they too had been killed.

More bad things were waiting for us. Toward dusk a group of four men were seen stealing up on our camp. We couldn't tell if they were soldiers or Cheyennes. Some of our men shot, and the four men were cut down. Too late we learned that these were our own men, Lean Elk and three others who had been outside the camp and were trying to rejoin us. Now they were dead, killed by their own comrades. When we realized what had happened to Lean Elk and his comrades our spirits were sick. It took Joseph to renew our courage. "Lean Elk was a brave and great man," he cried out. "The Great Spirit will welcome him. He was ready to die. Do as he would want you to and continue to fight as men." So Joseph gave us courage, and we fought on.

When night came we strengthened our defenses. Men and women used knives, captured bayonets, pots and pans to deepen our rifle pits and dig holes in which the women, children, and wounded would be safe. We made everything ready for the battle that we knew would resume again in the morning.

It was well that we did so, for in the morning the big thunder gun began to fire at us. At first the shells went harmlessly over our heads. Then the soldiers upended the gun so the shells went high into the air and then fell in our midst. Again and again they fired the big gun and the shells sent fragments everywhere. One woman and her child were buried alive and died. But we had done our job well. Not even the big gun could find and kill the rest of us, and safe behind our fortifications we could hold the soldiers at bay.

But the cold did find us. All night we could hardly sleep because of it, and when the day dawned it was bleak and icy. The wind continued to blow from the frozen wastes to the north. Snow fluttered down and made us damp and chill. We had only dried meat to eat. There were not enough blankets. The wounded suffered silently, the children cried, the brave women did all they could to help them and keep their men supplied with food, water, and ammunition. And we warriors lay in our frozen rifle pits peering out at the enemy, firing when one of them was rash enough to show his head. We held them back, but our suffering was greater and greater with each passing moment.

Who were these soldiers in front of us? Would I see my enemy? No, it couldn't be, for these soldiers were not from the army of One-arm Howard, whom we knew to be far away; they were other soldiers we had never seen before, from another army of the white man—it seemed he had limitless armies—that had come from we did not know where. I gave up hope now of finding my enemy. I thought I would die there in my cold rifle pit and that my enemy, safe and secure somewhere, would have the final laugh.

One bit of hope remained and broke through our despair from time to time to renew our spirits like the sun breaks through after a summer thunderstorm. The Sioux might come! For Joseph—so wisely!—had sent messengers to Sitting Bull imploring him to come to our aid. He had not trusted Looking Glass's confidence that we wouldn't be attacked, and as we neared the border to Grandmother's Country he had sent messengers to the great Sioux chief. Sitting Bull was not far away. In one, maybe two suns' travel he could reach us, and he had two thousand undefeated Sioux warriors with him, all those who had been too fierce and too proud to submit to the white man and who had fled for refuge to Canada. So as we fought we also looked to the north, from which direction the Sioux might come.

Two suns after the battle had started, a white flag went up over the soldiers' lines and a voice cried out in an Indian dialect, "Colonel Miles would like to see Joseph." This was the first time we knew for sure whom we were facing. We had heard of Miles from other Indians, who called him "Bear Coat." We didn't know he had an army nearby. We were not ready to surrender because of our hope of relief from Sitting Bull and because our fighting spirit was still up, but we decided to find out what Miles would say. So a Delaware Indian half-breed who understood some English went out to parley with the white general. The two agreed that if Joseph would come and talk, Miles would meet him halfway between the lines.

Joseph, with two other warriors, went to meet Miles, who came with a small group of soldiers. They met and talked on a buffalo robe placed halfway between the lines. I don't know exactly what was said, but evidently the talk broke down, for after some time Joseph turned and began to walk back toward our lines. Then that general did a bad thing, something that must surely have been against the heart of the Great Spirit. He called Joseph back—making some excuse—and when Joseph returned, his soldiers made him a prisoner. That was all he cared for his word and the white flag!

We were extremely angry when we saw what happened, but we could do nothing. We couldn't shoot for fear of hitting Joseph, and we had to watch as the soldiers took him away. We were like a raging mountain lion on a chain, full of fire but unable to act.

But Miles made a mistake. He sent one of his officers to look over our lines to see if we were stacking up our arms to surrender as he had demanded. That officer came too close to us and suddenly some of our warriors leaped out and seized him and dragged him down inside our lines. Now we had a prisoner too! And we wouldn't release him until Miles released Joseph. Shuslum Hihhih and other warriors, filled with anger, wanted to kill this officer, but White Bird wouldn't let them, for it was only because we held the officer a prisoner that we had a chance of getting Joseph back.

That night the officer was well treated by us. He was allowed to eat the food sent in to him from his own camp. He was made as comfortable as any of us were that cold night. Not so with Joseph. Later we learned that our chief was bound hand and foot, rolled in a blanket, and thrown in to sleep with the mules.

The next day we allowed communications to be sent between Miles and his captured officer, and when Miles learned how well we had treated his officer he relented and began to treat Joseph better too. Later that day, it was agreed to exchange the prisoners. We led the officer out to the halfway point between the lines, and soldiers brought Joseph out. We were ready to kill that officer instantly if they tried treachery again, but there was no trick this time. The officer returned with the soldiers, and Joseph came back with us. I imagine Bear Coat treated his officer badly that night; it was because of his carelessness that Miles's trick had not worked.

The sun rose and set four times, and still we held out in our bleak shelters and rifle pits. Not many people were being killed now on either side; neither soldier nor warrior dared show his face. It was not an open battle now, but a siege, and the advantage lay with the soldiers, for our suffering was greater than theirs, and they could also expect the troops of One-arm Howard to arrive soon and then they would have fresh supplies and overwhelming numbers. Still we hung on and waited and looked to the north for help. And then we saw it!

As I was lying on the cold ground, shivering in the wind-driven snow, I heard a shout from one of our men. "Sitting Bull! Sitting Bull! To the north! He comes!" We all looked to the north and sure enough, in the distance could be seen a swarm of rushing horses. Sitting Bull charging to our rescue! How our hearts sang then, for not only would we be rescued, but now we could catch those soldiers between us and crush them, for the Sioux on one side and the Nez Perce on the other would be like the jaws of a grizzly bear. At the same time we heard a cry of dismay from the soldiers closest to us; they too had seen the approaching animals, and some were already scrambling to get to the rear of their lines.

Then the sound from the soldiers changed from a cry of fear to a shout of their own. We looked again: It was not Sitting Bull and his mounted warriors, but a herd of buffalo stampeding through the flying snow! Our spirits that had soared so high now plunged low, like a stone that falls into the lake and sinks out of sight. After that there was talk of surrender. What had happened to Sitting Bull? I had no way of knowing at that time, but I would find out later.

Still we didn't want to surrender. Had we not stood off the charge of the horse soldiers? Had we not held the foot soldiers at bay in their rifle pits? Had they defeated us and taken our guns? No. We were not defeated; why should we surrender? Yet we could see that the women and children and wounded, and warriors too, suffered dreadfully. It was then that Bear Coat Miles sent two of the Christian Nez Perce who were with him as scouts to talk with us.

Jokais and Meopkowit were known to us, for they had daughters in our camp who had been with us during all our long march. These men had joined the whites so they could be closer to their daughters and maybe help them. Some of our warriors were angry at the Christian Nez Perce and wanted to kill Jokais and Meopkowit as they approached us, for they felt betrayed by them, but the chiefs restrained them. Jokais and Meopkowit were not bad men. They had never fired on us in the battles. There was no point in killing them now.

So we let them come and speak to us, and they told us the words of Bear Coat Miles: If we gave up our guns there would be no trials and no executions. We would be treated honorably as prisoners of war, and in the spring we would be sent back to the reservation at Lapwai, where we would join the rest of our nation. When we gave up our guns the soldiers would give us food and blankets and medicine for the wounded. These were the terms given us by Bear Coat if we would give up the fight.

I heard those terms, and I believed them, except for the part about no executions. I couldn't believe those white settlers back in the Salmon River country would let any of the warriors live who had taken part in that raid. Actually, almost all of those who had been in the raid had already been killed, but how about me? I was not in the raid, but others supposed that I had been. What would the white people believe about me?

The chiefs met to talk. Joseph spoke first, and he was in favor of agreeing to Miles's terms. Speaking with great power, this chief, youngest of all in years but greatest in wisdom, spoke out for the cause of the women and children. "Bear Coat wishes to make an agreement with us. His agreement is good. It would not be surrender if we agree to his terms, for has he not promised to send us back to our country? Is this not what we have been fighting for all this time? It would mean that we had won and made the white people agree that this is what should be. We can accept Miles's terms. There is no point in fighting any more while our people are hungry and freezing; the women are suffering with cold, the children crying with the chilly dampness of the shelter pits, and the wounded have no medicine for their wounds. For myself I do not care. I'm willing to die, and if we were all warriors I would say, 'Let us break out!' But because of the suffering of the People I say we must agree to the terms Miles gives us."

Chief White Bird spoke next. "You may surrender, Joseph, if you wish, but I will never surrender. The young men who started this war were almost all from my band. If I surrender I will be executed in spite of what has been promised to us, and many of my band too. If I am to die it will not be by the white man's rope, so I will escape with those who wish to go with me."

Then Looking Glass spoke, and he was full of hatred for the white man. "I am older than you, Joseph, and I have had too many experiences with the Long Knives. They have two faces and two tongues. If you surrender you will be sorry; and in your sorrow you will want to be dead, rather than to suffer from their treachery."

Looking Glass's words were strong, but they were the last

words he ever spoke. Right after this, as he was lying in one of the rifle pits, someone told him they could see an approaching Indian. Hoping that this was a courier from the Sioux, Looking Glass sprang up recklessly to get a better look. As he did so a distant soldier fired. The bullet struck Looking Glass in the forehead, and the fighting chief fell dead, instantly killed, falling like a great tree falls when struck by lightning.

This was the last casualty of the war, and Looking Glass was the only warrior to be killed after the first day's battle. In spite of his failings, Looking Glass was a great chief and the son of a great chief. His death was like the end of an age for us, the age in which we were a free people whose lives were guided by wise chiefs from great families. Now they were almost all gone: Looking Glass, Ollokot, Too-hool-hool-Sote, Lean Elk—all the great chiefs dead except White Bird and Joseph. True, Looking Glass had made bad mistakes. Except for him we would have escaped to Grandmother's Country. It was his arrogance that led to the disaster at Big Hole. It was his ts'ayta'nin, his extreme self-confidence, and his refusal to listen to Wottolen's warning dream that led to our encirclement here at Snake Creek. Still, he was a fighting chief and his courage never wavered, and though we were angry at him for his errors his death affected us so profoundly that some of the people, deeply distressed, slipped away from the camp and set out for the hills, even though they didn't know where they were going, even though they had no food and no blankets.

We stretched out Looking Glass's body on the ground and covered it with grass as best we could; we would bury it later, though when and how we did not know. Now, except for the sounds of muffled grief, there was no sound in our trenches. The cold wind whistled among us like an evil spirit. The skies were heavy and gray like our hearts. The few people who had blankets pulled them closely around

251

their bodies. I was shivering miserably as I sat not far from Joseph and White Bird. Then White Bird rose and looked intently at Joseph. And then Joseph stood also and the two men gazed into each other's eyes. White Bird spoke. "I am going to get ready to leave tonight, Hin-mah-too-yah-lat-kekht. You must stay with the women and the children. You are now the leader." Joseph embraced the old chief with a mighty embrace. They parted, and did I not see the tears in their eyes as they did so? Each knew that he would never see the other again.

Then Joseph called briskly to Jokais and Meopkowit to come to him. "Tell the white chief," he said, "that I accept his terms. Tell him to be ready to meet me. Go quickly and give him these words, for my people are cold and hungry and tired."

I watched as Jokais and Meopkowit galloped away to the soldiers' camp, while Joseph made ready to go, and his horse was brought by the two warriors who would accompany him, and the people watched with the first signs of hope on their faces that they had shown for many days. Joseph mounted, his rifle across the pommel of his saddle, a blanket draped around his broad shoulders, and his long black braids falling down almost to his moccasin leggings. Then to my surprise Joseph looked at me. "Teeto Hoonod," he said, "come with me. I will need you to be sure that the words that are spoken between Miles and me are true." Then with a kick of his heels Joseph spurred his horse out of our camp and toward the soldiers; the two warriors followed on foot, while I stumbled to my feet and ran to catch up with them.

The snow was falling so hard now we could not see the enemy lines. I held my head down against the wind, but Joseph held his head high and looked straight ahead as his horse plodded on. Then there they were, suddenly looming up through the snowy gloom of that day: Colonel Miles, standing in the center of a group of three officers, a man who proved to be the white man's interpreter, and, beside Miles, another white chief who must have been important or he would not have had such a place of honor. I was soon to learn that he was General Howard, our long-time pursuer and adversary. He had caught up with us at last.

Joseph rode ahead; the warriors waited behind, but I hurried forward and stood beside Joseph so I could listen to the words. Our chief dismounted. Holding his rifle in his two hands he walked to Howard and thrust the rifle forward for him to take, but Howard motioned that Joseph should give it to Miles instead.

Then Joseph stood back and spoke as follows to the white interpreter: "Tell General Howard I know his heart. What he told me before I have in my heart. I am tired of fighting. Our chiefs are killed. Looking Glass is dead. The old men are all killed. It is the young men who say yes or no. He who led the young men is dead. It is cold and we have no blankets. The little children are freezing to death. My people, some of them, have run away to the hills and have no blankets, no food; no one knows where they are, perhaps freezing to death. I want time to look for my children and see how many of them I can find. Maybe I shall find them among the dead. Hear me, my chiefs, I am tired; my heart is sick and sad. From where the sun now stands, I will fight no more forever."

Now Howard spoke, and I translated the words for Joseph. His voice was full of kindness: "You have your life. I am living. I have lost my brothers. Many of you have lost brothers, maybe more than on our side. I do not know. Do not worry more."

And Miles spoke too: "No more battles and blood. From this sun, we will have a good time on both sides, your band and mine." And then he spoke again the terms of the surrender: The Nez Perce would no longer fight, and the soldiers would take us to a safe place until spring, when we would be returned to our homes. These were his words, and I myself was there to hear them.

Joseph stayed in the white man's camp. He rode away with Miles and Howard and disappeared among the soldiers, who stood silently and respectfully as he passed among them. The two warriors with me followed him. I hesitated, not knowing what to do. Then Joseph paused and turned back to me and waved to me to return to the camp. I knew what he meant: I was to tell the people what had happened. It was good, for I did not want to surrender, and I did not want to leave Rising Moon.

So I returned to our camp and all gathered around me and I told them what Joseph had said, and I told them what Howard and Miles had said. Soon other warriors began to cross the lines. They went slowly at first, by twos and threes, to turn over their rifles to the soldiers. I saw Shuslum Hihhih go too, riding proudly on one of the few horses left to us. Now the women and children began to trek over the barren ground under the gun-barrel-gray skies. Now I could see fires lit in the soldiers' camp, and I could see the Indians who had given up the fight warming themselves, and the soldiers, who had been firing at us a short while ago, were now friendly. Soon food would be set out by the soldiers, and after five long suns with empty stomachs there would be plenty of food and warm blankets under which to sleep that night. What was at first a trickle of people going over to the soldiers now became a stream until hundreds had given up the fight and were now in the soldiers' camp.

But only a handful of these were from White Bird's band, for that fighting old chief still had fire in his heart and had not given up to the white man, and many of those in his band had decided to try to escape with him to Grandmother's Country as soon as night had fallen. And Rising Moon and I? Which way would we turn? Which path would we follow?

As I stood with Rising Moon silently watching the People trek across the barren ground to the soldiers' camp, my heart was filled with grief. Was this the way it was going to end for us? Was this the end of our beautiful tribe, this sad surrender of our freedom to the soldiers? For no matter how Joseph had bravely said, "We did not give up!" it was clear that we had lost the battle and the war.

My thoughts took flight and carried me on their wings back to our homeland in the Wallowa Valley. I saw the lively streams of clear mountain water, the rich, fertile valleys with our horses grazing in them peacefully, the cozy villages with smoke curling up from the lodges, and the high, snow-capped, forested mountains that embraced us on every side, sheltering us like the arms of our Mother the Earth. I saw again how it was in the winter as we passed the time in talk and rest and storytelling in the warmth of our lodges, how it was when the season-of-the-new-grass came and the flowers pushed their way up through the newly warmed earth to burst forth in their song of life. I remembered the summer, when the bands gathered from all over our country for the feasting, dancing, and games at Camas Prairie, and how it was in the season-of-the-falling-leaves when the hunting was good and the leaves of the trees were painted yellow and red by the Great Spirit and the air was crackling and sparkling with the clear, invigorating chill of the mountain air. We were a wealthy and happy people then, with thousands of horses, warm clothing, and plenty of food for all. We were a proud people too. Undefeated in war, we were the leading people of the whole region, and we led our lives as we wished to lead them, for there was no one who could tell us where to go or how we must live. Now, were we reduced to this? Our horses gone, our bravest warriors killed, nothing left to us but the rags on our backs, with other people telling us what to do? I knew as I watched the People march to the soldiers' camp and stack up their arms that I was watching the end forever of the old ways.

A voice broke in on my musings. It was Rising Moon. "Teeto Hoonod, if you are going with Joseph and the others you should leave now while it is still light. It will be night soon and here there is no warmth, no food, no fires. Those who remain here are White Bird's people. Aren't you going to join Joseph and the others?"

I was so absorbed in my own thoughts that I had momentarily forgotten the presence beside me of the slender, warriorlike young woman who had become as a wife to me. "Rising Moon, you ask me these questions, but what of yourself? You too are from Joseph's band. I don't see you preparing to make the walk to the soldiers' camp."

Rising Moon's dark eyes met mine and they flashed with a fierce spirit. "No, Teeto Hoonod, I will not live under the white man's rule. I don't trust the words of their generals. I think the People will never see their land again, and they will die in a strange place. I will not go with them. I will throw in my lot with White Bird, and ask the Great Spirit to help me, and hope to live free with the Sioux in Grandmother's Country to the north."

I felt hurt. "And don't you care about me, Rising Moon? And about the life of our child? Don't you want me with you?"

Tears welled up in Rising Moon's eyes as she answered, "I care about you, Teeto Hoonod. You and our child are all I have in this world. But I can't hold you back if you wish to go. And if you go, I can't go with you, much as my heart would wish to, for the spirit within me says that I must remain free."

Like the great waters that rise and surge in the Yellowstone River through which we had passed, so my own emotions rose and surged within me. I reached out to Rising Moon and held her. "You see, Rising Moon, I am still here. I have not walked to the white man's camp. My spirit feels as your spirit feels. I too will not go the white man's way. We will go tonight, together, and pray that the Great Spirit will see our plight and guide us safely."

Rising Moon said nothing at first, but I could tell from the look in her eye that she was glad. Finally she said simply, "It is good. Let us get ready to go."

So we joined those from White Bird's band who were preparing to escape. I checked my rifle and the revolver of my soldier enemy. We placed ammunition securely in our belts. What food we could find was eaten to give us strength. Then we waited until the darkness deepened, when the coldness of the night would force the soldiers into their blankets and their exhaustion would bring sleep to them. White Bird had chosen our direction: Straight toward the star-which-does-not-turn-in-the-sky. We would head this way and try to find a place where the soldiers' line was thin, where we could slip through and make our way onto the open prairie beyond. But even if we succeeded we would not be safe, for roving bands of horse soldiers would be scouting the plains, and fierce Cheyennes too, looking for those of us who had gotten away. If they caught us we would be treated as prisoners, or we might be killed on the spot. And while we were on foot, they would be mounted. Still, we were going to try.

There were about twenty of us in the little band that stole away from the camp at Snake Creek in the dead of night. Most were warriors, a few were women and children. White Bird was in charge. Each man carried a rifle with ammunition. The women carried what food was left. There were not enough blankets to go around, and the night was bitterly cold. The children had been carefully instructed not to utter so much as a sound. Brave little boys and girls! Though they were hungry and cold and frightened, not one of them cried out. The courage of these little people filled me with pride and made me think of our unborn child, safely held in Rising Moon's womb.

Scouts had been sent out in advance to find a path we

could follow in the dark. Our greatest dangers were running into soldiers or getting lost. The clouds were breaking up now, and we were able to take a sight on the star-that-does-not-move and knew that as long as we headed for this star we would be going in the direction of Grandmother's Country. It was a pitch-dark night. White Bird hoped we could use the darkness as cover until we left the soldiers behind, and then have the advantage of the daylight to speed us on our way. To keep from getting separated, each person held on to the person in front; Rising Moon and I were toward the rear of the column. Off we went into the blackness, slowly making our way up a small ravine that led out of the creek bed and offered us some concealment.

Soon we were on the gently rolling ground beyond the creek. There was little or no cover here. No trees, only occasional clumps of bushes and a few rocks. Somewhere out here were the soldiers who surrounded our camp. Would we run into them? We had to take this chance. On we crept. Absolute silence now, for we had to move quietly, coyote-like, making no sounds. Suddenly our little column came to a halt. This meant that the warriors leading us suspected that soldiers were near. We waited for what seemed like an endless time while the cold made its way deeper into our bones. Finally we were in motion again, even more slowly and silently this time. On we crept, and then I saw off to my left, faintly outlined in the dim starlight, a small camp of soldiers. They were asleep, lulled by their warm blankets and, perhaps, the belief that everyone had surrendered. We crept past them not more than a few yards away and yet they didn't waken! In another moment I saw White Bird standing beside me. He motioned to me in sign language and made me understand: If the white soldiers awoke I was to remain here as one of a rear guard while the others got away. I felt Rising Moon's hand tighten on mine as White Bird gave me this assignment.

258

We inched on step by step. We were past the soldiers now. The sun was beginning to make its way over the distant hills. The light was faint, but we could see. It was our moment of greatest danger. Then it happened! One of the children made a misstep and stones rattled noisily down a small decline. In the stillness it sounded like an avalanche, and the noise wakened the soldiers. One yelled something I couldn't understand. Had they seen us? We were beyond them now. If they had not seen us, we would be safe. But then a shot whistled over our heads, and another and another. We had been seen! White Bird barked out the order to move ahead rapidly. I seized my rifle and dropped to one knee. To Rising Moon I said, "I remain here. You go on with the rest of the band. I'll catch up later." And I thought I saw Rising Moon swiftly steal away as I turned to meet the soldiers coming up behind us.

In the increasing light of the dawn I saw that there were ten of them, and they were throwing saddles on their horses. The delay enabled our little band to get farther away, but the horses of the soldiers would give them the power to catch up once there was enough light to ride. The soldiers must be held back long enough for our group to escape, so I prepared to fire as soon as they tried to pursue us. Now I became aware that there were other warriors with me. I supposed White Bird had told them to join me as the rear guard.

Now the soldiers came. Closer and closer, walking their horses slowly because it was still only half-light and the horses might stumble. I raised my arm as a signal to the others when to fire. Then down my arm flashed as the horse soldiers neared us, and three rifles went off at once. A soldier dropped to the ground, and a horse, hit by our fire, stumbled and fell. The other soldiers wheeled their horses around. They were frightened because they couldn't see us and didn't know from exactly what spot the firing had come. I heard an officer bark an order: The soldiers were not to mount but to proceed on foot. Wise order. Mounted on their horses they would be easy targets. But that was good for us too, for this would delay them and give our little band more time to get away.

The soldiers crept forward, and we lay still, and when we saw one move we fired. In order to advance upon us the soldiers had to expose themselves, but we could remain hidden, hugging the ground and hiding behind rocks. This gave us an advantage, and soon the soldiers dared not advance farther. We had them pinned down. Our rear guard was succeeding, but when it was light they would see us, and since they were more numerous we would be in bad trouble. Besides, more soldiers would come to join them. There was only one hope: We must get their horses.

I motioned to the other warriors with me to remain where they were. I could see the horses. They were behind the soldiers, guarded by one man. Carefully, stealthily, hugging the ground like a snake, I made my way around the line of soldiers in front of us. I went in a wide arc, then swung back behind the soldiers' line. I was going to try to capture those horses, or at least run them off. It was a desperate plan, just desperate enough to succeed. As I went I was aware that one of the warriors in the rear guard had chosen to come with me, but it was still so dark, and my attention so focused on the soldiers and the horses, that I couldn't see who it was.

Now the horses were closer. Still I crept on. The firing behind me was desultory so I knew our men still had those troopers pinned down. Closer I came to the waiting horses. I motioned to the person with me to be ready to charge. I prepared to give him the signal: We would fire at the soldier guard, then rush the horses, steal two for ourselves, and run the rest of them off. I turned to give the order—and saw Rising Moon!! It was she who had stayed with me, she who was with me now! Silently I uttered bad words to myself.

260

She could see the anxiety and anger in my face, but I dared not speak to her. Too late to send her back. She must act now as a warrior with me.

I gave the signal and fired my rifle at the soldier guard. He was taken completely by surprise, and while my bullet didn't kill him, it did send him running desperately away from us. I gave the signal to Rising Moon for us to run for the horses. We were on our feet now, and I quickly seized two horses and then we were astride them. A few shots at the feet of the remaining horses sent them flying. It would take those soldiers a long time to catch them again! Our escaping band would be safe.

Waving exultantly to Rising Moon I drove my horse forward as swiftly as was possible in the gray light of dawn. It was a good animal, and Rising Moon was now beside me on hers. We turned and looked at each other and smiled, but I knew we were not yet out of danger. There might be other soldiers nearby, other dangers we didn't know.

We rode a little way, and then, with the speed of a snapping tendon, it happened: Two soldiers suddenly rose up from behind some rocks, and we were riding straight toward them! One of them raised his rifle to his shoulder. Before I could act he fired twice in rapid succession. A bullet whizzed harmlessly past me, but Rising Moon dropped from her horse with a little cry and fell to the ground. I heard her call out to me, "Teeto Hoonod, I'm hit. Ride! Ride!"

But I wouldn't ride. I reined in my horse and dropped to the ground a little distance from her and tried to get those soldiers in the sights of my rifle. Yes, there was the soldier who had shot Rising Moon coming toward us! He didn't see me where I had jumped to the ground; perhaps he thought his first shot had killed me. I raised my rifle to my shoulder, took careful aim, and squeezed the trigger with a sense of fierce, vengeful exultation. Nothing! The rifle jammed! That gun wouldn't fire! I was helpless as the soldier raised his rifle to his shoulder and took dead aim at my beloved, wounded Rising Moon. I struggled desperately with my rifle and at last freed the faulty catch, but a knifelike stab of agony went through me because I was too late; the soldier was about to fire, and at that range he couldn't miss.

Then suddenly I saw that the second soldier was standing beside the first one, and as that first soldier was about to shoot, the second soldier hit his rifle with his outstretched hand. The gun went off, but the bullet sped off harmlessly into the air. I raised my rifle again. I would get them both! I fired at the first soldier and he dropped to the ground like a stone, and I was about to fire at the second soldier, who stood there like a perfect target, when suddenly I saw his face. It was the face of my enemy!

I was exultant! At last I had him! He was completely exposed in the increasing light of dawn. One shot from my rifle would drop him, he who had killed my beloved brother, the one for whom I had searched for so many moons; at last the Great Spirit had delivered him into my hands! But with the speed of flashing lightning I also realized that he had saved Rising Moon; he had deflected the rifle of that first soldier and made the bullet go wild. I was torn in two, like a man between two straining horses. One half of me still drank from the cup of revenge; the other half didn't want to hurt this man who had for some reason been impelled to save the woman whom I loved. No, I *would* fire! I gave the order to my hand to pull the trigger and kill this hated enemy. But my fingers refused to obey; they wouldn't squeeze the trigger. Slowly I lowered my rifle helplessly. I couldn't believe it. After all this time I had let my enemy go unharmed.

There would not be another chance, for I heard the sound of soldiers coming. They had heard the firing of the rifles and would soon be upon us. Rising Moon was lying wounded on the ground, but there was nothing I could do to help her. We couldn't both escape on one horse even if I should succeed in getting her astride my horse with me before the soldiers came upon us. If I remained there it would be death for me, and for Rising Moon as well. I had to act quickly. With a cry of grief catching me in my throat I swung up on my horse, kneed him hard, and dashed off. A glance behind me showed me the form of my enemy. He was standing beside Rising Moon looking at me. His rifle was in his arms and he could have shot, but he made no move to fire. Behind him I could see the other soldiers closing in. Rising Moon was now a prisoner! I would escape, but it was only my body that was free, for as long as Rising Moon and my unborn child were in the soldiers' hands I was a prisoner too.

CHAPTER SIXTEEN

The Long Journey Ends

The next day I rejoined White Bird and his band and learned what had happened to them after they left me. Our fight with the soldiers had given them a head start, and when Rising Moon and I stampeded the soldiers' horses they easily escaped. But that had not been the end of their troubles, for although they saw no more soldiers, they did run into a war party of Assiniboin Indians. White Bird thought these Indians would be friendly, but instead they were attacked by them. Perhaps these Assiniboin Indians thought that White Bird and his band were helpless refugees and they could swoop down on them like vultures come to devour a dead carcass, but they soon found that old White Bird was far from dead, for the chief and his warriors gave them a sound thrashing. They also took a prisoner, and from him they learned that many of the Nez Perce who had fled singly or in small groups had been attacked by the ravenous Assiniboins and killed. From him White Bird learned why Sitting Bull hadn't come to our rescue: The six messengers that Joseph sent came upon an Assiniboin village. They were welcomed and led to believe they were among friends, but when they were asleep they were killed for the sake of their fine breech-loading rifles. Because he gave White Bird this information, the life of this Assiniboin prisoner was spared; he was only beaten, made to eat the dust, and then released to join the remnants of his comrades.

When we camped that night we lit no fires because of fear of our enemies. It seemed as though Americans and Indians alike looked upon the Nez Perce now as animals to be hunted down, and White Bird took no chances. We rested for several hours, but before the sun was up White Bird had us groping our way northward in the dark, until, just as the sun began to warm the earth, we came upon another group of Indians. We approached cautiously, not sure who they were, but then we saw they were not Assiniboins, but Crees. White Bird decided to take a chance and approach them, for we had used up all our food and were fiercely hungry, and so he let the Crees see us. As soon as they saw who we were, they sent a delegation to welcome us. They brought us food, water, and blankets and invited us to join them in their village. We believed they were sincere and, putting aside the suspicion that had been deeply ingrained in us these last many suns, we joined them. The Crees were as good as their word. They gave generously of their warm food, their women cared for our hungry and frightened children, and their men made sure we had ample ammunition. Soon we were refreshed and ready to resume our journey. I will never forget the kindness of those Crees; I hope the Great Spirit saw what they did for us that day and rewarded them.

We traveled the rest of the day and at last crossed the invisible line that separates the land of the Americans from Grandmother's Country. Now we were safe, free from the soldiers at last! On we traveled into a land that was new and strange to us, and we had not gone far before we were met by a band of Sioux warriors. How grand they looked on their fine horses, and how ragged was our band of weary exiles.

We fingered our rifles nervously. How would the Sioux receive us? We had often fought them in times past and quarreled with them over hunting rights in the Buffalo Country. Would they come to us now as friends, or bent upon revenging old wrongs? White Bird stepped forward boldly to meet them, and when the Sioux saw him come their own chief rode out to meet the sturdy old man. We watched as the two talked in sign language, the Sioux on his great war horse, White Bird standing alongside. Then we saw the Sioux chief climb off his horse and embrace White Bird, and we knew that the quarrels of the past were dead and that we were one in the face of our common enemy. The Sioux chief remounted his horse and motioned for White Bird to leap up behind him. With a wave to us to come ahead he spurred his horse back to his party, and soon all of us were riding behind the Sioux on their horses toward the camp of Sitting Bull, the famous Sioux chief who, like us, had refused to surrender.

The fires were warm and ready for us in the village of the Sioux; how grand it was to stand beside a brightly burning fire without fear. Sioux women, with friendly, smiling faces, brought us buffalo robes, and served us hot food, and comforted our women, and embraced our children. Here too we were met with the embrace of our Nez Perce friends who had fled from Snake Creek at the first charge of the soldiers and had reached the Sioux camp many days before. Over two hundred of us had escaped from Miles, about half of these having fled at the beginning of the battle and the other half, like us, having slipped away from the camp in small groups during and after the fighting. But there were also the faces of friends we looked for in vain, and when we didn't see them we knew they must have been killed by the Assiniboins.

The Nez Perce who reached the Sioux earlier told what happened with them during the days the battle of Snake Creek was being fought. It was a long while before Sitting Bull knew of our plight because Joseph's messengers had been murdered, but eventually some of our fleeing people reached Canada and brought the Sioux chief word of the disaster and our need for help. Unfortunately, Sitting Bull had misunderstood them, for the Nez Perce and Sioux didn't understand each other's language and had to talk in sign language, and he thought the battle was being fought on the Missouri River. That was too far away for his warriors to come to our rescue, so Sitting Bull did nothing. When he realized that we were only forty miles south of the border he quickly organized a war party and rode to our assistance, but before they had gone very far, more Nez Perce fleeing the battleground brought word that Joseph had surrendered, and so the Sioux chief turned back.

So we were free. Not all the People were prisoners! There were some of us left to live with a free spirit. As for myself, only my body was free, not my spirit. My heart ached for my own tribe, my own language, my home and land, and I realized as I talked with others that it was this way with them also. The Sioux were gracious to us. They shared with us what they had. They gave us a place in their village and we lived as one of them. Our women helped their women prepare the food, and our young men joined their young men in the hunt. But we were in a strange land, and there was not one among us who had not left behind a friend, wife, husband, or child with the main group who had stayed with Joseph. Yes, Joseph! I missed him greatly. Somehow where Joseph was, that was where our nation was. We had no home, but we had Joseph. He had become in our minds a symbol of the People and the only source of hope that one day we might all be reunited in our own land.

But the greatest agony for me was the unknown fate of Rising Moon. Many suns passed. The time of the falling leaves came and went and the time of the snow and cold arrived. We were comfortable in the village, but it seemed that not a moment passed when I didn't wonder what had happened to her. Had she died from her wound or was she healing? Were the soldiers mistreating her, or was she in the friendly hands of our people? Joseph once said that no wounded or sick Indian ever survived among the white men. Was this true with Rising Moon? And what of our unborn child? Was the child's life safe, or had the child perished when its mother was wounded?

Finally the warm weather began to break through the cold, and the ice on the streams started to crack and float away in great chunks in the rushing, gurgling, swirling waters of snow-fed creeks as they began their long journey to the faraway sea. Tiny flowers, such as Wali'ms loved, began to push their way stubbornly through the melting snow, and the spirit within the homesick Nez Perce began to yearn for their own land again. So it was that once the warmer weather was here to stay some of the Nez Perce began to leave. They went in groups of two and three, six and a dozen, with thanks to their benefactors, who wished them well. A few decided to find and rejoin Joseph, but most decided to return to the Idaho country and try to rejoin their Christian kinsmen on the reservation. Perhaps, they thought, they could slip into that land unnoticed by the soldiers and live once more on their own ground.

My heart yearned to return, not to our homeland but to Rising Moon, wherever she was. But I dared not leave Grandmother's Country, for I was sure I was wanted for the murders that had started the war. White Bird himself warned me, "If the Long Knives capture you, they will hang you because they believe you were one of those who killed the settlers on the Salmon River, and if they find me they will kill me, for those raiders were from my band." Yet to stay here with Sitting Bull, homeless, filled with anxiety for Rising Moon, was not to live at all. No, I would leave! I would try to find her no matter what the cost—if she still lived.

But where was she? Perhaps she was with the rest of the Nez Perce. Maybe she had survived her wound and the soldier whom I had called my enemy had taken her to be with Joseph. We had learned through the Indian grapevine that Joseph and the others had been taken by Bear Coat Miles to a white man's fort in Kansas, there to spend the winter. I must try to find out if Rising Moon was with them.

One day one of our people was getting ready to leave the camp, planning to rejoin Joseph in order to be with his family, for his heart, he said, could no longer stand to be apart. I asked him when he reached the others to find Shuslum Hihhih and ask him to send me word of Rising Moon. I knew Shuslum Hihhih would do this for he, like myself, could write the English language, and we both knew of the white man's way of sending messages in letters long distances from one town to another. I asked my friend to beg Shuslum Hihhih to send me such a letter and gave him the name of a town not far from our Sioux camp to which the letter to me could be sent. It seemed my only hope.

I waited until I thought the warrior had time to rejoin Joseph and then began, every few days, to make the trip to the place in the nearby town where the white man sent his letters to ask if one had come for me. The days went by and no letter came. The white man who ran the place of letters looked at me curiously when I came in, but he was friendly, and when I came back again and again he promised to look out with special care for any message that might arrive. But the season of the breaking ice came and went, and the season of the new grass came, and still there was no letter. I began to despair of ever hearing from Shuslum Hihhih. After all, the Nez Perce who was to take him my message might not have made it, or Shuslum Hihhih himself might be dead. In my despair I decided that I must set out alone to find Joseph, risking all in the hope that Rising Moon would be there and that the Americans would not find out who I

269

was and make me a prisoner. But first I went one last time to the letter place.

This time the man who kept the letters said to me warmly, "So here you are! I've been looking for you. Two days ago it came—the letter for you." Eagerly I thanked him. The address was in English, and so were the words inside. Shuslum Hihhih was taking no chances that the white man might intercept the written message, decide it was from hostile Indians, and discard it. The words were hard to read, but this is what they said:

To my friend, Teeto Hoonod,

Our spirits have been many places since you and I parted at Snake Creek. At first the soldiers were good to us. They fed us and gave us warm blankets. Bear Coat was the leader of the march, but Joseph was our leader. We all looked to him for hope and encouragement. His spirit never ceased working on our behalf. Two suns after we surrendered at the soldiers' camp, Bear Coat started the march. We needed that much time to bury the dead and chant our songs of grief. We were going to Fort Keogh, where we were to spend the winter. Then, so we understood, when the warm weather came we would return to the Lapwai Reservation and our own land. It was a hard journey, but the hardest thing of all was to see the Cheyennes on our horses. Bear Coat had given each of them five of our ponies in return for their help. Eight suns we traveled; then we reached the Yellowstone River and Fort Keogh.

When we arrived a band played for the soldiers to welcome them back, and for us too. Miles was treated as a hero by his people, but they also treated Joseph as a hero. This seemed strange to us, but the Americans are a strange people. First they treat us as enemies, then they make a hero out of Joseph. When I asked them why they did this, they said Joseph's name had been in the newspapers, and people all over the country knew of him.

270

All this time our spirits were strong, for we believed we would stay here until time to return home. But we didn't stay. After about fourteen suns Bear Coat said he had received orders from chiefs more powerful than he to take us down the Yellowstone River to another fort the whites called Fort Buford. This made us nervous, for this place was farther from our home. It was not part of our original agreement. But still we trusted Bear Coat Miles. Had we not made an agreement with him?

Soon we were on the way again. The strongest of us marched, and the rest—the wounded, the sick, the old, and the children—traveled on flatboats down the Yellowstone until we reached Fort Buford at the junction of the Yellowstone and Missouri Rivers. We were not here long before we were on the march again, this time still farther away, to a place called Fort Lincoln. Our fears increased, for the soldiers at Fort Buford were not friendly like those at Snake Creek and we were treated more like prisoners, and the Mandan Indians we met along the way were allowed to abuse us. Our hopes fell and we began to lose trust in Bear Coat.

Finally we found out that we were to be sent, not home as promised but to Indian territory in Oklahoma. This tore our hearts apart. Many of our people lost spirit so badly they began to be sick. Joseph was angry and said, "When will the white man learn to tell the truth!"

Not long after we arrived at Fort Lincoln we were on the way again. This time we rode in cars on the white man's iron horse, and our destination was Fort Leavenworth. We weren't asked if we wanted to go, we were ordered to go. No freedom was left to us, and no explanation given why Bear Coat Miles's promise was being broken. Joseph tried to talk to the white chiefs about the broken promise. He said, "I do not know who is to blame [that the promise is not being kept], but there are some things I want to know, which no one seems able to explain. I cannot understand how the government sends a man

271

out to fight us, as it did Colonel Miles, and then breaks his word. Such a government has something wrong with it. It seems white men have too many chiefs."

We arrived at Fort Leavenworth as the cold season began and were placed on a campground between a swamp and the Missouri River. This is where we are now as I write this letter to you. We have been here over four moons now. The ground is low. There is much disease in this place and bad spirits. Many of our people are sick, and some have already died. There is nothing for us to do, and our spirits have sunk low. Only Joseph works on our behalf. He sent a letter to the great white chiefs at Washington and asked to talk with them, but the war chief, General Sherman, disapproved it. Joseph will keep trying. He is our only hope.

We now understand that when warm weather comes we will be sent to another place in Indian territory. There it will be hot and we will have to try to farm poor land. Other Indians are already there and they will resent our coming for they will have to share what they have, which is all too little. To us this seems like death itself. When our people heard this news, many more became sick and died.

There is another bad thing that is happening: None of the children who have been born since our surrender at Snake Creek have lived. Still we have hope, for Joseph continues to try to talk with white people. He seems to have earned the respect of some of them, but, as he said, the white people have too many chiefs, and while some listen to him, and even come to visit him, others are against him.

Now for the news that you are most anxious to hear. Your message was that you want news of Rising Moon, that she was wounded as you escaped from Snake Creek and you don't know where she is. I have waited this long time to answer your question because I have to tell you she is not here. I have not seen her since Snake Creek. I have asked many people, "Have you seen Rising Moon?" All shake their heads sadly. Perhaps *she has died. Perhaps she is somewhere else, but other Indians who were wounded were sent to rejoin us. It saddens my heart to have to give you this news, but I must tell you the facts as they are.*

Shuslum Hihhih

I read my friend's letter twice, despair gripping my heart like the ice of winter grips the warm water of a lake. The People were dying in a strange land! The promise made to them by Bear Coat Miles had not been kept, and they would not be returning to our homes in the Idaho Country! And there was no word of Rising Moon. Where was she? I fought back my emotions in order to keep my mind clear to face the possibilities. In my desperation I called upon Qotsqo'tsn and thoughts came to me: *Teeto Hoonod, you must not despair. Think. Be cool.*

With an effort I turned my mind to the possibilities. Perhaps Shuslum Hihhih was mistaken and she had been sent by the soldiers to join the People and he had overlooked her presence? But no, this would not be possible. True, there were several hundred of the People and an individual could be there and not be known to Shuslum Hihhih. But Rising Moon and I were Shuslum's friends. He was one of the first persons she would seek out if she had been taken to join the others. Perhaps she was dead? That was the unthinkable thought that I now had to ponder. Of course it was far the most likely possibility. The shot from the soldier had wounded her badly; I had seen for myself the place where the bullet had torn through her shoulder. She had been left in the hands of the soldiers and, as Joseph had said, Indians do not recover their strength in the hands of the Americans. Probably she died out there on that forlorn, bitter cold prairie, and it was over for her and our unborn child, and I would never see her again. This thought, which I had been pushing away from me for many moons, could be pushed

273

away no longer. I had to think it; I had to face it.

Still, I didn't *know* she was dead; perhaps somehow she still lived. How could I find out? Where could I go to find out the truth about Rising Moon and her fate? My mind turned here and there for an answer. Slowly a thought became clear to me like the sun burning through the morning fog: There was only one person who might know the fate of Rising Moon, and that person was the soldier who had saved her from certain death by deflecting the rifle of his companion. This soldier, whom I had longed to kill and had searched for through many battles, the same soldier who killed Hohots Illpilp, was the only one who could tell me what had happened to her.

There was no other recourse; I must somehow find him and ask about Rising Moon. But how could I, who was wanted by the government for the murder of the settlers on the Salmon River, find this soldier and safely approach him?

I spent the rest of the day alone in deep thought. As I pondered my problem, it seemed as though Qotsqo'tsn became alive inside of me and began to talk to me and whisper ideas into my mind, and a plan slowly took shape within me. I would leave the friendly Sioux and the refuge I had found here in Grandmother's Country and make my way back to the land of the Americans. I would travel alone, and avoid contact with the whites as much as I could, until I made my way to the white man's forts. Here I would try to find out the location of the cavalry unit to which my enemy belonged. Then, when I found where his unit had been sent, I would go there and ask for this man. How would I know his name to ask for him? His revolver, of course. I took out the handsome pistol and looked on the handle where the name had been carved: H. HUNTER, SERGEANT, FIRST CAVALRY. That was the man for whom I would ask.

Of course I would be looked at suspiciously. An Indian

coming around white forts and asking questions! There would be questions asked of me, and the soldiers would certainly wonder if I were not a Nez Perce. If my identity was discovered I could only expect punishment or death. But I had one way to fool those soldiers: I would speak Shoshone, Wali'ms's language, and not Nez Perce. If I encountered white soldiers wise in the ways of the Indians they would know I was not truly Shoshone, but if I met soldiers who knew little about the Indians and their differences I could fool them. For most soldiers one red man is like another. Their ignorance of us might be my salvation.

But even then they would want to know why I, a wandering Shoshone, would want to know the whereabouts of one of their soldiers. For this a story must be devised. Of course, his revolver again. It was such an excellent weapon, with his name clearly marked on it. I would tell these soldiers I had come across it at the battlefield of Clearwater where I had been scouting for white troops left behind to guard the land after Howard marched his troops away. I would say that I wanted to return the weapon, hoping of course for a reward. It was a flimsy, unlikely story, but perhaps just because it was so unlikely I would be believed and would be given the information I sought.

So it was that I bade farewell to my Nez Perce and Sioux friends and set out on my journey alone. When asked where I was going I told them I was homesick for our own land and had decided to return to the Idaho Country. Of course I didn't tell anyone my real plans, for this would only increase the chance that my true identity would become known to my enemies.

I still had the good horse I had taken from the soldiers. I had a rifle of my own, and the revolver. I had enough ammunition to defend myself if attacked and to kill game for food, and a single blanket to protect myself against the chill of the northern spring nights. I was alone, a solitary figure traveling over the windswept prairie, but I was sustained by the desperate hope that somehow, somewhere, Rising Moon and our child were alive.

First I had to find out where the soldiers had gone who had been with Howard and fought the battle against us. I knew that Howard had joined Miles toward the end of the battle at Snake Creek. There might, therefore, be some persons in the area of that battle who would know where the soldiers had gone. I had to be extremely careful. Many of our people had been murdered by unfriendly Indians in this land through which I must travel. I remembered with horror the Assiniboins who had killed the six messengers sent by Joseph to the Sioux. The Assiniboins were not to be trusted, nor were the Cheyennes, who had fought against us in the final battle, nor the Crow, many of whom had tried to steal our horses. But the Crees were friendly, and others might prove friendly too.

When I thought hostile Indians were near I traveled by night, making my way slowly southward, always keeping the star-that-does-not-move at my back. Then my progress was painfully slow as I went on foot, leading my horse, guarding against a mishap in the dark. At other times I risked travel by day. These were glorious spring days when the new grass was thrusting up from the once-frozen earth, and the flowers were bursting forth in their mantle of color. The new life from my Mother the Earth gave me hope, but at night when the air grew chill and I huddled in my fireless camp, my spirits would sink again and I would have despairing thoughts of ever finding Rising Moon alive.

I received my first news from a small group of Crow whom I found not far from the Snake Creek battleground. I saw their camp one night. It wasn't hard to spot because their fires lit up the blackness for half a mile; clearly they were Indians who had nothing to fear. I waited not far from them until the next day. Then, leaving my horse and rifle in a hiding place, I took the chance of walking into their camp. I thought to myself, If I have nothing of value it is not so likely that they will harm me.

I came into their group not long after the sun had risen, as they were making ready to break camp. They eyed me suspiciously. There was no deceiving these Indians with my story of being a Shoshone; it was evident to them that I was a Nez Perce, so I made no pretense to the contrary. It was difficult to speak with them, for we spoke different tongues, but with the help of sign language, a few words of Nez Perce known to them, a fragment of Shoshone with which they were familiar, some words of Crow I had picked up, and many gestures, I made my wishes known. I told them I was a Nez Perce and continued, "I escaped to Grandmother's Country but was homesick for my people. I am journeying now, alone and without wealth of any kind, to find the People." Did they know which way the soldiers had gone? Did they know where the People had been taken?

They believed my story. Why not? A lot of it was true. I began to relax. It was evident they held no ill will toward me, and, since I had nothing to take, there was no point in their killing me. Yes, they knew where the People had been taken and which way the soldiers had gone. This is what I learned from them: Miles had led the People to the place where the Milk and Missouri rivers joined. There, so they thought, he had been joined by the rest of Howard's command. These soldiers, the troopers to whom my enemy belonged, had not returned the way they had come but had turned toward the northeast. Of course their movements had been carefully watched by the Crow who lived in that land. It was supposed that they had gone that way to join other white soldiers, though for what purpose was not known.

The Crow became friendly as we talked. (It is strange how people who might be enemies become friends if they begin

277

talking with each other.) I remained with them until they broke camp and moved on to the west. When they left I set out in an easterly direction, toward the junction of the two rivers. Once safely out of sight, for I still was taking no chances, I turned back, found my horse and cache of arms and food, and resumed my journey. This time I had a destination: the soldiers' camp at the place where the two rivers met.

I traveled many suns before I was near the place where the Crow had told me Howard's troops had joined those of Miles. As I approached the junction of the two rivers, I realized I was coming to a fort. Around the fort were small groups of Indians who made their home at the fringe of the white man's world. These Indians lived like camp dogs off what the white man chose to give them, and though I despised them I had no need to fear them. From them I learned what I needed to know. The fort was called Fort Peck, and there were about a hundred soldiers who made up the garrison. About one moon after the battle at Snake Creek, Howard's troops had met Miles's troops here, just as the Crow had said, but then Howard's troops had marched away, and these Indians didn't know where they had gone. "Much coming and going of soldiers," they said, "and who went where we don't know, but only a small company of the walking soldiers are left here." So there was no choice left to me: If I was to find Howard's soldiers I must risk an encounter with the soldiers. Only they could tell me.

I made my preparations carefully. Some distance from the Indians' encampment I found a hiding place in a ravine and hid my rifle in one place and the revolver in another. Then I tethered my horse a farther distance away in as concealed a place as I could find. I wouldn't enter the soldiers' fort with the revolver, even though I knew I would have to show it eventually to an officer, for fear I would be searched and the weapon taken from me. Then I invented a Shoshone name for myself and recalled the name of a Shoshone village that lay to the south of our homeland in the upper reaches of the Snake River. I approached the fort as casually as I could, with my heart pounding inside of me. At first the soldiers hardly noticed me. They were used to having "tame" Indians wandering in and out of the fort compound and were too ignorant of Indian ways to notice that I was different from the others. But when I finally halted one soldier and spoke to him in English he was at once surprised and suspicious.

"I need to talk with your officer," I said as calmly as I could.

The trooper looked me over carefully. He hesitated, not knowing what to do. Then he shrugged his shoulders, beckoned to another soldier to help him, and the two of them marched me off to a small log building in the midst of the fort. We entered the front room and one of the soldiers disappeared into a second room. The wait seemed endless. Finally he came back and beckoned to the second soldier to bring me in. Within moments I found myself standing, the two soldiers beside me, in a bare, austere room, and seated at a desk in front of me was a great bearlike man whose uniform proclaimed loudly that he was an officer of the army. The officer kept me standing as he looked me over suspiciously. He impressed me as a powerful, canny fellow, not a man to be taken lightly or a man to be trusted, and certainly more knowledgeable than the soldiers. My heart sank. I had hoped to meet an honest sort of person, more inclined to help his fellow man, but my instincts told me this man was a rogue.

Finally the officer spoke. "Well, what is it that you want?"

I was relieved at his question because he had not first asked me who I was. That meant that he was not yet suspicious that I might be a renegade Nez Perce. But why should he be suspicious of this? Would anyone like myself show up deliberately in a soldiers' fort? The very audacity of my plan was working for me, allaying the man's suspicions.

I answered him as coolly as I could. "I have come to ask the whereabouts of the soldiers who were with General Howard, those who pursued the Nez Perce and now, surely, must be somewhere nearby." This was a bold statement. Where any troops were located was certainly no business of a wandering Indian. I had to count, however, on the boldness of my plan to work for me.

It did work. The big officer was so startled that before he knew what he was saying he exclaimed, "The First Cavalry! Gone long ago. Taken by steamer to St. Louis back to their stations in the west, though where these are I don't know." Then suddenly his tone changed, as he realized what I had asked. "But what business is it of yours?" he asked roughly. "Who are you that you come here asking questions about matters that don't concern you?"

I had been waiting for this question, of course, and I answered by giving him the Shoshone name I had invented for myself, and the name of the Shoshone village in the Snake River country that I recalled from my childhood. I added, "The Shoshone have always been the white man's friends. Our chief, Chief Washakie, has led us in the ways of peace with the white man, and this is why I have felt free to approach you."

The officer pressed me further. "Where did you learn your English? You speak it too well to have learned it in some filthy Shoshone village."

"From the missionary schools," I answered, speaking truthfully for once. "Chief Washakie said that since we were the white man's friends someone among us should know English, and he sent me to school to learn."

Then one of the two soldiers spoke up; evidently he wanted to seem important. "He don't look like a Shoshone to me, Captain," he said. "I was stationed near the Sho-shone once, and he don't look like one of them."

There was an uneasy silence for a moment. I didn't know what to say. I had not expected interference from the soldier. Then the officer broke in. "Speak to the soldier here in Shoshone," he demanded.

Then I did a strange thing. To this day I don't know why I did it. Surely the trickster spirit of Coyote got into me, and that rascal could have been my undoing. I turned to that soldier dutifully and in my very best Shoshone said, "Your captain is a fool, and you do not have the sense of my horse." This I said to show my derision of these soldiers! But when I realized what I had done I almost panicked with fright.

I needn't have bothered to be afraid. The soldier said to his captain, "He's speakin' Shoshone all right, Captain." I heaved an inward sigh of relief. The soldier was a showoff; he hadn't understood a word I said.

The captain seemed satisfied. "For just a moment," he said, "I thought you might be one of them Nez Perce, up to some mischief or other, though why you would come here I don't know. But why do you ask about Howard's soldiers? What is it you're up to?"

So now I had to produce my story, this tale I had invented about having been with the army for a while as a scout, and after the battle of the Clearwater having gone over the bat-tlefield where I found this soldier's revolver, and now I had come to this country and wanted to return the revolver to the soldier hoping, of course, for a reward. It was an unlikely tale but I had two advantages. First, parts of it were true, so as I told it my voice had a ring of truth in it. But more important for me, the captain, in spite of all his suspicious questions, had believed what I had told him so far. When a man believes the first thing you tell him, he is likely to believe the second, and the next thing after that too, even though what you are now saying is more and more unlikely. Still, when I told him my wild tale he couldn't help but be suspicious again.

"This revolver you say you've got. Where is it?"

Accompanied by the two soldiers, I made my way back to the place where I had hidden the revolver. Of course I didn't disclose to them the whereabouts of my rifle or my horse. Guarded now like a prisoner, I was escorted back to the officer, the pistol carried by one of the soldiers. The captain was waiting for me. He was curious now and, as I was soon to learn, greedy too.

The officer took the revolver and examined it carefully, reading out loud the name on it: "H. Hunter, Sergeant, First Cavalry. You say you found it where the army fought the Nez Perce by the Clearwater River, do you? A likely story! Yet there is no record of Sergeant Henry Hunter having been killed. You didn't kill him for this gun." He seemed to be reasoning with himself now. "If you had you wouldn't be here now, would you? Not even a redskin would be that foolish. God knows how you ever got this weapon, but since you've returned it I'll keep it. I don't know where Hunter is, but maybe we can find him and I can return it."

My heart sank. If the captain kept the revolver, what hope did I have of ever finding Sergeant Hunter? But quickly I recovered my poise. I knew I must play my role to the end. "A reward?" I managed to gasp out.

The burly captain snorted. "A reward? Your reward is that I won't lock you up in the guardhouse for stealing a soldier's gun. Now be gone with you quickly, before you find yourself in trouble."

Now it struck me what had happened: This rogue wanted that fine revolver for himself. My freedom in return for the gun; that was the bargain. If he pressed some charge against me, of course he couldn't keep the revolver for himself. That was why he was letting me go. But I hadn't found out the whereabouts of the mysterious Henry Hunter, nor would I find out from that captain, for with a wave of his hand he dismissed me, and the next thing I knew the soldiers were leading me out of his office and into the compound.

But the Great Spirit must have been looking out for me that day, for if the officer was greedy, so were the soldiers. As I was led to the gate of the fort, one of them said, "So you want to know about Hunter, do you? What's it worth to you?"

"You know about Hunter?" I rejoined quickly.

"Well," the soldier said cannily, "we might. Word gets 'round 'bout these things, y'know."

Then the soldiers began to tease me. The first one said to the second, "Hunter? Yes, he's the one who refused to march with his company any longer. Said he wouldn't obey no more orders. Somethin' 'bout the Nez Perce. Wanted out of the service."

The second answered, "Might've gone badly with him, except he'd put in his years and had a good record. So Howard decided to dismiss him from the service. Just let him go without pay and that was the end of the matter. We all thought 'im pretty strange. Imagine giving up your pay just because of some Indians!" This he said to needle me, of course. Then he added, "But where's he now? Where d'ya think he went?"

It cost me my fine repeating rifle and my horse to get more information from those soldiers. Of course by now they knew I was no ordinary Shoshone and was up to something, but they asked no questions, for we were accomplices now, and since they had what they wanted from me they wanted to get rid of me as quickly as they could. I feared that once they had my horse and rifle they wouldn't tell me what I wanted to know, but they kept their bargain. That was in their interest too, for the sooner I knew where Hunter was,

283

the sooner I would be gone and the less danger there was that their deal with me would be exposed. So they told me.

"Hunter left the army and headed for Montana. Said he was going to go to the country at the northeast end of Yellowstone. At least, that's where he said he was going. Wanted a little bit of land and a new start."

Then the soldiers left and I was alone. I had the information I needed, but that was all I had, and as I made a cold and lonely camp that night on the prairie I reflected to myself: The revolver is gone, my rifle is gone, my horse is gone. My brother is dead, Kapoochas is dead, my wife and daughter are dead, the nation I belong to is destroyed, Joseph and my friends are in exile. I have nothing but my bare bones. And I fell into a despair assuaged only by an exhausted sleep.

But when I woke in the morning there was with me a sliver of determination and a bold thought. I'm in a bad place, I thought, so I'll do a bad thing. In the faint light of early morning I slipped up on the encampment of Indians around the fort and made off with one of their horses. It wasn't much of an animal, but it was better than nothing. Those tame Indians were so sleepy they didn't even wake up. It was probably days before they even realized that one of their miserable animals was gone.

Now I traveled many suns, heading west toward the Yellowstone, living off the land the best I could. Again I was grateful for Wali'ms, for I knew from her which of the plants could be eaten, and once I managed to trap a rabbit with a snare and that was a great feast for me. It was hard, but somehow I kept going until I finally reached some small settlements near the Yellowstone land and began to inquire about the white man called Henry Hunter.

The way I did it was this. I would go to a white town or ranch and ask if there was any work. Usually I was just brushed aside, but if there was I did it. Then I asked, rather casually, "Do you know a man named Henry Hunter?"

Sometimes the people just sent me away; sometimes they asked me why I wanted to know. If they did, I lied. "I have information for him from his comrades at Fort Peck." I asked and asked in this way, but no one knew anything about Hunter, so I kept moving on, working when I could, living off the land when I couldn't, and though some people were suspicious no one bothered me. They were too busy with their own affairs to get involved with one stray Indian who had no gun and nothing worth taking.

Finally, near a little town called Red Lodge, I came to a ranch that, as luck would have it, was lived in by a lone woman. She was a sturdy soul whose husband had been killed the year before when he stumbled onto a grizzly sow with her cubs. To my surprise she was not afraid of me and gave me work to do. I liked this woman, and she liked me, and I stayed and worked there for several days because I could see that she needed me. Then, one cloudy evening when we huddled in the cabin for shelter, I asked her my question about Hunter.

"Henry Hunter!" she exclaimed. "Of course. He was in the army. Came here half a year ago. Works hard. Lives alone. Needs a woman, that man does. You'll find him up the road about three miles, on your left, just beyond where the road crosses a small stream."

My heart leaped up within me! A tiny mouse, tucked away among bushes and rocks, thinks it can escape the probing eyes of the eagle as it circles high above in the great blue sky. But the eagle sees that mouse wherever it is because its eyes miss nothing. So I had been looking for one man, a tiny speck of life lost in the great vastness of forests and mountains. But the Great Spirit is like an eagle high above, and the Great Spirit knows where everything is in his creation. It was he who knew where Henry Hunter was and led me to him, he who caused my feet to follow in the path that would lead me to the spot where this man was.

So I thanked the woman and set off alone again up the mountain road those last weary miles. It was evening now, and the great dark clouds of a storm that had been gathering all day began to send a cold rain upon me. I drew my blanket more closely about me as I urged my horse along, my body weary but my spirit enlivened by the hope that you, Henry Hunter, would have the answer I was seeking. At last I arrived here at your cabin and knocked at the door. You opened the door to me, and though I was a rain-drenched stranger, you allowed me to come inside and sit by your fire and tell you my story. Now you know why I have come. Now you know who it is who sits before you and what strange mission it is that brings me on this wild night to your lonely cabin.

CHAPTER SEVENTEEN

Henry Hunter's Story

The fire had died down to glowing embers as I concluded my story. I had talked throughout the night. The white man in front of me rose and threw fresh logs on the fire to dispel the numbing chill that was creeping through the cabin. Then he turned to me and spoke.

"I am indeed Henry Hunter, the man you come to now as the only one who can tell you the fate of your woman. I am the man who killed your brother in that godforsaken battle by the Clearwater River. And it was indeed my revolver that you recovered, dropped in the heat of the battle. That moment lives in my mind as fresh as a new-fallen snow: There I was heading my platoon, stopped from advancing by you and Hohots Illpilp, your courage and your deadly shots. Then your brother exposed himself for one moment and I brought him down with a bullet from my rifle. . . ."

We both fell silent. I felt my heart pound as I heard him tell of the death of Hohots Illpilp. I looked at the man who had killed him, and I could tell that he felt great sorrow too; I felt no anger, only a sickness at the pit of my stomach.

He continued. "After the battle I followed you and your people over the Lolo Trail and arrived with an advance detachment of Howard's army shortly after the dreadful battle at Big Hole had ended. When I saw the corpses of the women and the children and the Bannock Indians mutilating the bodies of your dead warriors, I began to doubt that what we were doing was right.

"I was there, too, at Camas Meadow when you cleverly ran off our mules. Howard was downcast, but I was relieved, for by then I was hoping that you would escape. In the Yellowstone Country, when everyone else was confident that you were caught in our net, I knew that somehow you would find a way through. But when Howard deliberately fell two days' march behind you as you made your way north to Canada I feared that you would be caught. For this was a ruse on his part. He hoped that when he slowed down his pursuit you would also slow down, which would give Miles's army time to come upon you from the east before you could reach the Canadian border.

"Now Howard had to send a message to Miles telling him of his plan and urging him to come as fast as he could to intercept you, and he chose me and another man to carry it. The other man went by horse, and I went by water. Am I going to tell you that I delayed my journey? Let's just say that the soldier in me obeyed the order, but the man in me dragged his feet. But that is why I was with Miles's command when he ordered the first cavalry charge against you and when we made a perimeter line around you to keep you from escaping."

Henry Hunter fell silent, gathering his thoughts. "I see," I said, and then, impatiently, "But how is it that you know of Rising Moon?"

"I will tell you. Once you were surrounded, Miles knew that some of you might try to escape toward Sitting Bull. So he sent some soldiers north of your camp to intercept any of you who tried to get away, and I was among them. That is why I was in your path on the fateful night when you and Rising Moon and your little band tried to make your way from Snake Creek to the safety of Canada."

We both fell silent for as long as it takes a howling wolf to

288

sing its song as we approached the moment when Rising Moon was shot. I felt the grief rise in me again, and Hunter himself seemed to be fighting back tears.

"And then what happened?" I asked.

"And then it was bad. I was positioned with another soldier to watch for signs of escaping Indians when we saw you. We heard you as you approached our position. My companion was a rough fellow, a soldier who only lived to fight and only understood fighting, and when he saw the two of you he quickly prepared to fire. I didn't know what to do, but when my companion fired the shot that struck your woman I fired a shot that went wildly into the air. When I saw that he had shot a woman I felt sick and knew I could no longer kill in that war. What point was there in killing any more people? So when this soldier raised his rifle to fire a second time and put an end to the woman he had already wounded, and who now lay helplessly on the ground, I flung up my arm and struck his rifle, making his shot go wild.

"So it was, Teeto Hoonod, that though I killed your brother, I also tried to save the life of your woman.

"Then you shot, and your bullet killed that other soldier instantly, but I just stood there helplessly. I knew I was a target for you too, but I didn't seem to have the power to move away. I even saw you raise your rifle, and yet I remained where I was. Then you hesitated, and in that instant I came to my senses and dropped to the ground.

"Soon I heard other soldiers approaching. They must have been drawn by the sound of the firing. As soon as you were gone I went over to your woman and saw that the bullet had made an ugly wound in her shoulder. She was badly hurt but not dead. I thought to myself how senseless it was that this woman was hurt, especially now the fighting was over.

"The other soldiers came up, and their officer wanted to

289

take Rising Moon as a prisoner, but I decided to take charge of her myself. I got her back to the main camp and sent for the surgeon. He did what he could for her, stemming the flow of blood and binding up the wound. The bullet had passed clear through her body, which meant he didn't have to cut it out, but it did a lot of damage on its way. Of course your woman and I couldn't talk together because we didn't know each other's language, but all this time she remained conscious, and she seemed to know that I was looking after her. Time and again she placed her hand on her abdomen and looked at me and tried to say something, and eventually I understood that she was pregnant. She didn't try to tell the army doctor that. He was a competent man, but gruff and curt with her, but because I was friendly I guess she wanted me to know.

"It took two days for all the dead at the battlefield to be properly buried, and then we were on the march again headed for Fort Keogh. Rising Moon was with the other Nez Perce wounded, but I found excuses to look in on her. In this way we came to know each other, even though we couldn't talk, and she got so she would smile at me weakly when she saw me coming. But I could see that each day she was losing ground. Her body, weak as it was, just couldn't stand the rigors of travel, and it seemed as though her spirit couldn't get strong again among all of us soldiers. As the days went by it became clear that she was going to die for sure if she remained with us much longer.

"So I decided to do something about it. One evening, just as darkness was falling, I came to the part of the camp where the wounded were grouped together and found Rising Moon. I gave her a look—right into her eyes—and she seemed to understand. Then I picked up her thin body and placed it on my horse and then mounted the horse myself, and she put her arms around my body and hung on as tightly as she could in her weakened condition. Just to be safe, I passed a rope around us so she couldn't fall off. No one paid any attention. There weren't any guards around, for these were wounded people and there was no need to guard them. It was so dark it was hard for anyone to see what we were doing anyhow, and if any of the wounded noticed us they said nothing. Then I rode out of the camp. A sentry saw me, and I waved at him and he said nothing; perhaps the very boldness of my action threw him off guard. The truth was, no one much cared about one wounded Nez Perce woman and what happened to her.

"After we had ridden a couple of hours in the darkness, I made camp and kept your woman warm with blankets during the cold night, and the next day when the sun had warmed things up I traveled on. I was looking for a group of Indians I could leave Rising Moon with. I hoped that if she could stay with Indian people she would make it—she and the baby inside of her. The first Indians I saw were Crow but I passed them by, for many of them had turned against you. But eventually I found a Cree village and I decided to stop there, for I knew the Crees were a kind people.

"You can imagine the surprise of those Crees when an army sergeant came riding into their camp with a wounded Indian woman behind him on his horse! Their warriors came out to meet me, full of suspicion, but when they saw I had a wounded woman with me they understood and sent for their own women. The Cree women took to Rising Moon at once. They immediately made a place for her, and in no time at all they realized that she was not only wounded but pregnant. They took her in like she was one of their own daughters, and I could see the look of relief on your woman's face as they made her comfortable, relief not just for herself but also for the child she was carrying. As soon as I knew she would be well cared for, I left and returned to my company.

"Of course I had been missed, and the captain gave me a

scolding and wanted to know where I had been. I told him I had gone out to do a bit of hunting and had lost my way. I knew he didn't believe me but he let the matter drop. Guess he didn't want any more problems. As for Rising Moon, none of the soldiers even knew she was gone. There were many wounded, and she was only one more anonymous face. And the other wounded Indians knew that somehow I was trying to do something for her, so they pretended they had seen nothing.

"After this I knew for certain that I could no longer be a soldier, and when we reached Fort Keogh I asked to be dismissed from the service. My enlistment was almost up anyway, and I had put in many years of service in the army. General Howard had other things on his mind and didn't want to be bothered with a recalcitrant trooper like myself, so he gave orders that I should be dismissed from the service, but without my last allotment of pay because I had not finished my term. I was sent away in some disgrace, I guess you could say, but in my heart I felt strong and free. Not that there was anything wrong with my comrades. They weren't bad people—neither better nor worse than the common run of humanity—but I no longer belonged there. I had had enough of killing, and as I rode away I finally felt at peace with myself.

"I decided I would return to this part of Montana. When we passed through the Yellowstone area I had seen and admired it. I liked the great mountains and forests and thought that maybe this was a place where I could start a new life. I decided to build a cabin for myself and see if I could make a living from the forest and the land. I also hoped that I might one day find a woman of my own and maybe have a family."

There was silence in the cabin for a few moments as I pondered the meaning of these eventful days. Then I asked him to conclude his story.

"You are wondering what happened to Rising Moon, of course. Well, as time went on I found that I was wondering too. I couldn't free my mind from thoughts of your strong-hearted, brave little woman whose man had, mysteriously, not shot and killed me when he could. So one winter day about the middle of our month of March, not too long ago now, I decided to find out. I left my cabin here in the mountains and went back to the Cree village. None of the Crees recognized me at first, of course, but by using sign language I was able to give them some idea of the reason for my visit, and they finally found an old Cree woman who had once lived with some white people and spoke a little English. I told her the reason for my visit and she listened carefully as I spoke. Then she told me.

" 'The Nez Perce woman you brought us was bad sick. Her body was torn to pieces by the bullet, and evil spirits were in her wound and their poison was going all through her. We did all we could for her. Our medicine women chanted and drummed for her, but we could see that her spirit was soon going to leave her body and that she would go to the land of the Great Spirit. Yet still she clung to life, and I knew she was hanging on because of her unborn child. She wanted the child she was carrying to live, and because of this her spirit was fierce and determined and would not give up in spite of all her hurt. Because of this she made herself get stronger so that her child could be born. At last the day came when the child's soul clamored to come into this world. I was one of the women who attended her when she gave birth to her baby. She was so ill and so weak it was all she could do to push against the baby and bring it into the world. Finally the baby came out! She came into the great world and uttered her first cry! Yes, it was a baby girl who was born, a little girl who would not be denied her right to live. We held the baby tightly and rejoiced; we clapped and sang and shouted because the birth of the child was a

293

great victory, and the little mother also rejoiced with us. For as long as it has taken me to tell you this story the Nez Perce woman smiled with us, and then there suddenly came a look across her face of terrible pain, and with that a gush of blood poured out of her wound and with a little cry she died.' "

Henry Hunter stopped. There was only silence in the cabin. Then I asked quietly, only a slight tremor betraying my emotion, "Did the Cree woman have anything else to say?"

"Yes. She said one other thing. 'If you ever find the man who loved this woman, tell him that we will keep the child and care for her as one of our own. Tell him not to grieve too greatly for the mother who died, that in her death she gave birth to life, and that she has gone now to a place where she is free of pain.' "

The fire had died down once more, and in the darkness of the cabin I could scarcely see the face of my host, although I could sense his emotion by his labored breathing. At last I spoke again. "The Cree village where the child lives—can you find it again?"

He answered confidently, "I can find it again. It's written forever in my memory. I can find the village and can take you to the place where your woman is buried and where, if God has so willed it, your child still lives."

"We will go together then?" I asked.

"We will leave this very day," he answered.

Now daylight was soon to come. And that is how it happened that a few hours later Henry Hunter, a white man, and I, an Indian, left on our strange mission. Riding two fresh horses, with two rifles and a supply of food, we went out together to find the child. As we went down the road that led away from the cabin toward the land of the Cree Indians, the last of the black clouds from the storm of the night were being chased from the sky by a warm and victorious sun. The earth smelled damp and rich, as it does after a healing rain has made it fruitful, and seemed to smile at us. As we rode away, the fiery red made by the risen sun was giving way to blue as the great yellow disk made its way higher into the sky, and from its perch in one of the forest bushes nearby a meadowlark burst into song.

Epilogue

The United States Government did not honor the agreement that Colonel Miles made with Joseph that the Nez Perce would be returned to their homeland. Instead they were exiled to Indian territory in what is now the state of Oklahoma. Their severe treatment was part of General Sherman's plan to "teach the Indians a lesson." In the hot and unhealthy climate of the lowlands of Indian territory, many of the dispirited Nez Perce died from disease and malnutrition, until only three hundred of the original five hundred who had surrendered remained. It is also said that not one child born to the Nez Perce while they were in Indian territory survived.

Joseph was the Nez Perce's remaining hope. He became a well-known personality and was visited by important government officials and others who were sympathetic to his cause. Sometimes he took part in public ceremonies, and several times he went to Washington, D.C., where he talked with Presidents Rutherford B. Hayes and William McKinley and pleaded the cause of his people. Finally, as a result of his personal diplomacy, the Government granted the Nez Perce permission to rejoin their Christian kinsmen in Idaho.

However, local sentiment in Idaho would not tolerate the presence of Joseph, who was still blamed for the murders on the Salmon River. So Joseph and some of the other Nez

Perce who wanted to continue to live according to the old religion were sent instead to the Indian Reservation at Colville, Washington. Here Joseph lived until his death in 1904. Today a town in Oregon and a large dam bear his name.

A resourceful and intelligent people, the descendants of the Nez Perce who fought the war of 1877 live on, most of them in or near the reservations in Washington and northern Idaho. Like most Indians in this country they face great problems, but because Coyote created them a "manly people," they have survived and made a place for themselves in what has been a hostile world.

Columbia

Pend Oreille

Pend Oreille Lake

Flathead Lake

ROCKY

Spokane
WASHINGTON

Coeur d'Alene

B
i
t
t
e
r
r
o
o
t

Clark Fork

Flathead

Missoula

Clark Fork

Palouse

Stevensville

Snake
Lewiston

PRESENT-DAY
RESERVATION
BOUNDARY

LOLO TRAIL

Lochsa

Lolo

Walla Walla

Fort Lapwai

Bitterroot

Cottonwood
JULY 4-5

Clearwater
JULY 11-12

Anaconda Range

Big Hole

Butte

NEZ PERCE

RESERVATION

Big Hole
AUG 9

Wallowa Mts

Whitebird
JUNE 17

Beaverhead

R
a
n
g
e

Salmon

GEN.

HOWARD

OREGON

Salmon River
Mountains

Fort Lemhi

Bannack

Lemhi

Range

Junction

Monida
Pass

I D A H O

Boise

Snake River Plain